Information Technology for Management

Driving Digital Transformation to Increase Local and Global Performance, Growth and Sustainability

Twelfth Edition

T0340742

Information Technology for Management

Driving Digital Transformation to Increase Local and Global Performance, Growth and Sustainability

Twelfth Edition

EFRAIM TURBAN

CAROL POLLARD
Appalachian State University

GREGORY WOOD
Canisius College

VP AND EDITORIAL DIRECTOR	Mike McDonald
PUBLISHER	Lise Johnson
EDITOR	Jennifer Manias
EDITORIAL ASSISTANT	Kali Ridley
SENIOR MANAGING EDITOR	Judy Howarth
PRODUCTION EDITOR	Umamaheswari Gnanamani
COVER PHOTO CREDIT	© Yuichiro Chino/Getty Images

This book was set in 9.5/12.5 pt Source Sans Pro by SPi Global.

Founded in 1807, John Wiley & Sons, Inc. has been a valued source of knowledge and understanding for more than 200 years, helping people around the world meet their needs and fulfill their aspirations. Our company is built on a foundation of principles that include responsibility to the communities we serve and where we live and work. In 2008, we launched a Corporate Citizenship Initiative, a global effort to address the environmental, social, economic, and ethical challenges we face in our business. Among the issues we are addressing are carbon impact, paper specifications and procurement, ethical conduct within our business and among our vendors, and community and charitable support. For more information, please visit our website: www.wiley.com/go/citizenship.

Copyright © 2021, 2018, 2015, 2013, 2011, 2010 John Wiley & Sons, Inc. All rights reserved. No part of this publication may be reproduced, stored in a retrieval system, or transmitted in any form or by any means, electronic, mechanical, photocopying, recording, scanning or otherwise, except as permitted under Sections 107 or 108 of the 1976 United States Copyright Act, without either the prior written permission of the Publisher, or authorization through payment of the appropriate per-copy fee to the Copyright Clearance Center, Inc., 222 Rosewood Drive, Danvers, MA 01923 (Web site: www.copyright.com). Requests to the Publisher for permission should be addressed to the Permissions Department, John Wiley & Sons, Inc., 111 River Street, Hoboken, NJ 07030-5774, (201) 748-6011, fax (201) 748-6008, or online at: www.wiley.com/go/permissions.

Evaluation copies are provided to qualified academics and professionals for review purposes only, for use in their courses during the next academic year. These copies are licensed and may not be sold or transferred to a third party. Upon completion of the review period, please return the evaluation copy to Wiley. Return instructions and a free of charge return shipping label are available at: www.wiley.com/go/returnlabel. If you have chosen to adopt this textbook for use in your course, please accept this book as your complimentary desk copy. Outside of the United States, please contact your local sales representative.

ISBN: 978-1-119-70290-0 (PBK)
ISBN: 978-1-119-71379-1 (EVALC)

Library of Congress Cataloging in Publication Data

Names: Turban, Efraim, author. | Pollard, Carol (Carol E.), author. | Wood, Gregory R., author.
Title: Information technology for management : on-demand strategies for performance, growth and sustainability / Efraim Turban, Carol Pollard, Appalachian State University, Gregory Wood, Canisius College.
Description: Twelfth edition. | Hoboken : Wiley, 2021. | Includes indexes.
Identifiers: LCCN 2020025488 (print) | LCCN 2020025489 (ebook) | ISBN 9781119713807 (cloth) | ISBN 9781119702900 (pbk) | ISBN 9781119713791 (evalc) | ISBN 9781119713784 (adobe pdf) | ISBN 9781119702917 (epub)
Subjects: LCSH: Management information systems.
Classification: LCC T58.6 .T765 2021 (print) | LCC T58.6 (ebook) | DDC 658.4/038011—dc23
LC record available at https://lccn.loc.gov/2020025488
LC ebook record available at https://lccn.loc.gov/2020025489

The inside back cover will contain printing identification and country of origin if omitted from this page. In addition, if the ISBN on the back cover differs from the ISBN on this page, the one on the back cover is correct.

SKY10075802_052324

Brief Contents

Contents

4 Networks, the Internet of Things (IoT), and Edge Computing 107

5 Data Privacy and Cyber Security 149

PART 2 Maximizing Growth with Data Analytics, Social Media and Omni-Channel Technology

6 Business Intelligence, Data Science, and Data Analytics 199

7 Social Media and Semantic Web Technology 249

8 Omnichannel Retailing, E-commerce, and Mobile Commerce Technology 294

14 IT Ethics and Local and Global Sustainability   537

Preface

Information Technology for Management discusses the importance of aligning business-IT strategies and explains how companies rely on data, digital technology, and mobile devices to support them in the on-demand and sharing economies and help them address the challenges of the COVID-19 pandemic. Our goal is to provide students from any business discipline with a strong foundation for understanding digital technology concepts and terminology and the critical role that it plays in facilitating business sustainability, profitability, and growth locally and globally. The text also seeks to equip students with the information they need to become "informed users of IT." Enabling technologies and related concepts, discussed in this text include the following:

- **Sustainability.** Cloud services, artificial intelligence, blockchain technologies, edge computing, and other disruptive technologies are fundamental to sustaining business profitability and growth in today's on-demand and sharing economies. These technologies play a critical role in developing and managing projects and sourcing agreements, addressing personal privacy, encouraging social responsibility and attracting, connecting with and engaging employees, customers, and partners across omnichannel technologies to promote sustainable business performance and growth.
- **Performance and Profitability.** Combining the latest capabilities in descriptive, predictive, and prescriptive data analytics, reporting, collaboration, search, and digital communication helps enterprises be more agile and cuts costs to optimize business performance and profitability.
- **Growth.** Strategic technologies enable business to create new core competencies, expand their markets, and move into new markets to experience exponential growth in the on-demand and sharing economies locally and globally.

In this twelfth edition, students learn, explore, and understand technology concepts and terminology and the importance of IT's role in supporting the three essential components of business performance improvement: *technology, business processes,* and *people*. This edition has a greater focus on the global impacts of IT and includes discussions of the impact of the COVID-19 pandemic on the ways technology is enabling organizations to connect with employees, customers, and partners and to use disruptive technologies in new and innovative ways to get the job done!

What's New in the Twelfth Edition?

In the twelfth edition of *Information Technology for Management*, we present and discuss concepts in a comprehensive, yet easy-to-understand format by actively engaging students through a wider selection of case studies, interactive figures, chapter summaries, 34 whiteboard animations, tech notes, self-check quizzes, online and interactive exercises, critical thinking questions, and crossword puzzles. We have enhanced the twelfth edition in the following ways:

Diverse Audience. *Information Technology for Management* is directed toward undergraduate, introductory MBA courses, and Executive Education courses in Management Information Systems and General Business programs. Concepts are explained in a straightforward way, and interactive elements, tools, and techniques provide tangible resources that appeal to all levels of students.

Strong Pedagogical Approach. To encourage improved learning outcomes, we continue to employ a blended learning approach, in which different types of delivery and learning methods, enabled and supported by technology, are blended with traditional learning methods. For example, case study and theoretical content are presented visually, textually, and/or interactively to enable different groups of students to use different learning strategies in different combinations to fit their individual learning style and enhance their learning. Throughout the book, general content has been reorganized and updated to reflect the current state of new and previously included topics and 100 new informative static or interactive figures and 29 new tables have been added to effectively visually demonstrate new and expanded concepts. In addition, all cases and IT at Work vignettes have been updated or replaced, and learning objectives have been updated to be more succinct and consistent with new content. Finally, a chapter summary linked directly to each learning objective has been added at the end of each chapter.

Leading-Edge Content. Prior to and during the writing process, we consulted with a number of vendors, IT professionals, and managers who are hands-on users of leading technologies, to learn about their IT/business successes, challenges, experiences, and recommendations. To integrate the feedback of these business and IT professionals, new or updated chapter opening and closing cases have been added to many of the chapters along with the addition of relevant, leading-edge content in the body of the chapters.

New Technologies and Expanded Topics. New to this edition are the topics of artificial intelligence, quantum computing, edge computing, cognitive knowledge management and blockchain technology. Also included are updates to the IT framework, expanded coverage of data science and advanced data analytics and the tools and techniques that support them, the newest systems developments methodologies, and expanded coverage of the Project, Program, and Portfolio Management framework. Table P-1 provides a detailed list of new and expanded topics.

Useful Tools and Techniques. The "IT Toolbox" feature provides a skills-based takeaway tool or technique that the students can use in future courses and their upcoming career. In the twelfth edition, it has been revised and/or updated to reflect new content in the text. New to this edition is a feature we call "Did You Know?" This feature appears at the beginning of the main text of each chapter and delivers some interesting and often "fun" facts related to the technologies discussed within the chapter content and is designed to more effectively capture the students' interest at the beginning of each chapter.

Engaging Students to Assure Learning

The twelfth edition of *Information Technology for Management* engages students with up-to-date coverage of the most important IT trends today. Over the years, this IT textbook has distinguished itself with an emphasis on illustrating the use of cutting-edge business technologies for supporting and achieving managerial goals and objectives. The twelfth edition continues this tradition with more interactive activities and analyses.

Real-World Case Studies. Each chapter contains numerous real-world examples illustrating how businesses use IT to increase productivity, improve efficiency, enhance communication and collaboration, and gain a competitive edge. Faculty will appreciate a variety of options for reinforcing student learning, that include three different types of **Case Studies** (opening case, business case, and video case), along with IT at Work vignette.

Interactive Figures. The unique presentation of interactive figures enhances the students' comprehension of concepts by actively engaging the students in their own learning to effectively reinforce concepts and learning objectives.

Whiteboard Animations. These features tied to chapter learning objectives reinforce understanding of the textual content of the book and provide a clearer path to understanding key concepts through a multimedia overview of each learning objective. The 34 whiteboard animations fit particularly well with the "flipping the classroom" model that has become increasingly important during the COVID-19 pandemic and complement additional functionality and assets offered throughout the twelfth edition.

Learning Aids. Each chapter contains various learning aids, which include the following:

- **Learning Objectives** are listed at the beginning of each chapter and repeated at the beginning of each relevant section to help students focus their efforts and alert them to the important concepts that will be discussed.
- **IT at Work** boxes spotlight real-world cases and innovative uses of IT.
- **Tech Note** boxes explore topics such as "Key Performance Indicators" and "Six Basic Systems Development Guidelines."
- **Career Insight** boxes highlight different jobs in the IT for management field.
- **Chapter Summary** directly tied to learning objectives is included to close out each chapter.
- **Key Terms** definitions appear in the margins throughout the book and listed at the end of each chapter.

End of Chapter Activities. At the end of each chapter, features designed to assure student learning include the following:

- **Critical Thinking Questions** are designed to facilitate student discussion.
- **Online and Interactive Exercises** encourage students to explore additional topics.
- **Analyze and Decide** questions help students apply IT concepts to business decisions.
- **Reinforce Your Learning** A crossword puzzle is available for each chapter in the online resources to reinforce and test the students' understanding of key terms.
- **Concept Check Questions** in the enhanced e-book test student comprehension of each learning objective within a chapter. To ensure that the students are "clear on the concepts" and provide immediate feedback on their performance.

Details of New and Enhanced Features of the Twelfth Edition

The textbook consists of 14 chapters organized into 4 modules. All chapters have new or updated cases and content, as shown in Table P-1.

TABLE P-1 Summary of New and Expanded IT Topics, Cases, and IT at Work Vignettes

Chapter	New and Expanded IT and Business Topics	New and Updated Cases and IT at Work
1. Digital Transformation Disrupts Companies, Competition, and Careers Locally and Globally	• IT's role in the sharing economy • IT impact on global economy • Technology mega trends	• Uber • Airbnb • Coca-Cola • Costa Coffee • Creating a Digital Vision • IoT • Kroger • Netflix
2. Information Systems, IT Infrastructure, and the Cloud	• IS concepts and framework • Information, information, knowledge, wisdom model • Software-defined data center	• Tommy Flowers, Father of Computing • Lufthansa Technik • Grupo AGORA
3. Data Management, Data Warehouses, and Data Governance	• Data lifecycle • Genomics and big data • Blockchain technology • Cognitive knowledge management	• ThyssenKrupp Elevator • PwC and Energy Sector • Master Data in Healthcare • Predictive Policing Systems • ERMS in Action • University of Washington
4. Networks, the Internet of Things (IoT), and Edge Computing	• Net neutrality status • Mobile networks and near-field communication • Internet of things • Edge computing	• Cedar Park Smart Water • Minnesota Twins Audio Network • Ericsson in Africa • Salvation Army • States Take on Net Neutrality • Carnival Cruise Lines
5. Data Privacy and Cyber Security	• Data breaches • Major sources of cyberthreats • Cryptojacking • Man-in-the middle attacks • SQL injection • Data privacy	• Yahoo • Google • Oregon DHS • Bayer • Kenya protects citizen data • Marriott
6. Business Intelligence, Data Science, and Advanced Data Analytics	• Social search technologies • Descriptive data analytics • Predictive data analytics • Prescriptive data analytics • Tools and techniques to support all levels of data analytics	• NASCAR
7. Social Media and Semantic Web Technology	• Social bookmarking • Social customer service moves from optional to essential • Role of APIs in development of new Web applications and functionality • The dominance of Facebook and the demise of Google+ • Semantic Web and semantic search technologies • Social commerce, video conferencing, and remote work during COVID-19	• Digital Campaigns • Google • Amazon Neptune • Best Buy • Facebook • Power Searching with Google

(Continued)

TABLE P-1 **Summary of New and Expanded IT Topics, Cases, and IT at Work Vignettes** *(Continued)*

Chapter	New and Expanded IT and Business Topics	New and Updated Cases and IT at Work
8. Omnichannel Retailing, E-Commerce, and Mobile Commerce Technology	• Role of convenience in shaping retail markets • Direct and marketplace B2B ecommerce • Grab and go retailing • Subscription-based retailing • In-store retail technology • Omnichannel retailing • Growth of mobile commerce • Fulfillment as a service (FaaS) • Mobile payment methods • Impact of 5G networks on retailing • Expanded use of digital voice assistants (DVAs) for retail search, research, and ordering	• Amazon • Kroger • Macy's • Personalizing E-commerce • Dunkin Donuts • Bay Area Relief • eBay • MVS
9. Functional Business Systems	• Cross-functional coordination and integration of systems	• Equifax • MAHLE and SAP • Chatbot Marketing • THULE • SaaS and Global HR • MAHLE • FUZE
10. Enterprise Systems	• Always-on supply chain • Enterprise social platforms	• Walmart • FUZE • UPS • 1-800-Flowers.com • CISCO • Lowes
11. Artificial Intelligence, Robotics, and Quantum Computing Technology	• Artificial intelligence (AI) • Ethical issues associated with AI • Robotics • Work automation • AI-powered sentiment analysis, predictive analytics and content management systems • Quantum computing	• HSBC • Facebook • HUBSPOT • Facial Recognition • Hanson Robotics • Recommendation Systems
12. IT Strategy, Sourcing, and Strategic Technology Trends	• IT sourcing strategies • Strategic technology trends	• San Diego County • Nations and Comparative Advantage • Balanced Scorecard • ESSA Academy • DOD and CBRN Technology
13. Systems Development, IT Service Management and Project, Program and Portfolio Management	• New systems development methodologies • DevOps • IT service management • Project, program, and portfolio management Framework	• VELCO • Oakley • Target • Steve Jobs • BER • Denver International Airport

TABLE P-1 Summary of New and Expanded IT Topics, Cases, and IT at Work Vignettes *(Continued)*

Chapter	New and Expanded IT and Business Topics	New and Updated Cases and IT at Work
14. IT Ethics and Local and Global Sustainability	• Sustainability in developing countries • Climate change update • Access to clean water • Food security • Impact of technology on various aspects of quality of life before, during, and after the COVID-19 pandemic • Tech-Clash and an increased need for a 'People First' approach to technology amid the COVID-19 pandemic • Disruptive Technologies to address the challenges of the COVID-19 pandemic	• Royal Bank of Scotland • Facebook • Users Leaving Social Media • Blockchain and Sustainability • La Liga

Supplemental Materials

An extensive package of instructional materials is available to support this twelfth edition. These materials are accessible from the book companion website at *www.wiley.com/go/turban/infotechformgmt12E*

- **Instructor's Manual.** The Instructor's Manual presents objectives from the text with additional information to make them more appropriate and useful for the instructor. The manual also includes practical applications of concepts, case study elaboration, answers to end-of-chapter questions, questions for review, questions for discussion, and Internet exercises.

- **Test Bank.** The test bank contains over 1,000 questions and problems (about 75 per chapter) consisting of multiple-choice, short answer, fill-ins, and critical thinking/essay questions.

- **Respondus Test Bank.** This electronic test bank is a powerful tool for creating and managing exams that can be printed on paper or published directly to Blackboard, ANGEL, Desire2Learn, Moodle, and other learning systems. Exams can be created offline using a familiar Windows environment, or moved from one LMS to another.

- **PowerPoint Presentations.** A series of slides designed around the content of the text incorporates key points from the text and illustrations where appropriate.

- **Chapter Summary Whiteboard Animations.** A library of 34 video animations—"chunked" by learning objectives in each chapter—summarizes the content of each chapter in an entertaining visual way to engage the students in grasping the subject matter and providing an easily accessible audio track for those who are visually impaired.

- **Crossword Puzzles.** A set of online crossword puzzles that test and reinforce student understanding of key terms in a fun and interactive way.

Acknowledgments

No book is produced through the sole efforts of its authors, and this book is no exception. Many people contributed to its creation, both directly and indirectly, and we wish to acknowledge their contributions.

First, a special thank you goes to the team at John Wiley, including Lise Johnson, Business Publisher and Jennifer Manias, Editor, who shared their expert and encouraging editorial insights, Judy Howarth, Sr. Managing Editor, who provided much appreciated project management leadership, Padmapriya Soundarajan, Senior Production Editor, who offered valuable guidance throughout the production process, and Aarthi Ramachandran, Permissions Specialist, whose extensive and expert research into the images used in the text greatly enhanced the overall "look" of this edition.

Many thanks also to our talented graphic designer and Appalachian State University alumni, Nathan Sherrill, who created the innovative Whiteboard Animations for Chapters 7, 8, and 11.

Their combined skill, patience, humor, and support during the development and production of this most recent version of the text made the process much easier.

Our sincere thanks go to the following reviewers of the twelfth edition whose valuable feedback, insights, and suggestions were invaluable in ensuring the accuracy and readability of the book:

Joni Adkins, Northwest Missouri State University

Ahmad Al-Omari, Dakota State University

Rigoberto Chinchilla, Eastern Illinois University

Michael Donahue, Towson University

Samuel Elko, Seton Hill University

Robert Goble, Dallas Baptist University

Eileen Griffin, Canisius College

Binshan Lin, Louisiana State University in Shreveport

Thomas MacMullen, Eastern Illinois University

James Moore, Canisius College

Beverly S. Motich, Messiah College

Barin Nag, Towson University

Luis A. Otero, Inter-American University of Puerto Rico, Metropolitan Campus

John Pearson, Southern Illinois University

Daniel Riding, Florida Institute of Technology

Josie Schneider, Columbia Southern University

Derek Sedlack, South University

Eric Weinstein, The University of La Verne

Patricia White, Columbia Southern University

Gene A. Wright, University of Wisconsin–Milwaukee

Last, but by no means least, we extend our very special thanks to our families, friends, and colleagues who provided enormous encouragement, support, and understanding as we dedicated the necessary time and effort to create this new edition amid the turmoil of the COVID-19 pandemic. Their unfailing support and the power of information and communications technology enabled us to bring the twelfth edition in on time and on budget!

CAROL POLLARD
GREGORY WOOD

Digital Transformation Disrupts Companies, Competition, and Careers Locally and Globally

LEARNING OBJECTIVES

1.1 Define the differences between the on-demand and sharing economies and the six business objectives IT should focus on to enhance organizational performance, growth, and sustainability.

1.2 Explain the role of IT in improving business processes. Understand the concepts of business process reengineering and competitive advantage.

1.3 Describe how IT is disrupting the way that companies operate, the IT megatrends that are driving organizational performance, growth, and sustainability and how COVID-19 is accelerating digital transformation.

1.4 Discuss what it means to be an "informed user" of IT and the ways in which IT can add value to your career path and job performance.

Case 1.1 Opening Case

Uber and Airbnb Innovative Digital Business Models Facilitate Global Expansion and Operational Resilience During the COVID-19 Pandemic

Almost every new startup wants to disrupt some traditional industry with a digital solution. Two of the most ingenious and most-valuable startups to achieve this goal are Uber and Airbnb. For example, most consumers who tap an Uber app to get a ride would never consider dialing an 800 number for a taxi. With all transactions performed by apps and automated processes, the entire process from hailing to paying for a ride is slick, quick, and easy and eliminates the use of cash or credit cards at the time of service. Similarly, Airbnb provides an easy-to-use digital platform to offer accommodations, dining, and leisure activities to guests worldwide with the click of a couple of buttons.

New Economies and COVID-19 Require New Digital Business Models

Uber and Airbnb are popular examples of companies that developed new digital business models to transform slow-to-innovative industries. A simple definition of a business model is the way a company generates revenue and makes a profit. On-demand and sharing (access-over-ownership) business models provide real-time fulfillment of goods and services, which have attracted millions of users worldwide. These models fit best when speed and/or convenience matter the most. The ground transportation, grocery, and restaurant industries are examples of hyper-growth categories in the on-demand world. The home-based accommodation and bicycle/scooter rental industries are good examples of high-growth categories in the sharing economy. Currently, forward-thinking companies that have reaped the benefits of rethinking their business models by applying digital solutions to reshape their industries are now adapting their business models by utilizing technology in even more new and creative ways to meet the demands and uncertainties of the COVID-19 pandemic. The sharing economy has been severely impacted by COVID-19 causing companies like Uber and Airbnb to make creative adjustments and develop new strategies to ensure their customers feel safe and how they will need to operate in the 'new normal.'

Uber On-Demand Business Model

Uber disrupted the taxi industry with a workforce that is essentially any person with a smartphone and a car. Location-aware smartphone apps bring drivers and passengers together, while in-app accounts make the cashless payment process effortless. By simply opening the Uber app and pressing the middle button for several seconds (a long press), customers can order a ride to their current location, selecting the kind of car they want. Payment is automatically charged to the credit card on file with receipts via e-mail.

The Uber concept developed in response to scarcity of taxies. It started on a snowy Paris night in 2008 when the two founders could not get a cab. They wanted a simple app that could get them a car with a tap. On June 1, 2015, the entrepreneurs celebrated Uber's fifth anniversary and announced that the company had grown into a transportation network covering 311 cities in 58 countries in North and South Americas, Europe, Africa, Asia Pacific, and the Middle East. By mid-2018, their global presence had grown tremendously over the past few years, and to achieve this phenomenal growth Uber has invested in new and developing technologies and partnerships. For example, the company partnered with Carnegie Mellon University to build robotic cars and purchased deCarta, a 40-person mapping start-up to reduce its dependence on Google Maps.

Airbnb Access-over-Ownership Business Model

Another disruption to a traditional industry occurred when Airbnb blindsided the hotel industry. Airbnb—probably the most global of the new startups—allows anyone with a spare apartment or room to run their own bed and breakfast by giving them a technology platform to market themselves to a global market. Just click a few buttons on Airbnb's website and type up a brief description of your property and its amenities, and your spare room can become a new source of income! By 2016, Airbnb hosts had accommodated 40 million guests in its 1.5 million listings in 34,000 cities in 190 countries. In mid-2018, Airbnb had accommodated over a whopping 150 million guests in 4 million listings—including 1,400 castles—in 65,000 cities and 191 countries around the globe. In comparison, Hilton, InterContinental, and Marriott, the largest hotel chains in the world, have less than one million rooms each.

Business Success of Uber and Airbnb in terms of Company Valuation, Growth, and Globalization

The ride-hailing app Uber and the housing rental app Airbnb are two of the most valuable start-ups, as displayed in **Figure 1.1.** Valuation of a company at its early stages is based heavily on its growth potential and future value. In contrast, the valuation of an established company is based on its present value, which is calculated using traditional financial ratios and techniques related to revenues or other assets.

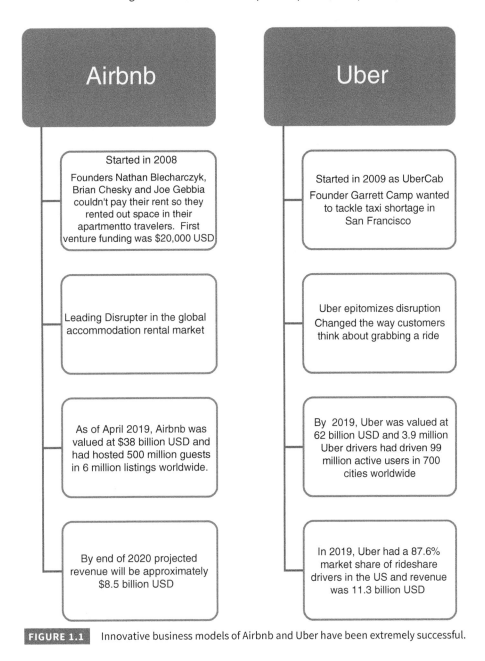

Airbnb

Started in 2008

Founders Nathan Blecharczyk, Brian Chesky and Joe Gebbia couldn't pay their rent so they rented out space in their apartmentto travelers. First venture funding was $20,000 USD

Leading Disrupter in the global accommodation rental market

As of April 2019, Airbnb was valued at $38 billion USD and had hosted 500 million guests in 6 million listings worldwide.

By end of 2020 projected revenue will be approximately $8.5 billion USD

Uber

Started in 2009 as UberCab

Founder Garrett Camp wanted to tackle taxi shortage in San Francisco

Uber epitomizes disruption Changed the way customers think about grabbing a ride

By 2019, Uber was valued at 62 billion USD and 3.9 million Uber drivers had driven 99 million active users in 700 cities worldwide

In 2019, Uber had a 87.6% market share of rideshare drivers in the US and revenue was 11.3 billion USD

FIGURE 1.1   Innovative business models of Airbnb and Uber have been extremely successful.

Uber's massive market value—estimated at $60 billion—is greater than 80% of all Standard & Poor (S&P) 500 companies, many of which have been around for 25, 50, or 100 years. Currently, investors value Airbnb at $31 billion—rivaling that of hotel giant Marriott International.

To achieve their phenomenal local and global growth, both Uber and Airbnb have used some interesting technology-enabled strategies. For example, Uber has been aggressive in going global. It uses "Ambassadors" who are paid to recruit new drivers from its competitor Lyft using an automated hiring, recruitment, and onboarding system that is far more efficient than the process used by traditional taxi companies. Ambassadors also offer free rides to new customers to advertise Uber by word of mouth in new cities, and drones are used to recruit new drivers and customers around the globe! Once a customer base has been established, Uber founder, Travis Kalanick, then actively lobbies governors worldwide to write new laws that favor Uber's business model.

However, globalization hasn't all been plain sailing for Uber. Since 2011, when Uber first expanded its services outside of the United States, Uber has encountered resistance in several countries such as

China, Russia, and Southeast Asia. Despite setbacks, it has been able to salvage market share in these countries by retaining a substantial share in joint ventures with local rivals such as Yandex.Taxi (https://taxi.yandex.ru) and Grab (https://www.grab.com/sg). More recently, Uber has shifted its focus to countries where it is convinced it can win, including India, Middle East, and North Africa, and has a particular interest in Saudi Arabia where Uber is focusing on recruiting female drivers who have only recently been allowed to drive there. Despite its optimism that its business model will be successful in these parts of the world, local competitors there also present undisputed barriers to Uber's ultimate success. For example, Uber sold its Chinese business to Didi Chuxing in 2016, putting an end to its very expensive, high-stakes battle over the lucrative Chinese market.

On the other hand, Airbnb growth strategies include developing new services to enhance their guests' travel experience, such as creating "Airbnb Plus - a listing of homes verified for quality and comfort" and identifying "Superhosts" who have consistently been rated highly by previous guests. They have also added "Travel Experiences" to allow their guests insider access to unexpected places together with a list of restaurants that have been recommended by many of their guests. But, Airbnb's most effective growth strategy has been increasing the number of countries where its services are offered. For example, since Airbnb unveiled its French platform in 2012, it has gone from strength to strength with a staggering 8.5 million French people using Airbnb properties between June 1 and August 31, 2019.

This strategy, however, has presented Airbnb organizers with some very interesting challenges that include handling a total of 65 different currencies, translating host listings between countries, dealing with foreign law agencies, and offering country-specific sign-up methods. For example, although Facebook or Google accounts work in the United States, these are not the best sign-up methods in other parts of the world, and just by allowing travelers to use Weibo (https://www.weibo.com/us) and WeChat (https://www.wechat.com/en), Airbnb is able to grow its customer base in China by 700%.

Uber and Airbnb Retool their Digital Business Models to Build Resilience during the COVID-19 Pandemic

While globalization has presented highly valued start-ups like Uber and Airbnb with huge opportunities for growth, the COVID-19 pandemic presented them with some daunting business challenges as people around the globe were told to stay home. In the early days of the pandemic, both Uber and Airbnb were faced with a significant downturn in demand as far fewer people took rides or sought accommodations for vacation or business, during COVD-19 lockdowns and Airbnb's plans to file a request to 'go public' were waylaid by pandemic-related turmoil in the stock market. This initial reaction has been followed by ongoing government and customer concerns about general health and safety issues associated with the pandemic. As a result, on-demand and sharing economy companies have been forced to make significant adjustments in response to unforeseen events and recent data show that their businesses are growing again thanks to agile thinking and creative adjustments they have made to their business models. For example, Airbnb made efforts to increase the variety of the accommodations they offer and use technology to broadcast their new offerings. In June

2020 Airbnb reported that bookings for entire homes and cabins and cottages in secluded areas increased significantly causing their gross booking value to grow for the first time since February 2020 and on August 19, 2020 it filed with the Security Exchange Commission (SEC) to 'go public'. In another creative move, Uber transformed itself from a solely ridesharing venture to a food delivery service. Consequently, their new mobile app 'Uber Eats' has become their key revenue generator amidst COVID-19. In creating Uber Eats, Uber offered restaurants a new way to connect with their customers and inject a modicum of positivity among the bad news plaguing the world during and after COVID-19. In quickly reacting to the unforeseen events of COVID-19, Uber and Airbnb have demonstrated the power of on-demand and sharing economy companies to make swift and significant adjustments to their business models by digitally transforming themselves.

At the end of the day, it is clear that technology plays a huge part in both enabling innovative products and services to facilitate local and global success by allowing gig workers and consumers in the on-demand and sharing economies to seamlessly connect with business services 24 hours a day, 365 days a year despite important cultural differences and the challenges of COVID-19.

Questions

1. In what ways are the Uber and Airbnb business models similar and different?
2. What challenges did Uber and Airbnb face when they went "global"?
3. What growth strategies are benefiting the global success of Uber and Airbnb? How do they differ?
4. How has technology helped or hindered Uber and Airbnb in the growth of their global business?
5. In what ways has the COVID-19 pandemic impacted Uber and Airbnb?

Sources: Compiled from Solomon (2016), Hawkins (2017), Henshall (2017), Domat (2018), Ledsom (2019), Airbnb.com, and Uber.com, Overstreet (2020).

 DID YOU KNOW?

*That **gig economy** is a new buzzword that refers to the rise in contracted work—or "gigs"—that aren't traditional jobs. Examples of these are ridesharing, home and apartment rentals, and food delivery and are made possible using apps and mobile devices. As many as one in every five jobs are currently contracted and it is estimated that over half of the U.S. workforce could find themselves doing contract or freelance work over the next decade. An example of "gig" work and how it affects the economy was offered in our opening case.*

IT architectures guide the process of planning, acquiring, building, modifying, and interfacing with deployed IT resources in a single department within an organization.

Legacy systems are older information systems that have been maintained over several decades because they fulfill critical needs.

Introduction

Many forward-thinking managers and entrepreneurs are digitally transforming their existing business models and reinventing their businesses. In a recent industry study, 87% of senior business leaders said digital transformation is a company priority and 79% of corporate strategists said they are reinventing their business and creating new revenue streams in new ways (Gartner, 2019). By no longer operating and maintaining outdated and complex **IT architectures** with a mix of **legacy systems** that can delay or prevent the release of innovative new products and services and absorb large portions of the information technology (IT) budget, companies can add value, increase their customer base, expand their business capabilities, and increase profits.

Companies such as Uber (https://www.uber.com), Airbnb (https://www.airbnb.com) Shyp (http://shyp.com), TaskRabbit (https://www.taskrabbit.com), and Lyft (https://www. lyft.com) are leveraging IT to create exciting new business models and revolutionize the way workers, businesses, and customers interact and compete. Peter Hinssen, a well-known business author, university lecturer, and digital consultant, described the change in digital technology as follows:

> Technology used to be nice. It used to be about making things a little bit better, a little bit more efficient. But, technology stopped being nice: it's disruptive. It's changing our business models, our consumer markets, our organizations. (MacIver, 2015)

As businesses continue to change their business models to accommodate the needs of the on-demand and sharing economies, IT professionals must constantly scan for innovative new technologies to provide business value, help shape the future of the business, and facilitate performance and growth in local and global markets. For example, smart devices, mobile apps, sensors, and technology platforms—along with increased customer demand for digital interactions and on-demand and shared services—have moved commerce in fresh new directions. We've all heard the phrase "there's an app for that," and that kind of consumer thinking drives the on-demand and sharing economies.

Business leaders today need to know what steps to take to get the most out of mobile, social, cloud, big data, analytics, visualization technologies, artificial intelligence and the Internet of Things (IoT) to move their business forward and enable new on-demand and sharing business models. Faced with opportunities and challenges, managers need to know how to leverage IT earlier and more efficiently than their competitors.

A goal of this book is to empower you to improve your use and management of IT by raising your understanding of IT terminology, practices, and tools and developing your IT skills to transform you into an informed IT user. Throughout this book, you will learn how digital technology is transforming business and society at all levels as the IT function takes on a key strategic role that determines an enterprise's success or failure. You will also be provided with an in-depth look at IT trends that have immediate and future capacity to influence products, services, competition, and business relationships. Along the way, we'll describe many ways in which IT is being used and can be used in business and provide you with the some of the terminology, techniques, and tools that enable organizations to leverage IT to improve their growth, performance, and sustainability.

In this opening chapter, you will learn about the powerful impacts of digital technology on people, business, government, entertainment, and society that are occurring today. You will also discover how leading companies are deploying digital technology and changing their business models, business processes, customer experiences, and ways of working. We will present examples of innovative products, services, and distribution channels to help you understand the digital revolution that is currently shaping the future of business, economy, and society and changing management careers. And, we'll explain why IT is important to you and how becoming an "informed user" of IT will add significant value to your career and overall quality of life.

1.1 | Doing Business in the On-Demand and Sharing Economies

LO1.1 Define *the differences between the on-demand and sharing economies and the six business objectives IT should focus on to enhance organizational performance, growth, and sustainability.*

The on-demand and sharing economies are revolutionizing commercial activities in businesses around the world. The businesses in these new economies are fueled by years of technology innovation and a radical change in consumer behavior. As companies become more highly digitized, it becomes more and more apparent that what companies can do depends on what their

IT and data management systems can do. For over a decade, powerful new digital approaches to doing business have emerged. And there is sufficient proof to expect even more rapid and dramatic changes due to IT breakthroughs and advances.

In market segment after market segment, mobile communications and technology stacks make it financially feasible for companies to bring together consumers and providers to purchase or share products and services. These capabilities have created the **on-demand economy** and the **sharing economy**. As Ev Williams, cofounder of Twitter (https://twitter.com/home) says,

On-demand economy is the economic activity created by technology companies that fulfill consumer demand through the immediate provisioning of products and services.

Sharing economy is an economic system in which goods or services are shared between private individuals, either free or for a fee, typically arranged through an online company or organization.

> *The internet makes human desires more easily attainable. In other words, it offers convenience. Convenience on the internet is basically achieved by two things: speed, and cognitive ease. If you study what the really big things on the internet are, you realize they are masters at making things fast and not making people think.*

The proliferation of smartphone-connected consumers, simple and secure purchase flows, and location-based services are a few of the market conditions and technological innovations that are propelling the explosion of on-demand and shared services.

Just as the rapid growth of online-only Amazon (https://www.amazon.com) and eBay transformed retail, the even faster growth of app-driven companies, such as Uber, Airbnb, and Grubhub (https://www.grubhub.com), has disrupted the taxi, hotel, and restaurant markets. As you read in the opening case, in six short years, Uber changed the taxi industry as it rose from start-up to the world's most valuable private technology company, and Airbnb tackled the fiercely competitive hotel market and attracted more than 60 million customers to become the third most valuable venture-capital-backed company in the world. Another example is Grubhub who became No. 1 in online food ordering, controlling over 20% of that $9 billion market. What today's successful technology businesses have in common are platform-based business models. Platforms consist of hardware, software, and networks that provide the connectivity for diverse transactions, such as ordering, tracking, user authentication, and payments. These business models are designed to serve today's on-demand economy, which is all about time (on-demand), convenience (tap an app), and personalized service (my way). For example, millennials want the ease of online payment over cash and insist on efficiency for all aspects of their lives, including shopping, delivery, and travel.

Key strategic and tactical questions that determine an organization's profitability and management performance are shown in **Figure 1.2.** Answers to each question require an understanding of the capabilities of mundane to complex IT, which ones to implement and how to manage them.

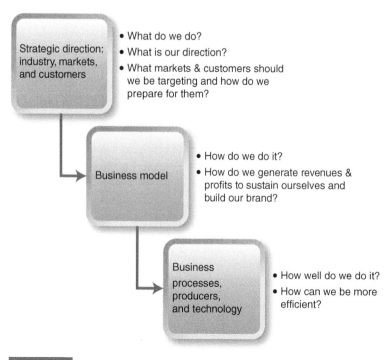

FIGURE 1.2 Key strategic and tactical questions.

Disruptive Digital Business Models

Digital transformation drives radical changes in **business models** to enable organizations to provide goods and services to customers in the way they want them delivered, when they want them, and where they want to have access to them.

Companies that adopt **digital business models** are better positioned to take advantage of business opportunities and survive. **Figure 1.3** describes seven highly disruptive business models and some of the companies that use them to differentiate their products and services.

Today, a top concern of well-established corporations, global financial institutions, born-on-the-Web retailers, and government agencies is how to design their digital business model to

- Deliver an incredible customer experience
- Turn a profit
- Increase market share
- Engage their employees

Business model is a company's core strategy for making a profit. It defines the products and/or services it will sell, its target market, costs associated with doing business, and the company's ongoing plans for achieving its goals.

Digital business model prescribes how businesses make money and meet their goals using digital technology, such as websites, social media, and mobile devices.

Business Model	• Description/Examples
Subscription	• Customer pays monthly payment for continued access to a specific product/service • *Netflix* • *Apple Music*
Freemium	• Customer gets 'basic' or free version of a product/service or a free trial. Has option to upgrade to a paid version of the product/service • *Linkedin* • *Dropbox*
Free	• Customer is the "product". Customer data is the most valuable part of the business along with his/her attention for advertisiing purposes • *Google* • *Facebook*
Access-over-Ownership	• Customer pays for temporary access to the product/service, but does not own it • *Zipcar* • *AirBnb*
Experience	• Customer is given a unique experience for which they are willing to pay a high price • *Tesla* • *Apple*
On-Demand	• Customer pays for a service they don't have time to do themselves, but is fulfilled by people with time, but short on money • *Uber* • *Taskrabbit*
Ecosystem	• Customer is sold an interdependent suite of products/services that when purchased, increase in value based on how many are owned • *Apple* • *Google*

FIGURE 1.3 Disruptive digital business models enable companies to engage customers to create value via websites, social channels, and mobile devices.

Customer experience describes the cumulative impact of multiple interactions over the course of a customer's contact with an organization.

In the digital (online) space, the **customer experience** must measure up to the very best the Web has to offer. Stakes are high for those who get it right—or wrong. There is a strong relationship between the quality of a firm's customer experience and loyalty, which, in turn, increases revenue. As a result, a firm's IT business objectives should be carefully and clearly defined.

IT's Role in the On-Demand and Sharing Economies

The 2018 IT Trends survey conducted by the Society of Information Management (SIM) reflects that the current state of IT management remains stable despite the massive changes present in the IT world today. Responses were analyzed from IT leaders in 793 highly digitized and tightly connected organizations. Results showed that companies are investing heavily in analytics, cybersecurity, cloud, application software development and maintenance, enterprise resource planning (ERP), and customer relationship management (CRM). These levels of investment are consistent with the top ten IT management concerns shown in **Table 1.1**, which clearly demonstrate a need for companies to continue to focus on strategic and organizational priorities such as cybersecurity, business–IT alignment, and **data analytics**.

Data analytics is the process of examining data sets to draw conclusions about the information they contain, usually with the aid of specialized information systems.

TABLE 1.1   Top Ten IT Management Issues

	IT Management Issues
1	Security, Cybersecurity and Privacy
2	Technology Alignment with the Business
3	Data Analytics
4	Compliance and Regulations
5	IT Cost Reduction & Controls
6	Business Cost Reduction & Controls
7	Innovation
8	Digital Transformation
9	Business Agility and Flexibility
10	IT Agility and Flexibility

Source: Adapted from Kappelman et al. (2019).

Respondents also indicated that in addition to cybersecurity, their most worrisome personal IT concerns centered around the skills shortage that has led to difficulties in finding and retaining highly skilled IT talent, the credibility of IT, and perception of IT leadership within an organization. On the business side, they listed alignment of business goals with IT goals, business continuity, and compliance/regulations as areas of concern. Once again, these findings point to one clear message—IT in the on-demand and sharing economies is all about safeguarding data and identifying and meeting customer needs. Each of these concerns will be addressed throughout the following chapters to help you understand how IT is managed to ensure corporate performance, growth, and sustainability goals are met.

IT—Business Objectives

Now, more than ever, IT must be responsive to the needs of consumers who are demanding a radical overhaul of business processes in companies across diverse industry sectors. Intuitive interfaces, around-the-clock availability, real-time fulfillment, personalized treatment, global consistency, and zero errors—this is the world to which customers have become increasingly accustomed. And, it's not just about providing a superior user or customer experience—when companies get it right, they can also offer more competitive prices because of lower costs, better operational controls, and open themselves up to less risk.

According to Chirantan Basu of Chron (Basu, 2017), to stay abreast of the ever-changing business landscape and customer needs, IT today must concentrate on the following six business objectives to enhance an organization's performance, growth, and sustainability:

1. **Product development**   From innovations in microprocessors to efficient drug-delivery systems, IT helps businesses respond quickly to changing customer demands.
2. **Stakeholder integration**   Companies use their investor relations websites to communicate with shareholders, research analysts, and others in the market.
3. **Process improvement**   An ERP system replaces dozens of legacy systems for finance, human resources, and other functional areas to increase efficiency and cost-effectiveness of internal business processes.
4. **Cost efficiencies**   IT allows companies to reduce transaction and implementation costs, such as costs of duplication and postage of e-mail versus snail mail.
5. **Competitive advantage**   Companies can use agile development, prototyping, and other systems methodologies to bring a product to market cost-effectively and quickly.
6. **Globalization**   Companies can outsource most of their noncore functions, such as HR and finance, to offshore companies and use Information Communication Technology (ICT) to stay in contact with its global employees, customers, and suppliers 24/7.

Every technology innovation triggers opportunities and threats to business models and strategies. With rare exceptions, every business model depends on a mix of IT, knowledge of its potential, requirements for success, and, equally important, its limitations.

Decades of technological innovation have given us smartphone apps, mobile payment platforms, GPS and map technology, and social authentication. These technologies are needed to build the infrastructure needed for on-demand services and sharing services.

This infrastructure—also referred to as a **technology platform** or **technology stack**—supports the exchange and coordination of staggering amounts of data.

In many consumer markets today, companies that do not have these mobile apps (Apple or Android) or other technology platforms that support the exchange of goods and services—no matter how useful their website—may find themselves losing their competitive edge. This often leads to customer dissatisfaction, which results in a considerably smaller customer base and inevitably leads to an inability to sustain performance and growth followed by decline and, in extreme cases, extinction.

These and many other technologies and their impact on how companies operate and compete will be discussed in the following chapters to enable you to understand the importance of IT for management and become a more informed user of IT.

Technology platform   is the operating system and computer hardware used as a base upon which other applications, processes, or technologies are developed.

Technology stack   is the multiple layers of hardware, software, network connectivity, and data analytics capability that comprise a technology platform.

IT at Work 1.1

Digital Transformation Drives Kroger's Mission to Improve Customer Satisfaction

Grocery store Kroger has long been a leader in customer satisfaction by creating unique, personalized shopping experiences that drive customer loyalty. Every year, they deliver more than 3 billion personalized recommendations to shoppers through their customer insights team and through their *Restock Kroger* project; they have created a seamless digital shopping experience for their customers to access anything, anywhere, anytime.

Promoting an omnichannel approach, Kroger offers its customers in-store and online experiences they don't distinguish between. Its goal is to deliver customers' needs at any point in time. Digital shelving, driverless grocery delivery, automated warehouse operations, on-demand delivery, and mini-grocery store setups in Walgreen's brick-and-mortar-pharmacies are just a few ways that Kroger is meeting customer needs through digital transformation.

Kroger CIO, Chris Hjelm, is proud of Kroger's commitment to data, innovation, and tech savvy initiatives that he has promoted during his time with the company. Some of the other innovative digital solutions already in place or being pilot tested at Kroger include the following:

- **Enhanced display for grocery environment (EDGE)** that displays prices, nutrition and allergy information along with videos and images on shelf-edge high-resolution screens to boost sales

- **Scan, Bag, Go** technology that allows shoppers to scan products using a provided handheld scanner or the Kroger mobile app

- **ClickList** online ordering services that offer targeted, personalized offers to shoppers

- **QueVision** that has lowered checkout times from an average of 4 minutes to less than 30 seconds and improved foot traffic management in stores by combining infrared sensors, predictive analytics, and management tools

- **Food at Safe Temperature (FAST) Alerts** that monitor temperature trends and alert store managers and facilities engineers of negative temperature trends before food safety issues arise

In his role as CIO of Kroger's $115 billion operation, Hjelm sees his key roles as twofold. He must "keep the trains running on time" and "create a sustainable competitive advantage by working on things that aren't being done elsewhere."

Sources: Compiled from The Kroger Co. (2018), Kroger 2019 Sustainability Report, and Zappa (2019).

Questions

1. Name four disruptive business models and describe what they offer to their customers.
2. How is IT contributing to the success of the on-demand and shared economies?
3. List the six IT business objectives.
4. What are the key strategic and tactical questions that determine an organization's profitability and management performance?
5. What is a business model?
6. What is a digital business model?
7. Give two examples of how companies are transitioning to digital business models.
8. What factors are driving the move to digital business models?

1.2 Business Process Improvement and Competition

Competitive advantage is when an organization differentiates itself by charging less and creating and delivering better quality products or services than its competitors.

Deliverables are tangible or intangible goods or services produced in a project and intended to be delivered to a customer.

LO1.2 Explain *the role of IT in improving business processes. Understand the concepts of business process reengineering and competitive advantage.*

One way that a company can gain a **competitive advantage** over its competitors is by improving business processes. Given that a company's success depends on the efficiency of its business processes, even small improvements in key processes can have significant payoff. All functions and departments in the enterprise have tasks they need to complete to produce outputs, or **deliverables**, in order to meet their objectives.

Before you can begin to improve something, you have to understand what it is you are improving. We'll start by defining a business process, looking at its characteristics, and then exploring ways in which a business process can be improved either incrementally or radically through business process reengineering (BPR).

What Is a Business Process?

In the simplest terms, a **business process** consists of activities that convert inputs into outputs by doing work.

Table 1.2 shows some examples of common business processes and the business units where they are used. In addition to business processes that are used within a business unit, some business processes can be **cross-functional** and involve two or more functions, for example, order fulfillment and product development, which is used in both sales and production/operations management.

Business process is a series of steps by which organizations coordinate and organize tasks to get work done within and across their different business functions.

Cross-functional business process involves two or more business functions.

TABLE 1.2 Examples of Business Processes in Business Units

Business Unit	Business Processes in Use
Accounting	Invoicing, reconciling accounts, auditing
Finance	Credit card or loan approval, estimating credit risk and financing terms
Human resources (HR)	Recruiting, hiring, assessing compliance with regulations, evaluating job performance
Information systems (IS/IT)	Generating and distributing reports, data visualizations, data analytics, data archiving
Marketing	Sales, product promotion, design and implementation of sales campaigns, qualifying a lead
Production and operations (POM)	Shipping, receiving, quality control, inventory management

Three Components of a Business Process. Business processes have the three basic components shown in **Figure 1.4**. They involve inputs, activities, and deliverables.

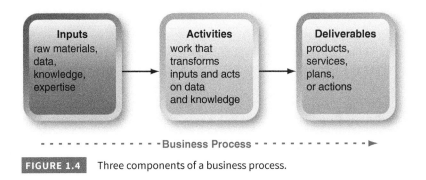

FIGURE 1.4 Three components of a business process.

Processes can be **formal** or **informal**. Routine formal processes are typically referred to as **standard operating procedures (SOPs)**. Although enterprises would prefer to formalize their informal processes in order to better understand, share, and optimize them, in many situations process knowledge remains in people's heads and is difficult to formalize.

Processes range from slow, rigid to fast-moving, adaptive. Rigid processes can be structured to be resistant to change, such as those that enforce security or compliance regulations. Adaptive processes are designed to respond to change or emerging conditions, particularly in marketing and IT.

Formal process is a process that has documented and well-established steps. For example, order taking and credit approval processes.

Informal process is a process that is typically undocumented, has inputs that may not yet been identified, and are knowledge-intensive.

Standard operating procedures (SOP) is a well-defined and documented way of doing something. An effective SOP states who will perform the tasks; what materials to use; and where, how, and when the tasks are to be performed. SOPs are needed for the handling of food, hazardous materials, or situations involving safety, security, or compliance.

Improving Business Processes

Designing an effective process can be complex because you need a deep understanding of the inputs and outputs (also known as deliverables), how things can go wrong, and how to prevent things from going wrong. For example, Dell had implemented a new process to reduce the time that tech support spent handling customer service calls. In an effort to minimize the length of the call, tech support's quality dropped so much that customers had to call multiple times to solve their problems. The new process had backfired—increasing the time to resolve computer problems and aggravating Dell customers.

The importance of efficient business processes and continuous process improvement cannot be overemphasized. Why? Because 100% of an enterprise's performance is the result of its processes. Maximizing the use of inputs in order to carry out similar activities better than one's competitors is a **critical success factor (CSF)**. Poorly designed, flawed, or outdated business processes waste resources, increase costs, cause delays, and aggravate customers. For example, when customers' orders are not filled on time or correctly, customer loyalty suffers, returns increase, and reshipping increases costs. The blame may not be employee incompetence, but a flawed order fulfillment process.

Critical success factor (CSF) is an element that is necessary to ensure the success of an organization or project, that is, access to adequate financial resources, clear definition of goals, realistic calendar of tasks and activities.

Don't Automate, Obliterate!

In today's on-demand economy, incrementally improving a business process isn't always sufficient to create the type of change required. Instead, radical changes need to occur to meet higher customer expectations. To do this, companies have to go beyond simply automating an existing process. They must reinvent the entire business process, including reducing the number of steps required, eliminating documents, developing automated decision-making, and dealing with regulatory and fraud issues. Operating models, skills, organizational structures, and roles need to be redesigned to match the reinvented processes. Data models should be adjusted and rebuilt to enable better decision-making, performance tracking, and customer insights.

Leading organizations have come to recognize that it can take a long time to see the benefits of traditional large-scale projects that migrate all current processes to digital and sometimes they don't work. Instead, successful companies are reinventing processes, challenging everything related to an existing process, and rebuilding it using cutting-edge digital technology. For example, rather than creating technology tools to help back-office employees type customer complaints into their systems, leading organizations create self-serve options for customers to type in their own complaints.

Business Process Reengineering. The process by which these types of radical process change can be achieved to improve productivity, **cycle time**, and quality is referred to as **business process reengineering (BPR)**. Its slogan is "Don't automate, obliterate!" (Hammer and Champy, 2006).

Cycle time is the period to complete one cycle of an operation or to complete a function, job, or task from start to finish.

Business process reengineering (BPR) is the radial redesign of core business processes to achieve a dramatic improvement in productivity, cycle times, and quality.

Consisting of the eight stages shown in **Figure 1.5**, BPR proposes that simply applying IT to a manual or outdated process does not always optimize it. Instead, processes need to be examined to determine whether they are still necessary. After unnecessary processes are identified and eliminated, the remaining ones are redesigned (or reengineered) in order to automate or streamline them. Next, the new process is implemented and put into operation and its performance is evaluated. Finally, the process is reassessed over time to continually improve it.

Business Process Reengineering

1. Develop Vision and Objectives
2. Understand Existing Processes
3. Identify Process for Redesign
4. Identify Change Levers
5. Implement New Process
6. Make New Process Operational
7. Evaluate New Process
8. Perform Continuous Improvement

FIGURE 1.5   Eight phases of BPR.

The goal of BPR is to eliminate unnecessary, non-value-added processes and simplify and automate the remaining processes to significantly reduce cycle time, labor, and costs. For example, reengineering the credit approval process cuts time from several days or hours to minutes or less. Simplifying processes naturally reduces the time needed to complete the process, which also cuts down on errors.

After eliminating waste, IT can enhance business processes by (1) automating existing manual processes; (2) expanding the data flows to reach more functions in order to make it possible for sequential activities to occur in parallel; and (3) creating innovative business processes that, in turn, create new business models. For instance, consumers can scan an image of a product and land on an e-commerce site, such as Amazon.com, selling that product. This process flips the traditional selling process by making it customer-centric.

With the help of **business process management (BPM)** software, business processes performed either by computers or manually can be mapped and new ones designed. The software includes built-in templates showing workflows and rules for various functions, such as rules for credit approval. These templates and rules provide consistency and high-quality outcomes. For example, Oracle's WebLogic Server Process Edition includes server software and process integration tools for automating complex business processes, such as handling an insurance claim.

However, BPM initiatives can be extremely challenging, and in order to be successful, BPM requires buy-in from a broad cross section of the business, the right technology selection, and highly effective change management processes. You will read more about optimizing business processes and role of BPM in the alignment of IT and business strategy in Chapter 13.

Business process management (BPM) consists of the methods, tools, and technology to support and continuously improve business processes.

Competition

Understanding trends that affect new ways of doing business and getting ahead of those trends by adding, deleting, and changing existing business processes gives organizations an important advantage over their competitors. Basically, this requires radically improving business processes to offer unique products or services or convince customers your business is a more attractive alternative to your competitors. Helping a company gain, maintain, and sustain a competitive advantage in the market is a very important function of IT, which will be discussed in detail in Chapter 12.

Influential industry leaders cite "new competition" as their biggest business challenge. Once an enterprise has learned to compete well in the market, it can only continue to excel by continually improving its business processes. Maintaining a competitive advantage requires forecasting market trends, staying abreast of industry changes, and developing innovative strategies to stay ahead of the competition. It also demands continuously tracking competitors and monitoring their future plans and promptly taking corrective action to outmaneuver them. To achieve this, an organization must have an IT function that is agile, flexible, and responsive (discussed in Chapter 12). IT agility, flexibility, and mobility are tightly interrelated and fully dependent on an organization's IT infrastructure and architecture, which are discussed in Chapter 2. **IT at Work 1.2** demonstrates how Coca-Cola transformed Costa Coffee by radically improving its business processes and completely replacing its IT architecture to meet and beat the competition.

IT at Work 1.2

Coca-Cola Gives Costa Coffee a Greenfield IT Opportunity to Ramp Up Global Retail Operations

Coca-Cola recently acquired 4,000-store Costa Coffee chain from Whitbread, a British Hospitality group, for $4.9 billion USD. The acquisition is part of Coca-Cola's strategy to build a coffee brand that will rival Starbucks in a global coffee shop market that is currently valued at $165 billion USD. The acquisition expands the existing Coca-Cola coffee lineup that already includes the market-leading Georgia brand in Japan, plus coffee products in many other countries.

In setting up Costa Coffee as a distinct entity, Coca-Cola also invested in a new foundation of digital platforms to fuel its ambitions of competing with Starbucks on a global scale. The acquisition gives Coca-Cola a strong, global coffee platform with a presence in more than 30 countries in Europe, Asia Pacific, the Middle East, and Africa and the potential for additional expansion. Founded in London, in 1971, Costa Coffee has become a major coffee brand across the world with nearly 4,000 retail outlets with highly trained baristas, a coffee vending operation, for-home coffee formats, and Costa's state-of-the-art Roastery.

Not many companies can create their IT organization from scratch, but with their acquisition by Coca-Cola, Costa Coffee was handed the golden opportunity to swap out its old legacy IT for new platforms, applications, and a ramped-up talent base. For Phil Scully, Costa's CIO, it was a dream come true. "It's as close to a greenfield IT opportunity as you'll ever get," he exuded, and "a rare opportunity that I'm hugely privileged to be able to take."

Usually, when companies are acquired, they must integrate their IT operations and services with those of the company acquiring them. In the Coca-Cola–Costa Coffee acquisition, that was not the case. Instead, Costa Coffee was offered the opportunity to build a brand-new IT function to connect to Coca-Cola's IT systems. To achieve this, Costa Coffee will have to work through a digital transformation to transition from the system it shares with its former parent, Whitbread, under a series of technology service agreements (TSAs) for Human Resources, Entity Resource Planning, CRM, Supply Chain, and other core systems.

Scully took over as Costa Coffee CIO in 2017 and since then he has taken huge strides in digital transformation, most of which has focused on enhancing customer and in-store capabilities. As Costa Coffee takes hold of its own IT destiny, the pressure will be on to build an advanced digital capability that will drive Coca-Cola's and Costa Coffee's goals. Cloud IT will be critical to their plan. Scully aims to move from a completely physical data center to the cloud to unlock opportunities such as fully upgrading its ERP systems to become a cloud-only business. The shift to the cloud is designed to provide IT, systems, and data management that is as consistent, repeatable, and high quality as its coffee is at its thousands of outlets around the world.

The transformation also demands a rapid ramp-up of talent. Scully is recruiting about 50% more IT professionals from around the world to create a blend of 130 to 140 permanent, contract, and outsourced IT staff to help him achieve his vision.

Sources: Compiled from Caballero (2018), Wood and Sweney (2018), MacIver (2019), and https://www.coca-colacompany.com.

Questions

1. What is a business process? Give three examples.
2. What is the difference between business deliverables and objectives?
3. List and give examples of the three components of a business process.
4. Explain the differences between formal and informal processes.
5. What is an SOP?
6. What is the purpose of BPM?

1.3 | IT Innovation and Disruption

LO1.3 Describe *how IT is disrupting the way that companies operate, the IT megatrends that are driving organizational performance, growth, and sustainability and how COVID-19 is accelerating digital transformation.*

Digital technology creates new markets, businesses, products, and careers. As digital technology changes the way consumers and retailers buy and sell products, companies must adapt and innovate to ensure their product offerings, platforms, technologies, and search options cater to these changing needs.

To qualify as a digital disruption, it must

1. Be a threat to personal or business goals in the short or long term
2. Must be digital, for example, related to the IoT, a mobile app, a new technology, or anything related to the digital evolution

Social–Mobile–Analytics–Cloud (SMAC) Model

We are in the era of **social–mobile–analytics–cloud (SMAC)** computing that is reshaping business strategies and day-to-day operations (**Figure 1.6**).

Social–mobile–analytics–cloud (SMAC) is the concept that the convergence of four technologies is currently driving business innovation and digital transformation.

Estimated 15 billion devices are connected to the Internet—forecasted to hit 50 billion by 2020 as more devices connect via mobile networks	Current 4.2 billion IoT devices projected to increase to 24 billion in 2020. This represents 73% of the total Internet-connected base
79% of online adults and 68% of all Americans use Facebook. Mobile use generates 30% of Facebook's ad revenue.	U.S. mobile commerce sales top $104.05 billion Facebook dominates all other social platforms with audience reach

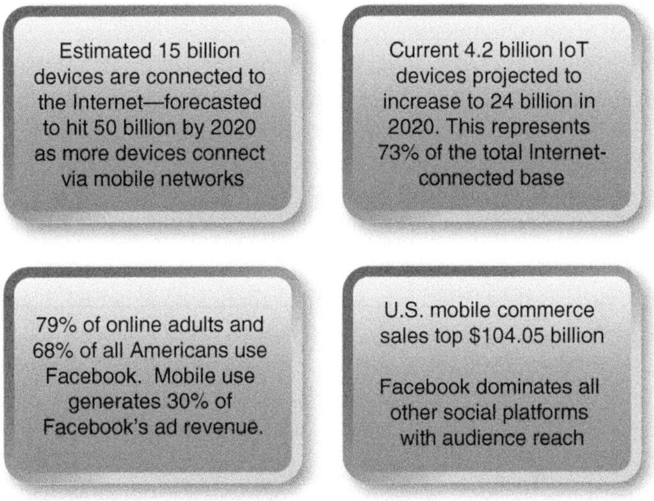

FIGURE 1.6   SMAC reshapes business strategies and day-to-day operations.

The cloud consists of huge data centers accessible via the Internet and forms the core by providing 24/7 access to storage, applications, and services. Handhelds and wearables, such as FitBit, Pebble, and Apple Watch, and their users form the edge. Social channels connect the core and edge. The SMAC integration creates the technical and services infrastructure needed for digital business. This infrastructure makes it possible to meet the expectations of employees, customers, and business partners given that almost everyone is connected (social), everywhere they go (mobile), gets the information they need (analytics), and has 24/7 access to products and services (cloud).

Here are three examples of SMAC's influence:

1. **Powerful social influences impact advertising and marketing**   Connections and feedback via social networks have changed the balance of influence. Consumers are more likely to trust tweets from ordinary people than recommendations made by celebrity endorsements. And, negative sentiments posted or tweeted can damage brands.

2. **Consumer devices go digital and offer new services**   The Nike+ FuelBand wristband helps customers track their exercise activities and calories burned. The device links to a mobile app that lets users post their progress on Facebook.

3. **eBay's move to cloud technology improves sellers' and buyers' experiences** The world's largest online marketplace, eBay, moved its IT infrastructure to the cloud. With cloud computing, eBay is able to introduce new types of landing pages and customer experiences without the delay associated with having to buy additional computing resources.

The balance of power has shifted as business is increasingly driven by individuals for whom mobiles are an extension of their body and mind. They expect to use location-aware services, apps, alerts, social networks, and the latest digital capabilities at work and outside work. To a growing extent, customer loyalty and revenue growth depend on a business's ability to offer unique customer experiences that wow customers more than competitors can.

Technology Mega Trends

For 21st-century enterprises, connectivity, big data and analytics, artificial intelligence, and **digitization** are technology **mega trends** that cannot be ignored. Business breakthroughs and innovation would be impossible without them. They also mark the difference between outdated 20th-century business models and practices and those of today's on-demand economy.

The most influential IT mega trends driving digital transformation of companies in the on-demand economy are discussed next.

Connectivity.
Companies need to connect with consumers and business partners across multiple channels and devices using digital platforms that consist of hardware, software (mobile apps), networks (social media), (embedded sensors), and **cloud computing**.

For example, rather than run applications or programs from software stored on a computer or server owned by the company, cloud computing allows companies to access the same kinds of applications through the Internet. Major business cloud computing providers include Amazon Web Services (AWS), Cisco Powered, Dell Cloud Solutions, Google Cloud, IBM Cloud Solutions, and Teradata Cloud. One of the many benefits of cloud is that it provides the flexibility to acquire or expand connectivity and computing power as needed for operations, business transactions, and communication.

Expanded connectivity supports smart products, which can sense, process, report, and take corrective action, such as smart clothing, watches, phones, to smart buildings and smart cities. This IoT is becoming a driving force in the on-demand and sharing economies

Connectivity pushes other sub trends, like **big data**, to create market opportunities for new products and services, such as social sentiment analysis, open innovation, new insurance business models, and micro personalized marketing and medicines.

Big Data and Data Analytics.
There is no question that the increasing volume of data can be valuable, but only if they are processed and available when and where they are needed. The problem is that the amount, variety, structure, and speed of data being generated or collected by enterprises differ significantly from traditional data. Big data stream in from multiple channels and sources, including the following:

- Mobile devices and machine-to-machine sensors embedded in everything from airport runways to casino chips (Later in this chapter, you will read more about the IoT.)
- Social content from texts, tweets, posts, blogs
- Clickstream data from the Web and Internet searches
- Video data and photos from retail and user-generated content
- Financial, medical, research, customer, and business-to-business transactions

Big data are 80% to 90% unstructured. **Unstructured data** do not have a predictable format like a credit card application form but may instead consist of large volumes of text. Huge volumes of unstructured data flooding into an enterprise are too much for traditional technology to process and analyze quickly. Big data tend to be more time sensitive than traditional (or small) data. Data collected from social, mobile, and other channels are

---

Digitization is the process of transforming any kind of activity or information into a digital format that can be collected, stored, searched, and analyzed electronically and efficiently.

Mega trends are forces that shape or create the future of business, the economy, and society.

Cloud computing is an Internet-based computing system consisting of many computers and other devices where computer infrastructure, access to applications, software, processing power, and so on are shared.

Big data is a process that is used when traditional data mining and handling techniques cannot uncover the insights and meaning of the underlying data that are usually unstructured (text), time sensitive, or extremely large.

Unstructured data is data that either does not have a predefined format or is not organized in a predefined manner. Unstructured data is typically text, although it may also contain some dates and numbers.

analyzed to gain insights and make smart decisions that drive up the bottom line. Machine-generated data from sensors and social media texts are main sources of big data.

Big data has been one of the most disruptive forces businesses have seen in a long time and impacts people, processes, and profits. When an enterprise harnesses its data and can act on analytic insights, it can turn the challenges into opportunities.

Artificial Intelligence and Robotics. To improve their ability to meet evolving customer expectations in a timely manner, digital innovators use technology to automate, streamline, or eliminate their processes. An example of this is robotic process automation that uses software and artificial intelligence to accelerate administrative activities. One bank saw its mortgage application time drop from 20 to 2 days after implementing technology to automate the document-intensive application process. It is estimated that by 2022, artificial intelligence and machine-learning systems will handle most customer interactions. These systems will be highly attuned to individual customer preferences and will tailor each engagement according to a customer's context and current need. Consequently, customers will quickly become accustomed to this level of valet service and won't stay with companies that do not anticipate their needs.

Digitization. Across industries, companies are attempting to transform their disconnected or disjointed approaches to customers, products, services, and operating models to an always-on, real-time, and information-rich marketplace. Some leaders are redesigning their capabilities and operating models to take full advantage of digital technologies to keep step with the "connected" consumer and attract talent. Others are creating qualitatively new business models—and tremendous value—around disruptive digital opportunities. In doing so, these companies secure not only continued relevance but also superior returns.

Digitization often requires that old wisdom be combined with new skills, for example, by training a merchandising manager to program a pricing algorithm and creating new roles, such as user-experience designer. The benefits of digitizing processes, through BPR, are huge. By digitizing information-intensive processes, costs can be cut by up to 90% and turnaround times improved by several orders of magnitude.

Examples span multiple industries. For example, one bank digitized its mortgage application and decision process, cutting the cost per new mortgage by 70% and slashing time to preliminary approval from several days to just one minute. A telecommunications company created a self-serve, prepaid service where customers could order and activate phones without back-office involvement. A shoe retailer built a system to manage its in-store inventory that enabled it to know immediately whether a shoe and size was in stock—saving time for customers and sales staff. An insurance company built a digital process to automatically adjudicate a large share of its simple claims.

In addition, replacing paper and manual processes with software allows businesses to automatically collect data that can be mined to better understand process performance, cost drivers, and causes of risk. Real-time reports and **dashboards** on digital-process performance enable managers to address problems before they get out of control. For example, quality issues in a company's supply chain can be identified and remedied more rapidly by monitoring customer buying behavior and feedback in digital channels.

Dashboards is an easy-to-read, often single-page, real-time user interface, showing a graphical presentation of the current status and historical trends of an organization's key performance indicators to enable instantaneous and informed decisions to be made.

Machine-to-Machine Technology. Sensors can be embedded in most products. Objects that connect themselves to the Internet include cars, heart monitors, stoplights, and appliances. Sensors are designed to detect and react, such as Ford's rain-sensing front wipers that use an advanced optical sensor to detect the intensity of rain or snowfall and adjust wiper speed accordingly. **Machine-to-machine (M2M) technology** and the **Internet of Things (IoT)** are widely used to automate business processes in industries ranging from transportation to health care. By adding sensors to trucks, turbines, roadways, utility meters, heart monitors, vending machines, and other equipment they sell, companies can track and manage their products remotely.

When devices or products are embedded with sensors, companies can track their movements or monitor interactions with them. Business models can be adjusted to take advantage of what is learned from this behavioral data. For example, an insurance company

Machine-to-machine (M2M) technology enables sensor-embedded products to share reliable real-time data via radio signals.

Internet of Things (IoT) refers to a set of capabilities enabled when physical things are connected to the Internet via sensors.

offers to install location sensors in customers' cars. By doing so, the company develops the ability to price the drivers' policies on how a car is driven and where it travels. Pricing is customized to match the actual risks of operating a vehicle rather than based on general proxies—driver's age, gender, or location of residence. **Table 1.3** lists several opportunities for improvement through the application of embedded physical things.

TABLE 1.3 Improvement Opportunities for Embedded Sensors

Industry Sector	Application	Payoff
Oil and gas	Exploration and development rely on extensive sensor networks placed in the earth's crust. Sensors can produce accurate readings of the location, structure, and dimensions of potential fields	Lower development costs and improved oil flows
Health care	Sensors and data links can monitor patients' behavior and symptoms in real time and at low cost, allowing physicians to more precisely diagnose disease and prescribe treatment regimens	Reduce hospitalization and treatment costs by $1 billion per year in the United States
Retail	Sensors can capture shoppers' profile data stored in their membership cards to help close purchases	Additional information and discounts at point of sale
Farming	Ground sensors can take into account crop and field conditions and adjust the amount of fertilizer that is spread on areas that need more nutrients	Reduction in time and cost
Advertising	Billboards can scan people passing by, assessing how they fit consumer profiles, and instantly change displayed messages based on those assessments	Better targeted marketing campaigns; flexibility; increased revenues
Automotive	Systems can detect imminent collisions and take evasive action, such as automatic braking systems	Potential accident reduction savings of more than $100 billion annually

COVID-19 Accelerates Digital Transformation

Recent developments surrounding the COVID-19 global pandemic have had a far-reaching effect on the global economy and the professional and personal lives of individuals. Consequently, companies in all industry sectors have had to act much more quickly to create new business models that address the regulatory requirements of COVID-19 lockdowns along with ensuing health and safety concerns and new purchasing habits of consumers, vendors and partners. Most companies have achieved this goal primarily by integrating new innovative information and communication technologies into their business models to increase personal engagement with consumers, vendors and partners, maintain a competitive advantage in the market and develop the operational resilience needed to safeguard their sustainability. As a result, the rate of digital transformation around the globe has increased significantly.

This accelerated digital transformation has not been limited to on-demand and sharing companies like Uber and Airbnb as described in our opening case. The unexpected events of COVID-19 have forced the pace of digital transformation to increase in all companies – large and small – and in all industry sectors as many struggle not only to compete, but also survive within uncertain times. In a recent survey of 2,500 enterprises across many different industry sectors the *COVID-19 Digital Engagement Report* shows that 97% of enterprise decision makers believed that the pandemic has accelerated companies' digital communications strategies by an average of six years; 95% are seeking new ways to engage customers, and 92% feel that transforming digital communications must be a priority in addressing current business challenges (Sil, 2020).

When people were asked to stay home and social distancing was shown to be the most effective way to slow the spread of the virus many companies saw their sales rapidly decrease, were unable to resume production and lost face-to-face contact with their customers. Small companies that were using limited technology prior to the pandemic have been particularly vulnerable to the impact of the pandemic. The mandated lockdowns and restricted activity caused their customers to engage in fewer activities outside of their own homes and began to replace face-to-face purchases of food, medications and clothing at 'bricks and mortar' establishments with e-commerce transactions for the first time. As a result, small firms have had to change their mindset and business models to include new and innovative technologies to sustain them. In addition, companies of all sizes have begun to rely heavily on Chatbots and other omni-channel technologies to provide online interactive customer service to consumers. To ensure continuity many companies have also relaxed their policies to allow employees to work from home using information communication technology (ICT) apps like WhatsApp, Skype and Zoom while securing their expanded networks with cloud security tools such as Data Network Solutions (DNS), DHCP, and IP Address Management. Interactions with vendors and partners have followed a similar pattern as sales meetings, stockholder meetings and industry conferences have necessarily evolved into virtual events.

The impact of COVID-19 has not been limited to private sector companies. Education, healthcare, and law enforcement and government agencies around the globe are also responding to the need to more rapidly digitally transform themselves. For example, schools at all levels from elementary to university are training teachers to use the same digital tools that private companies are using to enable an effective and secure virtual learning experience for their students. This transition has not come without issues. For example, one South Carolina county recently had to suspend its entire virtual learning program because of a ransomware attack.

In healthcare more and more patients are being offered 'tele-health' visits and IBM is exploring how artificial intelligence and robotics can be used to drastically speed up timelines to develop drugs and therapies to lessen the severity of COVID-19 when contracted by those in high risk groups.

In law enforcement, agencies are employing innovative technologies to deploy contactless crime investigation techniques. For example, agencies around the globe are intensifying their use of aerial drones to identify and eradicate illegal drug crop production, illegal fishing, contraband smuggling and human trafficking, and in some countries robots and drones are even being used to identify people who are not wearing masks in public places.

Government agencies at all levels have closed their doors and are relying heavily on maintaining virtual communications with their constituents. In many cases this has made the decision process for creating and enforcing public policies more widely available and transparent to constituents with both positive and negative consequences. These and other innovative technologies are discussed in detail in subsequent chapters.

Lessons Learned

Those companies that have adapted quickly to change by exploiting digital technology and software are outperforming their peers. Companies that change the way they view and use technology from being a cost center and operational function to be a genuine competitive differentiator will reap the benefits. The five factors companies attribute these benefits to can be summed up in the following Lessons Learned:

1. **Exploit the power of software**   Become "app-centric" and extend core business functions to include software development.
2. **Develop, deliver, disrupt—quickly!** Embrace agile development techniques and broadly implement DevOps.
3. **Boost speed and efficiency with automated programming interfaces (APIs)**   Take a managed approach to use APIs for building full-function Web applications (particularly mobile apps) and for integrating back-office systems.
4. **Leverage third-party innovation**   Take a more managed approach to use APIs for integrating third-party services into applications and enable external develop access to systems and data.
5. **Maximize returns with smarter IT investments**   Get smarter at assessing and prioritizing IT investments to maximize return on investment and put portfolio management in place to prioritize and track IT programs.

Business opportunities presented by today's technology innovations are being realized on an unprecedented scale. **Cloud services**, big data, mobility, digitization, and the IoT are just a few of the emerging technologies that will build operational resilience, disrupt many industries and shake up competitive positions.

Cloud services   is any computing resource that is provided over the Internet on demand.

In the pandemic and post-pandemic era, innovation through disruptive technology is necessary for any company to thrive in an on-demand and sharing economy where increased competition, expanded global markets and empowered customers define success. **IT at Work 1.3** demonstrates how one company successfully triumphed over its competition by using disruptive technology to disrupt itself!

IT at Work 1.3

Netflix Digitally Disrupts Itself!

In its first incarnation, Netflix simply provided a better way to rent DVDs. Going head to head with the then giant Blockbuster Video, a company that charged high late fees for DVD returns, Netflix allowed its customers to rent DVDs by mail with no late fees! Although the Netflix model didn't offer the instant gratification of taking home a DVD from a local store, it was simpler to rent from Netflix, and customers preferred the affordability Netflix offered. In this way, Netflix had seriously disrupted Blockbuster's business.

The subsequent introduction of Netflix's subscription streaming service also seriously disrupted major television networks such as ABC, CBS, and NBC. Until a few years ago, viewers could only watch TV shows on their television sets. As a result, TV moguls ABC, CBS, and NBC were able to charge high advertisement rates and high subscription rates. When Netflix came on the scene, traditional TV broadcasting companies had to completely reshape how they delivered their offerings. In doing so, their business operations were

significantly disrupted. They no longer had the bulk of the market, their advertisement revenues dropped substantially, and their costs have increased to provide Webcasting services such as video-on-demand and Web delivery of content. However, Netflix didn't stop at disrupting other competitors—it went on to disrupt itself!

With the entry of more and more digital Webcast services such as HULU, ROKU, Sling TV, Amazon Prime Video and Netflix were facing increasingly stiff competition. To survive and prosper, Netflix separated its first-run movie rental offerings from its Web streaming services and runs two business models simultaneously. In its latest incarnation, Netflix is focusing on edging out its competition with original programming. At the 2018 Emmy Awards, Netflix had more Emmy nominations than premium cable giant HBO and took home 23 prestigious awards! In creating a new market, Netflix has avoided being displaced by its competitors and is one of the rare companies that has successfully disrupted itself.

Sources: Compiled from Muck (2017), Romero (2019), and netflix.com.

Questions

1. What are the benefits of cloud computing?
2. What is M2M technology? Give an example of a business process that could be automated with M2M.
3. Describe the relationships in the SMAC model.
4. What impacts does the SMAC model have on business?
5. Why have mobile devices given consumers more power in the marketplace?
6. Explain why connectivity is important in today's on-demand economy.
7. In what ways is IT disrupting business?
8. In what ways has COVID-19 accelerated digital transformation?

1.4 IT and You

LO1.4 Discuss *what it means to be an "informed user" of IT and the ways in which IT can add value to your career path and job performance.*

Today, IT and information systems touch nearly all aspects of our lives. IT is a part of our social life, our work, and every business process, and it is no longer the sole responsibility of the IT department. Just think about much of your day you spend interacting with technology—your iPad, PC, and smartphone. The 2018 Global Mobile Consumer Survey reported that American consumers check their smartphones an average of 52 times each day (Spangler, 2018). Aggregated across the estimated 270 million American smartphone users, that's 12.69 billion "looks" per day!

These findings leave little doubt that IT impacts the way you work, the way you learn, the way you communicate and socialize, and the way you entertain yourself. Today, success in any field, be it health care, marketing, finance, accounting, law, education, sports, entertainment, etc. requires much more than a cursory knowledge of IT. IT is and will remain the foundation of the global economy and is especially important in the on-demand economy.

On-Demand 'Gig' Workers

Currently, approximately 57 million Americans participate as gig workers either through primary or secondary jobs and it is projected that by 2023 more than half of the US workforce will either be gig economy workers or have worked independently (Mitic, 2020). In a recent survey of managers, internal employees and external workers conducted by SHRM and SAP SuccessFactors (Bolden-Barrett, 2019), nearly 20% of all gig workers said they preferred the flexibility and autonomy of gig work and managers also favor gig work because it allows staffing levels to easily be adjusted according to changes in the economy. Approximately one-third also said they earn more as an external worker that they did as an internal employee. The three top reasons respondents gave for becoming gig workers were:

- Want to be an independent contractor, freelancer, temporary worker or consultant (49%).
- Want to choose the number of hours they work (40%).
- Want to be able to work from any location (33%).

Other reasons include work-life balance and family and health concerns which are becoming more pressing amid the COVID-19 pandemic.

Many on-demand workers also have a strong entrepreneurial drive and are working in the on-demand and sharing economies to build a business. This entrepreneurial spirit is reflected in the ways that on-demand workers are compensated. While the 40-hour work week is still alive and well, sources of income have changed. Instead of one paycheck, on-demand workers typically receive their income from three different sources:

1. On-demand work
2. Contracting and consulting
3. Running a business

Along with the start-up companies typically associated with on-demand work, such as Uber, Lyft, Door Dash and TaskRabbit, some of today's largest companies have also begun to incorporate on-demand workers into their growth strategies to cultivate a more nimble, competitive, and specialized workforce that provides higher quality and faster work outcomes at a lower overall cost. A growing number of apps offer excellent work opportunities and the decreased need for a physical presence 'at work', is making it easier than ever for workers to have multiple simultaneous jobs and what was once considered a fringe form or employment is now becoming the 'new normal' because of the increased demand created by the COVID-19 pandemic. Technology platforms where you can post, find, and perform on-demand work include Avvo, Catalant, Field Nation, Kelly Services, OnForce, TaskRabbit, Upwork, and Wonolo.

Changes in Work Status. While the on-demand and sharing economies provides positive opportunities, they can also offer limited benefits and inferior infrastructure. Take, for example, the "contractor" model that companies like Uber use. Initially, Uber set the standard for on-demand business by labeling its drivers "independent contractors" and essentially claiming that all its drivers were self-employed. This pushed many of the costs of doing business onto the independent contractors' shoulders and deprived them of baseline labor protections such as worker's compensation, social security contributions, minimum wage, and discrimination protections.

This business model also allowed companies using the Uber model to sidestep federal, state, and county taxes and insurance premiums and undercuts competitors that used a traditional W-2 hiring model. However, not all on-demand and sharing economy businesses use the Uber model.

Some companies treat their workers as employees from the start, while others have switched to the W-2 model, and both approaches are reaping benefits. Shyp CEO Kevin Gibbon posted on LinkedIn that the move to employee status was "an investment in a longer-time relationship with our couriers, which we believe will ultimately create the best experience for our customers." After moving to the W-2 model, Shyp had only 1 out of 245 employees quit and customer complaints decreased at the package delivery company. And Instacart, a food shopping and delivery service, offered its shoppers the option to convert to part-time employees so they could offer training to ensure a consistent customer experience and greater customer satisfaction.

Regardless of their work status, most gig workers appear to be highly satisfied with their work environment, perhaps because it fits a unique need. Intuit's on-demand economy survey reported the following:

- 70% of on-demand workers are satisfied with their work.
- 81% plan to continue working with the same provider over the next year.
- 63% are happier to be working in the on-demand economy.

Overall, gig workers are forward-looking, eager to embrace new opportunities, and want to take charge of their careers. **Table 1.4** describes eight industries that are poised for disruption by on-demand workers.

TABLE 1.4   **Eight Industries Poised for Disruption by On-Demand Workers**

Industry	Characteristics	Advantages of On-Demand Workers
IT tech and field services	IT field service technicians are hired to install, repair, and maintain IT hardware. Equipment is often decentralized, needs are unpredictable, and fast response times are demanded to maintain connectivity	Lower costs Reduced response time Improved customer satisfaction
Retail	Geographically dispersed; fluctuating markets; challenging to balance service level needs	Help fill service level gaps Automation quickly identifies and implements optimal coverage
Health care	Growing demand for at-home care; increasing health-care costs	Access to specialists as needed Help with everyday tasks Greater flexibility and control
Media/marketing	Develop content to drive sales; lack of reliable resources at right time and place	Lower cost, flexibility, availability
Oil and gas	Lack of talent, high overall labor costs, challenge of transferring knowledge of retiring workers, highly specialized skill set, workload imbalances	Lower labor costs Prevent corporate brain drain
Education	Long history of substitute teachers, need for new educational models	Online teaching and tutoring Personal and professional freedom
Property management	Customers demand immediate response times, online payments, and service requests	Right person for the right job at the right time Decrease vacancy rates, increase retention

IT Adds Value to Your Performance and Career

Whether you join the ranks of the gig workers or choose to stay in a traditional job, IT can greatly enhance your performance at work as you move through your career path. Staying current in emerging technologies is an essential skill for knowledge workers, entrepreneurs, managers, and business leaders—not just IT staff and the CIO. This has become particularly true during the COVID-19 pandemic where the ability to use IT has allowed many workers to retain their jobs and income level while working within the safety of their own homes. Despite this, in the current marketplace, organizations are finding it particularly difficult to find qualified IT talent, as illustrated in **IT at Work 1.4**.

IT at Work 1.4

Scott Zulpo Is Facing Stiff Competition

He's adding a senior project manager, a network analyst, and a help desk worker to his 55-member IT staff at BCU, a Vernon Hills, Illinois-based credit union where he is vice president of IT. And, Zulpo will need to add even more people to keep up with an increasing demand for tech-driven innovations.

"The challenge is twofold—first finding talent, and then determining if that talent has the skills, experience and personality to thrive in the position," says Zulpo, who's mindful that "the cost and impact of not hiring an 'A' player is huge."

Zulpo has his work cut out for him. He's hiring at a time when very few IT professionals are out of work. Consequently, competition for tech talent is fierce. The unemployment rate for tech workers is less than 2%, according to reports on recent data from the U.S. Bureau of Labor Statistics (2019).

And, Zulpo isn't the only one who's having a difficult time finding good IT talent. Many of his fellow IT leaders are seeking the same skills. A recent report by Tech Republic and ZDNet listed both network analyst and technical support among the top ten most sought-after skills in the next decade.

"The IT labor market is still very hot. The candidate is very much in the driver's seat," says Jason Hayman, market research manager for IT staffing firm TEKsystems.

Hayman cites a government report that estimates that 500,000 to 1 million IT jobs go unfilled every year and notes that some analysts say the figure is closer to 2 million. He says there's a classic supply-and-demand scenario working here, with demand for talent far exceeding supply.

The takeaway is there are not enough IT workers!

Sources: Compiled from Tech Republic/ZDNet (2017) and Bureau of Labor Statistics (2019).

IT as a Career Locally and Globally. Fueled by corporate growth, systems expansion, need for competitive or unique services to increase business and security initiatives, companies are increasing their IT hires. Companies need new tech hires who have a background in both technology and business and who can articulate IT's value in meeting business goals. In particular, companies are seeking IT employees with skills in programming, application development, technical support, security, cloud, business intelligence, Web development, database administration, and project management. According to the U.S. Department of Labor, IT job growth in the United States is estimated at 12% from 2018 to 2028, faster than the average for all occupations. This increase translates into roughly 546,200 new jobs in the next decade.

> *Demand for tech workers continues to grow at a pace that's unmatched in other industries.*
> *Raj Mukherjee, Senior Vice President of Product, Indeed.com*

As more companies undergo digital transformation, in-demand IT roles will shift by 2020 to include positions focused on advanced technologies such as IoT and block chain technology discussed in Chapter 4, data analytics in Chapter 6, and artificial intelligence and robotics in Chapter 11.

Managing and Interpreting Big Data Are High Demand Skills

Concerns about the analytics skills gap have existed for years. It is increasingly clear that the shortage isn't just in data scientists but also in data engineers, data analysts, and even the executives required to manage data initiatives. As a result, organizations and institutions are expanding their efforts to train, hire, and retain data professionals. Here are two of those skill sets that are in high demand.

Big data specialists manage and package big data collections, analyze, and interpret trends and present their findings in easy- to-understand ways to "C"-level executives. Those who can present the data through user-friendly data visualizations will be particularly sought after. Skills required of these big data professionals include big data visualization, statistical analysis, big data reporting and presentation, Apache Hadoop, Apache Spark, NoSQL database skills, and machine learning.

Business intelligence (BI) analysts use tools and techniques to go beyond the numbers of big data and act based on the findings of the big data analyses. Successful BI professionals use self-service BI platforms, such as Tableau, SAP, Oracle BI, Microsoft BI, and IBM Cognos, to create BI reports and visualizations to streamline the process and reduce reliance on additional staff. Additional skills of critical thinking, creative problem-solving, effective communication, and presentation skills further enhance their attractiveness to employers (Doyle, 2020).

According to a recent report by Tech Republic and ZDNet, other IT jobs that will be most in demand in 2020 are as follows:

1. Computer vision engineer
2. Machine learning engineer
3. Network analyst
4. Security analyst
5. Cloud engineer
6. App developer
7. BI analyst
8. DevOps lead
9. Database administrator
10. User support specialist

A description of these and other computer and IT occupations, education requirements, and 2018 median pay can be found in the Bureau of Labor Statistics Occupational Outlook Handbook (https://bls.gov/ooh/computer-and-technology/home.htm).

According to the 2019 Global Knowledge survey (Goodison, 2019), global annual wages for IT professionals are at their highest levels ever, averaging $89,732. By region, North American IT professionals earn $109,985 on average—23% higher than the worldwide average—followed by Europe, the Middle East, and Africa at $70,445; the Asia-Pacific region at $65,738; and Latin America at $41,465.

Other than IT executives, cloud computing professionals had the highest paid positions, earning an average of $115,889 per year globally. This is 29% higher than the global IT average annual salary. Of these, cloud architects and cloud engineers were the most popular cloud computing roles listed. Other top-paid IT roles were IT architecture and design with an average annual salary of $98,580, followed by project and program management at $98,344 and cyber-security at $97,322. The lowest global IT position was service desk and IT support with an average annual salary of $55,689 globally.

About 85% of the surveyed professionals had at least one IT certification, with North America being the only region falling below the average at 81%. In all regions, salaries of certified professionals surpassed that of those without any certifications, and those with more than one certification earned more than those with a single certification.

Career Insight 1.1

Security Analysts Are in High Demand

Cybersecurity analysts are already in great demand, and this demand is expected to continue well into the future as cyberattacks grow more sophisticated and technologies to fight them mature Government, private, and nonprofit organizations all rely heavily on technology. Hackers steal data and/or disrupt operations. Security analysts actively engage in a game of wits between organizations and cyber criminals to out-hack the hackers! Without security analysts, companies can be vulnerable to devastating attacks.

What Does a Security Analyst Do?

A security analyst detects and prevents cyber threats to an organization by planning and carrying out security measures to protect the company's software, hardware, and networks. IT security analysts are heavily involved with creating their company disaster recovery plan, a procedure that IT employees follow in case of emergency. IT security analysts must stay up to date on IT security and on the latest methods cyber attackers are using to infiltrate computer systems. As a security analyst, in the morning you might be researching how effective new security measures are. In the afternoon, you might be dealing with an active security threat.

A security analyst also needs to research new security technology to decide what will most effectively protect company data. As technologies become more sophisticated, the role of security analysts will likely evolve to include more data skills and artificial intelligence skills as the present reactive security approach changes to a more proactive one.

Up the Ante with Certification

Security analysts generally need a bachelor's degree in an IT-related area, and certifications are advantageous in securing, and advancing in, a position. Take, for example, Certification of Ethical Hacker (CEH), a computer certification that indicates proficiency in network security, especially in preventing malicious hacking attacks through preemptive countermeasures, is advantageous in securing a job. The CEH credential is a vendor-neutral certification for IT professionals who want to specialize in stopping and identifying malicious hackers by means of the same knowledge and tools the cyber criminals use. Before the CEH was introduced, private firms and government agencies hired reformed malicious hackers to secure their networks. The CEH is built on this model, which requires that those who earn the certification to agree in writing to abide by the law and honor a code of ethics. The CEH is sponsored by the International Council of E-Commerce Consultants (EC-Council), whose goals are to establish and maintain standards and credentials for the profession of ethical hackers and to educate IT professionals and the public on the role and value of security analysts. In addition to the CEH certification, the EC-Council offers several other security-related certifications, including secure programming and computer forensics. Certification proficiency levels range from entry level to independent contractor.

Growing Need for Security Analysts

Currently, it has been estimated that there are about 112,000 IT security analysts in the workforce, and the demand for IT security analysts is expected to grow by 32% from 2018 to 2028, resulting in an additional 35,500 jobs. The median annual pay for IT security analysts in 2018 was $98,350.

Sources: Bureau of Labor Statistics (2019) and EC-Council Certification (2019).

IT Job Prospects. In 2020, less than 2% of all IT workers in the United States are unemployed. Going forward, workers with specialized technical knowledge and strong communications and business skills, as well as those with an MBA with a concentration in an IT-related area, will have the best prospects. According to the Bureau of Labor Statistics (https://www.bls.gov), job openings will be the result of employment growth and the need to replace workers who transfer to other occupations or leave the labor force because they are reaching the retirement age.

Dow Chemical (www.dupont.com) set up its own social network to help managers identify the talent they need to carry out projects across its diverse business units and functions. To expand its talent pool, Dow extended the network to include former employees and retirees.

Other companies are using networks to tap external talent pools. These networks include online labor markets such as Amazon Mechanical Turk (https://www.mturk.com) and services such as InnoCentive (https://www.innocentive.com) that help solve business problems.

- Amazon Mechanical Turk is a marketplace for work that requires human intelligence. Its Web service enables companies to access a diverse, on-demand workforce.

- InnoCentive is an "open innovation" company that takes R&D problems in a broad range of areas such as engineering, computer science, and business and frames them as "challenge problems" for anyone to solve. It gives cash awards for the best solutions to solvers who meet the challenge criteria.

Becoming an Informed IT User

Informed user is a person knowledgeable about information systems and IT.

Knowing how best to use IT and how and when to interact with IT personnel, and they with you, will help you perform better at home and at work and enable you to become an **informed user** of technology.

The department or functional area that handles the collection, processing, storing, analysis, and distribution of information using a computer-based tool can be referred to by many names—some companies refer to it as information technology (IT), while others refer to it as information systems (IS), management information systems (MIS), IT support, IT services, or computer information systems (CIS). Whatever the name, its purpose is the same—to support a company's information needs by developing, operating, securing, and maintaining one or more information systems.

To become an informed IT user, you will learn how the six components of an information system—hardware, software, procedures, people, networks, and data—interact to provide you with the information that you need, when you need it, and in the format you need. These IT components will be discussed in detail in Chapter 2.

By reading this book, you will not only learn about the many aspects of IT acquisition, use, operation, and maintenance and how IT impacts organizations, but you will also become an informed IT user to improve your on-the-job performance and widen your career opportunities. For example, you will

- Understand how using IT can improve organizational performance
- Understand how and why IT can benefit organizational growth
- Understand how business can use IT to enhance the customer experience
- Understand how companies use IT to analyze business data and offer important insights
- Be able to offer input into the development and use of IT
- Be able to recommend and select IT applications at work
- Know how to find emerging technologies to make radical improvement in business processes
- Understand how IT can facilitate teamwork and improve individual productivity
- Appreciate the importance of ethical behavior when using IT and explain the associated risks and responsibilitiesFoster your entrepreneurial tendencies to start your own on-demand business.

Questions

1. How does IT enable business process engineering?
2. Is on-demand work a viable option for you? Explain.
3. What types of IT careers have the most potential in the current hiring market?
4. Why is IT a major enabler of business performance and success?
5. Why do you think it is beneficial to hold an IT certification?
6. Why do you think IT job prospects are so strong? Explain.
7. Why is important for you to be an "informed user" of IT?

Chapter Summary

LO1.1 *Define* the differences between the on-demand and sharing economies and the six business objectives IT should focus on to enhance organizational performance, growth, and sustainability.

The on-demand economy is the economic activity created by technology companies that fulfill individual consumer demands through the immediate provisioning of products and services. In the sharing economy, goods or services are *shared* between private individuals through an online company or organization.

The six business objectives that IT should focus on are as follows:

1. **Product development** to help businesses respond quickly to changing customer demands
2. **Stakeholder integration** to communicate with shareholders, research analysts, and others in the market
3. **Process improvement** to increase efficiency and cost-effectiveness of internal business processes
4. **Cost efficiencies** to reduce transaction and implementation costs
5. **Competitive advantage** to bring a product to market cost-effectively and quickly
6. **Globalization** to stay in contact with its global employees, customers, and suppliers 24/7

LO1.2 *Explain* the role of IT in improving business processes. Understand the concepts of business process reengineering and competitive advantage.

Outdated and complex application architectures, with a mix of interfaces, can delay or prevent the release of new products and services, and maintaining these obsolete systems absorbs large portions of the IT budget. As a result, managers and entrepreneurs must integrate digital disruptive technology into their products and services to improve their business processes and stay competitive. BPR is the concept of using IT to radically improve processes rather than simply making incremental positive changes. Competitive advantage is when an organization differentiates itself by charging less and creating and delivering better quality products or services than its competitors.

LO1.3 *Describe* how IT is disrupting the way that companies operate, the IT megatrends that are driving organizational performance, growth, and sustainability and how COVID-19 is accelerating digital transformation.

Disruptive technology has a powerful impact on people, business, government, entertainment, and society. IT enables leading companies to change their business models, business processes, customer experiences, and ways of working. Through examples of innovative products, services, and distribution channels, the digital revolution is currently shaping the future of business, the economy, and society and how it is changing management careers. IT megatrends that are driving performance, growth, and sustainability in organizations include connectivity, big data and data analytics, digitization, artificial intelligence and robotics, machine-to-machine learning, and IoT.

The COVID-19 pandemic has significantly accelerated the rate of digital transformation in public and private companies around the globe. In response to the unexpected events of the pandemic, companies in all industry sectors have had to act much more quickly to create new business models that address the regulatory requirements of COVID-19 lockdowns and ensuing health and safety concerns and new purchasing habits of consumers, vendors and partners. They have achieved this primarily by integrating new innovative information and communication technologies into their business models to increase personal engagement with consumers, vendors and partners, maintain a competitive advantage in the market and safeguard their sustainability.

LO1.4 *Discuss* what it means to be an "informed user" of IT and the ways in which IT can add value to your career path and job performance.

As an informed user, people have a better understanding of where IT fits in management today and are able to keep up with changes in IT as they evolve. Consequently, they will be better equipped to make recommendations about the adoption and productive use of new technologies at work or when starting their own business. Many career opportunities are available in the IT world that are either managerial or technical in their focus. People who choose not to take up IT jobs can still add significant value to their career and overall quality of life by just learning technology terminology and how to use technology to improve their work performance and overall quality of life.

Key Terms

big data 16
business model 7
business process 11
business process management (BPM) 13
business process reengineering (BPR) 12
cloud computing 16
cloud services 19
competitive advantage 10
critical success factor (CSF) 12
cross-functional business process 11
customer experience 8

cycle time 12
dashboards 17
data analytics 8
deliverables 10
digital business model 7
digitization 16
formal 11
informal 11
informed user 26
Internet of Things (IoT) 17
IT architecture 4

legacy systems 4
machine-to-machine (M2M) technology 17
mega trends 16
on-demand economy 6
sharing economy 6
social–mobile–analytics–cloud (SMAC) 15
standard operating procedures (SOPs) 11
technology platform 9
technology stack 9
unstructured data 16

Assuring Your Learning

Discuss: Critical Thinking Questions

1. Why are businesses experiencing a digital transformation?

2. More data are collected in a day now than existed in the world 10 years ago. What factors have contributed to this volume of data?

3. Assume you had no smartphone, other mobile device, or mobile apps to use for 24 hours. How would that mobile blackout disrupt your ability to function?

4. Name three highly disruptive digital technologies. Give an example of one disruption for each technology.

5. Why are enterprises adopting cloud computing?

6. What is the value of M2M technology? Give two examples.

7. Starbucks monitors tweets and other sources of big data. How might the company increase revenue from big data analytics?

8. Select three companies in different industries, such as banking, retail store, supermarket, airlines, or package delivery, that you do business with. What digital technologies does each company use to engage you, keep you informed, or create a unique customer experience? How effective is each use of digital technology to keeping you a loyal customer?

9. Describe two examples of the influence of SMAC on the financial industry.

10. What is the potential impact of the IoT on the health-care industry?

11. Why does reducing the cycle time of a business process also help to reduce errors?

12. Research firm Gartner defines competitive advantage as a difference between a company and its competitors *that matters to customers*. Describe one use of M2M technology that could provide a manufacturer with a competitive advantage.

13. What IT careers are forecasted to be in high demand? Explain why.

14. Why or how would understanding the latest IT trends influence your career?

Explore: Online Exercises

1. Research the growing importance of the IoT. Find two forecasts of its growth. What do they forecast?

2. Go to "9 Successful Digital Disruption Examples" (https://www.itbusinessedge.com/slideshows/9-successful-digital-disruption-examples.html) on the IT Business Edge website. Close the pop-up to view the slideshow and read the descriptions of each of the ways in which technology is disrupting our lives. Answer the following questions:

   a. Which of the disruptions resonated best with you and your lifestyle? Explain.

   b. Which of the disruptions was most surprising to you? Why?

   c. Rank order the disruptions in their order of importance to you. Write a short report explaining your rankings.

3. Go to "The Impact of COVID-19 on digital transformation" (https://v2.itweb.co.za/event/itweb/the-impact-of-covid-19-on-digital-transformation/) and watch a webinar of your choice. Write a short narrative in which you describe the content of the webinar and discuss how it helped you understand how companies' must digitally transform during and after the COVID-19 pandemic.

Analyze & Decide: Apply IT Concepts to Business Decisions

1. A transportation company is considering investing in a truck tire with embedded sensors. Outline the benefits of this investment. Would this investment create a long-term competitive advantage for company?

2. Visit the website of UPS (https://www.ups.com/us/en/global.page), Federal Express (https://www.fedex.com/en-us/home.html), and one other logistics and delivery company.

   a. At each site, describe what information is available to customers before and after they send a package.

   b. Compare the customer experiences of these three companies. Which one do you prefer? Why?

   c. Based on your experiences, if you want to send a package to another country, which company would you use? Why?

3. Visit Dell.com (https://www.dell.com/en-us) and Apple.com (https://www.apple.com/mac) to simulate buying a laptop computer. Compare and contrast the selection process, degree of customization, and other buying features. What factors are preventing companies from entering into this market, based on what you learned from this exercise?

Reinforce: Ensure Your Understanding of the Key Terms

Solve the online crossword provided for this chapter.

Web Resources

More resources and study tools are located on the student website. You'll find useful Web links and self-test quizzes that provide individualized feedback.

Case 1.2

Business Case: The IoT Comes to Sports

People love sports statistics and the more the better. Responding to this customer demand, the NFL and other sports agencies increased the quality and quantity of statistics available to coaches and fans with radio frequency identification (RFID) chips and football helmets designed to guard against brain injuries.

Player RFID Project

When the New England Patriots hosted the Pittsburgh Steelers in their season opener a few years back, each player was equipped with a set of RFID sensors. Each sensor, about the size of a quarter, will be embedded in players' shoulder pads and emits a unique radio frequency. Every stadium used by the NFL will be equipped with 20 receivers to pick up the RFID signals and pinpoint every player on the field. It also records speed, distance traveled, acceleration in real time, and the direction the player is facing.

The NFL plans to use the data it collects to power an Xbox One and Windows NFL apps to allow fans to call up stats for each player tied into the highlight clips posted on the app. The data will also be fed to broadcasters, leveraged for in-stadium displays, and provided to coaching staff and players.

"We've always had these traditional NFL stats," says Matt Swensson, senior director of Emerging Products and Technology at the NFL. "The league has been very interested in trying to broaden that and bring new statistics to the fans. Along the way, there's been more realization about how the data can be leveraged to make workflow more efficient around the game."

Zebra Technologies Software Vendor

The NFL's technology partner in its IoT push was Zebra Technologies of Lincolnshire, Illinois.

Zebra was well known for its manufacturing and selling marking, tracking and printing technologies such as thermal barcode label and receipt printers, RFID smart label printer/encoders, and card and kiosk printers. As it moved into IoT and M2M applications, Zebra launched its MotionWorks Sports Solution, which powers the NFL IoT initiative. Zebra was able to develop RFID tags that blink up to 85 times per second to track motion of athletes in sub-seconds. Then it had to find a customer for the product—so it turned to the biggest fish in the pond—the NFL. Zebra trialed the tags by equipping more than 2,000 players, 18 NFL stadiums and officials, markers, and pylons. Over the course of the season, more than 1.7 billion sets of XY player coordinates were measured, transmitted, and stored during the games. Every stadium was connected to a command station in San Jose, California, that controls when the data are collected and where they are sent and stores them in the cloud.

The Need for the Right People

An important lesson that Zebra learned is that generic data scientists were not sufficient to gain insight into the data. Zebra needed football experts. "When you look at analytics in football, you really need people. We had to go out and hire football people. The analytics from manufacturing weren't the same as the analytics from football. We could see correlations in the data that seemed important and then found out they weren't. We had to bring in people that had the football expertise who could say 'Look, this is why it matters,'" said Jill Stelfox, Zebra Technologies Vice President and General Manager, Location Solutions.

This IoT initiative has even been integrated into NFL's fantasy football offerings and college football.

New Developments—Helmet Sensors

The latest development in the use of this technology is in college football. College football programs across the United States are investing in new cutting-edge helmet technology to measure the hits players take during practice. The helmets have a set of sensors that record the hits taken by players in terms of G-forces, location, direction, and severity. Data from the hit are then sent to a handheld sensor used by training staff. Two types of helmets that are currently gaining favor with college football coaching staff are the Riddell InSite and VICIS Zero 1.

Questions

1. Why did NFL equip its players with RFID tags?
2. What factors contributed to the success of the IoT initiative at the NFL?
3. What are the benefits and drawbacks of using helmet sensors in college level sports?
4. What other types of IoT applications you think of that could be used in professional and college-level sports stadiums?

Sources: Compiled from Lee (2018), Macleod (2018), Moriarty (2018), http://www.riddell.com/insite, and https://vicis.com.

Case 1.3

Video Case: Creating a Digital Vision to Transform a Company and Improve the Customer Experience

Go to the website to view the video on how to create a vision for digital transformation of your company in which Dr. Jeanne Ross, Principal Research Scientist at the MIT Center for IS Research, discusses the need for companies to transform themselves by improving their customers' experience and remain competitive in the digital era. The video is accessible from https://www.techrepublic.com/videos/5-building-blocks-your-company-needs-for-successful-digital-transformation

and runs for 5 minutes 15 seconds. After watching the video, answer the following questions:

Questions

1. Why is creating a clear vision of how a company will better engage with customers and solve their problems a major challenge for most companies?

2. What are the five building blocks of a digital transformation?

3. What was the most important thing that you learned from the video?

References

Basu, C. "The Six Important Business Objectives of Information Technology." *Chron*, 2017. http://smallbusiness.chron.com/six-important-business-objectives-information-technology-25220.html; Bolden-Barrett, V. "Research Debunks Myth that most Gig Workers Can't Find Full-Time Jobs." *HRDive*, June 26, 2019.

Bureau of Labor Statistics. *Occupational Outlook Handbook*. U.S. Department of Labor, 2019–2020.

Caballero, M. "Coke Acquires Costa Coffee for $5B." *Bevnet*, 2018.

Domat, C. "Uber's Fight Goes Global." *Global Finance,* 2018.

Doyle, A. "Important Business Intelligence Skills with Examples." *The Balance Careers*, February 5, 2020.

EC-Council Certification. "Hair on Fire? Polish Your Security Skills with CEH Certification." 2019. https://cert.eccouncil.org/certified--ethical-hacker.html.

Gartner Group. "Speed Up Your Digital Business Transformation." 2019. https://www.gartner.com/smarterwithgartner/speed-up--your-digital-business-transformation.

Goodison, D. "Global IT Salaries Hit New High: 2019 IT Skills and Salary Report." 2019. https://www.crn.com/news/global-it-salaries--hit-new-high-2019-it-skills-and-salary-report?itc=refresh.

Hammer, M. and J. Champy. "Re-engineering the Corporation: A Manifesto for Business Revolution." Updated and revised edition. Harper Business Essentials, 2006.

Hawkins, A. "The Ride-Sharing App That Beat Uber in China Is Available in English for the First Time." *The Verge*, 2017.

Henshall, A. "The Aggressive Processes Uber Is Using for Global Expansion." *Business 2 Community*, 2017.

Kappelman, L., R. Torres, E. McLean, C. Maurer, V. Johnson, and K. Kim. "The 2018 SIM IT Issues and Trends Study." *MIS Quarterly Executive*, 2019, *18*(1), Article 7.

Kroger. "Kroger's 2019 Sustainability Report." Available from www.sustainability.kroger.com. Accessed on May 23, 2020.

Ledsom, A. "Airbnb and Its Second Largest Global Market; Can France Rein the Travel Giant In? *Forbes*, 2019.

Lee, B. "How This New Football Helmet Is Designed to Protect the Train." *Forbes*, 2018.

MacIver, K. "Digital Business in an Era of Disruptive Innovation." *I-CIO.com*, November 2015.

MacIver, K. "Costa Coffee Brews a Fresh Digital Blend to Fuel Its Global Ambitions." *Intelligence for the CIO*, 2019.

Macleod, R. "New Football Helmet Sensors Monitor Brain Injuries." *The Global and Mail*, 2018.

Mitic, I. "Gig Economy Statistics 2020: The New Normal in the Workplace." *Fortunly*, May 19, 2020.

Moriarty, J. "Some College Football Teams Are Using Cutting-Edge Helmet Technology to Monitor Hit Data by Position." *SBNation*, 2018.

Muck, A. "From Blockbuster to Netflix: The History of Disruption in Entertainment." *Forbes*, June 5, 2017.

Overstreet, K. "The Future of the Sharing Economy in the COVID-19 Aftermath." *Archdaily*, August 14, 2020.

Pofeldt, E. "On-Demand Work: The New Social Safety Net." *Forbes*, February 21, 2017.

Romero, A. "Everything We Know About Netflix's 2019 Original Series." *Refinery* 29, April 20, 2019.

Sil, D. "97% Enterprises Claim COVID-19 Boosted Their Digital Transformation Efforts: Twilio Report." *Entrepreneur*, July 21, 2020.

Solomon, B. "How Airbnb Expanded to 190 Countries by Thinking Global." *Forbes*, 2016.

Spangler, T. "Are Americans Addicted to Smartphones?" *Variety*, November 14, 2018.

Tech Republic/ZDNet. "IT Jobs in 2020: A Leader's Guide." *ZDNet*, 2017. https://www.zdnet.com/article/the-10-it-jobs-that-will-be--most-in-demand-in-2020.

The Kroger Co. "Kroger to Outline Restock Kroger Growth Model at 2019 Investor Conference." Press Release 2018. Available from http://ir.kroger.com/file/Index?KeyFile=395518885. Accessed on May 23, 2020.

U.S. Bureau of Labor Statistics. "Computer and Information Technology Occupations." 2019. https://www.bls.gov/ooh/computer-and--information-technology/home.htm.

Wood, Z. and M. Sweney. "Coca-Cola Buys Costa Coffee from Whitbread for £3.9bn." *The Guardian*, August 31, 2018.

Zappa, J. "Kroger CEO Offers Closer Look at Grocery Giant's Tech Innovation at NRF 2019." *Street Fight*, January 21, 2019.

CHAPTER 2

Information Systems, IT Infrastructure, and the Cloud

Case 2.1 Opening Case The Amazing Story of Tommy Flowers—Creator of the First Programmable Computer

The History Collection/Alamy Stock Photo

Steve Vidler/Alamy Stock Photo

MGPhoto76/Alamy Stock Photo

If you were asked to name the father of computing you'd probably say, Alan Turing. And, if you were asked to name the first programmable computer, you'd say ENIAC. In each case you would be wrong! To find out why, we need to go back in history to the Allied Forces D-Day Landings of WWII.

On June 6, 1944 Allied Forces landed on the beaches of Normandy, France, and ended German domination in France during WWII. Known as Operation Overlord, the ambitious Allied Forces military operation engaged 150,000 troops from 12 countries, 5,000 ships, and 11,000 airplanes in what is still the largest recorded military operation in history.

The success of D-Day and other Allied operations during WWII can be attributed primarily to one man—telecom engineer and computer pioneer Tommy Flowers. Flowers designed and built Colossus, the world's first electronic programmable computer that broke complex German codes at lightning speed to enable the Allies to gain valuable military information and significantly shorten the duration of WWII.

The Father of Computing

Tommy Flowers was born in London's East End on December 22, 1905. At the age of 16, he began an apprenticeship in mechanical engineering and earned a bachelor's degree in electrical engineering at the University of London. In 1926, he joined the telecommunications branch of the General Post Office (GPO) and in 1930 he was moved to the research station at Dollis Hill on the northwest side of London and later to Bletchley Park in Buckinghamshire. Flowers was particularly interested in the use of electronics for telephone exchanges and by 1939, he was convinced that an all-electronic system was possible. This background in switching electronics would prove crucial for his computer design in WWII.

The First Electronic Programmable Computer

Flowers was initially asked to build a decoder for the Turing–Welchman relay-based Bombe system (https://www.tnmoc.org/bombe) designed to break Enigma codes used by the Germans to send messages within the Third Reich. However, when the Germans began to use the far more complicated Lorenz SZ rotor stream cipher machines, the Bombe system proved to be ineffective. Since the Germans changed their codes at midnight every day, it was essential codes were cracked within a relatively few hours. If not, the information gleaned by the Allies was useless. The Bombe system assisted by the Tunny and Heath Robinson machines (https://www.tnmoc.org/tunny-heath-robinson) could not decode the highly sophisticated Lorenz codes quickly enough for its results to be of use. So, Flowers

proposed a radical new design—the use of valves rather than electromechanical switches. His new machine contained over 1,500 thermionic valves rather than the 150 valves used in the most complicated previous electronic device. This departure from electromechanical switches initially caused heated debate since glass valves had proved to be less reliable than the electromechanical switches currently in use. Using his knowledge of electronic switching, Flowers proved that large numbers of electronic circuits could be made to perform reliable calculations at speed by creating a stable environment where the system ran continuously, rather than turning it on and off. The innovative system also used one tape rather than two, thus saving more time by eliminating the need to synchronize the tapes.

Flowers had to use his own money to get the project off the ground when management at the Bletchley Park codebreaking center proved skeptical and encouraged Flowers to continue alone rather than prioritizing the project. Flowers' persistence paid off. He was soon assigned staff and priority access to resources that enabled his development of Colossus, the first electronic programmable computer.

How Does Colossus Work?

When Colossus began operating at Bletchley Park in February 1944, it ran a startling five times faster than its rival, the Heath Robinson electromechanical switch machine!

To decode the German High Command messages, a system of wheels on Colossus guided the single punched paper tape, containing the encrypted message, through an optical reader as a repetitive loop of punched paper tape in 5-bit teleprinter code. Characters on the tape were repeatedly read into Colossus at an astonishing rate of 5,000 characters per second.

When the paper tape was set up and the machine configured, it took no more than four hours to output the results of the statistical analysis of the message. These useable results, together with further work by the Bletchley Park codebreaker team, resulted in breaking the German Lorenz cipher to reveal the strategic message it disguised within an advantageous time frame.

Colossus in WWII and Beyond

On June 1, 1944, when Allied commanders were trying to determine when and where to launch Operation Overlord, a new version of Colossus that contained 2,500 valves and used shift registers to greatly increase processing speed, was pressed into service. Colossus II immediately provided vital intelligence regarding the D-Day landings.

On June 5, 1944, the almost instant information provided by Colossus revealed that Hitler was refusing to send troops into Normandy because he was convinced that any Allied landings would occur at Pas-de-Calais, almost 500 km north of the Normandy beaches. This information prompted Colonel Dwight D. Eisenhower, Commander-in-Chief of Operation Overlord, to immediately order the Allied Forces to land at Normandy the next day—June 6, 1944.

Colossus I and Colossus II continued providing vital intelligence until the end of the war and historians estimate that their use shortened WWII by as much as two years, saving thousands of lives. A total of 10 Colossus units were operational during World War II. All but 2 were dismantled after the war.

Years of Silence

During his lifetime, Flowers never received full recognition for his monumental accomplishments. Flowers' work during WWII was a closely guarded secret. It was tied to the Official Secrets Act administered by Britain's Secretary of Defense and all information related to his vital work for the war effort in WWII was kept secret until the late 1970s. At that time, Flowers was given limited permission to release a technical description of Colossus. The British Government didn't release any information about the functions that Colossus performed during WWII until June 2000, two years after Flowers died. Even Flowers' family didn't know the amazing achievements he had attained and the positive impact he had made on the duration of WWII. All Flowers was allowed to tell them was that his work was "secret and important."

Consequently, the nonclassified work of computer scientist and cryptanalyst, Alan Turing and the February 1946 public announcement of ENIAC, an electronic general-purpose computer designed by the U.S. Army's Ballistic Research Laboratory, led to their designation as firsts in the information technology field.

Recognition

Today, however, the place of Colossus as the first electronic programmable computer is assured, and Tommy Flowers, who was awarded the prestigious distinction of Member of the Order of the British Empire (MBE) for his groundbreaking work during WWII, has been officially acknowledged as the legitimate Father of Computing.

Tommy Flowers died on October 28, 1998 in London, England. He was 92 years old. Colossus II lives on through the Colossus II Rebuild, displayed in the original room where Colossus 9 stood during WII, at the National Museum of Computing (https://www.tnmoc.org/colossus) in Block H, Bletchley Park, Milton Keynes, England.

Questions

1. Why was Alan Turing's work acknowledged and Flowers' work was kept secret?
2. Why was it important that Flowers' work be kept secret?
3. How do you think Flowers came up with the idea to use electronic valves?
4. How did Colossus succeed in breaking the Lorenz codes where previous machines had failed?

Sources: Compiled from McFadden (2018), Centre for Computing (2019a,b), Crypto Museum (2019), and Sparks (2019).

 DID YOU KNOW?

The cloud has dramatically changed how IT professionals go about provisioning the IT infrastructure and how app developers approach projects, collaborate on them, and create software.

Introduction

To stay ahead, corporate leaders are constantly seeking new ways to grow their business in the face of rapid technology changes, increasingly empowered consumers and employees, and ongoing changes in government regulation. To do this, they launch new business models and strategies. Because these new business models, strategies, and performance capabilities frequently result from advances in technology, the company's ability to leverage technological innovation over time depends on its approach to its IS and their IT infrastructure, architecture and enterprise architecture.

In this chapter, you will first be introduced to the six components of an IS. Next you will learn about the different categories of IS and in which level of the organization each category of IS is used to solve business problems in businesses of all sizes throughout the global economy. You will also begin to learn the terminology of IT and be able to define and differentiate between IT terms such as IT infrastructure, IT architecture, and enterprise architecture and learn how they are developed, operated, and evaluated. Finally, you will be introduced to the concepts of data centers, cloud computing, and cloud services and how their use improves the performance, growth, and sustainability of businesses around the globe. With this knowledge, you will be able to help your organization more effectively leverage its IT capabilities to achieve sustainable competitive advantage and growth and more effectively and efficiently use IT in your personal life.

2.1 IS Concepts and Classification

LO2.1 Identify *the six components of an information system, the various types of information systems to the level of support needed, and the difference between data, information, knowledge, and wisdom.*

As we begin to explore the value of information technology (IT) to an organization, it's useful to understand what IT is, what it does, what level of systems is typically put in place at different levels of an organization, and how it impacts an organization's performance, growth, and sustainability.

First, let's look at the value that an **information system** can add in an organization. You probably already know that technology supports organizations and almost every business unit within an organization. The following three examples show how different business units in companies around the globe have improved their performance thanks to technology.

IT Adds Value

Marketing. Utilizing IBM software, Bolsa de Comercio de Santiago (https://sseinitiative .org/fact-sheet/bcs) a large stock exchange in Chile, can process its ever-increasing, high-volume trading in microseconds. The Chilean stock exchange system can do the detective work of analyzing current and past transactions and market information, learning, and adapting to market trends and connecting its traders to business information in real time. Immediate throughput in combination with analytics allows traders to make more accurate decisions.

Sales. Hospital readmissions are a leading topic of health-care policy and practice reform because they are common, costly, and potentially avoidable events. According to the *New England Journal of Medicine*, one in five patients suffers from preventable readmissions, which cost taxpayers over $17 billion a year. In the past, hospitals have been penalized for high readmission rates with cuts to the payments they receive from the government. To meet the current changes and future expectations, organizations are turning to IT for potential strategies to reduce readmissions. Using effective management information systems (MISs), the health-care industry can leverage unstructured information in ways not possible before, according to Matt McClelland, manager of information governance for Blue Cross Blue Shield of North Carolina (https://www.bluecrossnc.com). With proper support, information governance can bridge gaps among the needs to address regulation and litigation risk, generate increased sales and revenue, and cut costs and become more efficient. When performed correctly, information governance positively impacts every facet of business.

Operations Management. Most financial transactions in Ireland start or travel through the Allied Irish Bank (https://aib.ie). This means that AIB plays a major role not just in its customers' lives but also in the Irish economy at large. As such it is heavily intertwined with the Irish quality of life. To serve its constituents and country, AIB uses the agility of a state-of-the-art mainframe computer to deliver open banking and added functionality to make financial transactions from banking to mortgage loans easier, faster, and more secure. Innovative mainframe technology, such as the IBM Z platform, is pivotal to the successful operations at AIB in terms of performance and provides the "behind the scenes" power for its online banking operations.

In addition to supporting decision-making, coordination, and control in an organization, an IS helps managers and workers analyze problems, visualize complex sets of data, and create new products. ISs collect (**input**) and manipulate data (**processing**), and generate and distribute reports (**output**) based on data-specific IT services, such as processing customer orders and generating payroll. Finally, ISs save (**storage**) the data for future use. In addition to the four functions of **IPOS**, an information needs **feedback** from its users and other stakeholders to help improve future systems as demonstrated in **Figure 2.1**.

Information system (IS) is a combination of information technology and people's activities using technology to support business processes, operations, management, and decision-making at different levels of the organization.

IPOS is the cycle of inputting, processing, outputting, and storing information in an information system.

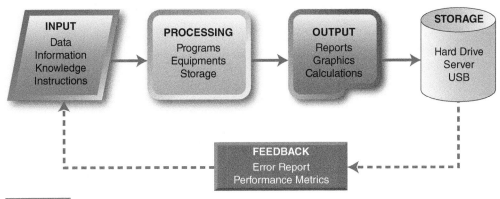

FIGURE 2.1   IPOS cycle.

The following example demonstrates how the components of the IPOS work together: To access a website, Amanda opens an Internet browser using the keyboard and enters a Web address into the browser (input). The system then uses that information to find the correct website (processing) and the content of the desired site is displayed in the Web browser (output). Next, Amanda bookmarks the desired website in the Web browser for future use (storage). The system then records the time it took to produce the output to compare actual versus expected performance (feedback).

Six Components of an IS

A computer IS consists of six interacting components. Regardless of type and where and by whom they are used within an organization, the components of an IS must be carefully managed to provide maximum benefit to the organization. Each of these IS components is shown in **Figure 2.2** and defined below.

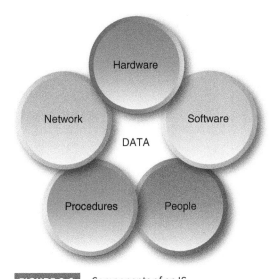

FIGURE 2.2   Components of an IS.

1. **Hardware**   Any physical device used in a computerized IS. Examples include central processing unit (CPU), sound card, video card, network card, hard drive, display, keyboard, motherboard, processor, power supply, modem, mouse, and printer.

2. **Software**   A set of machine-readable instructions (code) that makes up a computer application that directs a computer's processor to perform specific operations. Computer software is nontangible, contrasted with system hardware, which is the physical component of an IS. Examples include Internet browser, operating system (OS), Microsoft Office, Skype, and so on.

3. **People**   Any person involved in developing, operating and using an IS. Examples include analysts, programmers, operators help desk, and end users.

4. **Procedures** Documentation containing directions on how to use the other components of an IS. Examples include operational manual and user manual.

5. **Network** A combination of lines, wires, and physical devices connected to each other to create a telecommunications network. In computer networks, networked computing devices exchange data with each other using a data link. The connections between nodes are established using either cable media or wireless media. Networks can be internal or external. If they are available only internally within an organization, they are called "intranets." If they are available externally, they are called "internets." The best-known example of a computer network is the World Wide Web.

6. **Data** Raw or unorganized facts and figures (such as invoices, orders, payments, customer details, product numbers, product prices) that describe conditions, ideas, or objects.

Data, Information, Knowledge, and Wisdom

As you can see in Figure 2.2, **data** is the central component of any information system. Without data, an IS would have no purpose and companies would find it difficult to conduct business. An IS processes data into meaningful **information** that is transformed into corporate **knowledge** and ultimately creates **wisdom** that fuels corporate strategy, as shown in **Figure 2.3**.

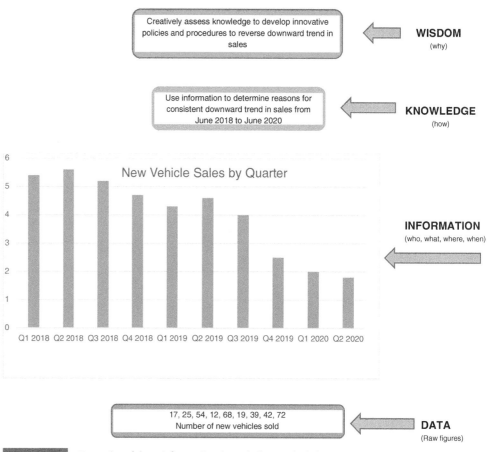

FIGURE 2.3 Examples of data, information, knowledge, and wisdom.

Data describe products, customers, events, activities, and transactions that are recorded, classified, and stored.

Information is data that have been processed, organized, or put into context so that they have meaning and value to the person receiving them.

Data are the raw material from which information is produced; the quality, reliability, and integrity of the data must be maintained for the information to be useful. Data are the raw facts and figures that are not organized in any way. Examples are the number of hours an employee worked in a certain week or the number of new Ford vehicles sold from the first quarter (Q1) of 2018 through the second quarter (Q2) of 2020 (Figure 2.3).

Information is an organization's most important asset, second only to people. Information provides the "who," "what," "where," and "when" of data in a given context. For example, summarizing the quarterly sales of new Ford vehicles from Q1 2018 through Q2 2020 provides information that shows sales have steadily decreased from Q2 2019.

Knowledge is used to answer the question "how" and is the fact or condition of knowing something with familiarity gained through experience or education. Knowledge is sometimes referred to as intellectual capital. In our example, it would involve determining how the trend can be reversed, for example, customer satisfaction can be improved, new features can be added, and pricing can be adjusted.

> **Knowledge** adds understanding, experience, accumulated learning, and expertise to information, as they apply to a current problem or activity.

There are two types of knowledge: explicit and tacit:

Explicit knowledge is the most basic form of knowledge and is easy to communicate, store, and distribute. When data is processed, organized, structured, and analyzed, the result is explicit knowledge. Examples include books, instruction manuals, policies and procedures, specifications, and Web content.

Tacit knowledge is the opposite of explicit knowledge and is difficult to transfer to others. It is personal, context-specific, and experiential. Tacit knowledge is not taught; it is learned by doing, watching, and experiencing. Examples include hands-on skills, specialized know-how, employee experiences.

Wisdom is more abstract than data and information (that can be harnessed) and knowledge (that can be shared). Wisdom adds value and increases effectiveness. It answers the "why" in a given situation. In the Ford example, wisdom would be corporate strategists evaluating the various reasons for the sales drop, creatively analyzing the situation as a whole, and developing innovative policies and procedures to reverse the recent downward trend in new vehicle sales.

> **Wisdom** is a collection of values, ethics, moral codes, and prior experiences that form an evaluated understanding or common-sense judgment.

ISs collect or input and process data to create and distribute reports or other outputs based on information gleaned from the raw data to support decision-making and business processes that, in turn, produce corporate knowledge that can be stored for future use. **Figure 2.4** shows how people interact with the IPOS cycle of an IS to convert raw data into more useful knowledge, information, and wisdom.

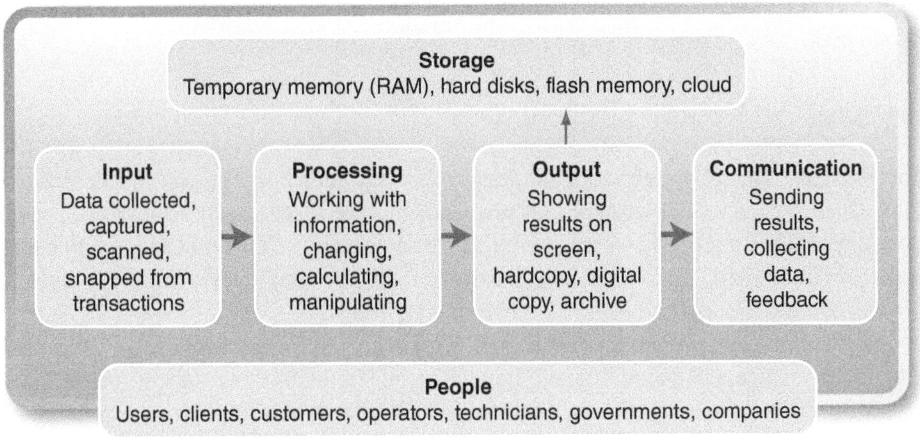

FIGURE 2.4   Data processing in the IPOS cycle.

Types of Information Systems

To ultimately transform raw data into wisdom, a hierarchy of different types of information systems (ISs) must be implemented. An IS may be as simple as a single computer and a printer used by one person, or as complex as several thousand computers of various types (tablets, desktops, laptops, mainframes) with hundreds of printers, scanners, and other devices connected through an elaborate network used by thousands of geographically dispersed employees. Similarly, the functions that business-driven IS perform to support business analysts and other departmental employees range from simple to complex, depending on the level of employees supported.

Figure 2.5 illustrates the classification of the various types of IS used in organizations, the organizational level at which they are used, the typical level of workers who use them and the types of input/output (I/O) produced by each. At the operational level of the organization, line workers use **transaction processing systems (TPSs)** to capture raw *data* and pass it along (output) to middle managers. The raw data is then input into office automation (OA) and MISs by middle managers to produce *information* for use by senior managers. Next, information is input into **decision support systems (DSSs)** for processing into explicit *knowledge* that will be used by senior managers to direct current corporate strategy. Finally, corporate executives input the explicit knowledge provided by the DSSs into executive information systems (EISs) and apply their experience, expertise, and skills to create *wisdom* that will lead to new corporate strategies.

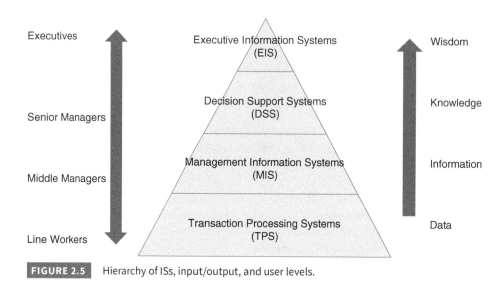

FIGURE 2.5 Hierarchy of ISs, input/output, and user levels.

In the next sections, we take a more in-depth look at these different types of IS and how they are used.

Transaction Processing System

Transaction processing is information processing that is divided into distinct, undividable operations called transaction. A **transaction processing system (TPS)** can be manual, as when data are typed into a form on a screen or automated by using scanners or sensors to capture barcodes or other data. TPSs are usually operated directly by frontline workers and provide the key data required to support the management of operations.

> **Transaction processing system (TPS)** is an information system that collects, monitors, stores, processes, and distributes specific types of data input from ongoing transactions.

Organizational data are processed by a TPS, for example, sales orders, reservations, stock control, and payments by payroll, accounting, financial, marketing, purchasing, inventory control, and other functional departments. The data are usually obtained through the automated or semiautomated tracking of low-level activities and basic transactions. Transactions are either:

Internal transactions are business transactions that originate within the organization or that occur within the organization, for example, payroll, purchases, budget transfers, and payments (in accounting terms, they are referred to as *accounts payable*); or

External transactions are business transactions that originate from outside the organization, for example, from customers, suppliers, regulators, distributors, and financing institutions.

TPSs are essential systems. Transactions that are not captured can result in lost sales, dissatisfied customers, unrecorded payments, and many other types of data errors with financial impacts. For example, if the accounting department issued a check to pay an invoice (bill) and it was cashed by the recipient, but information about that transaction was not captured, then two things happen. First, the amount of cash listed on the company's financial statements is incorrect because no deduction was made for the amount of the check. Second, the accounts payable (A/P) system will continue to show the invoice as unpaid, so the accounting department might pay it a second time. Likewise, if services are provided, but the transactions are not recorded, the company will not bill for them and thus lose service revenue.

Real-Time Processing Versus Batch Processing.
Data captured by a TPS are processed and periodically stored in a database (Chapter 3); they then become available for use by other systems. Processing of transactions is done in one of two ways:

1. **Real-time processing**   When airlines or theaters need to process seat reservations in real time to verify that seats are still available, they use **real-time processing**. OLTP uses client servers so that transactions can run on multiple computers on a network to process the transactions in real time. Data are accessed directly from the database and reports can be generated automatically (**Figure 2.6**).

Real-time processing   also referred to as online transaction processing (OLTP)—occurs when transactions are processed as they occur to keep account balances and inventories up to date and ensure the system always reflects the current status of the data.

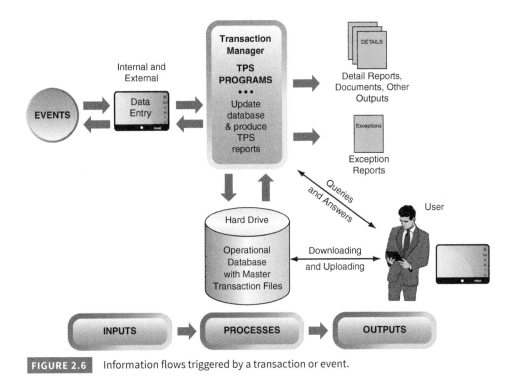

FIGURE 2.6   Information flows triggered by a transaction or event.

2. **Batch processing**   When transactions for a day, shift, or other time period are processed as "batched" data and updated in the data store, it is called **batch processing.** For example, payroll processing done weekly or biweekly is an example of batched data. Batch processing costs less than real-time processing. A disadvantage is that data are inaccurate some of the time because they are not updated in real time.

Batch processing   occurs when data are collected over a period of time and processed together at a predetermined time, such as hourly, daily, or weekly.

Processing Impacts Data Quality.
As data are collected or captured, they are validated to detect and correct obvious errors and omissions. For example, when a customer sets up an account with a financial services firm or retailer, the TPS validates that the address, city, and postal code provided are consistent with one another and also that they match the credit card holder's address, city, and postal code. If the form is not complete or errors are detected, the customer is required to make the corrections before the data are processed any further.

Data errors detected later may be time-consuming to correct or cause other problems. You can better understand the difficulty of detecting and correcting errors by considering identity theft. Victims of identity theft face enormous challenges and frustration trying to correct data about them.

Management Information System

Management information system (MIS) is a general-purpose reporting system whose objective is to provide managers with scheduled reports to track operations, monitoring, and control.

A **management information system (MIS)** is built on the data provided by TPSs. MISs are management-level systems that are used by middle managers to help ensure the smooth running of an organization in the short to medium term. The highly structured information provided by these systems allows managers to evaluate an organization's performance by comparing current with previous outputs. Functional areas or departments—accounting, finance, production/operations, marketing and sales, human resources, and engineering and design—are supported by ISs designed for their specific reporting needs.

Typically, a functional system provides reports about such topics as operational efficiency, effectiveness, and productivity by extracting information from databases and processing it according to the needs of the user. Types of reports include the following:

Periodic reports are created or run according to a preset schedule. Examples are daily, weekly, and quarterly.

- **Periodic reports** are easily distributed via e-mail, blogs, internal websites (called *intranets*), or other electronic media. Periodic reports are also easily ignored if workers do not find them worth the time to review.

Exception reports are generated only when something is outside the norm, either higher or lower than expected.

- **Exception reports** are created in unusual circumstances. These might include when generator sales immediately prior to a hurricane are much higher than the norm or when sales of fresh produce drops during a food contamination crisis. Exception reports are more likely to be read because workers know that some unusual event or deviation has occurred.

Reports generated by an MIS typically include graphs and charts, like the column and pie charts shown in **Figure 2.7**.

Damir Karan/iStockphoto.com

FIGURE 2.7   Sample report produced by an MIS.

Decision Support Systems

Ad hoc or on demand reports are unplanned reports. They are generated to a mobile device or computer *as needed*. They are generated on demand to learn more about a situation, problem, or opportunity.

A **decision support system (DSS)** is a knowledge-based system used by senior managers to facilitate the creation of knowledge and allow its integration into the organization. More specifically, a DSS is an interactive application that supports decision-making by manipulating and building upon the information from an MIS and/or a TPS to generate insights and new information in **ad hoc reports**.

Configurations of a DSS range from relatively simple applications that support a single user to complex enterprisewide systems. A DSS can support the analysis and solution of a specific problem, evaluate a strategic opportunity, or support ongoing operations. These systems support unstructured and semistructured decisions, such as make-or-buy-or-outsource decisions, or what products to develop and introduce into existing markets.

Structured decisions are relatively straightforward and made on a regular basis, and an IS can ensure that they are done consistently.

Degree of Structure of Decisions.   Decisions range from **structured** to **unstructured**. **Structured decisions** are those that have a well-defined method for solving and the data necessary to reach a sound decision. An example of a structured decision is determining whether an applicant qualifies for an auto loan, or whether to extend credit to a new customer—and the terms of those financing options. On the other hand, **unstructured decisions** include deciding which new products to develop or which new markets to enter. Semistructured decisions fall in the middle of the continuum. DSSs are best suited to support these types of decisions, but they are also used to support unstructured ones. To provide such support, DSSs have certain characteristics to support the decision-maker and the overall decision-making process.

Unstructured decisions are decisions that depend on human intelligence, knowledge, and/or experience—as well as on data and models to solve.

The main characteristic that distinguishes a DSS from an MIS is the inclusion of models. Decision-makers can manipulate models to conduct experiments and sensitivity analyses, for example, **what-if** and **goal seeking**. For example, what-if sales forecasts can be based on increases in customer demand, where current demand would be replaced by a projected change—maybe 5%—with higher and/or lower estimates to determine *what* would happen to sales *if* demand changed by 5%. On the other hand, **goal seeking** is a method of making decisions where the decision-maker has a specific outcome in mind and needs to determine how that outcome could be achieved and whether it is feasible to achieve that desired outcome. A DSS can also estimate the risk of alternative strategies or actions. Some of the benefits of implementing a DSS can be seen in **IT at Work 2.1**.

What-if analysis refers to changing assumptions or data in the model to observe the impacts of those changes on the outcome.

Goal seeking is the ability to calculate backward to obtain an input that would result in a set output.

IT at Work 2.1

California Pizza Kitchen (CPK) Uses a DSS to Support Inventory Decisions

White-collar criminal defense attorneys Larry Flax and Rick Rosenfield in Beverly Hills, California created California Pizza Kitchen (https://www.cpk.com) in 1985. Famously known for its hearth-baked barbecue-chicken pizza, the "designer pizza at off-the-rack prices" concept thrived.

Currently, CPK has over 250 locations in 30 U.S. states and 11 countries, including 17 California Pizza Kitchen nontraditional, franchise concepts designed for airports, universities, and stadiums. Maintaining optimal inventory levels at all its restaurants was challenging and time-consuming. In the early days, CPK used

an MIS to keep track of its financial information. However, maintaining inventory of all restaurants at optimal levels was challenging and time-consuming and as CPK managers' needs for quick, ad hoc reports to guide their daily ordering and operations, the inflexibility of the MIS proved to be a problem. To address this increased need for just-in-time reports and inventory updates, CPK replaced its MIS with a DSS. The ad hoc reporting capability of the DSS made it much easier for the chain's managers to maintain updated records, generate reports as and when needed to support inventory decisions at the corporate and restaurant levels. Many CPK restaurants reported a 5% increase in sales after the DSS was implemented.

Executive Information System

An **executive information system (EIS)** is typically used to identify long-term trends and to plan appropriate courses of action. The information in such systems is often weakly structured and comes from both internal and external sources. EISs are designed to be operated directly by executives without the need for intermediaries and easily tailored to the preferences of the individual using them. An EIS organizes and presents data and information from both external data sources and internal MIS or TPS in an easy-to-use dashboard format to support and extend the inherent capabilities of senior executives.

Executive information system (EIS) is a strategic-level information system that helps executives and senior managers analyze the environment in which the organization exists.

Initially, EISs were custom-made for an individual executive. However, a number of off-the-shelf EIS packages now exist and some enterprise-level systems offer a customizable EIS module. The characteristics of the various types of ISs are described in **Table 2.1**.

TABLE 2.1 Characteristics of Types of IS

Type	Characteristics	Type	Characteristics
TPS	Used by **operations** personnel	DSS	Used by **senior** managers
	Use internal and external data		Use internal and external data from MIS plus data added by the decision-maker who may have insights relevant to the decision context
	Crunch data to produce information for other ISs		Support semistructured or unstructured decisions
	Efficiency oriented		Contain models or formulas that enable sensitivity analysis, what-if analysis, goal seeking, and risk analysis
			Predict the future
MIS	Used by **lower and middle** managers	EIS	Used by **C-level** managers
	Based on internal information from TPS		Use internal data from lower level IS and external data sources
	Support structured decisions		Support unstructured decisions
	Inflexible		Very flexible
	Lack analytical capabilities		Easy-to-use, customizable interface
	Focus on past and present data		Focus on effectiveness of the organization

Here's an example of how these ISs are used together to add value in an organization. Day-to-day transaction data collected by the TPS are converted into prescheduled summarized reports by middle managers using an MIS. The findings in these reports are then analyzed by senior managers who use a DSS to support their semistructured or unstructured decision-making. DSSs contain models that consist of a set of formulas and functions, such as statistical, financial, optimization, and/or simulation models. Corporations, government agencies, the military, health care, medical research, major league sports, and nonprofits depend on their DSSs to answer what-if questions to help reduce waste in production operations, improve inventory management, support investment decisions, and predict demand and help sustain a competitive edge.

Customer data, sales, and other critical data produced by the DSS are then selected for further analysis, such as trend analysis or forecasting demand and are input into an EIS for use by top level management, who add their experience and expertise to make unstructured decisions that will affect the future of the business.

Figure 2.8 shows how the major types of ISs relate to one another and how data flow among them. In this example,

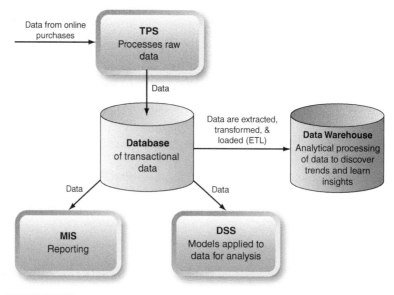

FIGURE 2.8 Flow of data from point of sale (POS) through processing, storage, reporting, decision support, and analysis. Also shows the relationships among different types of ISs.

1. Data from online purchases are captured and processed by the TPS and then stored in the transactional database.

2. Data needed for reporting purposes are extracted from the database and used by the MIS to create periodic, ad hoc, or other types of reports.

3. Data are output to a DSS where they are analyzed using formulas, financial ratios, or models.

ISs Exist within Corporate Culture

It is important to remember that ISs do not exist in isolation. They have a purpose and a social (organizational) context. A common *purpose* is to provide a solution to a business problem. The *social context* of the system consists of the values and beliefs that determine what is admissible and possible within the culture of the organization and among the people involved. For example, a company may believe that superb customer service and on-time delivery are critical success factors. This belief system influences IT investments, among other factors.

The business value of IT is determined by the people who use them, the business processes they support, and the culture of the organization. That is, IS value is determined by the relationships among ISs, people, and business processes—all of which are influenced strongly by organizational culture.

In an organization, there may be a culture of distrust between the technology and business employees. No enterprise IT architecture methodology or data governance can bridge this divide unless there is a genuine commitment to change. That commitment must come from the highest level of the organization—senior management. Methodologies cannot solve people problems; they can only provide a framework in which those problems can be solved.

Questions

1. Name the six components of an IS.
2. Describe the differences between data, information, knowledge, and wisdom.
3. Define TPS and give an example.
4. Explain why TPSs need to process incoming data before they are stored.
5. Define MIS and DSS and give an example of each.
6. What characteristic distinguishes a DSS from an MIS?
7. What level of personnel typically uses an EIS?
8. What factors determine IS value?

2.2 IT Infrastructure, IT Architecture, and Enterprise Architecture

LO2.2 Describe *IT infrastructure, IT architecture, and enterprise architecture (EA) and their roles in guiding IT growth and sustaining long-term performance and growth.*

Every enterprise has a core set of ISs and business processes that execute the transactions that keep it in business. Transactions include processing orders, order fulfillment and delivery, purchasing inventory and supplies, hiring and paying employees, and paying bills. To most effectively utilize its IT assets, an organization must create an IT infrastructure, IT architecture, and an **enterprise architecture (EA)** as shown in **Figure 2.9**.

Enterprise architecture (EA) is a conceptual blueprint that defines the structure and operation of an organization's strategy, information, processes, and IT assets.

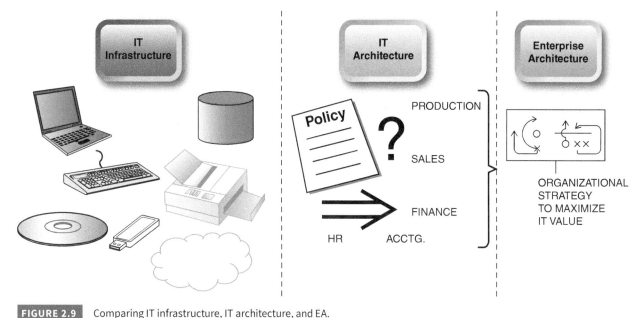

FIGURE 2.9 Comparing IT infrastructure, IT architecture, and EA.

IT infrastructure is an inventory of the physical IT devices that an organization owns and operates. It does **NOT** include the people or process components of an information system.

IT architecture guides the process of planning, acquiring, building, modifying, interfacing, and deploying IT resources in a single department within an organization.

The IT infrastructure describes an organization's entire collection of hardware, software, networks, data centers, facilities, and other related equipment used to develop, test, operate, manage, and support IT services.

The IT architecture offers a way to systematically identify technologies that work together to satisfy the needs of the departments' users. The IT architecture is a blueprint for how future technology acquisitions and deployment will take place. It consists of standards, investment decisions, and product selections for hardware, software, and communications. The IT architecture is developed first and foremost based on department direction and business requirements.

A well-developed EA reviews all the information systems across all departments in an organization to develop a strategy to organize and integrate the organization's IT infrastructures to help it meet the current and future goals of the enterprise and maximize the value of technology to the organization. It also enables the achievement of business objectives by providing graphic and text descriptions of strategies, policies, information, ISs, and business processes and the relationships between them to show a holistic view of the organization.

Adding Value with an EA

The EA adds value to an organization in that it can provide the basis for organizational change just as architectural plans guide a construction project. Since a poorly crafted EA can also hinder day-to-day operations and efforts to execute business strategy, it is more important than ever before to carefully consider the EA within your organization when deciding on an approach to business, technology, and corporate strategy. Simply put, EA helps solve two critical challenges: *where* an organization is going and *how* it will get there.

To get the most out of its EA, business leaders must understand, and more importantly measure, how the EA helps enable the organization to achieve sustainable growth in the most cost-effective and efficient way, while building in-house capabilities. The EA teams often struggle with measuring and communicating the value of their function since the EA function differs from company to company based on culture, funding levels, and the role IT plays in the enterprise. While it is typical to think of measuring success in solely financial terms, such as profitability and return on investment (ROI), measuring nonfinancial indicators, such as improved customer satisfaction, faster speed to market, and lower employee turnover is typically important, as diagrammed in **Figure 2.10**.

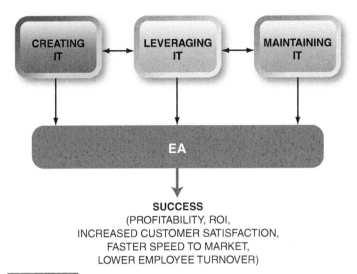

FIGURE 2.10 EA success.

Measuring EA Success

The success of EA in an organization is calculated by measuring a set of **key performance indicators (KPIs)**. KPIs present data in easy-to-comprehend and comparison-ready formats to gauge or compare performance in terms of meeting an organization's operational and strategic goals.

KPIs help reduce the complex nature of EA performance to a small number of understandable measures such as capabilities, operational performance, project performance, and financial performance as shown in **Figure 2.11,** and their importance to measuring the EA function is demonstrated in **IT at Work 2.2.**

Key performance indicators (KPIs) are a set of quantifiable measures used to evaluate factors that are critical to the success of an organization.

Capabilities

- Percentage of EA awareness
- Number of standards developed

Operational Performance

- Number of apps reused by more than one BU
- Number of apps purchased vs. built
- Percentage of reduction of repetitive data entry
- Percentage of increase in sharing data via Web services

Project Performance

- Percentage of reduction of development costs
- Number of projects using EA guidance
- Percentage of reduction in app development time
- Percentage of project architecturally aligned

Financial Performance

- Annual savings from digitization and enhanced process efficiency
- Percentage of cost reduction associated with adopting enterprise-wide standards
- Cost savings through reuse of software components and standardized purchase agreements
- Total cost savings to investment as result of EA
- Total cost avoidance to investment as result of EA

FIGURE 2.11 Enterprise architecture KPIs.

IT at Work 2.2

A New EA Improves Data Quality and EIS Use

Executives at a large chemical corporation were supported by an EIS that was specifically designed to meet their needs. The EIS was designed to provide senior managers with internal and external data and KPIs that were relevant to their specific needs. As with any system, the value of the EIS depended on the quality of the data it holds.

Too Much Irrelevant Data

Unfortunately, the EIS was a failure. Executives soon discovered that only half the data available through the EIS related to their level of analysis and decision-making at the corporate level. A worse problem was that the data they needed were not available when and how they wanted them. For example, executives needed to analyze current detailed sales revenue and cost data for every strategic business unit (SBU), product line, and operating business to compare performance. Unfortunately, data were not in standardized format as needed, making analysis difficult or impossible. A large part of the problem was that SBUs reported sales revenues in different time frames (e.g., daily, weekly, monthly, or quarterly), and many of those reports were not available when needed. As a result, senior management could not get a *trusted* view of the company's current overall performance and did not know which products were profitable.

There were two reasons why EIS failed:

1. **IT architecture was not designed for customized reporting** The design of the IT architecture had been based on financial accounting rules. That is, the data were organized to make it easy to collect and consolidate the data needed to prepare financial statements and reports that had to be submitted to the SEC (Securities and Exchange Commission) and other regulatory agencies. These statements and reports have well-defined or standardized formats and only need to be prepared at specific times during the year, typically annually or quarterly. The organization of the data (for financial reporting) did not have the flexibility needed for the customized ad hoc (unplanned) data needs of the executives. For example, it was nearly impossible to generate customized sales performance (nonfinancial) reports or do ad hoc analyses, such as comparing inventory turnover rates by product for each region for each sales quarter. Because of lags in reports from various SBUs, executives could not trust the underlying data.

2. **Complicated user interface** Executives could not easily review the KPIs. Instead, they had to sort through screens packed with too much data—some of interest and some irrelevant. To compensate for poor interface design, several IT analysts themselves had to do the data and KPI analyses for the executives—delaying response time and driving up the cost of reporting.

Solution: New EA with Standardized Data Formats

The CIO worked with a task force to design and implement an entirely new EA. Data governance policies and procedures were implemented to standardize data formats companywide. Data governance eliminated data inconsistencies to provide reliable KPI reports on inventory turns, cycle times, and profit margins of all SBUs.

The new architecture was business-driven instead of financial reporting-driven. It was easy to modify reports—eliminating the costly and time-consuming ad hoc analyses. Fewer IT resources are needed to maintain the system. Because the underlying data are now relatively reliable, EIS use by executives increased significantly.

EA and Sustainability

As you read in Chapter 1, the volume, variety, and speed of data being collected or generated have increased dramatically over the past decade. As enterprise ISs become more complex, long-range IT planning for sustainability is critical. Companies cannot simply continue to add storage, new apps, or data analytics on an as-needed basis and expect those additional IT assets to work with existing systems.

The relationship between complexity and planning is easier to see in physical things such as buildings and transportation systems. For example, if you are constructing a simple holiday cabin in a remote area, there is no need to create a detailed plan for future expansion. On the other hand, if you are building a large commercial development in a highly populated area, you're not likely to succeed without a detailed project plan. Relating this to the case of enterprise ISs, if you are building a simple, single-user, nondistributed system, you would not need to develop a well-thought-out growth plan. However, this approach would not be feasible to enable you to successfully manage big data, copious content from mobiles and social networks, and data in the cloud. Instead, you would need a well-designed set of plans, or blueprints, provided by an EA to align IT with business objectives by guiding and controlling hardware acquisition, software add-ons and upgrades, system changes, network upgrades, choice of cloud services, and other digital technology investments that you will need to make your business sustainable.

There are two specific strategic issues that the EA is designed to address:

1. **IT systems' complexity**   IT systems have become unmanageably complex and expensive to maintain.
2. **Poor business alignment**   Organizations find it difficult to keep their increasingly expensive IT systems aligned with business needs.

Business and IT Benefits of EA.   Having the right EA in place is important for the following reasons:

- EA cuts IT costs and increases productivity by giving decision-makers access to information, insights, and ideas where and when they need them.

- EA determines an organization's competitiveness, flexibility, and IT economics for the next decade and beyond. That is, it provides a long-term view of a company's processes, systems, and technologies so that IT investments do not simply fulfill immediate needs.

- EA helps align IT capabilities with business strategy—to grow, innovate, and respond to market demands, supported by an IT practice that is 100% in accord with business objectives.

- EA can reduce the risk of buying or building systems and enterprise applications that are incompatible or unnecessarily expensive to maintain and integrate.

Developing an EA

Developing an EA starts with the organization's goals, for example, *where does it want to be in three years?* and identifies the strategic direction in which it is heading and the business drivers to which it is responding. The goal is to make sure that everyone understands and shares a single vision. As soon as managers have defined this single shared vision of the future, they then consider the impact this vision will have on the business, technical, information, and solutions architectures of the enterprise. This shared vision of the future will dictate changes in all these architectures, assign priorities to those changes, and keep those changes grounded in business value.

Microsoft suggests four different perspectives be included in an EA as shown in **Table 2.2**.

It is important to recognize that the EA must be dynamic, not static. To sustain its effectiveness, it should be an ongoing process of aligning the creation, operation, and maintenance of IT across the organization with the ever-changing business objectives. As business needs change, so must the EA.

TABLE 2.2   Components of an EA

Business architecture	How the business works. Includes broad business strategies and plans for moving the organization from where it is now to where it wants to be. Processes the business uses to meet its goals
Application architecture	Portfolio of organization's applications. Includes descriptions of automated services that support business processes; descriptions of interactions and interdependencies between the organization's ISs
Information architecture	What the organization needs to know to perform its business processes and operations. Includes standard data models; data management policies and descriptions of patterns of information production and use in an organization
Technology architecture	Hardware and software that support the organization. Examples include desktop and server software; OSs; network connectivity components; printers, modems

EA Must Be Dynamic and Evolving

In order to keep IT aligned with the business, the EA must be a dynamic plan and changes in priorities and the business direction must be continually reflected in the target architecture to help keep IT aligned with them.

As shown in the model in **Figure 2.12**, the EA evolves toward the target architecture, which represents the company's future IT needs. According to this model, EA defines the following:

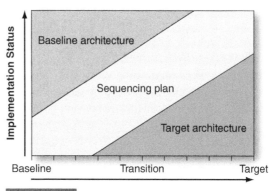

FIGURE 2.12   The importance of viewing EA as a dynamic and evolving plan.

1. The organization's mission, business functions, and future direction
2. Information and information flows needed to perform the mission
3. The current baseline architecture
4. The desired target architecture
5. The sequencing plan or strategy to progress from the baseline to the target architecture.

In essence, an IT infrastructure inventories physical IT devices, an IT architecture guides the acquisition, use, and disposal of them and the EA integrates the two to create IT strategy.

Questions

1. What is the purpose of the IT infrastructure?
2. How is the IT infrastructure different from the IT architecture?
3. What is the purpose of an EA?
4. What are the business benefits of an EA?
5. Explain why it is necessary to ensure that an EA maintains alignment between IT and business strategy?
6. What four categories of KPIs are typically used to measure the success of an EA? Give two examples of each.

Data center   is a large group of networked computer servers typically used by organizations for the remote storage, processing, or distribution of large amounts of data. A data center can also refer to the building or facility that houses the servers and equipment.

Cloud computing   is a model of networked online storage where data are stored in virtualized pools generally hosted by third parties.

2.3 | Data Centers and Cloud Computing

LO2.3 Understand *the different types of data centers, cloud computing and cloud services, and how they each add value in an organization.*

Data centers and **cloud computing** are types of IT infrastructures. In the past, there were few IT infrastructure options. In the early days of computing, companies owned their servers, storage, and network components to support their business applications, and these computing resources were located on their premises. Now, there are several new choices for an IT infrastructure strategy—including cloud computing. As is common to IT investments, each infrastructure configuration has strengths, weaknesses, and cost considerations.

Data Centers

Traditionally, data and database technologies were kept in data centers that were typically run by an in-house IT department (**Figure 2.13**) and consisted of on-premises hardware and equipment that store data within an organization's local area network.

Oleksiy Mark/Shutterstock

FIGURE 2.13   A row of network servers in a data center.

Today, companies may own and manage their own on-premises data centers or pay for the use of their vendors' data centers, such as in cloud computing, data virtualization, and software-as-a-service arrangements (**Figure 2.14**).

Michael D Brown/Shutterstock

FIGURE 2.14   Data centers are the infrastructure underlying cloud computing, virtualization, networking, security, delivery systems, and software-as-a-service.

In an on-premises data center connected to a local area network, it is easier to restrict access to applications and information to authorized, company-approved people and equipment. In the cloud, the management of updates, security, and ongoing maintenance are outsourced to a third-party cloud provider where data is accessible to anyone with the proper credentials and Internet connection. This arrangement can make a company more vulnerable since it increases exposure of company data at many more entry and exit points. Here are some examples of data centers.

- **National Climatic Data Center** The National Climatic Data Center (https://www.ncdc.noaa.gov/) is an example of a public data center that stores and manages the world's largest archive of weather data.

- **U.S. National Security Agency** The National Security Agency (https://www.nsa.gov/) houses its data center, shown in **Figure 2.15**, in Bluffdale, UT. It is the largest spy data center for the NSA. People who think their correspondence and postings through sites like Google, Facebook, and Apple are safe from prying eyes should rethink that belief. You will read more about reports exposing government data collection programs in Chapter 5.

EPA/epa european pressphoto agency b.v. /Alamy Stock Photo

FIGURE 2.15 The NSA data center in Bluffdale, UT.

- **Apple** has a 500,000-square-foot data center in Maiden, NC, that houses servers for various iCloud and iTunes services. The center plays a vital role in the company's back-end IT infrastructure. The data center has earned the highest level rating system for energy-efficient buildings, using 14% recycled materials in its construction process, diverting 93% of construction waste from landfills and sourcing almost 50% of purchased materials within 500 miles of Maiden to reduce the environmental impact from trucking materials over long distances.

Since only the company owns the infrastructure, a data center is more suitable for organizations that run many different types of applications and have complex workloads. A data center, like a factory, has limited capacity. Once it is built, the amount of storage and the workload the center can handle does not change without purchasing and installing more equipment.

When data centers fail, all operations, regardless of who owns the data center, can be seriously disrupted. These outages point to the risks of maintaining the complex and sophisticated technology needed to power data centers used by millions or hundreds of millions of people. Sometimes, enterprises' duplicated data are stored in many different or remote locations. While this might be useful for data that needs to be available in multiple locations to enable a quick response to queries, doing this can create data chaos at times. For example, the data needed for planning, decision-making, operations, queries, and reporting may be scattered or duplicated across numerous servers, data centers, devices, and cloud services. However, for the organization to function effectively, this disparate data must be unified or integrated.

Data Virtualization

Data virtualization is the process of abstracting, transforming, merging, and delivering data from disparate sources to provide a single point of access.

As organizations have transitioned to a cloud-based infrastructure, data centers have become virtualized. For example, Cisco (https://www.cisco.com) offers **data virtualization,** which gives greater IT flexibility. The main goal of data virtualization is to provide a single point of access to the data. By aggregating data from a wide range of sources, users can access applications without knowing their exact location. Using data virtualization methods, enterprises can respond to change more quickly and make better decisions in real time without physically moving their data, which significantly cuts costs.

Cisco Data Virtualization makes it possible to:

- Have instant access to data at any time and in any format
- Respond faster to changing data analytics needs
- Cut complexity and costs

Compared to traditional (nonvirtual) data integration and replication methods, data virtualization accelerates time to value with:

- **Greater agility** Speeds 5–10 times faster than traditional data integration methods
- **Streamlined approach** 50–75% time savings over data replication and consolidation methods
- **Better insight** Instant access to data

Software-Defined Data Center. Data virtualization has led to the latest development in data centers—the **software-defined data center (SDDC)**. An SDDC facilitates the integration of the various infrastructures of the SDDC silos within organizations and optimizes the use of resources, balances workloads, and maximizes operational efficiency by dynamically distributing workloads and provisioning networks. The goal of the SDDC is to decrease costs and increase agility, policy compliance, and security by deploying, operating, managing, and maintaining applications. In addition, by providing organizations with their own private cloud, SDDCs provide greater flexibility by allowing organizations to have on-demand access to their data instead of having to request permission from their cloud provider (see **Figure 2.16**).

Software-defined data center (SDDC) is a way to dramatically configure and provision apps, infrastructure, and IT resources, allowing a data center to be managed as a unified system.

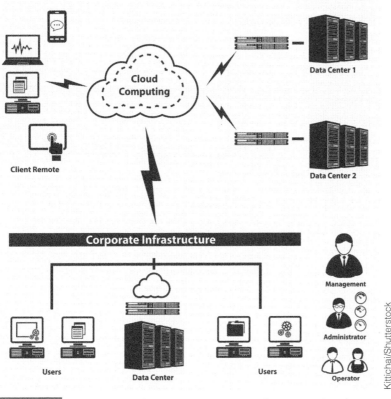

FIGURE 2.16 Corporate IT infrastructures can consist of an on-premises data center and off-premises cloud computing.

The base resources for the SDDC are *computation, storage, networking, and security*. Typically, the SDDC includes limited functionality of service portals, applications, OSs, VM hardware, hypervisors, physical hardware, software-defined networking, software-defined storage, a security layer, automation and management layers, catalogs, a gateway interface module, and third-party plug-ins (**Figure 2.17**).

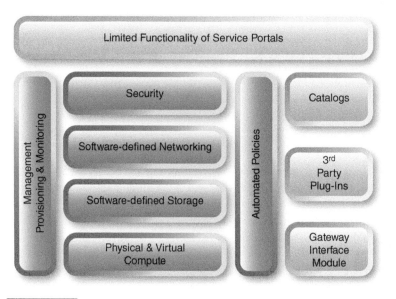

FIGURE 2.17 SDDC infrastructure (adapted from Sturm et al., 2017).

The SDDC market is expected to experience rapid growth over the coming years with a rise in the demand for advanced data management solutions for monitoring and ensuring the safety of enterprise data. As the use of SDDCs grows, data center managers will be called upon to scale their data centers exponentially at a moment's notice. Unfortunately, this is impossible to achieve using the traditional data center infrastructure. In the SDDC, software placement and optimization decisions are based on business logic, not technical provisioning directives. This requires changes in culture, processes, structure, and technology. The SDDC isolates the application layer from the physical infrastructure layer to facilitate faster and more effective deployment, management, and monitoring of diverse applications. This is achieved by finding each enterprise application an optimal home in a public or private cloud environment or draw from a diverse collection of resources.

From a business perspective, moving to an SDDC is motivated by the need to improve security, increase alignment of the IT infrastructure with business objectives and provision of applications more quickly.

Traditional data centers have dedicated, isolated hardware that results in poor utilization of resources and very limited flexibility. By consolidating virtualized servers, second-generation virtualization data centers use fewer resources and reduce the steps needed to decrease the time it takes to deploy workloads. This facilitates the definition of applications and resource needs. The flexible SDDC environment enables enterprise applications to be quickly reconfigured and supported to provide infrastructure as a service (IaaS). In this way, transitioning to an SDDC enables an organization to optimize its resource usage, provide capacity on demand, improve business-IT alignment, improve agility and flexibility of operations, and save money (**Figure 2.18**).

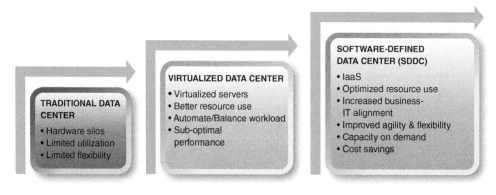

FIGURE 2.18 Evolution of data centers (adapted from Sturm et al., 2017).

Cloud Computing

In a business world where first movers gain the advantage, IT responsiveness and agility provide a competitive edge and lead to sustainable business practices. Yet, many IT infrastructures are extremely expensive to manage and too complex to easily adapt. A common solution is cloud computing. Cloud computing is the general term for infrastructures that use the Internet and private networks to access, share, and deliver computing resources.

Cloud systems are *scalable*. That is, they can be adjusted to meet changes in business needs. At the extreme, the cloud's capacity is unlimited depending on the vendor's offerings and service plans. A drawback of the cloud is control because a third party manages it. Unless the company uses a **private cloud** within its network, it shares computing and storage resources with other cloud users in the vendor's **public cloud**. Public clouds allow multiple clients to access the same virtualized services and utilize the same pool of servers across a public network. In contrast, private clouds are single-tenant environments with stronger security and control for regulated industries and critical data. In effect, private clouds retain all the IT security and control provided by traditional IT infrastructures with the added advantages of cloud computing.

private cloud delivers cloud computing services over the Internet or a private internal network to only select users instead of the general public.

public cloud is based on the standard cloud computing model in which a service provider makes resources, apps, or storage available to the general public over the Internet either free or on a pay-per-usage model.

Cloud Infrastructure

The cloud has greatly expanded the options for enterprise IT infrastructures because any device that accesses the Internet can access, share, and deliver data. Cloud computing is a valuable infrastructure because:

1. **It is dynamic**, not static and provides a way to make applications and computing power available on demand. Applications and power are available on demand because they are provided *as a service*. For example, any software that is provided on demand is referred to as **software as a service (SaaS)**. Typical SaaS products are Google Apps and Salesforce.com (https://www.salesforce.com). SaaS and other cloud services are discussed in more detail later in this section.
2. **Helps companies become more agile and responsive** while significantly reducing IT costs and complexity through improved workload optimization and service delivery.

software as a service (SaaS) is a widely used software licensing and delivery model in which software is licensed to users on a subscription basis and is centrally hosted.

Move to Enterprise Clouds.   A majority of large organizations have hundreds or thousands of software licenses that support business processes, such as licenses for Microsoft Office, Oracle database management, IBM CRM (customer relationship management), and various network security software. Managing software and their licenses involves deploying, provisioning, and updating them—all of which are time-consuming and expensive. Cloud computing overcomes these problems.

Enterprise Clouds is a special case of using cloud computing for competitive advantage through cost savings, increased speed and agility, and vastly improved collaboration among business partners and customers.

Moving Workloads from the Enterprise to the Cloud

Building a cloud strategy is a challenge and moving existing applications to the cloud is stressful. Despite the business and technical benefits, the risk exists of disrupting operations or customers in the process. With the cloud, the network and WAN (wide area network) become an even more critical part of the IT infrastructure. Greater network bandwidth is needed to support the increase in network traffic. And, putting part of the IT architecture or workload into the cloud requires different management approaches, different IT skills, and knowing how to manage vendor relationships and contracts.

Infrastructure Issues.   There is a big difference because cloud computing runs on a shared infrastructure, so the arrangement is less customized to a specific company's requirements. A comparison to help understand the challenges is that outsourcing is like renting an apartment, while the cloud is like getting a room at a hotel.

With cloud computing, it may be more difficult to get to the root of performance problems, like the unplanned outages that occurred with Google's Gmail and Workday's human resources apps. The trade-off is cost versus control.

Increasing demand for faster and more powerful computers, and increases in the number and variety of applications are driving the need for more capable IT architectures.

Cloud Services

Cloud computing is often referred to as a stack or broad range of services built on top of each other under the name cloud. Cloud services can advance the core business of delivering superior services to optimize business performance. Cloud can cut costs and add flexibility to the performance of critical business apps. It can improve responsiveness to end-consumers, application developers, and business organizations.

Cloud services are services made available to users on demand via the Internet from the servers of a cloud computing provider instead of being accessed through an organization's on-premises servers.

Traditional approaches to increasing database performance—manually tuning databases, adding more disk space, and upgrading processors—are not enough when you are dealing with streaming data and real-time big data analytics. **Cloud services** help to overcome these limitations. Cloud services are outsourced to a third-party cloud provider who manages the updates, security, and ongoing maintenance and are designed to provide easy, scalable access to applications, resources, and services and are fully managed by a cloud services provider. Each of these concepts, collectively known as Anything-as-a-Service (XaaS) models, are described in the following section, and the way in which one company used private and public cloud services to accelerate its digital transformation strategy is demonstrated in **IT at Work 2.3**.

IT at Work 2.3

Lufthansa Technik Philippines Accelerates Digital Transformation with Private and Public Cloud Services

Demand for air travel in the Asia Pacific grew by almost 9% in 2018, more than 2% faster than in Europe and 3.5 faster than in North America. This growth is creating huge potential for companies such as Lufthansa Technik Philippines (LTP) who provide airline maintenance, repair, and overhaul services (MRO). To fuel theses ambitions, LTP rethought its traditional model of running its IT infrastructure and development in-house and turned to Fujitsu, a hosting and managed-services company to create a hybrid IT model of public and private cloud services and existing systems. In this way, LTP was able not only to gain greater efficiencies and reliability but also to freed up resources in its IT group to concentrate on exploiting emerging new technologies.

As a result, the operation and maintenance of LTP systems have become more reliable and less labor intensive. Instead of having to manage their applications day to day, Fujitsu manages their core systems. In the highly regulation industry in which it operates, safety is LTP's number one priority and it wants to make sure the airplanes it maintains and repairs are returned to service in the safest condition possible. For this to happen, reliability of IT is key. Now, LTP is planning to blend its new private cloud with a set of public cloud apps it can use for less sensitive applications.

By moving to cloud services, LTP has also experienced a reduction of IT costs. It no longer needs to invest heavily in training and has been able to move people to other, more exciting lines of work including analytics, artificial intelligence (AI), robotics, and the Internet of things (IoT). All in all, the blend of cloud services that LTP has chosen has turned into a game changer for the company, that aspires to become the MRO of first choice in Asia.

Sources: Compiled from MacIver (2019), Martin (2019), and https://www.lufthansa-technik.com.

Anything-as-a-Service (XaaS) Models

The cloud computing model for on-demand delivery of and access to various types of computing resources also extends to the development of business apps. **Figure 2.19** shows five "as a service" solutions based on the concept that the resource—software, platform, infrastructure, data, or technology—can be provided on demand regardless of geolocation. As these as-service solutions develop, the focus is changing from massive technology implementation costs to business-reengineering programs that enable anything-as-a service (XaaS) platforms.

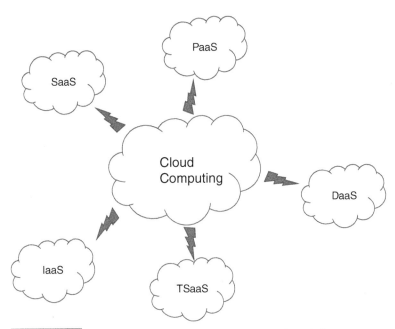

FIGURE 2.19   Five as-a-service solutions: software, platform, infrastructure, data, and technology solutions as a service.

Software as a Service.

SaaS is a rapidly growing method of delivering software and is particularly useful in applications in which there are considerable interactions between the organization and external entities that do not confer a competitive advantage, for example, e-mail and newsletters. It is also useful when an organization is going to be needing a particular type of software for a short period or for a specific project, and for software that is used periodically, for example, tax, payroll, or billing software. SaaS is not appropriate for accessing applications that require fast processing of real-time data or applications where regulation does not permit data being hosted externally.

Other terms for SaaS are *on-demand computing* and *hosted services.* The idea is basically the same: Instead of buying and installing expensive packaged enterprise applications, users can access software applications over a network, using an Internet browser. To use SaaS, a service provider hosts the application at its data center and customers access it via a standard Web browser. SaaS services can be licensed o customers as on-demand, through a subscription, as a pay-as-you-go model, or free of charge where revenue can be generated by other means, such as through sale of advertisements.

The SaaS model was developed to overcome the common challenge to an enterprise of being able to meet fluctuating demands on IT resources efficiently. It is used in many business functions, primarily customer relationship management (CRM), accounting, human resources (HR), service desk management, communication, and collaboration.

There are thousands of SaaS vendors. Salesforce.com is one of the most widely known SaaS providers. Other examples are Google Docs and collaborative presentation software Prezi. For instance, using Google Docs you use a browser to log in instead of installing Microsoft Word on your own computer, and then loading Word to create a document. This way, only the browser uses your computer's resources.

Platform as a Service (PaaS).

Platform as a service provides a standard unified platform for developing, testing, and deploying software over the Web. This computing platform allows the creation of Web applications quickly and easily without the complexity of buying and maintaining the underlying infrastructure. Without PaaS, the cost of developing some applications would be prohibitive.

Examples of PaaS include databases, Web servers, development tools, and execution runtime. PaaS is particularly useful when multiple software developers are working on a software development project when other external parties need to interact with the development process and for when developers want to automate testing and deployment services. It is less

Platform as a service (PaaS) is a computing platform that enables the quick and easy creation, testing, and deployment of Web applications without the necessity of buying and maintaining the software and infrastructure underneath it. It is a set of tools and services that make coding and deploying these applications faster and more efficient.

useful in those instances where application performance needs to be customized to the underlying hardware and software or an application needs to be highly portable in terms of where it is hosted. Some examples of PaaS include Microsoft Azure Service, Force.com, and App Engine.

Infrastructure as a Service (IaaS).

Infrastructure as a Service (IaaS) is a way of delivering servers, storage, networks, workload balancers, and OSs as an on-demand service.

Rather than purchasing all the components of its IT infrastructure, organizations buy their computing resources as a fully outsourced **Infrastructure as a Service (IaaS)** on demand. Generally, IaaS can be acquired as a public or private infrastructure or a combination of the two (hybrid).

A public IaaS is one that consists of shared resources deployed on a self-service basis over the Internet. On the other hand, a private IaaS is provided on a private network. And, a hybrid IaaS is a combination of both public and private. IaaS is useful where organizations experience significant highs and lows in terms of demand on the infrastructure, for new or existing organizations who have budgetary constraints on hardware investment and in situations where an organization has temporary infrastructure needs. Some IaaS providers you may be familiar with include Amazon Web Services (AWS) and Rackspace.

Data as a Service (DaaS).

Data as a Service (DaaS) is an information provision and distribution model in which data files (including text, images, sounds, and videos) are made available to customers over a network by a service provider.

Data as a Service is a relatively new entrant into the XaaS arena. DaaS enables data to be shared among clouds, systems, apps, and so on regardless of the data source or where they are stored. Data files, including text, images, sound, and video, are made available to customers over a network, typically the Internet. DaaS makes it easier for data architects to select data from different pools, filter out sensitive data, and make the remaining data available on demand.

A key benefit of DaaS is that it transfers the risks and responsibilities associated with data management to a third-party cloud provider. Traditionally, organizations stored and managed their data within a self-contained storage system; however, as data become more complex, it is increasingly difficult and expensive to maintain using the traditional data model. Using DaaS, organizational data are readily accessible through a cloud-based platform and can be delivered to users despite of organizational or geographical constraints. This model is growing in popularity as data become more complex, difficult, and expensive to maintain. Some of the most common business applications currently using DaaS are CRM and enterprise resource planning (ERP).

Technology Solutions as a Service—The New Kid on the Block.

Technology solutions as a service (TSaaS) combines software, hardware, networks, and telecommunications to provide specialized technology solutions that allow companies to adopt new technologies and transform their business.

Technology solutions as a service (TSaaS) is the newest entrant into the XaaS arena. Technology services are professional IT services designed to make the use of customizable and scalable technology accessible to all sizes of organizations.

The beauty of TSaaS is that it makes it easy for companies to optimize, manage, and automate their traditional IT environments by seamlessly integrating the latest technologies without the upfront financial burden of purchasing brand new equipment. By customizing the right level of service for an organizational environment, TSaaS provides the flexibility that companies need to focus on their core business and respond in real time to their clients' needs. Companies that provide TSaaS include ASD (https://www.asd-usa.com/technology-as-a-service) and ATSG (https://www.atsg.net/technology-solutions-as-a-service).

As-a-Service Models Are Enterprisewide and Can Trigger Lawsuits.

To achieve the benefits of cloud computing and XaaS, there must be IT, legal, and senior management oversight because a company still must meet its legal obligations and responsibilities to employees, customers, investors, business partners, and society. For example, the various As-a-service models are used in various aspects of business such as CRM and HR management and are also being used for operational and strategic purposes. Companies are frequently adopting software, platform, infrastructure, data management, and starting to embrace *mobility as a service* and *big data as a service* because they typically no longer have to worry about the costs of buying, maintaining, or updating their own data servers. Both hardware and human resources expenses can be cut significantly. Service arrangements all require that managers understand the benefits and trade-offs—and how to negotiate effective CSAs. Regulations mandate that confidential data be protected regardless of whether the data are on-premises or in the cloud. Therefore, a company's legal department needs to get involved in these IT decisions. Put simply, moving to cloud services is not simply an IT decision because the stakes around legal and compliance issues are very high.

Selecting a Cloud Vendor

Because cloud is still a relatively new and evolving business model, the decision to select a cloud service provider should be approached with even greater diligence than other IT decisions. As cloud computing becomes an increasingly important part of the IT delivery model, assessing and selecting the right cloud provider also become the most strategic decisions that business leaders undertake. Providers are not created equally, so it is important to investigate each provider's offerings prior to subscribing. When selecting and investing in cloud services, there are several service factors a vendor needs to address. These evaluation factors are listed in **Table 2.3.**

TABLE 2.3	Service Factors to Consider When Evaluating Cloud Vendors or Service Providers
Factors	**Examples of Questions to Be Addressed**
Delays	What are the estimated server delays and network delays?
Workloads	What is the volume of data and processing that can be handled during a specific amount of time?
Costs	What are the costs associated with workloads across multiple cloud computing platforms?
Security	How are data and networks secured against attacks? Are data encrypted and how strong is the encryption? What are network security practices?
Disaster recovery and business continuity	How is service outage defined? What level of redundancy is in place to minimize outages, including backup services in different geographical regions? If a natural disaster or outage occurs, how will cloud services be continued?
Technical expertise and understanding	Does the vendor have expertise in your industry or business processes? Does the vendor understand what you need to do and have the technical expertise to fulfill those obligations?
Insurance in case of failure	Does the vendor provide cloud insurance to mitigate user losses in case of service failure or damage? This is a new and important concept.
Third-party audit or an unbiased assessment of the ability to rely on the service provided by the vendor	Can the vendor show objective proof with an audit that it can live up to the promises it is making?

Vendor Management and Cloud Service Agreements. The move to the cloud is also a move to vendor-managed services and **cloud service agreements (CSA).**

Staff experienced in managing outsourcing projects may have the necessary expertise for managing work in the cloud and policing SLAs with vendors. The goal is not building the best CSA terms, but negotiating the terms that align most closely with the business needs. For example, if a server becomes nonoperational and it does not support a critical business operation, it would not make sense to pay a high premium for reestablishing the server within one hour. On the other hand, if the data on the server support a business process that would effectively close down the business for the period of time that it was not accessible, it would be prudent to negotiate the fastest possible service in the CSA and pay a premium for that high level of service.

Cloud service agreements (CSA) is also referred to as cloud service-level agreements (SLAs); the CSA or SLA is a negotiated agreement between a company and a service provider that can be a legally binding contract or an informal contract.

The Cloud Standards Customer Council (CSCC) first published the *Practical Guide to Cloud Service Agreements, Version 2.0*, in April 2015, to reflect changes that have occurred since 2012 when it first published the *Practical Guide to Cloud Service Level Agreements*. The new guide provides a practical reference to help enterprise IT and business decision-makers analyze CSAs from different cloud service providers. The main purpose of a CSA is to set clear expectations for service between the cloud customer (buyer) and the cloud provider (seller), but CSAs should also exist between a customer and other cloud entities, such as the cloud carrier, the cloud broker, and even the cloud auditor. Although the various service delivery models, that is, IaaS, PaaS, SaaS, and so on, may have different requirements, the guide focuses on the requirements that are common across the various service models (Cloud Standards Customer Council, 2015, p. 4).

Implementing an effective management process is an important step in ensuring internal and external user satisfaction with cloud services. **Table 2.4** lists the 10 steps that should be taken by cloud customers to evaluate cloud providers' CSAs in order to compare CSAs across multiple providers or to negotiate terms with a selected provider. You can review a sample CSA used by IBM by visiting http://www-05.ibm.com/support/operations/files/pdf/csa_us.pdf.

TABLE 2.4   10 Steps to Evaluate a CSA

1. Understand roles and responsibilities of the CSA customer and provider
2. Evaluate business-level policies and compliance requirements relevant to the CSA customer
3. Understand service and deployment model differences
4. Identify critical performance objectives such as availability, response time, and processing speed. Ensure they are measurable and auditable
5. Evaluate security and privacy requirements for customer information that has moved into the provider's cloud and applications, functions, and services being operated in the cloud to provide required service to the customer
6. Identify service management requirements such as auditing, monitoring and reporting, measurement, provisioning, change management, and upgrading/patching
7. Prepare for service failure management by explicitly documenting cloud service capabilities and performance expectations with remedies and limitations for each
8. Understand the disaster recovery plan
9. Develop a strong and detailed governance plan of the cloud services on the customer side
10. Understand the process to terminate the CSA

Questions

1. What is a data center?
2. What is the difference between on-premises data centers and cloud computing?
3. What is an SDDC?
4. What are the advantages of using an SDDC?
5. How can cloud computing solve the problems of managing software licenses?
6. What factors should be considered when selecting a cloud vendor or provider?
7. When are private clouds used instead of public clouds?
8. Explain three issues that need to be addressed when moving to cloud computing or services.

2.4 | Virtualization and Virtual Machines

LO2.4 Describe *the various types of virtualization and the ways in which an organization can benefit from it.*

Managers want streamlined, real-time, data-driven enterprises, yet they may face budget cuts. Sustaining performance requires the development of new business applications and analytics capabilities, which comprise the *front end* and the data stores and digital infrastructure, or back end, to support them. The back end is where the data reside. The problem is that data may have to navigate through a congested IT infrastructure that was first designed decades ago. These network or database bottlenecks can quickly wipe out the competitive advantages from big data, mobility, and so on.

Virtualization is one of the most cost-effective, hardware-reducing, energy-saving techniques used by cloud providers that allows the sharing of a single physical instance of an IT resource or app among multiple customers and organizations. It does this by assigning a logical name to a physical device and providing a pointer to that physical resource when demanded. There are many types of virtualization, such as virtual storage devices, virtual desktops, virtual OSs, and virtual servers for network virtualization.

You might ask why organizations want to virtualize their physical computing and networking devices. The answer is a gross underutilization of inefficient use of resources. Computer hardware had been designed to run a single OS and a single app, which leaves most computers vastly underutilized. Take, for example, the payroll app for a very large company that is run only once a month. Virtualization is a technique that creates a virtual (i.e., nonphysical) layer and multiple virtual machines (VMs) to run on a single physical machine. The virtual (or virtualization) layer makes it possible for each VM to share the resources of the hardware. **Figure 2.20** shows the relationship among the VMs and physical hardware.

Virtualization allows the sharing of a single physical instance of an IT resource or app among multiple customers and organizations

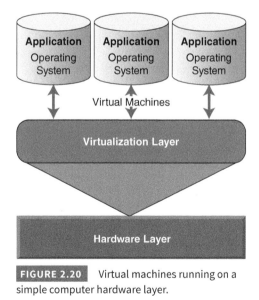

FIGURE 2.20   Virtual machines running on a simple computer hardware layer.

What Is a Virtual Machine?   Just as *virtual reality* is not real, but a software-created

world, a virtual machine is a software-created computer with a virtual server that sends and receives signals just like a physical one, even though it doesn't have its own circuitry and other physical components.

Technically, a **virtual machine (VM)** is created by a software layer, called the *virtualization layer,* as shown in Figure 2.20. That layer has its own Windows or other OS and apps, such as Microsoft Office, as if it were an actual physical computer.

virtual machine (VM)   is an emulation of a computer system based on computer architectures and provide functionality of a physical computer.

A VM behaves exactly like a physical computer and contains its own virtual—that is, *software-based*—CPU, RAM (random access memory), hard drive, and network interface card (NIC). An OS cannot tell the difference between a VM and a physical machine, nor can applications or other computers on a network tell the difference. Even the VM thinks it is a "real" computer. Users can set up multiple real computers to function as a single PC through virtualization to pool resources to create a more powerful VM.

Types of Virtualization

Almost any element of an IS can be virtualized, i.e., hardware, software, server, storage, network and desktop. In general, virtualization separates business applications and data from hardware resources. This separation allows companies to pool hardware resources—rather than dedicate servers to applications—and assign those resources to applications as needed. As a result, the most popular and widely used type of virtualization is hardware virtualization. The different types of virtualization are shown in **Figure 2.21** and defined below.

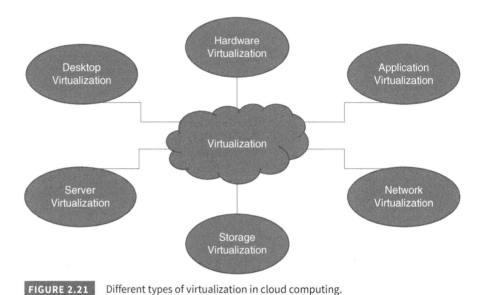

FIGURE 2.21 Different types of virtualization in cloud computing.

- **Storage virtualization** is the pooling of physical storage from multiple network storage devices into what appears to be a single storage device managed from a central console.
- **Server virtualization** consolidates multiple physical servers into virtual servers that run on a single physical server.
- **Desktop virtualization** is software technology that separates the desktop environment and associated application software from the physical machine that is used to access it.
- **Application virtualization** is the practice of running software from a remote server rather than on the user's computer.
- **Network virtualization** combines the available resources in a network by splitting the network load into manageable parts, each of which can be assigned (or reassigned) to a particular server on the network.
- **Hardware virtualization** is the use of software to emulate hardware or a total computer environment other than the one the software is actually running in. It allows a piece of hardware to run multiple OS images at once.

IT at Work 2.4 demonstrates one example of how virtualization can help an organization provide higher levels of customer service and improve productivity to ensure business continuity.

IT at Work 2.4

Virtualization and Business Continuity Go Hand in Hand at Liberty Wines

Liberty Wines (https://www.libertywines.co.uk) is one of the United Kingdom's foremost wine importers and distributors. It supplies wine to restaurants, supermarkets, and independent retailers from its headquarters in central London. It has earned multiple international wine awards, including the International Wine Challenge on Trade Supplier of the Year for two years running. As the business expanded, the existing servers did not have the capacity to handle increased data volumes, and maintenance of the system put a strain on the IT team of two employees. Existing systems were slow and could not provide the responsiveness that employees expected.

Liberty Wines had to speed up business processes to meet the customer needs in the fast-paced world of fine dining. To provide the service their customers expect, employees at Liberty Wines needed quick and easy access to customers, order, and stock information. In the past, the company relied on 10 physical servers for applications and services, such as order processing, reporting, and e-mail.

Liberty Wines deployed a virtualized server solution incorporating Windows Server 2008 R2. The 10 servers were replaced with 3 physical servers, running 10 virtual servers. An additional server was used as part of a backup system, further improving resilience and stability.

By reducing the number of physical servers from 10 to 4, power use and air conditioning costs were cut by 60%. Not only was the bottom line improved, but the carbon footprint was also reduced, which is good for the environment.

The new IT infrastructure cut hardware replacement costs by £45,000 (U.S. $69,500) while enhancing stability with the backup system. Applications now run faster, too, so employees can provide better customer service with improved productivity. When needed, virtual servers can be added quickly and easily to support business growth.

Virtualization increases the flexibility of IT assets, allowing companies to consolidate IT infrastructure, reduce maintenance and administration costs, and prepare for strategic IT initiatives. Virtualization is not primarily about cost-cutting, which is a tactical reason. More importantly, for strategic reasons, virtualization is used because it enables flexible sourcing and cloud computing.

The characteristics and benefits of virtualization include the following:

1. **Memory-intensive** VMs need a huge amount of RAM (random access memory, or primary memory) because of their massive processing requirements.
2. **Energy-efficient** VMs minimize energy consumed running and cooling servers in the data center—representing up to a 95% reduction in energy use per server.
3. **Scalability and load balancing** When a big event happens, such as the Super Bowl, millions of people go to a website at the same time. Virtualization provides load balancing to handle the demand for requests to the site. The VMware infrastructure automatically distributes the load across a cluster of physical servers to ensure the maximum performance of all running VMs. Load balancing is key to solving many of today's IT challenges.

Virtualization consolidates servers, which reduces the cost of servers, makes more efficient use of data center space, and reduces energy consumption. All of these factors reduce the total cost of ownership (TCO). Over a three-year life cycle, a VM costs approximately 75% less to operate than a physical server.

Questions

1. What are the main types of XaaS?
2. What are the advantages of using cloud computing?
3. How might companies risk violating regulation or compliance requirements with cloud services?
4. In what ways is a virtualized information system different from a traditional information system?
5. Describe the different types of virtualization.
6. What is load balancing and why is it important?

Chapter Summary

LO2.1 *Identify* the six components of an information system, the various types of information systems to the level of support needed, and the difference between data, information, knowledge, and wisdom.

The six components of an information system are: hardware, software, networks, people, procedures, and data. Of these, the data component is the most important since without data an information system would have no content or purposes. When working with information systems, data are distinguished from information in that data are raw facts and figures and information is processed data that is presented in a meaningful way to answer the questions "who, what, when, where." Similarly, knowledge is differentiated from information such that knowledge has added value. By adding user experience, knowledge can answer the question "how" something happens. Wisdom is more abstract than data and information that can be collected and knowledge that can be shared. It adds value to lower-level data, information, and knowledge and enhances the effectiveness of the organization by answering the question "why" based on user expertise and past experiences in a given situation.

Transaction process systems (TPSs) are used at the operational level where raw data are input into the system to create content that will be used by another higher-level IS. At the middle manager level, the most commonly used system is an MIS that processes and manipulates information transmitted from the lower-level TPSs to produce scheduled periodic reports. Decision support systems (DSSs) are typically put into operation to support senior-level managers and it is common to see what-if analyses performed using spreadsheet software in a DSS to help them make on-demand decisions that affect tactical decisions. At the C-level, managers are provided with executive information systems (EISs) that use dashboards and other graphical interfaces to visually show trends over time to assist in strategy setting and executive decision making at the strategic level.

LO2.2 *Describe* IT infrastructure, IT architecture, and enterprise architecture (EA) and their roles in guiding IT growth and sustaining long-term performance and growth.

The IT infrastructure takes a holistic view of the organization's IT assets by providing an inventory of all the physical IT devices an organization owns or leases, excluding its people or procedures. On the other hand, the IT architecture creates policies to guide the process of planning, acquiring, building, modifying, interfacing with, and implementing IT resources within a single department. The most complex of these is the enterprise architecture (EA). It is the EA that integrates the IT infrastructure with the multiple IT architectures from the different business units to create an organizational strategy to maximize IT value. The EA adds value by helping address two critical challenges: where an organization is going and how it will get there. With the right EA in place, an organization can cut IT costs, increase productivity, determine an organization's competitiveness, help IT align its capabilities with the business strategy, and reduce the risk of buying or building systems and enterprise apps

that are incompatible or unnecessarily expensive to maintain and integrate. In essence, an IT infrastructure inventories physical IT devices, an IT architecture guides the acquisition, use, and disposal of them, and the EA integrates the two to create IT strategy.

LO2.3 *Understand* the different types of data centers, cloud computing and cloud services, and how they each add value to an organization.

Traditionally, data centers were located on-site and were connected to a local area network to enable companies to restrict access to apps and information to authorized internal employees. In the cloud, data is stored at a third-party site and is accessible to anyone with the proper access permissions. To further decrease costs and increase agility, policy compliance and security, organizations are turning to software-defined data centers that add even more value to organizations by improving security, increasing IT infrastructure alignment with business objectives and provisioning apps more quickly.

Cloud computing delivers scalable computing and storage resources as a service to end-users over a network. Public clouds make resources available to the general public over the Internet. Private clouds limit sharing of resources to persons within the organization over a private network and offer stronger security and control for regulated industries and sensitive corporate data. Cloud computing adds value in an organization through its dynamic provisioning of apps and data and helps companies become more agile and responsive while significantly reducing IT costs and complexity through improved workload optimization and service delivery.

Cloud services are services made available to users on demand via the Internet from cloud computing providers' servers. In the anything as a service (XaaS) model, on-demand delivery of cloud services provides access to various types of computing resources, including infrastructure (IaaS), software (SaaS), data (DaaS), technology solutions (TSaaS), and platform (PaaS). SaaS is a rapidly growing method of delivering software and is particularly useful in apps where there is considerable interaction between the organization and external entities that are not competing or for apps that are used for periodically or for a specific project.

LO2.4 *Describe* the different types of virtualization and the ways in which an organization can benefit from it.

There are many types of virtualization including storage, server, desktop, apps, network, and hardware. A virtual machine (VM) is an emulation of a computer system based on computer architectures and provide functionality of a physical computer. A VM behaves exactly like a physical computer and contains its own virtual—*software-based*—CPU, RAM (random access memory), hard drive, and network interface card (NIC). Virtualization and VMs increase the flexibility of IT assets and allows companies to consolidate its IT infrastructure, reduce maintenance and administration costs, and better prepare for strategic IT initiatives. The scalability and load balancing they offer also enable organizations to handle fluctuating demands, reduces energy consumption, and increases the flexibility of their IT assets.

Key Terms

Ad hoc or on demand reports   40
batch processing   39
cloud computing   48
cloud service agreements (CSAs)   57
Cloud services   54
Data   36
Data as a Services   56
Data center   48
data virtualization   50
decision support system (DSS)   40
enterprise architecture (EA)   43
Enterprise Clouds   53
Exception reports   40
executive information system (EIS)   41
goal seeking   41

Hardware   35
Information   36
information system   34
Infrastructure as a Service (IaaS)   56
IPOS   34
key performance indicators (KPIs)   45
Knowledge   37
management information system (MIS)   40
Network   35
People   35
Periodic reports   40
Platform as a service   55
private cloud   53
Procedures   35
public cloud   53

real-time processing   39
Software   35
software as a service (SaaS)   53
software-defined data center (SDDC)   51
Structured decisions   40
Technology solutions as a service (TSaaS)   56
The IT architecture   44
The IT infrastructure   44
transaction processing system (TPS)   38
unstructured decisions   41
Virtualization   59
virtual machine (VM)   59
what-if analysis   41
Wisdom   37

Assuring Your Learning

Discuss: Critical Thinking Questions

1. Why is a strong market position or good profit performance only temporary?

2. Assume you had:

   a. A tall ladder with a sticker that lists a weight allowance only 5 lb more than you weigh. You know the manufacturer and model number.

   b. Perishable food with an expiration date two days into the future.

   c. A checking account balance that indicates you have sufficient funds to cover the balance due on an account.

   In all three cases, trusting the data to be correct could have negative consequences. Explain the consequences of trusting the data in each instance. How might you determine the correct data for each instance? Which data might not be possible to verify? How does dirty data impact your decision-making?

3. If business data are scattered throughout the enterprise and not synched until the end of the month, how does that impact day-to-day decision-making and planning?

4. Assume a bank's data are stored in silos based on financial product—checking accounts, saving accounts, mortgages, auto loans, and so on. What problems do these data silos create for the bank's managers?

5. Why do managers and workers still struggle to find information that they need to make decisions or act despite advances in digital technology? That is, what causes data deficiencies?

6. According to a Tech CEO Council Report, Fortune 500 companies waste $480 billion every year on inefficient business processes. What factors cause such huge waste? How can this waste be reduced?

7. Explain why organizations need to implement an EA.

8. What two problems can EA solve?

9. Why is it important for data to be standardized? Give an example of unstandardized data.

10. Why are TPSs critical systems?

11. Discuss why the cloud acts as the *great IT delivery frontier.*

12. What are the functions of data centers?

13. What factors need to be considered when selecting a cloud vendor?

14. What protection does an effective CSA provide?

15. Why is a CSA a legal document?

16. How can virtualization reduce IT costs while improving performance?

Explore: Online Exercises

1. When selecting a cloud vendor to host your enterprise data and apps, you need to evaluate the CSA.

   a. Research the CSAs of two cloud vendors, such as Rackspace, Amazon, or Google.

   b. For the vendors you selected, what are the CSA uptime percentages?

   c. Does each vendor count both scheduled downtime and planned downtime toward the CSA uptime percentage?

   d. Compare the CSAs in terms of two other criteria.

   e. Decide which CSA is better based on your comparisons.

   f. Report your results and explain your decision.

2. Visit eWeek.com Cloud News and Reviews at https://www.eweek.com/cloud and select one of the articles. Prepare an executive summary of the article.

3. Visit the website for Rackspace professional services (https://www.rackspace.com/professional-services) and choose two cloud-related services. Describe each of those cloud solutions and list the benefits organizations can enjoy from their use.

4. Visit Solarwinds Virtualization Manager (https://www.solarwinds.com/virtualization-manager) and view their interactive demo.

5. Visit YouTube.com and search for two videos on virtualization. For each video, give the title and date of the video and report what you learned.

Analyze & Decide: Apply IT Concepts to Business Decisions

1. Financial services firms experience large fluctuations in business volumes because of the cyclical nature of financial markets. These fluctuations are often caused by crises—such as the subprime mortgage problems, the discovery of major fraud, or a slowdown in the economy. These fluctuations require that executives and IT leaders can cut spending levels in market downturns and quickly scale up when business volumes rise again. Research SaaS solutions and vendors for the financial services sector. Would investment in SaaS help such firms align their IT capacity with their business needs and also cut IT costs? Explain your answer.

2. Despite multimillion-dollar investments, many IT organizations cannot respond quickly to evolving business needs. Also, they cannot adapt to large-scale shifts like mergers, sudden drops in sales, or new product introductions. Can cloud computing help organizations improve their responsiveness and get better control of their IT costs? Explain your answer.

3. Identify four KPIs for a major airline (e.g., American, United, Delta) or an automobile manufacturer (e.g., GM, Ford, BMW). Which KPI would be the easiest to present to managers on an online dashboard? Explain why.

Reinforce: Ensure Your Understanding of the Key Terms

Solve the online crossword provided for this chapter.

Web Resources

More resources and study tools are located on the student website. You'll find useful Web links and self-test quizzes that provide individualized feedback.

Case 2.2

Business Case: Grupo AGORA Upgrades IT to Quench the Thirst of Millions Throughout Spain

Grupo AGORA has been making alcoholic and nonalcoholic beverages for the past 160 years! AGORA is a fully independent 100% family-owned group of companies with fifth and sixth generations of the family running the business. AGORA employs over 1,000 people and offers a diverse portfolio of quality brands including Ambar, Moritz, La Pantera, Agua de Lunares and Konga.

Traditionally, Grupo AGORA's drink market was limited to the northern area of Spain and the region around Barcelona, as a result it wasn't easy to find one of their drinks in other parties of the country. Recently, they began to plan a countrywide expansion to bring their products to people in all corners of Spain. Growing a business, while exciting, also brought challenges. To support their planned growth, AGORA quickly realized that it would need to upgrade its slow, aging IT hardware solutions that would severely hinder its planned expansion.

Moves to Upgrade

To achieve the much-needed IT upgrade, AGORA partnered with LENOVO to implement a state-of-the-art IT infrastructure that would maximize performance and give them the highest level of reliability on their storage network. This combination of hardware, networks, and storage components coupled with cloud software has enabled AGORA to better allocate resources according to actual demand by providing real-time information reliability and share it companywide at the touch of a button.

Benefits Achieved

These changes have proved to be incredibly helpful. AGORA can now efficiently manage stock levels, plan marketing campaigns, and prepare to deal with a sudden spike in demand because of unseasonably high temperatures or an upcoming city festival, such as the San Fermin bull-running festival in Pamplona when shops and bars need to stock extra supplies for the week-long event. In addition, sales and marketing teams can now refine and tweak predictions and strategies on a day-to-day basis by cross-checking information provided by the new systems. With the new IT solution, AGORA is well on its way to pursuing its business expansion plans.

Questions

1. List three reasons why Grupo AGORA wanted to expand its market.
2. What were the consequences to AGORA of having a slow, aging IT solution?
3. In which business functions is real-time information reliability helpful at AGORA? Explain.
4. Why is it important for AGORA to have up-to-date information about its products?

Sources: Compiled from Newsbyte (2018) and http://www.agoragrupo.com/en.

Career Insight 2.1

Becoming an Enterprise Architect

Enterprise architects need much more than technology skills. On a daily basis, an enterprise architect's activities can change quickly and significantly. Ideally, enterprise architects should come from a highly technical background. Even though enterprise architects deal with many other factors besides technology, it is still important to keep technical skills current. The job performance and success of such an architect—or anyone responsible for large-scale IT projects—depend on a broad range of skills.

- **Interpersonal or people skills** The job requires interacting with people and getting their cooperation.
- **Ability to influence and motivate** A large part of the job is motivating users to comply with new processes and practices.
- **Negotiating skills** The project needs resources—time, money, and personnel—that must be negotiated to get things accomplished.

- **Critical-thinking and problem-solving skills** Architects face complex and unique problems. Being able to expedite solutions prevents bottlenecks.
- **Business and industry expertise** Knowing the business and industry improves the outcomes and the architect's credibility.
- **Process orientation** Thinking in terms of process is essential for an enterprise architect. Building repeatable and reusable processes as artifacts from the work they do and how they work themselves.

The most common function an enterprise architect will perform is that of overseeing a large-scale program. Programs are a group of related projects, and as such, managing EA implementations requires someone who can handle multiple aspects of one or more projects at one time. Program management is discussed in detail in Chapter 13.

References

Centre for Computing History. "Tommy Flowers." 2019a. http://www.computinghistory.org.uk/det/1078/Tommy-Flowers/.

Centre for Computing History. "The Colossus Mark 1 Computer Is Delivered to Bletchley Park." 2019b. http://www.computinghistory.org.uk/det/6014/The-Colossus-Mark-1-computer-is-delivered-to-Bletchley-Park.

Cloud Standards Customer Council. "Practical Guide to Cloud Service Agreements, Version 2.0." 2015.

Crypto Museum. "Tommy Flower. Inventor of the First Electronic Computer." *Crypto Museum*, 2019.

McFadden, C. "Tommy Flowers: The Man Who Built Colossus." *Interesting Engineering*, January 6, 2018.

MacIver, K. "Setting a Hybrid IT Flight Path to Digital Transformation." *Global Intelligence for the CIO*, 2019.

Martin, S. "Cloud vs. On-Premises vs. Hybrid – Which Is Best?" *Service Muse,* 2019.

Newsbyte. "Lenovo and Nutanix Help AGORA Group Quench the Thirst of Millions in Spain." 2018. http://www.sccnewsbyte.co.uk/lenovo/lenovo-and-nutanix-help-agora-group-quench-the-thirst-of-millions-in-spain.

Sparks, K. "Tommy Flowers British Engineer." *Encyclopedia Britannica*, October 24, 2019.

Sturm, R., C. Pollard, and J. Craig. *Application Performance Management in the Digital Enterprise*. Elsevier, March 2017.

CHAPTER 3

Data Management, Data Warehouses, and Data Governance

Case 3.1 Opening Case

ThyssenKrupp Elevator Saves $1.5 Million and 900 Trees by Digitizing Documents

The Company

ThyssenKrupp Elevator (**https://www.thyssenkruppelevator.com/**) is part of ThyssenKrupp AG, a globally diversified industrial group formed in 1811. With 155,000 employees in nearly 80 countries, ThyssenKrupp AG develops high-quality products and intelligent industrial processes and services that promote sustainability. ThyssenKrupp Elevator engineers, delivers, and maintains high-quality elevators, escalators, moving walks, and passenger boarding bridges to move people safely, comfortably, and efficiently. By innovatively applying technology to address customer needs, ThyssenKrupp engineers and highly skilled technicians develop advanced solutions to reshape the elevator industry and transform cities into the best places to live. They accomplish this by providing higher transport capacity and efficiency, more efficient use of building floor space, reduced energy consumption, and maximum availability of existing passenger transportation solutions.

The Problem

Elevator construction is a data intensive process. Approximately 700 documents are created, processed, and stored during the installation of one elevator. Multiply 700 by the 2,100 elevators that ThyssenKrupp produces annually, add in manufacturing escalators, moving walks, passenger-boarding bridges, and stair and platform lifts and they have to handle almost ONE MILLION documents per year!

At ThyssenKrupp, the data collection process was largely paper-based. This made it very difficult for employees to quickly find important information in documents that were constantly being shipped back and forth between its 100+ branch and service locations in a physical "red folder." To add to the confusion, as the project progressed, members of a project team manually added their own paper documents. This caused wasted time, lack of visibility into jobs, and delays in product delivery.

According to Mike Fuller, a ThyssenKrupp developer/analyst, "we faced several ongoing challenges, as the cost and time to manage our document-heavy processes increased continually."

Further problems were caused when documents were attached to emails in internal systems that weren't well managed. In addition, ThyssenKrupp was having to spend $25,000 per month to ship hard copies of the documents between its 100+ branches throughout the United States and Canada.

The use of shared network folders also contributed to the problem. File structures stored on multiple servers often had more than nine levels, folder path names frequently exceeded the system-maximum of 255 characters, and documents were inconsistently stored and used a lot of different naming conventions. This method of storing data led to lost files, duplicate documents, and version-control issues and cost ThyssenKrupp even more time and money.

Damon Rodkey, IT Manager at ThyssenKrupp, summed ThyssenKrupp's data problems by saying that he often felt that finding oil in his backyard would be easier than trying to find a particular document in ThyssenKrupp's shared network folders.

The Solution

ThyssenKrupp assigned a cross-functional team of engineers, coordinators, managers, and drafters to review the document management process and explore different solutions. The team mapped existing business processes and created a vision for an ideal system that would quickly find and track document.

The team's goal was twofold—digitize ThyssenKrupp's paper-based systems and automate document and information discovery. To achieve this, they needed a custom software application that was designed for manufacturing companies. They found their answer in M-Files (**https://www.m-files.com/en**), an intelligent content and document management platform. The M-Files platform is designed to improve grouping and management of content and unstructured information, using metadata to tag key attributes in a document's content, such as location, customer number, document type, date, etc. This gives the user a 360-degree view across all systems to show "what" a document is and not just "where" it is stored.

M-Files also triggers workflows, such as ThyssenKrupp's drawing submittal and approval process, to ensure drawings are properly reviewed before approval. Other features of M-Files that ThyssenKrupp finds useful in its global business are deployment in the cloud or on-premises and real-time security updates to ensure ThyssenKrupp's data are always current and secure. Performance improvement metrics ensure that ThyssenKrupp can track ongoing enhancements to its speed and accuracy in data management.

Mike Fuller expressed approval of the team's solution by saying, "the combination of configurability, scalability, ease-of-use and low implementation cost made M-Files a clear fit for our (ThyssenKrupp's) stage of digital transformation."

The Outcome

Thanks to M-Files, ThyssenKrupp is now managing its almost 100 million documents, across 500 users in seven departments in a far more efficient and effective way. Nicole Harris, Repair Coordinator at ThyssenKrupp commented that, "Now we file documents tagged by certain names, job numbers and branches. This make finding documents a lot simpler and most importantly, faster."

New workflows have been introduced. The outdated physical red folder has been replaced by new highly efficient automated workflow processes. ThyssenKrupp has also implemented an automated workflow to create and name standard multi-file documents containers for drawings and another to initiate the process of automatically assigning drawings based on requests. In this way, deliverables and schedules can be more easily and quickly tracked within the system. Transmittal of documents to internal and external sources was also automated within M-Files. These efficient new workflows have eliminated unnecessary papers costs, eliminated lost paper-based and electronic documents, removed more than 13 physical document handoffs between staff and across numerous departments, and increased project transparency.

Project delays also have been significantly reduced through the addition of an analytics-based workflow tracker that document tasks and processes in the building of an elevator. The tracker notifies team managers, project managers, and management of any missed deadlines so they can act upon them.

Finally, to replace emails that were difficult to manage and track, ThyssenKrupp now tracks communication among team members related to common project questions. Team members can create questions within a database and synchronize them with M-Files workflows to track and resolve queries more easily and faster. This enables ThyssenKrupp to continually improve its processes by eliminating frequently asked questions as roadblocks to more efficient workflows.

Their innovative approach to streamlining workflows and enriching them with metadata has made ThyssenKrupp a stellar example of effective data management through digital transformation.

Questions

1. How many documents does ThyssenKrupp have to process to build one elevator?

2. How did using M-Files benefit ThyssenKrupp?

3. What consequence did ThyssenKrupp face because of project delays?

4. For what tasks does ThyssenKrupp Elevator use M-Files?

Sources: Compiled from IQ BG, Inc. (2018), Bitpipe (2019), and ThyssenKruppelevator.com.

 DID YOU KNOW?

Database management and data governance have never been more important. With the advent of social media, the Web, big data, and the Cloud, organizational data is scattered everywhere—on-site and off-site. Without proper visibility and control of their data, companies risk big revenue and productivity losses and might even be faced with the prospect of bankruptcy!

Introduction

Collecting and maintaining trusted data is a critical aspect of any business. With the advent of computers, the amount of data collected and stored by organizations has grown exponentially over the past 20 years along with exciting new technologies to support it. Managing these vast amounts of data is an important challenge for today's organizations. Knowing how and where to find data, store it efficiently, analyze it in new ways to increase the organization's competitive advantage, and enable the right people to access it at the right time are all fundamental components of managing the ever-increasing amounts of corporate data. The reliability of business decisions depends on access to high-quality, timely, easily accessible data and the quality of the data depends on the dependability and effectiveness of the organizations' data management approach.

Data management is a technique that helps companies improve productivity by ensuring that people can find the data they need without conducting a long and difficult search. The goal of data management is to provide the infrastructure and tools to transform raw corporate data into useable high-quality information and knowledge. Just as you need to learn how to identify, control, protect, analyze, and invest financial assets, you also need to learn how to manage corporate data assets.

Databases, data management, and database technologies provide the tools that business needs in the new **biz-tech ecosystem** characterized by an increased interdependency between business and IT, cooperation within and without the enterprise and behaviors based on trust.

In this chapter you will learn database terms and the technologies that support large and small databases. You will also learn how information and knowledge are managed to maximize the benefits of existing and emerging database technologies and how the database function is governed.

Biz-tech ecosystem demands that business treat IT as an equal partner and IT steps up to the mark.

3.1 Data Management

LO3.1 Describe *the fundamentals of data management and how database management systems, including blockchain technology, help companies improve performance.*

Data management oversees the end-to-end lifecycle of data from creation and initial storage to the time when it becomes obsolete and is deleted. Due to the incredible volume of data that the typical organization creates, effective data management is vital to prevent storage costs from spiraling out of control and controlling data growth while supporting greater performance.

The goals of effective data management include:

Data management is the management of the flow of data from creation and initial storage to the time when the data become obsolete and are deleted.

1. Mitigating the risks and costs of complying with regulations.
2. Ensuring legal requirements are met.
3. Safeguarding data security.
4. Maintaining accuracy of data and availability.
5. Certifying consistency in data that come from or go to multiple locations.
6. Ensuring that data conform to organizational best practices for access, storage, backup, and disposal.

Typically, newer data, and data that is accessed more frequently, is stored on faster, but more expensive storage media while less critical data is stored on cheaper, slower media.

Benefits of data management include:

- greater compliance
- higher security
- less legal liability
- improved sales and marketing strategies
- better product classification
- improved data governance to reduce risk.

Database Technologies

The following data management technologies are fundamental to data management to keep users informed and support an organization's diverse business demands:

- **Database**   A collection of data sets or records stored in a systematic way.
- **Database management system (DBMS)**   Software that integrates with data collection systems such as TPS and business apps to store data in an organized way and provide facilities for accessing and managing data.

- **Data warehouse** Large data set that integrates data from multiple databases and data silos across the organization, and organizes them for complex analysis, knowledge discovery, and to support decision-making. For example, data are extracted from a database, processed to standardize their format, and then loaded into a data warehouse at specific times, such as weekly. As such, data in data warehouses are nonvolatile and ready for analysis.

- **Data mart** A small-scale data warehouse that supports a single function or one department. Enterprises that cannot afford to invest in data warehousing may start with one or more data marts.

Each of these database technologies are discussed in the following sections.

Databases

Transaction is a single logical unit of work that accesses and possibly modifies the contents of a database.

Atomicity means that any modifications to the database (insert, update, delete) are either completely made or discarded.

Consistency refers to leaving all data in a consistent state at the end of a transaction to maintain the integrity of the database.

Isolation makes a transaction separate from and independent of any other transaction.

Durability requires that a completed transaction, once committed, becomes part of the database and is not reversible.

Prior to the advent of databases, unrelated files were used to manually store, retrieve, and search data. It was a tedious process that adversely affected organizational performance, growth, and sustainability. At a time when organizations were struggling with maintaining data integrity, reducing data inconsistencies, and ensuring data security, databases were a welcome relief and an exciting step forward in the age of digital technology. Databases store data generated by business apps, sensors, operations, and transaction-processing systems (TPS). In a database every statement is executed as a **transaction**. Transactions access data using read/write operations. To ensure the integrity of a database, all data must meet the ACID test described in **Tech Note 3.1**.

Tech Note 3.1

The Data ACID Test

All data collected, monitored, and stored in a database and processed and distributed by a database must meet four criteria—**Atomicity**, **Consistency**, **Isolation**, and **Durability** (ACID).

A simple example shows how the ACID properties of a database work.

Imagine that you want to transfer some funds from your checking account and deposit them into your savings account. To perform this transaction, a journal entry must be made for auditing purposes. In this instance, *Atomicity* means funds can't be taken out of your checking account without being subsequently deposited into your savings accounts. If the transfer was interrupted for any reason, your checking and savings account balances would remain unchanged. *Consistency* ensures that a record of your transaction is made in a journal. If the journal is full, or the entry cannot be recorded for some other reason, then the transfer is cancelled, and your account balances return to their original amounts. *Isolation* ensures your transfer cannot be affected by any other transaction. Other transactions to alter your checking balance must wait until your current transaction is complete. *Durability* assures that the transaction is not lost once it is saved or committed. So, a power outage or a system crash won't cause any of your data to go missing.

Centralized database stores all data as a unified body in a single central computer such as a mainframe or server in one physical location.

Distributed database stores portions of the database on multiple computers controlled by a database management system (DBMS) within a network in a client-server configuration.

Centralized and Distributed Database Architectures
Medium and large enterprises typically have databases that are classified as **centralized** or **distributed**, as shown in **Figure 3.1**.

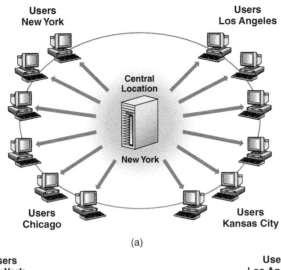

(a)

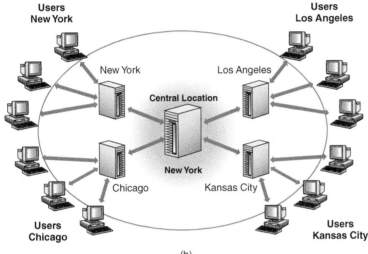

(b)

FIGURE 3.1 Comparison of (a) centralized and (b) distributed databases.

Centralized Databases

The traditional approach for storing data in larger enterprises is on a centralized database platform. In a centralized database, data are stored and maintained on one mainframe computer in a single physical location. Users access the single source of data from multiple points over a network (**Figure 3.1**). As the volume of data grew, this centralized configuration became unwieldy and caused bottlenecks in accessing data.

Benefits of a centralized database architecture include:

1. **Better control of data quality** Data consistency is easier when data are kept in one physical location because data additions, updates, and deletions can be made in a supervised and orderly fashion.

2. **Ease of use** Easier to maintain and back up in one physical location.

3. **Better IT security** Data are accessed via the centralized host computer, where they can be protected more easily from unauthorized access or modification.

4. **Better data integrity** Data stored in a centralized database are not duplicated in other places.

Disadvantages of centralized databases include:

1. **Transmission delay** When users are geographically dispersed the central computer can be slow to respond due to variations in data transfer rates.

2. **Security** The integrity of the data could easily be compromised if someone gained access to the central computer and data could be added, changed, and removed.

Scalability is the ability of the system to increase in size to handle data growth or the load of an increasing number of concurrent users, that is, scalable systems efficiently meet the demands of high-performance computing.

3. **Reliability**   A large number of simultaneous requests could cause the central computer to become overloaded and no longer respond.

4. **Scalability**   It is difficult to scale a centralized computer that has a limited capacity and cannot handle an infinite number of requests

Distributed Databases

Distributed databases were introduced to overcome speed and accessibility issues associated with the centralized database approach. In a distributed database, corporate data are stored on multiple servers controlled by a database management system (DBMS), as shown in **Figure 3.2**. The servers reside in the company's data centers, a private cloud, and/or a public cloud and users access the various servers via a wide area network (WAN). The most popular DBMSs are Oracle (**https://www.oracle.com/index.html**), IBM Db2 (**https://www.ibm.com/analytics/db2**), and Microsoft QuickBase (**https://www.quickbase.com/**).

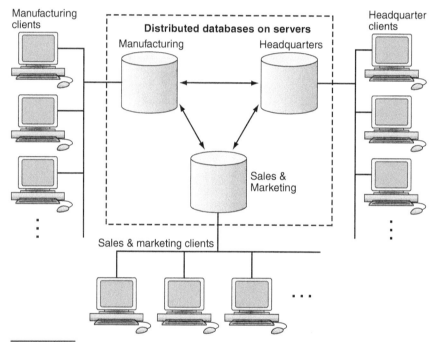

FIGURE 3.2   Distributed database architectures for headquarters, manufacturing, and sales and marketing.

Advantages of a distributed database include:

1. **Security**   The distributed database is controlled by a single, designated authority that authenticates a client's credentials before providing access to the database.

2. **Reliability**   If one site crashes, the system will keep running.

3. **Speed**   It's faster to search a part of a database than a single unified body of data.

4. **Scalability**   The load is shared between several computers. Consequently, the server resources are much greater than in a centralized database.

Disadvantages associated with distributed databases include:

1. **Availability**   If there's a problem with the network the distributed database is using, it can be difficult to access the data when needed.

2. **Expense**   The appropriate hardware and software can be expensive to purchase.

3. **Security**   If the security of the designated authority is compromised, data can be modified or even deleted.

Database Management System (DBMS)

To get the most out of a database that can automatically load, retrieve, or modify existing data from the system, a software package designed to define, manipulate, and manage the data must be used. This software package is called a database management system.

A database management system is basically a computerized data-keeping system that provides an accurate and consistent view of data throughout the enterprise to enable informed, actionable decisions that support the business strategy. Functions performed by a DBMS to help create such a view are shown in **Figure 3.3.**

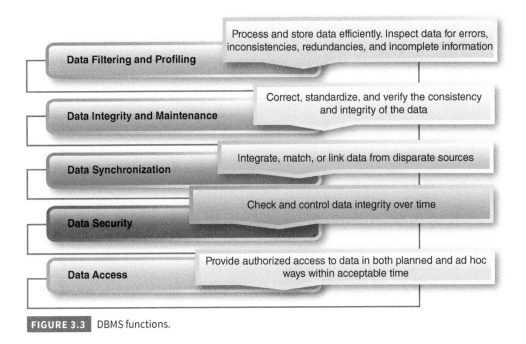

FIGURE 3.3 DBMS functions.

Online Transaction Processing versus Online Analytics Processing When most business transactions occur, that is, an item is sold or returned, an order is sent or cancelled, a payment or deposit is made, changes are made immediately to the database. Users of a DBMS can carry out four basic operations to either make these changes to the data stored in the database or manage the actual structure of the database. These four operations are known by the acronym **CRUD**—create (add), read, update and delete.

A DBMS records and processes these transactions in the database and supports queries and reporting. Given its function, a DBMS is referred to as an **online transaction processing (OLTP)** system. OLTP databases can process millions of transactions per second.

Databases are not the best tool for working with large, complex data sets—**online analytics processing (OLAP)**, and decision support. These limitations have led to the introduction of data warehouse technology. Data warehouses and data marts are optimized for OLAP and decision support.

To recap, databases are best used for extremely fast transaction processing and query processing. On the other hand, data warehouses and data marts are more appropriate for analysis of complex data and will be discussed further in Section 3.2.

Online transaction processing (OLTP) is a database design that breaks down complex information into simpler data tables to strike a balance between transaction processing efficiency and query efficiency.

Online analytics processing (OLAP) is the analysis of complex data from a data warehouse.

Elements of a DBMS

There are four important elements in any DBMS. These are: data structure, data modeling language, data query language, and transaction mechanisms. Each of these elements is described next.

Data structure To efficiently collect, retrieve, and modify data it must be structured in an organized fashion. Any data structure is designed to organize data to suit a specific purpose so that it can be accessed, modified, and used in appropriate ways.

Data structure is a specialized format for organizing and storing data. General data structures include, file, record, table, tree, and so on.

In **Figure 3.4**, a file (STUDENTS) is a collection of related records (CAVEY, SPENCER) and a record is a collection of related fields. Each data field holds a single fact or attribute (MAJOR, GPA, ID) about the entity that is described in a record. If there are 250 students, each student would have a record and the collection of all 250 records would constitute the file STUDENTS.

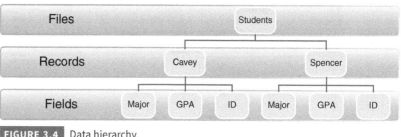

FIGURE 3.4 Data hierarchy.

Database query language refers to any computer programming language that finds and retrieves data from a database and information system by processing user queries.

Data modeling language

Over the years, several popular approaches to the modeling language of the DBMS have been developed. These include hierarchical, network, relational, and object-oriented. Of these, the relational database has become the mostly commonly used database model adopted by most enterprises.

Take the example of a customer order for multiple products. In this instance, an order (parent) can have many products (child) and a product (child) can appear on many orders (parent). This many-to-many relationship defeats the rules of hierarchy and consequently makes it very difficult, if not impossible, to model using the hierarchical approach. Since this type of relationship often occurs in business processes, it was important to overcome this limitation of the **hierarchical database** model (**Figure 3.5**).

Hierarchical database has a tree-like structure based on a one-to-many parent-child relationship between data elements. Every record, except the initial node that is called the root, has one parent and each parent record has one or more child records.

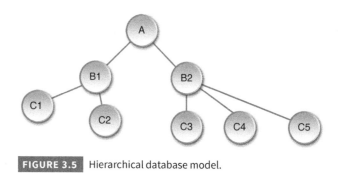

FIGURE 3.5 Hierarchical database model.

Network data model is a data model that allows multiple records to be linked to the same parent.

Network

The **network data model** was created to get around the limitations of the hierarchical model by allowing each child to have multiple parents (**Figure 3.6**). The network approach still had its issues, though. Computer programmers soon discovered that gaining a meaningful understanding of the data structure to make the network model efficient was extremely time-consuming and the complexity of the many-to-many relationships was difficult to implement and maintain.

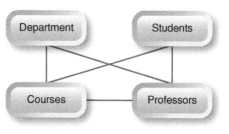

FIGURE 3.6 Network database model.

Relational data model is an approach to managing data using a structure and language that involves the use of data tables to collect groups of elements into relations.

Relational

The next iteration of database models attempted to get around the issues related to their predecessors is the **relational data model**. Instead of having to navigate through the database structure, a **relational database** stores data in tables (files) consisting of rows (records) and columns (fields), similar to the format of a spreadsheet. By doing this, it dispenses with the parent–child relationship dilemma and allows any file to be related to another through a common field that uniquely identifies an individual record.

In **Figure 3.7** the tables called Product and Invoice are related through the common field "product_num". By connecting files through these direct relationships, there is no need to trace a time-consuming, circuitous path to and from individual files and new relations can easily be added to any file as the need arises.

Product

Product_num	Item	Price
A123	8" x 11" paper, ream	3.00
B345	Epson 63XL black	54.00

Invoice

Invoice_num	Product_num	Qty.
10001	A123	3
10001	B345	2

FIGURE 3.7 Relational database model.

Object-Oriented (OO)

Object-Oriented (OO) The next database model to emerge was the **object-oriented database management system** (OODMS) that supports the creation and modeling of data as objects as used in object-oriented programming. An individual object (record) bundles attributes (fields) with operations and processes them together **(Figure 3.8)**.

An **object-oriented database management system** is a data model that supports the modelling and creation of data entities as objects that contain both data and the relationships of those data.

Student	Object Name	Course
ID (key) Name D/Birth GPA Address Phone	List of Attributes	Course Code (key) Course_title Course_hrs
Register-for (course) Calc-GPA () Cal-Age ()	List of Operations	Enroll ()

FIGURE 3.8 Object-oriented database model.

An object-oriented database is a more specialized type of data model and is best used in business applications in complex environments that require high performance processing. Examples of industries with a high demand for this type of database model can be found in the fields of engineering, telecommunications, specialized financial services, and scientific research.

Blockchain

Blockchain Blockchain is the most recent database model **(Figure 3.9)** and has the potential to change the way companies arrange, record, and verify transactions. **Blockchain** was originally designed to timestamp digital documents so that they couldn't be backdated or altered. It was later adapted by Satoshi Nakomoto to create digital cryptocurrency, Bitcoin. So, what is a blockchain—how does it work, what problems does it solve, and how is it being used today?

A **blockchain** is a distributed ledger represented by a sequential chain of data blocks that records transactions, establishes identity of the user, and establishes contracts.

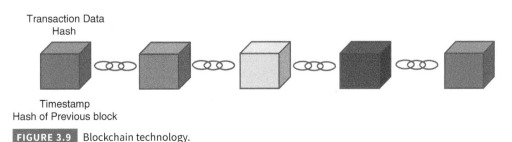

Transaction Data
Hash

Timestamp
Hash of Previous block

FIGURE 3.9 Blockchain technology.

Blockchain can replace the traditional roles carried out by bankers, auditors, lawyers, and financial advisors. With blockchain, you can eliminate these "middlemen" and greatly increases efficiencies and security.

Although it is implemented as a distributed database blockchain is different from the relational and O-O database models in several ways. In a blockchain many users can write entries into a database and a community of users controls how the data is amended and updated, instead of the third-party assigned administrator in a relational model.

Blockchains are also designed to be secure and build trust. The security is built into a blockchain system through the distributed timestamping server and peer-to-peer network. The result is a database comprised of a sequential chain of blocks of data that is managed autonomously in a decentralized way. The sequential chain of blocks allows anyone to send value anywhere the blockchain file can be accessed. The blocks in a blockchain are chained together using cryptographically created keys (**hash**).

The hash is the backbone of blockchain technology. Each block has its own hash, a timestamp, transaction data, and the hash of the previous block as shown in **Figure 3.9**. It is the hash of the previous block that links the chain of blocks and it's this technique that makes the blockchain so secure (immutable). If a block is somehow removed from the chain, all subsequent blocks will contain incorrect hashes and the corruption of the blockchain will be evident to all its users. The first block has no hash of a previous block and is known as the genesis block.

To edit a block, users must provide their own hash and the cryptographically created key (hash) of the previous block. With that information a user can transfer the value of whatever is stored in the blocks they are editing. Users can only edit block(s) they own and edits not verified by the two keys are rejected and the transaction is aborted. Blocks are never replaced. Instead, when a block is edited, a new block is created. In this way, a complete history is maintained of all transactions within the blockchain and the security of the data is assured. For example, a data breach in a pharmaceutical company could put protected health information of millions of patients at risk. Blockchain's random code (hash) required to encrypt information means there is nothing to decrypt as information cannot be altered once it is entered, creating a far more secure environment than possible before.

Proof-of-work and **peer-to-peer network** are two other mechanisms that are used to boost the security of the blockchain. Proof-of-work slows down the creation of new blocks when data are changed in an existing block to discourage tampering. The peer-to-peer network allows anyone to join the blockchain and sends a full copy of the blockchain to each user. When a new block is created the block is sent to everyone on the network and each user checks the new block to make sure it hasn't been altered. If the majority of the users verify the new block each user adds it to their own blockchain. This is called consensus and controls which blocks will be added to the blockchain and which ones will not. The most recent development in blockchains is "smart contracts." These are instructions stored on the blockchain to automatically perform repeat transactions based on certain conditions. Somewhat akin to "auto pay" in financial applications.

Blockchain technology is generating significant interest in global industries. For example, Walmart and its food suppliers are using blockchain to track their leafy greens through its entire manufacturing and logistics processes to ensure customers get what they want and have confidence in its quality. In addition to retail, blockchain technology is being used for far-reaching applications in finance, health care, media, government, and other industries. Bernard Marr (2018) recently published some interesting real-world examples of blockchain use in various industries, which include:

- **Health care** The Centers for Disease Control and Prevention (**https://www.cdc.gov/**) is putting disease outbreak data into a blockchain to increase the effectiveness of disaster relief and response.
- **Finance** Barclays Bank (**https://home.barclays/**) has launched several blockchain initiatives to track financial transactions, compliance, and combat fraud.
- **Manufacturing** A business-led community project based in Brooklyn, NY, allows members to locally produce and sell energy to reduce costs in energy distribution.
- **Government** The UK Department of Work and Pensions (**https://www.gov.uk/government/organisations/department-for-work-pensions**) is investigating the use of blockchain technology to record and administer benefit payments.
- **Non-Profit** Save the Children (**https://www.savethechildren.org/**), The Water Project (**https://thewaterproject.org/**), and Medic Mobile (**https://medicmobile.org/**) are

Hash is a function that takes an input value and outputs a unique fixed-size hexadecimal number that is the cryptographically created key for the data.

exploring the use of blockchain to provide greater transparency and create clearer links between donations and project outcomes.

- **Retail** OpenBazaar is using blockchain to build a decentralized market (**https://open bazaar.org/**) where goods and services can be traded with no middle-man.
- **Real estate** Ubiquity (**https://www.myubiquity.com/**) is creating a blockchain-driven system to smooth out the complicated legal process that creates friction and expense in real estate transfer.
- **Transport and tourism** Arcade City (**https://www.facebook.com/ArcadeCityHall/**) moves ride sharing and car hiring onto the blockchain to offer drivers choice of payment including Bitcoin, to compete with Uber.
- **Media** Kodak (**https://www.kodak.com/**) is developing a blockchain system for tracking intellectual property rights and payments to photographers.

In all industry sectors, the level of trust and security that currently only blockchain can offer is critical to a secure **supply chain**. A single data breach can undermine consumer confidence in a company, threaten intellectual property, put team members at risk, create potential compliance violations, and contribute to severe consequences within specific supply chains such as those encountered in Walmart's food supply chain and in health care.

> **Supply chain** is a network consisting of a company and its suppliers, vendors, warehouses, transportation companies, distribution centers, and retailers to produce and distribute a product or service.

IT at Work 3.1 describes how Blockchain use is showing tremendous potential in the energy and utility sectors, where benefits are being seen in:

- Reducing costs
- Promoting environmental sustainability
- Increasing transparency for stakeholders while not compromising privacy

---

IT at Work 3.1

Blockchain Promotes New Business Models in Energy and Sustainability

Pricewaterhouse Cooper (PwC), a large multinational professional services network (**https://www.pwc.com/**), has identified the energy sector as one of the industries where blockchain could have the biggest transformative and disruptive impact. The World Economic Forum, Stanford Woods Institute for the Environment, and PwC recently released a *joint report* identifying numerous ways in which blockchain has and will benefit the energy sector. One of the industries it can help is oil and gas. Siloed infrastructures and problems with transparency, efficiency, and optimization are negatively impacting oil and gas companies. For example, petroleum is one of the most traded commodities and requires a complex network of refiners, tankers, jobbers, governments, and other regulatory bodies. Unfortunately, this network contains siloed infrastructures and innumerable process inefficiencies. To address these problems, large oil and gas companies are investing in blockchain technology to reduce costs and reduce harmful environmental impacts. Oil and gas company concerns around privacy and trade secrets make private blockchains with features like data permissions and smart contracts.

Utilities companies like PG&E (**http://www.pgecorp.com/**), a large Northern California utility company, also have a few issues that blockchain can help with. Using blockchain, PG&E hopes to maintain a distributed ledger to track the chain of custody of grid materials. Serving 16 million Californians requires a massive portfolio of installed power infrastructure that currently result in inefficiencies. The company also supports 340,000 solar rooftops with 6,000 new ones joining each month. This means customer-sited equipment

shows up and interacts with their energy grid. So, they need better tools to account for electrical production and consumption. A blockchain distributed ledger can help do this by tracing chain of custody for grid materials to enhance PG&E's visibility into the status of its own assets and reduce the costs of tracking them manually. The first project PG&E implemented is tracking steel reels that carry overhead cables. If this works, they plan to expand blockchain to track transformers, gas pipes, and electric poles. The confidence built by these distributed ledgers could provide an important link between customer behavior and transactions with third parties.

Companies are also using blockchain solutions to enhance sustainability around the globe. For example, in the Netherlands, Circularise (**https://www.circularise.com/**) created a blockchain coupled with peer-to-peer technology and cryptographic techniques to build a decentralized information storage and communication platform that provides accurate pricing for recycled materials and tracks how many times the product has been recycled. For example, it can transmit information about the recycled materials between participants in a supply chain while allowing them to remain anonymous to disclose how they are supporting sustainability. In Norway, Empower (**https://www.circularise.com/**)—an economic development startup—uses blockchain tokens to encourage donation-based recycling. For every Euro dollar donated by an organization Empower commits to retrieve the same amount of plastic waste (in kgs) by weight to help clean up the environment and reduce poverty.

Sources: Compiled from Clawson (2018), PwC (2018), Spector (2018), World Economic Forum (2018),Consensys (2019), Peshkam (2019), and pgecorp.com.

Data Query Language

To get access to and modify the data in a database you need software that can interface with the database. This is where data **query** languages come into play. A database query language enables users to ask questions about the data and allows for maintaining the security of the database by monitoring login data, assigning access rights to different users, and providing protocols to add data to the system.

Structure Query Language (SQL) is the most widely-used mainstream **declarative language** that works with any database to simplify data access by requiring that users only declare what data they want rather than tell the DBMS how to get it. You are probably using SQL without even knowing it. For example, if you search an online catalog on a website that takes your input on a form or by a few mouse clicks, in all probability when you press the submit button, it will compose an SQL query to retrieve any records that match your search terms, retrieve the information, and generate a Web page specific to your search term(s). SQL is a relatively easy programming language to learn and proficiency in SQL is currently in high demand by employers.

Figure 3.10 illustrates an SQL request for three lists of employees (1) who were hired between June 1, 2012 and December 15, 2012; (2) live in Seattle, Tacoma, or Redmond; and (3) were NOT hired between June 1, 2012 and December 15, 2012, using three simple SQL commands (SELECT, FROM, WHERE).

Query is an ad hoc (unplanned) user request for specific data.

Structured Query Language (SQL) is a standardized query language for accessing databases.

Declarative language is a high-level programming language that allows the user to express what they want without specifying how to get it, thus separating the process of stating a problem from the process of solving it.

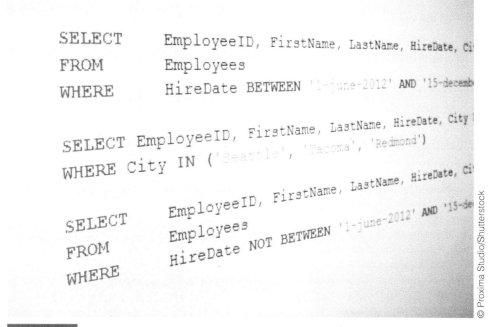

FIGURE 3.10 An instance of SQL to access employee information based on date of hire or city.

To ensure consistency in a SQL database, before and after a transaction is executed all data is tested against the four ACID database properties, described earlier in **Tech Note 3.1** to ensure changes to the database are saved in a consistent, safe, and robust manner.

Not Only SQL (NoSQL)

NoSQL is a non-relational database query language. Unlike SQL, NoSQL is **not** a high-level declarative query language. Instead, it has no predefined schema, avoids joins, is easy to scale, and can easily handle unstructured and unpredictable data. NoSQL is designed for distributed databases with very large-scale data needs and is used by corporations who have huge numbers of daily transactions like Facebook, Twitter, Amazon, LinkedIn, and Google. There are four main types of NoSQL databases: Key-value stores; column-oriented; graph; and document-oriented. Each of these has its own specific attributes and applicability as shown in **Figure 3.11.**

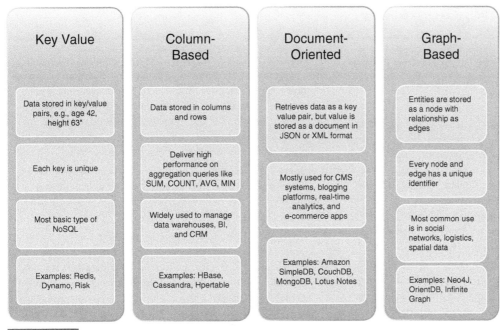

FIGURE 3.11 Types and characteristics of NoSQL distributed databases.

No single NoSQL solution is better than any other, however, some NoSQL databases are better at solving specific problems, such as: Instead of following the ACID requirements of SQL, NoSQL is guided by the **CAP theorem** (**consistency**, **availability** and **partition tolerance**) that acknowledges that it is only possible for a distributed database to meet two of its three components. As a result, some NoSQL databases are AP (availability, partition tolerance) compliant while others meet the tests of CA (consistency, availability) or CP (consistency, partition tolerance).

The **advantages** of NoSQL include:

- higher performance
- easy distribution of data on different nodes, which enables scalability and **fault tolerance**
- greater flexibility
- simpler administration

> **Fault tolerance** means that no single failure results in any loss of service.

With most NoSQL offerings, the bulk of the cost does not lie in acquiring the database, but rather in implementing it.

NewSQL is the latest type of scalable database that supports a SQL interface. It combines the reliability of SQL and the speed and performance of NoSQL to provide better functionality and services and provide database administrators with ACID performance guarantees. NewSQL works well in organizations interested in migrating existing applications to big data platforms, developing new applications on highly scalable online transaction processing systems, and wanting to capitalize on their existing knowledge of online transaction processing (OLTP).

Transaction Mechanism There are two main transaction mechanisms. A transaction can be committed or rolled back. *Committing* a transaction occurs when permanent changes are performed within the transaction. A *rollback* of a transaction occurs when any changes to data that have been performed within an uncommitted transaction are undone.

> **Transaction mechanism** is a set of logical operations used to help ensure integrity and concurrency and eliminate multiplicity.

Benefits of a DBMS

Database management systems benefit organizations by reducing data latency, volatility, and consistency. They are also useful in reducing query response time, increasing the predictability of queries and processing them in real-time to enable faster, more confident decision making. These factors should be assessed to determine the effectiveness of a DBMS as explained in **Tech Note 3.2**.

Tech Note 3.2

Factors That Influence the Performance of a DBMS

Factors to consider when evaluating the performance of a database management system include:

- **Data latency.** The elapsed time (or delay) between when data are created and when they are available for a query or report can significantly impact database performance. A low latency database experiences small delay times, while a high latency database experiences long delays. Applications have different tolerances for latency. For example, to perform well a stock market database needs low latency, while a higher latency is acceptable in a retailer's customer database. Database systems tend to have shorter latency than data warehouses.

- **Volatility.** The database needs adequate processing power to handle the volatility of the data. The rate at which data are added, updated, or deleted determines the workload the database must be able to control to prevent problems with the response rate to queries.

- **Data consistency.** Data must be consistent. There are two types of data consistency. **Immediate consistency** means that as soon as data are updated, responses to any new query will return the updated value. This method offers up-to-date consistent data but requires high latency. **Eventual consistency** means that not all query responses will reflect data changes uniformly and operates well at a low latency. In this model, the data will become consistent eventually, but in the meantime, inconsistent query results could cause serious problems for analyses that depend on accurate data.

- **Query response time.** The volume of data impacts response times to queries and data explorations. Many databases *pre-stage data*—that is, summarize or pre-calculate results—so queries have faster response rates.

- **Query predictability.** The greater the number of ad hoc or unpredictable queries, the more flexible the database needs to be. Database or query performance management is more difficult when the workloads are so unpredictable that they cannot be prepared for in advance. The ability to handle the workload is the most important criterion when choosing a database.

- **Query processing capabilities.** Database queries are processed in real time and results are transmitted via wired or wireless networks to computer screen or handheld devices.

DBMS Vendor Rankings

The top five enterprise database management systems of 2019 are Oracle's Database 18c, Microsoft SQL Server 2019, IBM DB2, SAP Sybase ASE, and PostgreSQL (Stroud 2019):

1. **Oracle Database 18c** consolidates and manages databases as cloud services via Oracle's multitenant architecture and in-memory data processing capabilities and can be rapidly provisioned.

2. **Microsoft SQL Server** ease of use, availability, and Windows operating system integration make it an easy choice for firms that choose Microsoft products for their enterprises.

3. **IBM Db2** is widely used in large data centers and runs on Linux, UNIX, Windows, IBM iSeries, and mainframes.

4. **SAP Sybase ASE** is a major force after 25 years of success and improvements. It supports partition locking, relaxed query limits, query plan optimization, and dynamic thread assignment.

5. **PostgreSQL** is the most advanced open source object-relational database, often used by online gaming applications and Skype and Yahoo! This database runs on a wide variety of operating systems including Linux, Windows, FreeBSD, and Solaris.

Questions

1. Describe the purpose and benefits of data management.
2. Define a database and a database management system (DBMS).
3. What are the four elements of a DBMS?
4. Explain what an online transaction-processing (OLAP) system does and which database technology is most appropriate for its use.
5. Describe the functions of a DBMS.
6. What is a relational database management system?
7. What are the main elements of a block in a blockchain?
8. What are the three mechanisms that help keep a blockchain secure?

3.2 Data Warehouses and Data Marts

LO3.2 Identify *the differences between a database, a data warehouse, and a data mart and why a company would move from a database to a data warehouse or data mart*

The huge number of transactions that occur daily in an organization require data in databases to be constantly modified or updated. The volatility of databases makes it impossible to use them for complex decision-making and problem-solving tasks. For this reason, data are extracted from the database, transformed (processed to standardize the data), and then loaded into a **data warehouse**.

Data warehouses are the primary source of cleansed data for analysis, reporting, and business intelligence (BI). Often the data are summarized in ways that enable quick responses to queries. For instance, query results can reveal changes in customer behavior and drive the decision to redevelop an advertising strategy. Data warehouses store data from various source systems and databases across an enterprise in order to run analytical queries against huge datasets collected over long time periods.

Data warehouse is a central depository of integrated data from one or more disparate sources.

The high cost of data warehouses can make them too expensive for a company to implement. **Data marts** are lower-cost, scaled-down versions of a data warehouse that can be implemented in a much shorter time, for example, in less than 90 days. Data marts serve a specific department or function, such as finance, marketing, or operations. Since they store smaller amounts of data, they are faster and easier to navigate and maintain.

Data mart is a small-scale data warehouse that supports a single function or one department.

Moving Data from a Database to a Data Warehouse or a Data Mart

The volatility caused by constant transaction processing makes data analysis difficult—and the demands to process millions of transactions per second consume the database's processing power. In contrast, data in warehouses are relatively stable, as needed for analysis. Therefore, select data are moved from databases to a data warehouse or a data mart. Consider a bank's database. Every deposit, withdrawal, loan payment, or other transactions executed by its thousands of users adds or changes the data. Specifically, data are moved in three main steps:

1. *Extracted* from designated databases.
2. *Transformed* by standardizing formats, cleaning the data, and integrating them.
3. *Loaded* into a data warehouse.

These three procedures—**extract, transform, and load (ETL)** are shown in **Figure 3.12.** In a data warehouse or data mart, data are *read-only* and are not changed until the next ETL cycle is performed.

© TechnoVectors/Shutterstock.com

FIGURE 3.12 Data enter databases from transaction systems. Data of interest are **extracted** from databases, **transformed** to clean and standardize them, and then **loaded** into a data warehouse. These three processes are called ETL.

Change data capture (CDC) processes capture the changes made at data sources and then apply those changes throughout enterprise data stores to keep data synchronized.

Data deduplication processes remove duplicates and standardize data formats.

Once the data are loaded into the data warehouse or data mart, two more operations—**change data capture (CDC)** and **data deduplication**—are carried out to prepare the raw data for analysis:

CDC minimizes the resources required for ETL processes by only dealing with data changes. Data deduplication helps to minimize storage and data synch.

Building and Using a Data Warehouse

Figure 3.13 diagrams how a typical database, data warehouse, and data mart architecture make data available for user access and analysis. The organization's data from operational transaction processes systems are stored in operational databases (left side of the figure). Not all data are transferred to the data warehouse. Frequently, only summary data are transferred. The warehouse organizes the data in multiple ways—by subject, functional area, vendor, and product. As shown, the data warehouse architecture defines the flow of data that starts when data are captured by transaction systems; the source data are stored in transactional (operational) databases; ETL processes move data from databases into data warehouses or data marts, where data are available for access, reporting, and further analysis by business intelligence (BI) and more advanced data analytics tools (discussed in detail in Chapter 6).

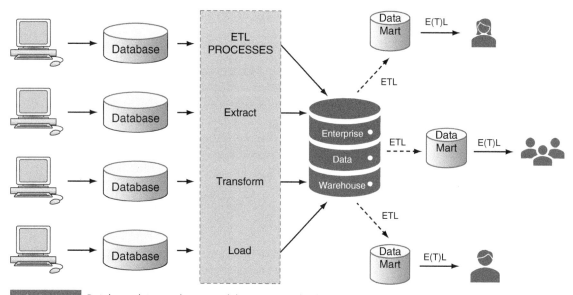

FIGURE 3.13 Database, data warehouse, and data marts make data available for user access and analysis.

Cloud data warehouse (CDW) is a database delivered in a public cloud as a managed service that is optimized for analytics, scale, and ease of use.

One recent data warehousing innovation is a **cloud data warehouse (CDW)**. CDWs are high-performance data warehouses built specifically for the cloud. CDWs make data collection easy and unlike traditional data warehouses, they enable rapid analytics and unlock the advantages of having a cloud-based data repository. Their logical arrangement of tables in a multi-dimensional database resemble the shape of a snowflake—hence the name. Centralized storage of data in the cloud eliminates the complexities associated with searching various data stores to locate individual records and make complying with required updates, changes, and deletions much easier to manager. CDWs are rapidly replacing on-site and hybrid data warehouse solutions because they offer rapid scalability, increased flexibility, lower costs, greater connectivity, and a high level of data security and encryption. Examples of CDWs include Snowflake, Oracle Autonomous Database, and Kintone.

Real-Time Support from an Active Data Warehouse

Early data warehouse technology primarily supported strategic applications that did not require instant response time, direct customer interaction, or integration with operational systems. ETL might have been done once per week or once per month. But, demand for information to support real-time customer interaction and operations leads to real-time data warehousing and analytics—known as an **active data warehouse (ADW).** Massive increases in computing power, processing speeds, and memory made ADW possible. ADWs are not designed to support executives' strategic decision-making, but rather to support operations.

> **Active data warehouse (ADW)** is the technical ability to capture transactions when they change and integrate them into the warehouse along with maintaining bath or scheduled cycle refreshes.

For example, shipping companies like DHL use huge fleets of trucks to move millions of packages. Every day and all day, operational managers make thousands of decisions that affect the bottom line, such as: "Do we need four trucks for this run?" "With two drivers delayed by bad weather, do we need to bring in extra help?" Traditional data warehousing is not suited for immediate operational support, but active data warehousing is. For example, companies with an ADW are able to:

- Interact with a customer to provide superior customer service.
- Respond to business events in near real time.
- Share up-to-date status data among merchants, vendors, customers, and associates.

Two examples of how companies in the retail and hospitality and tourism industries are benefitting from the use of ADW are described in **IT at Work 3.2**.

IT at Work 3.2

Companies Use Active Data Warehousing to Improve the Customer Experience

Retail: a **leading privately-held grocery supermarket chain** that operates more than 300 stores in three states across the southeast USA wanted real-time insight by implementing continuous integration between various point-of-sale systems across its stores into an ADW. For years, the grocery chain had used batch processing of its POS data from its 300 stores into the corporate data warehouse on a nightly basis. However, its increasingly high data volume from transactions of 5,000 items at 300 stores amounted to about 40–50 million transactions a day. These high transaction volumes led to huge delays in reporting, analysis, and decision making, that often rolled over into the next day. This held up transactions from subsequent days from being loaded adding complexity to the process. Data loads often failed and users were faced with highly unreliable reports and analysis. Despite the data problems, the grocery chain had fierce customer loyalty and efficient operation and sales capability of its merchandising and store management personnel, but this was being undermined with the reports and analysis delays and preventing the chain from making timely and effective responses to changing market conditions. The solution was a software from TIBCO and Teradata that together delivered a reliable, fault-tolerant, and load-balanced ADW. The solution offered three different ways to prevent failure at different levels to efficiently deliver data to the ADW. The ADW provided business users with several benefits, which included: generating sales data within 60 minutes; refining real-time inventory at stores and warehouses; and providing store managers with a real-time view of sales data and enabled them to create flex events based on real-time data.

Hospitality and Tourism: Travelocity (https://www.travelocity.com/) uses an ADW to find the best travel deals especially for you. The goal is to use "today's data today" instead of "yesterday's data today." The online travel agency's ADW analyzes your search history and destinations of interest; then predicts travel offers that you would most likely purchase. Offers are both relevant and timely to enhance your experience, which helps close the sale in a very competitive market. For example, when a customer is searching flights and hotels in Las Vegas, Travelocity recognizes the interest—the customer wants to go to Vegas. The ADW searches for the best-priced flights from all carriers, builds a few package deals, and presents them in real time to the customer. When customers see a personalized offer they find really interesting, the ADW helps generate a better customer experience. The real-time data-driven experience increases the conversion rate and sales.

Sources: Phillip (2019), XTIVIA (2019), **https://www.tibco.com/solutions/** retail, and **https://www.teradata.com/Products/Software/Integrated-Data-Warehouses**.

Data warehouse content can be delivered to decision-makers throughout the enterprise via the cloud or company-owned intranets. Users can view, query, and analyze the data and produce reports using Web browsers. These are extremely economical and effective data delivery methods.

Data Warehousing Supports Action as Well as Decisions

Many organizations have built data warehouses because they were frustrated with inconsistent data that could not support decisions or actions. Viewed from this perspective, data warehouses are infrastructure investments that companies in a variety of industries make to support ongoing and future operations, including the following:

- **Marketing** Keeps people informed of the status of products, marketing program effectiveness, and product line profitability; and allows them to take intelligent action to maximize per-customer profitability.
- **Pricing and contracts** Calculates costs accurately in order to optimize pricing of a contract. Without accurate cost data, prices may be below or too near to cost; or prices may be uncompetitive because they are too high.
- **Forecasting** Estimates customer demand for products and services.
- **Sales** Calculates sales profitability and productivity for all territories and regions; analyzes results by geography, product, sales group, or individual.
- **Financial** Provides real-time data for optimal credit terms, portfolio analysis, and actions that reduce risk or bad debt expense.

Data warehouses that pull together data from disparate sources and databases across an entire enterprise are called **enterprise data warehouses (EDWs)**.

One of the major drivers of change in the data management market is the increased amount of data to be managed. Enterprises need powerful DBMSs and data warehousing solutions, analytics, and reporting. The vendors that dominate this market to respond to evolving data management needs with more intelligent and advanced software and hardware. Advanced hardware technology enables scaling to much higher data volumes and workloads than previously possible, or it can handle specific workloads. Older general-purpose relational DBMSs lack the scalability or flexibility for specialized or very large workloads but are very good at what they do.

Table 3.1 summarizes several successful applications of data warehouses.

Enterprise data warehouses (EDWs) are data warehouses that integrate data from many different databases across an entire enterprise.

TABLE 3.1 Data Warehouse Applications by Industry

Industry	Applications
Airline	Crew assignment, aircraft deployment, analysis of route profitability, and customer loyalty promotions
Banking and financial	Customer service, trend analysis, product and service services promotions, and reduction of IS expenses
Credit card	Customer service, new information service for a fee, fraud detection
Defense contracts	Technology transfer, production of military applications
E-business	Data warehouses with personalization capabilities, marketing/shopping preferences allowing for up-selling and cross-selling
Government	Reporting on crime areas, homeland security
Health care	Reduction of operational expenses
Investment and insurance	Risk management, market movements analysis, customer tendencies analysis, and portfolio management
Retail chain	Trend analysis, buying pattern analysis, pricing policy, inventory control, sales promotions, and optimal distribution channel decision

Data Lakes

A major drawback of data warehouses is the need to structure/model the data before storing it. Using a **data lake** that can store huge quantities of raw structured, semi-structured, and unstructured data in their natural state, the transform operation of the ETL process can be avoided and not performed until requirements for the data are defined as needed **(Figure 3.14)**. A data lake can also include raw copies of source system data such as blog postings, product reviews, customer data, and product sales, as well as transformed data used for tasks such as reporting, visualization, advanced analytics, and machine learning. The flexibility of data lakes is particularly appealing to data analysts and data scientists who can easily configure and reconfigure their models, queries, and apps on-the-fly. Two examples of data lake software include Microsoft Azure Data Lake and IBM Data Lake.

Data lake is a single store of structured, semi-structured, and unstructured enterprise data stored in its natural format.

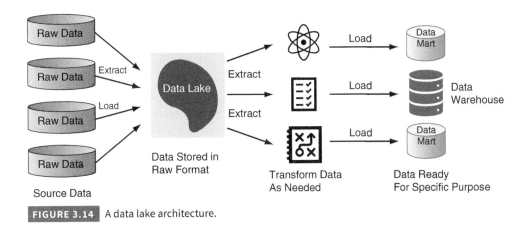

FIGURE 3.14 A data lake architecture.

Questions

1. What are the differences between databases and data warehouses?
2. What are the differences between data warehouses and data marts?
3. Explain ETL.
4. Explain CDC.
5. What is an advantage of an enterprise data warehouse (EDW)?
6. Why might a company invest in a data mart instead of a data warehouse?
7. What levels of an organization benefit most from a data warehouse?
8. How is a data lake different from a data warehouse?

3.3 | Data Governance and Master Data Management (MDM)

LO3.3 Describe *the importance of data governance in providing trusted data available when and where needed and why master data management (MDM) is an important data governance initiative.*

Strong data governance and MDM are needed to ensure data are of sufficient quality to meet business needs.

Data Governance

A sound data governance program includes a governing body, a defined set of procedures, and a plan to execute those procedures.

Data governance is the overall management of the availability, usability, integrity, and security of data used in an enterprise.

The success of every data-driven strategy or marketing effort depends on effective data governance that has highly developed formal policies and procedures to control enterprise data. **Data governance** policies must address structured, semistructured, and unstructured data to ensure that employees and business partners are provided with high-quality data they can trust and access on demand.

This is particularly important in the service industries. For example, strong data governance is necessary to comply with the strict governmental accountability requirements imposed on the health-care sector. Data governance programs, sometimes referred to as enterprise data governance, verify that data input into electronic health records and clinical, financial, and operational systems are accurate and complete and that only authorized edits can be made and logged.

With an effective data governance program, managers can determine where their data are coming from, who owns them, and who is responsible for what. Data governance is an enterprise-wide project because data cross boundaries and are used by people throughout the enterprise. New regulations and pressure to reduce costs have increased the importance of effective data governance. Governance eliminates the cost of maintaining and archiving bad, unneeded, or inaccurate data. These costs grow as the volume of data grows. Governance also reduces the legal risks associated with unmanaged or inconsistently managed information.

Three industries that rely heavily on data governance to comply with regulations or reporting requirements are the following:

- **Food industry** In the food industry, data governance is required to comply with food safety regulations. Food manufacturers and retailers have sophisticated control systems in place so that if a contaminated food product, such as spinach or peanut butter, is detected, they can trace the problem back to a particular processing plant or even the farm at the start of the food chain.

- **Financial services industry** In the financial services sector, strict reporting requirements of the Dodd–Frank Act are leading to greater use of data governance. The Dodd–Frank Act is an important piece of consumer protection regulation that was passed to enforce transparency and accountability in response to the 2008 financial crisis. Although some of its regulations have been rolled back, today consumers still benefit from many of the protections the Act put in place including the formation of the Consumer Financial Protection Bureau (CFPB).

- **Health-care industry** Data are health care's most valuable asset. Hospitals have mountains of electronic patient data. New health-care accountability and reporting obligations require data governance models for transparency to defend against fraud and to protect patients' information.

When developing a data governance program, it's important to present a strong business case to get buy-in from top executives and stakeholders. A crucial part of the business case is an estimate of the data governance program's return on investment (ROI) to show how it will add value to the company. You will need to justify the ROI based on both business and IT strategy to ensure that available funds are used to best meet the business objectives.

To do this you will need to carefully analyze the IT infrastructure about how different components of the IT infrastructure work together to support business processes, how data needed by one system can be received and used by another, and how easily data can be communicated and/or repurposed. You will also need to factor in risks and adverse events such as costs associated with rework in data collection, costs associated with unreliable or unfit data, and delays associated with untimely or unavailable data. Next these costs must be quantified and your level of confidence in the corporate data must be calculated to ensure your business case accurately reflects the value of a data governance program. **Tech Note 3.3** explains how to measure the value of data governance to assess its strength.

Tech Note 3.3

Accurately Measuring the Value of Data Governance

One metric used to make this calculation is the *confidence in data-dependent assumptions* metric, or CIDDA (Reeves & Bowen, 2013). The CIDDA identifies specific areas of deficiency.

So, to sum up, when building a data governance model, it is necessary to:

1. Establish a leadership team
2. Define the program's scope
3. Calculate the ROI using the CIDDA.

CIDDA is computed by multiplying three confidence estimates using the following formula:

$$CIDDA = G \times M \times TS$$

where

$G =$ Confidence that data are *good* enough for their intended purpose

$M =$ Confidence that data mean what you think they do

$TS =$ Confidence that you know where the data come from and trust the source.

CIDDA is a subjective metric for which there are no industry benchmarks, yet it can be evaluated over time to gauge improvements in data quality confidence.

To ensure your understanding of this IT Toolbox item, calculate the CIDDA of Company A over time, using the stated levels of confidence in the different aspects of its corporate data over Q1–Q4 2020:

$$Q1\_2020 : G = 40\%, M = 50\%, TS = 20\%$$
$$Q2\_2020 : G = 50\%, M = 55\%, TS = 30\%$$
$$Q3\_2020 : G = 60\%, M = 60\%, TS = 40\%$$
$$Q4\_2020 : G = 60\%, M = 70\%, TS = 45\%$$

The importance a strong data governance program can best be appreciated by considering the characteristics and consequences of weak or nonexistent data governance listed in **Table 3.2.**

TABLE 3.2   Characteristics and Consequences of Weak or Nonexistent Data Governance

- Data duplication causes isolated data silos.
- Inconsistency exists in the meaning and level of detail of data elements.
- Users do not trust the data and waste time verifying the data rather than analyzing them for appropriate decision-making.
- Leads to inaccurate data analysis.
- Bad decisions are made on perception rather than reality, which can negatively affect the company and its customers.
- Results in increased workloads and processing time.

Master Data and Master Data Management (MDM)

As data become more complex and their volumes explode, database performance degrades, and organizations are turning to the optimization of **master data**. Master data are fundamentally different from the high volume, velocity, and variety of **big data** and traditional data. For example, when a customer applies for automobile insurance, data provided on the application become the master data for that customer. In contrast, if the customer's vehicle has a device that sends data about his or her driving behavior to the insurer, those machine-generated data are transactional or operational data. Master data entities are the main entities of a company, such as customers, products, suppliers, employees, and assets.

Master data is the term used to describe business-critical information on customers, products and services, vendors, locations, employees, and other things needed for operations and business transactions.

Figure 3.15 shows how master data serve as a layer between transactional data in a database and analytical data in a data warehouse.

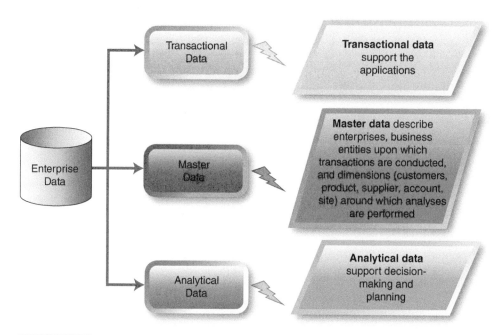

FIGURE 3.15 An enterprise has transactional, master, and analytical data.

Enhancing the customer experience is one example of an urgent business priority that relies on leveraging master data (O'Kane and Moran, 2018). An effective data governance strategy that can help organizations achieve this is referred to as **master data management.**

Master data management (MDM) integrates data from various sources or enterprise applications to create a more complete (unified) view of a customer, product, or other entity.

Data entity is anything real or abstract about which a company wants to collect and store data.

Master file is a collection of records describing one of the main entities in a database, such as customers, products, employees, and vendor. It is usually periodically updated.

Master Reference File and Data Entities

Master data are typically quite stable and typically stored in several different systems spread across the enterprise. Master data management (MDM) links and synchronizes all critical data from those disparate systems into one file called a **master file,** to provide a common point of reference. When the MDM consolidates data from various data sources into this master reference file or index, the MDM then feeds data back to the applications, thereby creating accurate and consistent data across the enterprise.

MDM solutions can be complex and expensive. Given their complexity and cost, most MDM solutions are out of reach for small and medium companies. Vendors have addressed this challenge by offering cloud-managed MDM services. For example, Dell Software offers its next-generation Dell Boomi MDM. Boomi provides MDM, data management, and data quality services (DQS) that are 100% cloud-based with near real-time synchronization (**https://boomi .com/content/video/demo/10min-demo/**).

Each department has distinct master data needs. Marketing, for example, is concerned with product pricing, brand, and product packaging, whereas production is concerned with product costs and schedules. A customer master reference file can feed data to all enterprise systems that have a customer relationship component, thereby providing a more unified picture of customers. Similarly, a product master reference file can feed data to all the production systems within the enterprise.

An MDM includes tools for cleaning and auditing the master data elements as well as tools for integrating and synchronizing data to make them more accessible. MDM offers a solution for managers frustrated by fragmented and dispersed data sources. **IT at Work 3.3** illustrates the master data management challenges faced by participants in the health-care supply chain in developing standards for the creation of an accurate and reliable master list of key data entities.

IT at Work 3.3

Standardizing Master Data Is a Challenge in Health Care

Health-care logistics are complex and depend on high-quality, trusted data. Unfortunately, accurate, standardized master data is a problem. An accurate master reference file of all products and services that a health-care system purchases (item master) is key to enabling tracking and tracing orders, strategic sourcing initiatives. Supplies, purchased services, and capital equipment represent about one-third of a hospital's operating expenses. It's estimated that a hospital's item master ranges from 18,000 to 200,000 items. Sadly, it is estimated that between 30% and 40% of item master files are inaccurate, creating waste across the supply chain and the health system.

Examples of waste resulting from inaccurate item master files include ordering off contract, ordering incorrect items, prolonged time to process orders, inability to capture commitments levels for contract pricing, and slow reimbursement due to missing data. Some industry experts estimate a 1.5% savings can be achieved by cleaning up the item master. Beyond this is the high investment in maintaining their item master to try to keep it as accurate as possible. Managing inaccurate data is estimated to waste 20% of current health-care buyers' time troubleshooting and fixing problems instead of strategically supporting the buying function. One small example is a cost-saving initiative begun by Kurt Knoth, VP, Supply Chain at Spectrum Health by which he reduced 30 different hand sanitizers used throughout the health-care system down to three. This resulted in a savings of $30,000 per year.

What is needed are industry-wide data standards that will ensure accurate product and pricing data that is categorized correctly along with barcodes/RFID tags that the system can use to tag items all the way to the smallest unit of use. Currently the FDA is supporting the UDI standards through the Association for Healthcare Resource and Materials Management (AHRMM), the premier membership group for health-care supply chain professionals, and GS1, an organization that designs and implements global standards for business communication, for example, the barcode, is helping focus the health-care industry around developing industry data standards.

The goal is to have a truck back up to the receiving dock at a health-care facility and the goods receiver has the correct product information, the packing, and the delivery information is easy to use for the track and trace team freeing them up to focus on strategic master data management initiatives to deliver the best patient care possible and save lives.

Sources: Compiled from Krieger (2018), Bagley (2019), Michigan State University (2019), ahrmm.org, and GS1.org.

Data governance combined with MDM is a powerful combination. As data sources and volumes continue to increase, so does the need to manage data as a strategic asset to extract its full value. Making business data consistent, trusted, and accessible across the enterprise is a critical first step in **customer-centric** business models. With data governance, companies can extract maximum value from their data by making better use of opportunities that are buried within behavioral data.

> **Customer-centric** is an approach to doing business that focuses on providing a positive customer experience at and after the point of sale to drive profit and gain competitive advantage.

Benefits of Data Governance and Master Data Management

Having highly developed and well-thought-out policies and procedures around data governance and master data management can lead to significant benefits in an organization, including:

1. **Improved regulatory compliance** Government regulations and compliance requirements have increased significantly in the past decade. Companies that fail to comply with laws on privacy, fraud, anti-money laundering, cybersecurity, occupational safety, and so on face harsh penalties.

2. **More efficient decision-making** Maximizes the use of data to make quicker decisions with greater certainty.

3. **Improved data understanding** When implemented well data governance provides a comprehensive view of all data assets along with greater accountability for specific data.

4. **Increased revenue** Better, faster decisions made with more certainty result in less costly errors such as false starts and data breaches so less money is spent managing PR and financial fallout.

Questions

1. Explain why it is important to develop an effective data governance program?
2. Explain the purposes of master data management.
3. Why has interest in data governance and MDM increased?
4. What are two ways that data is used in business?
5. What are three benefits of data governance.

3.4 Information Management

LO3.4 Explain *the concept of information management and why it is important for an organization to follow good information management practices.*

Almost everyone manages information. You manage your financial, social, and cloud accounts across multiple mobile devices and computers. You update or synchronize ("synch") your calendars, appointments, contact lists, media files, documents, and reports. Effective planning and decision-making tasks such as these depend on systems being able to make data available in usable formats on a timely basis. Your productivity also depends on the compatibility of devices and applications and their ability to share data. Not being able to transfer and synch whenever you add a device or app is bothersome and wastes time. For example, when you switch to the latest mobile device, you might need to reorganize content to make dealing with data and devices easier. To simplify add-ons, upgrades, sharing, and access, at a personal level you might leverage cloud services such as iTunes (**https://www.apple.com/itunes/**), a media player, media library, internet radio broadcaster and mobile device management app, or Instagram (**https://www.instagram.com**), a photo and video-sharing social networking service. At work you might use Diigo (**https://www.diigo.com/**), a powerful research tool and knowledge-sharing community and Box (**https://www.box.com/**), a cloud content management and file-sharing service for businesses.

In organizations complex **information management** situations arise every day and require a continuous plan to guide and control IT investments. This plan is known as information management and it is guided by the data cycle and data principles.

> **Information management** is the process of collecting, storing, managing, and maintaining data that is accurate, timely, reliable, valid, available, unique, and relevant to an organization.

Data Life Cycle and Data Principles

The data life cycle is a model that illustrates the way data travel through an organization as shown in **Figure 3.16**. The data life cycle begins with storage in a database, to being loaded into a data warehouse for analysis, then reported to knowledge workers or used in business apps. Supply chain management (SCM), customer relationship management (CRM), **knowledge management** (KM), and other enterprise applications that require up-to-date, readily accessible data to function properly and are discussed in detail in Chapter 10.

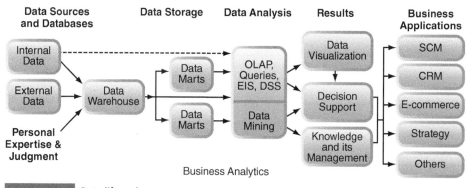

FIGURE 3.16 Data life cycle.

Three general data principles relate to the data life cycle perspective and help guide IT investment decisions. These are:

1. **Principle of diminishing data value**   The value of data diminishes as they age. This is a simple, yet powerful principle. Most organizations cannot operate at peak performance with blind spots (lack of data availability) of 30 days or longer. Global financial services institutions rely on near real-time data for peak performance.

2. **Principle of 90/90 data use**   According to the 90/90 data-use principle, a majority of stored data, as high as 90%, is seldom accessed after 90 days (except for auditing purposes). That is, roughly 90% of data lose most of their value after three months.

3. **Principle of data in context**   The capability to capture, process, format, and distribute data in near real time or faster requires a huge investment in data architecture (Chapter 2) and infrastructure to link remote POS systems to data storage, data analysis systems, and reporting apps. The investment can be justified on the principle that data must be integrated, processed, analyzed, and formatted into "actionable information."

Providing easy access to large volumes of information is just one of the challenges facing organizations. The days of simply managing structured data are over. Now, organizations must manage semistructured and unstructured content from social and mobile sources even though that data may be of questionable quality. Issues around information access, management, and security demand that information degradation and disorder must be addressed.

Harnessing Scattered Data

Business information is generally scattered throughout an enterprise, stored in separate systems dedicated to specific purposes, such as operations, supply chain management, or customer relationship management. Major organizations have over 100 data repositories (storage areas). In many companies, the integration of these disparate systems is limited—as is users' ability to access all the information they need. As a result, despite all the information flowing through companies, executives, managers, and workers often struggle to find the information they need to make sound decisions or do their jobs.

Breaking Down Data Silos

Companies worldwide are struggling to integrate thousands of siloed global applications and align them with their business strategy. **Data silos** exist in the workplace when departments and business units work within themselves and rarely, if ever, collaborate with other departments or business units **(Figure 3.17)**. The silo effect occurs when separate departments or teams don't have a system to communicate effectively with each other, data is trapped in departmental data silos, and productivity suffers. For example, when two departments are working on the same initiative and neither is aware that the other is working on it.

Data silo   are stand-alone data stores. Their data are not accessible by other ISs that need it or outside that department.

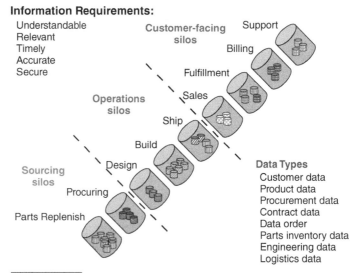

FIGURE 3.17 Data (or information) silos are ISs that do not have the capability to exchange data with other systems, making timely coordination and communication across functions or departments difficult.

Data silos are often found in service organizations, such as health-care and government. For example, in many hospitals, each line of business, division, and department has implemented its own IT apps, often without a thorough analysis of its relationship with other departmental or divisional systems. This arrangement leads to the hospital having IT groups that manage a particular suite of apps or data silos for a particular department or division.

Since silos are unable to share or exchange data, they cannot consistently be updated. When data are inconsistent across multiple enterprise applications, data quality cannot (and should not) be trusted without extensive verification. Data silos exist when there is no overall IT architecture to guide IT investments, data coordination, and communication. Data silos support a single function and, as a result, do not support an organization's cross-functional needs.

Even though technology connects more employees than ever before, the silo effect continues to be a concern in organizations of all types and sizes. Here are some interesting statistics that were collected in a recent survey (Marchese, 2019) on collaboration at work.

- 39% of surveyed employees believe people in their own organization do NOT collaborate enough
- 75% rate team work and collaboration as "very important," BUT only 18% get communication evaluations as part of their performance review
- 49% of millennials support social tools for workplace collaboration
- 97% of employees and executives believe lack of alignment within a team impacts the outcome of a task or project
- 86% of employees and executives cite lack of collaboration or ineffective communication for workplace failures
- 90% of employees believe that decision-makers should seek opinions of other before making a final decision, BUT 40% of employees believe that decision-makers consistently failed to seek another opinion
- Less than 50% said that their organizations discuss issues truthfully and effectively

Culture Must Change

If companies want to kill innovation, productivity, and healthy internal collaboration all they must do is discourage collaboration and continue to promote the information silo culture (Christman, 2018). So, how do you break down silos and promote sharing and collaboration to increase communications across functions? The first thing to realize is that moving from silos to collaboration requires a culture change. You are asking people to change the way they work and think differently. KAI Partners, Inc. (**https://kaipartners.com/**), a consulting firm, has a few suggestions:

1. **Publicly acknowledge shared goals**   Create a unified vision and form cross-unit teams where shared goals were publicly announced and shared victories celebrated.
2. **Embrace the "why"**   Encourage people to ask questions. People need information to get things done. Spur creativity and imagination to encourage innovation.
3. **Culture comes from the top**   Leading by example is the best way to model the change you want others to make. Don't' just encourage staff to be the "silo busters." Make sure upper management, including C-level professionals, lead change efforts.

By shifting from silos to collaborative systems organizations can overcome barriers to innovation that lack of communication can foster.

Garbage In, Garbage Out

In business, data are used for two reasons: to run a business (transaction and operational use) and to improve a business (analytic use). Both depend on high-quality trustworthy data. Regardless of how data are collected, they need to be validated so users know they can trust them. Unfortunately, a sizable amount data is neither validated nor trustworthy. You're probably familiar with the classic expression that sums up this situation—"garbage in, garbage out" (GIGO). To guard against this happening, companies must put safeguards in place, such as data integrity checks. For example, when you fill in an online form, it will not accept an e-mail address or a credit card number that is not formatted correctly. This type of data is referred to as **dirty data**.

Dirty data   are data of such poor quality that they cannot be trusted or relied upon for decisions.

When applications are not well managed, they can generate terabytes of irrelevant data, causing companies to drown in bad data. This data chaos could lead to errors that could put the company at risk. In the effort to manage excessive and massive amounts of data, there is increased risk of relevant information being lost (missing) or inaccurate.

Inaccurate Data   Too often managers and information workers are constrained by data that cannot be trusted because they are incomplete, out of context, outdated, inaccurate, inaccessible, or so overwhelming that they require weeks to analyze. In such situations, the decision-maker is facing too much uncertainty to make intelligent business decisions.

Bad decisions resulting from inaccurate data lead to increased costs, decreased revenue, and legal, reputational, and performance-related consequences. For example, if data are collected and analyzed based on inaccurate information because advertising was conducted in the wrong location for the wrong audience, marketing campaigns can become highly skewed and ineffective. Companies must then begin costly repairs to their datasets to correct the problems caused by dirty data. This creates a drop in customer satisfaction and a misuse of resources in a firm.

It is widely accepted that service organizations, like health-care systems, are drowning in inaccurate data. For example, an unintended consequence of Electronic Health Records is that data may not be as accurate and complete as expected. Incorrect lab values, imaging results, or physician documentation lead to medical errors, harm patients, and damage the organization's accreditation and reputation. This is particularly troubling since data collected from physician notes, registration forms, discharge summaries, documents, and more are doubling every five years. Unlike structured machine-ready data, these are messy data that takes a lot of time and effort for health-care providers to put it into a system to include in their business analysis. So, valuable but messy data are often routinely left out. As a result, millions of insightful patient notes and records are inaccessible or unavailable because historically there has been no easy way to input and analyze the information they contain.

Missing Data   Data can get lost in transit from one system to another. Or, data might never get captured because of inadequately tuned data collection systems, such as those that rely on sensors or scanners. Or, the data may not get captured in sufficient detail, as described.

Table 3.3 lists the characteristics typically associated with dirty or poor-quality data.

TABLE 3.3   Characteristics of Poor-Quality or Dirty Data

Characteristic of Dirty Data	Description
Incomplete	Missing data
Outdated or invalid	Too old to be valid or useful
Incorrect	Too many errors
Duplicated or in conflict	Too many copies or versions of the same data—and the versions are inconsistent or in conflict with each other
Nonstandardized	Data are stored in incompatible formats—and cannot be compared or summarized
Unusable	Data are not in context to be understood or interpreted correctly at the time of access

Poorly Designed Interfaces   Despite all the talk about user-friendly interfaces, some ISs are horrible to deal with. Poorly designed interfaces or formats that require extra time and effort to figure out increase the risk of errors from misunderstanding the data or ignoring them.

Nonstandardized Data Formats   When users are presented with data in inconsistent or nonstandardized formats, errors increase. Attempts to compare or analyze data are more difficult and take more time. For example, if the Northeast division reports weekly gross sales revenues per product line and the Southwest division reports monthly net sales per product, you cannot compare their performance without converting the data to a common format. Consider the extra effort needed to compare temperature-related sales, such as air conditioners, when some temperatures are expressed in degrees Fahrenheit and others in Centigrade.

Outdated Data   Information that decision-makers want keeps changing and it changes faster than IS departments can respond to because of the first four reasons in this list. Tracking tweets, YouTube hits, and other unstructured content requires expensive investments, which managers find risky in an economic downturn.

The Cost of Dirty Data

On average, an organization experiences 40% data growth annually, and 20% of that data is found to be dirty. The costs of poor-quality data spread throughout a company and affect systems from shipping and receiving to accounting and customer service. Data errors typically arise from the functions or departments that generate or create the data—and not within the IT department. When all costs are considered, the value of finding and fixing the causes of data errors becomes clear. In a time of decreased budgets, some organizations may not have the resources for such projects and may not even be aware of the problem. Others may be spending most of their time fixing problems, thus leaving them with no time to work on preventing them. The benefits of ensuring that data is accurate, timely, complete, consistent, and unique are well worth the effort. It is 10 times more expensive to correct dirty data than it is to prevent it.

Dirty data are costing U.S. businesses hundreds of billions of dollars a year and affecting their ability to ride out the tough economic climate. Incorrect and outdated values, missing data, and inconsistent data formats can cause lost customers, sales, and revenue; misallocation of resources; and flawed pricing strategies. Examples of these costs include:

- **Lost business**   Business is lost when sales opportunities are missed, orders are returned because wrong items were delivered, or errors frustrate and drive away customers.
- **Time spent preventing errors**   If data cannot be trusted, then employees need to spend more time and effort trying to verify information in order to avoid mistakes.
- **Time spent correcting errors**   Database staff need to process corrections to the database.

The cost of poor-quality data may be expressed as the following formula:

$$\text{Cost of Poor-Quality Data} = \text{Lost Business} + \text{Cost to Prevent Errors} + \text{Cost to Correct Errors}$$

- Using this formula, consider the example of costs of correcting errors in an organization:
  - **a.** Two database staff members spend 25% of their workday processing and verifying data corrections each day:

    $$2 \text{ people} \times 25\% \text{ of } 8 \text{ hours/day} = 4 \text{ hours/day correcting errors}$$

  - **b.** Hourly salaries are $50 per hour based on pay rate and benefits:

    $$\$50/\text{hour} \times 4 \text{ hours/day} = \$200/\text{day correcting errors}$$

  - **c.** 250 workdays per year:

    $$\$200/\text{day} \times 250 \text{ days} = \$50,000/\text{year to correct errors}$$

It is difficult to calculate the full cost of poor-quality data and its long-term effects. Part of the difficulty is the time delay between the mistake and when it is detected. Errors can be very difficult to correct, especially when systems extend across the enterprise. Another concern is that the impacts of errors can be unpredictable, far-reaching, and serious. **IT at Work 3.4** looks at how dirty data reportedly can impact discrimination in the criminal justice system.

IT at Work 3.4

Beware of Dirty Data in Predictive Policing Systems

With law enforcement agencies coming under increased scrutiny in recent years for disproportionate aggression toward minority suspects, it has been speculated that predictive policing software might help moderate these types of behavior. Recently researchers at New York University set out to test this theory and came up with some disturbing results.

It has been reported that at least 13 jurisdictions in the United States are currently using predictive policing systems to forecast criminal activity and allocate police resources. Unfortunately, in many of these jurisdictions, these systems are built on data based on flawed, racially charged, and sometimes outright unlawful practices. This may include system wide data manipulation, falsified police reports, unlawful use of force, planted evidence, and unconstitutional searches. Researchers at the AI Now Institute and New York University recently conducted a study of predictive policing systems. In it they compared substantiated evidence and other findings of unlawful or biased police practices collected during Department of Justice investigations or federal court adjudications with publicly available information regarding when the jurisdiction had used a predictive policing system. The results of the comparison were then used to determine whether police data used to train or implement the predictive policing systems were generated during periods of documented unlawful and biased police.

Strong evidence suggests that Chicago, New Orleans, and Maricopa County, AZ use predictive policing systems based on dirty data, although in New Orleans, the lack of transparency and accountability mechanisms made it difficult to discover the true extent of the problem and to properly assess risks associated with the flawed data in the predictive policing systems.

For example, the Chicago Police Department was under federal investigation for unlawful police practices when it implemented a computer system that identifies people at risk of becoming a victim or offender in a shooting or homicide. The NYU study revealed that resident who had the same demographics as those identified by the DOJ as targets of Chicago's policing bias matched those who were identified in the predictive policing system.

These findings strongly suggest that implementing predictive policing systems in jurisdictions with an extensive history of unlawful police practices increase the risks that dirty data will lead to flawed or unlawful predictions of criminal behavior. In turn, this can perpetuate additional harm to citizens via feedback throughout the criminal justice system.

Lead researcher Rashida Richardson was quick to point out that "Even though this study was limited to jurisdictions with well-established histories of police misconduct and discriminatory police practices, we know that these concerns about policing practices and policies are not limited to these jurisdictions, so greater scrutiny regarding data used in predictive policing technologies is necessary globally."

Their findings suggest that predictive policing systems must be treated cautiously and that it is critical that mechanisms be put in place to allow the public across the globe to be aware of such systems and assess and reject them.

Sources: Compiled from Richardson, Schultz, and Crawford (2019), Data Ethics (2019), and McClain (2019).

The overall goal of information management is to eliminate that struggle through the design and implementation of a sound data governance program and a well-planned enterprise architecture (EA). Another goal of information management is data security and compliance.

For example, organizations must be in compliance with continually evolving regulatory requirements, such as Sarbanes-Oxley Act, Basel III, the Computer Fraud and Abuse Act (CFAA), the USE PATRIOT Act, and the Health Insurance Portability and Accountability Act (HIPAA).

Benefits that can be derived from the use of information management include:

1. **Improved decision quality** Decision quality depends on accurate and complete data.
2. **Improved accuracy and reliability of management predictions** It is essential for managers to be able to predict sales, product demand, opportunities, and competitive threats. Management predictions focus on "what is going to happen" as opposed to financial reporting on "what has happened."
3. **Lower time and cost** of locating and integrating relevant information.
4. **Better data quality** Standardization of data results in more reliable and consistent data

Questions

1. What are the stages of the data lifecycle?
2. What is the function of master data management (MDM)?
3. What are the consequences of not cleaning "dirty data"?
4. What is the "silo effect" and how does it affect business performance?
5. What three factors are driving collaboration and information sharing?
6. What are the business benefits of information management?
7. Why is it important to have good information management practices?

3.5 Electronic Document, Record, and Content Management

LO3.5 Define the terms electronic document, electronic record, and electronic content and how the technologies that manage them are being used to make organizations more effective and efficient.

Electronic content is a collection of documents, records, and unstructured data available as a broad range of digital assets, such as audio, video, flash, multimedia files, and so on.

Electronic document is any paper, electronic form, file, email, fax, contract, lease, and so on actively being worked on.

Electronic record is any document that has been made final and is no longer meant to be altered.

Information and knowledge are stored in a database in the form of electronic documents, records, and content. Pricewaterhouse Coopers (PwC), a large professional services network, recently reported that that over four trillion paper documents are produced in the United States alone and this number is growing at an alarming 22% each year! They also found that 7.5% of documents get lost, 3% of the remainder get misfiled, and the average document gets copied 19 times. They also estimated that companies spend $20 in labor to file a document; $120 to find a misfiled document, and $220 to reproduce a lost document. This translates to the loss of millions of trees and billions of dollars spent in time and money. Consequently, companies are turning more and more to electronic documents, records, *and* content management as a solution.

First, it's useful to understand the differences between an electronic document, an electronic record, and electronic content. Next we will explain how each are managed and describe the software that supports them. The important differences between an **electronic document** and an **electronic record** is that documents are being *actively worked on* and *can be changed*. In contrast, records are *finished work* and are *not intended to be changed*. The different stages in the lifecycle of an electronic record are shown in **Figure 3.18. Electronic content** not only covers written documents and records, but also includes data that are maintained in different formats including audio, video, flash, and multimedia files.

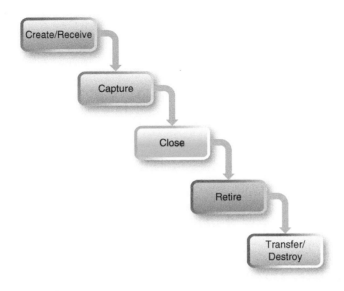

FIGURE 3.18   Five stages of the record lifecycle.

Electronic Document Management

The purpose of **electronic document management** is to systematically *create, share, organize, and efficiently retrieve* in-process or "living" documents. The information in document management is *transient content*, such as invoices that are signed and sent on to the next signatory or an older draft of a document discarded for a revised one. It is *content-driven* in that document repositories are typically organized to efficiently find documents by keyword or title and group documents by customer name or product. The goal of document management is *efficiency*: reduce paper, reduce lost and misfiled documents, provide easier, faster access and retrieval; reduce costs and storage space, and streamline information and workflow.

Electronic document management is the electronic storage, maintenance, and tracking of electronic documents and electronic images of paper-based information.

Electronic Document Management Systems

Software to support the management of electronic documents is called an **electronic documents management system (EDMS).** An EDMS is used by a broad range of users across the organization to perform their daily job functions. Since an EDMS handles "living" documents that are versioned and require frequent approvals, electronic review and approval are key features of an EDMS. While managing an EDMS creates overhead for users importing and creating documents, its power is quickly realized when users across the organization can easily find documents.

Electronic document management system is a software system for creating, organizing, storing, and retrieving different kinds of electronic documents.

Electronic Records Management

On the other hand, **electronic records management** focuses on *archiving* records to help an organization avoid penalties imposed by regulators, auditors, and other governing bodies. Archiving includes classifying, storing, and securing records and having a plan to determine what, when, and how records should be destroyed or preserved (in the case of important historical records). Records management is comprised of *historical content* and is *context-driven*, as in type of document and retention schedules. Government agencies are already expected to manage all permanent records electronically in preparation for the fast-approaching December 31, 2022 deadline when the National Archives and Records Administration (NARA) will no longer accept paper documents from government agencies. David Miller, Director of Records Management services for NARA's Federal Records Center Programs, warns that government agencies with permanent record collections "need to think about either getting those records into federal records centers ahead of the deadline or finding some way to do large-scale digitization of the content" (Goldstein, 2019). The goals of electronic records management are business continuity and compliance. To ensure this it must control the volume and quality of records;

Electronic records management establishes policies and standards for maintaining diverse types of records.

simplify storage of, maintenance of, and access to records; simplify locating a correct record when needed; ensure security; determine required retention time and develop a destruction system for records at the end of the retention time.

An effective electronic records management system (ERMS) captures all business data and documents at their first touchpoint—data centers, laptops, the mailroom, at customer sites, or remote offices. Records enter the enterprise in multiple ways—from online forms, bar codes, sensors, websites, social sites, copiers, e-mails, and more. In addition to capturing the entire document, important data from within a document can be captured and stored in a central, searchable repository. In this way, the data are accessible to support informed and timely business decisions.

Legal Duty to Retain Business Records

Companies need to be prepared to respond to an audit, federal investigation, lawsuit, or any other legal action against them. In the United States alone, more than 10 federal records management laws and regulations must be followed when managing government records.

Add to this regulations in the financial sector imposed by the Securities and Exchange Commission (SEC), the Health Insurance Portability and Accountability Act (HIPAA) in the health-care industry, and the Family Educational Rights and Privacy Act (FERPA) in education discussed in **IT at Work 3.5**, and organizations have a plethora of compliance standards to contend with. Types of lawsuits include doctor–patient confidentiality, student rights, parents' rights, patent violations, product safety negligence, theft of intellectual property, breach of contract, wrongful termination, harassment, discrimination, and many more.

IT at Work 3.5

Electronic Records Management Systems (ERMS) in Action

Here are some examples of how companies use ERMS in the health-care, finance, and education sectors:

- **Health care:** Anne Arundel Medical Center (AAMC) is a regional health system headquartered in Annapolis, Maryland and serves an area of one million people. Like many hospital systems, AAMC has made information available to employees to enable better decision-making for patients and AAMC. To do this, they implemented an electronic medical record system for patient care and billing. They also use multiple tools for reporting and leveraging information collected as part of normal patient care and hospital operations. Using these new technologies, IT analysts at AAMC actively created new reports. Unfortunately, employees often found it challenging to find the data they needed.
- **Finance:** American Express (AMEX) uses TELEform, developed by Alchemy and Cardiff Software, to collect and process more than one million customer satisfaction surveys every year. The data are collected in templates that consist of more than 600 different survey forms in 12 languages and 11 countries. AMEX integrated TELEform with AMEX's legacy system,

which enables it to distribute processed results to many managers. Because the survey forms are now readily accessible, AMEX has reduced the number of staff who process these forms from 17 to 1, thereby saving the company more than $500,000 a year.

- **Education:** Many higher education institutions including Princeton, University of Cincinnati and the University of Texas at Austin maintain their student records, as defined by FERPA, in an ERMS. To make best use of it, they rely on electronic written communication media, such as email, instant messaging, discussion boards, and chat sessions, to communicate with students and each other. Under FERPA, students dissatisfied with services they receive can file claims of lack of service, incorrect information, and faculty bias and then petition to view their records. To reduce institutional risk, university faculty, staff, and administrators try to maximize effective communication with their students by keeping careful electronic notes of how they delivered a service as well as documenting the knowledge and assistance they provided to the student.

Sources: Compiled from Green (2018), ECM Connection (2019), Michalowicz (2019), Steinberg (2019), Princeton University Records Management (2019), University of Cincinnati (2019), and University of Texas at Austin (2019).

Because senior management must ensure that their companies comply with legal and regulatory duties, managing electronic records (e-records) is a strategic issue for organizations in both the public and private sectors. The success of ERM depends greatly on a partnership of many key players, namely, senior management, users, records managers, archivists, administrators, and most importantly, IT personnel. Properly managed, records are strategic assets. Improperly managed or destroyed, they become liabilities.

In recent years, governing bodies such as the Association for Information and Image Management (AIIM), National Archives and Records Administration (NARA), and ARMA International (formerly the Association of Records Managers and Administrators) have created and published industry standards for document and records management. Numerous best practices articles, and links to valuable sources of information about document and records management, are available on their websites. The IT Toolbox describes ARMA's eight generally accepted recordkeeping principles framework.

Electronic Records Management Systems

Software to support an ERM is called an **electronic records management system (ERMS)**. ERMSs are currently the most widely implemented of the three systems and have the added functionality of disaster recovery, business continuity, and compliance. Because of this, applications of ERMS are often found in companies that are required by law to retain documents, such as health records that must be kept for a specified period, financial documents for a seven-year period, product designs for many decades, and e-mail messages about marketing promotions for a year. The multilayered access capabilities of an ERMS, that vet users as to their right-to-know information, make sure that employees can access and change only the documents they are authorized to handle.

> **Electronic records management system (ERMS)** is the technology tool used to electronically manage the creation and maintenance of records within classification schemes, apply retention and disposal schedules, and control access and use.

When companies select an ERMS to meet compliance requirements, they should ask the following questions:

1. Does the software meet the organization's needs? For example, can the ERMS be installed on the existing network? Can it be purchased as a service?
2. Is the software easy to use and accessible from Web browsers, office applications, and e-mail applications? If not, people will not use it.
3. Does the software have lightweight, modern Web and graphical user interfaces that effectively support remote users?
4. Before selecting a vendor, it is important to examine workflows and how data, documents, and communications flow throughout the company. For example, know which information on documents is used in business decisions. Once those needs and requirements are identified, they guide the selection of technology that can support the input types—that is, capture and index them so they can be archived consistently and retrieved on-demand.

Departments or companies whose employees spend most of their day filing or retrieving documents or warehousing paper records can reduce costs significantly with an ERMS. These systems minimize the inefficiencies and frustration associated with managing paper documents and workflows. However, they do not create a paperless office as had been predicted.

An ERMS can help a business to become more efficient and productive in the following ways:

- Enabling the company to access and use the content contained in documents.
- Cutting labor costs by automating business processes.
- Reducing the time and effort required to locate information the business needs to support decision-making.
- Improving the security of content, thereby reducing the risk of intellectual property theft.
- Minimizing the costs associated with printing, storing, and searching for content.

When workflows are digital, productivity increases, costs decrease, compliance obligations are easier to verify, and green computing becomes possible. Green computing is an initiative to conserve our valuable natural resources by reducing the effects of our computer usage on the environment. You can read about green computing and the related topics of reducing an organization's carbon footprint, sustainability, and ethical and social responsibilities in Chapter 5.

Enterprise Content Management

Enterprise content management is the capture, storage, retrieval, and management of a diverse set of digital assets including documents, records, emails, electronic communications, images, video, flash, audio, and multimedia.

Enterprise content management is the umbrella under which electronic document management and electronic records management exist and can be viewed as *document management on steroids*. In some ways it is like electronic document management, which is a sub-set of enterprise content management, but also includes handling many more different types of digital assets. The management of the enormous amount of content being collected electronically offers even more added value when it is integrated and stored in data warehouses where it can be easily analyzed.

Enterprise Content Management Systems

Enterprise content management system (ECMS) captures, preserves, and manages structured and unstructured a wide variety of digital assets and secures them digitally in compliance with policies.

Software to support enterprise content management is called an **enterprise content management systems (ECMS)**. An ECMS is much more than just a means of storing and managing organizational documents. Just as an EDMS can be thought of as a digital filing cabinet, the ECMS is more like a digital assistant that can automatically recognize the content within a digital asset and know who, where, and when to send it. An ECMS is particularly useful for companies seeking to manage and configure large volumes of structured and unstructured data and handling alternative media. Its goal is business continuity.

Choosing an EDMS, ERMS, or ECMS

When choosing an EDMS, ERMS, or ECMS it is important to match the strategic needs of the company with the capabilities of the system. To make an informed choice, you must understand the functional similarities and differences between the three.

Business continuity is the ability of a company to maintain essential functions during, as well as after, a disaster has occurred.

As you have read, a shared goal of electronic document management, electronic records management and enterprise content management is **business continuity.** If one of them fails, the entire organization could be at risk. However, when all achieve their goals, the future of the organization is assured.

Critical differences between an EDMS and an ERMS exist because EDMS users need to check in and check out stored documents quickly and easily and unlock them for future revision, while maintaining version tracking and histories of access.

On the other hand, ERMS users require that records be kept in their original format for retrieval for compliance or legal reasons. Just storing files on an organization's shared hard drives is insufficient to meet these industry compliance standards.

Another difference is that in an ERMS, records need to be placed in indexes determined by external rules, usually imposed by governmental or regulatory agencies. Consequently, this storage is often duplicated in both on-site and off-site records centers for safety reasons since software security is essential in an ERMS, but only desirable in a EDMS.

An ECMS has a broader mission. It differs from EDMS and ERMS in that it is designed to facilitate record lifecycle management, information governance, and collaboration. An ECMS also provides a single source of trusted information. It also provides version control and synchronization, along with intuitive search and discovery functions. An ECMS also can integrate with other applications to deliver viewable content across multiple platforms, along with security and optimized business processes in its content storage and retrieval systems (Trust Radius, 2019).

The major EDMS, ERMS, and ECMS tools are workflow software, authoring tools, scanners, and databases. These tools have query and search capabilities so documents can be identified and accessed like data in a database, records can be archived and easily retrieved, and content of all kinds can be made easily accessible on demand. Systems range from those designed to support a small workgroup to full-featured, Web-enabled enterprisewide systems. Examples of widely used electronic document, record, and content management systems include IBM e-File Laserfiche (**https://www.laserfiche.com/**), eFile Cabinet (**https://www.efilecabinet .com/**), M-Files (**https://www.m-files.com/en**), and NAVEX Global (**https://www.navexglobal .com/en-us**).

Questions

1. Define the term "electronic content."
2. Describe the main differences between an electronic document and an electronic record.
3. Why do companies use an electronic records management system?
4. Names three types of lawsuits that can be brought against a company related to their electronic records.
5. What characteristic of an ERMS allows employees to access and change only the documents they are authorized to handle?
6. What is the difference between an electronic document management system (EDMS) and an electronic record management system (ERMS)?
7. What is the shared goal of EDMS, ERMS, and ECMS?

Chapter Summary

LO 3.1 *Describe* the fundamentals of data management and how database management systems, including blockchain technology, help companies improve performance.

Data management oversees the end-to-end lifecycle of data from creation and initial storage to the time when it becomes obsolete and is deleted. Due to the incredible volume of data the typical organization creates, effective data management is vital to prevent storage costs from spiraling out of control and controlling data growth while supporting greater performance. Several data management technologies keep users informed and help support various business needs. They include a database, database management system (DBMS), data warehouses, and data marts. Databases store data generated by business apps, sensors, operations, and TPS. Medium and large enterprises typically have centralized or distributed databases. To get the most out of a database, a software package designed to define, manipulate, and manage the data must be used. This is called a database management system (DBMS). Database management systems benefit organizations by reducing data latency, volatility, and consistency. A well-designed DBMS can also reduce query response time, manage the predictability of queries and process them in real-time to enable faster, more confident decision-making. The newest entry into DBMS is blockchain technology. Blockchain adds far greater security and trust to a database through its immutable structure, permissionings and smart contracts. Blockchain technology is being used in innovative ways in many industry sectors.

LO 3.2 *Identify* the differences between a database, a data warehouse, and a data mart and why a company would move from a database to a data warehouse or data mart.

Databases work well with smaller data sets but lack the scalability or flexibility for specialized or very large workloads. When an organization has very large volumes of complex data, it needs to consider a data warehouse or a data mart. Data warehouses and data marts are used when the data set cannot efficiently process the data and the volatility of the database makes it impossible to use it for complex decision-making and problem-solving. Many organizations built data warehouses because they were frustrated with inconsistent data that couldn't support corporate decisions and customer interactions. A data warehouse or data mart is the primary source of cleansed data for analysis, reporting, and decision-making. The high cost of data warehouses can make them too expensive for smaller companies to implement.

Data marts are lower-cost, scaled-down versions of a data warehouse that can be implemented in a shorter timeframe. Date warehouses and data marts improve the overall customer experience and can be delivered to decision-makers through the enterprise via the cloud or company-owned intranets to enable faster, more accurate decisions.

LO 3.3 *Describe* the importance of data governance in providing trusted data available when and where needed and why master data management (MDM) is an important data governance initiative.

Data governance is an enterprisewide project because data cross boundaries and are used by people throughout the enterprise. Strong data governance and MDM are needed to ensure data are of sufficient quality to meet business needs. Industries rely heavily on data governance to help them comply with regulations or reporting requirements. MDM is an important part of data governance.

MDM offers a solution to management frustrated by fragmented and dispersed data sources. Data governance combined with MDM is a powerful combination. The need to manage data as a strategic asset to unlock its full value becomes more and more important as data sources and volumes continue to increase. Benefits of data governance and MDM include improved regulatory compliance, more efficient decision-making, improved understanding of data, and increased revenues.

LO 3.4 *Explain* the concept of information management and why it is important for an organization to follow good information management practices.

Information management is the process of collecting, storing, managing, and maintaining data that is accurate, timely, reliable, valid, available, unique, and relevant to an organization.

In business, data are used for two major reasons: to run a business and to improve a business. Both of these depend on easy and fast access to high-quality trustworthy data that is accurate, timely, reliable, unique, and relevant. Consequently, two important initiatives of information management are eliminating data silos and reducing "dirty data" that is, inaccurate, missing, or outdated data stored in nonstandard data formats and accessed through poorly designed interfaces. Dirty data can put the company at risk and are very costly to maintain resulting in lost business, time spent preventing errors, and time spent correcting errors. Data silos create barriers to collaboration and communication and can result in poor decision-making based on insufficient information. Good information management can improve decision quality and the accuracy and reliability of management predictions. It can also reduce the time and cost of locating and integrating relevant information and results in better data quality.

LO 3.5 *Define* the terms electronic document, electronic record, and electronic content and how the technologies that manage them are being used to make organizations more effective and efficient.

An electronic document refers to a document that is being actively worked and can be changed. An electronic record, on the other hand, is a finished document that is not intended to change, and electronic content is similar in nature, but also includes video, images, audio, flash, and multimedia files. Electronic documents are managed by an electronic documents management system (EDMS) to systematically *create, share, organize, and efficiently retrieve* living documents. An EDMS is used by a broad range of users across an organization to perform daily work and can be thought of as a digital filing cabinet that enables users to easily find documents anywhere, anytime. An electronic records management system (ERMS) is different. It focuses on *archiving* records to help with compliance and regulatory requirements imposed by auditors and other governing bodies. In addition, it simplifies storage, maintenance, and access to important records, determines retention time schedules, and develops a destruction system for records at the end of their life cycle. Content management is the umbrella under which electronic document management and electronic records management sit. It is similar in nature to electronic document management but includes handling many more different types of digital assets. An enterprise content management system (ECMS) provides value beyond just storing and managing organizational documents. It acts as a digital assistant that automatically recognizes content within a digital asset and knows to whom, where, and when to send it. An ECMS is particularly valuable to organizations that have large volumes of structured and unstructured data in several alternative digital media that must be managed and configured.

Key Terms

active data warehouse (ADW)   83
Atomicity   70
big data   87
biz-tech ecosystem   69
Blockchain   75
business continuity   100
Centralized database   70
change data capture (CDC)   82
cloud data warehouse (CDW)   82
customer-centric   89
Database   69
Database management system (DBMS)   69
Database query language   74
data deduplication   82
Data entity   88
Data governance   86
data lake   85
Data latency.   80
Data management   69
Data marts   81
Data modeling language   74
Data silo   91
Data structure   73
Data warehouses   81
Data Warehousing Supports Action as Well as Decisions   84

declarative language   78
dirty data   93
Distributed database   70
Electronic content   96
electronic document   96
electronic document management   97
electronic documents management system (EDMS)   97
electronic record   96
electronic records management   97
electronic records management system (ERMS)   99
Enterprise content management   100
enterprise content management systems (ECMS)   100
enterprise data warehouses (EDWs)   84
Eventual consistency   80
extract transform and load (ETL)   81
fault tolerance   79
hash   76
hierarchical database   74
Immediate consistency   80
information management   90
knowledge management   90
master data   87
Master data management (MDM).   88

master file   88
Master Reference File   88
Network   74
network data model   74
Not Only SQL (NoSQL)   78
object-oriented database management system   75
online analytics processing (OLAP)   73
online transaction processing (OLTP)   73
peer-to-peer network   76
Proof-of-work   76
query   78
Query predictability.   80
Query processing capabilities.   80
Query response time   80
relational database   74
relational data model   74
Scalability   72
Structure Query Language (SQL)   78
supply chain   77
transaction   70
Transaction Mechanism   79
Volatility.   80

Assuring Your Learning

Discuss: Critical Thinking Questions

1. What are the functions of databases and data warehouses?

2. How does data quality impact business performance?

3. List three types of waste or damages that data errors can cause.

4. What is the role of a master file?

5. Give three examples of business processes or operations that would benefit significantly from having detailed real-time or near real-time data and identify the benefits.

6. Name two industries that depend on data governance to comply with regulations or reporting requirements. Given an example of each.

7. Select an industry. Explain how an organization in that industry could improve consumer satisfaction through the use of data warehousing.

8. Explain the principle of 90/90 data use.

9. Why is master data management (MDM) important in companies with multiple data sources?

10. Name one challenge facing organizations regarding information management

11. What are the operational benefits and competitive advantages of using electronic document and records management?

12. How can a cognitive knowledge management system decrease operating costs and increase revenue?

Explore: Online and Interactive Exercises

1. Many organizations initiate data governance programs because of pressing compliance issues that impact data usage. Organizations may need data governance to comply with one or more regulations, such as the Gramm–Leach Bliley Act (GLB), HIPAA, Foreign Corrupt Practices Act (FCPA), Sarbanes–Oxley Act, and several state and federal privacy laws.

   a. Research and select two U.S. regulations or privacy laws.

   b. Describe how data governance would help an enterprise comply with these regulations or laws.

2. Research two electronic records management vendors, such as Iron Mountain.

   a. What are the retention recommendations made by the vendors? Why?

   b. What services or solutions does each vendor offer?

3. View the Microsoft QuickBase video at **https://www.quickbase. com/video-demo-watch**. Explain the benefits of this app that replaces Microsoft Access and explain whether or not you think QuickBase is an improvement over its predecessor.

Analyze & Decide: Apply IT Concepts to Business Decisions

1. Spring Street Company (SSC) wanted to reduce the "hidden costs" associated with its paper-intensive processes. Employees jokingly predicted that if the windows were open on a very windy day, total chaos would ensue as thousands of papers started to fly. If a flood, fire, or windy day occurred, the business would literally grind to a halt. The company's accountant, Sam Spring, decided to calculate the costs of its paper-driven processes to identify their impact on the bottom line. He recognized that several employees spent most of their day filing or retrieving documents. In addition, there were the monthly costs to warehouse old paper records. Sam measured the activities related to the handling of printed reports and paper files. His average estimates were as follows:

   a. Dealing with a file: It takes an employee 12 minutes to walk to the records room, locate a file, act on it, refile it, and return to his or her desk. Employees do this 4 times per day (five days per week).

   b. Number of employees: 10 full-time employees perform the functions.

   c. Lost document replacement: Once per day, a document gets "lost" (destroyed, misplaced, or covered with massive coffee stains) and must be recreated. The total cost of replacing each lost document is $200.

   d. Warehousing costs: Currently, document storage costs are $75 per month.

   Sam would prefer a system that lets employees find and work with business documents without leaving their desks. He's most concerned about the human resources and accounting departments. These personnel are traditional heavy users of paper files and would greatly benefit from a modern document management system. At the same time, however, Sam is also risk averse. He would rather invest in solutions that would reduce the risk of higher costs in the future. He recognizes that the U.S. PATRIOT Act's requirements that organizations provide immediate government access to records apply to SSC. He has read that manufacturing and government organizations rely on efficient document management to meet these broader regulatory imperatives. Finally, Sam wants to implement a disaster recovery system.

   Prepare a report that provides Sam with the data he needs to evaluate the company's costly paper-intensive approach to managing documents. You will need to conduct research to provide data to prepare this report. Your report should include the following information:

   1. How should SSC prepare for an ERMS if it decides to implement one?

   2. Using the data collected by Sam, create a spreadsheet that calculates the costs of handling paper at SSC based on average hourly rates per employee of $28. Add the cost of lost documents to this. Then, add the costs of warehousing the paper, which increases by 10% every month due to increases in volume. Present the results showing both monthly totals and a yearly total. Prepare graphs so that Sam can easily identify the projected growth in warehousing costs over the next three years.

   3. How can an ERMS also serve as a disaster recovery system in case of fire, flood, or break-in?

   4. Submit your recommendation for an ERM solution. Identify two vendors in your recommendation.

2. You are working for a national clothing chain. Several of the buyers have been having a lot of problems obtaining well-designed reports from your organization's sales and marketing departments on their activities by state over the past year. They want to be able to create

reports as needed and access them anytime, anywhere. The buyers need this knowledge to help them plan future purchases and think that a knowledge management system would help improve the retrieval of information from the company's data warehouse. You have been asked to research KM software packages and to report back to your colleagues. View a list of the top 10 KM software packages at the Capterra website (**https://www.capterra.com/sem-compare/knowledge-management-software?utm_source=bing&utm_medium=cpc-**). Choose at least three KM software tools from the list and go to their websites and take the demo. Write a report describing and comparing the KM tools that you demoed. Discuss the pros and cons of each of them and identify your favorite. Explain your choice.

Reinforce: Demonstrate Understanding of the Key Terms

Solve the online crossword to test your understanding of Key Terms in this chapter.

Web Resources

More resources and study tools are located on the student Website. You'll find useful web links and self-test quizzes that provide individualized feedback.

Case 3.2

Business Case: Dirty Data Jeopardize University Fundraising Efforts

Founded in 1861, the University of Washington (UW) is a multi-campus public research university located in Seattle, Tacoma, and Bothell, as well as a world-class academic medical center. The university has a total enrollment of more than 47,000 students in 16 colleges and schools. It offers 1,800 undergraduate courses each quarter to more than 32,000 students and annually confers more than 12,000 bachelor's, master's, doctoral, and professional degrees through 140 academic departments.

Beware of Dirty Data

Universities like UW know that fundraising can mean BIG money. At UW, however, dirty data hampered their fundraising efforts and instead of a significant opportunity they had a recipe for disaster: UW collects contact information from multiple sources and this was resulting in copious data errors and duplicate records in their huge donor database that houses the names, addresses, and other relevant information about more than 900,000 student, faculty, staff, alumni, and sports event attendees. They also knew that the contact information in UW's donor records quickly became outdated, especially for students and younger alumni who tend to be transient (relocating to new jobs, marrying—changing names). Taken all together, the University had a plethora of dirty data that resulted in large volumes of undeliverable mail, wasted postage and excessive production costs, and worst of all a loss in fundraising opportunities. For example, in one direct mail test, UW discovered that almost 10% of its mail was not delivered resulting in thousands of dollars in waste and lost funding. Mike Visaya, Associate Director of Information Management (IM) Strategic Technology Initiatives, lamented that because of the huge amount of data they had to handle UW "knew it was important to bring in an expert on data quality."

Improving Data Quality

To improve the quality of its donor database the University worked with Melissa Data (**https://www.melissa.com/**), a data collection and verification group. Together they implemented an extensive proactive data quality program to address the inaccurate data issues and ensure the consistency of student and alumni records in their primary donor database. Using Melissa's Data Quality Suite, UW updated the way in which it handled address, phone, and email verification and name parsing in such a way that caused Mike Visaya to proclaim that "now our data makes sense." To find and prevent data duplication, UW used Melissa Data's advanced record matching and deduplication solutions.

Melissa Data's geocoding service also helped UW analyze location-specific relationships in its data. For example, UW wanted to know if its football season ticket holders were big contributors to university academic programs and were surprised to discover that they are. Shawn Drew, Director of IM for the Office of Development, was impressed. He thought the database solutions allowed UW to "connect the dots, find new relationships and capitalize on the many ways our supporters wanted to contribute."

Identifying New Opportunities

Improvements to data quality also allowed the University the opportunity to go after international donors. Before implementing the solution, the University rarely mailed internationally. Now, with their new technology, UW can easily standardize and collect international contacts to increase their global fundraising efforts.

Thanks to their new data quality solution, UW went from the nightmare of dirty data quality and lost fundraising opportunities, to fulfilling their dream and raised a whopping $2.7 billion in one fundraising effort.

Questions

1. Why was there dirty data in the UW database?
2. What were the consequences to UW of the dirty data?
3. How did UW address the problem of dirty data?
4. What were the benefits they experienced from improving the quality of their donor database?
5. What new opportunity was identified by the new system?

Sources: Melissa Data (**2019**) and University of Washington (**2019**).

IT Toolbox

Framework for Generally Accepted Recordkeeping Principles

The Framework for generally accepted recordkeeping principles is a useful tool for managing business records to ensure that they support an enterprise's current and future regulatory, legal, risk mitigation, environmental, and operational requirements. The framework consists of eight principles or best practices, which also support data governance. These principles were created by ARMA International (formerly the Association of Records Managers and Administrators) and legal and IT professionals.

1. **Principle of accountability** Assign a senior executive to oversee a recordkeeping program; adopt policies and procedures to guide personnel; and ensure program audit ability.
2. **Principle of transparency** Document processes and activities of an organization's recordkeeping program in an understandable manner and available to all personnel and appropriate parties.
3. **Principle of integrity** Ensure recordkeeping program is able to reasonably guarantee the authenticity and reliability of records and data.
4. **Principle of protection** Construct the recordkeeping program to ensure a reasonable level of protection to records and information that are private, confidential, privileged, secret, or essential to business continuity.
5. **Principle of compliance** Ensure recordkeeping program complies with applicable laws, authorities, and the organization's policies.
6. **Principle of availability** Maintain records in a manner that ensures timely, efficient, and accurate retrieval of needed information.
7. **Principle of retention** Maintain records and data for an appropriate time based on legal, regulatory, fiscal, operational, and historical requirements.
8. **Principle of disposition** Securely dispose of records when they are no longer required to be maintained by laws or organizational policies.

References

Bagley, R. "The Data Supply Chain Is Critical to the Success of Healthcare Providers." *Logistics Tech Outlook*. 2019.

Bitpipe. "Saving $1.5 Million with New Workflows and Document Digitization." Retrieved from: https://media.bitpipe.com/io_14x/io_145881/item_1863016/Case%20Study%20-%20thyssenkrupp%20Elevator.pdf on November 10, 2019.

Christman, A. "It's Not Easy Being Lean: How to Break Down Silos and Promote Collaboration." *KAI Partners*. 2018. Retrieved from https://kaipartners.com/its-not-easy-being-lean-how-to-break-down-silos-and-promote-collaboration/ on November 6, 2019.

Consensys. "How Will Blockchain Benefit the Energy Industry?" Retrieved from: https://consensys.net/enterprise-ethereum/use-cases/energy-and-sustainability/ on November 10, 2019.

Data Ethics. "US Experience with Predicting Policing and 'Dirty Data': Treat It with Skepticism." *Data Ethics*, February 2019.

ECM Connection. "A Customer-Satisfying Experience." Retrieved from https://www.ecmconnection.com/doc/a-customer-satisfying-experience-0001 on November 9, 2019.

Goldstein, P. "What Is an Electronic Document Management System and Why Do You Need One?" *FedTech*, August 9, 2019.

Green, J. "Three Common Barriers to HER Implementation and How to Avoid Them." *Modernizing Medicine*, April 12, 2018.

IQ BG, Inc. "ThyssenKrupp Elevator Automates Document and Information Discovery with M-Files." 2018.

Krieger, K. "Spectrum Health Recognized for Supply Chain Services." *Spectrum Health Newsroom*, 2018.

Marchese, K. "How the 'Silo Effect' Is Hurting Cross Team Collaboration." *Trello*, October 23, 2019.

Marr, B. "35 Amazing Real-World Examples of How Blockchain Is Changing Our World." *Forbes*, January 22, 2018.

McClain, J. "With Dirty Data, Predictive Policing Can Make Bias Worse." *Futuritys*, March 8, 2019.

Melissa Data. "University Improves Fundraising Efforts Ten-Fold with Powerful Data Quality Solutions from Melissa Data." Retrieved from https://www.melissa.com/pdf/dqt-uw-casestudy.pdf November 9, 2019.

Michalowicz, M. "How to Use Surveys to Assess Customer Satisfaction." *American Express*, July 15, 2019.

Michigan State University. "Changes and Challenges in the Healthcare Supply Chain." *Michigan State University Online*, 2019.

O'Kane, B. and Moran, M. "MDM Is Critical to Maximizing CRM and Customer Experience." *Gartner*, December 12, 2018.

Phillip, B. "The Compleat Traveler: Active Data Warehousing Trumps the Traditional for Travelocity by Supporting Event-Based Decisions." *CRM Magazine.* Retrieved from https://www.questia.com/magazine/1G1-151051872/the-compleat-traveler-active-data-warehousing-trumps on November 9, 2019.

Pricewaterhouse Cooper. "The Developing Role of Blockchain in the Energy Sector." *PwC*, New Zealand. 2018.

Princeton University Records Management. "Email and Other Electronic Records." Retrieved from https://records.princeton.edu/records-management-manual/e-mail-and-other-electronic-records on November 8, 2019.

Reeves, M.G., and Bowen, R. "Developing a Data Governance Model in Health Care." *Healthcare Finance Management*, vol. 67(2): 82–86, 2013.

Richardson, R., Schultz, J., and Crawford, K. "Dirty Data, Bad Predictions: How Civil Rights Violations Impact Police Data, Predicting Policing Systems and Justice." *Social Science Review Network*, 2019.

Spector, J. "For Utilities Exploring Blockchain, There's Beauty in the Mundane." *GTM*, September 12, 2018.

Steinberg, S. "5 Ways to Help Get Crucial Insights and Data From Your Customers." *American Express*, November 4, 2019.

Stroud, F. "Top 10 Enterprise Database Systems of 2019." *ServerWatch*. Retrieved from https://www.serverwatch.com/server-trends/slideshows/top-10-enterprise-database-systems-to-consider-2019.html on November 3, 2019.

Thyssenkrupp. thyssenkruppelevator.com.

University of Cincinnati. "Public Records Requests." *University of Cincinnati, Office of General Counsel*, Retrieved from https://www.uc.edu/gencounsel/public-records.html on November 9, 2019.

University of Texas at Austin. "Educational Records." Retrieved from https://catalog.utexas.edu/general-information/appendices/appendix-c/educational-records/ on November 9, 2019.

University of Washington. "BeBoundless for Washington/ for the World." Retrieved from https://www.washington.edu/giving/ on November 9, 2019.

World Economic Forum. "Building Block(chain)s for a Better Planet." *Fourth Industrial Revolution for the Earth Series*. 2018.

XTIVIA. "Retail Active Data Warehouse." Retrieved from https://www.xtivia.com/media/eim_casestudy_Retail-Active-Data-Warehouse-ADW.pdf on November 9, 2019.

CHAPTER 4

Networks, the Internet of Things (IoT), and Edge Computing

Case 4.1 Opening Case

SEC PLANNING , LLC, https://www.secplanning.com/project/entr-signs-txdaot-beautification/

Hagai Nativ/Alamy Stock Photo

Cedar Park, Texas Improves Customer Communications to Empower Them to Conserve Water through Its New Smart Water Network

It has been estimated that 36% of U.S. households won't be able to afford water in the next five years because of rising utility costs and scarcity of water resources.

To address this concern, the City of Cedar Park, Texas, USA is doing its part by changing the way it communicates water consumption information to its 23,000 customers.

The City of Cedar Park

Founded in 1887, Cedar Park is one of the fastest growing cities in the Lone Star State where folks are friendly, businesses prosper, and residents are happy. Currently, Cedar Park's population stands at approximately 79,000. The city was founded by a group of courageous pioneers who endured countless hardships and challenges. Although times have changed, the pioneering spirit of its founders has endured to transform the park that was a rail stop in the late 1800s into the bustling high-tech employer hub that it is today.

The Problem

Since the city experienced a drought in 2015, the City of Cedar Park has been finding it more and more difficult to keep up with the level of transparency expected by its increasingly tech-savvy customers who were demanding greater accuracy in billing processes and improved transparency. The problem was that Cedar Park was using outdated water meters to collect water consumption data. Twice a month, Cedar Park's technicians drove by each customer location to collect data from automated drive-by meter readers and the City had no real-time data on water leaks. This not only led to dissatisfied customers, but also to response delays and wasted water.

Consequently, Cedar Park customers were frustrated by the limited analytics provided in their monthly bill because it didn't show why their bill fluctuated from month-to-month and they had limited confidence in the data it generated. In addition, customers were inconvenienced when major water leaks occurred.

To learn about the challenges and benefits of implementing smart water technology and find a workable solution to their problem, Cedar Park sought advice from 50 other municipal water districts.

The Solution

To eliminate outdated mailed invoices and phone enquiries, Cedar Park upgraded to digital water meters and a FlexNet® communication network, a two-way system that allows city staff to remotely monitor water usage and increase billing accuracy. Also known as Advanced Metering Infrastructure (AMI), the digital water meters provide customers with accurate near real-time data on their individual water usage and helps them gain deeper insight and understanding about how and when they use water.

Digital water meter readings are encrypted and transmitted from the meter to the utility company's database. The meter data display looks a lot like a car odometer and has nine digits. The digits represent the number of gallons consumed to 1/100th of a gallon. The last two digits can be used as leak indicators to detect water flow through the meter and are not used for billing purposes.

The FlexNet® communication network securely transmits and receives customer usage data, including water meter readings, meter identification number, and diagnostic information to verify the automated digital meter is working correctly. This safe and secure automated network uses a private radio frequency channel. The radio frequency operates at a much lower level than smartphones, microwaves and wireless routers and is registered by the Federal Communications Commission (FCC). Only key authorized City of Cedar Park personnel can access a customer account.

To facilitate customer access, Cedar Park added a web portal accessible from any PC, laptop, tablet, or mobile device to its Smart Water Network. Once a customer registers with a unique username and password they get a secure account login. This enables them to set and receive water consumption threshold alerts, view comparative data, get leak alerts, and receive notifications from the City. Customers can even set a vacation alert that tells them if water usage occurs when they are away from home or if their water consumption exceeds a given dollar amount in a billing cycle. Customers receive these updates every four hours.

Monitoring volume of water, or flow rate, is another useful feature of the Smart Water Network. Flow measurement monitors the volume of flowing water running through the digital water meter to accurately detect usage. In addition to providing accurate data for billing purposes, having a better understanding of the rate of water flow provides the City of Cedar Park with insights into potential damage and waste from water leaks and enable them to monitor potential lost revenue associated with broken pipes.

The Outcome

To meet customer demands and promote water conservation, Cedar Park turned to new technology to change their processes to offer real-time billing, electronic flow measurement, and leak detection to deliver immediately value to its 23,000 customers.

Now customers can use their smartphones to see how much water they are using and the impact on their monthly bill. As a result, customers are proactively managing their water consumption to save both money and water.

City records also show alerts triggered by leaks ranging from 20 to 300 gallons per hour, have saved customers thousands of dollars on their water bills and conserved tens of thousands of gallons of water by detecting and repairing the leaks much earlier than was possible before installation of the smart meters.

In the future, the City of Cedar Park plans to use the Smart Water Network to compare citywide meters reads to the production of their water treatment plants. This will enable them to estimate daily losses across the system and help them make long-term plans for citywide conservation and loss estimation.

Questions

1. Why was the City of Cedar Park attempting to address the way in which it communicated water consumption information to its customers?
2. Why were City of Cedar Park customers frustrated?
3. What is the Flexnet® communication network?
4. When City of Cedar Park customers access the intelligent water app on their smartphones what statistics can they get?

Sources: Compiled from City of Cedar Park (2019), Genardo (2019), Pinney (2019), Water Finance and Management Staff (2019a), and Water Finance and Management Staff (2019b).

 DID YOU KNOW?

Walmart prints QR codes on their receipts that price-match your purchases with other local retailers to build a cashback-like balance that can be redeemed for future purchases at Walmart.

Introduction

The experience at Cedar Park illustrates some of the powerful capabilities and opportunities computers networks provide to companies and their customers. To keep their business up and running, enterprises are becoming increasingly dependent on wired and wireless computer networks and mobile computing to communicate with their 23,000 customers, clients, vendors, partners, and employees seamlessly and quickly (Genardo, 2019). Today networks are changing significantly in their capacity and capabilities. For example, the Internet of Things (IoT), edge computing, software-defined networking, artificial intelligence (Chapter 11) and DevOps (Chapter 13) are changing the way business is conducted in all types and sizes of organizations. As a result, many IT professionals are realizing the processes they once relied on to manage critical areas of their IT networks have become outdated. In this chapter, you will learn about the latest developments in the different types of networks and how networks impact the way businesses communicate, collaborate, and manage relationships with customers, vendors, and other businesses. You will also learn how the largest network, the Internet, is enabling massive automatic data collection efforts from "things" rather than people and how this explosion of networked smart devices is leading to the growth of edge computing that brings data physically closer to where it is needed.

4.1 | Network Fundamentals

LO4.1 Describe *the different types of wired networks and their principal components and how a computer network supports basic business functions.*

To run a successful business, companies must communicate quickly and efficiently with their customers, suppliers, partners, and employees. To do this, they must have a well-designed **computer network**.

To make intelligent network investment decisions that impact operations and competitive position today's managers in large and small companies need to understand both the management and the technical sides of computer networks. In this section, you'll learn the functions that business networks support and the different applications and types of computer networks. You will also understand the different network components and how they work together.

Computer network   is a set of computers connected together for the purpose sharing resources.

Business Functions Supported by Computer Networks

Computer networks are designed to support five basic business functions (**Figure 4.1**):

- Communication
- Search
- Mobility
- Collaboration
- Relationships

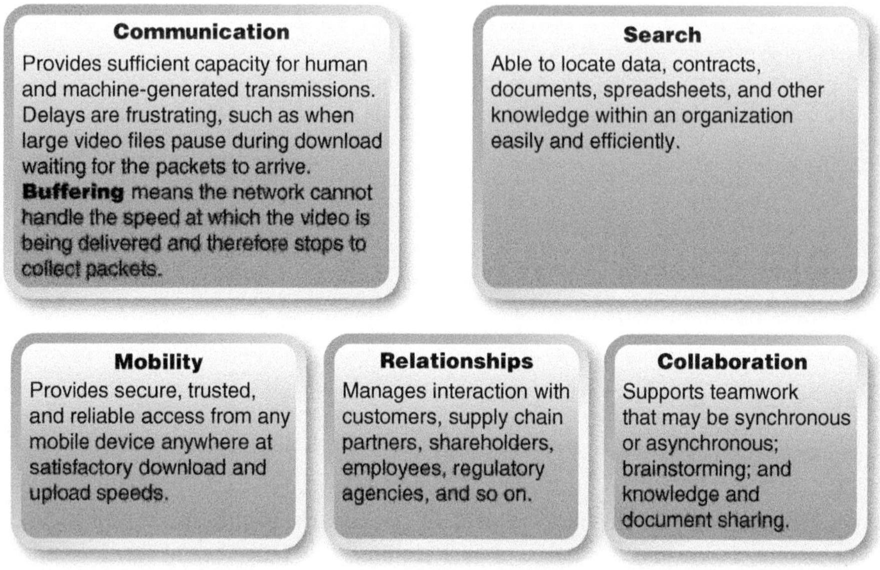

Communication
Provides sufficient capacity for human and machine-generated transmissions. Delays are frustrating, such as when large video files pause during download waiting for the packets to arrive. **Buffering** means the network cannot handle the speed at which the video is being delivered and therefore stops to collect packets.

Search
Able to locate data, contracts, documents, spreadsheets, and other knowledge within an organization easily and efficiently.

Mobility
Provides secure, trusted, and reliable access from any mobile device anywhere at satisfactory download and upload speeds.

Relationships
Manages interaction with customers, supply chain partners, shareholders, employees, regulatory agencies, and so on.

Collaboration
Supports teamwork that may be synchronous or asynchronous; brainstorming; and knowledge and document sharing.

FIGURE 4.1 Basic functions of business networks.

To facilitate these five basic business functions, a network provides data and file sharing, resource sharing, data protection and reduction of data duplication, simplified administration of the IT infrastructure, improved internal communications and better distribution of computing power. Examples of the benefits that companies derive from a well-developed network architecture include:

Instantaneous Data and File Sharing Files can be shared instantaneously across a network, regardless of the number of users. Employees can *collaborate* on documents, *search* for and exchange background material, revise spreadsheets and make simultaneous changes to a single document.

Simultaneous Resource Sharing Networks allow the simultaneous sharing of printers, servers, scanners, high-speed copiers and eliminates the need for expensive resource redundancies.

Secure Data Protection and Redundancy Preventing critical data loss saves businesses millions of dollars worldwide annually. A network automatically gathers documents from every computer in a network and securely backs them up in central systems (both on and off site) to protect data from accidental deletion or physical computer damage.

Streamlined Administration Before networks, each computer had to be updated one at a time. Now a network administrator can initiate an upgrade from a server and automatically duplicate the upgrade throughout the network simultaneously. This saves time and effort and makes sure that everyone in the company has the same software, protocols, and security measures.

Rapid Internal Communications   Network email can be instantaneously delivered to all users, voice mail systems can be hosted over a network and collaborative software and employees can coordinate meetings and work activities using network-hosted program management tools.

Distributing Computer Power   Tasks can be broken into smaller operations and distributed to multiple computer across the network. Each computer then completes the operation it has been sent and returns the results to the network controller that collects the results savings time and effort and often results in a superior outcome.

Types of Networks

In its simplest form, a computer network consists of two or more computers physically connected by hardware, software, and a communication medium.Computer networks are typically categorized by their scope. There are many types of networks as shown in **Table 4.1**. These include several variations of the two most widely used types of networks—the local area network (LAN) and the wide area network (WAN).

TABLE 4.1   **Types of Networks**

Acronym	Type	Characteristics	Example
LAN	Local Area Network	Connects network devices over a relatively short distance Owned, controlled, and managed by one individual or organization	Office building School Home
WAN	Wide Area Network	Spans a large physical distance Geographically dispersed collection of LANs Owned and managed by multiple entities	Internet Large company
SD-WAN	Software-Defined Wide Area Network	Spans a large physical distance to deliver economical and easier-to-manage WAN technology	Internet Large company
WWAN	Wireless Wide Area Network	WAN based on Wi-Fi wireless network technology	Internet Large company
WLAN	Wireless Local Area Network	LAN based on Wi-Fi wireless network technology	Internet Large company
MAN	Metropolitan Area Network	Spans a physical area larger than a LAN but smaller than a WAN Owned and operated by a single entity, e.g., government agency, large company	City Network of suburban fire stations
SAN	Storage Area Network Server Area Network	Connects servers to data storage devices	High-performance database
CAN	Campus Area Network Cluster Area Network	Spans multiple LANs but smaller than a MAN	University Local business campus
PAN	Personal Area Network	Spans a small physical space, typically 35 feet or less. Connects personal IT devices of a single individual	Laptop, smartphone, and portable printer connected together

The local area network (LAN) and wide area network (WAN) are described in more detail next.

Local Area Network (LAN)

A **local area network (LAN)** connects network devices over a relatively short distance and is typically owned, controlled, and managed by a single person or organization. For example, a

Local area network (LAN)   is a group of computers and other devices that share a communication line or wireless link to server within a limited geographic area.

Bus network configuration has a main channel to which nodes or secondary channels are connected in a branchlike structure.

LAN can serve anywhere from two users in a home-office to several hundred users in a corporation's central office. You're probably already familiar with the most common LAN. It is called the Ethernet. The devices on a LAN can be connected together in three difference ways. The LAN **bus**, **ring**, and **star** network configurations are illustrated in **Figure 4.2**. Of these, the bus configuration is the most common.

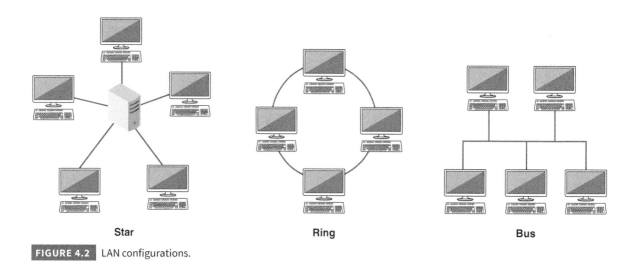

Star   Ring   Bus

FIGURE 4.2   LAN configurations.

Ring network configuration is one in which each computer is connected to two adjoining computers to form a closed circuit.

Star network configuration is one in which each computer is directly linked to a central computer and indirectly to each other.

Wide area network (WAN) is a communication network that spans a large geographic area.

Wide Area Network (WAN)

While a single LAN is suitable for a small business, it is insufficient for larger firms. A large company with many locations and thousands of employees needs a more complex network that covers larger distances and can transmit larger volumes of data. A **wide area network (WAN)** is designed to permit two or more LANs located over a large-scale geographic area (cities, states, and countries) to communicate with each other **(Figure 4.3)**. WANS are not owned by one

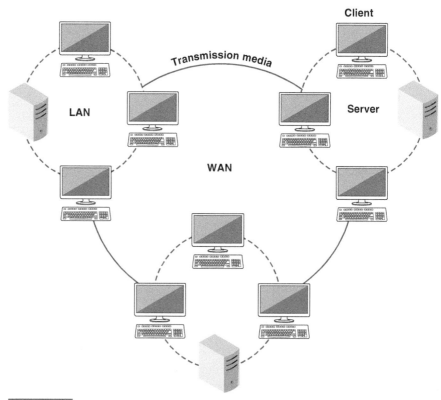

FIGURE 4.3   WAN configuration.

organization. They are collectively owned, distributed, and managed over long distances, often by an **internet service provider (ISP)**. A WAN can be private or public and works in a similar fashion to a LAN, but on a much larger scale.

A private WAN connects parts of a business, such as cloud services, main office and smaller branch offices networks, and other services. An enterprise WAN allows users to securely share access to apps, services and other centrally located resources. A public WAN has two or more of its LANs connected over the public Internet.

Typically, a router or other physical device is used to connect a LAN to a WAN. Connectivity and security between WAN sites are facilitated by a **virtual private network (VPN)**, discussed in the next section. The transmission medium used in many WANs include high speed digital subscriber lines (DSL) and fiber optic cables that are made up of glass fibers clad in a glass layer secured in a buffer tube to protect the cladding and finally covered with a jacket layer to protect the individual strands.

An **SD-WAN** utilizes a virtual WAN architecture to allow companies to leverage any combination of data transmission services to securely connect their users to apps. It does this by automatically setting optimal paths for network traffic based on real-time conditions to aggregate multiple public and private WAN links and save time and effort usually expended by network managers. SD-WANs are gaining in popularity because they are inexpensive to operate, offer increased flexibility, simplify efficient network operations, and provide network administrators with a 360-degree view of all devices, users, and apps from a single location.

Internet Service Provider (ISP) is an organization that provides services for accessing, using or participating with the Internet.

Virtual private network (VPN) is a service that allows safe and private network access by routing connections through a server and hiding the online actions.

Software-defined WAN (SD-WAN) is managed by one central app that efficiently distributes network traffic across a WAN over the Internet or cloud-based private networks.

Intranets, Extranets, and Virtual Private Networks

Intranets are LANs or WANS used internally within a company for data access, sharing, and collaboration between predefined users. An intranet can be viewed as a company's digital workspace where employees and colleagues work together to document, converse, and work on projects. For example, colleges and universities rely on intranets to provide services to students, faculty, and staff. Using screensharing and other groupware tools, intranets can support teamwork where no outside parties are involved.

Benefits of intranets include streamlining daily activities, organizing people and data, improving internal communications, and increasing collaboration between employees.

An **extranet**, on the other hand, is a WAN that facilitates a company's communication with external and widely distributed users such as suppliers, vendors, partners, or customers. Often an extranet is a network that connects two or more companies so they can securely share information and conduct business. Since authorized users remotely access content from a central server, extranets can drastically reduce storage space on individual hard drives.

Benefits of an extranet include: communicating and collaborating more effectively with clients, customers, and vendors over a secure network, integrating supply chains, reducing costs, improving business relationships, improving customer service, and securing communications. Extranets can be expensive to implement and maintain because of hardware, software, and employee training costs if hosted internally rather than by an internet service provider (ISP).

Virtual Private Network (VPN) Companies are always concerned about network security. Network transmissions can be intercepted or compromised and put a company at risk. One solution is to use a virtual private network (VPN), which encrypt the packets before they are transferred over the network. VPNs consist of encryption software and hardware that encrypt, send, and decrypt transmissions, as shown in **Figure 4.4**. A VPN facilitates a company's connectivity and security between WANs. In effect, instead of using a leased line to create a dedicated, physical connection, a company can invest in VPN technology to create virtual connections routed through the Internet from the company's private network to the remote site or employee.

Intranet is an internal portal or gateway that provides easy and inexpensive browsing and search capabilities for employees and colleagues within a company.

Extranet is a WAN that can be logged into remotely via the Internet to facilitate communication with clients and vendors.

FIGURE 4.4 Virtual private networks (VPNs) create encrypted connections to company networks.

Benefits of VPNs include increased online privacy and security, ad and tracker blocking, and bypassing ISP bandwidth throttling to ensure smoother browsing or streaming.

Transmission Media and Speed

All networks need physical transmission media to move data from source to destination. A signal is the term used for the data we want to send. Every signal is composed of a combination of 1s and 0s. The signal is measured in **hertz** or number of cycles per second. The more 1s and 0s transmitted within one second is, the higher the capacity of the transmission media will be.

Frequency is the capacity of a transmission media.

Bits per second (bps) is the speed at which data are transferred over a network.

Bandwidth of a media is the maximum amount of bps that can be transmitted over the media and it varies by media type.

Frequency consists of the volume of data that can be transmitted and is measured in **bits per second (bps)**. The range of frequencies a transmission media can accommodate without experiencing significant loss in performance is known as a frequency band or **bandwidth** as demonstrated in **Figure 4.5**. Upon ideal conditions, it is possible to reach maximum capacity in a connection although this seldom happens. The wider the range of frequencies a transmission media can accommodate is, the greater the bandwidth and the higher the transmission capacity will be. Wired networks typically use twisted pair cable, Ethernet, ISDN, DSL, or fiber optic transmission media.

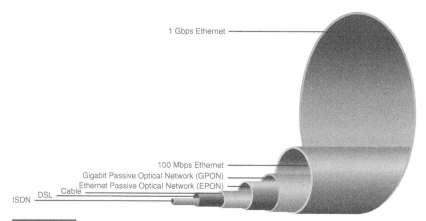

FIGURE 4.5 Bandwidth variation by transmission media type.

Network Components

In addition to understanding the different types of networks in organizations and their transmission media, as an informed user of IT, it's useful to become familiar with the physical network components and how they all work together.

Circuit Switching vs. Packet Switching

An important network component is the **switch**. All generations of wired and wireless networks use switches to establish a connection for data to be transferred. The two basic types of switching are circuit switching and packet switching.

- **Circuit switching**. In the past, when a call was placed between two landline phones, a circuit or connection was created that remained until one party hung up. This is called **circuit switching**. Circuit switching is an older technology that originated with telephone calls. It is not very efficient for digital transmission. 1G, 2G, and 3G networks had a circuit-switched subsystem.
- **Packet switching** **Packet switching** is faster than circuit switching. In a packet switched subsystem, files are broken into **packets**, numbered sequentially, and routed individually to their destination. When received at the destination, the packets are reassembled into their proper sequence. 4G was the first network generation to be based purely on packet switching. The result was significantly improved performance. Wireless networks use packet switching and wireless routers whose antennae transmit and receive packets.

Other main network components you should be familiar with are defined as follows:

- **Client** is the name used for a computer on a network.
- **Server** is a central repository of data and various programs that are shared by users in a network.
- **Router** links computers to the Internet to enable users to share a network connection. It acts like a dispatcher, choosing the best paths for data packets to travel from their source to their destination based on IP addresses.
- **Wireless Router** is a device that works as a router to forward data between network devices and serves as both a wireless access point and a router.
- **Hub** is a hardware device where data from many directions converge and are then sent out in many directions to multiple devices in a network. Hubs are commonly used to connect segments of a LAN.
- **Switch** is a controller that enables networked devices to talk to each other efficiently by transmitting data packets based on IP addresses. It connects the computers, printers and servers within a building or a company to create the network. It is more sophisticated than a hub.
- **Network Interface Card (NIC)** is a circuit board or chip installed in a computer to enable it to connect to a wired or wireless network.

A typical network in which each of these components are configured is shown in **Figure 4.6**.

Circuit switching   occurs when there is a dedicated connection between a source and destination.

Packet switching   occurs when data or voice is transferred in packets.

Packets   are individual pieces of a message that are collected and re-assembled with the other pieces of the same message at their destination. To improve communication performance and reliability, each larger message sent between two network devices is often subdivided into packets.

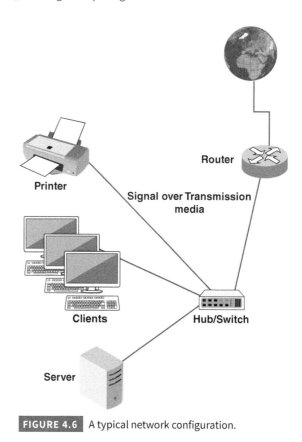

FIGURE 4.6   A typical network configuration.

Pure network applications are developed expressly for use by two more devices that help transfer data and communicate across a network.

Standalone network applications were originally developed for use on a single device and their functionality retooled to allow them to run on networks.

Network Applications

Companies use two main types of software to operate and maintain networks: **pure network applications** and **standalone network applications**. Example of pure network applications are shown in **Table 4.2**. Examples of standalone network applications include word processors, spreadsheets, database management systems, presentation graphics, etc.

TABLE 4.2   **Examples of Pure Network Applications**

Application	Purpose	Example Products
Email	Allows users to type messages at their local node and send them to someone on another node across the network.	Mailchimp; Salesforce Marketing Cloud; Yahoo; Outlook Express; Gmail; Mozilla Thunderbird
File Transfer (FTP)	Facilitates file transfer from one computer to another through download or upload.	Filezilla Client Free; AceFTP; CoffeeCup Free FTP; FTP Voyager; WinSCP; Cyberduck
Terminal Emulation (TELNET)	Allows workstation to access the server for an application program to allow uses to control the server and communicate with other servers on the network.	Cmder; ZOC Terminal Emulator; ConEmu Console Emulator; Mintty Console Emulator
GroupWare	Facilitate groupwork and improve on productivity. Can be used to communicate, cooperate, coordinate, problem solve, compete and negotiate.	
(a) Video Conferencing	Conduct a conference between two or more participants over a computer network to transmit audio and/or video data.	GoToMeeting; Zoom; Microsoft Teams; Intermedia Unite; RingCentral Meetings; Zoho; ClickMeeting
(b) Chatting	Establishes a real-time communication between two users online at the same time via the network.	Zendesk; Freshchat; LiveChat; ZohoSalesIQ; Zoho Desk; Intercom; Drift; Olark; LivePerson

Adapted from Kamau (2019)

IT at Work 4.1 describes how a new audio network platform and network management software has significantly enhanced the experience of major league baseball fans at Minnesota Twins Target Field.

IT at Work 4.1

Target Field Hits a Fan Home Run with New Audio Network

Target Field is home to Major League Baseball team Minnesota Twins and can hold more than 39,000 fans. The stadium is a three-tier grandstand with club seats, luxury suites, a press box, and the Budweiser Roof Deck featuring a fire pit, bar, city skyline view, bleacher seats and standing room. In addition to acting as a baseball venue, Target Field also hosts a variety of other events, including: football and soccer games, outdoor concerts and non-sports based corporate events. All of these require a high-quality audio system that can not only distribute audio signals to various areas throughout the stadium, but also pull signals back to the control room for mixing and processing.

Target Field management was looking for an easy and inexpensive solution and settled on a Dante audio network platform from Audinate. Dante is a digital media networking technology that allows users to send uncompressed, multi-channel audio over a single Ethernet cable and is widely adopted by the majority of pro audio-visual manufacturers. Dante also allowed Target Field to tap into the existing networking structure without having to install extra infrastructure to get audio where it needs it. With a Dante network in place, the next natural step was to deploy Dante Domain Manager (DDM) to the network to add control and security. DDM is network management software that enables user authentication, role-based security and audit capabilities to the network. DDM allows Target Field audio technicians to scale and segment its audio networks, defining specific AV device groupings by room, building and site, ensuring the stadium's audio is playing where it's wanted.

With DDM, Jeff Pederson, Lead Audio Technician, Minnesota Twins Baseball can be sure Target Field's audio is running smoothly and at a reasonable cost.

Sources: Compiled from Convergent (2018), Daley (2018), and PSW Staff (2019).

Questions

1. Describe the basic functions of business networks.
2. Name three different types of network configurations.
3. Why would a company choose to use a WAN rather than a LAN?
4. What is the difference between an intranet and an extranet?
5. How does a virtual private network (VPN) provide security?
6. How do investments in network infrastructure impact an organization?
7. How is an SD-WAN different from a WAN?
8. What are three different transmission media used in wired networks?

4.2 Wireless Networks and Standards

LO4.2 Identify *the different generations of wireless networks, the standards that drive them and the technologies that support them.*

A wireless network uses wireless data connections between network components and enables businesses avoid the costly process of introducing cables into a building or as connections between various locations. Over the past 30+ years, wireless networks have become faster, can cover wider distances and are more reliable. Typically, a new generation of wireless networks is introduced every ten years. Most recently, wireless networks have evolved from 4G networks designed for voice and data to 5G networks that support broadband. In the next section, we compare 4G and 5G networks and the standards that have been developed to guide their deployment and operation.

Differences Between 4G and 5G Networks

4G networks are digital or IP networks that enable relatively fast data transfer rates.

4G networks were introduced in 2010 and deliver up to 10 Mbps. The latest version of 4G is 4G LTE-A that can theoretically deliver speeds from 300 Mbps to 1 Gbps, with an average speed of 15–50 Mbps. 4G LTE-A is the most widely used network technology on today's mobile networks. Unlike its predecessors, 2G and 3G that have a circuit-switched subsystem, 4G is based purely on packet switching.

Improved network performance offered by 4G networks, measured by its data transfer capacity have provided fantastic opportunities for mobility, mobile commerce, collaboration, supply chain management remote work, and other productivity gains.

5G networks are designed to support the escalation in mobile data consumption, with users demanding higher data speeds and traffic volumes expected to increase by hundreds or even thousands of times over the next 10 years.

5G networks offer huge gains in both speed and capacity over existing 4G networks. 5G are currently being offered in limited geographical areas that will steadily expand and are up to ten times faster than 4G LTE-A—topping out at 10 Gbps. To put it into perspective, you can download a two-hour movie in 3.6 seconds on 5G. It takes 6 minutes on 4G. Although 5G builds on the foundation created by 4G, it's important to note that 5G is not an incremental or backward-compatible update to existing mobile communications standards. 5G completely breaks away from what has previously existed in mobile phone networks and uses different kinds of antennas, operates on different radio spectrum frequencies, connects many more devices, minimizes throttling, and dramatically increases the speed at which data are transferred across the network (Fisher, 2019a).

Advantages and Disadvantages of 5G

On the positive side, 5G offers huge gains in both speed and capacity over existing 4G and 4G LTE networks—along with opportunities at the operations and strategic levels. 5G promises to bring larger channels, higher speeds, larger packets of data, exponentially faster response time and the ability to connect many devices from a single location. In the short term, the 5G infrastructure build-out will create new jobs. In the longer term, 5G will create entirely new markets and economic opportunities driven by superior mobile capabilities in industries ranging from health care to automotive. On the negative side, the infrastructure needed to support 5G is expensive and privacy and security issues surrounding 5G have not yet been solved. Another concern about 5G is the *health risks* caused by its use of extremely high frequency (1 Billion cycles per second) microwaves. Almost 200 scientists and doctors in almost 40 countries have warned about 5G health risks in Resolution 1815 of the Council of Europe. This resolution calls for the halt to "the roll-out of 5G until potential hazards for human health and the environment have been fully investigated by scientists independent from industry" (Wagner, 2019).

There Is a Growing Need for 5G

As the Internet of Things (IoT) creates billions of new devices for remote sensing, telemetry, and control applications, which will lead to huge numbers of machine-to-machine and person-to-machine interactions, mobile networks will no longer be concerned primarily with person-to-person communications. To be efficient, these machine-to-machine connections will need the significantly faster speeds of 5G. Although 5G is still in its infancy, many organizations have already invested in the infrastructure required to run this new mobile wireless standard and all four major carriers are already offering 5G mobile devices. Apple has chosen to wait until 5G moves beyond its preliminary stages to offer a more consistent experience for its users (Welch, 2019). Currently 5G availability is extremely limited with a few telecommunications companies offering fixed 5G and mobile 5G services in a small number of cities throughout the United States (AndroidGuys, 2019; Fisher, 2019b) but with more to come (Bouma, 2019).

In the short term, the build out of the 5G infrastructure is creating new jobs. In the long-term, 5G will create entirely new markets and economic opportunities driven by superior mobile capabilities in industries ranging from health care to automotive to smart cities.

IT at Work 4.2 describes how one telecommunications company is successfully delivering sustainability in Africa through a combination of 4G and 5G connectivity.

IT at Work 4.2

Ericsson Delivers Sustainability in Africa

Connectivity is a critical enabler of social and economic change. The introduction of 5G and the expansion of existing LTE networks across Africa is expected to exponentially accelerate this process by facilitating delivery of next-generation mobile broadband and providing support for massive Internet of Things (IoT) deployment. In 2018, Ericsson (**www.ericsson.com**), a Swedish-based telecommunications company, announced a partnership with MTN South Africa—a South African multinational mobile telecommunications network provider—to deploy its first 5G technology. The first step was to deploy a customer trial of a fixed wireless access site. The site was located at the Midrand headquarters of Netstar (**www.netstar.co.za**), South Africa's leading vehicle tracking company situated between Johannesburg and Tshwane, South Africa. The trial included local customers and Netstar employees who could connect through different Wi-Fi access points. The 5G solution used in the trial operates on 28 GHz broadband with a total operating bandwidth of 100 MHz. The Intel 5G mobile trial platform provided fixed wireless access.

The push to 5G is seen as a wonderful opportunity to put South Africa on par, or ahead, of other countries while at the same time expanding the 4G capabilities already in place to extend high speed internet access to all South Africans and further drive down the cost of communicating.

One year later, MTN South Africa has hired Ericsson to supply 5G products and solutions with rollout expected to begin in 2020. Ericsson will also upgrade MTN South Africa's existing LTE and legacy radio access networks as part of a three-year deal.

Sources: Compiled from Aginam (2018), Back (2019), Sharma (2019), and Zacks (2019).

6G networks—the coming generation of broadband technology. Work is already underway on the development of 6G mobile telephone networks. 6G will be able to use higher frequencies than 5G networks and provide substantially higher capacity with much lower latency. 6G is not expected to be available before 2030.

Wireless Network Standards

As different generations of network are developed, network standards are needed to ensure the compatibility and interoperability of products manufactured by different vendors that are deployed in a network. They define the rules of communication among devices to make sure that the assorted networking hardware and software can work together seamlessly. Without standards, it would be difficult to create networks that can share information easily and reliably. Standards also enable companies to purchase hardware and software from multiple vendors to keep the marketplace healthy and keep prices competitive. The Institute of Electrical Electronic Engineers (IEEE) is a global group of engineers, scientists, and researchers who have developed network standards, known as the IEEE802 standards (**TechNote 4.1**).

Tech Note 4.1

The IEEE802 standards for wireless LANs and wireless WWANs, like the Internet, are what we commonly known as Wi-Fi.

- **IEEE 802.11ax** also known as "high-efficiency wireless," 802.11ax was released in September 2019. It is designed to handle the ever-increasing demand for faster multi-user data rates and has high single-user data rates 37% faster than 802.11ac. Although it pushes data speed to almost 10 Gbps, 802.11ax focuses more on real-world Wi-Fi performance and offers four times the throughput per user in highly congested areas, offers better power efficiency and boosts device battery life. It is also referred to as Wi-Fi 6.

- **IEEE 802.11ac** utilizes dual-band wireless technology and support simultaneous connections on both the 2.4 and 5 GHz Wi-Fi bands. 802.11ac offers backward compatibility to 802.11b/g/n and bandwidth rated up to 130 Mbps on 5 GHz, plus up to 450 Mbps on 2.4 GHz. It is also referred to as Wi-Fi 5.

- **IEEE 802.11a** runs on 12 channels in the 5-GHz spectrum in North America, which reduces interference issues. Data are transferred about 5 times faster than 802.11b, improving the quality of streaming media. It has extra bandwidth for large files. Since the 802.11a and b standards are not interoperable, data sent from an 802.11b network cannot be accessed by 802.11a networks.

- **IEEE 802.11n** improves upon prior 802.11 standards by adding multiple-input multiple-output (MIMO) and newer features. Frequency ranges from 2.4 to 5 GHz with a data rate of about 22 Mbps, but perhaps as high as 100 Mbps.

- **IEEE 802.11g** runs on three channels in the 2.4-GHz spectrum, but at the speed of 802.11a. It is compatible with the 802.11b standard.

- **IEEE 802.11b** shares spectrum with 2.4-GHz cordless phones, microwave ovens, and many Bluetooth products. Data are transferred at distances up to 100 meters or 328 feet. 802.11 was the first wireless IEEE standard to be released.

New Standards Needed for 5G   Because 5G characteristics don't overlap with those of 4G it cannot be delivered to existing phones, tablets or wireless modems by means of existing towers or software updates. Consequently, there are currently no firm 5G technology standards. The primary standards bodies working on 5G standards are the 3rd Generation Partnership Project (3GPP), the Internet Engineering Task Force (ITEF), and the International Telecommunication Union (ITU). Of these, 3GPP successfully completed the first implementable specifications that define the first phase of the global 5G standard in December 2017 with more expected by mid-2020.

Wireless Connectivity

There are five main ways that devices can connect wirelessly: Wi-Fi, WiMAX, LTE, wireless local area network (WLAN), and wireless wide area network (WWAN). These are discussed next.

Wi-Fi connects computers and smart devices to a network via a single access point like a router.

Wi-Fi hotspot is a wireless access point that provides Internet access to mobile devices like laptops and smartphones.

Wi-Fi is the standard way computers connect to wireless networks. Nearly all computers have built-in Wi-Fi chips that allow users to find and connect to wireless routers within a range of no more than 300 feet. The router must be connected to the Internet in order to provide Internet access to connected devices. Wi-Fi is based on the IEEE802.11 standards. Wi-Fi technology allows devices to share a network or Internet connection without the need to connect to a commercial network. Wi-Fi operates in the microwave frequency range to beam packets over short distances using part of the radio spectrum, or they can extend over larger areas, such as municipal Wi-Fi networks. See **Figure 4.7** for an overview of how Wi-Fi works. One way to connect through Wi-Fi is using a **Wi-Fi hotspot**, typically found in public locations such as hotels, cafes, airports, libraries, and hotels.

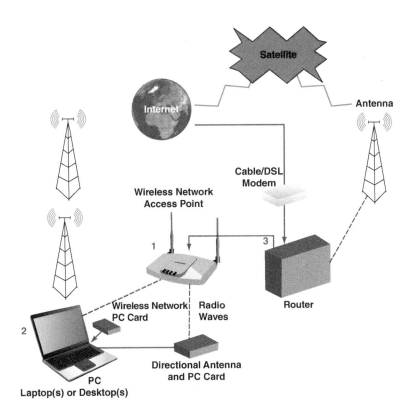

1. Radio-equipped access point connected to the Internet (or via a router). It generates and receives radio waves (up to 400 feet).
2. Several client devices, equipped with PC cards, generate and receive radio waves.
3. Router is connected to the Internet via a cable or DSL modem, or is connected via a satellite.

FIGURE 4.7 Overview of Wi-Fi.

WiMAX is a much faster way to connect wirelessly and covers much greater distances than Wi-Fi. Its range is 20–30 miles from its base station and it doesn't require a clear line of sight to function. MiWAX operates at a speed of approximately 70 Mbps. This is particularly useful in rural areas where users don't have access to Wi-Fi or a fixed broadband connection. WiMAX is based on the newer IEEE 802.16 set of standards and is usually deployed by service providers, whereas Wi-Fi can easily be deployed by individual end users. **Figure 4.8** shows the different components of a WiMAX/Wi-Fi network and how they work together.

WiMAX stands for worldwide interoperability for microwave access and was developed to overcome the short-range limitations of Wi-Fi.

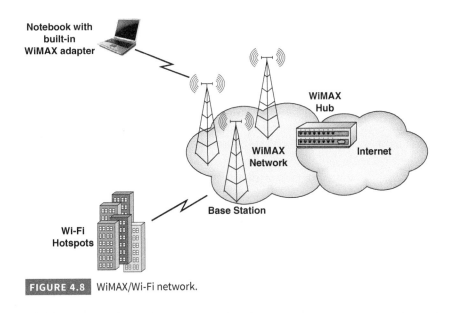

FIGURE 4.8 WiMAX/Wi-Fi network.

LTE is the fastest and most consistent cellular technology.

LTE-A is a version of LTE cellular technology that more closely follows the IEEE 802.11ac wireless network standard.

A **Wireless local area network (WLAN)** typically extends an existing wired LAN by attaching a wireless AP to a wired network.

A **Wireless wide area network (WWAN)** has a wider range than a local area network and can cover a group of buildings.

Wireless transmission media is a form of unguided media that does not require physical links between two or more devices.

Long Term Evolution (**LTE**) is a Global System for Mobile Communications (GSM) based technology that provides the fastest and most consistent download speeds and most closely follows the UN technical standard for 4G networks. The latest and fastest version of LTE is long term evolution advanced (**LTE-A**).

WLAN A wireless LAN uses high-frequency radio waves to communicate between computers, devices, or other nodes on the network with a single building.

WWAN The range of a WWAN depends on the transmission media and the wireless generation, which determines which services are available.

Wireless Networks Use Different Transmission Media

Several types of **wireless transmission media** can be used when installing wiring is impossible or impractical. Example of wireless transmission media include radio waves, microwaves, infrared, Bluetooth, and communication satellites.

Wireless transmission can be *omnidirectional*—waves are sent in all directions, or *directional*—point-to-point focused beams are used. The distance covered by wireless transmission media ranges from several meters to thousands of miles. Each wireless network generation uses more powerful frequency bands to offer faster and more reliable data transfer.

Radio Waves are a type of electromagnetic radiation that travels at the speed of light. This means that a radio wave can travel to the moon and back in 2 ½ seconds. A radio wave is generated by a transmitter and detected by a receiver using an antenna that allows the transmitter to send energy into space and to pick energy up from space. Transmitters and receivers are typically designed to operate over a limited range of frequencies. The low-frequency kilometer band (30–300 KHz), medium-frequency hectometer band (300 KHz–3 MHz), and the high-frequency decameter band (3–30 MHz). An advantage of radio waves is that they have the longest wavelengths of all known electromagnetic waves and can carry data over very large distances. A disadvantage of radio waves is that they cannot transmit large of volumes of data simultaneously because they operate at relatively low frequencies. Another is that continue exposure to large amounts of radio waves can cause health issues including cancer.

Microwaves are extremely high frequency radio waves that correspond to band frequencies of 30–300 GHz. This rand of frequencies is known as the millimeter band. Microwave transmission involves sending and receiving microwave radio waves over a microwave link made up of a strong of microwave radio antennae located at the top of towers at various microwave sites. Like infrared, microwave is classified as a "line of sight" transmission media. Unlike infrared, microwave transmissions can cover long distances. Advantages include high capacity and long-distance transmissions. In addition, to its line of sight limitation, disadvantages of microwave transmissions include expense, vulnerability to bad weather and electromagnetic interference from electric motors, electric power transmission lines, and wind turbines that can cause transmission degradation.

Infrared transmission requires a line-of-sight transmission where the sender and receive are aligned so that nothing obstructs the path of infrared light wave. It is an airwave, rather than a conducted-transmission system. The infrared frequency band is the largest part of the electromagnetic spectrum and corresponds to a radio frequency range of 300 GHz to 430 THz. Using an infrared connection, a computer, equipped with an inexpensive IR sensor, transfers files and other digital data over short-range wireless signals. Although infrared offers substantial bandwidth, there are interference risks. Advantages that infrared offers include price, low power consumption, easy to use, and rapid deployment as there are no licensing requirements. Disadvantages include line-of-sight requirement, cannot go through walls, devices cannot move during transmissions, and short transmission distance of 35 to 100 feet. In addition, exposure to high numbers of radio waves has been shown to cause cancer and other health issues.

Bluetooth transmission is an open wireless technology standard for transmitting fixed and mobile electronic device data over short distances.

Bluetooth helps link two devices via a wireless network. Disadvantages of Bluetooth include its limited range ranging from 10 meters to 100 meters depending on the class of radio it is using.

Satellite transmission involves line-of-sight transmission to and from communication satellites in the sky. There are three types of satellites. As their names imply, a geostationary-Earth-orbit (GEO) satellite is farthest from the Earth, a medium-Earth-orbit (MEO) satellite is closer to the Earth, and the low-Earth-orbit (LEO) orbit is closest to the Earth. An example of an MEO is a geographical positioning system (GPS) used by navigation systems in smart devices.

The **mashup** of a satellite-enabled geographical positioning systems (GPS) and a short-range wireless technology, such as Bluetooth can provide unprecedented intelligence. These technologies create opportunities for companies to develop solutions that make a consumer's life better. They could, for example, revolutionize traffic and road safety. Intelligent transport systems being developed by car manufacturers allow cars to communicate with each other and send alerts about sudden braking and will even allow for remote driving in the future. In the event of a collision, the car's system could automatically call emergency services. The technology can also apply the brakes automatically if it was determined that two cars were getting too close to each other or alert the driver to a car that is in their blind spot in the next lane.

> **Mashup** is a general term referring to the integration of two or more technologies.

Wireless Network Technologies

A wireless network infrastructure consists of the integration of technology, software, support, standards, security measures, and devices for the management and delivery of wireless communications. The most commonly used is Wi-Fi.

Other technologies that support networking are internet protocol communication standards and application program interface (API).

Internet Protocols (IP) Regardless of the generation, the basic technology that makes global communication possible is a network **protocol** commonly known as an **Internet Protocol (IP)**. Even the simplest network must use these protocols to communicate. For example, before transmitting data, a computer might be required to signal it's "ready to send" and then has to wait for the other to signal it's "ready to receive." When computers share a network, the protocol might specify that a computer can only "talk when it is your turn."

Each device attached to a network has a unique **IP address** that enables it to send and receive files. For example, each computer or device on an Ethernet has a 48-bit IP address. This address is used to send and receive transmissions using network protocols. Files are broken down into blocks known as **packets** in order to be transmitted over a network to their destination's IP address. Initially, networks used **IP Version 4 (IPv4)**. In April 2014 ARIN, the group that oversees Internet addresses, reported that IPv4 addresses were running out—making it urgent that enterprises move to the newer **IP Version 6 (IPv6) (Figure 4.9)**.

> **Internet Protocol** is a rule or procedure for transmitting data between computers and other electronic devices.
>
> **IP address** is a unique identifier for each device that communicates with a network that identifies and locates each device. An IP address is comparable to a telephone number or home address.

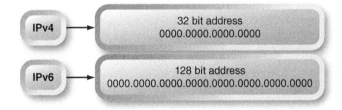

FIGURE 4.9 IPv4 addresses have 4 groups of four alphanumeric characters, which allow for 2^{32} or roughly 4.3 billion unique IP addresses. IPv6 addresses have 8 groups of alphanumeric characters, which allows for 2^{128}, or 340 trillion, trillion, trillion addresses. IPv6 also offers enhanced quality of service that is needed by the latest in video, interactive games, and e-commerce.

IP Version 4 (IPv4) has been Internet protocol for over three decades, but reached the limits of its 32-bit address design. It is difficult to configure, it is running out of addressing space, and it provides no features for site renumbering to allow for an easy change of Internet Service Provider (ISP), among other limitations.

IP Version 6 (IPv6) is the most recent version of the Internet Protocol. IPv6 and has replaced IPv4 because of IPv4's limitations in number of IP addresses it can generate. IPv6 has a 128-bit address and allows 7.9×10^{28} times as many addresses as IPv4, which provides about 4.3 billion addresses.

The IPv6 Internet protocol has features that are not present in IPv4. For example, IPv6 simplifies aspects of how addresses are assigned, how networks are renumbered and places responsibility for packet fragmentation when packets are processed in routers. The IPv6 protocol does not offer direct interoperability with IPv4, instead it creates a parallel, independent network. Fortunately, several transition mechanisms, such as NAT64 and 6rd, have been developed to allow IPv6 hosts to communicate with IPv4 servers.

Network protocols serve the following three basic functions:

1. Send data to the correct recipient(s).
2. Physically transmit data from source to destination, with security protected as needed.
3. Receive messages and send responses to the correct recipient(s).

The capacity and capabilities of data networks provide opportunities for more automated operations and new business strategies. M2M communications over wireless and wired networks automate operations, for instance, by triggering action such as sending a message or closing a valve. The speed at which data can be sent depends on several factors, including capacity, server usage, computer usage, noise, and the amount of network traffic. Transfer rate or speed is an instantaneous measurement.

Transmission Control Protocol/Internet Protocol (TCP/IP) TCP/IP is the most widely used and most widely available protocol suite. It is a layered architecture where each layer depicts the functionality of the protocol.

TCP/IP Packets use the **Transmission Control Protocol/Internet Protocol (TCP/IP)** protocol to carry data across the network. TCP/IP is the most widely used and most widely available protocol suite. It is a layered architecture where each layer depicts the functionality of the protocol. TCP/IP is a four-layer suite that consists of:

- **Application Layer**—top layer of TCP/IP includes applications or processes that use the transport layer to deliver data to destination computers. Application layer protocols include the hypertext transfer protocol (HTTP), file transfer protocol (FTP), simple mail transfer protocol (SMTP), and simple network management protocol (SNMP).

- **Transport Layer**—backbone of the TCP/IP that allows data to flow between two hosts. The Transport layer receives data from the application layer and transports it across the network. The two most commonly used transport layer protocols are Transmission Control Protocol (TCP) and the User Datagram Protocol (UDP). TCP divides the data received from the application layer into appropriate-sized chunks and pass them onto the network. It is a reliable connection that acknowledges received packets and sets timeouts to resend packets if acknowledges are not received. UDP is a simpler, but less reliable protocol that sends packets from one host to another without ways to ensure data sent is received by the target host.

- **Network (Internet) Layer**—organizes and handles the routing (movement) of data over the network. The main network layer protocol is a set of rules governing the format of data sent over the Internet or other network, known as the Internet Protocol (IP). Other protocols used at the network layer include the Internet Control Message Protocol (ICMP) that transfers control information about the status of the network, rather than application data (i.e., a ping) and Internet Group Multicast Protocol (IGMP) that allows a host to advertise its membership in a group of receivers that expresses an interest in receiving a particular stream of data (multicast) group to neighboring switches and routers, are also used at this layer.

- **Data Link (Network Interface) Layer**—normally consists of device drivers in the operating system (OS) and the network interface card attached to the system that take care of communication details of the media used to transfer data over the network. The media is usually cables of some sort, for example, Ethernet, twisted pair, coaxial, and fiber optic. The main protocols used at the Data Link Layer are the Address Resolution Protocol (ARP) and the Point to Point Protocol (PPP).

Application Program Interfaces (APIs) and Operating Systems

When software developers create applications, they must write and compile the code for a specific operating system (OS). **Figure 4.10** lists the common OSs. Each OS communicates with hardware in its own unique way; each OS has a specific API that programmers must use. Video game consoles and other hardware devices also have **application program interfaces (APIs)** that run software programs.

Application program interface (API) An interface is the boundary where two separate systems meet. An API provides a standard way for different things, such as software, content, or websites, to talk to each other in a way that they both understand without extensive programming.

Common Mobile OS	Common Desktop OS
Android	Windows
iOS	Mac OS X
Windows Phone	Linux

FIGURE 4.10 Common mobile and desktop operating systems. Each computer OS provides an API for programmers. Mobile OSs are designed around touchscreen input.

What Is an API?

An API consists of a set of functions, commands, and protocols used by programmers to build software for an operating system (OS). The API allows programmers to use predefined functions or reusable codes to interact with an OS without having to write a software program from scratch. APIs simplify the programmer's job.

APIs are the common method for accessing information, websites, and databases. They were created as gateways to popular apps such as Twitter, Facebook, and Amazon and enterprise apps provided by SAP, Oracle, NetSuite, and many other vendors.

Automated API

The current trend is toward automatically created APIs that are making innovative IT developments possible. Here are some examples of the benefits of automated APIs:

- Websites such as the European Union Patent office (**https://www.epo.org**) uses a **REST API** to map and update every one of their pages whenever a new page is published or an existing page is changed.

- McDonald's, along with Unilever and Gatorade, use automated API's to bring advertisements to Snapchat users. The social network app is using an auction-based system and targeting to choose which users see which advertisements.

- Amazon's Alexa **List Skills API** enables software developers to increase the efficiency of Alexa's list feature which allows users to add items to their lists within Alexa. Developers don't have to create their own list the Amazon List Skills API provides a standardized voice interaction model instead.

REST API the Representational State API is used to build Web services that are lightweight, maintainable and scalable. It provides a way to access resources in a particular environment.

List Skills API has a bi-directional interface that updates lists each time users make Shopping list or To Do requests.

API Value Chain in Business

APIs deliver more than half of all the traffic to major companies like Twitter and eBay. APIs are used to access business assets, such as customer information or a product or service, as shown in **Figure 4.11**. IT developers use APIs to quickly and easily connect diverse data and services to each other. APIs from Google, Twitter, Amazon, Facebook, Accuweather, Sears, and E*Trade are used to create many thousands of applications. For example, Google Maps API is a collection of APIs used by developers to create customized Google Maps that can be accessed on a Web browser or mobile devices.

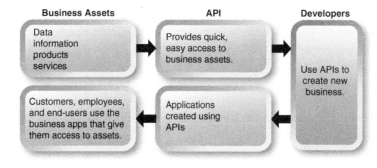

FIGURE 4.11 API value chain in business.

A typical network configuration with added wireless components is illustrated in Figure 4.12.

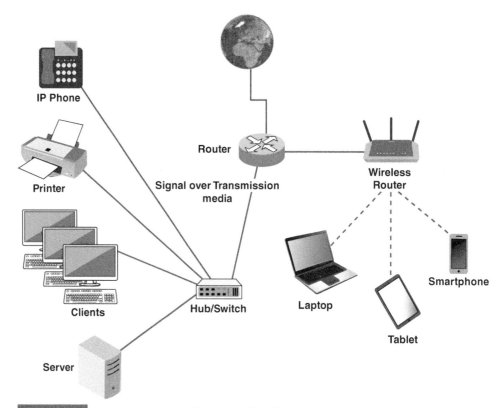

FIGURE 4.12 A typical network configuration with added wireless components.

The API value chain takes many forms because the organization that owns the business asset may or may not be the same as the organization that builds the APIs. Different people or organizations may build, distribute, and market the applications. At the end of the chain are end-users who benefit from the business asset. Often, many APIs are used to create a new user experience. The business benefits of APIs are listed in **Table 4.3**.

TABLE 4.3 Business Benefits of APIs

Characteristic	Benefit
APIs are channels to new customers and markets	APIs enable partners to use business assets to extend the reach of a company's products or services to customers and markets they might not
APIs promote innovation	Through an API, people who are committed to a challenge or problem can solve it themselves
APIs are a better way to organize IT	APIs promote innovation by allowing everyone in a company to use each other's assets without delay
APIs create a path to lots of Apps	Apps are going to be a crucial channel in the next 10 years. Apps are powered by APIs. Developers use APIs and combinations of APIs to create new user experiences

Questions

1. Why has IPv6 become increasingly important?
2. What is the difference between IPv4 and Ipv6?
3. What is the purpose of an IP address?
4. What is an API and what are the benefits of using an API?
5. What is the difference between 4G and 5G?
6. Why is 5G not widely available?
7. What benefits does a 5G network offer businesses?
8. What is the difference between circuit switching and packet switching?

4.3 Mobile Computing and the Internet of Things (IoT)

LO4.3 Explain *the growth in mobile data traffic and the benefits companies can gain from the Internet of Things (IoT) and edge computing.*

One of the basic functions of networks is mobility. The evolution of network technologies and standards has led to a declining need for a fixed-location computer, and an increased use of mobile devices. Mobile computing is a generic term that refers to a variety of devices that allow people to access data and information from anywhere, anytime. Mobile computing transfers data, voice and video over a network via a mobile device such as a laptop, computer tablet, smartphone or wearable, like a Fitbit or AppleWatch. Mobile devices are typically connected through a LAN or a WLAN. Mobile computing is designed for workers who travel outside the physical plant of their company, including sales personnel, repair people, service employees, etc. It transforms the way that companies conduct business. Improved network performance provides fantastic opportunities for mobility in mobile commerce, collaboration, supply chain management, work in remote geographical areas, and other productivity gains. Cisco (2019) predicts that global mobile traffic will grow exponentially from the 12 **exabytes** per month reported back in 2017 to 77 exabytes per month in 2022.

By equipping employees with a mobile device, companies enable them to initiate real-time contacts with customers, vendors and corporate systems anywhere, anytime without having to sit down at a desktop computer or use a modem. Mobile computing provides the basis for mobile commerce discussed in Chapter 8.

Exabyte is one quintillion bytes (1,000,000,000,000,000,000 Bytes) which is the equivalent of 1,000 petabytes of data or 7 trillion online video clips. Five Exabytes is equal to all words ever spoken by humans.

Mobile Network Drivers

Demand for high-capacity networks to support mobile computing is growing at unprecedented rates. Currently five main factors drive mobility as illustrated in **Figure 4.13** and are described in more detail next.

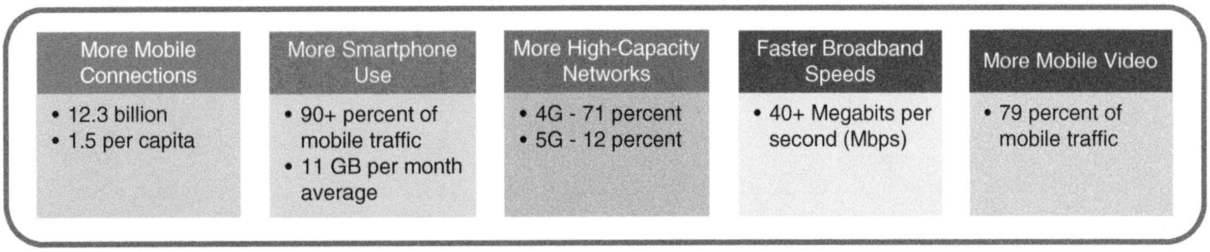

More Mobile Connections	More Smartphone Use	More High-Capacity Networks	Faster Broadband Speeds	More Mobile Video
• 12.3 billion • 1.5 per capita	• 90+ percent of mobile traffic • 11 GB per month average	• 4G - 71 percent • 5G - 12 percent	• 40+ Megabits per second (Mbps)	• 79 percent of mobile traffic

FIGURE 4.13 Factors driving mobility.

More Mobile Connections The global mobile population has recently exceeded 56% of the entire population of the globe. This translates to more than 4 billion unique users., mobile devices, excluding tablets, generate almost 49% of all global website traffic (Clement, 2019a, 2019b). Approximately 3.5 million active mobile social media users make social networking one of the most popular activities that causes them to look for more ways to connect. Currently, WhatsApp is the most popular messaging app with more than 1.6 billion monthly active users and Facebook Messenger is the second most popular. More connections are also needed as online shopping choices multiply.

More Smartphone Use

More and more mobile connections are being accessed by smartphones. By 2022, smartphones are expected to account for a mind-boggling 90+ percent of global mobile traffic.

More High-Capacity Networks

Voice over IP (VOIP) networks carry voice calls by converting analog (voice) signals to digital signs that are set as data packets.

The increase in mobile network connections is also leading to ever-increasing demand for high-capacity mobile networks. Examples of high-capacity networks are 4G and 5G wireless mobile, satellite, wireless sensor, and **VoIP (voice over Internet Protocol)** such as Skype and WhatsApp. Using VOIP, voice and data is transmitted in packets over telephone wires. Improved productivity, flexibility, and advanced features make VoIP a popular technology.

Faster Broadband Speeds

In today's global economy, advanced 4G and 5G mobile networks are the foundation for the global economy. For any nation to stay competitive and prosperous, it is imperative that investment and upgrades in these technologies continue to advance to satisfy demand. Mobile traffic is not distributed equally among all regions of the world. Some countries report wider mobile internet adoption than others. For example, some developing digital markets are "mobile-first" having skipped the acquisition of an expensive desktop PC network infrastructure. This can be witnessed in Asia and in African countries, like Nigeria where mobile devices generate more than 73% of its web traffic. It therefore follows that those countries with the highest average mobile internet speed will benefit most. As of August 2020, the country with the fastest average mobile internet speed was South Korea, with an average of 113.01 Mbps. **Table 4.4** lists the highest average internet speeds of the top 10 countries.

TABLE 4.4 **Top Ten Countries with Fastest Average Internet Speeds**

Country	Speed in MbPS
South Korea	113.01
China	111.26
UAE	111.13
Qatar	88.07
Saudi Arabia	77.55
Netherlands	75.4
Norway	74.34
Canada	69.46
Australia	68.23
Bulgaria	67.79

Adapted from O'Dea (2020).

More Mobile Video

Consistent with the increase for high-capacity networks is the demand for more mobile video. Mobile network users watch more than 62% of all digital video titles on their mobile devices. Netflix ranks among the worldwide higher grossing entertainment app titles, followed by Tencent Video and IQiYi Video.

Benefits of Mobile Computing

Companies benefit in three main ways from equipping their personnel with mobile computing devices:

- **Connectivity**—employees can stay connected to all sources, at all times.
- **Social Engagement**—employees can interact with customers, vendors, suppliers, partners, and each other via the Internet to create beneficial relationships.

    Personalization—mobile computing can be tailored to individual needs of all users to enhance the online experience.

Mobile Technologies

Enterprises are moving away from the ad hoc adoption of mobile devices and network infrastructure to a more strategic planning build-out of their mobile capabilities. As technologies that make up the mobile infrastructure evolve, identifying strategic technologies and avoiding wasted investments require more extensive planning and forecasting. Factors to consider are the network demands of multitasking mobile devices, more robust mobile OSs, and their applications.

Advancements in networks, devices and transmission media are changing enterprise information infrastructures and business environments dramatically. Mobile computers with built-in scan engines and voice recognition allow employees to travel and move about while collecting data. A good example of this would be an insurance agent who has to travel to an insurer's location after a hurricane to assess damage and collect audio, video and documentary data while talking to the insured and making a physical inspection of the property.

Three mobile network technologies that have created new ways of working and make a real difference to these types of data collection efforts and business operations are QR code, radio frequency identification (RFID), and near-field communication (NFC).

QR Code. If you've requested a return to Amazon, you've probably been provided with a **QR code** to show to UPS on your smartphone to authorize the shipment of your item **(Figure 4.14)**.

Quick Response (QR) Code is a two-dimensional barcode usually in a square structure with information stored in a black and white geometric symbol.

Manop Lohkaew/123RF

FIGURE 4.14 QR codes are collected by smart devices.

QR code is a member of the barcode family. Unlike the original one-dimensional barcode, QR code is two-dimensional, that is, horizontal and vertical. As a result, QR code is much more robust than the barcode typically found on food packaging that can only record basic product information. The two-dimensional QR code enables it to provide additional detailed product information without having to access a separate database to find it. The QR code can be automatically identified and read by an image input device or image scanning device.

QR codes have many business applications. To increase their competitiveness, some retailers have created their own QR code to enable shoppers to scan it into their mobile phones so they can bookmark a webpage, get coupons, view videos, purchase products, process order, and pay for goods to name a few. For instance, Starbucks and Dunkin Donuts use QR codes for mobile payment. The main difference between the two is that Starbucks customers pay with a Starbucks loyalty card they can load in advance and use to earn Stars that give them free drinks on future visits. Starbucks is also experimenting with QR scan-enabled augmented reality at their roasting facilities to enhance the customer experience. Other companies, like Dollar General, are in the planning stages. Dollar General is presently researching a scan-and-go system like the ones already in use at Costco and Sam's Club that lets shoppers scan item with their smartphone camera using the Dollar General app and scan a QR code at checkout to pay for their items.

QR codes are creating exciting new opportunities not only in retail, but also in other industry sectors. Publishing companies use them in magazines, photographers use them in table books of photographs, companies put them on web pages, and they can even be displayed on a billboard. Product and event marketers trying to get their message out are even screen printing QR codes on tee-shirts to link to a URL so potential customers can visit the page.

Advantages of a QR code which is printed on the product package, is its negligible cost and heightened security features. A disadvantage of the QR code is that it must be read individually. If you have multiple items to scan, it can be quite time-consuming and is appealing to individual consumers, but probably not as advantageous to suppliers and business partners, particularly if you think about using it in a warehouse environment.

As companies identify new ways to use them and adoption of QR codes increases it is expected that the simplicity and ease of use QR codes offer will continue to drive innovation and put even more new life into the bricks-and-mortar shopping experience.

Radio frequency identification (RFID) allows users to automatically and uniquely identify and track inventory and assets by using wireless contactless radio waves to capture encoded digital data on small RFID tags or smart labels to and from an RFID reader.

The purpose of an RFID tag is to gather identification information about people, devices, or objects, that is, a serial number.

There are two types of RFID tags—passive and active.

- **Passive tags** have a range of approximately 3–5 meters and can read at a rate of 10 or more times a second. They receive their energy to run from the RFID reader and do not have an internal battery and are extremely thin. RFID passive tags cost less than a dollar.
- **Active tags** have a range of approximately 100 meters. They have an internal power source that gives them their longer range but limits their life span. Active tags are bulkier than passive tags because of their internal battery. RFID active tags are more expensive than passive tags.

The RFID reader converts reflected or transmitted information from tags into useful digital data that can be processed by software running on a computer. The costs of RFID readers have dropped drastically in recent years from thousands of dollars to a current price range of $500 to $700, making RFID technology affordable to all sizes of companies. Prices range widely based on the frequency at which they operate.

RFID tags are generally reliable and while some RFID readers are designed to read one tag at a time, others can read many tags. Some functional problems that occur with the use of RFID technology include:

- Placing multiple RFID readers near each other can cause system interference.
- Noisy power supplies can degrade RFID performance. It's important to ensure that power sources are clean and regulated.

- Life-of-sight between the reader and the tag, while not required, can improve performance.
- An external antenna can improve the read range of RFID technology.
- Typically, the smaller the tag, the shorter the read range. Larger tags give better performance overall.

RFID delivers a number of benefits in a wide variety of industries. Retailers use RFID to track assets all the way to point of sale. Automotive companies use RFID to link a tag with a car's VIN to make sure repairs or recall work are carried out correctly and expediently. It can also track a car from manufacturer to dealer to ensure it is being transported to the correct destination. In manufacturing, products from beer to petroleum to chemicals can be tagged. In construction, RFID can be used to track prefabricated sections of large buildings that arrive onsite to be integrated into a new structure to shorten project timelines and lower labor costs.

Near-Field Communication (NFC) If you've used AirDrop on your smartphone you've used **near-field communication (NFC)**, a subset of RFID technology. NFC is a location-aware technology that allows two-way communication and is more secure than Bluetooth and Wi-Fi. An NFC tag contains small microchips with tiny aerials which can store a small amount of information for transfer to another near-field communication (NFC) device, such as a smartphone.

On the surface, Bluetooth and Wi-Fi might seem similar to near-field communication. All three allow wireless communication and data exchange between digital devices like smartphones **(Figure 4.15)**. The difference is that near-field communication utilizes electromagnetic radio fields while technologies such as Bluetooth and Wi-Fi focus on radio transmissions instead.

> **Near-field communication (NFC)** enables two devices within close proximity to establish a communication channel and transfer data through radio waves.

FIGURE 4.15 A location-aware NFC can be used to transfer photos and files, make purchases in restaurants, resorts, hotels, theme parks and theaters, at gas stations, and on buses and trains.

Examples of NFC Applications and Their Potential Business Value

Everyday near field communication is enabling companies to announce new ways in which they can make it easier and faster for customers to interact with them and help them stay ahead of their competition. Some effective applications include:

- The Apple iWatch wearable device with NFC communication capabilities is ideal for mobile payments. Instead of a wallet, users utilize their iWatch as a credit card or wave their wrists to pay for their Starbucks coffee. With GPS and location-based e-commerce services, retailers could send a coupon alert to the iWatch when a user passes their store. Consumers would then see the coupon and pay for the product with the iWatch.

- The self-healthcare industry is being radically transformed by the growing use of NFC technology. Wearable devices such as Fit-Bits, smart glucose monitors, and electrical nerve stimulators are becoming increasingly cheap and popular due to the proliferation of NFC technology. Some devices not only monitor, but also provide "automated or remote treatment" to provide smarter preventive care without the need for doctor or hospital visits and increase the well-being of users who have chronic illnesses.

- Passengers on public transportation systems can pay fares by waving an NFC smartphone as they board.

- Customers can pay for goods by waving an NFC-enabled credit card at the cash register.

- Customers can prove they have genuine Golden Goose Yeah sneakers because of the NFC tags that the upmarket manufacturer has embedded in their latest $600+ sneakers.

Another interesting NFC application is described in **IT at Work 4.3** that describes how the Salvation Army has simplified giving by adding NFC chips to its Red Kettles used in its annual Christmas fundraising campaign.

IT at Work 4.3

Salvation Army Simplifies the Act of Giving

The Salvation Army Red Kettle campaign is one of the oldest and largest charitable campaigns in the world. With the help of thousands of volunteers throughout the world, it has been operating the Christmas fundraiser for the past 129 years and has raised millions of dollars that provide children with Christmas toys and after-school programs, the homeless with clothes and shelter and the hungry with food.

This year, the Salvation Army added NFC chips to all 25,000 of its iconic Red kettles to enable shoppers to just tap their smartphone to make a donation to this worthwhile fundraiser. Kettle Pay was developed over the past two years and piloted last year in four markets before going nationwide in 2019.

NFC tags and stickers with a QR code, along with Apple Pay and Google Pay logos will be attached to the Red Kettles. Tapping the tag or scanning the code automatically opens a customer Salvation Army donation page on the donors' smartphone. They then select the amount of their donation and use Apple Pay or Google Pay to complete the transaction.

The donation is then automatically distributed to the donor's local Salvation Army unit based on their billing ZIP code and an email receipt is sent directly to their phone.

Twenty-five of those Red Kettles will be placed outside 21 stores in Bloomington, Illinois, where Salvation Army Lt. Justin Tracy and Chris Ayers, chair of the Salvation Army advisory board dropped the ceremonial first coins on November 14, 2019 to kick-off the local Red Kettle campaign. The goal of the Bloomington campaign is $520,000 and it's hoped that the new NFC-enabled Red Kettles will simplify the act of giving and help them reach their goal.

Sources: Compiled from Clark (2019), Fitzgerald (2019), Moran (2019), and Swiech (2019).

The Internet of Things

Internet of Things is the network of physical objects or "things" embedded with electronics, software, sensors, and network connectivity, that enables these objects to collect and exchange data.

The proliferation of data and the increased use of embedded sensors has led to the creation and rapid rise of the **Internet of Things (IoT)**—a giant network of connected people and things that collect and share data about how they are used and about the environment in which they exist. It is estimated there are approximately 30 billion IoT devices worldwide. By the year 2025, it is expected that there will be more than 75 billion (Nick, 2019). IoT is everywhere—in gadgets, machines, buildings, and other devices that connect to the Internet.

The IoT can best be described as a collection system that collects data from millions of data sensors embedded in everything from cars to power meters to refrigerators to airplanes to create KPIs and business insights for use in formulating business strategy (**Figure 4.16**). The IoT is the interconnection of any device that has an on/off switch. IoT devices have embedded electronics, software, sensors, and network connectivity to create a more cohesive and informed user experience. This includes everything from everyday items such as smartphones, coffee makers, washing machines, lamps, thermostats and headphones to industrial applications in an ambulance, airplane jet engine oil rig drill, smart traffic signals, smart parking meters, traffic congestion monitors, air pollution sensors, potable water monitors, and river, dam, and reservoir water level monitors. In other words, *if it can be* connected, it *will be* connected.

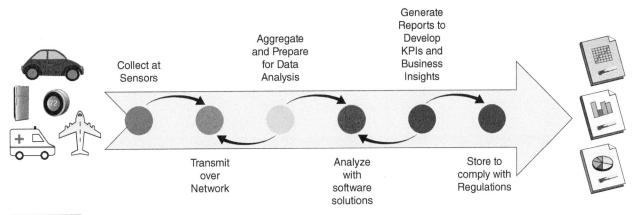

FIGURE 4.16   Data movement through the IoT system.

Factors Driving IoT

The primary driver for IoT is the broader adoption and deployment of sensors and smart devices. However, several things have created the "perfect storm" for the creation and growth of the IoT. These include:

- development of IPv6
- introduction of 5G networks
- more widely available broadband Internet
- lower cost of connecting
- overwhelming popularity of the smartphone
- development of more smart devices with Wi-Fi capabilities
- development of embedded sensors

IoT Architecture

IoT is a multi-layer technology used to manage and automate connected devices. The many layers of IoT technology form the IoT platform. There are more than 40 emerging technologies that play an important role in IoT (Lueth, 2019).

Building an IoT platform requires choices about hardware—including sensors, node devices, gateway devices, network infrastructure to name a few—and software solutions. These decisions are driven by questions asked and answered about the data about how and where it is collected, transferred, processed, analyzed, reported and ultimately stored.

- This requires the answers to several questions, including:
- what types of data will be collected?
- where will the data be collected from?
- how much date will be collected?
- how quickly does data have to be transferred?
- where will be data be kept?
- how reliable does data have to be?
- how timely does data have to be?
- what types of data analysis will be done?
- what are the compliance regulations that apply to the data?
- where will data be stored?
- how long does data need to be stored?

Once a company has answers to these questions, more informed decisions can be made concerning choice of sensors, nodes and gateways, network specifications, storage capacities (onsite or in the cloud), data analytics and reporting software solutions, etc.

IoT Analytics has published a useful Emerging IoT Technologies Radar (Lueth, 2019) to serve as a guide to anyone contemplating an IoT deployment or seeking to improve an existing one **(Figure 4.17)**.

	IoT Software	**IoT Hardware**	**IoT Connectivity**
Fairly Mature	Cloud computing	CPU Security Chips Edge gateways	WLAN WPAN Cellular IoT (2G/3G/4G) WNAN
Nearing Maturity	IoT Platforms Edge Analytics IoT-based streaming analytics Supervised Machine Learning Unsupervised Machine Learning Containers		LPWAN Pub/Sub
Coming Up	IoT Marketplaces Digital Twins Container Security IoT Security platforms Real-time databases Serverless/FaaS Deep Learning	Graphic Processing Units Non-Volatile flash memory (NAND) Application-specific Integrated Circuit (ASIC) Dynamic Random-Access Memory (DRAM) Field Programmable Gateway Array (FPGA) Neuro-synaptic chips	eSIM Network Virtualization 5G WiFi 6 Time Sensivive Networking
Years Out		Smart sensors ML-optimized gateways Energy harvesting for LPDs Cloud-connected sensors	LiFi Satellite IoT
Far On the Horizon		Quantum Computing	6G

*A sample of the full "State of the IoT 2019 Q1/Q2 report" and the database can be downloaded from **https://iot-analytics.com/sample-request-state-of-iot-update-2019-q1-q2**.

FIGURE 4.17   Emerging IoT Technologies Radar 2019.

The Growth of IoT

The popularity and use of IoT is growing. In 1990, there were 300,000 connected IoT devices, in 2019 there were 14.2 billion, and it is predicted that the number of IoT connections will grow to 25 billion in 2021 (Cook, 2019). In dollar terms, IoT Analytics reports that the global IoT market is expected to increase from over $150 billion in 2018 to more than $1.5 trillion by 2025 (Lueth, 2018). In a recent survey on IoT use (IoT Analytics, 2019), 82% of IT professionals from a diverse array of industries and companies of varying sizes around the world reported that they had either implemented IoT, are currently running a pilot program or are considering implementing IoT.

IoT is being implemented in many different industries, including healthcare, energy, agriculture, construction, and government and is shaping new rules for competitiveness **(Figure 4.18)**. Some industries have had IoT in place for quite some time, for others it is an entirely new concept. The use of smaller sensors, compared to the larger traditional IT infrastructure, is enabling more and more large and small companies to increase their computing capabilities and reduce power consumption to save money and increase performance, promote growth and facilitate sustainability. The many applications include:

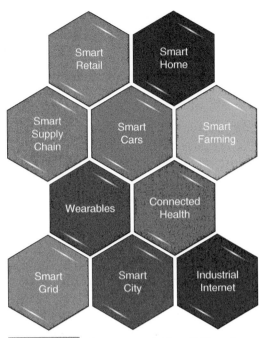

FIGURE 4.18   The Internet of Things (IoT) can be applied in many industries and product lines.

Smart Homes   Every month more than 60,000 people look for smart home devices such as thermostats, smart door bells, irrigation systems, and smart power outlets. Companies like Nest, Ecobee, Haier, Belkin, Ring, and AlertMe are among the more than 250 companies and startups that are enabling smart home IoT services.

Wearables   like Fitbit, AppleWatch, LookSee bracelet, and the Myo gesture control are some of the most popular fitness, message alert, smart jewelry and remote presentation control devices available today. They allow consumers to stay healthier and better informed.

Connected Health   has various functions including remote monitoring of equipment, to personal health sensors like heart monitors to surgical boots. It has the potential to improve not only how health professionals deliver care, but also to keep patients safe and healthy and allow patients more time interacting with their physicians and clinicians.

Smart Retail   has been adopted by retailers to compete more effectively by improving store operations, increasing purchases, reducing theft, enabling inventory management and enhancing the overall shopping experience of their customers.

Smart Travel   covers the entire spectrum of the travel experience from beginning to end. IoT assists in before travel activities such as online planning, booking and payments to services at transportation facilities that include travel status, direction to gates, electronic bag tags and lounge access. It also makes the trip more enjoyable with sensors embedded in seats that can monitor passenger body temperature, hydration level and anxiety level. On arrival at your destination IoT-enabled apps enable hotels to customize setting for each guest. Room temperatures, lights, and audio-visual components can be set and controlled remotely. Room sensors also indicate whether a room is empty or occupied at any given time and if there is a need for additional guest services. During the trip, online help with location transportation, attractions and events enhances the travel experience.

Connected Cars   use a complex network of sensors, antennas, software, and technologies to make decisions about the consistency, accuracy, and speed of cars. The reliability of this technology becomes more critical as automobile manufacturers move toward driverless vehicles that are currently being tested. Tesla is a good example of a connected car.

Smart Farming is a new application of IoT, that matches well with IoT's capabilities given the typically remote and large numbers of livestock that farmers deal with.

Smart Supply Chain offers solutions to problems of tracking good in transit and helping suppliers exchange inventory information. Embedded sensors in factory equipment can communicate pressure, temperature, and use of the machine and process workflow and adjust equipment settings to optimize performance.

Industrial Internet involves connected power generation, oil, gas, utilities, and health-care machines and devices that monitor unplanned downtime and system failures that can result in life-threatening situations.

Smart Grids A combination of smart meters, wireless technology, sensors, and software have create the smart grid that allows utility companies to accurately track power grids and cut back on energy use when the availability of electricity is stressed. It also provides consumers with valuable insights into their power consumption to make more intelligent decisions about energy conservation. For example, a fully deployed smart grid has the potential of saving between $39.69 and $101.57, and up to 592 pounds of carbon dioxide emissions, per consumer per year in the United States, according to the Smart Grid Consumer Collaborative (SGCC).

Smart Cities IoT is not limited to individual and industry use. On a broader scale, the IoT can be applied to things like "smart cities" that can help reduce waste and improve efficiency. Applications include water distribution, traffic management, waste management and environmental monitoring designed to remove the discomfort and issues with city living such as traffic congestion, noise and air pollution and personal safety.

Advantages and Disadvantages of IoT

To understand how IoT will impact their business, organizations have to consider both its advantages and disadvantages.

Organizations can expect to gain from using the IoT in several ways, for example, expected benefits from using IoT include:

- Monitoring performance, quality, and reliability of products and services
- Gaining insight into potential new products and service
- Support sales
- Better understand product use
- Remote troubleshooting of products
- Deliver revenue-generating post-sales service
- More efficiently deliver post-sales services

Similarly, there are disadvantages to using IoT and the responsibilities associated with collecting and analyzing massive amounts of data. The top two IoT disadvantages are network security and data privacy:

- **Network security** concerns center around the fact that currently companies often don't have control over the source and nature of the software and hardware being used in IoT initiatives. With billions of devices connected together there are a multitude of end-points where security breaches can occur and individuals or organizations can be hacked.
- **Data privacy** is becoming an increasing concern as more and more companies consider brokering data for profit. In 2018, Gartner (2018) reported that thirty-five (35%) of companies who had IoT initiatives were already selling or planning to sell data collected by their products and services and predict that by 2023 data brokering will become an integral part of many IoT platforms.

Other IoT *disadvantages* that organizations must consider include:

1. Data analysis capabilities
2. Data collection capabilities
3. Realistic efficiency opportunities
4. Realistic new revenue opportunities
5. Cost

Edge Computing

The cost of bandwidth and the explosive growth of IoT devices along with new apps that need real-time computing time such as data analytics, connected cars and connected health is driving **edge computing**. Edge computing is a new networking technology that brings the data closer to where it is being used and is being enabled by the new, faster 5G networks. It is essentially a local source of data processing and storage.

By bringing data storage closer to the devices where it's being collected, rather than relying on a central location that could be hundreds of miles away, edge computing reduces network latency issues that can affect apps performance. Edge computing also save money by analyzing these large amounts of data locally and eases overall network congestion. Once the data are processed locally, a much smaller volume of data that needs to be retained is transmitted to **fog nodes** and ultimately an even smaller volume of data is transmitted to cloud data centers for long-term storage. In this way, edge computing assists with cost of equipment and storage, transmission time and costs of latency sensitive data, multi-faceted transitory data and high-quality data and provides time-critical data when and where needed (**Figure 4.19**).

Edge Computing is part of a distributed computing topology where information processing is located close to the edge—where things and people produce or consume the information.

Fog node is the physical device where fog computing is deployed. Examples are servers, routers or switches.

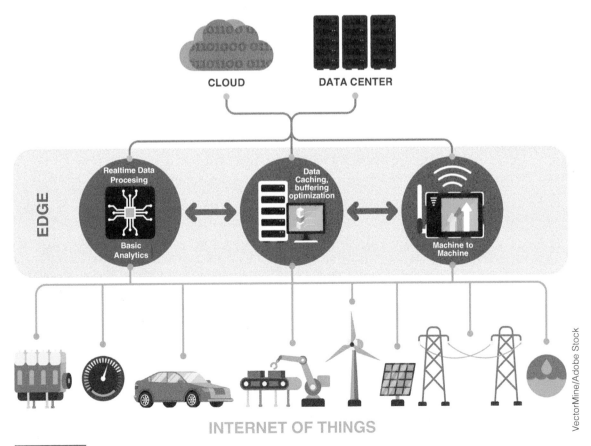

FIGURE 4.19 Edge computing.

Edge Architecture and Apps

Edge computing uses a distributed, open IT architecture with decentralized processing power. Data can be processed in the device itself or by a local computer or server rather than being transmitted to a data center. Edge technologies are becoming increasingly smaller and can be built into very small devices, such as drones, robots and medical devices, such as heart monitors.

Edge computing software comes in all shapes and sizes. Any company that is considering deploying edge computing needs to consider the business problem that has prompted them to consider edge computing in the first place, for example, network latency, coverage reliability, bandwidth cost, security. Then it must look at how edge computing can address the problem and how they would implement it for optimum benefit.

Industry Applications of Edge Computing

A good example of how edge computing can help with network traffic congestion and at simultaneously save time and money might be at a vineyard where an industrial sensor has been placed on a wine barrel that must be kept within a certain temperature range to prevent the wine from spoiling. To continuously monitor the wine barrel, the sensor is set to generate multiple alerts per minute and transmit the data to a data center for analysis. If this was at a very small vineyard where there are just a few wine barrels, this wouldn't be a problem, but if is at a very large Napa valley vineyard there might be thousands of wine barrels and this translates into millions of alerts every day with very few of them requiring that any action be taken. If instead the data are processed by an edge device that can analyze, filter, and compress the data locally, the constant flood of relatively insignificant raw data can be distilled into a much more manageable volume of relevant, aggregated data that can be periodically sent to the cloud or an inhouse data center.

Edge computing is particularly very useful in environments with unreliable network connectivity, such as airplanes, cruise ships (see Business Case 4.2), offshore oil rigs, rural agricultural sites, and remote military outposts. With local edge network resources, users at these locations are no longer at the mercy of the hit and miss connections to the cloud. For example, a jet engine generates a huge volume of performance and safety data during each hour of flight that requires massive onboard data storage, and for safety reasons, some on-plane analysis of the data. With edge-enabled local processing and analysis, this operation becomes much more seamless, reliable and secure.

Choosing Mobile Computing Solutions

As discussed earlier in this chapter, many different mobile computing technologies are available to help businesses improve their interactions with their customers, vendors, and partners to compete in the marketplace. The purpose, advantages, and disadvantages of each option need to be carefully evaluated before making a choice. Once a choice of solution has been made (e.g., QR codes, RFID, NFC, IoT, and Edge), the many pieces that make up that option also need to be assessed. For each technology, there is a host of available hardware, network, and software options. **Figure 4.20** lists four important characteristics that organization must consider when choosing mobile computing solutions and the technologies that support them.

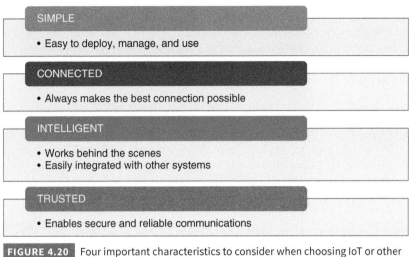

FIGURE 4.20 Four important characteristics to consider when choosing IoT or other mobile computing solution.

Networks Support Communication, Search, Collaboration and Relationships

The other four basic business functions that networks support are communication, search, collaboration, and relationships. *Communicating* over wired, wireless or mobile networks helps businesses *search* for information that helps them *collaborate* to get work done and develop business *relationships*. Company managers and staff communicate over networks and use search engines to collaborate with their suppliers and partners to make decisions as they develop and manufacture products, plan social media marketing strategies, make financial and IT investments, determine how to meet compliance mandates, design software, and so on. To assist in many of these decision-making processes, companies are increasingly turning to computer networks to make it easier for them to share files and to collect and analyze huge volumes of data produced by the proliferation of IoT sensors, RFID and NFC tags. Today, employees are often required to work in teams that are provided with copious digital documents and information and are expected to make complex decisions.

Teamwork can be quite dynamic and complex in the best of situations depending on the following factors:

- Group members may be in different geographic locations and/or work at different times.
- Group members may work for the same or different organizations.
- Needed data, information, or knowledge may be several different sources, several of which are external to the organization.

These factors can make it difficult for organizations to solve complex problems and make effective decisions. To overcome these concerns, companies are deploying more complex and more easily accessible networks to help them work together to share information over time and distance. Many leading businesses report that virtual collaboration enabled by increasingly fast, reliable and secure networks is particularly beneficial in managing their supply chain interactions and facilitate the development of beneficial relationships with suppliers and vendors. Several industry examples are listed below.

Collaborative Problem Solving Between Manufacturers and Transporters
Ford Motor Company began relying on UPS Logistics Group's data networks to track millions of cars and trucks and to analyze any potential problems before they occurred. As a result, Ford realized a $1 billion reduction in vehicle inventory and $125 million reduction in inventory carrying costs annually.

Sharing Information Between Retailers and Suppliers One of the most publicized examples of information sharing exists between Procter & Gamble (P&G) and Walmart. Walmart provides P&G with access to sales information on every item Walmart buys from P&G. The information is collected by P&G on a daily basis from every Walmart store, and P&G uses that information to manage the inventory replenishment for Walmart.

Facilitating Retailer–Supplier Collaboration: Asda Corporation European supermarket chain Asda has rolled out Web-based electronic data interchange (EDI) technology to 650 of its suppliers. Web EDI technology is based on the AS2 standard, an internationally accepted HTTP-based protocol used to send real-time data in multiple formats securely over the Internet. It has improved the efficiency and speed of traditional EDI communications, which route data over third-party, value-added networks (VANs).

Lowering Transportation and Inventory Costs and Reduced Stockouts: Unilever Unilever's 30 contract carriers deliver 250,000 truckloads of shipments annually. Unilever's Web-based database, the Transportation Business Center (TBC), provides these carriers with site specification requirements when they pick up a shipment at a manufacturing or distribution center or when they deliver goods to retailers. TBC gives carriers all the vital information they need: contact names and phone numbers, operating hours, the number of dock doors at a location, the height of the dock doors, how to make an appointment to deliver or pick up shipments, pallet configuration, and other special requirements. All mission-critical information that Unilever's carriers need to make pickups, shipments, and deliveries is now available electronically 24/7.

Reducing Product Development Time Caterpillar, Inc. is a multinational heavy-machinery manufacturer. In the traditional mode of operation, cycle time along the supply chain was long because the process involved paper—document transfers among managers, salespeople, and technical staff. To solve the problem, Caterpillar connected its engineering and manufacturing divisions with its active suppliers, distributors, overseas factories, and customers through an extranet-based global collaboration system. By means of the collaboration system, a request for a customized tractor component, for example, can be transmitted from a customer to a Caterpillar dealer and on to designers and suppliers, all in a very short time. Customers also can use the extranet to retrieve and modify detailed order information while the vehicle is still on the assembly line.

Currently there more than 2.5 million mobile computing apps that cover the entire gamut of mobile applications from fitness, travel and banking to games for all ages. Those that relate to communication, search, collaboration and relationship building support business in the following ways:

Search for documents and files that are stored in diverse locations becomes much easier and more efficient over a network. Search engines are a valuable tool that allows managers, vendors and customers to search for content on the World Wide Web by entering keywords or key phrases. In return, they receive a list of Web content in the form of websites, images, videos or other online data that helps them find information to support decision-making, finding, and prioritizing websites. Examples include Google, Yahoo, Bing, and Chrome.

Messaging includes older communications media such as e-mail and texts. More recently VOIP is a network technology that has grown to become one of the most used and least costly ways to communicate one-on-one along with apps that support videoconferences. Apps related to email include Gmail and Hotmail; to VOIP include Skype and WhatsApp, and to videoconferencing include WebMeeting and Google Hangouts.

Online Collaboration tools enable corporate and individual users to share, edit, plan, and communicate online. Examples of apps that help employees collaborate across departments, locations, and business apps include Office 265, Slack, and Asana.

Brainstorming ideas is no longer limited to a roomful of people offering their ideas that are written on sticky notes and placed on a whiteboard or posters. Instead, companies are choosing an alternative in the form of online brainstorming applications, many of which are cloud-based. Examples of brainstorming apps include xMind, iThoughtsX, and MindNode.

Mindmapping   is a creative and logical way to represent ideas and concepts. It creates a diagram that helps structure information to help you better analyze, understand, synthesize, recall, and generate ideas by connecting information around a central topic or subject and builds branches that emanate from it. **Figure 4.21** shows a sample Mindmap that was developed to encourage and generate ideas about how to combat global warming.

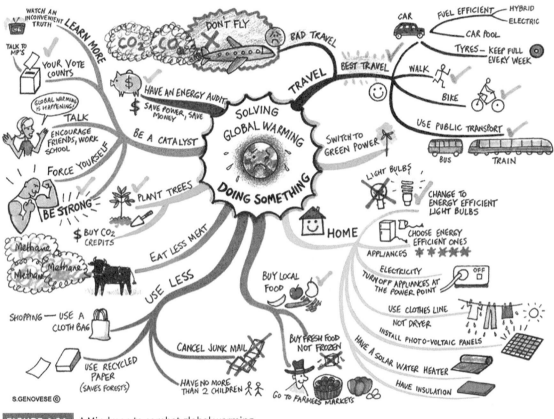

FIGURE 4.21   A Mindmap to combat global warming.

In contrast to traditional notetaking, information in a mindmap is structured in a way that more closely resembles how your brain works. Online mindmapping helps streamline teams work processes, minimize information overload, generates new ideas, and boosts innovation. Examples of mindmap apps include MindNode 6, SimpleMind+, and iThoughts.

Questions

1. What are the factors driving mobile computing?
2. Why is mobile global traffic increasing?
3. How is NFC different from RFID?
4. What are the two components of a wireless network infrastructure?
5. What are three types of wireless network transmission media?
6. What factors should be considered when evaluating mobile networks?
7. What types of industry sectors are using IoT?
8. How does a network help communication, collaboration and relationships between companies and their vendors?
9. What is edge computing and what networking problems does it address?
10. How can a Mindmap be used to structure a problem?

4.4 Network Quality of Service

LO4.4 Describe *the importance of evaluating the quality of a network and the current status of Net Neutrality.*

Quality of Service is a network's ability to achieve maximum bandwidth, optimize network performance elements like latency, error rate, uptime and downtime and control and manage network resources by setting priorities for specific types of data on the network.

Regardless of the type of networks companies deploy, one important business decision that must be made about their operation and maintenance is the issue of network **quality of service** (QoS). If a data packet gets lost or acknowledgement is not received the data must be retransmitted, wasting valuable business resources. Similarly, the delay of a message from source to destination can adversely impact business operations. This is particularly important for delay-sensitive data such as real-time voice and high-quality video. Bandwidth-intensive apps are important to certain business processes, but they also strain network capabilities and resources. The higher the required QoS, the more expensive the technologies needed to manage organizational networks.

While network quality of service addresses these issues of reliability, delay and bandwidth, QoS is also concerned with traffic prioritization and resource control mechanisms. This means that QoS measures the ability to assign different priorities to different apps, users or data to guarantee a certain level of performance to the speed at which data is transferred.

Regardless of the type of traffic, networks must provide secure, predictable, measurable, and sometimes guaranteed services for certain types of traffic. The principles of QoS can be applied in two ways:

Latency-sensitive apps are apps that are expected to respond quickly to specific events.

Traffic shaping is the ability to prioritize and throttle network traffic.

- **Prioritize traffic** Data and apps that are time-delay-sensitive or **latency-sensitive apps**, such as voice and video, are given priority on the network.
- **Throttle traffic** Other types of traffic need to be held back (throttled) to give latency-sensitive apps priority.

Peer-to-Peer (P2P) allows shared access to files and peripherals without the need for a central server in a network where each computer can act as a server for the others.

Traffic shaping delays the flow of less important network traffic, such as bulk data transfers and **Peer-to-Peer (P2P)** file-sharing programs, including **BitTorrent** traffic.

Traffic shaping creates a two-tier system in which certain customers or services get traffic priority for a premium charge. For example, time-sensitive data would be given priority over traffic that can be delayed briefly with little-to-no adverse effect. Certain applications are more sensitive to delays than others, such as streaming video and Internet phone services. Managing data transfer makes it possible to assure a certain level of performance or quality of service.

BitTorrent is a communication protocol for P2P file sharing used to distribute data and electronic files over the internet, such as movies and music.

In a corporate environment, business-related traffic may be given priority over other traffic by paying a premium price for that service. Proponents of traffic shaping, including AT & T and Times Warner, argue that ISPs should be able to charge more to customers who want to pay a premium for priority service. Traffic shaping is at the core of the hotly debated issue of **Net Neutrality**.

Net neutrality is a principle that Internet service providers (ISPs) and their regulators treat all Internet traffic the same way.

Net Neutrality

Net Neutrality essentially ensures equal opportunity for Internet speeds and access to website with no unfair fast or slow lanes and no blocking of anything that's legal on your phone, computer, or tablet.

Those who support the need for Net Neutrality favor the one-tier system in which all Internet data packets are treated the same, regardless of their content, destination, or source. Its supporters include the major Internet companies who provide the content you read and watch online, including Facebook, Netflix, Twitter, and Vimeo. They don't want to be discriminated against by network owners like AT&T, Comcast, Time Warner Cable, and Verizon who favor the two-tiered system and are fighting against Net Neutrality. These opponents of Net Neutrality argue there have always been different levels of Internet service and that a two-tiered system would enable more freedom of choice and promote Internet-based commerce.

Over the years, Net Neutrality battle has had its ups and downs, as demonstrated in **IT at Work 4.4**

IT at Work 4.4

States Take on the Net Neutrality Battle

Over the past decade, Net Neutrality has been a hotly debated topic that has evolved from Semi-Net Neutrality to Net Neutrality to the Restoring Internet Freedom Order—the latest regulation on Internet content access - which ironically allows the already free Internet to be restricted in new ways, to No Net Neutrality. To find out why it's now up to individual states to take up the battle for net neutrality, we need to look at the timeline associated with the various attempts to establish Net Neutrality at the Federal Levels.

- **December 21, 2010**—The Federal Communications Commission (FCC) *approved* a compromise that created two classes of Internet access: one for fixed-line providers and the other for the wireless Net. This effectively created Net Semi-Neutrality, since the FCC banned any outright blocking and unreasonable discrimination against websites or apps by fixed-line broadband providers but did not explicitly ban "paid prioritization" which allowed ISPs to charge companies that requested faster data transmission.

- **January 14, 2014**—A DC Circuit Appeals Court effectively *struck down* the FCC's 2010 Net Neutrality ruling by finding that under broadband's current *classification* as a Title I information service, the FCC had no authority to adopt Net neutrality regulations based on the concept of "common carriage." This allowed ISPs to create a two-tiered Internet but under close supervision to avoid anti-competitive practices and banned unreasonable discrimination against providers.

- **May 15, 2014**—The FCC voted 3–2 to *reinstate* Net Neutrality and prohibit behavior harmful to consumers or competition limiting the openness of the Internet. The new Rules, did however, allow network owners to charge extra fees to content providers.

- **February 26, 2015**—The FCC *reclassified* broadband as a Title II telecommunications service that effectively held broadband providers to many of the requirements of the traditional telephone network and gave the FCC greater powers to regulate broadband traffic.

- **December 14, 2017**—The FCC voted 3–2 to once again *repeal* the Net Neutrality Rules and overturned the reclassification of broadband as a Title II telecommunications service. This decision enabled ISPs to charge extra fees and block and/or censor content and users. Attorney Generals from 22 states and several activist groups filed suit appealing the FCC's decision.

- **June 11, 2018**—Net Neutrality Rules officially were *taken off the books* and the Restoring Internet Freedom Order went into effect overturning earlier net neutrality requirements on ISPs and banned states from protecting consumer rights by enacting their own Net Neutrality regulations. Several state legislators responded by introducing net neutrality legislation at the state level, including California that has the strictest net neutrality regulations. In turn, the DOJ filed lawsuits against states to overturn state level regulations.

- **October 1, 2019**—A panel of three judges at the DC Circuit Court of Appeals voted to deregulate companies like Comcast and Verizon and *officially repealed* Net Neutrality. However, the court also found the FCC had overstepped its authority when it banned states from enacting their own open internet rules to open the door for states to enact their own protections and uphold those already in place.

In response to the October 1, 2019 DC Circuit Court of Appeals ruling supporting state's right to enact their own Internet protections, some states have chosen to continue to do nothing, while others are at different stages of proposing and introducing new Rules, reviewing them in committee, or have already passed state-level regulations. California, New Jersey, Oregon, Vermont, and Washington have already enacted legislation to protect net neutrality.

In the 2019 legislative session, 29 states introduced Net Neutrality legislation. In all, 34 states plus the District of Columbia are in various stages of introducing and reviewing net neutrality regulations. As you might imagine, all this discontinuity makes it difficult for individual users, companies, and private telecommunications companies to keep track of new Net Neutrality requirements at the state level.

Sources: Compiled from Federal Communications Commission (FCC, 2019), Bode (2018), Bode (2019), Rogers (2018), Ulloa (2018), CBS News (2019), Morton (2019), and Reardon (2019).

Is the Net Neutrality Case Closed?   Not necessarily. Unless Congress passes legislation for or against Net Neutrality, things could drag on for a long time with either side appealing to the U.S. Supreme Court or asking the DC Circuit Court of Appeals for an "en banc" hearing that allows the full panel of justices to hear the case. In the meantime, the current assignment of broadband to the control of the Federal Trade Commission (FTC)—who is not authorized to police ISPs—rather than the FCC who has authority to police ISPs, has strengthened the case of those who oppose Net Neutrality (Mack 2019). Conversely, those in favor of reinstating Net Neutrality have been encouraged by the recent passing of the *Save the Internet Act* by the House. This Act would reinstate 2015 Net Neutrality rules and once again make the FCC the agent in charge of policing broadband. In the meantime, the tug-of-war continues.

Quality of Service Models

Two models are used to evaluate the quality of service of a network based on integrating or differentiating services.

The **Integration Services Model (IntServ)** is based on measuring how data flows through a network from source to destination and the resource needs of all routers in the network. This is achieved through a resource reservation protocol (RSVP) that provides a signaling mechanism to make a reservation to transfer data. This is done through a resource specification that defines the resources needed to make the reservation, including bandwidth, and a traffic specification that defines the traffic priority of the data flow. In the concluding step, the router decides to admit or deny the service based on previous commitments and current availability of resources. The integrated services model offers two classes of service—guaranteed and controlled load. The guaranteed service class is designed for real-time traffic that needs minimum end to end delay such as audio or videoconferencing. The controlled load service class is designed for email or file transfers that can accept some delays but are sensitive to overloading the network and to the possibility of lost data packets.

The **Differentiated Services Model (DiffServ)** was designed by the Internet Engineering Task Force (IETF). By marking the class of each packet directly on the packet, DiffServ eliminates the need for a signaling protocol that tells the routers which flows require special QoS treatment. For example, it might reduce the latency in voice or streaming video traffic while providing best effort service to file transfers. In the DiffServ, individual data packets are marked with information about the level of service required, other nodes in the network read the information and respond by providing the requested level of service. Once a data packet has been transferred its traffic flow information is no longer needed.

To summarize, the IntServ is limited to two classes of service and requires each router to remember information about each flow. In the DiffServe, there is no requirement to collect information about each flow. This makes the DiffServ more appropriate for large networks like the Internet where reserving paths and remembering state information would be onerous. The IntServ is more appropriate for smaller private networks where this type of overhead does not impact the operation of the network. Some organizations have both types of networks so it's important to remember that the two models are not mutually exclusive. They can and are used side by side. The most important thing to remember is that a QoS model must be used to ensure an organization is realizing optimal value from its networks.

Questions

1. Why has group work becoming more challenging?
2. What might limit the use of face-to-face brainstorming?
3. How can online brainstorming tools overcome those limits?
4. List ways in which virtual collaboration can be used in business.
5. What devices do you have that take advantage of the IoT? Describe how they impact the way that you live and work.
6. What is driving the rise of the IoT?
7. What is the main concern that organizations have about the IoT?
8. Do you think the advantages outweigh the disadvantages of the IoT? Explain.
9. Where do you stand on the issue of Net Neutrality?
10. How do you think the state level Net Neutrality regulations are going to impact ISPs?

Chapter Summary

LO4.1 *Describe* the different types of wired networks and their principal components and how a computer network supports basic business functions.

A computer network supports five basic business functions: communication, search, mobility, collaboration, and relationships. It can support these businesses function by providing data and file sharing, resource sharing, data protection and reduction of data duplication, simplified administration of the IT infrastructure, improved internal communications and better distribution of computing power. There are many types of networks, but the most commonly used are local area networks (LANs) and wide area networks (WAN). LANs have one owner and can be configured in three ways: bus, star and ring. WANs are more complex networks that cover larger distances and can transmit larger volumes of data. WANs are owned and managed by more than one organization and often requires the assistance of an internet service provider (ISP). WANs can be private or public. A modification of a WAN is the SD-WAN that is managed by a single central app. LANs and WANs can be classified as intranets or extranets. VPNs address network security concerns between WANs by encrypting data packets before they are transmitted over the network. All networks are constrained by the transmission media they use and whether they use circuit or packet switching. Other physical network components include client, server, wireless router, hub, switch and network interface card.

LO4.2 *Identify* the different generations of wireless networks, the standards that drive them and the technologies that support them.

A new network generation is released approximately every 10 years. 4G is the most commonly used network generation although the new 5G is much faster. 4G LTE-A run in internet protocols (IP) and operates at up to 1Gbps. 5G offer speeds up to 10 Gbps. is still in the early stages of adoption because it operates with different kinds of antennas, operates on different radio frequencies, connects many more devices, minimizing traffic throttling and dramatically increases the speed at which data are transferred across the network. New devices have to be developed to support 5G. The smartphones that run on 4G cannot accommodate the requirements of 5G. 4G devices are much more available than 5G devices and 5G is only available in limited areas. All generations of network are guided by a set of IEEE standards to ensure compatibility and interoperability of network products manufactured by different vendors. The latest standard is IEEE 802.11ax known as "high efficiency wireless" and referred to as Wi-Fi 6. It offers better power efficiency and boosts the battery life of devices. IEEE 802.11 standards support 4G networks, but new standard will be needed for 5G. Those standards are in the early stages of development. Wireless networks can connect through Wi-Fi, WiMAX, WWANs, and WLANs. Wi-Fi is the most common way in which wireless networks connect. Every network has to be connected through one of many wireless transmission media, ranging from radio waves to satellites. The wireless network infrastructure includes technology, software, support, standards, security measures and devices. Internet protocols (IPs) are used to allow the network to communicate. TCP/IP protocols carry data cross the network and Application Program Interfaces (APIs) are code compiled for a specific operating system (OS) that allows the OS to communicate with hardware in its own unique way.

LO4.3 *Explain* the growth in mobile data traffic and the benefits companies can gain from the Internet of Things (IoT) and edge computing.

The evolution of network technologies and standards has led to a declining need for fixed-location computers and an increased use of mobile computing devices. Examples of high-capacity networks are wireless mobile, satellite, IoT, and VoIP. The global mobile population has recently exceeded 56% of the entire world's population. This translates to more than 4 billion unique users of mobile devices. Companies benefit in three main ways from equipping personnel with mobile computing devices: connectivity, social engagement and personalization. QR codes, RFID, and NFC are three technologies that have promoted mobile computing by the benefits they provide to organizations using them. The IoT is probably the most rapidly growing mobile computing application. Its many applications include smart homes, wearables, connected health, smart retail, smart travel, connected cars, smart farming, smart supply chain, industrial internet, smart grids and smart cities. Through its use companies can expect to gain insight into potential new products and services, monitor performance, quality and reliability of products and services, support sales, better understand product use, eliminate the need for troubleshooting products, deliver revenue-generating post-sales service and most efficiently deliver those post-sales services. Caution needs to be exercised when dealing with extremely sensitive data since IoT does have some security and privacy issues. IoT can also be expensive and its data analysis, data collection and efficiencies can be overstated. Edge computing is the latest network technology. It brings data processing closer to where the data is needed to offer cost and efficiency benefits.

LO4.4 *Describe* the importance of evaluating the quality of a network and the current status of Net Neutrality.

All technology needs to assess as to the quality of traffic prioritization and traffic throttling. Network quality of service (QoS) can be classified in two ways: Integrated Services (IntServ) and Differentiated Services (DiffServ). Both models have their good points, but DiffServ is more appropriate for larger networks like the Internet and IntServ works better in smaller private networks. It's important to remember that the models are not mutually exclusive and can be used side by side in companies that have both types of networks. Net Neutrality has been a hot topic of debate for the past 10 or more years. If you follow its timeline you'll readily see the on again, off again nature of Net Neutrality and appreciate the battle that has raged for and against it. Currently, Net Neutrality at the Federal level has been eliminated and it is up to the individual states to enact their own Net Neutrality regulations.

Key Terms

Assuring Your Learning

Reflect: Critical Thinking Questions

1. Explain how network capacity is measured.

2. How are devices identified to a network?

3. Explain how digital signals are transmitted.

4. Explain the functions of switches and routers.

5. Traffic shaping creates two tiers of traffic. What are those tiers? Give an example of each type of traffic.

6. What are the differences between 4G, and 5G networks?

7. What are the two models of quality of service and how are they different?

8. Discuss two applications of near-field communication (NFC).

9. What are the benefits of APIs?

10. Describe the components of a mobile communication infrastructure.

11. What is the range of WiMAX? Why does it not need a clear line of sight?

12. Why are VPNs used to secure extranets?

13. How can group dynamics improve group work? How can it disrupt what groups might accomplish?

14. What are the benefits of using software to conduct remote brainstorming in the cloud?

Explore: Online and Interactive Exercises

1. Visit the Google apps website. Identify three types of collaboration support and their value in the workplace.

2. Compare the various features of broadband wireless networks (e.g., LTE-A, Wi-Fi, and WiMAX). Visit at least three broadband wireless network vendors.

a. Prepare a list of capabilities for each network.

b. Prepare a list of actual applications that each network can support.

c. Comment on the value of such applications to users. How can the benefits be assessed?

Analyze & Decide: Apply IT Concepts to Business Decisions

1. Go to the Aila website (**https://ailatech.com/blog/ten-retailers-using-qr-codes-for-in-store-payments**) and read their article on 10 Retailers who are using QR codes. Choose two of the retailers and compare their experiences. Would you use this type of app? Explain your answer.

2. Go to Analytics Vidhya website (**https://www.analyticsvidhya.com/blog/2016/08/10-youtube-videos-explaining-the-real-world-applications-of-internet-of-things-iot**) and choose two of the industry sector IoT videos. View the videos and write a report about what

you learned about IoT use. What surprised you the most? What information was new to you?

3. Visit the AT&T website (**https://www.business.att.com/content/dam/attbusiness/reports/what_need_know_iot_networks.pdf**) and read the article "What you Need to Know about IoT Wide Area Networks." Write a short report discussing the benefits of each type of network that can be used in an organization's IoT and make a choice for your "business."

Reinforce: Demonstrate Your Understanding of the Key Terms

Solve the online crossword provided for this chapter.

Web Resources

More resources and study tools are located on the student Website. You'll find useful web links and self-test quizzes that provide individualized feedback.

Case 4.2

Business Case: Carnival Seeks to Keep Passengers Happier at Sea with IoT, NFC, and Edge Computing

Two years after Carnival Corporation, introduced its OceanMedallion, a Star Trek-like communicator device, it has become an important part of the Princess Cruise experience and has significantly improved its passengers' satisfaction level. To date, OceanMedallion and its accompanying Internet of Things (IoT) architecture has been deployed on five Carnival's cruise ships. The Caribbean Princess, Regal Princess, Royal Princess, Crown Princess and Sky Princess. The Caribbean Princess was the first ship fully outfitted with the OceanMedallion but it's a lengthy process that involves not only technology but also MedallionClass service—a whole new service level tier needed to support the IoT model.

The OceanMedallion is about the size of a U.S. quarter. It connects customers with the ship's various services in a personalized way, regardless of where it is used on the vessel. The OceanMedallioin is mailed to the passenger prior to their arrival on the ship and they can wear it as a pendant, in a clip, on a sports band or on a bracelet. It's essentially a wearable IoT device that connects to Princess Cruises' shipboard sensor and data network. Its micro-antennae enable both Bluetooth and near-field communication (NFC) to communicate with various sensors, kiosks and other connective devices on Carnival MedallionClass ships and is touted to be waterproof, sunproof and sandproof. Unlike previous devices provided by the cruise company that included swipe cards, keys and other devices synced to individual ships' services, OceaMedallion connects to everything from the passenger's cabin door to all the games in the casino.

The MedallionClass component of the technology is an example of edge computing. Deployed sensors and mobile data collection devices on the ship perform their operations close to where the data orginates and interacts rather than sending every transaction all the way to a centralized database in the cloud. This reduces latency. Speeds up data analytics, enables a wider range of customized smart devices and reduces network traffic. All of this adds to making the passenger happier Security is paramount, too. Each interaction with the OceanMedallion uses a two-factor authentication process (customer ID and the OceanMedallion ID). One example of all of this is when a passenger checks in to board the ship. When they tap their OceanMedallion on an NFC reader at a kiosk it verifies them based on both the token and their ID number. This proves their identity and helps speed up the boarding process, getting the passenger to their cabin faster.

By incorporating technology like OceanMedallion, Carnival has gone a long way to eliminate friction in the passenger experience while minimizing the obtrusiveness of technology. This way, John Padgett, Chief Experience and Innovation Officer at Carnal says, "guest can be freed up to enjoy the experience more and consume more experiences." To enhance the passenger experience of even more of its guests, Carnival expects to deploy the OceanMedallion on six more ships in 2020.

Questions

1. Why did Carnival Cruise Line think the OceanMedallion would help increase their cruise sales?
2. What was the services component of the OceanMedallion called and what technologies did it us?
3. How many Carnival cruise ships is the OceanMedallion used?
4. What services does the OceanMedallion Class offer to passengers?
5. What benefits do passengers enjoy from using an OceanMedallion?

Sources: Compiled from Horowitz (2019), Hubbell (2019), Saltzman (2019), and princess.com.

IT Toolbox

Conducting a Technology Assessment

If you or your company are thinking of retiring any of your current network equipment or planning to buy new hardware or software sometime soon, you need to use a step-by-step approach to conduct a technology assessment.

Step 1.   Analyze your workflow. The first thing that needs to be done is understand how you or others work with the technology. Look at workflow and identify bottlenecks, inefficiencies, or recurring concerns about current workflows. Find out what an ideal workflow would look like.

Step 2.   Inventory and Review Existing Technology. Before you buy anything new, look at what you have. What technology do you have? How is the technology used? What are the strengths and weaknesses of the hardware and software you already have? How does the technology impact the workflow problems that you identified in Step 1.

Step 3. Generate Recommendations. Conduct a focus group to find out which technologies should be updated or replaced. Identify the business processes that will benefit from these changes.

Step 4.   Research—Research—Research. Go online and talk to your IT professionals and technology vendors about products that meet your needs. Check online forums and product reviews.

Step 5. Repeat as Necessary. A technology assessment is not a one-off event. Business needs and technology products change. Make sure that you regularly conduct a technology assessment to gauge where the company is and whether it is using the best technology to keep it on track to meet its goals.

Adapted from: Red Key Solutions (2019).

References

Aginam, E. "MTN, Ericsson Begin First 5G Customer Trial Deployment in South Africa." *Vanguard*, November 16, 2018.

AndroidGuys. "AT&T 5G: Where Is It Available and Which Phones Offer Support? *AndroidGuys*, September 3, 2019.

Bode, K. "Why Feds Can't Block California's Net Neutrality Bill." *The Verge*, October 2, 2018.

Bode, K. "Ajit Pai Whines About the Numerous State-Level Net Neutrality Laws He Just Helped Create." *Techdirt*, October 23, 2019.

Bouma, L. "AT&T Plans to offer True 5G Internet Nationwide by the First Half of 2020." *Cord Cutters News*, August 8, 2019.

BusinessTech. "MTN and Ericsson Begin 5G Customer Trial in South Africa." *BusinessTech*, November 15, 2018.

CBS News. "Net neutrality court battle pits tech firms, states against fed." *CBS News,* February 1, 2019, accessed at https://www.cbsnews.com/news/net-neutrality-court-battle-pits-tech-firms-states-against-feds/ Accessed on July 6, 2020.

Cisco. "Cisco Visual Networking Index: Global Mobile Data Traffic Forecast Update, 2017–2022." *Cisco*, February 18, 2019.

City of Cedar Park. "AMI Digital Water Meters Information." 2019. https://www.cedarparktexas.gov/departments/water-utility-billing/ami-smart-meters-information

Clark, M. "Salvation Army Adds NFC Chips to Red Kettles." *NFC World*, November 5, 2019

Clement, J. "Global Mobile Data Traffic from 2017 to 2022." *Statista*, August 9, 2019a.

Convergent. "Target Field Hits a Fan Experience Home Run with New, High-Quality Audio Network." November 29, 2018.

Cook, S. "60+ IoT Statistics and Facts." *Comparitech*, April 25, 2019.

Daley, D. "Target Field Audio Gets a Boost with Dante Networking." *SVG News*, December 20, 2018.

Fisher, T. "How Are 4G and 5G Different?" *Lifewire*, November 9, 2019a.

Fisher, T. "Verizon 5G: When and Where You Can Get It." *Lifewire*, November 11, 2019b.

Fitzgerald, K. "Salvation Army Adds a Contactless Payment Tags to Kettles Nationwide." *PaymentsSource,* November 4, 2019.

Gartner. "Gartner Identifies Top 10 Strategic IoT Technologies and Trends." November 7, 2018.

Genardo, K. "Cedar Park Streamlines Customer Communication through Sensus Solutions." *Bloomberg*, January 17, 2019.

Horowitz, B. "Carnival Looks to Keep Passengers Happier at Sea with the IoT." *PC Magazine, September* 13, 2019.

Hubbell, R. "Princess Cruises MedallionClass Experience Review." *Sugar and Soul*, April 26, 2019.

IoT Analytics. "IoT Platforms End User Satisfction Report 2019". https://iot-analytics.com/product/iot-platforms-end-user-satisfaction-report-2019/ Accessed on July 6, 2020.

Lueth, K. "40+ Emerging IoT Technologies You Should Have on Your Radar." *IoT Analytics*, September 3, 2019. https://iot-analytics.com/40-emerging-iot-technologies-you-should-have-on-your-radar/ Accessed on: February 27, 2020.

Lueth, K. "State of the IoT 2018: Number of IoT Devices Now at 7B – Market Accelerating." *IOT Analytics*, August 8, 2018.

Kamau, P. "Applications of Computer Networks." *TurboFuture*, February 7, 2019.

Mack, Z. "Net Neutrality was Repealed a Year Ago – What's Happened Since? *The Verge*, July 9, 2019.

Moran, J. "Salvation Army's Red Kettle Campaign Goes Digital." *The Center Square, November* 12, 2019.

Morton, H. "Net Neutrality 2019 Legislation." *NCSL*, December 21, 2019.

Nick, G. "How Many IoT Devices Are There?" *Techjury*, February 19, 2019. https://www.ncsl.org/research/telecommunications-and-information-technology/net-neutrality-2019-legislation.aspx Accessed on July 6, 2020.

O'Dea, S. "Countries with the fastest average mobile internet speed 2020." *Statista*, November 9, 2020.

Pinney, D. "Water Utilities Continue to Raise the Bar on How They Use Data." *Water Finance and Management*, January 3, 2019.

PSW Staff. "Tech Focus: Dante Domain Manager Deployed at Target Field." *ProSoundWeb*, May 20, 2019.

Reardon, M. "Net Neutrality Court Ruling: States Can Set Own Rules." *C/Net*, October 1, 2019.

Red Key Solutions. "Steps in Conducting a Technology Assessment." *Red Key Solutions IT Blog*, May 14, 2019.

Reed, E. "What Is Net Neutrality and Why Is It Important in 2019?" *The Street*, December 27, 2018.

Rogers, K. "Which States Have Net Neutrality Laws?" *Vice*, 2018.

Saltzman, D. "Princess Medallion-Class Cruise Ships." *Cruise Critic*, October 10, 2019.

Sensus. "Texas Water Provider Improves Customer Communication with Sensus." 2019.

Sharma, R. "MTN SA, Ericsson Run South Africa's First 5G Customer Trial." *The Fast Mode*, January 2019.

Swiech, P. "Needs Increasing in McLean County, Salvation Army Announces Red Kettle Goal." *Pentagraph*, November 14, 2019.

Ulloa, J. "California Enacts Strongest Net Neutrality Protections in the Nation – and the Trump Administration Sues." *Los Angeles Times*, September 30, 2018.

Wagner, P. "5G Health Risks: The War Between Technology and Human Beings." *Gaia*, May 14, 2019.

Water Finance and Management Staff. "City of Cedar Park, Texas, enhances customer communications with Sensus AMI." *Water Finance and Management*, January 21, 2019a.

Water Finance and Management Staff. "'Intelligent water' could save U.S. water utilities $17.6 billion." June 19, 2019b.

Welch, C. "Apple's iPhone 11 Doesn't Have 5G Because 5G Isn't Ready For The iPhone." *The Verge*, September 12, 2019.

Zacks Equity Research. "Ericsson to Modernize MTN South Africa's Network for 5G Era." *Yahoo! Finance*, November 24, 2019.

Data Privacy and Cyber Security

Case 5.1 Opening Case

olexanderkozak/Adobe Stock

Yeamake/Adobe Stock

Marzky Ragsac Jr./Adobe Stock

Yahoo Is Fined $117.5 Million for Worst Data Hacks in History

Thanks to a recent class-action lawsuit settlement, you might be entitled to two years of free credit monitoring services by AllClear ID or up to $358.80 cash. If you had a Yahoo account between January 1, 2012 and December 31, 2016, and are a resident of the United States or Israel you can file a claim at www.yahoodatabreachsettlement.com by July 20, 2020 to compensate you for your losses. The class-action lawsuit was brought against Yahoo because of not just one, but two of the largest known data breaches in history. The settlement award was three years in the making.

It wasn't until Fall 2016 that Yahoo alerted its users and the public to a huge data breach of its users' personal information that had occurred 2–3 years earlier. On September 22, 2016, Yahoo publicly disclosed that over 1 billion Yahoo account records had been stolen some time in 2014. In December 2016 Yahoo announced another hack dating back to 2013, which they said affected 1 billion user records. The impact of the second hack was subsequently updated in an October 2017 news release when Yahoo revealed that 3 billion Yahoo accounts had actually been breached, making it the largest data breach in history. The delay in reporting is partly because Yahoo itself did not know of the breach until shortly before releasing these statements to the public. The information leaked in the attacks included e-mail accounts, telephone numbers, street addresses, unencrypted security questions and answers, but no financial information.

To further compound the problem for Yahoo, who was in negotiations with mega-corporation Verizon to acquire Yahoo for $4.83 billion, Verizon said that the initial announcement could have a negative impact on their purchasing decision. The December 2016 release caused Verizon to further review the financial implications of the two breaches and reduce its offer to acquire Yahoo by $350 million.

The 2013 breach was conducted by an unknown unauthorized third party. The information stolen in the 2014 attack was sold by a "state-sponsored actor" on the Dark Web for 3 Bitcoins (approx. $1,900). The actor, who used the name "Peace", is of Russian origin and attempted to sell data from 200 million Yahoo users online. Yahoo urged all its users to change their passwords and security questions and to review their accounts for suspicious activity. To date, little information has been released on the 2013 breach, but more is known about the incident that occurred in 2014.

How the Second Attack Was Carried Out

The data theft was similar to the way in which a typical online attack of a database is carried out. The protections used for database containing the login and personal information were insufficient to protect against the advanced methods used by the hackers. In this case, the encryption method employed in the database was broken by the hacker. Additionally, cybercrime analyst Vitali Kremez maintains that the hacker stole the information from Yahoo slowly and methodically so as to not draw attention to the breach taking place.

Since the breach was not immediately detected, the hacker had plenty of time to leverage the information in a financially, personally, or politically beneficial manner. It is not clear if the seller is the original hacker.

Impact of the Data Breach

Since the breaches were so devastating and far reaching to most of Yahoo's customer base, Verizon is having second thoughts about the acquisition. Craig Silliman, general counsel to Verizon, said Verizon has "a reasonable basis" to believe that the data breach will have a significant impact on the deal proceedings and the likelihood that it will happen (Fiegerman, 2016). He furthers to explain that Yahoo will have to convince Verizon that the breach will not affect future processes in the company and that more security features have been and will be implemented. Also, the incidents could make the Yahoo deal worth about $200 million less than the $4.8 billion initially settled upon. In addition to the decreased value of Yahoo's core assets, the company's stock fell about 2% after the comments by Craig Silliman.

Justice Is Served

On March 17, 2017, the U.S. Department of Justice indicted two Russian Intelligence agents and two state-sponsored hackers, Alexsey Belan and Karim Baratov, for the theft of the Yahoo user data in 2014. Belan, one of the FBI's most notorious criminal hackers, had been previously indicted in two other cases. In the indictments it was revealed that the targets of the theft included Russian journalists, United States and Russian government officials, military personnel, and private-sector employees of financial, transportation, and other companies. The case against Yahoo was finally settled in October 2019 when Yahoo was ordered to pay $117.5 million dollars in restitution to its users. The settlement is pending final court approval set for April 2, 2020.

Questions

1. Why do you think Yahoo was targeted for these data breaches?

2. Why did Yahoo keep the breaches from the public eye? How did their nondisclosure affect Yahoo's relationship with its customers and partners?

3. In addition to the data theft, what else was damaged by this incident?

4. Were these cybersecurity incidents foreseeable? Were they avoidable?

5. Assuming that the CEO and CIO were forced to resign, what message does that send to senior management at Yahoo?

Sources: Compiled from Fiegerman (2016), Hackett (2016a), Kan (2016), Lee (2016), Matwyshyn and Bhargava (2016), Murgia (2016), Sterling (2015), Balakrishnan (2017), Clement (2019), Colby (2019), and Tyko (2019).

 DID YOU KNOW?

*Almost everyone has had an e-mail account hacked through their password. To check to see if you're one of the few whose account hasn't been compromised you can enter your e-mail address at **https://haveibeenpwned.com/**. If you're one of the many who have had an account compromised, you'll be able to review the list of breaches.*

Introduction

In today's interconnected world, it is essential that the data and networks discussed in Chapters 3 and 4 be protected against unauthorized access, tampering, and destruction. Our opening case is just one example of the blatant disregard that some companies can have for an individual's data privacy and the inexcusable behavior of the hackers who stole the data for fame or profit. Several of today's toughest data privacy and security challenges did not even exist at the start of this decade. The latest technologies such as social, mobile, and the cloud are powerful forces that can compromise the privacy of personal information and circumvent the security measures that need to be taken to protect it. While businesses, governments, and users greatly benefit from their use, these technologies can have harmful effects—not all of which are obvious yet.

As a result, organizations need to have a deeper understanding of how and when cyberattacks can occur and combine it with business context, valuation techniques, and financial quantification to establish the true costs of their losses. Applying this more accurate knowledge of potential business impacts, leaders can be much more effective in managing and controlling cyber risk and improve their ability to recover from a cyberattack.

Are you and your company prepared to deal effectively with privacy issues and corporate responsibilities that social, mobile, big data, and analytics technology create in business? Anecdotal research suggests the answer is "No"! Many often don't even recognize when privacy issues are present. If people and companies can't recognize the issues, then it is hard to imagine how they can act responsibly to combat them.

In this chapter you will learn about several IT privacy concerns and how companies and governments are dealing with them. These issues will be examined within the context of regulations, research findings, and case examples. Of course, there are no easy answers to the demise of privacy, piracy, and theft of intellectual property. There are no easy fixes, clear-cut judgments or solutions. As informed users, you need to be able to recognize privacy issues when they arise and know the types of security measures and risk management initiatives that need to be put in place to protect employees, customers, and stakeholders.

You will also learn about cybersecurity terminology, the rising number of data breaches, sources of cyberthreats, types of damage caused by cybercriminals' aggressive tactics, and their impacts on organizations. Finally, you will learn how organizations can defend against cyberattacks, correctly assess the damage they cause, and ensure that risk management initiatives needed for business continuity are implemented and regulatory requirements met.

5.1 Data Privacy Concerns and Regulations

LO5.1 Describe *the four main data privacy concerns, define the privacy paradox, and describe how data privacy regulations are protecting consumers.*

Data privacy is the right to self-determine what information about you is made accessible, to whom, when, and for what use or purpose.

Data privacy is becoming a priority for individuals, organizations, and governments around the globe. Data privacy issues can develop around data collected from many sources, including health-care records, driver's licenses, vehicle citations, criminal investigations, transactions with financial institutions, biological information (such as DNA), and residence and geographic records. A single large organization may possess personal information of millions of customers. To ensure it maintains a good reputation, the company must make sure that their customer information stays as safe and protected as possible.

Data privacy ensures that individuals, groups, and companies have freedom of choice and control over the personal information that companies collect about them, including what they do or do not want shared with or used by others and centers around the following four main concerns:

1. How data are **shared** with third parties
2. How data are **collected** and stored
3. How data are **used**
4. How data are **regulated**

The amount of shared personal information is a decision that individuals continuously make. This is an important concept since online content can hang around for an entire lifetime. Private content that uninhibited teenagers with bad judgment posted or sent cannot be made to disappear when they apply for jobs requiring security clearance or intense background checks or run for public office. A poor decision about the kind of information that a person shares can come back to haunt them later in life.

Confused, Concerned, and Out of Control

In a 2019 national privacy survey (Auxier et al., 2019), of 4,272 U.S. adults, Pew Research (www.pewresearch.org) reported that the majority of Americans are deeply concerned about data privacy. For example, the majority do not think it is possible to go through daily life without being tracked by companies and government agencies, that online data collection poses more risks than benefits, and they feel they have little or no control over how companies and government uses their personal data ranging from their physical location to social media posts. In addition, the greater majority have little or no confidence that companies will admit mistakes and take responsibility if they misuse or compromise their personal information. This same level of lack of confidence was reported when asked if they thought companies were using their personal information in ways they were comfortable with **(Figure 5.1)**.

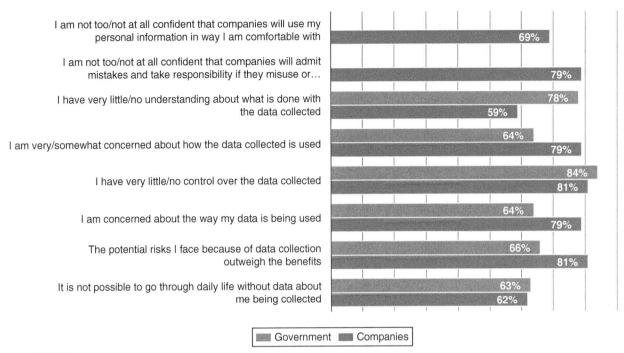

FIGURE 5.1 Americans are concerned, confused, and feel out of control about the collection of their personal information.

Despite this widespread concern for data privacy, few consumers are actually taking steps to share less information or delete data being collected about them online. For example, many acknowledged they pay little or no attention to privacy policies and terms of service. While almost all said they had been asked to approve a privacy policy only one in five said they *always* or often read a company's privacy policy before agreeing to it. Slightly more than one-third said they *sometimes* read it and about the same percentage said they *never* read a company's privacy policy (**Figure 5.2**). Of those who read the company's private policy, only one in five read it all the way through before agreeing to its terms.

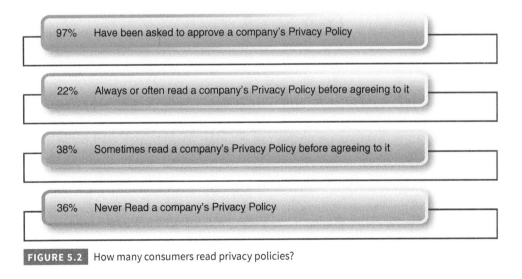

FIGURE 5.2 How many consumers read privacy policies?

Although many online users don't even take the time to read a privacy policy, many continue to disclose highly personal details of their everyday lives, including incriminating or illegal content, in their profiles or posts. For example, despite being at the heart of privacy scandals, in a single day Facebook has more than one billion users who share photos and details about their personal lives and users send nearly 32 million messages and upload almost 300 hours of videos to YouTube every minute. Online shopping is also on the increase, as reflected by online mega-shopping site Amazon that reported total assets of $199.1 billion for the quarter ending September 30, 2019—a 38.56% increase over 2018.

The Privacy Paradox

Privacy paradox is the disconnect between how important people say their online privacy is versus how they actually behave in real life.

The inconsistency between the competing demands to use IT and have an online presence, while guarding against potential threats to personal safety and privacy resulting from misuse of personal information is known as the **privacy paradox**. The privacy paradox occurs when social media users and online consumers are concerned about privacy, but their behaviors contradict these concerns to an extreme degree.

It can be reasoned that the privacy paradox can be attributed to the fact that 78% of people still don't really understand how their personal information is being collected and used by companies and a slightly lower percentage for information being collected and used by the government (see **Figure 5.1**). It can also be argued that the privacy paradox may be accounted for by the fact that social sites have become so embedded in the social lives of users that they disclose information about themselves even though it has become common knowledge that these sites do not provide adequate privacy controls and are willing to accept the consequences.

Privacy Rights Are Civil Rights

Data collection and analytics are increasingly vital to operating a business and are becoming integral to the way businesses deliver products and services to their customers. As a result, everything that is done online generates data much of which is tracked. Tracked data is fed into powerful algorithms to deliver personalized ads and other services that appear on websites that we visit. While these are sometimes beneficial, these same algorithms can be used to facilitate discrimination in employment, housing lending, e-commerce, and voting.

Consider for example, predictive hiring algorithms that reveal patterns of inequity based on past hiring decisions and past employment evaluations, or targeted discriminatory advertisements based on Facebook postings that that lead to the exclusion of applicants based on protected characteristics like race, gender, and sexuality. In retail and lending a UC Berkeley study found that online mortgage lenders were systematically charging Black and Latino borrowers more for loans, and companies like Home Depot and Staples were charging people higher prices for the same products in different locations basing their online pricing on where a buyer lived. And, we are all familiar with the online foreign interventions that occurred in the 2016 election designed to sway public opinion in favor of one candidate over the other.

All these behaviors disregard the civil-rights protections awarded to protect these types of discrimination including the Civil Rights Act of 1964, the Voting Rights Act of 1965, and the Fair Housing Act of 1968.

U.S. Consumer Protection Data Privacy Regulations

Breach of privacy is the loss of, unauthorized access to, or disclosure of, personal information.

Privacy is a business-critical discipline for many organizations, enforced by multiple regulations. To protect the privacy rights and civil rights of consumers the governments around the world have created regulations and enacted laws to ensure that data are collected, shared, and used only for the purpose for which the data were made available in the first place (**Figure 5.3**). Any unauthorized disclosure of personal information to third parties is normally considered a **breach of privacy**.

Global Government Regulations for Protection of PII*

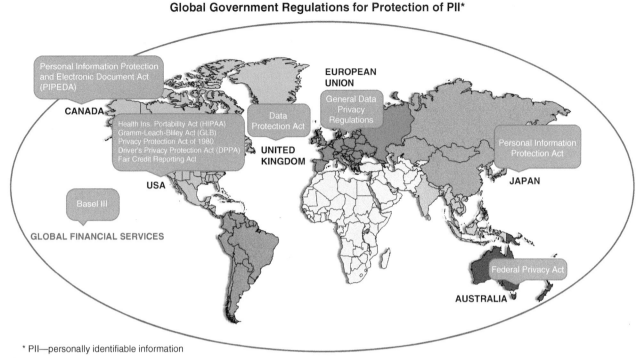

* PII—personally identifiable information

FIGURE 5.3 Global government regulations of PII.

In the United States, at the federal level, the power to enforce data protection regulations and protect data privacy rests with the U.S. Federal Trade Commission (FTC). U.S. Federal consumer protection data privacy regulations currently in place include those that protect data related to health care, finance, government, licenses, and credit:

- **Health Insurance Portability and Accountability Act (HIPAA)** protects the privacy of medical records and other personally identifiable healthcare information unless it's to a person who needs the information because they are involved in the person's care, processing payment for care, or the information is necessary to facilitate health-care operations.

- **Gramm-Leach-Bliley Act** requires financial institutions that offer consumers financial products such as loans, financial or investment advice, or insurance to explain their information-sharing practices to their customers and to safeguard sensitive data.

- **Privacy Protection Act of 1980** makes it unlawful for a government officer or employee, in connection with the investigation or prosecution of a criminal offense, to search for or seize any work product materials possessed by a person reasonably believed to have a purpose to disseminate to the public a newspaper, book, broadcast, or other similar form of publication, in or affecting interstate or foreign commerce.

- **Driver's Privacy Protection Act (DPPA)** protects the personally identifiable information of licensed drivers from improper use or disclosure.

- **Fair Credit Reporting Act** governs how a credit reporting agency can collect, access, use, and share credit information to ensure the accuracy, fairness, and privacy of the information in consumer credit bureau files.

U.S. State-Level Privacy Laws

Although the FTC has a broad level of authority over the enforcement of data protection regulations, there is no federal data privacy law or central data protection authority responsible for compliance with those regulations. Instead, most regulation is at the state level and the state attorneys general play a key role in enforcement. The number of state-level data privacy laws enacted across the United States is growing. All 50 U.S. states have adopted data breach notification laws. At least 35 states and Puerto Rico have data disposal laws and 25 states have enacted data privacy laws (Brooks, 2019).

The most recent and noteworthy of these is the **California Consumer Privacy Act** (CCPA) that became effective on January 1, 2020 (Germain, 2020). It is an updated version of a less effective act that was passed by California State Legislature on June 28, 2018 and grants California residents much more powerful new privacy protections, some of which could be extended to consumers across the United States. The CCPA offers several basic consumer privacy rights including the right to know what personal information is being collected; the right to access that data; the right to know who it's being sold to; and the right to opt out of those data sales. Most importantly, the CCPA also guarantees California residents the right to delete the data that companies have collected about them. Now, instead of companies like Google and Facebook being able to say no to consumers who asked that their data be deleted or charge for it, the CCPA provides individuals with the legal right to demand that companies delete their data or face the consequences of the new privacy act. If you live in California, be sure to look for the new "Do Not Sell My Personal Information" opt-out link that the CCPA now requires companies place on their Web pages if they have a policy of selling customer data.

European Union's General Data Protection Rules (GDPR)

Recently, the European Union's **General Data Protection Rules (GDPR)** spearheaded a global movement of evolving privacy and data protection laws with very strict requirements. The GDPR (**https://gdpr-info.eu/**) is an EU-wide consumer Bill of Rights enacted in May 2018 that empowers EU consumers by forcing retailers, marketers, and others to explicitly tell consumers how they are collecting, using, and storing consumers' personal data. In doing so, it guarantees data protection safeguards are built into products and services from the earliest state of development, providing "data protection by design" in new products and technologies. The GDPR unifies data protection laws across all 28 member nations of the EU plus Ireland, Lichtenstein, Norway, and Switzerland to give users more rights and control over information that can be pieced together to identify an individual, including location and biometric data, IP addresses, and any other information shared online.

By giving individuals more control over their personal information and the opportunity to interact safely with online websites the new law reins in technology giants and provides a safe but strict framework for conducting business online (Fogg, 2019). The GDPR applies not only to businesses that operate within the EU but also to businesses all over the world that target EU consumer data and protects the data of all EU citizens, regardless of whether they currently live in the EU.

Companies that violate the GDPR face a maximum fine of $23 million (€20 million) or 4% of their annual global turnover, whichever is larger. **IT at Work 5.1** describes how Google was fined $56.8 million (€50 million) for not fully informing users how their data would be used. Multiple countries outside the EU are being inspired by the GDPR principles to implement similar regulations of their own.

IT at Work 5.1

Google Is Fined $56.8 Million for Violating GDPR

Just one week after the GDPR went into effect, France's privacy regulator, the National Data Protection Commission (CNIL) imposed an unprecedented fine of $56.8 million (€50 million) on Google for disregarding the essential GDPR principles of transparency, information, and consent. The fine was one of the highest profile regulatory actions taken under the new GDPR rules. Specifically, Google was accused of forcing users to agree to new privacy policies and not having the legal basis to process user data for personalized advertisements. CNIL said the lack of transparency violation stemmed from Google users not being able to easily tell all the information Google collects about them when signing up for its services.

The French ruling focused on how easy to find and how complete the consumer-consent information provided by Google was. It found that full information about data processing purposes and data storage time was not all presented in the same place, but instead required as many as five or six clicks. It also said that some boxes giving consent were pre-checked violating the law.

Under the old European privacy rules, the maximum fine that could be levied on an offending company was $170,500 (€150,000). When the GDPR went into effect on May 25, 2018 national privacy regulators were given the power to fine companies as much as 4% of their global annual sales for the most serious violations. In using its powers to levy the hefty penalty for the first time, the French authorities said they felt the fine was "justified by the severity of the infringements observed regarding the essential principles." Google had come under scrutiny many times under the old rules before the new GDPR rules came into effect but had never been handed a fine anywhere near as high as the current one.

Under GDPR rules, Google cannot appeal the fine until it has handed over the $56.8 million (€50 million). Still, Google should consider itself lucky given that the company made $33.74 billion in the last quarter of 2018. If they had been fined the allowable maximum of 4% of its annual global turnover, the fine could have been more than $1 billion!

Sources: Compiled from Enright (2018), Bloomberg News (2019), Bondini (2019), Grothaus (2019), Porter (2019), and Schechner (2019).

The EU-U.S. Privacy Shield

Under the GDPR rules the EU does not allow the transfer of data on its citizens outside of the country unless the country is deemed to have adequate data privacy laws. The EU does not consider the data privacy laws currently in place in the United States to be adequate, so U.S. businesses must work around this requirement by adhering to the EU-U.S. Privacy Shield. A similar mechanism is available between Switzerland and the United States.

The EU-U.S. and Swiss-U.S. Privacy Shields are designed to provide companies on both sides of the Atlantic with a mechanism to comply with GDPR data protection requirements when transferring personal data from the European Union (EU) and Switzerland to the United States in support of transatlantic commerce. By becoming a conforming member of the privacy shields participating U.S. companies are considered to have adequate data protection to facilitate the transfer of EU data (Fugairon, 2019). At a recent meeting of the World Economic Forum (**https://www.weforum.org/**), Microsoft's CEO Satya Nadella voiced support for the GDPR and expressed the hope that the United States will take a similarly strict approach to protecting the privacy of its users' data (Dark Reading, 2019).

Public Lack of Understanding

As governments around the globe continue to work to protect the handling and privacy of their citizens' data by adopting more powerful laws, organizations are being required to reconsider how they collect, store, and process personal information. Unfortunately, these data privacy regulations and laws that have been put in place to protect consumers are generally not well understood by the general public. For instance, two-thirds of users surveyed in the 2019 Pew Research Report (Auxier et al., 2019) claimed they understood very little or nothing about the laws and regulations currently in place to protect their data privacy. Hopefully the information provided in this section has increased your awareness and understanding of them.

Questions

1. What are the four main concerns of data privacy?
2. Why is it important for you to know how your online data is handled?
3. What is the name of the phenomenon where users are concerned about data privacy, but their behaviors contradict these concerns?
4. Who has responsibility for data privacy laws at the U.S. federal level?
5. Name three U.S. consumer protection data privacy regulations.
6. What is the name of the new California data protection law?
7. Is an EU citizen who does not live in the EU protected under the GDPR?
8. Why is the United States not considered part of the GDPR?
9. What is the name of the mechanism that brings the United States under the jurisdiction of the GDPR?

5.2 | Extent and Cost of Cyberattacks and Cyber Threats

LO5.2 Identify *the extent and cost of cyberattacks and the 12 different types of intentional and unintentional cyberthreats.*

Cyber criminals use the Internet and private networks to hijack large numbers of records and systems including PCs, mobile devices, servers, and Internet of Thing (IoT) devices to spy on users, spam them, disrupt businesses, and steal identities. It is important to protect against these attacks because of the unprecedented volume of sensitive data the government, military, corporations, financial institutions, and medical organizations are collecting, processing, and storing on computers and other devices. Much of this data includes personally identifiable information, intellectual property, financial data, medical records, and other sensitive information and would result in negative consequences to its owners if it were accessed by unauthorized persons.

Cyberattack is an actual attempt to expose, alter, disable, destroy, steal, or gain unauthorized access to a computer system, infrastructure, network, or any other smart device.

In the 2019 Pew Research Report (Auxier et al., 2019) 70% of the 4,272 adults surveyed felt their personal data is *less* secure than it was five years ago, with only 6% believing their data is *more* secure than it was in the past. In the digital economy, organizational data are typically available on demand 24/7 to enable companies to benefit from opportunities for productivity improvement and data sharing with customers, suppliers, and business partners. This concept of data on demand is an operational and competitive necessity for global companies, but unfortunately, it also opens the door for **cyberattacks** that use several different types of **cyber threats** to execute them.

Cyber threat is the method used to commit a cyberattack that seeks to damage data, steal sensitive data, or disrupt digital life in general.

Cyberattacks often include breaches in data privacy like the ones experienced by Yahoo in the opening case and unfortunately are becoming a common occurrence. **Table 5.1** lists the top five largest data breaches on record as of July 2019.

TABLE 5.1 Top Five Largest Data Breaches

Rank	Company	Records Exposed	Year	Cause
1.	Yahoo	3 billion	2013	Hacking
2.	First American Financial Corporation	885 million	2019	Poor Security
3.	Facebook	540 million	2019	Poor Security
4.	Yahoo	500 million	2014	Hacking
5.	Marriott	500 million	2018	Hacking

Source: CNBC (2019).

The obvious issue surrounding the Yahoo data breaches discussed in the opening case is a lack of sophisticated **cyber security** measures. Simple username, password, and security questions simply were not enough to keep hackers at bay. UC Davis professor Hemant Bhargava notes that two-factor authentication (TFA) is successful in many other companies and that Yahoo should have followed suit (Matwyshyn & Bhargava, 2016). An example of TFA would be where a user is asked to enter information such as username and password, then a mobile app generates and sends a random number code for the user to enter before being granted access to his or her account. Both the Yahoo account and the mobile app are linked to a common, secure account. This method is exceptionally popular and useful since over 50% of Web users access the Web through their mobile phones. Unfortunately, many companies do not take adequate measures to secure personally identifiable information (PII). Failure to do so often results in cyberattacks such as those described in the following examples:

> **Cyber security** is the discipline dedicated to protecting information and systems used to process and store it from attack, damage, or unauthorized access.

- After detecting a network hack, credit card processing company Global Payments, Inc. spent 14 months investigating the resulting data breach that exposed 1.5 million U.S. debit and credit card accounts. Global's damages totaled $93 million. This loss consisted of $36 million in fraud losses and fines and $77 million for the investigation, remediation, credit monitoring, and identity theft insurance for affected consumers.
- Capitol One announced a data breach that put 100 million U.S. consumers and 6 million Canadian consumers at risk. The credit card company released a statement citing "unauthorized access by an outside individual" had occurred.
- Equifax, one of the three largest credit reporting agencies in the world, announced it had suffered a data breach of more than 148 million consumers' personal credit records.
- Federal Trade Commission alerted the public to a social security scam where a caller claiming to be from the Social Security Administration (SSA) informs you that there has been suspicious identity theft activity involving your SSN. You are then urged to purchase a prepaid debit card or other reloadable funds card and transfer all your money out of your bank accounts onto that card to keep the hackers from getting your money. At a later time, the caller calls again and asks for the card's account number and PIN to record it for safekeeping in your SSA record. Once they have that information, they drain the funds off the card and all your life savings are theirs!
- Just three weeks after Australia's Notifiable Data Breach (NDB) scheme went into effect the Office of the Australian Information Commissioner (OAIC) received 31 notifications of data breaches (Barbascgow, 2018).

Cyberattacks like these focus primarily on what companies are required to report publicly, that is, theft of personally identifiable information (PII), payment data, and personal health information (PHI). Consequently, the costs commonly associated with a cyberattack only take into consideration these more easily understood impacts. But these are not always an attacker's objective. Rarely brought into full view are theft of intellectual property (IP), espionage, data destruction, attacks on core operations, or attempts to disable critical infrastructure. These attacks can have a much more significant impact on organizations. But the damage they cause is not widely understood and is much more difficult to quantify.

In their Annual Data Breach Report, the Identify Theft Resource Center (ITRC) reported that data breaches increased by 17% in 2019. A total of 1,473 breaches were reported and 164,683,455 sensitive records were exposed (ITRC, 2020). The industry sectors that were most heavily targeted by the cyberattacks are shown in **Figure 5.4**. The types and extent of cyberattack experiences that companies suffered ranged from attempts to successful malicious attacks with organizational impacts such as data corruption, unrecoverable data, and tech-related business disruption with organizational impact as shown in **Figure 5.5** (CIO, 2019).

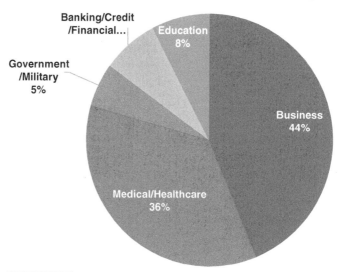

FIGURE 5.4 Number of 2019 U.S. data breaches by industry sector (adapted from ITRC, 2019).

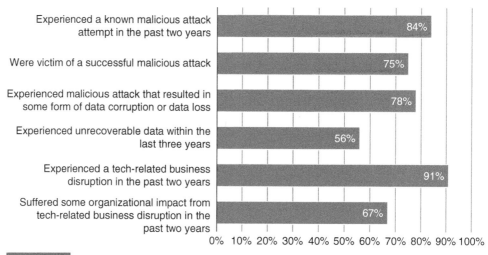

FIGURE 5.5 Percentage of companies across all industry sectors that have experienced cyberattacks (adapted from CIO, 2019).

Data breach is the *successful retrieval* of sensitive information by an unauthorized individual, group, or software system.

Vulnerability is a gap in IT security defenses of a network, system, or application that can be exploited by a cyber threat to gain unauthorized access.

attack vector is a path or means by which a computer criminal can gain access to a computer or network server in order to deliver a malicious outcome.

These **data breaches** can expose everything from usernames to passwords to Social Security numbers and are caused by the successful exploitation of **vulnerabilities** in information systems by a cyber threat (risk = cyber threat × vulnerability).

Vulnerabilities exist in networks, operating systems, applications, databases, mobile devices, and cloud environments. These vulnerabilities are referred to as **attack vectors** or entry points for malware, hackers, hacktivists, and organized crime. Mobile devices and apps, social media, and cloud services introduce even more attack vectors for malware, phishing, and hackers. As a result, new ways to commit cyberattacks are on the horizon.

Examples of vulnerabilities include lack of controls around people (user training, inadequate policies), process (inadequate separation of duties, poor process controls), or tools (lack of technical controls enforcement or monitoring). Vulnerabilities threaten the confidentiality, integrity, or availability (CIA) of data and information systems and leave organizations open to several types of unintentional and intentional cyber threats.

Unintentional Cyber Threats

Not all cyber threats are intentional. Unintentional, insider-originated security breaches can be the result of simple negligence, inattention, or lack of education on the part of administrators, employees, computer operators, and computer programmers. They can also be technology-related such as unintended software bugs or system configuration errors. The causes for these unintentional cyber threats fall into three major categories: human error, environmental hazards, and computer system failures.

- **Human error** can occur in the design of the hardware or information system. It can also occur during programming, testing, or data entry. Neglecting to change default passwords in applications or on systems or failing to manage patches creates security holes. Human error also includes untrained or unaware users falling prey to **social engineering** like phishing scams or ignoring security procedures. Human errors contribute to most **internal control (IC)** and information security problems.

- **Environmental hazards** include volcanoes, earthquakes, blizzards, floods, power failures or strong fluctuations, fires (the most common hazard), defective heating, ventilation and air-conditioning (HVAC) systems, explosions, radioactive fallout, and water-cooling-system failures. In addition to the primary damage, computer resources can be damaged by the side effects of a hazard, such as smoke and water. Such hazards may disrupt normal computer operations resulting in extended data inaccessibility and exorbitant restoration and recovery costs.

- **Computer systems failures** can occur as the result of poor manufacturing, defective materials, or poor maintenance. Unintentional malfunctions can also occur for other reasons, ranging from administrator inexperience to inadequate testing.

Intentional Cyber Threats

On the other hand, intentional security breaches are overt and direct actions designed to disrupt a system and include data theft such as inappropriate use of data (e.g., manipulating inputs); theft of computer time; theft of equipment and/or software; deliberate manipulation in handling, entering, programming, processing, or transferring data; sabotage; malicious damage to computer resources; destruction from malware and similar attacks; and miscellaneous computer abuses and Internet **fraud**. Twelve common cyber threats are described next.

Hacking   A common term used when a cyberattack occurs is that the system has been "hacked." **Hacking** is a very profitable industry that is a big part of underworld cybercrime, and a way for **hacktivists** to protest. Both the anonymity of the Internet and lack of international treaties provide hackers with a feeling of near invincibility because they face very low risk of capture and punishment.

In the Hacker culture there are three classes of Hackers, shown in **Table 5.2**.

Hacking is broadly defined as intentionally accessing a computer without authorization or exceeding authorized access. Various state and federal laws govern computer hacking.

Hacktivist is short for hackeractivist or someone who performs hacking to promote awareness for or otherwise support a social, political, economic, or other cause. Hacking an application, system, or network without authorization, regardless of motive, is a crime.

White hat Computer security specialist who breaks into protected systems and networks to test and assess their security.

Gray hat Person who may violate ethical standards or principles, but without the malicious intent ascribed to black hat hackers.

TABLE 5.2   Three Classes of Hackers

Type	Characteristics	Outcome
White hat	Computer security specialist who breaks into protected systems and networks to test and assess their security.	Use their skills to improve security by exposing vulnerabilities before malicious hackers (black hats) can detect and exploit them.
Black hat	Person who attempts to find computer security vulnerabilities and exploit them for personal financial gain or other malicious reasons.	Can inflict major damage on both individual computer users and large organizations by stealing personal financial information, compromising security of major systems, or shutting down or alerting the function of websites and networks.
Gray hat	Person who may violate ethical standards or principles, but without the malicious intent ascribed to black hat hackers.	May engage in practices that are less than ethical, but are often operating for the common good, e.g., exploits a security vulnerability to spread public awareness that the vulnerability exists.

An Inside Look at How the Hacking Industry Operates

Hacking is an industry with its own way of operating, a workforce, and support services. **Contract hackers** are available for hire or complete hack attacks can be bought. Hacking help desks provide 24/7 support—making sophisticated attacks easier to manage and execute. Hackers use social networks, underground forums, and the Deep Web to rate and promote services, share exploits, and recruit others. In certain forums and in the Deep Web, hackers can purchase the use of any number of services such as:

- Educational services
- Software platforms for building and distributing hacking tools and malware/ransomware
- Sale or purchase of stolen data ranging from items as simple as e-mail accounts to credit cards, PII, and corporate data.

Humans are easily hacked, making them and their social media posts high-risk attack vectors. For instance, it is often easy to get users to infect their corporate network or mobile devices by tricking them into downloading and installing backdoors.

Social Engineering

Experts believe that one of the greatest cybersecurity dangers over the next few years will involve a hacker's clever use of deception or manipulation of people's tendency to trust, be helpful, or simply follow their curiosity on social media. This phenomenon is called social engineering and it is difficult for even the most powerful IT security systems to defend against what can be made to appear to be authorized access.

Notorious cybercriminal Kevin Mitnick used social engineering as his primary method of gaining access to computer networks and discusses a wide range of social engineering attacks in his book, "The Art of Deception." In most social engineering exploits the criminal never comes face-to-face with the victim, but communicates via the phone or e-mail. **Phishing** is the oldest tools in a hacker's arsenal and still the most effective social-engineering technique. In a phishing attack, the attacker sends an e-mail to gain the victim's trust by evoking a sense of curiosity, urgency or fear, to steal confidential information. This is done by the attacker posing as a known person or legitimate organization, such as PayPal, a bank, credit card company, or other trusted source and asking the user to perform an action that would expose his or her computer to a cyber-threat or reveal credentials, personal, financial, or business-related private information. Phishing messages are either sent in mass campaigns or they are specifically targeted at a particular group of people or an individual person. The former requires no front work to gain context for the target but relies on sheer volume of messages (millions to tens of millions) to achieve returns.

The latter requires more effort to gather relevant context about the message target and is therefore sent out in far smaller batches but has a higher rate of return on both the number of opened messages and the payback per message for that effort. The latter approach is discussed later in this section.

Phishing messages include a request to respond with information of some kind or a link to a fraudulent website that often looks like an authentic site the user works with. When the user clicks the link to the site, he or she falls victim to a malware download, drive-by attack, or information skimming such as being asked for a credit card number, Social Security number, account number, or password.

Spear phishing is a type of phishing that targets select groups of people who have something in common. They can work at the same company, bank at the same financial institution, use a specific Internet provider, or attend the same church or university. The scam e-mails appear to be sent from organizations or people the potential victims normally receive e-mails from, making them even more deceptive.

Here is how spear phishing works:

1. Spear phishers gather information about people's activities, social groups, companies, and/or jobs from general media announcements, social media, or compromised accounts, applications that are poorly designed and leak information or they can steal it from websites, computers, or mobile devices they have compromised, and then use that information to customize messages.

2. Then they send the customized e-mails to targeted victims, creating some sort of pretext requiring the user to act or respond. These can be threats of account closure, loss of access or privilege, loss of funds or additional charges, legal actions impact to friends or family members, and so on. With the background information gained the message creates a very legitimate-sounding and compelling explanation as to why they need your personal data.

3. Finally, the victims are asked to click on a link inside the e-mail that takes them to a phony but realistic-looking website, where they are asked to provide passwords, account numbers, user IDs, access codes, PINs, and so on.

When spear phishing targets are executives or persons of significant wealth, power, influence, or control the activity is known as "whaling."

Malware refers to various levels of intrusive or malicious software that can run undetected in the background on an IS or personal computer. Less intrusive malware has more nuisance value than malicious intent. More hostile malware is specifically designed to disrupt computer or mobile operations, gather sensitive information, and gain access to private computer systems.

Today's hostile malware is often designed for long-term control of infected machines. Malware can attach itself to other software programs and replicate itself across systems or hide in useful apps. Advanced malware sets up outbound communication channels in order to upload stolen data, download payloads, or do reconnaissance. A malware's **payload** is code that is dropped on the system that performs any or all the following functions: facilitates the infection or communicates with the command and control server or downloads more code. In doing so, the payload carries out the purpose of the malware. The payload could cause damage that is visible or operate in stealth mode to remain undetected.

Types of intrusive, but not necessarily, malicious software include:

- *Cookie*—a small piece of data sent from a website and stored in a user's Web browser while the user is browsing a website. Each cookie can be stored in a small individual file or all cookies from one source, such as those used by Firefox, are stored in a single file. The purpose of a cookie is to deliver personalized service such as storing passwords and User ID for repeated use. While cookies are not technically malicious, it is what sites do with them that determines whether they are harmless. There is a concern that cookies can be privacy risks if they are used to track a user and they use valuable computer resources that can slow down a computer's efficiency.

- *Spamware*—software that enables attackers to search, sort, and compile a list of e-mail addresses, generate random addresses, insert fake headers into message, and use multiple mail servers simultaneously to broadcast unsolicited messages to unsuspecting recipients.

- *Adware*—software that embeds advertisements in the application. It is considered a legitimate alternative offered to consumers who do not wish to pay for software.

- *Spyware*—tracking software that is not designed to intentionally damage or disable a system. For example, an employer may install spyware on corporate laptops to monitor employee browsing activities, or an advertiser might use cookies to track what Web pages a user visits in order to target advertising in a marketing campaign.

Types of hostile malware include:

- *Zero-Day*—the most dangerous type of malware and the fastest growing cyber threat. According to a Q3 2019 Internet Security Report put out by WatchGuard, a global leader in network security and intelligence **zero-day** malware accounts for almost 50% of all malware attacks (Warfield, 2019). Zero-day exploits prey upon system vulnerabilities that an attacker finds, but that the organization hasn't yet discovered. In a zero-day exploit, organizations have no time to react increasing the likelihood of its success. The malicious malware takes advantage of the vulnerability to cause extensive damage to networks, apps, individual computers, or enable data breaches. Many of these attacks come in through e-mail or the Internet in suspicious e-mails or attachments. In most cases, once the vulnerability is exposed by the zero-day exploit a patch can fix the problem, but the damage is done. A zero-day exploit can result in severe consequences to organizations of all types and sizes.

- *Backdoor*—also a difficult to detect malicious computer program used to provide an attacker with unauthorized remote access to a compromised PC by exploiting security vulnerabilities and works in the background hidden from the user.

- *Rootkit*—a set of software tools that enables an attacker to gain control of a computer system without being detected.

- *Boot Record Infector*—attaches itself to the master boot record on a hard disk where it's loaded into memory when the system is started and can replicate itself to other drives or computers.

- *File Infector*—attaches itself to executable code (.exe files) and is installed once the code is opened.

- *Keylogger*—a piece of software or hardware that logs every key pressed on a computer keyboard. It can capture personal messages, passwords, credit card numbers, and anything that is typed.

- *Virus*—infects apps like Microsoft Word where it executes instructions once opened before transferring back control to the app.

- *Worm*—doesn't attach itself to a host, like a virus, but these self-contained programs can replicate themselves across computers and networks.

- *Trojan*—hides in a useful program to infect the victim's system. Trojans don't self-replicate but can be used to establish backdoors that are explored by attackers.

- *Remote access trojans (RATS)*—a form of Trojan horse that creates an unprotected backdoor into a system through which a hacker can remotely control that system. As the name implies, a backdoor provides easy access to a system, computer, or account by creating the access that may or may not require authentication. Storm worm, which is spread via **spam**, is a backdoor trojan embedded inside over 25 million computers. Storm's combined power has been compared to the processing might of a supercomputer. Storm-organized attacks can cripple any website.

Most viruses, worms, and trojans are activated when an attachment is opened, or a link is clicked. But when features are automated, they may trigger malware automatically. For example:

- If an e-mail client, such as Microsoft Outlook or Gmail, is set to allow scripting, then virus infection occurs by simply opening a message or attachment.

- Viewing e-mail messages in HTML, instead of in plain text, can trigger virus infections.

Malware Assaults Are Part of Everyday Operations

IT security researchers discover almost one million malicious programs every day and malware attacks are becoming more prevalent. In a recent report WatchGuard reported that malware attacks had increased 30% from Q2 to Q3 2019 (Warfield, 2019).

Malware creators often use social engineering to maximize the effective distribution of their creations. For example, the *ILoveYou* worm, used social engineering to entice people to open malware-infected e-mail messages. It successfully attacked tens of millions of Windows-based computers when it was sent as an e-mail attachment with the subject line: ILOVEYOU. Within nine days, the worm had spread worldwide, crippling networks, destroying files, and causing an estimated $5.5 billion in damages.

Botnets

When you string together several computers that are infected with malware you have a **botnet**. The term botnet is derived from the words ro**bot** and **net**work. Cyber criminals use trojan viruses to breach the security of several user computers, take control of each computer and organize all of the infected machines into a network of "bots" they can remotely control for malicious purposes. Botnets are typically used to send spam and phishing e-mails and launch DDoS attacks. Botnets are extremely dangerous because they scan for and compromise other computers, which then can be used for every type of crime and attack against computers, servers, and networks.

Ransomware is designed to block access to a computer system until a sum of money has been paid. The use of ransomware began on a fairly small scale, targeting individual users, but the ransomware cyberthreat is growing and attacks have become large scale. Now, some executives fear entire companies will be shut down by ransomware until they pay up, or risk losing all their data.

Ransomware works by first infiltrating a computer with malware and then encrypting all the files on the disk. The malware used to encrypt files can be difficult to defend against, and the encryption in most cases can't be broken. Then, the user is presented with a limited time offer: Lose all your data or send money with the promise the data will be unlocked. The fee typically varies from a few dollars to hundreds of dollars and often must be transmitted in Bitcoin. One hospital in Los Angeles, whose electronic medical record system was locked out for 10 days, was forced to pay cyber attackers 40 Bitcoins to get its system unlocked when law enforcement and computer experts were unable to help in restoring the hospital's data files.

Computer security experts have theorized that this type of attack has a higher rate of success versus other cybercrime activity that has become more difficult. The best insurance against ransomware is to have offline or segregated backups of data.

Cryptojacking is a way that cybercriminals can make money with minimal effort. It is a ransomware-like scheme to use other people's devices without their consent or knowledge to secretly syphon off cryptocurrency at the victim's expense. By getting the victim to click on a malicious link in an e-mail that loads a few lines of code on their computer or by infecting a website or online ad with JavaScript code that auto-executes once loaded in the victim's browser, the cryptojacker hijacks the victim's computer and gets away with the cryptocurrency tokens. The victim then must bear the cost of the computations and electricity that was expended to get the tokens.

SQL Injection is one of the most dangerous vulnerabilities of a network app since attackers can use SQL injection to bypass application security measures. The intent is to execute SQL code inside an app or Web page for personal gain or simply to be destructive. By inserting malicious code into SQL statements, an attacker can manipulate an SQL query and force the query to return different data than was intended by the authorized user. For example, when a website requires a user to login with a username and password on a Web form, an attacker intercepts the request and inserts an SQL statement that runs on the database undetected changing any subsequent query results.

Man-in-the-middle (MitM) attacks are on the rise. They occur when cyber criminals insert themselves between two-parties in a transaction with the intention of stealing data. One common MitM point of entry is an unsecured public Wi-Fi. Once malware has breached a system, the attacker can install software to process the victim's information. **Figure 5.6** shows the three common MitM attacks:

Session Hijacking

- The attacker hijacks a session between the victim and a trusted network server.

IP Spoofing

- The attacker convinces the victim's computer system that it is communicating with a trusted, known entity to provide the attacker with system access.

Replay

- The attacker intercepts messages and saves them with the intention of sending them later impersonating one of the trusted message participants.

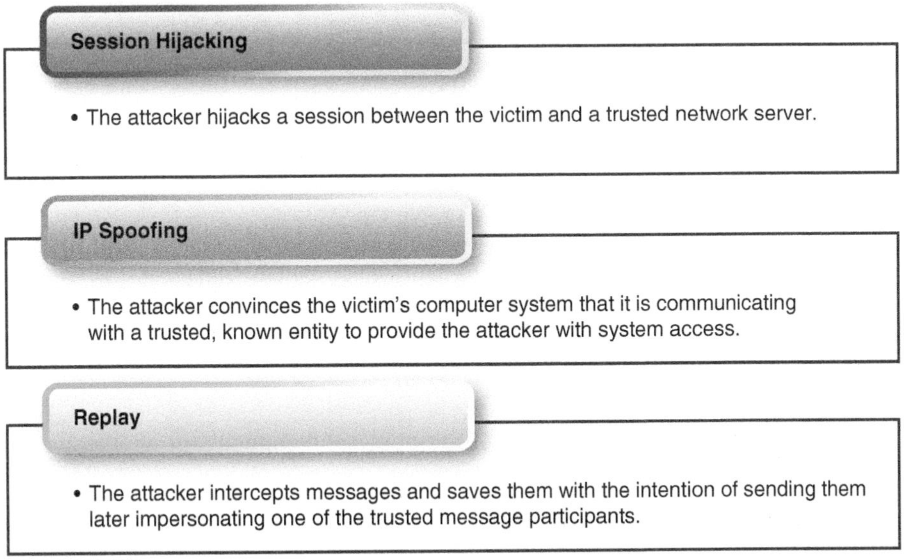

FIGURE 5.6 Three common MitM attacks.

One example of a MitM attack is active eavesdropping where the attacker makes an independent connection with two victims and relays messages between them to make believe they are talking directly to each other in a private conversation when in fact the entire conversation is controlled by the attacker. The attacker intercepts all relevant messages passing between the two victims and interjects new ones to his advantage. Typically the attackers in a MitM attack are looking for payment requests they can intercept and profit from.

Denial-of-Service (DoS) threats are also on the rise and need to be a top priority for organizations according to cyber security experts. DoS threats come in several "flavors," depending on their target. The three most prominent forms are described in **Figure 5.7**.

Distributed Denial-of-Service (DDoS)

- Crashes a network or website by bombarding it with traffic (i.e., *requests for service*) and effectively denying services to all those legitimately using it and leaving it vulnerable to other threats.

Telephony Denial-of-Service (TDoS)—

- Floods a network with phone calls and keeps the calls up for long durations to overwhelm an agent or circuit and prevents legitimate callers such as customers, partners, and suppliers from using network resources.

Permanent Denial-of-Service (PDoS)—

- Completely prevents the target's system or device from working. This attack type is unique. Instead of collecting data or providing some ongoing perverse function its objective is to completely prevent its target's device(s) from functioning. The damage PDoS causes is often so extensive that hardware must be rein-stalled or reinstated. PDoS is also known as "phlashing."

FIGURE 5.7   Three forms of DoS.

A "chilling" example of the havoc that PDoS can cause was demonstrated when a PDoS attack took the building management system offline in a block of residential apartments in Finland. The system's Internet connection was blocked causing the system to repeatedly try to reconnect by rebooting itself. During this downtime, the system was unable to supply heat at a time when temperatures were below freezing! Fortunately, the energy company was able to find alternate accommodations for residents until the system was brought back online.

Insider Threats

Not all cyber attackers are carried out by people outside an organization. **Insider threats** and misuse of privileges threats are a major challenge largely due to the many ways an employee or contractor can carry out malicious activities. These people may be able to bypass physical security (e.g., locked doors) and technical security (e.g., passwords) measures that organizations have put in place to prevent unauthorized access. Why? Because defenses such as firewalls and intrusion detection systems (IDSs) are primarily designed to protect against external threats. A method often used by insiders is **data tampering**, a common means of cyberattack that is overshadowed by other types of attacks. Data tampering is extremely serious because it may not be detected.

Two cyber threats that can be categorized both as intentional and unintentional are physical theft or loss and miscellaneous errors.

Physical theft or loss is the threat of an information asset going missing, whether through negligence or malice, that can send companies into a panic. The "miniaturization" of computing has led to an increase in physical theft or loss. Laptops, tablets, modems, routers, and

Data tampering is a cyberattack during which someone enters false or fraudulent data into a computer, or changes or deletes existing data.

USBs are much more easily transportable than mainframes or servers! When a laptop or tablet with unencrypted sensitive documents on it goes missing it's difficult to determine if a data breach has actually occurred, but precautions must always be taken. Theft of laptops occurs primarily in victims' own work area or from their vehicles. Theft is more likely to be related to the procurement of USB drives and printer paper. On the positive side, lost items are much more prevalent than theft.

Miscellaneous errors can also be the cause of data breaches. The main concern related to this source of cyberthreat is a shortage of capacity that prevents information from being available where and when needed. Other threat actions shown in **Table 5.3** that fall within this category of miscellaneous errors are less common.

TABLE 5.3   **Threat Actions Classified as Miscellaneous Errors**

Threat Action	Description
Shortage of Capacity	Insufficient computer capacity is available to make information available where and when needed
Misdelivery	Information delivered to the wrong person, when e-mails or documents are sent to the wrong people
Publishing error	Information published to an unintended audience, such as the entire Internet, enabling them to view it
Misconfiguration	A firewall rule is mistyped allowing access to a sensitive file server from all internal networks rather than a specific pool of hosts
Disposal error	A hard drive is not "wiped" on decommissioned devices
Programming error	Code is mistyped or logic is flawed
Date entry error	Data is entered incorrectly or into the incorrect file or duplicated
Omission	Data is not entered; document is not sent

IT at Work 5.2 illustrates how insider threats can unwittingly result in catastrophic consequences.

IT at Work 5.2

Oregon Department of Human Services Employees Fall for Phishing Scam

In January 2019, nine Oregon Department of Human Services (ODHS) were fooled by e-mails that were the product of a large targeted spear-phishing campaign. Initially, the breach was reported to have affected 350,000 patients, but later it was disclosed that a total of 645,000 people who had signed up for benefits with the ODHS had had their personal information inadvertently exposed to hackers.

A day after the attack the nine ODHS employees had trouble accessing their e-mail accounts and a subsequent investigation discovered the breach. ODHS hired a third-party security team to investigate the incident who determined no malware had been installed on the ODHS systems but the attackers had been able to access over two million e-mails. The e-mails contained file attachments with personal and medical data of more than 645,000 patients who had enrolled for various benefits. It took ODHS staff 20 days to secure the accounts after the hackers first attacked the system during which time the hackers had access to patient names, addresses, dates of birth, social security numbers, case number, and other protected health information. To secure the system, ODHS officials initiated a password reset to stop any further unauthorized access and remote access to the compromised accounts was terminated. Fortunately, the investigation did not find evidence that the attackers had copied the data from the ODHS system. ODHS was quicker than most affected targets making the breach public just three weeks after it occurred. In return for the security breach, ODHS patients were offered the opportunity to enroll in a free program that gives them one year of identity theft monitoring and recovery services.

Following the attack ODHS stressed they have cyber security measures in place to protect patient data, including security updates, up-to-date patching, independent security assessments, special security software, and routing employee training around phishing. A state hearing held as a result of the attack brought to light the frequency with which hackers have been targeting these types of government agencies over the past several years and the lack of staffing and resources facing many health-care and government entities that make these types of cyberattacks difficult to deter and detect.

Sources: Compiled from Anonymous (2019b), Chaffin (2019), Cimpanu (2019), Davis (2019a), Davis (2019b), and Rajagopal (2019).

Table 5.4 lists some way that organizations can guard against the various intentional and unintentional cyberthreats we have discussed.

TABLE 5.4 How to Guard Against Intentional and Unintentional Cyberthreats

Source/Type	Solution
Hacking	Train your staff Change password frequently Have "strong" passwords
Social engineering	Don't trust. Validate the source.
Phishing	Train your staff Monitor activity
Spear Phishing	Use a verbal password; implement a quality spam filter Only allow e-mail from authorized server
Malware	Use antimalware/AV software Patch promptly
Ransomware	Monitor change and watch key indicators; back-up system regularly Capture data on attacks Practice principle of least privilege
Cryptojacking	Add an extension to Web browser like NoCoin, minerlLock or NoScript
SQL Injection	Use a type-safe parameter encoding mechanism Validate input strings on server side
Man-in-the-Middle	Use strong encryption between client and server
Denial-of-service	Segregate key servers Choose your providers carefully Test your anti-DDoS service
Insider and privilege misuse	Monitor user behavior Track mobile media usage Know your data
Physical theft	Encrypt your data Train your staff Reduce use of paper
Physical loss	Encrypt your data Train your staff
Miscellaneous errors	Learn from your mistakes Strengthen controls Ensure all assets go through a rigorous check by IT before they are decommissioned or disposed of

What Motivates Cybercriminals?

Cyber criminals have different reasons and take different approaches when conducting a cyberattack. Some groups or individuals like to conduct "high-profile" attacks while others prefer to work "under-the-radar." The difference between these two approaches is explained next.

"High Profile" Cyberattacks

Hackers and hacktivists with personal agendas carry out high-profile attacks to gain recognition and notoriety. Hacktivist groups, such as Anonymous, a loosely associated international network of activist and hacktivist entities and its spin-off hacker group, LulzSec, have committed daring data breaches, data compromises, data leaks, thefts, threats, and privacy invasions. Consider the following three examples:

- **Philippine Commission on Elections** A few months before a Philippine election, the hacker group Anonymous tapped into the commission's website and released personal information on 55 million registered voters. The demonstration was in response to the Philippines' lax security measures around its voting machines; 1.3 million overseas voters' information, which included passport numbers, were included in the breach.
- **Combined Systems, Inc.** Proudly displaying its hacktivist flag, Anonymous took credit for knocking Combined Systems, Inc. offline and stealing personal data from its clients. Anonymous went after Combined Systems, which sells tear gas and crowd-control devices to law enforcement and military organizations, to protest war profiteers.
- **CIA** Twice in one year, Anonymous launched a DoS attack that forced the CIA website offline. The CIA takedown followed a busy week for the hacktivists. Within 10 days, the group also went after Chinese electronics manufacturer Foxconn, American Nazi groups, AV firm Symantec, and the office of Syria's president.

"Under the Radar" Cyberattacks
Not all cyber criminals seek notoriety. Some are profit motivated like **advanced persistent threat (APT)** attackers who typically operate in stealth mode. APTs operate under the radar so they can monitor network activity and steal data rather than cause damage to the network or organization, as described in **IT at Work 5.1**.

APTs typically target corporate and government secrets. Most APT attacks are launched through phishing. Typically, this type of attack begins with some reconnaissance on the part of attackers. This can include researching publicly available information about the company and its employees, often from social networking sites. This information is then used to create targeted phishing e-mail messages. A successful attack could give the attacker access to the enterprise's network.

APTs' purpose is long-term espionage. Once installed on a network, APTs transmit copies of documents, such as Microsoft Office files and PDFs, in stealth mode. APTs collect and store files on the company's network; encrypt them; then send them in bursts to servers often in China or Russia. This type of attack has been observed in other large-scale data breaches that exposed significant numbers of identities.

Advanced persistent threat (APT) is a prolonged and targeted cyberattack in which an attacker gains access to a network and remained undetected for a period of time.

How Much Does a Cyberattack Really Cost an Organization?

In 2019 the global average total cost of a data breach was $3.92 million. The average size of a data breach was 25,575 records, the cost per record lost was $150 and it took an average of 279 days for companies to identify and contain a breach. Companies in the United States reported the highest average cost of a breach at $8.19 million (up from $7.91 million in 2018) and health care had the highest industry average cost of $6.45 million (IBM Security, 2019).

Some costs are easy to see and quantify such as falling share prices, financial penalties, and federal and state government fines assessed because of inadequate cyber security. However, the largest contributor, loss of business, can have severe negative effects that can linger for years, resulting in a wide range of intangible costs tied consumer backlash, damaged reputation, disruption of operations, and loss of IP or other strategic assets. Some of these are difficult to measure since they are not easily quantifiable.

When assessing the damage caused by a cyberattack, along with the all-important loss of business there are three other major costs categories to be factored into the total cost of a data breach. These are:

1. Detection and escalation—costs to conduct activities that enable a company to detect the breach and report it to the appropriate personnel
2. Notification—costs to perform activities that enable the company to notify regulators and individuals who had their data compromised in the breach
3. Post data breach response—costs to create, operate, and maintain processes set up to help customers communicate with the company, such as call centers, as well as costs associated with redress and reparation.

Questions

1. Define and give an example of an intentional threat and an unintentional threat.
2. Why might management not treat cyberthreats as a top priority?
3. Describe the differences between distributed denial-of-service (DDoS), telephony denial-of-service (TDoS), and permanent denial-of-service (PDoS).
4. List and define three types of malware.
5. What are the risks caused by data tampering?
6. Define what a trojan is and explain why it is dangerous.
7. Why are MitM attacks on the rise? How might companies guard against MitM attacks?
8. What is cryptojacking? How can you protect yourself from being a victim of cryptojacking?

5.3 Cyberattack Targets and Consequences

LO5.3 Discuss *the six most deadly targets of cyberattacks and provide an example of how each impacts consumers and organizations.*

Every enterprise has data that profit-motivated criminals target. Customer data, networks, websites, proprietary information systems, and patents are examples of valuable digital assets that need to be protected. However, even high-tech companies and market leaders appear to be somewhat detached from the value of the confidential data they store and the ways in which highly motivated cyber criminals will try to steal them.

One of the biggest mistakes that managers make is underestimating IT vulnerabilities and threats. For example, workers use shadow IT like personal laptops and mobile devices for both work and leisure, and in an era of multitasking, they often do both at the same time. Yet off-time or off-site use of devices remains risky because, despite policies, employees continue to engage in dangerous online and communication habits. Those habits make them a weak link in an organization's otherwise solid security efforts.

Most Prevalent and Deadly Cyber attack Targets

The most prevalent and deadly targets that cybercriminals attack in companies and governmental agencies include: weak passwords, critical infrastructure; theft of IP; identity theft; shadow IT; bring your own device (BYOD) and social media.

Weak Passwords One of the greatest cybersecurity weaknesses that cyber criminals like to target is users who ignore the dangers of weak passwords and password reuse. The capture and misuse of credentials, such as user's IDs and passwords, is one of the foundation skills hackers use them execute numerous types of cyberthreats, such as phishing, leaving organizations open to data breaches. For example, an attacker can inject some SQL code into a Web form input box such as submit box or editable payment textbox to gain access to a user's account to gather resources or make changes to data. Given the huge number of global data breaches that are occurring, it is very likely that every user has at least one site or app that has been compromised. Proper credential management is essential to security since breaches of user passwords can be dangerous. Even the most secure password can become ineffective if it is used on every website and in every app. To guard against this, a strong password policy needs to be put in place as a form of "due diligence" to protect consumers and to avoid lawsuits. The password policy should include enforcing strong passwords for all Web apps and performing regular testing for weak passwords.

Critical Infrastructure   Hackers, hacktivists, crime syndicates, militant groups, industrial spies, fraudsters, and hostile governments continue to attack networks for profit, fame, revenge, or an ideology; to wage warfare and terrorism, fight against a terrorist campaign, or disable their target. For example, the Department of Homeland Security (DHS) Industrial Control Systems Cyber Emergency Response Team (ICS-CERT) warned that attacks against critical infrastructure are growing. The most affected industry is the energy sector.

A new form of malware, called Industroyer has been developed to target critical infrastructure in the energy sector. Industroyer takes direct control of electricity substation circuit breakers using industrial communication protocols. This means that power stations, transportation control systems, and water and gas plants are all potential targets of this powerful tool.

Figure 5.8 shows the 16 critical infrastructure sectors whose assets, systems, and networks, whether physical or virtual, are considered so vital that their incapacitation or destruction would have a debilitating effect on a country's security, national economic security, national public health or safety, or any combination thereof.

Critical infrastructure is defined as, "systems and assets, whether physical or virtual, so vital to a country that the incapacity or destruction of such systems and assets would have a debilitating impact on security, national economic security, national public health or safety, or any combination of those matters" (Department of Justice, 2001).

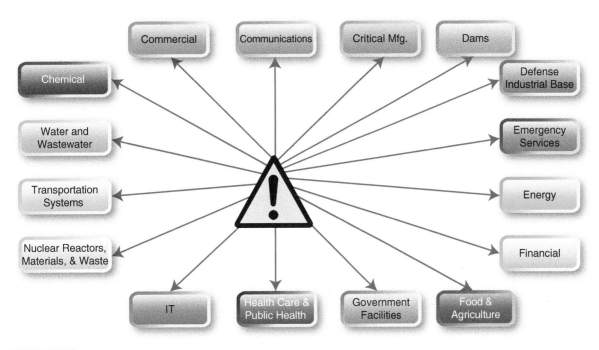

FIGURE 5.8   Critical infrastructure sectors.

Attacks on critical infrastructure sectors can significantly disrupt the functioning of government and business—and trigger cascading effects far beyond the targeted sector and physical location of the incident. These cyberattacks could compromise a country's critical infrastructure and its ability to provide essential services to its citizens.

For example, the first cyberattack against a nation's power grid occurred in December 2015, when a cyberattacker successfully seized control of the Prykarpattyaoblenergo Control Center (PCC) in the Western Ukraine leaving 230,000 citizens without power for up to six hours. The attackers carefully planned their assault over many months. They studied the networks and siphon operator credentials and finally launched their devastating synchronized assault in the middle of winter. The PCC operated a supervisory control and data acquisition (SCADA) system, which is a common form of industrial control system, that distributed electricity. The critical devices at 16 substations became unresponsive to any remote command by its operators after attackers overwrote its firmware. This type of control system is surprisingly more secure than some used in the United States since they have robust firewalls that separate them from control center business networks.

Governments around the world have plans in place to deal with the consequences of natural disasters, yet none have disaster relief plans for a downed power grid. Clearly, this must change. Local and state governments must work together with their national counterparts to produce and quickly implement plans to address future attacks. Examples of other critical infrastructures that have already been compromised include:

- Wolf Creek Nuclear Operating Corporation, Kansas, United States—spear phishing techniques were used to target individuals who had access to critical controls of the plant
- Rye Brooke, NY Dam—attacked the command-and-control system using a cellular modem
- Pivichna Substation near Kiev, Ukraine—supervisory control and data acquisition cyberattack caused an hour-long blackout to surrounding areas

In response to the consistently growing number of cyberattacks over the past decade, the Inter-American Committee Against Terrorism (CICTE) issued a formal declaration to protect critical infrastructure from emerging threats and a Presidential executive order was signed in May 2017 to strengthen the cybersecurity of Federal networks and critical infrastructure. The five countries who have shown the highest commitment to cyber security are the United Kingdom, United States, France, Lithuania, and Estonia.

Intellectual property (IP) attacks are increasing. This is particularly troubling since IP can represent more than 80% of a company's value and as such is a critical part of all 21st-century organizations. Losing customer data to hackers can be costly and embarrassing but losing IP, commonly known as trade secrets, could threaten a company's existence. On a country-level, nation-state actors continue to mount attacks on IP to gain valuable information from other countries, their military and private companies.

Theft of IP has always been a threat from corporate moles, disgruntled employees, and other insiders. While some IP may still be obtainable exclusively through physical means, digitization has made theft easier. Advancements in technology, increased mobility, rapid globalization, and the anonymous nature of the Internet create growing challenges in protecting IP. Hackers' preferred modus operandi is to break into employees' mobile devices and leapfrog into employers' networks—stealing trade secrets without a trace.

Cybersecurity experts and government officials are increasingly concerned about breaches from other countries into corporate and government networks either through mobile devices or other means. For example, China's Ministry of State Security and People's Liberation Army (PLA) have a mandate to steal U.S. industrial and trade secrets and have been particularly effective in these kind of attacks against the United States. Currently there is no sign that threats to U.S. IP and digitally based assets are slowing down (Underwood, 2019).

In May of 2016, President Barack Obama signed the Defend Trade Secrets Act (DTSA) to allow "the owners of trade secrets to bring a civil action in federal court for trade secret misappropriation" (Gibson Dunn, 2016). Until the signing of the DTSA, corporations had to rely on state law regarding trade secrets. Now, every American corporation is equally protected under federal law. Moreover, it extends the power of the federal government in regulation of trade secrets through interstate and foreign commerce while maintaining existing trade secret laws.

A classic example of theft of IP is the APT attack named Operation Aurora perpetrated against Google and described in **IT at Work 5.3.**

Intellectual property is a work or invention that is the result of creativity that has commercial value, including copyrighted property such as a blueprint, manuscript, or a design, and is protected by law from unauthorized use by others.

IT at Work 5.3

Operation Aurora Targets Major Financial, Defense, and Technology Company Networks

Operation Aurora was a counterespionage operation being run by the Chinese government. It was a series of cyberattacks conducted by APTs with ties to the People's Liberation Army in China. Attackers successfully accessed a database that flagged Gmail accounts marked for court-ordered wiretaps to gain insights into active investigations being conducted by the FBI and other law enforcement agencies that involved undercover Chinese operatives.

To access IP, Operation Aurora exploited security flaws in e-mail attachments to sneak into the networks of major financial, defense, and technology companies and research institutions in the United States by performing six steps, as described in **Figure 5.9**.

Standard IT security technologies at Google failed to prevent these six steps from occurring and neither Google nor its Gmail account holders knew they had been hacked.

Once the APTs gained access to Google's internal systems (Step 6), they were free to steal corporate secrets. Reportedly, over 30 other large companies from a wide range of industries were similarly targeted by Operation Aurora.

Most hack activities do not become headline grabbers until after the incidents are detected and reported. Even then, victimized companies are reluctant to discuss them, so statistics are scarce. In the case of Operation Aurora, the attack was not discovered until almost one year after the fact!

Sources: Compiled from Corbin (2013), Schwartz (2013), Gordon (2014), and Cyware (2016).

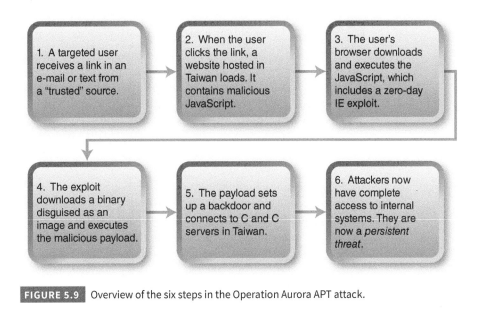

FIGURE 5.9 Overview of the six steps in the Operation Aurora APT attack.

Identity Theft Identity theft is also on the rise. Thefts where individuals' Social Security and credit card numbers are stolen and used by thieves are not new. Criminals have always obtained information about other people—by stealing wallets or dumpster diving. But widespread electronic sharing and databases have made the crime worse. Because financial institutions, data-processing firms, and retail businesses are reluctant to reveal incidents in which their customers' personal financial information may have been stolen, lost, or compromised, laws continue to be passed that force those notifications. Identity theft can result in frustration and a gross inconvenience to the victim in terms of wasted time and resources.

Shadow IT, sometimes known as **stealth IT**, introduces security risks when unsupported hardware and software used by individuals or departments circumvent IT security measures that apply to approved technology. Originally shadow IT included easily controlled items like unapproved Microsoft Excel macros and boxed software employees bought at an office supply store to use at work are some simple examples of Shadow IT. Nowadays, shadow IT has grown to include cloud apps that are outside an organization's firewall, like Dropbox and Google Docs for file sharing and data storage and Twitter, Facebook, WhatsApp WebEx, Salesforce, and Google Hangouts Chat to facilitate collaboration between team members.

Users bringing their personal mobile devices and mobile apps to work and connecting them to the corporate network is part of the larger trend to consumerize information technology and

Shadow IT is the use of IT-related hardware or software by an individual or a department without the knowledge of the IT department within the organization.

is a significant issue related to hardware-related shadow IT. When IT hardware like unapproved personal smartphones, portable hard drives, tablets, and large-capacity USB thumb drives are not specified and deployed by the IT department an organization's data can be especially vulnerable to attack and raise compliance concerns when corporate data is not stored in a secure location. Other organizational concerns related to shadow IT include negative effects on bandwidth and create network and software application protocol conflicts. **Figure 5.10** summarizes how shadow IT apps, mobile devices, and cloud services can put organizations at a greater risk of cyberattack.

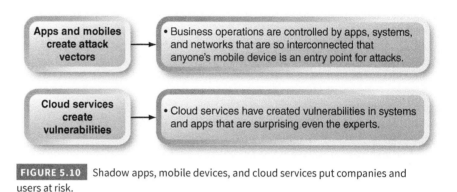

FIGURE 5.10 Shadow apps, mobile devices, and cloud services put companies and users at risk.

Opinions on Shadow IT are mixed. On one hand, management worries that in addition to security issues, it will create end user data silos and limit the free flow of information throughout the organization. Others believe that Shadow IT can be useful in a fast-changing business world and that IT must acknowledge that it exists and create acceptable-use policies for its oversight and use. Advances are being made in this area with the introduction of shadow IT policies.

Roughly 87% of U.S. organizations are either already using or planning to allow employees to "bring your own device"—BYOD. It's an appealing concept because BYOD enables companies to cut costs by not having to purchase and maintain employees' mobile devices. Unfortunately, many companies have rushed into it without considering how these policies relate to IT security. Mobile devices make easy targets since they rarely have strong authentication, access controls, and encryption even though they connect to mission-critical data and cloud services.

The BYOD trend is driven by employees using their own devices for business purposes because they are more powerful than those the company has provided. Another factor is mobility. In the past, and before the BYOD push, employees worked at their desks on a landline and on a computer plugged into the wall with a network cable. This change in exposure requires greater investment to defend against BYOD risks. As more and more people work from home and on the go, the office-bound traditional 9-to-5 workday has become a thing of the past.

BYOD Raises Serious and Legitimate Areas of Concern

Enterprises take risks with BYOD practices that they never would consider taking with conventional computing devices. One possible reason is that new devices, apps, and systems have been rolled out so quickly. As a result, smartphones are not being managed as secure devices. In fact, employees expected instant approval of (or at least no disapproval of) and support for their new tablet computers within hours of the product's release.

Hackers break into employees' mobile devices and leapfrog into employers' networks—stealing secrets without a trace. New vulnerabilities are created when personal and business data and communications are mixed together. All cybersecurity controls—authentication, access control, data confidentiality, and intrusion detection—implemented on corporate-owned resources can be rendered useless by an employee-owned device. The corporation's mobile infrastructure may not be able to support the increase in mobile network traffic and data processing, causing unacceptable delays or requiring additional investments.

Another serious problem arises when an employee's mobile device is lost or stolen. The company can suffer a data breach if the device is not adequately secured by a strong password and the data on the BYOD is not encrypted.

Social media cyberattacks are predicted to continue to be a major threat for business (Walker, 2019). Companies' poor social media security practices put their brands, customers, executives, and entire organizations at serious risk.

Social networks and cloud computing increase vulnerabilities by providing a single point of failure and attack for organized criminal networks. Critical, sensitive, and private information is at risk, and like previous IT trends, such as wireless networks, the goal of connectivity, take precedence over concern for security. As social networks increase their offerings, the gap between services and information security also increases. For example, virus and malware attacks on a well-established service such as e-mail have decreased as e-mail security has improved over the years. Unfortunately, malware is still finding ways to successfully disrupt new services and devices, such e-readers, netbooks, Google's Chrome OS, Facebook, YouTube, Twitter, LinkedIn, and other cloud-based social media networks.

For example, in Twitter and Facebook, where users build relationships with other users, cybercriminals are hacking in using stolen logins. These types of attacks that take advantage of user trust are very difficult to detect. Facebook recently reported that it disabled almost 1.3 billion fake accounts, Twitter suspended 70 million accounts, and LinkedIn openly admitted they have no reliable system for identifying and counting duplicate or fraudulent accounts.

To combat these types of cyberthreats, Web filtering, user education, and strict policies are key to preventing widespread outbreaks.

Networks and Services Increase Exposure to Risk An overriding reason why networks and services increase exposure to risk is the **time-to-exploitation** of today's sophisticated spyware and mobile viruses. That time has shrunk from months to minutes so IT staff have ever-shorter timeframes to find and fix flaws before they are compromised by an attack. Some attacks exist for as little as two hours, which means that enterprise IT security systems must have real-time protection.

When new vulnerabilities are found in operating systems, applications, or wired and wireless networks, patches are released by the vendor or security organization. Microsoft, for example, releases **patches** that it calls service packs to update and fix vulnerabilities in its operating systems, including Vista, and apps, including Office 2016. **Service packs** can be downloaded from Microsoft's Service Pack and Update Center (**https://support.microsoft .com/en-us/help/14162/windows-service-pack-and-update-center**).

Despite the best technology defenses, information security incidents often occur because users do not follow secure computing practices and procedures.

Time-to-exploitation is the elapsed time between when a vulnerability is discovered and when it is exploited.

Patch is a software program that users download and install to fix a vulnerability.

Questions

1. What is a critical infrastructure?
2. List three types of critical infrastructures.
3. How do social networks and cloud computing increase vulnerability?
4. Why are patches and service packs needed?
5. Why is it important to protect IP?
6. How are the motives of hacktivists and APTs different?
7. Explain why data on laptops and computers need to be encrypted.
8. Explain how identity theft can occur.

5.4 Defending Against Cyberattacks and Managing Risk

LO5.4 Identify *six cyber defense strategies and four risk management approaches and the IT defense tools that can be used to protect organizations from cyberattacks.*

Organized crime groups quickly learned that cybercrime has better payoffs with substantially lower risks to life, limb, and liberty than other activities like human trafficking, smuggling, extortion, and the drug trade. They have become virtually untouchable by law enforcement because often no one sees the crime and if it is identified, the lack of international treaties and cooperation make capture and trial between those non-extradition countries virtually impossible. Given this, it is not surprising that almost every survey identifies the same troubling trend—the recovery costs and frequency of cybercrimes are increasing while the costs of execution are declining. Just two examples of this are a 2013 security breach of Target Corporation's databases in which personal information of millions of customers was stolen resulting in the company agreeing to pay $18.5 million to settle the investigation by dozens of states and the billion-dollar lawsuit and regulatory investigation brought against Equifax. To deter cyberattacks companies must take the security of their data more seriously and implement stronger IT security practices and defenses.

To effectively guard against cyberattacks, top management must sponsor and promote security initiatives and fund them as a top priority. What most business leaders don't understand is how to design, implement, and manage effective cyber security strategies and risk management plans to prevent data breaches and protect IT and business resources. Cyberattacks on high-tech companies like Yahoo, LinkedIn, Google, Amazon, eBay, and Sony, and top security agencies like the CIA and FBI are proof that no one is safe.

On a global level, Verizon's 2019 Data Breach Investigations Report (Verizon, 2019) examined 41,686 incidents, of which 2,013 were confirmed data breaches. Of these 71% were financially motivated and 25% were motivated to gain a competitive advantage. The report also showed 69% of the cases were perpetrated by external sources, 39% were fueled by organized criminal groups, and 56% of the breaches took months or longer to be discovered. By the time the security failures were discovered and fixed, the damage was already done.

In view of this, managers must no longer question whether their networks will be the target of a cyberattack, but instead they need to determine "*when* will it happen?", "*how much* damage will be done?", "*how long* will the investigation take?", "*how high* will the costs of investigation and fines be?" and most important of all "how do we *protect* our systems against attack?"

The Information Security Forum (**https://www.securityforum.org/**), the leading authority on cyber, information security, and risk management that includes many Fortune 100 companies, compiled a list of the top information security problems and discovered that nine of the top 10 incidents could be summed up in three risk factors:

- Mistakes or human errors leading to misconfigured systems, applications, or networks
- Malfunctioning systems
- Failure to patch or otherwise properly maintain software on existing systems

The first step in a cyber security initiative is to choose a cyber defense strategy, then adopt risk mitigation strategies specific to different types of assets and deploy robust security measures that are not just the responsibility of IT and top management, but the ongoing duty of everyone in an organization. The cyber security field—like sports and law—has its own terminology, which is summarized for quick reference in **Table 5.5**.

TABLE 5.5   Cyber Security Terminology

Term	Definition
Access control	Security feature designed to restrict who has access to a network, IS, or data
Asset	Something of value that needs to be protected, such as customer data, trade secrets, proprietary formulas
Audit	Procedure of generating, recording, and reviewing a chronological record of system events to determine their accuracy
Authentication	Method (usually based on username and password) by which an IS validates or verifies that a user is really who he or she claims to be
Biometrics	Methods to identify a person based on a biological feature, such as a fingerprint or retina
Ciphertext	Encrypted text
Encryption	Transforming data into scrambled code to protect them from being understood by unauthorized users
Exploit	A program (code) that allows attackers to automatically break into a system through a vulnerability
Exposure	Estimated cost, loss, or damage that can result if a threat exploits a vulnerability
Fault tolerance	The ability of an IS to continue to operate when a failure occurs, but usually for a limited time or at a reduced level
Firewall	Software or hardware device that controls access to a private network from a public network (Internet) by analyzing data packets entering or exiting it
Plaintext or clear text	Readable text
Risk	Probability of a threat exploiting a vulnerability and the resulting cost of the loss, damage, disruption or destruction risk is a function of threat, vulnerability and cost of impact

Cyber Defense Strategies

The primary objective of IT security management is to defend all the components of an information system, specifically data, software applications, hardware, and networks against attacks. To do this a company must gather strategic and tactical intelligence to develop a customized cybersecurity defense. **Strategic intelligence** informs HOW an organization will defend itself. This includes analyzing the gaps in an organization's cyber security tools and processes to ensure they can adequately defend themselves against aggressive cyberthreat and make it easier for an organization to protect against threats before they occur. **Tactical intelligence** informs WHAT an organization needs to do when it is attacked. This might include identifying threatening domains, malware, and IP addresses and getting information from other organizations who have suffered similar cyberattacks.

Before forming a customized plan, cyber security personnel must understand the requirements and operations of the business. The defense strategy chosen depends on what needs to be protected and a cost–benefit analysis of the asset and the consequences of protecting it. That is, companies should neither underinvest nor overinvest. When choosing a cyber defense strategy, a company must keep in mind its major objectives (see **Table 5.6**).

TABLE 5.6 Cyber Defense Strategies

Prevention and Deterrence

- Properly designed controls may prevent errors from occurring, deter criminals from attacking the system, and, better yet, deny access to unauthorized people. These are the most desirable controls.

Detection

- The earlier an attack is detected, the easier it is to combat, and the less damage is done. Detection can be performed in many cases by using special diagnostic software, at a minimal cost.

Containment

- Mimize or limit loss once a malfunction has occurred. It is also called damage control. This can be accomplished, for example, by including a *fault-tolerant system* that permits operation in a degraded mode until full recovery is made. If a fault-tolerant system does not exist, a quick and possibly expensive recovery must take place. Users want their systems back in operation as fast as possible.

Recovery

- A recovery plan explains how to fix a damaged information system as quickly as possible. Replacing rather than repairing components is one route to fast recovery.

Correction

- Correcting the causes of damaged systems can prevent a problem from re-occurring.

Awareness/Compliance

- All organization members must be made aware and educated about the hazards and must comply with security rules and regulations.

Managing Risk

Risk is a situation involving exposure to danger.

The higher the value of the asset to the company and to cybercriminals, the greater the **risk** is to the company and the higher the level of security needs to be. To do this, a company can use one of four risk management approaches to assess its risk tolerance relative to different computing resources and their environment.

Risks mitigation is the action taken to reduce threats and ensure resiliency.

Figure 5.11 identifies and describes the four different **risk mitigation** strategies that apply to business continuity and disaster recovery. They are *acceptance, avoidance, limitation,* and *transference*.

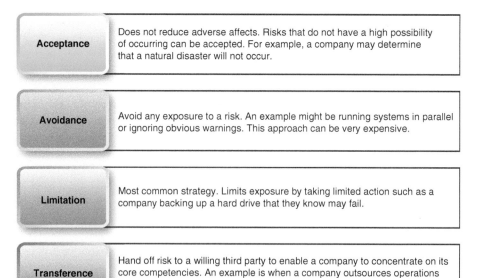

Acceptance — Does not reduce adverse affects. Risks that do not have a high possibility of occurring can be accepted. For example, a company may determine that a natural disaster will not occur.

Avoidance — Avoid any exposure to a risk. An example might be running systems in parallel or ignoring obvious warnings. This approach can be very expensive.

Limitation — Most common strategy. Limits exposure by taking limited action such as a company backing up a hard drive that they know may fail.

Transference — Hand off risk to a willing third party to enable a company to concentrate on its core competencies. An example is when a company outsources operations such as payroll or customer service.

FIGURE 5.11 Risk mitigation strategies.

Not all companies will choose to mitigate risk in the same way. It is important for each organization to choose one or more risk mitigation strategies that best fits its needs. The best approach is to choose the appropriate risk mitigation strategy that allows a company to successfully protect its most valuable assets rather than trying to protect all assets in the same way.

Securing Systems

Cyber security is an ongoing, unending process—something akin to painting the Golden Gate Bridge in San Francisco—and not a problem that can be easily solved with just hardware or software. Hardware and software security defenses cannot protect against irresponsible business practices. It is becoming more important than ever to view cyber security as a high priority as the growth of mobile technologies and IoT threaten to provide attackers with new opportunities.

Cyber Defense Tools   Since cyber criminals use many attack methods and strategies, multiple tools are needed to detect them and/or neutralize their effects. Four effective cyber defense tools are:

a. *Antivirus Software* Anti-malware tools are designed to detect malicious codes and prevent users from downloading them. They can also scan systems for the presence of worms, trojans, and other types of threats. This technology does not provide complete protection because it cannot defend against zero-day exploits. Antimalware may not be able to detect a previously unknown exploit.

b. *Intrusion Detection Systems (IDSs)* As the name implies, an IDS scans for unusual or suspicious traffic. An IDS can identify the start of a DoS attack by the traffic pattern, alerting the network administrator to take defensive action, such as switching to another IP address and diverting critical servers from the path of the attack.

c. *Intrusion Prevention Systems (IPSs)* An IPS is designed to take immediate action—such as blocking specific IP addresses—whenever a traffic-flow anomaly is detected. An application-specific integrated circuit (ASIC)-based IPS has the power and analysis capabilities to detect and block **distributed denial-of-service (DDoS) attacks**, functioning somewhat like an automated circuit breaker.

d. *IP Intelligence Services*. Being able to detect and block cyberthreats before they occur is a huge advantage in protecting a network against attack. IP intelligence service providers can help organizations significantly reduce malicious network activity to significantly reduce risk of online fraud, mitigate compliance risk, minimize time and effort spent processing bad traffic, and increase efficiency of data centers.

Protecting Against Malware Reinfection, Signatures, Mutations, and Variants   Malware is very difficult to remove from infected computers. When a host computer is infected, attempts to remove the malware can fail and the malware may reinfect the host for two reasons:

1. **Malware is captured in backups or archives**   Restoring the infected backup or archive also restores the malware.

2. **Malware infects removable media**   Months or years after the initial infection, the removable media may be accessed, and the malware could attempt to infect the host.

Most antivirus (AV) software relies on **malware signatures** to identify and then block malware. Detecting and preventing infections from the existing millions of malware signatures is not always a possibility. **Zero-day exploits**—malware so new their signatures are not yet known—are an example. Malware authors also evade detection by AV software and firewalls by altering malware code to create *variants*, which have new signatures. But not all procedures or AV tools can remove every trace of the malware. Even if the malicious parts of the infection can be cleaned from a system, the remaining pieces of code could make the system unstable or expose to future infection.

Malware signature   is a unique value that indicates the presence of malicious code.

zero-day exploit   is malicious software that exposes a vulnerability in software or hardware and can create complicated problems well before anyone detects it.

IT at Work 5.4 describes how one company successfully contained a malicious malware attack and covertly monitored and analyzed it.

IT at Work 5.4

Bayer Successfully Contains Malware Attack by Mercenaries

German drug maker Bayer (**https://www.bayer.com/**) recently contained a cyberattack it believes originated in China. Bayer found malware on its computer networks and covertly monitored and analyzed it for a year. After a year of self-espionage Bayer cleared the threat from its systems and disclosed the attack. Bayer confirmed "a significant hacking attempt" had taken place but there appeared to be no evidence of data theft or that the personal data had been compromised.

The group of hackers is thought to be part of the China-based Wicked Panda group, but Gerhard Schindler, former head of German's BND foreign intelligence service said it was very difficult to determine the hackers' location. The group had installed WINNTI malware on to Bayer's systems to spy on Bayer providing clear evidence that the complex and sophisticated malware had been used in a targeted, sustained espionage effort.

Citing at least four other WINNTI attacks in Germany, Andreas Rohr of the DCSO, a cyber security group, said the Wicked Panda Group is a very active group of hackers that can carry out multiple international attacks in parallel. While it's not possible to say for sure that Wicked Panda was responsible for the Bayer attack, Rohr said the method used bore the hallmark of Chinese mercenaries who carry out targeted cyberattacks and campaigns for money.

Sources: Compiled from Anonymous (2019a), Hashim (2019), and Weiss and Burger (2019).

Protect Mobile Devices   At a minimum there are several security defenses that must be put in place for mobile devices. These include mobile biometrics, voice biometrics, rogue app monitoring, remote wipe capability, and encryption.

> **Biometric control**   is an automated method of verifying the identity of a person, based on physical or behavioral characteristics. The most common biometrics are a thumbprint or fingerprint, voice print, retinal scan, and signature.

- **Mobile biometrics,** such as voice and fingerprint biometrics, can significantly improve the security of physical devices and provide stronger authentication for remote access or cloud services. **Biometric controls** have been integrated into e-business hardware and software products. Biometric controls do have some limitations: They are not accurate in certain cases, and some people see them as an invasion of privacy. Most biometric systems match some personal characteristic against a stored profile.

- **Voice biometrics** is an effective authentication solution across a wide range of consumer devices including smartphones, tablets, and TVs. Future mobile devices are expected to have fingerprint sensors to add another authentication factor. When Apple acquired Siri, Inc., the voice-based personal assistant Siri was integrated into its Apple's operating system; Siri gave Apple the potential to move into voice biometrics.

- **Rogue application monitoring** is used to detect and destroy malicious applications. Several vendors offer 24/7 monitoring and detection services to monitor major app stores and shut down rogue applications to minimize exposure and damage.

- **Mobile kill switch** or **remote wipe capability** as well as encryption are needed in the event of loss or theft of a device. All major smartphone platforms have a remote erase capability and encryption option.

- **Encryption** is process of converting information or data into a code and is essential to prevent unauthorized access to sensitive information transmitted online.

In the case of employees who travel for work, do-no-carry rules maybe an additional essential defense. In response to mobile security threats, many U.S. companies and government agencies are imposing do-not-carry rules on mobiles to prevent compromise. Travelers can bring only "clean" devices and are forbidden from connecting to the government's network while abroad.

Develop Do-Not-Carry Rules   The U.S. Chamber of Commerce did not learn that it and its member organizations were the victims of a cybertheft for months until the FBI informed the Chamber that servers in China were stealing data from four of its Asia policy experts, individuals who frequently travel to Asia. Most likely, the experts' mobile devices had been infected

with malware that was transmitting information and files back to the hackers. By the time the Chamber hardened (secured) its network, hackers had stolen at least six weeks of e-mails, most of which were communications with the largest U.S. corporations. Even later, the Chamber learned that its office printer and a thermostat in one of its corporate apartments were communicating with an Internet address in China. The Chamber did not disclose how hackers had infiltrated its systems, but its first step was to implement do-not-carry rules.

U.S. companies, government agencies, and organizations are now imposing **do-not-carry rules**, which assume that devices will inevitably be compromised according to Mike Rogers, current chairman of the House Intelligence Committee. For example, House members can bring only "clean" devices and are forbidden from connecting to the government's network while abroad. Rogers said he travels "electronically naked" to ensure cybersecurity during and after a trip.

Becoming IT Resilient
IT resilience involves effectively mitigating the risk to data and apps of any kind of planned or unplanned disruption. A recent survey conducted by IDC (CIO, 2019) showed that while most firms see IT resilience as a necessary prerequisite to achieving successful digital transformation, 90% of them do not consider themselves IT resilient and few have existing or planned IT resilience initiatives **(Figure 5.12)**. This IT resilience paradox is somewhat akin to the privacy paradox discussed earlier in the chapter and equally disconcerting.

> **IT resilience** is the ability to protect data and apps from any planned or unplanned disruption to eliminate the risk of downtime to maintain a seamless customer experience.

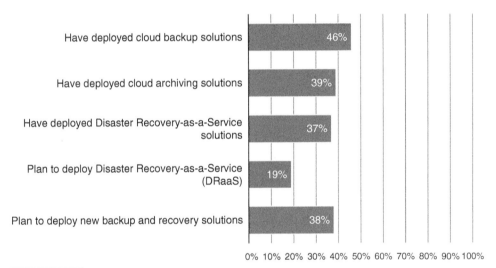

FIGURE 5.12 Companies deployed and planned IT resilience initiatives (adapted from CIO, 2019).

Backup and Recovery

Backup and recovery of IS and data are essential security operations for any business. For the past twenty or more years, tape systems have typically been the go-to backup technology, but using it requires the intervention of frequently overburdened IT staff to recognize an issue, diagnose it, come up with an effective solution, take timely action, and ensure recovery efforts are successful. This manual intervention takes time and puts the organization at risk. To combat cyberattacks in real-time software companies, like Zerto (www.zerto.com) and Veritas (www.veritas.com), offer sets of IT resilience tools and apps that automatically act to protect data and apps from just about any type of cyberattack.

But, becoming IT resilient is not just about technology. It is as much about people as it is about technology. In addition to making sure that the right technology is in place an organization needs people who understand their roles and clear policies and procedures to guide them about how to respond to a disruption or disaster to get the organization up and running again as quickly as possible. An effective IT resilience strategy should consist of four elements:

- **Availability**—keep customers continuously connected to their data and apps.
- **Mobility**—be able to move apps and workloads while keeping them fully protected.

- **Agility**—maintain the freedom to choose your own cloud and be able to move to, from and between clouds.
- **Training**—IT and non-IT employees must understand their roles in case of a disruption or disaster and been trained in how to respond.

Measuring IT resilience can be difficult, but it's something that most companies want to achieve and is increasingly important given the almost daily reports of cyberattacks that can have devastating results for those unprepared to effectively respond to them.

Policies and Procedures for IT Resilience and Disaster Recovery.

Business policies, procedures, and disaster recovery plans around computing resources are critical to IT resilience and cybersecurity. For example, insider incidents can be minimized with a layered defense-in-depth strategy consisting of security procedures, **acceptable use policies** (AUPs), and technology controls. In the United States the director of the Bureau of Consumer Protection at the Federal Trade Commission (FTC) warned that the agency would bring enforcement action against any small business that lacked adequate policies and procedures to protect consumer data. **Table 5.7** lists the characteristics of an effective cybersecurity program.

> **Acceptable use policy** is a document that lists the constraints and practices a user must agree to for access to a corporate network or the Internet.

TABLE 5.7 **Characteristics of an Effective Cybersecurity Program**

Make data and documents available and accessible 24/7 while simultaneously restricting access.
Implement and enforce procedures and AUPs for data, networks, hardware, and software that are company or employee owned, as discussed in the opening case.
Promote secure and legal sharing of information among authorized persons and partners.
Ensure compliance with government regulations and laws.
Prevent attacks by having network intrusion defenses in place.
Detect, diagnose, and respond to incidents and attacks in real time.
Maintain internal controls to prevent unauthorized alteration of data/records.
Recover from business disasters and disruptions quickly.

Business Continuity Planning

Risk management is not complete without a **business continuity plan** that has been tested to verify that it works. Business continuity refers to maintaining business functions or restoring them quickly when there has been a major disruption. The plan covers business processes, assets, human resources, business partners, and more. Fires, earthquakes, floods, power outages, malicious attacks, and other types of disasters hit data centers. Yet, business continuity planning capabilities can be a tough sell because they do not contribute to the bottom line—that is, until it is too late. Compare them to an insurance policy: If and only if a disaster occurs, the money has been well spent. And spending on business continuity preparedness is an ongoing process because there is always more that could be done to prepare better.

The purpose of a business continuity plan is to keep the business running after a disaster occurs. Each function in the business should have a feasible backup plan. For example, if the customer service center or call center was destroyed by a storm or lost all power, would anyone know how the reps would continue to answer customer calls? The backup plan could define how to provide necessary network access to enable business to continue. It is also important to revisit the business continuity plan from time to time and make adjustments that reflect the current state of the business and its environment.

To supplement and strengthen a business continuity plan the following strategies can be put in place to help reduce the impact of a disaster or disruption.

- Direct individual employees to make regular off-site backups of their files that can be accessed remotely with a secure username and password
- Deploy a cloud-based Email Continuity Solution, like Securence (**https://www.securence .com/solution/email-continuity-solution/**), to provide uninterrupted access to e-mail.
- Make sure you have cross-device software compatibility so that business can continue on employee mobile devices.
- Unify communications on a secure off-site cloud server that will keep operating in the event of a power outage, natural disaster or other disruptions.
- Establish a service-level agreement with your provider that offers fast support, emergency backup and routing to alternative servers when necessary.
- Put processes in place to ensure that IT teams can act quickly without approvals in case of a disaster or disruption.
- Make sure enough resources are allocated in the IT budget for adequate business continuity and disaster recovery services

Disaster Recovery Services

Another effective way to recover normal computer and network operations disrupted by a natural or other disaster such as a hurricane, earthquake, or explosion is to set up a secure, off-site disaster recovery space. Sites can be permanent or portable, such as an outfitted trailer that can be set up in the disaster area.

To ensure business continuity, an organization can either build and operate its own internal recovery site or lease an external site from a third party. If an organization does not have the funding or resources to build its own disaster recovery site, maintaining an annual contract with a commercial disaster recovery service is an effective way to protect against major business disruptions. For example, if a data center becomes inoperable a company can quickly and easily move its data processing operations to one of three types of disaster recovery sites and continue normal operations. The three types of sites are:

A **hot site** has all the necessary equipment including office space, furniture, communications capabilities and computer equipment. It also includes staffing to manage and monitor the equipment. Consequently, a hot site is fully functional and allows immediate recovery from a disaster. It is also the most expensive.

A **warm site** provides a fully equipped physical data center, but it has no customer data. The warm site is a less expensive option than the hot site and is typically used when primary data centers are attacked. After a disruption at the primary data center, an organization introduces its own customer data to restore normal business operations. The warm site takes longer to deploy than a hot site, but less time than a cold site.

A **cold site** provides office space but requires the customer to provide and install the equipment needed to continue operations. It is the least expensive option, but it takes longer to get an organization back up to full operation. A cold site is a good option when time to recovery is not critical.

In addition, to the monthly service charges established under the annual contract, daily fees and other incidental fees are also charged for use of all sites. Some of these companies also offer data backup services with or without a hot, warm, or cold site contract.

Whether an organization uses an internal or external disaster recovery site it is critical that it is located a sufficient distance from the organization's primary operations so that it is not affected by the same disaster. It's also essential that it's not on the same power grid.

Questions

1. Explain why it is becoming more important for organizations to make cyber risk management a high priority?
2. Name three IT defense tools.
3. What is the purpose of rogue application monitoring?
4. Why is a mobile kill switch or remote wipe capability an important part of managing cyber risk?
5. Why does an organization need to have a business continuity plan?
6. Name the three essential cybersecurity defenses.
7. What is the difference between hot, warm, and cold sites?
8. When and why do companies impose do-not-carry rules?

5.5 Regulatory Controls, Frameworks, and Models

LO5.5 Define *the five major general defense controls, eight major application defense controls, and the cyber security regulations and frameworks that help protect consumers and guide IT governance.*

To maintain a secure computing environment, it is important for organizations to set up a set of security controls specific to the resources and its environment. **Figure 5.13** illustrates the three major categories of cyber defense controls that used to guide the execution of a cyber defense strategy. **General defense controls** are established to protect the system regardless of the specific application. For example, protecting hardware and controlling access to the data center are independent of the specific application. **Application defense controls** are safeguards that are intended to protect specific applications. Each of these sets of controls are discussed next.

FIGURE 5.13 Major cyber defense controls.

General Defense Controls

The five major categories of general defense controls are physical controls, access controls, data security controls, communication controls, and administrative controls.

Physical controls protect physical computer facilities and resources. This includes protecting computers, data centers, software, manuals, and networks. They provide protection against most natural hazards as well as against some human hazards. Appropriate physical security may include several physical controls such as:

- Appropriate design of the data center. For example, the data center should be noncombustible and waterproof.
- Shields against electromagnetic fields.
- Well-designed fire prevention, detection, and extinguishing systems, including a sprinkler system, water pumps, and adequate drainage facilities.
- Emergency power shutoff and backup batteries, which must be maintained in operational condition.
- Properly designed and maintained air-conditioning systems.
- Motion detector alarms that detect physical intrusion.
- Badges for authorized persons.

Access control is the major line of defense against unauthorized insiders as well as outsiders. It is a security technique that dictates who is authorized to use an organization's computing resources. One example of an access control is an access list that specifies who can access a network, database, file, or data. Restricted access is achieved through a two-step process of (1) user authentication to identify different users on the network and (2) user authorization that grants or denies specific access permissions. Authentication methods include:

- Something only the user *knows*, such as a password
- Something only the user *has*, for example, a smart card or a token
- Something only the user *is*, such as a signature, voice, fingerprint, or retinal (eye) scan; implemented via biometric controls, which can be physical or behavioral

Authorization methods can be discretionary, mandatory, or role-based.

Data security controls are needed to protect sensitive data throughout the five stages of its lifecycle from creation to disposal. At *creation*, data must be classified based on how critical and sensitive it is and a data owner should be assigned. During *distribution* "data in motion" is vulnerable to compromise and appropriate safeguards such as encryption or data loss prevention technologies need to be used to prevent accidental or intentional unauthorized distribution of sensitive data. During *use*, data must be controlled so that it can be accessed only on classified systems by authorized users who have appropriate permissions. When the data is stored, or "at rest," appropriate controls must be implemented and regularly audited to make sure that the confidentiality, integrity, and availability of the data is ensured during storage and that it is backed up appropriately and regularly. During *disposition*—the final stage of the data lifecycle—controls need to specify how data will be properly destroyed according to corporate and regulatory retention and disposal policies. Without proper data security controls, organizations are leaving themselves open to lawsuits and regulatory data privacy fines.

Communications controls restrict access to devices on the network to endpoint devices that comply with the organization's security policy and secure the flow of data across networks. Typical communication network controls include firewalls, anti-malware systems, encryption, and virtual private networks.

Administrative controls deal with issuing guidelines and monitoring compliance with an organization's security guidelines. Examples of administrative controls are:

- Appropriately select, train, and supervise employees, especially in accounting and information systems
- Foster company loyalty

- Immediately revoke access privileges of dismissed, resigned, or transferred employees
- Require periodic modification of access controls, such as passwords
- Develop programming and documentation standards to make auditing easier and to use the standards as guides for employees
- Insist on security bonds or malfeasance insurance for key employees
- Institute separation of duties, namely, dividing sensitive computer duties among as many employees as economically feasible in order to decrease the chance of intentional or unintentional damage
- Perform periodic random audits of the system

Application Defense Controls

An application defense control is a security practice that blocks or restricts unauthorized apps from executing in ways that put data at risk. It ensures the privacy and security of data that is input, processed and transmitted between apps and restricts use to authorized users. Application controls include:

- Completeness checks to ensure records processing from start to finish
- Validity checks to ensure only valid data is input or processed
- Authentication to identify users
- Authorization to ensure appropriate permissions
- Input controls to ensure data integrity of all data entered
- Availability to ensure that the app is available as needed
- Whitelisting to document appropriate apps
- Blacklisting to block inappropriate apps

Auditing Information Systems

Auditing is another form of control. Some companies rely on surprise audits. But being proactive about searching for problems is more effective and can stop authorized use early on, before losses mount. An **audit** is an important part of any control system. Auditing can be viewed as an additional layer of controls or safeguards. It is considered as a deterrent to criminal actions, especially for insiders. Auditors attempt to answer questions such as these:

- Are there enough controls in the system?
- Which areas are not covered by controls?
- Which controls are not necessary?
- Are the controls implemented properly?
- Are the controls effective? That is, do they check the output of the system?
- Is there a clear separation of duties of employees?
- Are there procedures to ensure compliance with the controls?
- Are there procedures to ensure reporting and corrective actions in case of violations of controls?

Auditing a website is a good preventive measure to manage the legal risk. Legal risk is important in any IT system, but in Web systems it is even more important due to the content of the site, which may offend people or be in violation of copyright laws or other regulations (e.g., privacy protection). Auditing e-commerce is also more complex since, in addition to the website, one needs to audit order taking, order fulfillment, and all support systems. The Information Systems Audit and Control Association (www.isaca.org) provides a detailed audit roadmap for auditors to follow.

Government Regulations

As cyber threats continue to evolve and gain momentum in other industries, more and more legislative bills are being proposed. At the federal level, in the United States, many of the privacy regulations discussed previously in this chapter (see **Figure 5.2**), have a cyber security component. Others that are more specifically focused on cyber security concerns include the **Federal Information Security Management Act (FISMA)** that requires federal agencies to develop, document, and implement an information security and protection program. Many states are also making cyber security measures a higher priority. The National Conference of State Legislatures reported that in 2019, at least 43 U.S. states introduced bills that dealt significantly with cyber security. Of these, 31 states enacted cyber security legislation. Key areas covered by the new legislation require government agencies and/or business to:

- Implement training or specific types of security policies and practices.
- Create cyber security task forces and commissions.
- Restructure government for improved security.
- Provide for the security of utilities and critical infrastructure.
- Study the use of blockchain for cyber security.
- Address the security of connected devices.
- Address cyber security threats to elections.
- Provide funding for improved security measures.

To ensure compliance with regulations in the United States, the Securities Exchange Commission (SEC) and FTC has advised it will impose huge fines for data breaches to deter companies from underinvesting in data protection. With this in mind, companies that have not previously been governed by cyber security regulations will need to evaluate their current cyber security capabilities and vulnerabilities and determine how to implement security controls such as encryption, authentication, authorization, and disaster recovery.

Risk Management and IT Governance Frameworks

Two widely accepted frameworks that guide risk management and **IT governance** are the **Enterprise Risk Management (ERM) Framework** and **Control Objectives for Information and Related Technology Framework (COBIT, 2019)**.

Enterprise Risk Management Framework ERM is a risk-based approach to managing an enterprise developed by the Committee of Sponsoring Organizations of the Treadway Commission (COSO). The ERM consists of eight components, listed in **Table 5.8**.

TABLE 5.8 **Enterprise Risk Management Framework Components**

Component	Description
Internal environment	Assess risk management philosophy and culture
Objective setting	Determine relationship of risk to organizational goals
Event identification	Differentiate between risks and opportunities; negative/positive impact
Risk assessment	Assess risk probability and impact
Risk response	Identify and evaluate risk responses
Control activities	Develop policies and procedures to ensure implementation of risk responses
Information and communication	Identify, capture, and communicate information
Monitoring	Conduct ongoing and separate evaluations of risk-related activities

These eight components can be viewed from a strategic, operations, reporting, and compliance perspective at all level of the organizations. Taking a portfolio view of risk, management must consider how individual risks are interrelated and apply a strong system of internal controls to ensure effective enterprise risk management. Those involved in ERM include management, Board of Directors, Risk officers, and internal auditors. ERM is intended to be part of routine planning processes rather than a separate initiative. The ideal place to start is with buy-in and commitment from the board and senior leadership.

The COBIT 2019 Framework. COBIT 2019 is a globally recognized governance framework that integrates security, risk management, and IT governance developed by ISACA—the International Systems Audit and Control Association (www.isaca.org) . It addresses the latest trends, technologies, and security needs of organizations and aligns IT with business objectives, to deliver value, and manage associated risks. Its purpose is to enable management, users, and IS audit, control, and security practitioners to bridge the gap between control requirements, technical issues, and business risks.

The COBIT 2019 framework has 40 governance and management objectives for establishing an IT governance program and is based on a conceptual model of six governance system and three governance framework principles and seven components necessary to build and maintain a governance program. It is open and flexible and aligned to other major standards. The nine principles and seven components of COBIT 2019 are illustrated in **Figure 5.14**.

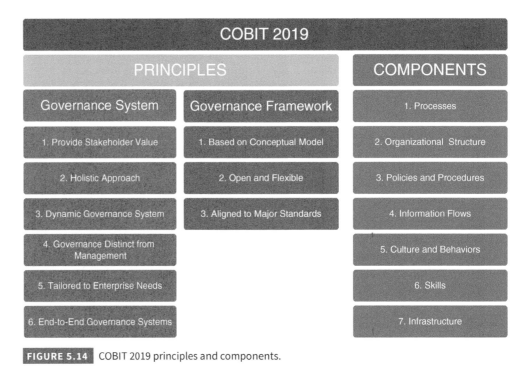

FIGURE 5.14 COBIT 2019 principles and components.

COBIT 2019 also includes focus areas and design factors that allow an organization to give an organization greater flexibility to tailor its IT governance system to its unique needs. It also adds many new features and user benefits such as implementation resources, practical guidance and insights, and comprehensive training opportunities.

The COBIT 2019 principles most applicable to cyber security:

1. A *system* needs to be in place that considers and effectively addresses enterprise information security requirements. At a minimum, this would include metrics for the number of clearly defined key security roles and the number of security-related incidents reported.

2. An established *security plan* has been accepted and communicated throughout the organization. This would include level of stakeholder satisfaction with the security plan, the number of security solutions that are different from those in the plan and the number of security solutions deviating from the enterprise security architecture that can lead to security gaps and potentially lengthen the time to resolve security or compliance issues.

3. Information security *solutions* are implemented throughout the organization. These should include the number of services and solutions that align with the security plan and security incidents caused by noncompliance with the security plan.

By following these three principles, using a specified set of IT-enabling processes, and taking additional steps to move from an application-centric focus to a data-centric focus, organizations that use COBIT 2019 can improve the governance and protection of their data and information.

While COBIT 2019 provides sound and comprehensive improvement recommendations to start the security governance journey, organizations clearly need to move beyond reactive compliance and security to proactively mandating the need for data privacy and security enterprise-wide. In this way data are always protected.

ERM and COBIT 2019 can be used separately or jointly. As with most improvement methodologies, the key to success is to start using them one step at a time.

Industry Security Standards

Industry groups impose their own standards to protect their customers and their members' brand images and revenues. One example is the **Payment Card Industry Data Security Standard (PCI DSS)** created by Visa, MasterCard, American Express, and Discover. PCI is required for all members, merchants, or service providers that store, process, or transmit cardholder data. PCI DSS requires merchants and card payment providers to make certain their Web applications are secure. If done correctly, this could reduce the number of Web-related security breaches.

The purpose of the PCI DSS is to improve customers' trust in e-commerce, especially when it comes to online payments, and to increase the Web security of online merchants. To motivate following these standards, the penalties for noncompliance are severe. The card brands can fine the retailer and increase transaction fees for each credit or debit card transaction. A finding of noncompliance can be the basis for lawsuits.

IT Security Defense-In-Depth Model

The Defense-in-Depth Model is based upon the premise that no organization can ever be fully protected by a single layer of security. However, when there are multiple levels of security defenses such as authentication and authorization, firewalls, malware scanners, intrusion detection systems, data encryption, auditing mechanisms, and user security training programs in place the gaps created by a single level of security can be effectively eliminated (**Figure 5.15**).

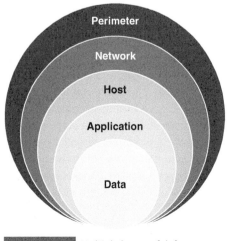

FIGURE 5.15   Multiple layers of defense.

The Model's objective is to provide redundancy to buy an organization more time in the event of a cyberattack or other vulnerability and involves people, processes, technology and the system's physical environment. The basic principle is that when one defense layer fails, another layer provides protection. For example, if a wireless network's security was compromised, then having encrypted data would still protect the data, provided that the thieves could not decrypt it.

The success of any type of IT project depends on the commitment and involvement of executive management, also referred to as the *tone at the top*. The same is true of IT security. An organization's information security stance makes users aware that insecure practices and mistakes will not be tolerated. Therefore, an IT security model begins with senior management commitment and support, as shown in **Figure 5.16**.

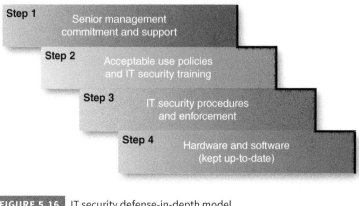

FIGURE 5.16 IT security defense-in-depth model.

To use the Defense-in-Depth Model an organization must carry out four major steps:

Step 1: Gain Senior Management Commitment and Support
Senior managers' influence is needed to implement and maintain security, ethical standards, privacy practices, and internal control. IT security is best when it is top-driven. Senior managers decide how stringent information security policies and practices should be to comply with laws and regulations. For example, financial institutions are subject to strict security and anti-money laundering (AML) rules because they face numerous national and international regulations and have high-value data. Advertising agencies and less regulated firms tend to have more lenient rules. Other factors influencing information security policies are a corporation's culture and how valuable their data are to criminals.

For instance, management may decide to forbid employees from using company e-mail accounts for nonwork purposes, accessing social media during work hours, or visiting gambling sites. These decisions will then become rules stated in company policy, integrated into procedures, and implemented with technology defenses. Sites that are forbidden, for instance, can be blocked by firewalls.

Step 2: Develop Acceptable Use Policies and IT Security Training
Organizations need to put in place strong policies and processes that make responsibilities and accountabilities clear to all employees. An **acceptable use policy (AUP)** explains what management has decided are acceptable and unacceptable activities, and the consequences of noncompliance. Rules about tweets, texting, social media, e-mail, applications, and hardware should be treated as extensions of other corporate policies—such as physical safety, equal opportunity, harassment, and discrimination. No policy can address every future situation, so rules need to be evaluated, updated, or modified. For example, if a company suffers a malware

infection traced to an employee using an unprotected smartphone connected to the company network, policies to restrict or prohibit those connections might be advisable.

Step 3: Create and Enforce IT Security Procedures and Enforcement

Secure procedures define how policies will be enforced, how incidents will be prevented, and how an incident will be responded. Here are the basic secure procedures to put in place:

a. **Define enforcement procedures** Rules that are defined in the AUP must be enforced and enforcement procedures must be applied consistently. Procedures for monitoring employee Internet and network usage are defined at this stage.

b. **Designate and empower an internal incident response team (IRT)** The IRT typically includes the CISO, legal counsel, senior managers, experienced communicators, and key operations staff. Minimizing the team size and bureaucracy can expedite decision-making and response. Because there may be significant liability issues, legal counsel needs to be involved in incident response planning and communication.

c. **Define notification procedures** When a data breach occurs the local police department, local office of the FBI, Securities and Exchange Commission (SEC), the U.S. Secret Service, or other relevant agency need to be notified immediately. Federal and state laws or industry regulations may define how and when affected people need to be notified.

d. **Define a breach response communications plan** Effective incident response communication plans include personnel and processes with lists, channels, and social media needed to execute all communications that might be needed.

e. **Monitor information and social media sources** Monitor Twitter, social media, and news coverage as a standard procedure to understand how people are responding to the incident and criticizing the company. Damage control procedures may be needed.

When an incident occurs, the organization is ready to respond intelligently—having the correct information to be honest, open, and accountable, and to communicate with consumers and other important audiences as quickly as possible.

Step 4: Implement Security Tools: Hardware and Software

The last step in the model is implementation of software and hardware needed to support and enforce the AUP and secure practices. The selection of hardware and software defenses is based on risk, security budget, AUP, and secure procedures. Every device that connects to an organization's network; every online activity and mobile app of employees; and each file sent or received are access points. Technology defense mechanisms need to be:

- able to provide strong authentication and access control of industrial grade
- appropriate for the types of networks and operating systems
- installed and configured correctly
- tested rigorously
- maintained regularly

No matter which frameworks, standards, and controls are used to assess, monitor, and control cyber risk, a balanced approach to measuring direct costs and intangible impacts associated with cyberattacks must be used to paint an accurate picture of the damage sustained and to guide the creation of increased security measures going forward. Some of the benefits that can be realized from passing cyber security and data privacy regulations can be seen in **IT at Work 5.5**.

IT at Work 5.5

Kenya Is Stepping up to Protect Its Citizens' Digital Data

It has long been acknowledged that African governments and companies have little concern for data security. The need for cyber security has been made more urgent with the rapid increase in number of mobile devices and apps and the increasing numbers of predatory attacks on consumers who are applying for credit online. This lack of concern provided social media giants Facebook, WhatsApp, and Google who are constrained in other parts of the world by existing cyber security and data privacy regulations with easy access to the personal information of consumers throughout Africa.

This situation changed in November 2019 when Kenya's president Uhuru Kenyatta stepped up and approved a new EU-inspired data protection law that is setting a high benchmark for the rest of the African continent. The new law complies with the EU's GDPR and sets out restrictions on data handling and sharing by Kenyan

government and corporations. Companies such as Kenya Airways and hotels as well as phone-based lender Safaricom will have to comply with the new data protection law when handling personal data from their clients. Any infringements of the new law will be investigated by an independent office with violators facing two-year prison sentences or maximum fine of $29,000.

The government feels that the new law is critical in encouraging new investments, particularly in the financial sector. It is already bolstering investment in its IT sector. Amazon Web Services has confirmed plans to build some of its infrastructure in Kenya and expand its operations. More stringent data protection also has benefits for the Kenyan government by dispelling concerns about how they store and handle citizen data and helping overcome widespread criticism of its plan to digitize its citizens' identities.

Sources: Compiled from Anonymous (2019), Kazeem (2019), Obulutsa and Miriri (2019), and Reuters (2019).

Questions

1. What is the purpose of general defense controls?
2. What is the purpose of application defense controls?
3. Name the five major categories of general controls.
4. Name four application controls.
5. Explain authentication and name two methods of authentication.
6. What are the six major objectives of a defense strategy?
7. What is the purpose of the PCI DSS?
8. What are the major elements in COBIT 2019?
9. What four components comprise the IT security defense-in-depth model?

Chapter Summary

LO5.1 *Describe* the four main data privacy concerns, define the privacy paradox, and describe how data privacy regulations are protecting consumers.

Data privacy issues can develop around data from many sources. The four main data privacy concerns are how the data is *shared, collected, used,* and *regulated.* The privacy paradox occurs when people say that they are concerned about the security of their data but do nothing to prevent it from being exposed and in fact, behave in ways that exacerbates the problem. U.S. consumer data privacy regulations include those related to healthcare, finance, government, licenses, and credit. At the federal level, the Federal Trade Commission (FTC) is responsible for enactment and enforcement of U.S. data protection laws, but responsibility for compliance with those laws falls to the

State Attorneys General. The major federal U.S. regulations currently in place include the Health Insurance Portability and Accountability Act (HIPAA), Gramm-Leach-Bliley Act, the Privacy Protection Action of 1980, Driver's Privacy Protection Act (DPPA), and the Fair Credit Reporting Act. At the state level, the most powerful data privacy protection law is the California Consumer Privacy Act (CCPA).

On a global level, the strictest data privacy regulation on the books at the present time is the European Union's General Data Protection Rules (GDPR). This newly enacted set or regulations empowers EU consumers by forcing retailers, marketers, and other to explicitly advise consumers how they are collecting, using, and storing consumer data. The GDPR unifies data protection laws against the 28 EU nations plus Ireland, Lichtenstein, Norway, and Switzerland to give consumers more rights and control over their information. The maximum fines that can be levied for violations of the GDPR are the highest of any data privacy regulations. The United States does not currently have adequate privacy laws, do not comply with GDPR requirements, and currently must work around this deficiency by adhering to EU-U.S. Privacy Shield and Switzerland-U.S. Privacy Shield requirements.

LO5.2 *Identify* the extent and cost of cyberattacks and the 12 different types of intentional and unintentional cyberthreats.

More and more cyberattacks are being reported worldwide daily and a large percentage of U.S. consumers feel that their data is less secure than it was five years ago. Examples of vulnerabilities in an organization that can lead to cyberattacks include lack of controls for people, processes, and technology. Several unintentional and intentional cyber threats are the cause of most cyberattacks. Unintentional cyber threats include human error, environmental hazards, and computer system failures. Intentional cyber threats include: hacking, phishing, installation of several types of intrusive and malicious malware, botnets, ransomware, cryptojacking, SQL injection, man-in-the-middle attacks, denial of service, insider threats, physical theft or loss, and miscellaneous errors.

LO5.3 *Discuss* the six most deadly targets of cyberattacks and provide an example of how each impacts consumers and organizations.

The six most prevalent and deadly targets that cybercriminals attack in companies and governmental agencies include: weak passwords, critical infrastructure, theft of IP, identify theft, bring your own device (BYOD), and social media. Weak passwords are one of the greatest weaknesses that can be used to execute numerous types of cyber threats. Attacks on critical infrastructure can significantly disrupt government and industry targets and can even compromise essential services in an entire country or area. Theft of intellectual property is increasing and particularly concerning since it can threaten a company's existence or expose a country's intelligence policies and procedures. Identity theft is also on the rise and can result in inconvenience and loss of time and resources. Another concern for organizations is the vulnerability caused when employees bring their own device (BYOD) to work. Mobile devices are easy targets for cyber criminals because of their weak authentications, lack of access controls, and inadequate or nonexistent encryption. BYOD allow hackers to break into mobile devices and leapfrog employer networks to steal sensitive data and company secrets. In addition, the corporation's mobile infrastructure may not be able to support the increase in mobile network traffic causing unacceptable delays or requiring investment in additional resources to keep up with demand. Finally, social media attacks are predicted to continue to be a major threat

for businesses. Social networks and cloud computing increases vulnerabilities by providing a single point of failure that leave it open to the installation of malware and other types of difficult to detect cyberattacks. These put the organization and its customer data at risk from exposure and theft.

LO5.4 *Identify* six cyber defense strategies, four risk management approaches, and the three essential IT defense tools.

There are six strategies that are effective defenses against cyberattacks. These are: prevention and deterrence, detection, containment, recovery, correction, and awareness/compliance. In determining a defense strategy, a company must determine the level of risk that it is willing to take in defending against cyberattacks. There are four risk mitigation approaches that can be taken: acceptance, limitation, avoidance or transfer, depending on the value of the asset being protected, and the consequences if the associated data is compromised. Three essential IT defense tools are useful in protecting against cyberattacks. These are: antivirus software, intrusion detection systems, and intrusion prevention systems. Antivirus software is designed to detect malicious codes and prevent users from downloading them and scan systems for worms, trojans, and other types of cyber threats. Intrusion detection systems scans for unusual or suspicious network traffic to alert network staff to take defense action. An intrusion prevention system is designed to take immediate action, such as blocking IP addresses and block DDoS attacks.

LO5.5 *Define* the five major general defense controls, eight major application defense controls, and the cyber security regulations and frameworks that help protect consumers and guide IT governance.

The five major general defense controls are physical, access, data security, communication, and administrative. The eight major application defense controls are completeness; validity, authentication, authorization, input controls, availability, whitelisting and blacklisting. Cyber security regulations have been put in place to protect consumers and safeguard companies from lawsuits as a result of data breaches and other types of cyberattacks. Regulations have been developed at federal and state levels. The Federal Information Security Management Act (FISMA) requires federal agencies to develop, document, and implement an information security and protection program, while the Enterprise Risk Management (ERM) Framework and COBIT 2019 focus on risk management and IT governance issues. The overarching IT Security Defense-in-Depth Model is a multilayered approach to security defense that includes authentication, authorization, firewalls, malware scanners, intrusion detection system, data encryption, and so on that are trigged at various layers of a system to provide fallbacks to another layer of protection in case of a cyberattack.

Key Terms

Interactive Exercises

Discuss: Critical Thinking Questions

1. Why is cybercrime expanding rapidly? Discuss some possible solutions.

2. In addition to hackers, what kinds of cybercriminals do organizations need to defend against?

3. What are the major motives of cybercriminals?

4. In what ways do users make themselves vulnerable to cybercrimes?

5. Why do malware creators alter their malware?

6. Why should you set a unique password for each website, service, and device that you use?

7. How can ransomware be stopped from stealing or disclosing data from an organization's network?

8. What impact might huge fines have on how much a company budgets for IT security defenses?

9. Why are BYOD, BYOA, and do-not-carry rules important to IT security? Why might users resist such rules?

10. Why do users refuse to use strong passwords even though they know how dangerous weak passwords are?

11. What factors should companies consider when they are choosing a risk management strategy?

12. Why should information control and security be of prime concern to management?

13. Explain what firewalls protect and what they do not protect.

14. Why are authentication and authorization important in e-commerce?

15. Some insurance companies will not insure a business unless the firm has a computer disaster recovery plan. Explain why.

16. Explain why risk management should involve the following elements: threats, exposure associated with each threat, risk of each threat occurring, cost of controls, and assessment of their effectiveness.

Explore: Online and Interactive Exercises

1. Visit **https://www.watchguard.com/wgrd-resource-center/security-report-q3-2019**. Read the two-page Introduction, Executive Summary, and Report Highlights of WatchGuard's Q3 2019 Internet Security Report. Summarize what you learned and write an opinion essay about the cyberattack statistics reported.

2. Visit **https://www.zdnet.com/article/this-new-ransomware-is-targeting-health-and-tech-companies-across-europe-and-north-america/**.

    a. View the video and read the article on ransomware attacks targeted on healthcare and technology companies in Europe, United States, and Canada.

    b. Explain the reasons for these breaches and discuss how they could have been avoided.

3. Visit **https://www.identityforce.com/resources/quiz** and take the Identity Theft Quiz. What was your score? Explain ways in which you could improve your score so that you are not as much at risk for identity theft.

4. Visit **https://www.cshub.com/content-hub/incident-of-the-week** and choose one of the major data breaches listed. Read about the data breach you chose. What lessons did you learn from the article? Describe your reaction to what you read.

Analyze & Decide: Apply IT Concepts to Business Decisions

1. Many firms concentrate on the wrong questions and end up throwing a great deal of money and time at minimal security risks while ignoring major vulnerabilities. Why?

2. Assessing how much a company is legally obligated to invest in cybersecurity remains a challenge. Since there is no such thing as perfect security (i.e., there is always more that you can do), resolving these questions can significantly affect cost.

   a. When are a company's security measures enough to comply with its obligations? For example, does installing a firewall and using virus detection software satisfy a company's legal obligations?

   b. Is it necessary for an organization to encrypt all of its data?

3. Assume that the daily probability of a major earthquake in Los Angeles is 0.07%. The chance of your computer center being damaged during such a quake is 5%. If the center is damaged, the average estimated damage will be $1.6 million.

   a. Calculate the expected loss (in dollars).

   b. An insurance agent is willing to insure your facility for an annual fee of $15,000. Analyze the offer and discuss whether to accept it.

4. Should an employer notify employees that their usage of computers is being monitored? Why or why not?

5. Twenty-five thousand messages arrive at an organization each year. Currently, there are no firewalls. On average, 1.2 successful hackings occur each year. Each successful hack attack results in a loss of about $130,000 to the company. A major firewall is proposed at a cost of $66,000. The estimated useful life is three years. The chance that an intruder will break through the firewall is 0.0002. In such a case, the damage will be $100,000 (30%), $200,000 (50%), or there will be no damage. There is an annual maintenance cost of $20,000 for the firewall.

   a. Should management buy the firewall?

   b. An improved firewall that is 99.9988% effective and that costs $84,000, with a life of three years and annual maintenance cost of $16,000, is available. Should this firewall be purchased instead of the first one?

Reinforce: Ensure your understanding of the Key Terms

Solve the online crossword provided for this chapter.

Web Resources

More resources and study tools are located on the student website. You'll find useful Web links and self-test quizzes that provide individualized feedback.

Case 3.2

Business Case: Multi-National Marriott Hotels Could Face Consumer Backlash and up to $1 Billion in Regulatory Fines and Litigation Costs for Massive Data Breach

Marriott is the world's biggest hotel operator of approximately 6,000 hotels in 127 countries around the world. In December 2018, Marriott discovered and reported an attack on its Starwood room reservation network that had occurred over a period four years! From 2014 to 2018 the personal details of as many as 500 million Marriott Hotel guests had been exposed making it one of the largest cyberattacks reported. Roughly 387 million contained sensitive personal information such as e-mails, dates of birth, passport number, physical addresses, and credit card details. Although Marriott claims that details such as credit

card numbers were encrypted it is believed that enough details were taken to allow the attackers to decrypt the information. Following the disclosure of the attack Marriott's shares fell 5.6% in pre-market trading and victims of the attack complained loudly on social media after finding out about the situation through the press before receiving any notification from Marriott.

While the size of the attack doesn't compare to that of Yahoo described in the opening case, the damage to Marriott's reputation is particularly devastating. Its guests rely on the hotel chain to keep them safe and secure in the real-world and the attack seemingly suggests that Marriott is incapable of ensuring its guests' digital safety and security. To add insult to injury, the company could face up to $1 billion in regulatory fines and litigation costs. To try to mitigate the impact of the reported attack, Arne Sorenson, Marriott's chief executive reached out to those affected by saying "We deeply regret this incident happening.

We fell short of what our guests deserve and what we expect of ourselves. We are doing everything we can to support guests, and using lessons learned to be better moving forward."

This latest attack is not the first for Marriott. Long before Marriott International disclosed the most recent cyberattack the hotel giant had already earned the dubious reputation of being an easy target for hackers. Hackers had skimmed credit cards, looted loyalty accounts, carried out elaborate schemes to trick Marriott employees into downloading malicious software, and in one particularly noxious attack dubbed 'Dark Hotel' networks at individual Marriott properties were hijacked to allow hackers to spy on corporate executives and politicians. In another attack, cyber criminals locked down rooms by seizing control of the keyless entry system and would not unlock them until the Marriott owner paid a ransom.

Shortly before the breach, Marriott said that it had begun to increase its investment in cyber security and had hired a new chief information security officer. The cyberattack on the Marriott hotel chain is thought to have been carried out by hackers working on behalf of the Chinese Ministry of State Security, China's communist-controlled civilian spy agency. The intelligence gathering effort that also hacked health insurers and security clearance files of millions more Americans hasn't been advertised on criminal marketplaces. This may be some consolation to the Marriott who may well face loss of business prompted by more significant backlash from its guests.

The hotel industry on the whole is not known for having robust cyber security technology. It is the third-most targeted industry after retail and finance. Hilton, Hyatt, Intercontinental, Trump, Radisson, and Mandarin Oriental have all been targets in part attacks. As hotel companies experiment with VOIP and Internet-connected rooms that could lead to the collection and storage of even more personal information, the cyberattack stakes are getting even higher.

Questions

1. Marriott had sustained several cyberattacks prior to the one described here. Why do you think it was still vulnerable to the current attack?

2. Give three reasons why you think Marriott failed to detect the current data breach for almost four years.

3. Would the sale of the personal data in criminal marketplaces affect the impact of this data breach on Marriott's reputation? Explain.

4. If you were a Marriott customer and were notified about loss of your personal data, how would you feel and what would you do?

Sources: Compiled from Bhaktavatsalam and Turner (2018), Clark (2018), Davies (2018), O'Flaherty (2018), and Kiesnoski (2019).

IT Toolbox

Conducting a Cost–Benefit Analysis

It is usually not economical to prepare protection against every possible threat. Therefore, an IT security program must provide a process for assessing threats and deciding which ones to prepare for, which ones to ignore and which ones to provide reduced protection against. Two commonly used cost–benefit analysis tools are risk assessment and business impact analysis. Risk assessment relies solely on quantitative measures, while the business impact analysis considers both qualitative and quantitative indicators.

- **Risk assessment**

    Risk assessments are done using an app or spreadsheet. The basic computations are shown here:

    $$\text{Expected loss} = P_1 \times P_2 \times L$$

    Where

    P_1 = probability of attack (estimate, based on judgment)
    P_2 = probability of attack being successful (estimate, based on judgment)
    L = loss occurring if attack is successful
    Expected loss = $P_1 \times P_2 \times L$

    Example:
    An organization estimates that the probability of a cyberattack is 2% and the attack has only a 10% chance of being successful.

If the attack is successful, the company estimates that it will lose $1 million.

This would be expressed as:

$$P_1 = 0.02, \ P_2 = 0.10, \ L = \$1,000,000$$

Then expected loss from this particular attack is

$$P_1 \times P_2 \times L = 0.02 \times 0.1 \times \$1,000,000 = \$2,000$$

- **Business impact analysis**

    A **business impact analysis (BIA)** estimates the consequences of disruption of a business function and collects data to develop recovery strategies.

    Potential loss scenarios are first identified during the risk assessment. Operations may also be interrupted by the failure of a supplier of goods or services or delayed deliveries. There are many possible scenarios that should be considered.

    The BIA identifies both operational and financial impacts resulting from a disruption. The financial impacts are easier to assess, but the operational impacts are more difficult to determine because of their qualitative nature. Several examples of operational and financial impacts to consider are shown in **Table 5.9**.

    The losses assessed using these two methods should be compared with the costs for possible recovery strategies to determine net risk. The BIA report should also prioritize the order of events for restoration of the business, with processes having the greatest operational and financial impacts being restored first.

TABLE 5.9   Business Disruption Qualitative and Quantitative Impacts

Type	Metric	Description
Financial	Quantitative	Lost sales and income
		Delayed sales or income
		Increased expenses (e.g., overtime labor, outsourcing, expediting costs)
		Regulatory fines
		Contractual penalties or loss of contractual bonuses
Operational	Qualitative	Customer dissatisfaction or defection
		Delay of new business plans

References

Anonymous. "Kenya Passes Data Protection Law to Ensure Digital Security." *International Finance*, November 15, 2019a.

Anonymous. "Phishing Attack Impacts 645,000 Oregon DHS Clients." *Prilock*, June 20, 2019b.

Anonymous. "Bayer Victim of a Cyber-attack: German Media." *PhysOrg*, April 4, 2019.

Auxier, B., Rainie, L., Anderson, M., Perrin, A., Kumar, M., and Turner, E. "Americans and Privacy: Concerned, Confused and Feeling Lack of Control Over Their Personal Information." *Pew Research Report*, November 15, 2019.

Balakrishnan, A. "U.S. Accuses Russia of Hacking Yahoo." *CNBC*, March 15, 2017.

Bhaktavatsalam, S. and Turner, G. "Marriott Cyber Attack Puts Data from 500 Million People at Risk." *Carrier Management*, November 30, 2018.

Bloomberg News. "Google Gets a $56.8 Million Fine from the EU's GDPR." *DigitalCommerce360,* January 21, 2019.

Bodoni, S. "France Uses New EU Privacy Law to Fine Google $56.8 Million." *Bloomberg*, January 21, 2019.

Brooks, R. "Data Privacy Laws by State. The U.S. Approach to Privacy Protection." *Netwrix*, August 27, 2019.

Chaffin, C. "Massive DHS Data Breach Raises Questions About Oregon's Cybersecurity Protocols." *The Oregonian*, June 24, 2019.

Cimpanu, C. "Data of 645k Oregonians Exposed After Nine DHS Employees Fell for a Phishing Attack." *ZD Net*, June 21, 2019.

CIO. "The Number Are in–IDC's 'State of IT Resilience Survey'." *CIO*, 2019.

Clark, P. "Marriott Breach Exposes Weakness in Cyber Defenses for Hotels." *Bloomberg*, December 14, 2018.

Colby, C. "Yahoo Data Breach: How to File for $358 or More as Part of Claim Settlement." *C/Net*, October 15, 2019.

Corbin, K. "Aurora Cyber Attackers Were Really Running Counter-Intelligence." *CIO*, April 22, 2013.

Cyware. "Everything You Need to Know About Operation Aurora." *Cyware*, 2019.

Dark Reading Staff. "Satya Nadella: Privacy Is a Human Right." *Dark Reading*, January 25, 2019.

Davies, T. "Marriott Hotel Chain Reveals Major Cyber Attack." *PrivSec Report*, December 3, 2018.

Davis, J. "Breach Tally of Oregon DHS Phishing Attack Reaches 645K Patients." *Health IT Security*, 2019a.

Davis, J. "350,000 Patients, 2M Emails Exposed in Oregon DHS Phishing Attack." *Health IT Security*, 2019b.

Enright, A. "GDPR Is Here." *DigitalCommerce360*, May 24, 2018.

Fiegerman, S. "Verizon Says Yahoo's Massive Breach Could Impact Deal." *CNN*, October 13, 2016.

Fogg, S. "What Is GDPR? The Basics of the EU's General Data Protection Regulation." *Termly*, June 26, 2019.

Fugairon, A. "How the GDPR and Privacy Shield Regulations Relate—and What They Mean for Your Business." *PivotPoint Security, January* 31, 2019.

Germain, T. "California's Privacy Law Is Finally Here. Now What?" *Consumer Reports*, January 2020.

Grothaus, M. "Google Has Been Fined $56.8 Million for Breaking the EU's GDPR Rules." *Fast Company*, January 22, 2019.

Hackett, R. "Yahoo's Titanic Data Breach Highlights Risk to M&A." *Fortune*, September 23, 2016a.

Hackett, R. "LinkedIn Lost 167 Million Account Credentials in Data Breach." *Fortune, May* 18, 2016b.

Hashim, A. "Pharma Giant Bayer Contained Cyber Attack Supposedly by a Chinese Hacking Group." *Latest Hacking News*, April 8, 2019.

ITRC. "2019 Data Breaches." Available from https://www.idtheftcenter .org/2019-data-breaches/ accessed on February 28, 2020.

Kan, M. "Hackers Now Have a Treasure Trove of User Data with the Yahoo Breach." *International Data Group*, September 22, 2016.

Kazeem, Y. "Kenya Is Stepping up Its Citizens' Digital Security with a New EU-Inspired Data Protection Law." *Quartz Africa*, November 12, 2019.

Kiesnoski, K. "5 of the biggest data breaches ever" CNBC. July 30, 1019. Accessed from https://www.cnbc.com/2019/07/30/five-of-the-biggest-data-breaches-ever.html on July 6, 2020.

Lee, D. "'State' Hackers Stole Data from 500 Million Users." *BBC*, September 23, 2016.

Matwyshyn, A., and H. Bhargava. "Will Yahoo's Data Breach Help Overhaul Online Security?" *Knowledge@Wharton: University of Pennsylvania*, September 27, 2016. Accessed from http://knowledge .wharton.upenn.edu/article/will-yahoos-data-breach-helpoverhaul-online-security/ on July 6, 2020.

Murgia, M. "Cyber experts look to usual suspects in Yahoo hack." *Financial Times*, September 25, 2016.

O'Flaherty, K. "Marriott Breach—What Happened, How Serious Is It and Who Is Impacted." *Forbes*, November 30, 2018.

Obulutsa, G. and Miriri, D. "Kenya Passes Data Protection Law Crucial for Tech Investments." *Reuters, November* 8, 2019.

Porter, J. "Google fined €50 million for GDPR violation in France." *The Verge*, January 21, 2019.

Rajagopal, A. "Incident of the Week: Oregon DHS Target of Phishing Attack." *Cyber Security Hub, June* 2, 2019.

Reuters. "Kenya Passes Data Protection Law Crucial for Tech Investments." *Economic Times CISO*, November 11, 2019.

Schechner, S. "Google Fined $57 Million in Biggest Penalty Yet Under New European Law." *The Wall Street Journal*, January 21, 2019.

Schwartz, M. "Google Aurora Hack Was Chinese Counterespionage Operation." *Dark Reading*, May 21, 2013.

Clement, J. "Number of Compromised Data Records in Selected Data Breaches as of May 2019." *Statista*, July 22, 2019.

Tyko, K. "Yahoo Data Breach Settlement 2019: How to Get up to $358 or Free Credit Monitoring." *USA Today*, October 14, 2019.

Verizon. "2019 Data Breach Investigations Report." Accessed from: https://enterprise.verizon.com/resources/reports/dbir/ 2019.

Walker, J. "Social Media has become an increasing cybersecurity risk for business." *SMPerth*, April 22, 2019.

Warfield, C. "Equifax Breach Vulnerability Surfaces as Top Network Attack in Q3 2019." *WatchGuard*, December 11, 2019.

Weiss, P. and Burger, L. "Bayer Contains Cyberattack It Says Bore Chinese Hallmarks." *Reuters*, April 4, 2019.

CHAPTER 6

Business Intelligence, Data Science, and Data Analytics

Case 6.1 Opening Case

NASCAR Pushes the Envelope by Combining Big Data with Augmented Reality in the World of Live Customer Engagement

The celebratory burnout after a NASCAR race has become a very popular way for NASCAR drivers to celebrate a victory, much to the delight of its fans. In fact, up to the mid-2010s there was even a contest prior to the NSCAR All-Star race that allowed drivers to compete for "best burnout"!

The Company

On December 14 1947, William Henry Getty France—an American race car driver known as "Big Bill"—met with a group of racing promoters, drivers, and mechanics to share his dream of establishing an organization to develop a set of rules and regulations to help promote stock car racing in America. Following a series of meetings, the National Association for Stock Car Auto Racing (NASCAR) was officially created on February 21, 1948. Today Jim France—son of Bill France Sr., the founder and first president of NASCAR—is NASCAR's Chairman and CEO. Although Daytona Beach had been running car races on its beach/road course since 1936, the first NASCAR sanctioned race was not run until February 15, 1948. Red Byron won the race in a Ford. "Big Bill" raced that day, too and finished fifth. Eleven years late, on February 22 1959, the first Daytona 500 race was run on the high-banked 2.5 mile Daytona International Speedway track. More than 41,000 fans were in attendance and the winner wasn't decided until 61 hours after the checkered flag was waved. Lee Petty was declared the winner—in a dramatic photo finish—by two feet. At the 62nd Annual Daytona 500 held on February 16, 2020 more than 250,000 fans cheered on America's top stock car drivers.

The Problem

Brad Keselowski, a NASCAR Cup Series champion is just one of the NASCAR drivers who felt the pressure "all the time" to provide exciting racing and attract new fans to NASCAR. He described his concern for the sport when he said, "The sport's going through its own set of struggles and the responsibility to increase NASCAR's audience falls in everybody's hands except for independent media." Many NASCAR drivers were seeing fans walk away and felt an urgent responsibility to attract new fans and bring long-lost ones back to stock car racing. Several longtime sponsors including Lowes and Target had left and although the Daytona 500 is always sold out, race attendance overall

was inconsistent and shrinking. For example, at the Food City 500 held in Spring 2019, the 150,000 capacity Bristol Speedway in Tennessee attracted a mere 38,000. The crowd was so small that speedway management didn't open some sections of the track to "enhance the fan experience" by bringing fans together in the straightaway sections on both side of the track. The TV ratings were also on the decline and had hit a record low following a pattern of decline over the past several years. Coupled with the recent retirement of some of NASCAR's biggest stars like Dale Earnhardt Jr., Jeff Gordon, and Tony Stewart it's clear that the sport is undergoing some big changes. It was agreed that NASCAR and its sponsors needed to make the sport more "fun and engaging" for its fans and drivers.

The Solution

NASCAR top management came up with the idea of bringing the experience of being at a race or at racing activities like burnouts to millions of fans who cannot attend an event in person. By integrating **big data** and **augmented reality** (AR) into front-end apps NASCAR saw a way to engage with its fans at a more personal level. The AR burnout simulation experience took many months of research and due diligence and in September 2019, NASCAR mobile app (**https://www.nascar.com/mobile**) users were able to use AR to get behind the wheel of their favorite NASCAR Playoff driver's car and perform burnouts in a 3D-rendered vehicle. The NASCAR AR burnout Experience driven by Goodyear was available to all users with AR-enabled devices through the end of the NASCAR playoffs. AR is a key area of development at NASCAR where the company is continually seeking new ways to bring immersive experiences to fans using next-generation technology. "Going into this project, we knew it was going to be 'leading edge,' so we leaned on business partners with established mobile delivery platforms such as Apple and Google, said Tim Clark, NASCAR senior vice president and chief digital officer, "We also employed a software development agency to assist us with developing the AR applications, and we had a team of around half a dozen developers and specialists on our own staff that we dedicated to the project." Since video data used for the burnouts was for simulations and not real-time video, the data was stored in an offline data repository. This data was optimized for performance so that bandwidth constraints with user mobile devices were minimized. The project involved capturing 3D renderings of cars and then creating a virtualization of burnouts that approximated the experience of being at a live burnout event.

In addition, to the AR burnout experience, NASCAR marshalled its cache of big data to create ten live 360-degree video streams to give viewers a look inside the race cars of various drivers during the races. The first was in driver Bubba' Wallace's car at the 2019 Daytona 500.

The Outcome

NASCAR now considers AR as an integral part of its customer outreach and marketing strategies. According to Clark "Augmented reality is helping us revolutionize the way NASCAR fans engage with the sport. Our goal is to bring fans as close to the sport as possible, and AR is an ideal medium to help us accomplish that . . ." Although it's too early to determine the long-time value of the NASCAR AR Burnout Experience and the 360-degree video streams, Clark added "we are just beginning to get feedback from fans . . . and the feedback has been very positive."

Questions

1. What issues were NASCAR dealing with that led it to consider using AR in its marketing strategy?
2. How did NASCAR approach the problem?
3. What benefits did AR offer to NASCAR fans?
4. What do you think NASCAR could do to further improve on its AR and big data initiatives?

Sources: Compiled from Eubanks (2019), Geekadmin (2019), Martinelli (2019), McCormick (2019), Meredith (2019), Patel (2019), Shacklett (2019), Staff Report (2019), and NASCAR (2020).

 DID YOU KNOW?

Data scientists come up with the craziest data-based facts! In a study of the most damaging hurricanes in the US during a six-month period, data scientists found that the ones with feminine names killed an average of 42 people compared to an average of 15 deaths reported from hurricanes with male names.

Introduction

The concept of using pictures or graphics to understand data has been around for centuries—from 17th-century maps and graphs to the invention of the pie chart in the early 1800s. In recent years, technology has brought the art and science of data visualization to the forefront, and it is changing the corporate landscape along with much more sophisticated data analytics methods and techniques and software that supports them.

Historically, data analytics was performed by statisticians, programmers, and data scientists who rarely interact directly with the business. However, easier-to-use data visualization, dashboard, and mashup technologies have changed this "experts-only" approach to data analysis and presentation. Today, data analytics are being pushed out into the business by advances that make it possible for employees at most levels of the organization to analyze data in a meaningful way. Vendors of enterprise-level analytics are also upgrading their analytics platforms previously designed for use by the statistical experts.

In this chapter, you will learn about three different levels of data analytics that range from business intelligence to data science and how they are being used to enhance performance, productivity, and competitive advantage in organizations around the globe. Later in this chapter, we expand on these topics to introduce you to the latest methods and techniques that are being used to conduct descriptive, predictive, and prescriptive data analytics including data mining, data visualization with dashboards and mashups, text mining, geospatial data mining, linear and time-series regression, and machines learning. We will also introduce you to data analytics software that offers drag-and-drop, automation, "show me" wizards, and easy-to-use dashboards that enable business users to develop their own interactive data visualization apps and dashboards. At one end of the spectrum data analytics software offers simple, point-and-click interfaces that do not require any particular coding knowledge or significant training. At the other end of the spectrum, data visualization software can be extremely powerful and complex. These more powerful data analytics apps enable business users to perform the kind of advanced analysis that could only have been performed by expert users of statistical software a few years ago. The combination of high-performance analytics and an easy-to-use data exploration interface enables different types of users to create and interact with graphs and charts to better understand and derive more value from their data faster than ever.

In Section 6.1, you will learn the fundamentals of BI and data science, how they add value in an organization, and the challenges associated with their use. We will also provide you with examples of BI software and the types of skills currently in high demand by organizations expanding their efforts to train, hire and retain competent BI professionals. In Section 6.2, you will learn how big data has led to advances in data analytics and how they add value in organizations to help them compete. In Section 6.3, you will learn about several descriptive data analytics methods and techniques that are used by organizations to make BI-guided decisions and in Section 6.4, you will learn some more advanced data analytics methods and techniques that drive predictive and prescriptive data analytics to give organizations powerful insights into their data stores and suggest actions they can take to improve organizational performance, growth and sustainability.

6.1 | Business Intelligence and Data Science

LO6.1 Define *the four phases of decision-making, the differences between business intelligence and data science and how each can be used to enable organizations gain a competitive advantage.*

Organizations are becoming increasingly dependent on analyzing data stored in IT systems to make important business-related decisions every day to make decisions about how to connect better with their customers, drive innovation and improve performance. Following a systematic step-by-step decision-making process helps managers make more deliberate and thoughtful decisions by collecting and organizing relevant data, gaining insights into the data and developing acceptable alternative solutions to an identified problem or opportunity.

Four Phases of Decision-Making

Decision-making occurs in four phases (**Figure 6.1**).

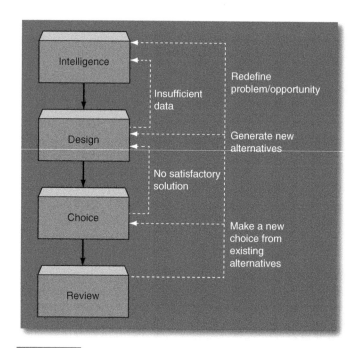

FIGURE 6.1   Four phases of decision-making.

- **Intelligence Phase**   Identify the problem or opportunity. Collect information. Establish a goal and assessment criteria.
- **Design Phase**   Specify various courses of action to solve the problem or exploit the opportunity. Analyze feasible alternatives. Evaluate each alternative against the criteria established in the intelligence stage.
- **Choice Phase**   Select an alternative course of action.
- **Review Phase**   (sometimes called the monitor, control, or implementation stage) Monitor and control the choice to ensure its proper execution. Return to any previous phase, including redefining the problem or opportunity if the solution fails.

Herbert Simon, a Nobel Prize winner in Economics, argued that when managers at all levels of an organization make decisions they are hampered by what he called "**bounded rationality**" Simon proposed that every decision is constrained by the cognitive limitations of the decision-maker, tractability of the decision and time available to make the decision and this leads to managers often **satisficing** rather than **optimizing** and a decision is made that is "good enough" but not optimal (Simon, 1956). On the whole optimizers achieve better outcomes than satisficers.

Data analytics is one way that decision-makers can more easily optimize their decisions by reducing huge volumes of data to a manageable amount of reliable, accurate and timely data presented in ways that are easy to understand.

Data Driven Decision-Making with Data Analytics

There are three levels of data analytics that vary in complexity and added value (**Figure 6.2**). The three levels are **descriptive**, **predictive**, and **prescriptive data analytics**.

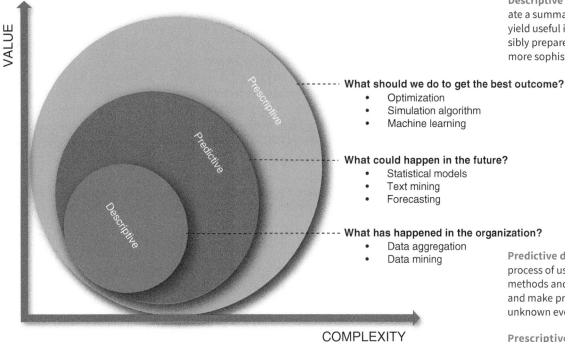

What should we do to get the best outcome?
- Optimization
- Simulation algorithm
- Machine learning

What could happen in the future?
- Statistical models
- Text mining
- Forecasting

What has happened in the organization?
- Data aggregation
- Data mining

FIGURE 6.2 Three levels of data analytics.

To help managers make optimal decisions in real-time data analysts and data scientists perform data gathering, preparation, analysis, and presentation tasks that range from descriptive **business intelligence (BI)** reporting to the more sophisticated predictive and prescriptive approach known as **data science**. BI is designed primarily to handle static and highly structured data from a single source such as numbers in a spreadsheet or database. Data science builds on BI's reporting capabilities to predict and prescribe by handling high-speed, high-volume, and complex multi-structured data from a wide variety of sources such as social media posts, IoT sensor data, text messages, images, and audio files. In addition to working with different types of data, BI and data science answer different types of questions (**Figure 6.3**).

Bounded rationality is the idea that rationality is limited by the tractability of the decision, cognitive limitations of the mind and time available to make the decision.

Satisficing is a decision-making strategy that involves searching through available alternatives until an acceptable solution is found. It is a composite of the words "satisfy" and "suffice".

Optimizing is the process of finding an alternative that is most cost effective or produces best achievable performance under given constraints by maximizing desired effects and minimizing undesired effect.

Descriptive data analytics create a summary of historical data to yield useful information and possibly prepare the data for future more sophisticated analysis.

Predictive data analytics is the process of using data analytics methods and techniques to model and make predictions about unknown events from data.

Prescriptive data analytics is dedicated to finding the best course of action among various choices given the known parameters.

Business intelligence (BI) is a set of best practices, software, infrastructure and tools to acquire and transform raw highly structured data into actionable insights to help managers at all levels of the organization make informed business decisions.

Data science is a multi-disciplinary field that uses domain expertise, scientific methods, programming skills, algorithms and statistics to extract knowledge and insights from structured, semi-structured and unstructured big data sets to predict future behavior and prescribe actions.

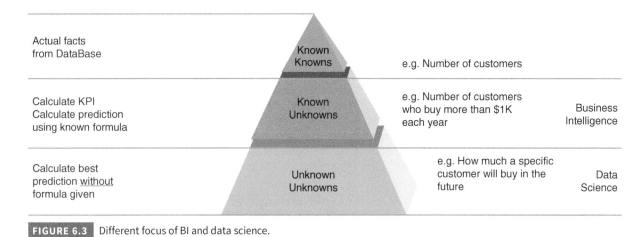

FIGURE 6.3   Different focus of BI and data science.

Known unknown is something we don't know, and we know we don't know it.

Unknown unknown is something we don't know, and we don't realize we don't know it.

Known known is something that we know, and we know that we know it.

The fundamental difference between the types of questions that business intelligence and data science is that traditional BI provides *new* values of things that we know that is **known unknowns** and although modern BI is gradually moving toward being able to handle questions that haven't been answered before, that is, **unknown unknowns**, data science is already proficient at answering these types of complex questions and transforming them into questions to which we already know the answer, that is, **known knowns**.

For example, in a traditional BI environment a manager might approach a BI developer with a formula or method that the manager understands and trusts to calculate customer lifetime value (CLV) and request the BI team to prepare a visual profile of the organization's most valuable customers and their buying preferences. In a data science setting, that same manager would bring their actual data and some questions that have never been answered before but wouldn't have a formula for calculating the answer. The data science team is then left to test multiple approaches, select the best ones based on environmental constraints and create a testable model to answer the business questions. Each of these concepts is discussed next.

Traditional and Modern Business Intelligence (BI)

Dashboard is a graphical user interface that provides at-a-glance views of relevant KPIs to an organization or department.

Data mashup the integration of two or more data sets from various business systems and external sources without relying on the middle step of ETL (extract, transform, and load) into a data warehouse or help from IT.

Data visualization is the process of representing abstract business or scientific data as images, diagrams, graphs, or animations that can aid in understanding the meaning of the data.

Before an organization can decide where it wants to go, it must know the current state of the business vis-à-vis its competitors on price, product quality, and market share. The demand for operational intelligence across multiple systems and businesses has increased dramatically as more and more people demand access to increasing amounts of data. Collecting data is relatively easy. Making sense of that data is not. Traditional BI provides managers with an easy to understand "snapshot" of what is happening now and what happened in the past to bring an organization to its current state. It is a relatively unsophisticated data analysis method that uses **dashboards**, **data mashups**, and **data visualization** (discussed in detail in Section 6.3) to allow managers to easily spot anomalies, outliers and trends in the data without sorting through pages of spreadsheets or lengthy reports. By providing managers with more interactive views of the data and empowering teams to analyze their own data, managers can better identify efficiencies and make more informed day-to-day decisions. Typical BI initiatives focus on the analysis of structured or semi-structured *historical* data to make it easier for users to ask data-related questions and integrate and deliver relevant and useful business information across an organization in an easy to understand format. Reporting is a central part of traditional BI and results are primarily descriptive analytics.

BI enables organizations to answer questions like:

- Which products have the highest repeat sales rate in the last six months?
- Do customer 'likes' on Facebook relate to product purchase?
- How does the sales trend break down by product group over the last five years?
- What do daily sales look like in each of my sales regions?
- How satisfied are patients with hospital healthcare services?

Modern BI is a more flexible and accessible than traditional BI. It is enabling BI to evolve as a more mature discipline that goes beyond just reporting and provides interactivity and mobile analytics for quick, fact-based decision-making along with large back-end functions for maintaining control and governance over reporting operations (Scherbak, 2019). Modern BI doesn't tell managers what to do and what will happen if a certain decision is made instead it enables managers to understand trends and develop insights from the data and expedites finding, merging and querying the data in real time. The focus of modern BI is to provide visual interactive **self-service analytics** to improve the speed and quality of decision-making at all management levels and add value to tactical and strategic management processes by supporting data access, interactivity, analysis, discovery, sharing and data governance. Reducing dependency on IT staff has a long history. For example, at one time, managers did not analyze data with spreadsheets, that work was carried out by the IT department, then Excel expertise became and the norm and managers were able to run their own reports in the format they wanted, when they wanted them.

Now, a modern BI solution with a flexible and personalized dashboard provides retailers with better visibility into inventory to make better decisions about what to order, how much, and when in order to prevent stock-outs or minimize inventory that sits on warehouse shelves or hospital administrators can benefit from using a BI dashboard like the one shown in **Figure 6.4** to visualize the patient experience through KPIs that provide insights into the patient experience and use that information to customize the patient experience, improve overall patient satisfaction and consequently improve efficiencies and profitability.

> **Modern BI** allows users to product reports and analysis on-the-fly and share data with other users to make decisions and optimize business results.

> **Self-service analytics** is a form of BI that enables and encourages managers and other users to perform queries and generate reports with nominal IT support.

FIGURE 6.4 BI metrics show how satisfied the patient was with their care, length of the average appointment, which department they visited, etc. to help provide more personalized healthcare.

Source: © Syncfusion Inc.

This latest generation of BI also includes "**embedded BI**" where dashboard reporting, data visualization and other analytics tools are seamlessly integrated into existing business apps to empower non-technical users with the ability to access data and build interactive dashboards and BI reports. This approach simplifies BI and leads to easier deployment, ability to tailor analytical functionality to the business and a specific situation, enable more seamless business processes and add value to existing software investments. Embedded BI also allows organizations to collect data from multiple streams of data and automate and merge it into one source of reliable information to quickly and easily answer business questions. Some forms of embedded BI extend functionality to mobile devices to ensure distributed workforces have access to BI support and enable real time collaboration.

> **Embedded BI** is the integration of self-service analytics tools and capabilities within commonly used business software apps.

Adding Value with Traditional and Modern BI

Companies and entire industry sectors are using BI's data visualization and interactivity to improve decision speed and quality—often with mobile displays - in the following ways.

Quick Detection and Decisions in Stock Markets

Wall Street firms, traders, wealth managers, risk analysts, and regulators rely on their ability to process and capitalize on market anomalies in real time. Because of the demanding pace of their decisions, capital market professionals use visualization for risk analysis, pretrade and posttrade checks, compliance monitoring, fraud detection, client profitability analysis, research and sales, and portfolio performance. Financial institutions not only need data visualization, but their executives and investors also expect the quality and excitement of visuals to make sense of dry financial data, such as real-time visual interpretation solutions that reflect opportunities, risk, and market changes.

Prompt Disaster Response by the Insurance Industry

The effectiveness of an insurer's response to a devastating hurricane or other catastrophic event depends on its ability to combine large amounts of data to fully understand the impact. Leading insurers are using Web-based data visualization and analysis technologies to better manage their responses to major disasters. In the days and weeks after a disaster, insurers face analysis and reporting bottlenecks. Analysts capable of creating maps and reports work frantically to respond to requests for information. Because new data continue being generated even after the event, the data have a short life span and reports need to be regenerated and redistributed. For example, when an earthquake occurs, workers throughout an insurance company access a Web-based (cloud) data app to visualize and analyze the impact. Users quickly determine which properties were subject to specific shake intensities and can visually build analyses on their own, rather than waiting for a report.

Pratt and Fruhlinger (2019) describe how some organizations are benefitting from using BI:

- **HelloFresh**—a BI solution saved a marketing analytics team 10–20 working hours per day by automating reporting processes and empowered the larger marketing team to develop regional, individualized digital marketing campaigns based on aggregate analyses of customer behavior.

- **REI**—increased its membership rates and member satisfaction by analyzing acquisition, retention and activation rates in their co-op membership database. They also improved shipping methods, member lifecycle management and product category offerings by analyzing customer segmentation.

- **Chipotle**—had disparate data sources that were hindering teams from seeing a unified view of its restaurants. A new modern BI platform allowed them to create a centralized view of operations to track restaurant operations at a national level. This led to better staff access to data and speed of report delivery for strategic projects has tripled from quarterly to month and saved thousands of hours of work.

- **Columbus Ohio School System**—used BI tools to examine numerous data points ranging from student attendance rates to student performance to improve student learning and high school graduation rates.

IT at Work 6.1 describes how Goodwill Industries of Denver uses BI to give back to the Community and more effectively and efficiently achieve its mission.

IT at Work 6.1

At Goodwill Industries of Denver, a Better Run Business makes for a Better Run World

Nonprofit organizations like Goodwill face some tough challenges but dealing with technology shouldn't be one of them. Goodwill Industries of Denver, Colorado is an independent member of Goodwill Industries International that recently merged with Colorado Springs-based Discover Goodwill of Southern & Western Colorado to create a $135 million nonprofit whose operations span the state. Its mission is to put people—including those with disabilities, the chronically unemployed, disadvantaged youths back to work by giving them education, career development, and mentoring. Retailing is their main business and they must keep sales and expenses under control, increase productivity and eliminate risk. However, too often budget and resource constraints limited them to using antiquated and inefficient business software on top of which the software was implemented on older technology and disparate systems. The company was analyzing their data through an internally created Excel database because it was cheap. In the words of Cindy Floyd, senior director of IT, they "needed a single pane of glass rather than separate shards located here and there and not fitting well together". In other words, to achieve their mission they needed to take advantage of next-generation applications and solutions and without adding more support staff.

To address these issues, Goodwill partnered with SAP to implement SAP's Business ByDesign software that would provide a single source for all Goodwill's data and allow managers to easily visualize sales levels at different locations, track warehouse expenses and determine headcounts they needed to maintain. Built-In Analytics is an essential capability of SAP's solution that drives transparency in the data and delivers analytical insights as an integrated part of business processes right out-of-the-box.

Before using SAP's Business ByDesign, Goodwill had several processes that were creating a lot of overhead that they have now brought under control. Now, instead of spending a lot of money on late payments, they can track and pay bills previously done on paper—that often got lost of forgotten—by easily tracking them in Business ByDesign and have already seen significant process performance improvements, increased productivity and cost savings. With Business ByDesign they can combine a lot of data and information to analyze it in ways not previously possible and are putting the savings they realize from using it back into the community. Providing people out in the community with new opportunities has proved to be very rewarding to Goodwill management and has enabled it to support its mission in a more efficient way.

Sources: Compiled from Campbell and Tully (2018), Kure (2018), Rodgers (2019), and SAP (2020).

Finding and Hiring BI Professionals

According to O*Net OnLine—a free online database that contains hundreds of occupational definitions—a BI professional "Produces financial and market intelligence by querying data repositories and generating period reports and devises methods for identifying data patterns and trends in available information sources." (O*Net Online, 2020).

One of the challenges organizations are struggling with is finding and hiring qualified data analytics professionals. Right now, there is a huge shortage of BI professionals who really understand big data even though it is one of the most exciting IT disciplines and future demand is expected to be even higher than it currently is.

BI professionals include BI analysts, BI developers, BI managers, BI consultants, and business analysts. For example, a BI analyst produces financial and market intelligence by querying data repositories and generating period reports. They also devices methods for identifying data patterns and trends in available data sources. Typical companies in a variety of industry sectors that employ BI analysts include Amazon, Boeing, USAA Insurance, Walt Disney Co., Banco Santander, and Sprint Nextel Corp. As of March 2020, the Bureau of Labor Statistics reports that the typical annual salary of a BI analyst ranges from $66,410 to $117,070 dependent on qualifications, experience and geographic location. **Career Insight 6.1** describes the job responsibilities and certifications available to BI analysts.

Career Insight 6.1

Becoming a BI Analyst

If the idea of discovering patterns in large volumes of data, interpreting the meaning of information for others and establishing and maintaining interpersonal business relationships appeals to you may want to consider a career as business intelligence (BI) analyst. As a BI analyst you would:

- Analyze competitive market strategies through analysis of related product, market or share trends.
- Synthesize current BI or trend data to support recommendations for action
- Stay abreast of industry and business trends.
- Manage timely flow of BI information to users.
- Collect BI data from available industry reports, public information, field reports or purchased sources.
- Prepare analytical reports and presentations.
- Develop information communication procedures to communicate with customers, competitors, suppliers, professional organizations, or other stakeholders.

- Use technology such as Alteryx, Tableau, Apache Hadoop; Teredata Database; Oracle PL/SQL, Amazon Redshift and Oracle JDBC, Apache Groovy, or Apache Tomcat.
- Perform statistical modeling using Python, R, SAS, or SPSS.
- Demonstrate proficiency in writing SQL, NoSQL or NewSQL BI queries, data modeling and data mining from multiple sources.

If you want to stand out from the crowd, The Bureau of Labor Statistics (**https://www.onetonline.org/link/summary/15-1199.08? redir=15-1099.10#Credentials**) lists 91 BI certifications that can be earned from 26 different sources (usually vendors) and the Data Warehousing Institute (TDWI) and the Institute for Certification of Computing Professionals (ICCP) have partnered to offer the Certified Business Intelligence Professional (CBIP) a vendor-neutral certification that tests applicant on their knowledge of information systems, data warehousing and a choice of business analytics, data integration, leadership and management, or data analysis and design. Holding this type of certification can result in a 10% to 20% premium in salary over those who do not have a BI certification.

Software to Support BI Professionals

BI software analyzes data, organizes it according to patterns and trends and visually presents the patterns to users—who may not be familiar with complex statistical analysis methods and techniques—so they can easily understand the information being presented. It is characterized by easy-to-use functionality that supports analytics workflow from data preparation to visual exploration and insight generation. Most user-friendly software has interactive elements and can pull data from Google Docs, Excel spreadsheets, Access databases, and other sources that most managers work with already to make it easy to see patterns and trends and identify opportunities for further analysis.

Modern BI software is evolving to provide business users with insights into fast changing markets where speed is valued over accuracy with an emphasis on self-service and augmentation. Trustmarque and Tableau (2020) describe the seven key attributes of modern BI software as:

- **Speed**—you can ask and answer questions in real-time even when working with massive and diverse data sets.
- **Visualization**—modern BI enables self-service analytics so users can ask more questions, **drill down** into the data and generate shareable dashboards.
- **Single source of truth**—massive volumes of data from difference sources can easily be combined blend different data sources in real-time with no upfront integration costs.
- **Real-time collaboration**—data is always live. Users can filter, sort, discuss, transform, and share data instantaneously.
- **Comprehensive governance**—views data governance as an important step in creating a safe and trusted environment for self-service analytics resulting in accurate, available and audited dashboards and reports.
- **Scalability**—start small and scale as needed. Modern BI supports all stages of an organization's analytical evolution.
- **Mobility**—Smartphone and tablet compatible to allow users to view, interact and share analytics regardless of device and location.

Figure 6.5 shows how BI has evolved from performance monitoring and KPI analysis to sophisticated self-service analytics platforms driven by artificial intelligence (AI). The major feature of modern BI that is proving to be a key competitive differentiator for vendors is

augmented analytics. Augmented analytics uses **machine learning** and artificial intelligence to automate data preparation, insight generation and insight explanation to augment how business managers and analysts explore, interpret and share data.

Augmented analytics is the use of machine learning and AI in BI tools to automate data preparation and help users discover and share insights.

Machine learning is scientific algorithms that identify patterns in big data to learn from the data and create insights based on the data.

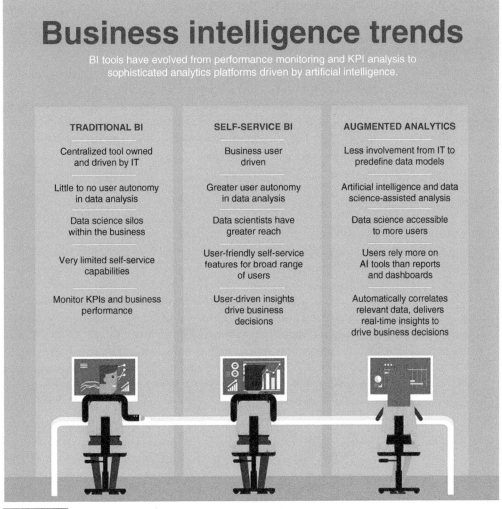

Business intelligence trends

BI tools have evolved from performance monitoring and KPI analysis to sophisticated analytics platforms driven by artificial intelligence.

TRADITIONAL BI	SELF-SERVICE BI	AUGMENTED ANALYTICS
Centralized tool owned and driven by IT	Business user driven	Less involvement from IT to predefine data models
Little to no user autonomy in data analysis	Greater user autonomy in data analysis	Artificial intelligence and data science-assisted analysis
Data science silos within the business	Data scientists have greater reach	Data science accessible to more users
Very limited self-service capabilities	User-friendly self-service features for broad range of users	Users rely more on AI tools than reports and dashboards
Monitor KPIs and business performance	User-driven insights drive business decisions	Automatically correlates relevant data, delivers real-time insights to drive business decisions

FIGURE 6.5   The evolution of BI.

It is expected that through the end of 2020 manual data management tasks will be reduced by 45 percent and more than half of major new business systems will use real-time context data to improve decision-making. Gartner (2020a) predicts that by 2022, augmented analytics technology will be mainstreamed in BI apps.

According to the 2020 Gartner Magic Quadrant for BI and Analytics (Gartner, 2020a), the current leaders in BI and descriptive data analytics platforms are:

- **Microsoft Power BI** (**https://powerbi.microsoft.com**)—offers easy-to-use data preparation, visual-based **data discovery**, interactive dashboards and augmented analytics. It is available on-site as an SaaS offering and has AI/machine learning functionality to offer context-aware insights.

- **Tableau** (**https://www.tableau.com**)—enables business users to access, prepare, analyze, and present results of data queries. It has augmented analytics and data governance capabilities along with natural language queries and automated insights. **Qlik** (**https://www.qlik.com**)—offers users at all levels to run Qlik Associative Engine—an integrating inference engine to replace the query-based approach, which divorces data from its context. Using an inference engine, users can input as much information as they have, and the software not only searches for the information provided but also will make associations with all other relevant data.

- **Thoughtspot** (**https://www.thoughtspot.com**)—has a search-based interface that supports complex questions with augmented analytics, including AI-driven crowdsourced-driven recommendations and autonomous monitoring of business metrics. It also has an in-database query option for Snowflake databases.

Data Visualization Consultants Respond to Demand In many organizations, data does not satisfy the four Vs. For example, many organizations still operate based on siloed data and cannot integrate data from different sources for quick or easy access, there is too much "dirty" data or they do not have personnel with the skills to leverage the full power of data analytics. To meet this need, data visualization consulting/service companies are bridging the gap between the organization, its data structures and lack of high-level data analysis skills. For example, xFusion Technologies provides a full range of IT services and solutions and seamless addresses the three roadblocks that obstruct the effective realization of data visualization: integration, interoperability and insight. Info-Matrix, a private, women owned small business, provides end-to-end BI data analytics tools and services (CIO Review, 2020).

Data Science

Oftentimes, BI is not enough. Instead of just *describing* the current status of primarily structured data, data science goes beyond the reporting functions of BI by using scientific methods and data modeling to *predict* future behavior and *prescribe* action to *optimize* processes based on unstructured, semi-structured and structured data **(Figure 6.6)**. Typically, historical data is used to build a mathematical model based on important trends. In data science, the model is then used on current data to predict what will happen next and prescribe actions to take for optimal outcomes. The goal of data science is to find patterns and trends in big data sets that lead to practical solutions to real-life data centric problems. To do this, data scientists combine critical thinking and scientific methods with a variety of data methods and techniques that enable them to easily understand and derive real meaning from the data.

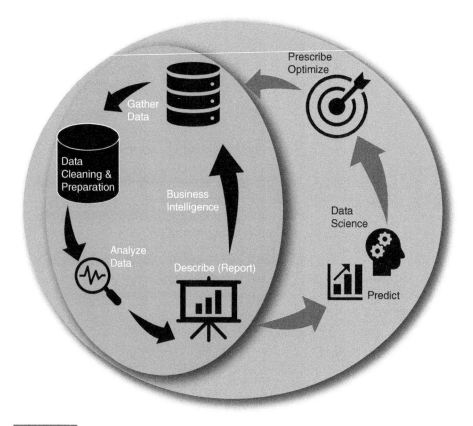

FIGURE 6.6 Data science goes beyond BI descriptions to predict and prescribe.

We describe the data science lifecycle as a seven-stage process (**Figure 6.7**). The activities that occur in each of the seven stages include:

FIGURE 6.7   Seven-stage decision science lifecycle.

- STAGE 1—CAPTURE DATA
  - Understand business requirements—understand which KPIs the business wants to focus on and optimize. Gain domain knowledge and understanding.
  - Gather, enter and extract data—Use tools and programming languages like Python, R, SQL, NoSQL and NewSQL to import data from multiple sources.

- STAGE 2—STORE DATA
  - Clean data—If data is not easy to read or has been compromised preliminary steps must be taken to "clean" the data that is, handling missing data, outliers, categorical data, standardizing naming conventions, etc. before it is input into models.
  - Ensure data security and integrity whether it is in Excel spreadsheets, data warehouses and/or across disparate sets and enable accessibility to authorized persons.

- STAGE 3—MODEL DATA
  - Create a Model—Select algorithms to use and populate them with prepared data. Using a baseline model compare performance of difference models against it. Keep it simple. If logistic regression offers 90% accuracy, there's no need to use neural nets which are much more complex, just to improve it to 91%.
  - Evaluate Model Performance—What is the goodness of fit of the model? Compare the model against the KPIs identified in Step 1. Make sure all business constraints are satisfied.

- STAGE 4—ANALYZE DATA
  - Perform exploratory data analysis.
  - Conduct confirmatory statistical data analytics (descriptive, predictive, and prescriptive) and perform visualization tests to discover patterns in the underlying data.

- STAGE 5—COMMUNICATE INFORMATION
  - Use business intelligence methods and techniques to report results to stakeholders.
  - Distribute data visualization reports and dashboards.
  - Get validation of how the model performs in a wide variety of business situations from all project stakeholders.
  - Manage stakeholder expectations.

- STAGE 6—DEPLOY DATA MODEL
  - Collaborate with data scientist, data engineers, software developers depending on the nature of the project.
  - Make sure there are no conflicts with other apps that are inter-dependent.
  - Test the model in the real-world production environment. If all KPIs react favorably, and all other business constraints are well under control we proceed to the next step, if not, identify problems and cycle through the previous steps again.
  - Gain business buy-in. This is the final check point. Core development work ends and support and maintenance come into play. The project is successful, and the outcome is a model that works to improve business efficiencies or competitiveness.

- STAGE 7—REITERATE PROCESS
  - Operate and optimize the data model as changes in the business degrade the effectiveness of the current model.
  - Monitor KPIs continuously—possibly through a visualization dashboard.
  - If model performance degrades, retrain the model using updated data.

Throughout its lifecycle, data science combines knowledge from many STEM disciplines including mathematics, statistics and computer programming and supplements it with domain knowledge about the topic of interest to use algorithmically supported scientific methods (**Figure 6.8**). Each of these are discussed in Section 6.4.

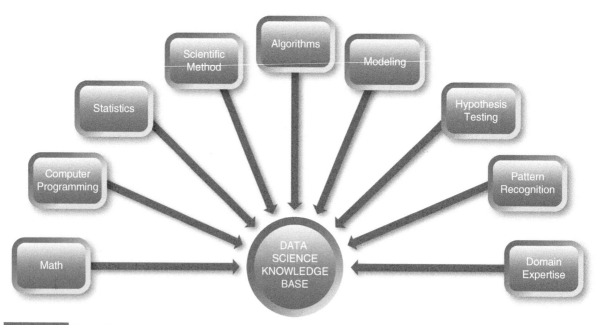

FIGURE 6.8 Data science is a composite of multiple STEM disciplines and domain knowledge.

Adding Value with Data Science

Insights gained through taking a data science approach can then lead to game-changing business decisions that impact revenue, the ability to compete, innovation and creativity, operational efficiencies and enhance the customer experience. Organizations that use data science to discover insights in their data stores to aid in corporate decision-making include:

- **Netflix**—**data mining** uncovers movie viewing patterns to understand what drives user interest and uses the algorithmically generated results to decide on topics for future Netflix original series.
- **Target**—identifies major customer segments within its customer base and analyzes the unique shopping behaviors of each segment to help them guide message content for different market audiences.
- **Procter and Gamble**—uses time series models to understand future consumer demand and help plan for optimal production levels across their extensive range of products.

Data science methods and techniques also develop "**data products**" like those created by recommendation engines that utilize user data to make personalized suggestions such as items to buy presented by Amazon, movie suggestions from Roku and music tips from Pandora.

> **Data product**   is a technical function that encapsulates an algorithm and is designed to integrate directly into core applications.

For example, it has been proposed that data science will drive the automotive industry in the future because of the vast quantities of big data generated by sensors as vehicles become more autonomous and that "traditional auto manufacturers will partner with non-automotive tech companies like Google, Apple, Uber, and Lyft to exploit their strengths and minimize their inherent weaknesses . . . to determine the trajectory of vehicle feature development" (Nerad 2019). Other industry sectors and business tasks that data science can be applied to include:

- **Aviation**   Real-time monitoring of the 'health' of aircraft by predicting performance of oil, fuel, liftoff and general aircraft mechanics.
- **Marketing**   Generating coupons at point of sale based on customer profiles and gaining valuable insights into customer behavior, including what content they want to read on a Web page or what products they are most likely to buy through a scientifically-generated data model and algorithms.
- **Financial Services**   Updating financial risk portfolios in a matter of minutes. Assessing credit risks through data modeling using machine learning and quantitative tools.
- **Healthcare**   Computer algorithms are already better than human doctors for analyzing medical images such as CT or PET scans and MRIs to more accurately identify abnormalities. Greater ability to classify and treat cancer and effects of medication. Using pattern-detection algorithms to identify asthma and COPD by recording and analyzing patient breathing and providing real-time feedback via a smartphone app.
- **Energy**   Forecasting electricity price and demand. Sophisticated models monitor plant availability, historical trends, seasonality and weather.
- **Manufacturing**   Predicting machinery failure through monitoring and predictive maintenance apps to reduce downtime and minimize waste.
- **Supply Chain**   Identifying improvement opportunities across the supply chain from procurement to in-store availability management.
- **Risk Management**   Detecting fraud or data tampering before it affects operations and analyzing risk for accurate forecasting of financial investment.
- **Hospitality and Tourism**   Algorithms that are heavily used in revenue management systems in which data about the weather, popularity of a flight, hotel room or restaurant or even surfing or skiing preferences are affecting prices and availability in real-time.
- **Law**   Legal AI software can read and scan judicial documents to find deviations and precedents.
- **Smart Devices and Cities**   Image recognition via remote cameras is being used in smart home surveillance and monitoring devices and in city analytics.

Building a Data Science Team

Every organization needs people who can analyze and find insights in data captured from a range of sources, including customer transactions, click streams, IoT sensors, social media, log files, and GPS plots. Large organizations have a separate data science team, whereas in small companies there may just be one person who has the necessary data analytic skills that were acquired through formal education or "on the job." As a team, members must have a combination of business and IT skills so it can build bridges with the business by applying the right level of technology to business problems.

Data science jobs are in extremely high demand. Dice.com showed the number of data science job postings on its website had increased about 32% during 2019 and indeed.com showed a 29% increase in the demand for data scientists. When a reference is made to data science jobs, people immediately think "data scientist", but the typical data science team consists of several people who each have a different set of skills. For example, data scientists need skills to unlock valuable and predictive insights to influence business decisions and spur competitiveness, while another data science team member is primarily a computer programmer and another is a statistics expert or serves as a liaison between IT and the business to ensure a good fit with current and ongoing business needs **(Table 6.1)**.

TABLE 6.1 **Data Science Roles and Skills**

Job Title	Role	Skills	Hiring Company Examples
Data and Analytics Manager	Manages data science team	Database systems (SQL and NoSQL) Leadership and project management Interpersonal communications Data mining and predictive modeling	Coursera Microsoft Slack Motorola
Data Scientist	Cleans, massages, and organizes big data	Distributed computing Predictive modeling Storytelling and visualizing Math, Stats, Machine Learning	Google Microsoft Adobe
Data Analyst	Collect, processes, and performs statistical data analysis	Spreadsheets (Excel) SQL and NoSQL databases	IBM HP DHL
Data Architect	Creates blueprints to integrate, centralize, protect, and maintain data sources	Data warehousing solutions In-depth knowledge of database architecture Data modeling Systems development	Visa Coca-Cola Logitech
Data Engineer	Develops, constructs, tests and maintains architectures	SQL and NoSQL database systems Data modeling Data APIs Data warehousing solutions	Spotify Facebook Amazon
Statistician	Collects, analyzes, and interprets qualitative and quantitative data with statistical theories and methods	Statistical theories and methods Data mining and machine learning Hadoop computing SQL and NoSQL database systems Cloud tools	LinkedIn Johnson and Johnson Pepsico
Database Administrator	Ensure database is available to all authorized users and it is performing well and is secure	Backup and recovery Data modeling and design SQL and NoSQL database systems Data security ERP and business knowledge	Tableau Reddit Twitter
Business Analyst	Improves business processes as intermediate between business and IT	Basic tools (e.g., Microsoft Office) Data Visualization (e.g., Tableau) Conscious listening and storytelling BI understanding Data modeling	UBER Dell Oracle

Sources: Adapted from KDNuggets (2015) and DeNisco Rayome (2019).

In January 2019, IBM partnered with The Open Group (**https://www.opengroup.org**) to develop a certification program that addresses the severe shortage of data scientists. Initially, they certified 140 new data scientists who were IBM employees. In September 2019, they announced the Open Group Certified Data Scientist (Open CDS) certification was available to the public. Open CDS is the industry's most comprehensive data scientist certification and is designed to verify that Data Scientist professionals have the qualities and capabilities required to produce effective analysis of data for the overall improvement of the business. In the next section you will learn about four important descriptive data analytics tools used in BI. **Career Insight 6.2** describes what a data scientist does in what Harvard Business Review referred to as "the sexiest job of the 21st century (Saxena 2019)."

Career Insight 6.2

Data Scientists Manipulate Big Data for Actionable Results

Big data, analytics tools, powerful networks, and greater processing power have contributed to growth of the field of data science. According to glassdoor.com (2020), the median annual salary for junior data scientists in the United States is $121,319 and $162,134 for senior data scientists. Facebook and Google were the highest paying companies for data scientists with salaries over $200K.

But, it's not just about the money—most data scientists really enjoy what they do. The job is interesting spanning many different aspects of the organization and in some cases involves analyzing company-supported community outreach programs. According to Gregg Gordon, VP Big Data practice group at Kronos, provider of workforce management solutions in the cloud being a data scientist is "not about sitting in a room all day—we take our work and apply it to customer problems. We're working and interacting with customers daily talking about real problems, then attempting to replicate, model and solve them."

An interesting example of what a data scientist does can be found by studying Jonathan Goldman, the person who transformed LinkedIn. At the time Goldman joined, LinkedIn had less than 8 million members. Goldman noticed that existing members were inviting their friends and colleagues to join, but they were not making connections with other members at the rate executives had expected. A LinkedIn manager said, "It was like arriving at a conference reception and realizing you don't know anyone. So you just stand in the corner sipping your drink—and you probably leave early." Goldman began analyzing the data from user profiles and looked for patterns to predict whose networks a given profile would land in. While most LinkedIn managers saw no value in Goldman's work, Reid Hoffman, LinkedIn's cofounder and CEO at the time, understood the power of analytics because of his experiences at PayPal. With Hoffman's approval, Goldman applied data science methods and techniques to test what would happen if members were presented with names of other members, they had not yet connected with but seemed likely to know. He displayed the three best new matches for each member based on his or her LinkedIn profile. Within days, the click-through rate on those matches skyrocketed and things really took off. Thanks to this one feature, LinkedIn's growth increased dramatically.

The most successful—and much sought after—data scientists possess a combination of analytical skills, technical prowess and business acumen needed to effectively analyze massive data sets while thinking critically and shifting assumptions on the fly, ultimately transforming raw intelligence into concise and actionable insights.

The LinkedIn example shows that good data scientists do much more than simply try to solve obvious business problems. Creative and critical thinking are part of their job—that is, part analyst and part artist. They dig through incoming data with the goal of discovering previously hidden insights that could lead to a competitive advantage or detect a business crisis in enough time to prevent it. Data scientists often need to evaluate and select those opportunities and threats that would be of greatest value to the enterprise or brand.

Sources: Altexsoft (2018), Bassa (2018), Szczecinski (2018), DeNisco Rayome (2019), BitDegree (2019), KDNuggets (2019), Korolov (2019), and Glassdoor (2020).

Software to Support the Data Science Team

The most commonly used computer programming languages that underly **advanced data analytics** solutions include:

- **Python**—a high-level object-oriented programming language. It has functional, dynamic type, and automatic memory management and is used by data scientists because it is extensible and provides several free data analysis libraries.

- **R**—an extensible, open source programming language that runs on Windows, Macintosh, Unix, and Linux platforms. R offers an extensive catalog of statistical and graphical methods and includes machine learning algorithms, linear and time series regression and statistical inference. R is an alternative to more traditional statistical packages like SPSS, SAS, and STATA.

- **Apache Hadoop**—Hadoop is an open source language that places no conditions on the structure of the data it can process and distributes computing problems across several servers. To store data, Hadoop uses its own distributed file system, *Hadoop File System* (HDFS). The HDFS is easily scalable. Servers and machines can be added to accommodate increasing volumes of data.

Resilient distributed dataset (RDD) is a fault-tolerant, immutable and distributed collection of objects that can be processed in parallel across a cluster.

- **Apache Spark** uses **resilient distributed datasets (RDDs)** and does not provide a distributed file storage system. It is most commonly used for computation and although it can run independently, it can also be used with Hadoop since it creates distributed datasets from files stored in the HDFS.

The major difference between Hadoop and Spark is speed. Spark's in-memory processing capabilities enable programs to iteratively run about 100 times faster than Hadoop in-memory and 10 times faster on disk. Despite Hadoop's shortcomings both Spark and Hadoop play major roles in big data analytics.

Using these programming languages as a foundation, user-friendly advanced data analytics software is intended for use by formally trained data science teams as well as individual business users and teams, sometimes referred to as "**citizen data scientists.**"

Citizen data scientist is an employee in an organization who can use advanced data analytic methods and techniques and software to create data models but has not been formally trained as a data scientist.

According to the 2020 Gartner Magic Quadrant for Data Science and Machine Learning Platforms (Gartner, 2020b), the leaders in advanced analytics software are:

- **Alteryx** (https://www.alteryx.com)—a user-friendly end-to-end analytics platform that allows data scientists and analysts to quickly solve business problems through its intuitive self-service visual interface with or without coding. Alteryx discovers, preps, analyzes, presents, and manages deployable analytic models by automating manual data tasks into repeatable analytic workflows.

- **SAS Visual Data Mining and Machine Learning** (https://www.sas.com/en_us/software/visual-data-mining-machine-learning.html)—offers end-to-end processing of raw data into actionable insights to empower organizations to solve complex analytical problems and see real results quickly and easily. It enables data science team members of all skill levels to handle tasks throughout the data science life cycle.

- **Azure Databricks** (https://azure.microsoft.com/en-us/services/databricks—a fast, easy and collaborative Apache Spark-based analytics service optimized for the Microsoft Azure cloud services platform. Databrick offers an interactive workspace that enables collaboration between data scientists, data engineers and business analysts.

- **Tibco** (https://www.tibco.com)—strong end-to-end capabilities from data management and preparation to deployment and production on a flexible and open platform that can integrate proprietary developed models using a wide range of open-source capabilities. Somewhat weak in augmented analytics.

- **Dataiku** (https://www.dataiku.com)—is an agile and flexible collaborative data science software platform for teams of data analysts, engineers and data scientists to enable self-service data analytics and operationalize machine learning. Dataiku offers programmers the ability to code in Pythron, R, Spark, etc. and citizen data scientists can choose a customizable drag-and-drop visual interface in the predictive workflow process from data preparation through analysis to modeling and presentation.

- **Mathworks** (https://www.mathworks.com)—a fully integrated platform where all new methods and techniques are seamlessly integrated within its carefully engineered environment from data preprocessing and model development to production and offers the possibility of automatically generating code.

In Sections 6.3 and 6.4, we will discuss the most commonly used analytics methods and techniques that are incorporated into the different levels of data analytics software from dashboards to machine learning.

Questions

1. What are the four phases of decision-making?
2. Why would an organization satisfice instead of optimize when making a decision?
3. What is BI and why is it important in an organization?
4. Why are human expertise and judgment important to data analytics? Give an example.
5. What is the relationship between data quality and the value of analytics?
6. How can manufacturers and health care benefit from BI level descriptive data analytics?
7. How does data science software for programmers differ from data science software for business users?

6.2 | Big Data and Advanced Data Analytics

LO6.2 Explain *how big data and advanced data analytics work together to predict organizational performance in the future and prescribe actionable insights.*

Building a data-driven business relies on developing advanced data analytics capabilities that convert data into valuable insights to drive real-time decision-making. On its own data have little value, it's what you do with the data that makes it interesting, and the more data you collect, the more insight into your business and its customers an organization can gain. Today greater volumes and more varied types of data are being collected and analyzed every day to help managers make good decisions across all industries and business units around the globe.

Big Data

When a data set is too large or complex to be analyzed using traditional methods it is called **big data**. Big data is the major factor driving the increased importance of advanced **data analytics** today. More and more managers and their teams are looking to big data to help drive successful decision-making and assist with critical job functions.

Big data is collected from a wide variety of sources. On the consumer side, a significant factor in increasing amount of big data is the boom in wearable technology—products like FitBit and the Apple Watch—smartphones and social media posts. On the public sector and enterprise side, sensor data and the Internet of Things (IoT) are being used to advance IT-enabled business processes like automated factories and distribution centers, semi-autonomous vehicles and smart cities. In addition, federal health reform efforts have pushed health-care organizations toward big data and analytics. These organizations are planning to use data analytics to support revenue cycle management, resource utilization, fraud prevention, health management, and quality improvement. **Table 6.2** shows the characteristics that differentiate "big data" from traditional or "small data."

Big data is a data set that is too large or complex to be analyzed using traditional data processing applications.

Data analytics is the process of examining data sets to draw conclusions about the information they contain, usually with the help of computer software.

TABLE 6.2 **The Differences Between "Big" Data and "Small Data"**

Category	"Big" Data	Traditional Data
Data Sources	Data generated outside the enterprise from nontraditional data sources. Include: • Social media • Sensor data • Log data • Device data • Video, images, etc.	Traditional enterprise data. Include: • Enterprise resource planning transactional data • Customer relationship management (CRM) systems • Web transactions • Financial data e.g., general ledger data
Volume	• Terabytes (10^{14}) • Petabytes (10^{15}) • Exabytes (10^{18}) • Zettabytes (10^{21})	• Gigabytes (10^{9}) • Terabytes (10^{12})
Velocity	• Often real-time • Requires immediate response	• Batch or near real-time • Does not always require immediate response
Variety	• Structured • Unstructured • Multistructured	• Structured • Unstructured
Value	• Complex, advanced, predictive business analysis and insights	• Business intelligence, analysis and reporting

The Four Vs of Big Data

To generate maximum business value from big data the right questions must be asked, and the appropriate level of analysis performed. To be effective in efficiently analyzing data, organizations must pay attention to the four main properties of big data that distinguish it from the data organizations previously generated. The four Vs of big data are Volume, Variety, Velocity and Veracity (**Figure 6.9**).

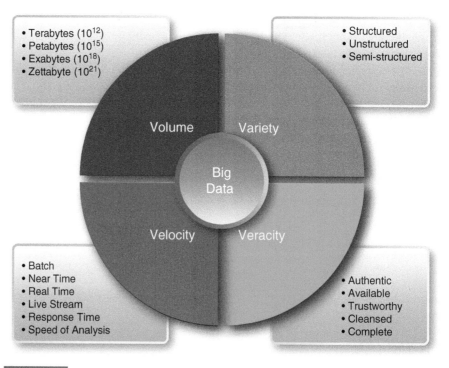

FIGURE 6.9 The four Vs of big data.

- **Volume**   To handle the sheer volume of "big data" and provide comprehensive analytics capabilities in the big data platform.

- **Variety**   The analytic environment has expanded from pulling data most structured data from a single enterprise data warehouse to include a variety of semi-structured and unstructured sources such as social medial posts, tweets, videos, images, sensor data, and customer service calls.

- **Velocity**   The speed with which data is stored, analyzed and reports generated. If the data are not processed in a timely manner, they may no longer be accurate or useful, for example, stock market data must be updated in real-time because of the volatility of the stock market as must inventory so that customers are not disappointed when an item that they ordered cannot be delivered as promised.

- **Veracity**   Data that are incomplete, missing or duplicated need to be repaired. Large data volumes and variety mean more dirty data that are harder to handle. If the wrong analysis or datasets are used, the output would be nonsense, as in the example of the Super Bowl winners and stock market performance. Stated in reverse, managers need context in order to understand how to interpret traditional and big data.

Big data can have a dramatic impact on the success of any enterprise or can be a low-contributing major expense. For example, many companies are collecting and capturing huge amounts of data but spending very little effort to ensure the veracity of data captured at the transactional stage or point of origin. Validating data not only increases confidence in the data, but also significantly reduce the efforts analyzing it and leads to better quality decisions. Successful use of the data depends also on ensuring that you avoid invalid assumptions, by testing any assumptions during analysis. Big data in and of itself is still just data—but lots more of it—and some of it will be relevant and some it won't.

In addition to the four Vs, **human expertise and judgment** must be added into the mix when analyzing big data. Data are worthless if they cannot be easily analyzed, interpreted, understood, and the results applied effectively in context. A common mistake that organizations make is to invest in the analytics foundation—quality data, data integration and data analysis tools—but overlook the most crucial component, which is the users' ability to interpret the visual reports. For example, one challenge is how to display the results of data analysis in a meaningful way that is not overwhelming to the user. For example, it may be necessary to collapse and condense the results to display graphs and charts in a way that decision-makers are accustomed to viewing them. Results may also need to be available quickly on mobile devices that are supported by different operating systems, browsers and user interfaces, and users may want to be able to easily explore the data on their own in real time. These types of decisions can't be made by the software, they require familiarity with the context and the capabilities and requirements of the user population—in short, they require human expertise coupled with the power of technology.

To successfully interpret the output from big data analytics human expertise and judgment must be applied along with high-quality data, data analytics methods and technique to optimize actionable insights. **IT at Work 6.2** describes how human expertise coupled with big data, data analytics, and collaboration have transformed how new drugs are developed.

IT at Work 6.2

Researchers Use Genomics and Big Data in Drug Discovery

Drug development is a high-risk business. Almost 90% of new drugs ultimately fail to reach the market. One of the challenges has been the amount, variety, and complexity of the data that need to be systematically analyzed. Big data technologies and private–public partnerships have made biomedical analytics feasible.

Biotechnology advances have produced massive data on the biological causes of disease. However, analyzing these data and converting discoveries into treatments are much more difficult. Not all biomedical insights lead to effective drug targets, and choosing the wrong target leads to failures late in the drug development process, costing time, money, and lives. Developing a new drug—from early discovery through Food and Drug Administration (FDA) approval—takes over a decade. As a consequence, each success ends up costing more than $1 billion. Sometimes much more! For example, by the time Pfizer Inc., Johnson & Johnson, and Eli Lilly & Co. announced their new drugs had only limited benefit for Alzheimer's patients in late-stage testing, the industry had spent more than $30 billion researching amyloid plaque in the brain.

Drug makers, governments, and academic researchers have partnered to improve the odds of drug success and after years of decline, the pharmaceutical industry is beginning to experience a greater rate of success with its clinical trials. Partnerships bring together the expertise of scientists from biology, chemistry, bioinformatics, genomics, and big data. They are using big data to identify biological targets for drugs and eliminate failures before they reach the human testing stage and many anticipate that big data

and the analytics that go with it could be a key element in further increasing the success rates in pharmaceutical R&D.

GlaxoSmithKline (GSK), the European Bioinformatics Institute (EBI), and the Wellcome Trust Sanger Institute established the Centre for Therapeutic Target Validation (CTTV) near Cambridge, England. CTTV partners combine cutting-edge genomics with the ability to collect and analyze massive amounts of biological data. By not developing drugs that target the wrong biological pathways, they avoid wasting billions of research dollars.

With biology now a data-driven discipline, collaborations such as CTTV are needed to improve efficiencies, cut costs, and provide the best opportunities for success. Other private–public partnerships that had formed to harness drug research and big data include the following:

- **Accelerating Medicines Partnership and U.S. National Institutes of Health (NIH)**   In February 2014, the NIH announced that the agency, 10 pharmaceutical companies, and nonprofit organizations were investing $230 million in the Accelerating Medicines Partnership.

- **Target Discovery Institute and Oxford University**   Oxford University opened the Target Discovery Institute in 2013. Target Discovery helps to identify drug targets and molecular interactions at a critical point in a disease-causing pathway—that is, when those diseases will respond to drug therapy. Researchers try to understand complex biological processes by analyzing image data that have been acquired at the microscopic scale.

Sources: Compiled from GSK (2017), Brown et al. (2018), Owens (2019), Qian et al. (2019), and Chen et al. (2020).

Big Data Goals and Challenges

Organization doesn't just collect and store big data. They need to use it to achieve business goals. Fortune 500 companies are investing billions of dollars in big data for two simple reasons—cut costs and gain market share by accurately predicting the future rather than using the proverbial WAG (wild-assed guess) approach. Other common goals associated with adopting big data include:

- Establish a data-driven culture.
- Create new ways to innovate and disrupt with technology.
- Accelerate speed of offering new capabilities and services.
- Launch new products and services.
- Improve processes.

Unfortunately, organizations are finding it particularly difficult to efficiently handle the volume, variety and veracity of big data generated by their customers who consume products and services digitally. Every industry—banking, finance, automotive, energy, manufacturing, hospitality and tourism, retail, etc.—faces big data challenges, but none more than "big pharma"—pharmaceuticals—and the broader healthcare industries. In their drug discovery programs, clinical trials, sales data, healthcare records, medical test results and genomics research and social media, the healthcare industry is handling masses of data. The big challenge is how to manage and store big data, decide what is relevant and what is not, how to access it and how to draw actionable insights. In a recent Big Data and AI Executive Survey of 65 leading companies, NewVantage Partners reported that 95% of the organizations surveyed said that changing the corporate culture is the biggest barrier to the adoption of big data and artificial intelligence (AI) (NewVantage Partners, 2019). This is supported by the finding that less than one-third of the C-level executives who completed the survey said they have a "data-driven organization" and even fewer claimed to have a "data culture." Cultural and technology-related challenges that organizations face include:

- Cultural
  - Encourage business units to share information across organizational silos.
  - Determine what internal and external, structured and unstructured data to use for different business decisions.
  - Find and hire experienced data science professionals.
  - Build high levels of trust between the data science team and the functional managers.
  - Gain top management support for investments in big data and training.
  - Create optimal way to organize big data programs.
  - Understand where big data investments should be focused in the organization.
  - Determine how to apply insights created from big data.

- Technology-related
  - Effectively handle the four Vs of big data.
  - Determine best way of presenting data analysis results (e.g., visualization, dashboards, augmented reality) to facilitate actionable decision-making.

To analyze big data sets, organizations turn to predictive and prescriptive data analytics—that go beyond the capabilities of traditional BI—to solve complex problems. Taken together these two high-level data analytics methods and techniques are referred to as **advanced data analytics**.

The key distinction between the results provided by BI's descriptive analytics and the more sophisticated predictive and prescriptive data analytics methods and techniques is that BI presents data insights through reporting, easy-to-use dashboards, and interactive visualizations while predictive and prescriptive data analytics use algorithms and scientific methods to statistically determine the relationships between data and make predictions and decide on the best course of action to help organization meet customer expectation, improve overall performance and stay competitive. These deeper insights combined with human expertise enable people to recognize meaningful relationships more quickly or easily; and furthermore, realize the strategic implications of these situations. Imagine trying to make sense of the rapidly accumulating and vast quantities of data generated by social media campaigns on Facebook or by sensors attached to machines or objects. For example, low-cost sensors make it possible to monitor all types of physical things and advanced data analytics makes it possible to understand those data in order to act in real time. For example, sensors data can be analyzed in real time to:

> **advanced data analytics** is the examination of data using sophisticated methods and techniques to discover deeper insights, make predictions and/or generate recommendations.

- monitor and regulate the temperature and climate conditions of perishable foods as they are transported from farm to supermarket.
- sniff for signs of spoilage of fruits and raw vegetables and detect the risk of *E. coli* contamination.
- track the condition of operating machinery and predict the probability of failure.
- track the wear of engines and determine when preventive maintenance is needed.

Predictive Data Analytics

To achieve the speed needed to handle big data, organizations are looking to more advanced analytical methods and techniques to dramatically reduce the time it takes to generate reports and come up with novel findings. For example, data scientists use predictive analytics to create a **predictive model** for forecasting future events based on probabilities of what might happen based on probabilities. In the energy sector utility companies need to forecast loads to predict energy demand. To do this, huge volumes of data imported from IoT sensors and business systems (in-house or in the cloud) are cleaned and aggregated. **Predictive modeling** develops a

> **predictive model** is based on several factors likely to influence future behavior and predicts at some confidence level the outcome of an event.
>
> **Predictive modeling** is a process that uses data mining and probabilities to forecast outcomes to create a statistical model to predict outcomes.

predictive model by statistically analyzing aggregated massive amounts of data from functional systems, enterprise wide systems and connected systems and applying data and text mining, linear or time-series regression, and machine learning (all discussed in detail in section 6.4). Then the model is integrated into a load forecasting system and coupled with business understanding to provide valuable actionable insights (**Figure 6.10**). Other predictive models might predict customer demand and purchasing preferences, airline traffic volume or fuel efficiency of different models of cars.

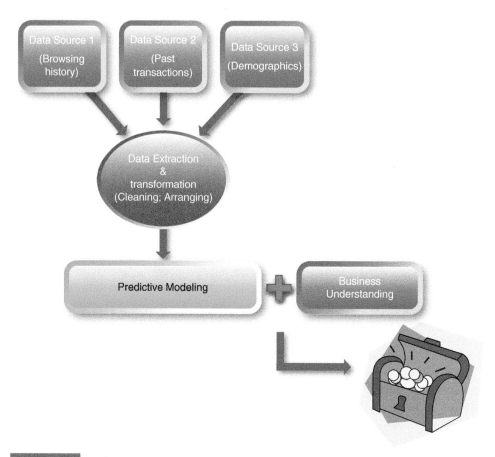

FIGURE 6.10 Predictive modeling.

Predictive analytics are frequently used in customer relationship management (CRM) systems to build sales campaigns and improve customer service. Now that customers can more easily compare services and products online companies are increasingly looking at patterns of purchasing behavior and service use to target marketing initiatives to encourage current customers to stay or entice potential customers to switch companies. Companies that have reported significant improvements in profits and their ability to compete as a result of using predicting modeling include:

- **Amazon** recommends products and services to users based on their past behavior. It is estimated that predicting modeling accounts for approximately 30% of all Amazon sales.
- **Macy's** combines browsing behavior within product categories and sends targeted emails for each customer segment. Macy's saw an 8–12% increase in online sales from their predictive modeling efforts.
- **Harley Davidson** targets potential customers, generates leads and closes sales by identifying potential high-value customers who are ready to make a purchase and following up with sales rep contact to walk them through the sales process.

- **Sprint** has significantly reduced its churn rate and increased its customer satisfaction ratings by identify customers at risk of leaving and proactively providing personalized retention offers using an AI-power algorithm.

Prescriptive Data Analytics

Prescriptive analytics is the third level of data analytics and the most powerful. Just as predictive analytics anticipate *what* will happen next, prescriptive analytics goes one step further to advise organizations *how to* react in the best way possible based on the prediction. Prescriptive analytics uses optimization technology and machine learning to solve complex decisions by suggesting multiple options for taking advantage of future opportunities or mitigating risks and the outcomes of each decision option. If issues are not just identified, but also solved, time and cost can be saved, and reliability and efficiency improved. The combination of predictive and prescriptive analytics produces the most beneficial results to an organization. For example, using pattern analysis, **Argo Corporation**, an agricultural equipment manufacturer based in Georgia, was able to optimize product configuration options for farm machinery and real-time customer demand to determine the optimal base configurations for its machines. As a result, Argo reduced product variety by 61% and cut days of inventory by 81% while still maintaining its service levels. In another example, when deadly cyclone Fani hit Odisha, India in May 2019, most people had been evacuated thanks to predictive analytics. Prior to the arrival of the storm, the Odisha meteorological department had predicted the arrival of the monstrous storm based on path, strength and timing of previous cyclones and used the results of their predictive analytics to make the decision to evacuate the potentially prone regions, saving thousands of lives.

Organizations in most industry sectors are using prescriptive analytics for a range of tasks from strategic planning to operational and tactical activities. Its usefulness goes beyond marketing and retail to address issues associated with cyber-security, fraud prevention, supply chain optimization and resource optimization.

Just a few examples of different industry sectors and the ways they can benefit from prescriptive analytics include:

- **Retail**—minimize customer churn. Gauge customer reaction to company actions. Optimize product offerings; inventory levels; customer satisfaction to increase customer retention and satisfaction; increase profits and reduce costs.
- **Travel and transportation**—optimize driver and route planning every 10 minutes to eliminate thousands of miles of unnecessary driving and improve driver retention; optimize fuel consumption to reduce costs and be more environmentally responsible; optimize crew schedules to increase employee morale and retain more pilots.
- **Manufacturing**—identify process improvements and optimizes production planning, scheduling, inventory and supply chain logistics to meet business requirements to offer major time and cost savings, increase agility and provide a greater return on investment (ROI).
- **Healthcare**—significantly improve patient transportation by optimizing hospital (location, specialization and available beds) and transport data to help dispatchers plan, manage and execute hundreds of daily patient transport requests every day. Improve radiation therapy by optimizing radiation treatment plans to enable clinicians to precisely target which radiation beams to turn on and predict when and for how long to deliver an optimal dose for each patient. On the administrative side, prescriptive analytics can ensure accurate staffing levels, plan support facilities location and capacity requirements, manage inventory levels and optimize home health service scheduling to increase patient and staff satisfaction and save considerable time and money.

Questions

1. What are the four Vs of big data?
2. What are the two biggest challenges associated with using big data?
3. What is predictive analytics?
4. What is prescriptive analytics?
5. How are predictive analytics adding value in organizations?
6. Name three industry sectors where prescriptive analytics are being used to add value.

---

data mining   is the process of using software to analyze unstructured, semi-structured and structured data from various perspectives, categorize them, and derive correlations or patterns among fields in the data.

data visualization   is the presentation of data in a graphical format to make it easier for decision-makers to grasp difficult concepts or identify new patterns in the data.

Digital dashboard   is a static or interactive electronic interface used to acquire and consolidate data across an organization.

6.3 | Descriptive Data Analytics Tools

LO6.3 Describe *four descriptive data analytics methods and techniques and how they are used.*

Four of the most important tools used in descriptive analytics are **data mining**, **data visualization**, **digital dashboards**, and **mashups**. Each of these tools is used to simplify sharing insights from data-driven decisions and enable organizations to provide users with an at-a-glance awareness of current business KPIs. Data mining is the first step in descriptive data analytics and involves software that analyzes data from various perspectives, categorize them and derive correlations or patterns among data fields. It enables organizations to analyze data to derive patterns and helps organizations make more informed decisions when and where needed; discover unknown insights from the data and automates and streamlines business processes. Data visualization provides a graphical representation of the data to make it easier to understand and digital dashboards use mashups to bring multiple data visualizations onto a single screen to provide an in-depth analysis of the data and provide a real-time snapshot of business productivity. Data visualization harnesses the power of BI and capitalizes on the way our brains work by providing users with an easy to understand graphical representation of historical data. A digital dashboard brings multiple data visualizations—ranging from a simple timeline to an interactive infographic—onto a single screen to provide an in-depth business analysis while providing a real-time snapshot of productivity that can be updated on-the-fly. Each of these descriptive data analytics tools are discussed next.

Data Mining is used as the first step in descriptive data analytics to identify previously unknown patterns in the data, that is, known unknowns. Using data mining software an organization can quickly and easily extract useful information from a vast quantity of data and present it as a report to management. Data mining easily handles structured data such as that found in databases or ERP systems.

Adding Value with Data Mining

Business value that organizations gain from data mining falls into three categories:

- Making more informed decision at the time they need to be made.
- Discovering unknown insights, patterns or relationships.
- Automating and streamlining or digitizing business processes.

For example, a food retailer might see that sales of pumpkin pies seem to spike just before Thanksgiving or a hammock retailer might see that more people visit its website when the weather is warmer. This gives them an opportunity to offer a promotion or a discount coupon to increase sales even further at times when demand isn't high and enables them to adjust their inventories to accommodate higher demand as needed. You're probably already familiar with a specialized data mining technique that Amazon uses called **affinity analysis**—to increased potential sales by recommending products of a similar nature to those already purchased.

Data Visualization Data visualization has become a very effective tool for organizations around the world to gain a comprehensive understanding of trends, market demands and needed process improvements. You've probably heard the saying "A picture is worth a thousand words"—interactive displays, charts with **drill down** capability, and **geospatial data** analysis do just that. They present data visually to enhance decision-making. For example, charts, graphs and maps can tell a much more compelling story than columns of numbers by effectively using visual cues that managers rely on to grasp and process huge amounts of information (**Figure 6.11**).

affinity analysis is a data mining technique that discovers co-occurrence relationships among activities performed by specific individuals or groups.

drill down is searching for something on a computer moving from general information to more detailed information by focusing on something of interest, for example, quarterly sales—monthly sales—daily sales.

geospatial data is data that have an explicit geographic component, ranging from vector and raster data to tabular data with site locations.

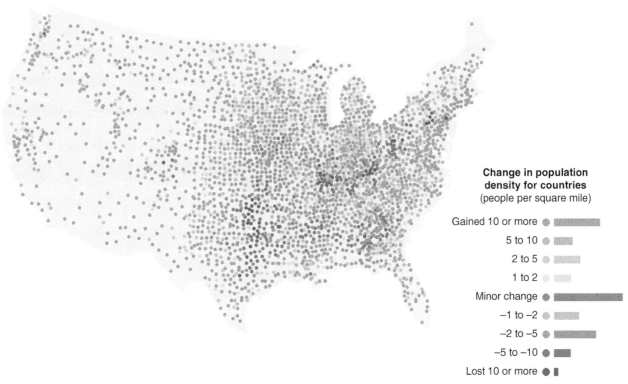

FIGURE 6.11 U.S. Census Bureau map shows easily identifiable changes in county population density. Different colors are used to indicate areas that gained and lost population. Intensity of color indicates extent of gain/loss.

Data visualization is a quick, easy way to convey concepts in a universal manner—and you can experiment with different scenarios by making slight adjustments. Visualizing data can save a business money, help communicate important points, and hold customer attention. Data visualization is important because of the way the human brain processes information. Using pie charts, histograms, bar graphs and maps to visualize large amounts of complex data is much easier than poring over spreadsheets or reports. Some useful business applications for data visualization include the following:

- Identifying areas that need attention or improvement.
- Clarifying which factors influence customer behavior.
- Helping understand which products to place where.
- Predicting sales volumes by location.

Adding Value through Learning, Exploration, and Discovery with Data Visualization

Data visualization enables learning that is the basis for continuous improvement. When companies in all industries, political parties, sports teams, or fund-raising agencies invest in marketing programs, campaigns, promotions, special events, or other projects, they use visualization to learn something from them. Data visualization is also used as a data explorer and **data discovery** tool. Companies, such as Safeway and PepsiCo, are discovering new relationships and learning how to improve performance using data visualization. Enterprise visualization apps for Androids, Apple iPads, and Surface tablets are replacing static business reports with real-time data, analytics, and interactive reporting tools. Visual displays make it easier for individuals to understand data and identify patterns that offer answers to business questions such as "Which product lines have the highest and lowest profit margins in each region?" Interactivity and drill-down capabilities are standard features that make visualization even more valuable.

data discovery is the process of using BI to collect data from various databases and consolidate it into a single source that can be easily and instantly evaluated.

Heat Maps In addition to charts, graphs, and timelines data visualizations also include heat maps. Heat maps are the most-used tool for representing complex statistical data and use a warm-to-cool color spectrum to show differences in classes of data. Doctors, engineers, marketers, and researchers use heat maps to make complex data sets easy to understand and actionable and manage content to cater to customer needs. Heat maps come in all types. The basic tricolor heat maps in **Figures 6.12 and 6.13** instantly alert the viewer to critical areas most in need of attention. Both heat maps cover the same data set, but it's interesting to see that the way in which the data are visually displayed depends on what you want to learn or convey. Figure 6.12 shows two more sophisticated types of heat maps that are particularly useful for analyzing the effectiveness of Web pages. The heat map on the left uses three colors (red, yellow, and green) to show how often the parts of a Web page are used to enable better content management. The more visitors click on an area of the Web page, the more red the area becomes, showing the "hotspots" that are clicked on most.

		Region			
Product Cate... Product Sub-Category		**Central**	**East**	**South**	**West**
Furniture	Bookcases	73	−10,151	−22,417	−676
	Chairs & Chairmats	37,920	33,583	34,026	44,409
	Office Furnishings	26,293	14,523	25,121	30,941
	Tables	−19,777	−50,677	26,172	−16,990
Office Supplies	Appliances	22,950	16,812	26,986	31,276
	Binders and Binder Accessories	73,951	71,420	69,530	92,273
	Envelopes	10,825	7,482	19,182	11,222
	Labels	2,429	4,041	3,479	3,740
	Paper	11,047	13,510	10,997	10,433
	Pens & Art Supplies	2,781	2,856	1,397	518
	Rubber Bands	−174	−238	156	178
	Scissors, Rulers and Trimmers	−1,765	−1,179	−2,903	−1,953
	Storage & Organization	−68	−7,233	11,836	−2,018
Technology	Computer Peripherals	11,971	14,808	30,475	37,280
	Copiers and Fax	513	67,254	63,598	35,997
	Office Machines	38,876	47,277	129,060	61,377
	Telephones and Communication	79,393	73,715	78,985	84,860

(a)

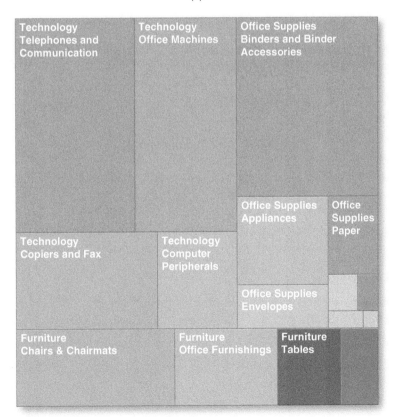

(b)

FIGURE 6.12 These basic heat maps represent the same data set using different colors (usually red and green) and color intensity to show the profitability of three product categories and their subcategories. In (a), data labels show detailed profit, while in (b), the area of each segment is used to make comparisons between profitability of product categories.

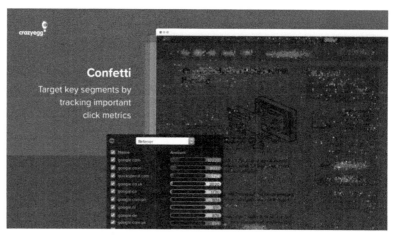

FIGURE 6.13 More sophisticated heat maps are useful for website visitor analysis, content management, and value of search engines by geographic area.

Source: Digital Marketing Agency, LLC, https://www.digitalmarketingagency.com/blog/heatmaps-benefits-common-issues-website-optimization/

The Confetti Heat Map on the righthand side of Figure 6.13 is a highly specific version of a traditional heat map that shows each individual user click on a website as a colored dot tied to the search engine that initiated the visit, for example, google.com, google.co.in, google.co.uk, google.ca (Crazy Egg, 2020).

Augmented Reality (AR) The highest level of data visualization currently available is **augmented reality (AR)** that compacts data into an easily digestible graphic or chart that can be visually projected with AR technology to fully engage the user. Some uses of augmented reality include:

augmented reality (AR) is the use of more contemporary 3-D visualization methods and techniques to illustrate the relationships within data including smart mapping, smart routines, machines learning, and natural language processing.

- **Coca-Cola** has developed an AR application that assists retailers in visualizing how a beverage cooler would fit into their stores.

- **Toys R Us** in Australia created a Virtual Easter Egg Hunt for its young customers. Using a computer table a child could follow Easter Bunnies around the store looking for digital eggs that were hidden around the store.

- **IKEA** uses augmented reality to assist customers with AR visualizations of how furniture will look in different living spaces.

- **Amazon View** lets online shoppers see how a product will look in their homes by clicking on the camera icon in the Amazon app and selecting products across categories like furniture, appliances, kitchenware and home décor.

- **Google** is trialing a new augmented reality feature for Google Maps. In this new feature, the app pickups up a person's location via GPS and uses Street View data to narrow it down to the user's exact location. It then displayed big arrows and directions on the screen for the user to follow **(Figure 6.14)**.

- **Bareburger** projects their new meatless Impossible Burgers onto their guests' virtual plate through the Snapchat app on their smartphones allowing Bareburger customers to view their lunch before ordering.

FIGURE 6.14   Google Maps is trialing an augmented reality feature.

John B Hewitt/Alamy Stock Photo

Companies such as NASCAR (in our opening case), Coca-Cola, IKEA, and Bareburger employed outside expertise to develop and launch its AR apps, and involved internal IT to facilitate knowledge transfer and ongoing application support. Many organizations are realizing that it's time to expand big data visualizations beyond "back office" analytics and into the real world of live customer engagement with video and AR streaming services that keep customers connected and engaged. For example, **IT at Work 6.3** describes how the U.S. Golf Association partnered with DeLoitte's Insight Studio program to shake things up by implementing two innovative visualization projects that allowed U.S. Open fans to engage with the sport in fresh new ways.

IT at Work 6.3

USGA "Reimagines" Golf with Data Visualization and Augmented Reality

With another U.S. Open on the way, the USGA needed to shake things up to engage fans at this major event. With the help of Deloitte's Insight Studio, United States Golf Association created a vision for major changes in its golf ecosystem and established a partnership to deliver greater value to its member golf clubs and facilities as well as the community of golfers it serves. As Sarah Hirshland, Senior Managing Director of Business Affairs with the USGA, put it "We're always thinking of ways to improve the fan experience to attract and better engage new fans. Deloitte helped us achieve both of these goals this year."

Insight Studio allows people form a wide range of business disciplines access to the world's most advanced analytics capabilities and with the help of its developers puts them together in a physical environment that enables them to engage in fresh unexpected ways. Between them Deloitte and the USGA designed wall-sized touchscreen data visualizations that invited more than 4,000 fans to explore US Open trivia and historical data about the golfers. It used real-time data from more than ten different sources to engage fans with relevant information in exciting new ways. Using the touchscreens fans quickly got answers to questions like, "What's the crowd density at hole #16?", "What's the best spot for viewing the action at hole #7", "How are fans moving in relation to <name of specific player>?" The highly visual data and intuitive access soon had fans flocking to use this new feature of the US Open.

Capitalizing on the success of Insight Studio, Deloitte developed another engaging and innovative digital experience for golf fans. At the 199th U.S. Open Championship at Pebble Beach Golf Links in California the U.S. Open Augmented Reality (AR) App was unveiled. Available from the Apple Store and Google Play Store the U.S. Open AR offers fans insights into player performance on the iconic 6th, 7th, and 18th holes in 3-D augmented reality. With the new app golf fans can follow the action in real-time on their own mobile device through a virtual map of the course. They can also compare player performance and see how competitors performed on the three iconic holes. To activate their augmented reality experience, fans aim their phones oat the AR image, available on-site in the tee times guide and a download from Deloitte. You can see more about how Deloitte did this by viewing three short videos at: **https://www2.deloitte.com/us/en/pages/about-deloitte/articles/usga-golf.html?id=us:2el:3fu:usgafy20:awa:greendot:051319**.

Sources: Compiled from Alderstadter (2019), Deloitte (2020a, 2020b), and USGA.com.

Dashboards Digital dashboard systems combine multiple data visualizations into a single screen to enhance data reporting and facilitate smooth business operations and decisions. Dashboards improve information integration by collecting multiple, disparate data feeds and sources, extracting features of interest, and manipulating the data, so the information is in a more accessible format. Users no longer need to log into multiple applications to see how the business is performing everything is presented in one place. Experts and novices can collect data quickly from disparate sources and then explore the data set with easy-to-use interactive dashboards (**Figure 6.15**). For example, a product might obtain data from the local operating system, from one or more apps that are running and from one or more remote sites on the Web and present it as though it all came from a single source. Drill-down paths are not predefined, which gives users more flexibility in how they view detailed data. When done well, a digital dashboard is a powerful tool that helps an organization efficiently develop analytical goals and strategies.

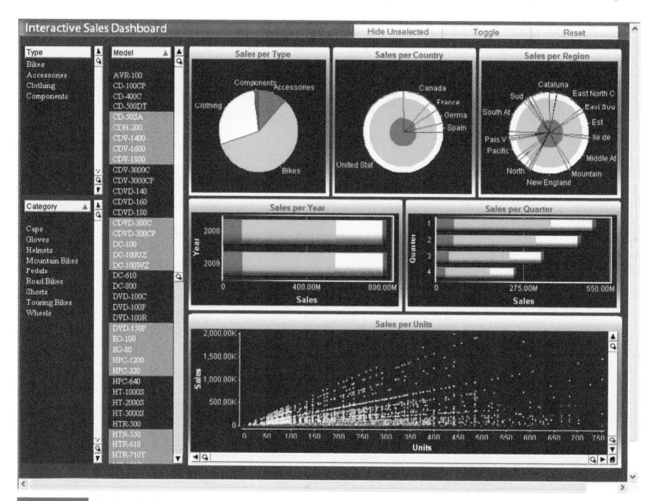

FIGURE 6.15 Dashboards allow users to interact with multiple corporate data sources on a single screen.

The major components of a dashboard are:

- **Design** The visualization method and descriptive captions to convey information so that they are correctly understood. Infographics are widely used because they convey information in interesting and informative ways.

- **Performance metrics** KPIs and other real-time content displayed on the dashboard. All dashboard data should reflect the current value of each metric.

- **API** APIs connect disparate data sources and feeds to display on the dashboard. The alternative is for users or IT to manually enter data to the dashboard. Dashboards created in this manner tend to fail because of the risk of incomplete, outdated, or wrong data, which users learn not to trust.

- **Access** Preferred access is via a secure Web browser from a mobile device.

Dashboards Are Real Time

Dashboards are often mistakenly thought of as reports consisting of various gauges, charts, and dials, but the purpose of business dashboards is much more specific and directed. The purpose of dashboards is to give users a clear view of the *current* state of KPIs, real-time alerts, and other metrics about operations. Dashboard design is a critical factor because business users need to be able to understand the significance of the dashboard information at a glance and have the capability to drill down to one or more levels of detail. Having real time, or near real time, data is essential to keep users aware of any meaningful changes in the metrics as they occur to make decisions in real time and take corrective actions promptly. Most dashboards today are interactive.

Dashboards work by connecting to business systems, such as accounting software, ERP, CRM, SCM, e-mail systems, website analytics programs, and project management software via APIs. **Table 6.3** lists some metrics that are commonly displayed on dashboards by function.

TABLE 6.3   **Example of Metrics Displayed on Dashboards by Function**

Dashboard Type	Metrics	Dashboard Type	Metrics
Accounting	• Net income • Net profits	Sales team	• Sales by lead source; which leads are most and least effective
	• Cash balance, actual vs. expected		• Number of leads and proposals per salesperson
	• Profit, current month projection		• Proposal close percentage
	• Changes in A/R and A/P		• Salesperson closing percentages
E-commerce	• Daily website visitors by traffic source		• Point at which prospective customers are being lost
	• Trend of mobile vs. tablet traffic	Advertising	• Number of leads generated by advertising; which advertising is most and least effective
	• Location where visitors are located		• Cost per lead, by advertising source
	• Top referring websites		• Advertising expense, as a percent of sales
	• Top keywords referring traffic		• Which advertising sources directly lead to sales
	• Revenue per website visitor	Order fulfillment	• Number of products manufactured, reworked
Finance	• Sales per day per channel		• On-time completion percent
	• How revenue is trending		• Changes in inventory levels
	• Days with the strongest sales, weakest sales		• Percent of on-time delivery per week, month
	• Products selling the best, worst		

Adding Value with Digital Dashboards

The interrelated benefits of business dashboards are as follows:

1. **Visibility**   Blind spots are minimized or eliminated. Threats and opportunities are detected as soon as possible.
2. **Continuous improvement**   A famous warning from Peter Drucker was "if you can't measure it, you can't improve it." Executive dashboards are custom designed to display the user's critical metrics and measures.
3. **Single sign-on**   Managers can spend a lot of time logging into various business systems and running reports. Single-sign-on dashboards save time and effort.

4. **Deviations from what was budgeted or planned** Any metrics, such as those listed in Table 11.3, can be programmed to display deviations from targets, such as comparisons of actual and planned or budgeted.

5. **Accountability** When employees know that their performance is tracked in near real time and can see their results, they tend to be motivated to improve their performance.

Data Mashups for Actionable Dashboards

Data mashups combine business data and applications from two or more sources that is typically a mix of internal data and applications as well as externally sourced data, SaaS (software as a service) and Web content to create an integrated experience. They enhance the interactive capabilities of dashboards, allow users to gain new insights, and spot trends within data in businesses of all sizes. The ability of enterprise mashups to quickly and easily consolidate data and functionality that is normally spread across several applications, onto a single Web page or mobile device screen, offers real business opportunities for companies of all shapes and sizes around the world. Because mashups can be developed in hours rather than days or weeks using preexisting technology, they do not require a huge investment and are a quick, cost-effective solution to a range of data analysis issues. With mashups users can filter down the data based on their needs so that only the information needed is provided by the available data services.

Unlike dashboards and drill-down capabilities that users actively engage with mashups remain behind the scene and are invisible because the data are presented as if coming from a single source. While combining disparate data sources is strength of a data mashup, they can also add value to an organization by combining data from a single source in new and unanticipated ways. Interactive dashboards and drillable reports can be rapidly built based on mashed-up data. Using mashups, digital dashboards pull data from disparate data sources and feeds to report KPIs and operational or strategic information on intuitive dashboards and interactive displays **(Figure 6.16)**. Enterprise mashups combine data from internal business sources (e.g., sales records, customer information, etc.) and/or information from external sources for enhanced usefulness and productivity. For instance, a bank may utilize an enterprise mashup to display a mortgage application from its own records, the property location on a Google map, and information from county government property tax records.

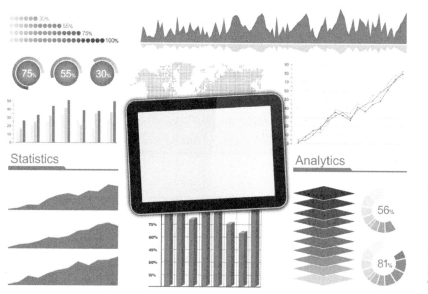

FIGURE 6.16 Dashboards pull data from disparate data sources and feeds, manipulate the data, and display the metrics.

Using self-service data mashup apps, nontechnical users can easily and quickly access, integrate, and display BI data from a variety of operational data sources, including those that are not integrated into the existing data warehouse, without having to understand the intricacies of the underlying data infrastructures or schemas.

In an enterprise environment, mashups can be used to solve a wide variety of business problems and day-to-day situations. Examples of these types of mashups are as follows:

1. **Customer**   A customer data mashup that provides a quick view of customer data for a salesperson in preparation for a customer site visit. Data can be pulled from internal data stores and Web sources, such as contact information, links to related websites, recent customer orders, lists of critical situations, and more.

2. **Logistics**   A logistics mashup that displays inventory for a group of department stores based on specific criteria. For example, you can mash current storm information onto a map of store locations and then wire the map to inventory data to show which stores located in the path of storms are low on generators.

3. **Human resource**   An HR mashup that provides a quick glance at employee data such as profiles, salary, ratings, benefits status, and activities. Data can be filtered to show custom views, for example, products whose average quarterly sales are lower than last quarter.

Point-and-click dashboard building is a common feature in data mashups. These mashup technologies provide visually rich and secure enterprise apps created from live data. They provide the flexibility to combine data from any enterprise app and the cloud regardless of its location. Users can build apps and dashboards that can be displayed on the Web and mobile devices.

Enterprise Mashup Architecture

Figure 6.17 shows the general architecture of an enterprise mashup app. Data from operational data stores, business systems, external data (economic data, suppliers; information, and competitors' activities), and real-time news feeds are integrated to generate an enterprise mashup.

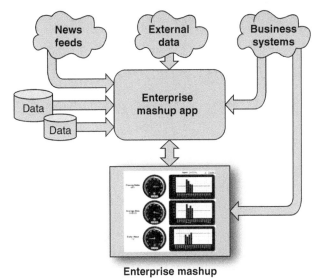

Enterprise mashup

FIGURE 6.17   Architecture of enterprise mashup application.

Adding Value with Mashups

Business users typically have a difficult time identifying current data needs. It is not realistic to expect them also to consider all the new sources of data that might be made available to them and the analyses they might perform if they had access to that data. With traditional BI and data warehousing systems, data sources must be identified, and some understanding of data requirements and data models is needed. For organizations, mashup apps decrease IT implementation costs over traditional, custom software development (discussed in Chapter 12) and significantly simplify business workflows—both increase the ROI (return on investment) of mashup implementations.

Enterprise mashups improve operational efficiency, optimize the sales pipeline, enhance customer satisfaction, and drive profitability. Within government, mashups have positively impacted strategic areas such as citizen engagement and satisfaction, financial transparency, project oversight, regulatory compliance, and legislated reporting. Mashup benefits can be summarized as:

- Dramatically reduces time and effort needed to combine disparate data sources.
- Users can define their own data mashups by combining fields from different data sources that were not previously modeled.
- Users can import external data sources, for example, spreadsheets and competitor data, to create new dashboards.
- Enables the building of complex queries by nonexperts with a drag-and-drop query building tool.

Questions

1. Why is data mining valuable to organizations?
2. How does data visualization contribute to organizational learning?
3. How do heat maps and tag clouds convey information?
4. Give two examples of data visualization for performance management
5. Why do you think dashboards must be in real time and customized for the executive or manager?
6. What are benefits of dashboards?
7. Explain why business managers need data mashup technology.
8. What are the three benefits of mashup technology to the organization?

6.4 | Predictive and Prescriptive Data Analytics Methods and Techniques

LO6.4 Identify *five predictive and prescriptive data analytics methods and techniques and how they are used.*

The most common predictive and prescriptive data analytics tools are text mining, spatial data mining, regression, optimization and rules-based decision-making, and machine learning. Each of these is discussed next.

Text mining is a specialized form of data mining. While data mining primarily focuses on analyzing structured numerical data, text mining interprets words and concepts in context. It is particularly useful in predictive analytics since today up to 75% of an organization's data consists of unstructured documents, social media, text messages, audio, video, images and diagrams, faxes and memos, call center or claims notes, etc. When customers freely express opinions and attitudes that are seen by millions of a company's current or prospective customers on social media, text mining helps companies tap into the explosion of these online customer opinions. Social commentary and social media are also being mined for **sentiment analysis** to understand consumer intent. Uncovering the opinions and concerns of customers and partners by tracking and analyzing social content has become a major focus of many organizations. Innovative companies know they can be more successful in meeting their customers' needs, if they understand them better.

Text mining is the process of deriving high quality information from text aided by software that can identify concepts, patterns, topics, keywords and other attributes in the unstructured data.

Sentiment analysis uses natural language processing, text analysis, computational linguistics and biometrics to systematically identify, extract and quantify affective stages and subjective information.

Methods and techniques for analyzing text, documents, and other unstructured content are available from several vendors. Combining text mining with data mining can create even greater value by analyzing structured data and unstructured text from both internal and external sources to provide the best view of what lies ahead.

Adding Value with Text Mining

Here are some examples of types of business value that organizations have created using text mining.

1. The mega-retailer **Walmart** wanted its online shoppers to find what they were looking for faster. Walmart analyzed clickstream data from its 45 million monthly online shoppers; then combined that data with product- and category-related popularity scores. The popularity scores had been generated by text mining the retailer's social media streams. Lessons learned from the analysis were integrated into the Polaris search engine used by customers on the company's website. Polaris has yielded a 10% to 15% increase in online shoppers completing a purchase, which equals roughly $1 billion in incremental online sales.

2. **McDonald's** bakery operation replaced manual equipment with high-speed photo analyses to inspect thousands of buns per minute for color, size, and sesame seed distribution. Automatically, ovens and baking processes adjust instantly to create uniform buns and reduce thousands of pounds of waste each year. Another food product company also uses photo analyses to sort every French fry produced in order to optimize quality.

3. **Infinity Insurance** discovered new insights that it applied to improve the performance of its fraud operation. The insurance company text mined years of adjuster reports to look for key drivers of fraudulent claims. As a result, the company reduced fraud by 75%, and eliminated marketing to customers with a high likelihood of fraudulent claims.

4. **ADP Corporation** is one of the largest payroll service providers in the world that processes data on 33 million workers. When ADP rolled out data visualizations with predictive analytics to improve its human resource (HR) function, it was surprised by what it found. After organizing the information and funneling it through an analysis program, the HR department found that ADP would soon face a serious retirement problem. To mitigate its foreseeable future talent gaps, ADP constructed new training programs to prepare the next generation of workers.

Organizations invest in text mining apps because they have features and capabilities beyond those offered by their legacy systems. Analytics vendors offer everything from simple-to-use reporting tools to highly sophisticated software for tackling the most complex data analysis problems.

Spatial Data Mining

Geographic information systems (GIS) and data mining software are naturally synergistic technologies. Together they can product powerful insights from vast quantities of disparate data to produce useful information. Everyday millions of decisions are made using a GIS. A GIS connects data with geography to understand *what* belongs *where*. For example, it's really difficult to visualize the locations of towns by their latitude and longitude coordinates listed in a spreadsheet, but it's easy to know where they are when you show these positions on a map **(Figure 6.18)**.

geographic information system (GIS)   is a computer-based tool that captures, stores, manipulates, analyzes, and visualizes geographic data on a map.

name	latitude	longitude
Seattle	47.5700	−122.3400
New York	40.7500	−73.9800
Miami	25.7876	−80.2241
Los Angeles	33.9900	−118.1800
Dallas	32.8200	−96.8400
Washington DC	38.9072	−77.0365

FIGURE 6.18 Longitude and latitude coordinates on a spreadsheet are much more difficult to visualize than when they are displayed on a map.

GIS is not just about mapping data, government, businesses, and individuals find GIS useful in solving everyday problems using **geospatial data**. For example, GIS can connect to location-tracking devices and apps. GIS software can link geospatial data—*where things or people are and where they are going*—with descriptive data—*what things are like or what customers are doing*. GIS's ability to track customers' movement and behavior in real space enables new strategies for marketing, retail, and entrepreneurship. Their ability to track products along the supply chain also offers opportunities in logistics and order fulfillment.

Collecting home and work addresses only paints a static picture of consumer locations. Their movements over time are not tracked. Data that are organized by zip code only cannot reveal customers' habits. By integrating GISs, businesses can more effectively solve problems such as organizing sales territories, pinpointing optimal locations, finding customers, managing campaigns, and delivering services. Geospatial data can also map competitors' actions.

Geocoding

In many cases, locations are already in existing data stores, but not in a format suitable for analytics. A simple process called **geocoding** can convert postal addresses to geospatial data that can then be measured and analyzed. By tapping into this resource, decision-makers can use the geographic or spatial context to detect and respond to opportunities.

Geocoding is the process of reading input text such as an address and converting it to output in the form of a latitude/longitude coordinate.

Case in Point: **GM** General Motors (GM) spends a staggering $2 billion a year on marketing. In the past, it shotgunned its ads at the general public. Now, it maps out which types of households will buy new cars, more accurately determines locations where people buy certain models, and channels its ads specifically to those areas. As a result, GM spends less money to generate higher sales.

GM managers use ESRI's ArcGIS software to view local demographics, location characteristics, regional differences, and the competitive brand environment to determine how a given dealership should be performing compared to actual results. The GIS makes it possible for GM to isolate demand, target its marketing efforts to local preferences, and position its dealerships to improve sales. With the intelligence provided by the GIS, GM has increased sales despite cutting the advertising budget.

GIS Is Not Your Grandfather's Map

Unlike a traditional flat map, a GIS-generated map is made up of many layers of information that provides users different ways to view a geographic space (**Figure 6.19**).

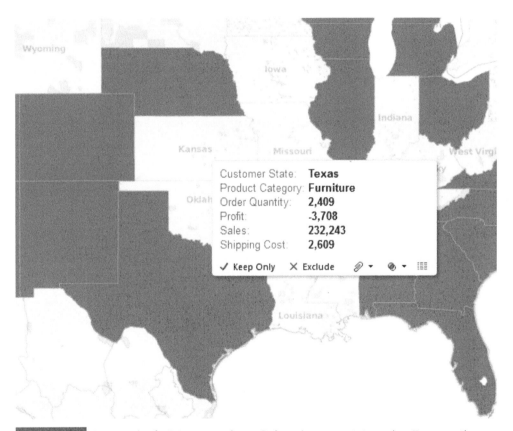

FIGURE 6.19 An example of a GIS-generated map. By hovering over a state, such as Texas, another layer of sales and financial data appears.

Imagine for a moment that you are a regional sales manager who needs to view sales data for one of your 75 stores distributed throughout the State of South Carolina. On a flat map of South Carolina, if you looked at retail store #50, you would see the name of the store and a dot showing where it is located on the map. However, if you view a GIS map of the United States on your computer, smartphone, or tablet, you can hover over South Carolina and when you click on retail store #50, up pops the store's location, store manager's name and phone number, weekly and monthly revenue, product categories, a photo of the storefront, and a virtual tour. As a highly paid, busy regional sales manager, this saves you time and your company money, increasing organizational effectiveness and efficiency.

Infrastructure and Location-Aware Collection of Geospatial Data

The infrastructure needed to collect geospatial data continues to expand. Cellular and Internet service providers, sensors, Google Earth, GPS, and RFID systems know the location of each connected user or object. Foursquare, Google Maps, and other mobile apps rely on GPS locations. With the Shopkick app, Macy's can track a shopper's every move within one of its stores and send the shopper notifications about deals and items of interest. iBeacon is a feature available in iOS 7 devices that uses a low-power Bluetooth transmission to broadcast a user's location. iBeacon allows Apple, or app developers leveraging Apple technology, to track users inside buildings where satellite transmissions may not reach.

Organizations can motivate customers to download a location-tracking app. Using GIS can help businesses target their customer markets more effectively and dynamically by engaging with them in real time.

Adding Value with Spatial Data Mining

GIS tools have made significant contributions to decision-making in finance, accounting, marketing, and other areas of business. Business applications include the following:

- **Analysts** can pinpoint the geographic areas where the highest performing stores are established.
- **Retailers** can learn how store sales are impacted by population or the proximity to competitors' stores.
- **A retail chain** with plans to open a hundred new stores can use GIS to identify relevant demographics, proximity to highways, public transportation, and competitors' stores to select the best location options.
- **Food and consumer products companies** can chart locations of complaint calls, enabling product traceability in the event of a crisis or recall.
- **Sales reps** might better target their customer visits by analyzing the geography of sales targets.

Geospatial Data Analysis Software

With current GIS, geospatial, and geocoding technologies and platforms, GISs can be easily incorporated and managed within data analytics and visualization software. Popular platforms include LandVision, Concept3D, GovPilot, PolicyMap, Thinkgeo MapSuite GIS Editor, and netTerrain OSP.

Regression Modeling

Linear regression is a statistical method that analyzes and finds relationships between a dependent variable and one or more independent (or explanatory) variables. Simple linear regression has one explanatory variable. Multiple linear regression has two or more explanatory variables.

Two types of regression modeling—linear and time series—are particularly useful in predicting future behavior and prescribing actionable insights. **Linear regression** modeling is used to predict the value of a variable that is dependent on the value of one or more other variables. The variable you want to predict is called the dependent variable. The variable(s) you are using to predict the other variable's value is called the independent (or explanatory) variable. Linear regression fits a straight line or surface that minimizes the discrepancies between predicted and actual output values.

Linear regression is used to make data-driven decisions rather than relying on experience and intuition. It is also useful in providing better insights by uncovering patterns and relationships that had gone unnoticed. For example, sales data can be analyzed to detect specific purchasing patterns on certain days of the week to help business managers anticipate when product demand is high or low and plan accordingly.

Figure 6.20 presents an example of a simple linear regression model that predicts expected test scores (dependent variable) dependent on hours studied (explanatory variable) for a class of 20 students. Each dot is a data point that reflects the actual test score and the number of hours actually studied. The straight line (regression) represents the expected values based on the average of test scores and hours studied taken from previous test data (historical data). Dots above the line indicate that students 1, 2, 6, 10, 12, 13, 14, 15, 16, and 19 performed better than expected. Dots below the line indicate that students 3, 4, 7, 8, 9, 11, 17, 18, and 20 performed worse than expected. Student 5 performed as expected.

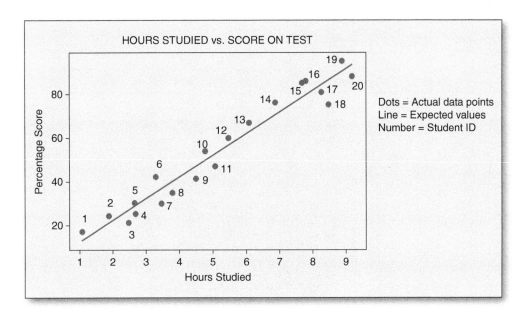

FIGURE 6.20　Simple linear regression model.

Time-Series Regression

A **time series** is a collection of data values over time. **Time-series regression** is performed by plotting a series of well-defined data points and attempting to predict what will happen to it in the future based on measuring the data at consistent time intervals over a specific period of time, such as monthly, quarterly or annually. The **trend line** shows the direction in which a variable is moving as time passes.

A time-series regression model estimates the direction a variable is trending over time.

Three ways data can be analyzed using a time-series regression are:

1. **Trend**—series of data points go up, down or stay flat over time
2. **Rate of Change**—the extent of relative change between data points over time.
3. **Cycles**—regularly repeating patterns in the data, such as at the end of a quarter when sales reps typically close sales out and see if they have made their target.

Figure 6.21 shows two types of time series regressions—**constant times series** and **trended time series**. A constant time series remains at about the same level over time, but a trended time series shows a stable linear movement up or down. Both constant and trended time series can fluctuate by season. For example, sales data may show that a business has more sales during certain holiday seasons than the rest of the year or that sales are lower at the beginning of the year than they are at the end of the year.

Constant time series is a time series in which the mean value of the time series is constant over time.

Trended time series is a time series in which the mean value of the time series can fluctuate by season.

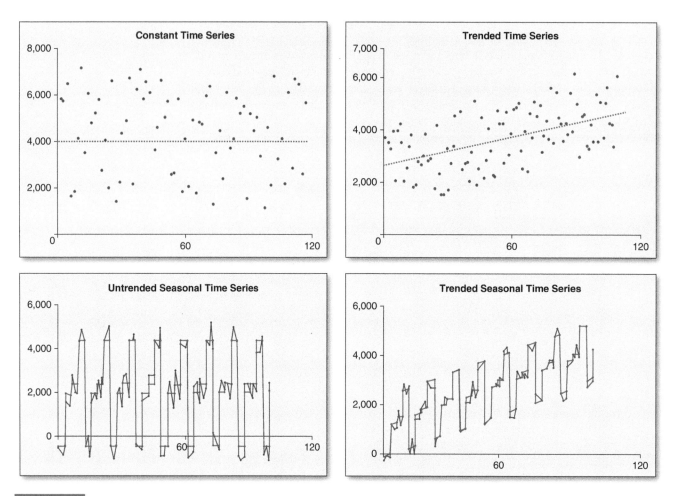

FIGURE 6.21 Example of time-series regression models.

You often see time series graphs in the newspapers or on the news. For example, stock and securities prices, stock market levels, unemployment rates and loan interest rates. Time series regression is a useful business tool that allows organizations to follow sales and profits to determine if they are increasing or decreasing over time; analyze inventory levels over time; perform economic forecasting, and project future workloads.

Adding Value with Regression

Regression modeling is a key component in making data-driven decisions at just about every level of an organization. It helps organizations understand the relationships between data points in their big data sets to make better decisions such as predicting sales or managing inventory levels based on supply on demand. Most customers use regression to understand a phenomenon such as "Why did customer demand for smartphones drop last month?" predict things about the future "What will smartphone sales look like next month?" or decide what action to take, "Should we decrease production of smartphones, stay as we are, or increase production?" In addition to forecasting, regression can also be used to understand patterns in the data that weren't known before, help identify and correct source of problems such as a launch of a new product or deployment of a new system that didn't go well, and optimize critical business processes.

Typically, business analysts and data professionals are tasked with extracting the relevant data, run regression analysis and create reports to guide and business managers, management teams, and sales units. Many of them use Microsoft Excel to generate simple (one independent variable) and multiple (more than one independent variable) linear and time series regression models as well as statistical software packages like IBM SPSS® Statistics that make it easy to produce regression equations, regression models and regression formulae.

Decision Optimization and Rules-Based Decision-Making—Business decision-makers need to optimize trade-offs multiple times a day. **Decision optimization** and **rules-based decision-making** tools can help them do this by identifying a course to prescribe the best outcomes from a myriad of options. With optimization and rules-based decision-making tools organizations can run complex models, analyze scenarios and factor in business rules and constraints to find the best course of action. Even seemingly simple decisions can require complex analysis. For example, a logistics company that owns a fleet of trucks needs to determine the most efficient route for one of its trucks as it makes deliveries to multiple locations. Even if the organization only had to deliver to 5 locations it would have to decide between 120 routes, but if it had 15 locations it would have a choice of 1.18345 trillion routes!

Decision optimization is the process of calculating values of variables that lead to an optimal value of the event under investigation.

Rules-based decision-making is decision-making that helps novices make decisions like an expert.

Adding Value with Optimization and Rules-Based Decision-Making

Decision-makers in all industry sectors are faced with decisions like this every day. Other examples include factory managers who must determine the best sequence for the manufacture of a product; airlines that must optimize schedules for aircraft, crews and maintenance personnel, and retailers who need to optimize their distribution networks. These decisions are far too complex for spreadsheets or descriptive analytics apps.

Decision optimization models use APIs, advanced mathematical and artificial intelligence techniques and optimization software like IBM Decision Optimization uses advanced offers powerful visualization features to help data scientists with the development process. They also enable them to communicate the benefits of optimization to line of business managers who can run multiple "what if" scenarios to rapidly adjust their plans if unexpected events occur. Optimization can be used with machine learning to address complex challenges and enable managers to make better decisions, improve profits and sustain a competitive advantage. One optimization example that we use every day is search engine optimization (SEO)—when we input a search term to look for websites that can inform us about a given topic on a search engine like Google, Firefox, or Chrome (more on this in Chapter 7).

Machine Learning. Another data analytics tool that is becoming popular for use with big data sets is machine learning. The technology that is used to implement machine learning is known as **cognitive computing**.

Cognitive computing is the technology that uses machine learning algorithms.

Adding Value with Machine Learning

Machine learning helps organizations identify images, personalize marketing campaigns, analyze genomics and "steer" autonomous vehicles. Machine learning creates models that provide accurate forecasts such as demand forecasts, and equipment failure predictions by manipulating real-time inputs and historical data. The four main tasks that machine learning applies known rules to include:

- Categorizing people or things.
- Predicting likely outcomes or actions based on identified patterns.
- Identifying previously unknown patterns and relationships.
- Detecting unexpected behaviors.

Machine learning and decision optimization are even more powerful when they are used together. For example, if a forecast from a machine learning model is input into a decision optimization model, the various tradeoffs and constraints can be assessed, and innovative solutions result to meet business goals. Likewise, if an action plan recommended by an optimization model has been implemented, the data from its use can be used as input for a machine learning model to improve forecasts and guard against risk. **IT at Work 6.4** describes one example of how a large energy company in Australia used machine learning to capture knowledge from its retiring employees and improve its corporate knowledge base.

IT at Work 6.4

Woodside Energy Beefs Up Its Knowledge Base with Machine Learning

Data get lost and experienced employees retire. This is a critical sustainability data problem many organizations face. It certainly was the case at Woodside Energy, the largest operator of oil and gas production in Australia that face the prospect of losing valuable corporate knowledge. This was a particularly daunting problem for Woodside since offshore energy is a particularly expensive undertaking. For example, a gas platform can cost $500,000 per day to operate and require real-time monitoring of thousands of inputs 24/7 by a crew living on top of 100,000 tons of steel in the middle of the ocean. The stakes in human lives, environmental safety and shareholder results are also incredibly high. That's why Woodside refers to its employees at "Heroes".

Thirty years of engineering and drilling knowledge vital to Woodside's business operations was buried in a mountain of unstructured data and in the minds of its most experienced engineers, many of whom were nearing retirement age. Without this knowledge, Woodside was facing the dilemma of losing meaningful insights into 30 years of complex engineering data to enable fact-driven decision-making on its complex projects. The answer was a cognitive assistant driven by machine learning.

Over the past several years, Woodside Energy has adopted a wide range of technology from data analytics and cognitive computing to 3D printing and AI in a bid to gain better insights into its huge volumes of data, help reduce costs and ensure high production performance and reliability. First, with the help of IBM's Watson, Woodside built a customized tool to allow its Heroes find detailed answers to highly specific questions even on remote oil and gas outposts 70 miles off the coast of Australia in the deep waters of the North West Shelf. To achieve this, Watson was fed the equivalent of 38,000 Woodside 100-page documents to create Willow, a cognitive assistant. It is estimated that a human working 24 hours a day would take more than five years to read all this information. Willow can process it and produce meaningful answers to questions posed by Woodside engineers in a matter of seconds.

Woodside estimates it has saved $10M AUD in employee costs because of faster access and more intuitive analysis of its engineering records. For example, its geoscience team has realized a whopping 75% reduction in time spent reading and searching through data sources. Willow has also created a different mindset for Woodside's Heroes who are now eager to have their knowledge recorded in the new system for future use by other engineers who might face similar challenges in the future.

To get even more benefits from predictive data analytics, Woodside is now looking at the other end of the hiring spectrum—recruiting. Once again, Woodside has partnered with IBM, this time to create a cognitive solution to simplify and improve its onboarding process. Overall, Woodside has deployed more than a dozen advanced data analytics solutions with the help of IBM and with Accenture Consulting Services to improve maintenance and process-control in its production operations. Woodside has even created its own data science team to work directly with asset engineering and operations to build a range of statistical and analytics tools using live streaming data for its facilities. In the past Woodside just reported on data. Now they create value from that data by analyzing and predicting outcomes.

Sources: Compiled from O'Brien (2017), CIO (2019), Accenture (2020), IBM (2020), and Woodside (2020).

Other companies that use machine learning to increase their capabilities include:

- **Under Armour** uses IBM Watson Cognitive Computing to provide the "Cognitive Coaching System"—a personal health assistant that provides users with real-time, data-based coaching using sensor and manually input data for sleep, fitness, activity and nutrition. The app has a rating of 4.5 starts from users and Under Armour has reported more than 51% growth in its customer base since implementing the Cognitive Coaching System.

- **Coca-Cola Amatil,** the largest bottler and distributor of non-alcoholic bottled beverages in the Asia Pacific region, uses Trax Retail Execution—an image-based technology—let's sales reps take photos of store shelves with their mobile devices. The images are then sent to the Trax Cloud and analyzed, returning actionable reports within minutes to sales reps who can quickly identify performance gaps and apply corrective actions in stores and providing more detailed online assessment to management. Within five months after implementing Trax Retail Execution Coca-Cola Amatil reported a gain of 1.3% market share in the Asia Pacific region.

- **Peter Glenn,** an outdoor apparel and gear retailer and wholesaler, uses AgilOne Advanced Analytics to gain insight into its customer profile and act on their findings. When they looked at trends between buyer groups they were able to make better segmentation decisions and when the company learned that more than 80% of its customer base had left, they were able to use that information to retarget and re-engage lost customers.

Questions

1. How are the methods and techniques used in predictive and prescriptive data analytics different from those used in descriptive data analytics?

2. How does text mining provide value? Give an example?

3. Give an example of how geospatial data would be useful to an organization?

4. Why does organization use regression analysis?

5. How do organizations benefit from using optimization and rules-based decision-making?

6. What is machine learning and why do organizations use it?

Chapter Summary

LO6.1 *Define* the four phases of decision-making, the differences between business intelligence and data science and how each can be used to enable organizations gain a competitive advantage.

The four phases of decision-making are intelligence, design, choice and review. In the intelligence phase a problem or opportunity is identified. In the design phase, various course of action are suggested. In the choice phase a course of action is selected and put into action where it is monitored and controlled in the review phase.

Traditional business intelligence is low level data analytics, but embedded BI and augmented analytics are enhancing BI capabilities. BI involves reviewing and analyzing historical data to report on the current status of an organization based on the analysis of structured data. The goal of BI is to drive profits by managing inventory and other assets and engaging customers in a smarter way. BI can allow for quick detection and decisions to take advantage of opportunities, risks and market changes. They can improve an HR function, lead to prompt disaster response by insurance companies and first responders, identify customer segments that can lead to higher profits, and increase membership rates and member satisfaction.

Data science is a more sophisticated form of data analytics. It goes beyond describing what has happened to predict future behavior and prescribing action to optimize processes and can handle multi-structured data. The goal of data science is to find patterns and trends in big data sets and added value when they lead to practical solutions for organizations related to increases in revenue, ability to compete, operational efficiencies and an enhanced experience for customers.

LO6.2 *Explain* how big data and advanced data analytics work together to predict organizational performance in the future and prescribe actionable insights.

When a data set is too large or complex to be analyzed using traditional methods it is called big data. Big data is a major factor driving advanced data analytics. The four major characteristics of big data are volume, variety, veracity and velocity. Big data is voluminous, it exists in various forms (e.g., numeric, text, audio, and images) and is collected from a variety of sources, it must be verifiable and be quickly accessible. Predictive data analytics is mid-level data analytics that analyzes multi-structured data from a variety of sources

to predict future behavior. Prescriptive data analytics is the highest level of data analytics and provides actionable insights taken from the results of descriptive and predictive data analytics to suggest viable alternatives for organizations to follow in making strategic decisions.

LO6.3 *Describe* four descriptive data analytics methods and techniques and how they are used.

The four most important descriptive data analytics tools are data mining, data visualization, digital dashboards and mashups. Data mining is the first step in descriptive data analytics and involves software that analyzes data from various perspectives, categorize them and derive correlations or patterns among data fields. Data visualization provides a graphical representation of the data to make it easier to understand and digital dashboards use mashups to bring multiple data visualizations onto a single screen to provide an in-depth analysis of the data and provide a real-time snapshot of a business productivity. Data mining helps organizations make more informed decisions when and where needed; discover unknown insights from the data and helps automate and streamline business processes. With data visualization business managers can make data-driven decisions faster and more confidently because the data is easier to understand. Organizations use visualization for process improvements, clarifying factors that influence customer behavior to improve the customer experience and predict sales by location to improve inventory management. Digital dashboards bring data together to create a more powerful visualization of multiple types of data and mashups integrate data from multiple sources adding to the power of visualization and digital dashboards. With these tools organizations can create strategies to reduce costs, increase revenue, improve products and performance to engage competitively in the market and enhance customer satisfaction.

LO6.4 *Identify* five predictive and prescriptive data analytics methods and techniques and how they are used.

The five major methods and techniques used in predictive and prescriptive data analytics are text mining, spatial data mining, regression, optimization and rules-based decision-making, and machine learning. Organizations use text mining to analyze clickstream data from online shoppers and integrate it with product popularity scores to increase their market share, and others analyze images to identify flaws in products to optimize product quality. Spatial data mining enables organizations to see the locations of their highest performing stores; learn how sales are impacted by population or proximity to competitor locations, identify highways, public transportation and competitor stores to select new locations and chart location of complaints to identify environmental variables that might be contributing to them. Predictive data analytics uses two types of regression modeling to predict future behavior. They are simple or multiple linear regression and time series regression. Regression model give a graphical representation of the data to show trends, rate of change and cycles that enable organizations to forecast sales, plan production and marketing campaigns and correct problems to improve a business process. Optimization and rules-based decision-making are used to optimize the multiple trade-offs that business manages have to consider every day. By running complex models, they can analyze scenarios and factor in business rules and constraints to find the best course of action. Machine learning uses cognitive computing technology to identify images for security purposes, personalize marketing campaigns, steer autonomous vehicles and detect unexpected behavior. Combining machine learning and optimization is a particularly powerful way to analyze date to predict and prescribe actional insights.

Key Terms

advanced data analytics   221
affinity analysis   225
augmented analytics   209
augmented reality (AR)   228
big data   217
bounded rationality   203
business intelligence (BI)   203
citizen data scientist   216
cognitive computing   241
constant time series   239
dashboard   204
data analytics   217
data discovery   226
data mashup   204
data mining   224
data product   213

data science   203
data visualization   224
data visualization   204
decision optimization   241
descriptive data analytics   203
digital dashboards   224
drill down   225
embedded BI   205
geocoding   236
geographic information system (GIS)   235
geospatial data   225
known known   204
known unknown   204
linear regression   238
machine learning   209
modern BI   205

optimizing   203
predictive data analytics   203
predictive model   221
predictive modeling   221
prescriptive data analytics   203
resilient distributed dataset (RDD)   216
rules-based decision-making   241
satisficing   203
self-service analytics   205
sentiment analysis   234
text mining   234
time-series regression   239
trended time series   239
unknown unknown   204

Assuring Your Learning

Discuss: Critical Thinking Questions

1. How people use, access, and discover data in business is being actively disrupted by tablets, which had been designed for consumers. Users have higher expectations for data displays and capabilities. Boring, static graphs and pie charts are unacceptable. Discuss how performance management—the monitoring of KPIs, for example—may be improved by providing managers with data visualizations. Now consider the opposite. In your opinion, would lack of data visualization hurt the ability to manage performance?

2. Lots of data are available to retailers to make good decisions—loyalty programs, Web analytics, and POS data. However, there is a big gap between having data and being able to leverage them for real-time decision-making. How can enterprise mashups close this gap?

3. Explain how executive dashboards can lead to better business insights. What are the limitations of dashboards?

Explore: Online and Interactive Exercises

1. Periscopic is a socially conscious data visualization firm that specializes in using IT to help companies and organizations facilitate information transparency and public awareness. From endangered species, to politics, to social justice, it is the goal of Periscopic to engage the public and deliver a message of responsibility and action. Its philosophy and tagline are "do good with data."

a. Visit http://periscopic.com and explore its recent work.

b. Discuss what types of data are currently being used to do good.

c. How effective is Periscopic's approach to public awareness and social justice?

2. Visit https://www.tibco.com/products/tibco-spotfire/learn/demos/boston-airbnb-explorer

Click on "Go To Demo."

a. Adjust filters on the left and Lasso to select a region of listings to see pricing heat map**c.** Describe the data visualization features in the demo and how the data visualization influenced your understanding of the data.

b. Explain the benefits of the application or analytics to your decision-making.

3. Visit https://www.klipfolio.com

a. Click on "Build my Dashboard" and start building your own dashboard.

b. Discuss your experience in building the dashboard. Was it difficult?

c. Describe the features of the dashboard that you felt were most useful.

4. Visit IBM's Watson Studio at https://dataplatform.cloud.ibm.com/registration/stepone?context=wdp&apps=all

a. Pick your region for apps and data.

b. Create an account.

c. In your opinion, what are the two most important benefits of this data discovery tool?

d. Would you recommend this tool? Explain your answer.

Analyze & Decide: Apply IT Concepts to Business Decisions

1. Qlik offers a complimentary e-book entitled "Turn your Excel Reports into Stunning Dashboards." Download the e-book. Write a report about what you learned.

2. Visit the website of software provider **Microstrategy** at https://www.microstrategy.com

a. Click on "Solutions."

b. Click "By Industry."

c. Scroll down to choose an industry that interests you and click on that Industry.

d. Choose a business application that interests you such as Distribution Center Operations, Digital Loyalty Card, Vendor Portal or Customer Analysis.

e. Click "Watch the Video."

f. Write a report describing what you learned.

Reinforce: Ensure Your Understanding of the Key Terms

Solve the online crossword provided for this chapter.

Web Resources

More resources and study tools are located on the student Website. You'll find useful web links and self-test quizzes that provide individualized feedback.

Case 6.2

Business Case: London Heathrow Airport Launches BI and Machine Learning to Improve Airfield Management, Predict Passenger Flow, and Transform Airport Security

Heathrow airport in London is the second busiest international airport in the world, second only to Dubai international airport in number of airplanes landing and taking off each day and the seventh largest in terms of total passenger traffic. Managing over 215,000 passengers every day is a challenging task and requires a high degree of coordination to manage passenger traffic and give passengers a smooth airport experience. Any unexpected disruptions in the smooth workflow in operations at Heathrow such as damaged runways, storms, delayed or canceled flights, shifts in jet streams, etc. would disturb the entire functioning of the airport, passengers and airport employees.

Data analysts at London Heathrow were using Excel spreadsheets to analyze its airfield, passenger and flight data and sorely needed a

centralized management system that would extract large volumes of data produced by airport operations and transform them into useful visual insights. Stuart Birrell, CIO at Heathrow was concerned that "We have tens of thousands of people who work around the airfield. Safety is critical. Adopting tools like Power BI makes life easier. It is the simple things. There is GPS in the airfield vehicles. If a driver finds a problem with the concrete, this can be recorded accurately." Heathrow chose Microsoft Power BI as their BI solution. The reporting produced by its BI tool ensured airfield safety, allowed airport staff to function better and improved passenger management.

The key was moving from a paper-based, reactive operations model to a more predictive, proactive planning model in which staff were dealt fewer surprises on a day-to-day basis that enabled them to change their plans on-the-fly. The answer was BI reports and dashboards that were made available to airfield managers, security officers, transfers and customer service staff and a machine learning model that accurately predicts passenger flow in 15-minute increments into each terminal. Birrell says it's possible to mash up historical scheduling data and a feedback loop to provide more accurate forecasts. With insights from these data analytics tools managers could plan staff breaks, open and close security lanes as needed and schedule staff shifts to balance passenger flow across the airport in peak times. As Birrell said, "For passengers, it is all about getting them to aircraft on time." The new system also helps manage arrivals. Under the old model, if several flights came into the airport an hour early because of tailwinds immigration and baggage staff would have to scramble to react to the sudden spike of arriving passengers. After the predictive model was deployed, the airport manager could share the insights with air traffic control and security

staff to better schedule immigration and security lanes and teams by knowing where passengers are arriving, how many of them are arriving and at what terminal to ensure the right number of immigration/security lanes are open and reduce time and stress for both passengers and airport staff.

For Birrell, the biggest challenges were not technology-related but were about a culture and mindset shift to get people onboard. "It's easy to do a bit of data analysis with one or two experts. It's more about how you deploy this around your organization; how do you get that security team of 4,000 to start using that data and change the way they're working," says Birrell. Now London Heathrow has people with its operations team who are deploying and building their own apps including one security officer who learned to build apps on his own with a little help from the IT department. So far, he has developed 12 apps to support his colleagues in security.

Questions

1. Why did London Heathrow need to move up from Excel to a business intelligence platform?

2. What are the benefits that London Heathrow passengers experienced as a result of the new approach to data analytics?

3. Describe one specific way in which machine learning improved London Heathrow operations.

4. What was the biggest challenge that CIO Birrell faced in deploying BI and machine learning at London Heathrow?

Sources: Compiled from Carey (2018), Saran (2018), Shah (2018), DataFlair (2019), and Microsoft (2020).

Case 6.3

Video Case: The Beauty of Data Visualization

TED Talks are influential videos of expert speakers on education, business, science, technology and creativity. Visit **https://www.ted.com/talks/anne_milgram_why_smart_statistics_are_the_key_to_fighting_crime** and listen to the Ted Talk by Anne Milgram, Attorney General of New Jersey on their use of data analytics to predict crime and deal with apprehension of criminals.

Questions

1. Explain why Milgram needed to used data analytics in her job.

2. Name some examples of the statistics that she used?

3. What results did she see from using the new analytics?

4. How did the change affect the profile of crimes they were dealing with?

IT Toolbox

Create a Dynamic Heat Map in Excel

Heat Maps are a fun and effective way to visually display the differences in different categories of data. Managers frequently use them to convey importance of data and prioritize actions. Making the heat map dynamic makes it much more effective so that when values change, the heat map will change.

Go to **https://trumpexcel.com/heat-map-excel/** and follow the steps to create your own dynamic heat map quickly and easily. Use the data shown on the TrumpExcel Web page or generate your own data such as hours spent on different sports activities each week; money spent on different categories of food by the month; number of minutes spent studying for different courses each week, etc.

References

Accenture. "Predictive Oil and Gas Analytics at Woodside." *Accenture Perspectives,* 2020.

Alderstadter, J. "USGA and Deloitte Launch U.S. Open Augmented Reality App." *USGA|U.S. Open*, June 4, 2019.

Altexsoft. "How to Structure a Data Science Team: Key Models and Roles to Consider." *Altexsoft*, September 25, 2018.

Bassa, A. "Managing a Data Science Team." *Harvard Business Review*, October 24, 2018.

BitDegree. "Data Scientist Salary Revealed." *BitDegree Tutorials*, December 6, 2019.

Brown, N. et al. "Big Data in Drug Discovery." *Progress in Medicinal Chemistry*, 2018, 57: 277–356.

Campbell, S. and Tully, A. "SAP Partner Enables Goodwill of Denver to Focus on What's Really Important." *SAP*, August 26, 2018.

Carey, S. "Heathrow Turns to Power BI to Predict Passenger Volumes Ahead of Time." *Computerworld*, October 17, 2018.

Chen, B., Garmir, L., Calvisi, D., Chua, M., Kelley, R. and Chen, X. "Harnessing Big 'Omics' Data and AI for Drug Discovery in Hepatocellular Carcinoma." *Nature Review Gastroenterology Hepatology,* 2020, 17(4): 238–251.

CIO Review. "Top Ten Data Visualization Consulting/Service Companies—2019." *CIO Review*, 2020.

Crazy Egg. "What Is a Heat Map, How to Create One, Examples and Case Studies." https://www.crazyegg.com/blog/understanding-using-heatmaps-studies. Accessed on February 24, 2020.

Dataflair Team. "Power BI Case Study—How the Tool Reduced Hassles of Heathrow & Edsby." *DataFlair*, September 19, 2019.

Deloitte. "Deloitte Insight Studio—Delivering outcomes by design." https://www2.deloitte.com/us/en/pages/deloitte-analytics/solutions/deloitte-insightstudio.html. Accessed on February 25, 2020a.

Deloitte. "Reimagining a Golf Ecosystem." https://www2.deloitte.com/us/en/pages/deloitte-analytics/solutions/deloitte-insight studio.html. Accessed on July 14, 2020b.

DeNisco Rayome, A. "How to Build a Data Science Team." *TechRepublic,* April 25, 2019.

Eubanks, M. "NASCAR: Despite Attendance Woes, NASCAR Continues to Roll On." *Fansided*, April 2019.

Gartner. "2020 Gartner Magic Quadrant for Analytics and Business Intelligence Platforms." *Gartner*, February 11, 2020a.

Gartner. "2020 Gartner Magic Quadrant for Data Science and Machine Learning Platforms." *Gartner,* February 11, 2020b.

Geekadmin. "How NASCAR Uses Augmented Reality and Big Data to Increase Customer Engagement." *Geek Denial*, October 12, 2019.

Glassdoor. 2020. https://www.glassdoor.com. Accessed on July 13, 2020.

GSK. (2017). "How Genomics is Driving a New Era of Drug Discovery." *GSK*. Available from https://www.gsk.com/en-gb/behind-the-science/innovation/how-genomics-is-driving-a-new-era-of-drug-discovery/. Accessed on July 13, 2020.

IBM. "Woodside Energy: Using IBM Watson Technology to Extract Decades of Experience from an Ocean of Data." https://www.ibm.com/case-studies/woodside-energy-watson-cognitive. Accessed on February 28, 2020.

KDnuggets. "How to Build Disruptive Data Science Teams: 10 Best Practices." *KDnuggets*, July 2019.

Kure, M. "Goodwill Industries of Denver Partners with Tech Leaders to Help Coloradans in Need." *SAP*, March 2, 2018.

Martinelli, M. "NASCAR Has a Problem, and Drivers Aren't Sure How to Fix It." *USA Today*, February 17, 2019.

McCormick, S. "Who Was Bill France, Sr. and Why Did He Start NASCAR?" *Liveaboutdotcom*, March 31, 2019.

Meredith, J. "Here's How Big Data Is Transforming Augmented Reality." *SmartDataCollective*, February 8, 2019.

Microsoft. 2020. https://powerbi.microsoft.com/en-us

Nascar. https://www.nascar.com/nascar-history. Accessed on February 18, 2020.

Nerad, J. "Data Science Will Drive Auto Industry in Future, Tata Consultancy Services Says." *Forbes*, August 27, 2019.

NewVantage Partners "Big Data and AI Executive Survey 2019." http://newvantage.com/wp-content/uploads/2018/12/Big-Data-Executive-Survey-2019-Findings-122718.pdf. Accessed on February 26, 2020.

O'Brien, J. "Woodside Beers Up Tech Play." *CIO,* March 2, 2017.

O*Net Online. Available from https://www.onetonline.org/link/summary/15-1199.08?redir=15-1099.10. Accessed on July 13, 2020.

Owens, J. "Big Data Analysis Approaches for Drug Discovery." *Technology Networks*, January 18, 2019.

Patel, S. "How NASCAR Is Using AR and 360-degree Video." *DIGIDAY*, February 15, 2019.

Pratt, M. and Fruhlinger, J. "What Is Business Intelligence? Transforming Data into Business Insights." *CIO*, October 16, 2019.

Qian, T., Zhu, S., and Hoshida, Y. "Use of Big Data in Drug Development for Precision Medicine: An Update." *Expert Review of Precision Medicine and Drug Development*, 2019, 4:1–12.

Rodger, J. "Discover Goodwill in Colorado Merges with Denver Organization to Form Statewide Entity." *The Gazette*, June 3, 2019.

Sanat. "Data Science Life Cycle." *Towards Data Science*. https://towardsdatascience.com/life-cycle-of-a-data-science-project-2973578b2f74. Accessed on February 18, 2020.

SAP "Goodwill Industries of Denver: Better Run World and Better Run Business." https://www.sap.com/about/customer-involvement/customer-stories.html?video=34a3377e-3b7d-0010-87a3-c30de2ffd8ff. Accessed on March 8, 2020.

Saran, C. "How Heathrow Transformed Using Analytics for the People." *ComputerWeekly.com*, October 18, 2018.

Saxena, A. "Is 'Data Scientist' the 'Sexiest Job of the 21st Century'? And How Do You Get One of Your Own?" *Entrepreneur*, January 30, 2019.

Scherbak, M. "Data Science vs. Business Intelligence: Same but Completely Different." *Towards Data Science*, March 25, 2019.

SelectHub. "Business Intelligence Software Tools Comparison." *SelectHub*. https://www.selecthub.com/business-intelligence-tools. Accessed on February 21, 2020.

Shacklett, M. "How NASCAR Uses Augmented Reality and Big Data to Increase Customer Engagement." *TechRepublic*, October 11, 2019.

Shah, S. "Heathrow CIO Stuart Birrell on Transforming Airport Security with Machine Learning." December 14, 2018.

Sharraf, S. "Woodside Energy Uses Cognitive Solution to Improve Onboarding." *CIO, October* 16, 2019.

Simon, H. "Rational Choice and the Structure of the Environment." *Psychological Review*, 1956, 63(2): 129–138.

Staff Report. "NASCAR Introduces Virtual Burnouts with New Augmented Reality Experience." *NASCAR*, September 13, 2019.

Szczecinski, M. "What Does a Data Team Really Do?" *Towards Data Science*, July 14, 2018.

Trustmarque and Tableau. "Seven Key Attributes of Business Intelligence." *Trustmarque Solutions, Ltd.*, 2020.

Woodside. "Data Science." https://www.woodside.com.au/innovation/data-science. Accessed on February 28, 2020.

Social Media and Semantic Web Technology

LEARNING OBJECTIVES

7.1 **Explain** how technological developments that define Web 2.0 created a fundamentally new experience for users.

7.2 **Describe** the most common Web 2.0 tools and applications and how businesses use them to accomplish their goals.

7.3 **Describe** how search engines work and identify ways that businesses gain competitive advantage by using search technology effectively.

7.4 **Explain** how Semantic Web technology enhances the accuracy of search engines results and how businesses can optimize their websites to take advantage of this emerging technology.

7.5 **Explain** how recommendation engines enhance user experience by predicting and recommending Web content, products, and services that might appeal to them.

Case 7.1 Opening Case

Fredex/Adobe Stock

dervish37/123RF

lkeskinen/123RF

The Darkside of Digital Campaigns: Disinformation and Foreign Influence

Background

While politicians and political organizations have had a presence on the Internet since its early days, it wasn't until 2008 and again in 2012 that we saw Barack Obama pioneer the use of Web 2.0 tools in a significant and decisive way. Since then, political campaigns and movements around the world have utilized the social Web to raise money, share their message, attract supporters, and win elections.

Nationwide digital campaigns are increasingly sophisticated, involving hundreds of workers that manage the campaign's online effort. Enterprise-level **collaboration platforms**, based on Web 2.0 technologies, help team members communicate and coordinate an increasing amount of digital activity as the campaign grows. These collaboration platforms are like private social networks, allowing team members to post messages, create online groups or committees, share multi-media content, send instant messages, video conference, and so on.

Web 2.0 Digital Campaign Tools

New Web technologies have created unexpected challenges to democracy, fairness, and the ability of governments to conduct elections free from the influence of disruptive domestic and foreign interference. Political campaigns must use several different social technologies in order to be competitive in today's technology-driven society. The following list contains the most essential components of a successful digital campaign strategy:

- **Website**—Campaigns create compelling and persuasive content on their website and drive traffic (users) to the website by posting links to the website on social media, digital advertising, and search engine results pages.

- **Search Marketing**—Digital campaign strategists work hard to increase the chances that the campaign's website will be listed when users search for certain kinds of information. This makes search marketing a critical component of any digital campaign.

- **Social Media**—Smart political campaigns use social media to "listen" to conversations of their followers as well as the discussions of people that disagree with them. Campaigns use social media to "build communities" of followers by connecting supporters with other people that share common values or political views. Social media can also be used to encourage users to visit the campaign website, download a campaign mobile app, or donate money to the campaign.

- **Digital Fundraising (crowdfunding)**—Web 2.0 technologies make it relatively easy and inexpensive for campaigns to solicit many, relatively small donations from lots of supporters as well as its traditional wealthy donors. In some cases, the small donations yield hundreds of millions of dollars and reduce the influence wealthy donors and special interest groups.

- **Digital Advertising**—Banner ads and graphic ads that appear on websites willing to host advertisements from online display networks like Google Ads or Yahoo! have at least two advantages to traditional mass media advertising. They are less expensive than most print, television, and radio ad campaigns and users can be targeted much more effectively based on gender, age, location, and interests.

- **Mobile Marketing**—Most Google searches are done on a smartphone. Campaigns should review how their search engine results pages (SERP) listing displays on mobile devices. Text and video messages designed to resonate with people in a particular state or town can be deployed via SMS technology or through a campaign mobile app. In the 2020 presidential campaign, the Bernie Sanders campaign used a mobile app called BERN that volunteers used to check public records to see if their friends were registered to vote. If the volunteer found an unregistered friend who might support Sanders, the volunteer was provided with suggestions for encouraging the friend to register to vote.

- **E-mail**—Sophisticated e-mail management software makes it possible for campaigns to send a large volume of e-mail that appears personalized to the interests and concerns of specific voters and manages the campaign's responses to those e-mails. When done effectively, this increases engagement with voters, leading to increased commitment, loyalty, and support.

- **Other Web 2.0 tools** including: online video streaming, podcasts, photo sharing, and the propagation of memes favorable to the campaign.

The Problem

It has become well known that in political campaigns, some candidates will "spin" or bend the truth, and in some cases tell outright lies. However, their ability to do this successfully is limited by the power of the news media and competing campaigns who will publicly call out disinformation when it occurs. Unfortunately, campaigns have learned to use Web 2.0 to significantly increase the impact of disinformation campaigns and conceal their attempts to influence people using false information. According to McKay Coppins, a journalist for *The Atlantic*, political campaigns can now sort voters into small, very distinct groups using a strategy called microtargeting. Specialized ads are then developed to speak to the interests, fears, and concerns of each microsegment. The problem with this practice, according to critics, is that only members of the microsegment see these ads. The messages, which may contain falsehoods, are not held up to the same scrutiny as those that are more widely broadcast on, say, television or radio. Campaigns can flood social media with large amounts of false information, delivered to people most likely to be affected by the specially crafted messages. The likelihood that competing campaigns or the news media will see these ads and be able to challenge or refute them in a timely manner is small. Furthermore, campaigns can not only target likely supporters, but also deliver misleading messages that discourage or create doubts in the minds of nonsupporters.

Perhaps even more disturbing is that foreign countries are using equally sophisticated methods to influence the outcome of elections, sow discord, and create doubts about the legitimacy of elections and democratic institutions. One strategy used by Russia in the 2016 election was the creation of websites that were used to publish false news stories. Thousands of fake social media accounts were then created to disseminate these "fake news" stories to mislead people and stoke division among the electorate. Hundreds of Russians were employed at so called "troll farms" where they produced and posted fabricated news and social media posts. Intelligence agencies have reported that Russia continues its effort to interfere in U.S. elections and is developing even more sophisticated methods for future elections in the United States and other democratic countries around the world.

The Outcome

Clearly the social Web has made it possible for political campaigns to more effectively engage users, raise money in ways that reduce the influence of wealthy and special interest groups, and spread their message to targeted groups of people most likely to favor the campaign's political views. However, Web 2.0 has also made it possible for enemies of democracy, both foreign and domestic, to influence and disrupt elections. The challenge for us, and people around the world who believe in democracy, is to find ways to defeat the disruptive and divisive impact of those who wish to weaken our democratic traditions and institutions.

Questions

1. Name three Web 2.0 tools that can be used by political campaigns to gain a competitive advantage.

2. Describe two ways that Russia attempted to interfere with the 2016 U.S. presidential campaign.

3. Describe how political campaigns can drive traffic to landing pages on their website.

4. Why is mobile marketing an increasingly important part of digital campaigning?

5. How has crowdfunding changed the nature of campaign financing? Are these changes considered good for democracy?

Sources: Compiled from Mayer (2018), Cadwallader (2019), Kendrick (2019), Stewart (2019), Chappell (2020), Coppins (2020), and Wikipedia Contributors (2020a).

 DID YOU KNOW?

Less than half of all global Internet traffic is generated by human beings. The rest is generated by bots, computer programs or scripts designed to run automated tasks online. Some of the bot-generated traffic comes from "good bots," like the bot spiders employed by search engines to crawl the Web looking for new websites, new webpages, and content updates so that we can find the most current online information. But "bad bots," which make up a sizable portion of overall Web traffic are used for a variety of nefarious purposes.

Introduction

Businesses are using the social Web for marketing, recruiting, research, collaboration on projects, or branding. And as you read in this chapter's opening case, social media is increasingly being used to influence political campaigns and people's views on a wide range of political and social issues that affect many aspects of our everyday life.

According to eMarketer (2019b), U.S. companies will spend over $129 billion on digital advertising, almost $20 billion more than they will spend on traditional media advertising (e.g., television, radio, print). Mobile ads account for approximately two-thirds of digital ad spending ($87.06 billion). Smartphones, tablets (e.g., iPads), and other mobile devices have replaced personal computers as the device used most frequently to access social media, search engines, and operate mobile apps.

Today the Web continues to evolve, and even newer technologies are creating Web 3.0—the Semantic Web. This latest evolution of the Web will enhance user experience by making it easier to find information using devices and applications that will let us talk to computers in the same way we talk to other people. Search engines will become better at understanding the kind of information we need and the reasons why we are searching for that information. Special kinds of search technology, called recommendation engines, will predict what information we might find interesting or what products and services might best match our needs and wants. Finally, we will discuss the ways that these emerging Web technologies present both challenges and opportunities for businesses.

7.1 Web 2.0—Social Web Technologies

LO7.1 Explain *how technological developments that define Web 2.0 created a fundamentally new experience for users.*

The Constantly Changing Web

One of the biggest changes in online retail is the use of social features by e-commerce sites. Most online retailers encourage customers to write reviews, rate products, and read reviews from others before deciding to buy.

Web 2.0 is a term used to describe a phase of World Wide Web evolution characterized by dynamic webpages, social media, mashup applications, broadband connectivity, and user-generated content.

Companies that have embraced the potential of **Web 2.0** technologies and the emerging social culture that characterizes our modern online experience. Smart entrepreneurs and established businesses are constantly looking for ways to leverage social technologies to develop new services that will attract customers and Internet users. Business professionals must devote time and resources to consistently monitoring technological innovation and related changes in consumer behavior in order to remain relevant and competitive in a constantly changing environment.

A Platform for Services and Social Interaction

The Web is a platform for all kinds of activity—shopping, entertainment, news, education, research, and business processes like logistics and electronic funds transfer (EFT). Homes maintain broadband wireless networks to connect multiple users simultaneously to the Internet from computers, smartphones, tablets, video game systems, and video-streaming devices like the Roku box. New technologies gave rise to websites with features and services that make it easy for people to interact with one another and the companies they choose to buy from. As a result, these services and technologies are collectively referred to as **social media** and the evolution of the Web that gave rise to social media is often referred to as Web 2.0 or the social Web (see **Table 7.1**).

TABLE 7.1 Web 1.0 Versus Web 2.0

Web 1.0—The Early Web	Web 2.0—The Social Web
Static pages, HTML	Dynamic pages, XML, and Java
Author-controlled content	User-controlled content
Computers	Computers, cell phones, televisions, PDAs, game systems, car dashboards
Users view content	Users create content
Individual users	User communities
Marketing goal: *influence*	Marketing goal: *relationships*
Data: single source	Data: multiple sources, for example, mashups

Emergence of Social Applications, Networks, and Services

Starting in 2000, a series of developments in the technology and business environment occurred that set the stage (infrastructure) for Web 2.0.

1. **Broad bandwidth (broadband)**   Internet access became faster and more widely available due to large-scale adoption of broadband technology, making it possible for large amounts of data to move from one place to another. Website load times shrank from a minute to instantaneous. Huge bandwidth is required to support byte-intensive music downloads and streaming video and movie services. As residential broadband connections became commonplace and public broadband connections increased in coffee shops, malls, college campuses, and other community centers, people began to rely on applications that required fast, high-volume data connections. These broadband connections increased the overall attractiveness and accessibility of the Internet—laying the foundation for interactivity and the social Web.

2. **Sustainable business models**   After the dot-com bust in the late 1990s when many badly conceived Internet businesses failed, a new breed of business emerged. These businesses had realistic revenue models. Companies like Amazon, Google, eBay, and others began to demonstrate that it was possible to create e-commerce and consumer service sites that could generate revenue and become not only self-sustaining, but also profitable.

3. **New Web programming technologies**   New Web programming languages and technologies were developed that made it possible for programmers to create dynamic and feature-rich websites. In some cases, these new features and website capabilities created new business opportunities, which in turn led to increased demand for Web access. Increased Web usage then led to larger potential markets for businesses with successful revenue models. These businesses frequently reinvested earnings into expanding their technological capabilities to attract even more customers. This cycle of enhanced technological features leading to greater value for the consumer/Web user and then to more people using the Web continues today. Some of these Web technologies are described in more detail in **Tech Note 7.1**.

Tech Note 7.1

AJAX Technologies and APIs

Asynchronous JavaScript and XML (AJAX) is a term referring to a group of technologies and programming languages that make it possible for webpages to respond to users' actions without requiring the entire page to reload. AJAX makes it possible for Web developers to create small apps that run on a page instead of a server. This capability makes programs run much faster, eliminating a key source of frustration with the early web. Another important programming development is the API, which acts as a software gateway that programmers can use to pass data back and forth between two or more applications, platforms, or websites (see **IT at Work 7.1**). With AJAX and APIs, website programmers can import data from other sources to create new functions and features that we have come to associate with social media applications (see the discussion of mashups later in this chapter).

AJAX technologies include JavaScript, extendable markup language (XML), document object model (DOM), hypertext markup language (HTML), XMLHttpRequest, and cascading style sheets (CSS), all of which are defined in **Table 7.2 (Hoffman,** 2019**)**.

TABLE 7.2   AJAX Technologies for Web 2.0

Hypertext markup language (HTML): The predominant language for web pages; it is used, along with CSS, to describe how things will appear on a web page.

Cascading style sheets (CSS): A language used to enhance the appearance of web pages written in a markup language.

Document object model (DOM): A programming API for documents. Programmers use it to manipulate (e.g., build, add, modify, delete, etc.) HTML documents.

Extensible markup language (XML): A set of rules and guidelines for describing data that can be used by other programming languages. It makes it possible for data to be shared across the web.

JavaScript: An object-oriented language used to create apps and functionality on websites. Examples of JavaScript apps include pop-up windows, validation of webform inputs, and images that change when a cursor passes over them.

XMLHttpRequest: A JavaScript object that serves as an API used by programs to retrieve data or resources from a URL without requiring a page load. It plays an important role in providing programmers with the ability to create dynamic and interactive web pages and applications.

Fetch API: Similar to XMLHttpRequest, but this API provides more powerful and flexible features.

Server-Sent Events: A function that allows the origin application to push data to the target application or website.

File Reader API: Allows data stored on a user's computer to be read asynchronously and used in the new web application.

HTML in XMLHttpRequest: This allows the XMLHttpRequest to process HTML data for use in a web application whereas only XML data could previously be used.

Sources: MDNContributors (2020), W3C (2015), Grigorik (2017), Buckler (2019), and Hoffman (2019).

IT at Work 7.1

Myntra Leverages Facebook APIs and SDKs for Success in Mobile Fashion Sales

Myntra is India's largest fashion e-commerce company, serving millions of customers and featuring over 2,000 of the world's top fashion brands. The company generates sales of over 200,000 items from its mobile app on any given day. Myntra is recognized as being the world's first mobile-only e-commerce platform and reportedly sold $500 million in gross merchandise volume in FY2015–16. Using Facebook's Open Graph API and SDK, the company was able to install features that let customers easily post information to their Facebook pages without leaving the Myntra website. This makes it possible for the company to leverage the social network of each customer to increase brand awareness and interest in the marketplace.

Using Facebook's SDK, the company implemented Facebook Login for its app as well as developed programs to access customer insight data and a range of analytics about the performance of their Facebook ads, conversion channels, and the success of various customer retention strategies. As a result of these integrations with Facebook, Myntra experienced significant growth and credits Facebook for as much as 25% of its sales revenue. In addition, Myntra improved the effectiveness of ad targeting and reduced advertising costs after learning that customers who use Facebook Login to access the e-commerce app were 32% more likely to convert (make a purchase) than other customers.

Sources: "Myntra—Best of Fashion" at **https://developers.facebook.com/**.

4. Application programming interfaces (API) and software development kits (SDK)   One of the big differences between Web 1.0 and Web 2.0 is the extent to which business organizations are willing to share information (data) with other organizations and developers who are creating new programs or services. For instance, Google Maps might allow a restaurant review website like *Yelp* to use its mapping application to create a feature showing restaurant locations. From a technology standpoint, two programming tools make this data sharing possible: APIs and SDKs.

Why Managers Should Understand Web Technology

Even those business managers who are not directly involved in managing an organization's website should be concerned about the underlying technology of Web 2.0 and social media. These technologies determine website features and capabilities. In other words, they determine what is possible on the Web. Understanding how Web technology is evolving helps managers identify strategic opportunities and threats as well as the ways in which a company might develop sustainable competitive advantages in the marketplace. Therefore, it is important to monitor the ongoing development of APIs, Web development languages, and other technologies that affect how the Web functions.

For instance, APIs associated with Facebook determine the nature of apps that can be written to interact with core Facebook features. Major changes to Facebook APIs are often rolled out with much fanfare because they define opportunities for developing new ways to create and share content on Facebook and across the Web, as described in IT at Work 7.1.

Plugins are buttons or features on non-Facebook sites that interact with Facebook in some way. For instance, the news website CNN might include a *Recommend* button on all its news articles. When a Facebook user presses the button, a link to the story is automatically created on the user's Facebook page. You don't have to be a Web programmer to follow and understand public announcements about API updates from Facebook, Google Maps, YouTube, and other popular social media platforms. These announcements help businesses identify opportunities for using social technology to make their own websites more attractive to users.

Communicating on the Web

Collectively, social media apps have shifted the locus of control for mass communications from large organizations to one shared with individual users. Now people as well as organizations share control over both the message and the medium. Instead of an organization broadcasting a single message to a mass audience using advertisements, a massive number of online conversations take place among any number of people and organizations.

No one has complete control over the message or the medium, yet anyone can play a part. Businesses used to focus on developing sophisticated ways of getting their message heard using advertising and public relations. But now companies must develop even more sophisticated strategies for listening and responding to what their customers are saying. They must figure out how to become part of the conversation.

Because of its relatively low cost and ease of use, social media is a powerful force for democratization; the network structure enables communication and collaboration on a massive scale. With traditional media, content is tightly controlled, and brand messages are "pushed" out to users, often in the form of an ad that interrupts whatever the user is doing. With social media, companies must figure out how to attract users by creating content that users will find helpful, interesting, entertaining, or informative. Content used to attract prospective customers can come in all types of media: infographics, blog posts, podcasts, video, photographs, and so on. Content can be delivered to users in a variety of ways, including websites, social networking services, sharing services (e.g., YouTube and Instagram), and e-mail. How content is delivered will often depend on the strategic goals of the company or brand. Users have greater freedom to decide if, when, and how they want to interact with such content. This new communication strategy is often referred to as **content marketing**.

Content marketing is a strategic marketing approach focused on creating and distributing valuable, relevant, and consistent content to attract and retain a clearly defined audience—and, ultimately, to drive profitable customer action. (*Source: The Content Marketing Institute.*)

content marketing   is a strategy that uses helpful or interesting information to attract and retain prospective customers, build brand awareness, and establish credibility leading eventually to purchase.

Characteristics of Social Media: What Makes It Different?

In order to understand what makes the modern Web so different from its earlier incarnation and other types of media, it is helpful to understand the differentiating features and changes made possible by XML, Java Script, APIs, and related technologies.

User-generated content (UGC)   In contrast to traditional media—TV, radio, and magazines—social media makes it possible for users to create and share their own content. Using social technologies, people share photographs, music, and video with the world. They express themselves using the written word in stories, articles, and opinion pieces that they publish on their own websites or other platforms. They rate products and write reviews. Many individuals and groups have become Internet celebrities because of the shows they created for YouTube. And because of YouTube's revenue-sharing policy, those that attract the largest audiences earn millions of dollars. These powerful technologies make it possible for individuals to communicate with the world, something that was previously only possible for large corporations and governments.

Content control   Most online content creation and sharing is done without editorial review. As a result, users decide for themselves what they want to create, share, and consume. Social technologies have shifted control of online content to a broad base of users. It is users who determine what content "goes viral" or becomes highly popular through sharing, not advertising agencies or companies with large advertising budgets.

Conversation With the advent of social media, a paradigm shift occurred in marketing communications from a broadcast (one-way) model to a conversation (two-way) model. Dialogue takes place in the form of one-to-one, one-to-many, and many-to-one formats. Social media websites contain features that allow people to talk back to corporations, governments, and each other in a variety of ways.

Community (common values, culture) Many social media technologies ultimately result in the creation of online communities. Like their offline counterparts, these online communities are made up of people who share a bond of common interests, values, norms, and even sanctions. Some communities are highly structured, whereas others may be more fluid and informal. As businesses learn to communicate on Web 2.0, some will attempt to create communities made up of consumers who have a strong interest in the company's brand. Social networking services (SNS) lend themselves to this type of strategy, but brand communities can be developed around blogs, **wikis**, **sharing sites**, and other types of social media.

Categorization by users (tagging)   Newer Web technologies allow users to decide for themselves how to categorize and label information they find online. This has created the potential for powerful forms of collaboration and information sharing as well as alternative forms of information search (see the discussion of social bookmarking later in the chapter).

Real people (profiles, usernames, and the human voice vs. the corporate "we")   Social media technologies allow people to express their individuality through the creation of online identities. In traditional media, communication and messages are broadcast in the form of advertisements or publicity (news stories or articles about a company or product). Web 2.0 provides individual people and groups with the tools to communicate with a global audience and create their own personal brands that characterize their personal, professional, or creative identity.

Connections (followers, friends, members, etc.)   There are many ways to establish various levels of connection that reflect different types of relationships. You can become someone's friend on Facebook. Follow someone on Twitter, or subscribe to a person's blog. Perhaps just as important, these connections can be severed when one party wants to end the relationship.

Constant updating (real time, dynamic)   Unlike the static Web of the 1990s, social technologies reflect our constantly evolving relationships, opinions, political views, religious beliefs, and values. The social Web is a constant stream of communications that never turns off and can sometimes be overwhelming. Popular examples of this characteristic include Twitter, Instagram, and Snapchat.

Content separated from form   Data from one source can be used or exported to other platforms. This allows users to organize and display content in ways they find most helpful. For instance, with a **really simple syndication (RSS)** aggregator, users can pull content from a number of sources into a single location, making it easier to follow news stories and blog updates from multiple sites. Someone writing about local restaurants can pull content from food critics, customer comments, and map location information from a variety of sources and aggregate this information into a single site, making it easier for users to get a complete picture of a restaurant without having to surf around to different sites.

Equipment independence   Increasingly, people access the Web from a variety of computers and mobile devices, including laptops, tablets, smartphones, video game systems, DVD players, and televisions. Soon, you might access the Web from things around your home like a refrigerator, your bathroom mirror, or kitchen countertop. (Check out the amazing new technology featured on videos by Corning Glass. Go to YouTube and search for "A Day Made of Glass" using the YouTube search engine.)

> **Really Simple Syndication (RSS)** is a technology that allows users to receive updates and shared information from websites in a standardized way. These updates can be in the form of blog posts, news, or video and audio recordings.

Challenges and Opportunities for Business

Successful companies are learning to engage customers in conversations as an alternative to the unidirectional or broadcast method of communication.

Forrester researchers Charlene Li and Josh Bernoff (2008) describe five key strategies that companies should use to leverage their social media interactions with consumers on the Web.

1. **Listening**   Monitoring what your customers say on social media. By listening to what customers say to your company and what they say to each other, organizations can gain valuable insights.

2. **Talking**   While listening is perhaps the most important priority, businesses still need to develop their message and communicate to their target audience(s).

3. **Energizing**   Using a variety of tactics, companies can create and maintain relationships with brand advocates who will support and promote the brand to their friends and followers on the Web. Energizing brand advocates is analogous to generating word-of-mouth communications in traditional marketing.

4. **Supporting**   Using social media to deliver effective and convenient customer service is one way to support your customers. Some businesses create communities where customers can help each other with product-related issues and questions.

5. **Embracing**   Many companies are utilizing social media to solicit new product ideas and suggestions for improving customer satisfaction from current customers. Managers are often surprised to learn that customers have great ideas for how the company can do better.

In addition, the constant and rapidly changing nature of the Web presents both a challenge and opportunity for businesses. The challenge is keeping up with the change by constantly monitoring technological evolution and potential competitors that may be more agile and tech savvy. This is one reason that technology companies invest heavily in talent acquisition, making sure they have the best people on their team to help in identifying ways that new Web technologies can be leveraged to gain competitive advantage.

In the rest of this chapter, we describe a variety of social media applications that are growing in popularity. We highlight some of the most attractive features and encourage you to explore them firsthand. Most are free, so they are easy to try. You are also encouraged to stay on top of new trends and applications by following online sources like Mashable, Social Media Today, and Social Media Examiner. The only way to understand the social media environment is to immerse yourself in it, experiencing it directly.

Questions

1. How has Web 2.0 changed the behavior of Internet users?
2. What is the purpose of an API? Provide an example of how a business might make use of an API.
3. Why is Web 2.0 referred to as the social Web?
4. What are some of the benefits or advantages that Web developers gain from using AJAX technologies?
5. What opportunities and challenges does Web 2.0 present for business organizations?

7.2 Social Web Tools and Applications

LO7.2 Describe *the most common Web 2.0 tools and applications and how businesses use them to accomplish their goals.*

In the previous section, we mentioned several tools and applications that are commonly available on Web 2.0. In this section, we will describe the most important of these tools and applications in more detail and provide examples of how they are utilized by individuals, groups, and organizations. **Table 7.3** lists the applications that will be covered in this section.

TABLE 7.3 **Web 2.0 Applications**

Application	Description
Social networking services (SNS)	An online platform or website that allows subscribers to interact and form communities or networks based on relationships, shared interests, activities, and so on.
Blogs	Online journal or informational web page or website featuring regularly updated articles or posts. Blogs that feature other types of media are called Podcasts (audio), Vlogs (video), and Plogs or Photoblogs (images).
Sharing sites	Websites that make it easy for users to upload and share digital content like photos, videos, music, or other digital content.
Mashups/RSS	Web applications that pull data from original sources to for use on a "host" website.
Social bookmarking/tags	An application for tagging or labeling online content for identification and/or later retrieval.
Wikis	A collaborative application that allows multiple people to create and edit online content.
E-commerce 2.0	Electronic buying and selling of goods and services that utilize, in part, social tools and applications.
Crowdsourcing	Leveraging large groups of users on the web to generate ideas, collect data, perform work, find solutions, do manual tasks, provide customer service, and so on.
Crowdfunding	Using the web to solicit funding or financing for charitable causes, business start-ups, new product development, and other purposes.
Collaboration platforms and tools	Social media technologies that make it possible for teams or groups of people to communicate, coordinate activity and share documents and files, and carry out other work-related activity.
Social monitoring services	Tools that monitor and analyze user activity on various social media websites and services.

Early descriptions of Web 2.0 would often identify the tools and applications listed in **Table 7.3** as distinct services or website functions. That is because in the early days of Web 2.0, new websites and Web businesses tended to focus on a single purpose or function. However, over the years as businesses grew and evolved to meet a growing number of user needs, feature convergence made it difficult to easily classify companies and their websites by a single function. For instance, Facebook started as a **social networking service (SNS)**, but now has features that span most of the other application descriptions in Table 7.3. It is a sharing site used by many to distribute photos and online content. It is increasingly common for people to tag or label photos with people's names, locations, the dates, and how they were feeling at the time the pictures were taken. Users can maintain blogs on their Facebook page or special group pages, and Facebook hosts thousands of apps that pull data from sources outside of the social network, making it a huge mashup app. While some single-purpose social media applications still exist on the Web today, thousands of newer applications have sprung up and continue to blur the lines of the original social media categories.

Social Networking Services (SNS)

As previously discussed, it can sometimes be difficult to distinguish social networking services from other types of social media where people join by agreeing to adhere to the website's **terms of service (TOS) agreement**, generate or share content, collaborate, or interact with each other in a variety of ways. Listed below are five characteristics that usually (but not always) differentiate social networking services from other types of online communities and social media services.

1. The development of a user's online **social network** is facilitated by the SNS when users connect their profile with that of other users, groups, or organizations.

2. User connections on an SNS tend to develop over time, one-by-one, and usually with the mutual consent of both parties. In other words, you aren't instantly connected with everyone else on the service when you join. Likewise, SNS users can discontinue their connections with other people, groups, or organizations on the SNS.

3. The creation, sharing, and consumption of user-generated content (UGC) plays a significant role in defining the nature of user behavior and activity on an SNS.

4. Users are typically linked to or identified by a site-specific profile containing a variety of information supplied by the user. Access to SNS content is not readily available to non-SNS members and UGC is not typically available to other members unless specifically permitted by the user that uploaded it to the SNS.

5. Social networking services are platforms or websites created with Web 2.0 or social media features and functionalities that allow users to interact with one another.

The number of SNSs has grown tremendously in recent years. Wikipedia.org maintains a regularly updated list of active SNS sites from around the world. Like other maturing product categories, the SNS industry has begun to separate into various segments and market niches. For instance, Facebook is a large, international, general SNS and Twitter is a large, international micro-blogging SNS. Qzone is the third largest SNS in the world but is primarily used by people who live in China where tight government controls on Internet activity prohibit people from using Facebook and Twitter. If a company wanted to create a public SNS, it would be extremely difficult to replicate the success Facebook. Among general-purpose SNS platforms, Facebook is the clear leader with over 2.5 billion active users and its dramatic growth over the past decade has been unparalleled in the social media world **(Table 7.4)**. However, the chances of building a successful SNS platform would be better if the company identified a segment or market niche of users that would be attracted to an SNS focused on a particular need or interest.

Terms of Service (TOS) agreement is a formal listing of the policies, liability limits, fees, user rights, and responsibilities associated with using an online service. Users are typically required to acknowledge they have read, understand, and agree to the TOS before they are allowed the service to use.

Social network is defined by a user's connections and interactions with other people. Users can have different types of social networks, such as family connections, connections of friends, school connections, professional connections, and so on.

TABLE 7.4 **Facebook Statistics as of December 2019**

2.5 billion monthly active users globally
1.65 billion daily active users globally. Daily active users make up 66% of monthly active users.
Facebook's revenue per user was $8.51 worldwide.
Facebook's revenue per user was $41.41 in the Unites States and Canada.
Approximately 88% of daily active users are outside the United States and Canada.
Facebook owns several other companies including Instagram (mobile photo-sharing), WhatsApp (mobile messenger app), Oculus (virtual reality), Moves (activity log), and Masquerade (selfie filters).
Over 2.89 billion monthly active users used one of Facebook's family of SNS services—Facebook, Instagram, Messenger, or WhatsApp at least once during a 30-day period through a mobile app or using a web or mobile browser.

Source: Facebook (2020).

As the category matures, SNS sites are differentiating themselves in a variety of ways, including:

- Target age group
- Geographic location of users
- Language
- User interests, for example, music, photography, gaming, or travel
- Social versus professional networking (see **IT at Work 7.2**)
- User interface, for example, profile page, mobile app, microblog, virtual world, and an emphasis on graphic versus text content

People today spend a significant portion of their time on social network services (see **Figure 7.1**). For better or worse, social media has changed the way we interact with others, how we communicate with companies and brands, how we learn about local and international events, and how we define relationships, reputation, privacy, group affiliations, and status.

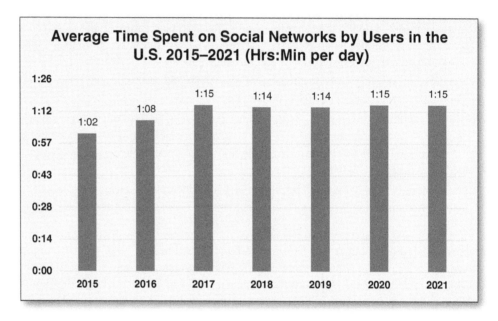

FIGURE 7.1 Since 2015, users 18 and over who access their social networking account(s) at least once a month have spent more than an hour a day on social networking apps or websites (adapted from eMarketer, 2019c).

How Businesses Use Social Networking Services

Social networking services have received increasing attention from the business community. Online communities can be used as a platform for the following:

- Selling goods and services
- Promoting products to prospective customers; for example, advertising
- Prospecting for customers
- Building relationships with customers and prospective customers
- Identifying customer perceptions by "listening" to conversations
- Soliciting ideas for new products and services from customers
- Providing support services to customers by answering questions, providing information, and so on
- Encouraging customers to share their positive perceptions with others, for example, by posting reviews of their experiences and satisfaction with products and services
- Gathering information about competitors and marketplace perceptions of competitors
- Identifying and interacting with prospective suppliers, partners, and collaborators

---

IT at Work 7.2

Recruiters Use Professional Networking Sites

Professionals use networking to form relationships with colleagues in similar or related fields to expand their effectiveness in an organization or industry. Employers use social media to find good prospective job applicants. It is no longer enough to post job openings on monster.com, indeed.com, and Careerbuilder.com. Job postings on these large sites often generate hundreds of applications from unqualified candidates. Reviewing all these applications can be overwhelming for recruiters and is very inefficient. Instead, many have turned to professional networking sites like LinkedIn. With over 760 million users, LinkedIn has been adding two new users every second for the past several years. Employers use LinkedIn to research candidates for employment and in some case, even before an applicant is selected for an interview, a recruiter will check them out on LinkedIn to see their accomplishments, connections, and recommendations. Applicants can make connections without ever having to pick up the phone or go to a recruiting office. Heathfield identified several ways that businesses recruiters use LinkedIn to increase their effectiveness:

- Identify potential candidates among their existing network of professionals.

- Ask their network to identify or recommend candidates for a position.

- Evaluate potential employees based on references and referrals from their existing network.

- Actively search for relevant keywords or qualifications in the profiles of LinkedIn users.

- Ask current employees to search among their LinkedIn networks for potential candidates.

- Post job openings on LinkedIn.

- Request introductions to potential candidates through their existing network of professionals.

- Use Inmail (the internal LinkedIn e-mail system) to contact potentially qualified individuals.

From the applicant's perspective, Ed Han of Balanced Careers points out that using LinkedIn allows applicants to grow and maintain their network, establish and control their own professional brand, and present an accurate picture of their resume, all of which are particularly appealing to recruiters. Patricia Lotich of Thriving Small Business recommends that professionals use every professional and social opportunity to meet and connect with new people and get to know them on a personal level. Leaving a positive impression, being optimistic, and excited about what you do and diligently returning e-mails and responding to social media posts helps maintain credibility.

Sources: Compiled from Heathfield (2012), Doyle (2019), Han (2019), Lotich (2019), and McKay (2019).

E-commerce 2.0 and Social Commerce

During the early days of Web 2.0, many companies that created social websites did not immediately embark on strategies and tactics designed to generate revenue and profit. Instead, their primary goal was to refine their product or service concept and demonstrate that it was something that would attract Internet users. The only sites with a clear and obvious method of generating income were online e-commerce sites like Amazon, eBay, Netflix, and Zappos. These companies were pioneers in the category of Business to Consumer (B2C) e-commerce. Eventually, other companies developed websites that served the product and service needs of businesses and other types of organizations. These companies engaged in what we call Business to Business (B2B) e-commerce. Eventually, many of these early online retailers began to incorporate social features on their websites. For instance, customers were encouraged to rate their satisfaction with the products they purchased, write product reviews, rate their satisfaction with the product seller's service, and share information about their purchases on social networking services. These kinds of features are referred to as e-commerce 2.0. But despite the growth and expansion of e-commerce Web businesses, it wasn't immediately clear how other social media websites would generate the revenue and profits necessary to remain in business. For instance, some people used to speculate that Facebook might become a subscriber website, where users would pay a monthly fee to use the popular SNS. However, over time it became clear that many social media websites would develop some version of an advertising business model.

Today, you will see advertisements in a variety of forms on Facebook and other social networking services. In addition, social media websites and services eventually discovered that data describing the online behavior of their users had value to other businesses who were willing to pay for access to this user data. In addition to advertising on SNS and other social websites, businesses learned that they could engage consumers organically (without paid advertisements) on many social websites. For instance, businesses can create their own Facebook pages and Twitter accounts and use these to communicate directly with customers and prospective customers. In some cases, they could use these tools to provide customer

Social commerce refers to a wide range of strategies and tactics used by business organizations to engage with consumers on the Web and social media apps to influence their purchasing behavior. This includes advertising, promotion, content marketing, organic (unpaid) interactions with consumers, and so on.

service, solicit customer feedback, and promote their products and services without paying anything to the social media companies that host their accounts. As a result, **social commerce** has become a widely used strategy for using social media to influence consumer behavior.

Private Social Networks

The ultimate niche community is a **private SNS**. Private SNSs use social technology to create a community restricted to members selected by the SNS's owner. Private SNSs allow a greater degree of control over the network. Companies can easily monitor activity on their own SNS platforms and track conversations taking place about their brands and products. However, managing a private SNS requires considerably more time, attention, and resources than maintaining a presence on a general SNS. Organizations need to understand up-front that they are making a substantial commitment with this strategy.

Most colleges and universities have Facebook pages. In addition, many institutions have developed private SNSs to engage students even before they set foot on campus. Students typically gain access to these private SNSs when they are admitted to the institution. On the system, they can interact with admissions counselors, current students, and other admitted students. Interactions that occur on these networks set the stage for relationships and engagement that are simply not possible with e-mail and phone calls.

While engaging customers on a private SNS can be time-consuming and potentially require significant staffing resources, the technological challenges associated with setting up a private SNS are relatively small. Several companies offer a combination of free and subscription-based pricing for individuals or organizations wishing to create a private social network. Basic SNS sites can be set up quickly for free. Search on "private social network services" for the latest information.

Engaging Consumers with Blogs and Microblogs

In their simplest form, **blogs** are websites (or sections of a website) where people or organizations regularly post content. Some personal blogs are simply online diaries or journals where people share their thoughts, reflections, or an account of their life. Other blogs are more sophisticated and professional in format, resembling online newspapers or magazines. Because blogging technology has become so commonplace, you may not always realize you are reading a blog when accessing online content. Many organizations have integrated one of the blogging platforms discussed later with their website. Blogging tools make it easy for organizations to provide website visitors with frequently updated content on pages with titles such as "What's New," "Company News," or "Product Updates." As a result, you may be a frequent blog reader without realizing it!

What Is the Purpose of a Blog?

Many professionals maintain a blog to establish their reputation and demonstrate their expertise. Corporate bloggers use the medium to tell stories about their brands and connect with customers. For businesses that practice content marketing, creating a blog is often the first step in a strategy that uses helpful and interesting information to attract prospective customers. The goal in content marketing is to think about the kinds of information that might be useful or interesting to customers, even if that information is not directly related to the company's products and services. For instance, a company that manufactures tools, might create a blog where articles are written about various do-it-yourself (DIY) home renovation and repair projects. This would make sense because the kind of person that will be interested in DIY home renovation and repair is probably the kind of person that will purchase tools for doing such work.

Blogging and Public Relations

Public relations (PR) professionals use a variety of strategies to generate awareness and a positive image for the organizations that they work for. One common PR strategy is to send information about a company or its brands to journalists in the hope that it will result in articles or news stories about the company in magazines, newspapers, and electronic media (radio and television). Because many blogs now reach such a large audience, public relations professionals have added popular blogs to the list of media that receive these kinds of announcements and information.

When a highly credible and influential blogger writes a positive story about a company, it can have a very positive impact on a brand's image. Bloggers can also have a negative impact if they write unfavorable posts about a company or its products. As a result, public relations professionals are learning how to identify and form positive relationships with influential bloggers with the goal of generating favorable coverage of companies and their products. Frequently, this will involve doing things like providing the blogger with information in advance of it being released to the public, providing access to company executives for interviews, sending the blogger samples of the company's product so that they can write from firsthand experience, and so on. For some companies, particularly those in the technology industry, building relationships with influential bloggers has become especially important.

Reading and Subscribing to Blogs

The best way to gain an understanding of the blogging phenomenon is to simply start reading blogs. You can use search engines like Google or Bing to find blogs on all kinds of topics. Just use the search phrase, "blogs about [topic]", replacing the word "[topic]" with what you are interested in. Most blogs make it easy to subscribe using RSS readers, discussed later in the chapter. Reading blogs is a great way to stay current on rapidly evolving topics related to technology and business.

Blogging Platforms

Selecting a **blogging platform** is an important decision when setting up a blog. Installing a platform when you are creating a blog is relatively easy. Converting to a new blogging platform after using another one for a while is not. Two of the most popular platforms are WordPress followed by Google's Blogger platform. Other blog platforms include TypePad, Movable Type, and Tumblr. The Tumblr platform is significantly different from traditional platforms in that it emphasizes easy posting of photos and light copy. As such, it is a microblogging platform and is discussed later in this chapter. WordPress is a feature rich platform and offers greater control over the blog's appearance while Blogger is simpler and easier to use, making it a good choice for beginning bloggers.

> **Blogging platform** is a software application used to create, edit, and add features to a blog. *WordPress* and *Blogger* are two of the most popular blogging platforms.

Microblogs

Microblogging is a way of sharing content with people by posting regular, often frequent, short messages. While most Web experts are familiar with the term, microblog is not a word most Web users are familiar with, even those that frequently use microblogging platforms like Twitter on a regular basis.

Most **microblog** content consists of text-based messages, although there appears to be an increase in people who are microblogging photos and video on sites like Instagram, Pinterest, and Tumblr.

> **Microblog** a blog that consists of frequent, but very brief posts containing text, pictures, or videos. Twitter is perhaps the most well-known example of a microblog.

Twitter

Twitter is often described as a social networking service just as much or more so than it is called a microblogging service. According to Twitter, approximately 500 million messages, or **tweets**, are sent each day by over 330 million active monthly users. People frequently attach descriptive keywords or **hashtags**, designated by the # sign, to their tweets to make them easier for others to find (e.g., #news, #politics, #fail).

> **tweets** a brief 140-character message or post broadcast on Twitter, a microblogging service.

> **hashtags** are terms proceeded by a hash sign (#) that people use to associate their message with a topic or theme.

Twitter has played a significant role in many global and domestic events. In countries where the media is largely dominated by government control, Twitter has proved to be an invaluable tool for activists engaged in organizing protests, debating political viewpoints, and broadcasting real-time information about significant events that might otherwise be ignored by the mainstream media. Twitter has become a primary channel for real-time updates on events and issues in politics, entertainment, social causes, and sports, for example, #Brexit—Britain's separation from the European Union, the #BlackLivesMatter movement, news about the popular television show #GameofThrones, and the U.S. presidential #Election2016 and #Election2020 where Twitter was used heavily by most candidates.

Many organizations have experimented with monitoring Twitter in cases where customers express frustration with a company or its products, and then quickly respond by offering to resolve customer complaints. In this way they learn about their business practices that frustrate or reassure consumers and use the service as a platform for customer service.

Over 65% of companies now use Twitter for marketing communications and are increasingly expanding their reach by encouraging employees to share relevant messages with their personal social networks. In addition to organic (unpaid) tweets, companies spend close to $3 billion a year on *promoted tweets*, or paid ads sent out over the network. Twitter is viewed by many companies as a good way to reach people on mobile devices.

Consumer Mashups and RSS Technology

Websites and mobile apps use AJAX technologies and APIs to pull data from a variety of sources and combines them to create a mashup that presents the information in a way that creates some new benefit or service. One of the most common examples of a consumer mashup that you are likely to encounter involves the integration of map data (from companies such as Google or MapQuest) with information like store names, locations, phone numbers, and consumer reviews from other websites. By combining this information in a single location or application, users enjoy a powerful and visually compelling service. *ProgrammableWeb.com* maintains a helpful directory of mashup applications.

RSS Technology

Another technology that extends control of Web content beyond the creator is really simple syndication (RSS). Traditionally, users had to visit multiple websites to view content at each location. This is time-consuming and difficult for users who are interested in following several different websites. RSS technology allows users to subscribe to multiple sources (e.g., blogs, news headlines, social media feeds, videos, and podcasts) and have the content displayed in a single application, called an "RSS reader" or "RSS aggregator." In effect, users can create a customized news and information site by personalizing how they want information from their news sources organized and displayed. Popular RSS aggregators include Feedly, NewsBlur, and The Old Reader. Many other free or freemium aggregators are available with a variety of features.

Social Metrics and Monitoring Tools

A fast-growing sector in the social technology field involves **social monitoring services**. Monitoring applications allow users to track conversations taking place on social media sites. The initial impetus for the growth of monitoring tools was the need for business organizations to better understand what people were saying about their brands, products, and executives (the "listening" strategy described in Section 7.1). Monitoring services can be used to identify industry experts, commentators, and opinion leaders who post regularly to social media sites. Once identified, public relations professionals can build relationships with these individuals and encourage them to become **brand advocates** who regularly portray the brand or company positively in their online writing and social media posts.

In the next section, we describe two categories of social monitoring tools: subscription-based services and free monitoring services.

Subscription Monitoring Services The most comprehensive social media monitoring tools require the user to pay a subscription or licensing fee. These tools not only monitor the social media environment for mentions of your brand or company name but also provide analytics and tools for measuring trends in the amount of conversation and the tone or sentiment (e.g., positive, negative, neutral) of the conversation, in addition to other aspects of online social interactions. Some of these tools are social media management platforms that help companies administer social media marketing campaigns and inbound marketing programs. The monitoring tools are just one of several features available in these enterprise-level applications.

Most high-end monitoring tools report information using a dashboard interface, which graphically represents the data it collects in real time. While prices for these high-end monitoring services can vary widely (typically, hundreds of dollars a month), they are usually beyond the budget of individual users.

Free Monitoring Services Fortunately, there are number of free monitoring tools that can be used by anyone. Some of these tools, like Twitter Search, are designed to monitor conversations on a single social media platform, while others, like Social Mention, are designed to provide feedback on activity across several social media platforms including Facebook, Twitter, and blogs.

Social Mention A popular free monitoring tool is Social Mention. This tool aggregates content from over 80 different social media sites including Facebook, YouTube, and Twitter. The best thing about Social Mention is that it provides users with four metrics that give insight into the nature of conversations taking place on the Web.

- **Strength**   The likelihood that a topic is being discussed on social media platforms
- **Passion**   The degree to which people who are talking about your brand will do so repeatedly
- **Sentiment**   The tone of the conversation; this metric helps you understand if people are feeling positive, negative, or neutral about the topic
- **Reach**   Measures the range of influence. It is the number of unique authors divided by the number of mentions.

Organizations can generate these statistics daily for a topic (e.g., brand name, public figure, current event) and record them in a spreadsheet. Over time, it becomes easy to see trends developing such as how many people are talking about a topic or how they feel about a topic. This is useful information for the social media marketer. Other free tools for monitoring Web activity include:

- **Twitter Search** is used to learn what people on Twitter are saying about a topic (see **https://twitter.com/explore**)
- **Hootsuite** is a popular social media management platform with specific tools for engagement, publishing, analytics, monitoring, and advertising across multiple social media channels. Users can open a free account to explore the service and upgrade to a larger range of features for as little as $10/month.
- **Google Alerts** is a useful monitoring tool that conducts automated Google searches for new Web content on topics specified by the user. The service sends regular e-mail updates listing Web content recently posted about the topic (see www.google.com/alerts).

Social monitoring tools play an essential role in helping marketers understand the conversations taking place on the Web. They represent a set of powerful tools in the arsenal of firms that seek to understand consumers, what they are interested in, what they are talking about, and what they are thinking. As such, it is important that you become familiar with these tools.

Enterprise 2.0: Workplace Collaboration and Knowledge Sharing

In today's competitive environment, businesses must be agile, able to respond quickly to a rapidly evolving marketplace. Employees must be able to work collaboratively, communicate clearly, reach consensus, make decisions, and implement their action plans effectively. Many businesses use intranets to deploy tools for employee collaboration and productivity. An **intranet** is a password-protected network that uses the same Web-based technologies (e.g., browsers, webpages, and hyperlinked text) found on the World Wide Web. Think of it as a private or internal Web. As organizations update their intranets, employees can now take advantage of many social features they have become accustomed to using on the Web. This trend is sometimes referred to as **Enterprise 2.0**. In Chapter 10, you will read about enterprise social platforms designed to facilitate collaboration and communication across an organization.

In this section, we review several social tools for collaboration that are available to everyone. Small businesses, startups, and nonprofits that lack resources to deploy modern Intranets can use these tools for increased productivity.

intranet is a computer network like the Internet except access is restricted by the intranet's owner, and users must sign into the intranet with a username and password. Many companies create intranets for their employees and business partners.

Collaboration Tools

Dialogue or **synchronous communication** is an important part of the collaborative process. Because of social distancing and other restrictions that resulted from the coronavirus pandemic that emerged in the spring of 2020, businesses and other organizations relied heavily on video conferencing apps such as Zoom, Skype, Fuze and GoToMeeting. Individuals also increased their use of free video conferencing apps like WhatsApp, Google Hangouts, and Facebook Messenger, that allow groups of up to 8, 10 and 50 participants to participate, respectively. Many of these video conferencing services have developed mobile apps so that users can participate in a video call from their smartphone or other mobile device. Many companies have announced that because of their successful experience with employees working from home during the pandemic, they plan to continue the practice in some form or another after the pandemic is over. As a result, we expect that demand for high quality video meeting apps and other collaboration technologies will continue to remain strong.

synchronous communication dialogue or conversation that takes place in real time, without the long delays between exchanges that occur, for instance, in e-mail or discussion board conversations.

Social Tools for Information Retrieval, Knowledge Management, and Sharing

When people work together as part of a group or team, they frequently need to find and share information with other members of the group. Search engines like Google and Bing are among the most frequently used tools on the Web for finding information. Enterprise search utilities can be used for knowledge management and accessing internal records that can be of value to the group. Later in this chapter you will read about search engines in more detail and learn how large search engine services use information culled from social media sites to improve the relevance of the search result listings. they provide. You will learn more about knowledge management in Chapter 10.

Discussion groups and Q&A websites can provide a forum for asking questions to groups of people. For instance, the American Marketing Association maintains a discussion group on LinkedIn that has over 52,000 members. Participants can ask questions and solicit input from other members of the group. Members can also monitor discussion groups, receiving periodic digests of group activity that can be scanned for material of interest. LinkedIn can be a particularly useful website for business professionals with questions that can be answered by experts or other business professionals. The popular website Reddit bills itself as a "a network of communities based on people's interests". Reddit, one of the most popular U.S. websites, maintains thousands of discussion groups or "subreddits" on a large variety of topics. Quora is considered a high quality, general Q&A website, which means that a wide array of topics are discussed on the site and the impact of disruptive users is limited by moderation, user profiles, website policy, and other controls that help maintain a constructive and useful environment.

Social Bookmarking Tools

Social bookmarking tools allow users to tag Web content with keywords of their choosing. Users later retrieve content by searching on one or more of these keywords. In addition to helping users retrieve the saved URLs of websites they want to return to, social bookmarking sites can sometimes be used as an alternative search engine, helping users search for and discover Web content tagged by other users. This is what makes the bookmarking system "social." Information searches on these sites will produce different results than Google or Bing because the websites are categorized based on a **folksonomy** (folk taxonomy). In other words, humans tag websites differently than the computer algorithms used by Google or Bing, and that is why the search will generate a different and potentially useful list of websites.

folksonomy   is a system of classifying and organizing online content into categories based on user-generated metadata such as keywords.

Diigo has developed several social bookmarking and collaboration tools, making it perhaps the best application in this category. While Diigo appears to be the most fully featured application in this category, other social media websites feature ways of tagging and saving Web-based content. Twitter, Pinterest, StumbleUpon, and Pocket are all services that allow for social bookmarking.

Content Creation and Sharing

Work groups, teams, and committees typically need to share documents and files as part of their collaborative efforts. In the past, large amounts of paper were consumed when everyone on the team was given a hard copy of the documents being used and discussed. With the advent of e-mail, workers began distributing documents electronically, which was perhaps the easiest way for working teams to share documents. Now business professionals are starting to experience the limitations of e-mail as a distribution and document storage system.

Dropbox is a **cloud storage service** that makes it easy to access your documents from any of the devices you work on. It is a shared hard drive for your computer, phone, and tablet computer. Dropbox also allows users to share files and folders with others, making it a great tool for collaboration. There are two Dropbox features that make it particularly attractive. First, saving files to Dropbox is just as easy as saving a file to your hard drive. Dropbox also maintains a version history record for documents, making it easy to see the changes made to a document and undo them if necessary. This is a great feature for teams working on collaborative writing projects. Dropbox prices its service based on the amount of storage space users anticipate needing. This makes Dropbox a good solution for students and small businesses. Business users typically purchase a premium plan that provides for much more space, enhanced security, and account administrative features as well as API access, which allows companies to integrate Dropbox with existing computer applications. Other cloud storage and document sharing services include Box, Google Drive, Microsoft OneDrive, and IDrive.

cloud storage services   provide users with the ability to save documents and other kinds of electronic media on servers connected to the Web. This makes it possible for users to access their data from multiple devices and to share files with other individuals.

Shared Content Creation with Wikis

A wiki is a social media content management application that allows teams to collaborate on the creation of webpages. Wikis can be used as a workspace for collaborative teams or they can become public websites built by groups of collaborators. The most popular wiki project is Wikipedia.org, the online encyclopedia (alexa.com, 2020). Businesses can create product wikis and encourage employees and customers to contribute information that will form a knowledge base resource for those who need information about the product.

Many organizations like MediaWiki and DokuWiki offer free software programs for creating, maintaining, and managing wikis. (MediaWiki is the wiki engine used by Wikipedia.org.) Other popular wiki programs like Confluence and Helpie Wiki are commercial wiki applications that charge users based on their need for Web hosting and the number of people that will be working on the wiki project. Wikis can be a particularly good way for a small business to distribute nonconfidential information to employees and business partners. Setting up a wiki is much easier than creating a full-featured website.

Leveraging the Power of the Crowd: Crowdsourcing and Crowdfunding

In recent years, several companies have created online communities for the purpose of identifying market opportunities through crowdsourcing. **Crowdsourcing** is a model of problem solving, production, and idea generation that marshals the collective talents of a large group of people that use the Web. Business organizations that have used social crowdsourcing websites include Fiat, Sara Lee, BMW, Kraft, Procter & Gamble, and Starbucks. See **Table 7.5** for a list of other examples.

TABLE 7.5   **Examples of Crowdsourcing Websites**

Category	Crowdsource Websites
R&D crowdsourcing	**InnoCentive**—Challenge-driven Innovation **Yet2**—Innovation and IP Marketplace **NineSigma**—Technology Problem Solving **Hypios**—Problem Solving for Advanced Technology
Crowdsourcing for marketing, design, and ideas	**Brand Tags**—Brand Identification from the Crowd **Guerra Creativa**—Logos and Designs **LeadVine**—Leads and Referrals **Challenge.gov**—Solutions to Government Problems
Crowdsourcing product ideas	**Procter & Gamble**—Crowdsource Product Ideas for P&G **Quirky**—Community Sourced Product Ideas **CafePress**—Buy, Sell, Create Your Product
Crowdsourcing HR & freelance work	**Amazon Mechanical Turk**—"A Marketplace for Work" **Clickworker**—Cloud-based Global Workforce **Topcoder**—Crowd Coding
Crowdfunding websites	**ArtistShare**—New Artist Projects **Kickstarter**—Large, General Crowdfunding Site **GoFundMe**—For Personal Fundraisers **Crowdrise**—Funding for Inspiring Social Causes
Peer-2-peer UGC websites	**Wikipedia**—Online Encyclopedia Produced by the People **Quora**—Answers from Experts, Amateurs, and Insiders, Voted Up or Down **Yahoo Answers**—Another P2P Question & Answer Site **Diigo**—Crowdsourced Web Bookmarks, Tags, and More

Adapted in part from BoardofInnovation.com (2020).

Crowdfunding

More recently, businesses and entrepreneurs have turned to the crowdsourcing model to finance business start-ups or projects. Several **crowdfunding** sites have become popular in recent years, including GoFundMe and Kickstarter. Each crowdfunding site is governed by different rules that establish the kinds of projects or organizations that can use them, and the types of crowdfunding allowed on the site **(Table 7.6)**. Crowdfunding sites typically collect a percentage of the money raised, but even this can vary, so it is important to read the terms of service carefully before selecting a site to raise money on. See **https://www.crowdfunding .com/** for a list of the most popular sites.

TABLE 7.6 **Types of Crowdfunding**

Donations	Often used by charities and political campaigns. Contributors do not receive anything tangible in exchange for their donation, just the knowledge that they are supporting a cause they like or believe in. (In some cases, contributors may be eligible for a tax write-off.)
Rewards	Contributors receive a benefit, reward, or thank-you gift. Often, it is something related to the project. For instance, people who contribute to a filmmaker's project may receive a copy of the finished work on DVD.
Credit	Contributors essentially make microloans to fund projects and expect to be repaid with interest.
Equity	Contributors make "micro investments" and receive a proportional ownership stake in the company or project. It is likely that regulatory agencies that oversee equities markets in the United States and other countries will establish rules governing or even restricting this type of crowdfunding.
Royalties	Contributors receive a percentage of the sales revenue generated by a project. For instance, people who contribute to a musician's recording project might receive royalties from the sale of the artist's music.

Sources: Outlaw (2013) and Wikipedia Contributors (2020b).

Social Media Is More Than Facebook, YouTube, and Twitter

Many people think that social media is limited to a few iconic companies or brand names like Facebook, Twitter, and YouTube. While those companies have certainly capitalized on the new technology and tend to dominate their respective market segments, social media is a term describing a wide range of technologies, features, functionalities, and services used across the Web and embedded in most of the websites and mobile apps you use today.

Although you may be familiar with using social media for recreational purposes or connecting with friends and family, businesses use social technologies for a wide variety tasks and functions. See **Table 7.7** below.

TABLE 7.7 **How Businesses Use Social Media Tools and Applications**

Business Task or Function	Social Media Tools and Applications
Collaboration and team management	Private SNS, Collaboration Tools and Platforms
Communication and engagement with customers	Blogs, Wikis, Email, SNS
Image and reputation management	Digital Public Relations, Social Media Monitoring Tools
Communication and engagement with employees and partners	Intranets, Blogs, Private SNS
Talent acquisition and recruiting	Professional SNS (i.e. LinkedIn)
Research and Development (R&D)	Search Engines, Online Databases, Discussion Forums, Q&A websites
Productivity and innovation	Crowdsourcing
Information utilities	Knowledge Management Tools and Search Engines and Enterprise Search Utilities
Content marketing and content management	Blogs, Wikis, RSS
Finance and fund raising	Crowdfunding
Selling goods and services online	B2C e-Commerce, Social Commerce
Finding suppliers and purchasing goods and services for business	B2B e-Commerce, Social Commerce

Questions

1. Why would a business want to create a private SNS? What are some of the challenges associated with doing this?

2. List the characteristics that differentiate an SNS from other types of online communities.

3. For what purposes do businesses use blogs?

4. Give an example of how a business might use a mashup application on its website.

5. Why are social bookmarking services superior to the traditional method of saving website links to a list of "favorites" or "bookmarks" in a Web browser?

6. Why is it sometimes difficult to differentiate between types of social media? For example, Twitter is often referred to as an SNS, a microblog, and a social bookmarking service. YouTube is often referred to as a video sharing site, an SNS, and a vlog (video blog) platform.

7.3 Using Search Technology for Business Success

LO7.3 Describe *how search engines work and identify ways that businesses gain competitive advantage by using search technology effectively.*

Search engines have developed into powerful tools used by individuals and business organizations for a variety of purposes. In this section, you will learn how search engines work and the role they play in generating revenue and consumer awareness for organizations. You will also discover how businesses use enterprise search technology to unlock hidden content within their organizations. Finally, you will read about how search and Internet technology is evolving to provide more accurate and useful results.

How Search Engines Work

Search engine is an application for locating Web pages or other content (e.g., documents, media files) on a computer network. Popular Web-based search engines include Google, Bing, Yippy, and Yahoo.

The term **search engine** is used to refer to many kinds of information retrieval (IR) services that find content on the World Wide Web. These services vary in significant ways. Understanding how these services differ can improve the quality of results obtained when conducting a search for online information. Listed below is a brief description of different IR services for finding Web content. Each type of search engine has distinctive strengths and weaknesses. Therefore, it is important to know the differences so you can select the best tool most likely to meet your objectives.

Spiders also known as crawlers, Web bots, or simply "bots," are small computer programs designed to perform automated, repetitive tasks over the Internet. They are used by search engines to scan webpages and return information that is later used to answer users' search inquiries.

- **Crawler search engines** rely on sophisticated computer programs called **spiders**, **crawlers**, or **bots** that surf the Internet, locating webpages, links, and other content that are then stored in the search engine's page repository. The most popular commercial search engines, Google and Bing, are based on crawler technology.

- **Web directories** list webpages organized into hierarchical categories. Originally, Web directories were created and maintained by human editors who decided how a website would be categorized. Today, many Web directories use technology to automate new website listings. Web directories are typically classified as "general" directories that cover a wide range of topical categories, or "niche" directories that focus on a narrow range of topics. Examples of popular general directories include Best of the Web, JoeAnt, and LookSmart. Wikipedia maintains a list of general and niche Web directories.

- **Hybrid search engines** combine the results of a directory created by humans and results from a crawler search engine, with the goal of providing both accuracy and broad coverage of the Internet.

- **Meta-search engines** compile results from other search engines. For instance, Dogpile generates listings by combining results from Google and Yahoo.
- **Semantic search engines** are designed to locate information based on the nature and meaning of Web content, not simple keyword matches. The goal of these search engines is to dramatically increase the accuracy and usefulness of search results.

How Crawler Search Engines Work

Since the most popular search engines (Google and Bing) are crawler search engines, we will describe in greater detail how these IR applications work. Behind the relatively simple interfaces of these two powerful search engines, a great deal of complex technology is at work (**Figure 7.2**). Because modern search engines use proprietary technology in the race to stay ahead of competitors, it is not possible to tell exactly how they decide what websites will appear in a SERP. However, it is possible to describe the basic process shared by most crawler search engines.

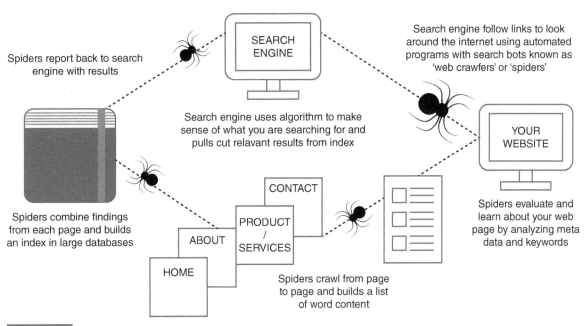

FIGURE 7.2 Components of crawler search engine.

1. The crawler control module assigns webpage URLs to programs called spiders or bots. The spider downloads these webpages into a **page repository** and scans them for links. The links are transferred to the **crawler control module** and used to determine where the spiders will be sent in the future. (Most search engines also allow Web masters to submit URLs, requesting that their websites be scanned so they will appear in search results. These requests are added to the crawler control queue.)

2. The **indexer module** creates look-up tables by extracting words from the webpages and recording the URL where they were found. The indexer module also creates an inverted index that helps search engines efficiently locate relevant pages containing **keywords** used in a search. (See **Figure 7.3** for examples of an inverted index.)

page repository a data structure that stores and manages information from a large number of webpages, providing a fast and efficient means for accessing and analyzing the information at a later time.

Crawler control module is a software program that controls several "spiders" responsible for scanning or crawling through information on the Web.

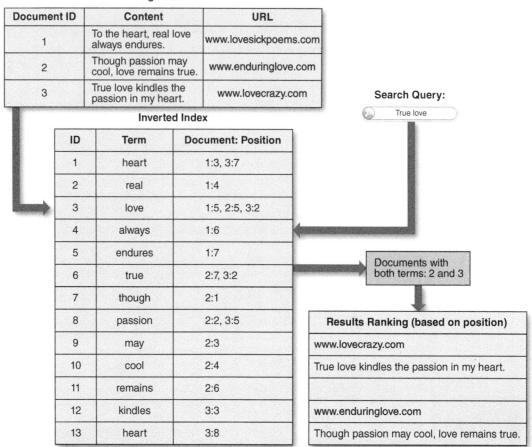

Page Index

Document ID	Content	URL
1	To the heart, real love always endures.	www.lovesickpoems.com
2	Though passion may cool, love remains true.	www.enduringlove.com
3	True love kindles the passion in my heart.	www.lovecrazy.com

Search Query:

True love

Inverted Index

ID	Term	Document: Position
1	heart	1:3, 3:7
2	real	1:4
3	love	1:5, 2:5, 3:2
4	always	1:6
5	endures	1:7
6	true	2:7, 3:2
7	though	2:1
8	passion	2:2, 3:5
9	may	2:3
10	cool	2:4
11	remains	2:6
12	kindles	3:3
13	heart	3:8

Documents with both terms: 2 and 3

Results Ranking (based on position)

www.lovecrazy.com
True love kindles the passion in my heart.
www.enduringlove.com
Though passion may cool, love remains true.

FIGURE 7.3 Search engines use inverted indices to efficiently locate Web content based on search query terms.

3. The **collection analysis module** creates utility indexes that aid in providing search results. The utility indexes contain information about things such as how many pages are in a website, the geographic location of the website, number of pictures on a webpage, webpage length, or other site-specific information the search engine may use to determine the relevance of a page.

4. The **retrieval/ranking module** determines the order in which pages are listed in a SERP. The methods by which search engines determine website listing order varies and the specific algorithms they use are often carefully guarded trade secrets. In some cases, a search engine may use hundreds of different criteria to determine which pages appear at the top of a SERP. Google, for instance, claims to use over 200 "clues" to determine how it ranks pages (Google.com, 2014).

5. Webpages retrieved by the spiders, along with the indices and ranking information, are stored on large servers (see **IT at Work 7.3**).

IT at Work 7.3

Google Data Centers Must Keep up With Growing Consumer Demand on the Web

Not only does Google maintain a copy of the Internet for its search engine services, it is also constantly updating a map of the entire planet for users of its popular Google Earth application. In addition, the company maintains a full-text, searchable copy of 25 million books, equal to 4 billion pages or 2 trillion words. And then there are applications like Gmail, serving roughly 1.5 billion people around the world and YouTube, where 500 hours of video are uploaded every minute! Add all this up, and Google is facing perhaps the biggest data storage challenge ever. So, where does Google store all this data?

Information collected by Google is housed on approximately 1 million servers spread across 21 different facilities worldwide. The facilities are large, factory-like installations containing row upon row of racked and stacked servers. Cooling systems, required to keep servers from overheating, are a significant component of any large data center (Figure 7.4). Google pioneered the software and hardware used in the data centers and is recognized as a leader in data center operations.

FIGURE 7.4 Pipes pass through the chiller plant at the Google, Inc., data center in Changhua, Taiwan. Google doubled its spending plan for its new data center in Taiwan to $600 million amid surging demand from Asia for its Gmail and YouTube services.

The company's data centers are built with energy efficiency, reliability, and performance in mind. As Google is a leading provider of Internet services, its data infrastructure must keep up with growing consumer demand for speedy performance and reliability. More recently, Google has had to contend with revelations that the U.S. National Security Agency (NSA) breached its server network security. This follows cyberattacks by hackers suspected of being associated with the Chinese government. Protecting company data from criminals and government powers is a significant challenge.

Industrywide, data centers used 70 terawatt-hours (70 billion kilowatts) of electricity in 2014, representing approximately 2% of the world's energy consumption. Since then global Internet use has rapidly increased, resulting in an 80% increase in data center traffic, and a 50% increase in data center workload. However, energy production has also increased along with significant improvements in the technological efficiency and sustainability of global data centers. The net result is that worldwide energy consumption by data centers has risen to 198 terawatt-hours, but represents a smaller percentage (only 1%) of the world's total energy consumption. Google is widely recognized as operating some of the most efficient data centers in the world (see Figure 7.5). Beginning in 2017, Google obtained 100% of its energy needs for offices and data centers from renewable sources. For additional information, see Google's data center Web page **https://www.google.com/about/datacenters**.

FIGURE 7.5 New, large-scale data centers being constructed for companies like Google, Microsoft, and Facebook house thousands of servers and are creating concern among environmentalists over increases in energy consumption.

Sources: Compiled from Cisco (2018), Masanet (2018), International Energy Assoc. (2019), and Google (2020).

---

6. The **query interface** is where users enter words that describe the kind of information they are looking for. The search engine then applies various algorithms to match the query string with information stored in the indices to determine what pages to display in the SERP.

Each search engine utilizes variations and refinements of the previously described steps to achieve superior results. The Web search industry is highly competitive and the proprietary advances in search technology used by each company are closely guarded secrets. For instance, even the first step in the process, crawling the Web for content, can vary greatly depending on the strategic goals of the search engine.

One of the many challenges faced by large commercial search engines is storage. In the simplest sense, the crawler approach to search requires a company to store a copy of the Web in large data centers. In addition to the petabytes of storage required to maintain this copy of the Web, the search engine must also store the results of its indexing process and the list of links for future crawls.

Why Search Is Important for Business

Search engines play an important role in our personal and professional use of the Web. They are free, easy to use, and become more powerful and effective every day. Most of us take them for granted and are generally unaware of the complex technologies that power these tools. For the average Web user, it may not be vitally important to understand how search technology is evolving. But for business managers, understanding the potential power of search technology is crucial and becoming more important every day. It has long been recognized that access to information is a competitive advantage. Search technology impacts business in each of the following ways:

- Enterprise search—unlocking the value of information within an organization
- Recommendation engines—presenting information to users without requiring them to conduct an active search
- Search engine marketing (SEM) and search engine optimization (SEO)—getting found by consumers on the Web
- Web search—finding crucial business information online
- Emerging search technologies—mobile search, IPA search, and the Semantic Web

Each of these important search technology applications are described below.

Enterprise Search

Enterprise search tools are used by employees to search for and retrieve information related to their work in a manner that complies with the organization's information-sharing and access control policies. Information can come from a variety of sources, including publicly available information, enterprise information (internal records) found in company databases and intranets, as well as information on individual employee computers. Enterprise search tools allow companies to gain competitive advantages by leveraging the value of internal information that would otherwise remain hidden or "siloed." Information can be inaccessible if an organization has incompatible technologies in various units, lack of coordination or cooperation between units, security concerns, and concerns about the cost of making information accessible.

In most organizations, a large portion of employees are "knowledge workers" (e.g., business analysts, marketing managers, purchasing agents, IT managers, etc.). Access to information has a significant impact on their productivity. Enterprise search tools allow workers to extract internal information from databases, intranets, content management systems, files, contracts, policy manuals, and other documents to make timely decisions, adding value to the company and enhancing its competitive advantage. There are three important aspects of enterprise search technology that business managers should understand.

1. **Structured versus unstructured data**.   Originally, enterprise search tools worked only with structured data. Many newer systems now claim to work with unstructured information as well, although there is some variability in terms of how well they accomplish this.

2. **Security issues in enterprise search.**   Unlike a Web search, enterprise search tools must balance the goal of making information widely available throughout the organization with the need to restrict access based on an employee's job function or security clearance. Enterprise search tools must contain features that manage access control and balance employee information needs with the firm's concerns about security breaches or limiting access to sensitive content.

3. **Enterprise search utilities.**   Manufacturers of enterprise search technology continue to develop improved and powerful tools for enterprise search. The most important features of new enterprise search utilities are their ability to handle unstructured data and the ability to manage access control.

Recommendation Engines

Recommendation engines represent an interesting twist on IR technology. Unlike Web search engines that begin with a user query for information, recommendation engines attempt to anticipate information that a user might find useful. Recommendation engines are used by e-commerce sites to recommend products; news organizations to recommend news articles and videos; Web advertisers to anticipate the ads people might respond to; and so on. They represent a huge potential for businesses and developers. While the use of recommendation engines is widespread, there is still much work to be done to improve the accuracy of these fascinating applications. You can read more about recommendation engines in Section 7.5.

Search Marketing

Most traditional advertising methods target customers who are not actively engaged in shopping for a product. Instead, they are watching television, listening to the radio, reading a magazine, or driving down the road, paying little attention to the billboards they pass. To most people, advertising represents an unwelcome interruption. On the other hand, people using search engines are actively looking for information. As a result, they are much more likely to be interested in product and service information found in SERPs if it is related to the topic they are searching for. Efforts to reach this audience are much more likely to produce sales. Search marketing is the umbrella term that refers to two different strategies for influencing how a website will appear on SERPs: search engine optimization (SEO) and search engine marketing (SEM).

Search Engine Optimization (SEO)   SEO involves designing a webpage to satisfy an ever-evolving list of user experience criteria set by search engines and programmed into an algorithm that determines how a company's website will appear in the SERP organic (unpaid) listings. Reportedly, Google uses over 200 on-page and off-page factors to determine how it will list a website on its results pages. On-page factors refer to things a company can do when designing its website, including regularly updating content, using appropriate keywords in the content, making sure the website displays quickly and correctly for different devices, and so on. Off-page factors refer to things like how many other websites link back to the company's website, or how often the website is mentioned on social media websites. **Social media optimization** refers to strategies designed to enhance a company's presence on social media sites. The idea behind these off-page factors is that good websites are more likely to show up on third party websites and mentioned by people using social media. SEO has a direct impact on the organic or unpaid listings SERPs. The typical goal of SEO is to get a website to rank as high as possible in organic SERP listings so that it will be more visible to search engine users.

Search Engine Marketing (SEM)   SEM is a strategy of purchasing ads that appear in specific locations on SERPs and are usually identified as ads to differentiate them from organic listings. Paid search listings are often referred to as **pay-per-click (PPC)** advertising because advertisers pay search engines based on how many people click on the ads. Managing an effective PPC ad campaign involves making strategic decisions about what keyword search queries will trigger the display of an ad. In addition, search engines use a pricing system that requires companies to bid on the keywords that will trigger placement of their PPC ads on SERPs. Therefore, budgeting for a PPC ad campaign can be challenging. However, SEM is an important strategy for gaining visibility on search results pages, especially if the company's website is new or is not ranked sufficiently high in SERP organic listings to be seen by prospective customers. SEO is critical for achieving high ranking in the organic listings, but it can take time for the effects of good SEO practices to take effect. For this reason, most experts recommend using a combination of SEO and SEM strategies to achieve the desired levels of Web traffic coming from search engines.

Growth of Search Marketing   As companies begin to realize the power of search marketing, more money is being spent on this highly effective strategy. The research firm eMarketer (2019b) estimates that spending on PPC search advertising by U.S. companies reached $55.17 billion in 2019, an increase of 18% from the year before. Google reportedly generated 73% of the total revenue from PPC search advertising (eMarketer, 2019a). By comparison, Microsoft's Bing search engine accounted for only 6.5% of the total search advertising spend. Both types of spending, SEO and PPC, illustrate how important search marketing is to businesses these days. Companies now spend more on SEM than they do on television or print advertising. Unlike most traditional advertising methods, return on investment (ROI) can be calculated for search marketing costs by tracking **click-through rates (CTRs)**, changes in site traffic, and purchasing behavior.

Click-through rates (CTRs) are the percentage of people who click on a hyperlinked area of a SERP or webpage.

Web Search for Business

Commercial search engines and Web directories are useful tools for knowledge workers in business. To use search engines effectively, workers should familiarize themselves with all the features available on the search engine they use. Since Google is the most popular search engine, we highlight some of those features in the following list. Focused search tools make it possible to search for information in different formats—Web pages, videos, images, maps, and the like—by selecting the appropriate navigation button on the SERP page.

- **Filetype.**   If you are looking specifically for information contained in a certain file format, you can use the "filetype:[file extension]" command following your keyword query. For instance, the search "private colleges filetype:xls" will produce links to MS Excel files with information related to private colleges. Use this command to find Adobe files (.pdf), MS Word files (.docx), MS PowerPoint files (.pptx), and so on.
- **Advanced search.**   To narrow your search, go to the Advanced Search panel. From this page, you can set a wide range of parameters for your search, including limiting the search to certain domains (e.g., .gov, .org, .edu), languages, dates, and even reading level. You can also use this to narrow your search to a particular website.
- **Search tools button.**   Allows you to narrow your results to listings from specific locations or time frames.
- **Search history.**   Have you ever found a page using a search engine, but later had trouble finding it again? If you are logged into your Google account while using the search engine, it's possible to review your search history. It will show you not only your search queries but also the pages you visited following each query.

These are just a few of the many features you can use to conduct a power search. While you are in college, take the time to become proficient with using different search engine features. Not only will it help with your immediate research needs, it will help you in your career as well. At the end of this chapter, we include information for a free online Power Search course offered by Google. This is a good way to enhance your ability to find the information you need.

Real-Time Search   Sometimes you need information about things as they happen. For instance, you may be interested in monitoring news stories written about your company or you might need to know what people are saying about your brand or a political candidate on Twitter. For these situations, you'll need a real-time search tool like one of the following:

- **Google Trends.**   This tool will help you identify current and historical interest in the topic by reporting the volume of search activity over time. Google Trends allows you to view the information for different time periods and geographic regions.

- **Google Alerts.**   Use Google Alerts to create automated searches for monitoring new Web content, news stories, videos, and blog posts about some topic. Users set up alerts by specifying a search term (e.g., a company name, product, or topic), how often they want to receive notices, and an e-mail address where the alerts are to be sent. When Google finds content that match the parameters of the search, users are notified via e-mail. Bing has a similar feature called News Alerts.

- **Twitter Search.**   You can leverage the crowd of over 650 million Twitter users to find information as well as gauge sentiment on a wide range of topics and issues in real time. Twitter's search tool looks like other search engines and includes an advanced search mode. In addition to real-time search, the Twitter search tool is also an example of social search, which was explained earlier in the chapter.

Emerging Search Technologies

Mobile Search and Mobile SEO   Mobile devices have become ubiquitous. With the emergence of smartphones and tablet computers, mobile devices now account for over half of all Web traffic. In some developing countries, mobile devices account for an even larger share of Internet use since they are less expensive than computers. Since more people are using mobile devices to surf the Web, it should come as no surprise that most Internet searches are conducted using mobile devices instead of computers. With the dramatic increase in mobile device usage, companies need to make sure their websites and content can be found via mobile search and that SERP listings and their websites will display properly on mobile devices.

Personal Assistants and Voice Search   Major Internet technology firms Apple, Amazon, Google, and Microsoft and a host of smaller firms have launched **intelligent personal assistant (IPA)** systems that threaten to disrupt conventional approaches to search marketing. IPA software is typically designed to help people perform basic tasks like turning on/off lights and small appliances, activating household alarm systems, and searching the Internet for music, videos, weather, and other types of information. While IPAs are still in the growth stages of the product life cycle, forecasted demand for the foreseeable future seems strong. Just as businesses once faced the challenge of reformatting website content for smaller screens on mobile devices, they must now determine how to serve up information in a format optimized to make it attractive to a variety of IPAs acting as proxies for their owners.

    Semantic technologies are powering another major evolution of the Web, what some are calling Web 3.0. This phase of Web development is characterized by technologies that will make it possible for computers to understand the meaning of Web content which in turn will improve the ability of computers to find the most helpful and meaningful information that we need. Web 3.0 will use Natural Language Processing (NLP) to make it possible for us to "talk" to our computers in the same way that we talk to other people. Artificial Intelligence will also play a key role in helping search engines and other Web applications to improve performance over time as they learn how to determine and predict the kind of information that will be most helpful to us depending on our objectives or intent for conducting a search.

Questions

1. What is the primary difference between a Web directory and a crawler-based search engine?
2. What is the purpose of an index in a search engine?
3. Why are companies increasingly interested in enterprise search tools capable of handling unstructured data?
4. What is the difference between SEO and PPC advertising?
5. Describe three different real-time search tools.

7.4 A Search for Meaning—Web 3.0 and Semantic Technology

LO7.4 Explain *how Semantic Web technology enhances the accuracy of search engines results and how businesses can optimize their websites to take advantage of this emerging technology.*

Earlier in this chapter you learned about the social technologies that gave rise to Web 2.0, the social Web. Today, the Web is evolving again, becoming what some might call Web 3.0, or the Semantic Web. The technologies that characterize this third major phase of Web development are designed to make Web tools and applications that are smarter and better able to understand us, the language we use, and the problems we are trying to solve.

The Semantic Web will use context, personalization, and vertical search to make content, commerce, and community more relevant and easier to access. With the addition of mobile technology, this Web well be more accessible than ever.

- Context defines the intent of the user; for example, trying to purchase music, to find a job, to share memories with friends and family.
- Personalization refers to the user's personal characteristics that impact how relevant the content, commerce, and community are to an individual.
- Vertical search focuses on finding information in a content area, such as travel, finance, legal, and medical.

What Is the Semantic Web?

Metadata is information that describes other types of data. For example, metadata attached to a file would describe the nature and format of the data in the file, making it easier for some programs to use.

Natural language processing (NLP) is a technology that allows users to interact with computers using their natural language instead of a predetermined set of commands and syntax structures.

Semantic refers to the meaning of words or language. The **Semantic Web** is one in which computers can interpret the meaning of content (data) by using **metadata** and **natural language processing (NLP)** to support search, retrieval, analysis, and information amalgamation from both structured and unstructured sources. Semantic technologies will create a new, richer experience for Web users. Tim Berners-Lee, creator of the technology that made the World Wide Web possible, described the Semantic Web as follows: "The Semantic Web is an extension of the current Web in which information is given well-defined meaning, better enabling computers and people to work in cooperation."

Much of the world's digital information is stored in files structured so they can only be read by the programs that created them. Metadata tags will describe the nature of the file's information, where it came from, or how it is arranged. At the risk of sounding dramatic, metadata transforms a connected, but largely uninterpretable, Web (network) of pages into a large database that can be searched, analyzed, understood, and repurposed by a variety of applications.

It is helpful to think about the Semantic Web against the background of earlier Internet functionality (see **Table 7.8**). The early Internet allowed programmers and users to access information and communicate with one another without worrying about the details associated with the machines they used to connect to the network and store the information. The Semantic Web continues this evolution, making it possible to access information about real things (people, places, contracts, books, chemicals, etc.) without knowing the details associated with the nature or structure of the data files, pages, and databases where these things are described or contained. This will greatly expand the ways in which we search for and find information related to our needs and interests.

TABLE 7.8   **Evolution of the Web**

Web 1.0—The Early Web	Web 2.0—The Social Web	Web 3.0—The Semantic Web: A Web of (Understandable) Data
Static pages, HTML	Dynamic pages, XML, and Java	Metadata tags; artificial intelligence, natural language processing; other semantic tools
Author-controlled content	User-controlled content	Computer-controlled content
Computers	Computers, cell phones, televisions, PDAs, game systems, car dashboards	Computers, IoT, and mobile devices
Users view content	Users create content	Users are provided with a more relevant, useful, and enjoyable web experience
Individual users	User communities	Individual users and user communities
Marketing goal: *influence*	Marketing goal: *relationships*	Marketing goals: *Understanding*—turns the web into a giant readable database by representing meanings and connecting knowledge.
Data: single source	Data: multiple sources, for example, mashups	Data: combines connected, linked data with intelligent content to facilitate machine understanding and processing of content, metadata, and other information

The Language(s) of Web 3.0

The early Web was built using hypertext markup language (HTML). Web 2.0 was made possible, in part, by the development of languages like XML and JavaScript. The Semantic Web utilizes additional languages that have been developed by *World Wide Web Consortium (W3C),* a group led by Berners-Lee. These include **resource description framework (RDF), Web ontology language (OWL),** and **SPARQL protocol and RDF query language (SPARQL).** RDF is a language used to represent information about resources on the Internet. It will describe these resources using metadata **uniform resource identifiers (URIs)** like "title," "author," and "copyright and license information." It is one of the features that allow data to be used by multiple applications.

SPARQL is a query language used to retrieve and manipulate data stored in RDF format. OWL is the W3C language used to categorize and accurately identify the nature of things found on the Internet. Used together, these languages will enhance the element of context on the Web, producing more fruitful and accurate information searches based on a user's intent.

IT at Work 7.4

Amazon Neptune—A Fast, Reliable Semantic Database in the Cloud

While most of us think of Amazon.com as a successful pioneer of retail e-commerce, the company is also one of the largest providers of cloud-based software as a service (SaaS) products. Amazon Web Services (AWS), a subsidiary of Amazon, provides several on-demand cloud computing platforms and APIs to individuals, companies, and governments. Among the company's products are business applications, database applications, media services, robotics applications, security services, storage, and several other types of cloud-based software services. In 2018, AWS announced the general availability of Amazon Neptune, a "fast, reliable and fully managed graph database service" designed to make it possible for customers to develop sophisticated applications that could query billions of relationships within milliseconds, something not possible with traditional relational databases.

What made the Amazon Neptune service different from other database products is that it was built using semantic technologies like RDF and SPARQL that powered the service's complex search and reporting features. Neptune is a graph database, which does a better job of representing the relationships between data points in addition to the data points themselves. This allows companies to gain greater insights from their existing data. Traditional relational databases are less capable of handling data relationships, making them rigid and less able to add different connections or adapt to new business requirements. Graph databases, on the other hand, are more flexible when adding expanded data models or changing business needs. In

addition, graph databases offer greater speed than relational databases, especially as the size of the database grows over time. Some example applications built using Neptune include:

- **Networking/IT Operations**—Neptune can store a graph (model) of a network and use it to more effectively manage operations. IT managers can easily detect the kind of activity taking place across the network and make timely decisions about how to address potential problems like the spread of malicious software or the detection of potential data breaches.

- **Social Networking**—Neptune can process large amounts of user profiles and interactions, making it easy to add a social networking component to applications based on the nature of the relationships contained in the graph database.

- **Recommendation Engines**—Neptune provides organizations with deep product collections with expanded ability to make recommendations to users based on their relationships with others in the database that may share interests, purchase history, and other relevant similarities.

- **Fraud Detection**—Neptune can easily identify aberrant or unusual financial transactions that are unlike transactions made by other users that share similarities with a specific user. These can then be flagged for further investigation. It also allows investigators to detect patterns of fraud across a network.

Sources: Compiled from Business Wire (2018), Rayome (2018), Baer (2019), and Amazon (2020).

Semantic Web and Semantic Search

As you have read, the Semantic Web is described by metadata, making it easier for a broad range of applications to identify and utilize data. One of the barriers to creating a Semantic Web based on metadata, however, is the tagging process. Who will tag all the data currently on the Web? How can we be sure that such data will be tagged correctly? Will people purposely tag data incorrectly to gain some advantage?

Semantic search engines can be programmed to take advantage of metadata tags, but their usefulness would be very limited if that was the only way they could understand Web content. Metadata tags, therefore, are just one approach used by semantic search engines to understand the meaning of online content. In addition to metadata tags, search engines are incorporating advanced technologies like Natural Language Processing and Artificial Intelligence. The goal is to make communicating with a search engine as easy or easier than you might communicate with another person.

Another goal of semantic search is to understand the context or intent of users looking for information to increase the relevance and accuracy of results. For instance, if a search engine understood the proper context of a search query containing the words "Disney World," it would know if the user was

- planning a vacation, or,
- looking for a job at the theme park, or,
- interested in the history of Disney World.

Semantic Search Features and Benefits   So, what can semantic search engines do that is so much better compared to search engines that work solely on keyword matching? Practical search features based on semantic search technology include.

Related searches/queries—The search engine suggests alternative queries (words and phrases) that may produce information related to the original query or may ask, "Did you mean: [search term]?" if it detects a misspelling.

Reference results—The search engine suggests reference material related to the query, such as a dictionary definition, Wikipedia pages, maps, reviews, or stock quotes.

Semantically annotated results—Highlighted search terms are returned along with related words or phrases that may not have appeared in the original query. These can be used in future searches simply by clicking on them.

Full-text similarity search—Users can submit a block of text or even a full document to find similar content.

Search on semantic/syntactic annotations—It allows a user to indicate the syntax such as part-of-speech (noun, verb, etc.)—or its semantic meaning, whether it's a company name, location, or event. For instance, a keyword search on the word "center" would produce too many results. Instead, a search query could be written using syntax such as the following:

<organization> center </organization>

This would only return documents where the word "center" was part of an organization's name (e.g., Johnson Research Center or Millard Youth Center). Google currently allows you to specify the kind of files you are looking for (e.g., filetype:pdf).

Concept search—Search engines could return results with related concepts. For instance, if the original query was "Tarantino films," documents would be returned that contain the word "movies" even though it is different than the word "films."

Ontology-based search—Ontologies define the relationships between data. An ontology is based on the concept of "triples": subject, predicate, and object. This would allow the search engine to answer questions such as "What vegetables are green?" The search engine would return results about "broccoli," "spinach," "peas," "asparagus," "Brussels sprouts," and so on.

Semantic Web search   takes advantage of content tagged with metadata as previously described in this section. Search results are likely to be more accurate than keyword matching.

Faceted search   provides a means of refining or filtering results based on predefined categories called facets. For instance, a search on "colleges" might result in options to "refine this search by . . ." location, size, degrees offered, private or public, and so on. Many e-commerce websites provide users with faceted search features, allowing shoppers to filter search results by things like price, average rating, brand name, and product features.

Clustered search—This is similar to a faceted search, but without the predefined categories. Visit *Carrot2.org* to better understand this concept. After conducting a search, click on the "tree map" option to see ways to refine your search. The refining options are extracted from the content in pages of the initial search.

Natural language search   tools attempt to extract words from questions like "How many countries are there in Europe?" and create a semantic representation of the query. Initially, this is what people hoped search engines would evolve toward, but Grimes wonders if we have become so accustomed to typing just one or two words into our queries that writing out a whole question may seem like too much work. As it turns out, many search engines process both kinds of search queries well. Try asking a question on the semantic search engine *SenseBot*. This search engine usually returns answers (and their source websites) to a question instead of just listing of websites where related information might be found.

Google and Bing have been building semantic technologies into their systems to improve the user experience. Other search engines with similar semantic search features include *Duck-DuckGo, Carrot2.org,* and *SenseBot.*

Semantic Web for Business

The most immediate challenge faced by businesses is the need to optimize their websites for semantic search. Because search engines are responsible for directing so much traffic to business websites, it will be important that companies take advantage of semantic technologies to ensure they continue to remain visible to prospective customers who use search engines. While the details of semantic SEO are beyond the scope of this book, one thing that businesses can do is to think about the issue of context when creating content on their websites. Page titles and keywords used in content should be selected for their ability to help search engines match the information with a user's intent or the context of the search. Extending an example used earlier in this section, a website with information about Disney World should use page titles and keywords to indicate if the information on a webpage is related to Disney World <u>vacations</u>, <u>employment opportunities</u> at Disney World, or <u>the history</u> of the famous theme park. This will increase the likelihood that the website is listed in the results if a search engine determines that the user is attempting to find information for one of these purposes.

Another example illustrates how websites optimized for semantic technology with metadata produce richer, more attractive listings on SERPs. Google calls these listings *rich snippets* (see **Figure 7.6**).

FIGURE 7.6 Rich snippets provide additional information about a website, increasing the chances that users will click on the listing when they see it on a search engine results page.

These enhanced search listings are more visually attractive (see Figure 7.6) and produce greater CTRs compared to traditional listings. Businesses need to stay up to date with advances in semantic search so that they can continuously optimize their sites to increase traffic coming from major search engines.

Questions

1. List five different practical ways that semantic technology is enhancing the search experience of users.
2. How do metadata tags facilitate more accurate search results?
3. Briefly describe the three phases of the World Wide Web's development.
4. Define the words "context," "personalization," and "vertical search." Explain how they make for better information search results.
5. What are three languages developed by the W3C and associated with the Semantic Web?

7.5 | Recommendation Engines

LO7.5 Explain *how recommendation engines enhance user experience by predicting and recommending Web content, products, and services that might appeal to them.*

Retail websites need an effective way of recommending their vast array of products to customers. Most e-commerce sites provide website search tools based on the technologies previously discussed in this chapter. Relying on customers to find products through an active search, however, assumes customers know what they want and how to describe it when forming their search query. For these reasons, many e-commerce sites rely on recommendation engines (sometimes called recommender systems). Recommendation engines proactively identify products that have a high probability of being something the consumer might want to buy. Amazon has long been recognized as having one of the best recommendation engines. Each time customers log into the site, they are presented with an assortment of products based on their purchase history, browsing history, product reviews, ratings, and many other factors. In effect, Amazon personalizes their website for each individual which in turns leads to increased sales. Consumers respond to these personalized pages by purchasing products at much higher rates when compared to banner advertisements and other Web-based promotions.

There are three widely used approaches to creating useful recommendations: content-based filtering, collaborative filtering, and hybrid strategies.

Content-based filtering recommends products based on the product features of items the customer has interacted with in the past (**Figure 7.7**). Interactions can include viewing an item, "liking" an item, purchasing an item, saving an item to a wish list, and so on. In the simplest sense, content-based filtering uses item similarity to make recommendations. For instance, the Netflix recommendation engine attempts to recommend movies that are like movies you have already watched (see **IT at Work 7.5**). Music-streaming site Pandora creates its recommendations or playlists based on the Music Genome Project©, a system that uses approximately 450 different attributes to describe songs. These detailed systems for describing movies and songs enhance Netflix's and Pandora's positions in highly competitive industries because of their ability to offer superior recommendations to their customers.

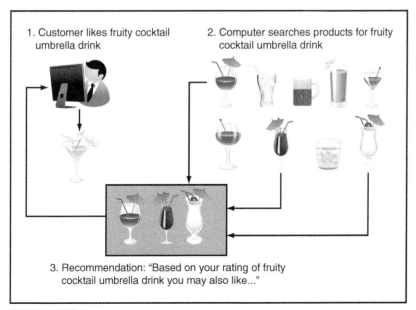

1. Customer likes fruity cocktail umbrella drink

2. Computer searches products for fruity cocktail umbrella drink

3. Recommendation: "Based on your rating of fruity cocktail umbrella drink you may also like..."

FIGURE 7.7   Content-based filtering produces recommendations based on similarity of product features.

IT at Work 7.5

Best Buy Uses Recommendations to Compete with Amazon

Prior to 2015, analysts were pessimistic about Best Buy's ability to stay in business. Remaining viable in the shadow of Amazon's growing e-commerce empire appeared to be a challenge that Best Buy wouldn't be able to win. Yet today, Best Buy is not only surviving, but according to Forbes, the electronic retailer is thriving. The value of the company's stock has increased six times over since 2012. What was the key to Best Buy's turnaround? The company embarked on a multi-pronged strategy called Renew Blue, specifically designed to counter competition from Amazon. The plan included price matching, placing greater emphasis on customer service to improve the in-store experience, development of special relationships with suppliers and investing heavily in its own online performance. A critical part of that last strategy, improving online performance was directly aimed at taking back sales and market share that had been lost to Amazon over the years. Amazon is widely recognized as having one of the best recommendation systems for suggesting products to its customers. Best Buy decided that to be competitive, they to needed to follow a similar strategy and in 2015, they launched a recommendation system for their e-commerce website.

Shortly after launching their recommendation system, Best Buy saw nearly five-fold increase in the growth rate of their e-commerce business, up 25% from just 5% in the year prior. The retailer earned $832 million from e-commerce during the first quarter of 2015, which represented almost 11% of its total U.S. revenue, up from 8.5%. Much of this improvement has been attributed to personalization based on the recommendation system's ability to provide meaningful and relevant product suggestions based on different types of criteria. Customers that logged into the site were shown a customized landing page full of products that the system determined would be most attractive to shoppers, including products that the customer had shown interest in previously. The company also streamlined its omni-channel operations, which allowed the in-store and website operations to coordinate their efforts to serve customers more effectively including letting customers order online, and then pick-up their purchases in a nearby store. Best Buy also created an API that allowed other websites and bloggers to post recommended products on their websites. In 2018, the company reported $42.1 billion in revenue, $2.72 in non-GAAP earnings per share, and an 11% dividend increase. Thanks to the implementation of a successful recommendation system and other key strategies, Best Buy's future looks much better today than it did just a handful of years ago.

Sources: Compiled from Business Insider (2016), Goodrich (2017), and Mourdoukoutas (2019).

Collaborative filtering makes recommendations based on a user's similarity to other people. For instance, when a customer gives a product a high rating, he or she may receive recommendations based on the purchases of other people who also gave the same product a high rating. Sometimes, websites will explain the reason for the recommendations with the message "Other people who liked this product also bought. . ." Many collaborative filtering systems use purchase history to identify similarities among customers. In principle, however, any customer characteristic that improves the quality of recommendations could be used (see **Figure 7.8**).

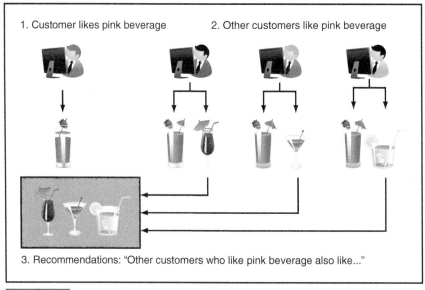

FIGURE 7.8 Collaborative filtering bases recommendations on similarity to other customers.

In an effort to develop increasingly better recommendation engines, developers are exploring a number of creative ways to predict what consumers might like based on patterns of consumer behavior, interests, ratings, reviews, social media contacts and conversations, media use, financial information, and so on.

In addition to content filtering and collaborative filtering, two other approaches to recommendation engines are mentioned in the literature: knowledge-based systems and demographic systems. Knowledge-based systems use information about a user's needs to recommend products. This kind of system is useful for developing recommendations for products that consumers do not shop for very often. For instance, an insurance company may ask a customer a series of questions about his or her needs, and then use that information to recommend policy options. Demographic systems base recommendations on demographic factors corresponding to a potential customer (i.e., age, gender, race, income, etc.). While similarity to other customers might play a role in developing these recommendations, such systems are different from collaborative filtering systems that typically rely on information about a person's behavior (i.e., purchase, product ratings, etc.).

Systems are being developed that leverage big data streams from multiple sources to refine and enhance the performance of current systems.

Limitations of Recommendation Engines

While recommendation engines have proven valuable and are widely used, there are still challenges that must be overcome. Four commonly cited limitations are described as follows:

Cold start or new user: Making recommendations for a user who has not provided any information to the system is a challenge since most systems require a starting point or some minimal amount of information about the user. Where a website does not have sufficient information of its own to make recommendations, consumers' existing social media profiles from sites like Facebook and Twitter can be used.

Sparsity: Collaborative systems depend on having information about a critical mass of users to compare to the target user to create reliable or stable recommendations. This is not always available in situations where products have only been rated by a few people or when it is not possible to identify a group of people who are similar to a user with unusual preferences.

Limited feature content: For content filter systems to work, there must be enough information available about product features and the information must exist in a structured format so it can be read by computers. Often feature information must be entered manually, which can be prohibitive in situations where there are many products.

Overspecialization: If systems can only recommend items that are highly similar to a user profile, then the recommendations may not be useful. For example, if the recommendation system is too narrowly configured on a website that sells clothing, users may only see recommendations for the same clothing item he or she liked, but in different sizes or colors.

Hybrid recommendation engines develop recommendations based on some combination of the methodologies described above (content-based filtering, collaboration filtering, knowledge-based and demographic systems). Hybrid systems are used to increase the quality of recommendations and address shortcomings of systems that only use a single methodology. To illustrate the potential complexity and variation in hybrid systems, four approaches are listed below:

- **Weighted hybrid**—Results from different recommenders are assigned a weight and combined numerically to determine a final set of recommendations. Relative weights are determined by system tests to identify the levels that produce the best recommendations.
- **Mixed hybrid**—Results from different recommenders are presented alongside of each other.
- **Cascade hybrid**—Recommenders are assigned a rank or priority. If a tie occurs (with two products assigned the same recommendation value), results from the lower-ranked systems are used to break ties from the higher-ranked systems.
- **Compound hybrid**—This approach combines results from two recommender systems from the same technique category (e.g., two collaborative filters), but uses different algorithms or calculation procedures.

Recommendation engines are now used by many companies with deep content (e.g., large product inventory) that might otherwise go undiscovered if the companies depended on customers to engage in an active search. To simplify our description of recommendation engines, most of the examples above have been based on e-commerce sites recommending products to customers. However, this technology is used by many kinds of business organizations, as illustrated in **Table 7.9**.

TABLE 7.9   Examples of Recommendation Engine Applications

Company	How It Uses Recommendation Engines. . .
Amazon	Recommends products using multiple filtering methods.
Netflix	Approximately 75% of Netflix movies are selected as a result of its recommendation system.
Pandora	This streaming music site creates playlists based on similarity to initial songs or artists selected by the user.
CNN, Time, Fast Company, Rolling Stone, NBCNews.com, Reuters, Us Weekly	These news and entertainment companies all use a recommendation engine (or "content discovery system") created by Outbrain.com to suggest additional articles related to the one site visitors initially viewed.
YouTube	YouTube uses a variation of Amazon's recommendation engine to suggest additional videos people might like to watch.
Goodreads	This social website for readers recommends books based on user ratings of books they have read.
Samsung	Uses recommendation engines built into its "smart TVs" to suggest television programming to viewers.
Facebook and LinkedIn	These social networking services use recommendation engines to suggest people that users may want to connect with.
Apple	Helps users find mobile apps they might enjoy.
Microsoft Xbox 360	Suggests new games based on what users have previously shown an interest in.
Tripadvisor	Recommends travel destinations and services based on destinations people have viewed or rated.
Stitch Fix	This fashion start-up uses a recommender system in conjunction with human stylists to select and ship clothing products to customers, before customers viewed or ordered them!

Questions

1. How is a recommendation engine different from a search engine?
2. Besides e-commerce websites that sell products, what are some other ways that recommendation engines are being used on the Web today?
3. What are some examples of user information required by recommendation engines that use collaborative filtering?
4. Before implementing a content-based recommendation engine, what kind of information would website operators need to collect about their products?
5. What are the four limitations or challenges that recommendation systems sometimes face?
6. What is a recommendation engine called that combines different methodologies to create recommendations? What are three ways these systems combine methodologies?

Chapter Summary

LO7.1 *Explain* how technological developments that define Web 2.0 created a fundamentally new experience for users.

Around the year 2000, a series of developments in the technology and business environment occurred that set the stage for the Web to enter a new phase of development, often referred to as Web 2.0 or the social Web. As a result of new programming languages (AJAX technologies), APIs and SDKs, websites began to develop new features that enhanced the ability of users to interact with one another in various ways. Collectively, these websites were referred to as social media. Social media websites gave people the ability to create user generated content (UGC), tag and bookmark Web content, import content from other websites to use in new applications, and access the Web from a variety of devices including computers, mobile devices, and gaming systems. Businesses had to learn new ways to interact with customers on the social Web. For instance, instead of broadcasting advertising messages to everyone, companies needed to learn that customers could "talk back" on social media, so businesses were forced to listen to consumers, and respond to their concerns. Many companies eventually figured out that Web 2.0 also presented many opportunities for engaging with customers. It is recommended that companies focus their efforts on five strategic activities when using the Web to connect with consumers: Listening, Talking, Energizing, Supporting and Embracing.

LO7.2 *Describe* the most common Web 2.0 tools and applications and how businesses use them to accomplish their goals.

The most common Web 2.0 tools and applications include: social networking services (SNS), blogs, sharing sites, mashups, social bookmarking tools, wikis, e-commerce 2.0, crowdsourcing, crowdfunding, collaboration platforms, and social monitoring tools. Each of these tools and applications were described and examples described how businesses make use of many of these social media applications.

LO7.3 *Describe* how search engines work and identify ways that businesses gain competitive advantage by using search technology effectively.

There are different types of search engines that people can use to find information on the Web including, Web directories, crawler search engines, hybrid search engines, meta search engines, and semantic search engines. The largest search engines, Google and Bing, are crawler search engines. Crawler search engines use computer programs called spider bots to crawl the Web looking for new and updated webpages. Information returned by the spider bots is processed and evaluated by a complex algorithm that ranks websites using over 200 different criteria to determine how websites are ranked on search engine results pages (SERPs) for queries containing different words and phrases. Because search engines are responsible for much of the traffic a website receives, businesses attempt to improve the way their website appears on SERPs by using search engine optimization (SEO) and search engine marketing (SEM). SEO is a strategy of "optimizing" an organization's website so that it will be positively evaluated by the search engine's ranking algorithm and appear at the top of a SERPs organic or unpaid listings. SEM involves purchasing Pay-Per-Click (PPC) ads that will appear in special advertising areas on SERPs.

Both strategies are considered important for organizations trying to improve the Web traffic they receive from search engines.

LO7.4 *Explain* how Semantic Web technology enhances the accuracy of search engines results and how businesses can optimize their websites to take advantage of this emerging technology.

Today, the Web continues to evolve, and we are experiencing what some might call Web 3.0, or the Semantic Web. According to Tim Berners-Lee, creator of the technology that made the World Wide Web possible, "The Semantic Web is an extension of the current Web in which information is given well-defined meaning, better enabling computers and people to work in cooperation." Perhaps the most immediate impact of new semantic technologies is a dramatic improvement in the way that search engines work. Among the semantic technologies being used to improve Web search is Natural Language Processing and Artificial Intelligence. These and other semantic technologies improve search engines' ability to better understand our search queries, and to do a better job of understanding the context of a search. Businesses need to optimize their website content based on the semantic technologies being used by search engines to determine how websites should be listed on SERPs.

LO7.5 *Explain* how recommendation engines enhance user experience by predicting and recommending Web content, products, and services that might appeal to them.

Recommendation engines proactively identify products that have a high probability of being something the consumer might want to buy. Recommendation engines are also used by companies to recommend content to users. For instance, news organizations will often use recommendation engines to suggest stories that a user might be interested in. YouTube uses a recommendation engine to queue up additional videos that a user might like to watch. Perhaps the most well-known recommendation engine is Amazon's search engine, which determines what products you'll see displayed when you log into the retailer's website. You read that recommendation engines rely on three different "filters" for determining what a user might be interested in: content-based filters, collaborative filters, and hybrid filters. Content filters tend to recommend things that are similar to other things you have selected before. Collaborative filters tend to recommend things that people similar to you have selected. Hybrid filters are, as you probably guessed, a blend of other types of filters. While recommendation engines have proven valuable to many business organizations, there is a lot of room for improvement, so we expect that recommendations will become even more accurate over time.

Key Terms

Assuring Your Learning

Discuss: Critical Thinking Questions

1. Explain the fundamental differences between Web 1.0 and Web 2.0.

2. Define social media and explain how the use of social technologies fundamentally changed how people and organizations used the World Wide Web.

3. Compare the communication practices of organizations using the broadcast model versus the communication practices of organizations using a conversation model and Web 2.0 technologies.

4. What are the four primary factors described in the text that set the stage for Web 2.0 or the social Web that we enjoy today?

5. What is an API? Why should marketing professionals monitor changes in the access and functionality of APIs used by website and application developers?

6. Explain Facebook's Open Graph Initiative. How do Facebook's social plug-ins play a role in the Open Graph program?

7. Briefly describe each of the following kinds of social media:

    a. social networking service

    b. blog

    c. microblogging service

    d. social bookmarking service

    e. RSS aggregator

    f. sharing websites

    g. mashups

    h. document storage and sharing service

8. Explain what is meant by "feature convergence" and how it blurs the distinction between different types of social media platforms.

9. Each of the following was listed as an element of social media. Describe each and explain its role in shaping and defining the social Web.

    a. user generated content

    b. content control

    c. conversation

    d. community (common values, culture)

    e. categorization by users (tagging)

    f. real people

    g. connections

    h. constant updating

    i. content separated from form

    j. equipment independence

10. If you were looking for a job or wanted to build your reputation as an expert in some area related to marketing, what social media tools would you use for your personal branding strategy and why?

11. How can companies utilize social media collaboration tools to become more competitive?

12. Describe how mashups create new benefits and functionality from existing data or information.

13. Describe some common ways that marketers can benefit by using social media monitoring tools.

14. Why is it important that businesses maintain a high level of visibility on SERPs?

15. Why are organic search listings more valuable than paid search listings for most companies over the long term? Even though organic search listings are more valuable, what are some reasons that companies should consider using PPC advertising as part of their search marketing strategies?

16. Explain the differences between Web directories, crawler search engines, and hybrid search engines.

17. Why do search engines consider their algorithms for rank ordering webpage listings on SERPs to be trade secrets? What would be the consequences of publicizing detailed information about how a search engine ranks its results?

18. Why do consumer search engines like Google and Bing require vast amounts of data storage? How have they addressed this need? What environmental issues are associated with the way large technology companies operate their data storage facilities?

19. Explain why enterprise search technology is becoming increasingly important to organizations. Describe how enterprise search applications are different from consumer search engines in terms of their functionality, purpose, and the special challenges they must overcome.

20. Explain why people are much more likely to view and pay attention to product and service information in SERPs compared to traditional mass media advertising? What strategies are businesses adopting to take advantage of this trend?

21. Why is it easier to measure the return-on-investment of resources spent on search engine marketing compared to mass media advertising?

22. How has the widespread adoption of mobile devices impacted the SEO practices?

23. The goal of Google, Bing, Yippy, and other consumer search engines is to provide users with a positive user experience. What recommendations would you make to a website owner about using website content to improve the site's rank on search result listings?

24. Explain how search engines determine if websites contain information relevant to a user's search inquiry.

25. Describe five ways that semantic search engines can enhance functionality for users. How will businesses benefit from the development of semantic search functions?

26. Recommender systems use different approaches to generating recommendations. Explain the difference between content-based filtering and collaborative filtering. Describe the kind of information required for each approach to work.

27. What are the alternatives to content-based filtering and collaborative filtering recommender systems? When is it most useful to use these alternatives?

28. Hybrid recommendation engines utilize two or more filtering strategies to create recommendations. Describe the four different approaches to creating a hybrid system.

Explore: Online and Interactive Exercises

1. Using online sources, research Facebook's Open Graph initiative. Make a list of "pros" and "cons" regarding these changes from the viewpoint of a Facebook user.

2. Using Google to find interesting and helpful blogs:

    a. Step 1 First go to Google.com and enter a search word(s) or phrase related to the topic you are interested in.

    b. Step 2 When the results page appears, click on the word "News" that appears under the left side of the search window. Then, click on the word "Tools" that appears under the right side of the search window.

    c. Step 3 After you click Tools, a new row of filter words will appear. Look for the words "All news". Click on "All news" and select Blogs from the drop-down list. This will limit the SERP listings to blog webpages.

    d. Step 4 Find a blog or two that seem interesting and read a few posts. Leave comments in the response section (if available). See if the blog author or other readers reply.

3. Set up an account on two different RSS readers (e.g., NewsBlur and Feedly.com). Use them to subscribe to some blogs that are of interest to you (see question 2 above for how to find blogs). Prepare a report or presentation comparing the strengths and weakness of each application.

4. Visit the LinkedIn page for college students: **https://students.linkedin.com/**. Using the information on this page, create a LinkedIn account and begin building your professional network. Search the Internet for additional tips on using LinkedIn to find jobs and prepare a brief report on your findings.

5. Using a search engine, find four examples of mashup applications. Prepare a report describing each one. If possible, identify the website(s) where data are pulled from to create the application.

6. Create an account on diigo.com, the social bookmarking site. Actively use it to tag and categorize webpages that you want to remember for future viewing. Use the search engine on diigo.com to find pages that other users have tagged. Compare the effectiveness of your searches to similar searches using Google and Yahoo.

7. Select a search query term or phrase based on a class assignment, a product you plan to purchase, or some area of personal interest. Use the query at each of the following search engines:

- Google.com
- Bing.com
- Carrot2.org
- SenseBot.com

    For each site, make the following observations:

    a. How relevant or useful are the websites listed on the first two pages of search results?

    b. What differences do you observe in terms of how the search engines list websites on the search results page?

    c. Do you see any indication that the search engine is using semantic technology to generate results (see "Semantic Search Features and Benefits" in Section 7.4)?

8. Use an existing account, or sign up for an account, at one of the websites listed in Table 7.9. Make a list of the ways the website recommends its content, goods, or services to you. Based on your observations, are you able to determine what kind of recommendation system is in use by the website?

Analyze & Decide: Apply IT Concepts to Business Decisions

1. Use *socialmention.com* to evaluate the nature of conversations people are having about three telecommunications companies: AT&T, Verizon, and Sprint. Based on the four metrics provided by Social Mention, decide which company is viewed most favorably and least favorably by the marketplace. Using Twitter search, read a sample of tweets where people discuss the companies. Can you draw any conclusions as to specific reasons why the companies are viewed favorably or unfavorably?

2. Your boss would like you to recommend a free service for storing and sharing documents in the cloud. Create accounts at *Box.com* and *Dropbox.com*. Explore each service so that you understand how it works. Make a recommendation and provide your reasons for the service you select.

3. The supervisor of your department recently read a story about companies that use Second Life to conduct virtual meetings on the service. Create an account on Second Life and spend a few hours learning how to use it. With a handful of other students, arrange to meet in Second Life for a brief discussion. Based on your experience, prepare a recommendation for your supervisor stating whether you think using Second Life for meetings would be a good idea. Justify your recommendation. (Note: This interesting project will probably require you to use a high-performance computer. Review the Second Life system requirements at **https://secondlife.com/support/system-requirements/**.)

4. The marketing manager in your department just read a story about the rapid growth Snapchat, a relatively new social media app. Because your company sells fashion items to women in the 18- to 34-year-old age group, the manger thinks this may be a good platform for promoting your company's brand. You are asked to research the advertising and promotional opportunities on Snapchat and come up with a list of ways to promote your brand on the app. After visiting **https://forbusiness.snapchat.com/** to conduct your research, you might also want to use a search engine to find additional websites with information about advertising on Snapchat. After collecting your information, prepare a brief memo outlining your recommendations.

5. Perform a search engine query using the terms "data center" + "environmental impact." Describe the environmental concerns that large-scale data centers are creating around the globe and steps that companies are taking to address these concerns. Read about Google's efforts at **https://sustainability.google/**. In your opinion, is Google making a satisfactory effort to minimize the negative impact of its business on the environment? Explain your answer.

6. Select a consumer product or service for which there are at least three popular brand names. For example, you might choose the category "cell phone carriers," which includes Verizon, AT&T, Sprint, and T-Mobile. On the **https://trends.google.com/trends/** page, type the brand names, separated by commas, into the search field at the top of the screen (e.g., Verizon, AT&T, Sprint, T-Mobile). The resulting chart will display the search query volume by brand, an indicator of how much interest each brand has received over time. Using the Google Trends data, answer the following questions.

    a. *Tip:* Before answering the questions below, use Google's search engine to find articles on "how to interpret Google trends." This will help you better understand the Google trends report and make it easier to answer the following questions.

    b. Using the date setting at the top of the *Google Trends* page, explore different periods of time. Briefly summarize how interest in each brand has changed over the last four years.

    c. In the *Regional Interest* section, you can see how interest in each brand varies by country or city. In which countries and cities is each brand most popular?

    d. In the *Related Searches* section, you will see a list of topics and query terms of interest to people who used one of the brand names in a search. How does the list of related topics change from one brand name to another? Do the topic and query term lists give you any insight into what kind of information people may be interested in relative to each brand?

    e. Using a search engine, see if you can find market share data for the product or industry you researched on Google Trends. If you find this information, does there seem to be any relationship between search volume and market share for the brand names you explored?

Reinforce: Ensure Your Understanding of the Key Terms

Solve the online crossword provided for this chapter.

Web Resources

More resources and study tools are located on the student website. You'll find useful Web links and self-test quizzes that provide individualized feedback.

Case 7.2

Business Case: Facebook Helps Songkick Rock the Ticket Sales Industry

Web 2.0 or social technology makes it possible for business to share information in mutually beneficial ways. Specifically, programming tools like APIs and SDKs make it possible for developers to create applications that will connect Facebook with other websites as well as applications that exchange data with applications on Facebook. For instance, Facebook has created several different programming tools that help organizations leverage the power of social networking data for attracting and engaging customers. When IT and marketing managers understand the capabilities of Facebook's programs, they are better able to imagine the myriad ways to leverage the technology for engaging customers, promoting brands, enhancing brand reputations, and reducing marketing expenses.

    Songkick is the world's second largest seller of concert tickets, sending out over a million geo-targeted concert alerts each day via e-mail and push notifications. In a crowded industry of ticket sellers, Songkick's unique mission is to be the ". . . world's leading independent artist-ticketing and concert discovery platform." Their strategy is to treat artists with respect, providing multiple ways for musicians and bands to promote their music, grow their fan base, and provide a simple, cost–effective program for selling concert tickets. Their vision is simple: they want every show to sell out! For music fans, the mission is not just to sell you tickets to concerts you already know about, but to alert you to artists and events that you might not otherwise be aware of. As a business strategy, the company's mission and vision are inspirational, empowering, and easy to understand. However, translating this simplicity into action requires a sophisticated combination of integrated technologies that rely heavily on APIs, SDKs, analytics programs, data sharing, and social media.

For Songkick's customers to find value in the concert alerts they receive, the company must understand its customer base and be able to predict the kinds of shows people are most likely to be interested in. When customers create their Songkick account prior to purchasing tickets, they use Facebook's Login instead of filling out forms with lots of questions. This not only makes it easier to set up a Songkick account, but it gives the company access to a rich set of demographic and behavioral data that will later help them make personalized recommendations about artists and events. The *Facebook Login* feature is created by developers using the *Facebook SDK*, which provides tools programmer's use to integrate the login feature with their own platforms. Approximately 50% of Songkick's customers use the feature to create or log in to their account.

To further expand their understanding of customers and their behavior, Songkick's developers used the *Facebook SDK* and the *App Events Export API* to connect with the Facebook *Analytics for Apps* program. This provided Songkick with an in-depth view of its audience, their preferences, and behaviors associated with patterns of engagement and retention. Based on insights from *Analytics for Apps* program, Songkick was able to identify new features and services for their app that improved its value to customers. Finally, Songkick programmers used the *Facebook SDK* and *APIs* to integrate with the *Facebook App Ads* program. This program connected Songkick ads that appear on Facebook with the Songkick app, providing analytics and improving customer engagement. For instance, Songkick can use what Facebook calls *Deep Linking* with their ads. Deep Linking makes it easier for new app installers (customers) to reach the information that originally inspired them to try the service. What this means in practice is that when a Facebook user sees a personalized Songkick ad promoting a Goo Goo Dolls concert, they will download and open the Songkick app, and be promptly taken to the app page for the Goo Goo Dolls concert, the reason they downloaded the app in the first place. Without Deep Linking, users would likely have to navigate several account setup and introductory screens before reaching the desired information. Deep Linking improves customer satisfaction, engagement, retention, and conversions.

As a result of Songkick's integration and data sharing with Facebook programs, the company experienced 7% more purchases by people using *Facebook Login* and a 15% increase in sales as a result of insights gained from *Analytics for Apps*. Furthermore, customers acquired from the Facebook network had a 35% higher lifetime value than customers acquired from other channels.

Questions

1. Why is Facebook motivated to share so much data about its users with other companies as well as creating ways for users to log in into other websites with their Facebook username and password?

2. What does Songkick gain by having customers use Facebook Login to create accounts and log in to their website or mobile app?

3. How does Facebook's Deep Linking program improve customer satisfaction and increased conversions (purchases)?

4. How did Songkick benefit from integrating its platform with Facebook's Analytics for Apps program?

5. How does Songkick use information it obtains from Facebook to effectively alert customers to artists and concert events they might not otherwise hear about? Couldn't they just as easily do that by sending information about all the upcoming concerts in a customer's geographic area?

Sources: Compiled from "Songkick Orchestrates a Sound Growth Strategy" at *developers.facebook.com* and *Songkick.com*.

Case 7.3

Video Case: Power Searching with Google

Google has created two easy-to-follow video courses designed to teach you how to use search engines more effectively: Power Searching and Advanced Power Searching. Each course contains a series of videos that you can view at your own pace. Following each video, you are shown a set of activities and small quizzes that you can use to test your knowledge. Start with the Power Searching course. Once you have mastered the basic skills discussed in that course, move on to the Advanced Power Searching course.

Visit Google's Search Education Online page **http://www.power-searchingwithgoogle.com/**. On this page, you will see links for the two self-guided courses: Power Searching and Advanced Power Searching.

Select the Power Searching link and begin viewing the course videos. After each video, do the related activities and test your knowledge with any online quizzes or tests that are provided. After you have completed the Power Searching course, go back and take the Advanced Power Searching course.

While it may take several days to complete both courses, we encourage you to do so. The time you invest in learning these power search techniques will pay off next time you need to use a search engine for a class- or work-related research project.

Question

1. Describe two or three search techniques you learned from these tutorial videos that you think will be particularly helpful.

IT Toolbox

How to Create a Blog

Setting up a blog is relatively easy. Making the effort to regularly write and post content that others will find interesting is more challenging. The following steps outline the process of setting up a blog.

1. Create a plan. Successful blogging requires a certain degree of organization and discipline. Your plan should answer questions like these:

   a. What are you going to blog about? What will be the focus or topic of your blog?

   b. Identify your target audience. For whom are you writing?

   c. How often do you intend to update your blog? Some bloggers post new material daily, some weekly, and some just a few times a month. As a rule, readers are more likely to follow blogs that are updated regularly. Avoid sporadic updates or only blogging when you feel like it. Successful bloggers frequently set up a publication schedule outlining topics and posting dates to keep themselves on track.

   d. Who else is blogging about the same topic? Identify bloggers you can interact with through your posts and comments on their blogs.

2. Determine if you will self-host your blog by purchasing a hosting plan and domain name (URL), or if your blog will use a free blogging service. Free services allow you to get up and running quickly and do not require any long-term commitments. This provides an easy, low-risk way to get started. While this might be the most convenient approach, you do not actually own your blog or the content you post there because it is on a domain owned by someone else. Your domain name in these situations is usually in the form of "myblogname.blogspot.com," which can appear less professional to some readers. Purchasing a hosting plan and domain name, however, is the better long-term strategy since it creates a unique identity for your blog.

3. Select a blogging platform. This is the software that will provide the look and feel of your site and give you myriad features you can employ to build a successful blog. Standard features in most blog platforms include a comment section, RSS buttons so readers can subscribe to your blog, and share buttons so readers can post links to your blog on other social media sites (e.g., Twitter, Facebook, Digg, etc.).

4. Set up your blog. Once you've set up your hosting and platform arrangements, you will need to create the aesthetic design for your site. Most platforms make this easy with a multitude of template options that you can further customize to give your blog a unique look.

5. Get started. Now comes the challenging part, writing your posts and regularly updating your blog to attract readers. You can read blogs about blogging to get great tips and advice.

References

alexa.com. "The Top 500 Sites on the Web." March 2, 2020.

Amazon. "Amazon Neptune". aws.amazon.com, accessed March 3, 2020.

Baer, T. "Catching up with Amazon Neptune". zdnet.com, November 26, 2019.

BoardofInnovation.com. "Open Innovation & Crowdsourcing Resources." boardofinnovation.com, March 3, 2020.

Buckler, C. "XMLHttpRequest vs the Fetch API: What's Best for Ajax in 2019?" sitepoint.com, February 19, 2019.

Business Insider. "Best Buy's e-commerce Business Is Surging." businessinsider.com, May 25, 2016.

Business Wire. "AWS Announces General Availability of Amazon Neptune." businesswire.com, May 30, 2018.

Cadwallader, C. "How Did Social Media Manipulate Our Votes and Our Elections?" Interviewed by Guy Raz, TED Radio Hour, National Public Radio, July 12, 2019 Transcript. https://www.npr.org/transcripts/740771021.

Chappell, B. "FEC Commissioner Rips Facebook Over Political Ad Policy: 'This Will Not Do'." npr.org, January 9, 2020.

Cisco. "Cisco Global Cloud Index: Forecast and Methodology, 2016–2021." cisco.com, 2018.

Coppins, M. "Behind the 'Disinformation Campaign' Backing Trump in the 2020 Election." Interviewed by Mary Louise Kelly, All Things Considered, National Public Radio, February 7, 2020, Transcript. https://www.npr.org/transcripts/803907482.

Doyle, A. "Recommendations on LinkedIn." Balance Careers, May 20, 2019.

eMarketer. "Google Dominates US Search, but Amazon Is Closing the Gap." emarketer.com, October 14, 2019a.

eMarketer. "US Digital Ad Spending Will Surpass Traditional in 2019." eMarketer.com, February 20, 2019b.

eMarketer. "US Time Spent with Social Media 2019." eMarketer.com, May 30, 2019c.

Facebook. "Facebook Q4 2019 Results." investor.fb.com, January 29, 2020.

Grigorik, I. "Constructing the Object Model." developers.google.com, February 9, 2017.

Goodrich, A. "Learning from Best Buy's Turnaround: 5 Tactics." salsify.com, June 8, 2017.

Google. "About Google Data Centers." google.com, 2020.

Han, E. "LinkedIn 101: Why You Should Use LinkedIn." Balance Careers, June 25, 2019.

Heathfield, S. "Use LinkedIn for Recruiting Employees." Human resources.com, accessed August 12, 2012.

Li, C. and J. Bernoff. "Groundswell: Winning in a World Transformed by Social Technologies." Cambridge, MA, Harvard Business Press, 2008.

Hoffman, J. "What Does AJAX Even Stand For?." thehistoryoftheweb.com, March 4, 2019.

International Energy Assoc. "Tracking Buildings." iea.org, 2019.

Kendrick, L. "5 Things Every Political Campaign Should Be Doing Digitally for 2020." *thecampaignworkshop.com*, August 5, 2019.

Lotich, P. "5 Advantages of Professional Networking." *Thriving Small Business*, July 9, 2019.

McKay, D. "How to Build and Maintain a Professional Network." *Balance Careers*, May 30, 2019.

Masanet, E. R., et al. *Global Data Center Energy Use: Distribution, Composition, and Near-Term Outlook*. Evanston, IL, 2018.

Mayer, J. "How Russia Helped Swing the Election for Trump." *newyorker.com*, October 1, 2018.

MDNContributors. "AJAX." *developer.mozilla.org*, February 17, 2020.

Mourdoukoutas, P. "Best Buy Is Still in Business–And Thriving." *forbes.com*, March 2, 2019.

Outlaw, S. "What Type of Crowdfunding Is Best for You?" *Entrepreneur.com*, October 3, 2013.

Rayome, A. "Amazon Neptune Is Here: 6 Ways Customers Use the AWS Graph Database." *techrepublic.com*, May 31, 2018.

Stewart, E., "Bernie Sanders Is Winning the Internet. Will It Win Him the White House?" *vox.com*, July 5, 2019.

Wikipedia Contributors. "Russian Interference in the 2016 United States Elections." *Wikipedia, The Free Encyclopedia*, 23 February, 2020a.

Wikipedia Contributors. "Crowdfunding." *Wikipedia, The Free Encyclopedia*, 24 February, 2020b.

CHAPTER 8

Omnichannel Retailing, E-commerce, and Mobile Commerce Technology

Case 8.1 Opening Case

cascadecreatives/123 RF

Shachima/Shutterstock.com

AP Images/Elaine Thompson

Amazon Pioneers New In-Store Retail Concept

Amazon is well known as one of the largest e-commerce retailers in the world. Since it began in 1994, Amazon has been an innovator of e-commerce business strategies and technologies that most of us take for granted today. More recently, the company has made an interesting foray into the world of brick-and-mortar retailing along with its reputation for technological innovation. In 2017, Amazon carved out a significant store-based retail footprint for itself when it acquired Whole Foods, a chain of 431 upscale grocery stores featuring organic and other healthy food products. Then in January of 2018, the company opened its first Amazon Go store to the public. Amazon Go stores are similar in size and product offerings to convenience stores. But what makes the new stores unique is Amazon's implementation of what some are now calling the *grab and go retailing* concept.

No Checkout Lines

The biggest difference between Amazon Go and other types of store-based retailers is the absence of checkout lines and registers in any of the stores. When customers enter an Amazon Go store, they simply fill their bags with products and walk out of the store. In addition to the elimination of checkout lines, the Amazon Go system also saves money by tracking inventory in real time, so employees know exactly what items need to be replaced on store shelves and what items need to be ordered from suppliers. This reduces labor costs, inventory, and supply chain costs as well as increasing sales revenue resulting from enhanced performance on product and convenience.

How It Works

When customers first walk into an Amazon Go store, they use an app on their smartphone to generate a **Quick response (QR) code** that is scanned at one of the store's entryway kiosks. The QR code identifies the shopper and their Amazon account credentials including a payment method like a credit or debit card. Cameras also capture an image of each customer at the kiosk scanner and begin tracking customer movements and product selections throughout the store. The Amazon Go cameras and product sensors also track when customers change their minds about a product by returning it to the shelf. Once customers have finished shopping, they simply exit the store and the system charges the customer's account for the products they selected.

Based on the success of its new "grab and go" system, Amazon has begun testing the technology in a larger grocery store format called Amazon Go Grocery (AGG). The technology appears to be successful in the AGG store even with products such as produce or packaged meat that don't always come in standardized units, sizes, and weights. Amazon says its "grab and go" system includes some of the same technologies used in autonomous cars—**computer vision (CV)**, **sensor fusion**, and **deep learning** (a type of artificial intelligence).

Financial Impact of the Grab and Go Concept

An analysis of the potential economic benefits for stores adopting this kind of technology was conducted by Focal Systems, a company that provides technology solutions for in-store retailers. Focal Systems estimates that compared to other convenience store operations, an Amazon Go store will save approximately $372,300 a year in direct labor costs (elimination of cashiers) and $40,000 a year by avoiding lost sales that occur because of stock-out situations. The company also estimates an additional $50,000 in savings because the systems collect data about employee productivity and supply chain efficiencies such as when new products should be ordered to avoid stock-out situations. Improved store performance is expected to yield an increase of about $173,000 in net profits compared to other convenience stores. Together, these items add up to $635,300 in annual benefit to each Amazon Go store.

The Future of Grab and Go Retailing

By the end of March 2020, Amazon had opened 26 Amazon Go stores and one AGG store. (Amazon has also increased the number of Whole Foods stores to 500, further increasing its stake in store-based retailing.) Amazon is also selling a variation of its sensor and tracking technology to other retailers under the name Just Walk Out that works without requiring customers to have an Amazon account, although presumably other retailers would require customers to have an account with them. Industry experts have speculated how Amazon's new grab and go concept might evolve. For instance, while Amazon Go and AGG stores have made things more convenient by eliminating checkout lines, they have introduced a new step at the beginning of the shopping experience by requiring shoppers to stop and scan their Amazon account information when entering a store. Might Amazon consider using facial recognition technology to link shoppers to their Amazon account information so that customers could simply walk into a store and be instantly recognized? While shoppers at Amazon Go stores have presumably accepted the technology that constantly tracks and monitors their every move while in the store, is this something that other shoppers will be comfortable with at other stores? We also don't know how many shoppers will by-pass grab and go stores because they don't want to set up digital accounts or feel uncomfortable with the intensive tracking systems required by grab and go technology. For now, Amazon appears to consider their experiment with grab and go retailing a success, and some have speculated that the company plans to expand the Amazon Go chain to as many as 2,000 stores.

Questions

1. Recent consumer surveys suggest that the three most important qualities of a retail operation are price, product (quality and selection), and convenience. Based on that information, how are customers likely to react to Amazon's grab and go retail strategy?

2. How will the data collected by the Amazon Go checkout system aid in the company's supply chain management?

3. Do you think that customers will prefer the company use facial recognition technology to link customers with their account instead of requiring shoppers to scan a QR code on their smartphone?

Would facial recognition technology make shopping at an Amazon Go store more convenient?

4. One of the things that Amazon could do with their advanced technology is to collect data about in-store traffic patterns, identifying how shoppers move through the store, what areas they spend the most time in, and how long a typical shopper spends in the store. How do you think store managers could use that kind of information to improve the shopping experience for Amazon Go customers?

5. Since Amazon Go shoppers must use their smartphone and an Amazon mobile app to enter a store, make a list of ways that Amazon Go store managers could influence shoppers using the Amazon app and other mobile technology.

Sources: Compiled from Medhora & Dastin (2016), Thompson (2017), Chaubard (2019), Schrager (2019), Machkovech (2020), and Statt (2020).

Quick response (QR) code   A machine-readable code typically used to store a link to a URL or Web page address that can be read by a computer scanner or mobile device.

Computer vision (CV)   is a technology for machines that can see and acquire information from images or multidimensional data.

Sensor fusion   involves combining data from different sources so that the result is less uncertainty than would exist if the separate data sets were used individually. Also known as multisensor data fusion.

Deep learning   is a subset of machine learning and artificial intelligence that employs artificial neural networks. These artificial neural networks are computer algorithms that loosely replicate the function of neurons in the human brain and are capable of learning from large, structured and unstructured data sets.

Showrooming   The practice of examining products in a traditional retail store, sometimes with the help of a salesperson, and then purchasing the product online.

 DID YOU KNOW?

Vending machines have been around a lot longer than you probably think. In 1892 you could buy divorce papers for $2.50 from a vending machine in the town of Corinne, Utah. It has been suggested that the earliest vending machine appeared in Alexandria, Egypt, during the first century A.D. and was used to dispense holy water in exchange for a coin! Vending machines also played a role in relatively new types of commerce. The first application of mobile commerce occurred in 1997 when two mobile-phone enabled Coca-Cola vending machines were installed in Helsinki, Finland. Thirsty customers could pay for their soda using text messages.

Introduction

Now is both an exciting and challenging time to be a retailer. Traditional brick-and-mortar stores face increasingly intense competition from other traditional retailers as well as from competitors in the online and mobile retail channels. Consumers, armed with mobile devices, have more information than ever before about products, prices, and alternative places to shop. A particular source of frustration for traditional retailers is the practice of **showrooming**, where consumers visit a store to look at merchandise, seek information and advice from salespeople, maybe even try on clothes, and then leave the store to make their purchases from an online retailer that offers lower prices.

Online retailers also face significant challenges. Maintaining an e-commerce website requires an ongoing investment in new technologies designed to enhance the online shopping experience, increase operational and logistical efficiency, and maintain high levels of customer satisfaction. Thanks to social media, dissatisfied customers now have numerous forums for complaining about frustrating experiences they might have with a company. It can be difficult meeting customer expectations that seem to grow more and more demanding every day.

Companies that are branching out into mobile commerce also face challenges. For years, industry pundits have said that mobile commerce, or m-commerce, is going to be huge. But those predictions failed to materialize for many years, leaving some to question their investments in mobile technology. However, mobile devices have finally begun to impact retailing in noticeable ways. Now retailers of all kinds are looking at new technologies such as artificial intelligence, virtual reality, recommendation systems, and new types of payment systems as possible ways to gain a competitive advantage. In this chapter, you will read about the forces that are shaping consumer shopping behavior and the ways that traditional, online, and mobile retailers are using technology to address the many challenges they face.

8.1 Omnichannel Retailing

LO8.1 Describe *how the concept of omnichannel retailing is changing the nature of shopping for consumers and the role convenience plays in determining where shoppers choose to shop.*

Life is not easy for managers in the retail sector these days. The challenges faced by retailers have never been more complex, frustrating, and fraught with peril. Consumers are demanding, price-conscious, and easily swayed by competitors. Technology is both a blessing and a curse. Countless new and innovative technology "solutions" to retailing problems are offered by a dizzying array of vendors. Many of the newest technologies promise to give retailers a competitive edge in the marketplace but are unproven. Budgets for technology are limited and making the wrong decision can lead to financial consequences, operational failures, and lost customers. However, because of intense competition, retailers cannot afford to be too conservative, or they risk losing out to competitors that use technology to enhance the shopping experience, reduce costs, integrate sales channels, and improve recordkeeping, data collection, and analysis of key performance indicators (KPIs).

Keeping Up with Consumer Demands and Behavior

Understanding and responding to consumer needs and behavior is the key to survival for the modern retailer. The challenge, however, is increasingly complex as retailers are confronted with several industry-wide challenges including new competitors, new technologies, and evolving consumer needs and demands. Faced with so many changes and challenges, knowing what factors to prioritize can seem overwhelming. Researchers at Deloitte Development LLC track the retail industry and have identified the following factors as critical areas for retailers to focus on at the beginning of this decade (Sides and Swaminathan, 2020).

Convenience   A recent study of holiday shoppers found strong evidence that two-thirds of all retail shoppers hold price, product selection, and convenience to be the most important factors in their buying decisions (Sides and Furman, 2019; Sides and Swaminathan, 2020). Because of enhanced price transparency, consumers are more empowered than ever to do price comparisons. Using the Web and mobile technology, consumers can easily look up price information from a variety of local and online retailers.. These same technologies also make it difficult for retailers to differentiate themselves on product selection and quality since most products are widely available from many different retailers.. This makes convenience the critical, or differentiating factor that determines where consumers choose to shop. Providing consumers with an easy shopping experience may sound simple enough until you realize that convenience means different things to different consumers.

For some shoppers, convenience means being able to find just the right product without spending a long time searching. For others, convenience might mean being able to pick up or return a product with little or no hassle. Or, convenience might mean being able to checkout or purchase products easily. As you read in the opening case, Amazon is putting this to the test with its new Amazon Go stores where customers avoid the checkout line altogether. Determining what convenience means for its customers is only the first step for retailers. The hard work comes in figuring out how to organize and coordinate everyone in the company to deliver on the promise of convenience. In other words, convenience must be sewn into the fabric of a retail organization, influencing managerial decision-making, adoption of critical technologies, employee actions, the way different units of a company work together, and so on.

Marketing Strategy: Differentiation Is Critical   Now more than ever, retail marketing strategies must start with knowing and understanding the retailer's target customers. For instance, some customers will say that speedy delivery is an important factor in their assessment of retail convenience, while other customers prefer a free delivery option, even if it means waiting a couple extra days to receive their products. Because it is often difficult, if not impossible to be all things to all people, retailers must understand the customers they wish to serve and organize their entire business around that segment's needs. Product and price are still important to shoppers, but delivering the product in ways that are convenient for the customer has become the critical battleground where retailers compete.

New tactics such as same day delivery, buy online pick-up in store, and curbside delivery are all examples of ways that retailers are trying to optimize convenience for their customers. Retailers are also experimenting with different business models such as **subscription-based retailing** (see **Table 8.1**), **fulfillment as a service (FaaS)**, **online marketplaces**, Web and cloud services, and so on. Retailers, especially small and mid-sized companies, often contract with third-party organizations for FaaS and e-commerce Web services so that they can focus on their retail business instead of trying to manage complex and highly technical functions outside their core areas of expertise (Busby, 2019; Puryear, 2020). This typically adds value to the customer by providing superior service at a lower cost. This strategy usually means that FaaS and online marketplace companies will be the ones to rely heavily on technology to accomplish their role in the retailing supply chain.

Subscription-based retailing is where a customer subscribes to receive a regular parcel of goods, usually on a monthly or quarterly basis.

Fulfillment as a service (FaaS) typically involves contracting with a third-party business to handle the tasks associated with fulfilling orders received by a retailer. FaaS companies employ sophisticated technology to manage inventory, warehousing, and complex logistical operations to deliver retail orders (and returns) with increasing speed and efficiency.

TABLE 8.1 Examples of Subscription-Based Retailing

Company	Product Category	Description
Amazon	General retail	Amazon Prime members can save money when ordering various types of products on a reoccurring schedule determined by the customer. For instance, a customer might subscribe to the purchase of coffee or tea to be automatically delivered every month. **https://www.amazon.com**
Target	Infant clothing	Parents can subscribe to Target's Cat & Jack private label boxes. For $40, customers receive a box of infant clothing based on baby's gender and age. Customers can return unwanted items to any Target store location or by mail. **https://www.target.com**
Boxed	Grocery, snacks, personal care, and more	Subscribers to the company's "Boxed Up" service can purchase a large variety of products that are frequently sold in bulk or large quantities. For an annual subscription fee of $49, customers enjoy free shipping on all orders, 2% cash rewards, and exclusive perks. **https://www.boxed.com**
Stitch Fix	Casual fashion	After submitting information about size and price limit, subscribers receive a box of clothing to try on and keep what they like. Unwanted clothing is returned to the company for a refund via prepaid envelope. **https://www.stitchfix.com**
Birch Box	Bath and beauty	Subscribers receive a monthly box of cosmetic and hair care product samples personalized for each user based on information they submit when signing up for the service. **https://www.birchbox.com**
My First Reading Club	Children's books	Each month subscribers receive a box with 3–4 age appropriate books for young children. **https://www.myfirstreadingclub.com**
Hungry Root	Vegan meals	Subscribers receive periodic shipments of ingredients for cooking a variety of vegan meals. **https://www.hungryroot.com**

Once a retailer understands how to prioritize the things that are most important to target customers, technology and people can be utilized to promote and deliver on the promise of convenience and other consumer needs that influence shopper's purchase decisions.

Retailers that want to be successful in today's highly competitive environment must develop strategies for:

Online marketplaces are websites that provide a platform for multiple retailers to promote and sell product and services, usually for a fee, commission, or other type of remuneration. Popular examples include Amazon, eBay, and Etsy.

- Collecting and analyzing consumer data to gain insights into customer needs and preferences.
- At the same time, being sensitive to growing concerns about privacy by consumers and government regulators.

- Tracking retail industry trends and innovations in the area's localized fulfillment and delivery tactics.
- Utilizing transparent pricing practices.
- Looking for consumer opportunities where shoppers are willing to pay a premium for personalized or convenience options.

Notice that all five of the above factors have something in common: using information to better understand and satisfy needs and wants of a target segment of shoppers. To be successful, the customer must be the focus of all retail strategies and tactics.

Digital Connections

Not too long ago, both experts and shoppers differentiated between the digital world of retailing (e-commerce) and the brick-and-mortar (or offline) retail environment. Increasingly, that divide has blurred. Technology plays an ever-increasing role in creating highly personalized, interactive, and convenient shopping experiences in all retail channels. In Chapter 7, you read about advances in Web technologies such as APIs, symantec search technology, digital voice assistants (DVAs), and recommendation systems that have all had an impact on the retail environment. In addition, advances in mobile technologies have changed the way that shoppers purchase goods and services. One of the biggest changes emerging today is the growth of 5G networks (discussed in Chapter 4), which will dramatically improve the speed that data travels over a network, reducing delays, and increasing connectivity (think more devices, more people, doing more things at the same time) (Campanaro, 2018). For example, a 5G network will make it possible for stores to use robots for mundane tasks such as stocking shelves or checking for spills. This kind of application would likely slow down a store's current 4G Wi-Fi network to a crawl. But a 5G network will be able to handle deployment of a robotic workforce without disrupting or slowing down other important operations on the store's Wi-Fi network (Dumont, 2019). Some estimates predict that superior performance of 5G networks could add as much as $12 billion in retail revenue by 2021 (Sides and Swaminathan, 2020).

Digital retail channels continue to evolve as advances are made in technology and retail strategy. Now, in addition to e-commerce (Web) and m-commerce (mobile), companies are exploring social commerce, where social networking services become platforms for retailing goods and services.

Consumers Still Love to Shop in Stores

Despite the impressive growth of e-commerce over the past two decades, approximately 85% to 90% of retail sales in 2019 were made by conventional retailers (Sentance, 2019; Sides and Swaminathan, 2020). But competition from e-commerce retailing has made innovation, focused on customer needs, even more important than ever for traditional location-based retailers. As previously noted, convenience is among the most critical factors influencing consumers, and traditional retailers have some advantages on this factor that are difficult for online retailers to replicate.

- **Empowered employees**   Store employees can and should be a key point of differentiation for traditional retailers when it comes to delivering on the convenience promise. But this doesn't happen all by itself. Competitive retail stores need to empower and guide store-level employees on ways to make the store shopping experience easy and hassle free. Technology can play a role in such actions by providing devices that make it easier for employees to answer questions, find information, locate products, and even help reduce checkout times by processing transactions anywhere in the store using mobile devices that can process payments.
- **Critical "node" in the supply chain**   Physical stores can serve as a valuable part of the retail supply chain by providing "last mile" order fulfillment services. For instance, across the country, many grocery stores now offer services directly, or through third-party

companies, that allow customers to order groceries online, and pick up their orders at curbside, or even have their orders delivered at home.

- **Optimize shopping history data** Many retailers have rich databases full of shopper history generated through shopper's club or loyalty/reward programs. Mining this data for ways to offer greater value and convenience to customers will be an important part of staying competitive.

Supply Chain Is More Important Than Ever

If you were to ask shoppers to name Walmart's biggest competitive advantage, most would probably say that the largest retailer in the world is best known for offering everyday low prices (see **Figure 8.1**). This is understandable since the company frequently promotes its competitive prices. However, low price all by itself is not a sustainable competitive advantage. That's because if one retailer lowers a price to attract customers, it is very easy for a competing retailer to do the same thing. While that might make customers happy, it ends up being a poor marketing strategy because the result is that both retailers end up with smaller profit margins. So, Walmart's sustainable competitive advantage is not its low prices. Instead, it is the company's very efficient and powerful supply chain. Walmart can afford to sell products at low prices because the supply chain delivers those products at a lower cost than what other retailers must pay for their products. And because it has taken Walmart many years to build the experience, relationships, and **logistical infrastructure** supporting its powerful supply chain, it would be very difficult for competitors to match Walmart's supply chain system.

Logistical infrastructure refers to the organization of a complex system of facilities, equipment, transportation, and other requirements necessary for the delivery of goods and services from the point of origin to the point of sale to the end user.

FIGURE 8.1 While customers enjoy Walmart's low prices, the real secret to its success is the supply chain that makes it possible for the retailer to maintain healthy profits margins even when selling products at "everyday low prices."

You might make a similar argument about Amazon. Is Amazon a successful e-commerce giant because they were among the first companies to start selling things online? More likely, the secret to Amazon's success is its ever-growing and sophisticated methods of order fulfillment—an important supply chain function. Amazon's supply chain is what enables it to promise next day delivery on a large portion of the products they sell. And while other companies might sell products online, not very many of them can match Amazon's expertise, technology, and logistical infrastructure that support the company's order fulfillment capabilities.

Retailers such as Walmart, Amazon, and others will continue to develop their supply chain, seeking ways to offer customers better pricing, product selection, and convenience. Retailers will employ emerging technologies like artificial intelligence and machine learning to find ways of reducing costs associated with inventory management, logistics, and other supply chain functions in order to enhance efficiency and create greater value for retailers and customers alike.

The Omnichannel Retailing Concept

As the retailing world continues to evolve because of digital, mobile, Web and Internet technologies, new channels have emerged that were initially considered to be separate and distinct. Most retailers and a large segment of the consumer market still view online shopping (**e-commerce**) and **mobile commerce** (**m-commerce**) channels as competing with traditional brick-and-mortar or store-based operations.

For instance, some retailers are frustrated by customer behaviors like *showrooming*, a practice described earlier in this chapter. However, as businesses learn about the full potential of mobile and other digital technologies, retailers are looking for ways to integrate and coordinate the customer experience across all channels. This new approach is called **omnichannel retailing** (Fontanella, 2020) and how it is being successfully used is illustrated in **IT at Work 8.1**.

E-commerce or "electronic commerce" is the buying and selling of goods and services on a computer network, such as the Internet or the World Wide Web.

M-commerce or "mobile commerce" is the buying and selling of goods and services using mobile devices (such as a smartphone) and a telecommunications or computer network.

Omnichannel retailing is a business strategy that provides customers with a seamless and integrated experience across multiple retail channels such as in-store, online, mobile and other sales and product distribution channels.

IT at Work 8.1

Kroger Adopts New Omnichannel Click and Collect Strategy

Kroger operates 40 different food processing plants and is a chain of almost 2,500 retail stores, operating under 12 different names, in 31 states, and enjoys annual sales of approximately $121 billion dollars. While Kroger enjoys a long and successful history as a traditional store-based business, the company didn't experience the kind of industry-wide disruption created by new online businesses in other industries. That is because the perishable nature of many grocery products prevented e-commerce retailers from developing an order-fulfillment and logistics infrastructure that could move products to the end user before becoming spoiled. However, companies are able to offer customers a wide range of retail food concepts and services from traditional, a la carte grocery shopping, delivery of uncooked, packaged meal ingredients, to several prepared food options that can be delivered to customers at home or the office. In order to stay competitive, Kroger, like other traditional store-based retailers, has developed a set of omnichannel retail strategies that combine e-commerce and store-based retailing to meet the ever-changing needs of its customers.

One of Kroger's successful new business practices is known across the industry as the "Click and Pick" or "Click and Collect" strategy. This omnichannel strategy allows customers to shop online for their groceries, and then drive to the nearest Kroger store to pick up their order. This approach to grocery retail is becoming increasingly popular with higher-income shoppers in the 35- to 44-year-old age bracket. Studies show that omnichannel services like Kroger's Clicklist® service have grown from 7% of all online purchases in 2015 to approximately 22% in 2019. What might seem like a relatively simple idea, letting customers pick up their online orders from a store, requires quite a bit of planning, coordination, and communication between the various departments and business partners that make the click and collect process work. For instance, there are different variations on the click and collect concept, and retailers must work hard to help customers know what

kind of service is being offered. Common variations on the click and pick process include the following:

- Picking up order at the register.
- Curbside pickup.
- Delivery to customer's automobile trunk.
- Picking up order from a locker inside the store.
- Remote pickup from an affiliated store or third-party location such as UPS, FedEx, or post offices.

Of these different variations, most customers use click and collect programs where an order is picked up at the register. However, 81% of customers have expressed an interest in using curbside pickup. Many customers are still in the process of determining what approach they are most comfortable with. That's good news for Kroger's Clicklist® service, because it is designed as a curbside pickup service. Kroger also learned that simply letting customers arrive to pick up their order whenever they wanted created all kinds of problems (remember, we're dealing with perishable products here like produce and ice cream!). With Kroger's service, customers can select a 1-hour time window as much as 3 days ahead of time. This allows Kroger to schedule employees and manage parking lot traffic to minimize customer wait times. In addition to its Clicklist® service, Kroger also gives customers the option of home or office delivery, shipping, and, of course, in-store shopping. Kroger has different guidelines and systems for each type of shopping experience. For instance, deliveries to home or office are made quickly, usually in about an hour, whereas Kroger's shipping service is like ordering other types of online products where delivery is sent via a package delivery service and can take anywhere between 1 and 3 days. Based on the popularity of Kroger's click and collect service, it looks like the company continues its tradition of evolving with the changing demands and conditions of the marketplace.

Sources: Compiled from Kats (2018), Kelso (2018), Progressive Grocer (2018), and Banton (2019).

As illustrated in **Figure 8.2**, many businesses operate separate retail channels. For instance, in-store product prices may be different from those the customer finds on the company's e-commerce website or direct mail catalog. Records of customer purchases from the e-commerce website may not be available to service personnel assisting the customer at the store level. But retail strategy is evolving. Most major retailers today understand that the goal is to offer consumers multiple and coordinated brand-based "touchpoints" that leverage the strengths of each channel. For instance, a company with a truly integrated or omnichannel strategy might spark a customer's interest using mobile advertising or direct mail catalogs. The customer then visits a brick-and-mortar store to examine the product firsthand and speak to a salesperson. In-store purchases might be made using one of the mobile payment methods discussed later in this chapter. If the store does not have the size or color of the product desired, the customer might order it by accessing the store's e-commerce site with their smartphone by scanning a **bar code** or QR code placed strategically on an in-store display. The product can then be purchased and delivered through the mail. Product returns can be handled through the mail or returned to a physical store, depending on what is most convenient for the customer. Customer service reps in a call center would have a record of the customer's purchase regardless of which channel the transaction had been completed through. The omnichannel strategy takes into consideration the potential impact of social media, where customers interact with the brand on sites such as Instagram or Twitter and share brand experiences with others in their social network.

Bar code A machine-readable code consisting of numbers and a pattern of thick and thin lines that can be scanned to identify the object on which the code appears.

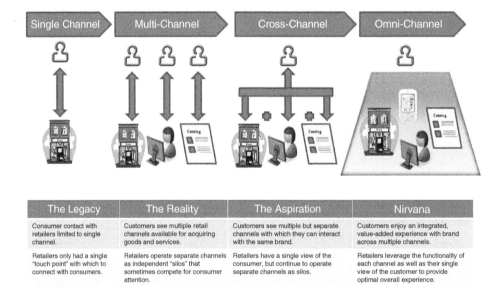

The Legacy	The Reality	The Aspiration	Nirvana
Consumer contact with retailers limited to single channel.	Customers see multiple retail channels available for acquiring goods and services.	Customers see multiple but separate channels with which they can interact with the same brand.	Customers enjoy an integrated, value-added experience with brand across multiple channels.
Retailers only had a single "touch point" with which to connect with consumers.	Retailers operate separate channels as independent "silos" that sometimes compete for consumer attention.	Retailers have a single view of the consumer, but continue to operate separate channels as silos.	Retailers leverage the functionality of each channel as well as their single view of the customer to provide optimal overall experience.

FIGURE 8.2 Retail strategy is evolving toward an omnichannel approach (adapted from National Retail Federation, 2011).

While omnichannel retailing is a well-known concept among retailers today, many are still challenged when it comes to creating and maintaining the service and convenience infrastructure required to deliver on the promise of an integrated, value-added experience across multiple channels.

Questions

1. Describe the three factors that are most likely to influence consumer shopping behavior.

2. List some examples of things that retailers (online or in-store) do to increase convenience for their customers.

3. Why are retailers likely to view technology as both a blessing and a curse?

4. What is subscription-based retailing? List a couple examples of how different companies are applying this concept.

5. Explain why omnichannel retailing provides a better shopping experience for consumers.

8.2 | In-Store Retail Technology

LO8.2 Explain *how consumer expectations and shopping behavior have changed during the last decade and ways that store-based retailers have evolved to meet changing customer demands.*

Changes in Consumer Shopping Behavior

As noted earlier in this chapter, most retail sales (85% to 90%) take place in traditional brick-and-mortar stores. That does not mean, however, that store-based retailers can be competitive without significant investments in technology, innovation, and strategic marketing. Remember that the three most important aspects of the retail experience for shoppers are product, price, and convenience. However, what we have observed over the past decade is that there are many ways for retailers to deliver on those three important areas, with some approaches clearly being more successful than others.

Before exploring the kinds of innovations and technologies being used by retailers, let's first review how customer shopping expectations and behavior have changed:

- Customers frequently make use of multiple channels to make a purchase. Even if they buy a product in a store, it is very likely that they have used the Web or mobile device to research their purchase. This just emphasizes the importance of omnichannel retailing.

- Increasingly, customers utilize mobile devices while shopping in a store. This doesn't always mean the customer is showrooming. Many customers prefer to get product information from their smartphone than asking a store employee.

- Customers that shop in stores want to be able to check out or pay for their purchase using some form of mobile payment.

- Most shoppers are willing to allow collection of data about their shopping and purchase behaviors, but only if there is a clear benefit for sharing this information. Consumers generally see this benefit in the form of discounts offered to members of store loyalty or reward programs that offer discounts to shoppers.

- Shoppers today, especially younger shoppers, are increasingly attracted to what some experts refer to as "experiential shopping" where consumer behavior is driven, in part, by the shopping experience (Wertz, 2018). Convenience can certainly be part of this experience, but stores are experimenting with a broad array of technologies that redefine the in-store retail environment.

In-Store Retailing Trends

Based on an understanding of the kinds of consumer behavior just described, it is possible to anticipate what retail innovations are most likely to be successful. For instance, it is very likely that store-based retailers will continue to benefit from innovations that enhance experiential and "frictionless" (convenient) shopping at scale (Lipsman, 2019). It is not enough for a brand or retailer to develop special services or experiential gimmicks that are only available at a flagship store in New York or Los Angeles. For an innovation to have a meaningful impact on sales across an entire company, it must be something that can be delivered to increasingly larger numbers of customers over time. Examples of successful innovations at store-based retailers include the growth of "click and collect" or "click and pickup" services, where customers order online and then pick up their order at a nearby store. Similar services where customers order using a mobile app and then pick up their order from a store are also expected to be successful. Grab and go retailing or cashierless stores like Amazon Go are expected to increase across the industry as retailers begin to see the value of the required technologies. **IT at Work 8.2** explains how Macy's is capitalizing on its use of innovative in-store retail technology.

IT at Work 8.2

Will Macy's Pioneering In-Store Technologies Save the Day?

Although Macy's publicly positions itself as an "omnichannel retailer with iconic brands" that offers its customers with a seamless across the store, online, and mobile channel experience, Macy's seems to distinguish itself with its pioneering in-store technology. Examples of Macy's innovative in-store retail technology include the following:

Interactive and engaging digital displays Macy's was among the first major retailers to develop in-store, eye-catching displays and screens, some of which were interactive, making it easier for shoppers to browse merchandise and find things they were interested in. Macy's recently announced plans for an in-store virtual mirror technology that will be used in their cosmetics and beauty departments. Combined with augmented reality, the novel mirror displays will make it possible for customers to try on over 250 different types of cosmetics and see how they look. These virtual makeovers will take much less time and be more convenient than applying cosmetics to the customer's face.

Embracing customer use of mobile devices Back when most store-based retailers became frustrated by customers using their mobile devices to compare prices with online retail websites, Macy's found ways of including mobile devices in its in-store shopping experience. Macy's has been a pioneer of mobile payment systems and product discovery applications. For instance, the company featured QR codes on signage next to fashion collections. When scanned by a customer, the QR code generated videos about the collection and designer(s). If a store is out-of-stock on a product, employees will show customers how they can find what they want and buy it using the store's mobile app. The company still considers that a win.

Novel and unique tech-based merchandising For several years, Macy's has used a variety of eye-catching and attractive shelving fixtures, display lighting, and interactive technology to create novel merchandising opportunities on the sales floor. Examples include Macy's B8ta merchandising concept that features cool new tech products that are likely to appeal to the young technology geek inside all of us. Or Macy's interactive Fragrance Bars, a merchandising concept that presents customers with perfume samples from each of the six different scents families, and screens next to the samples that display product information and branding messages. The Market @ Macy's is another merchandising concept that uses pop-up style fixtures that feature several unique and interesting products from smaller, sometimes cause-centered organizations and manufacturers. As part of the promotion for this merchandising concept, Macy's has partnered with Facebook, clearly an attempt to hopefully engage with customers via social media.

Augmented and virtual reality Macy's was an early adopter of augmented and virtual reality for in-store retailing. Some of its more recent applications include a furniture shopping experience called "Visualize Your Space," which allows customers to place pieces of furniture they see in the store into the customer's living space by projecting images of them from their smartphone, to provide a more realistic estimation of how the furniture will look at home. Aside from engaging customers with a novel and interesting technology, Macy's expects that the tool will reduce the amount of product returns to the furniture department.

Mobile payment systems Over the years, Macy's has encouraged customers to use mobile payment and experimented with different systems as mobile payment technology evolved. Currently, the mobile-friendly retailer is promoting Macy's "My Wallet," a mobile wallet app that customers can use to manage payment information, promotions, and Macy's coupons. Mobile payment is also available to customers using the Scan & Pay feature on the Macy's store app.

Despite Macy's omnichannel strategy and its liberal use of emerging technologies, the company has struggled over the last decade and has forced to close many of its store-based operations. Some retail experts question if Macy's can survive in this ever-changing and competitive retail marketplace given its roots as a department store retailer. That suggests there might be structural problems with the company's business model that can't be fixed by showing off the latest, coolest tech to today's customers.

Sources: Compiled from Amato-McCoy (2018), ARPost (2018), Verdon (2019), and Bohannon (2020).

In-Store Tech Improves Convenience and Enhances the Shopping Experience

To describe all the different technologies used by store-based retailers today would be a monumental task. Many important computer technologies used in stores would likely be perceived as relatively mundane by most people. Take, for instance, the modern cash register used to record all the transactions that take place when large numbers of shoppers purchase their products prior to leaving the store. Most electronic cash registers are essentially dedicated computer workstations linked to a store's network and are responsible for transferring data to one or more data warehouses where it can be used for accounting, inventory management, customer relationship management (CRM), and so on. These are important, even critical functions for the success of the business, but electronic cash registers are probably not going to be something that differentiates a retailer in today's environment. Many of the standard or traditional technologies used by retailers today are described in other parts of this textbook. In this section, you will read about emerging and innovative technologies that are relatively new to store-based retailers, with a special emphasis on technologies designed to improve a retailer's performance on product, price, or convenience, the three factors identified earlier as being most important for a majority of shoppers (Gilliland, 2019).

Free, In-Store Wi-Fi to Aid Shoppers Using Mobile Devices   Store managers were initially frustrated by consumers empowered by mobile devices. Now, stores that have adopted omnichannel retail systems have adapted. Many stores offer free Wi-Fi connections to customers, allowing stores to collect useful data from consumers that connect to their in-store network. This allows retailers to track customer behavior across all channels—store, Web, and mobile. Stores can also study traffic patterns to learn where customers spend time in the store, what attracts their attention, and how shoppers navigate through the different parts of a store.

Autonomous Shopping Carts   Some traditional retailers are looking at technology such as autonomous shopping carts that follow a customer instead of having to be pushed around a store. This could certainly make shopping more convenient for some shoppers, but this type of technology is still considered experimental.

Nike Speed Shop   In its NYC flagship store, Nike introduced a service where consumers could go online to select the different shoes they wanted to try on. Then, Nike employees would collect those shoes and place them in a special locker for the customer, saving the customer time and effort during in-store shopping experience (Wertz, 2018).

Increased Use of In-Store Digital Displays   Retailers today are finding many novel ways to use in-store digital displays. Sometimes, the application is something as simple as a large screen monitor that displays slide shows or videos of products. But more innovative applications involve interactive displays. Bloomingdales in NYC placed large screens in their display windows that featured fashion products by Ralph Loren. Customers could interact with the screen via a touch pad and/or products on the display using their mobile phone. Customers didn't even have to go into the store. Other fashion retailers have experimented with a variety of "Smart Dressing Room" concepts that feature different kinds of interactive, touch-screen-style displays. Some have displays that make it easier for customers to scroll through images of different products, explore different colors or matching items, and determine if items are in-stock and where they product can be found in the store. Other dressing room applications feature touch screen displays that are built into mirrors or use augmented and virtual reality to show customers how they might look wearing different fashions without going through the drudgery of actually trying clothes on. In some stores, customers can use the displays to request additional clothes to try on or even order a beverage or a snack while selecting their new wardrobe. Another type of novel display is something you might see in a grocery store. The digital shelf edge is a small, but very long digital display that can be attached to the customer facing edge of a retail shelf. The unusually shaped screen constantly displays images related to the products that are next to it on the shelf. The images are constantly moving, which is specifically designed to be eye-catching.

Novel Payment Systems   One area that retailers have been working on for some time now is how to make payment easier and more convenient for shoppers. Most of the innovation in payment systems has been based on advances in mobile technologies that you will read about in Section 8.5 later in this chapter. As previously discussed, Amazon's cashierless stores are another example of innovation in how shoppers pay for their products. Another payment innovation that is becoming more commonplace is handheld devices that store employees can use to process customer transactions. These devices are sometimes replacing larger, traditional cash registers in smaller shops and restaurants, or are being used in larger stores as a way for employees to step in and quickly help customers when the regular checkout lines become too long.

Questions

1. When evaluating new services and/or technologies that might attract shoppers to a store-based retailer, what criteria should managers consider when evaluating innovations? In other words, what areas of performance should innovations be expected to improve in today's competitive retail environment?

2. If you were a retail manager, how would you evaluate the Nike Speed Shop service described in this section? Is this the kind of service that can scale over time? Would it become a sustainable competitive advantage for retailers who decided to provide the service?

3. What are some examples of experiential retail that are likely to appeal to younger shoppers in their late teens and early 20s?

4. Why does it make sense to offer free in-store Wi-Fi connections given the way that people like to shop these days?

5. Out of the three most important factors that influence where people shop, why is convenience probably the one that retailers should focus on the most (instead of product and price)?

8.3 E-commerce—Online Retailing

LO8.3 Identify *the different markets served by online retailers and the strategies and technologies they use to conduct e-commerce.*

During the late 1990s, the idea of purchasing things online was still a novel concept. People who purchased books and other low-priced items from websites were innovators. Nowadays, shopping for things online and comparing prices among different retailers are common consumer behaviors. In the past decade, the variety of goods and services available through e-commerce sites has skyrocketed. If you look through older textbooks in the IT field, you will find examples of authors predicting that e-commerce will only be successful with small, low-priced consumer goods. But we now know this is simply not the case. People today purchase everything from toothpaste to cars, houses, and diamond rings online. E-commerce in the business-to-business (B2B) sector is even larger than it is in the business-to-consumer (B2C) marketplace.

E-commerce is now used in almost every industry and marketplace. In this section, we briefly describe the major online markets where e-commerce is used.

Types of E-commerce Markets

Business to Consumer (B2C) B2C e-commerce takes place when a retail business sells products or services online to end users. Many e-commerce businesses are **pure play e-commerce retailers**. However, traditional retailers that used to only operate in physical stores are now creating online retail websites, and e-commerce retailers have begun to branch out into store-based retailing. When a retailer operates in both e-commerce and store-based channels, it creates opportunities for omnichannel retail practices that consumers say they like. Most of the top 10 U.S. e-commerce retailers also have physical store-based operations (see **Figure 8.3**).

Pure play e-commerce retailers are retailers that only operate online (the Web) and do not use other channels such as mobile or in-store retailing.

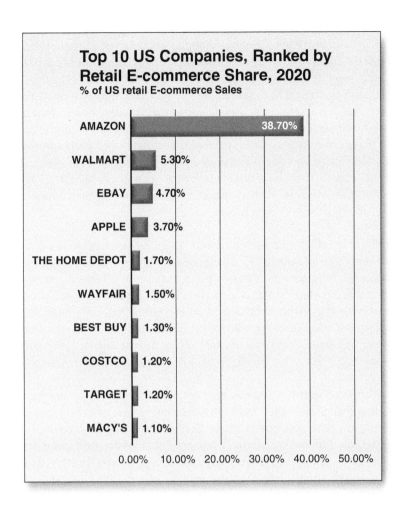

FIGURE 8.3   The relative market share of the top e-commerce retailers (adapted from WARC, 2019).

Many of the technologies used for e-commerce were originally developed for the online B2C market before being utilized in other commerce markets. Some of the relatively new e-commerce trends occurring today are listed in the following sections (Ahlenius, 2019).

Mass Personalization   Personalization involves a variety of strategies for making customized advertisements, product recommendations, pricing, and delivery options based on information about a consumer's preferences, context, browsing, and shopping behaviors. Two examples illustrate how online retailers might use personalization to increase sales. First, retailers might use data about a customer's past purchases and the purchase behavior of other demographically similar customers to recommend new products. Second, instead of using uniform pricing, the retailer might develop personalized prices based on information about individual customers. Unlike store-based retailers, e-commerce retailers can collect a lot of information about individual shoppers and then use that information to develop personalized offers where the products, prices, and promotional messages might vary from what is offered to other customers. The accuracy and value of these personalized offers can then be tested (see A/B Testing below) to see if further adjustments can be made to optimize the yield from these personalized offers.

It is well known that Amazon and other e-commerce retailers personalize the products displayed on their websites based on the company's recommendation system. Online advertisers also have the capability of presenting different messages to customers based on what they know about a shopper's behavior. In fact, it is the ability to target individuals or small groups of individuals with customized offers that makes e-commerce and digital marketing so attractive to businesses.

Clearly, not everyone is comfortable with the amount of information that e-commerce businesses collect and distribute about our shopping and Internet use behaviors. Companies face significant challenges when using personalization strategies. On one hand, personalization provides Internet users and shoppers with more relevant information in the form of products and advertisements that might have something to do with our interests and needs. However, companies also risk consumer trust and confidence if they use data in ways that people feel is invasive or overly self-serving. One way that some companies have attempted to be more transparent about the use of consumer data is to create loyalty or reward programs that customers can opt-in to and receive benefits in exchange for the use of their data (Heist, 2020). These benefits typically come in the form of discounts, premiums, or other special treatment. Studies have shown that consumers are much more accepting about sharing their data when given the opportunity to opt-in to these kinds of programs.

Use of Artificial Intelligence Applications Because it is possible for e-commerce companies to collect so much information about individual shoppers, it can be challenging to identify patterns and trends in large data sets that are able to guide decision-making. Artificial intelligence applications, specifically machine learning, can be used to sort and analyze big data and guide strategic decision-making on product offerings, pricing, promotion, and personalization efforts. Other types of artificial intelligence applications can power various types of work automation and customer service features such as chat bots that can use natural language processing to answer customer questions online. Artificial intelligence will be discussed in detail in Chapter 11.

Recommendation Systems As you read in Chapter 7, many e-commerce retailers use recommendation engines to suggest products that customers are most likely to find attractive. Online retailers have even developed tools for personalizing product recommendations that shoppers see when visiting an e-commerce website. Recommendation systems typically use information about the shopper to create these customized product recommendations. Some of the data used by recommendation systems includes information about the shopper's past purchases, search history, demographic characteristics, and information about other shoppers that share things in common with the target customer. **IT at Work 8.3** describes how companies from hair care to travel agencies are successfully using the weather to personalize items for their customers to increase revenue and improve customer satisfaction.

IT at Work 8.3

Companies Personalize E-commerce Based on the Weather

Recently, a variety of companies have been experimenting with adding users' local weather to the list of data points used by a company's recommendation system. As you will read in this IT at Work, this approach seems to have had a positive impact on sales at the websites where this new approach has been used.

Fashion brand Burton used a weather API on its website to determine the weather conditions at a user's location. Based on the weather information, product images matching the user's weather condition were displayed on the Web page (e.g., sweaters and wool coats and gloves for people in snowy and cold weather, lighter shirts and light weight jacket when the weather was warm and sunny). As a result of using weather-based targeting, Burton saw an 11.6% uptick in website conversions.

Pantene, maker of hair care products, chose to focus on weather-related hair conditions. The company first determined what weather-related phenomena caused bad hair days (e.g., things like high humidity or dry heat). Then, the company partnered with The Weather Channel (TWC) to run ads during forecasts that involved these kinds of weather condition likely to cause concern for the appearance of one's hair. Along with the Pantene ads, customers received coupons and directions to the nearest store. Pantene reported a remarkable 28% increase in sales during the campaign.

TUI, a British Travel Company, wanted to increase bookings for holiday vacations. TUI partnered with an online weather service used by people to get weather forecasts. According to the plan, whenever the weather at a user's location was cold, rainy, with snow, or wind, a TUI ad was displayed that featured images of sunny, warm weather at the beach. As a result, the company reported a significant increase in vacation bookings and returned to the weather website for an extension of the original campaign.

Sources: Compiled from Brebion (2016), Kacmaz (2016), Huff (2017), Alexis (2018), Hall (2020), and Morris (2020).

Based on a somewhat limited number of use cases, it appears that weather can in fact influence consumer interest and behavior. Other companies that have experienced positive results from weather-based personalization include Lipton Iced Tea, BMW, Molson, and the clothing brand "George." Therefore, using weather information to determine the nature of the ads or products featured on an e-commerce website makes sense. While recommendation engines have already proven their value, there is still a lot of work that can be done to improve the performance of existing recommendation systems.

A/B Testing of Product, Price, and Promotional Tactics Another advantage that e-commerce retailers have compared to store-based retail is that they can more easily optimize various aspects of what they offer to customers. A common example of this is the use of A/B testing with digital advertising. An e-commerce retailer can run two different digital ad messages (A and B) to see which one attracts more customers to their website. After tracking the performance of each ad over a period of time, the retailer determines which ad was most successful and uses it to replace less successful advertisements. Some retailers are constantly engaged in testing as a way of continuously improving marketing performance and customer experience.

Consumer Use of DVAs for Search, Research, and Ordering As you read in Chapter 7, people are increasingly using DVAs. E-commerce retailers are still learning how to use DVAs to increase online sales. But voice assistant technologies seem to be popular, and, therefore, we anticipate that online retailers will look for ways to leverage these systems to improve online sales. You can see how marketing executives from around the world think about the importance of DVA and other emerging technologies in **Figure 8.4**.

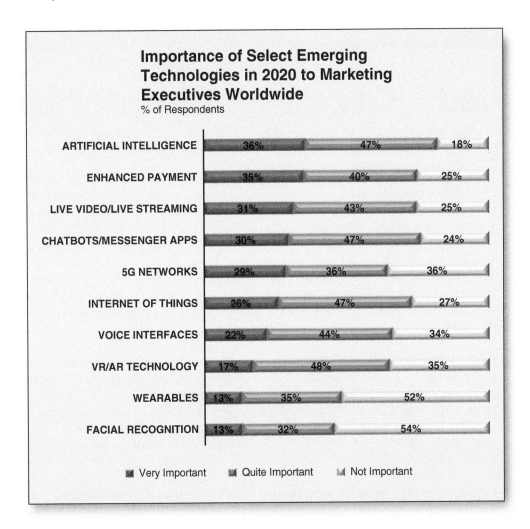

FIGURE 8.4 How marketing executives around the world view the importance of emerging technologies (adapted from WARC, 2019).

Business to Business (B2B) E-Commerce

In B2B e-commerce, the buyers, sellers, and transactions are conducted between organizations. It covers applications that enable an organization to form electronic relationships with its distributors, resellers, suppliers, customers, and other partners. By using B2B e-commerce, organizations can restructure their supply chains and partner relationships. Forrester reports that **business-to-business (B2B) e-commerce** will reach $1.8 trillion and account for 17% of all B2B sales in the United States by 2023 (Bonde et al., 2018). Compared to other types of e-commerce, B2B comprises a striking 85% of all e-commerce dollar volume.

There are several business models for B2B e-commerce applications. The major ones are sell-side marketplaces and e-sourcing (the buy-side marketplace) and are described next.

Sell-Side B2B Marketplaces

There are basically two types of e-commerce in sell-side B2B markets: direct and marketplace. In the **direct e-commerce** model, the buyer organization is expected to come to a single seller's site to view catalogs and place an order. In **marketplace e-commerce**, the products of multiple companies are offered for purchase by one marketplace operator. The marketplace model creates much greater competition for the companies that sell their products on the site and therefore creates an advantage for buyer organizations. For this reason, some sellers prefer the direct model. A recent introduction of a B2B marketplace website is Amazon Business. Alibaba is an example of a B2B marketplace e-commerce site that primarily sells products from Chinese manufacturers to other companies around the world. Other marketplace B2B platforms include DHgate, eWorldTrade, and TradeKey.

> **Direct e-commerce** involves organizations selling their products or services directly to other organizations from their own private website or one managed by a third party.
>
> **Marketplace e-commerce** is where product or service information is provided by multiple third parties and transactions are processed by one marketplace operator.

To avoid the cut-throat competition that can be produced by marketplace e-commerce sites, some B2B sellers are integrating back-office solutions to their direct e-commerce sites that add extra value to their buyers and create exit barriers for customers. For example, integrated B2B solutions can include things such as:

- Digital order writing for fields sales staff.
- Automated order sync that integrates orders with accounting or other administrative software.
- Integrations with Enterprise Resource Planning (ERP) systems. These integrated solutions can streamline the procurement process, saving the buyer time and money, giving them a reason to stay with a seller that offers these benefits.

B2B e-commerce websites are used by hundreds of thousands of companies. This strategy can be especially powerful for companies with superb reputations. The seller can be either a manufacturer (e.g., IBM), or a distributor (e.g., avnet.com is an example of a large distributor in IT), or a retailer (e.g., Office Depot). The seller uses e-commerce to increase sales, reduce selling and advertising expenditures, increase delivery speed, and reduce administrative costs. Some B2B sellers such as Dell Computers use auctions extensively. In addition to auctions from their own websites, organizations can use third-party auction sites, such as eBay, to liquidate items. Companies such as Overstock help organizations auction obsolete and excess assets and inventories.

E-Sourcing (Buy-Side Marketplaces)

E-sourcing refers to many different procurement methods that make use of an electronic venue for identifying, evaluating, selecting, negotiating, and collaborating with suppliers. The primary methods are online auctions, RFQ (request for quote) processing, and private exchanges. E-sourcing also applies to many other secondary activities, which add to the cycle time and transaction costs when performed using traditional methods. Secondary activities include trading partner collaboration, contract negotiation, and supplier selection.

E-Procurement

Corporate procurement, also called **corporate purchasing**, deals with the transactional elements of buying products and services by an organization for its operational and functional needs. Organizations procure materials to produce finished goods, which is referred to as **direct procurement**, and products for daily operational needs, which is referred to as **indirect procurement**. **E-procurement** refers to the reengineered procurement process using e-business technologies and strategies. Strategies and solutions linked to e-procurement have two basic goals:

- **Control costs.** The first goal is to control corporate spending. Organizations want to spend intelligently for procurement activities to maximize the value of their spending, that is, to ensure that money spent to procure items results in procuring the right products at the best value. Corporate e-procurement constitutes a substantial portion of an organization's operational spending. For example, it is common for large manufacturing organizations to spend millions of U.S. dollars procuring products and services. Organizations thus design e-procurement systems to facilitate and control overall procurement spending.
- **Simplify processes.** The second goal is to streamline the procurement process to make it efficient. Inefficiencies in the procurement process introduce delays in ordering and receiving items and tax internal resources.

The two goals of cost control and streamlining can be met in three ways:

1. Streamline the e-procurement process within an organization's value chain. Doing so reduces the number of employees needed to process purchasing, reduces the procurement cycle time to order and receive items, and empowers an organization's staff with enough information about the products and services to enable them to make intelligent decisions when procuring items.

2. Align the organization's procurement process with those of other trading partners, which belong to the organization's virtual supply chain. Alignment can be achieved by automating the process from end to end, including trading partner's systems, and simplifies the buying process. This enables suppliers to react efficiently to buyers' needs.

3. Use appropriate e-procurement strategies and solutions. Organizations analyze spending patterns to improve spending decisions and outcomes.

Electronic Data Interchange (EDI) Systems   EDI systems are typically set up by large companies for the efficient procurement of products from an assortment of established vendors. While EDI technologies predate large-scale use of the Internet, most EDI systems now use the Internet as the primary method of transmitting data. EDI systems are designed to efficiently exchange documents, eliminating many of the costs associated with processing paper documents. As such, they lend themselves to buyers and suppliers that need to convey information to each other in the form of purchase orders, invoices, bills of lading, customs documents, shipping status documents, payment documents, and so on. While EDIs use the Internet for data transmission, they are not accessible to the public. Instead, only approved or authorized vendors are given access to a company's EDI system.

Other E-commerce Markets   While B2C and B2B e-commerce account for most online sales today, other types of e-commerce marketplaces are emerging. The **direct-to-consumer (D2C) marketplace** is composed of businesses that ship their products directly to consumers without using wholesalers, distributors, or other middlemen that play a role in other retail channels. Examples of popular D2C brands include Dollar Shave Club, BarkBox (dog toys and treats), Bonobos (men's clothing), Casper (mattresses), and Warby Parker (glasses and prescription eyeglasses). Many D2C companies have been pioneers of the subscription marketing business model.

Another online market is the **peer-to-peer (P2P) marketplace**. Broadly defined, P2P business model is based on exchanges that occur between two individuals (Erne, 2018). In the P2P marketplace, there are several examples of different types of P2P e-commerce. For instance, eBay and Craigslist are two established platforms designed to facilitate exchanges or transactions between individuals. They essentially replace garage sales, classified newspaper ads, and small shops that sell collectible items. That said, there are many examples of entrepreneurs who have discovered ways to also use these marketplaces as part of their business enterprise. Airbnb and ride-sharing services such as Uber and Lyft are newer P2P brands that have become very popular and are part of what some people refer to as the gig economy. Supporting P2P transactions are systems that make it easy for individuals to transfer money to each other. Examples of P2P payment systems include services like Zelle, Venmo, and the Square Cash App.

Challenges to E-commerce

Despite the tremendous growth of online retailers, many face challenges that can interfere with business growth. Major issues include the following:

1. **Resolving channel conflict** Sellers that are click-and-mortar companies, such as Levi's or GM, face a conflict with their regular wholesale and retail distributors when they circumvent those distributors by selling online directly to customers. (These distributors are other businesses that carry the company's product.) This situation is called **channel conflict** because it is a conflict between an online selling channel and physical selling channels. Channel conflict has forced some companies to limit their B2C efforts or not to sell direct online. An alternative approach is to try to collaborate in some way with the existing distributors whose services may be restructured. For example, an auto company could allow customers to configure a car online but require that the car be picked up from a dealer, where customers could also arrange financing, warranties, and service.

2. **Resolving conflicts within click-and-mortar organizations** When an established company sells online directly to customers, it creates conflict with its own offline operations. Conflicts may arise in areas such as pricing of products and services, allocation of resources (e.g., advertising budget), and logistics services provided by the offline activities to the online activities (e.g., handling of returns of items bought online). To minimize this type of conflict, companies may separate the online division from the traditional division. The downside is that separation can increase expenses and reduce the synergy between the two organizational parts.

3. **Managing order fulfillment and logistics** Online retailers face tough order fulfillment and logistics problems when selling online because of the need to design systems that accept and process a huge volume of small orders, to physically pick items from warehouse shelves and put them into boxes, to be sure that the correct labels are applied, and to accept returns. The return process is referred to as reverse logistics.

4. **Determining viability and risk of online retailers** Many pure play online retailers went bankrupt in the early days of online retailing, the result of problems with cash flow, customer acquisition, order fulfillment, and demand forecasting. Online competition, especially in commodity products such as CDs, toys, books, or groceries, became very fierce due to the ease of entry into the marketplace. As Porter's (2008) five competitive forces model explains, low entry barriers intensify competition in an industry. A problem most new and established online retailers face is to determine how long to operate while still losing money and how to finance those losses.

5. **Identifying appropriate revenue (business) models** During the early days of Internet based business, many companies failed to articulate a clear business model. Venture capital firms, entrepreneurs, and technology visionaries all had very high expectations for companies that did business online, but many of these firms did not have a clear plan for monetizing their activities, and because the Internet was so new, many investors and venture capital firms weren't quite sure how to value Internet based businesses. Eventually, a lot of companies closed, and a lot of early investments were lost. Today, most companies have a clear idea of how they plan to make money and investors are much more knowledgeable about the challenges that online businesses face and the different business models they can use to generate revenue and profits.

Channel conflict Competition between a manufacturer's distribution partners who sell through different channels. Channel conflict can occur at the wholesale, retail, or internal sales department level.

E-commerce Business and Strategic Planning

The process of online marketing planning is very similar to the development of any other marketing plan. Unfortunately, organizations don't always follow best practice and instead devise separate online and offline plans, which is contrary to the holistic way in which customers perceive a business. Here are several online business and planning recommendations:

1. Build the marketing plan around the customer, rather than on products.
2. Monitor progress toward the one-year vision for the business in order to identify when adjustments are needed, and then be agile enough to respond.
3. Identify all key assumptions in the marketing plan. When there is evidence that those assumptions are wrong, identify the new assumptions and adjust the plan.
4. Make data-driven, fact-based decisions and plans.

Questions

1. Explain the differences between the various types of e-commerce marketplaces.
2. Why does channel conflict sometimes occur when companies sell their products through both traditional and online channels?
3. Explain the challenges faced by e-commerce companies that use personalization strategies to customize the advertisements and product recommendations that customers see when shopping online. How do some companies try to increase transparency regarding how they use consumer data?
4. Describe some of the new technologies being used by e-commerce retailers to improve service, convenience, and user experience.
5. List three online marketing planning recommendations.

8.4 | Mobile Commerce

LO8.4 Understand *how mobile technologies are creating opportunities for new forms of commerce in both new and established industries.*

Ever since the late 1990s, industry experts and pundits have been predicting that mobile commerce was about to become "the next big thing" in marketing and the sale of consumer goods. Before we explore how mobile commerce has evolved since 1997, let us define some terms related to this topic:

Mobile commerce or m-commerce   The buying or selling of goods and services using a wireless, handheld device such as a smartphone or tablet (slate) computer.

Mobile e-commerce   The use of a wireless, handheld devices, to order and/or pay for goods and services from online vendors. For example, a customer can order a pair of shoes from Zappos.com using a mobile app or purchase music from iTunes from their smartphone.

Mobile retailing   The use of mobile technology to promote, enhance, and add value to the in-store shopping experience. For example, a customer can use a coupon on their smartphone when paying for their meal at the Hard Rock Café, or "check in" to a retail location using a mobile app from ShopKick.com or Foursquare.com.

Mobile marketing   A variety of activities used by organizations to engage, communicate, and interact over Wi-Fi and telecommunications networks with consumers using wireless, handheld devices. For example, a company can send special offers to customers who have opted-in to receive discounts via SMS text message or advertise a brand on a popular mobile game app.

These four terms are not mutually exclusive. Mobile e-commerce, mobile retailing, and mobile marketing are all forms of mobile commerce. Mobile e-commerce emphasizes the use of mobile apps and mobile websites for carrying out transactions and does not necessarily involve interaction with a traditional retail store. Mobile retailing, on the other hand, emphasizes in-store shopping using a mobile device but could include situations where the customer ultimately orders from a website or mobile app. Mobile marketing is the term used to describe promotional strategies and tactics that encourage both mobile e-commerce and mobile retail. This overlap reflects the evolution toward the omnichannel retail concept discussed earlier in this chapter.

Although there have been some interesting and even successful examples of m-commerce since 1997, predictions about mobile technology becoming a pervasive force in consumer retailing have proven overly optimistic until recently. There are several reasons why consumers and businesses have been slow to embrace m-commerce:

- Relatively primitive mobile devices (compared to modern smartphones and tablets)
- Concerns about privacy and security
- Slow network connection speeds
- Limited market size
- Limited and inconvenient mobile payment options
- Lack of technological standardization (devices, OSs, browsers, etc.)

However, many of these barriers have been reduced or eliminated. As you read in the previous section, the number of people who now own mobile devices, particularly smartphones, has grown dramatically. According to one widely quoted statistic, more people own smartphones today than own toothbrushes! Telecommunications carriers have expanded their coverage of populated areas using high-speed networks. Modern smartphones and tablet devices have features that make shopping via bright colorful screens fun and easy. Mobile devices have become the dominant way that people engage in many types of Internet activity, such as social media, and Web search. In many countries, far more people own mobile devices compared to those who own personal computers. While security will always be an evolving concern, consumer comfort with completing transactions on mobile devices continues to grow. Several mobile payment methods are emerging that are more convenient than traditional transaction methods. So finally, after years of waiting, it appears that earlier predictions about m-commerce are finally coming true. In this section, we describe some of the many ways businesses and consumers are using mobile technologies to buy and sell goods and services.

Mobile Advertising

Because mobile smartphones and other handheld devices have become ubiquitous, it makes sense for companies to find effective ways of advertising to customers on the mobile screen. Some advertisements are analogous to television advertisements. For instance, many "free" mobile apps are supported by in-app advertisements, like the ads you might see while playing a game on your smartphone, or ads you might see while watching YouTube videos on a mobile device. Frequently, mobile app developers will offer two versions of an app. One will be free, but feature advertisements during use, and the other will require payment for the app that can then be used without displaying ads. Another type of advertisement is unique to mobile devices. Location-based advertisements can be pushed out to a user's home screen or text message app when certain criteria are met. For instance, if a customer has a mobile app from a chain of coffee restaurants, and they happen to walk near one of the restaurants, the app might push out a message ad that that encourages customers to come to the store for a holiday beverage or a special offer. Advertisers can also send promotional text messages to customers that have opted in to receive advertising messages from the company.

Mobile Apps

Many retail businesses can benefit by encouraging customers to download brand specific mobile apps. Successful apps typically provide features that provide enhanced convenience and service to customers using the app. For instance, many companies in the travel industry have developed apps that make it easy for travelers to purchase tickets, make reservations, check-in at the airport or hotel, make it easier to by-pass the counter at rental car agencies, and so on. Many companies that have developed and distributed apps have found that they can increase brand value to customers, enhance brand loyalty, and boost company sales and profits.

Information: Competitive Advantage in Mobile Commerce

As you can see from reading **IT at Work 8.4**, integrating mobile technology with a brand's retail and e-commerce strategy provides another important benefit to business: customer information and identification. When customers interact with a brand using a mobile device, information is collected about the customer that can be used to optimize the interaction. For instance, when customers use a brand's mobile app to shop for products, their shopping experience can be customized based on the company's knowledge of previous purchases, payment methods, product preferences, and even location.

IT at Work 8.4

Dunkin Donuts Mobile Marketing

Founded in 1950, Dunkin Donuts has more than 12,900 restaurants in 42 countries worldwide. Many people take their coffee and donuts to go, and so it was natural for the popular restaurant chain to develop a mobile marketing strategy that reflected its customer's increasing use of mobile technology. Dunkin was an innovator and pioneer in mobile marketing. In 2009, Dunkin created a mobile social network called Dunkin Run based on the premise that single individuals are often tasked with picking up a group's order from one of the chain's restaurants. The mobile app allowed different people to tell the person making the Dunkin Run what kind of food or beverage they wanted. In the early days of mobile retailing, this was an impressive first step for the company.

Nowadays, Dunkin's mobile strategies are more complex and exciting. Dunkin Donuts customers cannot only place orders from the company's mobile app, but as of 2018, customers also place voice orders using either an iPhone or an Android phone. In addition to placing orders, customers can use the app to rack up points in the company's reward program, called DD Perks Rewards. Like other loyalty programs, the purpose of the program is to encourage customer retention and visits to the restaurant chain. While only a small portion of Dunkin Donut's customers use the mobile device to place orders, the company has learned that customers that use the app save the company money by simplifying the order process. Also, orders that come from the app only take about 30% of the time it takes for people to order in person. As a result, the app does a good job increasing the company's ability to serve people and get them out of the store quickly.

Dunkin Donuts expects to continue being a leader in the use of innovative but practical technologies that aid them in providing good products efficiently to their customers.

Sources: Compiled from Olenski (2017), Dunkin Donuts (2018, 2019), Liffreing (2018), and Peterson (2018).

In-Store Tracking In-store shopping experiences can be optimized through mobile technology that can track a customer's movement through a retail store. This is analogous to e-commerce sites that track the pages a customer looks at to better understand consumer interests and to make decisions about website design. Tracking how a customer moves through a store, noting what displays the customer looks at, or what departments the customer spends the most time in can be extremely helpful for understanding individual consumer preferences as well as creating optimal store layout. Systems for tracking customers based on signals emitted from smartphones and other mobile devices are being deployed. However, stores must be cautious about how they use these systems because consumers generally respond quite negatively to the idea when asked.

Consumers generally do not trust stores to keep their data private or secure. Recent news stories about data breaches involving credit card and other information at large retailers suggest there is reason for concern. Stores that use "opt-in" methods, receiving the customer's permission in exchange for some defined benefit, are more likely to get a positive reception. Those that opt-in typically expect to receive discounts or some form of meaningful convenience benefit. Some will only agree to **in-store tracking** in exchange for free products. Consumer acceptance is sometimes accomplished through loyalty programs that offer discounts and special premiums to customers who opt-in.

Not all tracking systems rely on user smartphones. Disney uses signal emitting wristbands to make everything in the Magic Kingdom more magical. The wristbands aid guests with hotel check-ins, replace tickets for park admission, make it easy to reserve times for popular rides, and even help Disney employees to deliver the correct dinners to hungry guests in large, crowded restaurants. Still, retailers and the makers of in-store tracking systems need to be concerned about consumer backlash related to this new technology since less magical applications are considered "creepy" by many shoppers. Therefore, it is important that brands involved in mobile e-commerce and mobile retailing have clear privacy statements and use an opt-in system to obtain permission from customers before tracking their online and offline shopping behaviors.

While relatively few businesses fully utilize mobile tracking and monitoring systems at present, as brands become more sophisticated with mobile technology, it is expected they will strive to gain a competitive advantage by using this information to provide better service, convenience, and a more personalized, enjoyable shopping experience, both online and in traditional stores.

QR Codes in Mobile Marketing

In Japan, QR codes are used in mobile marketing more often than in the United States. Consumers in that country frequently use their mobile devices to scan QR codes using the camera and bar code reader apps. QR codes frequently contain links to a Web page with product information. The QR code is supposed to be an easier alternative to typing a URL address into a **mobile browser** (see **Figure 8.5**). While QR codes have not been as popular in the United States as they are in Asia, marketers have used them in print advertising and direct mail ads with some success. Charitable organizations use QR codes on the outside of direct mail solicitations. Scanning the code takes the user to a video explaining the mission of the organization and typically makes a more compelling request for a donation than is possible through print media. Additionally, responses to the QR code promotions can be tracked and used to evaluate program effectiveness.

Mobile browser A Web browser that is optimized to display Web content effectively on a small mobile device such as a smartphone.

FIGURE 8.5 Smartphone users can scan QR codes that help them easily access product information on the Internet without the hassle of typing a URL code into a mobile browser.

Some experts believe, however, that QR code technology will never be as popular in the United States as it is in Asia. They cite studies reporting that many smartphone users simply do not know what to do with a QR code. Other research suggests users think that the scanning process is inconvenient or that QR codes frequently direct users to pages that do not really contain anything of interest. For QR codes to become something American consumers use frequently, businesses will have to prove that they help mobile users find content that is interesting and valuable.

Mobile Entertainment

Mobile entertainment is expanding on wireless devices. Many mobile apps have been created for music, movies, videos, games, adult entertainment, and gambling. Sports enthusiasts enjoy many apps and services on their mobile devices. Apps exist to check game scores; track news about specific athletes, teams, or sports; take part in fantasy team contests such as fantasy football; and participate in sports-oriented social networking services. Several sports-related games such as mobile golf and sports trivia apps are widely available. There are even apps designed to provide tips and information for improving your own athletic performance. Apps are available to record workout times, schedule training exercises, record heart rates and a variety of other information related to athletic training. The iPhone even has an app that analyzes a person's golf swing and provides advice for improving performance.

ESPN is widely acknowledged as a leader in mobile marketing to the sports fan. It offers several popular branded mobile apps that deliver information and entertainment to its target audience. It also utilizes well-designed mobile websites and has a large database of fans that have opted in to receive sports-related news alerts sent to their phones via text messages.

Industry analysts predict that recent improvements in mobile devices will lead to an even bigger increase in the number of people who watch video clips, movies, and television programming on their mobile devices. The screen size of tablet computers makes watching video programming more attractive than on a smartphone. However, the number of people viewing video on smartphones seems to be increasing, while at the same time smartphone screen sizes are increasing. Popular fee-based video streaming services such as Netflix, Amazon, and Hulu now offer mobile apps for most mobile devices.

The iTunes Store, Google, and Amazon continue to be leading distributors of digital music, movies, TV shows, e-books, and podcasts available to consumers. Mobile users can also access music from digital streaming sites such as Pandora and Spotify. Both services offer free streaming music. Users can upgrade their accounts by paying a subscription fee, which then reduces the amount of advertising they are exposed to.

While still relatively small, the mobile gambling industry is expected to grow substantially over the next few years. Some predict that this type of mobile commerce could generate as much as $20 billion soon. Primary growth of this market is expected to take place in Japan and other Asian countries, such as horse racing in Hong Kong. Current laws in the United States prohibit most forms of online gambling; consequently, gambling via mobile devices is largely unavailable in the United States.

Many mobile apps are available for consumers interested in home-based entertainment activities. The Food Network offers an app with tips and recipes for fine dining and entertaining. Martha Stewart publishes articles about home entertainment and lifestyle apps while several bartending apps with numerous cocktail recipes can be found on iTunes and Google Play.

Hotel Services and Travel Go Wireless

In recent years, smartphones and other mobile devices have become essential travel aids. Most major airlines, hotel chains, and Internet travel agencies have developed mobile apps to help travelers manage their arrangements. Airlines frequently give passengers the option of receiving up-to-date information about their flights through an app or via **short message service (SMS)** text messaging. Google Maps is perhaps one of the most popular apps used by travelers, because it offers different directions and options for people depending on how they are

Short message service (SMS) is a technology installed on most mobile phones for sending and receiving brief text messages.

traveling: by car, public transportation, bicycle, walking, or even air travel. The mapping app also shows travelers where they can find restaurants, hotels, stores, and other helpful services. Even AAA, the automobile club, has a mobile app that helps drivers plan their trips and an app for drivers who need roadside assistance. Other interesting mobile travel tools include apps that translate voice or text when traveling abroad, apps for finding nearby Wi-Fi hotspots, and apps created by several popular travel guides.

Most large hotel chains, independent hotels, and inns offer guests in-room, wireless high-speed Internet connections, although this is not always a free service. Some of these same hotels offer Wi-Fi Internet access in public areas such as the lobby and meeting rooms. Larger hotel chains have apps that allow guests to make reservations, check their bills, and locate hotel services using a mobile app. Starwood, Hilton, and other hotels have mobile check-in programs whereby guests use their mobile devices to gain access to their rooms. This makes it possible to check in to the hotel without having to stop first at the front desk. Most airlines now offer travelers the option of loading a boarding pass onto their mobile devices as demonstrated in **Figure 8.6**.

FIGURE 8.6 Travelers use mobile apps to book reservations, find directions, and locate reviews and recommendations for a wide range of travel and hospitality services.

Mobile Social Networking

More people access social media from social apps than from personal computers now. As a result, Facebook and other popular social media sites have added mobile features in recent years to stay competitive. Some social media sites, such as the popular Snapchat platform, is entirely app based. All the most popular social networking sites offer apps that allow users to access their accounts from a smartphone or other mobile device, making social media a primary driver of growth in the mobile app industry.

Questions

1. Describe some of the ways that people are using mobile devices to shop for products and services.
2. What are some ways in which traditional brick-and-mortar retailers can use mobile technology to enhance a customer's in-store shopping experience?
3. List four to five types of mobile entertainment apps that are widely available to consumers today.
4. List some ways that travelers and travel-related businesses are using mobile technology.
5. How are companies using QR codes to promote products and services to mobile consumers? Why are QR codes not as popular in the United States as they are in Asia and other parts of the world?
6. Explain why the mobile gaming market represents such a lucrative market opportunity for advertisers.

8.5 | Mobile Payment and Financial Services

LO8.5 Recognize *how mobile payment methods benefit both consumers and retailers.*

Mobile Payment Systems

Increasingly, consumers are using mobile devices to pay for products. Mobile payment is accepted by many retailers and is popular with consumers who now can use a variety of payment and P2P money transfer apps available on iTunes, Google Play, and from banks, credit card companies, and even smartphone manufacturers such as Samsung. Some forms of mobile payment represent an attractive option for consumers who do not have credit cards. Mobile payment is particularly important in third-world countries where many people do not have access to banking services. Additionally, retailers may benefit from new payment options that carry lower transaction costs compared to the service fees charged by many banks and credit card companies.

Proximity mobile payments, a common method based on RFID (Radio Frequency Identification) technology, typically allow consumers to transfer payment authorization to a vendor by simply tapping on or passing their phone over the vendor's mobile payment terminal.

While most consumer mobile payment systems are based on the use of a smartphone and related technologies such as SMS text messaging, some companies are building mobile payment into wristbands, key fobs, watches, and similar wearables. Lyle and Scott, a Scottish knitwear brand, has even built mobile payment into the wrist cuff of their jackets.

As mobile commerce grows, demand has increased for payment systems that make transactions from mobile devices convenient, safe, and secure. Several businesses have attempted to meet this demand using a variety of technologies. There are two basic transaction types of interest: using a mobile device for the online purchase of goods and services (e.g., ordering a book from Amazon.com) and for payment of goods and services in a traditional brick-and-mortar store. Here are examples of some approaches under development or in use today:

Charge to phone bill with SMS confirmation   This e-commerce payment solution is a lot easier than entering credit card and other information on a small mobile handheld device. It requires users to set up an account with a payment company such as Boku (**https://www.boku.com**). The amount of the charge is then added to the payer's phone bill, and the telecom carrier remits this amount to the payee. Telecom companies may deduct a service charge from the amount paid.

Near-field communication (NFC)   NFC is a high frequency form of RFID technology. Unlike other types of RFID technology, NFC devices are capable of both sending and receiving information with other NFC devices. At checkout, the mobile user simply passes or taps their phone next to a merchant terminal and payment is transferred. Users sometimes receive an SMS text message confirmation. NFC technologies can be used in conjunction with other payment systems like mobile wallets or store-specific payment apps. NFC systems are sometimes referred to as contactless payment systems.

Mobile wallet systems   Mobile wallet apps let a user enter information from one or more credit cards. To make a payment, the shopper uses a password or fingerprint to open the payment app and then selects the credit card account they wish to pay with. The mobile wallet app uses an NFC connection to transfer payment information to the retailer as described above. Examples of popular mobile wallet systems include PayPal, Apple Pay, Google Pay, and Samsung Pay, all of which only work on NFC-enabled mobile devices. Venmo, a subsidiary of PayPal, is a popular new mobile wallet designed as a P2P payment system and should work on any smartphone capable of sending and receiving SMS text messages. Venmo is currently available only to people who are physically in the United States and have a U.S. smartphone number.

QR code systems   Several companies are developing mobile payment systems that generate a QR code on the user's phone, which is, in turn, scanned by the retailer to complete the transaction. Other systems work by having the retailer generate a QR code, sometimes printed on a receipt, that is then scanned by the customer's mobile payment app. Finally, P2P payment apps require both users to open the payment app on their phone, and money is transferred when one user scans the code on the other user's phone. Walmart, Target, Dunkin Donuts, Dollar General, Macy's, and 7-Eleven are just a few of the many retailers that have adopted QR code payment systems (Staff, 2019).

SMS and secure payment screens   While not as popular in the United States, SMS payment systems are quite popular in other parts of the world. Payment is initiated when the retailer sends a text message to the purchaser's phone (purchasers can also initiate payment by sending a text to the retailer's short code). Once the order has been placed, the retailer sends a text message containing a link to a secure payment page created by the payment processing company. Users complete the process by entering their payment information on the secure page.

Mobile phone card reader   (See Square.com and Paypal.com) This novel approach requires retailers to connect a card reader device to their mobile phone or tablet. In the alternative, both companies offer other types of card readers that can process credit card security chips, or NFC payment devices. The card reader, which resembles a small cube (Square) or pyramid (PayPal), allows retailers to accept credit card payments using a mobile phone or tablet. Retailers can send receipts to customers via e-mail.

Almost all the payment systems thus described are illustrated by a variety of videos on Youtube.com. Interested readers are encouraged to view these video resources for a more complete explanation of how the different mobile payment systems work.

Wireless payment systems transform mobile phones into secure, self-contained purchasing tools capable of instantly authorizing payments over the cellular telecommunications network. One advantage of many mobile payment systems over traditional credit card systems is the ability to handle **micropayments** or transactions involving relatively small sums of money. The ability to make micropayments allows individuals to use their mobile devices to do things such as purchase a beverage from a vending machine or make a payment to a municipal parking meter. Many cities in Europe, and a growing number in the United States, have adopted mobile phone payment systems for parking and report dramatic increases in revenue because of the reduction in loss due to theft and broken meters and the reduced expense associated with collecting cash from traditional meters.

Mobile bill payments Many banks have created mobile banking apps with features that allow customers to access the bank's online bill pay service with their mobile device. As a result, customers can pay their regular bills for things such as utilities, phone service, and medical bills from a mobile device.

Mobile Banking and Financial Services

Mobile banking is generally defined as using a handheld device to perform banking transactions and other related activities. The services offered include bill payments and money transfers, depositing checks, account administration, balance inquiries, accessing account statements, and so on.

People access financial services using a combination of mobile media channels including SMS text messaging, mobile Web browsers, and customized banking apps. Mobile banking is a natural extension of online, or Web-based banking services, which have grown in popularity over the last decade.

To remain competitive, most banks in the United States offer some type of mobile banking service. As a result, almost 90% of banking customers report using a mobile banking app. The number rises to 97% when looking only at millennial customers. That said, customers of all ages have clearly adapted to mobile banking technology. While most mobile banking apps allow customers to perform common banking transactions, leaders in the industry are hard at work developing advanced banking apps with features such as the following:

- Using ATM machines with a mobile device instead of an ATM card.
- Customized text message alerts to warn customers of things like low account balances, large withdraws, or potentially fraudulent transactions.
- Applying for loans using a mobile banking app.
- Filling in "known information" on applications for loans or new accounts. Entering a lot of information on a mobile device can be challenging, so banks and credit unions that input information they already have about their customers will improve the bank's performance and make things more convenient for customers.
- Money management, credit management, and financial wellness tools that can be accessed from a mobile device.
- Integration with DVA systems. There is speculation that banks may eventually link their online and mobile banking systems to DVAs. If that happened, you might be able to say "Alexa, transfer $100 from my checking account to my savings account." Or you could ask Siri, "How much do I have in my savings account today?" Experts predict that tens of millions of people will use DVA-enabled banking transactions over the next five years (Phaneuf, 2019; Van Dyke, 2019).

Short Codes

Banks and financial service organizations have two basic options for providing mobile services. Smartphone users can download dedicated apps to conduct banking transactions. The other option is to provide service through SMS text message technology. As you know, text messaging is widely popular. Many mobile financial services make use of short codes for designating the recipient of SMS text messages. A **short code** works like a telephone number, except that it is only five or six characters long and easier to remember. Businesses lease short codes from the Common Short Code Association (CSCA) for $500 to $1,000 a month. The lower price is for randomly assigned codes, whereas companies that want a specific short code pay a higher monthly rate. Once a company has leased its short code, it can begin using that code in promotions and interactive exchanges with customers.

Short codes are used for a wide variety of SMS text services, not just financial services. For example, voting on the popular television show *American Idol* is done with short codes. Each contestant is assigned a specific short code, and viewers are encouraged to send text messages indicating which performer they like the best. The annual MTV Movie Awards also uses short code voting, which allows viewers to pick the winning entry in certain prize categories. On some telecommunications networks, ring tones are sold using short codes and SMS texts. **IT at Work 8.5** demonstrates how one not-for-profit organization successfully used short codes in its SMS-driven fundraising activities.

IT at Work 8.5

Bay Area Fire Relief Fund Surpasses Fundraising Goals with SMS Donation Strategy

Over the last few areas, California has experienced an increased number of wildfires, affecting tens of thousands of people, resulting in fatalities, property damage, and has cost the state billions of dollars in fire suppression efforts and aid to victims. The 2017 wildfire season was the worst year on record at the time, resulting in over 9,000 fires burning through more than 1.3 million acres of land. Over 10,000 structures were destroyed or severely damaged and 47 people (45 civilians and 2 firefighters) lost their lives. Tragically, the situation became even worse in 2018 when 8,527 fires destroyed almost 1.9 million acres, 22,751 buildings, and 97 civilians and 6 firefighters were killed.

Many different charitable organizations have responded to the situation by raising money to provide support for victims of wildfires. To aid victims of wildfires in nearby communities, the Bay Area Fire Relief Fund (BAFRF) was created. Working with other community businesses and organization, the fund spread the word that people could aid wildfire victims by donating to the fund using text messaging. Mobile giving has increased over the past decade, so fund organizers were hopeful the strategy would help them raise desperately needed funds to help wildfire victims.

So how do charities raise money using SMS technology? First, the charity must decide which of two donation strategies they will use in their fundraising efforts. The two options are (1) text to give and (2) text to donate. While both options might sound similar, there are important differences. With the text to give option, the charities establish a standard donation amount. Fundraisers will often choose an amount designed to get the most participation possible. For example, they might select an amount of $5, $10, or $20. Whatever amount they choose, that is what each donation will bring in. When donors hear or see a message about the campaign, they will be told to text a key word to a specific short code to donate. The key word should be something relatively brief and easy to remember. In this situation, organizers could have chosen a word like firefund, or they could have used the acronym for the organization, "BAFRF." Charitable organizations often work with professional fundraising consultants that help them get a dedicated short code or one that is shared with other charity groups. Once the keyword and short code have been determined, the charity can start promoting its campaign to encourage donors to give using the SMS technology on their phones.

The text to donate strategy also uses a keyword and short code. However, instead of a standard donation being collected when the text message is sent, the donor receives a link to a secure donation page hosted by a payment processor like PayPal. The donor then enters the amount they wish to donate and submits the information to complete the donation.

The Bay Area Relief Fund decided to use a text to donate campaign that would let individual donors decide how much they wished to contribute. They partnered with several radio stations and other business organizations to promote the campaign to residents of the Bay Area. During a three-month period that included the Christmas season, the fund raised over $500,000, surpassing their original goal. Mobile donations were a good strategy for this organization because the technology infrastructure required to run the campaign was relatively simple and easy to set up, making it possible to get the campaign up and running in a timely manner.

Sources: Compiled from Inside Radio (2017), Cumulus Media (2018), Morand (2018), and Bryant (2019).

Security Issues Questions

At present, the benefits associated with mobile banking seem to outweigh potential security threats. However, as the number of people who engage in mobile banking increases, the likelihood that criminals will target mobile financial activity is sure to grow as well. What kinds of threats exist to mobile banking? **Table 8.2** lists the most common threats to mobile banking.

TABLE 8.2 **Mobile Banking Security Risks**

Cloning	Duplicating the electronic serial number (ESM) of one phone and using it in second phone, the clone. This allows the perpetrator to have calls and other transactions billed to the original phone.
Phishing	Using a fraudulent communication, such as an e-mail, to trick the receiver into divulging critical information such as account numbers, passwords, or other identifying information.
Smishing	Similar to phishing, but the fraudulent communication comes in the form of an SMS message.
Vishing	Again, similar to phishing, but the fraudulent communication comes in the form of a voice or voicemail message encouraging the victim to divulge secure information.
Lost or stolen phone	Lost or stolen cell phones can be used to conduct financial transactions without the owner's permission.

Questions

1. What are the two basic technologies used for mobile banking and financial services?
2. Why have e-wallets not been widely adopted and what will makers of e-wallets need to do to make this payment method more attractive to consumers?
3. What are the most common types of mobile banking activities consumers perform?
4. What are the most common security risks associated with online retailers?
5. Research some of the mobile payment systems currently available to merchants and consumers so that you understand how each system differs from others.
6. What are micropayments and why is it beneficial to consumers and businesses that mobile payment systems can process these types of transactions?

Chapter Summary

LO8.1 _Describe_ how the concept of omnichannel retailing is changing the nature of shopping for consumers and the role convenience plays in determining where shoppers choose to shop.

In this chapter, you learned that product (quality and selection), price, and convenience are the three most important factors that determine where consumers choose to purchase product and services. Shoppers today have more retail channels to select from than ever, including traditional store-based retailers, e-commerce websites, and mobile channels. Historically, retailers operated these channels as separate and distinct entities. However, to enhance convenience for customers, retailers have been moving to omnichannel retailing, a strategy designed to let consumers move seamlessly across channels for different stages of the retail purchasing experience. For instance, consumers might look at products and get information at a brick-and-mortar store, then use their mobile phone to determine where the product is sold for the lowest price, and then return home to discuss the purchase with family members and purchase the product from an e-commerce website using a computer. Omnichannel retailers allow returns and follow-up service through multiple channels. Finally, you learned that supply chain management is a critical function that has a significant impact on a retailer's ability to optimize performance on product, price, and convenience.

LO8.2 _Explain_ how consumer expectations and shopping behavior have changed during the last decade and ways that store-based retailers have evolved to meet changing customer demands.

In this section, you learned that retailers are exploring ways of using in-store technology to improve the convenience of shopping and enhance the experiential nature of the shopping experience. Some examples of emerging in-store technology tactics include autonomous shopping carts, "grab and go" stores (no checkout lines), free in-store Wi-Fi, in-store lockers stocked with products that shoppers have selected online prior to coming to the store, increased use of digital and interactive displays, and mobile payment methods.

LO8.3 _Identify_ the different markets served by online retailers and the strategies and technologies they use to conduct e-commerce.

In this section, you learned about online retailing (e-commerce) and the different types of markets where e-commerce takes place. Today businesses engage in e-commerce to serve consumers in the B2C, B2B, D2C, and P2P markets. Currently, the B2B market is the largest of these four, followed by the B2C market. E-commerce B2C retailers are using strategies like mass personalization of websites and advertisements, recommendation engines, new artificial intelligence apps., continuous A/B testing of product, price, and promotion tactics, and digital voice assistants. The P2P market is perhaps the fast-growing sector because of innovative new services that connect buyers and sellers. Examples include popular new companies like Airbnb and ride-sharing services like Uber and Lyft. Also supporting the growth of P2P markets are new P2P payment systems like Zelle, Venmo and the Square Cash App.

LO8.4 _Understand_ how mobile technologies are creating opportunities for new forms of commerce in both new and established industries.

In this section, you read about the long-awaited growth of mobile commerce or m-commerce, and some of the ways that companies are attempting to leverage shoppers' use of mobile devices to increase sales. Two big factors contributing to the growth of mobile commerce is the significant adoption rates of mobile smartphones and other handheld devices and the increasing performance of telecommunications networks (specifically the evolution from 4G to 5G networks). Some of the strategies used by companies include mobile advertising, use of QR codes on product labels and advertisements, use of customer identity for personalization and in-store tracking, and the development of brand-specific mobile apps. Since most people access social media using mobile devices, many companies have developed social marketing strategies that increase engagement with customers using mobile devices.

LO8.5 _Recognize_ how mobile payment methods benefit both consumers and retailers.

In this section, you read about the different ways that people can now pay for goods and services using a mobile app. Mobile wallet apps are designed primarily for people to use when shopping at stores and are an alternative to using cash or credit/debit cards. Other apps make it easier for people to purchase products online, or transfer money to other people. Some retailers have developed brand-specific apps that shoppers can use to pay for products in their stores and online. The banking industry has been quick to embrace the use of mobile apps that can be used to conduct all sorts of transactions. Most banks today offer mobile banking, and some banks have chosen to be leaders in

this field by developing the most full-featured apps that customers can use for things such as applying for loans, money management, and mobile bill payment. Many charities have had success with fundraising campaigns that encourage people to donate using the SMS (text messaging) apps on their phones.

Key Terms

bar code   302
channel conflict   312
cloning   322
computer vision (CV)   295
Corporate procurement   310
deep learning   295
direct e-commerce   310
direct procurement   310
E-commerce   301
E-procurement   311
E-sourcing   310
fulfillment as a service (FaaS)   298

indirect procurement   311
in-store tracking   316
logistical infrastructure   300
lost or stolen phone   322
m-commerce   301
marketplace e-commerce   310
micropayments   320
mobile browser   316
mobile marketing   313
omnichannel retailing   301
online marketplaces   298
peer-to-peer (P2P) marketplace   311

phishing   322
pure play e-commerce retailers   306
quick response (QR) code   295
sensor fusion   295
short code   321
short message service (SMS)   317
showrooming   296
smishing   322
subscription-based retailing   298
vishing   322

Assuring Your Learning

Discuss: Critical Thinking Questions

1. What is showrooming? Are customers who engage in it acting ethically? Provide reasons for your answer.

2. What are some creative and constructive ways for traditional retailers to respond to showrooming?

3. Why do you think Amazon felt compelled to start engaging in store-based retailing?

4. Why is mobile technology potentially important to the banking industry? What consumer needs does it fulfill?

5. Identify and describe five key challenges faced by online retailers in the market today.

6. Why is the online B2B market so much larger than the online B2C market?

7. Explain the fundamental difference between vertical and horizontal exchanges in the online B2B market.

8. What is the difference between a direct and a marketplace B2B e-commerce website? Why do sellers find marketplace websites challenging?

9. What are the two primary goals of companies who engage in e-procurement and what strategies do they use to achieve those goals?

10. What is the purpose of an EDI procurement system?

11. How do direct B2B e-commerce sites attempt to make their sites more attractive to business buyers?

12. Explain how mobile computing technology is being used by brick-and-mortar retailers to enhance the in-store shopping experience.

13. QR codes are extremely popular in Japan and other parts of Asia. Manufacturers place QR codes on product packages and

advertisements, making it easy for consumers to access information about the products using a mobile device. Why do you think QR codes are not popular with U.S. consumers? Do you think QR codes will eventually become accepted by U.S. consumers? Why or why not?

14. How are people using mobile devices to conduct banking and other financial services?

15. Evaluate the various mobile electronic payment processes described in this chapter. Which one do you think is likely to emerge as the dominant method for mobile payment? Explain your answer.

16. What are some of the risks faced by consumers who use mobile devices for banking and other financial transactions?

17. What are the key benefits of using a mobile wallet? Do you think new improvements to this mobile application will make it more attractive to end-users?

18. How has mobile computing changed the retail shopping behavior of consumers?

19. Describe the mobile entertainment market and the ways people can use their mobile devices to have fun.

20. How do travelers use mobile technology when flying, using hotels, and traveling in foreign countries?

21. How is mobile computing creating an attractive opportunity for advertisers? Will consumers be receptive to this type of communication? Why or why not?

22. List some location-based services and explain their value to both businesses and mobile device users.

Explore: Online and Interactive Exercises

1. Assume that you are interested in buying a car. You can find information about financing and insurance for cars at MSN Autos or Autobytel (see links below). Decide what car you want to buy. Configure your car by going to the car manufacturer's website. Finally, try to find the car at Autobytel. What information is most supportive of your decision-making process? Was the experience pleasant or frustrating?

Automobile Websites

- MSN Autos: **https://www.msn.com/en-us/Autos**
- Autobytel: **https://www.autobytel.com**

2. Visit Amazon (link below) and identify at least three specific elements of its personalization and customization features. Browse specific books on one subject, leave the site, and then go back and revisit the site. What do you observe? Are these features likely to encourage you to purchase more books in the future from Amazon.com? How does the "One-Click" feature encourage sales from mobile devices?

- Amazon website: **https://www.amazon.com**

3. Read Google's new privacy policy. What types of information does Google collect about people who use its services? How can people either restrict or avoid having Google collect information about them? How does Google say it uses the information it collects about people who utilize its services?

- Google Privacy Policy: **https://policies.google.com/privacy?hl=en-US**

4. Conduct a study on selling diamonds and gems online. Each group member investigates one company such as Blue Nile, James Allen, Ritani, Diamonds Direct, or Rare Carat.

    a. What features are used in these sites to educate buyers about gemstones?

    b. How do the sites attract buyers?

    c. How do the sites increase trust in online purchasing?

    d. What customer service features are provided?

    e. Would you buy a $5,000 diamond ring online? Why or why not?

Diamond/Jewelry Websites

- Blue Nile: **https://www.bluenile.com**
- James Allen: **https://www.jamesallen.com**
- Ritani: **https://www.ritani.com/diamonds**
- Diamonds Online: **https://diamondsdirect.com**
- Rare Carat: **https://www.rarecarat.com**

5. If you have a smartphone, download the Shopkick shopping app. Use the app for a few weeks and then prepare a report or presentation about your experience. Describe how Shopkick uses behavioral reinforcement to encourage specific kinds of shopping behaviors (e.g., store visits, looking for promotional products, participating in marketing surveys). Explain whether you think you will continue using this application.

- Shopkick website: **https://www.shopkick.com**

Analyze & Decide: Apply IT Concepts to Business Decisions

1. What is the National Automated Clearing House Association (NACHA)? What is its role? What is the Automated Clearing House (ACH)? Who are the key participants in an ACH e-payment? Describe the "pilot" projects currently under way at ACH.

- **https://www.nacha.org**

2. Use an Internet search engine such as Google or Bing to identify a list of online banks. Form teams and have each team research one of the banks. Each team should attempt to convince the class that its e-bank activities are the best.

3. As an independent IT contract worker, you must often arrange travel to and from your clients' places of business. You do not typically have time to always explore every travel website when planning travel, so you wish to identify the one that over time will work the best for you. Working in a small group of three to four people, use the Internet to explore the following travel sites: orbitz.com, travelocity.com, kayak.com, concierge.com, and expedia.com (search "online travel sites" for additional options). Select a handful of travel destinations and see how helpful each site is in terms of:

    a. Finding the lowest airfare.

    b. Identifying hotels for business travel.

    c. Recommendations for dining and other location-based services.

    d. Evaluate the site for its ability to aid in international travel arrangements.

    e. Availability and usefulness of travel tips, advisories, and other helpful information.

    f. Prepare a report comparing how each site performed in terms of its ease of use, helpfulness, and best overall deal. Which site would you recommend?

Travel Websites

- Orbitz: **https://www.orbitz.com**
- Travelocity: **https://www.travelocity.com**
- Kayak: **https://www.kayak.com**
- Expedia: **https://www.expedia.com**
- Concierge: **https://www.concierge.com**

4. Using Youtube.com or any other video-sharing site, watch examples of AR mobile apps and promotional campaigns. Write a brief report describing your reaction to this new technology and predict if it will become more commonplace in the future.

Reinforce: Ensure Your Understanding of the Key Terms

Solve the online crossword provided for this chapter.

Web Resources

More resources and study tools are located on the student website. You'll find useful Web links and self-test quizzes that provide individualized feedback.

Case 8.2

Business Case: eBay—An E-commerce Pioneer Faces New Challenges

The online auction website eBay was one of the early pioneers in e-commerce, opening for business in 1995 with the name "Auction Web." Founded by Pierre Omidyar, the company managed to survive the dot-com bubble in the late 1990s and eventually changed its name to eBay. Today it is among the largest 15 e-commerce companies based on 2018 annual revenue of $10.75 billion and a market capitalization of approximately $34.5 billion. While eBay is clearly a major player in the online B2C and B2B marketplace, it has struggled in the last five years to achieve the kind of growth expected by investors (see **Figure 8.7**).

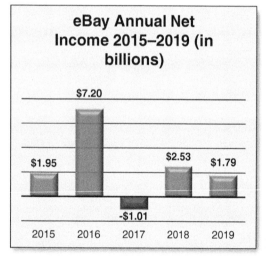

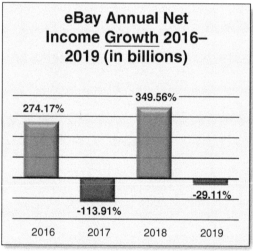

FIGURE 8.7 eBay's annual net income and income growth from 2015 to 2019.

While eBay initially positioned itself as an online auction site focusing on P2P transactions, many small and medium-sized businesses discovered that the platform also worked well for B2C and B2B markets. In 2016, it launched "eBay Business Supply," a separate area on its website to provide improved service for business buyers and sellers. The B2B service includes special tools for procurement professionals and employees and an area that promotes wholesale transactions between qualified sellers and buyers. While businesses have recognized eBay's potential for providing an effective online marketplace for their products, it is unclear if buyers recognize the companies expanded position.

Reasons for Lackluster Growth

On a market call for investors, eBay's interim CEO Scott Schenkel stated, "For 2020 and beyond, change is needed to improve the underlying health of the Marketplace's business." The company has struggled to grow its GMV, a metric that describes the volume of sales, in dollars, made by an e-commerce company. Market analysts have suggested that several factors have impacted eBay's performance in recent years including a nationwide implementation of an Internet sales tax, decline of GMV across the industry, and competition from other e-commerce retailers, especially Amazon whose GMV for third-party sellers has been above 20%. eBay recognizes that change is needed to improve its performance and plans to borrow a few strategies from the dominant e-commerce company's playbook.

Strategies for Improving Performance

Large e-commerce websites such as eBay and Amazon are challenged by the size and breadth of their product offerings because they make it difficult for buyers to find products they want to buy.

Amazon has addressed the problem with strong website search tools and recommendation systems. To improve its performance, eBay plans to make it easier for sellers to provide more details about the products they are selling. This, in turn, will improve the search process for buyers. This is particularly important because eBay prides itself on offering unique products that buyers are less likely to find on other e-commerce sites. eBay needs to create features like Amazon's buy box, a box on many of Amazon's product pages that features other sellers offering the same merchandise, sometimes for lower prices. Third-party sellers on Amazon compete to be listed in the buy box by offering super competitive prices, excellent service, and positive customer feedback. eBay needs to develop something similar to help their best sellers succeed and to convince buyers they are finding the best deals.

Another company creating competition for eBay is a smaller company called Etsy that was founded in 2005. Etsy has a more narrowly defined audience than eBay, focusing largely on boutique items, handmade crafts, vintage fashions, and craft supplies. While Etsy is much smaller than eBay, it is growing at a much faster rate due in large part to its expertise in marketing, better search tools, and product discovery. Product discovery refers to a range of strategies that help customers find products. While search engines are part of product discovery, it also includes things like how products are categorized on a website, recommendation engines that suggest products, development of landing pages for product collections, and strategies for promoting "related products" (e.g., selling water filters to people that bought Keurig coffee makers). Etsy also has developed features of its search engine that help the business estimate user context (buyer intent) that can provide more relevant search results.

eBay also plans to increase its use of artificial intelligence. In January 2018, the company hired Jan Penderson who has 30+ years of experience developing search, deep learning, machine learning, and other artificial intelligence applications for companies like Twitter, Microsoft, Yahoo, and Amazon. As VP of Artificial Intelligence, he will oversee the roll-out of eBay's AI-powered applications. For instance, the company plans to develop tools based on computer vision, a branch of AI that enables computers to "see" images and understand what is in the pictures. This could be used to enhance product search tools. Customers could use images as their search queries, essentially telling the eBay search tool to "find me something that looks like this." The company also plans to use AI for dynamic pricing and personalization strategies. eBay also wants to use AI and artificial reality technology to make the shopping experience more fun and is using machine learning to improve contextual advertising designed to bring more customers to the site.

Questions

1. eBay is trying to get consumers and sellers to view the website as more than just an auction site. Instead, they are trying to get the market to understand that eBay is also a good source for new products and B2B products. In your opinion, is this strategy succeeding?

2. What are some ways that eBay is trying to improve its performance by using AI to create new and helpful applications designed to make shopping more fun?

3. Why is website search so important for large e-commerce websites?

4. What is product discovery and why is it important?

5. Even though eBay is one of the original online retailers, and is one of the largest e-commerce firms, why do financial experts feel the company is struggling?

Sources: Compiled from Cochran (2017), Hickey (2018), Chaffey (2019), Katariya (2019), Levy (2019), Ballard (2020), Laxner (2020), and Marketwatch (2020).

Case 8.3

Video Case: Searching with Pictures Using Mobile Visual Search

Earlier in the chapter, you read that U.S. consumers were not responding to QR code marketing with the same enthusiasm as Asian consumers. In response, some companies are experimenting with an alternative to QR codes called **mobile visual search (MVS)** technology. MVS is an image recognition technology that proponents claim will be more attractive to consumers.

With an MVS app, users scan the pictures they find on product labels, catalogs, or advertisements. This initiates a search function that returns information to the user. Depending on the MVS app used, the search information might be general in nature, like what you get when conducting a search on Google. Or, the app may return specific information, for instance, a page where the user can order the product. This technology has spawned a new industry of MVS services.

Find and watch videos of three different MVS applications on YouTube or other video-sharing sites. To help you get started, try a couple of the search phrases listed below. Simply go to YouTube and type the phrases into the YouTube search tool. Sometimes, the developer websites have some amazing video illustrations that show how their mobile apps work. To find those websites, simply enter the same search phrases below, but use the Google or Bing search engine:

- Pond5
- Google Lens
- Shopgate Mobile Shopping
- BlipparCamFind

You may find videos about other MVS apps by entering "mobile visual search" into the YouTube search engine. Get the latest news and information about MVS by searching on the phrase "mobile visual search" using Google or another search engine. Compare and contrast MVS with marketing strategies using QR codes.

Questions

1. If consumers begin to use MVS on a large-scale basis, how should businesses adjust their marketing practices to take advantage of this technology?

2. Based on the videos and additional research, how do the MVS services differ from one another?

References

Ahlenius, T. "5 Trends for B2C Ecommerce in 2019." *americaneagle.com*, January 2020.

Alexis, C. "How to Use Personalization without Being a Creep." *moveableink.com*, July 27, 2018.

Amato-McCoy, D. "Macy's Adding More In-Store Technology, Partnering with Facebook." *chainstorage.com*, September 17, 2018.

ARPost. "Macy's Uses Immersive Technology to Enhance In-Store Shopping Experience." *arpost.co*, September 21, 2018.

Ballard, J. "Amazon Is Not the Biggest Threat eBay Faces." *fool.com*, January 4, 2020.

Banton, C. "The World's Largest Grocery Store Chains." *thebalancesmb.com*, July 23, 2019.

Bohannon, C. "How Macy's Combines Fashion, Mobile Technology to Target Younger Shoppers." *retaildive.com*, March 16, 2020.

Bonde, A. et al. "US B2B eCommerce Will Hit $1.8 Trillion By 2023." *forrester.com*, January 28, 2019.

Brebion, A. "Deliver Better User Experience through Weather Based Personalization." *abtasty.com*, March 30, 2016.

Bryant, E. "How Text-to-Donate Unlocks the Power of Your Donors." *gmg.cm*, July 27, 2019.

Busby, A. "Fulfillment as a Service, Why the Future of Delivery Is in the Clouds." *forbes.com*, October 23, 2019.

Campanaro, A. "What Is 5G? The Next Wireless Revolution Explained." *nbcnews.com*, March 12, 2018.

Chaffey, D. "eBay Case Study." *smartinsights.com*, January 14, 2019.

Chaubard, F. "Analysis of Amazon Go Platform and Its Implications on Large Format Grocery Stores." *focalsystems.com*, July 29, 2019.

Cochran, T. "eBay Marketing Case Study." *ukessays.com*, September 18, 2017.

Cumulus Media. "Cumulus Media/San Francisco Cluster Raises Half-Million for Bay Area Relief Fund." *allaccess.com*, January 2, 2018.

Dumont, J. "In-store Robots Could Get Smarter with 5G Connectivity." *grocerydrive.com*, July 31, 2019.

Dunkin Donuts. "Dunkin' Donuts Integrates On-the-Go Mobile Ordering with the Google Assistant." *news.dunkindonuts.com*, March 4, 2018.

Dunkin Donuts. "Dunkin' Rolls Out Two Major Mobile App and DD Perks® Enhancements to Provide Greater Access for Guests Nationwide." *news.dunkindonus.com*, September 19, 2019.

Erne, M. "Peer to Peer Business Model in E-Commerce." *newyorkecommerceforum.com*, April 14, 2018.

Fontanella, C. "15 Examples of Brands with Brilliant Omnichannel Experiences." *hubspot.com*, February 28, 2020.

Gilliland, N. "12 Examples of Digital Technology in Retail Stores." *econsultancy.com*, January 23, 2019.

Hall, H. "15 Smart Ecommerce Personalization Examples That Boost Sales." *optinmonster.com*, January 3, 2020.

Heist, G. "Why Hyper-Personalization Demands a Fair Value Exchange." *marketingland.com*, March 10, 2020.

Hickey, A. "eBay Charts Tech-Heavy 2018 with New AI Chief and Upcoming AR Tool." *ciodrive.com*, February 14, 2018.

Huff, M. "How Amazon's Weather Personalization Tool Spotlights a Hot Trend in Marketing." *the-gma.com*, June 1, 2017.

Inside Radio. "Cumulus SF Cluster Halfway to $500K Fire Relief Goal." *insideradio.com*, October 20, 2017.

Kacmaz, G. "4 Reasons You Should Use Weather-Based Personalization." *kameloon.com*, April 5, 2016.

Katariya, S. "eBay's Platform Is Powered by AI and Fueled by Customer Input." *tech.ebayinc.com*, March 13, 2019.

Kats, R. "Consumers Continue to Be Enticed by Click and Collect." *emarketer.com*, February 12, 2020.

Kelso, A. "Consumers Are Growing More Comfortable with Click and Collect, Study Finds." *grocerydive.com*, August 23, 2018.

Laxner, E. "The Amazon Buy Box: How It Works for Sellers, and Why It's So Important." *bigcommerce.com*, March 20, 2020.

Levy, A. "eBay Needs Some Changes to Compete with Amazon." *fool.com*, October 26, 2019.

Liffreing, I. "How Dunkin' Donuts Turns to Voice to Boost Mobile Orders." *digiday.com*, March 19, 2018.

Lipsman, A. "The Future of Retail 2020: 10 Trends That Will Shape the Year Ahead." *emarketer.com*, December 19, 2019.

Machkovech, S. "Amazon Made a Bigger Camera-Spying Store—So We Tried to Steal Its Fruit." *artstechnica.com*, February 26, 2020.

Marketwatch. "Annual Financials for eBay Inc." *marketwatch.com*, March 30, 2020.

Medhora, N. and Dastin, J. "Amazon Opens Line-Free Grocery Store in Challenge to Supermarkets." *reuters.com*, December 5, 2016.

Morand, T. "The Ultimate Guide to Text-To-Give Fundraising." *wildapricot.com*, October 4, 2018.

Morris, T. "Companies Face a 'Paradox' between Digital Personalization and Data Privacy." *retaildive.com*, February 25, 2020.

National Retail Federation. "Mobile Retailing Blueprint: A Comprehensive Guide for Navigating the Mobile Landscape." January 4, 2011.

Olenski, S. "Time to Make the Donuts: How the Dunkin' Donuts Brand Stays Relevant." *forbes.com*, March 6, 2017.

Peterson, R. "20 Best Digital Marketing Case Studies of 2018 to Inspire in 2019." *barnraisersllc.com*, December 16, 2018.

Phaneuf, A. "State of Mobile Banking in 2020: Top Apps, Features, Statistics and Market Trends." *businessinsider.com*, August 14, 2019.

Porter, M. "The Five Competitive Forces That Shape Strategy." *Harvard Business Review*, 86, no. 1, January 2008, pp. 86–104.

Progressive Grocer. "Kroger Changes Name of Click-and-Collect Service to Avoid Confusion." *progressivegrocer.com*, September 27, 2018.

Puryear, C. "Selling on Online Marketplaces: Best Platforms for Selling Your Products." *bigcommerce.com*, March 10, 2020.

Schrager, A. "We Wouldn't Have Ecommerce without Amazon." *qz.com*, October 22, 2019.

Sentance, R. "20+ Stats That Show How Online Retail Is Changing." *econsultancy.com*, July 25, 2019.

Sides, R. and Furman, B., "2019 Retail Outlook: Transition Ahead." Deloitte Development LLC, 2019.

Sides, R. and Swaminathan, N. "2020 Retail Industry Outlook: Convenience as a Promise." Deloitte Development LLC, 2020.

Staff, A. "10 Retailers Using QR Codes for In-Store Payments." *ailatech.com*, February 20, 2019.

Statt, N. "Amazon Is Expanding Its Cashierless Go Model into a Full-Blown Grocery Store." *theverge.com*, February 25, 2020.

Thompson, D. "Why Amazon Bought Whole Foods." *theatlantic.com*, June 16, 2017.

Van Dyke, D. "Soon Nearly a Third of US Consumers Will Regularly Make Payments with Their Voice." *businessinsider.com*, June 23, 2017.

Verdon, J. "Smells Like Innovation: Macy's Blends Online and In-Store Experience at Digital Fragrance Bars." *uschamber.com*, July 29, 2019.

WARC. "The Marketer's Toolkit 2020." *warc.com/toolkit*, December 2, 2019.

Wertz, J. "5 Trends That Will Redefine Retail in 2019." *forbes.com*, November 28, 2018.

Functional Business Systems

LEARNING OBJECTIVES

9.1 Identify the four traditional functional business units and how business-driven functional business systems support functional and cross-functional process improvement.

9.2 Define productions and operations management and the various types of functional business systems that support the POM function.

9.3 Describe the sales and marketing management function and how sales and marketing management systems impact sales management procedures and tasks and the two major functional activities of marketing management.

9.4 Define the accounting and finance functions and the management systems that help organizations meet local and global regulatory compliance requirements and facilitate capital budgeting and forecasting.

9.5 Identify the purpose of human resource management and the ways in which HRIS can improve the HR function.

Case 9.1 Opening Case

Business Case: Equifax Data Breach Highlights Need for Regulatory Compliance Changes in Financial Management

On December 5, 2019, lawyers for consumers damaged by a major data breach at Equifax, Inc. filed a motion in federal court in Atlanta for final approval of the settlement of one of the largest lawsuits concerning consumer financial data in history. The settlement was based on a lawsuit brought against Equifax because of a massive September 2017 breach at Equifax in which the financial data of half the US population was stolen. Consumer anger at the company could lead to legislative reform that fundamentally changes the credit report and lending industry and how consumer financial data is managed.

Company Background

Equifax is a global data analytics and technology company headquartered in Atlanta, GA. The company has over 11,000 employees and operates in over 24 countries throughout the Americas, Europe, and Asia Pacific. The company uses unique data, innovative analytics, technology, and industry expertise to power organizations and individuals around the world by transforming knowledge into insights that help make more informed business and personal decisions. Equifax is a member of the S&P 500 and its stock is traded on the NYSE. The company analyzes data on 820 million consumers, 91 million businesses worldwide, and its database includes employee data contributed from more than 7,100 employers. Equifax along with Experian and TransUnion are the three major credit reporting agencies in the United States, responsible for the creation and handling of consumer credit reports and scores.

Problem

"Equifax sits on the crown jewels of what we consider personally identifying information," says Jason Glassberg, cofounder of the corporate security and penetration testing firm Casaba Security. "My hope is that this really becomes a watershed moment and opens up everyone's eyes, because it's astonishing how ridiculous almost everything Equifax did was." Even though Equifax became aware of the hack in July, consumers were not notified until September, giving identity thefts a large window to wreak havoc unnoticed. Equifax was able to delay reporting the hack because current state laws do not adequately specify fast disclosure windows. An article in the Harvard Business review stated emphatically

"Current measures do not work. When data breaches occur, consumers are urged to check a website to see if they were affected. They are offered time-limited credit monitoring services and encouraged to check credit reports for stray transactions. This protocol has done little to stem the rise in data breaches and identity thefts in the United States." Equifax's response was far worse than the already lacking norm for major breaches. The company's official Twitter account directed customers to a phishing website FOUR times. The authentic website Equifax created to address the attack asked consumers to disclose the last 6 digits of their social security number at a time when confidence in Equifax handling of security was at an all-time low. To make public relations even worse, Equifax used the theft notification website to attempt to disclaim liability for the breach. "These are all indicators of a company that had a horrible security culture," says Tinfoil Security's Michael Borohovski. "Unfortunately, the only word for it is negligence." Security expects were galled to learn the attack was done using a known security vulnerability that had a patch availability. Other signs of a culture of inept security was the discovery that the company's security credentials for employees in Argentina was simple "admin, admin". Recovering from stolen identity credentials is difficult. Cancelling a credit card is comparatively easy compared to changing a social security number or birthdate.

Need for Regulatory Compliance Reform

Congress has introduced half a dozen bills to introduce much needed reforms with titles ranging from the innocuous Protect Act to the more pointed Freedom from Equifax Exploitation Act. Many of the solutions are themed around giving consumers more control of their data. Currently consumers can request a credit freeze for a fee that prevents companies from accessing their credit data and subsequently preventing identity thefts from fraudulently opening new credit accounts. Legislation hopes to make credit freezes quick, easy, and free. Credit freezing would become the standard, with consumers only unlocking their credit when they need to apply for a loan. Currently companies can access credit data at any time only getting access from a credit agency without the need for consumer consent to their data being released. Other solutions in multiple bills include phasing out the use of Social Security numbers by the major credit agencies by 2020. The bills also aim to heighten standards for accuracy in reports and better legal protections for consumers when reports have errors. This is a badly needed reform as the three major credit agencies have more complaints against them than any other company according the US Consumer Protection Bureau. When errors are reported, the agencies only correct them 20% of the time. If successful, these reforms should give consumers more control over their financial information as well as holding credit agencies more accountable for errors.

Outcome

On January 13, 2020, a Final Order and Judgment was issued. The settlement requires that Equifax pay $380.5 million into a fund for class benefits, attorney fees, expenses, service awards, and notice and administration costs; up to an additional $125 million if needed to satisfy claims for certain out-of-pocket losses, and potentially $2 billion more if all 147 million class members sign up for credit monitoring. The need to reform credit reporting is heightened as new tools such as consumer scoring become common. New practices like consumer scoring "scrape" websites and social media accounts to create a profile of a consumer that is sold to third parties. These new technologies still suffer from the same issues that credit scores have been criticized about for decades, inaccurate financial data and discriminatory lending decisions. Regulations should consider these new regulatory compliance technologies in legislation and utilize security best practices including algorithmic transparency and data minimization to ensure consumers are more protected from breaches in the future.

Sources: Compiled from Brewster (2017), Newman (2017), Rotenberg (2017), Uchill (2017), Anderson (2019), Puig (2019), Meltzer (2019), Piovesan (2019), Stewart (2020), Equifaxbreachsettlement.com (2020), LaCroix (2020), and St. John (2020).

 DID YOU KNOW?

That . . . it has been predicted that the average person will soon hold more conversations with chatbots than with their spouse! Driven by the promise of intelligent round-the-clock digital sales and marketing support, a growing number of companies are using chatbots to engage with customers alongside phone, e-mail, and social media.

Introduction

Every business has several traditional functional business units that support different aspects of the business. Consider the case of an electronics company. The finance function is responsible for acquiring capital needed for research and development (R&D) and other investment processes. The marketing function is responsible for product promotion and pricing, identifying target customers, and improving the customer experience (CX). The operations function plans and coordinates all the resources needed to design, manufacture, and transport products. The IT function is responsible for the technology infrastructure, data management, and social, mobile, and cloud services. Accounting manages assets and meets compliance mandates. Human resource (HR) recruits, trains, and develops a talented workforce. These business functions involve complex processes that depend on access to data, collaboration, communication, and data analysis to pinpoint what must be done and employees' workflows to make that happen.

In this chapter you will learn about different traditional functional business units and the various functional and cross-functional information systems designed to help employees and managers make better decisions and improve efficiency and performance in the different functional areas of a typical business organization and contribute to overall organizational growth and sustainability.

9.1 | Functional and Cross-Functional Business Processes

LO9.1 Identify *the four traditional functional business units and how business-driven functional business systems support functional and cross-functional process improvement.*

An organization is divided into several functional business units—sometimes known as functional silos—that it depends on to meet its goals. The main reason business processes are separated into functional business units is to allow each to operate within its area of expertise to build efficiencies and effectiveness across the business as a whole. Traditionally, these functional business units include production and operations, sales and marketing, accounting and finance, and human resources **(Figure 9.1)**.

FIGURE 9.1   The four major business units.

Each of these functional business units are responsible for business processes throughout the production of a product as services. These processes include:

1. **Production and operations:**   materials purchasing, quality control, scheduling, shipping, receiving, manufacturing resource planning, manufacturing execution.

2. **Sales and marketing:**   pricing, social media promotions, market research, demand forecasts, sales campaign management, order tracking, online and mobile order processing and sales, customer relationship management, salesforce automation.

3. **Accounting and finance:**   order processing, accounts receivable, accounts payable, general ledger, budgeting, inventory control, payroll, cash management, asset management, credit management, investment management, capital budgeting, financial forecasting, financial statement reporting to comply with federal and industry-specific regulations and government agencies.

4. **Human resources:**   payroll, recruitment and hiring, succession planning, employee benefits, training, compensation, performance appraisal, compliance with federal and state employment regulations.

Not all organizations are structured around functional business units that are controlled and coordinated by top-level management, some develop a project-based structure centered around different products or projects, while others develop a matrix structure that combines functions and projects (matrix) in which employees report to both a functional business unit manager and one or more project leaders. In addition to the four major functional business areas, larger organizations frequently expand this list to include Strategic Planning, Business Development, R&D, Customer Service, and Information Technology.

Information Systems to Support Functional Business Units

To efficiently and effectively perform and control the business processes related to a given business unit, each functional business unit needs a variety of **functional business systems** to support it. Some of these support processes that are performed solely within a business function while others support cross-functional business processes across two or more business units.

Functional Business System (FBS)   is an IS designed to improve the efficiency and performance of a specific functional area within an organization.

While most organizations focus on external entities such as customers, partners, and government, business success also depends on internal factors like the efficiency and effectiveness of managers, employees, core business processes, and the use of innovative technology to improve business processes. To achieve this, organizations provide their employees, consumers, business partners and regulators in each functional business unit with a wide range of business-driven technologies to support core processes, problem-solving, decision-making, and comply with local and global regulatory requirements **(Figure 9.2)**. Within each functional business unit there are specialized FBS for the different levels of workers and managers including the transaction processing systems (TPS), management information systems (MIS), decision support systems (DSS), and executive information systems (EIS) that you learned about in Chapter 2.

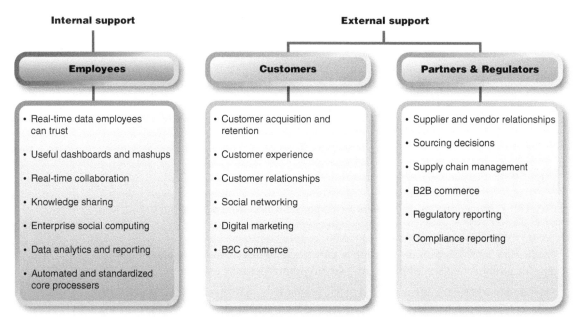

FIGURE 9.2 Comparison of the IT capabilities that organizations provide to employees, consumers, business partners, and government regulators.

Functional business systems provide a foundation for the more sophisticated enterprise-level systems discussed in Chapter 10. As data from transaction processing systems (discussed in Chapter 2) are fed into functional systems they in turn must efficiently and effectively integrate with external systems and support systems at the enterprise level as shown in **Figure 9.3**.

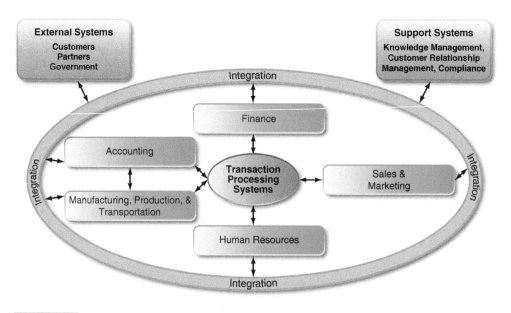

FIGURE 9.3 Data from functional area ISs support enterprise apps.

Breaking Down Functional Business Silos
Originally, information systems were designed to only support the accounting function. Systems for other functions were rolled out later. This fragmented roll-out approach created data silos where information was effectively trapped in one functional area of the business and could not support cross-functional business processes. For example, accounting systems record sales, payments, customer profile information, product pricing, promotional expenses, and so on. To effectively evaluate the impact of past promotional activities and pricing decisions, the marketing department must be able to analyze the relationship between the product's price, promotional expenditures, and sales volume during a specific time period. In addition, the marketing unit might need to analyze the revenue generated by each customer to determine how the salesforce should prioritize accounts. However, if this information is trapped in the accounting system, it may not be available to the marketing unit. In some cases, employees in marketing may not be granted access to the accounting system, or even more problematic, the system may only be programmed to use the data for creating standard accounting reports and statements and might not permit retrieval of information in ways that are useful to the marketing department or other units in the company.

Cross-Functional Coordination and Integration
Cross-functional business systems reflect the fact that the business unit they support should, as much as possible, connect with other business units seamlessly to best serve the customer. **Cross-functional business processes** occur when different departments within the same organization work together to achieve a common goal. For example, an operational-level TPS in the sales department that contains customer order information will be needed by several different business units areas such as accounting, production and operations, and sales and marketing. In today's fast-paced, competitive business environment, departments or functions must be able to coordinate in the development of strategic plans and the performance of operations-level actions. Uncoordinated workflows and data flows between departments can result in delays, errors, poor customer service, and higher costs. When FBSs allow for cross-functional coordination, it becomes possible for the company to monitor and evaluate progress toward goals and objectives established during the strategic planning process. It also becomes easier to identify problems or barriers to achieving objectives and develop solutions to those problems.

> A **cross-functional business system** integrates the end-to-end activities of an entire business process and cross departmental boundaries.

Data Requirements
The data requirements of functional business units at the operational level are extensive and relatively routine because they have fixed sources of input and tasks that follow **standard operating procedures (SOPs)**. An FBS helps companies and employees adhere to easily automated SOPs. SOPs are an integral part of a quality control (QC) system because they provide individuals with information to perform jobs properly. A key benefit of SOPs is that they minimize variation and promote quality through consistent implementation of a process or procedure within the organization, even if there are temporary or permanent personnel changes. For example, SOPs are written for handling purchase orders, order fulfillment, customer complaints, recruitment and hiring, emergency response, and disaster recovery. Data that are lost or compromised have financial implications. As such, it is critical that businesses have SOPs to maintain three related data properties in its IS. These three properties are:

> **standard operating procedures (SOPs)** is a set of written instructions on how to perform a function or activity. SOPs provide the framework for complex processes to be managed more effectively.

Data security Data security refers to the protection of data from malicious or unintentional corruption, unauthorized modification, theft, or natural causes such as floods. The purpose of data security is to maintain data integrity.

Data validity Data validation involves tests and evaluations used to detect and correct errors, for instance, mistakes that might occur during data entry in fields such as customer name and address.

Data integrity Data integrity refers to the maintenance of data accuracy and validity over its life cycle including the prevention of unintended modification or corruption.

While each of the three organizational structures and additional functional areas make important contributions to the success of an organization, our goal in this chapter is to describe the different types of information systems that are used throughout an organization within the traditional functional business units listed above. In the following sections, the most common types of information systems that support the four traditional functional business units are described.

Questions

1. Define the five traditional functional business units.
2. Describe the processes that each traditional functional business unit performs.
3. Define what an SOP is and give an example.
4. Explain the relationship between TPSs and FBSs.
5. Name the three data properties that an IS must have.

9.2 Production and Operations Management Systems

LO9.2 Define *productions and operations management and the various types of functional business systems that support the POM function.*

The **productions and operations management (POM)** function is responsible for processes that transform inputs into value-added outputs, as shown in **Figure 9.4**. These inputs include capital investments, human resources (workers, staff, and managers); facilities, supplies, equipment, materials, IT, and information along with the time and energy needed to manage them. These are transformed through inspection and alteration and subsequent transportation and/or storage. The outputs are the goods and services that an organization produces.

FIGURE 9.4 Production and operations management (POM) systems process and transform inputs into outputs.

POM provides information on the production activities of an organization to facilitate the decision-making processes of production managers. Historically, the production and operations area focused primarily on activities within the company related to the manufacture of products and services. Considerable emphasis was placed on increasing product quality and reducing manufacturing costs, believing that these were critical factors in business success. More recently, businesses have developed a broader perspective, understanding that customer value is a more critical success factor. Significant advances in customer value require more than just improvements in product quality and reduced costs.

Basically, a **production and operations management (POM) system** helps an organization estimate, plan, and schedule resources, that is budgeting, inventory, and time tracking/scheduling. At a higher level, it facilitates managing, controlling, tracking, and communicating progress and resource allocation and facilitates collaborative, documentary, and administrative tasks to inform decision makers.

The main objective of POM software is to optimize workflow in the production of goods and/or the delivery of services. With rising complexity and specialization of work, software that helps manage these responsibilities is in high demand due to its potential to dramatically increase work efficiency, conserve resources, and improve the overall quality of products and services.

A wide variety of POM systems focus on various aspects of operations management that are heavily used across virtually all business functions from project management (discussed in detail in Chapter 13), to distributing and managing workloads to fully integrated enterprise-level solution such as a supply chain (SCM) system or enterprise resource planning (ERP) system (discussed in detail in Chapter 10). The major categories of POM systems are discussed next.

> A **production and operations management system** assists in the operation, planning, execution, and ongoing management of an organization.

Inventory Control Systems

Inventory control systems are important because they minimize the total cost of inventory while maintaining optimal inventory levels to support production and operations. Inventory levels are maintained by reordering the quantity needed at the right times in order to meet demand. POM departments keep **safety stock** as a hedge against **stockouts**. Safety stock is needed in case of unexpected events, such as spikes in demand or longer delivery times. One of the crucial decisions involved in inventory management is weighing the cost of inventory against the cost of stockouts. Stockouts of materials and parts can slow or shut down production while stockouts of final products result in reduced sales. Both of these situations can have significant short- and long-term financial consequences that need to be balanced against the potential savings associated with lower inventory levels.

Managing inventory is important to profit margins because of numerous costs associated with inventory, in addition to the cost of the inventory. Inventory control systems minimize the following three cost categories:

- Inventory carrying costs
- Inventory ordering costs
- Cost of shortages

To minimize the sum of these three costs (see **Figure 9.5**), the company must decide when to order and how much to order. One inventory model that is used to answer both questions is the **economic order quantity (EOQ)** model. The EOQ model takes all costs into consideration.

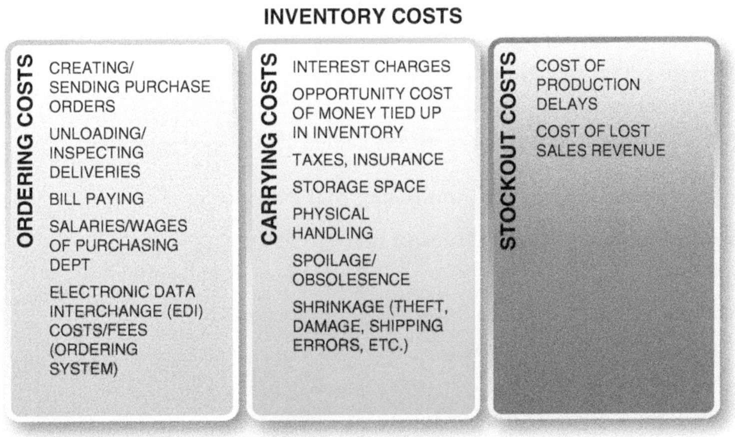

> **Inventory control systems** is an IS that controls stock or inventory management.
>
> **safety stock** is extra inventory used as a buffer to reduce the risk of stockouts. It is also called buffer stock.
>
> **stockouts** inventory shortage arising from unexpected demand, delays in scheduled delivery, production delays, or poor inventory management.

INVENTORY COSTS

ORDERING COSTS	CARRYING COSTS	STOCKOUT COSTS
CREATING/SENDING PURCHASE ORDERS	INTEREST CHARGES	COST OF PRODUCTION DELAYS
UNLOADING/INSPECTING DELIVERIES	OPPORTUNITY COST OF MONEY TIED UP IN INVENTORY	COST OF LOST SALES REVENUE
BILL PAYING	TAXES, INSURANCE	
SALARIES/WAGES OF PURCHASING DEPT	STORAGE SPACE	
ELECTRONIC DATA INTERCHANGE (EDI) COSTS/FEES (ORDERING SYSTEM)	PHYSICAL HANDLING	
	SPOILAGE/OBSOLESENCE	
	SHRINKAGE (THEFT, DAMAGE, SHIPPING ERRORS, ETC.)	

FIGURE 9.5 Inventory control systems help companies balance inventory ordering and carrying costs against the costs of inventory shortages.

Capterra (**www.capterra.com**) provides examples of Inventory Management Systems that include QuickBooks Enterprise (**https://quickbooks.intuit.com/**), NetSuite (**https://system .na0.netsuite.com/pages/customerlogin.jsp**), Inventory Cloud (**www.waspbarcode.com**) and Skubana (**https://www.skubana.com/multi-channel-inventory-management/**).

Just-in-Time Inventory Management Systems In manufacturing, customer demand for high quality at a low cost is a major concern. Price pressure can be overwhelming especially when an organization is competing globally. **Just-in-time (JIT) inventory management** is a widely used method of manufacturing used to minimize waste and deal with the complexity of inventory management. With JIT, costs associated with carrying large inventories at any given point in time are eliminated. However, the trade-off is higher ordering costs because of more frequent orders. Because of the higher risk of stockouts, JIT requires accurate and timely monitoring of materials' usage in production.

> **Just-in-time (JIT) inventory management** involves minimizing holding costs by not taking possession of inventory until it is needed in the production process.

Everything in the JIT chain is interdependent, so coordination and good relationships with suppliers are critical for JIT to work well. Any delay can be very costly to all companies linked in the chain. Delays can be caused by labor strikes, interrupted supply lines, bad weather, market demand fluctuations, stockouts, lack of communication upstream and downstream in the supply chain, and unforeseen production interruptions. In addition, inventory or material quality is critical. Poor quality causes delays, for example, fixing products or scrapping what cannot be fixed and waiting for delivery of the reorder.

JIT was developed by Toyota because of high real-estate costs in Tokyo, Japan, which made warehousing expensive. It is used extensively in the auto manufacturing industry. For example, if parts and subassemblies arrive at a workstation exactly when needed, holding inventory is not required. There are no delays in production, and there are no idle production facilities or underutilized workers, if parts and subassemblies arrive on schedule and in usable condition. The use of JIT needs to be justified with a cost–benefit analysis. For example, JIT requires that inventory arrive on schedule and be of the right quality.

Despite potential cost-saving benefits, JIT is likely to fail in companies that have the following:

- Uncooperative supply chain partners, vendors, workers, or management.
- Custom or nonrepetitive production.

Lean Manufacturing Systems Lean manufacturing has its roots in Toyota's JIT inventory management practices. A company that practices lean manufacturing concentrates not only on obtaining inventory when needed, but also concentrates on minimizing wasted steps within its manufacturing process while simultaneously maximizing productivity. The main objective of lean manufacturing is to eliminate waste of any kind by eliminating any step in the manufacturing process that does not add value to the final product. Holding inventory that is not needed very soon is seen as waste, which adds cost but not value is one way to do this. Lean manufacturing adds to this by empowering workers to improve production processes so that production decisions can be made by those who are closest to the processes.

As shown in **Figure 9.6**, the five core "Principles of Lean Management" are:

- **Value.** Specify value from the standpoint of the customer
- **Map Value Stream.** Identify steps in the value stream and eliminate steps that do not create value.
- **Create Flow.** Ensure smooth flow of product to customer by completing value-creating steps in a tight sequence.
- **Establish Pull.** Use flow to let customers pull value from the next upstream activity.
- **Seek Perfection.** Repeat above cycle until perfect results are achieved.

Production and Operations Management Systems

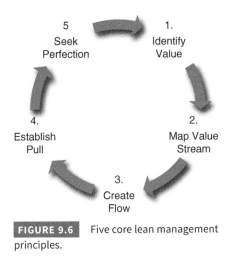

FIGURE 9.6 Five core lean management principles.

Lean manufacturing is not suitable for all types of organizations. For example, in organizations that are subject to bad weather or frequent labor strikes, lean manufacturing is difficult to achieve.

A **lean manufacturing system** transforms planning, scheduling and execution of processes on the factory flow by creating a demand-driven manufacturing process that controls replenishment of resources, helps utilize and open up capacity and enables manufacturers to react to changes in customer needs. It also enables suppliers to deliver small lots on a daily or frequent basis, and controls production so that machines are not necessarily run at full capacity.

Oracle Lean Scheduling (**https://www.oracle.com/applications/primavera/solutions/lean-scheduling/features.html**), Siemens Lean Manufacturing (**https://siemensmfg.com/custom-solutions/lean-manufacturing/**), SYSPRO (**https://us.syspro.com/business-software/business-needs/lean-manufacturing/**), Synchrono (**http://www.synchrono.com/category/lean-manufacturing-software/**), and other vendors offer JIT and demand-driven lean manufacturing systems.

> A **lean manufacturing system** streamlines efficiency and processes by connecting production line machinery and warehouse management systems to maximize productivity.

Quality Management Systems (QMS)

Quality management ensures the quality of products and services and is critical to meet customer expectations and maintain customer loyalty. **Quality management systems (QMS)** provide quality planning, quality assurance, quality control, and quality improvement and how to achieve it. A QMS can be stand-alone systems or part of an enterprise-wide **total quality management (TQM)** effort. QC systems provide data about the quality of incoming materials and parts, as well as the quality of in-process semi-finished, and finished products. These systems record the results of all inspections and compare actual results to expected results.

The main components of a QMS include:

> A **quality management system (QMS)** is a formalized integrated system that documents processes, procedures, and responsibilities to achieve quality policies and objectives to consistently meet customer requirements while also satisfying regulatory and development requirements.

- **Compliance control** including documenting, processing, scheduling, correction, and auditing reports related to QC activities.
- **Analytics tools** to achieve effectual planning, scheduling, and executive of quality review processes.
- **Customer satisfaction management** to report issues in product quality.
- **Document management** to provide a centralized system for easy access to important quality-related documents and effectively manage a large volume of data to enhance interactions between cross-functional departments.
- **Real-time data** to provide real-time analytics and data displayed through graphical dashboards.
- **Risk management tools** to report quality-related risks and predict service failures and consequent financial impacts.

The main objectives of a QMS include improved internal processes, lower costs, optimization of resource utilization, continuously improved customer satisfaction, and data management. Data for a QMS may be collected by sensors or radio frequency identification (RFID) systems and interpreted in real time, or they can be stored in a database for future analysis. Reports on the percentage of defects or percentage of rework needed can keep managers informed of performance among departments. KIA Motors introduced an intelligent QMS system to analyze customer complaints, so it could more quickly investigate and make corrections.

Examples of QMS and auditing systems include isoTracker (**https://www.isotracker .com/**), QMS Guru (**https://www.qms.guru/**), Inspect2GO (**https://inspect2go.com/**), and MasterControl (**https://www.mastercontrol.com/**).

Computer-Integrated Manufacturing Systems

Computer-integrated manufacturing is a management approach that uses computers and automation systems to control the entire manufacturing and production process. It encompasses all activities in the production system from planning and design of a product through manufacturing and quality control. This integration of people, technology, and processes allows for the exchange of information between individual processes and initiates actions based on information received. CIM is comprehensive and flexible, which is especially important in the redesign or elimination of business processes. Prior to the introduction of CIM in the early 1980s, production managers were given many pieces of information such as time, attendance, receiving reports, inspection reports, and so on to figure out how to accomplish production tasks. The information was frequently late, rarely current or reliable, voluminous, and extremely difficult to assimilate. CIM helps production managers better use information to execute manufacturing plans. It uses computers and communication networks to transform automated manufacturing systems into interconnected systems that cooperate across all organizational functions.

The goal of CIM is to remove all barriers between functions within an operation and encourage marketing, order entry, accounting, design, manufacturing, quality control, shipping, and other departments to work closely together throughout the process. As a result, CIM data-driven automation affects all systems or subsystems within the manufacturing environment: design and development, production, marketing and sales, and field support and service.

CIM systems simplify manufacturing technologies and techniques, automate as many of the manufacturing processes as possible, and integrate and coordinate all aspects of design, manufacturing, and related functions. CIM systems can perform production monitoring, scheduling and planning, statistical process monitoring, quality analysis, personnel monitoring, order status reporting, and production lot tracking. They provide information by linking each operation task, giving decision makers access to needed information. Tasks are performed in parallel not in sequence, saving time. You may know the technology associated with CIM as CAD/CAM (**computer-aided design** and **computer-aided manufacturing**). Today, CIM systems extend the capabilities of CAD/CAM beyond the engineering function to all business functions of the firm from customer order through design and production (CAD/CAM) to quality control, product shipment, and customer service.

Advantages gained from using CIM systems include:

- Reduction in costs
- Improved quality and customer satisfaction
- Greater production control
- Reduced inventory requirements
- Improved product development cycles to enable faster response to market pressures
- Support for manufacturing of small lots

Computer-integrated manufacturing (CIM) is the integration of manufacturing operations by integrating people, technology, and manufacturing processes.

computer-aided design is the use of computer systems to assist in the creation, modification, analysis, and optimization of a design.

computer-aided manufacturing is the capability of a computer system to process, store, and display large amounts of data representing part and product specifications.

Robots have become a vital element in CIM and can contribute significantly to making production and manufacturing processes more efficient and reliable. For example, arc-welding robots are common in steel production and automobile manufacturing plants. They are also frequently used on assembly lines in organizations that practice lean manufacturing and picking and packing products can be performed much faster and more efficiently used robots. An interesting use of robots can be found in electronics and optical companies that are sensitive about contamination. They use clean-room robots to perform tasks in an isolated, sealed, and insulated environment. You will learn much more about robotics in Chapter 11.

Implementing a CIM system is not without its challenges primarily because CIM requires a change in management attitudes. For example, a lack of understanding of the technology and how it impacts the organization and its employees can contribute to a manager's failure to support CIM implementation. As a result, CIM implementation must start with top management commitment to provide the necessary time, money, and other resources needed to make required changes, encourage careful planning of each technical element, and establish an appropriate training program. The existing structure of the organization also must change to facilitate cooperation and information sharing between all the different functional business units. Finally, many companies experience difficulties in justifying the cost of implementing CIM, but need to keep in mind that without CIM, it may become necessary to make large investments to change existing ISs to fit new processes in response to intense competition and time to market pressures.

Two examples of commonly used CIM systems CIM Systems, Inc. (**http://cimrobotics .com**) and CIM Industrial Systems (**http://cim.as**).

Manufacturing Execution Systems

Manufacturing execution systems (MESs) can be viewed as a subset of CIM. They manage operations on the shop floors of factories. Some MESs schedule a few critical machines, while others manage all operations on the shop floor. Functions of MES programs include compiling a bill of materials, resource management and scheduling, preparing and dispatching production orders, preparing work-in-progress (WIP) reports, and tracking production lots. For instance, an MES can schedule and track each step of the production phase of a particular job and then print out the bill of materials for the operator and the production steps to complete at each phase. It repeats this process for each operator and each step until a particular job is complete.

Unlike CIM, an MES is based much more on standard reusable application software, instead of custom-designed software programs on a contract-by-contract basis. An MES tries to eliminate the time and information gap of early years on the shop floor by providing the plant with information in real time. Corporate business functions are given timely plant information to support business planning decisions.

MESs are generally installed on-premises, but cloud-based solutions are becoming available. MES is a subset of enterprise resource planning (ERP) systems, which you will read about in Chapter 10.

Examples of leading MES include SAP ME (**https://www.sap.com**), Oracle Manufacturing Cloud (**https://www.oracle.com/applications/supply-chain-management/manufacturing/**), and Shopfloor-Online (**https://www.lighthousesystems.com/mes-mom-software**).

In **IT at Work 9.1** you will see how industry and software vendors are forming long-standing partnerships to revolutionize the production and operations management processes.

Manufacturing execution systems manage, monitor, and synchronize the execution of real-time, physical processes involved in transforming raw materials into intermediate and/or finished goods and execute work orders with production scheduling and enterprise-level systems.

IT at Work 9.1

International Parts Supplier Partners with SAP to Digitalize Its Production Development Processes Around the Globe

MAHLE, a German automotive partners manufacturer based in Stuttgart, Germany, is one of the largest automotive suppliers worldwide with 79,000 employees at 160 production locations in 30 different countries around the globe. MAHLE is also well known as a technology innovator in mobility for the future. In February 2020, MAHLE announced its latest digital transformation project in which it will partner with SAP, an enterprise resource planning software developer, on six strategic projects that span its entire value chain. These include standardizing its complete product development process across its 160 locations around the globe and the roll out of several direct and indirect innovative purchasing solutions. "Digitalization is the key to securing MAHLE's innovative edge in the global competitive field – in IT as well as in vehicle technology," declared Dr. Jörg Stratmann, CEO and Chairman of the MAHLE Management Board.

The new central digital SAP-based platform titled the "Digital Backbone" will standardize MAHLE's data and processes and will be continuously developed and optimized specifically for the automotive industry. The partnership between MAHLE and SAP is setting new standards in terms of standardization and agility in POM and will give its customers and partners in the automotive industry valuable insight into how the company make themselves "future proof." It's a partnership between industry member and software vendor that benefits both parties. Michael Frick, CFO and member of the MAHLE Management Board responsible for IT Services, feels that "The strategic partnership between MAHLE and SAP bring together two innovation drivers. Together we'll set new standards." And Thomas Saueressig, Member of the Management Board of SAPSE responsible for Board area SAP Product Engineering, agrees that the joint production development effort indicates that, "The automotive industry is showing impressive momentum in its digital transformation and we at SAP can support our customers with our in-depth knowledge of the sector."

Sources: Compiled from MAHLE (2020), Parsons (2020), Warburton (2020), and Wesseler (2020).

Transportation Management Systems

Within POM, transportation management systems (TMSs) are relied on to handle transportation planning, which includes shipping consolidation, load and trip planning, route planning, fleet and driver planning, and carrier selection to gain significant cost savings and provide better customer service. TMSs also support vehicle management and accounting transactions.

inbound logistics refers to receiving inventory.

outbound logistics refers to shipping inventory.

Shipping Consolidation Logistics management is a subset of TMS that deals with the coordination of several complex **inbound logistics**, and **outbound logistics** processes, focused on integrating processes for procuring, producing, and shipping products and/or services.

Logistics management systems automate warehousing operations, along with shipping and other logistical functions. They also monitor the flow of products from supplier to end user. The main functions of logistics management systems are:

- Optimize transportation operations.
- Coordinate with all suppliers.
- Integrate supply chain technologies.
- Synchronize inbound and outbound flows of materials or goods.
- Manage distribution or transport networks.

These systems enable real-time monitoring and tracking of supply chain shipments, schedules, and orders. For example, a logistics management system can enable customers, suppliers, and carriers to collaborate to compare rates and choose the best carrier for each shipment. It does this by supporting all modes of transportation allowing an organization to connect parcel, truckload, rail, ocean, and air carriers to seamlessly meet its shipping needs.

Example of logistics systems include Freight Pop (**https://www.freightpop.com/features**), Roserocket (**https://www.roserocket.com/**), Shippo (**https://goshippo.com/**), and Kuebix TMS (**https://www.kuebix.com/kuebix-tms/**).

Load and Trip Planning, Route Planning, Fleet and Driver Planning, and Carrier Selection
Supporting field workers and vehicle fleet managers is an important part of transportation management. Software that supports these functions is referred to as a field service management (FSM) system. FSM systems optimize routing and effective fleet use through automatic territory management, map visualization, calendar management, and appointment scheduling. They also supply customer forms or notifications such as traffic and weather updates provided through client dashboards. Some more advanced solutions offer GPS-tracking, auto-dispatching, and offline report. FSM systems are often used on mobile devices and are accessible through a Web interface.

Trends in TMS Growth
Four factors that are currently contributing to the growth of TMS are as follows:

1. **Need to upgrade or replace outdated transportation systems** Many systems were installed over 10 years ago—before tablet computers and mobile technologies had become widespread in business. They are considered legacy (old) systems, and are inflexible, difficult to integrate with other newer systems, and expensive to maintain.

2. **Growth of intermodal transport** Intermodal transportation refers to the use of two or more transport modes, such as container ship, air, truck, and rail, to move products from source to destination. Many more companies are shipping via intermodals, and their older TMSs cannot support or deal with intermodal movement, according to Dwight Klappich, a research vice president for Gartner. When brick-and-mortar manufacturers began selling online, for example, they learned that their existing TMSs were inadequate for handling the new line of business. Shippers that expand globally face similar challenges when they try to manage multiple rail, truck, and ocean shipments. Thus, there is a growing need for more robust TMSs to handle multidimensional shipping arrangements.

3. **TMS vendors add capabilities** The basic functions performed by a TMS include gathering data on a load to be transported and matching those data to a historical routing guide. Then the TMS is used to manage the communication process with the various carriers. New feature-rich TMSs are able to access information services to help the shipper identify optimal routes, given all current conditions. For example, the latest TMSs can interact directly with market-data benchmarking services. An automated, real-time market monitoring function saves shippers time and errors and cuts costs significantly.

4. **TMSs handle big data** Transportation tends to generate a high volume of transactional data. Managing the data is not easy. TMS vendors are developing systems that make valuable use of the big data that are collected and stored. By drilling down into specific regions or focusing on particular market trends, for example, shippers can use their big data to make better decisions.

Examples of FMS include Microsoft Dynamics 365 Field Service (**https://dynamics .microsoft.com/en-us/field-service/overview/**), Oracle Mobile Field Service (**https://www .oracle.com/applications/ebusiness/products/mobile-field-service/**), SAP (**https://www .sap.com/products/transportation-logistics.html**), and Synchroteam (**https://www .synchroteam.com/**).

In **Case 9.2: Business Case** at the end of this chapter you will read how MAHLE (introduced in IT at Work 9.1) initially partnered with SAP to successfully deploy a TMS to improve its logistics processes.

Other POM Technologies

Many other areas of production/operations are improved by ISs and tools. Production planning optimization tools, product routing and tracking systems, order management, factory layout planning and design, and other tasks can be supported by POM subsystems. For example, a Web-based system at Office Depot matches employee scheduling with store traffic patterns to increase customer satisfaction and reduce costs. Schurman Fine Papers, a manufacturer/retailer of greeting cards and specialty products, uses special warehouse management software to improve demand forecasting and inventory processes. Its two warehouses efficiently distribute products to over 30,000 retail stores.

Questions

1. What is the function of SCM in an organization?
2. What trends are contributing to the growing use of TMS?
3. Define logistics management.
4. What are the three categories of inventory costs?
5. What are the objectives of JIT?
6. Explain the difference between EOQ and JIT inventory models.
7. What is the goal of lean manufacturing?
8. What is CIM?

9.3 Sales and Marketing Management Systems

LO9.3 Describe *the sales and marketing management function and how sales and marketing management systems impact sales management procedures and tasks and the two major functional activities of marketing management.*

Significant changes have occurred in the field of marketing over the last decade due to the evolution of information systems and particularly the Web. Not only has technology created entire new service and product categories, but also many traditional marketing functions including product development, pricing, distribution, and promotion have changed. ISs and digital networks that have emerged in the last 10–15 years have resulted in new revenue streams, new business models, new retail, promotion and distribution channels, and entirely new ways of interacting with and support customers.

In general, sales and marketing systems support the following:

- Customer relationships (sales and support)
- Digital advertising
- Social media monitoring and promotions
- Automated ad placement and media buying
- Market research
- Intelligence gathering
- Distributing products and services to customers
- Order tracking
- Online and mobile order processing
- Online and mobile payment methods

Various sales and marketing management systems are depicted in **Figure 9.7**. In Chapters 7 and 8 we already discussed some sales and marketing strategies including omnichannel retailing, e-commerce, and mobile commerce. In addition, although managing the customer is a critical component of sales and marketing management, CRM is typically treated as an enterprise-level system and you will learn about this important aspect of sales and marketing management in Chapter 10 where we discuss it in detail.

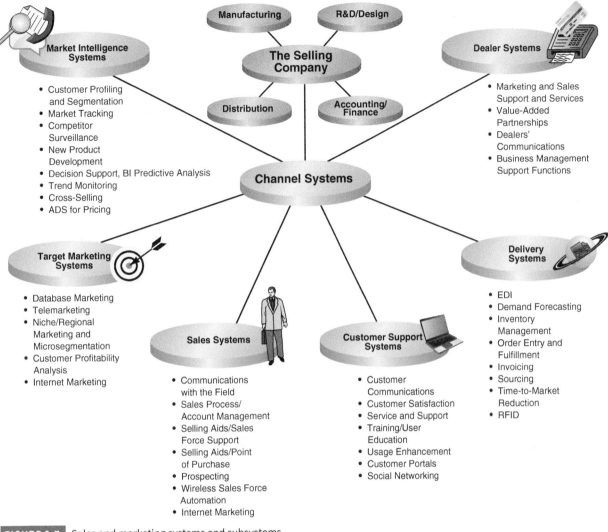

FIGURE 9.7 Sales and marketing systems and subsystems.

In this chapter our focus is on sales and marketing management at the functional level and how IT supports these two business functions.

Sales Management Systems

Sales management involves sales procedures and tasks from the generation of leads and quotes and moving to customer conversion, purchases, returns, and support. **Sales management systems** combine different sales procedures and tasks to provide a detailed overview of a sales team's work on different products, services, location, and customers to accelerate the tracking of sales flow and help an organization achieve its sales targets faster. Benefits of sales management systems include:

- Provides feedback on sales team members performance
- Boosts repeat selling
- Increases social media marketing

There are many different types of sales management systems. Features include summarizing leads, reporting, collaboration, predicting analysis, pricing optimization, online product promotion, tracking the entire sales cycling, and even custom branding. For example, an organization can collect the performance of its salespeople in a sales management system and use it to compare performance along several dimensions, such as time, product, region, and even the time of day. Or, actual current sales can be compared to historical data and to expectations providing actionable insights. Then, sales productivity can be boosted by Web-based call centers.

When a customer calls a sales rep, the rep can look at the customer's history of purchases, demographics, services available where the customer lives, and more. This information enables reps to provide better customer service.

Sales management systems can be deployed in three ways ranging from basic solutions that are free to much more sophisticated and costly offerings:

1. **On-premise**   Covered by a single license and hosted on the client's local server, these are the most expensive since they require complex set up and possibly some hardware installing.
2. **Software-as-a-Service (SaaS)**.   Usually paid for by the month and hosted on the vendor's server, the user organization is not responsible for installation, updating, or maintenance. It is generally a less expensive option.
3. **Cloud-hosted**.   Most of these sales management systems offer free basic plans and are the last expensive option due to universal access and the absence of any responsibility for the user organization to update them or pay for maintenance.

Capterra (**https://www.capterra.com/**) provides us with a useful list of sales management software offerings and reviews that include Brightpearl (**https://www.brightpearl.com/**), HubSpot Sales (**https://www.hubspot.com/**), Pipedrive (**https://www.pipedrive.com/**), and Infusionsoft (**https://keap.com/infusionsoft**). Sales management software that is especially helpful to small businesses, enabling them to rapidly increase sales and growth includes Zendesk sell, Oracle NetSuite, and AmoCRM (Software Advice, 2020).

Marketing Management Systems

The American Marketing Association defines **marketing management** as the process of planning and executing the creation, pricing, promotion, and distribution of ideas, goods, and services to create market exchanges that satisfy customers and organizations. It is essentially a process that allows organization to determine which products or services are of interest to its customers and what strategy they should use in generating sales and communication with customers. Marketing managers plan, organize, control, and implement marketing programs, policies, and strategies to create and satisfy the demand for the organization's products or services and maximize profits.

The two main function-level activities involved in marketing management are pricing of products or services and profitability analysis.

Pricing of Products or Services   Sales volume as well as profits are determined by the prices of products or services. Pricing is a difficult decision, particularly during economic recessions. ISs used in conjunction with data collected from online markets helps companies maximize profits using a variety of yield management practices. For instance, online retailers can personalize the Web pages shown to individual customers and display a combination of products and prices customized to entice that customer to make a purchase. The automated decisions about what products and prices to display to a customer are determined by a complex algorithm based on the customer's previous purchases, Web viewing history, activity on social media, and product searches. While airlines have been charging different ticket prices for the same flight for years, the practice is now employed by many different businesses as part of a mass-customization strategy made possible by information and computing technologies. Another example of technology-driven pricing and promotional strategies includes flash sales designed to engage customers and trigger a quick spike in sales. Flash sales work by offering customers an incredible deal for a very short time, usually announced via mobile text message, e-mail, or social media.

Profitability Analysis   In deciding on advertising and other marketing efforts, managers need to know the profit contribution or profit margin (profit margin = sale price − cost of good) of certain products and services. Profitability metrics for products and services can be derived from the cost-accounting system. For example, profit performance analysis software available from IBM, Oracle, SAS, and Microstrategy is designed to help managers assess and improve the profit performance of their line of business, products, distribution channels, sales regions, and other dimensions critical to managing the enterprise. Several airlines, for example, use automated decision support systems (DSS) to set prices based on profitability.

Marketing managers use a variety of metrics to measure progress against objectives to guide a firm's marketing plan. To achieve this, they use a marketing management system to systematically collect and report accurate data obtained through market research, survey, and customer feedback.

Traditional **marketing management systems** benefit an organization by providing:

- Easier access to customer information
- Improved account planning
- Visual schedules to prioritize work
- Easier communication with other members of the marketing team
- Anytime, anywhere access to customer information, schedules, and reports

Examples of marketing management systems include Salesforce Pardot (**https://www.pardot.com/**), Hubspot Marketing (**https://www.hubspot.com/products/marketing/get-started**), Sharpspring (**https://sharpspring.com/**), and TechTarget's Target ROI (**https://www.techtarget.com**).

Social Media as a Marketing Management Strategy

Entire marketing efforts are going digital to facilitate greater streamlining and automating of marketing tasks. As a result, more and more marketing managers are using social media marketing to generate awareness about their brand and promote their goods and services. One of the main features that attracts them to use social media as a marketing tool is its faster, spontaneous, and systematic form of communication. Social media provides easy access to a huge diverse population that is searching for good online content. For example, in the finance industry, where time is money, social media outlets like Twitter, Facebook, and Instagram are great marketing tools for reaching customers quickly and easily as well as enabling marketing managers to gather valuable, free market knowledge. This not only saves time, but also makes sure that the business is put in front of its target audience. Social media has also been shown to increase revenue and increased brand loyalty.

One feature of social media that is gaining a lot of traction as a particularly useful marketing tool is a **chatbot**. Chatbots enable conversational marketing via auditory or textual methods (**Figure 9.8**).

A **chatbot** is a service powered by rules and sometimes artificial intelligence that simulates a conversation (or chat) with a customer using a chat interface.

Zapp2Photo/Shutterstock.com

FIGURE 9.8   A chatbot verifies a customer order.

They provide customers with assistance and access to information 24/7 and are proving to be more effective at improving customer satisfaction and giving marketing managers better insights into customer behaviors, preferences, and complaints than the more established virtual help desks. By responding to requests faster chatbots can positively impact the customer relationship and free up customer support teams to apply their knowledge to more complex queries. Interestingly, a recent survey on the state of conversational marketing reported that as customers become more familiar with using chatbots, only 38% of consumers prefer to talk to a human when making enquiries (Kilens, 2019). Coupled with the right machine learning tools, a chatbot can also analyze feedback and other information it gathers from customers giving marketing managers value information to guide marketing strategy. From a financial standpoint, a recent Deloitte study reported that by 2022 chatbots are projected to save organizations billions of dollars by streamlining customer service and bot-based commerce (Robinson et al., 2017). **IT at Work 9.2** describes how Universal Studies is using chatbots to market its experience rather than a physical product.

IT at Work 9.2

Chatbot Marketing Improves Customer Relationships at Home, on Vacation, and at Sporting Events

DOM. If you're sitting at home watching TV and feel like a late-night snack, instead of picking up the phone or going to their website all you have to do is access Domino's Pizza Facebook page, interact with its chatbot—DOM—and voila! your favorite pizza will appear at your door in a matter of minutes. Using the chatbot you can custom order pizzas just like you would by phone or online, but the ability to save and repeat orders make is much easier to score your favorite pie without having to leave the couch. Although online order is nothing new, ordering through a chatbot eliminates the need to download an app or create an account.

One of the unique aspects of Universal Studios adoption of chatbots is that it supports a customer experience rather than a product or service. Guests at Universal Studios can now interact with chatbots to do more than book reservations and buy tickets. They can get practical information while on-the-ground at one of its parks. For example, guests can find out ride wait times in real-time

rather than rely on a third-party app to see whether they are faced with long wait lines so they can adjust their plan of attack as to what rides to go on next. It's this kind of real-time information on demand that makes chatbots so valuable to a business.

ROBOT PIRES. To get closer to its global fanbase, Arsenal FC, an English powerhouse soccer team based in London, introduced an official chatbot to liaise with fans. The quirky Arsenal chatbot—dubbed "Robot Pires" after one of its most revered players who later returned to the club as a coach—operates across social messaging channels including Facebook Messenger, Slack, Skype, and Telegram to give Arsenal supporters easy access to breaking news and timely content delivery of schedules, results, videos player stats, and ticket information. For example, Robot Pires sends out score reports for users who can't watch soccer matches in real-time along with upcoming match schedules, team line-ups, and news articles to make it about so much more than traditional customer service.

Sources: Compiled from Bell (2018), Barnhart (2019), Kilens (2019), Rathod (2020), and Domino's Pizza (2020).

Questions

1. Explain push-through marketing and pull-through marketing.
2. List two sales and distribution channels.
3. Describe challenges associated with pricing products and services.
4. Describe profitability analysis.
5. What are the differences between sales management and marketing management?
6. How do some online businesses determine the prices they will charge to individual customers?

9.4 | Accounting, Finance, and Regulatory Compliance Systems

LO9.4 Define *the accounting and finance functions and the management systems that help organizations meet local and global regulatory compliance requirements and facilitate capital budgeting and forecasting.*

Accounting and finance departments are responsible for controlling and managing cash flows, assets, liabilities, and net revenues (profit) as well as ensuring that an organization remains compliant with local and global regulatory requirements. Financial accounting is a specialized branch of accounting that keeps track of a company's financial transactions and prepares financial statements, such as balance sheets and **income statements**. Using standardized guidelines, business transactions are recorded, summarized, and presented in a financial report or financial statement such as an income statement or a balance sheet. However, the objective of financial accounting is not simply to report the value of a company. Rather, its purpose is to provide sufficient and accurate information for others to assess the value of a company for investment or other purposes. Investors, regulators, and others rely on the integrity and accuracy of external financial statements. As a result, accounting and finance departments must comply with generally accepted accounting principles (GAAP) and with the requirements of the **Financial Accounting Standards Board (FASB)**. Corporations whose stock is publicly traded must also comply with the reporting requirements of the Securities and Exchange Commission (SEC), a regulatory agency of the U.S. government.

In this section you will learn how accounting, financial planning and budgeting, and regulatory compliance systems help support the accounting and finance functions achieve their objectives.

> **Income statements** summarizes a company's revenue and expenses for one quarter of a fiscal year or the entire fiscal year. It is also known as a P&L (profit and loss) or earnings statement.

> **Financial Accounting Standards Board (FASB)** establishes financial accounting and reporting standards for public and private companies and not-for-profit organizations.

Accounting Systems

Accounting software is a foundational technology for many companies, and as a business grows, powerful and effective accounting solutions are critical. Most accounting software packages offer the same basic features necessary for managing finances: accounts receivable (A/R), accounts payable (A/P), general ledger, billing and invoicing, purchase and sales orders, and reporting. In addition to basic functionality, the top accounting solutions offer additional features to give users more power, flexibility, and customization. Often, accounting solutions are closely integrated with enterprise systems, such as ERP systems that include an extensive accounting module.

Many vendors offer cloud-based accounting solutions. SaaS accounting software solutions include the features of traditional systems, with the added benefit of anytime, anywhere accessibility and updating.

Financial Planning and Budgeting Systems

The management of financial assets is a major task in financial planning and budgeting. Financial planning, similar to any other functional planning, is tied to the overall organizational planning and to other functional areas. It is divided into short-, medium-, and long-term horizons, much as activities planning. **Financial planning and budgeting systems** help companies create and manage budgets, improving the organization's ability to monitor performance and quickly identify departures from planned financial activity when they occur.

Knowing the availability and cost of money is a key ingredient for successful financial planning. Especially important is projecting cash flows, which tells organizations what funds they need and when and how they will acquire them. In today's tough economic conditions with tight credit and limited availability of funds, this function has become critical to most companies' survival. Inaccurate cash flow projection is the main reason why many small businesses go bankrupt. For example, the inability to access credit led to the bankruptcy of investment bank Lehman Brothers some years ago.

Five activities that are central to financial planning and budgeting are budgeting, forecasting, financial ratio analysis, and profitability analysis and cost control.

Budgeting   The best-known part of financial planning is the annual budget, which allocates the financial resources of an organization among participants, activities, and projects. The budget is the financial expression of the enterprise's plans. Management allocates resources in the way that best supports the mission. IT enables the introduction of financial logic and efficiency into the budgeting process. Several software packages, many of which are Web-based, are available to support budget preparation and control.

Capital budgeting is the process of analyzing and selecting investments with the highest return on investment (ROI) for the company. The process may include comparing alternative investments, for example, evaluating private cloud versus public cloud computing options.

Forecasting As you read, a major reason why organizations fail is their inability to forecast and/or secure sufficient cash flow. Underestimated expenses, overspending, financial mismanagement, and fraud can lead to disaster. Good planning is necessary, but not sufficient, and must be supplemented by skillful control. Control activities in organizations take many forms, including control and auditing of the systems themselves. IT plays an extremely important role in supporting organizational control, as we show throughout the text.

Financial Ratio Analysis A major task of the accounting/finance department is to watch the financial health of the company by monitoring and assessing a set of financial ratios. These ratios are also used by external parties when they decide whether to invest in an organization, extend credit, or buy it.

The collection of data for ratio analysis is done by the financial planning and budgeting system, and computation of the ratios completed through financial analysis models. Interpretation of ratios and the ability to forecast their future behavior require expertise.

Profitability Analysis and Cost Control Companies are concerned with the profitability of individual products or services, product lines, divisions, or the financial health of the entire organization. Profitability analysis software allows accurate computation of profitability and allocation of overhead costs. One way to control cost is by properly estimating it. This is done by using special software. For example, Oracle Hyperion Profitability and Cost Management software (**https://www.oracle.com/applications/performance-management/ solutions/profitability-cost-management.html**) is a performance management app that provides insights into costs and profitability. This app helps managers evaluate business performance by discovering the drivers of cost and profitability and improving resource alignment. Sophisticated business rules are stored in one place, enabling analyses and strategies to be shared easily across an enterprise.

IT at Work 9.3 describes how Thule used a budgeting and planning system to upgrade its recordkeeping from Excel spreadsheets and increase the confidence of its finance team in its budgeting process.

IT at Work 9.3

THULE Gets a Single Source of Truth for Its Financials

You're probably familiar with the name Thule. The Thule Group helps you transport your sporting equipment—bicycle, skis, snowboard, fishing rods and more—safely, easily, and in style. The Thule group is based in Malmo, Sweden and has more than 2,200 employees at more than 40 production and sales locations around the world. Thule Vehicle Accessories North America is a division of Thule and is committed to high quality and continuous innovation in their products. Unfortunately, until recently budgeting and planning in the North America Division were sub-par. Individual sales and department managers kept their budget data in Excel spreadsheets and shared them by e-mail. This means that each month, when the finance department gathered up data, someone had spent at least one full workday keying the actual into Excel spreadsheets. This manual process was time-consuming and prone to human error. Most important, the data was inconsistent. Sales and expense forecasting were cumbersome at best and if Sales was likely to miss one of its targets, the typical response was to cut back on spending without specifying where. On top of this, the organization was growing, which made managing expense budgets even more challenging.

To address the problem, the finance department took the lead in searching for more capable software. The solution they settled on was Planful, an easy-to-use, cloud-based financial planning and budgeting system that would not overburden the Thule IT team. Planful allowed Thule to produce its next annual budget in less than half the time it had taken previously. The person who did the data entry was freed up to do more valuable work and Planful provided a single point of access to consistent data shared by all users. In addition, using Planful's easy-to-use templates Finance and Sales collaborated to develop a rolling sales forecast that is updated every month to extend Thule's yearly financial horizon. As a result, Thule now has a forecast that people can actually sit down and discuss, and they have far better visibility into important financial issues related to their customers, promotions, and expense management.

Mark Cohen, VP of Finance at Thule Vehicle Accessories North America, summed up the success of the project when he said, "Before we were lucky just to get the numbers. Leveraging Continuous Planning with Planful we get the numbers and the whole story." In December 2019, Thule announced the acquisition of Denver Outfitters to expand Thule's portfolio of products focused on an active lifestyle to include fly fishing rod vaults. Thanks to its more efficient and effective budgeting and planning practices the acquisition is not expected to have a material impact on the quarterly results or financial status of the Thule Group.

Sources: Compiled from Backbone Media (2020), Planful (2020), Prevedere (2020), and thule.com (2020).

Finance and budgeting management systems make it easy for individuals and organizations to stay on top of their finances, both from a savings perspective and from a debt management standpoint to reduce debt and free up savings for investment purposes. The major benefits of using budgeting software are that it can reduce the time and effort involved in the budget process, explore and analyze the implications of organizational and environmental changes, facilitate the integration of corporate strategic objectives with operational plans, make planning an ongoing continuous process, and automatically monitor exceptions for patterns and trends.

Planning, budgeting, and forecasting are three features that assist organizations in gaining an insight into the health of the company and speed up cycle times. While many organizations still use Excel-like spreadsheets in their the financial planning process others—like the Thule Group in **IT at Work 9.3**—have significantly improved their financial processes by moving to more sophisticated cloud-based solutions that allow users to view their financial data on a single screen and drill down into cell values to get a deeper understanding of the data **(Figure 9.9)**. This allows organizations to react more quickly to market changes and capitalize on new opportunities. Many of the cloud-based offerings are a good fit for finance departments that need to increase accountability and accuracy and help them align their budget with their organization's strategic plan.

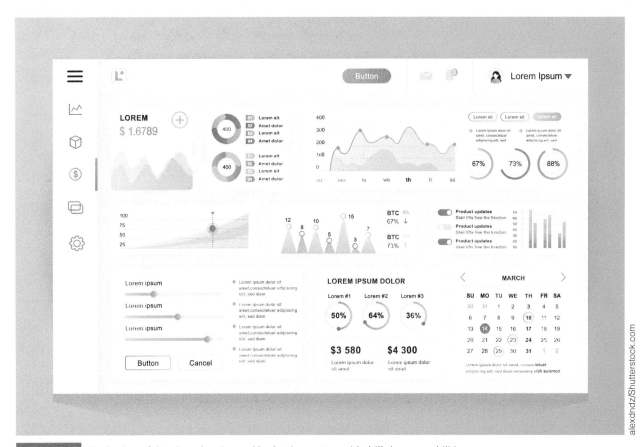

FIGURE 9.9 Single view of data in a planning and budgeting system with drill-down capabilities.

alexdndz/Shutterstock.com

Capterra (**https://www.capterra.com/**) provides examples of planning and budgeting software including Adaptive Insights (**https://www.adaptiveinsights.com/**), Planning Maestro (**https://www.centage.com/products/planning-maestro/**), Planful (**https://planful .com/**), and XLERANT (**https://xlerant.com/**).

Regulatory Compliance Systems

Regulatory compliance systems are designed to help organizations understand what regulations, policies, and obligations are applicable to them locally and globally to manage changes to applicable financial, data, environmental, and health and safety regulations. They help eliminate compliance issues and risk and their features can vary widely from one solution provider to another. Financial disclosure is an important task for any accounting and finance department. As part of an organization's compliance obligations, the accounting function must attest (verify) that there are no material weaknesses in internal controls. A weakness in an internal control is a major cause of monetary fraud and mishandling of data, which is also known as white-collar crime.

Financial Misrepresentations

financial misrepresentations occurs when a company has intentionally deceived one or more other parties.

Financial Misrepresentations The prevention, detection, and investigation of fraud are needed to reduce the risk of publicly reporting inaccurate information. The classic high-profile examples of **financial misrepresentations** are Bernard L. Madoff Investment Securities (2008), Lehman Brothers (2008), Enron (2001), and many related to the subprime mortgage crisis. **Table 9.1** describes three of the worst accounting fraud cases of all time. The FBI investigates white-collar crime and reports on the subject at its website FBI.gov.

TABLE 9.1 Three Worst Accounting Scandals of All Time

Company and Fraudsters	Damages	How They Did It	Penalties
Bernie Madoff Investment Securities LLC (2008) Bernie Madoff, his accountant David Friehling, and CFO Frank DiPascalli	Tricked investors out of $64.8 billion through the largest Ponzi scheme in the history.	Investors were paid returns out of their own money or money from other investors—rather than from profits.	150 years in prison for Madoff + $170 billion restitution. Prison time for Friehling and DiPascalli.
Lehman Brothers (2008) Lehman executives and the company's auditors, Ernst & Young	Hid over $50 billion in loans disguised as sales.	Allegedly sold toxic assets to Cayman Island banks with the understanding that they would be bought back eventually. Created the impression that Lehman had $50 billion more in cash and $50 billion less in toxic assets than it actually had.	Forced into the largest bankruptcy in U.S. history.
Enron (2001) CEO Jeffrey Skilling and former CEO Ken Lay	Shareholders lost $74 billion, thousands of employees and investors lost their retirement accounts, and many employees lost their jobs.	Kept huge debts off its balance sheets.	Lay died before serving time; Skilling received 24 years in prison. The company filed for bankruptcy. Arthur Andersen was found guilty of fudging Enron's accounts.

The SEC's financial disclosure system is central to its mission of protecting investors and maintaining fair, orderly, and efficient markets. Since 1934, the SEC has required financial disclosure in forms and documents. In 1984, the SEC began collecting electronic documents to help investors obtain information, but those documents made it difficult to search for and find specific data items.

To eliminate that difficulty and improve how investors find and use information, the SEC now requires public companies, called filers, to submit their financial reports as *tagged interactive data files* (FASB.org, 2012) formatted in **eXtensible Business Reporting Language (XBRL)**. In addition, data in the reports must be tagged according to standards established by the Financial Accounting Securities Board (FASB). Each year, FASB updates the list of over 15,000 computer readable tags known as the **GAAP Financial Reporting Taxonomy**. Annual updates reflect changes in accounting standards and other enhancements designed to improve the reporting process and usability. **Tech Note 9.1** explains how tagged interactive data files can be created using XBRL tagging.

Tech Note 9.1

Creating XBRL Documents

XBRL is a language for the standards-based exchange of business information between business systems. Each item, such as cash or depreciation expense, is tagged with descriptive metadata or labels, such as calendar year, audited/unaudited status, currency, and so on, as defined by the GAAP Financial Reporting Taxonomy. The taxonomy is like a data dictionary that defines financial concepts and the relationships between various types of data that might be included in a financial report. The **XBRL language** and data tags make it possible for the reports to be read by any software that includes an XBRL processor. Interactive (tagged) data make it easier for investors to analyze and compare the financial performance of public companies, increasing the efficiency and transparency of reporting processes, and the ability to consolidate financial data from different operating systems.

Prior to XBRL, reports were noninteractive. Investors who wanted specific data had to manually search lengthy corporate annual reports or mutual fund documents. As more companies use interactive data, sophisticated analysis tools used by financial professionals are now available to average investors.

Creating XBRL documents does not require XML computer programming. As requirements for XBRL reporting become increasingly common around the world, more vendors are developing software products for marking up reports, tagging data, submitting reports to various recipients, as well as receiving and analyzing tagged data from other sources. **Figure 9.10** shows how XBRL documents are created. XBRL helps companies:

- Generate cleaner data, including written explanations and supporting notes.
- Produce more accurate data with fewer errors that require follow-up by regulators.
- Transmit data more quickly to regulators and meet deadlines.
- Increase the number of cases and amount of information that staffers can handle.

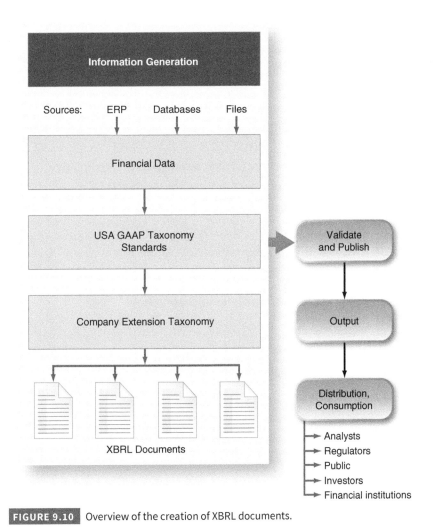

FIGURE 9.10   Overview of the creation of XBRL documents.

XBRL Reporting Compliance

In addition to the public companies required by the SEC to submit their financial reports as XBRL documents, other businesses are being required to use XBRL-formatted reporting. For instance, the SEC requires mutual funds to submit risk return summaries in XBRL format, and banks in the United States must submit certain types of XBRL reports to the Federal Deposit Insurance Corporation (FDIC). Globally, regulators in many other countries require companies to file reports using XBRL. When international firms file XBRL reports, they will oftentimes use the International Financial Reporting Standards (IFRS) Taxonomy created by the International Accounting Standards Board (IASB). We anticipate that XBRL reporting will increase over time as regulatory agencies, investors, and organizations responsible for setting accounting standards increasingly argue that XBRL reporting is good for both business and the economy.

Mishandling Data

Another important aspect of regulatory compliance is the monetary consequences of mishandling customer data. This is clearly demonstrated in our opening case where Equifax did not adequately protect the data of over 147 million people from a cyberattack. As you read, the financial consequences to Equifax will be dire and will result in a significant negative impact on consumer and stockholder confidence levels.

Common elements found in regulatory compliance software includes:

- Support for widely adopted standards such as ISO 9000 (quality management); ISO 14000 (environmental management); IS) 31000 (risk management) and OHSAS 18000 (Occupational health and safety management).
- Identify and management regulatory requirements including permits and reports by country or world region.
- Provide access to regulatory content and compliance requirements of regulatory agencies.
- Ability to measure compliance and product reports for delivery to agencies, customers, suppliers, shareholders, etc.
- Management and planning of compliance audits, including scheduling, task assignments, tracking, and report.
- Measure and assess risk associated with noncompliance.
- Document change to provide a history of regulatory compliance.
- Measure costs of fulfilling regulatory compliance requirements.

Some examples of leading regulatory compliance software include MetricStream (**https://www.metricstream.com/**), MASTERCONTROL (**https://www.mastercontrol.com/**), IBM OpenPages with Watson Regulatory Compliance Management (**https://www.ibm.com/us-en/marketplace/governance-risk-and-compliance?mhsrc=ibmsearch_a&mhq=openPages**), and QUANTIVATE (**https://quantivate.com/**).

Questions

1. Identify five activities that are central to financial planning and budgeting.
2. Name three features that assist organizations in gaining an insight into the health of the company and speed up cycle times.
3. What types of regulatory compliance are organizations responsible for?
4. What is eXtensible Business Reporting Language (XBRL)?
5. Why does the SEC mandate data disclosure, whereby data items are tagged to make them easily searchable?
6. Identify three common elements found in regulatory compliance software.

9.5 | Human Resource Information Systems (HRIS)

LO9.5 Identify *the purpose of human resource management and the ways in which HRIS can improve the HR function.*

Retaining high-performance people requires monitoring how people feel about the workplace, their compensation, value to the company, and chances for advancement—and maintaining workplace health and safety. To this, companies must find, recruit, motivate, deploy, train, and assess employees to succeed in their workplace (**Figure 9.11**).

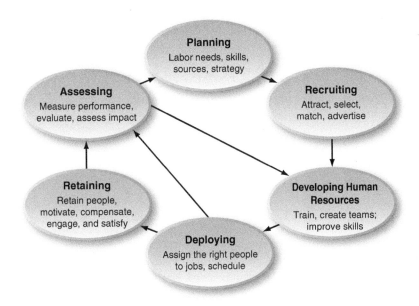

FIGURE 9.11   Illustrates the management activities HR carries out in acquiring, developing, and managing talented people.

The main goals of **human resource management** are to support various facets of the employment process including **recruitment**; **employee development**; **HR planning, control, and management**; and **HR compliance**.

To reduce the workload and improve the effectiveness of the HR function, organizations need reliable **human resource information systems (HRIS)** that support and improve each of these HR activities and reduces the workload of the HR team to allow them time to deal one-on-one with personnel issues in a more personalized way.

Recruitment   Many companies flooded with applicants still have difficulty finding the right people. LinkedIn, Indeed.com, and Monster.com are widely used social media sites for recruitment and headhunters. In fact, some reports suggest that over 90% of U.S. companies use LinkedIn as their primary source of identifying job candidates. HR managers using LinkedIn must become familiar with the website's search tools for finding candidates that meet certain criteria for the position they are trying to fill. Using the advanced search features, HR managers can develop search queries that screen user profiles on the basis of things such as current job title, current industry, seniority level, and years of education. Keywords can be used to find candidates with specials, training, or experience. Job hunters should consider the search strategies HR professionals are likely to use when searching for candidates and include information in their profiles that will increase the chances of being included in search results.

human resource management is a field that deals with employment policies, procedures, communications, and compliance requirements.

recruitment is the process of finding potential employees with the skills and talent needed by the company, testing them, and deciding which ones to hire.

employee development is a joint endeavor between employee and employer to update the existing skills and knowledge of an individual employee.

HR planning, control, and management is the continuous process of systematically forecasting future human resource requirements and determining the extent to which existing human resources can be most effectively utilized to meet those requirements.

HR compliance is the process of defining policies and procedure to ensure lawful employment and work practices in line with the company's human capital resource goals.

a **human resource information systems (HRIS)** provides a centralized repository of employee master data that the HR management group needs for completing HR processes.

Employee Development

Once recruited, employees become part of the corporate HR talent pool, which needs to be maintained and developed. Activities associated with employee development typically include:

Performance Evaluation Employees are evaluated periodically by their immediate supervisors. Peers or subordinates may also evaluate others. Evaluations are usually recorded on paper or electronic forms. Using such information manually is a tedious and error-prone job. Once digitized, evaluations can be used to support many decisions, ranging from rewards to transfers to layoffs. For example, Cisco Systems is known for developing an IT-based human capital strategy. Many universities evaluate professors online. The evaluation form appears on the screen, and the students fill it in. Results can be tabulated in minutes. Corporate managers can analyze employees' performances with the help of intelligent systems, which provide systematic interpretation of performance over time. Several vendors provide software for performance evaluation, such as HalogenSoftware.com and Capterra.com.

Training and Human Resources Development Employee training and retraining are important activities of the HR department. Major issues are planning of classes and tailoring specific training programs to meet the needs of the organization and employees. Sophisticated HR departments build a career development plan for each employee. IT can support the planning, monitoring, and control of these activities by using workflow applications.

HR Planning, Control, and Management

In some industries, labor negotiation is an important aspect of HR planning, and it may be facilitated by IT. For most companies, administering employee benefits is also a significant part of the HR function. Here are several examples of how an HRIS can help.

Personnel Planning and HR Strategies The HR department forecasts requirements for people and skills. In some geographical areas and for overseas assignments, it may be difficult to find particular types of employees. In such cases, the HR department plans how to locate sufficient HR or develop them from within.

Benefits Administration Employees' contributions to their organizations are rewarded by salary/wage, bonuses, and other benefits. Benefits include those for health and dental care as well as contributions for pensions. Managing the benefits system can be a complex task, due to its many components and the tendency of organizations to allow employees to choose and trade off benefits. In large companies, using computers for self-benefits selection can save a tremendous amount of labor and time for HR staff. Providing flexibility in selecting benefits is viewed as a competitive advantage in large organizations. It can be successfully implemented when supported by computers. Some companies have automated benefits enrollments. Employees can self-register for specific benefits using the corporate portal or voice technology. Employees self-select desired benefits from a menu. Payroll pay cards are now in use in numerous companies, such as Payless Shoes, which has 30,000 employees in 5,000 stores. The system specifies the value of each benefit and the available benefits balance of each employee. Some companies use intelligent agents to assist employees and monitor their actions.

Employee Relationship Management In their effort to better manage employees, companies are developing human capital management, facilitated by the Web, to streamline the HR process. These Web applications are more commonly referred to as employee relationship management. For example, self-services such as tracking personal information and online training are very popular in ERM. Improved relationships with employees result in better retention and higher productivity.

HR Compliance   In today's legal environment, effective HR compliance programs are a "must have" for all organizations to monitor workplace and employment practices to ensure compliance with federal, state, and local regulatory requirements related to recruitment and employment. These include the Fair Labor Standards Act (FLSA), Occupational Health & Safety Agencies (OSHA), and the antidiscrimination and sexual harassment laws along with seven other employment laws to protect against discrimination are listed in **Table 9.2**.

TABLE 9.2   **HR Monitors Compliance with Antidiscrimination Employment Laws**

Title VII of the Civil Rights Act of 1964	Prohibits discrimination on the basis of race, color, religion, national origin, and sex. It also prohibits sex discrimination on the basis of pregnancy and sexual harassment.
Civil Rights Act of 1966	Prohibits discrimination based on race or ethnic origin.
Equal Pay Act of 1963	Prohibits employers from paying different wages to men and women who perform essentially the same work under similar working conditions.
Bankruptcy Act	Prohibits discrimination against anyone who has declared bankruptcy.
Americans with Disabilities Act	Prohibits discrimination against persons with disabilities.
Equal Employment Opportunity Act	Prohibits discrimination against minorities based on poor credit ratings.
Age Discrimination in Employment Act (ADEA)	Prohibits discrimination against individuals who are age 40 or above.

HR managers are expected to understand and take steps to ensure compliance with all federal, state, and local regulatory requirements. These laws and regulations change frequently, which makes remaining compliant on an ongoing basis a difficult task. An HRIS can help HR managers comply with these regulations and make the process of gathering, synthesizing, and reporting relevant information much less arduous and time consuming. An HRIS helps an organization keep up with constantly changing regulations and laws by continually providing updated information about laws affecting a particular business, sometimes automatically and may even be capable of sending alerts when regulations or compliance requirements change. Compliance-related benefits that an organization gains from an HRIS include:

- Making HR paperwork completion, storage, and organization easier and faster
- Helping with wage and hour law compliance
- Allowing better compliance oversight
- Mitigating errors that may result in noncompliance
- Avoiding penalties from being noncompliant

HRIS Move to the Cloud

In the past few years, HRIS have been moved to intranets and clouds—wherein HR applications are leased in SaaS arrangements. Using intranets, HR applications have shifted many routine tasks to employees who log in to manage their retirement benefits, payroll deductions, direct deposits, health-care benefits, and the like. When employees manage their own HR services, HR professionals can focus on legal and compliance responsibilities, employee development, talent management, hiring, and succession planning.

   IT at Work 9.4 demonstrates how innovative SaaS HRIS solutions are enabling global organizations to transform their HR functions.

IT at Work 9.4

SaaS Benefits Global HR Transformation Efforts

Three real-world examples illustrate the benefits of tying SaaS to global HR transformation efforts:

- A **global medical device manufacturer** needed to create an independent HR system as it divested from its parent company. Cloud computing was at the core of its new global HR delivery model, which reduced the demand on internal business and IT resources. The company was able to establish fully independent HR operations within 10 months.

- A **national nonprofit foundation** with a fast-growing employee population wanted to improve the effectiveness of HR operations. The organization selected a cloud-based solution, which dramatically improved time to value without overstretching internal IT resources. Because little front-end investment was required, the foundation hit its budget target.

- A **global entertainment company** needed a learning management system that could deliver content varying from instructor-based training to 30-second video how-to snippets. It chose to deploy a new learning management system in the cloud. With this approach, it quickly got the new system up and running.

- A **global provider of recruitment staffing services** implemented a SaaS system including Bullhorn ATS—an applicant tracking system that automates an organization's recruiting and staffing operations and provides a central repository for candidate resumes and applications—to improve its HR capabilities.

- A **leading global health technology company** implemented Deloitte's global HR SaaS solution to support its HR transformation and help to drive innovation. The result was standardized and simplified core staffing processes and the introduction of real-time people analytics to drive better recruiting decisions.

Sources: Compiled from Deloitte (2016) and HR Solutions (2020).

Questions

1. What are the key HR functions?
2. What are the benefits of moving HRISs to intranets or the cloud?
3. What concerns have deterred companies from implementing SaaS HR?
4. How can companies reduce the cost of recruiting qualified employees?
5. Describe IT support for HR planning and control.

Chapter Summary

LO9.1 *Identify* the four traditional functional business units and how business-driven functional business systems support functional and cross-functional process improvement.

The four traditional functional business units found in most organizations are production and operations; sales and marketing; accounting and finance; and human resources. Each functional business unit uses a variety of functional business systems to support core processes, problem solve, make decisions, and comply with local and global regulatory requirements. FBSs provide a foundation for more sophisticated enterprise-level systems by feeding information to external systems and to enterprise-level systems with the organization. Data silos can inhibit effective decision making across functional business units. Cross-functional business processes allow organizations to monitor and evaluate progress toward its goals and objectives established during the strategic planning process and makes it easier to identify problems or barriers to achieving objectives and develop solutions.

LO9.2 *Define* productions and operations management and the various types of functional business systems that support the POM function.

Productions and operations management (POM) facilitates the decision-making processes of production managers by transforming inputs into value-added outputs. These inputs include capital investments, human resources (workers, staff, and managers), facilities, supplies, equipment, materials, IT, and information along with the time and energy needed to manage them. These are transformed through inspection and alteration and subsequent transportation and/or storage. The outputs are the goods and services that an organization produces. POM uses a wide variety of systems including inventory control systems, just-in-time inventory management systems, lean manufacturing systems, quality management systems, computer-integrated manufacturing systems—include CAD/CAM—manufacturing execution systems and transportation management systems.

LO9.3 *Describe* the sales and marketing management function and how sales and marketing management systems impact sales management procedures and tasks and the two major functional activities of marketing management.

Sales and marketing management focuses on customer sales and support, advertising, market research, order tracking, and online mobile order processing and payments. Over the past 10–15 years improvements in technology, and particularly in the Web have created new revenue streams, new business models, new retail, promotion and distribution channels, and entirely new ways of interacting with and support customers. Sales management systems are offered as an on-premise, cloud-based, and SaaS solution. Their features include summarizing leads, reporting, collaboration, predicting analysis, pricing optimization, online product promotion, tracking the entire sales cycling, and even custom branding. They improve sales procedures and tasks by providing feedback on sales team member performance, boosting repeat sales, and increasing social media marketing. They also help sales teams provide better customer service. Marketing management systems at the functional level focus on pricing or products or services and profitability analysis. They allow the systematic collection and reporting of accurate data obtained through market research, survey, and customer feedback along with profitability metrics from cost accounting systems. Marketing management systems make it easier for marketing teams to access customer information, improve account planning, provide visualized schedules to prioritize work, and enable easier communication with other marketing team members anywhere, any time.

LO9.4 *Define* the accounting and finance functions and the management systems that help organizations meet local and global regulatory compliance requirements and facilitate capital budgeting and forecasting.

Accounting and finance departments are functional business units that are responsible for controlling and managing cash flows, assets, liabilities, and net revenues. However, the objective of financial accounting is not simply to report the value of a company. Rather, its purpose is to provide sufficient and accurate information for others to assess the value of a company for investment or other purposes. Investors, regulators, and others rely on the integrity and accuracy of external financial statements to validate that an organization is compliant with local and global regulatory requirements. Acco unting, financial planning

and budgeting, and regulatory compliance systems help support the accounting and finance functions.

Accounting software is a foundational technology for many companies, and as a business grows, powerful and effective accounting solutions are critical. Most accounting software packages offer the same basic features necessary for managing finances: accounts receivable (A/R), accounts payable (A/P), general ledger, billing and invoicing, purchase and sales orders, and reporting.

Financial planning and budgeting systems help companies create and manage budgets, improving the organization's ability to monitor performance and quickly identify departures from planned financial activity when they occur. Activities they support include budgeting, capital budgeting, forecasting, financial ratio analysis, and profitability analysis and cost control.

Regulatory compliance systems are designed to help organizations understand what regulations, policies, and obligations are applicable to them locally and globally to manage changes to applicable environmental and health and safety regulations. To do this, they use mandated XBRL tagging and reporting. Regulatory compliance systems help eliminate compliance issues and risk and their features can vary widely from one solution provider to another.

LO9.5 *Identify* the purpose of human resource management and the ways in which HRIS can improve the HR function.

The purpose of the HR department is to support various facets of the employment process including recruitment, employee development and HR planning, control, and management. Human resource (HR) management is a field that deals with employment policies, procedures, communications, and compliance requirements. Effective HR compliance programs are a necessity for all organizations in today's legal environment. HR needs to monitor workplace and employment practices to ensure compliance with the Fair Labor Standards Act (FLSA), Occupational Health & Safety Agencies (OSHA), and the anti-discrimination and sexual harassment laws.

Human resource information systems (HRIS) are transforming the HR function by facilitating employee performance evaluation, training and HR development, personnel planning, benefits administration and access, and reducing the workload of the HR team to allow them time to deal one-on-one with personnel issues in a more personalized way.

Key Terms

Assuring Your Learning

Discuss: Critical Thinking Questions

1. Discuss the need for sharing data among functional areas.

2. How does waste increase costs? Give three examples.

3. What is the value of lean manufacturing?

4. What is the objective of EOQ?

5. What are the risks of JIT management?

6. Explain the value of finance and budgeting management systems.

7. Push-through ads use data about a person to determine whether the ad should appear. What marketing opportunities does this capability create?

8. Explain why the SEC requires that filers use XBRL.

9. Discuss how IT facilitates the capital budgeting process.

10. Discuss the role IT plays in auditing.

11. Explain the role and benefits of SaaS in HR management.

12. How does digital technology improve the recruitment process?

Explore: Online and Interactive Exercises

1. Visit the Oracle website at **https://www.oracle.com/index.html**

   a. Search for "*Peoplesoft*"

   b. Select *Peoplesoft 9.2 Human Capital Management* and review the HR applications.

   c. Write a 300-word piece describing three benefits of PeopleSoft Human Capital Management.

2. Search for a recent (within two years) video or demo that explains EOQ. Explain the formula.

3. Visit the Oracle website at **https://www.oracle.com/index.html**.

   a. Search for and select *Financial Management System*.

   b. Read the page and watch the short video (1m 15s).

   c. Write a 500-word opinion piece describing how a Financial Management System works and how it adds value in an organization.

4. Examine the capabilities of two POM software packages: Prepare a table that clearly compares and contrasts their capabilities.

5. Choose one of the sales and marketing management systems listed in the chapter. Visit the website and demo the offering. What functional support does the software provide? How easy was it to use?

Analyze & Decide: Apply IT Concepts to Business Decisions

1. Research and analyze

   a. Choose one company that is the subject of an IT at Work from this chapter. Research the company and find reports on how they are using functional business systems **other than the one** that is described in the IT at Work. Write a two-page paper explaining the system(s) they are using and list the advantages/disadvantages associated with its use.

Reinforce: Ensure your understanding of the Key Terms

Solve the online crossword provided for this chapter.

Web Resources

More resources and study tools are located on the student website. You'll find useful Web links and self-test quizzes that provide individualized feedback.

Case 9.2

Business Case: MAHLE GmbH Partners with SAP and MHP to Digitalize Its Logistics and Product Development Processes

If you drive a car, odds are your engine system and components were made by MAHLE GmbH—a leading international development partner and supplier to the passenger and commercial automotive industry and a mobility pioneer. MAHLE's products are installed in at last every second vehicle worldwide. MAHLE components and systems are also used in rail transport and marine applications and stationary applications like mobile machinery. Headquartered in Stuttgart, Germany, MAHLE currently has 79,000 employees in over 30 countries at 160 production locations. It also has 16 major research and development centers in Germany, Great Britain, Luxembourg, Spain, Slovenia, USA, Brazil, Japan, China, and India where more than 6,000 development engineers and technicians work on innovative solutions for the mobility of the future. In 2018, MAHLE reported annual revenues of $14 billion (€12.8 billion). As a company it is committed to making transportation more efficient, more environmentally friendly, and more comfortable. It is continuously optimizing the combustion engine, driving forward the use of alternative fuels, and laying the foundation for the widespread acceptance and worldwide introduction of e-mobility.

The Problem

In 2018, MAHLE was faced with a real dilemma—it was a transportation-based company with a major logistics problem! MAHLE didn't have a good sense of how efficient its shipping processes were and how much they were spending to ship goods. As a result, its use of resources was well below optimal levels and planning horizons were too short to let them manage their logistics proactively. To deal with these issues MAHLE needed a cost-effective, repeatable, and fully transparent method for distributing its components for combustion engine and electric vehicles. Simply put, MAHLE's logistics processes needed a major digital transformation.

The Solution

To remedy their logistics dilemma, top management at MAHLE chose to work with consultants from MHP Management. They turned to SAP and MHP because both had a well-grounded understanding of the global automotive industry with an emphasis on logistics. SAP and MHP were also experts in end-to-end integrated processes and scalable solutions and were leaders in digital transformation innovations

and had lots of highly satisfied customers. With their help, MAHLE implemented SAP's Transportation Management software (SAP TM) to get much the needed visibility into its logistics processes. SAP TM is a stand-alone app that enables organizations to manage all inbound and outbound domestic and international freight in the same environment and provides traceability and visibility of orders, shipments, items, and logistics processes. The implementation of SAP Transportation Management is allowing MAHLE to reduce costs, make better use of resources, improve overall operational performance, improve communications with carriers, and get the full transparent transport network it needed to enable productions and operations managers to better plan, control, and optimize it. Specific value-driven results MAHLE achieved include:

- A new transport cockpit for quick access to an up-to-date overview for logistics planners
- Reduce planning horizon to six weeks
- Almost doubled inbound load capacity use
- Significantly decreased inbound transfer costs

Since SAP Transportation Manager was put in place, Dr. Markus Lohrey, Head of Logistics Europe at MAHLE claims, "We were able to lower transportation costs by proactively planning transfers and managing load capacity – with full transparency at every step of the shipping process." He further commented that, "Our ability to plan for optimal resource use increased exponentially and we significantly lowered costs for shipping Europe with SAP Transportation Management."

Questions

1. What was the dilemma that MAHLE was facing?
2. Why did MAHLE seek out SAP and MHP to help with its logistics problems?
3. What benefits did MAHLE receive from implementing the SAP Transportation Management?
4. What processes does the second phase of MAHLE's digital transformation project involve?
5. What is the outcome of the partnership between MAHLE and SAP?

Sources: Compiled from Isaak (2018), SAP (2018, 2019), **https://www .mahle.com** (2020), MAHLE (2020), Parsons (2020), Warburton (2020), and Wesseler (2020).

Case 9.3

Video Case: Fuze Increases Its Sales and Marketing Success with an Account-Based Marketing System

Marketing managers must deliver real results fast. To do this, they must not only target the right accounts, they must target the right people at the right time and gather reliable business intelligence that tells them what, where, and when "deals" are being made in the market. Fuze is a leading global communications and collaborations software vendor that combines voice, chat, and video. To increase their

market, Fuze needed to find a way to efficiently get the right message to companies who were actively looking for a communications and collaboration tool at the right time and to provide them with better insights about those accounts to accelerate its sale and marketing process and increase revenues. To do this, they adopted Tech Target's Priority Engine to identify and purchase accounts with real purchase intent and leverage the data into ROI-driving marketing and sales. Visit the Techtarget website at: **https://www.techtarget.com/customers/ fuze/** and watch the video (2m 44s).

1. What was it about Tech Target's Priority Engine that immediately engaged the attention of Fuze marketers?

2. What is the prime consideration for Fuze to ensure adoption of a marketing tool?

3. Which business functions are typically involved in the decision-making process when Fuze adopts a new marketing system, and why?

4. How is TechTarget's Priority Engine helping Fuze to identify new accounts with real purchase intent?

References

Anderson, R. "You're Not Getting Your $125 Claim from Equifax After All." *Thrillist*, December 20, 2019.

Backbone Media. "Thule Group Expands Its Growing Outdoor and Adventure Camping Category with Fly Fishing Rod Vaults via the Acquisition of the Leading North American Player Denver Outfitters." *Newsroom*, December 30, 2019.

Brewster, T. "A Brief History of Equifax Security Fails." *Forbes*, September 7, 2017.

Barnhart, B. "11 Chatbot Marketing Examples to Boost Your Bot Strategy." *SproutSocial*, February 11, 2019.

Bell, R. "Arsenal Enhance Fan Experience with AI-powered 'Robot Pires' Chatbot." *Bdaily News*, October 14, 2018.

Deloitte. "A New Global HR Software Solution Supports HR Transformation and Drives Innovation at Philips." *Deloitte*, 2016.

Domino's Pizza. https://www.dominos.com/chat-pizza-order/, 2020. *Equifaxbreachsettlement.com*, 2020.

"US GAAP Financial Reporting Taxonomy." *fasb.org*, 2012.

FTC. "Equifax Data Breach Settlementa." *Federal Trade Commission*, January 2020.

HR Solutions. "Project Solutions." Available from http://hrxgurus.com/hr-project-activities. Accessed on March 22, 2020.

Isaak, S. "Building a Foundation for the Future: One PLM at MAHLE." *Cenit*, July 26, 2018.

Kilens, M. "2019 State of Conversational Marketing." *Drift*, July 16, 2019.

LaCroix, K. "Equifax Data Breach-Related Securities Suit Settled for $149 Million." *The D&O Diary*, February 17, 2020.

MAHLE. "MAHLE and SAP: Strong Partners for Digitalization." *Mahle.com*, February 12, 2020.

Meltzer, M. "Equifax Nears 'Historic' Data Breach Settlement That Could Cost up to $3.5B." *Atlanta Business Chronicle*, December 9, 2019.

Newman, L. H. "Equifax Officially Has No Excuse." *WIRED*, September 14, 2017.

Parsons, B. "MAHLE and SAP: Strong Partners for Digitalization." *Company News HQ*, February 12, 2020.

Piovesan, C. "Cyber Breach Planning: Lessons from the Equifax Breach." *Forbes*, April 15, 2019.

Planful. "Thule Achieves a Unified View with Planful." *Planful*, 2020.

Prevedere. "3 Real-World Market Demand Forecasting Success Stories." Available from https://www.prevedere.com/3-real-world-market-demand-forecasting-stories/. Accessed on March 24, 2020.

Puig, A. "Equifax Data Breach Settlement: What you Should Know." *Federal Trade Commission Consumer Information*, July 22, 2019.

Rathod, A. "Why Chatbots Play a Mission-Critical Role in Marketing More than Even Before." *Nimble*, 2020.

Robinson, M., J. Gray, A. Cowley, and R. Tan, "Adopting the Power of Conversational UX Chatbots." *Deloitte Digital*, 2017.

Rotenberg, M. "Equifax, The Credit Reporting Industry and What Congress Should Do Next." *Harvard Business Review*, September 20, 2017.

SAP. "How Do You Build High-Performance Logistics Processes for High-Performance Automotive Parts?" *SAP Business Transformation Study*, 2018.

SAP. "SAP Transportation Management at MAHLE Behr GMBH & Co. KG." Available from www.sap.com. Accessed on March 23, 2020.

St. John, A. "Justice Department Charges Chinese Nationals with Equifax Data Breach." *Consumer Reports*, February 10, 2020.

Stewart, M. "All the Ways Equifax Epically Bungled Its Breach Response." *WIRED*, 2020.

thule.com, 2020.

Uchill, J. "House Panel Hits Equifax with Long List of Investigation Demands." *The Hill*, November 17, 2017.

Warburton, S. "MAHLE and SAP team on Digitalisation." *Just Auto*, February 13, 2020.

Wesseler, B. "SAP baut "Digital Backbone" für Mahle." *IT-Zoom*, February 14, 2020.

Enterprise Systems

LEARNING OBJECTIVES

10.1 Describe six types of enterprise systems and the major drivers and challenges associated with migrating to them.

10.2 Define the purpose of an ERP and the key factors that lead to a successful ERP implementation.

10.3 Identify the three supply chain management (SCM) flows and major capabilities of SCM systems.

10.4 Define the five phases of the customer relationship management (CRM) process and the role of a CRM system in customer acquisition, retention, and customer lifetime value.

10.5 Explain the purpose of enterprise knowledge management (EKM), enterprise content management (ECM), and enterprise social platforms (ESPs) and their impact on communication and collaboration in an organization.

Case 10.1 Opening Case

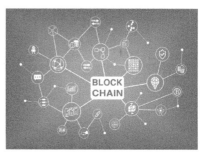

High-Profile Food Recalls Prompt Walmart to Create a Safer, More Transparent, and More Efficient Global Food Supply Chain

The Company

Walmart is one of the world's biggest retailers and most well-known and valuable brands around the globe. Over the last 70 years Walmart has grown from a single five and dime store—Walton's 5-10—in Bentonville, Arkansas, into a global digital enterprise. It has a total of 11,766 stores in 27 countries around the world and employs 2.2 million associates in approximately 400 million square feet of sales area. In 2019, Walmart reported worldwide annual revenues of more than $514 billion, of which $22.4 billion were online sales—almost double the $11.5 billion reported in 2018.

The Problem

Food safety is a huge worldwide social and economic problem. In a recent report, the World Health Organization (WHO) reported that an estimated 600 million people worldwide fall ill after eating contaminated food every year and 420,000 of them die. This includes foodborne illnesses at restaurants, hotels, convenience stores, and other food service organizations, as well as food recalls and other food safety issues. In the United States alone, in 2019, the food industry had losses between $55.5 and $93.2 billion related to unsafe food. That's a 20% increase over the past four years.

These statistics are particularly worrisome problem for retail giants like Walmart who operate on such a large scale. Frank Yiannas, VP of food safety at Walmart, was becoming increasingly concerned about recalls of food products like the one linking romaine lettuce grown in Arizona to the E. coli virus. In that recall, the Centers for Disease Control and Prevention reported that 210 people in 36 U.S. states had fallen ill, 96 of whom were hospitalized and 5 died. In addition to health issues, the recall resulted in millions of bags and heads of romaine lettuce to be removed from store shelves (whether tainted or not) and consumers lost confidence in the product, regardless of where it was grown, which impacted the livelihood of many suppliers and farmers. Yiannas realized that Walmart's current supply chain management system could not quickly identify a food product's origin. The current system only used a one-step up and one-step back model of food traceability, making it "outdated for the 21st century." The current food traceability system that took several days to weeks to trace the origin of a food item purchased from a Walmart store was woefully inadequate. Walmart wanted to get to a point where a customer could scan a bag of salad and know with certainty where it came from.

On closer inspection Yiannas realized that effective and efficient collaboration between Walmart and its food producers and consumers was also hindering food safety efforts. For example, some of Walmart's suppliers kept their data in siloed databases that were inaccessible by other members of the supply chain. This was making it difficult to retrieve data and share it among other supply chain partners. In addition, with food supply chains across multiple national borders, Walmart need to be able to stay compliant any new government regulations that were instituted in the different countries where they operated. The current situation in food safety was also completely at odds with Sam Walton's original vision to help people live better by saving them money, and top management agreed that significant improvements in their outdated technology were necessary. Charles Redfield, Executive VP of food for Walmart U.S., clearly spelled out Walmart's philosophy: "Customers trust us to help them put quality food on their tables . . . We have to go further than offering great food at an everyday low price. Our customers need to know they can trust us to help ensure that food is safe."

The Solution

In response to the food safety issues, Walmart launched the "Walmart Food Traceability Initiative." Its goal was to create a user-friendly, low-cost, blockchain solution that met Walmart's traceability requirements and at the same time created shared value for its suppliers across the entire food supply chain. To achieve this goal, Walmart partnered with IBM and some of Walmart's partners in its food supply chain to develop technology that would enable food products to be traced back to the source quickly during a recall and minimize the impact on consumer health and reduce losses of uncontaminated products incorrectly linked to the recall. Walmart chose to work with IBM, because it was fast being recognized as the leader in blockchain technology development and deployment. IBM's reputation was particularly high in logistics that is founded on traceability and transparency in the supply chain. More importantly, IBM was working with the world's leading retailers and food companies to explore how blockchain could address food safety worldwide through its Food Trust Network (https://www.ibm.com/blockchain/solutions/food-trust). It seemed like the perfect choice.

The partnership involved implementing IBM's digital ledger that relies on IBM blockchain technology powered by Hyperledger Fabric (https://www.hyperledger.org/projects/fabric). IBM's blockchain technology is unique in its capability to immediately connect users through a permissible and permanent shared record of the details of a food's origin. It uses a decentralized model to share food supply chain information, including food origin details, processing data, and shipping data among members in its permissioned blockchain network. Each node on the blockchain is controlled by a separate entity and all data on the blockchain is encrypted. Organizations uploading information continue to own the data and are the only ones that can authorize permission for the information to be seen or shared.

After collaborating with IBM for 18 months and pilot testing the IBM Food Trust Network with numerous suppliers, Walmart found that by using IBM's blockchain technology they could cut the time it takes to track a food item from one of its stores back to source in seconds instead of days or even weeks. However, Walmart understood that although the technology provided critical end-to-end visibility its value would be greatly diminished without proper connection to other supply chain systems and use by all parties in the supply chain. Consequently, the successful deployment of the blockchain technology was highly dependent on the involvement of all its suppliers. In September 2018, Walmart and Sam's Club put their "leafy green" suppliers on notice that they had one year to capture digital traceability event information using the IBM Food Trust Network and be up and running on the network. Walmart also posted a list of FAQs on its website along with prerecorded webinars to explain the new requirements and how suppliers could comply.

The Outcome

Walmart's Food Traceability Initiative is a resounding success. It has provided Walmart customers with a renewed peace of mind that its produce is safe to eat, and the blockchain-enabled end-to-end visibility has also restored customer trust. Customers also benefit from better accuracy and timeliness of availability of the leafy greens they want—when they want them. It also offers Walmart and its supply chain partners with faster processing times, real-time stock level updates, improved shelf-life management, a higher level of trust between supply chain partners through information sharing and lower compliance costs. Now everyone within Walmart's blockchain can build transparency by sharing information and validating it almost instantaneously without sacrificing security in a trusted environment. Over the past two and one-half years, IBM's Food Trust Network has expanded to more than 80 members and has tracked over 1,300 food products to increase food safety and reduce food waste.

Walmart's latest foray into applying blockchain technology is at Walmart China where it recently partnered with VeChain Thor blockchain technology. The new partnership is expected to include over 125 product lines covering more than 10 product lines such as fresh meats, rice, mushroom, and cooking oil. By the end of 2020, Walmart expects to trace 50% of its fresh packaged meats and 40% of its fresh packaged vegetables. Other Walmart China initiatives is to optimize its supply chain logistics to include enhanced data storage and analytics and the development of a customized perishable food distribution center that can store and process more than 4,000 kinds of temperature-regulated, refrigerated, or frozen goods simultaneously.

Questions

1. Why did Walmart turn to blockchain technology to improve its food supply chain?

2. Why did Walmart choose to partner with IBM?

3. What is the significance of Walmart's deployment of blockchain technology in its food supply chain to world health?

4. What do you consider was the most important outcome of Walmart's deployment of the IBM Trusted Food Network?

5. As a customer, are you more comfortable purchasing "leafy greens" and other food from Walmart after reading about their involvement in the IBM Food Trust Network? Explain.

Sources: Compiled from Aspa (2018), Gagliordi (2018), Redman (2018), Shaw (2018), Dimitrov (2019), Gupta (2019), O'Callaghan (2019), Walmart (2019), O'Connell (2020), Smith (2020), and VeChain.org.

DID YOU KNOW?

That . . . . A walking package-delivery robot is now available! In January 2020, U.S. startup Agility Robotics announced that Ford—the automobile manufacturer—had purchased two of its bipedal robots, Digit, to test on the "last-mile" of their supply chain. Digit is approximately the height and shape of a small adult human and navigates semiautonomously with the help of LIDAR—a radar-enabled detection system—and other IoT sensors. Digit can carry boxes in its arms up to 40 lb (18 kg) and can be used in logistics and warehouses.

Introduction

An important challenge for business leaders is how to seamlessly integrate the data stored in their many different types of functional systems liked the ones described in Chapter 9 to better meet the needs of their customers, achieve business objectives, and improve security.

This dilemma is widespread in the business community since many organizations are still have antiquated, siloed mainframe computers, software implemented 20 to 30 years ago and data stored in outdated databases and data centers. These systems are difficult and expensive to maintain, update, integrate, and interface securely with leading-edge business apps. When companies decide to update their IT infrastructure, they must invest in tightly integrated enterprise systems that offer seamless data handling between all the different types of systems and are easier to secure. With these enterprise systems, companies can operate at optimal efficiency levels and make better informed decisions consistent with the corporate strategy. Enterprise systems fall into several categories: enterprise resource planning (ERP), supply chain management (SCM), customer relationship management (CRM), knowledge management (KM), and enterprise social platforms (ESPs). These enterprise systems are integrated by their connection to a central data repository that enables them to synchronize and share corporate data from all departments and functional areas so that employees can simultaneously view and work with enterprise wide data.

In this chapter, you will learn about the benefits, limitations, and risks of investing in and implementing the different types of enterprise systems that support all three levels of a business—strategic, managerial, and operational—and how these systems affect relationships with suppliers, vendors, and customers.

10.1 | Intro to Enterprise Systems

LO10.1 Describe *six types of enterprise systems and the major drivers and challenges associated with migrating to them.*

Enterprise systems are large-scale application software packages that support business processes, information flows, reporting, and data analytics in complex organizations.

Enterprise systems are large-scale application software packages that support business processes, information flows, reporting, and data analytics in complex organizations. They enable organizations to gain company-wide access to business knowledge, increase employee productivity, improve customer and supplier engagement, and minimize duplication of data. They can integrate business processes such as sales, financial management, human resources and inventory/order management into a single platform to make access to key data and completing work processes easier. The core strength of enterprise-wide systems is their integration and functionality across the organization. Enterprise-wide systems not only integrate systems within the organization but also link organizations with their suppliers, business partners, and customers. Enterprise systems offer benefits in terms of easier business planning, improved record keeping, and high productivity. For example, to increase employee productivity, enterprise systems automate **core business processes** such as sending out sales flyers, generating customer orders, or processing payroll for consistency and efficiency because of their accessibility to a central data repository. Or improve customer satisfaction by overcoming problems that can arise such as if a customer called an order into the ordering department, there was no easy way to transfer customer order data to manufacturing or order fulfillment who in turn were unable to transfer data to shipping when the product was ready for delivery to the customer. And, of course, tracking the order was impossible because there was no automated process in place to connect shipping with transportation companies. These are great improvements that enterprise systems offer over their legacy equivalents that operated in isolation from each other and had few if any mechanisms that allowed them to share data between systems.

Core business processes include accounting, finance, sales, marketing, human resources, inventory, productions, and manufacturing.

Types of Enterprise Systems

Table 10.1 lists and describes the six main types of enterprise systems typically implemented to integrate and improve business processes and functions.

TABLE 10.1   Enterprise Systems and Their Functions

Name	Acronym	Function
Enterprise resource planning	ERP	Integrates an enterprise's internal applications, supports its external business processes, and links to its external business partners. Integrate business processes, including supply chains, manufacturing, financial, human resources, budgeting, sales, and customer service. Used primarily in the manufacturing industry
Supply chain management	SCM	Supports the steps in the supply chain—procurement, sourcing, manufacturing, storage, inventory control, scheduling, order fulfillment, and distribution. Improves decision-making, forecasting, optimization, and analysis
Customer relationship management	CRM	Helps create a total view of customers to maximize share-of-wallet and profitability. A business strategy to segment and manage customers to optimize customer lifetime value
Enterprise knowledge management systems	EKMS	Help organize company knowledge about business productivity, competitive business models, business intelligence. It is made up of different software modules linked by a central user interface
Enterprise content management system	ECMS	Provides capability for multiple users throughout an organization with different permission levels to manage a website or a section of the content
Enterprise social platforms	ESPs	Enhance social networks, both within the enterprise and across key members of the enterprise's supply and distribution chains. An important method for enhancing communication, coordination, and collaboration for business purposes

ERP, SCM, CRM, KM, CM, and ESPs are integrated by their connection to a central data repository that enables them to sync and share the latest data, as illustrated in **Figure 10.1**. For example, the integration of ERP and SCM improves inventory management and increases performance throughout the supply chain. A CRM enables workers in all relevant departments to be aware of the status of customer orders and KM and ESP enhance knowledge handling, communication, and collaboration throughout the organization.

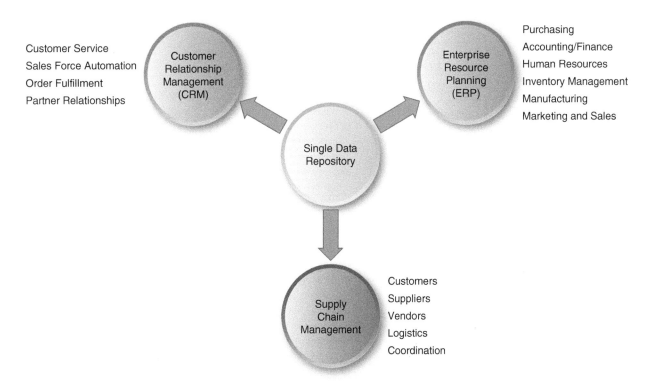

FIGURE 10.1   Integration of enterprise-wide systems is achieved via access to shared data.

Interface means to connect to and exchange data with apps and systems.

Legacy systems are older information systems (ISs) that have been maintained over several decades because they fulfill critical needs.

Integrating Legacy Systems

While enterprise systems are considered a boon to many organizations, seeking to integrate a host of disparate, siloed legacy systems can disrupt an organization because enterprise systems change the way in which data are stored and accessed and can lead to resistance. Integrating legacy systems with cloud-based enterprise systems is complex, as described in **Tech Note 10.1**. Much of the complexity is due to getting new apps or system modules to **interface** with existing or legacy systems that are several generations older.

Tech Note 10.1

Data Transfers to Mainframes

Enterprise systems require data transfers—often to mainframes. Designing enterprise-level systems involves a variety of components that had been implemented on mainframes, midrange computers, networks, or cloud environments. In most large enterprises, mainframes are the workhorse systems that run the majority of business transactions. In contrast, customer interfaces through customer service; ERP, CRM, and SCM apps; websites; and business-to-business (B2B) interactions are usually on distributed systems or in the cloud. Many times seemingly well-planned projects fail and require extensive reworking because integration issues had not been properly planned.

Some enterprises choose to avoid the challenges of integration by creating a new system that replaces the full functionality of the old one. This option is the most expensive, difficult, and risky. An advantage is that this option offers a longer-term solution that is agile to respond to changing business needs. Despite that potential pay-off, complete replacement requires a large up-front investment for development, poses difficulties in duplicating behavior of the **legacy system**, and increases the risk of complete software project failure.

Companies tend to migrate to an enterprise solution when limitations caused by their existing systems interfere with performance or the ability to compete. **IT at Work 10.1** is an example.

IT at Work 10.1

Organic Valley Does Business Better with Enterprise Systems

Organic Valley Family of Farms (**https://www.organicvalley.coop/ our-farmers/small-family-farms**) is the largest U.S. cooperative (co-op) of organic farmers and one of the nation's leading organic brands. The co-op represents over 1,300 family farms in 34 states and Canada. Its mission is to keep small and mid-sized farmers farming. Organic Valley produces over 200 organic foods, including organic milk, soy, cheese, butter, eggs, produce, juice, and meats, which are sold in supermarkets, natural foods stores, and food co-ops and as ingredients for other organic food manufacturers nationwide. One of the biggest challenges for Organic Valley had been managing growth in the face of increasing competition from larger companies.

Organic Valley needed to consolidate its disparate systems into one enterprise solution to improve operating efficiencies and maintain the high quality of its line of perishable food products. The company had been doing planning using spreadsheets; separately, it completed its financials, order management, and inventory on an enterprise system designed for discrete manufacturing. As operations expanded, it needed to make a major leap in business systems.

Organic Valley also needed a solution with enough flexibility and versatility to manage the company's dairy, produce, meat, and egg lines of business, all of which have different and unique requirements.

Organic Valley hired a consultant during the selection process to help identify the most important functions and features, such as shelf-life management and expiration date management. Based on these requirements, three possible vendors were identified. Organic Valley and its consultant agreed that the solutions offered by the vendor Infor best fit its business.

The company now has one integrated system to support all business processes across all its lines of business. With the Infor enterprise solution, Organic Valley is much more agile on the technical side, and this has given it the ability to support rapid business growth. The company projects savings of $2 million per year through improved supply chain planning and other operational efficiencies.

Major reasons why companies replace all or parts of their legacy systems or supplement their existing systems with enterprise systems include the following:

1. **High maintenance costs**   Maintaining and upgrading legacy systems are some of the most difficult challenges facing chief information officers (CIOs) and IT departments.
2. **Inflexibility**   Legacy architectures were not designed for flexibility. These huge systems cannot be easily redesigned to share data with newer systems, unlike modern architectures.
3. **Integration obstacles**   Legacy systems execute business processes that are hardwired by rigid, predefined process flows. Their hardwiring makes integration with other systems such as CRM and Web-based applications difficult and sometimes impossible.
4. **Lack of staff**   IT departments find it increasingly difficult to hire staff who are qualified to work on mainframes and applications written in languages no longer used by the latest technologies.
5. **Cloud**   The cloud has lowered up-front costs. Cloud-based enterprise systems can be a good fit for companies facing upgrades to their legacy ERP and other enterprise systems.

Migrating to enterprise systems involves changing the current management of people, processes, and existing technology. Three typical situations where changes are most needed in an organization are as follows:

1. **Changes in how people perform their jobs**   Jobs and how they are performed will change to accommodate the new processes. Enterprise systems require retraining users whose productivity will drop initially as they adjust to a new way of doing their jobs.
2. **Redesign of business processes**   Processes need to be simplified and redesigned so that they can be automated, either totally or partially. Tasks that are no longer necessary are removed from the processes.
3. **Integration of many types of uncoupled legacy systems**   Integrating legacy systems is necessary so that data can flow seamlessly among departments and business partners. Automated data flows are essential to productivity improvements.

For example, manual document-intensive processes such as order entry and billing create major headaches for workers. These processes require users to manually review documents for approval, enter data from those documents into a back-office system, and then make decisions. Automated order entry systems track customer orders from the time of initial order placement through the completion of those orders and perform backorder processing, analysis, invoicing, and billing.

Questions related to enterprise systems that an organization should also itself to evaluate the current state of their enterprise systems and their potential include the following:

- **Are our current apps tightly aligned?**   One of the IT function's most important roles is to provide and support applications that enable workers to access, use, and understand data. These applications need to be tightly aligned with well-defined and well-designed business processes—a standard that few organizations can presently achieve.
- **Who are our most important customers?**   Customer loyalty helps drive profits, but only for customers who are profitable to the company. Many companies do not know how to recognize or encourage the kind of customer loyalty that is worth having. Using data about buying behaviors (e.g., amount spent per month; purchase of high-margin products; return activity; and demands for customer service) helps a company identify its loyal customers and which ones are profitable.
- **How much have we invested or are we willing to invest in enterprise systems?**   Companies worldwide spend billions of dollars in the design and implementation of enterprise systems. For example, organizations make huge investments in ERP systems from vendors such as SAP, Oracle, Sage ERP, Infor, and NetSuite to create an integrated global supply chain. Interorganizational ISs play a major role in improving communication and integration among firms in a global supply chain.

Companies don't always have the resources to replace all their legacy systems at the same time, so the migration to a full suite of enterprise systems is typically an incremental process based on business priorities. In the next sections, each of the six major enterprise systems will be explained in detail.

Questions

1. Explain the purpose of an enterprise system.
2. Describe six types of enterprise systems.
3. What are the five major reasons organizations migrate to enterprise systems?
4. What are two challenges of legacy systems?
5. Why do companies not replace all of their legacy systems?
6. Why is it difficult to implement enterprise systems?
7. Explain the three types of changes needed when an enterprise system is implemented.

10.2 Enterprise Resource Planning

LO10.2 Define *the purpose of an ERP and the key factors that lead to a successful ERP implementation.*

ERP is all about automation of workflows and accounting processes to analyze a business and forecast development decisions. To better understand what ERP is, think about all the various processes needed to run a business. These might include inventory and order management, finance and accounting, human resources (HR), CRM, SCM, and e-commerce. ERP software integrates all these various functions into a single system to streamline processes and information across the entire organization.

Automating ERP

Enterprise resource planning (ERP) is business process management software that allows an organization to use tightly integrated applications to manage business and automate business processes related to services, technology, and human resources.

According to a report published by Allied Market Research the 2018 **enterprise resource planning (ERP)** software market was valued at $35.81 billion and is projected to reach $78.40 billion by 2026 (Allied Market Research, 2019). The biggest user of ERP is the manufacturing sector. This is not surprising, since ERP systems were originally designed to facilitate manufacturing business processes such as managing raw materials, controlling inventory and order entry, and handling product distribution. The current increase is attributed to the increasing number of pharmaceutical, automotive, garment, and consumer electronics companies who are entering manufacturing markets.

The central feature of all ERP systems is a shared database that supports multiple business functions used throughout an organization so that employees in different divisions, such as accounting, HR, and sales, can rely on the same information for their different purposes. An ERP can integrate all parts of an operation, including manufacturing/production, CRM, human resources, finance and accounting, SCM, and corporate service management into a single platform (**Figure 10.2**).

FIGURE 10.2 ERP modules.

ERP software also offers some degree of synchronized information reporting. Instead of forcing employees to maintain separate databases and spreadsheets that must be manually merged to generate reports, some ERP solutions allow staff to pull reports from a single system. For instance, with sales orders automatically flowing into the financial system without any manual rekeying, the order management department can process orders more quickly and accurately, and the finance department can close the books faster. Other common ERP features include a portal or dashboard to enable employees to quickly understand metrics of the firm's KPIs. The most used ERP functions reported in the 2018 Allied Market Research study were finance and human resources, followed by inventory management, customer management, and supply chain and manufacturing.

ERP and the IT Infrastructure

From a technology perspective, ERP is the software infrastructure that links an enterprise's internal applications and supports its external business processes. Departments stay informed about what is ongoing in other departments that impact its operations or performance. Knowing about problem situations and being able to work around them save time and expense and preserve good customer relations. For example, using ERP, a manufacturer shares the database of parts, products, production capacities, schedules, backorders, and trouble spots. Responding quickly and correctly to materials shortages, spikes in customer demand, or other contingencies means that small initial problems are solved instead of allowing them to be amplified down the line.

Figure 10.3 demonstrates how an ERP fits into an enterprise's IT infrastructure. The core ERP functions are integrated with other systems or modules, such as SCM and CRM. An **enterprise application integration (EAI)** layer enables the ERP to interface with legacy apps. EAI is middleware that connects and acts as a go-between for applications and their business processes.

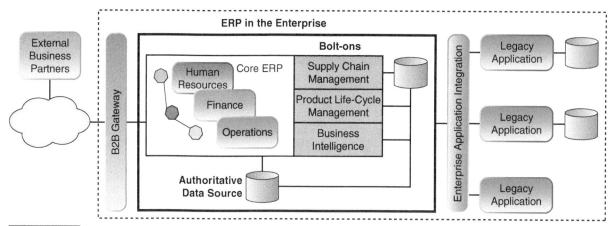

FIGURE 10.3 Overview of the complexity of ERP and its interfaces with other enterprise systems (U.S. Army Business Transformation Knowledge Center, 2009).

Acquiring an ERP ERPs are not usually built in-house or built using proprietary software because the costs and time to do so would be staggering. Typically, ERP systems are acquired by purchasing or leasing in a software-as-a-service (SaaS) arrangement. (You will read more about IT outsourcing in Chapter 12.) All ERPs must be customized to the company's specifications. Here are two examples of how ERP acquisitions can be customized:

1. **Boers & Co Fine Metalworking** in the Netherlands has been manufacturing fine mechanical parts, high-precision assembly, and sheet metal products for over 100 years. The company implemented Epicor ERP to access real-time data for everything from the shop floor to finance. All business operations from the front office through production, receiving and shipping, to order entry and cash receipts are handled by the ERP.

2. **Peters Ice Cream** was an independently owned Australian ice cream producer and distributor with an excellent reputation for high-quality products and on-time deliveries. When Peters was acquired by food giant Nestlé, it also came under the control of Nestlé's current ERP that used batch processing. Unfortunately, Nestlé's ERP was not tailored for the specific needs of an ice cream company and did not interface well with Peters' legacy systems. Peters' network of freezers extends throughout Australia. To get the ice cream flavors where and when they are needed, it is essential that information on stock levels and deliveries be accurate, which meant they had to be updated in real time. To help meet their requirements, Peters turned to Infor's M3 QuickStep Food and Beverage ERP solution. QuickStep came with 70% of Peters' business processes preconfigured, enabling them to implement their new ERP system in just eight months.

Choosing an ERP Solution ERPs are complex, but they are becoming more user friendly. Other options are hosted ERP solutions, such as ERP SaaS, and cloud-based ERP. Still, ERPs are expensive, time-consuming implementations that require a lot of planning. Four rules to consider when selecting an ERP solution or software package are listed in **Table 10.2**.

TABLE 10.2   **ERP Selection Rules**

Selection Rule	Description
1. **Select** an ERP solution that targets the company's requirements.	ERP packages are tailored for organizations based on their size and industry. Midmarket solutions have more sophisticated capabilities than packages for small businesses; large enterprise packages are the most complex. It is important to choose an ERP that can support critical functions of the organization, such as accounting or inventory management.
2. **Evaluate** potential ERP vendors' strengths and weaknesses.	Check how many customers each vendor has; its financial health (you do not want to select a vendor on the brink of bankruptcy); experience in the specific industry, and how the ERP can scale as the company grows.
3. **Meet** with each vendor and get a hands-on demo of its ERP solutions.	Demos allow employees to experience the usability of each ERP module and how well the ERP would support business processes.
4. **Calculate** ERP's total cost of ownership (TCO).	The cost of the ERP or the monthly SaaS fee is only the beginning of the calculation. The TCO also includes implementation, customization, management services, training, additional hardware and networks, additional bandwidth for a Web-based product, and IT staff.

ERP Implementation Critical Success Factors

In order to successfully implement an ERP, an organization must consider the key factors that increase the likelihood of ERP success and minimize the risk of problems. Many managers assume that success or failure depends on the software and, furthermore, that a failure is the fault of the software that is purchased or licensed. In reality, 95% of a project's success or failure lies in the hands of the company that is implementing the software, not the software vendor.

The results of a survey to identify the factors ERP experts considered most important to successful ERP projects are shown in **Figure 10.4**.

Most Important Factors for ERP Project Success

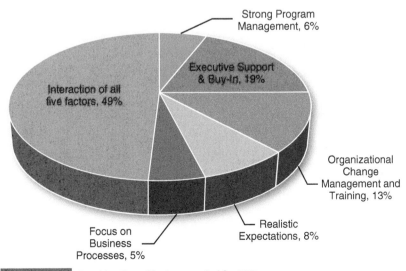

FIGURE 10.4   Combination of factors needed for ERP success.

Nearly half of the experts indicated that the failure of any one of the factors significantly increases the risk of ERP failure. Each of the key factors is described next.

1. **Focus on business processes and requirements** Too often, companies get caught up in technical capabilities or platforms on which the ERP runs. But compared to business processes, none of this really matters. What matters is how managers want business operations to run and what the key business requirements are. Once management and IT have defined them, they can intelligently choose the software, modules, and vendor that fit their unique business needs.

2. **Focus on realistic expectations** Developing a business case to get approval from upper management or the board of directors is essential, but not sufficient. You must have a realistic goal in mind before establishing key performance measures, setting baselines and targets for those measures, and then tracking performance after going live. The performance results are proof of how well the ERP meets the expectations that had been listed in the business case.

3. **A strong program management approach** An ERP project depends on how it is managed and what resources are available. Responsibility for the management of the ERP implementation project cannot be transferred to vendors or consulting firms. Because of the business disruption and cost involved, ERP projects require the full-time attention and support of high-profile champions on the key functions for a long period of time, from 6 to 12 months on average. It is also known that ERP projects cannot be managed by people who can be spared. They must be managed by people who are indispensable. Without powerful champions, commitment of necessary resources and an adequate budget (discussed next), expect the ERP to fail. Program management will be explained in detail in Chapter 13.

4. **Obtain executive support and buy-in** Any project without support from top management will fail. No matter how well run a project is, there will be problems such as conflicting business needs or business disruptions that can only be resolved by someone with the power and authority to cut through the politics and personal agendas.

5. **Invest in change management and training** Another key principle to understand is that when you design an ERP, you redesign the organization. ERP systems involve dramatic change for workers. ERPs lose value if people do not understand how to use them effectively. Investing in training, change management, and job design are crucial to the outcome of any large-scale IT project.

Once each of these key factors are in place, it is important to take time to plan and prepare before starting any ERP implementation project. An ERP vendor's motive is to close the deal as fast as possible. The company needs to make sure it correctly defines its needs and what it can afford to achieve in order to intelligently evaluate and select the best vendor. Do not be rushed into a decision. Take your time! Too often, companies jump right into a project without validating the vendor's understanding of business requirements or their project plan. The principle of "measure twice, cut once" applies to vendor selection. The more time the company spends ensuring that these things are done right at the start, the lower the risk of failure and the less time spent fixing problems later. Filing a lawsuit against a vendor is not a fix. Lawsuits are both expensive and risky and contribute nothing to the company's performance.

Lessons Learned

The success of an ERP depends on organizational and technological factors that occur prior to, during, and after its implementation. Managers and other decision-makers tend to think that if an enterprise system works for leading companies, it will work for them as well. But that is not necessarily true. In fact, several of the best companies have suffered devastating consequences that led to multimillion dollar losses, bankruptcy, or lawsuits.

Most often when an ERP implementation fails, the ERP is eventually fixed and remains in use. This can give the false impression that the ERP was successful from the start. Knowing what to do and what not to do are important. Failures usually teach the most valuable lessons, as you will learn.

ERP Implementations Are Complex and Risky   Planning, deploying, or fine-tuning these complex business software systems for your company is such a large undertaking that such projects fail more than 50% to 70% of the time. Those are not encouraging statistics. ERP failures have made it impossible to ship products and, at the extreme, have led to bankruptcy. Many ERP projects have ended up in litigation, the headlines, and out-of-court settlements. Dell canceled an ERP system after spending two years and $200 million on its implementation. Hershey Food Corp. filed highly publicized lawsuits against its ERP vendors for a failed implementation.

The following ERP failures led to lengthy lawsuits against vendors or consulting firms. Unfortunately, lawsuits do not turn a disastrous ERP implementation into a successful one.

- **Bait-and-switch: ScanSource vs. Avanade**   A half-million lines of custom code were not enough to produce a viable Microsoft Dynamics AX ERP system for point-of-sale and RFID products distributor ScanSource, according to a lawsuit filed by ScanSource against Avanade. AX is one of four ERP products sold under the Dynamics brand and is aimed at larger companies. The project was estimated to cost $17 million and take 11 months, but the cost estimate grew to a staggering $66 million, and it failed to "go live" after three years. Avanade misrepresented the skills of its consultants in order to win the contract; then sent in a continually changing cast of consultants without the expertise to do the job or familiarity with AX—hence, the allegation of "bait-and-switch" tactics. ScanSource terminated the contact with Avanade and hired another company to fix the problems at an additional cost of $58 to $72 million.
- **Unmet obligations: Dillard's, Inc. vs. JDA Software Group**   Dillard's alleged that i2 failed to meet obligations regarding two software-license agreements for which the department store had paid $8 million. JDA Software Group Inc. was ordered to pay $246 million in damages.
- **Bankruptcy bound: FoxMeyer Drugs vs. SAP and Andersen Consulting**   FoxMeyer Drugs was a $5B company and the nation's largest distributor of pharmaceuticals before its ERP failure that led to a $500M lawsuit against SAP and Andersen Consulting. FoxMeyer's ERP could not process the transactions needed to supply its customers with their orders. FoxMeyer had been processing 425,000 invoice lines per day on its legacy software. The company's ERP was limited to 10,000 invoice lines per day. This quickly decreased order processing capability, sent the company into bankruptcy protection, and ultimately shut down the business. Implementation was troubled almost from the start. Despite warnings from Woltz Consulting, during the early stages of the project, that a schedule for the entire implementation to be completed in 18 months was totally unrealistic, FoxMeyer went ahead with the vendor's planned implementation.

The most important lesson to be learned from these examples of ERP failures is that when it comes to ERP selection, you either get it right or pay the price for years to come!

Be aware that reading vendor white papers and viewing Webcasts or demos may give you a biased view of the benefits of ERP software. You need to conduct your own research to learn the full story behind an enterprise system implementation. Problems may be skipped over or ignored. While blogs and YouTube posts may be good sources of objective data, many vendors have blogs and YouTube videos that are designed to appear neutral, when in fact they are not.

What's New in ERP Systems?

As we have discussed, ERP systems can be deployed on the premises, in the cloud, or as a managed service depending on business needs and customer expectations. The latest ERP solutions are designed with a focus on social collaboration, deployment flexibility, faster response, and accessibility from mobile devices. They have touch-enabled user interfaces designed to work with all touch-screen devices. New apps and mobile add-ons enable the following:

- Sales associates to process orders, take payments, and collect signatures with an iPad app
- Field technicians to provide customer service from anywhere
- Marketing to manage every aspect of ongoing customer relationships using a smartphone app
- Production to access to the real-time information needed to reduce stockouts and excess inventory
- Customers to access, pay, and view invoices online

Selecting an ERP Vendor, Value-Added Reseller or Consultant

Value-added reseller (VAR) customizes or adds features to a vendor's software or equipment and resells the enhanced product.

The complexities and time requirements to implement an ERP typically requires the help of an ERP vendor, **value-added reseller (VAR)** or consultant. Much of the complexity is due to getting new apps or system modules to interface with existing or legacy systems that are several generations old.

ERP vendors　An **ERP vendor** develops ERP software and implements and supports its own product(s). There are almost 200 ERP vendors in the martketplace. The two largest ERP vendors are SAP and Oracle. In the 2018 worldwide ERP software market, SAP remained a clear ERP market leader in licenses, maintenance, and subscription revenues. SAP accounted for 6.8% of the market share, followed by Oracle, Intuit, FIS Global, and Fiserv, who each represented approximately 3% of the ERP market share.

To help organizations evaluate different ERP vendors, the website at Technology Evaluation Centers (**https://www.featuredcustomers.com/vendors?q=ERP**) provides side-by-side comparisons of ERP products, along with impartial software reviews, software demos, and pricing.

Value-added resellers (VARs)　VARs purchase ERP software at a discount from a vendor, customize its features for a specific client or industry sector, and add services to it before selling to a client. A VAR can represent several different vendor products and can help compare the advantages and disadvantages of different ERP products for individual clients. VARs are informed about best practices and procedures for ERP implementation and can offer years of experience and up-to-date knowledge about ERP products.

Independent ERP consultant　Enlisting the advice of a highly experienced independent ERP consultant or consulting firm can also increase the chances of a successful ERP implementation (see **Career Insight 10.1**). An ERP consultant offers customized consulting services that include identifying and vetting different ERP options, selecting the best ERP for the task at hand, and implementing and supporting the ERP when it is in operation. Unlike VARs, independent ERP consultants do not partner with specific ERP vendors.

Career Insight 10.1

ERP Consultant: What Skills Do You Need?

According to the Bureau of Labor Statistics, the role of ERP consultant is becoming a high-demand job in the U.S. economy. ERP consultants currently earn a median pay of $83,802 and can demand top income of $123,000 (payscale.com).

What do ERP consultants do all day? They write design specifications and estimates for programs, based on requirements; participate in decision-making to optimize and improve IT management; analyze and understand existing software; and assist technical teams using change management and technical skills.

What specific skills do ERP consultants need? According to **Morgan McKinley**, a large online recruiting service, if you envision becoming an ERP consultant, you will need to have the following experience and skills:

1. Business process analysis experience including requirements gathering, ability to identify defects and stakeholder management
2. Excellent organizational skills including ability to deal with ambiguity, juggle multiple priorities, and meet goals and deadlines
3. Exceptional interpersonal skills and the ability to influence people
4. Ability and willingness to share knowledge as a trainer or mentor to end users

To help find a VAR or consultant, the Manifest (**https://themanifest.com/erp/consultants**) publishes an annual list of its top 25 ERP consulting companies.

To simplify and reduce the cost of the ERP software evaluation, comparison, and selection processes, an annual event called the ERP Vendor Shootout (VSO) (**http://www.vsoforerp.com/home.html**) is held and geared toward ERP selection teams and decision-makers for companies with manufacturing, distribution, or project-oriented requirements.

IT at Work 10.2 describes how Energy drinks implemented a Sage Accpac ERP with the help of a New York–based ERP consulting firm.

IT at Work 10.2

FUZE Adopts a Smart ERP with Help of Pyramid Consulting

FUZE Energy Drinks is the producer of "smart age" beverages, and its production and inventory demands were expanding so fast that its outdated legacy systems couldn't keep up. Joseph Ramilla, FUZE chairman, was particularly concerned about lack of information about current inventory levels. As he pointed out, "If any component of our inventory expires or is out of stock, were' dead in the water." In addition to concerns about management of their rapidly growing stocks and inventory, other processes that existing systems were failing included the following:

- Planning and managing production to keep up with supply and demand
- Not keeping up with reporting of financial decisions

FUZE desperately needed an integrated, cost-effective, and easy-to-maintain ERP solution that would put their manufacturing and distribution processes back on track. Pyramid Consulting, a New York– based firm had a well-deserved reputation for providing turnkey, cost-effective solutions for the beverage industry and was the perfect partner to help FUZE find an ERP that meet its requirements. FUZE had some tight time constraints. Because of the urgency of the situation, FUZE imposed a tight one-month deadline on the project. Pyramid recommended and implemented Sage Accpac—a Web-hosted ERP to help FUZE fully automate its financial, inventory, and production areas. In just three weeks, Pyramid had completed the implementation, flawlessly transferred all FUZE data from its legacy systems, and begun training FUZE employees on the use of Sage Accpac. Under Pyramid's expert guidance, FUZE quickly saw multiple benefits from Sage Accpac's capabilities, including seamless integration of its financial and production reporting, order entry, inventory control, accounts payable and receivable. The new system allowed FUZE to concentrate on its core competencies and the project was delivered on time at a reasonable price. Ramilla was delighted with the end result and is enjoying the maintenance-free Web-hosted environment in which Sage Accpac operates.

Sources: Compiled from Seth (2018), Sage Accpac (2020), fuzebev.com, and sage.com.

10.3 Supply Chain Management

LO10.3 Identify *the three supply chain management (SCM) flows and major capabilities of SCM systems.*

Supply chain starts with the acquisition of raw materials or the procurement (purchase) of products and proceeds through manufacture, transport, and delivery—and the disposal or recycling of products.

Having the best **supply chain** possible is becoming more important as manufacturers and retailers recognize its role as a strategic tool for business performance and growth rather than as the support role that it has been relegated to in the past. It is a network of raw material suppliers, distributors, manufacturers or assemblers, order fulfillment and logistic providers, and retailers that participate in the production, delivery, and sale of a product to the customer (**Figure 10.5**). The supply chain is like a pipeline that tracks movement of products and materials from plant, to warehouse, to store, to customer and is composed of multiple companies that coordinate activities to differentiate themselves from their competitors.

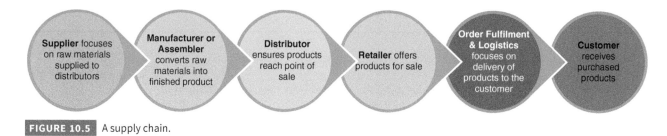

FIGURE 10.5 A supply chain.

Supply chains vary significantly depending on the type, complexity, and perishability of the product. For example, in a simplified sense, the food supply chain begins with the livestock or farm, moves to the manufacturer, then through the distribution centers and wholesalers to the retailer and final customer. A supply chain must be managed carefully to get the right products in the hands of a company's customers at the appropriate time to ensure customer satisfaction and higher revenues.

Supply chain management (SCM) centralizes the management of the flow of goods and services to maximize customer value, achieve competitive advantage, and enhance collaboration between vendors, producers, suppliers, and customers. The purpose of managing a supply chain is to help companies meet customer demand as efficiently and cost-effectively as possible to give them an advantage over their competitors. To optimize performance, many organizations are automating their supply chain by implementing powerful supply chain management systems (SCM system). Items managed might include raw materials used in the production of goods, partially finished goods, and finished products. Think of the chain in terms of its links (Figure 10.5) because the entire chain is not managed as a single unit. A company can only manage the links it touches. That is, a company manages only those partners who are one-back and one-up from them in the supply chain.

Supply chain management (SCM) is the efficient management of the flows of material, data, and payments among companies in the supply chain, from suppliers to consumers.

Automating the Supply Chain

An SCM system is software that manages and supports each one-up, one-back linkage in a supply chain, i.e., manufacturing, inventory and control, scheduling, and transportation. SCM systems allow organizations to manage supply chains, vendor relationships, and distribution channels to better track resources, improve efficiency, and increase customer satisfaction through improved decision-making, forecasting, optimization, and analysis. Businesses benefit from an SCM system by identifying inefficiencies in supply and distribution channels, optimizing warehouse storage, tracking the provenance of their products, and automating purchases.

SCM software focuses around improving business functions such as the following:

- **Inventory optimization** to minimize overhead costs and ensure uninterrupted delivery. Inventory can be tracked using bar codes, serial number, or RFID tags (**Figure 10.6**).

- **Warehouse management** to track materials and goods within a warehouse or distribution center.

- **Forecasting** to reduce uncertainty and variability associated with supply and demand.
- **Optimal cycle time and customer service** by increasing control over processes.
- **Supplier management** to track performance and compliance, measure risk, etc.
- **Procurement** by managing and automating purchase orders and receipts, creating a transparent audit trail and integrating financial management systems.
- **Logistics planning** to ensure that ready-to-ship items are delivered to the customer as quickly as possible and are handled carefully to ensure they are undamaged.

FIGURE 10.6 A digital supply chain using RFID tags.

SCM software solutions allow businesses to integrate multiple tools into an existing system or offer a single software suite to manage individual supply chain and logistics processes. For example, SCM suites, such as *JDA Supply Chain Now, Streamline Shipping Solutions,* and *Supply Vision*, manage the entire SCM process, while other products focus on specific processes within the supply chain. For example, *JDA's Demand Planning* focuses on giving users data for inventory and revenue forecasts and helping decision-makers plan for the future; *Dr. Dispatch* manages trucking and brokerage, including cash flow, company growth, dispatching, and equipment scheduling; and *Bellwether BPM* allows companies to manage inventory and purchases, including requisitions, purchase order management, approval routing, receiving, invoice matching, etc.

Managing the Three Supply Chain Flows

A supply chain has three flows that an SCM system can optimize within a business. These are materials, information (data), and money. Descriptions of these three main flows are as follows:

1. **Material or product flow** This is the movement of materials and goods from a supplier to its consumer. For example, Ford supplies dealerships that, in turn, sell to end users. Products that are returned make up what is called the **reverse supply chain** because goods are moving in the reverse direction.

Reverse supply chain is a series of activities required to retrieve a used product from a customer to either dispose of it or reuse it.

2. **Information flow** This is the movement of detailed data among members of the supply chain, for example, order information, customer information, order fulfillment, delivery status, and proof-of-delivery confirmation. Most information flows are done electronically, although paper invoices or receipts are still common for noncommercial customers.

3. **Financial flow** This is the transfer of payments and financial arrangements, for example, billing payment schedules, credit terms, and payment via **electronic funds transfer (EFT)**. EFT provides for electronic payments and collections. It is safe, secure, efficient, and less expensive than paper check payments and collections.

Electronic funds transfer (EFT) is the electronic transfer of money from one bank account to another, either within a single institution or across multiple institutions using a computer-based system and without direct intervention of bank personnel.

Order fulfillment is the set of complex processes involved in providing customers with what they ordered on time and all customer services related to on-time delivery of a product.

Logistics entails all processes and information needed to efficiently move products from origin to destination.

Back-office operations supports accounting, inventory management and shipping processes in the fulfillment of orders.

Front-office operations involve order fulfillment activities visible to the customer, like sales and advertising.

Electronic data interchange (EDI) involves electronically communicating information such as purchase order and invoices.

Electronic Data Interchange in the Order Fulfillment and Logistics Process

The **order fulfillment** process is one of the most critical and challenging parts of SCM and provides an excellent example of how these three flows work can be automated in the supply chain. The order fulfillment and **logistics** process consists of all the steps an organization must take from the time they receive an order until the finished items is placed in the hands of the customer. Order fulfillment is complex because it involves **back-office operations**, such as accounting, inventory management, and shipping and is closely aligned with **front-office operations** or customer-facing activities.

The key objective of order fulfillment is to deliver materials or products at the right time, to the right place, and at the right cost. For example, a customer who has ordered a new appliance from Lowe's Home Improvement—a large U.S. retail company specializing in home improvement, appliances, and services—via its website expects to receive it as scheduled, undamaged, with assembly and operating instructions, warranty and return information. If it is back ordered, the customer will be advised. If it is damaged in transit or the customer is not satisfied with the appliance, it will be returned and restocked at a regular or discounted price.

It is imperative that the order fulfillment and logistics process be carried out in a consistent way, that the outcomes are reliable, that frequent and effective communication are maintained with all participants and that materials and products are organized for easy retrieval. The main challenges related to the order fulfillment process are forecasting, inventory management, optimization, and logistics. All of these directly align with the major strengths of an SCM system including the use of **electronic data interchange** (EDI) capabilities throughout the nine steps. For example, EDI facilitates the flow of orders in and out of the supply chain and improves accuracy and efficiency of the process by eliminating many complex, time-consuming activities and seamlessly connecting all involved parties such as suppliers, logistics providers and retailers. Many large retailers require their suppliers to use EDI because it enables more reliable and consistent B2B transactions. Think about the thousands of products carried by large retailers like Walmart, Target, Lowe's, Home Depot, and Best Buy. EDI was most likely used to stock those shelves and in the case of online orders, get them delivered to customers' homes.

The nine-step order fulfillment process depicted in **Figure 10.7** and explained in **Tech Note 10.2** provides a typical example of how supply chain flows, actions, and participants work together to achieve a successful outcome using an SCM system.

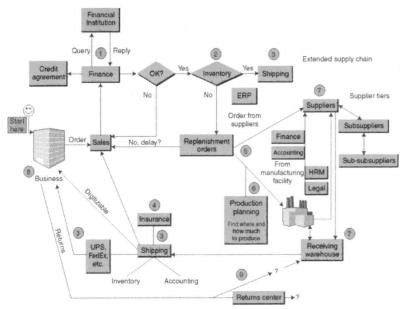

FIGURE 10.7 On-demand forecasts, inventory management, optimization, and logistics activities are conducted at various points throughout the nine-step order fulfillment and logistics process.

Tech Note 10.2

The Nine-Step Order Fulfillment and Logistics Process

Step 1: Make sure that the customer will pay Depending on the payment method and prior arrangements with the customer, verify that the customer can and will pay and agrees to the payment terms. This activity is done by the finance department for B2B sales or an external company such as PayPal or a credit card issuer such as Visa for business-to-customer (B2C) sales. Any holdup in payment may cause a shipment to be delayed, resulting in a loss of goodwill or a customer. In B2C, the customers usually pay by credit card, but with major credit card data theft at Target and other retailers, the buyer may be using a stolen card.

Step 2: Check in-stock availability and reorder as necessary As soon as an order is received, either through a website, file import, mobile sales, or EDI, the stock is checked to determine the availability of the product or materials. If there is not enough stock, the ordering system places an order, typically automatically using EDI. To perform these operations, the ordering system needs to interface with the inventory system.

Step 3: Arrange shipments When the product is available, shipment to the customer is arranged (otherwise, go to Step 5). Products can be digital or physical. If the item is physical and available, packaging and shipment arrangements are made. Both the packaging/shipping department and internal shippers or outside transporters may be involved. Digital items are usually available because their "inventory" is not depleted. However, a digital product, such as software, may be under revision and thus unavailable for delivery at certain times. In either case, information needs to flow among several partners.

Step 4: Insurance The contents of a shipment may need to be insured. Both the finance department and an insurance company could be involved, and again, information needs to be exchanged with the customer and insurance agent.

Step 5: Replenishment Customized orders will always trigger a need for some manufacturing or assembly operation. Similarly, if standard items are out of stock, they need to be produced or procured. Production is done in-house or outsourced.

Step 6: In-house production In-house production needs to be planned, and actual production needs to be scheduled. Production planning involves people, materials, components, machines, financial resources, and possibly suppliers and subcontractors. In the case of assembly and/or manufacturing, several plant services may be needed, including collaboration with business partners. Production facilities may be located in a different country than the company's headquarters or retailers. This may further complicate the flow of information.

Step 7: Source from suppliers A manufacturer may opt to buy products or subassemblies from suppliers. Similarly, if the seller is a retailer, such as in the case of Amazon.com or Walmart.com, the retailer must purchase products from its manufacturers. In this case, appropriate receiving and quality assurance of incoming materials and products must take place.

Once production (Step 6) or purchasing from suppliers (Step 7) is completed, shipments to the customers (Step 3) are arranged.

Step 8: Contacts with customers Sales representatives keep in contact with customers, especially in B2B, starting with the notification of orders received and ending with notification of a shipment or change in delivery date. These contacts are frequently generated automatically.

Step 9: Returns In some cases, customers want to exchange or return items. The movement of returns from customers back to vendors is reverse logistics. Such returns can be a major problem, especially when they occur in large volumes.

Virtual Collaboration in the Supply Chain

Leading businesses are moving quickly to realize the benefits of virtual collaboration in the supply chain. Several examples of organizations that are benefiting from sharing information appear below.

B2B retailers: Inventory replenishment   One of the most publicized examples of information sharing exists between Procter & Gamble (P&G) and Walmart. Walmart provides P&G with access to sales information on every item Walmart buys from P&G. The information is collected by P&G on a daily basis from every Walmart store, and P&G uses that information to manage the inventory replenishment for Walmart.

Retailer–supplier: Virtual collaboration   European supermarket chain **Asda** has rolled out Web-based EDI technology to 650 suppliers. Web EDI technology is based on the AS2 standard, an internationally accepted HTTP-based protocol used to send real-time data in multiple formats securely over the Internet. It promises to improve the efficiency and speed of traditional EDI communications, which route data over third-party, value-added networks (VANs).

Manufacturer–contract carriers: Lower transportation and inventory costs and reduced stockouts   Unilever is one of the world's leading manufacturers and suppliers of fast-moving consumer goods sold in more than 190 countries and used by 2.5 billion consumers. Their 400+ brands include Lipton, Knorr, Dove, Hellman's, Suave, Brooke Bond, and Omo. To deliver these goods to retailers efficiently, Unilever sources contract carriers. To manage this large transportation network, Unilever uses Bravo Solution's Transportation Business Center (TBC) to feed routing guides, support supply chain planning, and monitor internal and carrier performance. The Web-based system provides carriers with site specification requirements when they pick up a shipment at a manufacturing or distribution center or when they deliver goods to retailers. TBC gives carriers all of the vital information they need: contact names and phone numbers, operating hours, the number of dock doors at a location, the height of the dock doors, how to make an appointment to deliver or pick up shipments, pallet configuration, and other special requirements. All mission-critical information that Unilever's carriers need to make pickups, shipments, and deliveries is now available electronically 24/7.

Manufacturer–suppliers–distributors–customers: Information sharing to reduce product development time   Caterpillar, Inc. is a multinational heavy-machinery manufacturer. In the traditional mode of operation, cycle time along the supply chain was long because the process involved paper—document transfers among managers, salespeople, and technical staff. To solve the problem, Caterpillar connected its engineering and manufacturing divisions with its active suppliers, distributors, overseas factories, and customers through an extranet-based global collaboration system. By means of the collaboration system, a request for a customized tractor component, for example, can be transmitted from a customer to a Caterpillar dealer and on to designers and suppliers, all in a very short time. Customers also can use the extranet to retrieve and modify detailed order information while the vehicle is still on the assembly line.

Achieving a Fully Digitized Supply Chain

Customers have come to expect unprecedented levels of service such as same-day delivery, free shipping, and real-time alerts about product availability or price changes. Using technology to increase speed, transparency and sustainability has become necessary if a company wants to grow and maintain its customer base and sustain a competitive advantage. Technology is the biggest factor in changing the traditional supply chain into a digitized, 24/7 supply chain, referred to as the **"always-on" supply chain**. Supply chain executives at more than half of the companies that responded to IDC's biennial supply chain survey said they are leveraging digital technologies and business innovations to manage the increasing complexity of today's global always-on supply chain.

In the past, supply chains were linear and companies tackled supply chain challenges primarily by focusing on internal cost reduction and improved operational efficiency. But traditional

Always-on supply chain is an integrated set of supply networks characterized by a continuous, high-velocity flow of information and analytics creating predictive, actionable decisions to better serve the customer 24/7.

approaches are less effective as supply chains become longer and more interconnected, and there are higher stakeholder expectations and more sources of risk. Always-on supply chains are more connected, intelligent, scalable, and agile. Driven by social media and the IoT, digitized supply chains have 50 times more data available to them than just five years ago, including doing things that could not have been done. For example, sensors that enable data collection and advancements in computing power have significantly improved predictive analytics. Supplemental tools, such as automation and wearables, are creating digital, continuously operating supply chains and an interconnected network of supply chain workers.

Recently, *MHI*, an international supply chain trade association and Deloitte US, an industry-leading audit and consulting firm, released the 2019 MHI Annual Industry Report "The Rise of Supply Chain Consciousness" (MHI and Deloitte, 2020). Based on responses from 1000+ respondents, in large and small companies across a wide range of sectors, the report revealed that several innovative emerging technologies are dramatically impacting the supply chain and the people who manage them.

The report focused on 11 technological innovations that are driving significant changes at each of the four stages of supply digitization.

Four Technology Stages of Digital Adoption

The MHI/Deloitte Report (2020) suggests that a company must go through a natural progression of adopting increasingly powerful technology to get the most out of its supply chain. To illustrate how this is done, they provide a guiding framework for organizations to follow. According to their "Four Technology Stages of Digital Adoption," organizations pass through four distinct stages as they move toward optimizing their supply chain—digital connectivity, automation, advanced analytics, and artificial intelligence (AI). The report describes a total of 11 technologies that can be used to achieve this, and each stage provides a necessary foundation for the next (see **Figure 10.8**). We have added three more technologies—AI-powered GPS, AI algorithms, and Machine Learning—to show how companies are using AI in their fully digitized supply chains. Each of the 14 technologies and their impact on supply chain effectiveness are described next.

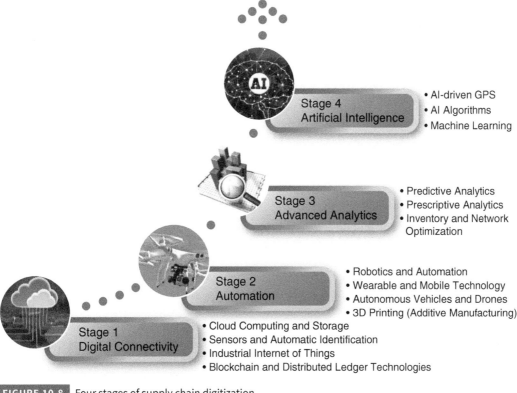

FIGURE 10.8 Four stages of supply chain digitization.

Stage 1: Digital connectivity involves collecting, validating, and organizing data from IoT, cloud computing, sensors and automatic identification, and blockchain technology to enable real-time, end-to-end visibility in the supply chain. 70% of companies in the MHI/Deloitte study were using at least one of these four technologies.

- **Industrial internet of things (IoT)** is the use of connected devices and smart electronics in industries such as manufacturing, transportation, power generation, and health care. It is an effective way to track and authenticate products and shipments using GPS and other positional technologies and can enable an Internet-driven fully connected industrial environment.

- **Cloud computing and storage** plays a critical role in the improvement of SCM by supporting an enterprise's efforts to share data with multiple, geographically dispersed partners. Benefits of cloud computing in the supply chain include improved collaboration among supply chain partners, cost-effective use of staff resources, and the ability to adapt to changing business needs quickly.

- **Sensors and automatic identification** are a means of delivering computing and communications power to everyday devices and businesses. The data they generate can lead to better business models and increased visibility in supply chains. By collecting data from objects, then communicating and aggregating that data into information that is presented to users, sensors can help users reach decisions about how to make, move, or change those objects. For example, by positioning a network of sensors throughout its plants, an automobile company can measure humidity in its buildings. If readings rise about those acceptable for paining vehicle bodies, the next car body on the line will automatically be routed to a different step of the manufacturing process that is not adversely affected by the humidity in the building. This process change reduces costs of repainting and downtime on the line.

- **Blockchain technology** Blockchain is the natural technology for providing greater security and transparency in the online supply chain, as demonstrated in our opening case. The purpose of the supply chain is to track a product from start to finish and that's exactly what blockchain does. As discussed in Chapter 3, blockchain is a ledger-based system that allows data entry in "blocks" to facilitate the process of immutably recording transactions and tracking assets in a business network, making it impossible to manipulate the supply chain by protecting it against falsified documents, transactions and other information.

Stage 2: Automation involves using automated systems, robotics, and augmented technologies to perform repetitive, resource-intensive tasks to streamline safer, faster, and more reliable operations. About 53% of responding companies were using automation tools in their supply chain.

- **Robotics and automation** Robotics and automation are revolutionizing supply chains across the globe. As technology becomes smarter, faster, and cheaper, it is being called upon to do more. Robots are increasingly able to demonstrate "human" capabilities and traits such as sensing, dexterity, memory, and trainability. They are being integrated into supply chains, taking on more human-oriented tasks, including picking and packaging, testing or inspecting products, and assembling electronics.

- **Wearable and mobile technology** Wearable technologies are devices incorporated into clothing and accessories that can be comfortably worn. These devices perform many of the same computing tasks as mobile phones and laptop computers and frequently can outperform them. Enterprise wearables from smart glasses to voice-directed hands-free wearable scanners and real-time views of every touchpoint within the supply chain are improving worker safety and increasing transparency within the supply chain and avoid potential bottlenecks. Increasing numbers of companies are piloting the use of smart glasses within their supply chains. One company used them to implement "vision picking" in their warehouse where displays on the smart glasses showed the task information during the pick process, including aisle, product location, and quantity. As a result, staff worked much faster and reduced errors, increasing efficiency by 25%.

- **Autonomous vehicles and drones** Driverless vehicles and drones use a variety of technologies, including sensors, cameras, and advanced driver assistance systems, to handle some or all functions of operating a vehicle. Drones can deliver significant value to businesses by improving supply chain operations. Companies can transform their operations by using drones to monitor functioning of plants, maintain security, and provide real-time data about a facility's surroundings. One large U.S. retailer has asked for permission to test drones for making deliveries to customers in its parking lots and at customers' homes. The retailer also wants to use the aerial technology enabled by drones to check on its buildings, warehouses, and distribution centers. The retailer has tested drones inside its facilities but now wants to do outdoor tests. To do that, it needs FAA permission.

- **3D Printing** Additive manufacturing could revolutionize production processes and have far-reaching future implications for product supply chains. A global aerospace and defense company deployed electronic beam melting, a 3D printing technology, and reduced production costs for aerospace components by 50% while still maintaining functionality and performance.

Stage 3: Advanced analytics is where mountains of data are converted into valuable insights using predictive analytics, prescriptive analytics, and inventory and network optimization tools to improve supply chain effectiveness. Only 30% of responding companies reported using predictive or prescriptive analytics in their supply chain operations. **Predictive analytics** Some of the most effective applications of predictive analytics focus on predicting patterns associated with consumer behavior. In the supply chain arena, predictive modeling allows managers to manage inventory better, plan more reliable transportation networks, and reduce variability in lead times. This can enhance service levels, lower costs, and improve the bottom line.

- **Prescriptive analytics** build on the results provided by predictive analytics and can be used to identify what is likely to happen if current activities are continued. In the supply chain, prescriptive analytics are extremely useful for making recommendations, for making more efficient and better-informed decisions, and for identifying adjustments needed to optimize strategy and operations.

- **Inventory and network optimization tools** Route planning, product flow path analysis, and asset optimization help companies streamline operations, improve inventory control, gain visibility, manage risk, and reduce costs. The ability to deploy assets and position inventory well is critical to delivering the right service at the right cost. Inventory and network optimization are powerful decision-support tools to model end-to-end supply chain costs and trade-offs. An equipment manufacturer who had excess inventory across its distribution network, as a result of lead-time discrepancies between similar parts from the same supplier, high variability of transportation lead times, and a highly complex product portfolio, constructed an integrated parts management framework consisting of inventory analytics and optimization, sales and customer insights, supply insights, and a parts business plan to reduce product and transportation costs and improve product placement and inventory balance.

Stage 4: Artificial intelligence is the highest level of business intelligence and analytics that involves using AI-powered GPS, AI algorithms, and machine learning to generate smarter supply chain insights and learning from itself by pattern matching, recording behaviors, and integrating feedback from digital and human interfaces.

- **AI-powered GPS** like the ones described in **IT at Work 10.3** can be used to create the most efficient routes for transportation company fleets to prevent drivers getting stuck in traffic or having to back-track.

- **AI algorithms** can forecast when orders will arrive and leave a warehouse. This is called "smart placement" and allows employees to put pallets of products in the best position for getting orders out the door. Instead of moving pallets around to get to the correct order, AI allows an organization to be smarter about where items are initially placed.

IT at Work 10.3

UPS Enhances Its Supply Chain with AI-Driven Continuous Delivery Route Optimization, Drones, and Autonomous Vehicles

UPS is a global leader in logistics and is a pioneer in supply chain digitization. To create even more operational efficiencies, UPS added UPSNav to its ORION route guidance platform in 2020. UPS-Nav is the most advanced routing technology that has ever been deployed by UPS and provides local delivery drivers with detailed turn-by-turn directions to guide them, not just to addresses, but to specific package drop-off and pickup locations, like loading docks that aren't visible from the street. The new SCM software feature is a huge improvement over the basic ORION route guidance platform UPS implemented in 2012 that provided its drivers with a static route at the start of their workday. UPSNav updates directions for drivers while they are on the road, based on changing weather and traffic conditions and work commitments. Optimizing delivery routes is extremely important at UPS. It save time, reduces carbon emissions, and reduces wear and tear on its vehicles. UPS estimates that using ORION alone has saved it over 100 million delivery miles and annual savings of $50 million since 2012. The benefits from USPNav are expected to far exceed those realized from ORION.

UPS Flight Forward is its drone subsidiary that currently delivers various medical products between health centers and labs by drones at University of California at San Diego Health. UPS is currently exploring new opportunities in this space related to delivery of essential health-care products to office-based dental and medical practitioners.

UPS is also on its way to using autonomous ground vehicles. On January 31, 2020, UPS ordered 10,000 electric vehicles that it will begin using in mid-2020 and at the same time partnered with Waymo—a U.S. autonomous driving vehicle development company—to test the efficacy of using Waymo's self-driving Chrysler Pacific minivans—with a trained operator on board—to pick up packages on a frequent basis from the UPS store location in Arizona and deliver them to a nearby UPS sorting hub. The goal is faster turnaround times in preparation for on-demand delivery. UPS has quietly been using autonomous trucks—through TuSimple, a startup trucking company—to haul cargo between Phoenix and Tuscon, Arizona, since May 2019. If these initiatives continue to be successful, UPS anticipates that it will benefit small to medium-sized businesses with faster movement of goods and help them realize significant cost savings.

Sources: Compiled from Morgan (2018), Hirsch (2019), O'Kane (2019), Condon (2020), Peterson (2020), Schmidt (2020), Yamanouchi (2020), and Zaccara (2020).

- **Machine learning** can be used to analyze production times and logistics to better predict delivery dates. Instead of relying on manufacturing and shipping schedules to estimate time of arrival, AI combines historical delivery information with customer feedback, weather reports, and logistics to provide information about product availability to sales associates and customers and accurately predict when a customer will get delivery of ordered products.

The Economist recently predicted that using AI in the supply chain will have a larger economic impact than any other application of technology and will affect a larger number of organizations (The Economist, 2018), and 79% of the respondents in the MHI/Deloitte study believe that AI will become a core supply chain competency by 2022. One company that has successfully achieved full supply chain digitization is UPS. IT at Work 10.3 describes how UPS is successfully using several forms of AI to increase customer satisfaction, reduce costs, and cut back on carbon emissions.

Lessons Learned

Changing business and customer requirements are putting new and greater pressures on organizations to improve on the "Always-On" supply chain by developing what some are calling the "NextGen" or "Thinking" supply chain. This new form of supply chain will be proactive, predictive, and prescriptive. It will be tightly connected to data sources such as social opinion and IoT outputs and will allow close collaboration with suppliers and customers through cloud-based commerce networks that offer a high level of security. All its links will be interconnected and synchronized to enable companies to gain the very highest levels of competitive advantage. The vast majority of respondents in the MHI/Deloitte study said they expect upcoming innovative technologies will have a significant impact on their supply chain over the next 10 years and believe that most will disrupt supply chain practices and create lasting competitive advantage for companies that use them and disadvantages those companies that don't. This means that business leaders will be enthusiastically embracing new and emerging technologies to provide improvements in supply chain visibility, reduce costs and enhance customer service, and determine how best to apply them to their future requirements of an efficient supply chain.

To gain familiarity with new technologies before investing heavily in them, organizations would be advised to take a test-and-learn approach along with sharing insights with other participants in their supply chain. The major barriers to adopting innovative supply chain technologies will be an organization's lack of a clear business case to justify investment, lack of talent to utilize the technology effectively, and a corporate culture that is risk adverse.

Moving forward, it's important to remember that digitally transforming the supply chain is not just about driving efficiency and effectiveness of an organization's bottom line, it is also about enhancing the customer experience and acting in a socially responsible way.

A sophisticated, fully digitized SCM system is an important tool that will enable organizations to shield itself against the digital disruptions of the future and achieve its goals.

Leading SCM Systems Developers

Each year Gartner Research conducts extensive research into many different technology markets to develop what is called "Magic Quadrant." Each Magic Quadrant positions technology vendors in a specific technology market as leaders, challengers, niche players, and visionaries (Gartner, 2020). The Magic Quadrant is intended to be a first step in helping organizations understand technology offerings in a specific market and how they align with its specific business objectives. According to Gartner's 2019 SCM-related Magic Quadrants—Sales and Operations Planning Systems, Management Execution Systems, Warehouse Management Systems, and Transportation Management Systems (Gartner, 2020)—the leading SCM software developers in 2019 included: Demand Solutions (**https://www.demandsolutions.com**), Logility (**https://www.logility.com**), SAP SCM (**https://www.sap.com/products/digital-supply-chain/scm.html**), Oracle (**https://www.oracle.com/index.html**), JDA Software Inc. (**https://jda.com**), OMP (**https://omp.com**), Anaplan (**https://www.anaplan.com**), High Jump (**https://www.highjump.com**), and Arkieva (**https://arkieva.com**).

Questions

1. What is a supply chain?
2. List four functions carried out by companies in a supply chain.
3. List and describe the three main flows being managed in a supply chain.
4. Describe SCM.
5. What are the top two strategic priorities of SCM executives?
6. What are the two major barriers preventing innovation in the supply chain?
7. What are the top innovative digital technologies impacting SCM?
8. Why would companies want to achieve a fully digitized supply chain?
9. What are the characteristics of the NextGen SCM?

10.4 Customer Relationship Management

LO10.4 Define the five phases of the customer relationship management (CRM) process and the role of a CRM system in customer acquisition, retention, and customer lifetime value.

Focusing on the customer is a vital part of doing business and an essential component of the supply chain. Managing customers should be a core competency of any business, whether they

Customer relationship management (CRM) is the process of choosing the most suitable and efficient approach to making and maintaining interactions with customer and clients.

are customer-facing such as health care, fitness, travel, or retail or supplier-facing such as manufacturing, wholesaling. A company that has a successful **customer relationship management (CRM)** strategy has a distinct advantage over its competitors. Effective CRM can provide managers with a 360-degree view of the customer relationship, enable real-time responses, and improve sales productivity and predictability.

The CRM Process

The CRM process is a series of activities in which organizations (1) identify new prospects and sales leads, (2) track and monitor in-person and online sales opportunities, (3) organize and engage current customers by getting to know their requirements and preferences, (4) establish a relationship with current customers by carefully managing customer communication, and (5) manage the customer life cycle to encourage repeat purchases and referrals, as shown in **Figure 10.9**. All these processes can be improved significantly by automating them.

FIGURE 10.9 Five key phases of the CRM process.

While technology plays an important part in optimizing performance in each of the five phases of the CRM process, CRM technology alone cannot transform or improve customer relationships. A survey conducted by Forrester Research revealed that technology and strategy are a necessary, but not sufficient condition for CRM project success. A total of 414 business professionals thought that business performance improvement depends on a combination of the right people, processes, strategy, and technology. See **Figure 10.10** to see how well you can estimate the percentage they attributed to each of these four factors.

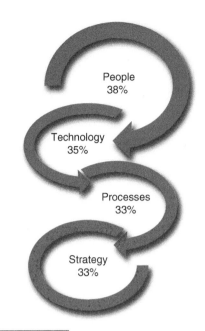

FIGURE 10.10 Four CRM critical success factors.

Changes in people's behavior, their commitment, attitude toward mandatory changes as well as process improvements make the difference between better bottom lines or a $100 million write-off. Buying the most suitable CRM is like buying a Ferrari or Porsche. You will not win any races simply because you bought a sports car and you won't become the next Lady Gaga or Elton John simply by owning a Steinway piano! To effectively compete in the marketplace, an organization must intelligently manage its customer relationships to ensure its processes, people, and strategy are aligned and fully consistent with its goals of increasing revenues and net profits and enhancing the customer experience. Just as inventory and supplier relationships need to be effectively managed in the supply chain, effective CRM is every bit as data-driven, complex, and continuously changing. For example, the growth of mobile sales channels, social networking, e-mail, and smartphones have made engaging customers across multiple touchpoints much more complex **(Figure 10.11)**. In addition, many companies have customer data in multiple, disparate systems that are not integrated—until they implement a CRM system.

FIGURE 10.11 Multiple touchpoints add to CRM complexity.

Automating CRM

A CRM system is a widely used and mature technology that can be deployed on the premises, in the cloud, or as on-demand SaaS. Numerous successful CRM implementations have helped transform the business, increased profit, and strengthened customer loyalty, and fierce competition among the big four CRM vendors—Salesforce.com, SAP, Oracle, and Microsoft—motivates innovation.

From a technology perspective, a CRM system is similar in some ways to an ERP. Both interface with and share data from other systems, are sold in modules, and are offered on the premises, in the cloud, or as SaaS. In practice, however, CRMs are different from ERPs whose users are often required to adhere to tight business rules and user practices. For example, ERPs are used by accounting, finance, and HR personnel who must comply with generally accepted accounting principles (GAAPs), the Securities Exchange Commission (SEC), labor laws, or other legal requirements. In contrast, CRMs are primarily used by sales and marketing personnel who tend to be less tolerant of inflexible rules of conduct. Instead, they are accustomed to being creative in finding customers and closing the deal. If the CRM system does not support them in a way that fits the way they think and act, sales and marketing can reject the CRM and cause total system failure.

CRM refers to the methodologies and software tools to leverage customer data in order to achieve the following:

- Identify the appropriate customer experience for a customer.
- Predict and prevent attrition (loss) of a customer, unless he or she is not worth retaining.
- Acquire new customers who are most likely to become profitable.
- Up-sell (sell more profitable products/services) or cross-sell (sell additional products/services) to unprofitable customers to move them to a profit position.
- Reduce inefficiencies that waste advertising dollars.

In 2019, the worldwide CRM software market was valued at $34.9 billion and is expected to reach $40.2 billion by 2023. Salesforce is by far the largest CRM vendor worldwide. Other CRM vendors who are recognized as leaders in the field include Adobe, Oracle, SAP, ServiceNow, Microsoft, Genesys Telecommunications Laboratories, Nice Systems, Pegasystems, Verint Systems, Inc., and Zendesk.

Customer Acquisition and Retention

CRM systems play a major role in the customer experience, and an enjoyable customer experience positively impacts customer acquisition and retention. For example, CRM technologies are invaluable in developing and automating marketing campaigns and promotions to attract new customers, increase sales to existing customers, or both. Attracting and acquiring new customers are expensive activities: for example, it costs banks roughly $100 to acquire each new customer. Newly acquired customers are unprofitable until they have purchased enough products or services to exceed the cost to acquire and service them. However, not all customers are worth retaining. Some customers can be unprofitable so it's important to determine each **customer lifetime value (CLV)**. This is where data analytics, sophisticated predictive analytics, and business intelligence (BI) are needed along with business rules that specify how to treat or manage customers based on their value score. In the IT Toolbox at the end of the chapter, you will learn how to determine CLV.

Retaining customers that generate revenues in excess of the costs (e.g., customer service, returns, promotional items, and the like) is critical. The purpose of loyalty or frequent purchase programs offered by online retailers, coffee shops, airlines, supermarkets, credit card issuers, casinos, and other companies is to track customers for CRM purposes and build customer loyalty to improve financial performance. Loyalty programs rely on data warehouses and data analytics to recognize and reward customers who repeatedly use services or products. **IT at Work 10.4** describes how worldwide florist 1-800-Flowers uses its loyalty program to attract and retains customers.

Customer lifetime value (CLV) is the value a customer contributes to the business over the entire lifetime of their relationship with the company.

IT at Work 10.4

Customer Engagement Blooms at 1-800-Flowers.com through Its Innovative Online Loyalty Program

1-800-Flowers.com is an Internet pioneer. Online sales are a major marketing channel in addition to telephone and fax orders. Competition is very strong in this industry. The company's success was based on operational efficiency, convenience (24/7 accessibility), and reliability. However, all major competitors essentially provide the same products and services. To maintain its competitive edge, the company transformed itself into a customer-centric organization, caring for more than 15 million customers.

One of 1-800-Flowers.com's most successful customer relationship initiatives is its Celebrations Passport loyalty program. The company partnered with Caesars Rewards to cultivate an attractive loyalty program in which its customer earn 30× reward credits for every $1 spent and are offered free shipping and no service charge on all purchases for one year across all their brands—Harry & David,

Cheryl's Cookies, Shari's Berries, Simply Chocolate, Wolferman's, and Personalization Universe. 1-800-Flowers uses AI, new augmented reality functions, additional payment options, mobile app upgrades, and elevated service features to introduce new and unique ways for customers to interact with the company while providing a significantly enhanced customer experience that is helping it stay competitive and deliver a more personalized experience for its customers.

Celebrations Passports is part of 1-800-Flowers.com's strategy to use more innovative integrated CRM technologies to deepen customer engagement while providing a one-stop shop for all of its customers' "celebratory" needs. Deepening customer relationships through its loyalty program has significantly helped raise the level of brand loyalty. In 2019 Q2, the company attributed a 9% increase in revenues and a 12% increase in new customer growth to its Celebrations Passport program.

Sources: Compiled from Tierney (2018), Mills (2019), Sherred (2019), Loyalty 360 (2020), CaesarsRewards.com, and 1800flowers.com.

CRM for a Competitive Edge

According to management guru Peter Drucker, "Those companies who know their customers, understand their needs, and communicate intelligently with them will always have a competitive advantage over those that don't" (1969). For most types of companies, marketing effectiveness depends on how well they know their customers: specifically, knowing what their customers want, how best to contact them, and what types of offers they are likely to respond to positively. Knowing your customers is critical, since a mere 5% increase in customer retention can improve profits by as much as 20%. Customer-centric business strategies strive to provide products and services that customers want to buy. One of the best examples is the Apple iPhone and iPod—devices that customers were willing to camp out on sidewalks to buy to guarantee getting one on the day of the release of its latest version. In contrast, companies with product-centric strategies need to create demand for their products, which is more expensive and may fail.

Implementing a CRM System

A formal business plan must be in place before any CRM project begins—one that quantifies the expected costs, tangible financial benefits, and intangible strategic benefits, as well as the risks. The plan should include an assessment of the following:

- **Tangible net benefits** The plan must include a clear and precise cost–benefit analysis that lists all the planned project costs and tangible benefits. This portion of the plan should also contain a strategy for assessing key financial metrics, such as ROI, net present value (NPV), or other justification methods.

- **Intangible benefits** The plan should detail the expected intangible benefits, and it should list the measured successes and shortfalls. Often, an improvement in customer satisfaction is the primary goal of the CRM solution, but in many cases, this key value is not measured.

- **Risk assessment** The risk assessment is a list of all of the potential pitfalls related to the people, processes, and technology that are involved in the CRM project. Having such a list helps to lessen the probability that problems will occur. And, if they do happen, a company may find that, by having listed and considered the problems in advance, the problems are more manageable than they would have been otherwise.

One of the biggest problems in CRM implementation is the difficulty of defining and measuring success. Many companies say that when it comes to determining value, intangible benefits are more significant than tangible cost savings and number of customers. Yet, companies often fail to establish quantitative or even qualitative measures in order to judge these intangible benefits that typically include increases in staff productivity (e.g., more deals closed), cost avoidance, revenues, and margin increases, as well as reductions in inventory costs (e.g., due to the elimination of errors). Other intangible benefits include increased customer satisfaction, loyalty, and retention.

For example, at Coca Cola Germany, its CRM software allows it to instantly respond to customer and supplier concerns. Using Salesforce, the Coca Cola Germany team can easily log issues and dispatch a field service technician in real time. The results have been a resounding 30% increase in productivity and a significant rise in customer satisfaction.

Lessons Learned

Given the high level of investment in CRM, it is obvious that companies want to get as much value as possible out of their systems. It is unfortunate, then, that so many of them make mistakes in selecting and implementing CRM software. There are several CRM mistakes that must be avoided at all cost. Five common CRM mistakes and actions to avoid them are explained in **Table 10.3.**

TABLE 10.3   CRM Mistakes: How to Avoid Them

CRM Mistakes	How to Avoid the Mistakes
Putting IT department in charge of the CRM project instead of the business users	The hands-on business users need to champion and lead the project initiative, with IT playing a supporting role. CRM is a software project whose success relies on users' input, which helps ensure that they actually will use it. Unlike other apps, salespeople do not have to use CRM. If the system is underused, companies will see only limited improvements.
Not getting the CRM requirements right by not involving key business stakeholders from the outset	CRM implementations need buy-in from the users and other business stakeholders, who can spread enthusiasm. Frequent communication about the project is important to engaging them in a meaningful way.
Making mobile CRM strategy an afterthought	Consider mobility a priority in the CRM project from the outset. Putting an existing CRM on mobile devices is a bad plan.
Taking wrong approach to CRM training	Make sure that the interface is intuitive enough that most users will not need hands-on training. When people sit in a classroom for an hour, they will only retain five minutes of what they hear. A learning program during lunch that focuses on one or two lessons is a much more effective adoption strategy.
Underestimating users' resistance to change	Users will not tolerate poorly designed systems. Frustrating users is a fast track to failure, or, at a minimum, suboptimal results.

Source: Adapted from All (2014).

Learning by Example   Citizen National Bank's experience is one example of a CRM failure that ultimately became a success when it changed vendors. The lessons learned, at a cost of $500,000, were as follows:

- Be absolutely clear on how the CRM application will add value to the sales process.
- Determine if and why salespeople are avoiding CRM.
- Provide incentives for the sales team to adopt CRM.
- Find ways to simplify the use of the CRM application.
- Adjust the CRM system as business needs change.

Questions

1. Explain the four critical success factors for CRM.
2. Why does CRM matter?
3. Discuss how CRM impacts customer acquisition and retention.
4. According to Peter Drucker, what does marketing effectiveness depend on?
5. Give three reasons why CRM fails.
6. How can an organization justify implementing a CRM system?

10.5 Communicating and Collaborating with Enterprise Knowledge Management Systems, Enterprise Content Management Systems, and Enterprise Social Platforms

LO10.5 Explain *the purpose of enterprise knowledge management (EKM), enterprise content management (ECM) systems, and enterprise social platforms (ESPs) and their impact on communication and collaboration in an organization.*

Two major types of enterprise systems are used to enable and facilitate communication and collaboration within an organization: EKM systems and ESPs.

What Is Knowledge Management?

Knowledge management (KM) is an extension of information management discussed in Chapter 3. The concept of KM was created by the management consulting community and prompted by the emergence of the Internet. With quick, easy way to access vast quantities information that could be shared among geographically dispersed departments through dashboards, expertise locators and databases created from best practices data, consultants soon realized they had a new tool they could market. That new tool's name was KM and the concept was rapidly embraced by organizations and professional associations around the globe in an age where **intellectual capital** was becoming more and more valued. According to the Garner Group, KM is defined as

> *a discipline that promotes an integrated approach to identifying, capturing, evaluating, retrieving, and sharing all of an enterprise's information assets. These assets may include databases, documents, policies, procedures and previously uncaptured expertise and experience in individual workers.* (Duhon, 1988)

Dr. Michael Koenig, an expert in the origins, goals, and fundamentals of KM, describes four operational KM components (Koenig, 2018):

- **Content management** The goal of KM is to capture knowledge, improve access, enhance its creation, transfer, and use and manage it as a corporate asset to help deal effectively with rapid changes, turnover, and downsizing.
- **Expertise location** KM is also about "rallying the troops" to get their buy-in and support in locating and retaining valuable expertise that may be lost. For example, when employees leave the company.
- **Lessons learned** KM is about education and learning from past experiences. It's a way to teach people about something they don't know, thus eliminating the need to "reinvent

Knowledge management (KM) is the process of creating, sharing, using and managing knowledge and information in an organization to make the best use of the knowledge.

Intellectual capital is the collective documented and undocumented knowledge of individuals in an organization or society that can be exploited for some money-making or other useful purpose.

the wheel" to save time and effort and ensure fewer mistakes are made. Fewer mistakes equate to less risk caused by lack of knowledge or sloppy work that can lead to dangerous long-term threats to organizational performance and reputation.

- **Community of practice (CoP)** is groups of people get together to share a common interest or passion and learn to perform common tasks better through knowledge sharing and regular interactions. KM can inspire people and CoPs to come up with innovative ways to see and do things differently and hopefully better.

Koenig's Three Stages of KM Development

According to Koenig (2018), each KM component must be managed in three stages to cultivate changes in the way that people interact with technology, with data, and with others in the organization, i.e., culture (**Figure 10.12**). The three stages are as follows:

- **Stage 1: Information technology** IT enables organizations to communicate in a more effective way. Deploying the Internet to achieve more effective use of information and knowledge is at the heart of KM. Management consulting companies jumped at the new possibilities offered by an EKM system and quickly realized that if they shared knowledge provided by the Internet, intranet, extranets, and databases across their own organizations, they could effectively stop duplicating work and underbid their competitors and make more profit.

- **Stage 2: HR and corporate culture** It soon became clear that a KM initiative would fail if people didn't use it and would require significant changes in corporate culture. KM extends beyond just collecting and structuring information and knowledge and makes it more accessible across the organization. The rewards for doing so must be examined and modified to encourage knowledge sharing. Stage 2 also involves the design of easy-to-use, user-friendly systems that consider human factors.

- **Stage 3: Taxonomy and content management** The technology must enable people to easily collect, store, and retrieve relevant content. After all, if people bought into the concept of KM, but then couldn't find and access the data they were looking for, enterprise-wide KM would fail. Today, data analytics (Chapter 6) and machine learning (Chapter 11) have become a major part of EKM development.

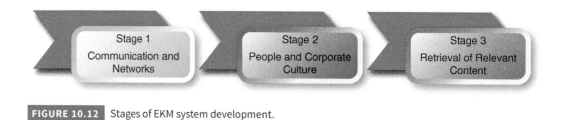

| Stage 1 Communication and Networks | Stage 2 People and Corporate Culture | Stage 3 Retrieval of Relevant Content |

FIGURE 10.12 Stages of EKM system development.

Automating EKM

Enterprise knowledge management is any solution or system that deals with organizing data into structures that create business knowledge out of existing assets while ensuring its security and managing access.

Enterprise knowledge management (EKM) system is an information system used to capture, organize and create knowledge to enhance organizational processes.

An **enterprise knowledge management (EKM)** system is a popular business tool that improves the flow of knowledge across all departments in an organization. Many large public and private companies relay on an EKM system as part of their business strategy to streamline workflows, leverage existing expertise, and reduce communication overhead called.

An **enterprise knowledge management (EKM) system** stores, retrieves, and shares information to help make processes more visible and reduces the problems associated with loss of knowledge, such as when a long-term employee retires or leaves the company for other reasons. An EKM system captures both explicit and tacit knowledge (discussed in Chapter 2). For example, explicit knowledge such as policies and procedures related to accounting principles, sales territories, and quote format might be incorporated into an EKM system to guide new sales personnel in the organization's prescribed approach to general account management. Likewise, an EKM system can capture the tacit knowledge of highly experienced and successful salespersons about how best to manage certain types of accounts and incorporate that knowledge into training videos.

A sophisticated EKM system also has powerful search and collaboration features and can integrate seamlessly with other systems to share important information with employees and customers. This makes employees more effective (business processes, policies, training manuals) and increases customer loyalty (user manual, white papers). To maintain an effective EKM system, an organization must regularly analyze and optimize its performance and continually update content.

IT at Work 10.5 illustrates how one large software company shares knowledge across its sellers and partners to increased productivity and profits.

IT at Work 10.5

Cisco Sales Connect Increases Sales Productivity at Home and on the Road

CISCO is the worldwide leader in IT, networking, and cybersecurity solutions. It develops, manufactures, and sells networking hardware, telecommunications equipment, and other high-technology services and products to help companies of all sizes transform how people connect, communicate, and collaborate. From its headquarters in San Jose, California, in the center of Silicon Valley, this American multinational technology conglomerate has leveraged KM technology to enable its sales representatives to better know their customers and meet their needs effectively and efficiently.

With knowledge content spread across a wide array of different systems throughout the organization, Cisco's 80,000 sales representatives were spending 15% to 25% of their time just trying to find the right information for their customer. This resulted in a huge loss of sales productivity. Clearly, its sales representative, who sells across its deep portfolio of product lines, needed an efficient way to find the most relevant information that would help them win new business.

Cisco created a "Tech Zone" that developed an application for smartphones and tablets. The app, called Sales Connect, offers the its sales representatives a dynamic experience that immediately provide sales team with the best information available to assist them through all stages of the sales process by offering them:

- **Intelligent search**—allows sellers to retrieve all relevant information on a given topic, through conventional search, discovery, or voice-enabled search powered by Nuance.

- **Featured content**—provides sellers with content related to key products and Cisco messages.
- **Personalized content**—pulls in CRM feeds to recommend relevant content to sales teams based on customer profiles, product portfolio, territory, behavior, etc.
- **Dynamic content**—automatically or manually bundles all relevant Cisco sales information related to a topic to create global sales kits.

Sales Connect has become a single source of trusted information for sales enablement content across departments, source systems, and product lines and has driven significant sales productivity gains. Internal and partner sales teams work smarter and more proactively with access to personalized information through a simplified, intuitive experience. Using this new system, Cisco saves millions of dollars in unproductive sales time every year.

For Cisco sellers and partners, there is the Cisco Sales Connect App for sales enablement available on iOS and Android mobile devices. It brings Cisco sales content straight to a handheld device so that sellers and partners can find demos, presentations, training, and proposals tailored to how they sell to close more business anytime, anywhere using their Cisco.com login.

Sources: Compiled from Zupan (2017), apple.com, and cisco.com.

Benefits of EKM System

An EKM system benefits companies in several ways, including:

- Better strategic management
- Increases productivity and productivity
- Increases collaboration, sharing, and teamwork
- Decreases gaps in learning
- Increases accumulation of corporate knowledge
- Accelerates productivity of new employees through better training based on existing expertise
- Standardizes processes to more easily access information to improve decision-making
- Protects intellectual capital

Today EKM systems come in all shapes, sizes, and prices. Many EKM systems are cloud-based and platform-independent. This leads to gains in efficiency and effectiveness driven by the newfound capabilities of employees and customers to read information anywhere, at any time on mobile devices such as laptops, computer tablets, and smartphones.

Currently, widely used dedicated EKM systems include Bloomfire (**https://bloomfire .com**), Document 360 (**https://document360.io**), and ProProfs Knowledge Base (**https:// www.proprofs.com/knowledgebase**). Other popular KM systems such as Zendesk (**https:// www.zendesk.com**) and Bitrix24 (**https://www.bitrix24.com**) also support closely related enterprise functions such as CRM, social networking, content management, and HR activities.

Techniques for Managing Knowledge in Group Work

Many managerial decisions are made based on group discussion and teamwork. These could be made when organizations are developing and manufacturing products, planning social media marketing strategies, making financial and IT investments, determining how to meet compliance mandates, and designing software. Several factors contribute to the complex group dynamics that occur in group work related to the creation of content for an EKM system.

- Group members may work in different places, at different times, and in different time zones.
- Group members may work for the same or different organizations.
- Needed data, information, or knowledge may be stored in many different sources, several of which are external to the organization.

Several group techniques have been developed to assist group work. Two of the most popular group techniques for sharing knowledge are **brainstorming** and **mindmapping**. These are both discussed next.

Brainstorming is a group problem-solving technique in which group members offer up spontaneous ideas for discussion to stimulate creative thinking and develop new ideas.

Mindmapping is a creative and logical method of note-taking that maps out ideas on a graph.

Brainstorming   Brainstorming is an informal group technique that is used to achieve a shared understanding of a business goal and its associated challenges through generation of creative ideas. The technique requires intensive open group discussion in which every member is encouraged to submit as many ideas as possible based on their domain knowledge by thinking out loud or writing an idea on a sticky note that is placed on a whiteboard. When all ideas have been presented, similar ideas are grouped together, and duplicates discarded. Following this, each main idea is discussed and actions are taken. Brainstorming used to be limited to a room full of people offering their ideas, but the introduction of technology has changed that. Companies now have a much more efficient way to hold brainstorming sessions using online apps, many of which are cloud based, and some are available on mobile devices.

Online Collaborative Brainstorming Tools   Electronic methods of brainstorming allow group members to access a document that serves as a "virtual whiteboard" stored on a central server or on a cloud-based system. After initial discussion about the concept or objective under discussion, each team member submits their individual ideas via their individual keyboard, and the individual ideas appear anonymously on the virtual whiteboard. Individual ideas are then automatically sorted into core concepts that are labeled with a single word or short phrase and duplicates removed.

After intensive group discussion, the group can vote on major ideas by placing "dots" on the concepts they consider to be most important and the concept with the most dots gets priority. Another method of voting is against predetermined criteria, such as importance and ease of implementation. Using the latter approach, an automatically generated two-by-two graph then guides the group to choose priorities for action and a report can be printed with results of the voting. All of this occurs in real time.

Automated brainstorming offers several advantages. For example, using sticky notes, ideas have to be typed up afterward, using an online brainstorming tool, group members type their own ideas into the system saving significant time and effort. It also allows group members who are lower on the totem pole can anonymously offer ideas and not be intimidated by those who are higher ranked in the organization; more knowledge can be captured in a shorter time frame; if members are geographically dispersed, travel expenses and time can be drastically reduced and constraints on the number of sessions a company can afford to hold become irrelevant.

Popular online brainstorming and collaborative meeting apps include GroupMap (**https://www.groupmap.com**), Stormboard (**https://www.stormboard.com**), PowerNoodle (**https://www.powernoodle.com**), ThinkTank (**https://www.groupsystems.com**), MeetingSphere (**https://www.meetingsphere.com**), and 1000Minds (**https://www.1000minds.com**).

Mindmapping   The purpose of a mind map is to stimulate clear, creative thinking. Mindmapping is a visual form of brainstorming that helps people think, collect knowledge, remember information, develop innovative ideas, and streamline group work. Unlike traditional brainstorming, a mind map is a graphical tool created with images, single words and lines. Mindmapping is structured in a way that more closely resembles how the human mind works and engages the brain in a much richer way that structured text. It particularly appeals to visual thinkers who feel constrained by text, leading to greater freedom of thought. The addition of colors and images in a mind map allow groups to more easily analyze, understand, integrate, and recall information to generate new ideas and boosts innovative thinking. The power of mindmapping is in its simplicity. In addition to decision-making, mindmapping is used for problem-solving, planning, researching, and consolidating information from multiple sources, presenting concepts in a clear and concise way, gaining insight into complex topics and jogging creativity in diverse personal and business-related situations.

Creating a Mind Map   A mind map starts with a blank sheet of paper or blank computer screen on which a central theme is drawn as a single word or image. Next, associated representations or major ideas, called first-level associations, are added. A maximum of seven first-level associations should be used. These are then connected back to the central concept with curved lines, and other second and third level associations are represented as branches that emanate from the related higher-level association. Since people who use color and images when learning have been shown to have better recall of events, color and images can be added to further stimulate imagination and creativity (**Figure 10.13**). Mindmapping can be accomplished individually and then shared with as a group (solo mindmapping), or collaboratively through the simultaneous creation of a mind map by multiple team members.

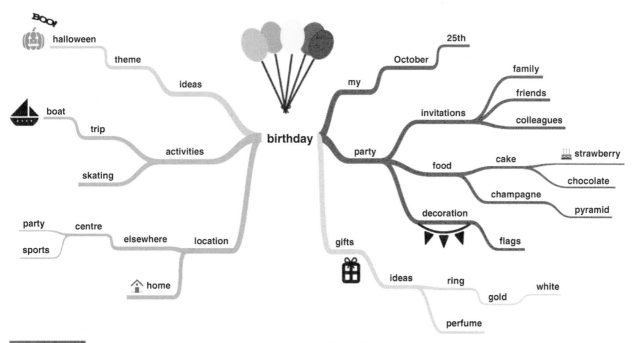

FIGURE 10.13   A mind map with color and images created with Simplemind.

Online Mindmapping Tools Several Popular mindmapping apps that offer solo mindmapping include MindMup 2.0 (**https://www.mindmup.com**), iMindMap Online (**https://app.imindmap.com**), Bubble.us! (**https://bubbl.us**). MindGenius (**https://www.mindgenius.com**) and Simplemind (**https://simplemind.eu**) are available for mobile devices for mindmapping on the go.

Teams can collaboratively and simultaneously create a mind map using Coggle (**https://coggle.it**), MindMeister (**https://www.mindmeister.com**), and WiseMapping (**http://www.wisemapping.com**).

Most companies offer a free edition of their software on their website.

Lessons Learned It is important to remember that the outcomes of collaborative activities such as brainstorming and mindmapping are only as good as the people who are invited to participate in the exercise. If the right number and mix of people are involved, chances are the outcome will be beneficial. If the people in the room do not have the domain knowledge or level of expertise required to generate creative ideas related to the topic at hand. Likewise, if too many people are involved, the outcome is not likely to provide the basis for a good decision. The most effective group sessions involve 3 to 10 people meeting for less than two hours.

KM, CM, and group work are constantly advancing. For example, in an age of big data, data analytics, AI, and machine learning, the concept of KM is evolving into a new concept called cognitive knowledge management. Cognitive knowledge management and its relationship to AI and machine learning are discussed in detail in Chapter 11. Collaboration through ESPs continues to evolve and will be an ongoing disrupting, but hopefully positive, influence on group processes, mobile apps, and the future of work.

Enterprise Content Management (ECM)

Enterprise content management is a set of defined processes, strategies, and tools that allow an organization to effectively obtain, organize, store, and deliver critical information to its employees, stakeholders, and customers.

Enterprise content management (ECM) is one of the operational components of KM. Before intellectual capital can be created to inform communities of practice, an organization must collect content, organize it for easy access, store it in a variety of places, and make it readily available for use. Most importantly, the content must be secure and accessible only by authorized persons. For example, the ability to access the correct version of a document at the right time can be critical to responding to customer or vendor requests and securing documents to be compliant with corporate policy and government regulations is essential to an organization's continuity. But, in a nondigitized environment, these processes can prove difficult, frustrating, and sometimes impossible. In order to be competitive, organizations need to reduce time, cost, and complexity of managing documents throughout their life cycle and help ensure compliance with record retention policies and regulations to reduce risk.

Purpose and Benefits of an ECM System

ECM systems enable an organization to securely store large quantities of content, distribute information, build and manage workflows, facilitate team collaboration, and integrate with other enterprise systems such as ERP, CRM, SCM, and ESP. ECM systems not only help companies collect, organize, manage, and distribute structured content like documents and reports but also seamlessly handle unstructured content including images, surveys, product information, PDFs, e-mails, instant messages, and website content. To do this, ECM systems must be compatible with most file types including office productivity suites such as (.doc, .xls. txt), image files (jpeg, tiff, png), e-mail, Web standards (HTML, XML), CAD files, and more.

By eliminating dependence on paper documents and organizing vast quantities of digitized unstructured information based on business needs, ECM systems empower organizations to work more efficiently. Other benefits of an ECM system include the following:

- Streamlining business processes by eliminating paper
- Driving improved customer service
- Increased productivity
- Reduced risk

Employees at every level of an organization can access and exchange information using an ECM system based on user privileges assigned by a system administrator. This streamlines information handling throughout its life cycle—from collection to disposal—and automates various business processing using automated embedded workflows.

Using an ECM System

The first step in using an ECM system is the digital capture and import of information such as vendor invoices, customer payments, job applicant resumes, vendor contracts, correspondence with customer and vendors, and research reports. This saves time, effort, and expense over manual collection of data that involves labor-intensive duplication, slow distribution, lost or misplaced documents and inconvenience of documents, and file retrieval from diverse and/ or off-site storage locations.

Next, business critical documents are stored in a digital repository where they can be viewed, edited, and organized.

Now documents can be retrieved based on a full-text search, specific words or phrases, and/or preset search options such as document creation date or names of previous users. This results in faster information retrieval that enables employees to quickly answer customer or vendor requests and provides almost instantaneous access to more complete information for better and quicker decision-making about issues that impact the business. The automated process also helps eliminate many manual tasks such as photocopying, hand delivering content, and repetitive drag and drop operations. With an ECM system, an organization can automatically route documents to the right people at the right time, alert staff members to documents that require attention, and recognize errors early in the document retrieval process.

Finally, an ECM system reduces organizational risk by providing a safe and secure repository for all corporate content. Compliance is becoming a greater liability for most organizations and optimizing records management by restricting access and monitoring system logins, document handling, and password changes allows an organization to protect information from unauthorized access or modification and reduces risk. For example, sensitive employee information is made accessible only to authorized HR department staff and financial data stay within the knowledge of authorized finance department staff members.

ECM systems provide digital document management and automated workflows to all size organizations, across all major industries such as manufacturing, retail, finance, health care, and government. They support multiple languages and are available on-site or in the cloud. Many have powerful AI and analytics capabilities

The most widely used ECM systems include Seismic (**https://seismic.com**), DocuWare (**https://start.docuware.com**), Laserfiche (**https://www.laserfiche.com**), eFileCabinet (**https://www.efilecabinet.com**), Xerox DocuShare (**https://www.docushare.com**), and Zoho Docs (**https://www.zoho.com/docs**).

Enterprise Social Platforms

In Chapter 7, you learned how organizations use social media to connect with their customers, vendors, and partners to promote their business. Within an organization, enterprise-wide communication and collaboration are equally important to help enable business leaders enhance productivity, teamwork, and employee satisfaction. Software that supports communication and collaboration on an enterprise level is referred to as an **enterprise social platform** (ESP) or an enterprise social media network **(Figure 10.14)**. Using an ESP, employees can connect and collaborate, exchange feedback, stay informed, build relationships, and share documents and data. Collecting real-time data and closing the gap between globally distributed teams can be critical to an organization's performance. With quick access to corporate knowledge through an ESP, organizations can resolve issues sooner, minimize costs, and attain a competitive advantage. Whether it's answering questions or sharing ideas, the open forum provided by an ESP flattens corporate hierarchies and motivates employees to share their opinions and creative thoughts.

Enterprise social platform is a private, company-owned social media software app that promotes social connectivity and collaboration with an organization and enhances productivity and employee satisfaction.

FIGURE 10.14   The many parts of an ESP.

Business performance depends on broadband data networks for communication, mobility, and collaboration that make it easier to share information and documents. For example, after Ford Motor Company began relying on UPS Logistics Group's data networks to track millions of cars and trucks and to analyze any potential problems before they occur, Ford realized a $1 billion reduction in vehicle inventory and $125 million reduction in inventory carrying costs annually. More and more people need to work together and share documents over time and distance. Teams make most of the complex decisions in organizations, and many teams are geographically dispersed and work in different time zones. This can make organizational decision-making difficult.

Growth in the ESP Market

It is estimated that the ESP market will reach $49.51 billion USD by 2021. This represents an 85% increase in market share within the last five years. Greater interest in ESPs can be attributed to five major factors (**Figure 10.15**):

1. **Networks**   Increased use of mobile devices and more widespread use of social networking websites.
2. **Employee productivity**   Growing need for improved enterprise efficiencies.
3. **Knowledge management**   Captures and reuses knowledge within the enterprise.
4. **Collaboration**   Maintains human connections across a disparate workforce.
5. **Employee pressure**   Pressure from workers to use the social technologies they prefer to use.

FIGURE 10.15 Major factors driving increased interest in ESPs.

To address these concerns, six general recommendations for realizing business value from enterprise social networking are listed in **Table 10.4**.

TABLE 10.4   **Recommendations to Realize Business Value from Enterprise Social**

1. **Make sure that management is listening**   Leaders and decision-makers need to monitor social chatter to keep informed and respond promptly.

2. **Provide visible feedback and rewards**   Employee participation is largely driven by the desire to be recognized by peers and managers.

3. **Brand the social network**   Employees want to feel that the company is behind the initiative. At Red Robin, for example, renaming Yammer to Yummer connected employees to the brand.

4. **Identify and leverage change agents**   Start with those employees most eager to participate, especially **millennials** who are looking for recognition and purpose.

5. **Introduce competitions and games**   Experience shows that people are more likely to engage when they are having fun.

6. **Make the rules of engagement simple**   Do not overengineer or control the social network. Make it easy to enroll and participate.

Millennials   is the term used to describe people born between the early 1980s and the early 2000s.

The increased use of ESPs reflects a trend toward more informal communication at work as more companies seek to integrate and embed social media into primary enterprise solutions to support business-critical decisions and create more social workflows as an alternative to existing formal communication channels.

Evolution of ESPs

Over the years, ESPs have evolved from older communications media such as e-mail, videoconferencing, fax, and texts—and blogs, Skype, Web meetings, and social media to the new more sophisticated and wide-reaching apps. Currently, ESPs come in a variety of shapes and sizes to facilitate real-time collaboration within and across enterprises with a broad range of social tools that seamlessly integrated business processes, activities, and enterprise apps. A selection of these apps is shown in **Table 10.5**.

TABLE 10.5 Examples of ESP Apps

Name	Website	Demo
SharePoint	https://www.microsoft.com/en-us/p/sharepoint/9nblggh510hb ?activetab=pivot:overviewtab	Yes
Yammer	https://www.yammer.com	Yes
Oracle's Social Network	Available on the App Store	Yes
IBM Connections	https://www.ibm.com	No
GoToConnect	https://www.goto.com/connect	No
Salesforce Chatter	https://www.salesforce.com/products/chatter/overview	Yes
tibbr	https://www.tibco.com/products/tibbr	Yes

SharePoint and Yammer are the two most widely used ESPs and are discussed next to demonstrate the different features of a typical ESP.

SharePoint SharePoint is a Microsoft collaboration and document management platform currently used by 85% to 90% of Fortune 500 firms. SharePoint is difficult to define because it is not a single software program, but rather a platform for multiple kinds of programs and apps. The platform is a back-end system that links employees' computers and mobile devices to make it easy to communicate and to synchronize their efforts. SharePoint has the following social capabilities:

- **Intranet and extranet** Intranets are the internal-facing sites everyone in a company logs into to find news, announcements, scheduled tasks, and access to files and data. Dashboards are customized by department and role to control access. SharePoint provides tools for setting up employee social network platforms and company wikis. SharePoint can be used to set up a secure, access-controlled extranet site to share with external partners in the supply chain.

- **Documents** SharePoint provides a shared space to store documents, so they are not siloed on any one person's hard drive or device. Documents stored on a collaboration and document management system can be accessed by anyone in the company—unless the administrator has limited access. They enable coworkers to work simultaneously on a single document, save previous versions, and track updates.

- **Collaboration and BI** An ESP makes it easy for users to stay up to date and to coordinate their efforts on projects from any desktop or mobile device and to discover patterns and insights into enterprise data.

Yammer **Yammer** is another widely used microblogging and ESP that allows private communication with users/employees within an organization and outside of an organization to facilitate collaboration across departments, locations, and business apps. Its interface is similar to that of Facebook including likes, newsfeeds, threaded conversation, and direct messaging and is sometimes referred to as a "Facebook for business." Yammer has emerged as an effective communication and problem-solving tool rapidly replacing e-mail in many businesses. Unlike public social media platforms such as Twitter and Facebook, Yammer only allows members to connect with other members who belong to the same e-mail domain. This private social channel helps employees, partners, and customers communicate; exchange information; and collaborate across departments, locations, and business apps.

At the first YamJam Conference in 2012, Yammer's CEO and founder introduced the new platform **Enterprise Graph**—calling it an enhanced way for business to be more social. Enterprise Graph tries to show how users are related to one another. It enables developers and customers to seamlessly connect people, conversations, and data across all their business services. With Enterprise Graph, Yammer solves the social network sprawl problem, which is when businesses end up interacting with multiple social networks inside their own company. The objective is to develop a standard that brings everything together and works off the same database.

Office Graph and Oslo App Microsoft's newer project, code-named Oslo, builds on the concept of the Enterprise Graph. One of the significant features of Yammer is how it maps the relationships between people and information by simply recording likes, posts, replies, shares, and uploads. Microsoft applied these capabilities to Office with Office Graph. Office Graph uses signals from e-mail, social conversations, documents, sites, instant messages, meetings, and more to map the relationships between people and concepts. By tapping into Office Graph, Oslo provides a natural way for users to navigate, discover, and search people, information, and knowledge across the enterprise.

Questions

1. What are the basic functions of an ESP?
2. What are the capabilities of SharePoint?
3. In what ways can enterprises realize value from Yammer or other enterprise social?
4. Why is KM important in an organization?
5. How does Salesforce Chatter enable workers to solve problems?
6. What are three advantages of online brainstorming?
7. How is mindmapping different from brainstorming?

Chapter Summary

LO10.1 *Describe* six types of enterprise systems and the major drivers and challenges associated with migrating to them.

The six major enterprise systems are enterprise resource planning (ERP), supply chain management (SCM), customer relationship management (CRM), knowledge management (KM), and enterprise social platforms (ESPs). Organizations migrate to these integrated systems because their existing legacy systems are outdated and no longer meet business needs. For example, legacy systems have high maintenance costs, they are inflexible, they only support rigid, predefined process flows, and the cost of the cloud is no longer a barrier to change. All of these drivers make it very attractive for an organization to move to enterprise systems. Challenges that organizations face in migrating to enterprise systems include changes in the way people work, redesign of business processes, and integration of diverse uncoupled legacy systems.

LO10.2 *Define* the purpose of an ERP and the key factors that lead to a successful ERP implementation.

An ERP automates workflows and accounting processes to analyze a business and forecast development decisions. ERPs are complex and expensive. Implementing them is a time-consuming process that is best guided by an ERP implementation specialist. The key factors that

increase the likelihood of ERP success and minimize risk include organizational change management and training, strong program management, realistic expectations, and a business process focus. Ideally, all these factors would come together to ensure the highest probability of a successful ERP implementation since the absence of just one of these factors can significantly increase the risk of failure.

LO10.3 *Identify* the three supply chain management (SCM) flows and major capabilities of SCM systems.

The three flows in a supply chain are material or product flow, information, and financial.

Supply chains vary significantly depending on type, complexity, and perishability of the product being moved. SCM system centralizes the management of the flow of goods and services to maximize customer value, achieve competitive advantage, and enhance collaboration between vendors, producers, suppliers, and customers by managing and supporting each one-up and one-back linkages in the supply chain. The purpose of managing a supply chain is to help companies meet customer demand as efficiently and cost-effectively as possible to give them an advantage over their competitors. To optimize performance, many organizations are automating their supply chain by implementing powerful supply chain management systems (SCM system).

LO10.4 *Define* the five phases of the customer relationship management (CRM) process and the role of a CRM system in customer acquisition, retention, and customer lifetime value.

The five phases of the CRM process are (1) identify new prospects and sales leads, (2) track and monitor in-person and online sales opportunities, (3) organize and engage current customers by getting to know their requirements and preferences, (4) establish a relationship with current customers by carefully manage customer communication, and (5) manage the customer life cycle to encourage repeat purchases and referrals. All these processes can be significantly improved by automating them. CRM systems play a major role in the customer experience by developing and automating marketing campaigns and promotions to attract new customers, processing data analytics to calculate CLV and identify customers who are worth retaining and supporting customers online through their life cycle to build customer loyalty through loyalty programs and the like. With all the data available in a CRM, an organization can really get to know customer preferences and gain a competitive edge in the market.

LO10.5 *Explain* the purpose of enterprise knowledge management (EKM), enterprise content management (ECM) systems, and enterprise social platforms (ESPs) and their impact on communication and collaboration in an organization.

EKM and ESPs are two major types of enterprise systems that are used to enable and facilitate communication and collaboration within an organization. KM is the process of collecting, storing, managing, and distributing diverse sources of information within an organization. Technology that marshals intellectual capital across an organization is called an EKM system. EKM systems help companies leverage the full value of corporate knowledge to drive strategic activities such as ERP, SCM, CRM, corporate decision-making, and business intelligence. They also enable greater and more effective collaboration, particularly in groups by automating brainstorming and mindmapping activities.

Content management is a subset of KM that focuses on organizing, storing, defining, and enforcing access rights and securing structured and unstructured information and knowledge for use by other enterprise systems. Enterprise content management systems impact organizations by streamlining business processes, driving improvements in customer service, increasing productivity, and reducing risk associated with noncompliance with corporate policies and government regulations.

Key Terms

always-on supply chain   382
back-office operations   380
brainstorming   396
core business processes   366
customer lifetime value (CLV)   390
customer relationship
    management (CRM)   388
electronic data interchange (EDI)   380
electronic funds transfer (EFT)   380
enterprise content management   398

enterprise knowledge management
    (EKM)   394
enterprise knowledge management
    (EKM) system   394
enterprise resource planning (ERP)   370
enterprise social platform   399
enterprise systems   366
front-office operations   380
intellectual capital   393
interface   368

Knowledge management (KM)   393
legacy system   368
logistics   380
millennials   401
mindmapping   396
order fulfillment   380
reverse supply chain   379
supply chain   378
Supply chain management (SCM)   378
value-added reseller (VAR)   376

Assuring Your Learning

Discuss: Critical Thinking Questions

1. Most supply chain professionals agree that one of the biggest barriers to successful collaboration is a slow *issue resolution* process. This has been identified as a systemic problem related to quality of information flow, in terms of both the level of detail and timeliness of shared data. In addition, almost all supply chain professionals agree that rapid problem resolution is part of good collaboration. True collaboration can be defined in terms of speed, both in problem-solving and in organizational learning. Many also indicate that speed of response in truly collaborative relationships is twice as fast or faster, with learning curve improvements more than 50% greater than in noncollaborative trading partner relationships.

a. Discuss why supply chain partners may not be able to resolve issues quickly. Consider *information flows* in your discussion.

b. What impacts might slow problem (issue) resolution have on the supply chain?

c. Based on your answer to (a), discuss which enterprise systems could speed up problem resolution.

d. What is meant by learning curve improvements?

2. Distinguish between ERP and SCM software. In what ways do they complement each other?

3. State the business value of enterprise systems and how they can be used to manage the supply chain more effectively.

4. What problems are encountered in implementing CRM systems?

5. Find examples of how an organization in two of the following industry sectors improve their supply chains: manufacturing, hospitals, retailing, education, construction, agribusiness, and shipping. Compare the benefits to each organization.

6. It is claimed that supply chains are essentially "a series of linked suppliers and customers; every customer is in turn a supplier to the next downstream organization, until the ultimate end-user." Explain this statement. Use a diagram.

7. What are the benefits of ESPs and why do organizations invest heavily in them?

8. KM emerged with the advent of the Internet. Discuss how Internet technologies have enabled organizations to more effectively manage knowledge.

Explore: Online and Interactive Exercises

Visit each of the following enterprise vendor websites. Write a brief report on the latest features of their ESPs, apps, or solutions.

1. SharePoint

2. Oracle

3. Salesforce

4. SAP SCM

5. DocuShare

Analyze & Decide: Apply IT Concepts to Business Decisions

1. Select an ESP vendor. Search and read a case study of one of the vendor's customers. Summarize the case and identify the benefits of the implementation.

2. Assess the costs and benefits of a cloud CRM. A large food-processing company would like to determine the cost–benefit of installing a CRM app in a private cloud. Create a report that contains these analyses:

  a. Calculate the tangible costs and benefits in a spreadsheet using the data provided.

  b. List two intangible benefits of moving to the cloud.

  c. Estimate the value of those two benefits

  d. List two risks associated with moving the CRM app to a public cloud.

Use the following tangible and intangible costs to perform your calculation

Tangible costs

- CRM in private cloud: $35 per user per month
- Technical support and maintenance: $250 per month

- Total number of users: 100 (90 salespeople and 10 supervisors)
- Training of 90 salespeople for five days: productivity loss $200 per day per person
- Training of five supervisors: productivity loss $300 per day per person
- Additional hardware, networks, and bandwidth: $15,000 per month

Tangible benefits

- Increase in average sales revenues = $6,000 per month per salesperson
- Increase in sales revenues from an improvement in customer retention = $5,000 per month
- Gross profit from sales revenues = 20%

3. Visit **https://comparisons.financeonline.com/zendesk-knowledge-vs-bloomfire-vs-document360**. View the free trial or demo for each of the three EKM systems and compare their advantages and disadvantages. Create a report of your findings.

Reinforce: Ensure Your Understanding of the Key Terms

Solve the online crossword provided for this chapter.

Web Resources

More resources and study tools are located on the student Website. You'll find useful web links and self-test quizzes that provide individualized feedback.

Case 10.2

Business Case: Lowe's Integrates Augmented Reality and Robot Assistants into Its SCM and CRM Programs

Lowe's Inc. is a retail company based out of Mooresville, NC, specializing in the sale of hardware, home appliances, and building materials. With over 285,000 employees, the company can serve nearly 15 million customers each week from over 1,800 stores in the United States, Canada, and Mexico. Lowe's provides both products and services to their customers, using the input–transformation–output (ITO) model. The ITO model is the center function of the supply chain that successful companies, such as Lowe's, use. With over 7,500 suppliers, Lowe's can decrease reliance on vendors and focus on providing its unique style of CRM.

Commitment to Customers

A large aspect of Lowe's supply chain is its commitment to ensuring that relationships with customers are maintained throughout the life cycles of the products the customers purchase.

To assist customers at the start of their shopping experience, Lowe's has introduced the LoweBot—a 5′ tall robot shopping assistant that understands and speaks seven languages. When customers come into a Lowe's store, the LoweBot detects them through a 3D scanner and asks them what they are looking for, directs them to the requested items, and displays location-based special offers and smart recommendations on its rear-facing display panel. The LoweBot also scan shelves and send up-to-date inventory information back to store associates as it travels through the store.

Its Omnichannel Approach to Retailing

In addition to meeting customer needs in the store, Lowe's has employed a method of reaching the mobile and online customer through omnichannel retailing to create a consistent experience for customers on mobile apps, websites, and in the store and cater to its many consumers who "window shop" online. This is where Lowe's sets itself apart in the hardware market with its ability to engage technology and the Internet of things in its operations. A significant contributor to the success of this model is that Lowe's controls 80% of its products in its own distribution channel. When coupled with omnichannel, Lowe's provides its customers products and services at the lowest cost and the highest convenience. Customers can order directly from Lowe's distribution centers, effectively eliminating the middleman, and to order products and services from the app, website, or physical store.

Enhancing the Customer Experience

In an effort to beat out its competitors, Lowe's rolled out Holoroom (**https://www.lowes.com/l/virtual-room-designer.html**), its virtual reality system that allows customers to visualize potential home improvement projects in the kitchen and bathroom. Customers of 19 U.S. stores, mainly in the Bay Area, were able to move products around in virtual rooms and see how they interact together.

Customers wear a virtual reality headset and select items from a library of Lowe's products and place them in the virtual environment to determine if they are desirable to place in one's house. Beyond visualizing product placement in one's house, the customers can employ different design patterns and paint colors.

To make the system personalized, customers first enter the dimensions of their rooms into Lowe's website or mobile app using the MyLowes feature. Using the dimensions as a template, Lowe's gives potential project and product recommendations to customers using the feature. As a follow-up to Holoroom, Lowe's more recently implemented HoloLens to demonstrate a variety of design options for kitchen cabinetry, countertops, backsplashes, and appliances in a visually rich and interactive way. To see their new kitchen, customers can wear an AV/VR headset to experience a holographic representation of their choices for a new kitchen, instantaneously change finishes and options and share their designs easily online.

In 2019, Lowe's added to its suite of CRM tools by implementing FloorLink, a cloud-based system for job tracking measure/estimating, installation scheduling, and sales management of its flooring products. The new software streamlines the flooring workflow process by making estimating flooring materials easier and more efficient for Lowe's employees to quote customers faster and refigure on the fly, results in a higher closing rate of flooring sales and increases collaboration between Lowe's store associated, installers, and its customers. In addition, FloorLink streamlines installer scheduling and saves Lowe's hundreds of dollars in printed paper and ink every day. These new features in its CRM have proved to be extremely successful in attracting more customers and significantly cutting costs. Other AV/VR apps that Lowe's is pilot testing include Holoroom How-To that immerses customers in a DIY project— such as tiling a shower—and gives them step-by-step instructions on completing the task, a variation for Lowe's employees, called Holoroom How To: Red Vest, and Holoroom Test Drive that allows customers to feel as though they are holding and using a power tool and "View in your Space," a mobile app that lets customer visualize a piece of furniture in their own living space.

Questions

1. What are the names of the two CRM modules that Lowe's implemented to improve its CRM processes?
2. How does Lowe's provide quality products and services through its supply chain system?
3. What is Lowe's approach to product life-cycle management?
4. Why does Lowe's focus so strongly on CRM?
5. What is Lowe's view on technology in its processes?
6. How does omnichannel retailing further connect Lowe's to the customer?

Sources: Compiled from Sun (2017), Trout (2017), Bhattacharyya (2018), Klein (2018), Martin (2018), Overby (2019), Waldron (2020), and lowes.com.

Case 10.3

Video Case: P&G—Creating Conversations with Global Consumers

The decline of traditional marketing channels forced changes in CRM transformation at Procter & Gamble (P&G). P&G's cloud environment allows for all consumer data to be in one location for fresh, relevant relationships with 4.8 billion consumers as they transition from one product to the next over the course of their lifetimes.

Visit **https://www.teradata.com** and search for the video entitled "P&G: Creating Conversations with Global Consumers." Watch the video and answer the following.

Questions

1. How does P&G maintain an ongoing dialog with a customer?
2. What were P&G's data challenges?
3. What is 1, Consumer Place? Where is it?
4. In your opinion, how does P&G try to maximize CLV?

IT Toolbox

Calculating Customer Lifetime Value

Imagine that you are the owner of a small fitness club and you want to increase your membership. One way that many gym owners do this is by offering a discounted one-year introductory membership to entice people to join. If you know what your typical club member spends over their "lifetime" at your fitness club you can calculate how much you need to charge a new member for an introductory membership to make sure you break even in a relatively short period time. This calculation is called the customer lifetime value (CLV). To calculate the CLV, you would use the following equation.

(Average Value of a Sale) × (Number of Repeat Transactions) × (Average Retention Time)

After reviewing your records, you determine that the typical gym club member stays with the club for an average of five years and spends $50 each month in membership fees. In this, the CLV calculation would be

$$\$50 \times 60 = \$3,000 \text{ in total revenue } (\$600 \text{ per year})$$

As owner of the gym, calculating the CLV of your typical member tells you that if you offered a new member a one-year introductory membership for less than $600 per year that new member would show you a profit in a short period of time. This calculation gives you a value based on your average customer, if you want to know each individual customer's CLV to offer them a customized offer to stay with the club, you'd need to use a CRM system to analyze not just their CLV, but also their purchases, behaviors, and preferred day and time to exercise.

References

All, A. "8 Common CRM Mistakes, and How to Avoid Them." *Enterprise Apps Today*, February 20, 2014.

Allied Market Research. "ERP Software Market Outlook to 2026." 2019. https://www.alliedmarketresearch.com/ERP-market.

Aspa, J. "Walmart and IBM to Launch Blockchain-Based Food Safety Solution." *Blockchain Investing News*, September 25, 2018.

Bhattacharyya, S. "Lowe's Is Using VR and AR to Get People into Stores." *Digiday*, July 25, 2018.

Condon, S. "Drones, Autonomous Driving and More: UPS's New Modernization Initiatives." *ZDNet*, January 30, 2020.

Dimitrov, B. "How Walmart and Others Are Riding a Blockchain Wave to Supply Chain Paradise." *Forbes*, December 5, 2019.

Duhon, B. "It's All in Our Heads." *Journal of Knowledge Management*, 1988, 9: 15–21.

Drucker, P. F. *The Age of Discontinuity*. New York: Harper & Row. 1969.

Gagliordi, N. "Walmart Implements IBM's Blockchain for Food Traceability." *ZDNet,* September 24, 2018.

Gartner Research. "The Gartner Magic Quadrant: Positioning Technology Players within a Specific Market." *Gartner,* 2020.

Gupta, A. "600 Million People Fall Sick Due to Contaminated Food; Check Out These Tips to Ensure Food Safety." *TimesNowNews.com*, December 9, 2019.

Hirsch, J. "UPS Invests in Autonomous Truck Developer TuSimple." *Trucks.com*, August 15, 2019.

Klein, K. "Lowe's Adapts Virtual Reality Tool to Train Workers." *Hardware Retailing*, February 19, 2018.

Koenig, M. "What Is KM? Knowledge Management Explained." *KM World*, January 15, 2018.

Loyalty 360. "1-800-flower.com Continues to Innovate." *Loyalty 360*, January 30, 2020.

Martin, C. "Lowe's Extends Virtual Reality Training from Shoppers to Employees." *Media Post – Connected Thinking*, February 6, 2018.

MHI and Deloitte. "2019 MHI Annual Industry Report: Elevating Supply Chain Digital Consciousness." Available from https://www.mhi.org/publications/report. Accessed on February 1, 2020.

Mills, P. "1-800-FLOWERS.COM Picks up Shari's Berries." *Loyalty 360*, August 8, 2019.

Morgan, B. "5 Examples of How AI Can Be Used Across the Supply Chain." *Forbes*, September 17, 2018.

O'Callaghan, L. "Traceability Revamp for Walmart." *FruitNet*, June 28, 2019.

O'Connell, B. "History of Walmart: Timeline and Facts." *TheStreet*, January 2, 2020.

O'Kane, S. "UPS Has Been Quietly Delivering Cargo Using Self-Driving Trucks." *The Verge*, August 15, 2019.

Overby, S. "Augmented Reality (AR): 4 Enterprise Use Cases." *The Enterprisers Project*, October 15, 2019.

Peterson, K. "UPS to Enhance ORION with Continuous Delivery Route Optimization." *MarketWatch*, January 29, 2020.

Redman, R. "Walmart Requires Suppliers to Use Traceability System for Leafy Greens." *Supermarket News*, September 25, 2018.

Sage Accpac. "FUZE Invigorates Business with Sage Accpac Web-Hosted Solution." Available from http://www.sagesoftware.com/pdf/accp/ss/accp_FUZE_ss.pdf. Accessed on February 1, 2020.

Schmidt, A. "UPS Buys 10,000 Electric Delivery Vans and Announces Waymo Partnership." *Yahoo! Finance*, January 30, 2020.

Seth, S. "Case Studies of Successful Enterprise Resource Planning." *Investopedia*, June 5, 2018.

Shaw, F. "The Tremendous Cost of Foodborne Illnesses, and What to Do about It." *QSR Outside Insights*, June 2018.

Sherred, K. "1-800-FLOWERS Reports Nearly 9% Q2 Revenue Bump, Thanks in part to Loyalty Program." *ConfectioneryNews.Com*, February 13, 2019.

Smith, C. "60 Amazing Walmart Statistics and Facts (2019): By the Numbers." *DMR Business Statistics*, January 24, 2020.

Sun, L. "Microsoft Sells 'Thousands' of HoloLens – What Now?" *The Motley Fool*, February 2, 2017.

The Economist. "How AI Is spreading Throughout the Supply Chain." *Special Report*, March 28, 2018.

Tierney, J. "Celebrations Passport Dials Up Enhanced Customer Engagement at 1-800-Flower.com." *Loyalty 360*, March 14, 2018.

Trout, M. "Lowe's: VR, The Future of Retail." *Digital Initiative*, April 25, 2017.

U.S. Army Business Transformation Knowledge Center. *army.mil/armyBTKC*, 2009.

Waldron, J. "Lowe's Is Augmenting Retail Reality with VR & Robot Assistants." *Future Stores*, January 2020.

Walmart. "Walmart Announces Plan to Invest $1.2 Billion to Upgrade Logistics in China." *Walmart Newsroom*, July 2, 2019.

Yamanouchi, K. "UPS Orders 10,000 Electric Delivery Trucks, Plans Test of Self-Driving Vans." *The Atlanta Journal-Constitution*, January 31, 2020.

Zaccara, G. "UPS Announces Numerous Products and Innovative Technology Programs to Help SMBs Grow and Compete." *MarketWatch*, January 29, 2020.

Zupan, J. "Know Your Customer: The Store of Cisco SalesConnect." *Attiv/o.* Available from https://www.attivio.com/blog/post/know-your-customer-story-cisco-salesconnect. Accessed on February 6, 2020.

CHAPTER 11

Artificial Intelligence, Robotics, and Quantum Computing Technology

Case 11.1 Opening Case

Boggy/Adobe Stock
adam121/Adobe Stock
Igor Zakharevich/123RF

HSBC Adopts Machine Learning Artificial Intelligence to Fight Money Laundering

HSBC Holdings is a British multinational investment bank and financial services holding company. With a history dating back to 1865, HSBC first opened its doors in Hong Kong where it hoped to finance trade between Europe and Asia. Its name comes from a company, formed in London by the Hong Kong and Shanghai Banking Corporation (HSBC), to act as a new group holding company in 1991. For more than 150 years, HSBC has prospered through many kinds of changes—revolutions, economic crises, and new technologies. Today, HSBC is Europe's largest bank, and the seventh largest bank in the world. It serves more than 40 million customers through its global business and has $2.251 (€2.055) billion in assets.

Money Laundering at HSBC

Despite HSBC's prominence in the banking world, its record has not gone untarnished during the past two decades. On four different occasions (in 2003, 2010, 2012, and 2015), the banking organization was cited for lax anti-money laundering practices by regulators in the United States, India, Argentina, Switzerland, and the United Kingdom. Not only did the bank fail to recognize the money laundering activities using its banking accounts, but in several situations, officers and employees of the bank played a direct role in money laundering, tax evasion, and other financial crimes. These lapses resulted in more than $1.94 billion in fines, a penalty that many regard as shamefully low, considering that HSBC's money laundering was connected to nuclear weapon development programs in Iran and North Korea, financing of terrorist organizations, and large-scale drug trafficking operations linked to fraud, organized crime, and murder.

To rehabilitate the bank's reputation for lax regulation and to discourage use of its operations by criminal and terrorist organizations, current HSBC executives have embarked on new efforts to detect and eliminate money laundering and tax evasion schemes. To help with their renewed commitment to fight money laundering activities and fraud, the bank has contracted with companies like Ayasdi, a Silicon Valley–based developer of machine learning artificial intelligence (AI) programs. Because of HSBC's size and extensive global network of banking operations, employees, and customers, traditional methods of monitoring transactions and account fluctuations for indications of illegal activity are inefficient given the sheer amount of financial data generated daily.

Anti-Money Laundering (AML) Applications

Traditionally, banks employed myriad rules that act as filters for spotting suspected activity. For instance, consider an account with an average monthly balance of $3000, and an average transaction amount below $250. If that account suddenly has a deposit of $20,000 followed by a transfer of these funds to an international account, the situation should raise flags. However, when transactions like this are buried in a seemingly endless sea of financial activity and dependent on human auditors to find these cases, it is likely that a great deal of questionable activity will go unnoticed, even when bank officers and employees are doing their best to identify suspicious activity. Anti-money laundering (AML) applications powered by AI have a much better chance of catching situations like this as well as more nuanced attempts to evade money laundering regulations.

AML Application Powered by AI

As a first step in the development of an AML solution, an Ayasdi data scientist used **feature engineering** to identify elements in HSBC's data that would be helpful training an AI application to identify cases of suspected money laundering activity. Then machine learning programs developed by Ayasdi applied several algorithms that sifted through HSBC's data to identify numerous patterns or clusters of financial activity. Ayasdi staff then worked closely with the bank's IT experts and a team of modeling specialists from HSBC to review and validate what the AI algorithms were predicting so that the patterns and clusters uncovered by the AML program could be explained. Because of the tight regulatory nature of the banking industry, it isn't enough to just have the AI point out data patterns or clusters related to fraud (an outcome sometimes called the "black box" effect of machine learning). Instead, bankers must be able to explain how the patterns were derived and why they are indicative fraudulent activity.

Results of Ayasdi AML Solution

In the end, the Ayasdi AML application was able to uncover several new patterns in the data directly related to new fraud cases as well as reduce HSBC's incidents of false positives (cases that would have been flagged as fraud, but were not really linked to illegal activity) by 20%.

Future of AI Applications in the Banking Industry

In addition to the use of machine learning AI to combat money laundering behavior, financial organizations today are using machine learning applications to uncover other types of criminal behavior such as fraudulent credit card transactions, and detection of unusual activity on a bank's computer system that might indicate penetration by a hacker or someone using an employee's account without permission. HSBC officers in charge of financial crime mitigation are actively working to harness technology and data with the goal of identifying criminal activity in real time. It is expected that the banking industry will embrace AI banking programs for many of the same reasons that banks have been rapid adopters of mobile technology in the consumer banking sector. AI promises to help banks enhance customer convenience, trust, and security, all of which are critical strategies for differentiating themselves from the competition.

Questions

1. Why would a bank like HSBC find it difficult to identify transactions and account fluctuations that should be clear signs of money laundering or other fraudulent behavior?

2. How did Ayasdi's machine learning AI help HSBC uncover cases of money laundering?

3. What is the purpose of "feature engineering" conducted prior to submitting data to the machine learning application?

4. What is the black box effect of machine learning applications?

5. Why are banks likely to adopt different kinds of AI technologies in the future? What do they hope to gain from this emerging area of technology?

Sources: Compiled from Irrera (2017), Arnold (2018), Faggella (2018a), Symphony Ayasdi (2019), and Worldwide Business Research (2020).

 DID YOU KNOW?

According to the New York Times, the average salary of an AI specialist is equal to the price of a luxury, Rolls-Royce automobile (between $300,000 and $500,000). By 2020, 85% of customer engagement will be non-human, and by 2030, 38% of all jobs in the United States will be replaced by AI. Experts predict that the global AI industry will grow from $2 trillion today, to $15.7 trillion in 2030, making it the largest single commercial opportunity worldwide. (Metz, 2017, Rao & Verweij, 2017, and Holmes, 2019).

Introduction

In this chapter, you will learn about some of the most exciting technological advances being made today in the fields of artificial intelligence, robotics, and quantum computing. The fields of artificial intelligence and quantum computing are still considered emerging technologies. In terms of practical applications, the field of quantum computing is still so new there really aren't very many applications at all. Quantum mechanics is a theoretical field that is still not completely understood by some of the brightest minds in the world of physics. Likewise, some of the brightest minds in the field of computer engineering are still a long way off from being able to create a workable, reliable quantum computer. Artificial intelligence is considerably farther along in its development, but most would agree that we are still at the beginning of turning theoretical understanding into practical application. But the applications we have today are amazing. Yet, these applications can still produce unwanted consequences when developers aren't careful, so part of our goal should be to create standards and guidelines to minimize unwanted consequences and optimize the benefits of the technology. Finally, robotic applications have been around for decades, but we still consider this an emerging technology because we can see that when robotics is used in conjunction with artificial intelligence and perhaps quantum computing in the near future, there is still a great deal of unrealized potential that exists for all three fields.

11.1 How AI Works

LO11.1 Explain *what artificial intelligence is and describe the different branches or technologies that comprise the AI field.*

Artificial intelligence is perhaps one of the most talked and written about technologies today. Research scientists and engineers are hard at work making advances in all branches of AI, while others are busy developing new AI applications that can carry out work currently performed by humans. AI is on the radar of most top executives in companies around the world who know the technology holds tremendous potential for improving the way their company does business.

However, despite all this attention, no one has yet developed a comprehensive definition for artificial intelligence that completely captures how AI applications work, what they do, and what we should expect from AI applications in the future. For our purposes, the Oxford University Press (2019) provides a good definition of artificial intelligence:

> *"The theory and development of computer systems able to perform tasks normally requiring human intelligence, such as visual perception, speech recognition, decision-making, and translation between languages."*

Part of the reason that experts have had trouble agreeing on a definition for artificial intelligence might be because experts have trouble agreeing on how to define human intelligence and other cognitive processes related to human intelligence.

Another approach to describing AI was proposed by Alan Turing (1912–1954), a noted mathematician and logician remembered for helping British intelligence crack the codes used to encrypt German military communications during the Second World War (Matthias, 2017). Turing described a test for intelligence in computers based on a machine's ability to engage in conversation. In what has become known as "The Turing Test," a computer would be placed in one room, and a human in a room next door. A second person, a judge, would be able to converse with both the computer and the human using a chat interface (like text messaging). After conversing with both rooms, if the judge cannot determine which room holds the computer and which room holds the human, it could be said that the computer was intelligent. While interesting, even the Turing Test falls short of fully capturing all types of AI under development today. Even though we might struggle to come up with a comprehensive definition of AI, one thing clear to most people is that AI technology is already beginning to have a significant impact on the global business environment. Some have even suggested that AI, along with the Internet of Things (IoT), robotics, quantum computing, and other emerging technologies will define the fourth Industrial Revolution (Marr, 2018a; Schulze, 2019). See **Figure 11.1**.

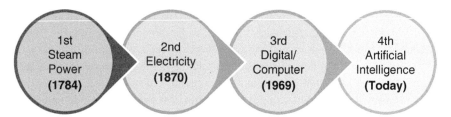

FIGURE 11.1 Evolution of Industrial Revolutions—periods of rapid social change brought about by rapid adoption of new technologies that replace previous methods of production and work.

To better understand the current scope of AI being developed today, we can start by looking at how the development of AI has evolved.

Stages of Artificial Intelligence Development

There are three stages of AI development used to categorize the sophistication and complexity of AI applications (Joshi, 2019b):

1. **Artificial narrow intelligence (ANI)** also known as "weak" AI, essentially current applications
2. **Artificial general intelligence (AGI)**, also known as "strong" AI, essentially future applications that will be on par with human capabilities
3. **Artificial super intelligence (ASI)** essentially, future applications with capabilities that surpass what humans are capable of.

- **Stage One.** Narrow or weak AI describes most current AI applications that are designed to carry out narrow, predefined tasks that usually draw on a single source of data. While narrow AI is the lowest stage of development, there are still many impressive applications today that fall into this category. For instance, Google Assistant is a virtual assistant powered by AI and available on most Android smartphones. It can carry out simple tasks such as searching the Internet, checking the weather, and scheduling events in a user's calendar. A similar application is Siri, Apple's virtual assistant, available on iPhones and other mobile devices made by Apple. Google translate is another helpful example. While these and other examples of weak AI technology represent our ability to create ever more powerful and helpful machines, these applications still fall far short of machines that can fully replicate human intelligence and capabilities.

- **Stage Two.**   General or strong AI describes applications that are on par with human capabilities including self-awareness, and the ability to understand, learn, and seek out solutions to problems and to engage in conversation and self-programming. While it is anticipated that AGI applications will be much more useful and beneficial than current AI technology, it also raises some interesting ethical and perhaps even legal questions. For instance, many believe that, strong AI applications will replicate such human qualities as consciousness, self-awareness, reasoning, and reflection. If that is true, then we might ask what ethical principles should guide the way we treat these new sentient beings (Schneider, 2017; Hildt, 2019)? Where do machines with consciousness fall on the spectrum of things, animals, and humans? Is it even ethical to create AGI applications? For now, these are interesting questions to think about, but not pressing since the creation of AGI applications is not likely to happen soon. While some speculate that the emergence of strong AI applications could appear as early as 2030, most experts don't expect the field to achieve this stage until we are closer to 2060 or even further in the future (Joshi, 2019a).

- **Stage Three.**   Super intelligence AI refers to applications that exceed human intelligence capabilities. Most experts in the field consider the development of ASI applications to be hypothetical, or at least something that will not take place until the far distant future. Most science-fiction stories about robots and machines taking over the world typically feature machines powered by ASI. Fortunately, most of us are not likely to be around to see the development of any ASI applications.

Types of Artificial Intelligence Machines

Another approach to understanding different types of AI is to categorize applications by the level of intelligence they require. Using this approach, we can describe four different types of AI (Fonseca, 2019; Joshi, 2019b). See **Figure 11.2**.

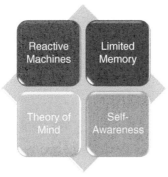

FIGURE 11.2   The four types of artificial intelligence machines.

Reactive Machines   The most basic type of AI machines cannot form memories or utilize experience from past events to better understand how they should react to current conditions. A common example of a reactive machine is Deep Blue, a super-computer developed by IBM to play chess. Deep Blue bested Russian Chess Grandmaster Gary Kasparov in 1997, becoming the first computer program to defeat a reigning world chess champion (Reynoso, 2019; Fonseca, 2019). **Reactive machines** are designed for one task and are unable to learn new tasks or even develop ways of performing their task better. At the heart of their programming is a set of rules that guide them in how to react to conditions they may encounter. As a result, reactive machines will always respond to a set of conditions in the same way.

Limited Memory Machines

AI applications in the limited memory category utilize a combination of programmed rules and memory of recent events to determine the correct action. Autonomous vehicles are often cited as an example of limited memory AI. Identification of things like lanes, street signs, and other common objects navigated by drivers are programmed into the car's AI. But memory is also used to help the car make good choices by remembering the speed limit sign it passed a few miles back, the position of vehicles surrounding the car, and what lane the car is driving in. By using a combination of programmed rules and memory of recent events, the car can process situations and conditions faster than if it was only using programmed rules. Prior to incorporating limited memory into autonomous vehicles, it could take as much as 100 seconds for a car to decide how to react to something on the road. Clearly a reaction time of 100 seconds is much too slow for safe and effective driving!

Theory of Mind Machines

While current AI applications fall into one of the first two categories, we have not yet developed a machine capable of the third category, theory of mind. Machines in this category are capable of developing representations of their environment and other agents or things in the world. A representation is the way we think or depict external things inside our minds. It is these representations that determine a machine's ability to react to and adapt to changing environmental stimuli (information). To create AI capable of this very human cognitive ability will be challenging and complex. A theory of mind machine will have the ability to converse, recognize emotions, and have thoughts and emotions that affect its behavior and understanding of its environment (Hintze, 2016). Machines in this category will be like the general or strong AI applications described previously.

Self-Awareness Machines

As you've probably already guessed, development of machines in this last category is a long way off in the future. Self-aware machines will not only be able to create representations of things in their environment, but also of themselves. Achievement of this level of AI will bring machines as close as possible to human intelligence and speculate that it might not be possible to achieve this level of AI (Fonseca, 2019). One of the challenges that researchers face is that before they can program consciousness into machines, they must first understand what it is in humans. As a steppingstone toward that goal, researchers are currently studying memory, learning, and how people use experience to determine current behavior. Understanding these processes in humans will aid development of AI applications in the future.

The Six Branches of Artificial Intelligence

The final approach to understanding the scope of artificial intelligence and the various applications being developed is to consider the different functions and processing capabilities of the different branches of AI applications being used today. Most experts agree that the field of AI consists of research and applications in the following areas (Lateef, 2017):

1. **Machine learning**—machines that can learn.
2. **Deep learning**—sophisticated learning machines that use neural networks.
3. **Natural language processing (NLP)**—machines that can communicate like humans.
4. **Expert systems**—machines that solve complex problems.
5. **Fuzzy logic**—machines that replicate the fuzzy logic reasoning abilities of humans.
6. **Robotics**—robots that use AI to learn, solve problems, and communicate.

1. **Machine Learning** As you read in Chapter 6, **machine learning (ML)** applications use statistical algorithms to find patterns in large data sets (including "Big Data"). Data can include all kinds of digital information including numbers, images, sounds, words, and so on. Programmers use these data sets to "train" their applications to perform a desired behavior. Let's take a simple example. Say we want to train our machine to recognize pictures of goldfish: Not whales, sharks, guppies, pollywogs, crabs, salmon, or other aquatic creatures; just goldfish. First, we would compile a structured data set containing hundreds of images. Images would also be tagged with a variable indicating if the image was a goldfish or something else (not a goldfish). We would start by feeding our goldfish identifier AI part of the data set so it could learn the difference between goldfish pictures and nongoldfish pictures. Once we have trained the goldfish identifier AI, we would then use the rest of our data to see how well it performs its task by showing it the new images and measuring how often it correctly identifies the images as goldfish or not goldfish. Once our new application achieves a target identification rate of, say, 99.8%, we can call it successful and begin to market it to all the businesses that need to identify goldfish pictures. While many helpful applications are variations on this simple task, machine learning applications can do much more complex things. For instance, recommendations systems that you read about in Chapter 7 have begun to use machine learning to refine and improve the recommendations they make over time. Search engines like Google also employ machine learning to improve the accuracy and context of search engine results. Machine learning is perhaps one of the more popular AI technologies being used by businesses today (Hao, 2018).

    There are three different approaches to machine learning in use today (Rimol, 2020):

    1. **Supervised learning**—this approach is analogous to providing the machine with a teacher, however the "teacher" is really the part of a data set containing the correct answer. In our example above, the teacher is the variable that identifies an image as containing goldfish or not.

    2. **Unsupervised learning**—with unsupervised learning, the machine is on its own to identify patterns and structures in the data used to categorize things. In our example above, we would be looking for the machine to correctly group the pictures into a goldfish group and a not-goldfish group, but the machine would not be able to label the groups, or tell us which one is the goldfish group.

    3. **Reinforcement learning**—with this type of learning, the computer learns by trial and error. From our example, the machine would begin by attempting to identify goldfish images. A correct answer would receive a score of +1 and an incorrect answer would receive a score of −1. By attempting to optimize reinforcements, the computer would become increasingly better at correctly identifying the goldfish pictures.

2. **Deep Learning** All machine learning applications use algorithms to learn from data. But deep learning applications use a special type of algorithm called neural networks (see **Figure 11.3**). Because of these neural networks, **deep learning (DL)** applications are believed to approximate human learning processes and are capable of much more complex and sophisticated learning challenges (Marr, 2018b; Grossfield, 2020). Neural networks are the critical feature of deep learning AI that distinguishes it from other types of machine learning. As with other machine learning applications, deep learning applications can be trained using supervised, unsupervised, and reinforcement methods.

    Figure 11.3 is a simplified illustration of what occurs in deep learning applications where many, many layers of nodes combine to create deep neural networks that find and amplify the patterns that exist in the data (Hao, 2018; Greenewald & Goldfeld, 2019). Neural networks used in deep learning always have an **Input Layer** (T_0), one or more **Hidden Layers** (T_1, T_2, T_3) and an **Output Layer** (T_4).

    - **The input layer** consists of data the machine is supposed to act upon, or in this case, pictures of cats and dogs.

    - **The output layer** is the action performed by the machine, or in this case, correctly sorting the images of cats and dogs.

    - **The hidden layers** represent the data processing that occurs in order to achieve the correct output.

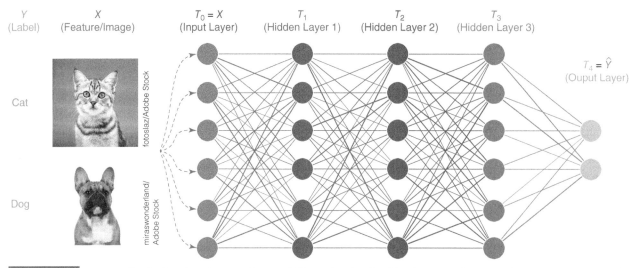

FIGURE 11.3 An example of a deep learning neural network illustrating the algorithm layers used to properly categorize pictures of cats and dogs.

Because deep learning AI can handle more complex tasks, neural networks are used in applications like autonomous cars, cybersecurity, fraud detection, customer service bots, and other applications that require language skills, and investment applications that can uncover patterns in large amounts of marketing and company specific data. There is tremendous interest in developing deep learning applications across many industries.

3. **Natural Language Processing (NLP)** Some AI applications use **natural language processing (NLP)** that allows them to interact with people using human language. Some applications, like Google Translate, can even take input in one language and translate it into another! Most NLP applications also rely on machine learning to teach language to machines.

NLP programs have two basic components, **natural language understanding (NLU)** and **natural language generation (NLG)**. The task of understanding language is more complex and challenging than the task of language generation. That is because languages (and the rules that govern them) are complex, ambiguous, and have many characteristics that are difficult to describe using rules, algorithms, and programming code (Le, 2018). Also, some languages present special challenges when it comes to spelling, grammar, pronunciation, and so on. For an NLP application to be useful, it must do much more than simply understand the definitions or meaning of individual words. Instead, NLP applications must be able to understand the nuances of a human language based on several aspects of language processing, some of which are listed below (see **Table 11.1**) (Garbade, 2018).

TABLE 11.1 **Aspects of Human Language Used in NLP Applications**

Aspect of Language Processing	Description
Syntax	The arrangement of words so that they make grammatical sense.
Semantics	Semantic analysis attempts to define the meaning of a single word or a group of words.
Pragmatics	A subset of semantic analysis that describes the way context (e.g., participants and their intentions) shape the meaning of certain words or phrases.
Phonetics/Phonology	Phonetics is the study of individual speech sounds. Phonology is the study of sound patterns (phonemes) associated with a certain language and the rules governing pronunciation.
Morphology/ Morpheme	The study of word structure and word formation including the role of morphemes, the minimal unit of words that still have meaning and can't be divided further.
Discourse	One of the most challenging problems in NLP is how to model ways that utterances in language stick together to form coherent discourse.
World Knowledge	The use of world knowledge to determine the correct meaning of words and phrases.

Sources: Mahler and Cheung (2017), Gupta (2017), Garbade (2018).

NLP applications can converse with humans. This capability has the effect of making people think that these machines, at least sophisticated NLP machines, have become more "human like" than other types of AI and are therefore more impressive. Also, NLP applications that can converse with humans are able to perform very complex tasks (Garbade, 2018) such as:

- customer service bots that can use both text and speech to assist customers
- increasingly "intelligent" digital voice assistants (like Alexa, Siri, and Cortana)
- translation work, turning written or spoken language into another language
- monitoring and analyzing conversations on social media, including conducting sentiment analysis that measures how humans feel about various topics, brands, organizations, and public figures
- complex information searches for both public (Internet) and private or company-owned information. Company-owned information can be structured (highly organized) and unstructured and might include things like internal records, e-mail, reports, financial data, audio recordings, video, and other types of documents and data

These are just a few of the many ways in which people and organizations are using NLP applications today. You can read about other examples of how Facebook is using NLP in **IT at Work 11.1**.

IT at Work 11.1

Facebook—A Social Intelligent Company

While most people are familiar with Facebook as the largest social network in the world, the company is actively going about the process of becoming a major player in the use of artificial intelligence applications. As you know, Facebook's revenue model is based on advertising—finding ways to learn about its users and packaging that information for its advertisers.

Facebook users regularly and freely divulge all kinds of information on Facebook. On each user's page there lies a treasure trove of data about user interests, what they like (and what they don't), pictures that show where they went to dinner, where they went on vacation, and who they went with. Users talk about the great and not so great experiences with local retailers and online shopping sites. All this information just sits there waiting to be gathered up and offered to advertisers so they can zero in on the consumers that best fit their target market customer profile. One problem that limits Facebook's ability to scoop up all this great information is that most of it is unstructured. To tackle this challenging problem, Facebook has developed an AI application based on natural language processing (NLP) and deep learning (DL), the AI technology that uses neural networks to solve particularly challenging problems. In this case, the deep learning application is turned loose on Facebook's data in order to develop a method for creating structured data out of unstructured data. This is even more impressive when you consider how much data Facebook is sitting on. Facebook is simultaneously using several different artificial intelligence applications, but this one is called "Deep Text," and is designed to focus on written content created by users. By converting the unstructured data to structured data, other programs will be able to move through the datamining process much quicker to find the essential data that will convince Facebook advertisers to continue connecting with Facebook's users. Facebook is using other AI Developments such as:

Facebook Translations—Back in the early days of Facebook, the company crowdsourced translation tasks to various users around the globe, people who were willing to spend a bit of time translating key parts of the Facebook website. Nowadays, that is considered old school. Facebook uses an NLP programs to provide instant translations to people around the globe.

Chatbots—Facebook now operates a chatbot on Messenger, appropriately called Messenger Bot. Users can also use Facebook's technology to create their own chatbot and experiment with different ways it can interact with others.

Mobile Video and Image Editing—Caffe2go is a mobile, AI-infused application that makes use of machine learning to filter video and images with special effects that make really cool and interesting new videos and images that can be shared with friends.

Preventing Suicide—On a much more serious issue, Facebook is using its AI resources to identify signals that could indicate that someone might be at risk of committing suicide. A lot of research has been conducted in recent years showing that machine learning apps are almost scary in their ability to pick up on emotional and mental health fluctuations in users. It isn't a perfect science, but it does perform well, and it allows Facebook to potentially help those might need it.

Finding the Naughty Stuff—Facebook has taken a beating in recent years about the amount of inappropriate content that slips by Facebook censors. Now it has a new weapon to combat content that is not welcome on the site, including nudity, fake accounts, scammers, advertisements for illegal products, and hate speech. In 2018 during a company earnings call, company CEO Mark Zuckerberg admitted that it was much easier to design AI that can recognize a nipple than it is to design AI to recognize the linguistic patterns in hate speech. But he promised that the company would keep on trying.

Sources: Compiled from Marr (2016), Biddle (2018), Nieva (2018), Kambria (2019), and Marr (2019).

4. **Expert Systems**   An **expert system (ES)** is a branch of AI that has been developed to solve complex problems in a specific discipline with greater speed and information processing capabilities than a human expert. ES applications typically have three components: (1) **knowledge base**, (2) **inference engine**, and (3) **user interface**. As the name implies, a knowledge base contains all the information (facts) the system has about the discipline or domain for which it was designed. Information for the knowledge base is derived from observation or interviews with subject matter experts and other sources by knowledge engineers. Newer expert systems are being developed with ML capabilities that can add information to their original knowledge base using experience, just like humans. The inference engine is the component of an ES that applies rules and information processing methods to information in the knowledge base. It is the component where problems are solved, decisions and predictions are made, explanations are developed, and alternative solutions are generated. Inference engines have two primary modes: forward chaining and backward chaining. Forward chaining is used when the ES utilizes multiple facts to arrive at a single output (i.e. decision, solution, or prediction). Backward chaining is used when the system begins with a single input, item, or event, and attempts to identify the various factors that explain, created, or caused the event. Modern ES programs have a deep learning component built into their inference engines. This allows the ES to go beyond simple rule-based reasoning to develop a solution, even when inputs are noisy or ambiguous. Deep learning helps the ES to come up with a probabilistic answer (i.e. ". . . there is a 70% chance of rain") whereas rule-based systems are limited to problems where all of the information required by a rule is available (Matthias, 2018). The user interface is the ES component that interacts with a user. A user interface might use natural language processing (NLP) so that a user can speak verbally with an ES or enter written instructions using a keyboard. NLP would also assist the ES with providing easy to understand output and explanations. Expert systems have been used in a wide variety of industries and applications including:

- Medical diagnosis
- Stock market trading
- Planning and scheduling (i.e., airline schedules, manufacturing processes, logistics)
- Process monitoring and control
- Facilities management and maintenance

5. **Fuzzy Logic**   Computers, and the software programs that run on them, typically require binary inputs—yes–no, true–false, 0–1, and so on. This creates a dilemma of sorts for AI programs that attempt to replicate human intelligence because humans are very comfortable dealing with probabilistic inputs and outputs. Many of the things we experience everyday fall into the "maybe zone" that lies between yes and no or true and false. **Fuzzy logic** AI attempts to replicate the fuzzy logic reasoning abilities of humans (Sayantini, 2019).

Applications of fuzzy logic AI show up quite often today in the control systems of consumer products. Some examples include air conditioners, automobile transmissions, vacuum cleaners, copy machines, drones, dishwashers, and many other everyday products used around the world. Industrial use of fuzzy logic AI includes things like control system engineering, mixing of industrial materials, industrial automation, robotics, and so on.

6. **Robotics**   It is difficult to find agreement among robotics engineers and developers on the definition of the terms, robotics, and robot. The Oxford English Dictionary (2019) defines the word robot as, "A machine capable of carrying out a complex series of actions automatically, especially one programmable by a computer." The field of robotics draws on knowledge from mechanical and electrical engineering, computer

science, and other disciplines, to create robots. Workers in the field of robotics design computer systems responsible for robot control, sensory feedback, and information processing. In Section 11.3 of this chapter we discuss this important topic in much greater detail including how robots (with and without AI) work and how they are used in business today.

Questions

1. Why have experts had trouble over the years coming up with a comprehensive definition of artificial intelligence?
2. Describe the three different levels of AI development. Which one describes most of the AI applications in use today?
3. What are the four different types of AI machines or applications? How do they differ?
4. Briefly describe the six different branches of AI technology.
5. What is the essential difference between machine learning and deep learning applications?

11.2 AI Applications in Business and Society

LO11.2 Describe *the factors affecting adoption of AI in business organizations and provide examples of AI applications being used in various industries and the public sector.*

Adoption of AI Business Applications

Now that you know about the different kinds of artificial intelligence and the way they work we will now look at how businesses are using or planning to use AI technologies. According to a report by the consulting firm Gartner (Goasduff, 2019), 48% of global companies are expected to implement AI applications before the end of 2020. However, there is still concern that business executives do not fully appreciate the potential of AI to contribute to their company's performance. For instance, there seems to be broad acceptance of the AI's ability to aid businesses with **work automation** (Manyika & Sneader, 2018). However, executives seem less aware of ways that AI can augment human decision making and interactions. AI can help human workers identify points in a company's customer interactions that are critical or add value. With enhanced classification and predictive skills, AI can uncover these critical points by analyzing large volumes of data and can do so at a higher rate and volume than humans (Pettey, 2017). AI can be used for things like identifying sensor malfunctions that could lead to shutting down an entire production line, or using AI predictive capabilities to forecast sales and inventory levels or even risk factors associated with a customer's ability to pay based on credit history and past payment record. Only using AI to automate work represents a tremendous under-utilization of this powerful technology (Panetta, 2019).

> **Work automation** is the term used to describe replacing a human worker with *machines or computer technology*.

AI Maturity in Organizations

Researchers at Gartner have developed a five-stage maturity model, which is shown in **Figure 11.4**. The model categorizes the various levels of organizational readiness for AI adoption (Panetta, 2019). Use of the AI Maturity Model can help organizations determine their readiness for implementation of AI technology and set realistic goals for moving forward in a sensible and systematic manner.

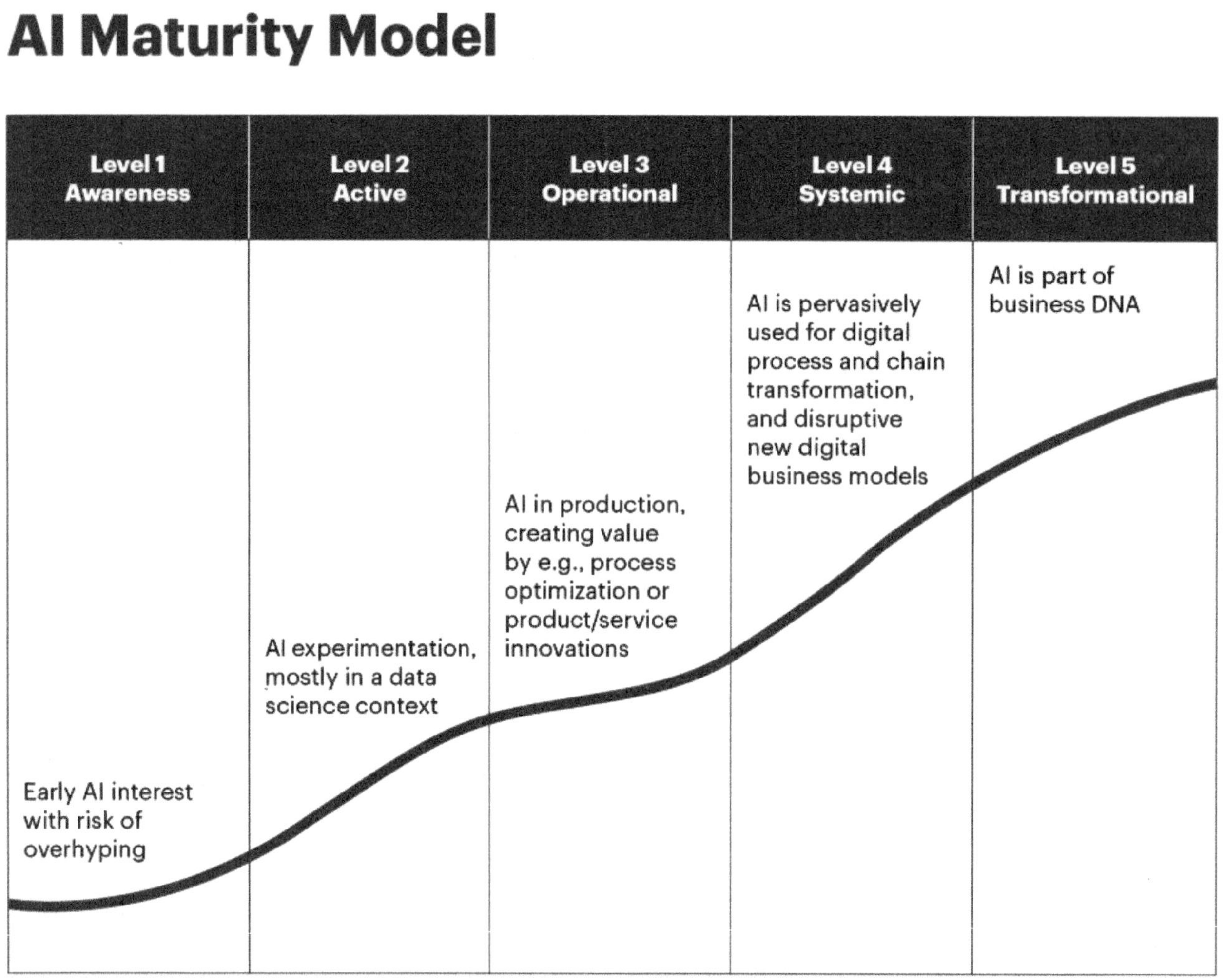

AI Maturity Model

Level 1 Awareness	Level 2 Active	Level 3 Operational	Level 4 Systemic	Level 5 Transformational
Early AI interest with risk of overhyping	AI experimentation, mostly in a data science context	AI in production, creating value by e.g., process optimization or product/service innovations	AI is pervasively used for digital process and chain transformation, and disruptive new digital business models	AI is part of business DNA

FIGURE 11.4 Gartner Five-Stage AI Maturity Model.

Source: Adapted from Panetta, 2019

Stage 1: Awareness—at this stage, AI is a topic that is being discussed across the organization, but not in a strategic or systematic way. There are no projects or pilot projects underway. Because executives have limited experience with AI, there is a risk that the potential for AI applications can be "over-hyped."

Stage 2: Active—at this stage, the company begins a more systematic exploration of AI adoption through the development of use cases, proof of concept, and pilot projects. Knowledge of AI begins to increase within the company.

Stage 3: Operational—a company has reached this stage when at least one AI project has moved to production. Experts and AI technology are accessible to the organization, while leaders and budgets have been assigned to guide and resource AI projects.

Stage 4: Systematic—AI adoption is prevalent throughout digitalized processes across the firm and supply chain operations while the organization evaluates options for taking advantage of new, potentially disruptive business models based on AI technology.

Stage 5: Transformational—organizations at this stage have already undergone a digital transformation and are using AI in all their business processes.

Currently, most companies are believed to be in the awareness stage of the Maturity Model and only a handful have reached the transformational stage. In the next section we'll explore how companies are using AI.

Current AI Use in Business and Society

While most people would correctly describe AI as an emerging technology, it sometimes seems like there are already endless examples of the ways that AI technology is being used by businesses, nongovernmental organizations (NGOs), and government agencies. In some cases, these AI applications have transformed the way business and other organizations operate.

For example, organizations today use technology to manage the process of transforming inputs into outputs to generate revenue. In doing this, huge volumes of data are created and the data generated by business processes has value. Specifically, it can be used by managers to understand what is going on throughout a business process and they can then use that understanding to guide their decisions about changes to improve the process. This typically results in an ability to generate more revenue and improve customer satisfaction. In fact, most businesses have figured out that collecting data about all aspects of their business processes can improve their understanding of their customers, suppliers, and stakeholders even more and lead to additional insights that will help them further improve the process. So, instead of only saving data in the form of bank statements, sales receipts, and other kinds of data that gets generated without much effort, companies have started actively collecting data related to parts of a business process that don't inherently generate data.

For instance, companies administer surveys to customers, and then save and analyze the data showing how customers responded to the survey. They attach sensors to the machines used in their production processes and collect the data from these sensors to figure out when a machine requires maintenance, service, or replacement.

Because we now live in "the digital age," a lot of our business process takes place on the Internet or on telecommunications networks. In Chapter 4 you read how companies have developed ways of collecting and retaining all the digital data generated by the activity and sales transactions that take place on these networks. In Chapter 6 you learned that the huge volume of data that is now collected on the Internet and telecommunications networks is referred as "big data" and you were introduced to the concept of AI. Two important aspects of AI that are contributing to organizational efficiency and effectiveness are the use of AI in **predictive analytics**, **sentiment analysis,** and **content management systems**.

Predictive Analytics
As you read in Chapter 6, predictive analytics are used by companies to identify patterns in data. Their use in customer relationship management (CRM) systems or customer transaction data make it possible to predict the likelihood of customer activity, such as making an investment, leasing a new car, or taking out a loan to pay for a child's college tuition. Banks and other financial services firms can use these applications to predict the life-time value of a customer, and tailor their services and fee accordingly. Many of these predictive analytics apps are AI-driven to help companies identify potential customer service problems by sifting through customer feedback forms, e-mail, messages, and even social media activity (Bharadwaj, 2019). Some interesting examples of how AI-driven predictive analytics apps are being used or are very close to deployment by organizations include:

- **Banks and other financial services firms** can use these applications to predict the life-time value of a customer, and tailor their services and fee accordingly. AI can help companies identify potential customer service problems by sifting through customer feedback forms, e-mail, messages, and even social media activity (Bharadwaj, 2019).
- **Credit card companies** use predictive analytics to detect fraud and predict the risk associated with loaning money to a customer using customer financial data, payment history, and social media data. These systems assign a risk value to customers that lenders can use to make decisions about extending credit, increasing or decreasing credit lines, or other decisions affecting future interactions and engagement with customers.

- **Large B2B companies** can use similar strategies to evaluate the credit worthiness of their customers, using predictive analytics to assess the likelihood that business customers might not pay their bills on time, and take appropriate action when deciding how much credit to extend to high-risk accounts.
- **Retailers,** especially e-commerce retailers, use AI-powered predictive analytics to identify when it is time to advertise certain products to customers, knowing which ones are close to making a purchase decision. And media organizations can recommend articles, book, or movies that customers might like based on recent browsing behavior, social media conversations, and past purchases.

Sentiment Analysis NLP programs that can understand written social media posts have been combined with machine learning technology that can sift through real-time and historical social media data to find posts that mention a company's name or product. These posts can then be extracted and categorized according to topic(s) discussed. The applications also use AI to understand both the meaning of the messages and also the sentiment or feelings expressed by the writer based on the number of positive or negative words used. These analyses provide valuable insights about consumer beliefs and feelings related to the topics mentioned in the consumer conversations. This is a valuable alternative to traditional consumer research where data is collected in small focus groups or large, structured response surveys that might not reflect real consumer sentiment and might present problems with generalizability or response validity.

Sentiment analysis is a widely used approach to understanding consumer attitudes and emotions in the era of social media.

Sentiment analysis essentially gives companies a way to listen in on conversations about consumer experience that were previously unavailable. It also provides powerful insights to the role that "word-of-mouth" communications play in influencing consumer behavior. Another methodology called social network analysis can estimate which relationships are most likely to influence the purchase and brand selection decisions related to different product categories. For instance, the manufacturer of a consumer product might be able to benefit from understanding which parent is most likely to influence the brand preference for their products. This in turn will have a likely impact on the marketing strategies and messages that firms use in their communications to take advantage of social influencers.

Content Management Systems With the increasing use of social media and business marketing strategies that are based on the regular publication of content related to customer interests and needs, companies have increased their investment in tools and personnel responsible for managing a vast collection of digital media in various formats. Content management systems are software programs used to curate a collection of digital content in a variety of formats. A large collection of original or curated content can be a valuable asset in today's business environment. However, even a modern CMS requires a great deal of human time and effort. Core features of a CMS include indexing search and retrieval, format management, revision control, and management. Large content collections can require considerable input by content managers who perform frequent but simple tasks related to the core features of the CMS. AI can significantly reduce the time spent by human agents on content management tasks by automatic image tagging, selection of content based on user interests and past content use, understanding both the meaning and tone of content and matching it with an appropriate audience, accelerated content creation, and voice controlled CMS. Other possibilities for AI enhancement include optimizing content for SEO, tagging content with advanced analytics, and interactions with other AI-enabled systems (Roe, 2019)

Thankfully, AI can solve these types of big data problems and help managers and top executives make better decisions. Underlying the ability to replicate all these impressive AI-generated human-like behaviors is its capacity to uncover meaningful patterns in the data that can lead to important insights about the business process that created the data. In other words, AI can help businesses use vast amounts of data to answer questions about the critical process used to make products that people are willing to buy.

Do All Businesses Need to Invest in AI?

AI technologies are a game-changer for organizations of all types and across all industries. Companies around the globe are asking themselves, "Should we invest in solutions that will help us understand how our businesses work as well as understanding things that might be hurting our business?" The answer is yes. Remember, we are long past the time when a typical organization used a simple process, only part of which generated data that a manager could use to consider ways of improving things. For businesses to thrive in this digital age with intelligent machines, they must adopt AI technologies to remain competitive with all the other smart managers who are already using AI to improve their business process in ways that regular humans can't even imagine.

The AI applications being used today are just the beginning for this powerful new technology. Because most companies are still in the awareness stage of AI maturity, it is exciting to think about the many ways that AI use will mature in the future, changing our lives, changing the businesses we work in, and changing the businesses that make the goods and services we purchase and consume.

In conclusion, when AI-driven machine learning and NLP technology are integrated with predictive analytics (Chapter 6), existing and new data sources can be used to predict the products customers will want and when they are most likely to act, allowing companies to tailor their marketing strategies and communications to take advantage of those predictions. **IT at Work 11.2** provides an explicit example of how an assortment of machine learning techniques are being used by a large inbound marketing company to increase its appeal to a wider range of prospective buyers.

IT at Work 11.2

HubSpot Uses AI Machine Learning for Inbound Marketing

Inbound marketing pioneer HubSpot is a pioneer in the application of machine learning (ML) technology for inbound marketing. HubSpot not only uses ML in its own business but has created applications that can be used by its customers. For those unfamiliar with the inbound marketing concept, the strategy is an alternative to traditional forms of advertising that interrupt consumers when they are engaged in activities like watching television, reading a magazine, or listening to the radio. Instead, inbound marketers attempt to attract prospective buyers by offering loads of interesting and useful content. The goal is to connect with customers using this content, and then nurture the relationship with even more content, tailored to the special interests and needs they can identify through a series of interactions. The goal is that this "soft sell" approach will build profitable relationships where traditional interruption advertising just irritates people. Examples of the way HubSpot is using machine learning include:

Content Strategy—Creating more traffic with more meaningful content. Machine learning applications can learn what content is most likely to resonate with prospective customers, resulting in a greater yield, which usually means directing more traffic to the company website with less content.

Predictive Scoring—HubSpot's ML applications are used to develop a model for scoring every lead in the company's Customer Relationship Management (CRM) database. These scores pinpoint customers that have the greatest probability of purchasing in the near future, allowing the sales team to focus their resources on those customers while at the same time, using other automated content strategies to maintain contact with prospective customers that aren't yet ready to purchase.

Data Enrichment—Everything HubSpot does is based on the information about each lead (prospective customer) listed in the CRM database. On top of this behavioral and field contact data, HubSpot enriches each record with lots of useful details about a contact and their company that can then be used in the predictive lead scoring and personalization of future interactions with prospects.

Adaptive A/B Testing—This is a classic strategy in all kinds of online communication like PPC search ads, online display ads, e-mail marketing, landing page design, titles on blog posts, and so on. The idea is simple, put to versions out in cyberspace, wait to see which one produces the best response after a period, and then pull the weaker performing content, leaving the stronger version online to do its magic. But when supercharged with machine learning AI, the standard A/B test turns into adaptive testing. Adaptive A/B testing starts out with four versions of a content, ad, or e-mail. Then instead of waiting to see which one "wins," the ML app constantly monitors the impact of each version, gradually promoting the use of "winning" versions and demoting the use of "losing" content. Solutions are reached must faster, testing covers four, not two variations, and fewer customers encounter sub-optimal content.

HubSpot's use of AI in these four areas supercharges an already effective inbound marketing system. And by drinking its own Kool-Aid, HubSpot shows it customers that it can practice what it preaches and succeed.

Sources: Compiled from Ørhøj (2018), McCraw (2019), Plaut (2020), and Hubspot (2020).

AI Use in the Public Sector

AI is successfully being used in a number of public sector service domains such as law enforcement and healthcare.

Law Enforcement and Public Safety

Many AI law enforcement applications have already been developed, and the technological barriers to adoption, such as the availability of hardware and software and the development of a data collection infrastructure are falling rapidly (Walch, 2019). Some of the most straightforward law enforcement applications of AI include:

- **Enhanced image and video search**—with the growing network of security cameras and **closed-circuit television (CCTV)** feeds, the amount and availability of image and video data is growing exponentially. A **law enforcement agency (LEA)** attempting to discover specific objects in this data using manual search methods would face a daunting if not impossible task. Fortunately, AI applications using **computer vision** can sift through vast amounts of image and video data to aid LEAs in finding patterns or images related to specific incidents that can be used for several purposes like locating missing persons, tracking known or suspected criminals, and identifying witnesses to crimes and documenting illegal behavior ranging from minor traffic accidents to homicide. Artificial intelligence is also used to enhance image quality quickly so that an LEA can extract important information (i.e., license plate number, a person's identity, etc.) from images that were originally too distorted to be helpful.

> **computer vision** is a field of artificial intelligence that trains computers to see using deep learning and cameras to identify objects in images and video and take appropriate action based on that information.

- **Facial recognition systems**—are a special application of AI-enhanced image and video search that can identify people by matching a person's image to images or video from security cameras and CCTV feeds. Facial recognition systems have been used for identifying and locating individuals from a vast amount of real-time image and video data and for surveillance of large public gatherings at schools, concerts, and sporting events and similar venues. While questions remain as to the technology's effectiveness and accuracy, use of facial recognition by LEAs creates great concern among citizens and government leaders about its impact on constitutionally guaranteed rights and freedoms (e.g., free association and free movement) as well as concerns about invasion of privacy. These important issues are discussed in Section 11.3 below.

  In a related use, facial recognition systems are increasingly being used in security systems that use **biometric input devices** that limit access to facilities and digital systems and files. For instance, some smartphones use facial recognition in place of a password or PIN code to unlock the device. Access to rooms, secure areas, and buildings can be based on a facial recognition systems scan of a person's face to determine if they should have access to secure facilities.

> **Biometric input devices** measure the unique physical characteristics of a person, typically for use in security devices designed to only allow access to specific individuals. Examples of commonly used visual biometric inputs include recognition of fingerprint, retina, iris, and facial features.

- **Detecting and preventing crime with data analysis**—a great deal of police work involves the collection and analysis of information or data. AI applications excel at processing large amounts of data and with greater speed and accuracy than humans. As a result, there is tremendous potential for AI to aid LEAs with situations where data can be used to identify patterns of data that are consistent with criminal behavior, such as the analysis of financial records to identify various types of fraud, money laundering, tax evasion, and other criminal behavior. Developers are working applications that might be able to predict where and when crimes are more likely to happen, allowing police agencies to make better decisions about where to focus deployment of police patrols.

Healthcare and Medicine

Many exciting new AI applications have been developed for the medical and healthcare fields. As in other industries, the most successful applications are programs that can reduce the need for medical professionals to perform routine or data-intensive processes, allowing them to shift their focus to aspects of treatment and patient care that require human capabilities.

- **Radiology**.   As you read earlier, medical AI applications have been developed to read x-rays, mammograms, and CT scans, allowing radiologists to refocus their time and attention on more important aspects of their jobs.

- **Electronic Medical Records.**   NLP technology is used in the development of voice recognition software, enabling workers to more easily update electronic medical records (EMR) or dictate patient care notes and instructions that can be transcribed into written records. These records can then conceivably be analyzed by other AI applications for possible problems. More complete and timely medical records reduce the chances of medical errors resulting from incomplete or unclear information.

- **Diagnosis**.   Information about a patient's symptoms and vital signs can be used to diagnose medical problems and common treatment options. These applications are particularly helpful in cases where standard diagnosis and treatment doesn't seem to be working. A 2017 study by Stephen Weng, an epidemiologist at the University of Nottingham in the United Kingdom compared diagnostic decisions made by a trained AI application with diagnoses made using standard diagnostic criteria used by physicians to predict heart attack risk. The results of the study showed that the AI program made better predictions (Hutson, 2017).

- **Medication Errors.**   AI technology is used to prevent medication errors by analyzing a patient's current medications and flagging potentially harmful interactions with new medications being prescribed by a physician.

- **Improved Care**.   Hospitals and other healthcare facilities can use AI to monitor, track, and analyze patient, provider, and facility data to improve care and reduce factors that might cause things like increased infection rates, poor treatment outcomes, and medical errors related to conditions at a facility.

- **Telemedicine.**   As you read in Chapter 9, AI-driven chatbots are being used for customer service but they are also proving to be a very useful feature in Web-based medical and telemedicine services.

- **Administration Issues**.   Important, but less-exciting, concerns like billing errors, recovery of third-party payments, staffing shortages, inefficiencies in medical supply inventories, and so on can also be discovered and solved with the aid of AI programs.

Barriers to AI Adoption and Use

Experts say that companies face three barriers to implementing AI solutions. They are *skills, fear of the unknown*, and concerns about the *full data scope or data quality* derived from AI.

Skills   New AI applications in companies will require a shift in worker skillsets. For instance, radiologists currently spend a great deal of time reading x-rays. Adoption of AI will reduce the time radiologists spend reading images. Instead, radiologists will refocus their time and energy on consultations with physicians about diagnosis and treatment options, performing image-guided medical procedures, and communicating with patients. Companies will need to anticipate the changes that AI will bring for their workers and be prepared to support and facilitate their evolution to new roles. Another skill-related concern is finding workers specifically skilled in the implementation and operation of AI applications.

Demand for workers with AI skills is greater than supply, so companies need to develop plans for successfully recruiting and retaining people with expertise in AI. Other options include purchasing developed AI applications that require less in-house expertise, providing opportunities for current employees to receive AI training, and buying or licensing AI from large technology companies that can provide support for their applications (Chui & Malhotra, 2018).

Fear of the Unknown One reason that work automation applications are popular is because it is relatively easy to estimate the cost–benefit analysis. But for other types of AI application, understanding both the risks and the benefits can be more challenging. Because adoption of AI solutions is likely to be a major undertaking for a company, executives will be expected to articulate and quantify both the costs and benefits associated with using new AI programs. Some things like "improved decision making" and the value of uncovering patterns in large consumer data sets might be difficult.

Concerns about the Full Data Scope or Data Quality Derived from AI It is widely understood that most AI applications require vast amounts of data from which they can draw information, make decisions, or predict probabilities of future events. This requires that organizations have a workable data collection infrastructure that can feed their AI machines. Without that infrastructure or without an understanding of the kind of data required, new AI projects will likely fail. Executives need ways of assessing these data-related questions prior to adoption (Goasduff, 2019).

11.3 AI and Society (Ethics)

LO11.3 Describe *the ethical and social challenges created by the emerging use of artificial intelligence by businesses and public sector organizations.*

For almost as long as scientists and researchers have been thinking about how to develop AI and build it into applications to provide a host of useful benefits, other scientists, researchers, philosophers, and regular, everyday people have voiced concerns, criticism, and debate about the potential downside of artificial intelligence. There has been speculation about the winners and losers in a world powered by AI. Advocates of AI suggest that while the world is certainly going to change, numerous opportunities will be created and available to those displaced by artificial intelligence applications, while others simply are not buying these explanations. AI experts acknowledge that some applications have the potential to create unintended consequences, and caution developers to take steps to avoid those outcomes, while others worry that without clear guidelines enforced by laws and regulations, businesses will throw caution to the wind and march out applications that systematically harm people in ways that are very real, but are not transparent or easily understood.

In this section, we identify three of the most pressings concerns about the impact that AI is likely to have on society and how those concerns should be addressed or mitigated.

Major Issues of Concern

The following list expresses the most common concerns that people have about the impact of artificial intelligences on work and society:

- Fear of job loss and financial ruin by AI work automation
- Privacy and civil rights violations caused by government and law enforcement AI applications
- Systematic bias resulting from ML algorithms and data

Work Automation and Job Loss

To assess the impact that AI is likely to have on various jobs, we need to look at the kind of jobs that are easy to automate and those that are not. Many people assume that blue collar jobs are the most at risk of being automated, perhaps because of the way that manufacturers have been so quick to replace production workers with robot-powered production lines. But that also sheds light on the kind of work that lends itself to automation. Work that is routine, and done the same way repeatedly, is more likely to be automated. But not all blue-collar work is easily automated. For instance, an electrician that wires new homes tackles a new challenge with each new house. Electricians that service existing homes perhaps face even more new situations. Since computers don't walk very well (yet) and find it difficult to pull new electrical wire through existing walls, many electrician jobs are probably safe from automation (Faggella, 2018b).

What might surprise some people is that many white-collar jobs are likely candidates for automation. Jobs that deal primarily with numbers and data are quite vulnerable to automation. For instance, consider the work of an accountant that specializes in preparation of tax returns for individuals. Today, many people have switched from taking their taxes to a local CPA, and instead are doing their taxes online with services like TurboTax, H&R Block, or CreditKarma (Cnet, 2020; Wang, 2019). Why? Because many of these online tax preparation services use artificial intelligence and do a very nice job walking people through a series of questions and answers that make tax filing relatively easy and oftentimes for a lower price than what they used to pay their human tax accountant. Also, these online systems don't get overwhelmed by the high volume of work that flows in during the month prior to April 15, the deadline for filing tax returns. In other words, they scale much easier than human tax services. A lot of jobs like this that people think are safe because they are white-collar jobs are in fact quite easy to automate (Faggella, 2019a).

So, it's clear that many jobs that exist today, both blue-collar and white-collar jobs, are probably good candidates for automation. It's hard to say exactly what percentage of jobs will eventually be automated, but some estimates suggest it could be close to 40%. And while this amount of upheaval in the job market is going to be disruptive and painful for lots of people, it is too late to put a halt to this trend. To coin a phrase, that train has already left the station.

For current workers, and those preparing to enter the workforce, the smart thing to do now is ask yourself if the kind of work you do, or plan to do is likely to be automated. If the answer is yes, then come up with a different plan. Recognize that this is not as easy as it sounds. People make huge psychological investments in their work and it is part of their identity. In some cases, these are careers that required significant investments in time, energy, and training or education. Change will be difficult, but not impossible.

One question that is sure to be vigorously debated is what role should government and business play in facilitating the workforce's transition from automated jobs to new jobs that are less subject to the forces of work automation? Advocates of social Darwinism might argue that the fate of workers should be left up to market forces to determine winners and losers. However, others might argue that it is in the best interests of society to help workers retrain and prepare for new jobs. Leaving 40% of the workforce lingering in unemployment and financial stagnation isn't good for the overall economy. That 40% represents a lot of consumers that will need to scale back on spending. Removing so many people from the consuming public will very likely have a negative impact on businesses. So, it probably makes sense for both government and business to develop a response to the coming upheaval caused by work automation. If individuals, businesses, and government each do their part, we might be able to achieve the bright future described by work automation advocates where artificial intelligence replaces automated jobs with an equal number of new opportunities in a golden age of intelligent machines. Time will tell if the workforce and the world's leaders in business and government will rise to the occasion and are able to make the transition smoothly.

Privacy, Civil Rights, and Government Use of Artificial Intelligence

One application of AI that probably inspires just as much concern as work automation is facial recognition technology. Facial recognition technology is something that many of us are exposed to everyday when we log into Facebook to share snapshots of fun times with family and friends or look at the photos shared by others. For years, Facebook has encouraged us to tag people in our pictures, something that for the most part seemed relatively harmless. Of course, what we've been doing is to help Facebook curate one of the largest ever collections of images tagged with facial identification data. Facebook's facial recognition software can now tell you who is in your photos with messages like, "It looks like this is a picture of Fred Johnson. Do you want to tag Fred in this picture?" While it isn't entirely clear what Facebook does or might do with their collection of facial identification data, it illustrates how easy it is for facial recognition technology to become an accepted part of our lives.

We've seen television shows and movies where high tech law enforcement agencies and national intelligence agencies are depicted using facial recognition technology to identify suspected criminals and terrorists trying to evade capture. The use of facial recognition technology is widespread in authoritarian countries like China, but in the United States, regulation of this technology varies across cities and states, with very little current regulation at the federal level (Crawford, 2019). But facial recognition technology isn't the only AI application that concerned citizens need to worry about. Faggella (2019b) describes other surveillance technologies in use around the world today including robotic birds and drones, and smart glasses equipped with facial recognition technology. It is expected that facial recognition combined with other types of AI that can be used for monitoring phone and voice conversations and e-mail and text messages will provide government and law enforcement agencies with an arsenal of high-tech surveillance tools. While some cities have enacted laws that limit or prohibit the use of facial recognition, very little has been done at the federal level to review these new technologies and the implications they have for people's constitutional rights. Until then, it will be difficult to say how such tools are being used today, and with what degree of oversight.

IT at Work 11.3

Facial Recognition—It Isn't All Bad

It seems that the more people learn about facial recognition and how it can be used by unknown forces to track and monitor your movements, the less comfortable people are about the government making widescale use of the technology. But here are examples of companies and healthcare workers that are using facial recognition for good (at least we think so).

1. Helping Faceless is a company started by Shashank Singh who was almost kidnapped by a stranger, but fortunately was saved by another stranger who was able to return him to his home. But many other children are not so lucky. Every eight minutes a child goes missing in India. With the Helping Faces app, people can upload pictures of missing children or children that are found alone, and the app attempts to connect the two using facial recognition. See the Helping Faces website: **http://www.helpingfaceless.com/**.

2. In a 2019 article published in the journal Nature Medicine, a U.S. company called **FDNA** (as in Face DNA) described how they developed an AI app to recognize cases of 200 genetic disorders that manifest themselves in various facial characteristics.

You can read more about their work on the company website: **https://www.fdna.com/**.

3. Another healthcare-related application involves medical facilities using FR technologies to streamline patient identification in acute cases. Medical errors in hospitals happen with alarming frequencies, for example, incorrect patient, incorrect site procedure, incorrect medication, and other errors. Researchers tested a facial recognition app used for patient identity. Whether patients were under anesthesia or unconscious, facial recognition verified all patients with 99% accuracy even after a surgery. See journal article: **https://mhealth.jmir.org/2019/4/e11472/**.

4. Facial recognition can be used instead of traditional methods for securing access to smartphones. Apple iPhone users can now use facial recognition technology to lock and unlock their smartphones, making it virtually impossible for thieves to use stolen or lost phones. Read more about Apple's facial recognition technology at: **https://support.apple.com/en-us/**

Sources: Compiled from Ansari (2016), Ghosh (2018), West (2019), and Jeon et al. (2019).

Unexpected Results When Bias Creeps into the Learning Process

Another concern that can negatively impact people is when some kinds of machine learning programs develop a bias in their decision-making ability. Perhaps the classical example of bias in machine learning is the COMPAS system used in Broward County, Florida to predict whether someone convicted and imprisoned for a crime would be likely to re-offend if released on parole. Judges used these risk scores in developing sentences, with tougher sentences being doled out to those with higher risk scores.

Developers followed standard protocols for developing the algorithms and data set used in the training of the program. Yet these ordinary development choices led to a biased system. What developers failed to consider was that their data was influenced by structural racism that was baked into the system. Questions used to calculate recidivism scores differentiated whites and African Americans but had little to do with recidivism. For instance, questions were asked about whether individuals had a job or not, whether they had a parent that spent time in jail or not, and how often they got into fights in school. African Americans have a higher probability of answering those questions in ways that increased their risk score, even though the questions were not at all predictive of recidivism. To add insult to injury, the reverse effect occurred for convicted white people. African Americans experienced an inordinate number of false positives and were incorrectly flagged as likely recidivists twice as often as whites. On the other hand, whites were incorrectly labeled as low risk more often than blacks. Eventually the activist group ProPublica was able to prove the COMPAS system was flawed, but by that time the damage had been done to many African Americans who received longer jail terms, paid higher fines, and experienced other negative consequences (McKenna, 2019; Angwin et al., 2016).

While the COMPAS case illustrates bias that emerged as a result of poor selection of questions used to develop risk scores, another case demonstrates how bias can emerge through interaction with biased individuals. In a well-known case, Microsoft developed an AI program that was supposed to use NLP and interaction with users on the social networking site Twitter. Developers were hoping to show that interaction with Twitter users would help the NLP AI to learn how to communicate with humans. Instead, "It took less than 24 hours for Twitter to corrupt an innocent AI chatbot." Instead of helping the chatbot to learn how to communicate through fun and playful conversation, users began to flood the chatbot with racist, misogynistic, and "Donald Trumpist" language. Unfortunately, the Chatbot learned quickly from the bad kids on Twitter and started spewing the kind of language it encountered on the social network (Vincent, 2016; Schwartz, 2019).

Other cases of bias have popped up in AI programs designed to identify loan applicants that are supposedly good risks for paying back their loans, and whether social services should remove children from their parents. Bias errors in these kinds of applications can have serious consequences and illustrate the importance of carefully evaluating ways that bias can creep into machine learning and other kinds of AI applications. In most cases, the biased outcomes of AI programs were unintentional, yet they illustrate the care that developers must use in applications, and the obligation they must be vigilant when bias might lead to such serious consequence.

Questions

1. Is the use of AI technology for work automation unethical? Why or why not?
2. What steps should workers take to determine if their jobs or intended career path has a higher risk of being automated?
3. Why should businesses and governments find ways of supporting workers that lose their jobs because of work automation?
4. Why are technologies like facial recognition and AI programs that monitor a large volume of phone calls and e-mail messages a concern for American citizens?
5. Give an example of how bias can creep into the training of a machine learning application, resulting in unintended but negative consequences.

11.4 Robotics

LO11.4 **Describe** *the different kinds of robots in use today, and how they benefit both businesses and individuals.*

robotics is the branch of technology that deals with the design, construction, operation, and application of robots (Oxford English Dictionary, 2019).

Robotics is an interdisciplinary field that draws from knowledge and research in mechanical, information, and electrical engineering, computer science, artificial intelligence, nanotechnology, bioengineering, and other fields. Robotic machines first appeared in the late 1950s and early 1960s. Since that time, the design, complexity, and sophistication of robotic machines has grown significantly (Ben-Ari & Mondada, 2018).

The use of robotics is fairly common in industry (production, assembly and packing, and warehousing), and have an increasing role in the military (combat and drone machines), medicine, transportation (autonomous vehicles), law enforcement (bomb disposal), and even entertainment (e.g., televised robot combat competitions, toys, amusement park rides, and so on) (Joshi, 2018). Robots are frequently used to perform repetitive and sometimes dangerous tasks not well suited to humans. They are also used in environments like space, underwater, and other places where humans would encounter unsafe or deadly conditions. Most robots today are used in some part of a manufacturing process, especially the automotive industry where robots weld, paint, assemble, and perform other production line tasks. That said, in the last decade there has been a considerable increase in robots capable of different types of work outside of the factory floor. For instance, robots are used in warehouses to store, move, collect, and manage inventory. New types of warehouses are being developed that will be completely run by robots. Use of robots in the medical field has resulted in surprising new applications like performing complex surgical procedures.

Robots are also beginning to be used in law enforcement. The use of robots in law enforcement today is still limited, although like other forms of AI, developers believe there is much potential for expanding their use. Law enforcement agencies currently use robots in situations like bomb disposal and exploring situations that may hold unknown risks for human officers. When AI is built into these types of machines, they can detect and recognize objects in their immediate environment, and react to changing situations autonomously, reducing reaction times choosing correct actions without having to wait for input from a remote human controller. AI-powered robots will be able to perform a wider range of useful tasks further reducing the need for a human officer to place themselves in harm's way.

Most robots do not use any type of AI and most AI applications are not connected to or part of a robot. However, when combined, AI-enhanced robots can both behave (action) and think (intelligence), to some extent like humans. This combination of the two disciplines can result in powerful and impressive machines that come quite close to the type of robots often described in science fiction books and movies. Robots that are useful or helpful can be made to have even greater value when the robot can solve problems, learn, communicate, and make decisions using the power of AI programming.

Types of Robotic Machines

Attempts to categorize the different types of robotic machines have proven to be difficult. Part of the problem is that today there are so many different types of robots and robotic technologies. Robots are also doing several kinds of work across many industries. In the section that follows, we will describe some of the more exciting ways that robots are being used today, and the technological advances that are making these new applications possible. Even though this will not be an exhaustive list of the different types of robots in use today, it should help you understand the current level of robotics development and the most common use cases for robotic technology.

Robotics and Work Automation As you read in the earlier in the chapter, work automation is a phenomenon that extends beyond robotics, since software programs can also be used to replace human workers. Work automation can be controversial when applied on a wide scale basis, disrupting the occupations of entire human work forces. Work automation is less problematic when applied to tasks that are repetitive, boring, dangerous, or physically exhausting. Robots are especially valuable in high tech and other industries where precision and clean-room production is required (i.e., production of semi-conductors, OLED displays, or pharmaceuticals).

Manufacturing and supply chain management are business functions where lots of activity generates lots of data. Therefore, AI applications are likely to be helpful to businesses that are seeking insights about these processes that were previously unavailable to researchers using traditional data analysis techniques. Perhaps one of the biggest ways that robotics and AI have transformed manufacturing in the past two decades in through work automation. In most industries, workers on the production line have been replaced by robotic machines designed to perform repetitive, sometimes dangerous tasks requiring strength, flexibility, and endurance that exceed what might reasonably be expected by most human workers. Robots are designed to perform seemingly contradictory tasks such as movement of heavy materials and equipment while at the same time operating with consistently high levels of precision required to meet exacting quality control standards. The capabilities play an important role in the optimization of on-time, error-free production processes that also minimize waste and defective products.

To achieve competitive levels of production volume and speed, as well as minimize the need for continuous monitoring and remote control of industrial robots, artificial intelligence is combined with robotic technology to produce smart or intelligent robots, capable of problem solving, decision making, the ability to see and recognize objects in their immediate environment, and the ability to learn from experience. While not all industrial robots require a full complement of AI capabilities, industrial robots programmed with AI skills relevant to their designated role on the production line will prove ever-more valuable than "non-intelligent" robotic machines. Industrial robots have been designed to use all branches of AI technology.

The most common use of robots for work automation is in the manufacturing sector of the economy. Industrial robots used in manufacturing and production applications can be categorized into six types based on the way they are configured (Technavio, 2018). While we describe each type of industrial robot below, it is highly recommended that you use a search engine to find images of these robots, since that is really the best way to understand the design and function of each type.

- **Cartesian**—these robots are also called rectilinear or gantry robots and have a rectangular configuration that allows for precise location of the arm by moving in three dimensions (i.e., left to right, forward or backwards, and up and down). They can be used in applications that require positional accuracy and flexibility in their configuration. They can be used in pick and place operations, loading and unloading, and material handling.

- **Cylindrical**—this type of robot has an arm that rotates around its base creating what is referred to as a donut-shaped work envelope, and another extendable arm that shifts back and forth as well as rotated. This type of robot is used for assembly operations, coating applications, machine loading/unloading, and transport of LCD panels.

- **SCARA**—Selective Compliance Assembly Robot Arm or SCARA robots have two connected arms that can rotate around a fixed base (referred to as a donut-shaped work envelope). The two connected arms allow for precise movement within a specified plane area. These robots are used in assembly, semi-conductor, and biomed production, packaging, and machine loading.

- **Delta**—these types of industrial robots get their spider-like look from three sets of parallel fore-arms whose movement can be coordinated for precision and connect to a common effector (the device at the end of a robotic arm that interacts with the environment). The design of the delta robot configuration allows for rapid pick and place operations transferring items from one place to another. They are used in a variety of industries including food, pharmaceutical, and electronics. See **Figure 11.5** below.

Fotoagentur WESTEND61/Westend61 GmbH/Alamy Stock Photo

FIGURE 11.5   The Delta industrial robot configuration is well suited to rapid pick and place tasks used in the food manufacturing and packaging industry.

- **Polar**—these types of robots are another configuration of two robotic arms attached to a fixed base. The arms can collapse into a parallel horizontal position, or straighten out to affect a longer reach, with an extendable rotating arm. Polar robot configurations are used for glass handling, injection molding, welding, and material handling.
- **Articulated**—one of the most common types of industrial robot, articulated robots, are configured like a big arm, with anywhere between two and ten rotary joints. Each additional rotary joint increases the degrees of freedom, or range of movement possible for the robot. These robots are used in a wide range of applications including food packing, arc welding, steel cutting, and handling glass and other materials.

Collaborative Robots   Another kind of robot that is increasingly being used in production applications is a **collaborative robots**. One of the goals for collaborative robots production systems is safety. Typically, the robot part of the working pair takes on aspects of the production process that may involve heavy lifting, repetitive or routine movements, or other steps in the processes that might be potentially unsafe to human workers. Collaborative robots are designed to mitigate these risks, while increasing productivity and quality control.

collaborative robots   also known as **Cobots**, work together with human workers to accomplish a task or set of tasks.

Medical/Surgical Robots   In healthcare, robots are being used in a variety of surgical procedures. Surgical robots are usually considered collaborative robots because instead of replacing the surgeon, the robots work with surgeons to execute surgical procedures that require extremely high levels of precision, the use of micro-instrumentation and other situations where robotics devices augment the skills and experience of human surgeons. Medical robots are designed to augment a surgeon's skill, knowledge, and expertise, by taking on surgical tasks that require extremely high levels of precision and stability over long periods of time. As surgeons grow older, their knowledge and experience increase, but they are also more prone to slight hand tremors that can have a negative impact on their ability to perform surgical procedures. Medical robots expand the length of a surgeon's career by eliminating hand tremors as a concern.

For example, laparoscopy is a type of minimally invasive surgery that is replacing traditional surgical procedures. Instead of making large incisions to access underlying tissue and organs, laparoscopy uses very small openings and special tools called endoscopes that make it possible to reach and operate on underlying tissue and organs through the small holes. Medical robots can perform endoscopy procedures with greater precision than human doctors who might be hampered by their inability to see the operating environment like they would in traditional surgical procedures. Minimally invasive procedures have important benefits for patients. The smaller incisions mean faster healing times, shorter hospital stays, lower risk of infections and complications, less pain and discomfort, and smaller scars.

Most medical robots draw on multiple artificial intelligence technologies to develop and carry out their surgical functions including using machine learning to achieve submillimeter precision and expand dexterity to reach more areas of the body (Anandan, 2018).

Service Robots   The term service robot covers a wide variety of use cases. Like industrial robots, professional service robots are designed to perform tasks that are repetitive, possibly boring, or may represent a potential risk to the health and safety of humans. The only difference is that professional service robots are used outside of production and factory environments. Instead, these service robots are used in a variety of professional and business settings. Some examples of professional service robots include:

- agricultural robots
- customer service robots
- construction robots
- demolition robots
- inspection robots

A fascinating type of service and collaborative robots is an exoskeleton robot that is currently being used in healthcare. These are robots that can be worn by a human and used to mimic or augment the body's own movements, while at the same time adding protective or strength features (Agence France-Presse, 2019) (see **Figure 11.6**). Exoskeleton robots are being studied for possible use by the military and already have obvious applications in work that requires heavy lifting and movement of materials, like the kind of tasks that might be required in warehouse settings.

John D. Ivanko/Alamy Stock Photo

FIGURE 11.6   Exoskeleton robots can be worn to mimic or augment the body's own movements.

At home, people are using personal service robots designed to perform tasks in a residential environment. They may be partially or fully autonomous. Some examples include robotic vacuum cleaners such as the Roomba, lawn mowing robots like Husqvarna's 115H robotic lawn mower, and the WORX WR150 Landroid, and surveillance robots like Nest, Lynx, and Erector Spykee. One area that developers are exploring is domestic service robots that can assist elderly individuals with healthcare and routine tasks around the house. As the number of senior citizens grows, the cost of hiring people to provide in-home assistance has become expensive, just as costs associated with assisted living facilities have also increased. Domestic service robots may extend the time that seniors can continue to live independently thanks to the help of robots that will be able to perform a variety of tasks that seniors are no longer able to do by themselves.

A **drone** is a flying robot that can be remotely controlled or fly autonomously through software-controlled flight plans working with onboard sensors and GPS.

Drones Another growth area in the field of robotics is aerial robotics or **drones**. In the public and private sectors, drones are being used to tackle everything from disease control to cleaning up the ocean to deliver pizza and helping fight wars. as more organizations are capitalizing on the commercial opportunities that drones offer it has been reported that the emerging global market for business services using drones is valued at over $127 billion (CB INSIGHTS, 2020). In business, a common use of aerial drones can be seen in RFID equipped warehouses where drones are used after normal work hours to scan products, perform inventory checks, track merchandise, map product locations, and perform other repetitive tasks. Drones are also being used to improve processes in many industry sectors including healthcare, agriculture, weather forecasting, waste management, mining, energy, construction and planning, insurance, and real estate to name a few. In late 2019, Amazon announced Prime Air—a delivery system that will use drones to deliver packages to residential addresses in 30 minutes or less.

In the military, drones are known as UAVs (unmanned aerial vehicles) or RPAS (remotely piloted aerial systems) and are used for surveillance and in offensive operations where manned flight is considered too risky or difficult. Currently 95 countries around the world already possess some form of military drone technology compared with approximately 60 countries 10 years ago. Law enforcement agencies and emergency response teams are increasingly using drones for surveillance and patrol. For example, Land Rover has partnered with the Austrian Red Cross to design a special operations vehicle with a roof-mounted, thermal imaging drone. The vehicle includes an integrated landing system that allows the drone to securely land atop the vehicle while it is in motion. Land Rover hopes that the custom drone-equipped Land Rover Discovery—it has dubbed "Project Hero"—will save lives by speeding up emergency response times. In addition, drones are proving invaluable in supporting the efforts of conservation agencies and disease control centers.

IT at Work 11.4

Sophia—Hanson Robotics' Animatronic Humanoid Robot

Hanson Robotics' animatronic humanoid robot is perhaps the most recognized robot in the world, at least among those who follow robotics news (see **Figure 11.7**). Using advance artificial intelligence programming, Sophia can carry on life-like conversations; she can listen and speak using natural language. She is the first robot to ever be made a citizen of a country (Saudi Arabia), and is the Innovation Ambassador for the United Nations. Unlike more robots with more functional designs, like the powerful, multi-purpose robotic arms used in factories and production lines around the world, Sophia was designed to look human. Specifically, designing Sophia was an attempt to see how far designers could go in terms of using the robot's appearance and functionality to mimic social behaviors and inspire feelings of love and compassion in return. Needless today, Sophia has a very different mission than, say, an industrial Delta class production robot. She has sat for interviews, appeared on television, and was featured on the cover of ELLE magazine. Despite these and many other public "firsts" for a member of the robot or humanoid race, Sophia is still a long way off from possessing the kind of advanced robotic state that she mimics. Self-aware robotic

characters in films and movies like Ex Machina or more recently, the television show West World, are still far beyond the abilities of Sophia's creators at Hanson Robotics. Still, she is perhaps the most impressive example of cutting-edge humanoid technology.

Sophia was recently joined at Hanson computing by a new little sister, appropriately named "Little Sophia." Just like big Sophia, Little Sophia was designed with the goal of being relatable or at least interesting to human girls. Hanson specifically designed Little Sophia hoping that the robot would help spark girl's interest in robotics and perhaps other STEM disciplines.

Despite these noble-sounding goals, Sophia and her developer, David Hanson, CEO and founder of Hanson Robotics, have come in for some criticism from people that don't consider Sophia to be a serious attempt to advance the field of intelligent robotics. Some question Hanson's understanding of artificial intelligence and hard-core computing given his formal training (a Bachelor of Fine Arts in film) and his previous career at Walt Disney. And while there may be some validity to some of these criticisms, we can't help but wonder what the other team's animatronic humanoid robot looks and sounds like?

Sources: Compiled from Greshko (2018), Urbi (2018), Hanson Robotics (2020), and Marr (2020).

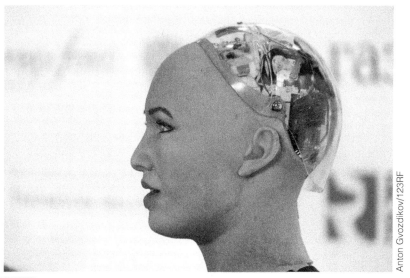

Anton Gvozdikov/123RF

FIGURE 11.7 Sophia is an example of an animatronic humanoid robot designed to mimic both the verbal and nonverbal communication skills of an adult female human.

Autonomous Robots Autonomous robots operate without a great deal of external control. They can be as simple as a Roomba or they may be larger, much more sophisticated machines that use various types of AI to guide their behavior. For instance, it might be an autonomous vehicle (AV), such as a passenger car, delivery van or a semi-trailer truck for transporting freight over long distances. Another type of autonomous robot that is showing up in warehouses and order-fulfillment services is a robotic picking machine. These robots can move around a warehouse or similar facility, selecting individual items from inventory that are needed to fulfill an order. Once all the items for an order have been selected, the robot drops off the items at a station for packing and returns to collect items for the next order. Order information is sent to the robots using a Wi-Fi network connection.

Another AV being used in warehouses is an autonomous forklift. These AVs can be directed to unload trucks parked at a loading dock and move freight to designated areas of the warehouse. Likewise, they can load a truck when given instructions to do so (Guillot, 2018).

Questions

1. How do industrial robots benefit companies that use them for production and manufacturing?
2. What has been the effect of advances in artificial intelligence on the field of robotics?
3. How are collaborative robots different from industrial robots that work without direct interaction with humans during the production process?
4. What advantages do surgeons and patients experience when medical robots are used during surgical procedures?
5. Describe some examples of autonomous robots.

11.5 Quantum Computing (QC)

LO11.5 Describe *how quantum computers are different from modern-day computers and explain how quantum computers are likely to impact business and society in the future.*

What Is Quantum Mechanics?

Quantum mechanics is a branch of science, more specifically a branch of physics that describes the behavior or movement of microscopic objects. Classical physics does a good job of explaining the behavior of larger objects that can be seen with the naked eye. But once you get down to the microscopic level, things behave in ways that can seem strange. Quantum physics is used to explain the behavior of things like atoms, electrons, and light. Scientists have found, for instance, that predicting the location of an electron as it moves around the nucleus of an atom can be difficult using classical physics. This is because electrons have a property called **superposition** (Katwala, 2020; Wired, 2020).

Superposition is the ability to be in two places at once.

Another quantum physics concept is **entanglement**. Entanglement describes the case where two things are connected, such as two entangled coins, such that when one lands on heads, the other lands on heads, and vice versa. Things that are entangled work as a kind of system. **Interference** is a third concept that describes the way that something can increase (constructive interference) or decrease (destructive interference) the behavior of another thing (Wired, 2020). Modern-day computers operate using bits, a series of switches that must always be in one of two positions, on–off, open–closed, or 0–1. Bits are organized into bytes, a series of eight connected bits. While the most basic component of a computer is a two-position bit, modern 64-bit computers can represent 2^{64} different values (over 18 quintillion) that allow us to do very complex things using computers and other digital devices. While our computers today work great for dealing with macroscopic phenomena, they still have a hard time with natural quantum phenomena that can't be represented by a two-position (0,1) bit.

Quantum Computers

Instead of the bits used in computers today, quantum computers use another kind of switch called a **qubit**. Qubits can hold a value of 0, 1, as well as values between 0 and 1. This third value represents the concept of superposition described above. Quantum computers also operate on qubits in ways that replicate other quantum concepts like entanglement and interference. Someday, quantum computers will be able to tackle problems that can't be solved by even the most powerful super-computers in use today. Some examples of these new advances include the following areas.

Artificial Intelligence As you learned earlier in this chapter, many artificial intelligence programs are already capable of processing exceptionally large data sets to train or learn how to do things like make decisions or identify objects. Other applications can sift through large data sets to uncover meaningful patterns or relationships in the data that would not be obvious to human agents. It is expected that integrating AI with quantum computing will increase the ability of AI applications to process even greater amounts of data at faster rates.

Cybersecurity　Cybersecurity professionals use various tools to detect data breaches and the unauthorized activity of hackers as they move around inside of a computer system or network. It is expected that quantum computers will be able to spot unauthorized activity much faster than is currently possible. Of course, cybersecurity will always be a challenge because it is likely that hackers and criminals will eventually find ways of using quantum computing to bypass security protocols on computers and networks. Modern security systems today use security systems that utilize mathematical operations such as prime factorization (breaking down large numbers as a product of smaller prime numbers) for data encryption and other protective features. But with a quantum computer, criminals will be able to easily break through these protective layers, including figuring out very complex passwords. Hopefully, new quantum computers will also facilitate the development of even more rigorous security systems (Sham, 2019).

Product Innovation　Development of new products, especially products based on chemistry or the mixing of materials should be enhanced by advances in quantum computing. That is because chemistry is based on the way that molecules of various substances will interact. Since molecules operate at the microscopic layer, quantum computers should have a definite advantage over traditional computers when it comes to identifying, developing, and testing things like new pharmaceutical medications, and fertilizers that improve crop yield without the negative environmental impacts caused by current products. Another area for innovation is the development of materials that can be used in the production of renewable energy sources, like solar panels that convert sunlight into greater amounts of electricity than current materials or smaller batteries that can store greater amounts of electricity than our batteries today.

Business, Market, and Financial Modeling　Business organizations will make use of quantum computers for all types of problems, such as predicting the future performance of equities markets or individual companies and modeling various alternatives in the development of a supply chain. For instance, a package delivery service should be able to determine the best methods of shipping and delivery routes in a way that increases performance and lowers costs.

Weather Forecasting and Climate Change　Today, meteorologists use statistical models to monitor weather systems and predict future weather. With quantum computers, they will be able to develop even better predictions as well as help determine the growing impact of climate change on different regions around the world.

Challenges in Quantum Computing

While the future for quantum computing is very exciting, it is expected that practical use and widespread availability of quantum computers is quite a way off. Many of the advances in quantum computing today are the result of academic research occurring in universities around the world. Two companies at the forefront of developing a quantum computer are IBM and Alphabet (Google), each of which is working hard to develop a quantum computing machine. Both companies have created prototype machines that have served to demonstrate many of the obstacles that need to be overcome in future quantum computers (Gibney, 2019). Another tech giant, Microsoft, is already developing a software language for programming quantum computers.

But current quantum machines are prone to errors resulting from noise, faults, and loss of coherence, a property critical to the operation of quantum computers. **Fault tolerance** is the ability of a computer or a network to keep working despite the failure of one of its components. Current quantum computers have extremely low fault tolerance. **Coherence** is the ability of a quantum computer to maintain information in qubits that are in a state of superposition (the "in-between 0 and 1" state that qubits can represent). Coherence is the property that makes it possible to develop algorithms capable of performing super-fast calculations much more rapid than modern-day computers. Coherence is also required for quantum entanglement, or the ability to represent the connected nature of two qubits in the superposition state. Loss of coherence, or **decoherence**, is caused by things like vibrations, temperature changes, and electromagnetic waves, to which current quantum computers are extremely sensitive. The quantum computers developed IBM and Google both have a little less than 55 qubits, but information from qubits in a superposition state deteriorates quickly, within tens of milliseconds. Even with a small number of qubits, the machines are surprisingly powerful, just not very reliable (Katwala, 2020). Future quantum machines will need to use more qubits and find solutions to the decoherence problem. Experts predict that the development of large-scale, error-free quantum computers is probably at least 10–20 years away (Wired, 2018; Pakin & Coles, 2019; Somma, 2020). **Tech Note 11.1** explains how you can learn more about the quantum computing prototypes and resources offered by IBM.

Tech Note 11.1

Quantum Computing at IBM

For reasons explained earlier in this chapter, there are no companies currently using quantum computers for business. The best you can do is learn about the prototype machines developed by Google and IBM. That said, both companies are very proud of their respective accomplishments, and are happy to share their experience with you from the pages of their websites. The IBM website is particularly impressive. The pages are full of explanations and tutorials designed to help people learn about quantum computing, quantum programming, and the challenges faced by workers in the quantum computing field. You can even run a program on IBM's quantum computer from your account on their website. Despite the complexity of quantum mechanics and quantum computers, IBM has done a good job of making the examples and tutorials on the website interesting and understandable for those of us that don't have PhDs in physics or computer science.

- To learn more about quantum computing on the IBM website, visit: **https://www.ibm.com/quantum-computing/learn/what-is-ibm-q/**
- To create an account, and run your programs on the IBM quantum computer, visit the IBM Quantum Computing Experience at: **https://quantum-computing.ibm.com/login**

Questions

1. How would you explain the quantum mechanics concept of superposition to a friend?
2. In quantum mechanics, what does it mean for two things to be in a state of entanglement?
3. In quantum mechanics, what is the difference between positive and negative interference?
4. Describe some of the fields or disciplines that are expected to be influenced by the development of workable and widely available quantum computers.
5. What is the difference between bits that are used in computers today, and qubits that are used in quantum computers?
6. What are three quantum states that can be replicated by qubits.
7. Why can't traditional bits perform operations similar to qubits?
8. What are the key obstacles facing computer engineers regarding the development of quantum computers?

Chapter Summary

LO11.1 *Explain* what artificial intelligence is and describe the different branches or technologies that comprise the AI field.

Artificial intelligence (AI) is the theory and development of computer systems that can perform tasks normally requiring human intelligence, such as visual perception, speech recognition, decision making, and translation between languages. AI development be classified into three stages of AI—weak, strong, and super intelligent. There are four types of AI machines: reactive machines, limited memory, theory of mind, and self-awareness machines. The different branches or technologies associated with AI include machine learning, deep learning, natural language processing, robotics, expert systems, and fuzzy logic.

LO11.2 *Describe* the factors affecting adoption of AI in business organizations and provide examples of AI applications being used in various industries and the public sector.

When adopting AI organizations pass through five phases of AI maturity. Currently, most organizations are in the AI awareness stage. When passing through the AI maturity phases companies face three barriers they must overcome: skills, fear of the unknown, and concerns about data scope and quality. Companies need to use AI applications to understand the complex nature of their business process as represented by big data. Three important aspects of AI that are contributing to organizational efficiency and effectiveness are the use of AI in predictive analytics, sentiment analysis, and content management systems. For example, predictive analytics are being used by banks and other financial service firms, credit card companies, large B2B companies, and retailers to evaluate the credit worthiness of their customers and suppliers, and identify when and where to target their advertising campaigns. Sentiment analysis used to understand consumers better and content management systems curate a collection of digital content that AI can use to reduce time spent by human agents.

LO11.3 *Describe* the ethical and social challenges created by the emerging use of artificial intelligence by businesses and public sector organizations.

The three areas of great concern regarding AI applications in business and society are (1) the implications of work automation and the impact on a large portion of the workforce, (2) privacy and civil rights concerns about the AI applications that might be used by government and law enforcement agencies, and (3) bias and other unintended consequences that might occur when AI applications are used to solve important problems.

LO11.4 *Describe* the different kinds of robots in use today, and how they benefit both businesses and individuals.

Several different kinds of robotic machines are in use today across all industry sectors. Robots are also used in the public sector by the military, law enforcement agencies, conservation agencies, and emergency response teams. Types of robots in use include industrial robots used in production and manufacturing, collaborative robots, medical robots, service robots, and autonomous robots like AVs and drones. Robots perform dangerous and mundane tasks to free up safer and more interesting work for humans. However, there is also a concern that robots are replacing humans who are no open to reskilling themselves.

LO11.5 *Describe* how quantum computers are different from modern-day computers and explain how quantum computers are likely to impact business and society in the future.

The field of quantum mechanics and quantum computing and the quantum phenomena describe the behavior of things at the microscopic level rather than at the macroscopic level. Instead of looking at the bit level of 0s and 1s, quantum computers work with qubits that can have any value from 0 to 1. Quantum computers are still in the development stage and these devices are being designed to capture or replicate quantum phenomena, such as the state of superposition, the state of coherence, state of entanglement, and the concept of interference. In the future, it is hoped that quantum computing will be useful in the areas of AI, cybersecurity, product innovation, business, marketing and financial modeling, weather forecasting, and climate change. Some of the practical obstacles faced by computer engineers in the design and development of quantum computers include their propensity to errors resulting from noise, faults, and loss of coherence.

Key Terms

artificial general intelligence (AGI) 412	expert system (ES) 418	natural language understanding (NLU) 416
artificial intelligence 411	facial recognition systems 424	qubit 436
artificial narrow intelligence (ANI) 412	fault tolerance 437	reactive machines 413
artificial super intelligence (ASI) 412	feature engineering 410	reinforcement learning 415
biometric input devices 424	fuzzy logic 418	robotics 430
closed-circuit television (CCTV) 424	inference engine 418	self-awareness machines 414
coherence 437	interference 436	sentiment analysis 422
collaborative robots 432	knowledge base 418	superposition 436
computer vision 424	law enforcement agency (LEA) 424	supervised learning 415
decoherence 438	limited memory machines 414	theory of mind machines 414
deep learning (DL) 415	machine learning (ML) 415	unsupervised learning 415
drones 434	natural language generation (NLG) 416	user interface 418
entanglement 436	natural language processing (NLP) 416	work automation 419

Assuring Your Learning

Discuss: Critical Thinking Questions

1. Using an Internet search engine, find information about the "fourth industrial revolution." What are the characteristics of an industrial revolution? What were the first three industrial revolutions and how did they change society? What are the potential benefits and threats facing society because of technologies that will define the fourth industrial revolution?

2. Discuss ethical issues associated with creating strong AI machines. Should they be treated any differently than machines without strong AI? Better or worse than animals? Better or worse than humans?

3. Why is data so critical to the development of machine learning applications? How is data used by machine learning developers?

4. Describe the first three industrial revolutions discussed in the text. Why do people believe that artificial intelligence will create a new age of industrial revolution?

5. The development stages of artificial intelligence are described as weak, strong, and super intelligent AI. Explain how applications in each stage will differ from those in other stages.

6. What is the critical difference between reactive and limited memory AI machines, and machines that are categorized as theory of mind and self-awareness machines?

7. List each of the six branches of artificial intelligence and briefly explain each one.

8. Machine learning and deep learning are both used today to create AI applications that can learn from "experience." What is the fundamental difference between the way each of these technologies learn?

9. When training a machine learning application, developers can use one of three different approaches: supervised learning, unsupervised learning, and reinforcement learning. Describe each strategy and explain how the data used in each process will differ from that used in the other two.

10. Natural language processing (NLP) applications can learn how to communicate verbally or in written form using language that looks and sounds very much like the way humans communicate. What are the six aspects of natural language that NLP applications must learn to develop their communication capabilities?

11. What are the three components of an expert system (ES) program? Explain what each component does.

12. Work automation is the practice of replacing human workers with technology (i.e., software programs or robots). Describe the impact that work automation is likely to have on business and society in the future. What type of jobs are most susceptible to being automated and what kind of jobs are resistant to work automation and why?

Explore: Online and Interactive Exercises

1. Explore the Internet to learn about NLP applications. Describe three NLP applications currently in use today.

2. Search the Internet to find articles about the way that social networking and social media services have begun to build AI into their operations. Explain how AI technologies are enhancing the services that these companies provide to users.

3. AI experts and philosophers have suggested that future advances in AI that might make it possible to create super-intelligent, self-aware machines raising a host of ethical issues because it would be very difficult to meaningfully differentiate these sentient machines from humans. Search the Internet for information about this issue and decide if you think these kinds of machines should be treated differently than we treat other machines. What rights or protections should these kinds of machines be given?

4. In May of 2017, the website hackermoon.com published a long list of artificial intelligence applications that could be used today. Visit the hackermoon.com website and look at the applications on their lists. Explore at least three of these applications and summarize your evaluation of each application in a paragraph.

- List 1: **https://hackernoon.com/a-list-of-artificial-intelligence-tools-you-can-use-today-for-personal-use-1-3-7f1b60b6c94f**
- List 2: **https://hackernoon.com/a-list-of-artificial-intelligence-tools-you-can-use-today-for-businesses-2-3-eea3ac374835**

5. The purpose of this exercise is not to criticize all the great companies described in Case 2.2, but rather, figure out if you can, why their recommendation systems don't work so well.

  a. Log into the website of each company listed in Case 2.2 (recommendation engines) and examine the recommendations that are made to you.

  b. Make a list, or better yet, keep a small journal. Each time you visit one of these sites, note the recommendations made to you and try to articulate why the recommendation does or doesn't work. Check out the friends you have in common with your Facebook recommendations, and ask yourself if those people are real friends or just Facebook friends? Or why don't you feel like watching some of the movies and shows recommended by Netflix? Why would you never have made those recommendations to yourself? Same thing with Amazon—why are the product recommendations so poor?

  c. After about a week, look over your notes and see if you can find any common problems. What was it about the recommendations you received that made them particularly bad ideas?

  d. Prepare a brief memo summarizing your observations and send them to the customer service department of one or more of the websites. Share any responses you get with your professor and fellow students.

Analyze & Decide: Apply IT Concepts to Business Decisions

1. In 1994, a company called Imagination Engines Inc. applied for a patent on its design of what they call an imagination engine, an artificial intelligence application that supposedly can generate ideas that businesses could use to develop new innovative products and services. Read a description of this company's approach to creating new ideas and determine if you would recommend its use by business

organizations. Explain your reasons for or against. To get started, visit this page: **http://www.imagination-engines.com/**

2. Explain how predictive analytics AI programs can be valuable to businesses. Select a business and using what you know about it, describe how those businesses might benefit from AI-powered predictive analytics.

3. Explain how companies can use sentiment analysis instead of traditional consumer research methods like focus groups and surveys.

4. Put yourself in the role of an administrator of a large healthcare organization or a health insurance company. Study the issue of medical robots being used for surgery. Develop a position on whether the use of surgical robots is something you should support or not. Create a list of positive and negative impacts this practice could have on your organization.

5. As businesses move to adopt AI in their operations, they face three barriers. Describe those barriers and ways that companies can overcome them.

6. If you were the CIO (chief information officer) for a large company, would you recommend that the company invest in the adoption of quantum computing technology soon?

Reinforce: Ensure your understanding of the Key Terms

Solve the online crossword provided for this chapter.

Web Resources

More resources and study tools are located on the student website. You'll find useful Web links and self-test quizzes that provide individualized feedback.

Case 11.2

Business Case: Recommendation Systems Powered by AI—Still Room for Improvement

Much has been written about the wonders of some of the most well-known recommendation systems in use today at companies like Amazon, Netflix, LinkedIn, Facebook, and YouTube. These recommendations are credited with giving their companies a significant competitive advantage and are said to be responsible for significant increases in whatever system the company uses to keep score. For Amazon, that would be sales dollars. The Amazon recommendation system is said to be responsible for 35% of sales, a figure that has been cited by several authors dating back to at least 2013 (MacKenzie, Meyer, & Noble, 2013; Morgan, 2018). The Netflix recommendation system is also believed to be one of the best in the business. Netflix counts success in terms of how many shows people watch, how much time they spend watching Netflix, and other metrics associated with engagement and time on channel. But the Netflix recommendation system is also credited with moving dollars to the company's bottom line to the tune of $1 billion a year (Arora, 2016).

In the realm of social media, score is kept a little differently, and in the case of Facebook and LinkedIn, recommendation systems are frequently used to suggest connections you might wish to add to your network. Facebook periodically show you friends of friends that you might be interested in "friending," while on LinkedIn, you are frequently shown the profiles of individuals that might make great professional connections. Finally, YouTube's recommendation system lines up a queue of videos that stand ready to fill your viewing screen once your current video finishes playing. Sometimes the relationship between your current video and the line-up of recommended videos is obvious. While watching a clip of a Saturday Night

Live sketch, you can see that several of the recommended videos waiting for you are also SNL clips. But not always, and that is probably where some cool recommendation engine juju comes into play, trying to figure out what will really grab your interest and keep you on-site for a few more minutes, watching new clips and the increasingly annoying advertisements that now seem to find multiple ways of popping up and interrupting your use of YouTube's platform without paying the price of admission.

While all of these companies are to be credited for pioneering recommendation technology that most likely generates beneficial results, it seems that more often than not, the recommendations we get are not as impressive as what so many blog writers would have us believe.

Today, all these recommendation systems have been infused and super-charged from their original creations with the power of artificial intelligence. The question is, has this really changed much in terms of the user experience? How many times do you really send a friend request to that person Facebook tells you share four friends in common? Would you accept a friend request from that individual if they sent one to you? How often do you try to connect with the professionals that LinkedIn recommends to you? Or do you find the whole process of deleting all those suggestions a pain? Finally, how often have you sat down to watch Netflix and after scrolling through all their movies and television shows, you end up watching another channel or maybe decide to go read a book. Or when was the last time you purchased an unsolicited product that was recommended to you on Amazon?

Sources: Compiled from MacKenzie, Meyer, and Noble (2013), Arora (2016), Adams (2017), Morgan (2018), and Pandey (2019).

References

"Artificial Intelligence," Oxford University Press, *lexico.com*, 2019.

"Robot," Oxford University Press, *lexico.com*, 2019.

"Robotics," Oxford University Press, *lexico.com*, 2019.

Adams, R. "10 Powerful Examples of Artificial Intelligence in Use Today." *forbes.com*, January 10, 2017.

Agence France-Presse. "Paralysed Man Walks Using Mind-Controlled Exoskeleton." *The Guardian*, October 4, 2019.

Anandan, T. "Robots and AI in the OR." *robotics.org*, November 26, 2018.

Angwin, J., Larson, J., Mattu, S., and Kirchner, L. "Machine Bias." *propublica.org*, May 23, 2016.

Ansari, A. "People Helping Faceless: This App Helps Lost Children Reconnect with Their Families." *topyaps.com*, May 4, 2016.

Arnold, M. "HSBC Brings in AI to Help Spot Money Laundering." *ft.com*, April 8, 2018.

Arora, S. "Recommendation Engines: How Amazon and Netflix Are Winning the Personalization Battle." *martech.com*, June 28, 2016.

Ben-Ari, M. and Mondada, F. "Elements of Robotics." *Springer*, Cham, 2018

Bharadwaj, R. "Business Intelligence in Finance—Current Applications." *emerj.com*, February 25, 2019.

Biddle, S. "Facebook Uses Artificial Intelligence to Predict Your Future Actions for Advertisers, Says Confidential Document." *theintercept.com*, April 13, 2018.

CB INSIGHTS. "38 Ways Drones Will Impact Society: From Fighting War to Forecasting Weather, UAVs Change Everything." *CB INSIGHTS Newsletter*, January 9, 2020.

Chui, M. and Malhotra, S. "AI Adoption Advances, but Foundational Barriers Remain." *mckinsey.com*, November 2018.

Cnet Staff. "Best Tax Software for 2020: TurboTax, H&R Block, TaxSlayer and More." *cnet.com*, March 20, 2020.

Crawford, S. "Facial Recognition Laws Are (Literally) All Over the Map." *wired.com*, December 16, 2019.

Faggella, D. "Artificial Intelligence for Government Surveillance—7 Unique Use-Cases." *emerj.com*, November 24, 2019b.

Faggella, D. "Artificial Intelligence Job Loss Is a Comparatively Minor Concern." *danfaggella.com*, May 1, 2018b.

Faggella, D. "Bank Reduces Money-Laundering Investigation Effort with AI." *emerj.com*, December 12, 2018a.

Faggella, D. "Three Factors for Job Security in the Age of Artificial Intelligence." *emerj.com*, October 13, 2019a.

Fonseca, L. "An Introduction to Artificial Intelligence: The Four Types of AI." *thedifferenceengine.tech*, November, 2019.

Garbade, M. "A Simple Introduction to Natural Language Processing." *becominghuman.ai*, October 15, 2018

Ghosh, M. "Use This Mobile App to Bring a Social Change in India: Stop Child Trafficking Now!" *trak.in*, May 23, 2018.

Gibney, E. "Hello Quantum World! Google Publishes Landmark Quantum Supremacy Claim." *nature.com*, October 23, 2019.

Goasduff, L. "3 Barriers to AI Adoption." *gartner.com*, September 18, 2019.

Greenwald, K. and Goldfield, Z. "Estimating Information Flow in Deep Neural Networks." *medium.com*, June 19, 2019.

Greshko, M. "Meet Sophia, the Robot That Looks Almost Human." *nationalgeographic.com*, May 18, 2018.

Grossfield, B. "Deep Learning vs Machine Learning: A Simple Way to Understand the Difference." *zendesk.com*, January 23, 2020.

Guillot, C. "4 Types of Autonomous Mobile Robots, and Their Warehouse Use Cases." *supplychaindive.com*, August 7, 2018.

Gupta, K. "Natural Language Processing: What Programming Languages Are Best Suitable?" *freelancinggig.com*, July 12, 2017.

Hanson Robotics. "Sophia 2020—A Vision for Robots Who Can Help People." *hansonrobotics.com*, January 14, 2020.

Hao, K. "What Is Machine Learning?" *technologyreview.com*, November 17, 2018.

Hildt, E. "Artificial Intelligence: Does Consciousness Matter?" *frontiersin.org*, July 2, 2019.

Hintze, A. "Understanding the Four Types of Artificial Intelligence." *govtech.com*, November 14, 2016.

Holmes, F. "AI Will Add $15 Trillion to the World Economy by 2030." *forbes.com*, February 25, 2019.

HubSpot. "Inbound Powered by Artificial Intelligence", *hubspot.com*, 2020.

Hutson, M. "Self-Taught Artificial Intelligence Beats Doctors at Predicting Heart Attacks." *sciencemag.org*, April 14, 2017.

Irrera, A. "HSBC Partners with AI Startup to Combat Money Laundering." *reuters.com*, June 1, 2017.

Jeon, B. et al. "A Facial Recognition Mobile App for Patient Safety and Biometric Identification: Design, Development, and Validation." *JMIR Mhealth Uhealth* 2019, 7(4).

Joshi, N. "7 Types of Artificial Intelligence." *forbes.com*, June 19, 2019b.

Joshi, N. "How Far Are We from Achieving Artificial General Intelligence?" *forbes.com*, June 10, 2019a.

Joshi, N. "Robotics Is Taking Over the Entertainment Industry." *allerin.com*, September 25, 2018.

Kambria. "How Facebook Uses Artificial Intelligence." *kambria.com*, June 5, 2019.

Katwala, A. "Quantum Computers Will Change the World (if They Work)." *wired.co.uk*, March 5, 2020.

Lateef, Z. "Types of Artificial Intelligence You Should Know." *edureka.co*, August 7, 2017.

Le, J. "The 7 NLP Techniques That Will Change How You Communicate in the Future (Part I)." *heartbeat.fritz.ai*, June 6, 2018.

MacKenzie, I., Meyer, C., and Noble, S. "How Retailers Can Keep up with Consumers." *McKinsey.com*, October 2013.

Mahler, T. and Cheung, W. et al. "Breaking NLP: Using Morphosyntax, Semantics, Pragmatics and World Knowledge to Fool Sentiment Analysis Systems." *Proceedings of the First Workshop on Building Linguistically Generalizable NLP Systems*, 33–39, Copenhagen, Denmark, September 8, 2017.

Manyika, J. and Sneader, K. "AI, Automation, and the Future of Work: Ten Things to Solve For." *mckinsey.com*, June 2018.

Marr, B. "4 Mind-Blowing Ways Facebook Uses Artificial Intelligence." *forbes.com*, December 29, 2016.

Marr, B. "Artificial Human Beings: The Amazing Examples of Robotic Humanoids and Digital Humans." *forbes.com*, February 17, 2020.

Marr, B. "The 10 Best Examples of How Companies Use Artificial Intelligence in Practice." *forbes.com*, December 9, 2019.

Marr, B. "The 4th Industrial Revolution Is Here—Are You Ready?" *forbes.com*, August 13, 2018a.

Marr, B. "What Is Deep Learning AI? A Simple Guide With 8 Practical Examples." *forbes.com*, October 1, 2018b.

Matthias, A. "Alan Turing (1912–1954)." *moral-robots.com*, May 11, 2017.

Matthias, A. "What are Expert Systems?" moral-robots.com, August 17, 2018.

McCraw, C. "How Predictive Lead Scoring Uses AI to Generate Sales Revenue." *getvoip.com*, December 10, 2019.

McKenna, M. "Three Notable Examples of AI Bias." *aibusiness.com*, October 14, 2019.

Metz, C. "Tech Giants Are Paying Huge Salaries for Scarce A.I. Talent." *nytimes.com*, October 22, 2017.

Morgan, B. "How Amazon Has Reorganized Around Artificial Intelligence and Machine Learning." *forbes.com*, July 16, 2018.

Nieva, R. "How Facebook Uses Artificial Intelligence to Take Down Abusive Posts." *cnet.com*, May 2, 2018.

Ørhøj, L. "6 Ways to Use Machine Learning Techniques in HubSpot." *avidlyagency.com*, November 28, 2018.

Pakin, S. and Coles, P. "The Problem with Quantum Computers." *blogs.scientificamerican.com*, June 10, 2019.

Pandey, P. "The Remarkable World of Recommender Systems." *towardsdatascience.com*, May 9, 2019.

Panetta, K. "The CIO's Guide to Artificial Intelligence." *gartner.com*, February 5, 2019.

Pettey, C. "Optimize IT Operations to Drive Business Value." *gartner.com*, April 3, 2017.

Plaut, A. "A/B Testing Is Dead, Adaptive Testing Is What's Next." *blog.hubspot.com*, January 15, 2020.

Rao, A. and Verweij, G. "Sizing the Prize: What's the Real Value of AI for Your Business and How Can You Capitalize?" *pwc.com*, 2017.

Reynoso, R. "4 Main Types of Artificial Intelligence." *learn.g2.com*, March 27, 2019.

Rimol, M. "Understand 3 Key Types of Machine Learning." *gartner.com*, March 18, 2020.

Roe, D. "The Role of AI in Content Management Systems." *cmswire.com*, October 23, 2019.

Sayantini. "What Is Fuzzy Logic in AI and What Are Its Applications?" *edureka.com*, December 10, 2019.

Schneider, S. "Is Anyone Home? A Way to Find Out if AI Has Become Self-Aware." *blogs.scientificamerican.com*, July 19, 2017.

Schulze, E. "Everything You Need to Know about the Fourth Industrial Revolution." *cnbc.com*, January 17, 2019.

Schwartz, O. "In 2016, Microsoft's Racist Chatbot Revealed the Dangers of Online Conversation." *spectrum.ieee.org*, November 25, 2019.

Sham, S. "The Impact of Quantum Computing on Cybersecurity." *okta.com*, July 12, 2019.

Simon, M. "The WIRED Guide to Robots." *wired.com*, May 17, 2018.

Somma, R. "Are We Ready for Quantum Computers?" *blogs.scientificamerican.com*, March 13, 2020.

Symphony Ayasdi. "Anti-Money Laundering Solution Deep Dive." *ayasdi.com*, 2019.

Technavio. "6 Major Types of Industrial Robots Used in the Global Manufacturing 2018." *blog.technavio.com*, August 31, 2018.

Urbi, J. "The Complicated Truth about Sophia the Robot — an Almost Human Robot or a PR stunt." *cnbc.com*, June 5, 2018.

Vincent, J. "Twitter Taught Microsoft's AI Chatbot to be a Racist Asshole in Less Than a Day." *theverge.com*, March 24, 2016.

Walch, K. "The Growth of AI Adoption In Law Enforcement." *forbes.com*, July 26, 2019.

Wang, G. "Tech Talk: Intuit's AI-Powered Tax Knowledge Engine Boosts Filers' Confidence." *intuit.com*, March 6, 2019.

West, J. "21 Amazing Uses for Face Recognition—Facial Recognition Use Cases." *facefirst.com*, September 15, 2019.

Wired. "Quantum Computing Expert Explains One Concept in 5 Levels of Difficulty." *YouTube.com*, June 25, 2018. https://www.youtube.com/watch?v=OWJCfOvochA

Worldwide Business Research. "Here's How HSBC Is Using Artificial Intelligence to Take Money Launderers to the Cleaners", *netfinance.wbresearch.com*, 2020.

CHAPTER 12

IT Strategy, Sourcing, and Strategic Technology Trends

Case 12.1 Opening Case

Stuart Miles/Adobe Stock
Svetocheck/Shutterstock.com
Tobrono/Adobe Stock

San Diego County's 20-Year Outsourcing Journey

Company Overview

The County of San Diego, California, is one of the most award-winning and innovative government agencies in the United States. Its Board of Supervisors runs it like a business and emphasizes accountability, efficiency, and customer service. The County's annual revenues are around $4 billion per year, and it is home to 3.3 million residents. The County of San Diego's mission is to be a national municipal leader and a strategic business partner for innovative technology solutions. To achieve this, San Diego County's vision is to provide high-quality technology and wireless services while driving strategic innovation through collaboration and partnership with city and regional stakeholders. The County Technology Office is responsible for the oversight of the County's IT, including strategic planning, contract oversight, and execution and operational support for over 18,000 County employees at more than 200 sites.

The Problem

Twenty years ago, San Diego County had an outdated IT infrastructure that needed a $100 million investment to update it. Systems weren't integrated; 50+ departments each had their own IT staff, and communication throughout its 300 County offices was poor.

The Solution

Instead of investing heavily in outdated IT infrastructure, San Diego County decided to outsource its entire IT function—hardware, software, networks, data centers, help desk—everything! It wanted a productive outsourcing arrangement that offered a state-of-the-art IT infrastructure, an IT governance structure that fits the County's needs, and strong interoffice communications. In 2020, San Diego County has achieved its goal and is a model for how to outsource government IT operations. But it wasn't easy getting there.

Outsourcing Contract #1   In October 1999, the San Diego County Board of Supervisors decided to outsource a radical upgrading of the County's IT function. On December 13, 1999, Tom Boardman, Chief Technology Officer for San Diego County, signed a $644 million, seven-year IT outsourcing contract with Pennant Alliance, a four-vendor team led by Computer Sciences Corporation (CSC). At the time it was the biggest, broadest outsourcing deal ever initiated by a regional government. Under the terms of the outsourcing contract, all County IT employees, hardware, and processes were moved to the

consortium. The entire IT function was centralized under a new County Technology Office (CTO) by replacing every component of the County's IT infrastructure and developing an aggressive enterprise resource planning (ERP) rollout plan to provide San Diego County's citizens with better access to its services.

Unfortunately, the first year of the contract didn't go smoothly largely due to the San Diego County's extremely high expectations. For example, the contract set the unrealistic requirement that Pennant correct 90% of reported application software problems within two hours and 99% within six hours. County employees cited one problem of waiting for weeks to receive reports and being billed several hundred dollars. Before outsourcing, the employee was accustomed to receiving a similar report in a maximum of three days and at no cost. Paperwork and administrative red tape also rose dramatically. One manager claimed that since outsourcing began, "We've had more system failures in the last three months than in the last three years."

At the end of two years, the outsourcing situation was an even bigger mess. The two principals who signed the deal had left, Michael Moore was the new San Diego County CIO, and the new day-to-day managers were embroiled in a bitter behind-the-scenes dispute over costs, service levels, and a late rollout of the promised ERP. By this time, Pennant had already exceeded its project investment by $10 million due to penalties and unforeseen upgrades to the County's creaky IT infrastructure and had added 300 extra people to hand hold County agency employees through the early days of the transition.

By the end of the contract, things were getting on a much more even keel. Seventeen separate help desks had been combined into one; five e-mail systems were integrated into a single system, and 800 or more servers distributed over 300 sites reduced to 520 housed in a single data center. Security had also been improved with the deployment of a common operating system for 12,000 County PCs that were refreshed every 36 months. The IT silos had disappeared, and in its place an integrated IT function.

Moore and his IT staff could now concentrate on strategic IT planning. Dramatic rewards were being realized from the new integrated IT infrastructure. Reliability was up and outages were down, and more effective security was designed in, rather than bolted on.

Outsourcing Contract #2   In January 2006, under its new CIO, Harold Tuck, San Diego County parted company with Pennant Alliance when it signed a seven-year $667 million outsourcing contract with

Northrop Grumman Information Technology (NGIT). Learning from previous mistakes, the new contract specified fewer service-level agreements and divided IT problems into two categories: priority one and priority two to enable faster response time requirements for higher-priority problems and more realistic response times for lesser-priority ones. The second contract recognized the diversity in the county's user base. Rather than a one-size-fits-all approach to an employee's "desktop package" a choice of resources was offered to ensure departments got the essential resources they used and didn't get ones they would never use. It also addressed disaster recovery and business continuity needs. Several years into contract things were going well primarily due to a significant increase in frequency and quality of communications between the parties and the more reasonable terms of the contract, so it came as a surprise when NGIT walked away from it and transferred ownership to HP Enterprise Services (HPE), who was a major subcontractor in the existing contract.

Outsourcing Contracts #3, #4, and #5   On May 1, 2011, HPE assumed its duties as sole contractor and the County entered into its third outsourcing contract. On November 15, 2016, current San Diego County CIO, Mikel Haas, entered into a second contract with HPE, now known as Perspecta. One of HPE's goals was to establish a long-term relationship with its client while delivering superior IT services. A third outsourcing contract was signed with Perspecta on July 16, 2019. Currently, Perspecta provides 300 people to support the county's IT and telecommunications services through a help desk, desktops, applications, network, and one local and two remote data centers.

Lessons Learned

San Diego County's outsourcing struggles and ultimate success offer some useful insights into what can go right and what can go wrong in an IT outsourcing relationship. One of San Diego's major problems was the overly ambitious scope of its first outsourcing contract with Pennant and its failure to consider the different needs of its diverse departments and agencies. By applying lessons learned from one contract to the next, San Diego County's 20-year outsourcing experience effectively moved its IT functions from chaos to stabilization and ultimately transformed it into its current steady state. It also resulted in development of a beneficial and trustworthy long-term relationship between the County and Perspecta that has enabled the County to concentrate on its core competency of serving its 3.5 million residents and successfully fulfill its mission to be a national municipal leader and strategic business partner for innovative technology solutions.

Questions

1. Why did the outsourcing contract with Pennant Alliance fail?
2. What two differences contributed to the success of the contract with NGIT?
3. What were the two most important outcomes of the contracts with Perspecta?
4. What is the most important lesson you learned from reading about San Diego County's 20-year outsourcing journey?

Sources: Compiled from Field (2001), Repsher-Emery (2001), Hanson (2005), Douglas (2010), Williams (2011), San Diego County (2016), Wood (2019), and San Diego County Technology Office (2020).

? DID YOU KNOW?

Business stakeholders are almost four times more likely to be highly satisfied with IT if there is an effective and visible IT strategy in place.

Introduction

Organizational performance depends on the quality and responsiveness of its IT infrastructure and information systems. IT strategy shapes the direction of an organization's IT investments over the next one to five years to maximize business value and shareholder wealth. As with all strategies, IT strategy defines priorities, provides a road map, establishes a budget, and develops an investment plan that must align with and support the business strategy. Deciding on a strategy entails making decisions about a future that can only be imagined. According to Roger L. Martin's article in *Harvard Business Review*: "True strategy is about placing bets and making hard choices. The objective is not to eliminate risk but to increase the odds of success" (2014). Strategy making is uncomfortable because it is about taking risks and facing the unknown.

Creating an IT strategy means deciding how to acquire, implement, maintain, and dispose of all IT assets needed to meet current and future organizational objectives along with methods to monitor, measure, and control how well things are working. An IT strategic plan also includes a tactical plan for acquiring or providing new technology and services. The tactical plan defines how to execute the IT strategic plan: for example, deciding on sourcing options such as **in-house development**, managed services, cloud computing, or software as a service (SaaS). Strategies are measured and evaluated continuously and revised annually during the strategic planning process. Some of these measures are quantifiable, and others are not. A tool that is used to evaluate both financial and nonfinancial metrics of an IT strategy is the balanced scorecard

In-house development   Information systems are developed by a company's own IT department or IT personnel.

(BSC). The BSC provides a much more comprehensive assessment of a company's performance than solely relying on numbers on a profit/loss statement.

Another important component of the IT strategy is the acquisition of newly emerging strategic technologies. Strategic technologies can change the way that a business operates and are important differentiators in determining future directions of a company in the digital economy.

In this chapter, we discuss the components of an IT strategy and the benefits it can offer. You will learn how a BSC helps evaluate the effectiveness of an IT strategy. You will also learn the different ways an organization can source IT and the advantages innovative strategic technologies can provide to ensure business continuity.

12.1 IT Strategy and Competitive Advantage

LO12.1 Define *five activities that can improve Business–IT alignment, the five forces in Porter's Competitive Forces Model and the five primary and four support activities of Porter's Value Chain.*

Aligning the IT strategy with the business strategy to improve business performance is still one of the most important challenges that CIOs face. An organization's **IT strategy** directs IT investment decisions that create, maintain, and sustain a competitive advantage and business value for the organization. To create an effective IT strategy that will improve the financial performance and/or marketplace competitiveness of an organization, a CIO must have a clear understanding of the **business strategy** and the environment in which the business exists. Armed with this understanding, the CIO can work toward making sure that the IT strategy is closely aligned with the overall business strategy to achieve **business–IT alignment**.

Aligning IT Strategy and Business Strategy

Economic and technical experts agree that the success and sustainability of an organization are heavily dependent on the extent to which an organization can achieve business–IT alignment by linking its IT strategy with its business strategy.

The first step in achieving business–IT alignment is to understand business objectives and how IT capabilities can best support business requirements; this way strategic planning will ensure that maximum IT dollars are spent on creating business value for the organization. It's important for IT to understand where the organization is headed and how technology can help it achieve its goals. Aligning technology with business processes is becoming increasingly important due to the pace of change in technology and the business. From business strategy planning to execution, digital technology has become the foundation for everything enterprises do.

Alignment is a complex management activity and calls for extensive communication and collaboration between IT and corporate leaders. Business–IT alignment can be improved by focusing on the following five activities:

1. **Commitment to IT planning by senior management** Senior management commitment to IT planning is essential to success.
2. **CIO is a member of senior management** The key to achieving business–IT alignment is for the CIO to attain strategic influence. Rather than being narrow technologists, CIOs must be both business and technology savvy. The skill set of CIOs is outlined in **Table 12.1**.
3. **Understanding IT and corporate planning** A prerequisite for effective business–IT alignment for the CIO is to understand business planning and for the CEO and business planners to understand their company's IT planning.
4. **Shared culture and effective communication** IT planning cannot occur in isolation. The CIO must understand and buy into the corporate culture. Frequent, open, and effective communication between the IT function and the business is essential to ensure a shared culture and keep everyone aware of planning activities and business dynamics.
5. **Multilevel links** Links between business and IT plans should be made at the strategic, tactical, and operational levels.

IT strategy is a plan of action to create an organization's IT capabilities for maximum and sustainable value in the organization, goals, and objectives and specifies the necessary financial requirements, budgets, and resources.

Business strategy sets the overall direction of an organization and defines how it will achieve its mission, vision, and organizational goals.

Business–IT alignment refers to applying IT in an appropriate and timely way that is consistent with business strategies, goals, and needs.

TABLE 12.1 **CIO Skills to Improve Business–IT Alignment**

- **Political savvy** Effectively understand managers, workers, and their priorities and use that knowledge to influence others to support organizational objectives.
- **Influence, leadership, and power** Inspire a shared vision and influence subordinates and superiors.
- **Relationship management** Build and maintain working relationships with coworkers and those external to the organization. Negotiate problem solutions without alienating those impacted. Understand others and get their cooperation in nonauthoritarian relationships.
- **Resourcefulness** Think strategically and make good decisions under pressure. Can set up complex work systems and engage in flexible problem resolution.
- **Strategic planning** Capable of developing long-term objectives and strategies and translating vision into realistic business strategies.
- **Doing what it takes** Persevering in the face of obstacles.
- **Leading employees** Delegating work to employees effectively; broadening employee opportunities; and interacting fairly with employees.

The Open Group Architecture Framework (TOGAF)

The Open Group Architecture Framework (TOGAF) (**https://www.opengroup.org/togaf**) is a useful IT strategy tool that is currently being used by more than 60% of Fortune 500 companies to align IT goals with overall business goals to improve business efficiency. TOGAF provides a systematic approach to designing, planning, implementing, and governing the enterprise IT architecture. By focusing on the business, applications, data and IT infrastructure, the TOGAF methodology (**Figure 12.1**) helps organizations define and organize business requirements before the start of a software development project and keeps the process moving quickly with few errors. TOGAF also helps organizations to plan their cross-departmental IT efforts. TOGAF is free for organizations to use internally.

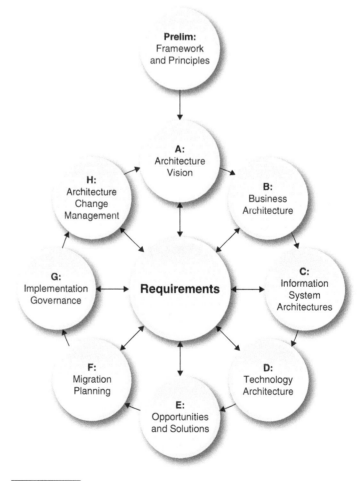

FIGURE 12.1 The Open Group Architecture Framework (TOGAF).

Resistance to Business–IT alignment

Even though firms instinctively expect benefits from business–IT alignment, many are still resistant to achieving alignment. According to a survey of business leaders by PwC Advisory, 87% of business leaders believe that IT is critical to their companies' strategic success, but not all of them work with IT to achieve that success. Less than 50% of business leaders reported that the IT function was very involved in the strategic planning process.

When the IT strategy is not aligned with the business strategies, there is a higher risk that the IT project will be abandoned before completion. Roughly 75% of companies abandoned at least one IT project and 30% abandoned more than 10% of IT projects for this reason. There are several possible reasons why a high percentage of IT projects are abandoned—the business strategy changed, technology changed, the project was not going to be completed on time or on budget, the project sponsors responsible did not work well together, or the IT strategy was changed to cloud or SaaS. Both strategies need to remain fluid to adapt to opportunities and threats. The fundamental principle to be learned is that when the business strategy changes, the IT strategy must change with it.

Achieving and Sustaining a Competitive Advantage—Locally and Globally

A well-thought-out and executed IT strategy that aligns with the business to develop, source, and put in place technology that best supports business processes and goals can give an organization a **competitive advantage** in the marketplace.

In business, as in sports, companies want to win customers, market share, position in the industry. Basically, this requires gaining an edge over competitors by being first to take advantage of market opportunities, providing great customer experiences, doing something well that others cannot easily imitate, or convincing customers why it is a more valuable alternative than the competition.

To create a competitive advantage, an organization must evaluate major four factors with the company and the environment in which it operates:

1. **Benefit**   What benefits does the company's product or service provide? What features does it have? What are its advantages over other similar products made by competitors? How do those advantages benefit the customer?

2. **Target market**   Who are the company's customer, where are they, and what are their needs? Understand who buys, where they are located, and how the company's product can make their life better.

3. **Globalization**   What benefits can we offer by buying and selling products and services in the global market? Can we benefit from current **free trade** agreements? Do we need a global business strategy? In today's connected world, an organization's target market and revenues no longer need to be confined within national borders or by country-centric trade policies. Even small firms in rural areas can adopt a global business strategy to benefit the global market.

4. **Competition**   Who are the company's direct competitors? Competitors aren't necessarily similar companies. On-demand businesses are changing the way that business is done—Marriott didn't realize that an online accommodation rental website such as AirBnB would take a large share of their market and now Marriott is fighting back by getting into the luxury online accommodation rental market.

When viewed together, these factors provide a company with a clear picture of the strategy it must take to *benefit* its *target market* and take advantage of opportunities in the *global marketplace* by offering products and services superior to those offered by its *competition*.

Competitive advantage   is an edge that enables a company to outperform its average competitor in ways that matter to its customers.

Free trade   is a policy by which a government does not discriminate against imports or interfere with experts by applying tariffs to import or subsidies to exports.

Competitive Advantage Tools

Two of the most widely used methodologies associated with gaining, maintaining, and sustaining a competitive edge are the Competitive Forces Model and Value Chain Model, which are discussed next.

Porter's Competitive Forces Model
Michael Porter's **competitive forces model**, also called the **five forces model**, is a simple but powerful strategic planning tool for understanding the strength of an organization's competitive position in its current environment and in the environment into which it's considering moving.

The model assumes that there are five important forces that determine competitive power in a business situation and influence a company's position within a given industry and the strategy that management chooses to pursue. Other forces, including new regulations, which affect all companies in the industry and have a rather uniform impact on each company in an industry, are not included in the model.

The Five Forces According to Porter, five major forces in an industry affect the degree of competition, which impact profit margins and ultimate profitability **(Figure 12.2)**. While each of the five forces needs to be assessed individually, it's their overall interaction that determines potential competitive advantage. For example, while profit margins for pizzerias may be small, the ease of entering that industry draws many new entrants. Conversely, profit margins for delivery services may be large, but the cost of technology needed to support the service is a huge barrier to entry into the market. The five industry (or market) forces are as follows:

1. **Threat of new entrants**   Industries that have large profit margins attract entrants into the market to a greater degree than industries with small margins. The same principle applies to jobs—people are attracted to higher-paying jobs, if they can meet the criteria or acquire the skills for that job. In order to gain market share, entrants usually need to sell at lower prices as an incentive. Their tactics can force companies already in the industry to defend their market share by lowering prices—reducing profit margin. Thus, this threat puts downward pressure on profit margins by driving down prices.

   This force also refers to the strength of the **barriers to entry** into an industry, which is how easy it is to enter an industry. The threat of entry is lower (less powerful) when existing companies have ITs that are difficult to duplicate or very expensive. Those ITs create barriers to entry that reduce the threat of entry.

   Barriers to Entry Economic obstacles to market participation such as a fixed cost that must be incurred by a new entrant into a market that existing market participants have not had to incur.

2. **Supplier power**   Bargaining power of suppliers is high when the supplier or brand is powerful, such as Apple, Microsoft, and auto manufacturers. Power is determined by how much a company purchases from a supplier. The more powerful company has the leverage to demand better prices or terms, which increase its profit margin. Conversely, suppliers with very little bargaining power tend to have small profit margins.

3. **Buyer power**   The bargaining power of customers, buyers, and distribution channels is an opposite force to the bargaining power of suppliers. This force is high when there are few large customers, buyers, or distribution channels like Walmart and government agencies in a market.

4. **Threat of substitute products or services**   Where there is product-for-product substitution, such as Kindle for Nook, there is downward pressure on prices. As the threat of substitutes increases, the profit margin decreases because sellers need to keep prices competitively low.

5. **Competitive rivalry**   Fierce competition between companies and their competitors leads to expensive advertising and promotions, intense investments in R&D, or other efforts that cut into profit margins. This force is influenced by all other four forces and most likely to be high when barriers to entry are low, the threat of substitute products is high, and suppliers and buyers in the market attempt to control it. That is why this force is placed in the center of the model.

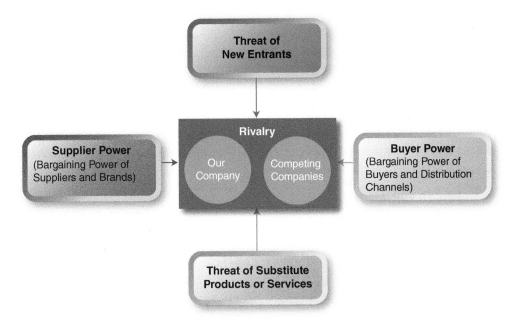

FIGURE 12.2 Porter's competitive forces model.

The strength of each force is determined by the industry's structure. Existing companies in an industry need to protect themselves against these forces. Alternatively, they can take advantage of the forces to improve their position or to challenge industry leaders or move into a new industry. The relationships between the forces are shown in Figure 12.2.

Companies can identify the forces that influence competitive advantage in their market-place and then develop their strategy to deal with each. Porter (1985) proposed three primary types of strategies companies can use to gain competitive advantage. They are *cost leadership*, *differentiation*, and *focus* (niche). In **Table 12.2**, Porter's three classic strategies are described first, followed by descriptions of nine other general strategies that can be used to gain a competitive advantage. Applying the right kinds of technology can enhance each of these strategies.

TABLE 12.2 **Strategies for Competitive Advantage**

Strategy	Description
Cost leadership	Produce product/service at the lowest cost in the industry.
Differentiation	Offer different products, services, or product features.
Niche	Select a narrow-scope segment (market niche) and be the best in quality, speed, or cost in that segment.
Growth	Increase market share, acquire more customers, or sell more types of products.
Alliance	Work with business partners in partnerships, alliances, joint ventures, or virtual companies.
Innovation	Introduce new products/services; put new features in existing products/services; develop new ways to produce products/services.
Operational effectiveness	Improve the manner in which internal business processes are executed so that the firm performs similar activities better than its rivals.
Customer orientation	Concentrate on customer satisfaction.
Time	Treat time as a resource, then manage it, and use it to the firm's advantage.
Entry barriers	Create barriers to entry. By introducing innovative products or using IT to provide exceptional service, companies can create entry barriers to discourage new entrants.
Customer or supplier lock-in	Encourage customers or suppliers to stay with you rather than going to competitors. Reduce customers' bargaining power by locking them in.
Increase switching costs	Discourage customers or suppliers from going to competitors for economic reasons.

Porter's Value Chain Model Another useful strategic management tool is Porter's Value Chain. The **Value Chain Model** identifies where the greatest value exists in an organization and how that value can be increased. Understanding how your company creates value and identifying ways to add even greater value are essential in developing a competitive strategy. Porter proposed a general-purpose value chain that any organization can use to examine all its activities and their relationships to each other. These activities fall into two major categories: primary and support.

Primary activities are those business activities directly involved in the production of goods. Primary activities relate directly to the creation, sale, maintenance, and support of a product or services. The five **primary activities** are as follows:

1. **Inbound logistics**—acquisition, receipt and control of raw materials and other inputs
2. **Operations**—manufacturing, packaging, production control and quality control
3. **Outbound logistics**—order handling, delivery, invoicing
4. **Sales and marketing**—sales campaigns, order taking, social networking, sales analysis, market research
5. **Servicing**—customer service including warranty and maintenance

Primary activities usually occur sequentially, from 1 to 5. As work progresses, value is added to the product in each activity. To be more specific, incoming materials (1) are processed (in receiving, storage, etc.) in activities called inbound logistics. Next, the materials are used in operations (2), where significant value is added by the process of turning raw materials into products. Products need to be prepared for delivery (packaging, storing, and shipping) in the outbound logistics activities (3). Then sales and marketing (4) attempt to sell the products to customers, increasing product value by creating demand for the company's products. The value of a sold item is much larger than that of an unsold one. Finally, after-sales service (5), such as warranty service or upgrade notification, is performed for the customer, further adding value.

Four main support activities feed into one or more of the primary activities:

1. **Accounting, legal and finance**—legal, accounting, financial management
2. **Human resources (HR) management**—personnel, recruitment, training, staff planning
3. **Product and technology development**—product and process design, production engineering, market testing, R & D
4. **Procurement**—supplier management, funding, subcontracting

Each support activity can be applied to any or all the primary activities. Support activities may also support each other, as shown in **Figure 12.3**.

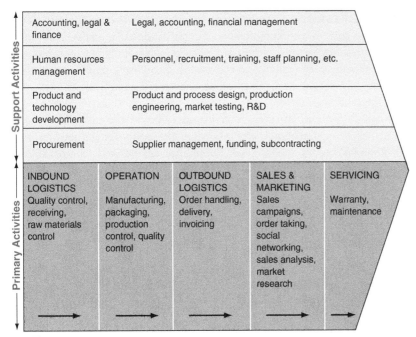

FIGURE 12.3 Porter's value chain. The arrows represent the flow of goods, services, and data in an organization.

IT Agility, Responsiveness, and Flexibility To be competitive, an organization relies heavily on IT **agility**, **responsiveness**, and **flexibility.** The benefit of IT agility is that it enables an organization to take advantage of opportunities faster and more effectively. The benefit of IT responsiveness is that IT capacity can be quickly increased or decreased as needed in a business.

The benefits of IT flexibility enable an organization to easily change its functions and processes. For example, wireless networks are more flexible than wired infrastructure. They can be set up, moved, or removed easily, without dealing with cables and other physical requirements of wired networks. Mass migration to mobile devices from PCs has expanded the scope of IT beyond traditional organizational boundaries—making location practically irrelevant.

IT agility, flexibility, and mobility are tightly interrelated and fully dependent on an organization's IT infrastructure and architecture, as discussed in Chapter 2.

Once an enterprise has developed a competitive edge, it can only be maintained and sustained by continually pursuing new and better ways to compete. Maintaining a competitive advantage requires forecasting trends and industry changes and figuring out what the company needs to do to stay ahead of the game. It demands continuously tracking competitors and their future plans and promptly taking corrective action. It's important to remember that while IT plays a key role in competitive advantage, that advantage is short-lived if competitors quickly duplicate it.

Agility means being able to respond quickly.

Responsiveness means that IT capacity can be easily scaled up or down as needed, which essentially requires cloud computing.

Flexibility means having the ability to quickly integrate new business functions or to easily reconfigure software or apps.

Competing Globally

Alongside their general business strategy, many organizations develop a global business strategy to compete in today's globalized economy. **Globalization** is a multifaceted phenomenon of cross-border trade and interconnectedness of the economics, politics, and culture among countries. Differences between culture and language, business practices, raw material supply chains, manufacturing and product specifications (imperial vs. metric), logistics (miles vs. kilometers; different national holidays), immigration policies, political and legal systems all affect the way companies must operate. While globalization increases opportunities in the marketplace, heightens competition, and increases revenue, it can also undermine whole country or industry sector economies because of skill and labor cost discrepancies in different countries around the world.

Globalization is the free trade of goods and services across national borders and cultures as the interdependence of nation's economies grows driven by people, technology, information, and cash flow.

IT Drives Globalization Five major drivers, all based on change—political, technological, market conditions, cost, and competition—lead organizations to globalize their operations. Of these, technology is now at the forefront of globalization creating new jobs, innovations, and networking sites to allow individuals and companies to connect globally. In today's connected world, IT and the Internet are enabling a new wave of globalization (**Figure 12.4**). To stay competitive in an international market, a company must use the latest technological innovations to produce and distribute goods and services in the most efficient and cost-effective way. With the help of IT and the Internet, an organization's target market and revenues need no longer be confined within national borders, enabling even the smallest companies to compete in global trade.

FIGURE 12.4 Riding the globalization wave.

Products, communication, and information sharing based upon or improved by IT are present in almost every aspect of life in industrial societies around the globe. For example, the Internet has transformed the way that organizations operate and have created entirely new ways for retailers and their customers to make transactions. The media and entertainment industries have been dramatically transformed with websites, blogs, instant messaging, e-mail, social media, and other Internet-based communication systems make it much easier for companies and professionals with common interests to connect, exchange information, and collaborate. Education at all levels is continually transforming thanks to innovations in communication, education, and presentation software. Some specific examples of IT-enabled globalization include the following:

- A smartphone has a body manufactured in Taiwan, assembled in China, runs software developed in the United States, and is sold at retail stores around the world.
- A small enterprise can sell goods to consumers in multiple countries on Amazon and eBay with no setup costs.
- Individual craftspeople can list their goods on Etsy to peddle their wares around the globe.
- A lecture given by a South African professor teaching in an Australian university via a Web conference transmitted to students in the United States.
- Companies set up Facebook pages to get customer feedback without the added expense of market researchers.

- The car you purchased in Canada is made of parts manufactured all over the world. An engine manufactured by robots in the United Kingdom, bodywork from India, headlights from the United States, tires from France, alloy wheels from Rumania, glass from Germany, bumpers and accessories from Spain, a drive system from Austria, and a suspension system from Sweden.

- Over the Internet people around the globe can read a breaking news story about the deadly Corona virus that started in China in real time and take necessary precautions about travel and how to stay healthy.

- Computer hardware produced in Asia is shipped to the United States for quality control before being shipped to a retailer in Canada.

While these technologies allow the spread of ideas to improve people's lives and increase company revenues, they can also widen the gap between those who have access and those who don't. However, those companies that don't have IT access are denied many of the opportunities to compete globally and the "digital divide" becomes even greater.

When Countries Compete

Globalization can occur at an individual level, company level, industry level, or country level. **Comparative advantage** is a term used when *countries* compete to gain an economic competitive advantage by producing products and services for a lower **opportunity cost** than other countries. This means that the cost of producing goods or services is less than the opportunity lost by not producing them. The concept of opportunity cost can be difficult to grasp. To help you understand it better, in **Tech Note 12.1** we present a simple example of a choice you've probably had to make at one time or another during your time in college.

> **Comparative advantage** is a country's ability to produce goods or services more efficiently and inexpensively than another.
>
> **Opportunity cost** is the benefit that is missed or given up when an individual, business, or country chooses one alternative over another.

Tech Note 12.1

How Does "Opportunity Cost" Work?

Opportunity cost is a concept that can be difficult to grasp. It not only applies to countries but also to organizations and individuals. To help you understand the concept, here's a simple example that you can relate to.

It's two days until the final exam in your information systems course. There are three different ways you can spend your time between now and then. You can work out at the gym, surf social media, or read this book. Ideally, you want to spend time doing all of these, but time is getting short and you must choose one way to spend your time. This means you will have to decide on your *next best choice*.

Right now, it's safe to say that instead of reading this textbook, you would prefer to work out at the gym to improve your body or surf social media to catch up with friends. However, choosing not to read this book might not be the best decision given that you've been struggling in the course and you need to improve your grade. One way of making the best decision in this situation is to evaluate the difference between what you are gaining and what you are giving up when you choose one decision over another. This difference is called the opportunity cost.

To calculate the opportunity cost of engaging in each activity—reading this book, surfing social media, or working out at the gym—we assign a number between 1 and 10 to reflect how much you value the outcome of each activity. Let's assume that in comparing your options you give reading this book to get a better grade a 9, surfing social media to catch up with friends a 6, and working out at the gym to improve your body an 8. Now, we can calculate the opportunity cost.

1. If you choose to **read this book,** you will improve your chances of getting a better grade on the final exam, but you will *give up* the opportunity to catch up with friends and improve your body. The opportunity cost would be the difference between a better grade (9) and the enjoyment gained by surfing social media (6) plus time lost working out at the gym to get a better body (8). In this case, the opportunity cost is $9 - (8+6) = 5$.

2. If you choose to spend your time **surfing social media**, you will enjoy catching up with friends, but you will *give up* the opportunity to earn a better grade and get a better body. The opportunity cost would be the difference between surfing social media (6) and a better grade (9) plus a better body (8). In this case, the opportunity cost is $6 - (8+9) = 11$.

3. If you choose to spend your time **working out at the gym**, you will get a better body, but you will *give up* the opportunity to get a better grade and catch up with your friends on social media. The opportunity cost will be a better grade and time lost hanging out with your friends on social media. The opportunity cost would be the difference between getting a better body (8) and getting a better grade (9) plus hanging out with friends on social media (6). In this case, the opportunity cost is $8 - (9+6) = 7$.

Comparing the trade-offs of each option in this example, your *next best choice* to spending time doing everything is reading this book. It has the lowest opportunity cost, which essentially means that the advantages you associate with getting a better grade are greater than the disadvantages you associate with not working out at the gym and surfing social media.

A country's comparative advantage usually comes from an abundance of natural resources or human capital that results in lower price, higher quality, or time savings. Traditionally, countries have gained a comparative advantage by producing *goods* to sell to other countries. For example, China's huge population enabled it to be a leader in producing a variety of products more cheaply than other countries. Japan's innovative process improvements in productivity based on the Japanese work ethics and culture enabled it to become the home to six of the top ten largest vehicle manufacturers in the world. Saudi Arabia gets its comparative advantage from its abundance of oil. Canada from its large quantities of lumber. Central American companies have a plentiful supply of bananas and the United States is a leader in computer software, quantum computing, and satellite technology because of its large numbers of highly skilled computer engineers and innovative researchers. Some developing countries such as Japan have benefited to such a great degree from a **goods-based comparative advantage** that they are now classified as developed countries.

Goods-based comparative advantage A situation in which a country can produce goods for a lower opportunity cost than other countries.

IT-Enabled **Service-Based Comparative Advantage**

Information technology has made the concept of global competition more relevant than ever for governments. For example, two types of technology—*information communications technology (ICT)* like the Internet, social media, smartphones, wireless mobile devices, and information kiosks and *support technology* like network servers, data centers, and cloud computing—play a particularly important part in changing a country's ability to compete in the world marketplace. It's not the availability of the actual technology that contributes to changes in the way that countries can gain a comparative advantage. It's the way it's being used to enable the creation of large-scale exportable business, financial, and entertainment *services* not previously possible, including call centers, knowledge portals, medical transcription services, electronic publishing, telemarketing, and help desks that is making the difference by providing countries with a **service-based comparative advantage**.

Service-based comparative advantage A country's capacity to produce and sell services at a lower opportunity cost than its trading partners.

The rising number of countries who are turning to services to gain a comparative advantage in world trade is particularly evident in developing nations where they are making particularly significant strides in becoming more active and more successful participants in the global economy and ICT makes comparative advantage more relevant than ever. The examples provided in **IT at Work 12.1** are just two of the many innovative IT-enabled services that are creating new opportunities for developed and developing countries to gain a comparative advantage, reduce trade barriers, and create a more integrated global economy.

IT at Work 12.1

India and Australia Use ICT to Gain a Comparative Advantage

India has a huge number of young educated English speakers in its population that can now be connected cheaply and instantaneously with the rest of the English-speaking world to provide cost-effective call center outsourcing services 24/7. If a company in another country considers that choosing a call center in India rather than maintaining one locally has a low opportunity cost, it will choose to outsource its services there. Currently, many companies in many different industry sectors buy services from call centers in India as a cheaper alternative to locally based call centers; in fact, having call centers in India has become the norm for many large-scale organizations around the globe. IT-enabled call centers offer India a comparative advantage based on volume, time, and cost.

When the Australian government committed to digitizing all its medical records, it led to the development of a large population of highly skilled medical transcriptionists. This has created a market for the worldwide large-scale export of Australian-based medical transcription services. This is how it works. At the end of a long day a radiologist in a Western Hemisphere Country such as the United States, Canada, or Latin America can send notes to a transcriptionist in Australia who will transcribe the notes during their work hours and return them via secure e-mail. By the time the radiologist reports to work the next morning, the radiology report is waiting for her. The fast turnaround not only saves time and cost (because of the favorable exchange rate between the AUD and the US dollar) but also enables a faster diagnosis that can result in more immediate treatment and better cure rates for the patient. Medical transcription is providing Australia with a comparative advantage based on human capital and time.

Questions

1. What is business–IT alignment?
2. Why would an IT department want to achieve business–IT alignment?
3. What is the difference between the goals of a business strategy and an IT strategy?
4. Name the five activities that organizations need engage in to improve business–IT alignment.
5. How does business–IT alignment help companies gain a competitive advantage in the marketplace?
6. What are the seven skills that a CIO needs to help improve business–IT alignment?
7. Name the five competitive forces in Porter's five forces model.
8. In what ways can ICT help a country achieve a comparative advantage?

12.2 IT Strategic Planning, Process, and Tools

LO12.2 Describe *the three levels of an IT strategic plan, identify the five components of an IT strategy, and describe two tools that are useful in the strategic planning process.*

Just as business strategic planning covers three levels of the organization—strategic, managerial, and operational—IT strategic planning must do the same. Management at each level operates within a different time frame. C-level managers focus on an organization's long-term strategic goals. Mid-level managers concentrate on medium-term objectives. Operational-level personnel work "in the moment" to complete shorter-term and daily tasks.

Industry, sector, and specific competitive environments as well as emerging technology trends all shape IT strategy. For an organization to be fully effective, strategic, managerial, and operational plans must be consistent, mutually supportive, and focused on achieving the organization's overall mission. In other words, they must be closely aligned. To closely align IT with business objectives, **IT strategic planning** must also focus on managing and aligning IT with all three levels of the organization. IT strategy directs all IT investments including social, mobile, analytics, cloud, and other digital technology resources as they relate to fundamental issues such as an organization's position in its industry, its available resources and options, and future directions. When an organization is developing an IT strategy, it should ask questions such as the following:

IT strategic planning is the process of defining an organization's strategy or direction in adopting, implementing, using, and disposing of its IT assets.

- What is the long-term direction of the business?
- What is the overall plan for deploying resources?
- What trade-offs are necessary? What resources will need to be shared?
- What is the company's position compared to that of its competitors?
- How does a company achieve competitive advantage over rivals in order to achieve maximize profitability?

The Five Components of an IT Strategy

Ideally, an IT strategy should include five components that cover all aspects of the IT function:

- Applications strategy
  - Plan the direction and principles concerning the development, operation, and maintenance of IT applications throughout the enterprise.
- Integration strategy
  - Consider how to connect all IT applications in a seamless way.
- Infrastructure strategy
  - Develop and maintain the IT infrastructure including its safety and security.
- Services strategy
  - Plan for, provide, and manage IT services when, where, and at what level the business and its different functional areas require.

- Sourcing strategy
  - Plan how to acquire IT infrastructure, software, and services either internally or with one or more external suppliers.

Identifying Value Drivers

Value driver enhances the value of a product or service to consumers, creating value for the company. Advanced IT, reliability, and brand reputation are examples.

To make targeted improvements business activities in core process areas that create significant value and work together with other factors to drive future revenue and profit at or above the current rate must be identified. These business activities are commonly referred to as **value drivers**.

Effective long-term strategic planning starts with a clear understanding of these value drivers. But, it's not sufficient to identify high-level value drivers such as *cost* and link them directly to daily business activities, since cost is almost always a value driver. For a value driver to be useful, it is necessary to drill down to identify the specific business activities that impact it. In the case of cost, this may supply and demand, cost of raw materials, cost of labor, cost of equipment, etc. The general types of value drivers are explained in **Table 12.3**. Since value drivers can have a limited life span, their value can diminish due to changes in the economy or industry. Consequently, it is important to regularly review the importance of each value driver to the business and replace them with more relevant value drivers as the need arises.

TABLE 12.3   **Three General Types of Business Value Drivers**

Type of Business Value Drivers	Definitions	Examples
Operational—Shorter-term factors	Factors that impact cash flow and the cash generation ability through increased efficiency or growth	Cost of raw materials, cost of providing service, cost per mile, sales volume, sales revenue
Financial—Medium-term factors	Factors that minimize the cost of capital incurred by the company to finance operations	Debt level, working capital, capital expenditures, day's receivables, bad debt expense
Sustainability—Long-term factors	Survival factors; factors that enable a business to continue functioning consistently and optimally for a long time	Government regulations, industry standards, federal and state environmental laws, privacy and security regulations

A Reactive Approach to IT Investments Will Fail

When an organization does not engage in IT strategic planning, systems are developed in a piece-meal manner and they don't effectively contribute to the overall strategic vision of the organization or enable it to respond to market changes. Making decision for IT investments based on an immediate need or threat—rather than on a carefully crafted IT strategy—might be necessary at times, but reactive approaches result in incompatible, redundant, expensive-to-maintain, or failed systems. These IT investments tend to be patches that rarely align with the business strategy.

Two of the biggest risks and concerns of top management are (1) failing to align IT to real business needs and, as a result, (2) failing to deliver value to the business. Since IT has a dramatic effect on business performance and competitiveness, the failure to create a well-thought out IT strategy to effectively manage IT seriously impacts business performance.

Developing an IT Strategic Plan

IT strategic plan is a formal document that details how the IT department will provide, support, and ensure ongoing business operations.

The end result of IT strategic planning is the development of a comprehensive **IT strategic plan** that will guide future investments in the acquisition, implementation, operation, maintenance, and eventual disposal of IT assets. The four objectives of the IT strategic plan are to

1. Improve management's understanding of IT opportunities and limitations
2. Assess current performance
3. Identify capacity and human resource requirements
4. Clarify the level of investment required

An effective IT strategic plan consists of three main components: *a long-range IT plan*, a *medium-term IT plan,* and an *IT tactical plan,* all of which should be closely aligned with the overall *strategic business plan* (**Figure 12.5**).

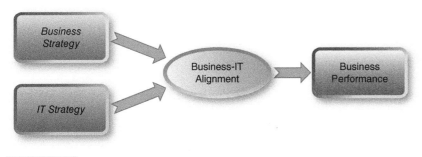

FIGURE 12.5   IT strategic plan components.

The **long-range IT plan**—sometimes referred to as the strategic IT plan—aligns with strategic-level business planning. The IT strategic plan starts with the IT vision and strategy, which defines the future concept of what IT should do to achieve the goals, objectives, and strategic position of the firm and how this will be achieved. The overall direction, requirements, and sourcing—either outsourcing or insourcing—of resources, such as infrastructure, application services, data services, security services, IT governance, and management architecture; budget; activities; and time frames are set for three to five years into the future. The planning process continues by addressing lower-level activities with a shorter time frame.

The **medium-term IT plan** more closely aligns with managerial or administrative level business planning. It focuses on general project plans in terms of the specific requirements and sourcing of resources as well as the **project portfolio**. The project portfolio lists major resource projects, including infrastructure, application services, data services, and security services, that are consistent with the long-range plan. Some companies may define their portfolio in terms of applications. The **applications portfolio** is a list of major, approved information system projects that are also consistent with the long-range plan. Expectations for sourcing of resources in the project or applications portfolio should be driven by the business strategy. Since some of these projects will take more than a year to complete and others will not start in the current year, this plan extends over several years.

The **tactical IT plan** aligns with operational-level business planning. It must be created to develop budgets and schedules for current-year projects and daily activities. Managers and supervisors at the operational level work closely with the workforce and customers to make sure employees have the resources necessary to carry out their roles and customers are well served and satisfied. Detailed data in real time or near real time is necessary for workers to do their job and close the deal. They need to be provided with data needed to track work schedules and employee performance; inventory levels; sales activity and order fulfillment; production output and delivery schedules; and resolve disruptions or deviations from expected outcomes. Since all other systems work from data captured or created at this level, ensuring the accuracy and consistency of operational data is vital.

IT Strategic Planning Process and Tools

To create an IT strategic plan, it's important to follow a prescribed IT strategic planning process. An effective IT strategic planning process is critical to an organization's long-term success and health and is essential to support consistent decision-making about IT investments at all levels of the business. An IT strategic planning process must be integrated, holistic, and sustainable. When IT activities are synchronized with the organization's strategic direction, the IT function has greater credibility and is considered a trust partner throughout the various departments in the organization. Demonstrating inclusiveness by consolidating expertise and ideas from across the organization and closely aligning IT investments with the organization's direction are the hallmarks of a holistic strategic planning process. An organization's goals and the environment in which it operates change over time. It is not enough to develop a one-time long-term IT strategic plan. It is critical that the plan be an ongoing process in which the changing needs of the business vis-à-vis the existing portfolio of IT assets are regularly evaluated. To be sustainable, the IT strategic plan must be reviewed on a monthly, quarterly, or annual basis to determine shifts in an organization's business direction or environment and update the IT strategic plan to stay abreast of any changes. To do this, strategic planning cycles should be established to identify potentially beneficial IT services, perform cost–benefit analyses, prioritize, and allocate resources to its list of potential projects.

Specifics of the IT strategic planning process, of course, vary among organizations. Each enterprise has its own way of conducting the strategic planning process and approach that fits its own culture and leadership style. For those companies that haven't yet established an IT strategic planning process or aren't seeing the benefits they'd hoped for from an already established process, Intel's IT Strategic Planning Process (**Tech Note 12.2**) provides an excellent model to follow.

Tech Note 12.2

Intel's Six-Step IT Strategic Planning Process

Intel uses a six-step IT strategic planning process that closely aligns IT investments and solutions to strategic planning at the corporate level. This business–IT alignment was achieved by bringing together a variety of perspectives from senior management, IT, and business groups in the planning stage as shown in steps 1 through 4 in **Figure 12.6**. To minimize time demands, the strategic planning team engaged subject matter experts at critical points instead of involving them at every step of the process.

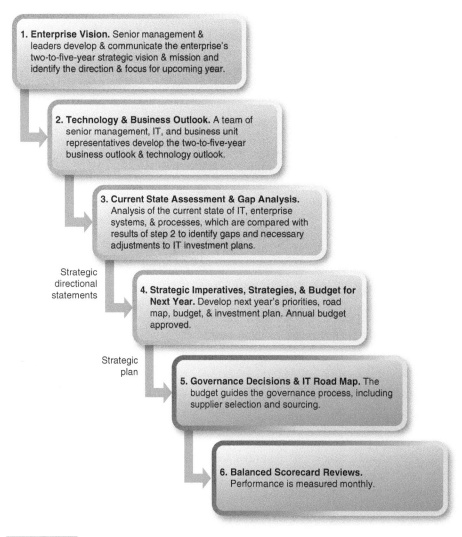

FIGURE 12.6 Model of Intel's six-step IT strategic planning process. Planning phase: steps 1 to 4. Decision-making phase: step 5. Measuring and evaluation phase: step 6.

The activities in the planning, decision-making, measuring, and evaluation phases of Intel's six-step process flow naturally from one step to the next. The business and IT strategic plans are evaluated and adjusted annually to keep pace with rapid changes in the industry. Using this IT strategic planning process, Intel has improved agility, performance, and sustainability. It has provided a clear and credible direction for the enterprise and supports consistent decision-making at all levels of the business.

Strategic Planning Tools

Various functions in the organization—such as manufacturing, R&D (research and development), and IT—are the most successful when their strategies are forward looking. Forward looking means an organization evaluates its full potential by conducting an analysis of its strengths, weaknesses, opportunities, and threats within the political, social economic, and technical environments in which it will be operating in the future. This is known as a SWOT analysis. Based on the result of the SWOT analysis, the organization is better equipped to decide on the best way to allocate resources to develop critical capabilities. In practice, competing agendas, tight budgets, poor interdepartmental communication, and politics can turn strategic planning discussions into bar room brawls—if they are not well managed.

SWOT Analysis The SWOT analysis is a useful evaluation tool that enables an organization to develop and confirm the goals of its corporate and IT strategies to increase business performance and profitability.

The SWOT analysis begins with the evaluation of internal **strengths** and **weaknesses** in your organization, followed by an examination of external **opportunities** and **threats** that may affect the organization based on the market and the overall environment of the organization. Examples of some of the strengths, weaknesses, opportunities, and threats commonly experienced by organizations are shown in **Figure 12.7**.

The primary purpose of a SWOT analysis is to help an organization become fully aware of all the factors that are involved in making a business decision. A SWOT analysis is the most useful when it is completed in the early stages of the strategic planning process. By performing a SWOT analysis before an organization commits to any sort of action, including setting new initiatives, revamping internal policies, or considering opportunities for new markets, it can develop effectives strategies by capitalizing on its strengths and opportunities to overcome its weaknesses and threats.

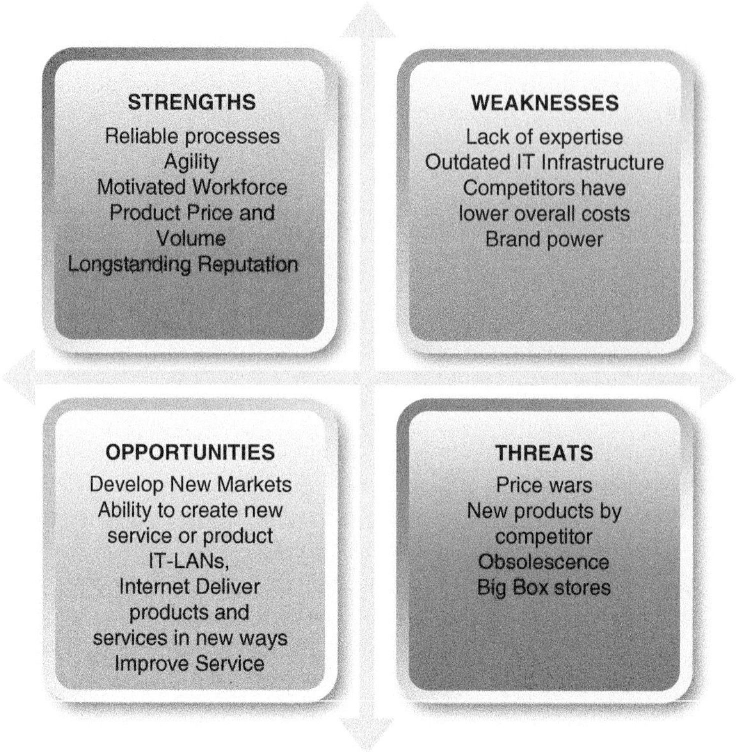

STRENGTHS
Reliable processes
Agility
Motivated Workforce
Product Price and
Volume
Longstanding Reputation

WEAKNESSES
Lack of expertise
Outdated IT Infrastructure
Competitors have
lower overall costs
Brand power

OPPORTUNITIES
Develop New Markets
Ability to create new
service or product
IT-LANs,
Internet Deliver
products and
services in new ways
Improve Service

THREATS
Price wars
New products by
competitor
Obsolescence
Big Box stores

FIGURE 12.7 SWOT analysis consists of a realistic evaluation of internal strengths and weaknesses and external opportunities and threats.

For example, any company looking to expand its business operations into a developing country must investigate that country's political and economic stability and critical infrastructure. In this case, strategic analysis might include reviewing the U.S. Central Intelligence Agency's (CIA) *World Factbook.*

The *World Factbook* provides information on the history, people, government, economy, geography, communications, transportation, military, and transnational issues for 266 world entities. Then the company would need to investigate competitors and their potential reactions to a new entrant into their market.

Equally important, the company would need to assess its ability to compete profitably in the market and impacts of the expansion on other parts of the company. For example, having excess production capacity would require less capital than if a new factory needed to be built. In the **IT Toolbox** at the end of this chapter, you will learn how to conduct a SWOT analysis of a business and of yourself.

Balanced scorecard is a strategic management methodology for evaluating performance based on both financial and nonfinancial metrics.

The Balanced Scorecard

The **balanced scorecard (BSC)** is another useful strategic planning tool that looks at all aspects of an organization from four unique perspectives. It helps organizations clarify and update their strategy, align the IT strategy with the business strategy, and link strategic objectives to long-term goals and annual budgets. The result is a visual blueprint that an organization can use to select strategic measures to improve business performance. Using a BSC also enhances strategic awareness and better align business and IT in both small and large companies.

The BSC methodology is typically used at the end of the strategic planning process to review performance on a regular basis. For example, Intel used a BSC approach to measure its business performance in the final step of its six-step IT strategic planning process (Figure 12.7). The BSC is used to translate strategic plans and mission statements into a set of **business objectives** and performance metrics that can be quantified and measured to evaluate how well objectives are being achieved.

Business objectives are the goals of an organization and the building blocks of a strategy.

Business objectives set out what the business is trying to achieve. They are action-oriented statements that define the continuous improvement activities that must be done to be successful, that is, achieve a return on investments (ROI) of at least 8% in 2020. Well-thought-out objectives should meet the five "SMART" criteria shown in **Figure 12.8**.

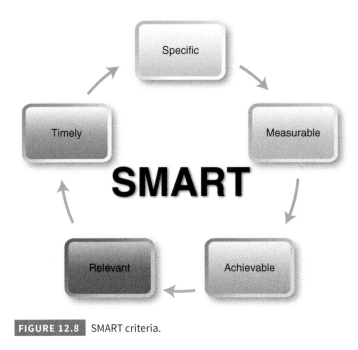

FIGURE 12.8 SMART criteria.

Traditionally, the typical business objective could be summed up simply as *to make a profit*. As a result, performance metrics have typically been based on quantitative measures such as the following:

- **P&L (profit and loss) reports**—revenue, expenses, net profit
- **Cash flow statements**—is there enough cash to cover current liabilities?
- **Balance sheets**—that reflect the overall status of finances at a certain date

These financial metrics are called **lagging indicators** because they quantify past performance. As such, they represent historical information and are not ideal tools for managing day-to-day operations and planning.

Lagging indicators confirm what has happened. They evaluate outcomes and achievements.

Today, many managers are frustrated by the inadequacies of traditional quantitative performance measures and have completely abandoned financial measures. However, most managers don't want to have to choose between financial and operational measures. Instead, they want a balanced presentation of measures that allow them to view the company from several perspectives simultaneously. The BSC provides this. Companies that use the BSC can improve their IT strategic planning process by

- **Clarifying** or updating a business strategy
- **Linking** strategic objectives to long-term targets and annual budgets
- **Integrating** strategic objectives into resource allocation processes
- **Increasing** companywide understanding of the corporate vision and strategy

The Four Different Perspectives of the BSC The BSC measures and evaluates an organization's performance from four different perspectives to ensure that limited resources are invested to achieve the highest possible ROI. These perspectives are as follows:

1. **Financial** To succeed financially, how should we appear to our investors and shareholders?
2. **Customer** To achieve our vision, how should we provide value to our customers?
3. **Business processes** To satisfy our shareholders and customers, what business processes must we focus on and excel at?
4. **Innovation, learning, and growth** To achieve our vision, how will we sustain our ability to innovate, learn, change, and improve?

The BSC method is "balanced" because it does not rely solely on traditional financial measures. Instead, it balances financial measures with three forward-looking nonfinancial measures, as shown in **Figure 12.9**.

The BSC is not a template that can be applied to business in general or even to an entire industry. Different market situations, product strategies, and competitive environments require different scorecards. Business units need to devise customized scorecards to fit their mission, strategy, technology, and culture. Some examples of measurement criteria that can be used within each of these perspectives are shown in **Table 12.4**.

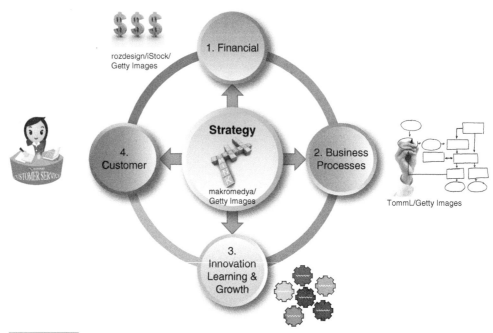

FIGURE 12.9 BSC uses four metrics to measure performance—one financial metric and three nonfinancial metrics.

TABLE 12.4 **Examples of BSC Measurement Criteria**

Perspective	Objective	Measurement
Financial	• Increase profits • Decrease costs • Increase revenue • Provide better value for stakeholders	• Revenue • Revenue growth rates • Earnings and cash flow • Asset utilization • Project profitability
Customer	• Produce better quality product • Provide top-quality customer service • Offer better value for money	• Market share • Customer acquisition, retention, loyalty • Customer relationships, satisfaction, likes, recommendations, loyalty • Brand image, reputation • Price–value relationship
Internal business processes	• Increase production • More efficiently use materials • Achieve excellence in quality control	• Cycle times, rate of defects • Production throughput, productivity rates • Cost per process • Cost per transaction • Safety Incident Index • Analysis of social network posts • Customer satisfaction survey
Innovation, learning, and growth	• Sustain our ability to change • Improve through training • Increase number of employee certifications • Hire better qualified personnel • Increase retention rate • Increase number of innovative products and processes	• Employee skills, morale, turnover, capacity for change • IT capabilities • Percentage of revenue from new products/services • Employee motivation • Employee qualifications • R & D results

The general steps to follow in the BSC methodology are

1. Establish the organization's vision for the future.
2. Identify BSC performance metrics that link vision and strategy to results (Figure 12.9)
3. Select meaningful strategic objectives (**Figure 12.10**).
4. Measure each objective (**Figure 12.11**).
5. Set target(s) for each objective (Figure 12.11).
6. Determine the action(s) and initiative(s) needed to achieve each target (Figure 12.11).
7. Implement necessary tracking, analytics, communication, and reporting systems, including sensors, data visualization, mashups, and dashboards via social and mobile channels.
8. Collect, analyze, and compare performance data with targets.
9. Revise actions to improve performance gaps and take advantage of new opportunities.

To help you better understand how the BSC methodology works in **IT at Work 12.2** we provide a real-world example of how a BSC adds value to the IT strategic planning process at a low-cost airline, starting with the business vision and strategy.

IT at Work 12.2

Applying the BSC at a Low-Cost Airline

To a large extent, low-cost airlines such as JetBlue and Southwest Airlines compete on price. But customers don't choose an airline based solely on price. They are also looking for a more enjoyable travel experience. To develop a strategy to fulfill these goals, an organization can use the BSC to identify other value drivers that will make a customer choose them as their preferred airline. In addition to financial objectives such as competitive pricing, lower costs, and increased revenue, an organization must view its goals from a customer, business process, and learning and growth perspectives. A simple subset of these factors might include the following:

- Percent of on-time flights (Customer perspective)
- Rapid ground turnaround time (Internal business process perspective)
- Synchronized and efficient ground crew (Learning and growth perspective)

When you place each of these *objectives* into one of the four BSC perspectives (financial, customer, business process, learning and growth) and choose a way to *measure* them against a specific *target* you can develop clearly defined *actions* to achieve the objective. In **Figure 12.10,** we show a simplified strategy map that a low-cost airline might use. **Figure 12.11** illustrates examples of measurements, targets, and actions that could be taken to achieve an airline's objective of rapid ground turnaround time.

Now, let's take a closer look at how differences in how each airline operates might positively or negatively affect this objective. JetBlue has a policy that allows one free checked bag, while Southwest allows two free checked bags. On the surface this may seem a simple incentive based solely on competitive pricing, but there's more to it than meets the eye. Surprisingly, the free checked bag policy relates directly to achieving the process improvement objective of rapid ground turnaround time. The time it takes to board passengers affects the ability to take off on time, which in turn impacts on the ground turnaround time at departure and arrival time at destination.

How does this work? JetBlue has assigned seats. This allows the terminal crew to control boarding starting at the back of the plane to minimize the bottlenecks in the aisle. In contrast, Southwest has open seating and passengers typically take seats beginning at the front of the airplane. This can clog the aisle. More checked bags mean passengers need more time to place their bags into the overhead bins. Less checked bags mean less time and reduces ground turnaround time and increases the likelihood of an on-time departure that could lead to an on-time arrival at destination and no missed connections. Now we can see that Southwest is attempting to offset the inconvenience of the extra time needed for the open-seating boarding process by reducing the number of carry-on bags and the time it takes for passengers to place them into overhead compartments.

By measuring how well the targets for on-ground times, for example, no more than 55 minutes and percent of on-time departures (85%) are being met, both airlines can determine if their actions are optimal or need to be revised. To clarify and update their strategy, align the IT strategy with the business strategy, and link strategic objectives to long-term goals and annual budgets, low-cost airlines like JetBlue and Southwest have successfully used the BSC methodology to develop a strategic vision, create an agreed-upon set of objectives and measures, identify and set targets, and develop actions appropriate for the company's business model.

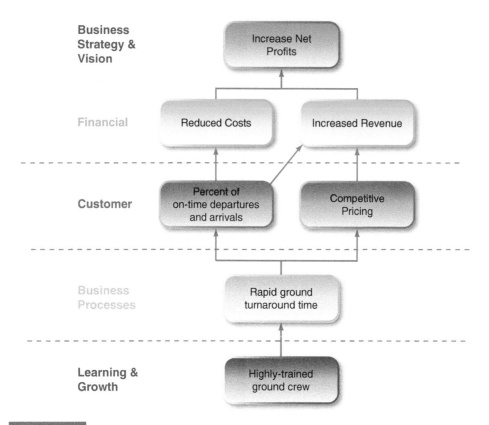

FIGURE 12.10 Overview of a low-cost airline's BSC objectives to fulfill business vision of profitability.

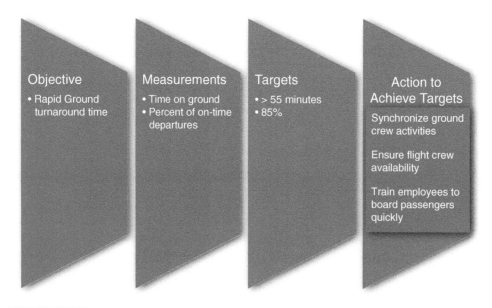

FIGURE 12.11 Examples of measurements, targets, and actions to achieve the objective of rapid ground turnaround time.

Process Deliverables   The deliverables from the IT strategic planning process should include the following:

1. An evaluation of the strategic goals and directions of the organization and how IT is aligned
2. A new or revised IT vision and assessment of the state of the IT department
3. A statement of the strategies, objectives, and policies for the IT department
4. The overall direction, requirements, and sourcing of resources

IT Steering Committee   The entire strategic planning process is often conducted by an IT steering committee. The **IT Steering Committee** is a team of managers and staff that represents various business units that establish IT priorities and ensures that the IT department is meeting the needs of the enterprise. The steering committee major tasks are listed in **Table 12.5**.

TABLE 12.5   **Five Tasks of a Steering Committee**

Task	Description
Set the direction	In linking the corporate strategy with the IT strategy, planning is the key activity.
Allocate scarce resources	The committee approves the allocation of resources for and within the information systems organization. This includes outsourcing policy.
Make staffing decisions	Key IT personnel decisions involve a consultation-and-approval process made by the committee, including outsourcing decisions.
Communicate and provide feedback	Information regarding IT activities should flow freely.
Set and evaluate performance metrics	The committee should establish performance measures for the IT department and see that they are met. This includes the initiation of SLAs.

The success of steering committees largely depends on the establishment of IT *governance*, formally established statements that direct the policies regarding IT alignment with organizational goals and allocation of resources. Not all organizations have a high-level IT steering committee. Instead, project priorities may be determined by the IT director, by his or her superior, by company politics, or even on a first-come, first-served basis.

Questions

1. What are the three levels of an IT strategic plan?
2. What is the purpose of the IT strategic planning process?
3. Why would an organization conduct a SWOT analysis?
4. What is the purpose of using the BSC in the IT strategic planning process?
5. How does the BSC approach differ from previous measurement approaches?
6. What are the four BSC perspectives?
7. What are the four deliverables of the IT strategic planning process?
8. What is the purpose of an IT steering committee?
9. What five tasks do the steering committee perform?
10. What are the three general types of business value drivers?

12.3 IT Sourcing Strategies and IT Service Management

LO12.3 Discuss *the two broad categories of IT sourcing strategies, the importance of IT service management, and the five phases of the outsourcing cycle.*

IT strategy guides an organization's IT investments decisions about how it will source the acquisition, support, and management of its information systems. Not all organizations are created equal. Some can hire the best IT workers available to develop their own systems, while others have limited resources that constrain their ability to even have a separate IT function. In very small companies, their entire "IT department" often consists of a worker in a non-IT department that has a natural aptitude for working with technology. In another, an organization may have the necessary IT resources, but can be more profitable or more customer focused by concentrating on its core competencies and leaving IT development to companies who specialize in systems development. In all cases, when acquiring and supporting technology, an organization must consider all its **IT sourcing** options.

> **IT sourcing** is the strategy used to acquire and maintain IT systems and IT services.

IT sourcing strategy options fall into two broad categories:

1. **In-house systems development.** Systems are developed or other IT work is done in-house by IT developers, IT operators, IT project managers, etc. Typically, IT that provides competitive advantages or that contain proprietary or confidential data are developed and maintained by the organization's own in-house IT function. Other nonsensitive in-house development might sometimes be carried out with the help of consulting companies or vendors.

> **Outsourcing** involves the development and maintenance of IT systems or IT services by an external service provider who is a third-party supplier or vendor.

2. **Outsourcing.** At most companies today, one or more types of outsourcing arrangements are used as part of their IT strategy. Strategies that can be used to outsource IT include the following:

   - *Offshoring* Systems development and/or support are provided by a supplier in a country that is different from the country of the sourcing organization.

   - *Onshoring* Systems development and/or support can be sourced to consulting companies or suppliers within the same country as the sourcing organization.

   - *Cloud services* IT services, from infrastructure to apps (Xaas), are delivered by a third-party vendor over the cloud.

In-house systems development is covered in detail in Chapter 13. In this chapter, we focus on describing IT offshoring, IT onshoring and cloud services.

IT Offshoring

> **Offshoring** is the practice of acquiring and maintaining IT systems and IT services from external third-party providers located in a different country from the company sourcing the systems and services.

Offshoring systems development has become a common practice due to global markets, lower costs, and increased access to skilled labor. About one-third of Fortune 500 companies outsource software development to software companies in India. It is not only the cost and the technical capabilities that matter. Several other factors to consider are the business and political climates in the selected country, the quality of the infrastructure, and risks such as IT competency, human capital, the economy, the legal environment, and cultural differences.

Duke University's *Center for International Business Education and Research* studied actual offshoring results. According to their study, Fortune 500 companies reduced costs by offshoring—63% of the companies achieved over 30% annual savings and 14% of them achieved savings over 50%. The respondents were overwhelmingly satisfied with their offshore operations. Three-quarters (72%) said their offshore implementations met or exceeded their expected cost savings. Almost one-third of the respondents (31%) achieved their service-level goals within the first five months of their contracts, while 75% did so within 12 months. The study concluded that "offshoring delivers faster results than average domestic improvement efforts." Even though these are very general results, offshoring success stories ease the fears about the risks of offshoring.

IT Onshoring

IT **onshoring** is the opposite of offshoring. It involves the relocation of business operations and processes to a lower-cost or high-quality location inside national borders to supply IT infrastructure, software, and services. IT onshoring is a good choice for organizations who need to seek outside resources but want to work with a supplier that is closer to home to get faster delivery of products and services. It is an advantageous and increasingly popular alternative to IT offshoring because it allows a company to increase efficiencies and productivity by concentrating on its core competencies, as demonstrated in our opening case.

The types of work that are ideal for onshoring include the following:

- Work that has not been routinized
- Work that if offshored would result in the client company losing too much control over critical operations
- Situations in which offshoring would place the client company at too great a risk to its data security, data privacy, or intellectual property and proprietary information
- Business activities that rely on an uncommon combination of specific application domain knowledge and IT knowledge in order to do the work properly

> **Onshoring** is the practice of acquiring and maintaining IT systems and services from external third-party providers located in the <u>same</u> country as the company sourcing the systems and services.

Cloud Services

As you have read in Chapter 2, in its simplest form, cloud computing is a way for companies to procure **anything as a service (XaaS)**, including infrastructure (IaaS), applications (AaaS), platforms (PaaS), and business processes, via the Internet. When legacy systems could no longer provide the functionality needed to solve the businesses problems, companies migrated to the cloud to connect core systems and apps. XaaS simplifies the deployment of IT and cut costs in organizations. It is a useful way to modernize operational and business models to be more efficient and engage customers, employees, and other stakeholders in new ways.

When they rely on XaaS, IT departments no longer have to make major capital investment or rely on employing highly skilled IT developers to get access to an IT resource. Instead, IT capabilities can be sourced, scaled on, and delivered on demand without physical location, labor, or capital restrictions. As a result, an enterprise's cloud strategy plays a role in its sourcing strategy and business growth.

Integrating Cloud with On-Premises Systems While the concept of cloud is simple, an enterprise's **cloud strategy** tends to be quite complex. Cloud is being adopted across more of the enterprise, but mostly in addition to on-premises systems—not as full replacements for them. Hybrid solutions create integration challenges. Cloud services—also referred to as **edge services**—have to integrate back-to-core internal systems. That is, edge services have to connect and share data with enterprise systems such as order and inventory management, ERP, CRM, SCM, legacy financial, and HR systems and on mobile and social platforms.

> **Cloud Strategy** A complex strategy to source scale and deliver IT capabilities on demand without physical location, labor, or capital restrictions in addition to on-premise systems.
>
> **Edge service** is a term that refers to a cloud service.

Tactical Adoption versus Coordinated Cloud Strategy Deploying cloud services incrementally results in apps and services that are patched together to create end-to-end business processes. This is a short-sighted **tactical adoption approach**. While this approach may have been sufficient in the recent past, cloud services are increasingly more sophisticated and numerous. Tactical approaches will cause difficult integration problems—as occurred with adoption of ERP, mobile, social, and big data systems. Cloud adoption needs to occur according to a coordinated strategy. Given the ever-changing cloud services, it will be tough to know how to design a sustainable cloud strategy. For example, a new class of cloud offerings is being built around business outcomes instead of as point solutions. In effect, this would be business outcomes as a service.

Determining cloud strategies and lease agreements that best support business needs may require hiring cloud consultants, such as Accenture, Booz Allen, Deloitte, Gartner, HP, IBM, or others.

Cloud Strategy Challenges From the outset, the top challenges about migrating to the cloud revolved around cybersecurity, privacy, data availability, and the accessibility of the service. The newer challenges relate to cloud strategy, including integration of cloud with on-premises resources, extensibility, and reliability of the cloud service. **Extensibility** is the ability to get data into and out of the cloud service. These cloud service challenges need to be addressed before deciding on sourcing solutions.

For example, when Nestlé Nespresso S. A. transitioned from a traditional coffee shop to an online distributor in the single-serving coffee machine category, Nespresso needed to replace its complex ERP. By deploying a cloud integration platform, Nespresso has integrated its ERP, warehouse management systems, and ordering tool. Nespresso now leverages its cloud and traditional IT solutions.

In another case, social network LinkedIn migrated to cloud services to support sales and CRM; it began by using noncustomized, out-of-the-box capabilities. As the company grew rapidly, the standard cloud services could no longer support the lines of business. Business processes increasingly needed to be integrated with ERP and proprietary systems to generate sales leads. LinkedIn switched to a cloud-based integration platform that is able to connect its lead generation, financial, and CRM systems and its proprietary apps and data warehouse. Integrating cloud and on-premises systems gives salespeople a single view of the data they need to do their jobs.

In both of the above examples, the migration was far from perfect at first, and hard lessons learned early helped achieve impressive results eventually. Companies have learned the following lessons about outsourcing:

1. **Manage change** by securing the commitment of senior leaders in an overt fashion and by recognizing subtle cultural differences that can undermine initial transition efforts.

2. **Assess organizational readiness** for a transition from a mental and technical standpoint and set realistic expectations and manage them actively.

3. **Anticipate risks and formulate a plan for mitigating them**, beginning with a strategy for dealing with "loss-of-control" threats, both real and imagined.

4. **Build project management infrastructure** that recognizes the "process of transition" needs to be managed as carefully as processes being transitioned. Mapping how the AP process should look post transition and how it will be managed end to end and by whom is important.

5. **Create a governance mechanism** that can discreetly collect feedback from the transition project manager and provide formal executive oversight and guidance. Form an executive steering committee that includes two senior managers from each organization and representation from all business units impacted by the outsourcing.

6. **Properly define how success will be measured,** both qualitatively and quantitatively. Identifying the right benchmarks for success and vigilantly measuring efforts against them over time are critical. eBay continued to outsource—transitioning its global vendor/supplier maintenance and general ledger activities.

Despite the challenges, today, the critical question is no longer whether cloud computing will be a fundamental deployment model for enterprise systems, such as ERP and SCM. Rather, the question is "How can companies profit from the capabilities that cloud computing offers?"

IT Service Management

The explosion of cloud-based apps and the anything-as-a service (XaaS) concept discussed in Chapter 2 has led to the IT function taking a strategic approach to the sourcing and management of **IT services** in support of business goals. **IT service management (ITSM)** not only delivers IT functionality but also focuses on co-creating business value by managing IT services, change requests, responding to problems and incidents, and managing IT assets and knowledge. To achieve this, ITSM focuses on two things: the services provided and the creation of a trusted **service relationship** among an organization's customers, vendors/suppliers and regulatory agencies and looks beyond technology to address issues related to people, processes, and governance (**Figure 12.12**).

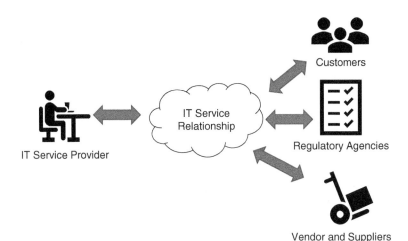

FIGURE 12.12 ITSM co-creates value among service providers, customers, vendors, suppliers, and regulatory agencies.

Levels and Types of IT Services

IT services can be sourced in three different ways—from a Type 1 **internal service provider**, a Type II **shared service provider,** or a Type III **external service provider**. As discussed above, when an organization gets its IT services from an external service provider, it is referred to as "outsourcing."

The complete set of services managed by a service provider is referred to as a **service portfolio**. The service portfolio consists of services that are currently being considered and developed, those that are currently supported, and those that are no longer offered. Any technology can be offered as a service to prevent an organization from having to install, manage, support, and operate technology and reduce upfront capital investment. An organization might source IT services such as support, management and self-service tools to configure and operate IT infrastructure, software apps, cloud database services, APIs, network services, data synchronization, data visualization, security, IoT monitoring, workflow and business process monitoring. One way in which organizations like University of Colorado at Colorado Springs, Lowes Home Improvement, Worcester Polytechnic Institute, Harley Davidson, and many others are getting the most benefit from their wide range of IT services is by taking a structured strategic approach to ITSM and establishing a formal IT Service Management Office (ITSMO). The overall goal of the IT function and the ITSMO is to implement the right processes, people, and technology to best meet strategic business objectives. To improve their ITSM initiatives, many organizations around the globe have adopted the IT Infrastructure Library (ITIL®).

ITIL®4   ITIL serves as a roadmap for process improvement to help IT professionals build a foundation for ongoing service excellence while meeting budget and regulatory requirements. Originally developed for the British Government, ITIL®4 is the most recent iteration that builds on earlier versions of ITIL to consider everything service providers and service consumers need to co-create business value efficiently and effectively. ITIL®4 is now controlled by AXELOS (**https://www.axelos.com/best-practice-solutions/itil**), a joint venture company created

---

IT services   is the application of business and technical expertise to enable organizations in creating, managing, optimizing, and accessing information and business processes.

IT service management (ITSM)   is a strategy by which IT systems are offered under contract to customers and performance is managed as a service to achieve greater business–IT alignment and smooth business processes and operations.

Service relationship   is the degree of cooperation between a service provider and service customers, vendors/suppliers, and regulatory agencies including service provision, service consumption, and service relationship management.

Internal service provider   delivers IT services to a single business unit in its own organization.

Shared service provider   provides IT services to different business units in its own organization.

External service provider   delivers IT services to customers outside the organization.

by the UK Cabinet Office and Capita, a public limited company, that manages, develops, and grows the Global Best Practice portfolio to help organizations become more effective in key business areas that include project, program, and ITSM.

ITIL®4 manages the IT life cycle and aligns IT resources with business needs to co-create value through the interaction of four different dimensions—organizations and people; information and technology; partners and suppliers; and value streams and processes that are each influenced by political, environmental, legal, technological, social, and economic factors (**Figure 12.13**).

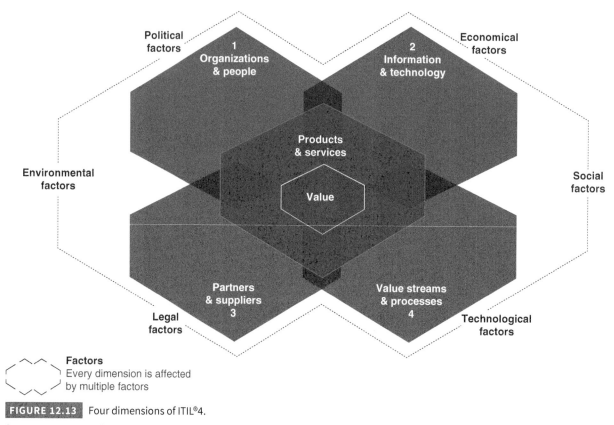

FIGURE 12.13 Four dimensions of ITIL®4.

(*Source:* Jouret, 2019).

Organizations and people   Organizational culture, systems of authority, roles, skills and competencies needed to plan, manage, and deliver IT services.

Information and technology   Information and technology needed to deliver IT services including servers, storage, networks, databases, etc. as well as that needed to manage the services such as tools, knowledge bases, configuration information, etc.

Partners and suppliers   No service provided can do everything. Partners and suppliers contribute in various ways to the services that are delivered. A service relationship must be nurtured to ensure effective service delivery.

Value streams and processes   All the activities, workflows, controls, and procedures necessary to provide high-quality on-time services to create value for customers and users.

To bring these four dimensions together and encourage service providers to work flexibly and cooperatively with them instead of working in silos, ITIL®4 uses a service value system (SVS) that promotes co-creation of value over optimization within each dimension and is directed by seven guiding principles (see **Figure 12.14**).

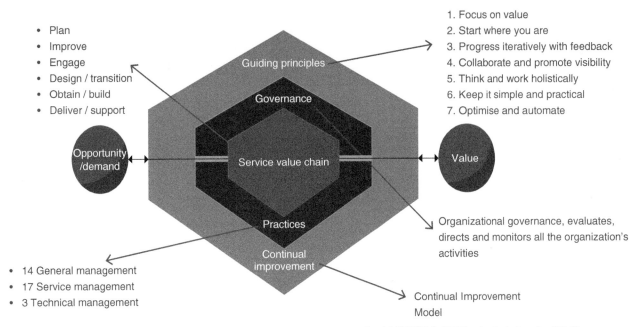

- Plan
- Improve
- Engage
- Design / transition
- Obtain / build
- Deliver / support

1. Focus on value
2. Start where you are
3. Progress iteratively with feedback
4. Collaborate and promote visibility
5. Think and work holistically
6. Keep it simple and practical
7. Optimise and automate

Guiding principles

Governance

Opportunity /demand

Service value chain

Value

Practices

Organizational governance, evaluates, directs and monitors all the organization's activities

Continual improvement

- 14 General management
- 17 Service management
- 3 Technical management

Continual Improvement Model

Copyright AXELOS Limited 2018 Reproduced under licence from AXELOS

FIGURE 12.14   ITIL®4 SVS.
(*Source:* Limited, 2019).

To begin the SVS, opportunities and demands trigger everything a service provider does. At the heart of the SVS is the service value chain that consists of six key activities that are needed to create and realize business value. These are given as follows:

1. **Plan**   Ensure a shared understanding of what the organization wants and how it will be done by creating plans, portfolios, architectures, policies, etc.

2. **Improve**   Create improvements initiatives to ensure continuous improvement of all products, services, and practices across all four ITSM dimensions.

3. **Engage**   Interact with stakeholders and understand their needs.

4. **Design and transition**   Create new and changes services and ensure stakeholders expectations around quality, cost, and time to market are met.

5. **Obtain/build**   Create service components, ensure they are available when and where needed, and ensure they meet agreed-upon specifications.

6. **Deliver and support**   Ensure services meet stakeholder delivery and support expectations.

To implement the SVS, ITIL®4 provides 34 practices to guide organizations in strategically planning, sourcing, and managing their IT services. The 34 practices are grouped into three major categories: general management (14), service management (17), and technology management (3). **Table 12.6** lists each of those 34 practices. A complete description of each of the 34 practices can be found in the Axelos publication "ITIL Foundation, ITIL 4 Edition" at **https://www.axelos.com/best-practice-solutions/itil/what-is-itil**.

TABLE 12.6 Thirty-Four ITIL®4 Governing Practices (Source: Limited, 2019)

General Management (14)	Service Management (17)	Technology Management (3)
Strategy mgmt.	Business analysis	Deployment mgmt.
Architecture mgmt.	Service catalog mgmt.	Infrastructure and platform mgmt.
Service financial mgmt.	Service design	Software development and mgmt.
Workforce and talent mgmt.	Service level mgmt.	
Continual improvement	Availability mgmt.	
Measurement and reporting	Capacity and performance mgmt.	
Risk mgmt.	Service continuity mgmt.	
Information security	Monitoring and event mgmt.	
Knowledge mgmt.	Incident mgmt.	
Organizational change mgmt.	Service request mgmt.	
Project mgmt.	Problem mgmt.	
Portfolio mgmt.	Release mgmt.	
Relationship mgmt.	Change enablement	
Supplier mgmt.	Service validation and testing	
	Service configuration mgmt.	
	IT asset mgmt.	
	Service desk	

Some examples of organizations that have improved their ITSM by following the ITIL guidelines include the following:

- Renault/Nissan Group car dealerships based in Switzerland and Austria were generating 750 service requests and 250 incident tickets per month. They had multiple local, in-country help desks with no consolidate view and fees charged per incident were high. When they implemented a single, central service desk that supported dealers and back-office functions to provide access to shared IS, a comprehensive view of user data and their demand for apps not only improved capacity management and measurement of service support but also a fixed incident management price saved them money (Billouz, 2020).

- A Global Financial Services organization had an unacceptably high rate of incidents being categorized as Severity 1 and many "problems" were being left unresolved for extended periods. These took up an inordinately large amount of senior executives' time and led to recurring incidents. When it was realized that most of these issues were being fueled by unauthorized and unplanned changes, a consulting agency was employed to upgrade the current ITSM tool set. By integrating ITSM processes and putting governance in place, 16 "quick win" projects saved 1,000 person-days per year and 200 services improvements were identified. In less than a year the IT function regained command of its operational challenges. Severity 1 incidents were reduced by 30%, Severity 2 incidents were reduced by 50%, and all changes were controlled by developing and implementing a Change Classification Hierarchy. Overall, improvements translated to savings of $250,000 per month (Hamblin, 2020).

- Harley-Davidson embarked on a five-year ITIL implementation plan to integrate their ITSM processes with a goal to have world-class industry best practices. At the time, processes were siloed—all teams were doing their own thing in terms of making up their own processes and people in complementary teams like database, networking, or hardware operating systems didn't know what was going on. As a result, work in response to incident and problem tickets was being duplicated repeatedly. To make things worse, sales offices in China, India, Brazil, and Australia each had their own system that in some cases was barely supported—if something broke, somebody would have to scramble to fix it. Harley-Davidson partnered with IBM Tivoli Software Group to integrate and align all its service processes and apps. They started with incident and problem management then they moved on to address request, changes, configuration management and release management. As a result of implementing ITIL, Harley-Davidson has achieved its goal of being one of the best in the business when it comes to managing IT services. It supports its locations around the globe from a central point and offers top-quality IT services.

Service-Level Agreement IT services typically operate under a **service-level agreement (SLA)** that guarantees the performance of their services. The SLA is a particularly important component of ITSM that serves as both the blueprint and warranty for the provision of IT services either by the internal IT function or by an external provider. It serves to make all parties aware of their responsibilities and when they may be held liable for failing to live up to those responsibilities. For example, a service provider might be held responsible to respond to an outage within two minutes 90% of the time and within five minutes 99% of the time. Or, agree to correct 95% of reported application software problems with two hours and 99% within six hours as was the case at the County of San Diego in the opening case at the beginning of this chapter. When services are delivered through the cloud, a cloud service agreement (CSA) is used as explained in Chapter 2.

> **Service-level agreement (SLA)** is a contract between a service provider and its internal or external customers that document services the provider will furnish and defines the service standards the provider is obligated to meet.

A strong SLA or CSA can help prevent many of the disruptions and dangers that can come with IT sourcing or migrating to the cloud. The provisions and parameters of the contract are the only protections a company has when terms are not met, or the arrangement is terminated. Neither contract should be signed without a thorough legal review.

There is no template SLA, and each cloud solution vendor is unique. Certainly, if a vendor's SLA is light on details, that alone may be an indicator that the vendor is light on accountability. Additionally, if a sourcing or cloud vendor refuses to improve its SLAs or negotiate vital points, then that vendor should not be considered. Unless the organization takes an informed and active role in the provisions and parameters of the SLA, it will typically be written to protect the service provider.

Benefits of Using a Structured ITSM Strategy

ITSM provides real benefits by helping the IT function become more adaptive, flexible, cost-effective, and service oriented. It drives change within the IT function, including how IT manages its processes, IT assets, vendor relationships, and IT personnel. ITSM shares commonalities with project management and IT governance and their supporting frameworks like business process reengineering (Chapter 1), COBIT2019 (Chapter 5), and PMBOK (Chapter 13). Benefits that can be expected from taking a strategic approach to ITSM are as follows:

- Lower IT operation costs
- Higher returns on IT investments
- Minimal service outages
- Ability to establish, well-defined, repeatable, and manageable IT processes
- Efficient analysis of IT problems to reduce repeat incidents
- Improved efficiency of IT help desk teams
- Clear expectations of service levels and service availability
- Risk-free implementation of IT changes
- Better transparency into IT processes and services

Top vendors of ITSM software includes BMC Helix ITSM v 19.02, ServiceNow, Ivanti Service Manager 2019.1, Cherwell Service Management v. 9.5.2, and Axios Systems assyst v11 (Gartner, 2019).

The Outsourcing Life Cycle

Regardless of what types of outsourcing an organization chooses or type of products or services an organization wants to outsource, such as production and operations, data center, applications management, call center, business process, or supply chain, there are multiple ways to proceed. As with any significant transformation of an organization's business model, it is always best to follow an organized and methodical approach. The exact approach chosen will be determined by many things, including the following:

- An organization's familiarity with outsourcing in any areas other than the one being currently considered
- What currently exists in-house that can be used as a foundation for the outsourcing process
- Level of outsourcing sophistication of the procurement and legal groups
- Whether an organization is just exploring the possibilities of outsourcing or has definite outsourcing objectives

The Five-Phase Outsourcing Life Cycle Jeff Richards of CIO Professional Services proposes a five-phase outsourcing life cycle **(Figure 12.15)**. The five phases are comprised of a total of 12 distinct stages (Richards, 2016). Using this structured, phased outsourcing strategy, organizations can optimize what, where, and when they acquire IT assets and services.

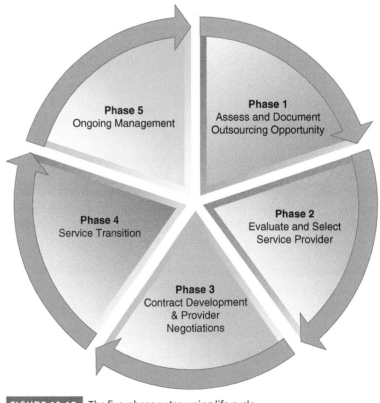

FIGURE 12.15 The five-phase outsourcing life cycle.

Here is a "top-level" description of each of the five phases of the outsourcing life cycle shown in Figure 12.15:

- **Phase 1**   This is the preparatory phase, where you assess opportunities and develop your overarching strategy and process- or geography-specific business cases for outsourcing.
- **Phase 2**   In this phase, you prepare and issue the **request for proposal (RFP)**, evaluate the proposals that are submitted, and select a service provider.
- **Phase 3**   Once a service provider has been selected, the next step is to develop and negotiate the **outsourcing contract** that will serve as a framework for your relationship with your new business partner.
- **Phase 4**   Once the contract is in place, it's time to plan and execute the service transition. This is the point at which all of your and the service provider's efforts either come to fruition or go off the track. Time invested in Phases 1 to 3 will mitigate that risk.
- **Phase 5**   Finally, with everything in place, the last phase is all about the ongoing management of the SLAs and managing the service provider relationship.

Depending on an organization's maturity, changing business conditions, or recognition of new information, it can choose to enter or exit the outsourcing life cycle at any point in the process. Just be aware that each entry or exit point has associated risks, costs, and benefits. In the next sections, we discuss RFPs, outsourcing contracts, SLAs, and how to establish and manage the SLAs and vendor relationship.

Request for Proposal (RFP)   To evaluate potential suppliers and vendors, an organization typically prepares and distributes an RFP document. The purpose of the RFP is to carefully articulate the requirements and objectives of the project and clearly state what is expected from the managed service provider or outsourcing company. The more proactive and prescriptive the RFP is, the easier it will be to negotiate a good contract. The requirements defined in the RFP document should include

- Service scope
- Technical architecture, vision, and strategic objectives
- Service delivery model, service management processes
- SLA
- Governance model and forums
- Commercial objectives
- Cost treatment and allocation
- Pricing model
- How assets will be treated
- Legal terms
- Employee transfer
- Risk and compliance

The RFP should be distributed to all vendors simultaneously along with a clearly stated timeline for response and key contact details. It is important to allow enough time for vendors to respond to the RFP, so that they can get a clear understanding of the project and due diligence requirements. The purpose of the RFP is to define "what" is expected of the supplier. The purpose of the response is for the managed services or technology supplier to explain "how" they propose to carry out the requirements of the project.

When the responses are received, all RFPs should be systematically compared to identify the best overall opportunity in terms of level of capability to meet the service and technology requirements of the project. Just as developing an IT strategy doesn't rely solely on cost indicators, the same is true when evaluating RFPs. It is not enough to rely on the most attractive

Request for proposal (RFP)   is a document issued by an organization to request third-party bids for products, solutions, and services.

Outsourcing contract   is a legal document that specifies what work will be handled by a third party, project deliverables, the schedule within which project deliverables will be delivered, and the consequences of non-performance.

total cost of ownership (TCO) savings. Instead, companies typically use a detailed supplier evaluation form that evaluates reputation, recent successes, existing relationship with the supplier, service delivery, technical quality, employee skill level, reliability, assurance of supply and risk, and reputation in the industry.

Once a supplier has been selected or a supplier shortlist has been developed, a draft contract with a full set of work schedules should be drawn up in consultation with key organizational stakeholders. The draft contract should be based primarily on company requirements stated in the RFP rather those proposed in the supplier responses to the RFP. When the draft contract is submitted to the vendor(s), they should be given a time limit within which to respond. Negotiations toward a final contract can now begin.

Outsourcing Contracts   An outsourcing contract is a legal agreement between a supplier (service provider) and an organization (service receiver) that is hiring it. It contains all the items and conditions of the business relationship between the two parties, including how and when project requirements will be met, and the consequences of nonperformance. The outsourcing contract is usually handled by the legal department. Outsourcing contracts typically involve extensive negotiations between the service provider and the service receiver.

Ask for "Proof of Concept" or a Trial Run

Proof of concept (POC)   is a vendor demonstration of a product to see how or how well it works.

During negotiations, it's often advisable to ask for a **proof of concept (POC)**. In simple terms, a POC is a vendor demonstration of a product to see how it works and how well it works. Requesting a POC of a vendor product, puts the adage "it worked in development" to the test in a production environment. This way an organization can ensure that the product under consideration can and will deliver as promised. The results of a POC need to be measurable for use in the decision-making process. For example, a certain performance level may be used as a threshold for acceptance of a product.

Trial run   is when a vendor product or service is tested in a pilot study or limited area of the business to confirm its usefulness to the company.

A **trial run**, or pilot, is little different. In this scenario, a vendor may offer the option to let you test their products or services in a pilot study or a small portion of the business to verify that it fits the company's needs.

In either case, if the vendor demo or test adds value on a small scale, then it should follow that the system can be successfully rolled out on a larger scale. If the supplier cannot meet the requirements in a POC or trial run, then the company avoids a failure.

Outsourcing contracts and SLAs should always be reviewed by a company's legal team.

Establishing and Managing IT Vendor Relationships

When sourcing IT projects, the starting point in building a positive and strong vendor relationship is vendor selection. If a company makes a bad selection or enters into a vaguely worded service contract, most likely the software, app, or implementation will fail, and the vendor will not be able to resolve the problems fast enough, if at all. Failures are usually followed by lawsuits.

Finding and Selecting a Vendor   To minimize interpersonal or technical conflicts with IT vendors, businesses need to thoroughly research the vendor. It is very important to ask questions about the services and products the vendor will provide and get as many specifics as possible. Also take the time to verify the vendor's claims about its products and check all references to make sure that the vendor has a proven track record of success. When selecting a vendor, two criteria to assess first are experience and stability:

- Experience with very similar systems of similar size, scope, and requirements. Experience with the ITs that are needed, integrating those ITs into the existing infrastructure and the customer's industry.
- Financial and qualified personnel stability. A vendor's reputation impacts its stability.

Of course, for innovative IT implementations, vendors will not have experience and one major failure—and the lawsuit that follows—can create instability. If those criteria are not met, there is no reason to further consider the vendor.

Research by McKinsey indicates that a majority of technology executives want to have stronger relationships with their IT suppliers, but they often act in ways that undermine that goal. In fact, many corporate customers lose out on the potential benefit of close relationships by an overemphasis on costs instead of value. Ideally, a customer/vendor relationship is a mutually beneficial partnership, and both sides are best served by treating it as such.

Vendors often buy hardware or software from other vendors. In order to avoid problems with the primary IT vendor, check secondary suppliers as well. Ask the primary vendor how they will deliver on their promises if the secondary vendors go out of business or otherwise end their relationship.

This example shows the importance of managing the sourcing process. A U.S. transportation company needed to make cuts immediately to its IT operating budget to reverse cost overruns. The company had a long-standing outsourcing contract with a top-tier service provider, but it had not implemented effective SLAs to control costs. Over the years, the service provider's costs increased significantly. As a result, the annual cost to outsource 750 terabytes of data more than tripled, an overinvestment that contributed to runaway IT outsourcing expenditures of $225 million a year. A companywide budget shortfall forced the IT division to cut $36 million from its 2020 budget—without harming quality of service. The CIO had to reexamine its data and infrastructure needs and take a more informed, proactive role in managing the relationship with its service provider.

The most important factor in managing a vendor is communication! A well-established, well-maintained, and frequently used line of communication will avoid misunderstandings and proactively address concerns before they turn into full-blown problems.

Managing Multiple Vendors
When it comes to sourcing and managing vendors, less is more. It is much easier to work with a single strategic vendor that help a company fulfill its business strategy than trying to juggle relationships between several different vendors. Even then, as we saw in our opening case, San Diego County ran into some major problems. In that case, you also saw that working with a single vendor can create a tighter connection between the vendor, the business, and IT and results in a closer alignment that result in time and money savings. Unfortunately, a company seldom enjoys the luxury of only dealing with one vendor at a time. Companies that have multiple IT vendors face the challenge of managing all these different relationships.

As companies increase outsourcing activities, a gap is created in their organizational structure, management methods, and software tools. At that point, some companies turn for help to an **outsource relationship management (ORM)** company. ORMs provide automated tools to monitor and manage the outsourcing relationships. ORMs monitor and manage SLAs.

Taking a Unified Approach to Vendor Management
When dealing with vendors, it's important to use a structured process right from the start. Dealing haphazardly with collecting RFPs can make it difficult to get formal contracts; make sure support is there when needed and avoid unpleasant disagreements about prices and warranties. Most importantly, this haphazard approach makes it almost impossible to align IT strategy with corporate strategy. A unified vendor management process administered through a **vendor management organization (VMO)** can help. Forester Research has found that a VMO is a driving force behind promoting best practices, providing contract and negotiation templates, facilitating communication, collaborating across finance and legal to negotiate more effective SLAs, and helping define vendor KPIs. Over the past several years, many organizations have begun to formalize their vendor management process through a VMO whose responsibilities can range from a dedicated staff that oversee and manage vendors down to a simple, but structured process for sourcing and managing vendor relationships. VMOs are becoming particularly popular as companies realize that it's almost impossible to manage vendors effectively if appropriate terms and requirements have not been included in their selection and contracts at the start.

Vendor management organization (VMO) is a business unit with an organization that is responsible for evaluating suppliers of goods and services and overseeing regular interaction and long-term relationships with vendors.

For example, at Cisco, their VMO manages its strategic vendors who supply IT infrastructure, software, storage, telecom services, and outsourced services. Its VMO is also tasked with closely following Cisco's corporate strategy while providing expertise in process and business development, asset management, and vendor engagement. With standard contracts in place worldwide, Cisco is now able to manage existing contracts and negotiate more effective new ones. In fact, their VMO saved Cisco $33 million in the first three quarters of its first year and $64 million over the life of the contracts put in place during that time. Cisco was also able to reduce its number of vendors and consolidate its contracts to reduce paperwork.

At the end of the day, its performance that counts. Like any other business unit, a VMO must be measured. Some useful ways to measure this include the following:

- Speed of response to vendor questions
- Consistency and transparency of reporting potential performance issues
- Higher-quality results at a lower cost from suppliers
- Improved key vendor relationships with business managers
- Improved business performance

Outsourcing Benefits

Organizations can realize several benefits from outsourcing their IT operations. One benefit is that by outsourcing some or all of its IT function, an organization can focus on its core competencies. Another might be that the new and improved services available through the cloud give an organization access to the most innovative new technologies to help it differentiate from its competitors. Another might be that outsourcing provides a small organization with the skilled IT personnel needed to operate and maintain the technology and a service provider can provide access to the IT and accompanying services at a much lower cost. A more extensive list of outsourcing benefits is given in **Table 12.7**.

TABLE 12.7　**Reasons Why Organization Outsource IT**

Generate revenue
Increase efficiency
Gain agility to respond to changes in the marketplace
Allow enterprise to focus on core competencies
Cut operational costs
Greater acceptance of offshoring as an IT strategy
Cloud computer and SaaS are proven effective IT strategies
Differentiate themselves from competitors
Reduce burden on internal IT department

Outsourcing Risks and Hidden Costs

As companies find that their business strategy is increasingly tied to IT solutions, the concerns about outsourcing risks increase. Risks associated with outsourcing are as follows:

- **Shirking** The vendor deliberately underperforms while claiming full payment, for example, billing for more hours than were worked and/or providing excellent staff at first and later replacing them with less qualified ones.
- **Poaching** The vendor develops a strategic application for a client and then uses it for other clients.

- **Opportunistic repricing**   When a client enters into a long-term contract with a vendor, the vendor changes financial terms at some point or overcharges for unanticipated enhancements and contract extensions.
- **Breach of contract by vendor**   The vendor fails to carry out the terms of the outsourcing contract.
- **Inability of vendor to deliver as promised**   Sometimes outsourcers represent themselves as being more skilled than they are and are unable to deliver the products or services that are promised in the outsourcing contract.
- **Vendor lock-in**   In the event that the outsourcing relationship does not go well, it can be difficult to get out of the outsourcing contract.
- **Loss of control over data**   Once the data is on the outsourcers' servers, the organization has little control over how and when that data can be accessed and by whom.
- **Lower employee morale**   IT employees may feel devalued as a result of development and services being performed by an outside source.
- **Relationship setup costs**   Depending on what is outsourced and to whom, an organization might end up spending 10% above the contract price to set up the relationship and manage it over time. The budgeted amount may increase even more when outsourcing is used— anywhere from 15% to 65% when factoring in costs of international travel and cultural differences.

Questions

1. What contributes to the complexity of a cloud strategy?
2. How does tactical adoption of cloud services differ from a coordinated cloud strategy?
3. What is onshore sourcing?
4. What are the major benefits and risks of outsourcing?
5. What needs to be done before signing a contract with an IT vendor?
6. What is the purpose of an RFP?
7. What is ITSM?
8. What are the four dimensions of ITIL®4?
9. What is the difference between an outsourcing contract and an SLA?
10. What is the purpose of a VMO?

12.4 Strategic Technology Trends

LO12.4 Explain *how organizations identify strategic technology trends to achieve their corporate vision and describe the five-step technology scanning process.*

To sustain a competitive advantage, companies need to strategically invest in emerging **strategic technology** to widen their set of core competencies and help them differentiate themselves in the market, expand their existing market, or move into different markets. This might include technologies with a high potential for disruption of the business, end users, or IT, significantly increase market share, or enable the creation of innovate new products.

IT at Work 12.3 describes how ESSA Academy in England uses strategic technologies to improve the student experience.

Strategic technology   has the potential to make significant impacts on an organization's long-term plans, programs, and initiatives.

IT at Work 12.3

Strategic Technology Transforms School from Failing to National Top 20% on Progress

Five years ago, ESSA Academy was a failing school. Now it is known as the first school in Britain to buy touch-screen devices for all its students and rated in the National top 20% of School on student progress. As a result, it has turned the fortunes of the school, its students, and teachers around and advises schools from Afghanistan to Australia on how to teach with technology.

Situated in Bolton, Lancashire, England, **ESSA Academy** has 877 students aged 11 to 16 years. To address concerns about failing students, when the school created its own vision of learning based on its students' needs, it strategically applied IT in the design of its customized curriculum.

As part of a whole school approach to transforming the learning environment, school–student relationship, and relationships between students, teachers, and parents, ESSA Academy administrators had a vision. Abdul Chohan, a director of the academy, wanted to use technology to create an environment in which students could enjoy learning and use computers for something other than playing games. He also wanted to encourage teachers to embrace new ways of understanding planning, classroom activities, and the learning process.

Inspired by this vision of a modern school, the ICT coordinator turned to strategically using consumer-level technology rather than educational solutions. The idea of giving expensive electronics to its mostly poor, ethnic-minority students was derided when the plans were announced in the local press. People saw it as a gimmick—a bribe to get students to come to the school.

From the start, ESSA's strategy involved the parents who made the new technology "family technology." In this way, parents were able to share learning experiences with their children "anytime, everywhere." And, teachers developed materials from lessons accessible from iTunes U and combined this with the use of apps and digital tools available on the iPad.

Then Chohan started to use iTunes U to curate content collaboratively and turn that content into textbooks that students can reference online rather than buying physical textbooks. This innovative approach enabled ESSA students to create, develop, and share resources in a collaborative way to further enhance their learning.

The gamble paid off initially and is continuing to pay off. In 2015, 54% of ESSA's graduating students achieved higher than national average scores on exit exams. In 2019, ESSA celebrated its best ever results when a record-breaking number of students achieved top grades in their 2019 GCSE examinations. This was confirmed when the UK government released its provisional "league tables" showing how well individual schools performed it reported that ESSA students had made above average progress and placed ESSA in the top 20% of schools nationally for progress. These results are made more meaningful when you consider that when these same graduating students first enrolled at ESSA their average grade was significantly below the national average. As Martin Knowles, Principal of ESSA Academy said, "The results are further testimony to the incredible work students, staff and parents/carers have put in over the past five years."

The move toward cloud technology, where most of the resources and communications between students, teachers, and parents are digital, has resulted in cost savings for most school departments and a feeling of liberation from physical constraints. Students are more motivated and engaged. There is a sense of enjoyment in learning to use their own technology, and students who have been encouraged to get involved in the new initiative are finding new apps to use in different classes—an activity that teachers highly value.

Sources: Compiled from Lee (2015), Pipe (2016), Chaudhari (2019), and www.essaacademy.org (2020).

Scanning for Strategic Technology Trends

The first step to considering and adopting new technologies is to find them. Approaches to finding trending strategic technologies include exploring the research and development activities of major research centers and IT consulting firms and attending technology industry conferences, such as COMDEX, IBM Inter-Connect, Google Next, Adobe Summit, and HIMSS.

Every year at its Symposium/ITxpo, Gartner, Inc.—a global consulting firm that provides information, advice, and tools for IT leaders—highlights top strategic technology trends that organizations should be following. Gartner's top 10 strategic technology trends for 2020 are described in **Table 12.8**.

TABLE 12.8 **Top 10 Strategic Technology Trends**

Trend	Strategic Technology	Description/Examples
1	Hyperautomation	Machine learning, packaged software and automation tools including Robots, autonomous vehicles, consumer electronics.
2	Multiexperience	Interfaces that will change how users perceive and interact with the digital world including virtual reality, augmented reality, and mixed reality. Conversational platforms such as Alexa, Siri, Cortana, Google Assistant.
3	Democratization of expertise	Technology that enables workers without special training to be able to make an impact. Citizen development, no-code models.
4	Human augmentation	Wearable or implantable devices. Smart glasses or contact lenses with augmented reality capabilities. RFID implants to provide building access or POS technology. DNA sequencing technology.
5	Transparency and traceability	IT needs to be trusted. AI, machine learning, data privacy, ownership and control; ethically aligned design.
6	The empowered edge	Edge computing will become a dominant factor across all industries as it is empowered with increasingly more sophisticated and specialized computing resources and more data storage. Complex edge devices are robots, drones, autonomous vehicles.
7	Distributed cloud	Distribution of public cloud services to different locations while originating public cloud provider assumes responsibility for operation, governance, updates to and evolution of the services.
8	Autonomous things	Technologies that exploit AI to deliver advanced behaviors that interact with their surroundings and people. Robots, drones, ships, appliances, aircraft, and cars.
9	Practical blockchain	Blockchain will become more mainstream with more practically applications. Smart contracts will be encoded into the blockchain itself.
10	AI security	Hackers are leveraging AI for nefarious purposes. Machine learning can be used to thwart attacks like phishing and malware.

Another approach is to scan printed IT publications and online offerings. There are hundreds of magazines, trade journals, newsletters, and e-zines covering the IT industry while others are focused on specific niches within the IT industry. Reading the best publications can help you stay current and offer opportunities for networking with peers and many of them allow you to sign up for daily feeds to an e-mail account to make it easier to keep up to date. Some of these publications are listed in **Table 12.9**.

TABLE 12.9 **Top IT Publications**

Name	Focus	Website
Computerworld	Current IT industry happenings	https://www.computerworld.com
Redmond Magazine	Independent voice of Microsoft IT community	https://redmondmag.com/Home.aspx
Network Computing	Information on networking infrastructure, messaging, security, and storage	https://www.networkcomputing.com
CIO Magazine	Issues faced by senior-level IT professionals and intersection of business and IT	https://www.cio.com
Certification Magazine	Technical certifications and training	http://certmag.com
Recode	Technology journalism	https://www.vox.com/recode
9to5Mac	Apple products	https://www.vox.com/recode
The Next Web	Information, updates, and insights around the globe about IT and its impact on every part of our lives	https://thenextweb.com
Dark Reading	IT security	https://www.darkreading.com

To achieve their corporate vision, some organizations have a more structured process in place to identify up-and-coming strategic technologies. In an era of rapid technological change, technology scanning is a critical strategic activity for any organization. To enhance their IT strategy, every organization needs to continually scan for emerging technologies. Understanding the performance improvements provided by new technologies, such as cost savings or service improvements, can range from incremental to revolutionary. Certain strategic technologies can create a basis for significant improvements, while other technologies may address relatively narrow needs and opportunities.

To be most effective, it's useful to establish a structured approach to strategic technology scanning. The five steps listed in **Table 12.10** provide a framework to guide technology scanning activities.

TABLE 12.10   **Five Steps to Technology Scanning**

Step	Activity
1. General Technology Search	Conduct a very broad review of new and emerging technologies that might be beneficial to the organization.
2. Technology Mapping	Conduct structured investigations into an organization's performance capabilities and identify the points of leverage for technological developments related to cost, reliability, safety, or capacity (for all competing modes).
3. Systems Modeling	Develop and maintain a set of models that can be used to evaluate technological improvements as they affect specific aspects of the organization.
4. Customer Requirements Analysis	Investigate the requirements of selected groups of customers and identify new ways of doing business; estimate resulting customer benefits in cost, speed, reliability, safety, and capacity.
5. Analysis of Specific Technologies	Examine for enhancing specific technologies performance identified as having potential.

Investing in Trending Strategic Technologies   Once appropriate new strategic technologies have been identified and assessed, companies need to make decision about strategically investing in IT that fits with business goals. Although this might include technologies with a high potential for disruption of the business and customers or require a major capital investment, being an early adopter of these technologies reduces the risk of falling behind the competition and it is money well spent.

Through carefully considered sourcing strategies, organizations can acquire emerging strategic technologies to enable them to gain the competitive advantage they need to flourish by widening their set of core competencies, expanding their existing market, or moving into different markets.

Questions

1. What are three ways that a company can identify and keep up with emerging strategic technologies?
2. Why would a company want to invest in strategic technologies?
3. What does an organization need to put in place to identify suitable strategic technologies?
4. What are the five steps in the technology scanning process?

Chapter Summary

LO12.1 *Define* five activities that can improve Business–IT alignment, the five forces in Porter's Competitive Forces Model and the five primary and four support activities of Porter's Value Chain.

The five activities that lead to business–IT alignment are commitment to IT planning by senior management; make sure the CIO is a member of the senior management team; understand IT and corporate planning; promote a shared culture and effective communication; and have multilevel links between business and IT plans at the strategic, tactical, and operational levels.

Porter's five forces model includes barriers to entry, bargaining power of suppliers, bargaining power of customers or buyers, threat of substitute products or services, and competitive rivalry.

Porter's value chain has five primary activities that describe the creation, sale, maintenance, and support of a product or service from start to finish. Inbound logistics focused on the acquisition and receipt of raw materials and other inputs. Operations include the manufacture and testing of a product. Outbound logistics includes its packaging, storage, delivery, and distribution. Service is the final link in the value chain and addresses the level of customer service provided. The four activities that support operations are a company's infrastructure—accounting, finance and management; human resource management; produce and technology development (R&D), and procurement.

LO12.2 *Describe* the three levels of an IT strategic plan, identify the five components of an IT strategy, and describe two tools that are useful in the strategic planning process.

The three levels of an IT strategic plan are the IT long-range plan, IT medium-term plan, and IT tactical plan. The long-range plan sets out the IT vision and overall strategy by describing the direction for resource requirements and sourcing, along with budget, activities, and time frames for the entire strategic plan. The medium-term plan defines the general project plans by determining resources needs and creating a product portfolio. The IT tactical plan is a current year plan that has a detailed budget and a specific schedule of activities and how they will be performed.

The five components of an IT strategy are the strategies related to IT applications, integration, infrastructure, services, and sourcing.

The SWOT analysis and BSC are two useful tools used in the strategic planning process. A SWOT analysis is used in the **early stages** of the strategic planning process to help an organization increase performance and profitability by enabling it to critically evaluate internal strengths and weaknesses versus external opportunities and threats. The results of the SWOT analysis are used to capitalize on the organization's strengths and opportunities to overcome its weaknesses and strengths. The balance scorecard methodology (BSC) is typically used at the **end** of the strategic planning process to review performance on a regular basis. The BSC looks at business objectives from four different perspectives: financial; customer; business processes; and innovation, learning, and growth. It can improve the IT strategic planning process by enabling an organization to clarify or update a business strategy; link strategic objectives to long-term targets and annual budgets; integrate strategic objectives into resource allocation; and increase enterprisewide understanding of the corporate vision and strategy.

LO12.3 *Discuss* the two broad categories of IT sourcing strategies, the importance of IT service management, and the five phases of the outsourcing cycle.

IT can be sourced in two main ways. Systems can be developed in-house or with the help of consultants and vendors to capitalize on IT that provides an organization's competitive advantage or contains proprietary or confidential data. Outsourcing is when IT operations and services are developed and maintained by a third-party supplier or vendor. Outsourcing can be accomplished by onshoring, offshoring, or cloud services.

IT service management is a strategic approach to managing IT services provided by an internal service provider, a shared services provider, or an external services provider. When IT services are not governed by an ITSM, program inefficiencies and unproductive processes can reduce performance and growth in an organization. ITIL®4 is an internationally accepted framework that guides ITSM by focusing on four dimensions—organizations/people, value streams/processes, information/technology, and partners/suppliers—and provides a SVS with 7 guiding principles and 34 practices to improve the management and support of IT services.

It's useful to use a five-phase structured approach to any type of outsourcing. These include preparation, RFP, outsourcing contract, service transition, and ongoing management of an SLA. In addition to enabling an organization to focus on its core competencies, outsourcing benefits enable an organization to generate more revenue; increase efficiency, gain agility to respond to change in the marketplace; lower operational costs; differentiate themselves from competitors; and reduce the burden of an internal IT department. Outsourcing also has some risks including suppliers who shirk their responsibilities, poach from other companies, engage in opportunistic repricing, do not fulfill its contract commitments, and overstate their abilities. Outsourcing can also result in vendor lock-in, loss of control over corporate data, lower employee morale, and the setup of a supplier relationship can cost more than was anticipated, over and above the price of the contract.

LO12.4 *Explain* how organizations identify strategic technology trends to achieve their corporate vision and describe the five-step technology scanning process.

To identify technology trends that can help an organization meet its strategic goals, an organization typically finds them by exploring R & D activities of major research centers and IT consulting firms, attending industry conferences, or scanning printed IT publications and online offerings. To effectively identify and evaluate the technologies, it is useful to use a structured five-step technology scanning process. The five steps are conduct a general technology search, map technologies onto business needs, evaluate potential improvements, analyze customer requirements, and systematically analyze technologies that show potential for improving business performance.

Key Terms

Assuring Your Learning

Discuss: Critical Thinking Questions

1. What are the three value drivers for a major retail store, such as Macy's or Home Depot? Do any of them have a limited life span? Explain.

2. What directs investments in social, mobile, analytics, cloud, and other digital technology resources?

3. What are the four objectives of an IT strategic plan?

4. What might be some reasons why companies use outsourcing instead of in-house development?

5. Compare the benefits of onshoring versus offshoring.

6. What are the risks of offshoring work/jobs to other countries, for example, to China or India?

7. Describe the six-step IT strategic planning process.

8. If there are conflicting priorities and disagreements among members of the IT steering committee, how might they be resolved?

9. Why is the BSC methodology "balanced"?

10. Why is it important to implement an ITSM program?

11. What are the four dimensions of ITIL®4?

12. Why has tactical adoption of IT become a risky approach compared to a coordinated cloud strategy?

13. Why are strategic technologies important to strategic planning?

14. Give three examples of strategic technologies and how they can influence organizational performance.

Explore: Online and Interactive Exercises

1. Visit Accenture.com and search for "outsourcing." Describe the IT outsourcing services offered by Accenture. Do the same for KPMG at kpmg.com, or PricewaterhouseCoopers at pwc.com. Create a table that compares the outsourcing services of two of these consulting firms.

2. Visit the Government Technology website at govtech.com. Search for "managing successful vendor relationships." Prepare a list of recommendations based on what you learn.

3. Visit the website of Deloitte US at **https://www2.deloitte.com/us/en/insights/focus/tech-trends.html** and watch the Video on the Tech Trends 2020. Compare and contrast Deloitte's list with Gartner's top ten strategic trends presented in the chapter. Discuss their similarities and differences.

4. Visit Gatekeeper's website at **https://www.gatekeeperhq.com/blog/vendor-management-case-study-inchcape-shipping-services** and read the Vendor Management case study of Inchcape Shipping Services. Describe how Inchcape chose Gatekeeper as its supplier and explain why you think Inchcape chose Gatekeeper. Would you have done the same? Why?

Analyze & Decide: Apply IT Concepts to Business Decisions

1. Visit **https://www.agreements.org/service-level-agreements .html** and read agreements.org has to say about SLAs. Compile a list of recommendations that you would make to your company if they were considering outsourcing, including what to do and what to avoid.

2. Netflix streams videos on TVs, personal computers, and smartphones using cloud services from Amazon Web Services (AWS). Its model is a direct challenge to traditional content distributors, which are limited by physical distribution and network broadcasting. In contrast, Netflix capitalizes on low cost and virtually unlimited cloud capacity to deliver content on demand almost anywhere. Research Netflix to learn more about its position in the industry in the on-demand economy and explain how it is currently using cloud technologies to create business value. Research another company in the on-demand media and entertainment space—for example, Amazon Prime, Roku, or Hulu. Compare the cloud strategies of Netflix and two of its competitors.

Reinforce: Ensure Your Understanding of the Key Terms

Solve the online crossword provided for this chapter.

Web Resources

More resources and study tools are located on the student website. You'll find useful Web links and self-test quizzes that provide individualized feedback.

Case 12.2

Business Case: Department of Defense (DOD) Evaluates Technology to Gain Help for Crisis Victims and Protect First Responders

The Department of Defense (DOD) serves as in innovative leader in sourcing technology to protect Americans and U.S. troops on and off the battlefield. DOD recognizes the importance of applying knowledge-based acquisition practices to improve the outcomes of their IT projects. When projects enter development with insufficient knowledge, negative effects often cascade throughout the acquisition cycle. The DOD's three acquisition phases— technology development, systems development, and production—align with three key points for demonstrating knowledge. In systems technology analysis, the DOD's needs are matched with the time, funding, and other resources required by the proposed technology. In systems development, the stability and performance of the technology are evaluated. In production, the schedule, costs, and quality targets are measured using the BSC methodology.

One critical area that serves both populations is crisis response. Crisis response teams like the Army National Guard and the 95th Weapons of Mass Destruction Civil Support Team out of northern California support civil authorities and incident commanders including fire and police chiefs while simultaneously protecting first responders.

The Maneuver Support Center of Excellence Homeland Defense/ Civil Support Office and Maneuver Support Battle Lab (MSCoE) is responsible for evaluating new crisis-response technologies and developing tools for crisis response teams. According to Gregg Thompson, MSCoE deputy to the commanding general, "We want our people—our No. 1 priority—to have the capability to assess hazardous environments without exposure to the hazards." Time-to-action, reliability of intelligence and safe-site assessment are critical components of crisis-response missions related to Chemical, Biological, Radiological, and Nuclear (CBRN) environments as well as natural disasters such as earthquakes, wildfires, hurricanes, and floods.

Recently, the DOD was tasked with developing a powerful crisis-response tool to add to their CBRN arsenal. The DOD's Test and Evaluation Master Plan (TEMP) is an important part of its sourcing process that lays out the process which technology is acquired, supported, and managed. Following TEMP's guidelines, the DOD conducted extensive market research into suitable technologies and chose three different private sector suppliers who could provide the following innovative technologies that could be used in the CBRN environment:

- **Blackbird** A drone with color and infrared cameras developed by Nightingale Security to assist ground teams in rapid communication, while thousands of military, law enforcement, and first responders simultaneously watch the drone's feed.

- **The X3 Finder** A mobile, mountable, and weather-resistant device developed by SpecOps Group, Inc. that can detect heartbeats and respiration through 18 inches of concrete to assist emergency-response crew locate victims of natural or man-made disasters.

- **FARO Focus S 350** A 3D mapping and scanning apparatus developed by FARO that can be used to relay 3D models of structures back to commanders so that they can see exactly what their troops are dealing with. The scanner can also perform a post-blast analysis, reconstruct a crash, and generate accurate incident documents to future learning.

Another TEMP requirement is that a structured test and evaluation of any acquisition must be conducted to ensure decision-makers have enough information to assess the technology's technical performance and determine that it is "operationally effective and suitable, survivable and safe for intended use." It further specifies that testing and evaluation should integrate modeling and simulation to "facilitate learning, assess technology maturity and interoperability, facilitate integration into fielded forces and confirm performance . . .". In keeping with these requirements, the DOD requested a joint Proof of Concept (POC) from Nightingale Security, SpecOps Group, Inc. and FARO to evaluate the combined effectiveness of the three search-and-rescue technologies. The POC was conducted at Fort Leonard Wood, a U.S. Army training installation in the Missouri Ozarks. The three suppliers demonstrated and tested the Blackbird, X3 Finder,

and FOCUS S 350 by simulating a 5.7-magnitude earthquake in which a building collapsed leaving role-playing victims "trapped" in a pile of rubble. During the test and evaluation, the three technologies performed well and the DOD decided to proceed with their purchase and implementation.

Questions

1. What three technologies was the DOD evaluating?

2. Why was the simulation a useful part of its acquisition process?

3. What would the consequences be if the DOD had not conducted a test and evaluation of using the three technologies?

4. What other measures could the DOD have taken to make sure that the three devices were reliable?

Sources: Compiled from Department of Defense (2011), AcqNotes (2018), Campbell (2019, 2020), and Department of Defense (2019).

IT Toolbox

SWOT Analysis

As discussed in the chapter, the primary purpose of the SWOT analysis is to identify and assign significant factors that affect the business to one of the four categories to analyze where it stands in the market and help guide an organization's strategic planning process.

Don't worry about elaborating on the nature of the strengths, weaknesses, opportunities, and threats; bullet points are sufficient at this stage of the analysis. Just capture the factors that are relevant in each of the four areas using two or three words to describe them.

After listing factors in all four areas, compare your lists side by side to get an overall picture of how the businesses is performing and what issues need to be addressed. Create four prioritized lists by prioritizing the issues by importance and ease of implementation by asking yourself "What needs to and can be addressed now?" and "What can and will have to wait until later?"

Finally, review the prioritized lists by asking:

1. How can we use our strengths to take advantage of the opportunities identified?

2. How can we use these strengths to overcome the threats identified?

3. What do we need to do to overcome the identified weaknesses to take advantage of the listed opportunities?

4. How can we minimize our weaknesses to overcome the identified threats?

When you have your finalized lists, the SWOT analysis is ready to guide the process of developing corporate and IT strategies. The value of a SWOT analysis depends on how well the analysis is performed. To gain the greatest value from performing a SWOT, carrying out the SWOT early on in the strategic planning process and following these rules helps:

- Be realistic about the strengths and weaknesses of your organization.
- Be realistic about the size of the opportunities and threats.
- Be specific and keep the analysis simple or as simple as possible.
- Evaluate your company's strengths and weaknesses in relation to those of competitors (better than or worse than competitors).
- Expect conflicting views because SWOT is subjective, forward-looking, and based on assumptions.

Have Fun with a Personal SWOT

To identify the actions you can take to best meet the requirements of the job or promotion you are seeking, conduct a personal SWOT analysis. To help you understand yourself, picture yourself as a competitive product in the marketplace, and list your strengths, weaknesses, opportunities, or threats from the perspective of a prospective "customer," that is, employer. Comparing your strengths and weaknesses to job requirements will help you identify gaps, prepare you to be the best candidate for the position you are seeking, and alert you to issues that could arise in the interview process.

References

AcqNotes. "Test and Evaluation Master Plan (TEMP)." 2018. Available from http://acqnotes.com/acqnote/careerfields/test-and-evaluation-master-plan-temp Accessed on January 26, 2020.

Billouz, D. "Service Desk: At the Heart of ITIL 4's Service Value Chain." *The Axelos Blog*, January 10, 2020.

Campbell, S. "Army Evaluates New CBRN—a Crisis-Response Technology." *Guidon*, October 24, 2019.

Campbell, S. "Army Salutes Earthquake to Evaluate Crisis-Response Tech." *U.S. Army*, 2020. Available from https://ftleonardwood-presscenter.com/army-evaluates-new-cbrn-and-crisis-response-technology Accessed on January 24, 2020.

Chaudhari, S. "GCSE Results 2019: Celebrations Continue with More First Class Results." *The Bolton News*, August 24, 2019.

Department of Defense. "Incorporating Test and Evaluation into Department of Defense Acquisition Contracts." 2011. Available from http://www.acqnotes.com/Attachments/Guide%20on%20Incorporating%20TE%20into%20DoD%20Acquisition%20Contracts.pdf Accessed on January 3, 2021.

Department of Defense. "Defense Acquisition Guidebook." 2019. Available from https://www.dau.edu/tools/dag. Accessed on January 3, 2021.

Douglas, M. "San Diego County CIO Shares Secrets Behind Success with It Outsourcing." *Government Technology*, June 13, 2010.

Field, T. "San Diego Outsourcing Update: A Rocky First Year of Transition." *IT World*, April 3, 2001.

Gartner. "Critical Capabilities for IT Service Management Tools." *Gartner*, September 4, 2019.

Hamblin, K. "Global Financial Services Organisation Banks on ITSM Process Improvement Programme." *Pink Elephant*, 2020.

Hanson, W. "San Diego County Nears Completion of 7-Year Outsourcing Contract, Prepares for Next Steps." *Government Technology*, February 11, 2005.

Jouret, S. "Everything You Wanted to Know About ITIL in One Thousand Words!" *Axelos Global Best Practice*, February 2019.

Lee, J. "This Bolton School Was Failing—Until It Gave Each Pupil an iPod." *The Telegraph*, January 2015.

Martin, R. L. "The Big Lie of Strategic Planning." *Harvard Business Review*, January–February 2014.

Pipe, M. "Seven Ideas for Using Education Technology." *SecEd*, July 2016. http://www.sec-ed.co.uk/best-practice/seven-ideas-for-using-educational-technology.

Porter, M.E. "Competitive Advantage: Creating and Sustaining Superior Performance". *The Free Press*. 1985.

Repsher-Emery, G. "Pennant Alliance Meets High Standards in San Diego." *Washington Technology*, March 14, 2001.

Richards, J. "Introduction to the Outsourcing Lifecycle." *CIO Professional Services*, July 2016. Available from https://www.ciops.com/blog/163-introduction-to-the-outsourcing-lifecycle#.XisKMG-5Fxpw Accessed on January 26, 2020.

San Diego County. "Information Technology and Telecommunications Services Agreement." 2016. Available from https://www.sandiegocounty.gov/content/dam/sdc/cto/docs/ito_contract/01%20-%20Base%20Terms%20and%20Conditions.pdf Accessed on January 22, 2020.

San Diego County Technology Office, "Outsourcing." 2020. Available from https://www.sandiegocounty.gov/cto/outsourcing.html Accessed on January 22, 2020.

Williams, M. "San Diego County Read for Hewlett-Package as New IT Outsourcing Partner." *Government Technology*, May 9, 2011.

Wood, C. "Ransomware Solution? Outsource All IT, Says Local Government Expert." *StateScoop*, July 2, 2019.

CHAPTER 13

Systems Development, IT Service Management and Project, Program and Portfolio Management

Case 13.1 Opening Case

Ruud Morijn/123RF

Vermont Electric Power Company Inc. and Vermont Transco LLC (collectively VELCO).

marcscott/123RF

VELCO Outsources Project Management and Brings in Politically Sensitive Capital Project $6 Million Under Budget

Sometimes companies lack the in-house project management expertise they need to complete very large projects. This was the case at Vermont Electric Power Company, Inc. (VELCO), an electrical assets transmission company that works with Vermont's 17 local utilities and the New England regional grid operator to meet high national and regional standards of reliability to ensure citizens of Vermont have a constant supply of electricity.

The Company

VELCO was formed in 1956 when Vermont's local utilities joined together to establish the nation's first statewide "transmission only" company to create and maintain an interconnected electric transmission grid capable of sharing access to clean hydro power. Currently, VELCO is responsible for 738 miles of transmission lines over 13,000 acres of rights-of-way that are maintained through its 55 substations, switching stations, and terminal facilities. VELCO's fiber-optic communication networks monitor and not only control the electrical system but also provide a key link to high-speed Internet access for customers throughout Vermont.

VELCO's 150 employees strive to give Vermont's utilities and their customers a reliable high-voltage grid and continued access to safe reliable, cost-effective electricity. VELCO is also very active in regional energy issues and collaboratively develops and advocates cost-effective reliability solutions related to system infrastructure, energy efficiency, or energy generation. VELCO's vision is to create a sustainable Vermont through its people, assets, relationships, and operative model.

The Problem

Throughout Vermont, massive ice storms and blizzards are not uncommon and power outages pose a danger, not just to business and property, but to life itself! To ensure electricity is always flowing to its customers, VELCO was required to provide a redundant electrical feed into the area to satisfy regional reliability standards. Unfortunately, a previous large transmission project had resulted in a firestorm of public outcry about the need, aesthetics, and cost of transmission projects in general. For the new project, dubbed the East Avenue Loop Project, to proceed, VELCO leadership would have to develop a strategy for anticipating and proactively addressing public concerns.

VELCO top management felt that if they could defuse the environmental and cost concerns on the East Avenue Loop Project, future projects would experience far fewer problems and delays. Cost was a major issue. The capital project was estimated to cost a staggering $35.7 million, so it would have to be carefully managed to meet cost and schedule estimates. VELCO also had to ensure that they honored the environmental commitments made to state regulators and its customers. As a relatively small business with limited project management expertise, VELCO would need outside help to pull off this expensive and politically sensitive major capital project.

The Solution

To manage this politically sensitive endeavor, VELCO selected PM Solutions, a global project management consulting company that helps business leaders apply best practice project and portfolio management to drive organizational performance and efficiency. PM Solutions' experts have an extensive network of company-backed resources and assets to draw from including extensive research and benchmarking that enable them to stay on the forefront of Project, Program and Portfolio Management (PPPM) trends and new approaches that positively impact its clients across industries and around the globe.

At VELCO, PM Solutions' first mission was to develop a public engagement process that proactively solicited input from the public and state regulators. A series of public and city council meetings were held to explain the project need, address issues, and build support. Much like a political campaign, the VELCO project was painted in its best light, and the concerns of stakeholders were listened to carefully, with strategies for response carefully crafted.

Meanwhile, PM Solutions addressed critical details that included the development of an accurate cost estimate and a realistic but demanding schedule. Strong project management governance practices were also established in VELCO's Project Management Office (PMO) to ensure success in this and future projects, along with innovative risk management and mitigation strategies. For example, when the team needed to access an island in the river to install large transmission line structures, they took advantage of adverse weather to build an ice bridge instead of a standard bridge, resulting in a $460,000 cost savings.

The Outcome

The East Avenue Loop Project was completed on time and $6 million under budget. As a result, customer satisfaction scores increased by 20%. The public outreach approach used in managing the project improved community relations, and the resulting agreements helped to eliminate hearings before the state utility regulatory board. This was the first project of its size to be approved by the Board without several days of hearings. As a result, the project was granted a board certificate to proceed six months earlier than previous large transmission projects, resulting in an exponential savings of time and money for VELCO.

Chris Dutton, VELCO's CEO, expressed delight with the outcome of the project:

> *Early stakeholder outreach and interested-party negotiation reduces project cost and the timeframe for project completion – results that increase system reliability, which is VELCO's primary responsibility. The PM Solutions' project manager for the East Avenue Loop Project embraced this approach and brought a higher, more disciplined level of project management practice, which helped us to save ratepayer dollars and successfully complete a critical project.*

PM Solutions continues to help lead and support large-scale capital projects for VELCO. Their expertise has added important political know-how and best practice project management to the business of electrical transmission construction in Vermont that will benefit the industry into the future.

Questions

1. What was the first thing that PM Solutions did when it was hired by VELCO?
2. Why was the VELCO project compared to a political campaign?
3. Why do you think VELCO was so successful in cutting the project budget?
4. Identify three positive results of VELCO's East Avenue Loop Project.

Sources: Compiled from PM Solutions (2020) and velco.com.

DID YOU KNOW?

Medical professionals may soon be able to give shots, inject drugs, and take blood samples in a new way thanks to 4D printing and innovative systems development techniques. Software engineers are currently developing tiny needles that mimic parasites that attach to tissues and could replace hypodermic needs. Systems developed with 4D printing use dynamic materials that can be programmed to change shape, color, and function in response to external stimuli such as based on a signal from a person or a reaction to changes in the environment such as water, light, heat.

Introduction

Systems development is the core activity of the IT function. As an informed user of IT, it's important for you to know how you should work with your IT department to develop information systems (ISs) and manage projects. A basic understanding of the principles of systems development will enable you to spot mistakes and make suggestions during the development process to increase the success of the project. If you are, or aspire to be, an IT professional, systems development is an integral part of your work. As you learned in Chapter 12, organizations can acquire their information systems in several different ways. The way a system is developed often depends on the number and skill level of IT professionals who are employed in an organization, expense, and availability. Sometimes systems are fully or partially sourced externally and sometimes they are developed in-house (Chapter 10). When they are developed in-house, an IT department can go about it in several different ways using an assortment of systems methodologies. Regardless of the method used to develop a system, there is one typical **systems development life cycle (SDLC)** that guides them through the process. In this chapter, you will learn the SDLC and the different systems development methodologies.

And, all systems development projects must be managed. When companies develop or build new products, services, markets, enterprise systems, or apps, they typically use a project management approach. Project management is a structured approach to plan, manage, and control the completion of a project throughout its life cycle.

Effective project management is gaining in importance for all types of projects because of technology complexity, tighter budgets, tougher competition, and shorter time-to-delivery requirements. The 2019 Pulse of the Profession survey (PMI, 2019a)—focused on transforming the high cost of low project performance—reported that organizations are still wasting almost 12% of their project investments due to poor performance. It also emphasized that project management is becoming increasingly dependent on technology to help get projects delivered on time, within budget, and according to specifications. The use of IT in project management is taking on a new urgency in an age of digital sustainability and the need to minimize risk of project failure. In short, companies need to increase the number of project successes to like the one reported in our opening case at VELCO. In this chapter, you will learn how systems are developed, how project success can be achieved by combining a structured project management approach with technology as well as the differences between levels of project management and the skill sets needed for each.

13.1 Systems Development

LO13.1 Identify *typical business drivers for systems development projects and the five phases of the systems development life cycle (SDLC).*

All **systems development** projects are prompted by a **business need**. Business needs are the basic drivers of high-level change in an organization that add value to a business such as reducing costs, increasing revenue, or decreasing time to market. Business needs are put into action by implementing projects and transforming operations.

Typical **business drivers** for systems development include the following:

- Globalization of the economy
- E-commerce, mobile commerce
- Security and privacy issues
- Communication, collaboration, and partnerships
- Knowledge management
- Continuous improvement and total quality management
- Business process redesign

The IT function can fulfill these business needs by creating systems that improve services, reduce costs, create stronger controls, lead to better performance, provide more and better information, offer strong support for new products and services, and provide secure data transfer and storage. After a business need has been identified, a system request is submitted to the IT department by a business unit and the SDLC can begin (**Figure 13.1**).

systems development is a set of activities, methods, best practices, deliverables, and automated tools to creating and maintaining IT architecture and software.

business need is a gap between the current state of a business and its goals.

A **business driver** is a condition, process, resource, or rationale that is vital for an organization to thrive.

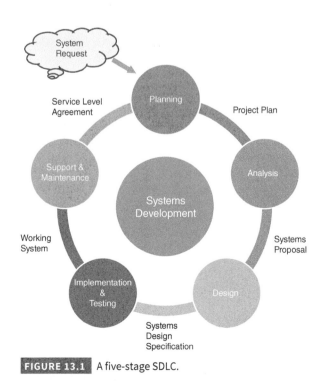

FIGURE 13.1 A five-stage SDLC.

The Systems Development Life Cycle

The SDLC is a multiple-stage approach used by IT professionals to develop high-quality ISs from planning and analysis through support and maintenance. The SDLC provides a framework for several different systems development methodologies (discussed later in the chapter). Typical SDLC activities include gathering the user requirements, determining budgets, creating a logical systems design, creating a physical systems system, building and testing the system, writing detailed user and developer documentation, training users, and maintaining the system. The activities performed during systems development vary depending on the size and complexity of the system. Systems are developed by people who are technically qualified, business oriented, and highly motivated. Systems developers must be good communicators with strong analytical and critical thinking skills.

The many activities of the SDLC are typically divided up into five to seven stages. We define the SDLC as a five-stage process. The five stages are planning, analysis, design, implementation/testing, and support/maintenance (Figure 13.1). Each stage consists of well-defined tasks based on the scope of the project. The five stages are described next.

Stage 1: Systems Planning To begin the SDLC, a business unit submits a systems request based on a business need and systems planning begins (Figure 13.1). The systems request begins the planning process by describing the problem or desired changes. The purpose of the planning stage is to perform a preliminary investigation and to find out if the request is feasible.

A feasibility study determines the probability of success of a proposed system and provides a rough assessment of its technical, economic, organizational, and behavioral feasibility. The feasibility study is critical to the systems development process because, when done properly, the study can prevent companies from making expensive mistakes, where systems are created that will not work, that will not work efficiently, or that people cannot or will not use. The Census Bureau case in **IT at Work 13.1** is another useful example. The various feasibility analyses also give the stakeholders an opportunity to decide what metrics to use to measure how a proposed system meets their objectives.

- Technical feasibility   **Technical feasibility** determines if the required technology, IT infrastructure, data structures, analytics, and resources can be developed and/or acquired to solve the business problem. Technical feasibility also determines if the organization's existing technology can be used to achieve the project's performance objectives.

IT at Work 13.1

Rapid Prototyping with 3D Printing Helps Oakley Get Products Out Faster

To get its sports, equipment, and eyewear products out the door as quickly as possible, Oakley, a California-based sports brand, needed to create prototypes of functional product parts during product development. To do this, Oakley uses HP's Multi Jet Fusion 3D printer in its development process. Using rapid prototyping with 3D printing, Oakley engineers create a 2D sketch and design a model with HP's Jet Fusion 580, and within 24 hours they have the physical part to test and refine. To differentiate between iterations of product development, each part can be created in multiple colors and the process repeated as needed. Use of rapid prototyping has enabled Oakley to reduce product development stages of its eyewear selection as well as other athletic equipment. As Nicolas Garfias, head of Design at Oakley, explained, "World-class athletes around the globe depend on Oakley to compete at the highest level. With HP's breakthrough 3D printing technology, we will not only accelerate our design to production timelines, but we will also conceptualize the way our products are made, pushing the boundaries of sports performance to new heights."

Using 3D printing additive manufacturing Oakley has streamlined its development process and optimized the shape of its sunglasses. Oakley also has used HP's Multi Jet Fusion for rapid prototyping in many of its other product lines including helmets and trophies. Overall, it has helped them deliver the highest design standards to millions of athletes around the world. Jeff Fawcett, 3D Printing Product Manager at HP, summed up its partnership with Oakley up by saying, "Together, we are transforming the sports performance community and changing the way the world designs and manufactures consumer products."

Sources: Compiled from Dignan (2019), Orr (2019), and Vialva (2019).

- Economic feasibility **Economic feasibility** determines if the project is an acceptable financial risk and if the company can afford the expense and time needed to complete the project. Economic feasibility addresses two primary questions: Do the benefits outweigh the costs of the project? Can the project be completed as scheduled?

Management can assess economic feasibility by using cost–benefit analysis and financial techniques such as time value of money, return on investment (ROI), net present value (NPV), and breakeven analysis. ROI is the ratio of the net income attributable to a project divided by the average cost of resources invested in the project. NPV is the net amount by which project benefits exceed project costs, after allowing for the cost of capital and the time value of money. Breakeven analysis calculates the point at which the cumulative cash flow from a project equals the investment made in the project.

Calculating economic feasibility in IT projects is rarely straightforward. Part of the difficulty is that some benefits are intangible. For a proposed system that involves big data, real-time analytics, or 3D printing, there may be no previous evidence of what sort of financial payback can be expected.

- **Legal and organizational feasibility** Are there legal, regulatory, or environmental reasons why the project cannot or should not be implemented? This analysis looks at the company's policies and politics, including impacts on power distribution and business relationships.
- **Behavioral feasibility** Behavioral feasibility considers human issues. All systems development projects introduce change, and people generally resist change. Overt resistance from employees may take the form of sabotaging the new system (e.g., entering data incorrectly) or deriding the new system to anyone who will listen. Covert resistance typically occurs when employees simply do their jobs using their old methods.

Behavioral feasibility is concerned with assessing the skills and the training needed to use the new IS. In some organizations, a proposed system may require mathematical or linguistic skills beyond what the workforce currently possesses. In others, a workforce may simply need to improve their skills. Behavioral feasibility is as much about "can they use it" as it is about "will they use it."

After the initial feasibility analysis has been completed, a **go/no-go decision** is reached. If it is a no-go decision, the project can be revised, put on the shelf until conditions are more favorable, or discarded. If the decision is "go," then the systems development project proceeds. The deliverable from the planning stage is a Project Plan.

Stage 2: Systems Analysis
Requirements analysis is critical to the success of the project. The purpose of systems analysis is to analyze and understand the problem identified in the planning stage by gathering user requirements. This can be accomplished by observing how the business process that the system will support is carried out, interviewing users, sending out a questionnaire, or applying knowledge gleaned in developing similar systems. During this stage, process models are created to establish the **logical design** of the system and explore alternative solutions to create the system. The **deliverable** from the systems analysis stage is the Systems Proposal.

Systems development practitioners agree that the more time invested in planning and analyzing the current system, business problem, or opportunity and understanding problems that are likely to occur during development, the greater the probability that the new system will be a success. Tools such as joint application development (JAD) and rapid application development (RAD), described in detail in Section 13.2, are used in this stage of systems development.

Stage 3: Systems Design
In the systems design stage, system developers utilize the design specifications to create the user interface and establish data requirements. It is in this stage that systems developers use tools like rapid prototyping that are described in Section 13.2. IT at Work 13.1 demonstrates how eye manufacturer Oakley uses rapid prototyping technology to get their product out as fast as possible. They also develop the **physical design** of the system

Go/no-go decision a determination to proceed with or abandon a plan or project.

logical design lists and describes all the information resources (data and processes) and the scope of duties and responsibilities of consumers of the information involved in the operation of the new system. It is business focused and always precedes physical design.

deliverable is any measurable, tangible, verifiable outcome, result, or item that is produced to complete a project or part of a project. Examples might be hardware, software, planning documents, or meeting minutes.

physical design transforms business requirements into a specific technological solution by identifying all physical servers and major technical components that will be used to support the desired business outcome.

by determining and acquiring the hardware and software needed to carry out the logical design of the system. Next, they create user and system documentation. During the design stage, management and user involvement is critical to ensure that business requirements are being met. The deliverable from the design stage is the System Design Specification.

Stage 4: Implementation and Testing

Implementation, or deployment, is the process of converting from the old system to the new system. During this stage of the SDLC, the system is actually put in place and tested. There are four ways that the new system can be installed. We call these the four "Ps" of systems conversion: plunge, parallel, pilot, and phased. Rapid prototyping is also useful in the implementation and testing stage.

In the **plunge conversion**, the old system is cut off and the new system is turned on at a specified time. This type of conversion is the least expensive, but it is the riskiest if the new system does not work as planned.

In a **parallel conversion**, the old system and the new system operate concurrently for a specified period of time. That is, both systems process the same data at the same time, and the outputs are compared. This type of conversion is the most expensive but least risky.

A **pilot conversion** introduces the new system in one location, or with one group of people, to test it out. After the new system works properly, it is rolled out to the entire organization.

A **phased conversion** introduces components of the new system, such as individual modules, in stages. Each module is assessed, and, when it works properly, other modules are introduced until the entire new system is operational.

Once the system is up and running, testing verifies that apps, interfaces, data transfers, and so on work correctly under all possible conditions. Testing requires a lot of time, effort, and expense to do properly. However, the costs and consequences of improper testing, which could possibly lead to a system that does not meet its objectives, are enormous.

Finally, users are trained in the use of the system and provided with the user documentation created during the design stage. The deliverable from the implementation and testing stage is the new working system.

Stage 5: Support and Maintenance

Once the new system's operations are stabilized, *audits* are performed during operation to assess the system's capabilities and determine if it is being used correctly. Maintenance must always be kept up rigorously. Users of the system should be kept up to date concerning the latest modifications and procedures.

This phase also involves supporting users in their use of the system according to any service-level agreements (SLAs) that may be in place. The deliverable from the support and maintenance stage is the SLA.

It is important to remember that the SDLC is an iterative process, not a linear one. This means that when results from one stage are assessed, they can be revised, if needed, and a previous stage can be revisited before continuing to the next stage. For example, since all systems need to be updated significantly or replaced after several years of operation, systems development activities are repeated as maintenance turns into "change" that leads to the development of a new system.

Questions

1. What are the five stages of the SDLC?
2. Name the deliverables from three of the five SDLC stages.
3. Explain the purpose of feasibility tests and why they are important in developing ISs.
4. Is the systems development process a linear or a cyclical process? Explain.
5. Name the four system conversion methods.

13.2 Systems Development Methodologies

LO13.2 Define *the different systems development methodologies, the major differences between them, and the tools and techniques used.*

While there is only one SDLC, many different systems development methods are used to create information systems. The major systems development methodologies are waterfall, object-oriented, Agile, and DevOps (**Table 13.1**). Each of these are explained next.

TABLE 13.1   **Comparing Systems Development Methodologies**

Method	People	Process & Tool Based	Flexible	Plan-Based	Communication and Collaboration	Contract Negotiation	Separation of Duties
Waterfall		x		x			x
Object-Oriented	x	x	X		x		x
Agile	x		X		x	x	x
DevOps	x	x	X	x	x	x	

Waterfall Model

The **waterfall model** was the first SDLC model to be used widely in systems development (**Figure 13.2**). Sometimes known as "structured analysis," the waterfall model is a *sequential, predictive approach*. It is very simple to use and understand but is quite inflexible. Using the waterfall model, each phase of the SDLC must be completed before the next phase can begin. There is no opportunity to go back to a previous stage and no overlapping in the phases. Recordkeeping is extremely important when using the waterfall model to keep everything on track within each clearly defined stage according to the project plan.

waterfall model   is a sequential, predictive systems development methodology that is simple to use and understand, but inflexible.

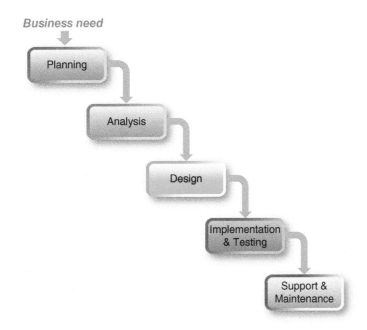

Business need
→ Planning → Analysis → Design → Implementation & Testing → Support & Maintenance

FIGURE 13.2   Waterfall method.

The waterfall model is particularly useful for small systems, short-term projects, when it is very unlikely that requirements will change and when there are no ambiguous requirements. A disadvantage of developing a system using the waterfall model is that it doesn't allow for much reflection or revision. This can be problematic since users are notorious for seeing opportunities for changing or adding features during development.

Object-Oriented Analysis and Design

object-oriented (O-O)   is an iterative systems analysis and design methodology that emphasizes modularity and reusability.

Unlike the sequential predictive waterfall model, **object-oriented (O-O) analysis and design** is an *iterative, adaptive* systems analysis and design method. O-O analysis and design is a popular approach for systems development that emphasizes modularity and reusability and encourages better communication between analysts, developers, and users. The introduction of the O-O approach in the 1970s marked a radical change in systems development. In O-O analysis, entities that interact with each other are grouped together to create a model that accurately represents the purpose of the new system using terminology that is close to that used in the users' everyday work.

O-O views a system as a collection of modular objects that encapsulate data and processes. Objects are such things as people, things, transactions, and events. For example, in a college admissions system, objects of interest might include student, course, and major. By keeping data and processes together, developers save time and avoid errors by using reusable program modules that have been tested and verified. And, the iterative nature of O-O allows changes to be made along the way.

A large part of O-O analysis is the unified modeling language (UML) and use cases. UML uses a set of symbols to graphically represent the various components and relationships within a system and is used primarily to support O-O analysis and develop object models. Use cases are a simple to construct and easy to understand graphical representation of the existing system early in the systems development process and reflect user requirements for the new system in later models.

Use-case model   is a list of actions or steps that define the interactions between a user and system to achieve an expected outcome.

Use-case diagram   is a graphic depiction of the major elements (use cases) within a system and its environment.

use-case description   is a text-based list of actions or steps that detail the interactions between users and the system needed to achieve the goal of the system.

Use-Case Model   Use cases show business events, who or what objects initiated the events, and how the system responds to the events. A use case has two parts: **use-case diagram**, which is a visual summary of several related use cases within a system; and a **use-case description**, which is a text-based description of the business event and how users will interact with the system to accomplish the task (**Figure 13.3**).

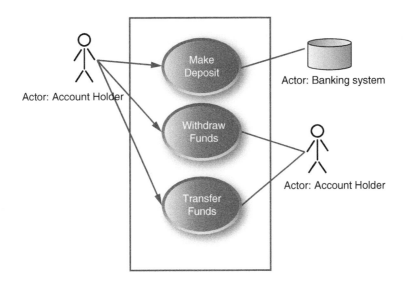

Use case name	States the use case name. Typically, the name expresses the objective or observable result of the use case, such as "Withdraw Cash" in the case of an ATM machine.
Brief description	Describes the role and purpose of the use case. i.e., Make Deposit
Actor(s)	Names of actor(s) involved in the use case. i.e., Account holder, banking system
Typical flow	Describes the ideal, primary steps involved in this use case.
Alternative flows	Describe exceptions or deviations from the basic flow, such as how the process works when the actor enters an incorrect user ID and the user authentication fails.
Special requirements	Specify any nonfunctional requirement that is specific to a use case but is not specified in the text of the use case flow of events. Examples of special requirements include: legal and regulatory requirements; application standards; quality attributes of the system, including usability, reliability, performance, and supportability; operating systems and environments; compatibility requirements; and design constraints.
Preconditions	A state of the system that must be present before a use case is performed, i.e., what triggers the use case?
Post conditions	A list of possible states for the system immediately after a use case is finished.
Assumptions	List the gaps in your information for this use case. What (if anything) did you have to assume when completing the description?

FIGURE 13.3 An object-oriented use-case model has two parts: the use-case diagram and the use-case description. Here's a simple example of an account holder interacting with a banking ATM.

Using O-O analysis and design methods to develop systems can potentially produce more reliable and useable systems. The O-O approach promotes a better understanding of a system, making information easier to use and reuse throughout a system, and developing a system that can be easily modified or changed to make maintenance easier. It also helps reduce the complexity of the systems development process.

Agile Systems Development Methodology

The **Agile** methodology is the most flexible of all systems development methodologies. Agile uses an *iterative, incremental approach* to overcome the disadvantages of the sequential waterfall model. The goal of Agile is to deliver software components early and often through a highly iterative process. Developers begin with a simplistic project design and begin to work

Agile is a very flexible iterative, incremental systems development methodology that overcomes the disadvantages of the waterfall model.

on small modules. The Agile methodology addresses the problems of rapid change occurring in the on-demand economy, such as changes in market forces, system requirements, and project staff. Agile methodologies minimize risk by breaking down the project into small manageable chunks called iterations and puts a strong emphasis on real-time communication and teamwork.

In doing so, Agile focuses on the collaboration and communication skills of its participants. For example, instead of Agile managers creating a structured contract with the project sponsor, they focus on creating a collaborative relationship. Using Agile, the emphasis is on competency rather than process where reaching the goal is more important than how you get there. As a result, teams in rigid organizations find it difficult to adjust to the fluidity of the Agile method.

The Agile process has four stages, sometimes called tracks, shown in **Figure 13.4**. These stages (warm-up, construction, release, and production) have many simultaneously occurring activities that cause them to be much less structured than activities in other types of systems development methodologies. So much so that some feel that a method as flexible as Agile shouldn't even have stages.

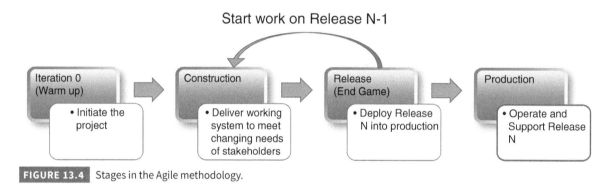

FIGURE 13.4 Stages in the Agile methodology.

Advantages of using Agile include ease of making changes, adding features, and incorporating client feedback and early identification of glitches in the system. Disadvantages include requirement of a good project manager and the absence of a definitive plan at the beginning of the SDLC that can cause the final product to be significantly different from that originally intended.

Created by the Agile Alliance, Agile systems development is the umbrella term used for several different Agile software development methods including Scrum, Kanban, Scrumban, and extreme programming. These are discussed next.

Scrum

Scrum is a framework that consists of small self-organizing, cross-functional Scrum Teams who work together to produce small pieces of a system iteratively and incrementally in **sprints** to maximize opportunities for feedback. Springs typically range from 7 to 30 days. Work is pulled through the system in batches called the sprint backlog. At the end of each sprint, project priorities are evaluated, and acceptance tests are run and evaluated. These short sprints allow for errors to be found and customer feedback that can be incorporated into the design before the next sprint is run. Every day, a 15-minute Daily Scrum is held to synchronize activities and create a plan for the next 24 hours. No changes are allowed mid-sprint.

The Scrum approach is centered around three tenets: *transparency* (sharing a common understanding of the work), *inspection* (users must be able to frequently inspect Scrum output and progress), and *adaptation* (if an inspection reveals one or more deviation outside of acceptable limits, it must be adjusted as quickly as possible to minimize further deviation). Scrum works best in products and development projects.

Kanban

Kanban is different from Scrum. It is a technique used for managing the creation of parts of a system with an emphasis on continuous delivery while not overburdening the development team. Its goal is to help teams to work together more effectively. Kanban is based

sprint is a set period of time during which specific work has to be completed and made ready for review.

Kanban is Japanese for a signboard. It is a visual process and project management methodology used in systems development projects.

on three principles: *visualizing* workflows; *limiting* the amount of work in progress, and employing a *pull system* to improve the flow of work by pulling in the next item on the backlog when the current task is completed.

Unlike Scrum, Kanban has no prescribed roles, focuses on continuous delivery rather than on sprints, pulls single pieces of work into the system rather than batching them in a sprint, uses specialized teams as well as cross-functional ones, and cycle time is emphasized over speed. Kanban works well when priorities are frequently adjusted and quick response to changes is required. When Scrum teams want to add a layer of visibility to their work, they sometimes adopt select Kanban principles to assist them. Kanban is best suited to the design stage of the SDLC.

Scrumban

Scrumban is a hybrid of Scrum and Kanban. Scrumban uses the prescriptive elements of Scrum and combines them with Kanban's more adaptive pull system to view and better understand workflows and continuously improve Scrum teamwork processes. Using Scrumban, team workflow is controlled by the status of current work and not by sprint content. Changes can be added as needed and an ongoing product backlog is created using just in time "kanbans" or timecards rather than waiting for the next sprint. Although there is a daily scrum, workflow is continuous and where necessary specialized team can be brought onboard. Scrumban works particularly well in the support and maintenance stage of systems development.

Scrumban is an agile systems development methodology that combines certain aspects of Scrum and Kanban originally designed as a way to transition from Scrum to Kanban.

Extreme Programming

Using **extreme programming**, software is developed in small pieces that make little sense on their own, but when put together, they form a system—somewhat like putting jigsaw pieces together to complete a jigsaw puzzle. The first step in developing a system using extreme programming is to create user stories in which use requirements are documented to understand what the user wants the system to do. Next, acceptance tests are conducted to make sure that the system produces the results that the user wants. Gaining verification of the functionality by the user in this way shifts the responsibility to the user. Finally, after user approval, small releases are delivered. Extreme programming works because it creates good communication between developers and users, designs are simple and efficient, feedback is obtained at every step of the project, and the methodology adapts well to changes.

extreme programming is a pragmatic systems development approach to Agile development that emphasizes business results first and takes an incremental approach to building software, using continual testing and revision.

The DevOps Approach to Systems Development

The latest development methodology to emerge is **DevOps**—short for software DEVelopment and IT OPerations. The goal of DevOps is to deliver an information system that meets all user requirements to business units in a timely manner and ensure the system runs without interruption or disruption. DevOps closely aligns itself with an organization's ITSM strategy. It emphasizes *communication and collaboration between software developers, operators, and testers* who are involved in both the development (Stages 1 through 4) and operations/maintenance (Stage 5). When other systems development methodologies are used, a development team gathers business requirements and hands them off to a separate quality assurance team that tests the systems that then passes the system on to operations, another separate department within the IT function to implement. This separation of duties has led to bottlenecks in the process and the deployment of systems that don't work the way users want them to and far too many systems that are technically perfect and "work in development," sit idle because they don't meet user needs or they function poorly.

Gaps created by this separation of duties between development, testing, and operations personnel can lead to nonuse or a low level of system use. DevOps was developed to address these communication and collaboration challenges by creating a cross-functional team to build, test, and run the system and develop a culture in which the building, testing, delivery AND support and maintenance of a system can happen quickly, frequently, and reliably (**Figure 13.5**). **IT at Work 13.2** describes how Target, a large U.S. retailer has successfully achieved a viable DevOps culture in their extensive IT department.

DevOps is a set of processes that encourages collaboration between system designers, developers, testers, and operators.

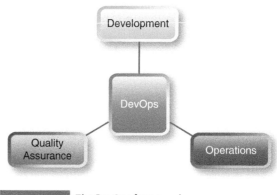

FIGURE 13.5 The DevOps framework.

IT at Work 13.2

DevOps at Target Goes from Good to Better to Best

According to Target technical architect Dan Cundiff, DevOps "started out in small corners of development and infrastructure teams" and has now "caught on like wildfire." With almost 1,800 stores across the United States and a huge online presence, Target is the second largest importer in the United States with 38 fulfillment centers across the United States. Target's IT function manages three data centers and leverage two leading public cloud providers. So, it takes a lot of IT to run them efficiently, and developing an effective DevOps initiative was considered critical to the success of its operations. According to Heather Mikman, Target's Sr. Director of Technology Services, DevOps is an integral part of helping Target keep up with the pace of change and innovation required to be a leading retailer. A major issue was that Target had a lot of organizational siloes, large investments in IT, and outdated processes that slowed down Target's ability to innovate. For example, in anticipation of the Christmas selling season, Target brings on 70,000 new team members to handle more than 170 million store transactions and 3 million in-store pickups that have to quickly learn how to operate its systems. To make sure that Target guests are "delighted", its systems must be stable and easy to use.

The answer to Target's problem began as a grassroots DevOps operation driven by a handful of change agents. The initiative soon got the attention of senior leadership who began to support DevOps and drive it across Target's large enterprise IT function—that consists of thousands of staffers. Finally, DevOps found a top management champion in its CIO Mike McNamara whose vision was that Target would be an Agile—DevOps shop with qualified IT staff to support it. At that point, the DevOps initiative began to build

out at scale and its skilled team adopted the mantra "no system will be deployed until it has the green light."

To get to this point, IT teams initially focused on continuous integration and building an empowered learning environment for its system developers and engineers. To continue to build momentum for DevOps, they started to host internal DevOps events. At the first event, there were over 100 attendees to help the organization share and learn what the DevOps team was doing. Next, they had middle and top managers attend a more formal on-site DevOps conference. They also started to discuss Target's DevOps success externally by presenting at local DevOps meet-ups in Minneapolis and hosted other external events. By this time, confidence in DevOps was growing as systems deployments rose from 10 to 80 deployments per week and incidents had been reduced to less than 10 per month—clearly things were getting better and better. A reduction in the ratio of contractor to internal staff came next, and Target established clear team priorities to give the members a clear focus of their responsibilities. Finally, systems were transitioned to a public cloud provider to return control to Target's internal IT systems. To get teams engaged with Agile and DevOps, Target set up an accelerated learning environment called "the Dojo" to support team members and refine, reinforce, and strengthen their engineering capabilities. Moving to Agile under Mike McNamara set in motion an incentive to change and think differently about how systems were developed, deployed, and maintained and contributed to establishing a DevOps culture at Target. Today, Target is continuing to learn from what went right and what could be improved in its DevOps initiative across its IT organization, and the new organizational culture is fully embracing DevOps principles and reaping its benefits.

Sources: Compiled from Brown (2017), Null (2020), and **https://dojo.target. com/mindsets/devops**.

DevOps focuses on the creation of an integrated team, including user representatives, that covers the end-to-end SDLC regardless of whether they use the waterfall methodology, take an object-oriented or Agile approach to systems development. DevOps isn't focused on speed and rapid development. Its goal is minimal disruption of the business and maximum performance reliability to lower the failure rate of new releases, shorten lead time between fixes, enable shorter time to market and mean time to recovery.

Organizations that use DevOps, including Amazon, Netflix, Facebook, and Twitter, have reported significant benefits such as shorter time to market, improved customer satisfaction, better product quality, more reliable release, improved productivity and efficiency, and the ability to build the right product.

Despite these success stories, organizations are encountering some major challenges in implementing a DevOps mindset. A closer look reveals that the majority of companies reporting huge successes from DevOps are digital by nature. Their employees are typically millennials and Generation Z, their processes are agile, and most of their technology is cloud based. They are very different from large manufacturers, financial firms, marketing agencies, retailers, healthcare agencies, and government agencies where employees tend to be much more of a mixed bag—Baby Boomers, Generation X and Y—who are less comfortable with IT, their approaches to systems development tend to be based on older, less flexible systems development methodologies and their technology is based on legacy systems combined with a few client/server or cloud apps. These differences are a critical factor in adopting DevOps, because to be successful it demands a major change in organizational culture. The DevOps methodology requires that employees in the somewhat incompatible business and IT departments of more traditional companies, who have different motivations and backgrounds work as a team. This has proved to be a stumbling block in moving the DevOps movement forward.

To build a DevOps culture that emphasizes communication and collaboration between users, software developers, system testers, and IT operations professionals, organizations are using team-building and engagement activities such as games, trust activities, and seminars. In addition, DevOps is heavily dependent on automation to ensure smooth development and deployment. A few examples of software that support DevOps in its entirety or at specific points in the SDLC include Buddy to build, test, and deploy software; TestRail for test management; QuerySurge for continuous data testing; and Jenkins to handle project changes.

Systems Development Tools and Techniques

There are several high-level tools and techniques that are used to decrease the time needed to design and implement information systems. These tools and techniques can be used independently or in combination depending on the complexity of the system and project deadlines. Some systems development techniques like prototyping, **joint application development (JAD)**, and **rapid application development (RAD)** rely heavily on end-user involvement, while others like integrated CASE tools and code generators focus more on the technical aspects of systems development, combined with some user involvement.

Joint Application Development (JAD) is a team-oriented technique used in the planning and analysis stages of the SDLC to collect business requirements.

Rapid Application Development (RAD) is an interactive process used throughout the SDLC continuing until the system is completely developed and all users are satisfied with the outcome.

Joint Application Development

JAD is built on the premise that end users have a vital stake in a new system and should participate fully in systems development. JAD consists of several collaborative workshops called JAD sessions that involve participants from the business and the IT function to determine consensus-based systems requirements. Its main purpose is to accelerate the SDLC through greater user involvement and group dynamics to enable systems developers to more accurately understand the user view of the business need and to jointly develop an effective IT solution.

In a JAD session, the business side is represented by users including top management, managers, and end users who provide insights into available support, explain how the project supports the business function, provide specifics of business requirements, and offer operation-level inputs about how the process currently works to support day-to-day tasks. On the IT side, a JAD project leader develops an agenda and leads the JAD session. Systems analysts and other IT staff provide technical assistance focused on security, backup, hardware, software, and network capability. Finally, an IT staff member acts as a scribe to document the results of the JAD sessions.

JAD can be successfully used when developing new systems, enhancing existing systems, converting systems, or purchasing a system. They JAD sessions can be both useful and a hindrance depending on the project. For example, JAD allows key users to participate effectively, issues can be resolved quickly, assumptions are documented and understood. JAD can also result in a more accurate statement of system requirements and provide a better understanding of the business needs, and buy-in associated with increased user participation can result in stronger commitment to the success of the new system. However, JAD can be expensive and cumbersome if the user group is too large or where business needs are not well defined, and if key users are not properly identified and included in JAD sessions, the outcome will not be optimal.

Rapid Application Development

RAD is like JAD, but in addition to user involvement it also relies heavily on prototyping, integrated CASE tools, and code generators. The goal of RAD is to radically cut development time and expense by involving users at every stage of systems development. RAD is not generally as structured and formal as JAD and focuses more on software development than JAD. In addition to workshops and prototyping (discussed in the next section), RAD uses early, reiterative user testing and existing software components. RAD is particularly useful in the development of systems that require a highly interactive or complex user interface.

One of the main advantages of RAD over the traditional SDLC tools is that it is focused on iteration and self-correction. This leads to systems that can be developed quicker at significant cost savings. However, less time spent in development and a primary focus on system mechanics at the expense of business needs can lead to lower business–IT alignment and issues associated with system quality, consistency, and design standards.

rapid prototyping is an iterative process used to quickly create an early sample, model or release of a system to test a concept or process.

A **prototype** is a working model of a system or part of a system usually built to demonstrate it to users, who can test it, and request rework as necessary.

Rapid Prototyping

Rapid prototyping is an iterative process typically used in the analysis and design stages of the SDLC to help developers build systems that meet business needs and are easy for users to use **(Figure 13.6)**. Time to market is critical to beating competitors and gaining market share. A **prototype** reduces precious time spent in systems development. Using an initial set of user requirements, systems developers build a prototype of a system or part of a system and demonstrate it to a group of users. Based on their feedback, developers refine the system as often as necessary to meet user requirements.

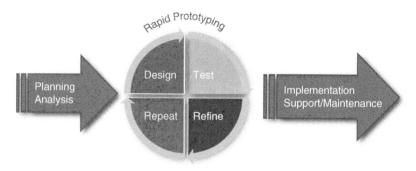

FIGURE 13.6 The rapid prototyping process within the SDLC.

Advantages of rapid prototyping include detecting errors early to save time and money; enhance collaboration with IT and the business; collect user feedback and test functionality and interactions within the system. Rapid prototyping is particularly useful in designing systems that have complex user interfaces, such as online forms, websites, and mobile apps. Rapid prototyping technology such as **3D printing** is used in manufacturing to enable fast fabrication of a scale model of a physical part of a new product using three-dimensional computer-aided design (CAD) to speed up product development, as previously described in IT at Work 13.1.

3D printing is a technology that uses additive manufacturing to quickly build physical objects layer-by-layer to create real-world objects.

CASE tools are software apps used by IT project managers, systems analysts, and systems developers to automate SDLC activities.

Computer-Aided Software Engineering (CASE) Tools

CASE tools refer to software used to automate systems development. A systems development project that relies heavily on CASE tools is often referred to as **software engineering**. There are three classes of CASE tools that automate many of the SDLC activities:

- **Upper CASE tools** Used in the planning and analysis stages of the SDLC to perform repetitive activities such as gathering requirements, diagramming processes, and presenting them in an organized way. Upper CASE tools include diagram, chart, and report generators such as VISIO, SmartDraw, and EDGE Diagrammer.

- **Lower CASE tools** Used in the design, implementation/testing, and support/maintenance stages of the SDLC to automatically generate code, test for functionality and defects, monitor implementation, and perform software maintenance activities. They include Java Case Developer v1.0, Code::Blocks IDE, and DB Designer Fork.
- **Integrated CASE tools** Used in the all stages of the SDLC from requirements gathering to testing and documentation. Examples include Visible Analyst and Artiso Visual Case.

All classes of CASE tools depend on a central repository that handles a store of common, integrated, and consistent data such as requirement documents, reports, diagrams, product specifications. By automating SDLC activities, CASE tools accelerate systems development to produce a high-quality system and uncover any analysis and design issues before moving on to the next stage of the SDLC. They also provide better system documentation that helps during operation and maintenance.

Source Code Generators
Source code generators are used in the design stage of the SDLC by computer programmers. Reusable source code generators use a library of high-quality prewritten common application source code modules to support a large percentage of the programming effort. To program a system, developers combine different source code modules and customize the result. Source code generators can be proprietary or open source. For example, SWIG is a free source code generator that connects programs written in C and C++. Others include Lazarus, JSToolNpp, and FreeBASIC Compiler.

A **source code generator** automatically generates common application source code in any computer programming language, for example, BASIC, VB, PHP, ASP. NET, SQL, C#, Java Script.

Low-Code Development Platforms
Low-code development platforms provide a graphical user interface for professional coders and nontraditional developers, such as IT-savvy users, to program a system quickly and easily with minimal coding. This reduces the time typically spent in traditional programming and minimizes the need for extensive coding knowledge or experience. They provide base-level code, scripts, and integrations, so an organization can prototype and build apps without developing complex IT infrastructures. Coupled with RAD, they are a powerful tool for developers and nondevelopers. The downside is that their ease of use can lead to security issues associated with shadow IT if users start developing new systems without the approval of their IT department (Chapter 5). Fortunately, most users like doing what they do and aren't interested in being developers. Low-code development platforms are also known Application Platform as a Service (aPaaS) or high-productivity application development platforms. Examples include OutSystems, Salesforce Lightning Platform, and Mendix.

A **low-code development platform** is software that provides developers and nondevelopers with an intuitive graphical user interface instead of a traditional computer programming environment to create apps.

Choosing a Systems Methodology or Tool

There is no hard and fast rule for the choice of a systems development methodology or tool. Each IT project is unique and depends on business needs, current processes, financial and HR resources, and organization culture. The choice of an appropriate methodology must take all these factors into account.

Questions

1. Name the different types of systems development methodologies.
2. What the is the main difference between the waterfall method and the Agile method?
3. Why is it important for an organization to be flexible when developing ISs?
4. Why is the concept of DevOps appealing to organizations?
5. How is RAD different from JAD?
6. What are the three classes of CASE tools?
7. What is a low-code development platform? What are its advantages and disadvantages?

13.3 Project, Program and Portfolio Management (PPPM)

LO13.3 Describe *the differences between project, program and portfolio management, the five phases of the project management life cycle, and the ten knowledge areas of project management.*

project is a temporary endeavor undertaken to create a unique product, service, or result.

program is a group of similar or related projects that are managed and coordinated as a group.

portfolio is group of unrelated programs within an organization that are managed holistically to achieve strategic goals.

Companies don't just deal with one project a time. They usually have multiple projects running simultaneously, which necessitates grouping them into several programs and one overarching portfolio. Over the years, project management has evolved from being a single **project**-centric profession to three distinct levels of management, that is, project, **program**, and **portfolio** management.

Project, program and portfolio management occurs at different levels of an organization's hierarchy. Management of individual projects occurs at the operational level of an organization. Programs are managed at the tactical level, and portfolio management is an integral part of business strategy (**Figure 13.7**).

FIGURE 13.7 Hierarchy of project, program and portfolio management.

In the next sections, you will learn more about project, program and portfolio management (PPPM), and the different roles that project, program and portfolio manager play, together with the processes, tools, and techniques they need to deliver projects, programs, and portfolio on time and on budget while adding value.

Project Management

Project management is the discipline of using established principles, procedures, and policies to successfully guide a project from start to finish to achieve specific goals and meet specified criteria within a specified period. A project is the lowest component in the hierarchy of project, program and portfolio management (PPPM). Unlike day-to-day operations, that is, ongoing work performed to sustain business, each project has a set time to start and a deadline for completion. Projects can range from small to large and can take anywhere from a few hours to many years to complete. For example, a small software development team may be asked to add a new feature to an in-house software app for the marketing department, a college decides to upgrade its IT infrastructure to provide wireless Internet to student dorms, or a public utility company revamps its entire state-wide network to meet high national and regional standards to ensure its constituents have a constant supply of electricity—as was the case at VELCO in our opening case.

Regardless of size or length of time they take to complete, every project must have a **project sponsor** who usually provides the direction and funding for the project, requires a variety of resources, has a budget and time frame that must be managed and involves certain elements of uncertainty and risk. The typical characteristics associated with a project are recapped in **Table 13.2**.

Project sponsor is a person or organization that approves and/or supports the allocation of resources for a project, defines its goals, and evaluates the success of the project at completion.

TABLE 13.2 **Distinguishing Characteristics of a Project**

- Clearly defined scope, deliverables, and results
- An estimated time frame or schedule that is subject to a high degree of uncertainty
- An estimated budget that is subject to a high degree of uncertainty
- The requirement of extensive interaction among participants
- Tasks that may compete or conflict with other business activities, which makes planning and scheduling difficult
- Risky but with a high profit potential or benefits

Project success is becoming increasingly reliant on four things:

- Engaged executive sponsors
- Projects aligned with organizational strategy
- Control over scope creep
- High **project management technology quotient (PMTQ)**

project management technology quotient (PMTQ) is a person's ability to adapt, manage, and integrate technology based on the needs of the project or the organization.

The Role of the Project Manager

The project manager is the central point of contact in a project. He/she acts as a conduit between the project team, project sponsor, end users, and all other project **stakeholders**. A project manager's responsibilities do not include hands-on project work—that is the responsibility of project team members. The project manager's main responsibility is to manage the triple constraint—scope, time, and cost—to meet project objectives while ensuring project quality. For example, a project manager is responsible for managing and controlling the progress of the project to make sure that project team members are on task and the project successfully fulfills the requirements set by the project sponsor on time and on budget. To achieve this, they must streamline processes, maintain project schedules and budget, and manage the interactions and work of a handful people to as many as hundreds of people. Successful project management is not only built on creating and managing systems and processes, but also requires developing and maintaining strong relationships with all project stakeholders.

stakeholders All interested parties in a project including program team members, project sponsors and end users.

Skills and Competencies   To be successful, project managers need a variety of skills to plan, execute, and control a project. Technical, business, and management skills are necessary, but not sufficient, to manage an IT project well. In addition to general technical knowledge and a high PMTQ needed to keep up with rapid changes in technology, successful project managers also must possess soft skills to manage people.

For example, along with identifying anticipated costs early on to develop a realistic budget, good project managers must be able to quickly resolve resource conflicts, optimize allocation of workers to minimize the effect of funding on operating capital, and keep all project stakeholders in the loop. It is also becoming increasingly important to have managers with high

PMTQ who know how to successfully leverage technology to coordinate tasks and clearly identifying goals or deliverables within each project phase and reduce inefficiencies in time management that can adversely affect the project budget. A list of important project manager skills and competencies is shown in **Figure 13.8**.

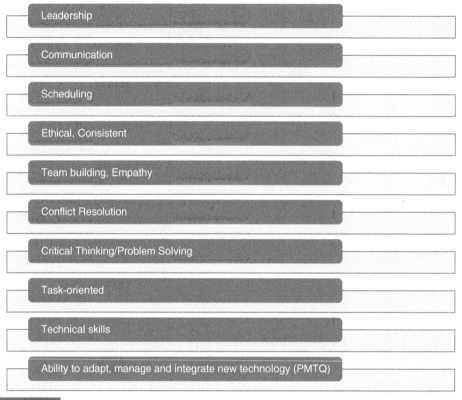

Leadership

Communication

Scheduling

Ethical, Consistent

Team building, Empathy

Conflict Resolution

Critical Thinking/Problem Solving

Task-oriented

Technical skills

Ability to adapt, manage and integrate new technology (PMTQ)

FIGURE 13.8 Ten essential project manager skills and competences.

Different types of project manager skills are needed in different situations. For example, in large projects, project managers must be good leaders, have strong project management experience, be adept at planning, and be capable of maintaining frequent and effective communications with team members and other project stakeholders. Most of all, they must have good team building skills. In smaller projects, prior project management experience is less important, but keeping open lines of communication and leveraging new technologies are always key.

To perform well as a project manager, it is also important to use a structured project management framework. In fact, not using a best-practice project management approach within a systems development project is considered the biggest mistake an IT project manager can make. **Tech Note 13.1** provides good advice on this topic.

Tech Note 13.1

Six Basic Systems Development Guidelines for IT Project Managers

1. Always develop a project plan.
2. Involve all stakeholders and listen carefully to them at all stages of the project.
3. Encourage teamwork and commitment to the project.
4. Use project management tools to identify tasks and milestones.
5. Perform accurate cost/benefit analysis.
6. Remain flexible.

The Project Management Institute (PMI) sums up the ideal skill set for project managers in its Talent Triangle:

- Technical project management
- Leadership capabilities
- Strategic and business management

In short, a project manager must be able to excel in working with technology and people while taking business goals into account.

Program Management

Program management occurs at the tactical level of an organization and is distinctively different from project management. While a project is a *single* undertaking with a set beginning and end, a program is a *group of related projects*. This means that a program doesn't always have a single, clearly defined deliverable or timeline. Projects within a program will have different timelines. Although it is still temporary in nature—when all projects are complete, the program is complete—a program is more ongoing than a project because it involves more than one project.

The concept of a program evolved to get around the challenges associated with efficiently managing resources in organizations that were running multiple projects simultaneously. These organizations soon realized that evaluating the viability of an individual project in isolation, making cost-effective resource allocation difficult if not impossible. Managing related projects as a group in an overarching program resulted in much better utilization of resources than a single project. For example, several advertising projects in the marketing department may require the same resources, such as materials, equipment, and people.

By grouping related projects, organizations soon realized that resources could be more easily and effectively allocated across the projects and time frames adjusted as needed throughout project life cycles. Benefits that an organization can realize from using a structured approach to program management include increased synergy between projects, optimal use of resources, less resource constraints, improved communication through better coordination among projects, and ultimately better business performance.

Another fundamental difference between programs and projects is the pattern of project activities. For example, programs typically demand a significantly greater amount of coordination and negotiation in addition to project planning, execution, monitoring and controlling, and a program involves a greater degree of risk and uncertainty.

The Role of Program Manager

Program manager is the next rung of the project management career ladder. Unlike the project manager who micromanages a single project, the role of the program manager is more tactical. Program managers don't manage projects. They provide oversight to ensure that each project in the program is completed effectively and efficiently to produce quality deliverables that meet stakeholder requirements. Their focus is on overseeing project work and resources in projects that are currently in their program. This focus on *current projects* ensures work and resources are moving between projects at the right time and that resource needs of all projects are met. It is also the role of the program manager to validate that the right projects are included in the program and that any projects not adding value to the business are either realigned or removed. To do this, a project manager creates a master schedule to manage the dependencies between project, a risk manager plan, and a communication strategy to ensure that any changes that are necessary because of a change in business strategy are communicated quickly and clearly to project managers and their teams.

Skills and Competencies   Typically, a program manager has several years of project manager experience and will have completed several very large, complex or risky projects. In addition to their basic project manager skills, a program manager must be particularly adept at multitasking and have particularly good communication and organizational skills to handle multiple projects at one time.

Portfolio Management

Portfolio management occurs at the strategic level of the organization and is the centralized management of all projects currently proposed, in progress, or *planned for the future* to identify investment synergies, resource and budget considerations between projects that will enable an organization to achieve its strategic objectives. Organizations have limited resources—people, money, facilities, and equipment—and while there are many projects that an organization could undertake at any one time, it isn't possible to do them all. Looking at projects holistically enables executive management to review portfolios and programs, to determine which projects are or are not necessary, and in what order they should be completed. In this way, an organization can see where money should be spent—now and in the future—prioritize projects, stage the start of new projects, spread resources appropriately, and track their progress. In the absence of strong portfolio management, it is difficult for top managers to make fully informed decisions to approve the "right" new projects, shut down projects with no hope for success and plan for future projects. While most organization have a single project portfolio, very large global organizations may have multiple project portfolios.

The Role of the Portfolio Manager   The portfolio manager provides insights into high-level budgets and resource allocation and helps an organization plan for future projects by giving business managers better insights into where investments will result in most value added. Portfolio managers are also responsible for identifying gaps in the current project portfolio and singling out current projects and programs that may prevent completion of future ones. Some of the responsibilities of the portfolio manager are as follows:

- Map proposed projects to overall organization objectives and strategies.
- Assess the value that a proposed project brings to the company.
- Assess the complexity of proposed projects.
- Prioritize project proposals for project selection.
- Prioritize programs to keep up with changing business strategies.

Skills and Competencies   A portfolio manager must have proven himself/herself as a successful project manager and program manager. In addition to the skills of a project manager and program manager, a portfolio manager must possess strategic management skills, have a record of making top-level decisions, and be able to manage the entire portfolio of an organization's project proposals, projects, and programs. This requires exceptional coordination, communication, collaboration, and negotiation skills as well as technical skills to fully utilize supporting tools and techniques.

Putting It All Together

To be effective, project managers, program managers, and portfolio managers must understand and respect each other's roles. **Figure 13.9** compares the importance of different project management skills and competencies at the project, program and portfolio management levels. While the project manager is managing multiple tasks, schedule, and resources within a single project, the program manager is focused on coordinating between related projects within a program, to evaluate which projects are working toward the same or similar goals, and identifying resource dependencies between them. At the top level, portfolio managers are choosing, monitoring, and controlling all programs within an organization through negotiation and collaboration to ensure they fulfill the current and future strategic objectives of an organization.

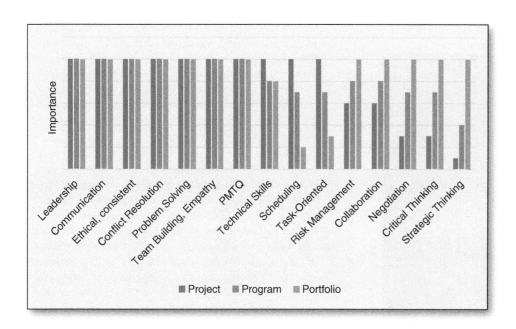

FIGURE 13.9   Comparison of importance of skills and competencies for project, program and portfolio management.

IT at Work 13.3 describes Steve Jobs' shared vision approach to project management that can be summed up as sharing the right information with the right people at the right time.

IT at Work 13.3

Great Project, Program and Portfolio Managers Share the Right Information with the Right People at the Right Time—All the Time!

As an entrepreneur, and sometimes as a project manager, you have one essential job—bring about the possible! This is what Steve Jobs of Apple computer fame and a few others have done. Steve Jobs (1955–2011) was an entrepreneur, industrial designer, and father of four who is regarded as the technology industry's most visionary leaders of our time (Figure 13.10). He cofounded Apple Inc. and reinvented the PC, music players, phones, tablets, and digital publishing. Jobs continuously managed remarkably

FIGURE 13.10 Steve Jobs, CEO and founder of Apple Computers and Pixar boss, was one of the greatest project managers.

innovative projects—extremely successful ones as well as many failures. Although widely recognized as a marketing and technology guru, Jobs was largely successful because of his project-based approach for managing his business and producing new products. His approach to executing projects ultimately changed the business world. Jobs' *shared vision* project management style offers lessons to help managers focus and motivate their team to get projects completed on schedule.

Shared vision and accountability A significant part of what made Jobs successful was his persistent push to keep projects moving while communicating with his team to ensure that they were working toward the shared vision. He stressed accountability and did not let anyone slide on that principle. He got to know everyone on the team and actively inspired them. Guy Kawasaki, Apple's chief evangelist and liaison to the Mac developer community, said Jobs appreciated great work. He was well known for giving employees feedback— publicly telling them if they were great or lousy. His bluntness infuriated some people but also motivated them to either do their best or leave.

Communication Structure, understanding, and inspiration depend on the one irreplaceable management skill: communication. Part of what made Jobs so successful was his constant push to keep projects moving while communicating with his team to ensure that they were working toward a shared vision. He held regular meetings to avoid wasting time with long e-mail chains and having to address the same concerns multiple times. As a project manager, your team members look to you for guidance. They mirror your emotions and if you can learn to communicate your vision with intense enthusiasm and certainty your team will follow suit and achieve the impossible before your faith inspires them.

Do not just listen—Understand! There is a big difference between listening and understanding. Jobs made sure that he understood everyone on his team and that they understood him. This is done by making people demonstrate that they understand and not simply asking them if they understand. When everyone confirms that they are on the same page, they will keep moving forward.

Sources: Compiled from Gallo (2015), Jimenez (2017), Peter Barron Stark Companies (2017), Congdon (2018), and Biography (2019).

Why Projects Fail

An important part of project management is knowing when to throw in the towel and declare an ongoing project a failure. Take, for example, the case of a Fortune 500 company that learned that six of its major projects were in trouble two months into a new project. In each case, it *seemed* as though the project failed overnight without warning. The CIO felt blindsided and executive management wanted to know who and what was to blame. The company's project management office (PMO) was asked to explain.

During the investigation, the PMO learned that the project staff felt strong but subtle pressure to keep problems to themselves. The six failing projects had executive sponsors who were politically powerful and known to attack people who delivered bad news. So, rather than report that their project was in trouble, staff worked harder, hoping to recover from missed deadlines, but deadlines were still missed.

Sometimes, the only right way to fix a project is to cancel it. If a project suffers from one or more of conditions listed in the following scenario, it has reached a point where its feasibility must be critically reexamined. It is very difficult to kill any project when millions of dollars have been spent to date—even when it is clearly the right decision.

> *The project is behind schedule. The scope changes almost daily. There were too few milestones identified during the planning stage to be able to monitor progress. Too many, or the wrong, resources were allocated. Because of the lack of regularly scheduled meetings, the project manager has no information on what the team members are working on at any given time. The team members are not communicating because they know that the project is on its deathbed and are afraid to say so. Many people in the company also know that the project is in trouble, except for senior management.*

The money already spent on the project, or **sunk costs**, should not be considered in the decision to cancel. The only relevant cost, from a financial point of view, is whether the total value from continuing is greater than the total cost of doing so.

sunk cost is a cost that has already been incurred and cannot be recovered.

The Project Management Office

Large organizations typically establish a **project management office (PMO)**. The overarching purpose of a PMO is to govern quality assurance, change management and in an IT environment, systems design and development (**Figure 13.11**).

project management office (PMO) is a group or department that defines and maintains standards for project management within an organization.

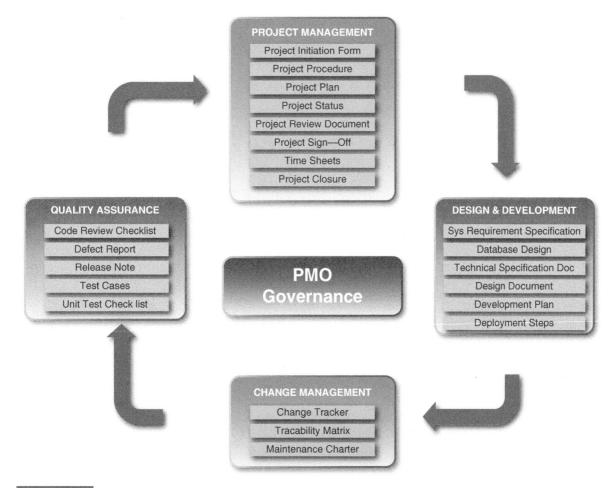

FIGURE 13.11 PMO governance in a systems environment.

A major role of the PMO is to define and maintain process standards by providing a framework for its PPPMs to follow to establish standard performance measures aligned with organizational objectives. The PMO also provides them with the necessary forms, templates, tools, and software as well as initial and ongoing training, expert advice, and a repository of lessons learned. By setting, maintaining, and ensuring standardization across all the projects in a company's portfolio, a PMO enables an organization to benefit from economies of scale, optimized consistency across projects, and resource sharing between projects to significantly improve how projects are managed.

PPPM Frameworks

Without a structured PPPM framework, organizations are likely to encounter unnecessary confusion, wasted resources, and miscommunications that can derail a project and adversely affect organizational performance, growth, and sustainability.

Typical benefits that organizations realize from using a structured PPPM approach are shown in **Figure 13.12**.

PPM Framework Benefits

- Better control of resources (people, money, facilities and equipment)
- Improved customer relations
- Shorter development times
- Lower Costs
- Higher quality and increased reliability
- Higher profit margins
- Improved productivity
- Better internal coordination
- Higher employee morale

FIGURE 13.12   Benefits of using a structured PPPM framework.

The two most widely used PPPM frameworks are the PMI Project Management Book of Knowledge, currently in its sixth edition (PMBOK6e) and PRINCE 2. Both methodologies are ideal in an IT environment since they both have an "agile" component. This makes both frameworks ideal for use in IT projects where the end product is often not well defined.

- **PMI® Project Management Body of Knowledge (PMBOK 6e)** is currently the definitive guide for managing projects of all types. Developed in the United States by the PMI, a highly regarded international nonprofit project management professional association, the PMBOK's use is widespread throughout the world. The most basic certification supported by PMI is the Certified Association Project Manager (CAPM), followed by Project Management Professional (PMP), Program Management Professional (PgMP), Portfolio Management Professional (PfMP), and specialized certifications focused on Agile, business analysis, scheduling, and risk management.

- **PRINCE2 (PRojects IN a Controlled Environment)** is a project management methodology developed by the Cabinet Office in the United Kingdom and currently managed and developed by AXELOS, a joint venture between Capita and the Cabinet Office. PRINCE2 is widely used in the UK private sector, Australia, and Western European Countries. Its certifications include PRINCE2 Foundation, PRINCE2 Practitioner, PRINCE2 Agile Foundation, and PRINCE2 Agile Practitioner. Currently, there are approximately 1 million people worldwide who hold a PRINCE2 certification.

These frameworks and certifications promote professionalism, quality standards, and ethics within the PPPM profession to enable project management professionals to work in virtually any industry, anywhere in the world.

In the next sections, the concepts, processes, tools, and techniques that lead to best PPPM practices are described in a framework based on the PMBOK 6e.

The Project Triple Constraint

Every project has three factors that must always be carefully managed throughout the project life cycle by the project manager as he/she works with project sponsors, the project team, and other stakeholders to meet project objectives and produce project deliverables. These three factors that must be managed effectively to facilitate successful completion and closure of any project are scope, time, and cost. Together they are referred to as the **triple constraint (Figure 13.13)**.

triple constraint is the combination of the three most significant elements of any project: scope, time, and cost. It is also known as the iron triangle.

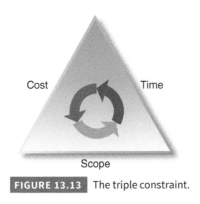

FIGURE 13.13 The triple constraint.

1. **Scope**   The project scope is the specification of what the project is supposed to accomplish—its outcomes or deliverables. Scope is measured in terms of the project size, goals, and requirements.

2. **Time**   A project is made up of *tasks*. Each task has a start date and an end date. The duration of a project extends from the start date of the first task to the finish date of the last task. Time needed to produce the deliverables is naturally related to the scope and availability of resources allocated to the project.

3. **Cost**   This is the estimation of the amount of money that will be required to complete the project. Cost itself encompasses various things, such as resources, labor rates for contractors, risk estimates, and bills of materials. All aspects of the project that have a monetary component are made part of the overall cost structure. Projects are often approved based on cost.

These three constraints are closely interrelated so that a change in any one of the three constraints manifests a change in the other two. For example, if the scope of work to be completed is changed, it will affect time and cost. Similarly, if the time in which a project must be completed is changed, it will affect the scope and cost of the project. And, if changes are made to the project budget, the amount of work (scope) that can be completed within a given amount of time will change. Ignoring the potential repercussions of adjusting project scope, time, or cost will lead to problems and may cause the project to ultimately fail.

Five Phases of the Project Management Life Cycle

The project life cycle starts with an idea or concept and a project plan. If the project is approved, then the project team proceeds; if not, it is either rejected, refined, and reconsidered or delayed. The life cycle of any project can be broken down into five major phases: Initiating, Planning, Execution, Monitoring/Controlling, and Closing (**Figure 13.14**). Each of these five phases consists of several procedures that must be completed to achieve a successful project outcome and produce the necessary documents to pass on so the next phase can begin. There are numerous procedures that must be performed during the project management life cycle, depending on the scope and complexity of the project. These procedures, inputs, outputs, and the tools and techniques used to produce them are discussed in detail in Sections 13.4 and 13.5 of this chapter.

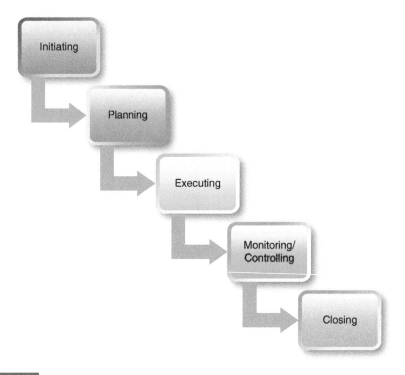

FIGURE 13.14 The five phases of the project management life cycle. All projects, IT or otherwise, move through five phases of the project management life cycle.

Ten Knowledge Areas of Project Management To efficiently and effectively move through every phase of the project management life cycle, project managers must effectively manage 10 key aspects of a project. Four reflect quality plus the triple constraint. These are commonly referred to as the "core" areas of a project. Five other areas "support" the core areas and one serves to "integrate" the core and support areas (**Figure 13.15**).

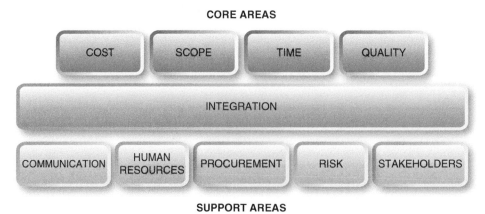

FIGURE 13.15 Ten knowledge areas of project management.

The areas that a project manager manages, monitors, and controls make sense when you think about what you need to pay attention to when completing a project. Let's take a simple example of organizing a tailgating party. Before you start, you must know the **scope** of the tailgating event you want to organize, how much *time* you have before the event needs to begin, and how much it will *cost* to achieve the desired outcome. Now, you'll want to make sure that everyone has a good time, so you'll want to make sure that you understand what's involved in creating and delivering a *quality* product. Once these areas of the project are understood, you'll need some support—**communication** will tell you how, when, and with whom to communicate, *human resources* will help you focus on who should be involved in the planning, execution, and monitoring of the event, a knowledge of HR will help you find the people that you need to organize the event, and *procurement* will help you find suppliers for items that you haven't already got, and you'll have to consider *risk*, just in case it rains or the game is canceled. Lastly, but certainly not least, you'll need to make sure that you understand how to handle all the people interested in the tailgating event, that is, your stakeholders.

> **scope**   is the body of work that needs to be completed within a project to achieve a desired outcome.

In the next two sections, you will learn how to apply a structured project management approach and integrated technology in the project management life cycle to improve the chances of project success. Walking through the project management life cycle stage by stage and learning about the tools and techniques that project managers use in each stage is a good way to understand the mechanics of project management.

Questions

1. What distinguishes a project from day-to-day operations?
2. What are the differences between PPPM?
3. In what ways are the roles of project, program and portfolio managers different?
4. What are the three components of the triple constraint?
5. What are the five phases in the project management life cycle?
6. Why is it important to use a structured project management approach?

13.4 Initiating, Planning, and Executing Projects

LO13.4 Discuss *the purpose of the initiation, planning, and execution phases of the project management life cycle and necessary documents and tools.*

While all five phases of the project management life cycle need to be carefully planned and executed, the first two phases of the project management life cycle are particularly important. If the existing business environment and project stakeholder needs are not considered and the project is not planned well, it is very unlikely that it will achieve its objectives.

Phase One: Project Initiating

Initiating involves deciding on what the project will produce and what work tasks need to be performed to produce the desired project deliverables. All organizations face the challenge of choosing which investments will add most value in a business and how to allocate scarce resources to competing projects. To do this, you must understand the business environment and the way it works. Typically, a senior manager identifies an opportunity, problem, or need and the desired business outcomes of the project.

Some of the key activities in the initiating stage include the following:

- Analyzing business requirements
- Identifying stakeholders and their roles
- Identifying stakeholder needs
- Evaluating business processes
- Reviewing financial reports and budgets
- Conducting a feasibility analysis
- Choosing a project manager
- Setting up the project team

During the initiating stage, you will create several documents to define a new project. Often a feasibility study (like the one described in the earlier part of this chapter) is performed and/or a **business case** is developed. Next, a statement of work (SOW) is prepared along with a project charter that will be signed off by stakeholders to launch the project.

business case is a presentation or document that outlines the justification for the start-up and funding of a project.

Preparing a Business Case
Projects start with an idea that is explained in a business case. To justify a project, a project manager, senior executive, or sponsor prepares a convincing business case for consideration. Since not all projects are viable and not all viable projects can be funded, business cases must be reviewed and prioritized. In the review process, projects compete for approval and funding. Project analysis methods are used to prioritize proposed projects and allocate the budget for maximum return. Budgeting decisions apply to all business investments, such as construction to increase manufacturing capacity, entering new markets, modernizing retail stores, R&D, and acquiring IT, apps, and enterprise systems. Investments in IT for marketing or manufacturing innovations compete head-on with investments needed to comply with new laws and regulations in finance, accounting, HR, and cybersecurity.

Statement of Work
If the business case is accepted, a **statement of work (SOW)** is prepared. The SOW is written as a definitive statement, which means that it defines the project plan but does not offer any options or alternatives in the scope. The project plan in the SOW is reviewed; a go or no-go decision is made; if a go decision is made, the project is initiated.

Project Charter
Another essential part of the initiating stage is the preparation of a **project charter (Figure 13.16)**. The project charter specifies the scope of the project, gives the project manager authority over the project, provides summary milestones, specifies the project budget, and identifies the source of project funding. Most importantly, the project charter formally approves the project so that it can progress to the planning phase.

Project Charter
ABC COMPANY
ACCOUNTS PAYABLE PROJECT

This Charter formally authorizes the Accounting Project Team to develop and implement a new accounts payment system for use in ABC Company's accounting group. A project plan will be developed and submitted to the Project Sponsor for approval. The project plan will include: scope statement; schedule; cost estimate; budget; and provisions for scope, resource, schedule, communications, quality, risk, procurement, and stakeholder management as well as project control. All resources will be assigned by the Project Sponsor, Tony Golembesky, National Accounts Director.

Project Scope

The purpose of the Accounts Payable project is to improve the timeliness and accuracy of accounts payable. This project meets ABC's need for improved efficiencies across all departments by reducing accounts payable cycle time and minimizing staffing required for accounts payable operations. The project deliverables shall include accounting system design, all coding, testing, implementation of an integrated system for use with existing IT infrastructure, and a user's guide. The objectives of the Accounts Payable project are to reduce accounts payable cycle time by 20% and reduce accounts payable staffing by 15%. High level risks for this project include ensuring implementation is completed without impacting ongoing accounts payable operations and ensuring there are no issues with migrating accounts from the legacy system to the new system. Success will be determined by the Project Sponsor once the system is implemented and one full accounts payable cycle has been completed that meets the objectives with no variances.

Project Manager

The Project Manager, Bruce Huester, is hereby authorized to interface with management as required, negotiate for resources, delegate responsibilities within the framework of the project, and to communicate with all contractors and management, as required, to ensure successful and timely completion of the project. The Project Manager is responsible for developing the project plan, monitoring the schedule, cost, and scope of the project during implementation, and maintaining control over the project by measuring performance and taking corrective action.

Milestone Schedule

The project plan will be submitted and approved in accordance with the milestone schedule below. Upon approval of the project plan resources will be assigned to the project and work will commence within 5 business days. The Project Sponsor must approve any schedule changes which may impact milestones. A detailed schedule will be included in the project plan.

The high level milestone schedule is:

Feb 1, 2021 – Project Plan Complete and Approved

Mar 31, 2021 – Accounts Payable Design Completed

May 31, 2021 – Coding Completed

June 30, 2021 – Testing Completed

July 31, 2021 – Beta Testing Completed

Sept 30, 2021 - Implementation Completed

Oct 15, 2021 – One Accounts Payable Cycle Complete and Project Completion

Project Budget

The budget for the Accounts Payable project is $730,000. The project is to be funded through the Accounting Technology Budget.

Sponsor Acceptance

Approved by the Project Sponsor

_____ Date: _____

Tony Golembesky, National Accounts Director

FIGURE 13.16   A sample project charter.

Once the business case has been reviewed and the project has received initial approval to proceed, it's time to move on to the project Planning phase, which is a much more complex phase of the project.

Templates are often used to create many of the project management documents, including the business case, the SOW, and the project charter. The **IT Toolbox** at the end of this chapter

template   is a sample document that already has some details in place.

contains a Business Case and an SOW template representative of those typically used in the initiating phase.

Phase Two: Project Planning

The planning phase further clarifies the project objectives and plans all necessary activities to complete the project. The planning phase focuses on time, schedule, costs, and allocation of resources. A project plan will be developed that addresses each of these items along with any associated risks that might occur during the execution and implementation of the project. Planning activities include the following:

- Identifying project deliverables
- Identifying tasks that need to be performed to complete the project
- Developing a list of tasks, called a work breakdown structure (WBS) to show the dependencies between the tasks
- Creating a schedule to carry out the task listed on the WBS
- Determining resources need to complete the project tasks
- Obtaining cost estimates for resources such as materials, equipment, and people
- Preparing a project budget
- Identifying potential risks and formulating appropriate responses to problems that could occur during the project

The WBS and risk register are two important documents that are prepared during the planning phase along with plans that consider how to manage each of the 10 knowledge areas.

Work Breakdown Structure The **work breakdown structure (WBS)** is a list of tasks that identify all work or activities that need to be performed, the order in which the work will be performed. An example of a WBS is shown in **Figure 13.17**. **Figure 13.18** shows a screenshot of a WBS (left side) developed using Microsoft Project. All project resources—people, equipment, facilities—are managed according to the tasks listed in the WBS.

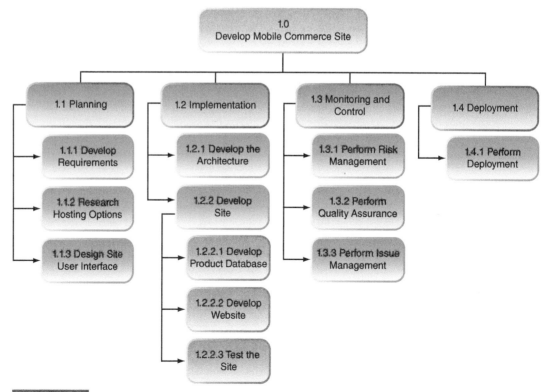

FIGURE 13.17 One segment of the WBS for a mobile commerce site project.

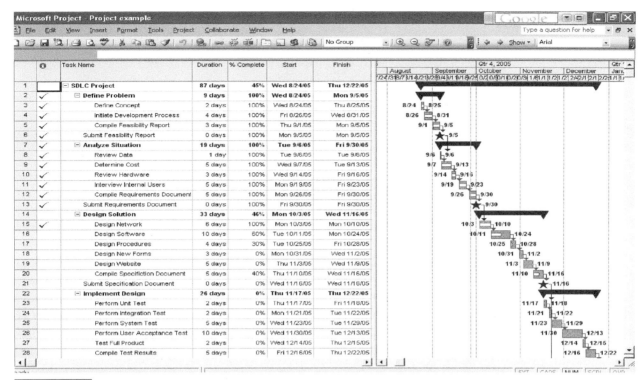

FIGURE 13.18 Microsoft Project screenshot of WBS (left side) and Gantt chart (right side).

Milestones The WBS breaks a project down into the tasks or activities that must be performed and defines the order in which they will be performed, to produce the deliverable or part of a deliverable at each milestone. Project **milestones** are very important scheduling and status devices because they enable the project manager to measure progress as the project proceeds through its planned life cycle. Lack of milestones has been a contributing factor in many project failures. Each milestone typically represents a deliverable (100% complete), but it may also signify the percent complete, such as 50% complete.

- **Milestone example** Assume that you are the project manager of a project for a client who wants to post a creative project on Kickstarter.com to raise funds using **crowdfunding**. You visit Kickstarter.com and do requirements analysis. You determine that you need to produce five deliverables: (1) a video, (2) a set of photos and illustrations, (3) a script that explains why the creative project deserves funding, (4) a set of pledge categories and rewards to backers, and (5) the final site with all deliverables uploaded to Kickstarter.com and tested. Each deliverable represents a milestone in your project plan. You then rely on your milestone schedule to verify that the project is on track or to warn of the need for corrective action. Milestones should be natural, important control points in the project and easy for everyone to recognize.

Risk Register During a project, many known and unknown risks can occur. Consideration of these risks needs to occur early in the project life cycle, during the planning phase. The **risk register** also lists the source of each risk, how you will respond to each risk, and the name of the person responsible for addressing the risk.

When the planning phase has been successfully completed, the project may be approved, sent back to the drawing board to be revised, or may be thrown on the rubbish heap and rejected. If it's approved, the real work of the project can begin.

Phase Three: Project Execution

It's during the execution phase of project management that the project team starts actual work on the project deliverable. Key activities listed on the WBS are carried out and the project plan

milestone is used to manage the project work effort, monitor results, and report meaningful status to project stakeholders.

crowdfunding is raising funds for a project from the public, or *crowd*, via the Web.

risk register lists all known risks and their source, an estimation of unknown risks and the response to be taken to each risk.

produced in the planning phase is put into action. Activities performed in the execution phase include the following:

- Allocating resources to tasks listed on the WBS
- Communicating and coordinating with key stakeholders
- Performing the tasks listed on the WBS
- Reporting progress that has been made in regular meetings

Gantt chart is a horizontal bar chart that graphically displays the project schedule.

Gantt Chart
A **Gantt chart** is a bar chart that is used to show the timeline of the project schedule, as shown on the right side of Figure 13.18. On a Gantt chart, the start and finish dates of all tasks and milestones appear as bars whose length represents its duration. Gantt charts are multipurpose visualization tools that are used in planning, execution, and monitoring phases and enable the project manager to prepare at-a-glance status reports.

Cost Estimation
While costs are not technically part of the WBS, the projects' estimated cost can be calculated from the WBS. Each task or activity has a start date and duration, which determine its finish date. For example, if a task starts on Monday, November 2, and takes eight workdays (excluding weekend days) to complete, the finish date is Wednesday, November 11. Assume that the resources—people, equipment, and materials—needed to complete the task and their costs are known. Project management software computes the cost of the project based on labor time (duration) of each task in the WBS and the cost of labor or other resource.

responsibility matrix lets everyone know who is responsible for completion of tasks.

Responsibility Matrix
If a resource is listed on the WBS, that means they are responsible for at least one project task. A **responsibility matrix** shows who has primary responsibility and who has support responsibility for each activity listed on the WBS. **Table 13.3** is an example of a responsibility matrix.

TABLE 13.3 **Responsibility Matrix Showing Primary and Support Responsibilities for WBS Tasks**

		Level of Responsibility				
WBS ID	**Activity**	**Anna**	**Bart**	**Beth**	**Fred**	**Don**
1.1	Storyboard video		S		P	
1.2	Recruit volunteers to act in video		S	P		
1.3	Record video segments				P	S
2.1	Select five photographs and images	P				S
2.2	Crop and edit photos	S				P

P = primary responsibility, S = support responsibility

13.5 Monitoring/Controlling and Closing Projects

LO13.5 Describe *the activities of the monitoring/controlling and closing phases of the project management life cycle and the increasingly important role of the project management technology quotient (PMTQ).*

Once the project work has begun, it's time to start monitoring performance, collecting feedback, and putting controls in place to correct any variances from the original project plan and eventually formally closing out the project.

Phase Four: Project Monitoring and Controlling

Project Monitoring and Controlling include tracking, reviewing, and managing the progress and performance of the project along with managing any necessary changes.

Monitoring and controlling occur continuously while the project work is being executed, so it overlaps with Project Execution. These phases, described in Figure 13.18, depend on the baseline, milestones, responsibility matrix, and other elements from the planning phase. They keep the project team informed of project status and help them cope with challenges they encounter. Except for short, simple projects, there are always risks and changes that need to be kept under control and documented.

Monitoring depends on prompt and candid feedback from the project team, as you read in the opening case. In-person visits, reports, and records are also useful monitoring tools. Project control depends on systems and decision rules for managing variances between the project's scope, cost, schedule, and quality and the realities of project implementation.

Throughout the project, the work must be tracked against the schedule to ensure that the project is on track. Doing this helps identify variances from the baseline target early so they can be addressed before the gap between actual and expected performance becomes too great. In this way, cost overruns and risk can be minimized and the probability of completing the project on time and on budget is maximized. Feedback is very important in this stage. While monitoring identifies problems, feedback enables controls to be put in place to "stop the bleeding." Activities during the Monitoring/Controlling phase include the following:

- Measuring extent and timing of task completion
- Comparing actual versus expected performance on all tasks
- Collecting feedback
- Taking appropriate action to correct problems and address issues
- Making report reports to appropriate stakeholders
- Documenting progress and updating the project plan, as needed

Project Status Report   To monitor the progress of a project, project status reports will be prepared and reviewed to check on the progress of the project. Status reports are typically prepared once a week. Status reports include a summary of the project status vis-à-vis planned performance; work planned; work completed; work planned; open issues; open risks; status of project milestones and deliverables; open change requests; project key performance indicators (KPIs); schedule status and cost status.

Scope Creep   During the project, it is almost guaranteed that requests will be made that change the scope of the work required to produce the project deliverable. **Scope creep** refers to the growth of the project, which might seem inconsequential—at least to the person who is requesting that change. It is imperative that scope is continuously monitored and that any change to the scope of the project be explicitly controlled by compensating for changes in the budget, the deadline, and/or resources. Consider the following scenario.

scope creep   is the piling up of small changes that by themselves are manageable but in aggregate are significant.

The project scope is to build a new online accounting application capable of processing at least 1,000 expense reports (in multiple currencies) per day, which has a budget of $200,000, and is expected to last three months. After the project is started, the scope expands to include processing of thousands of sales commissions per day. The project manager needs to renegotiate the project's duration and budget for the added functionality, testing, and user training, making sure that any requested change, no matter how small, is documented and accompanied by approval.

Information system design is highly susceptible to scope creep for many reasons. Intended users ask for additional features. People who were not intended users ask to be included. Technology changed from the time the business case was written and systems development began. The actions of a competitor, supplier, or regulatory agency triggered additional requests for functionality. Because scope creep is expensive, project managers impose controls on changes requested by users. These controls help to prevent *runaway projects*—systems development projects that are so far over budget and past deadline that they must be abandoned, typically with large monetary loss.

Integrated Change Control Quite often, changes occur as the project proceeds. Changes tend to have a trickle-down effect because of task dependencies and shared resources. For example, consider the following three activities from Table 13.3:

1.1 Storyboard a video.

1.2 Recruit volunteers to act in the video.

1.3 Record video segments.

Activity 1.3 is dependent on the completion of activities 1.1 and 1.2. Video recording cannot start until after the video has been storyboarded and actors are available.

Integrated change control processes help to manage the disruption resulting from requested changes and corrective actions across the project life cycle (**Figure 13.19**). Integrated change control processes are always documented and saved in the event of project failure or lawsuits related to the failure. These documents are needed to defend decisions—what did and did not happen, such as the following:

- Approved change requests
- Rejected change requests
- Updates to the project plan
- Updates to the scope
- Approved corrective and preventive actions
- Approved defect repair
- Validated defect repair

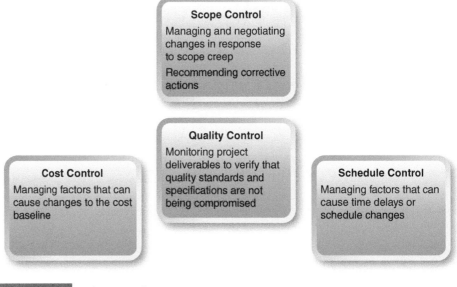

FIGURE 13.19 Project controls.

Critical path is the shortest time possible to complete all tasks required to finish the project. A delay of any task on the critical path will delay the project.

Critical Path Analysis All projects have a **critical path** that extends the length of the project and determines the shortest path along which all projects tasks must be completed in order to finish the project. Project management software shows the critical path on the Gantt chart, as in **Figure 13.20**. Each task or activity on the critical path is called a **critical task** or activity. Critical tasks must finish on schedule because delays will delay the project unless something is done to compensate. While it may seem that adding new people to a project is an obvious solution, in fact, it may initially slow it down. If any noncritical tasks get delayed enough, they could go critical, so both critical and noncritical paths need to be monitored.

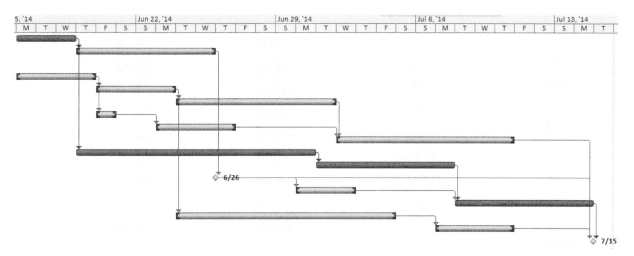

FIGURE 13.20 The critical path is shown as red (dark) bars. The critical path consists of all tasks from project start to finish that must be completed on time for the project to finish on time.

Project Baseline Plan When the project plan is finalized and accepted, the accepted plan becomes the **baseline** or master plan. The baseline is used for monitoring and controlling. Any change to the baseline is a deviation, or **variance**, to the plan—and it needs to be documented. Using project management software, you can save the WBS as the baseline. From then on, deviations will automatically be documented as variances from the baseline, as shown in **Figure 13.21**.

baseline is a specification of the project plan that has been formally reviewed and agreed upon. It should be changed only through a formal change control process.

Work			
Scheduled:	680 hrs	Remaining:	581.2 hrs
Baseline:	528 hrs	Actual:	98.8 hrs
Variance:	152 hrs	Percent complete:	15%

Costs			
Scheduled:	$14,104.00	Remaining:	$11,751.60
Baseline:	$10,624.00	Actual:	$2,352.40
Variance:	$3,480.00		

Task Status		Resource status	
Tasks not yet started:	7	Work resources:	4
Tasks in progress:	9	Overallocated work resources:	4
Tasks completed:	0	Material resources:	0
Total tasks:	16	Total resources:	8

FIGURE 13.21 Work and cost variances from the agreed-upon project baseline are documented by project management software.

Once all work has been monitored and controlled and the project deliverable has been completed, it's time to move on to the final phase of the project management life cycle and formally close the project.

IT at Work 13.4 describes the major problems the occurred when the Berlin Brandenburg Airport (BER) project was completely botched and delayed for more than 10 years.

IT at Work 13.4

Project Management Mistakes Delay Berlin Airport Opening by Nine Years

In 2019, Berlin had 35.65 million passengers going in and out of its two airports—Berlin Schönefeld in the southeast section of the city and BFG Berlin-Tegel in the northwest. Passengers should have been flying into the new Berlin Brandenburg Airport (BER), but its opening has been delayed over eight years because of bungled project management practices.

When construction of BER started in 2006, it was originally scheduled to open in 2011. The actual grand opening of BER was to take place on June 2012, with Willy Brandt, Germany's ex-Chancellor and Angela Merkel, current German Chancellor as guests of honor. Thousands of volunteers had conducted trial runs leading up to the big day. The media had prepared round-the-clock coverage of the opening and Lufthansa was ferrying in one of its newly acquired Airbus A380s for the inaugural flight to Frankfurt. Fast forward to February 2020 and the world is still waiting for BER to open. But the event never happened. In mid-May 2012, the opening of BER was called off because of "technical issues" that were initially attributed to a faulty fire-protection system. As time went by, other problems were found including wiring that overheated—and eventually led to 800 wiring violations, escalators that were too short, and serious structural faults. Technical issues weren't the only problems at the ill-fated BER. There were allegations of corruption, several key contractors were fired, and several legal disputes emerged around project financing. Andreas Speath, a German aviation industry analyst bemoaned that "There was never a central management installed to oversee and properly monitor the project as a whole." At present, the airport is still a huge construction site, and problems with the fire protection system still have not been resolved.

In all, the deadline has been pushed back six times due to various project management problems. Currently, BER is scheduled to open on October 31, 2020—nine years after its originally scheduled opening—and registration is currently underway for 20,000 volunteers who will trial the airport. However, some people believe the airport will never open. Thosten Dirks, a Lufthansa board member, stated that BER "will be torn down and built anew."

Throughout the duration of the project, there have several construction freezes because of inadequate funding and at one point a whopping $897 million (€750 million) was needed to keep the project going. The original budget for BER was $3.1 billion (€2.83 billion) now it is in excess of $5 billion (€7 billion) and the ongoing delays are costing taxpayers $1,085 million (€l million) per day. It also now appears that the new airport will be too small to handle current volumes of air traffic in and out of Berlin. While Tegel and Schönefeld jointly served more than 33 million travelers in 2019, the new BER is only initially equipped to handle 27 million. In addition to gross inconveniences to the general public, German aviation authorities, and the forced resignation of Mayor, Klaus Wowereit, BER delays have been partly blamed for the insolvency of at least one German airline. Air Berlin was relying on using BER as a hub for more lucrative long-haul flight connections to expand its operations.

All in all, the BER project has turned out to be a true planning, monitoring, and controlling disaster that has become a running joke with the residents of Berlin and tarnished Germany's reputation for engineering prowess and efficiency.

Sources: Compiled from Haines (2017), Reuters (2017), Ros (2017), Daily Sabah Tourism (2018), Massey (2019), Schumacher (2019), and Flughafen Berlin Brandenburg (2020).

Phase Five: Project Closing

At closing, the project manager declares the project complete. In keeping with the saying, "It ain't over until the fat lady sings," project closing can't occur until the project sponsor signs off the final project deliverable and formally accepts the project outcome. During the closing phase of the project life cycle, the project manager confers with the project team, project sponsor, and other project stakeholders to conduct a **postmortem** in which they document lessons learned to improve future projects.

Activities that occur during closing include the following:

postmortem is a method for evaluating project performance, identifying lessons learned, and making recommendations for future projects.

- Delivering the final project deliverable
- Obtaining and documenting formal stakeholder acceptance of the project deliverable
- Documenting and archiving all project documents
- Documenting "Lessons Learned" to inform upcoming projects
- Formally releasing all resources

Lessons Learned Report   An important document that is created during project closing is the Lessons Learned report. The **Lessons Learned** enables future project teams to learn from the project team's positive and negative experiences. The Lessons Learned identify the reasons the project was successful or not, strengths and weaknesses of the project plan, how problems were detected and resolved, and how the project was successful in spite of them.

Here are three common lessons learned that are frequently documented during the project closing phase.

- **Communication is king**   The most important skill that a project manager can learn is good communication. Timely, frequent, and targeted communication to all key stakeholders is paramount to keeping a project on track. Make sure that you communicate early and often to the right people in the right way!

- **Set realistic and detailed project plans with adequate time and resources**   Projects are subject to unanticipated and uncontrollable events, so they need to have slack time built into the schedule and budget. However, project teams can be pressured to cut project costs. In response, they might reduce the time and budget allocated to training, testing, and change management. These cuts result in poor quality and low user acceptance.

- **Encourage timely feedback and be willing to listen**   All projects encounter difficulties. Make sure that employees know they will not be punished for raising concerns, even if other project members deny that problems exist. Fear blocks the flow of useful information.

- **Manage risk with regular project status reviews**   For the most part, no one likes formal project reviews, but they are necessary to identify and address current and potential problems.

Achieving a High PMTQ

Project professionals no longer just work with people, they also must be proficient in using technology, that is, must have a high PMTQ. PMTQ is similar in concept to IQ and EQ, but instead of measuring intelligence or emotional quotients, PMTQ focuses on how "tech savvy" a person or organization is. A high PMTQ helps organizations adapt to rapidly changing technology, acknowledge its central role in the business, and view IT as a means of achieving improved performance and growth.

A large number of organizations are seeing significant improvement in their project success rates after deploying PPPM software and are working hard on improving their PMTQ by integrating more sophisticated software apps and hardware into their projects. However, many others still fall back on apps such as Excel to manage projects. Often, this is because project managers and/or team members have limited experience with dedicated project management software tools that offer more advanced features and far more reliable results. However, as technology becomes a more integral part of project management practices, those that don't take advantage of it will lose their ability to compete.

In stressing the importance of creating and maintaining a high PMTQ in combination with a structured project management framework, the PMI (2019b) encourages organizations to achieve a high PMTQ by engaging in the following activities:

- **Encourage always-on curiosity**   Try out new project delivery approaches, new ideas, new perspectives, and new technologies by integrating emerging project delivery practices, such as AI, without chasing every new digital trend.

- **Practice all-inclusive leadership**   Manage technology as well as people, including those who know how to manage technology and some who are digital employees like robots. Advocate for technology and enlist support from "digital ambassadors."

- **Create a future-proof talent pool**   Recruit and retain project professionals with good technology skills who can keep up with changing technology and are willing to update their skills accordingly. Invest in training current project professionals before hiring new ones.

Today, there are hundreds of PPPM apps designed specifically to assist in the activities of different project management phases mentioned earlier in this chapter. Project management software packages fall into the three main classes, and a sampling of apps that fall into each of these categories is shown in **Table 13.4**.

TABLE 13.4 **Improve Your PMTQ with Software**

Class	Focus	Product	Website
Low end	Single or small projects	Trello	https://trello.com
		Zoho Projects	https://www.zoho.com/projects
		Liquid Planner	https://www.liquidplanner.com
		Mavenlink	https://www.mavenlink.com
Mid-range	Multiple projects and users	Microsoft Project 2019	https://products.office.com/en-us/project/project-management-software
		monday.com	https://monday.com
		Celoxis	https://www.celoxis.com
		Wrike	https://www.wrike.com
High end	Large projects PPM	Clarity PPM	https://www.broadcom.com/products/software/business-management/clarity-project-portfolio-management-software
		SAP Portfolio	https://www.sap.com/products/project-portfolio-management.html
		Project Portfolio Office	https://www.go2ppo.com
Open source	Varied	Asana	https://asana.com
		Freedcamp	https://freedcamp.com
		ProjectLibre	https://www.openproject.org
		Redmine	http://www.projectlibre.com
			https://www.redmine.org

Low-end modern project management software that is Web based is particularly useful to small companies. It enables projects to be managed regardless of location and time differences and facilitates communication among project managers and their team members. These types of apps are usually charged by user per month and can be very cost-effective, particularly if it's being used for a one-off project.

More sophisticated project management apps are offered on-site, cloud-based, or online and continue to be improved with advanced features and the ability to integrate with other technologies. Along with project professional technology skills, the decision of which project management software to use depends on project needs, company's needs, size of business, and industry. For example, if an organization is developing a new marketing campaign or revamping a website, these are relatively straightforward initiatives with only a few tasks, and a low-end or open-source app would be sufficient to do the job. On the other hand, taking a new product line to market might involve hundreds of interdependent tasks performed by many people over several months, or consider the myriad of people and tasks involved in the development of BER over the past eight years described in IT at Work 13.4. In these larger projects, more sophisticated software is needed to provide a central repository for project documents, schedules, charts, and reports.

However, PMTQ goes beyond just integrating software into PPPM processes. It also includes incorporating some innovative systems development techniques such as DevOps, Agile, and prototyping and some of the new innovative emerging technologies like robotics, machine learning and drones. By 2030, Gartner (2019) predicts that 80% of today's project management tasks will be eliminated as AI and virtual reality are integrated into PPPM software to perform the data collection, analysis, and report tasks that make up a large percentage of PPPM work.

Questions

1. What processes help ensure that the impacts resulting from requested changes and corrective actions are managed across the project life cycle?

2. What happens when a task on the critical path is delayed?

3. What are the three attributes that must be managed effectively for successful completion and closure of any project?

4. Why are lessons learned from a completed project identified?

5. Why is the evaluation of a project's success or failure somewhat subjective?

6. What are three best practices to keep projects on track?

7. Why are IT projects high susceptible to scope creep?

8. Why is it important for an organization to have a high PMTQ? And, how can they maintain it?

Career Insight 13.1

Becoming a Project Manager

Project management is a high-level skill and a demanding career choice. The most successful upper-level project managers typically have an MBA or other business degree, a recognized project management certification, and financial background to plan and manage the project budget. A typical job description for an IT project manager is as follows:

Responsible for the coordination and completion of projects within the information technology department. Oversees all aspects of projects and project budgets. Sets deadlines, assigns responsibilities, and monitors and summarizes progress of project. Builds and maintains working relationships with team members, vendors, and other departments involved in the projects. Prepares reports for upper management regarding status of project. Requires a bachelor's degree, two to four years of experience, and knowledge of project management software. MBA is preferred. Leads and directs the work of others. A wide degree of creativity and latitude is expected. Typically reports to a senior manager or head of a unit/department.

Chapter Summary

LO13.1 *Identify* typical business drivers for systems development projects and the five phases of the systems development life cycle (SDLC).

Typical drivers for systems development include globalization, e-commerce, security, communication, collaboration and partnerships, knowledge management, continuous improvement, and business process redesign. The five phases of the systems development life cycle (SDLC) are systems planning, analysis, design, implementation/testing, and maintenance/support.

LO13.2 *Define* the different systems development methodologies, the major differences between them, and the tools and techniques used.

The major systems development methodologies are waterfall, object-oriented, Agile, and DevOps. The waterfall method is sequential and predictive, whereas O-O analysis and design is an iterative process that emphasizes modularity and reusability and encourages communication between analysts, developers and users. The Agile method is more flexible than the waterfall model and O-O and collaborates closely with system users, working in short sprints to stay current with user requirements and minimize risk. Agile emphasizes competency over process. DevOps closely aligns itself with an organization's ITSM and emphasizes integration between systems developers and IT operations personnel. DevOps' goal is minimal disruption of the business and maximum performance reliability rather than speed and rapid development. Tools used in systems development include JAD, RAD, rapid prototyping, CASE tools, source code generators, and low-code development platforms.

LO13.3 *Describe* the differences between project, program and portfolio management, the five phases of the project management life cycle, and the ten knowledge areas of project management.

Project management is the discipline of using established principles, procedures, and policies to successfully guide a single project from start to finish to achieve specific goals and meet specified criteria within a specified period. **Program management** involves overseeing and controlling a group of related projects and focused on current project. **Project portfolio management** involves the centralized management of all proposed, current, and future projects in an organization. Project management occurs at the operational level of the organization. Program management occurs at the tactical level of the organization and provides oversight of project managers. Project portfolio management is a strategic-level initiative that closely aligns with the business strategy and future goals and provides oversight of project and program managers. The five phases of the project management life cycle are initiating, planning, execution, monitoring/controlling and closing. The ten knowledge areas of project management are time, cost, scope, quality, integration, human resources, risk management, procurement, communication, and stakeholders.

LO13.4 *Discuss* the purpose of the initiation, planning, and execution phases of the project management life cycle and necessary documents and tools.

Initiating a project involves deciding on project objectives and what work tasks need to be performed in order to achieve the desired outcome. During the initiating phase, the project manager creates several documents to define a new project. Often a feasibility study (like the one described in the earlier part of this chapter) is performed and/or a business case is developed. Next, a SOW is prepared along with a project charter that will be signed off by stakeholders to launch the project. Templates are often used to create these documents. Project planning further clarifies project objectives and plans all necessary activities to complete the project. The planning phase focuses on time, schedule, costs, and allocation of resources. A project plan will be developed that addresses each of these items along with any associated risks that might occur during the execution and implementation of the project. The WBS and risk register are two important documents that are prepared during the planning phase along with plans that consider how to manage each

of the ten knowledge areas. In the execution phase of project management, the project team starts actual work on the project deliverable. During the execution phase, software that supports Gantt charts, cost estimation and responsibility matrices improves speed, consistency, and accuracy.

LO13.5 *Describe* the activities of the monitoring/controlling and closing phases of the project management life cycle and the increasing role of the project management technology quotient (PMTQ).

Project monitoring and controlling include tracking, reviewing, and managing the progress and performance of the project along with managing any necessary changes. Monitoring and controlling occur continuously while the project work is being executed, so these phases overlap with project execution. Monitoring depends on prompt and candid feedback from the project team, as you read in the opening case. In-person visits, reports, and records are also useful monitoring tools. Project control depends on systems and decision rules for managing variances between the project's scope, cost, schedule, and quality and the realities of project implementation. Project baseline plan, status reports, and integrated change control are essential elements of monitoring and controlling projects. Tools used include software that supports critical path analysis and project baseline plan tracking. In the closing phase of the project life cycle, the project manager confers with the project team, project sponsor, and other project stakeholders to conduct a postmortem in which they document lessons learned to improve future projects. PMTQ is becoming increasingly important in PPPM as more and more apps are developed with greater abilities to automate and integrate project management tasks. Those companies that don't embrace PMTQ by providing technical training to project professionals and adopting PPPM software will be disadvantaged.

Key Terms

3D printing   504
Agile   499
baseline   525
behavioral feasibility   495
business case   518
business drivers   493
business need   493
CASE tools   504
communication   517
critical path   524
critical task   524
crowdfunding   521
deliverable   495
DevOps   501
economic feasibility   495
extreme programming   501
Gantt chart   522
go/no-go decision   495
integrated CASE tools   505
integrated change control   524
Joint Application Development (JAD)   503
Kanban   500
legal and organizational feasibility   495
lessons learned   527
logical design   495

low-code development platform   505
lower CASE tools   505
milestones   521
object-oriented (O-O)   498
parallel conversion   496
phased conversion   496
physical design   495
pilot conversion   496
plunge conversion   496
portfolio   506
portfolio management   510
postmortem   526
program   506
program management   529
project   506
project charter   518
project management   529
project management office (PMO)   513
project management technology quotient (PMTQ)   507
project portfolio management (PPM)   529
project sponsor   507
prototype   504
Rapid Application Development (RAD)   503
rapid prototyping   504

responsibility matrix   522
risk register   521
scope   517
scope creep   523
Scrum   500
Scrumban   501
Software engineering   504
source code generator   505
sprint   500
stakeholder   507
statement of work (SOW)   518
sunk cost   513
systems development   493
systems development life cycle (SDLC)   492
technical feasibility   494
template   519
triple constraint   515
upper CASE tools   504
use-case description   498
use-case diagram   498
use-case model   498
waterfall model   497
work breakdown structure (WBS)   520

Assuring Your Learning

Discuss: Critical Thinking Questions

1. Business cases take a long time to research and write. As a result, they are also time-consuming to review. Explain why business cases require so much effort and detail.

2. What risks might the use of project portfolio management (PPM) minimize? Do you think PPM can guarantee honest and unbiased project approvals or not? Explain your position.

3. Why should each deliverable be made a milestone?

4. Why is the critical path an important monitoring tool?

5. How does diagramming the triple constraint as a triangle clearly demonstrate how time, scope, and cost are interrelated?

6. Refer to the Center for Project Management's list of seven IT project management mistakes. Select two of these mistakes and explain how they contribute to project failure.

7. Why should the go/no-go decision be made more than once in a project's life cycle?

8. If a project is started without a documented baseline, what risks might the project and project team face?

9. Explain how control activities are, in effect, risk management activities.

10. Why is it tough to ignore sunk costs when evaluating a failing project?

11. Why are IT projects so susceptible to scope creep?

12. What leads to a runaway project?

13. What feasibilities are needed prior to IT project approval?

14. Explain the stages of the SDLC.

Explore: Online and Interactive Exercises

1. ProjectLibre Cloud is the open-source replacement of Microsoft Project. Visit the ProjectLibre website at **www.ProjectLibre.org**.

   a. Download the free software.

   b. Assume that you are the project manager on a project of your choice that you are able to manage. Several project examples are delivering a tailgate party for 50 people, remodeling a kitchen, creating a YouTube video for advertising a new product, or implementing a new cloud accounting IS.

   c. Use the software to plan a project of your choice. Create a WBS and Gantt chart.

2. Research and compare the current top three open-source project management tools. What are their limitations?

3. Research the software packages of three project management vendors listed in Table 13.4 and find a review of each one. Write a report that compares the features of the packages, including prices, and that summarizes the reviews.

4. Assume that you are a member of a project team working on a project with a six-month timeline. The materials your team needs to complete their first set of tasks will arrive three days later than their promised delivery date. The delay has a 10% chance of delaying completion of the project. You know that no one will tell the project manager of the delayed delivery because it is the first month of the project so it does not seem important enough to report. Would you inform the project manager of the delay? Explain your decision. Now assume that you did not report the delay and such delays happened in each month afterward. What would you do and when? In your opinion, should the entire team present these problems? Explain your decisions.

Analyze & Decide: Apply IT Concepts to Business Decisions

1. You are the project manager and need to compose an SOW for clients who want you to develop a Kickstarter.com site for their project, as discussed in the chapter.

   a. Start off by composing an SOW using a standard SOW template that you found and downloaded from the Internet.

   b. Use **Tom's Planner** (https://www.tomsplanner.com) or other free Gantt chart software to create a Gantt chart for your project.

   c. Assume that after your clients review your SOW and Gantt chart, they request that you discount the price 20%. Based on the triple constraints, how would you respond?

2. Explore project management software on vendors' websites. Select a single project management package, download the demo, and try it. Make a list of the important features of the package. Be sure to investigate its cloud and collaboration features. Report your findings.

3. Managing a project with Microsoft Project is often the approach to IT project management, but many users still prefer to use Microsoft Excel instead. The main reasons are that MS Project is too expensive, wastes too much time to set up and keep updated, and is tough to use. The debate between Excel and Project has valid arguments for either approach. Research the reviews of Excel and MS Project as project management tools. Write a business case for the use of each.

Reinforce: Ensure Your Understanding of the Key Terms

Solve the online crossword provided for this chapter.

Web Resources

More resources and study tools are located on the student website. You'll find useful Web links and self-test quizzes that provide individualized feedback.

Case 13.2

Business Case: It Took 10 Years and More Than $600 Million to Realize That Big Muscles, Not Computer, Can Best Move Baggage

Second only to the ongoing saga of BER, described in IT at Work 13.4, one of the most classic examples of project management failures on record is the development and deployment of an expensive automated airport baggage system that never worked and delayed the opening of DIA, one of the busiest airports in the United States, by 16 months. Twenty-five years later, it's getting a new one!

In 1995, the management of the soon-to-be-opened Denver International Airport strode boldly into the future when it purchased one of the first ever computerized baggage-handling systems. That ill-fated system immediately had 21 miles of track—mostly underground—became known for its inability to protect and deliver practically every piece of baggage assigned to it. To add insult to injury, the absence of a working baggage handling system meant that the state-of-the-art airport could not open on time or anytime reasonably close to its projected opening date.

The new $200 million baggage-handling system was designed to be the state of the art. Conventional baggage-handling systems are manual, and each airline operates its own system. DIA wanted an automated one-baggage-system-fits-all configuration that it could lease back to multiple airlines.

The system would consist of 100 computers, 56 laser scanners, conveyor belts, and thousands of motors. The system would contain 400 fiberglass carts, each carrying a single suitcase through 22 miles of steel track. Operating at 20 miles per hour, the system would deliver 60,000 bags per hour from dozens of gates. The system was designed to carry luggage from airplane to baggage carousel in less than 10 minutes. The goal was that the luggage would be waiting at the carousel for deplaning passengers. No more waiting for baggage at the end of a long trip—so customer satisfaction would soar.

The city of Denver selected two companies to assist in the project management process. Greiner Engineering—an engineering, architecture, and airport planning company—and Morrison-Knudsen Engineering—a design-construction organization. The City of Denver, Greiner, and MKE made up the project management team that coordinated schedules, controlled costs, managed information, and administered approximately 100 design contracts, 160 general contractors, and more than 2,000 subcontractors.

A review of the project timeline and project management mistakes that were made provides some insight into the difficulties that contributed to the failure of the project

- **DIA Construction starts**   November 1989.
- **Ignored experts**   In 1990, the City of Denver hired Breier Neidle Patrone Associates to do a feasibility analysis to build a fully integrated baggage system. Reports advised that complexity made the project unfeasible despite this a decision is made to go ahead with the DIA project and the DIA project management team asked for bids for the automated baggage-handling system.
- **Underestimated complexity**   Fall 1991: Of the 16 companies included in the bidding process, only 3 responded. None could complete the project in time for the October 1993 opening. All three bids were rejected, and the urgent search for a company that would meet the deadline continued.
- **Poor planning and impossible expectations**   In April 1992, DIA went to contract with BAE Systems to complete the project in time for the October 1993 opening—ignoring expert evidence that the timeline was impossible to achieve.
- **Lack of due diligence**   Contract terms between DIA and BAE and project specifications were hammered out in only three meetings. The rush to contract ignored the feasibility analysis. The pressure to move quickly drove them to skip critical due diligence steps.
- **Excluded key stakeholders**   BAE and the airport project management team excluded airline representatives during the negotiations.
- **Scope creep**   1992–1993: Numerous changes in the scope of the project were made. For instance, Continental Airlines requested ski equipment handling facilities be added to its concourse, and the scope of the baggage-handling system expanded from handling only Concourse "B" baggage to handling baggage for the entire airport.
- **Ignored interface design**   Baggage-handling system had to interface with the airport rather than the other way round because the design of the building was started before the baggage system design was known. The designers of the physical building only made general allowances for where they thought the baggage system would go. DIA had sharp corners that required turns that baggage carts could not navigate. To keep carts from falling off the rails, the speed of the system had to be decreased to 30 cars per minute thereby eliminating DIA's competitive advantage of fast baggage turnaround time.

As a result of the mistakes made, the project was a spectacular failure that teaches us a lot about the importance of involving the right stakeholders at the right time, making sure project communication flows and that scope creep is carefully controlled. When the project was abandoned in 2005—10 years after it was begun—the project costs had jumped from the initial $200 million to $600 million and the underground tunnels are used by airport employees to move baggage between the terminal and concourses using reliable tugs and carts.

Despite the massive setbacks and huge cost overruns of the original system, in January 2020 DIA announced that two new automated baggage systems are on track to be completed in 2021. Let's hope they have learned from their past mistakes and have better luck this time around.

Sources: Compiled from Johnson (2005), Weiss (2005), Harden (2015), Montgomery (2017), Sylte (2019), and Vendituoli (2020).

Case 13.3

Demo Case: Mavenlink Project Management and Planning Software

Mavenlink is a vendor that provides easy-to-follow video tutorials and online project management resources through the World's First Unified Project Delivery Cloud. With Mavenlink, you can track project timelines, collaborate on tasks, manage team activities, and integrate with Google Apps, QuickBooks, and Salesforce from a single workplace environment.

Visit Mavenlink's website **http://Mavenlink.com**. Read about the company and its project management products. Search for the

Mavenlink Tutorial by Michelle on YouTube and watch the video. (The video runs for 12:54 minutes.)

Questions

1. What Mavenlink features support project planning?
2. What Mavenlink features support project monitoring and control?
3. How does Mavenlink support change management supported?
4. If you were a project manager, would you choose Mavenlink to manage your projects? Explain.

IT Toolbox

Project Management Templates

One of the tools typically used by project managers is a set of templates. Templates, or standardized forms, are usually created by an organization's PMO in larger firms or senior project manager in a small firm. Templates serve two main purposes. (1) Templates standardize the content of documents across all projects. (2) Templates minimize time and effort required of project managers and portfolio managers in creating and reviewing the multitude of documents used in project management.

A full set of project management templates organized by stages of project management life cycle are available online from **Project Management Docs**. Go to their website and check them out.

Following are two templates for documents prepared during Project Initiation. These easy-to-use business case and SOW templates will help get you started on your project management journey.

Business Case Template

Project Overview Statement

Executive Summary

Project Name:

Department:

Date:

Author(s):

Project Manager(s):

Executive Sponsor(s):

Describe the pertinent facts of the project in a clear and concise way.

PROJECT BUSINESS CASE

Project Overview

Describe what is involved in executing the project.

Business Issue/Opportunity

Describe expected benefits and how the project fits within the company's business strategy and contributes toward its goals and objectives.

Project Business Goal

Clearly identify the opportunity, need, or problem facing the company and why the project is necessary. Discuss the drivers that have triggered the project proposal and link them to the business need.

Primary Project Objectives

List and describe the objectives of the project.

1. *Objective 1*
2. *Objective 2 . . .*
3. *Objective n . . .*

Project Benefits and Cost–Benefit Analysis

Describe the key benefits from implementing this project.

1. *Benefit 1*
2. *Benefit 2 . . .*
3. *Benefit n . . .*

Based on the costs established for each option, describe how those costs are weighed against the benefits. Conduct the cost–benefit analysis for each option taking into account costs, benefits, and risks.

PRIMARY PROJECT DELIVERABLES

Milestone 1

1. *Deliverable name: Description of the deliverable*
2. *Deliverable name: Description of the deliverable*

n. . . .

Milestone n

1. *Deliverable name: Description of the deliverable*
2. *Deliverable name: Description of the deliverable*

n. . . .

Project Interdependencies and Inputs

Explain other projects in process or planned that have a relationship to this proposed project. List inputs that other projects may have to this project development.

- *[input]*
- *[input]*
- *[input]*

Project Assumptions and Constraints

List and describe all underlying technical, environmental, and resource availability assumptions upon which the project and benefits are based. List and describe constraints that can come from external or internal factors.

Project Risks

Describe known risks that apply to this project.

Project KPIs

List and describe project KPIs or critical success factors.

Project Duration Estimates and Deliverables			
Project Milestone		**Date Estimate**	**Confidence Level**
Project Start Date			*[High/Medium/Low]*
Milestone 1			*[High/Medium/Low]*
Milestone *n*			*[High/Medium/Low]*
Project Completion	Date		*[High/Medium/Low]*

APPROVALS

Prepared by

_____

Project Manager

Approved by

_____

Project Sponsor

_____

Executive Sponsor

_____

Client Sponsor

Statement of Work Template

Date	[Insert date]
Client	[Insert client's name]
Job Name	[Insert project name]
Requested by	[Insert client sponsor's name]
From	[Insert project manager's name]
Summary and Objectives	A high-level description of the project and objectives
Project Scope	Description of the project scope, deliverables, and the process for how it will be performed
Schedule and Work Breakdown Structure (WBS)	List of tasks in sequential order, resources allocated to each task, and schedule
Cost or Pricing	Description of the cost (pricing) for all types of resources—labor costs, materials, equipment, overhead expenses; discussion of payment terms, including a payment schedule and if payments are based on a milestone/deliverable or a schedule, if appropriate
Key Assumptions	A crucial part of an SOW—any assumptions made when scoping and estimating the project need to be documented

Acceptance

The client named below verifies that the terms of this statement of work are acceptable. The parties hereto are each acting with proper authority of their respective companies.

Company name	Company name
Full name	Full name
Title	Title
Signature	Signature
Date	Date

References

Biography. "Steve Jobs Biography." *Biography*, August 21, 2019.

Brown, D. "Target CIO Explains How DevOps Took Root Inside the Retail Giant." *The Enterprisers Project*, January 16, 2017.

Congdon, L. "Distorting the Truth to Advance Your Vision." *Entrepreneur*, May 25, 2018.

Daily Sabah Tourism. "Chaos-plagued Berlin Airport Needs over 750 Million Euros Before Opening." *Daily Sabah Tourism*, January 8, 2018.

Dignan, L. "Oakley Expands Prototyping with HP 3D Printers." *ZDNet*, December 16, 2019.

Flughafen Berlin Brandenburg. "Airport Company Seeks 20,000 Volunteers for BER Trial Operation." *BER*, January 27, 2020.

Gallo, C. "How Steve Jobs Inspired People to 'Dream Bigger'." *Entrepreneur*, October 9, 2015.

Gartner. "Gartner Says 80 Percent of Today's Project Management Tasks Will Be Eliminated by 2030 as Artificial Intelligence Takes Over." *Gartner Press Release*, March 20, 2019.

Grimes, R. A. "11 Signs Your IT Project Is Doomed." *Computerworld. com*, May 6, 2013.

Haines, G. "The Farcical Saga of Berlin's New Airport – Whatever Happened to Germany Efficiency?" *The Telegraph*, June 1, 2017.

Harden, M. "DIA20: The High-Tech Airport Baggage System That Failed to Launch." *Denver Business Journal*, February 23, 2015.

Jimenez, C. "Steve Jobs' Shared Vision and His Project Management Style." *Modern Technology, Ecology and Empowerment*, June 8, 2017.

Johnson, K. "Denver Airport Saw the Future. It Didn't Work." *The New York Times*, August 27, 2005.

Massey, A. "When Will Berlin's Brandenburg Airport Actually Open?" *Simple Flying*, April 20, 2019.

Montgomery, H. "Denver International Airport to Begin Construction on Baggage Handling System Modifications." *Flydenver.com*, July 31, 2017.

Null, C. "10 Companies Killing It at DevOps." *TechBeacon*, 2020.

Orr, T. "Rapid Prototyping: Increasing Proficiency in Design." *Lumitex*, May 23, 2019.

Peter Barron Stark Companies. "How to Communicate Your Vision Like Steve Jobs and the Best-of-the-Best." *PeterBarronStark Companies*. Available from https://peterstark.com/communicate-vision-steve-jobs. Accessed on February 11, 2020.

PM Solutions. "Vermont Electric Power Company, Inc. (VELCO) Delivers Capital Initiative $6 Million Under Budget." Available from https://www.pmsolutions.com. Accessed on February 13, 2020.

PMI. "Pulse of the Profession 2019." 2019a. Available from https://www.pmi.org/learning/thought-leadership/pulse/pulse-of-the-profession-2019. Accessed on February 14, 2020.

PMI. "The Future of Work: Leading the Way with PMTQ." 2019b. Available from https://www.pmi.org/-/media/pmi/documents/public/pdf/learning/thought-leadership/pulse/pulse-of-the-profession-2019.pdf?v=ff445571-0b23-4a2b-a989-44eb20df55bd&sc_lang_temp=en. Accessed on February 14, 2020.

Reuters. "Berlin's New Airport to Finally Open in October 2020." *Reuters*, December 15, 2017.

Ros, M. "The Ongoing Saga of Berlin's Unfinished Airport." *CNN Travel*, December 5, 2017.

Schumacher, E. "New Berlin Airport to Finally Open Next October." *DW*, November 29, 2019.

Sylte, A. "New Question: Has There Been Any Effort to Resurrect DIA's Failed 'Baggage System from Hell'?" *9NEWS.com*, July 9, 2019.

Vendituoli, M. "DIA's 2 New Baggage Systems Are On Track to Be Completed in 2021." *Denver Business Journal*, January 9, 2020.

Vialva, T. "Oakley Selects 3D Printing as Prototyping Partner for Sports Equipment." December 18, 2019.

Weiss, T. "United Axes Troubled Baggage System at Denver Airport." *Computerworld*, June 10, 2005.

IT Ethics and Local and Global Sustainability

LEARNING OBJECTIVES

14.1 Describe the three basic tenets of business and IT ethics and how IT-related unethical behavior impacts business, employees, customers, shareholders, and the civil rights of protected classes.

14.2 Discuss the three facets of sustainability and how ICT impacts profits and the six elements of quality of life in developed countries before and during the COVID-19 pandemic.

14.3 Explain how ICT production and use is impacting climate change and the two main sustainability issues in developing countries and the barriers to improving them.

Case 14.1 Opening Case

mino21/Adobe Stock

stanciuc/Adobe Stock

Doug Houghton/Alamy Stock Photo

Royal Bank of Scotland Leverages Technology to Fulfill Its Strategy to Build a More Sustainable Bank

When it comes to sustainability, technology has been called the great enabler. At the Royal Bank of Scotland (https://www.rbs.com/), technology is one of the major influences on its strategic initiative to build a more sustainable bank.

The Company

The Royal Bank of Scotland (RBS) was founded in Edinburgh, Scotland by Royal Charter on May 31, 1727. RBS opened its first branch office in Glasgow, Scotland in 1783. In its early days, RBS branches were mainly located in Scotland. It opened a branch office in London, England in 1874 and throughout the years have established a major presence in many large towns and cities throughout England and Wales and to a lesser extent in the United States. In addition to banking, RBS offers insurance, mortgages, and personal loans to its customers. Currently RBS is one of the world's top ten financial groups with approximately 140,000 employees across 30 countries and operates out of more than 2,000 sites worldwide. RBS is part of the RBS Group, headquartered in Edinburgh, Scotland, which consists of other subsidiary banks including NatWest, Lombards, First Active, Citizens Financial Group, and insurance groups such as Direct Line and Churchill.

RBS grew rapidly through the early 2000s when it made a series of bad mistakes that culminated in the crisis of 2008. Since then, the bank has been working to put things right. Technology has been at the forefront of those efforts to rebuild resilience, trust, and shareholders value.

The Problem

RBS' major problems began in 2007, when it sought to enter emerging international markets by forming a consortium with Belgian-Dutch bank Fortis and Banco Santander of Spain to acquire Dutch Bank ABN Amro. The consortium paid 71 billion Euros ($80.3 billion), which was three times the book value of the Amsterdam-based bank. By the time that RBS had secured the deal, ABN Amro had already sold its Chicago-based LaSalle unit (the asset most prized by the consortium) to Bank of America and RBS was left with an underperforming London-based investment banking franchise and a handful of small Asian operations. The deal literally "broke the bank" and led to the resignation of then chief executive Fred Goodwin.

To stay afloat, RBS was forced to seek a government bailout just six months after it had bought ABN Amro, introduced deep cost-cutting measures, and changed its focus back to the UK market. Today, RBS is still 71% government-owned but the Treasury's 2018 Fall budget indicated the government will start selling off its stake in RBS by March 2019. In rebuilding the bank, RBS has focused its efforts on using technology to do business in a more responsible way by building a more sustainable bank that is transparent on environmental, social, and ethical issues.

The Solution

RBS Chairman Howard Davies considers digital maturity critical to the future success of RBS. He recognizes the potential for technology to significantly disrupt traditional banking business models and wants RBS to be at the forefront of this exciting change in the banking industry. His agenda is increasingly dominated by new technology-driven initiatives and digital innovation. Using a technology-driven approach, RBS is working hard to reduce costs and provide better services for its large and still very loyal customer base in a way that matches their preferences and lifestyles. This increasingly means faster responses, delivered digitally, 24/7.

One such technology-driven initiative was the launch of ESME, a digital platform that provides extremely rapid loan approvals for RBS' small and medium-sized business customers. RBS is also working with Fujitsu to provide support for forms of sustainable banking that harness the huge potential for technology in the sustainability space. RBS has already embarked on a successful Fujitsu-powered desktop transformation program that has resulted in huge cost and energy savings. Fujitsu has also worked with graduates of RBS' Sustainable Banking Graduate Training Program who have proposed solutions to sustainability issues including devising plans for chatbots for mental health and gamification programs to encourage RBS employees to compete with each other on achievements that support RBS' responsible and sustainable business commitments.

Other successful technology-related RBS' customer-focused sustainability initiatives include:

- Protected customers from nearly 600,000 fraud attempts, that would have resulted in approximately 252 million British pounds being stolen.

- Trained over 150,000 colleagues and customers as part of "Friends Against Scams" commitment to provide training to one million people across the UK by the end of 2020.

- Located a TechXpert at every branch to empower customers to take advantage of digital and mobile banking.
- Provided an award-winning mobile app that has been used by more than 6.3 million RBS customers.
- Implemented CORA, an AI-powered digital assistant, that has given answers to customer 24/7 queries in more than 4.3 million online conversations.
- Launched the UK's first paperless mortgage application.
- Helped more than 6.5 million young people learn about money through their use of MoneySense on RBS' website.
- Published their Annual Statement on their corporate website to improve transparency.

In March 2018, RBS entered its first acquisition since the fateful purchase of ABN Amro, when it acquired Edinburgh-based company Free Agent for 53 million British pounds ($70 million). Free Agent provides cloud-based accounting software to small companies, freelancers, and their accountants. Free Agent integrates everything from invoices, expense management, and project management to sales tax. This new acquisition allows RBS to offer its business customers a much greater assortment of valuable online services. The use of Free Agent is offered free of charge to all RBS business banking customers. Its use not only saves customers time and money but importantly will enable them to be in compliance with Making Tax Digital (MTD), a bold new British government initiative that requires all VAT-registered businesses to report their Value Added Tax (VAT) transactions through the fully digital real-time MTD tax system effective April 1, 2019.

The Outcome

RBS no longer has ambitions for world domination! Instead they are seeking a viable future as a community-oriented private sector bank in a more competitive market. Thanks to its innovative technology use, RBS has already created a sound foundation on which to rebuild the trust of its customers and is well on its way to creating the most efficient, reliable, and sound bank that it can.

Distinctions earned to date include RBS' approach to disclosure that has earned it the independent AA1000 Assurance kitemark, a leading indicator of reporting good practice. RBS' mobile banking app has also been voted "Best Banking App" at the British Bank Awards for the last two years.

To further show support for the sustainability of its community, RBS uses 100% green electricity in all its buildings in the UK and Ireland, reduced its carbon footprint by 210,000 tonnes of CO_2 (36% of its total footprint), and has committed $104 million (£80 million to energy saving measures across its properties). In December 2019, new RBS CEO Alison Rose and more than 100 RBS employees slept out under the stars at the World's Big Sleep Out, to help to raise money to end homelessness and RBS donated $328,750 (£250,000) to Giving Tuesday in the UK to support several employee- and customer-supported charities. Most recently in January 2020, Royal Bank of Scotland launched a new $9 million (£7 million) program to help support communities and organizations across Scotland. Sustainability has taken a strong foothold at RBS and its customers and communities are enjoying the benefits.

Sources: Compiled from Horn (2018), Withers (2018), Building Sustainability (2019), Britz (2020), Davies (2020), and rbs.com.

 ## DID YOU KNOW?

People in the world's poorest countries are more likely to have access to mobile phones than to working toilets or clean water. In most countries, the majority of people spend less than 30 minutes collecting water or have a piped supply within their home. But, in some regions of sub-Saharan Africa many spend more than an hour on each trip to collect water. According to water. org, *785 million people live without access to safe water and 2 billion people live without access to improved sanitation. These unsanitary conditions result in the deaths of one million people each year and an annual loss in time and income of $260 billion dollars.*

Introduction

Privacy and security (Chapter 5) concern themselves primarily with protecting the data, hardware, software, and network components of an IS. In this chapter, we discuss ethics and sustainable development that focus on the people and procedures components of an IS. We are living in an age where technology is capturing and processing the details of everything we do through our interconnected devices in real time. While users, businesses, and governments benefit greatly from the use of the latest social, mobile, cloud, and information management technologies to collect data about their customers and employees, this practice presents ethical dilemmas. On one hand, this data collection can lead to ethical behavior that benefits both organizations and their customers or employees, and on the other hand, it can lead to unethical behavior on the part of organizations who are eager to garner as much information as they possibly can, regardless of its negative impact. Anecdotal evidence suggests that many people do not always recognize these sorts of ethical dilemmas or their potential impacts.

Sustainability is another issue that affects all of us. Global warming is causing an increase in the density, strength, and location of ferocious tornadoes, uncontrollable wildfires, and sea level rise that can lead to catastrophic floods, tsunamis, and larger numbers of disastrous hurricanes. Lack of access to clean water, proper sanitation, and food security most directly affect those in developing countries. Technology can help alleviate and even remedy some of these concerns.

In this chapter you will learn how IT-related ethics, accountability, legal responsibilities, and sustainability issues can impact organizational performance and global well-being. Both negative and positive consequences of the production and use of technology will be discussed as they relate to you as an informed user of IT, to organizations, and to the world at large. These issues will be examined within the context of ethical and sustainability dilemmas, laws, regulations, research findings, and case examples. Of course, even widely publicized guidelines cannot provide easy answers to the demise of computer-related fraud, unemployment and displacement, misuse of computers, or the negative impact of the latest digital devices on quality of life, social discrimination, and sustainability. There are no easy fixes, clear-cut judgments, answers, or solutions. Our objective is to enable you as an informed user of IT to recognize computer-related ethical and sustainability development issues when you are confronted with them and hopefully tip the balance toward more ethical behavior and social responsibility by promoting more effective use of technology.

14.1 An Introduction to Ethics

LO14.1 Describe *the three basic tenets of business and IT ethics and how IT-related unethical behavior impacts business, employees, customers, shareholders, and the civil rights of protected classes.*

Ethics are the moral compass of a person, organization, or country. They prescribe the kind of behavior an ethical company or person should engage in. In business, people base their trust in a company on how ethical it is. **Ethical behavior** is good for business and involves demonstrating respect for the key moral principles that govern behavior.

Ethics are particularly important in the use and administration of information systems since they deal with sensitive personal and corporate information and misuse can impact the lives and well-being of so many. Any discussion about data collection and digital devices raises ethical questions that might include:

- Does the availability of data justify their use?
- Should shoppers be able to keep their buying habits private?
- Can people keep their entertainment, online gaming, and other legal activities confidential?
- Do media have the right to publish or post highly private text messages of politicians and celebrities?

These types of questions about data access, collection, mining, tracking, monitoring, privacy, and profiling point to examples of IT capabilities that have ethical consequences. Consider the following IT-related ethical dilemmas.

- A database of health-care electronic records is compromised and the breach undetected for an extended period. If vital medical data disappear or are unavailable when and where needed, patient care can be severely adversely affected.
- Unethical behaviors have been intentionally or inadvertently introduced into software by developers putting companies at risk.
- A system's integrity has been repeatedly breached or questioned, making people naturally hesitant about using an organization's Internet-based and e-commerce services.

Ethics are the values and customs of a particular group that identify what is considered right and what is considered wrong.

Ethical behavior is acting in ways consistent with the accepted values of society and individuals.

The Three Basic Tenets of Business and IT Ethics

Ethical behavior is guided by various sets of principles and tenets of ethics. In business, there isn't one consistent set of ethical principles that all companies must follow. Each company has the right to develop its own standards that are particularly meaningful to its organization and its employees. Several sets of ethics principles have been proposed and include terms like justice, beneficence, fairness, and common good, but the overall concept is the same and regardless of the set of ethical principles you choose to follow, they can all be summed up in three basic tenets described in **Figure 14.1**.

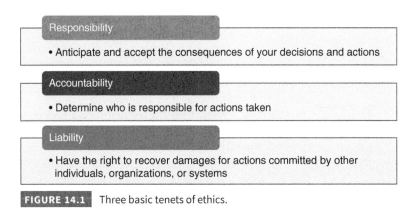

- Responsibility
  - Anticipate and accept the consequences of your decisions and actions
- Accountability
  - Determine who is responsible for actions taken
- Liability
  - Have the right to recover damages for actions committed by other individuals, organizations, or systems

FIGURE 14.1   Three basic tenets of ethics.

Tech Note 14.1 presents a comprehensive set of ethical principles widely used by organizations worldwide to govern ethical behavior in the workplace. The set was created by the Joseph and Edna Josephson Institute of Ethics, a highly regarded nonprofit organization established to champion character education for youth and ethical conduct in business, government, policing, journalism, sports, healthcare, and law.

Tech Note 14.1

Twelve Ethical Principles for Business Executives

1. **Honesty.** *Be honest in all communications and actions.* Ethical executives are honest and truthful in all their dealings and do not deliberately mislead or deceive others by misrepresentations, overstatements, partial truths, selective omissions, or any other means.

2. **Integrity.** *Maintain personal integrity.* Ethical executives demonstrate personal integrity and the courage of their convictions by doing what they think is right even when there is great pressure to do otherwise. They are principled, honorable, and upright and will fight for their beliefs. They will not sacrifice principle for expediency, be hypocritical, or be unscrupulous.

3. **Promise-Keeping and Trustworthiness.** *Keep promises and fulfill commitments.* Ethical executives are trustworthy. They are candid and forthcoming in supplying relevant information and correcting misapprehensions of fact, and they make every reasonable effort to fulfill the letter and spirit of their promises and commitments. They do not interpret agreements in an unreasonably technical or legalistic manner in order to rationalize noncompliance or create justifications for escaping their commitments.

4. **Loyalty.** *Be loyal within the framework of other ethical principles.* Ethical executives are trustworthy, demonstrate fidelity and loyalty to persons and institutions by friendship in adversity, and demonstrate support and devotion to duty; they do not use or disclose information learned in confidence for personal advantage. They safeguard the ability to make independent professional judgments by scrupulously avoiding undue influences and conflicts of interest. They are loyal to their companies and colleagues and if they decide to accept other employment, they provide reasonable notice, respect the proprietary information of their former employer, and refuse to engage in any activities that take undue advantage of their previous positions.

5. **Fairness.** *Strive to be fair and just in all dealings.* Ethical executives are fair and just in all dealings; they do not exercise power arbitrarily, and do not use overreaching or indecent means to gain or maintain any advantage or take undue advantage of another's mistakes or difficulties. Fair persons manifest a commitment to justice, the equal treatment of individuals, and tolerance for and acceptance of diversity; they are open-minded; they are willing to admit they are wrong and, where appropriate, change their positions and beliefs.

6. **Concern for Others.** *Demonstrate compassion and a genuine concern for the well-being of others.* Ethical executives are caring, compassionate, benevolent, and kind; they help those in need, and seek to accomplish their business objectives in a manner that causes the least harm and the greatest positive good.

7. **Respect for Others.** *Treat everyone with respect.* Ethical executives demonstrate respect for the human dignity, autonomy, privacy, rights, and interests of all those who have a stake in their decisions; they are courteous and treat all people with equal respect and dignity regardless of sex, race, or national origin.

8. **Law Abiding.** *Obey the law and comply with regulations.* Ethical executives abide by laws, rules, and regulations relating to their business activities.

9. **Commitment to Excellence.** *Pursue excellence at all times in all things you do.* Ethical executives pursue excellence in performing their duties, are well informed and prepared, and constantly endeavor to increase their proficiency in all areas of responsibility.

10. **Leadership.** *Exemplify honor.* Ethical executives are conscious of the responsibilities and opportunities of their position of leadership and seek to be positive ethical role models by their own conduct and by helping to create an environment in which principled reasoning and ethical decision making are highly prized.

11. **Reputation and Morale.** *Build and protect the company's good reputation and employee morale.* Ethical executives seek to protect and build the company's good reputation and the morale of its employees by engaging in no conduct that might undermine respect and by taking whatever actions are necessary to correct or prevent inappropriate conduct of others.

12. **Accountability.** *Be accountable in all dealings.* Ethical executives acknowledge and accept personal accountability for the ethical quality of their decisions and omissions to themselves, their colleagues, their companies, and their communities.

Sources: Compiled from Harker (2014), Josephson (2015), Luism75 (2019), and **http://josephsononbusinessethics.com/2010/12/12-ethical-principles-for-business-executives/**.

Code of Ethics

In a workplace, employees are expected to uphold certain outlined ethical behaviors. To do this, every organization should have a code of ethics regardless of whether it is legally mandated. An introduction to a company's code of ethics should be part of an employee's "onboarding" process and is designed to help them understand the level of ethical behavior expected of them when interacting with computer resources, customer and colleagues during their employment with the company. Sometimes known as ethical standards of conduct, a **code of ethics** refers to areas of activities that can create ethical dilemmas and risks. It is developed to provide employees guidance about how to act and make the right decision in uncertain situations.

A code of ethics has two main purposes. It serves as an internal guide and as an external statement of an organization's values and commitments. A company's code of ethics should:

- Show employees the company operates in a responsible way
- Show customers that the company values integrity
- Prevent unintentional violations of ethical behavior
- Provide a clear point of reference if enforcement of corrective action is necessary

Some large IT-related companies that have a code of ethics that you can find online include:

- Amazon
- Apple
- Dell
- Facebook
- Google
- Intel
- LinkedIn
- Microsoft
- Twitter
- Yahoo

> **code of ethics** is a set of principles and rules used by individual and organizations to govern their decision-making process, as well as to distinguish right from wrong.

IT Professionals' Code of Ethics

IT professionals and the systems they develop play an important role in our lives and the operation of organizations so it's important that they comply with a mandatory code of ethics like those of other professions, such as healthcare, finance, and law. The increasing number of computer-related incidents in the workplace has prompted many organizations to implement an IT code of ethics. Professional IT associations also have their own clearly prescribed code of ethics for their members. For example, the following list includes the guiding principles of several IT-related professional associations.

- **Association of IT Professionals (AITP) Code of Ethics and Standards of Conduct** that expands on its Code of Ethics by providing specific statements of behavior in support of each element of the code. AITP stresses that "they are not objectives to be strived for, they are rules that no true professional will violate" (www.comptia.org).
- **Project Management Institute (PMI) Code of Ethics and Professional Conduct** sets the standard for the profession of project management about what behaviors are right and honorable. It also articulates ideals to which project managers aspire as well as behaviors that are mandatory.
- **Society of Information Management (SIM) Code of Conduct** requires its members to maintain a culture in which the highest principles and values are not just respected but are practiced with honesty and integrity.
- **American Medical Informatics Association (AMIA) Code of Professional Ethical Conduct** promotes a strong ethical framework for its members to keep pace with the dynamism in the field of medical informatics. It requires members to uphold its principles and guidelines related to the collection, sharing, and storage of data and for dealing ethically with patients and their families, colleagues, institutions, and employers.
- **Australian Computer Society Code of Ethics** requires its members to advance the honor, dignity, and effectiveness of the IT professions through the primacy of public interest and enhancement of quality of life, honesty, competence, professional development, and professionalism.

- **British Computer Society Code of Conduct and Practice** sets the professional standards of competence, conduct, and ethical practice for computing in the UK. It directs its members to endeavor to discharge principal duties relating to the public interests, employers, clients, and the profession and to maintain a certain level of professional competency and integrity in their professional lives.

- **Computer Society of South Africa Code of Ethics** promotes consistent standards of professionalism and service in the IT industry and requires its members to act in a professional manner in their relationships with their customers, employees, fellow members, and the public.

While the principles and guidelines included in these Codes of Ethics and Codes of Conduct are reassuring, not all IT professionals are bound by them because membership in IT societies and associations is not mandatory. To overcome this disparity and promote more ethical behavior, organizations should encourage their IT employees to join professional associations.

Developing an Ethics and Compliance Program

To formalize the process, every organization should have an ethics and compliance program that ensures **comprehensive reporting, clear accountability,** and **full and effective oversight** by top management.

Comprehensive Reporting
In the United States, **Sarbanes–Oxley Act (SOX)** mandates more accurate business reporting and disclosure of violations and advocates "an organizational culture that encourages ethical conduct and a commitment to compliance with the law" as a precondition to the establishment of "effective compliance and ethics" programs. The SOX requires that companies promote work ethics by proving that their financial applications and systems are controlled (secured) to ensure financial reports that can be trusted. It is intended to discourage increase accountability, encourage corporate responsibility, and reduce fraud.

Section 302 of the SOX deters corporate and executive fraud by requiring that the CEO and CFO verify that they have reviewed the financial report, and, to the best of their knowledge, the report does not contain an untrue statement or omit any material fact. To motivate honesty, executive management faces criminal penalties including long jail terms for false reports. Section 805 mandates a review of the Sentencing Guidelines to ensure that "the guidelines that apply to organizations . . . are sufficient to deter and punish organizational criminal conduct."

Among other measures, SOX requires companies to set up comprehensive internal controls. There is no question that SOX, and the complex and costly provisions it requires public companies to follow, have had a major impact on corporate financial accounting. For starters, companies have had to set up comprehensive internal controls over financial reporting to prevent fraud, catching it when it occurs. Since the collapse of Arthur Andersen, following the accounting firm's conviction on criminal charges related to the Enron case, outside accounting firms are tougher with clients they are auditing, particularly about their internal controls.

Accountability
Employees must be aware of what is expected of them with respect to their interactions with corporate computer resources and of the enforcement and consequences they will face if they engage in unethical behavior. SOX and the SEC direct that if controls can be ignored, there is no control. Therefore, fraud prevention and detection require an effective monitoring system. If a company shows its employees that it can find out everything that every employee does and use that evidence to prosecute a wrongdoer to the fullest extent possible under the law, then the likelihood of any employee adopting an "I can get away with it" attitude drops drastically.

Every individual who works with an information system should be assigned specific roles and responsibilities. The tasks for which an employee is responsible should be clearly stated in an information security plan and readily measurable by someone with managerial responsibility for cyber security. For example, an organization might have a policy that all employees must avoid installing their own software on a company-owned computer or network. To ensure compliance with the policy, regular checks would be carried out to be certain the policy is being followed. Individuals must be aware of what is expected of them and guide continual improvement.

Once implemented, it is imperative that a company strictly applies with its provisions. Any lapse or failure to do so may result in confusion within the company that can ultimately adversely affect employee and customer satisfaction.

Full and Effective Oversight   An enterprise-wide approach that combines risk, security, compliance, and IT specialists greatly increases the prevention and detection of ethical infringements. Prevention is the most cost-effective approach, since detection and prosecution costs are enormous in addition to the direct cost of the loss. It starts with **corporate governance**, culture, and ethics at the top levels of the organization.

IT can play an important role in a company's efforts to ensure full and effective oversight. For example, IT monitoring and control demonstrate that the company has implemented effective corporate governance and fraud prevention measures. Regulators look favorably on companies that can demonstrate best practices in corporate governance and operational risk management since roughly 85% of occupational fraud could be prevented if proper IT-based internal controls had been implemented and followed. Management and staff would then spend less time worrying about regulations and more time adding value to their brands and business.

A strong board of directors is another effective tool for governance of an organization's ethics and compliance and program. In overseeing the program, it is the board's responsibility to review any complaints and prioritize, effectively mitigate and respond to risks being attentive to both negative events and identifying opportunities for improvement. To ensure checks and balances, shareholders should be responsible for monitoring the effectiveness of the board and recommending any needed changes.

> **corporate governance**   is a structure of rules, practices, and processes used to control and operate a company.

Ethics Training in the Workplace

To make employees aware of their responsibility to act ethically at work, employee ethics training must be a part of any ethics and compliance program. Unfortunately, it is an area of employee training that sometimes gets overlooked. It is critical to enable employees understand its importance to help them make ethical decisions that in turn help the company achieve its goals. Workplace ethics training helps build strong teams, foster professionalism, and increase productivity at work. Situations involving ethics need to be dealt with expediently, so it is important to have a set of rules and policies that give employees a tangible reference for what a company considers "ethical behavior."

Ethics training can range from a simple conversation with an HR professional or a full-blown training program that discusses potential ethical dilemmas that an employee may encounter in the workplace such as customer privacy, employee and customer data protection, fraud, customer relations, and general employee behavior and presents the best course of action in each situation. It is also important that an ethics training program not only stresses the disadvantages of engaging in unethical behavior but also discusses the advantages of behaving ethically. It also needs to specify the controls that are in place to encourage the prompt reporting of unethical behavior. These should include a **whistleblower** policy consistent with the Occupational Safety and Health Act's (OSHA) Whistleblower Protection Program that protects employees from retaliation for disclosing unethical behavior in the workplace such as violating a law, rule, or regulation, gross mismanagement, gross waste of company funds, abuse of authority, or significant dangers to public health and safety.

> **whistleblower**   is an employee, supplier, contractor, client, or any other individual who has and reports insider knowledge of illegal activities occurring in an organization.

IT-Related Unethical Behavior

The flip side of ethical behavior is **unethical behavior**. Unethical behavior can have far-reaching and negative impacts on organizations, industries, and society. As you read in

> **unethical behavior**   is an action that is not considered morally right or proper carried out by a person, a profession, or an industry.

Chapter 5, security breaches occur not only because of cyberattacks by hackers or APTs, but also because of unethical or negligent employees who can bring entire industries to a halt by delaying or shutting down operations or exposing sensitive data about the company and its customers.

Unethical behavior can lead to very serious consequences that can cost a company time and money in trying to repair their reputation, cost millions of dollars and even prison time, and adversely affect its sustainability. These real-world examples of scandals that resulted from unethical behavior by companies or employees demonstrate the dire consequences of unethical behavior.

- **Volkswagen** installed software on 11 million of its diesel vehicles worldwide that allowed the cars to falsely pass emissions tests. The "defeat device" was discovered by the Environmental Protection Agency (EPA) and the deception could cost Volkswagen as much as $87 million. Volkswagen reportedly set aside $7.3 billion to deal with the fallout from the scandal that could include compensating owners for loss of value to their vehicles, fixing the emissions problems, and settling civil and criminal lawsuits.

- **A former Goldman Sachs programmer**, Sergey Aleynikov, was convicted of downloading proprietary software that the bank used in its trading program to his personal computer, laptop, and a portable memory device immediately before joining a competing firm. Aleynikov unsuccessfully tried to cover up the theft of intellectual property by deleting his computer history. When officials at Goldman Sachs were alerted to uploads of large amounts of data from their system, they discovered that Aleynikov had used his work desktop on at least four occasions to transfer about 32 MB of proprietary source code to an external website. He was convicted of theft in 2011 and served 11 months in federal prison before being released when the sentence was overturned. Although further criminal actions were brought against him, no further prison time was recommended.

In the following sections examples contain several types of IT-related unethical behavior you might have already encountered.

Risky or Unethical Behavior in Mobile Apps

In 2018 global spending on mobile apps was $101 billion. Of the more than 2.8 million mobile apps, it has been reported that approximately 50,000 of them engage in unethical or risky behaviors as more reports about privacy and security issues associated with mobile apps come to light weekly. **Table 14.1** lists several types of risky mobile app behaviors.

TABLE 14.1 **Mobile App Risky Behavior**

Location tracking
Accessing device's address book or contact list
Identifying user or phone unique identifier (UDID)
Recording in-app purchases
Sharing data with ad networks and analytics companies

whitelisted apps is an approved app or executable file that is permitted to be present and active on a computer system.

blacklisted apps is a malicious app that mimics a reputable, highly downloaded app.

The number of malicious apps is growing at an alarming rate. In 2018, the number of blacklisted apps increased by 20% over the previous year (Help Net Security, 2019). Malicious apps can serve up trojan attacks, other malware, or phishing attacks and with a single click, users can inadvertently launch a targeted attack against their organizations. Many companies try to counter potential threats from mobile apps by identifying **whitelisted apps** and **blacklisted apps**. Unfortunately, they are not always effective in getting employees to exclusively using whitelisted apps and avoiding the blacklisted apps.

Many blacklisted apps are found in unreliable third-party stores. Legitimate app stores that offer **whitelisted apps** for online banking, retail shopping, gaming, and other functions might be unaware of blacklisted apps lurking in their app stores. Despite their best efforts, legitimate app store operators cannot reliably police their own catalogs for rogue apps that are continually being introduced into the market by unethical developers.

Tech-Savvy Individuals and Scalpers Exploit Artificial Intelligence

As discussed in Chapter 11, artificial intelligence (AI) was designed to make our lives better and more efficient, but that is not always the case. For example, buying event tickets online is more stressful and near impossible in some instances than ever before due to AI.

Tech-savvy individuals create macros, which are computing apps that allow users to input one instruction that coincides with a long list of instructions to be completed automatically by the program, to instantly and automatically buy as many tickets to popular events and shows as possible. Acting alone or in collaboration with "scalpers," they resell the tickets at immensely inflated prices since the original tickets are sold out.

One example of this type of unethical behavior was evident in tickets sales for one of Canadian hip-hop star Drake's concerts in Greenwich, UK. To the consternation of many Drake fans who had roused themselves from sleep in the middle of the night to buy tickets, the concert sold out online almost immediately. With original ticket prices ranging from $60 to $145 (€55 to €132), scalpers sold tickets for up to $900 (€800). It is estimated that one macro developer profited by more than $28 million (€25 million) using this method.

Distracted Driving

At any given time, approximately 660,000 Americans are using or manipulating an electronic device while driving. Safety experts at the National Highway Traffic Safety Administration (NHTSA) warn that using a cell phone to access a GPS app, surf the Web, view social media, or text while driving is more dangerous than driving under the influence (DUI). The delay in a driver's reaction time when using a hand-held or hands-free cell phone is equivalent to that of a person with a 0.08% blood alcohol concentration. A driver can safely take his eyes off the road for no more than two seconds. Sending a text while driving takes your eyes off the road for approximately 5 seconds. At 55 mph that's like driving the length of an entire football field with your eyes closed (NHTSA, 2018).

In 2019, the Department of Transportation reported that texting while driving is a primary or contributing factor in as many as 16% of all police-reported traffic accidents, 58% of crashes involving teen drivers, and 14% of fatal crashes. In a 2019 Zendrive survey of the driving behaviors and attitudes of 2,000 Americans, 36% of the respondents admitted to texting while driving, 60% said they were likely to use a GPS, and 19% said they surf the web while driving. Thirty-seven (37%) percent of the drivers in the 18–34 age range also reported that they felt a high degree of pressure to respond to work-related messages while driving compared to 25% of the national average among all age groups. These types of behavior were directly attributed to the death of 4,637 people in car accidents in 2018. In addition to loss of lives, texting while driving has a huge economic impact. Distracted drivers cost employers and society $129 billion per year in medical costs, legal costs, vehicle damage, property damage, time lost from work, and increased insurance rates (The Zebra, 2019).

Forty-seven of the 50 U.S. states have banned texting while driving and 16 states have banned drivers from using hand-held cell phones for any purpose (Kitch, 2018). Distracted driving carries mandatory fines of up to $500. In some states, such as California and New York State, drivers charged with texting while driving face fines **and** have their driving license suspended. If driving while distracted causes injury or death to others, violators face jail time.

Additive Manufacturing Dilemmas (3D Printing and Bioprinting)

Another trendy technology that has sparked ethical and other debates is the 3D printer and 3D bioprinting. For instance, a surgeon used a 3D-printed model of a baby's skull in an intricate surgery to correct a serious birth defect. Bioprinting of aortic valves and 3D bioprinting technology have been used by researchers at Cornell University to fabricate living heart valves that possess the same anatomical architecture as the original valve.

Despite benefits, the medical application of bioprinting to produce living tissue and organs is expected to spark major ethical debates about whether lives are being saved or redefined. For example, 3D-bioprinted human organs may be subject to conflicting religious, political, moral, and financial interests. The 3D printing of nonliving medical devices, such as prosthetic limbs, is expected to be in high demand because of longer life spans and insufficient levels of health care in various countries. A major hurdle is determining who is legally responsible for ensuring the quality of the resulting organs and devices? Without medical malpractice insurance covering these new applications, they cannot proceed. As 3D medical printing becomes a normal procedure it raises several ethical questions concerning accessibility in healthcare settings, testing for its safety and effectiveness, and whether it will be used to create enhancements that go beyond what is considered normal.

Unfortunately, 3D printers can exert impacts on the environment worse than those of standard manufacturing. For instance, the carbon footprint can be greater depending on what is being made and the type of printer being used. 3D printers use a lot more energy than conventional milling machines. 3D printers can use 100 times more electricity to produce a part than would have been used to produce the same part by nonadditive manufacturing.

Despite the ethical challenges it poses, the use of 3D printing is growing, and its future growth will be driven by organizations who recognize the need to get aboard the 3D printing bandwagon in order to stay competitive.

Insider Fraud

It is a crime with severe financial consequences. Fighting fraud is an ethical duty—and essential to public trust and the integrity of a company's brand. **Insider fraud** is a term that refers to a variety of criminal behaviors perpetrated by an organization's employees or contractors against an employer. Other terms for this crime are internal, employment, or occupational fraud.

Fraud is a nonviolent crime using deception, confidence, and trickery to secure resources for personal gain.

computer-related fraud is the use of computers, the Internet, and other IT devices to defraud people or organizations of resources.

Fraud in the workplace is a serious problem for most organizations and technology compounds the problem by facilitating access to information. According to the latest Annual Global Fraud Survey, 81% of organizations have been victims of **computer-related fraud** perpetrated by insiders. Of these, 36% were carried out by senior or middle managers and 45% were attributed to junior employees. Only 23% of the reported frauds resulted from actions of an agent or outsider access to corporate networks.

Why Fraud Occurs

Fraud occurs because internal controls to prevent insider fraud—no matter how strong—will fail on occasion. **Fraud risk management** is a system of policies and procedures to prevent and detect illegal acts committed by managers, employees, customers, or business partners against a company's interests. Although each corporation establishes its own specific procedures, fraud risk management involves assessing a company's exposure to fraud; implementing defenses to prevent and detect fraud; defining procedures to investigate, prosecute, and recover losses from fraud. Analyzing why and how fraud could occur is as important as detecting and stopping it. This analysis is used to identify necessary corporate policies to deter insider fraud and fraud detection systems when prevention fails.

Fraud Risk Factors

Factors that increase a company's exposure to fraud are illustrated in **Figure 14.2.** ISs are implemented to protect companies against these factors. Companies make themselves targets of fraud because of the interaction of these four factors:

1. A high level of trust in employees without enough oversight to verify that they are not stealing from the company
2. Relying on informal processes of control
3. A mindset (belief) that internal controls and fraud prevention systems are too expensive to implement
4. Assigning a wide range of duties for each employee, giving them opportunities to commit fraud

FIGURE 14.2 Factors that make companies targets for fraud.

For instance, when a small manufacturer was the victim of theft of intellectual property, the computer network logs identified the computer that had been used to commit the alleged crime. But there was no way to connect that computer to one specific individual. A manager's conviction that he knew who had perpetrated the crime was insufficient evidence. The lesson learned was that the internal control—*separation of duties*—is important not only to fraud prevention but also to fraud prosecution and recovery of losses. Since employees had shared computer accounts, they were not able to link the fraud to the person who committed it.

Fraud Prevention and Detection Designing effective fraud response and litigation-readiness strategies (post-incident strategies) is crucial to be able to do the following:

- Recover financial losses.
- Punish perpetrators through lawsuits, criminal charges, and/or forfeited gains.
- Stop fraudsters from victimizing other organizations.

History has shown that if the punishment for committing fraud is not severe, the fraudster's next employer will be the next victim. Trying to keep fraud hidden can mean either *doing nothing* or simply firing the employee. These approaches to dealing with fraud are not sustainable because they erode the effectiveness of fraud prevention measures and produce a **moral hazard**, that is, they take the risk out of insider fraud.

One of the most effective fraud prevention techniques is that of detection and punishment. The fear of being caught and prosecuted is a strong deterrent. IT can play a major role in detecting fraud to support a strong corporate governance program and facilitate the internal audits and controls essential to the prevention and detection of occupational fraud. If employees are made aware that fraud will be detected by IT-monitoring systems and punished, with the attacker possibly turned over to the police or FBI the attitude that "I can get away with it" drops drastically.

The paradox is that many companies prevent a successful fraud diagnosis or forensic accounting investigation by deploying insufficient resources to protect against fraud even though they know they cannot afford the unrecoverable losses that might ensue.

Several examples of occupational fraud, their characteristics, and the extent to which they impact corporate financial statements are illustrated in **Table 14.2**.

moral hazard is the risk that a party to a transaction has not entered into a contract in good faith or has provided misleading information.

TABLE 14.2 Types, Impact, and Characteristics of Occupational Fraud

Types of Fraud	Impacts Financial Statements?	Typical Characteristics
Operating management corruption	No	Occurs off the books. Median loss due to corruption is six times median loss due to misappropriation
Conflict of interest	No	Breach of confidentiality, such as revealing competitor bids Often occurs coincident with bribery
Bribery	No	Uses positional power or money to influence others
Embezzlement or "misappropriation"	Yes	Employee theft Employee access to company property creates the opportunity for embezzlement
Senior management financial reporting fraud	Yes	Involves massive breach of trust and leveraging of positional power
Accounting cycle fraud	Yes	Also called "earnings management" or "earnings engineering" Violates generally accepted accounting principles (GAAP) and all other accounting principles; see aicpa.org

Intelligent Analysis and Anomaly Detections Most detection activity can be handled by intelligent analysis engines using advanced data warehousing and analytics techniques. These systems take in audit trails from key systems and personnel records from the HR and finance departments. The data are stored in a data warehouse where they are analyzed to detect anomalous patterns, such as excessive hours worked, deviations in patterns of behavior, copying huge amounts of data, attempts to override controls, unusual transactions, and inadequate documentation about a transaction. Information from investigations is fed back into the detection system so it learns of any anomalous patterns. Since insiders might work in collusion with organized criminals, insider profiling is important to find wider patterns of criminal networks.

Internal Controls In companies with lax accounting systems, it is too easy for employees to misdirect purchase orders and payments, bribe a supplier, or manipulate accounting data. When senior managers are involved in a fraud, preventing fraud is extremely tough. Consider Bernie Madoff, who committed a record-setting fraud scheme for many years even after the Sarbanes–Oxley Act was passed in 2002 to help prevent financial fraud.

In a much smaller but still serious fraud case involving a New York-based nonprofit, a volunteer was responsible for counting cash receipts at the annual fundraiser. The volunteer had performed this task for 30 years. One year, an accountant was assigned to assist the volunteer with the count. The volunteer offered the accountant a "cut" of the cash in exchange for her silence about the theft.

Strong internal controls, which depend on IT for their effectiveness, consist of the following:

- **Segregation of duties** tops the list of best practices in control procedures. When handling a company's assets, the work of managers and employees needs to be subject to approval or authorization. For example, any attempt to issue a check to a vendor not in the database of approved vendors will be prevented by the accounting IS.

- **Job rotation** More than one person should be familiar with each transaction cycle in the business wherever possible. Rotation of jobs helps prevent overreliance on a single individual—and is a way to expose fraudulent activities.

- **Oversight** Management—whether a single owner or a team of individuals—must monitor what is actually happening in the business. Auditing ISs are part of a strong oversight function. Unannounced periodic walk-throughs of a process or review of how things are really being done can reveal existing or potential problem areas.

- **Safeguarding of assets** It is essential to a fraud prevention program. Access to networks, financial systems, and databases must be controlled with strong passwords and other security measures. Similarly, bank checks, petty cash funds, and company credit cards need to be locked up when not in use.

- **IT policies—understand your IS** Heavy reliance on IT staff can open up opportunities for fraud. Establish a computer use policy and educate employees on the importance of securing information. Strictly enforce the use of separate logins and keep passwords confidential. Install firewalls, e-mail scanners, and biometric access.

Regulatory Controls In the early 2000s, the U.S. business economy was significantly impacted by fraud scandals that involved senior executives at several major corporations. Lawmakers believed that the scope of these crimes destroyed the public's confidence in the country's financial systems and markets. To combat this, several laws were passed that heightened the legal responsibilities of corporate management to actively guard against fraud by employees, established stricter management and reporting requirements, and introduced severe penalties for failure to comply. As a result, fraud management became a necessary functional process. These frauds played a role in the SEC's rule for XBRL data reporting that was discussed in Chapter 9.

To protect clients, customers, and constituents, all public and private enterprises are subject to federal and state laws and regulations including:

- **Foreign Corrupt Practices Act (FCPA)**—a U.S. federal law that addresses accounting transparency requirements under the Securities Exchange Act of 1934 and bribery of foreign officials.

- **Federal Sentencing Guidelines**—a set of nonbinding rules to federal judges to consider when they are sentencing a person for a federal crime. They are designed to provide consistent and fair ranges of sentences for determining the length of a prison sentence for felonies and serious misdemeanors in the U.S. federal court system.

- **Dodd-Frank Wall Street Reform and Consumer Protection Act**—a U.S. Federal law that overhauled financial regulation enacted to help prevent a repeat of the 2007–2008 financial crisis. It made changes affecting all federal financial regulatory agencies and almost every part of the U.S. financial services industry. The law also acts as a consumer watchdog to prevent mortgage companies and pay-day lenders from exploiting consumers.

- **Consumer Protection Act**—it shields consumers and their financial records from abuse by ensuring that the rights of all involved parties are protected by regulating the activity undertaken and ensuring that ethical and legal practices are employed.

- **UK Bribery Act of 2010**—an Act of Parliament that relates to criminal law concerning bribery. It is designed to ensure that UK businesses do not fuel corruption in different markets around the world. Offenders may be imprisoned for up to 10 years depending on the severity of the bribery offense and the sentence may also include a monetary fine.

- **Federal Trade Commission (FTC) Social Media Guidelines for Financial Institutions**—the FTC has focused on curtailing deceptive practices, even if unintentional, by businesses engaged in online commerce. As discussed in Chapter 5, companies expose themselves to harsh sanctions by federal agencies when they do not fulfill the terms of the privacy policies that their customers rely upon. While businesses should always ensure that their online advertisements are truthfully conveyed, a business with a social media presence should take particular note of the FTC's recent efforts to enforce truth in online advertising, privacy policies, and security measures.

- **Federal Financial Institutions Examination Council (FFIEC)** released guidelines entitled *Social Media: Consumer Compliance Risk Management Guidance* to help financial institutions effectively manage the current risks caused associated with their use of social media. Key social media guidelines for financial institutions that protect consumers against unethical behavior are listed in **Table 14.3**.

TABLE 14.3 Key Social Media Guidelines for Financial Institutions

Guidelines	Issue	Solution
Institute policies to comply with advertising, communications, and other consumer protection laws	No policies in place; need a social media risk assessment tool.	Implement social policies to prevent issues such as spam. For example, staff should know how to react when a customer posts confidential information such as a bank number on their social profiles.
Use monitoring tools	Financial institutions have added social channels that can expose their brand to additional feedback.	Use social monitoring tools to identify issues that may cause a negative reaction and respond quickly. The use of social monitoring tools also helps banks refute inaccurate statements, protecting their brand reputation.
Train employees	Whether or not employees represent your brand on social media, their public social comments may be seen to reflect the financial institution.	The best way to reduce risk is to train employees on how to use social networks professionally.

Unfortunately, this increased legislation has not been very successful in deterring occupational fraud.

Discrimination in Social Media Recruiting

An interesting but concerning area where IT has opened several new avenues for **discrimination** at work is the use of social media for recruiting. Social media can provide employers with a cost-effective and efficient way to attract prospective candidates and reach those who aren't actively looking to change jobs in the elusive search for the "ideal candidate." In order to cast a wide net for potential candidates, social media has become the method of choice when companies recruit new hires. It was recently reported that 94% of employers are using social media for recruiting (Robert Half 2018). In today's interconnected world, employers have more options than ever before to recruit new hires online. Recruiters see LinkedIn as the world's largest resume database and Zip Recruiter, Monster.com, and Career Builder specialize in talent acquisition and serve as quasi-classified pages. Employers also can use popular social media channels, such as Facebook, LinkedIn, Instagram, and Twitter to find the best candidate for a position.

Employers use social media for multiple reasons: to engage employees, to share knowledge among employees, and for recruitment and hiring of new employees. Engaging in unethical and illegal social media snooping that results in bias when recruiting new hires is known as **social media discrimination**.

Social media has become a hotbed of discrimination in recruitment and is a serious topic for HR managers and recruiters who use Facebook, Amazon, LinkedIn, Twitter, and Instagram and chat room platforms like Workplace by Facebook, Microsoft Teams, and Salesforce Chatter. There is a fine line between ethical **microtargeting**, a marketing strategy that uses consumer data and demographics to create targeted subsets or market segments, and unethical social media discrimination that uses protected class information to vet individual candidates and puts employers in jeopardy of breaking the law.

social media discrimination occurs when a potential employer or recruiter uses social networking websites to research a person's character, behaviors, and social circles and treats them less favorably than another person based on the information they gather.

Unethical and Illegal Practices in Social Media Recruiting Career Builder reports that 70% of employers are using social media to vet their recruiting prospects (Hayes 2018). Most of these background checks are well-intentioned. Unfortunately, some are not and result in bias and social media discrimination making social media a hotbed for recruiting discrimination. Depending on how job candidates control their privacy and how much they reveal through check-ins and posts, recruiters can learn a great deal more about a candidate than they should use in their decision to interview, recommend, or hire someone. The improper use of information scraped from social media sites may be discriminatory and illegal. The problem starts with members who post age, race, gender, and ethnicity information—or enable it to be learned from content on their sites.

Recruiting through social media often involves searching information the job candidate did not want considered or that is illegal to use in the hiring process. In the past, employment law attorneys dealt with this risk by advising companies to avoid using social media in their hiring and recruitment process to avoid legal risk. However, that proposal is not realistic. By opting out of social media, recruiting firms lose a productive way to find candidates, which could cost them millions of dollars and background checks must be conducted to protect a company against being charged with **negligent hiring**.

Negligent Hiring   As discussed earlier in this chapter, employers have a legal obligation to make the best effort to protect their employees and customers when they make hiring decisions. For example, a victim of violence in the workplace may have a cause of action for negligent hiring against their employer if they can show that the employer was aware of the attacker's termination from a previous position for the same behavior. To avoid the risk of negligent hiring most employers conduct some form of background screening.

To balance the competing risks of social discrimination and negligent hiring, a company can conduct the steps shown in **Figure 14.3**

> **Negligent hiring**   is the hiring of an employee when the employer knew or should have known about the employee's background which, if known, indicates a dangerous or untrustworthy character.

Ask candidate to sign a disclosure statement
- Let candidates themselves disclose information found on social media. Explain to them the reason for the disclosure statement.

Create a standard process and document it
- A consistent and well-documented process is necessary to ensure and demonstrate compliance if there is an EEOC employment investigation.

Avoid coercive practices
- Ensure recruiters do not pressure candidates to disclose protected information via social media by requiring them to disclose passwords or relax privacy setting for purposes of review by the employer.

Train, Train, Train
- Training and repeated reminders and refresher courses are important to emphasize that management intends to comply with all employment and hiring laws and regulations.

FIGURE 14.3   Steps to balance social discrimination and negligent hiring.

Social Stalking   Recruiters that use social media can also be social stalkers! Almost half of the recruiters in the Jobvite survey said that they regarded photos of alcohol consumption and marijuana use on social networks negatively. Interestingly, they were also negatively influenced by bad spelling in social media posts! Facebook members who expose too much information about themselves through social posts are vulnerable to employers and recruiters who use social content in the hiring process. Although laws forbid the use of certain types of social media information, it's hard to monitor its effect on hiring practices.

civil rights are the rights of citizens to political and social freedom and equality.

protected class is a group of people with characteristics that cannot be targeted for discrimination and harassment such as age, race, disability, gender, marital status, national origin, genetic information, and religion.

Civil Rights and Protected Classes Two critical issues that can arise relative to social media discrimination is when an employer's use of information violates a candidate's **civil rights** or is based on their **protected class** in a hiring decision.

In the United States, an individual's **civil rights** are protected by federal law. If a person's civil rights are interfered with by another, the person can seek legal action for the injury. Examples of civil rights include:

- freedom of speech
- freedom of the press
- the right to peaceful assembly
- the right to vote
- the right to equality in public places

Discrimination also occurs when a person receives different treatment because of their membership in a particular group or **protected class**. Social media discrimination based on protected class information is illegal in the United States and many other countries. Various jurisdictions have enacted statutes to prevent discrimination based on protected classes that include a person's race, sex, religion, age, previous condition of servitude, physical limitation, national origin, and, in some instances, sexual orientation.

Title VII of the Civil Rights Act of 1964, the **Age Discrimination in Employment Act** of 1967 (ADEA), the **Americans with Disabilities Act** of 1990 (ADA), and **Genetic Information Non-discrimination Act** of 2008 (GINA) make it illegal to discriminate based on protected class information in any aspect of employment, including recruitment, hiring, and firing. GINA, the latest of these laws, was passed when results from the Human Genome Project started raising ethical dilemmas.

Protected class information that is interesting and useful to recruiters is readily available on social media. Protected class information such as age, marital status, political affiliations or religion is often unwittingly shared through message and photos on social media sites and chat room apps like Facebook, LinkedIn, Workplace by Facebook, Microsoft Teams, and Salesforce Chatter. For example:

- A woman with a small child posts that she is losing time from work because of her child's illness.
- A candidate posts messages vigorously supporting or opposing impeachment of President Donald Trump.
- A man posts compromising photos of himself and another man in a chat room for homosexuals.
- A candidate posts a message about his 50th High School Reunion that reveals his age.

When information about protected classes is used to weed out candidates, it can lead to class action social media discrimination lawsuits brought on behalf of the large number of people who allegedly were precluded.

Recruiting Regulations

The **Equal Employment Opportunity Commission (EEOC)** is the primary governmental agency that enforces federal laws prohibiting discrimination in employment. Other agencies and legislatures that govern and monitor workplace discrimination include the **National Conference**

of State Legislatures that passed summary legislation preventing employers from requesting passwords to personal Internet accounts to get or keep a job. To date, 25 states have enacted such laws. Other states have such laws pending, and there are several proposals before Congress to do the same on a federal level.

Proving Social Media Discrimination

Unlike data privacy cases, social media discrimination is not always obvious, and it is much more difficult to prove. When companies violate privacy regulations (discussed in Chapter 5) that their customers rely upon, these are clear-cut cases that are relatively easy to detect and prosecute. For example, when the FTC charged SnapChat for lying to its customers about its disappearing messages services it was an obvious violation of "unfair and deceptive trade practices." Unfortunately, things are not so clear cut in social media discrimination cases. Consider, for example, the following social media recruiting scenario:

In the course of recruiting a new hire a recruiter reviews a candidate's activity on social media platforms. During this activity, the recruiter discovers the following information about him, passes it along to the employer and they use the information in their decision not to hire him.

1. The candidate checks in via Foursquare at Woodsman Gym once or twice a day usually around 7 a.m., noon, or 6 p.m.
2. His Facebook album is filled with party photos, showing what might be considered excessive drinking.
3. His resume suggests that he is in his early 30s, but his social profile about high school indicates that his real age is late 40s.
4. His posts describe his religious beliefs and customs, family's serious medical conditions, financial stress, and desire to spend as much time as possible snowboarding.
5. He makes fun of and posts insulting cartoons of people who follow a dress code at work.

Like other job seekers, this candidate is posting, tweeting, and blogging information he probably would not want a recruiter or prospective employer to know about. While party photos might not show *illegal* behavior, when they are posted on a social network, they could easily influence a potential employer's evaluation of a job applicant as well as disclose information about race, gender, age, and other protected class information. If a company uses these photos and postings to piece together a profile of his age, religion, or genetic condition and rejects him based on what they found, the company has committed social media discrimination and is very likely in violation of other laws. However, proving that their hiring decision was based on this information may not be easy.

The major social media platforms often try to place responsibility for unethical recruitment microtargeting solely on the employer. **IT at Work 14.1** shows one example where the courts didn't agree. When Facebook was faced with multiple class action lawsuits alleging social media discrimination by microtargeting applicants based on age and gender, the social media platform was also held accountable.

IT at Work 14.1

Facebook Agrees to $3 Million Settlement in Multiple Lawsuits for Enabling Online Race, Age, and Gender Discrimination in Recruitment Ads

The Civil Rights Act of 1964 specifically prohibits discriminating against a person because of "race, color, religion, sex or national origin." The law applies to every stage of employment, including recruitment. On March 21, 2019, Facebook announced that it had reached a settlement in several discrimination lawsuits brought by the Communication Workers (CWA) and the ACLU.

Facebook first came under scrutiny for civil rights abuse in 2016 when a ProPublica investigation found that companies could buy ads that targeted users based on their race—a practice that is illegal in the context of employment advertising. This triggered lawsuits from the National Fair Housing Alliance, the ACLU, and the Communication Workers of America (CWA) representing 700,000 media workers across the United States. As a result, Facebook developed a new system to prevent employers from buying ads that screened users based on "ethnic affinity" but continued to allow advertisers to filter out characteristics linked to other protected classes including gender and age.

As a result, another class action lawsuit was filed in December 2017 alleging that Facebook had allowed companies like T-Mobile, Cox Communications, and Cox Media Group to adjust the settings for their online job ads to target people under 40 years of age. They were able to do this by using Facebook's paid advertisement platform that was programmed to allow advertisers to microtarget their ads to exclude people from receiving jobs based on gender, race (by zipcode), or age in violation of Federal civil rights laws. For example, by checking certain boxes, an employer could microtarget ads to younger, male workers while excluding others from seeing the ads. These findings support a statement made by Nancy Lea-Mond, executive VP of AARP, that age discrimination is alive and well in the digital era. AARP is the largest advocate group for older Americans. Along with two top members of the U.S. Senate Special Committee on Aging it is calling for employers and technology companies to stop limiting recruitment ads on Facebook and other online sites to younger workers.

In September 2018, another lawsuit was filed with the EEOC in which the ACLU charged Facebook and 10 other employers of discrimination based on gender. ACLU charged that employers used Facebook's microtargeting tool to exclude all but male prospective applicants from receiving job advertisements and opportunities.

In March 2019, even before the EEOC made its ruling, Facebook announced that it would no longer sell targeted ads that potentially discriminate against women, people, or color or the elderly. To achieve this goal, Facebook removed over 5,000 targeting options for advertisers if the ads are related to housing, employment, or credit offers. Ads related to other products and services will not be affected by the changes.

Sources: Compiled from McDevitt (2017), Campbell (2018), Fetherolf, Allen, and Romer-Friedman (2018), Nguyen (2018), Romer-Friedman (2018), Valentino-DeVries (2018), Vanian (2018), Campbell (2019), and Gruenberg (2019).

Protecting Companies and Candidates from Social Media Discrimination

Companies that have not implemented formal processes for the use of social media in recruiting and selection may put themselves at risk of legal complaints because of inconsistent practices. For example, although a job applicant might not know whether their social media profiles have been screened, there are several ways they can find out. For instance, an applicant might be tipped off after receiving a suspicious friend request or by talking with current employees and hiring managers who disclose the information—either purposely or accidentally—during the interview.

To guard against committing social discrimination when using social media to recruit, it's advisable that **companies** protect themselves in several ways, shown in **Table 14.4**.

TABLE 14.4	Corporate Strategies to Protect against Social Discrimination on Social Media
Only use HR personnel or external recruiters who are trained in employment and recruiting law.	
Make sure ads are not targeted in a manner that excludes potential applicants based on protected class information.	
Have either a third party or a designated person within the company who does not make hiring decisions do the background check.	
Use only publicly available information. Do not friend someone to get access to private information.	
Do not request username or passwords for social media accounts.	
Consider tracking and analyzing applicant flow generated by social media ads to identify any adverse impacts and adjust accordingly.	
Make sure overall recruitment efforts are inclusive and encourage a diverse range of applicants.	

Steps that **candidates** should take to protect themselves against social discrimination in social media are shown in **Table 14.5**.

TABLE 14.5	Steps for Candidates to Protect against Social Discrimination on Social Media
Ensure your social media account is set to private, not public.	
Don't accept any people you don't know.	
Manually remove any inappropriate, embarrassing, or negative content from your profile, or better yet, don't post it in the first place.	

Don't forget that although social media can be used against you, it can also be a valuable job search resource. If you present yourself as a smart, talented individual who's enthusiastic about beginning a new career and will be an excellent addition to any company, your chances of being successfully recruited will increase significantly.

Providing a Secure and Respectful Workplace

An ethical company treats its employees and stakeholders fairly and is a good neighbor and community member, locally and globally. No company can stay in business for long if it consistently treats its employees poorly and behaves in unethical ways toward its customers and stakeholders. The importance of management creating a culture that promotes an ethical and sustainable climate within the workplace cannot be overstated. It is the responsibility of every organization to establish a secure, respectful workplace for its employees by reducing their exposure to risks such as bullying, harassment, fraud and bribery, and discriminatory practices. If an incident of fraud or bribery occurs, organizations must provide a safe environment in which employees can come forward with information. If discriminatory practices occur, an employee must have recourse. Company responsibilities include:

- being intolerant of disrespectful, untrustworthy, hostile, or bullying behavior
- setting clear expectations of respectful behavior
- responding to ideas, concerns, complaints, and feedback with empathy, fairness, dignity, and respect
- offering an ethics training program

- offering a formal conflict resolution process
- setting up ethics, fraud, and whistleblower hotlines for anonymous reporting of unethical behavior

Employees also have a measure of responsibility in building and maintaining a secure, respectful, and sustainable workplace and must act conscientiously to:

- treat each other with respect and consideration
- act inclusively
- value others
- accept differences in other people
- recognize the efforts and achievements of others
- consider impact of their behavior on others
- report unethical behavior

The Ethical Dilemma of Competing Responsibilities

In some situations, there is no clear-cut framework for deciding what is ethical and what is not. In these cases, we are faced with an **ethical dilemma**. For example, most major retailers, from supermarket and drug store chains to major investment banks rely on predictive analytics to understand consumer shopping habits and their personal habits to market themselves more efficiently. In some cases, police departments use them to prevent crime by identifying persons of questionable character.

Although privacy invasion is typically considered unethical, situations like this can present competing corporate responsibilities and trade-offs relating to personal data. On the one hand, an ethically conscious corporate attitude sounds politically correct; on the other hand, managers have a responsibility to perform well for their stakeholders and police officers have an obligation to protect law-abiding citizens. From one side of the argument, monitoring may be (or seem to be) the ethical thing to do. From the other it may not.

Globalization, the Internet, and connectivity have the power to undermine moral responsibility. It becomes much easier to ignore harm that might result from unethical behavior when the perpetrator is physically distant from a faceless victim. Despite the challenges and lack of clear answers, instilling good ethical values is important because relying on the law alone to safeguard civil rights and society is insufficient. The law has its limits in large part because it changes so slowly.

Questions

1. What are the three tenets of ethical behavior?
2. Why is it important for a company to have a code of ethics?
3. What are three ways in which the production, development, and use of IT is causing unethical behavior?
4. Name three protected classes.
5. How is social media depriving protected classes of their civil rights?
6. Why is it important that a company provide its employees with a secure and respectful workplace?
7. What types of behavior can a secure and respectful workplace help deter?
8. What is insider fraud? What are some other terms for insider fraud?
9. What four factors increase the risk of fraud?
10. What is the difference between social media discrimination and negligent hiring?

14.2 ICT and Local Sustainability

LO14.2 Discuss *the three facets of sustainability and how ICT impacts profits and the six elements of quality of life in developed countries before and during the COVID-19 pandemic.*

Sustainability is an issue confronting all organizations today, regardless of their size or place in the marketplace. Increasingly, companies are finding that embracing sustainable practices leads to better corporate culture, more reliable products, greater long-term profitability, and a better work life for their employees. While ethics focus on the principles, standards, rules, and codes of conduct that make cooperation, justice, and freedom of expression possible on a day-to-day basis **sustainability** goes beyond the day-to-day operations. It addresses conserving the natural environment, strengthening the economy, and improving social conditions to not only meet the needs of the present but to ensure that the needs of future generations will not be compromised.

The three facets of sustainability focus on the economy, society, and environment and are often informally referred to as profits, people, and planet. In terms of *profits* and business continuity, ongoing sustainable business practices might simply mean that the overall corporate strategy and policies are not self-defeating or dangerous to an organization's long-term well-being and reputation. In terms of *people*, sustainable employment practices might include ensuring employees are provided with a secure and respectful workplace, paid adequately, and given enough benefits to build families and contribute to their communities. In terms of the *planet*, sustainability might mean ensuring that natural resources are replaced or conserved for the long term and that the environment and its ecosystems are not harmed in the creation, operation, and use of an organization's products and services.

To be sustainable an organization must not only judiciously manage profits, people, and planet as separate entities but must also responsibly manage the interactions between the three. The interaction between people and profits is referred to as **fair trade**. The interaction of profits and planet is known as **eco-efficiency** and then people with the planet should be striving for **environmental justice (Figure 14.4)**. Each of these concepts are explained below:

sustainability is the ability to create and maintain conditions that enable humans and nature to exist in productive harmony to support present and future generations.

Fair trade means pricing products and services in an affordable and equitable manner, providing employees with decent working conditions in all locations, and offering fair terms of trade to farmers and workers in developing countries.

Eco-efficiency involves the creation of more and better goods and services while using fewer resources and creating less waste and pollution.

Environmental justice focuses on the fair treatment and meaningful involvement of all people regardless of race, color, national origin, or income with respect to the development, implementation, and enforcement of environmental laws, regulations, and policies.

FIGURE 14.4 Three facets of sustainability.

By responsibly managing the three facets of sustainability and their interactions, an organization is much more likely to continue to stay in business and lower costs over the long term, while improving internal and external relations and better managing competition and risk.

The Triple Bottom Line and Sustainable Development

triple bottom line is a process by which companies manage their financial, social, and environmental risks, obligations, and opportunities.

The sustainability of an organization is often assessed by how it manages the three facets of sustainability. For accounting purposes this is referred to as the **triple bottom line**. The triple bottom line is not just an accounting method, it is a way of thinking about corporate social responsibility and expands the notion of organizational performance evaluation beyond merely accounting for the traditional financial bottom line to measuring a company's social and environmental responsibility.

sustainable development is an initiative to create long-term stakeholder value through implementing a business strategy focused on doing business in an ethical, social, environmental, cultural, and economically responsible way.

To achieve sustainability companies and governments must engage in **sustainable development** activities that recognize this inseparable link between profits, people, and planet. A corporate sustainable development program creates policies that foster longevity, transparency, and appropriate employee development.

Addressing sustainability is an imperative that is being embraced by leaders in many industry sectors. Every year, Corporate Knights, a specialized media and investment research firm based in Toronto, Canada, releases its Global 100 report that lists the most sustainable corporations in the world. In developing their list, Global Knights track the sustainable practices of companies in several measurable ways including environmental factors such as how much energy and water are consumed and how much emissions and waste are generated. It also includes human factors such as ratio of CEO compensation to that of company employees, worker safety and turnover, and representation of women in board and management positions. The top five companies in the 2019 Global 100 who have been rated as being the best corporate protectors of the planet and its resources are shown in **Table 14.6.**

TABLE 14.6   **Top 10 World's Most Sustainable Corporations**

Rank 2019	Rank 2020	Company	Industry Type	Country	Overall Score
1	4	Orsted A/S	Wholesale Power	Denmark	85.20%
2	1	Chr. Hansen Holding A/S	Food and Other Chemical Agents	Denmark	83.90%
3	3	Neste Oyj	Petroleum Refineries	Finland	83.64%
4	14	Cisco Systems Inc	Communications Equipment	United States	83.59%
5	48	Autodesk Inc	Software	United States	82.84%
6	58	Novozymes A/S	Specialty and Performance Chemicals	Denmark	82.70%
7	35	ING Groep NV	Banks	Netherlands	82.53%
8	–	Enel SpA	Wholesale Power	Italy	81.77%
9	8	Banco do Brasil SA	Banks	Brazil	81.72%
10	–	Algonquin Power & Utilities Corp	Electric Utilities	Canada	80.89%

Source: Corporate Knights 2020 Global 100 Ranking (corporateknights.com)

Benefits companies can realize from embarking on sustainable development programs include:

- Acquisition and retention of sustainability-conscious customers who are driven to purchase goods and services from companies who have proven themselves to be sustainable
- Attraction and retention of socially responsible investors who respond to sustainability-conscious customers and invest in companies with strong sustainable development programs

- More dedicated sustainability-conscious employees who enhance the company's reputation through social media
- Attraction and retention of sustainability-conscious talent
- Short-term and long-term cost savings
- Increase in market share through building a brand image based on sustainability and differentiating products from those of competitors

In the following sections, you will learn how IT impacts profits, people, and planet and how companies are leveraging technology in their sustainable development programs amid the concerns of the COVID-19 pandemic.

Profits: "Green IT" Trumps Greenbacks

Profit is an essential component of any analysis of sustainability regardless of the way an organization trades in the exchange of goods and services. Sustainable profitability for a business means that an organization provides a service or product that is both profitable and environmentally friendly. To stay in business and remain profitable in the long term, companies must consider the viability of consumers continuing to purchase their product at a price they can afford and suppliers continuing to make the product, or supply the materials required to make it, at a cost that provides a healthy profit. To help do this an organization must source materials that can be certified as environmentally friendly from companies that engage in ethical practices and must not engage in business with countries or companies with bad reputations.

There is a common misconception that focusing on expensive "green" initiatives means that profits must suffer. Researchers at the Massachusetts Institute of Technology refute this claim. The results of an eight-year study showed that sustainability and profit are far from mutually exclusive. Thirty-seven (37%) percent of organizations reported a profit from sustainability and upwards of 50% have adapted their business model to take advantage of sustainability opportunities.

The most recent survey conducted by JUST Capital shows similar results. They measured worker pay, well-being, customer treatment, privacy, beneficial products, environmental impact, job creation, strong community involvement, and ethical leadership to create a ranked index of 428 "sustainable" companies. When the performance of the 428 JUST Index companies were compared to the Russell 1000 companies over the period from 2007 to 2018 it found that the ROI reported by the JUST Index companies was almost 2% higher (10.4% compared to 8.7%) than the ROI of the Russell 1000 companies. A comparison limited to the last five years, showed the difference in ROI increased to 7% higher for the JUST Index companies (Volkov 2019).

Another way a company can benefit financially from sustainability is by investing in sustainable companies. More and more companies are investing in securities associated with sustainability and corporate responsibility as part of their sustainable development programs. In their latest report, the U.S. Forum for Sustainable and Responsible Investment reported that **sustainable, responsible, and impact investing (SRI)** had grown to $12 trillion. This means that more than 25% of all dollars under professional management in the United States are being invested to promote advances in social, environmental, and governance practices motivated by personal values, corporate mission, and the demands of sustainability-conscious clients, stakeholders, and/or constituents.

Efficient use of IT and more specifically information communications technology (ICT) as it is often referred to in sustainability reports can be an important enabler in ensuring sustainable profits. In findings reported by The Climate Group—working alongside the Global e-Sustainability Initiative (GeSI) discussed earlier—it was shown that improvements in the way people and companies produce and use ICT can deliver energy efficiency savings to global businesses of over $800 billion (€500 billion) by reducing GHG emissions.

sustainable, responsible, and impact investing (SRI) is an investment strategy that considers environmental, social, and corporate governance (ESG) criteria to generate long-term competitive financial returns and positive societal impact.

People: Preserving Quality of Life

In the age of COVID-19 people are using technology to stay connected to others more than ever before as more and more carry smartphones, tote tablets and jump from one ICT app to the other. New technologies develop quickly and continuously, and society is becoming more adept at using these new technology innovations to help enhance their quality of life. However, while technology has significantly improved quality of life, in some ways it would seem it has only given the illusion of improving quality of life, without actually doing so (Bontrager 2018). In a recent report by MarketWatch (**https://www.marketwatch.com/story/an-estimated-107-- million-americans-could-miss-work-the-monday-after-the-game-of-thrones-finale-2019-- 05-16**), it was estimated that approximately 27.2 million American workers were absent, late, or distracted at work the day after the "Game of Thrones" final episode costing $3.3 billion in lost productivity. It is important to understand the power technology can have over our quality of life and more importantly understand the possible consequences that can result if we do not responsibly control its use. Consequently, as an informed user you need to consider several ethical and social issues associated with technology that is primarily meant to improve communication, relationships, productivity at work and overall **quality of life**.

quality of life   is the general well-being of individuals and societies, including physical health, family, education, employment, wealth, safety, religious beliefs, and the environment.

The six elements of quality of life that information technology impacts in positive and negative ways are *communications, relationships, work–life balance, healthcare, education,* and *travel.* Each of these elements are discussed next.

Communications
There is no doubt that ICT significantly improved communications-related quality of life issues for individuals and organizations during the COVID-19 lockdowns and quarantines. The use of ICT has been an interesting journey. Twenty-five years ago, before the advent of the Internet, people corresponded with friends and family by letters processed by the post office. These could take days or in the case of international mail, weeks, to reach the intended recipient and a similar amount of time to send/receive a response, or people talked over expensive and often unreliable telephone landlines. Now, people can use their smartphone to text back and forth around the globe receiving responses to questions or comments in a matter of seconds, and free international telephone call apps that offer video as well as audio communication such as Skype, WhatsApp, Facebook, and other mobile apps are freely available. Documents can also be transmitted with equal ease. Instead of unreliable international transmittal by snail mail, or even courier, documents attached to or scanned into an e-mail can be sent to an intended recipient almost instantly. Most recently, during the COVID-19 pandemic lockdowns and quarantines, being able to adopt video communications apps has become particularly important. Consequently, communication technologies such as Zoom, Cisco Webex, GoTo Meeting, and Google Hangouts Meet have become invaluable to maintaining effective communications at work and at home. At work, this type of technology has proved to be particularly useful in facilitating engagement among individuals and different departments by enabling employees to discuss topics of interest and share ideas using various online channels and forums anytime, anywhere without face-to-face interactions. In social settings, these technologies have become a lifeline for isolated family members, friends, and social groups.

Communicating Safely, Anytime, Anywhere
In the midst of the COVID-19 pandemic, communicating safely through technology enables people to stay in touch with friends, family, and work colleagues to help prevent spread of the disease. As a result, individuals and groups can communicate with ease regardless of location and the move from closed communications between very small numbers of people to communicating in larger groups—by interest or project—is steadily becoming the norm. In addition, in organizations, virtual teams, agile talent, and remote work have become necessary to sustain companies as they navigate their way through unchartered waters during the pandemic and prepare for a new way of communicating in the future. As a result, time zones and office hours have become less and less relevant, and ICT is increasingly enabling companies to communicate, make decisions, and seek information across the globe, around the clock, seven days a week.

Empowering Remote Workers Before, During, and After COVID-19   While it is estimated that 37% of all jobs could be performed remotely, before the COVID-19 pandemic only 7% of all U.S. workers worked at home, while Europeans were much more likely to engage in remote work. In a recent study of 30 European countries, Denmark reported 23%, The Netherlands reported 21%, and Sweden reported 18% of their working population worked remotely (Ojala and Pyoria, 2018). Before COVID-19, remote work was a highly sought-after benefit. Those who had access to a "flexible workplace" considered it a luxury offered primarily to knowledge workers such as executives, IT managers, financial analysts, and accountants (Desilver, 2020). From a technology perspective, remote work is enabled by technologies such as virtual private networks (VPNs), voice over internal protocols (VoIP), virtual meetings, cloud technology, work collaboration tools, and facial recognition technologies.

During the early stages of the COVID-19 pandemic when public health organizations strongly encouraged people to social distance to inhibit the spread of the virus, remote work was one major tactic that was available to companies to help avoid large groups of people working in close quarters. Not surprisingly, in May 2020, the Society for Human Resource Management (SHRM) issued a COVID-19 Business Index 2020 that showed the number of U.S. remote workers had increased drastically (SHRM, 2020). It reported that 64% of salaried employees and 49% of hourly employees were working from home most of the time, compared to 3% and 2% respectively in January 2020. Organizations around the globe are similarly being forced to allow millions of employees to work from home to avoid contagion.

The COVID-19 pandemic has and will continue to drastically change the face of remote work and "normal" business operations. More and more companies extend the option of remote work to employees as confinement rules are relaxed and lifted, and executives and managers are being confronted with the daunting task of empowering and coordinating a much larger remote workforce. One of the main drivers of this decision to ramp up remote work is economic. Monitoring a remote worker costs approximately $7 per month and having an employee work from home just half the time can result in savings of more than $10,000 per year in increased productivity, lower real estate costs, and reduced absenteeism (Global Workplace Analytics, 2020). Technologies that help employers track the productivity of their remote workers include Active-Trak, Teramind, Time Doctor, and Work Examiner. According to Dreyfuss (2020) monitoring software can track keystrokes, e-mail, file transfer, apps used, and time spent on each task.

For some, this is a completely new experience that can be fraught with uncertainty. Despite advantages such as greater employee productivity, reduced office costs, access to a wider talent pool and high retention rates, remote work also presents challenges to both employers and employees when offered on a large scale to a wider range of employees. These include information security, privacy, and the lack of timely technology support—as evidenced by a recent class action against Zoom. When weighing up the pros and cons of remote work, it seems clear that if companies want to remain competitive in the market, keep their current top performing employees and attract new talent they will have to rely on the technologies and IT services that make remote work possible for those employees who are in jobs that can be done remotely

Dangers of Off-the-cuff, Impulsive, Emotion-based Messaging   Not all impacts of information communications technology are positive. Unfortunately, the increased speed of workplace communications also has a downside. Because of the technology, people and organizations have come to expect instant responses. Electronic messages and comments can be off-the-cuff, impulsive, and emotion-based, with employees and politicians often blurting out messages that just pop into their mind. When little time is spent in crafting a carefully worded comment or response or a message is misdirected, it can lead to devastating consequences. Nowhere is this more disconcerting than when top-level politicians engage in this type of off-the-cuff method of communicating much to detriment of their citizens.

Relationships   Individuals experience both positive and negative impacts when they are linked through technology to a 24/7 workplace. Working remotely and being connected to mobile devices saves employers time and money. Telecommuters don't need an office or physical space to work in and even those who work onsite don't have to travel to as many meetings.

Challenges to Establishing Close Relationships   While technology has enhanced the speed, ease, and feasibility of communication to increase productivity, it has also made it more challenging for companies to establish and maintain close relationships with employees, customers, vendors, and suppliers enabled by the face-to-face communication methods they used in pre-Internet times. Electronic communication methods in the workplace have evolved from fax machines, voicemail, and simple e-mails to videoconferences, online newsletters, instant messages, a private company intranet, and even social media.

Adverse Effects on Socialization   Unfortunately, workplace technology can adversely impact users' abilities to socialize as remote or onsite employees see less and less of their employers and colleagues. You don't even need to walk across to the next office to discuss something with a colleague—just send them a text or an e-mail and you'll have an instant answer! This can lead to a highly disengaged work environment that brings with it worsening mental health problems. These include suicide and depression, that are being connected to a decrease in real, meaningful human interaction as people become more attached to their devices and less connected to the world around them.

Work–Life balance
Technologies in the digital age blur work, social, and personal time. ICT keeps people connected with no real off switch. Many people live and work in a state of continuous partial attention as they move through their day—loosely connected to friends and family through various apps on mobile and wearable devices. Just look around when you are in a coffee shop, doctor's office, or even a restaurant—people are more connected to technology than they are to each other! For example, consider what devices you use to stay informed and how often you glance at them. You might not have noticed the gradual increase in the amount of data and information that you receive or check routinely until one day you realize how much they overwhelm your time and attention.

- How many more things do you check today compared to a year ago?
- How long can you go without checking your devices without experiencing anxiety?
- When do you put down your mobiles and concentrate on one thing at a time?

Your answers may indicate digital or connectivity overload or even obsession and your tolerance level for distractions.

Digital Distractions and Loss of Focus Leads to Loss of Productivity   People do not need to be reminded how their lives are being taken over by tweets, texts, e-mail, social media, and annoying electronic static. It is all too easy to jump from checking e-mails to Facebook and the next thing you know you've wasted an hour scrolling through posts. Interestingly, this phenomenon isn't limited to millennials or Generation Z, older users are just as distracted as younger users. At home and at work users are more likely to suffer from too much data, rather than from data scarcity. This condition, known as **cognitive overload**, interferes with our ability to focus and be productive.

cognitive overload   occurs when too much information or too many tasks are assigned or undertaken, resulting in an inability to process the information.

It is important to be able to focus. Nobel Prize-winning neuroscientist Eric Kandel wrote in his book *In Search of Memory* that only by intensely concentrating can a person link new ideas and facts "meaningfully and systematically with knowledge already well-established in memory" (Kandel 2006). He explained the importance of mental discipline to successful performance. If your mind is free of distraction, your mind is better able to absorb data, interactions, and trends and synthesize the new information with what you already know. As a result, you are more likely to come up with innovative ideas. If you are multitasking or are trying to function with only partial attention, your ability to synthesize information may be compromised.

How big is the distraction problem and how much does it cost? Some researchers estimate that distraction costs hundreds of billions of dollars a year in lost productivity. According to a 2018 survey conducted by Udemy (**https://research.udemy.com/research_report/udemy-depth-2018-workplace-distraction-report/**), more than 70% of workers reported feeling distracted on the job and 16% said they almost always feel unfocused (Kuligowski 2019). According to Atlassian, the main culprit is excessive e-mails (**https://www.atlassian.com/ time-wasting-at-work-infographic**). On average, employees said they received 304 business e-mails each week, checked their e-mail 36 times per hour and spent 16 minutes refocusing after handling incoming e-mail. On a personal level, this results in the equivalent of missing one night's sleep and a lowering of IQ by 10 points. At an organizational level, loss of employee productivity translates to $1,250 spent handling spam, $1,800 handling unnecessary e-mail, and $2,100 to $4,100 in composing poorly written, ineffective communications. This all adds up to an annual loss in productivity that ranges from $5,150 to $7,150 per employee. Needless to say, digital distraction and lack of focus in the workplace are getting the attention of senior management. When Inc. called the CEOs of technology companies Instagram, Box, and Zumba, they confirmed that the lack of focus on the job is one of their biggest concerns.

Combatting Digital Distractions   To overcome digital distractions on the job, organizations are using focus management techniques to help employees find ways to balance their workday and find ways to focus. For instance, senior management at Google, SAP, Instagram, Box, and Zumba are experimenting with new ways to diminish cognitive overload in order to help their employees stay focused. Google employees take courses that help to sharpen their attention skills and the founders of Zumba and Box have developed their own methods to carve out focus time, such as putting aside large blocks of time to think undisturbed. Several ways that organizations can combat workplace distractions are shown in **Figure 14.5**.

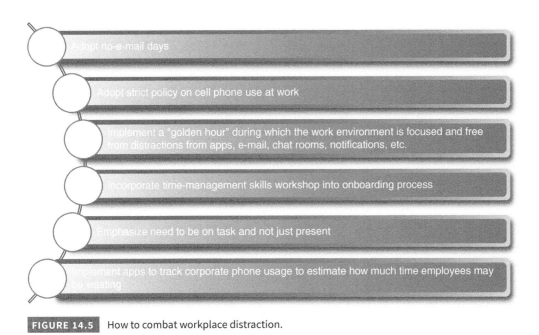

FIGURE 14.5   How to combat workplace distraction.

IT at Work 14.2 demonstrates how some groups of individuals across various interest sectors are attempting to improve their work/life balance. For companies, the key is to create a balance between technology and the human element. Whenever a company invests in technology, improving the employee, customer, and stakeholder experience must always be at the forefront of any corporate strategy.

IT at Work 14.2

Tech Workers, Journalists, and Politicians Seek to Restore Work/Life Balance by Resolving to Quit the "Always On" Culture in 2020

Top social media sites including Twitter and Facebook are being peppered with thousands of posts from users who say they are looking to delete or reduce their dependence on social media apps in 2020. The #deleteFacebook tag re-emerged on Twitter on New Year's Eve 2019 with hundreds of users sharing tweets imploring others to take a break from social media to read a book or connect with people face-to-face. Many expressed their feelings of being fed up with what they view as vitriolic and antagonistic behavior from strangers on the Web and are ready to disengage. Ironically, many of those posting are technology workers who are determined to pick up new hobbies like painting, playing board games, and learning a language or playing a musical instrument to alleviate the stress and anxiety increasingly associated with being "always on." Former Google director of engineering Ankit Jain is one those vowing to renew his passion for music by picking up his saxophone instead of continually checking his smartphone, while others in the tech field seek to restore their emotional health and wellbeing by reducing their reliance on social media and detach themselves from the opinions of strangers on the Internet.

In Canada, Keith Gerein, a journalist for the Edmonton Journal, points out that politicians and journalists are increasingly using social media platforms to "insult, vilify, stoke, mislead, and make outrageous claims" and implores them to be far less aggressive in their tweeting and posting that evoke varying degrees of bigotry, misogyny, and threats of violence from their opponents and members of the general public.

Thankfully, journalists are heeding the call to find a better work/life balance for themselves and those who are affected by their postings. CBS News president Susan Zirinsky said she is "resolved to do everything in my power to help everyone tune out the noise and focus on what's important," while Charlie Sykes, one of the founders of The Bulwark, an American conservative news and opinion website, resolved to "Read more. . . tweet less. Spend more time with grandkids and dogs." NPR "Morning Edition" co-host Steve Inskeep proclaimed that he intends to "better pace myself. Get proper sleep, delete social media on weekends, think about one thing at a time when the job allows," and Tanzina Vega, the host of The Takeaway, a one-hour daily NPR news show that reveals unexpected insights into the day's news, resolved "to figure out a work/life balance even if it means asking for help."

Politicians are also not immune to the effects of social media on their quality of life and that of their constituents. On January 1, 2020 Moses Kuria, Gatundu South Member of Parliament and one of the most vocal Kenyan politicians on social media sites, promised to deactivate all his social media accounts, except WhatsApp, as part of his new year resolutions. He said that he intends to use the time he would usually spend on social media to focus on other things that are more important to his constituents and that his example will prompt others to follow suit. Kuria's resolution to take a break from social media for a full year came as a surprise to many Kenyans considering his obsession with posting rebel-rousing and insensitive insults against his critics and political opponents that often caused a public uproar.

If you can't follow suit and give up your social media accounts entirely, at least try some of these tips to improve your day-to-day quality of life. Check social media just once a day. Change your notifications to get them less frequently. Use Google Alerts to find relevant links and articles via daily or weekly digest or use Trello to make a digital to-do list. Learn a new social media skill to help you in your work, and finally, use the 80/20 rule—80% of outputs result from 20% of all inputs for a given event—when gathering new information via social media.

Sources: Compiled from Gerein (2019), Malley (2019), Farr (2020), Mabonga (2020), and Stetler (2020).

To offer insights into overall employee online activity, an employee monitoring system like Activity Monitor (**https://www.business.com/reviews/activity-monitor/?_ ga=2.49197286.1574916442.1577997800-1674760721.1577997800**) can be implemented. However, if this type of monitoring is used, it is essential that the monitoring is both ethical and transparent. An organization must be forthcoming about how the monitoring aligns with company goals and employees must be made aware of official company policy about nonwork use of company equipment so as not to breach employee rights. The critical thing about any anti-distraction strategy is to avoid micromanaging employees. It may be counterproductive if employees feel "big brother" is constantly watching over their shoulder and they are not being trusted to use their time wisely.

Healthcare
No one can deny that technology has brought about many improvements in physical health and comfort. However, the impact of technology on health is not always positive.

Continually Evolving Medical Technology Innovations
The use of new technology in healthcare has led to some major breakthroughs including lower infant mortality rates, new cures for diseases, innovative new medical equipment, orthotic devices and drugs, 3D printed human organs, and tele-medicine that is particularly beneficial for patients who live in rural and undeveloped areas. Technology also offers a better way to improve communications between doctors and patients and helps us stay fit by pushing us to engage in more activity.

Mental Health and Technology Addiction On the flip side, it has been theorized that technology can be detrimental to mental health. The fear of missing out (FOMO) on social information and work information can cause anxiety and even panic attacks sometimes with serious consequences to a worker's health and productivity. For example, in highly developed countries where technology use is high, significantly higher suicide and depression rates are being reported and psychotherapy programs are needed to help patients recover from computer addiction.

Attention Deficit Syndrome Ten years ago, many believed that the Internet sharpened cognitive skills. Gaming required fast thinking and good motor skills. In contrast to widely held assumptions, the subjects who were heavy online users scored poorly on the cognitive test. One explanation for their poor performance was that they had attention deficit syndrome that results in less control over their attention. Because of their inability to concentrate for long, they were not able to distinguish important information from trivia. Researchers continue to study whether chronic media multitaskers are born with an inability to concentrate or are damaging their cognitive control by willingly taking in so much at once. Science also shows that the best strategy to improve focus is to practice doing it.

Michael Merzenich, a neuroscientist, gave a biological explanation of the impacts of multitasking on focus ability. He explained that the more you focus, the more your brain releases a chemical called noradrenaline, which helps you concentrate on the task at hand.

Even brief mental blocks created by shifting between tasks can cost as much as 40% of someone's productive time—that's 16 hours out of every work week!

Education
According to Chad Stevens, former Chief Education Strategist for CDW-G, a leading provider of multi-brand technology solutions serving higher education and K-12 institutions, IT and education go together like peanut butter and jelly (Stevens 2020). However, teachers can be frustrated with the quality of their IT services and IT teams exasperated by teachers' demands. As a result, there is a pressing need for both sides of the aisle to sit down together to discuss what one side wants and what the other can provide.

Education Delivery Many educators see educational technology as an integral and useful part of their pedagogical toolkit. In organizations, online training programs have become a critical part of education efforts to upskill employees and move new recruits seamlessly through the onboarding process. ICT can cater to almost all learning styles, including visual, tactical, and auditory.

Anytime, Anywhere Learning Technology enables training to be offered at will to individual employees or teams irrespective of day or time and wherever employees are located.

Preserving Past Knowledge and Experience ICT provides a way to capture corporate knowledge and expertise that can easily be passed along to others and overcome the brain drain of highly experienced employees who retire or leave the company for other reasons. Now corporate knowledge about customers and the cumulative knowledge of communities of practice such as medical specialists, engineers, environmentalists, and academics can be easily accessed and taught in a variety of ways. Knowledge and experience stored in information systems such as customer relationship systems, supply chain management systems and AI-based cognitive computing platforms like IBM's Watson can be valuable tools in improving an employee's knowledge and education.

Loss of Skills Machines and robots are attractive to organizations because they are more efficient and produce more consistent results than their human counterparts. When technology, such as software, a machine, or robot replaces the work of a human being less employment opportunities exist, and human talent can get lost.

Travel   The right to freedom of movement is highly valued in our society. Everyone wants to be able to go wherever they want when they want.

Disrupting the Travel and Tourism Industry   ICT has severely disrupted the travel and tourism industry particularly in the ways that companies interact with their customers. Local travel agents used to play a dominant role as the communication hub between travelers, hotels, airlines, care rental agencies, and tour operators, but now they have been replaced by a new generation of expedient online self-service platforms operated by the airlines, rental car companies, and on-demand startups like Airbnb and Booking.com. Innovative IoT technologies like the Carnival Cruise Medallion (described in the closing business case in Chapter 4) and the Walt Disney customizable, wearable RFID-equipped MagicBand have also become game changers in the tourism industry by providing a more personalized travel experience to their guests.

Reducing Traffic Congestion   Automatic traffic control systems on the autobahn in Germany and other major roadways in other countries regulate speed limits in relation to weather conditions and volume of traffic. This can ease traffic congestion and increase road safety but also infringes on the rights of those who wish to drive at higher speeds regardless of weather conditions and traffic congestion allowing workers to arrive at work on time and more relaxed. Another way that IT can address travel-related quality of life issues is by allowing companies to save money and increase employee satisfaction by permitting a large percentage of their workforce to work from home. In addition to easing traffic congestion, telecommuting also eases air pollution, traffic accidents and driver stress.

Enjoying a Safer and More Stress-Free Driving Experience   Major technology companies are partnering with the automotive industry to deliver more advanced, safer, and more comfortable vehicles. Cars have essentially become large smart devices. To reduce driver stress and improve road safety, manufacturers are turning to **driver-assisted technology** like advanced emergency braking capabilities, adaptive cruise controls, lane change assist, and mapping technology. To save owner time, they offer **predictive vehicle technology** in the form of sensors that inform the owner when the vehicle needs to be serviced and can estimate its performance, set up appointments in real time, and inform users of any safety hazards linked with a malfunctioning car due to company recalls.

In the future, we might even see a fully **autonomous vehicle (AV).** The combination of AI, big data, and a decrease in the size and price of IoT sensors is fueling concept designs of AVs with no steering wheel and no driver. The Cybernetic AI Self-Driving Car Institute is already developing AI systems specifically for self-driving cars. This deep learning software will enable AVs to become better drivers by learning from its experiences on the road to deal with difficult situations. IoT sensors will be positioned throughout the car to collect big data and perform and monitor actions and sound alerts. The combination of AI, big data, neural networks, algorithms, and IoT technology could enable cars that make it easier for people to travel without the hassles of airport check-in, security checks, delayed flights, and cramped airline seats. Imagine the possibilities offered by the revolutionary design of the Volvo 360c concept vehicle (**https://www.volvo-cars.com/intl/cars/concepts/360c**)—a fully self-driving electric car that acts as a mobile office, living room, entertainment space, and sleeping environment. In January 2020, Honda and GM unveiled working models of their AVs that are not as versatile as the Volvo 360c but are breaking new ground in the automotive industry with no steering wheel, no pedals, and no driver seat.

In the meantime, hybrid and electric vehicle (EV) manufacturers are using a series of IoT sensors, radar, cameras, and GPS to provide a safe auto-driving experience that allows drivers to arrive more refreshed at their destinations and experience lower levels of stress while driving.

Reducing the Need to Travel   Technology is a huge factor in saving corporate funds and natural resources by reducing the amount of travel that employees need to engage in. Using teleconferencing in place of face-to-face meetings is a common use of technology. This benefits not just the company but also positively impacts the employee's quality of life because they are required to spend less time traveling for work and more time at home and their environment is less polluted.

Questions

1. What is the triple bottom line?
2. How does ICT affect the profits of a company?
3. Why would a company want to become sustainable?
4. What are the six aspects of quality of life?
5. How does the use of ICT impact communications?
6. Why would you purchase an electric vehicle?

14.3 ICT and Global Sustainability

LO14.3 Explain *how ICT production and use is impacting climate change and the two main sustainability issues in developing countries and the barriers to improving them.*

Being profit-motivated without concern for damage to the planet is unacceptable. To protect the planet, the four factors illustrated in **Figure 14.6** must be judiciously applied to air, energy, waste, water, and biodiversity around the globe. To do this, companies are turning to technology to reduce global warming, recycle product packaging, reduce, recycle, and reuse waste, reduce water and power usage through recycling and recovery, and measure their overall effect on the environment.

FIGURE 14.6   The four "Rs" of environmental sustainability.

Intel takes the four "Rs" of environmental sustainability seriously. Intel has a track record of taking a proactive approach to issues related to sustainability both economically and environmentally. Reduce–reuse–recycle–recover is an important part of Intel's business strategy and long-term goal. From an economic standpoint, Intel has mitigated risks, saved costs, protected brand recognition, and developed new products and market opportunities. From an environmental perspective, Intel has addressed climate issues, diversity in the workforce, employee safety, set up an ethical work environment, conducted supply chain audits, and established and supported community service volunteer programs.

Sustainable IT is one of the main drivers of Intel's sustainability program. Chief information officer (CIO) Diane Bryant seized the opportunity for ICT to play a key role in enabling Intel to achieve its corporate sustainability goals when the chief executive officer (CEO) Paul Otellini announced his ambitious goal to reduce environmental impacts in key areas including energy efficiency, water conservation, and a 20% emissions reduction, Bryant committed ICT to help the business deliver their objectives through the use of sustainable ICT to reduce environmental impacts of IT operations and help transform the overall Intel organization by the following:

- Aligning all IT processes and practices with the core reduce, reuse, and recycle principles of sustainability
- Identifying innovative ways to use IT in business processes to delivery sustainability benefits across the enterprise

To better manage sustainability initiatives and effect change within IT and across Intel, Bryant established the IT Sustainability Program Office (SPO). The task of the SPO was to develop a sustainability strategy to educate and provide leadership to the organization on the principles and importance of sustainable business practices. First, necessary metrics, strategies, and processes were defined and implemented internally. To do this, they focused on the core metric of carbon footprint (CO_2) reduction, as well as reducing water, energy, and other resource consumption, and adopted internal IT goals to manage Intel's IT energy footprint and contribute to energy reduction.

Moving forward, the SPO's key challenge was to embed a sustainability focus in decision-making activities and best practices throughout Intel's daily business activities and transform sustainability from a program to a mind-set.

Climate change (global warming) is the most pressing sustainability issue that is currently capturing the attention of environmentalists and other scientists relative to sustainability of the earth. Over the past 60 years, every decade has been hotter than the previous one and unfortunately, people at the bottom of the socioeconomic ladder are most adversely affected. Extreme heat increases health problems, ravages crops and make it dangerous for workers to work outside. In many parts of the world, where water and electricity - to power fans and air conditioners - is non-existent or in short supply the impact is particularly devastating. To improve quality of life, companies and governments must work together to protect the world's natural resources and control the damage already done by making water and electricity more accessible, by planting trees to bring down the rising temperatures in major cities and by changing labor laws so that people don't have to work as many hours in the intense heat.

While winds and forest management play a role in the intensity and frequency of many natural disasters such as hurricanes, tsunamis, floods, crop damage, and forest fires, there is mounting evidence that climate change is a significant contributor to their size, intensity, frequency, and level of damage sustained. For example, warmer oceans are fueling the rapid intensification and frequency of hurricanes and a warmer and wetter atmosphere is intensifying rainfall. Stronger rainstorms make inland flooding worse and crop damage and rising sea levels are leading to more severe coastal flooding. In the United States heat and drought, much of which can be attributed to global warming, have more than doubled the cumulative forest fire area burned since 1984. Glaciers are melting at a more rapid pace than many scientists expected to see for decades and the amount of Artic sea ice has declined so quickly that we may see ice-free summers in that region by the 2030s (Fountain 2019). Apocalyptic wildfires destroyed millions of acres in Southeast Australia, destroying homes, threatening and taking the lives of citizens, and killing half-a-billion animals in 2020.

Climate change is closely associated with an increase in fossil fuel use and **greenhouse gas (GHG)** emissions that can lead to worsening air quality, water pollution, warming and rising oceans, and an increase in natural disasters. GHGstrap the sun's heat within the earth's atmosphere, warming it and keeping it at habitable temperatures. **Figure 14.7** illustrates how GHGs such as CO_2, methane (CH_4), and nitrous oxide (N_2O) absorb infrared radiation (IR) and reradiate it back to contribute to the **greenhouse effect**.

greenhouse gas (GHG) emissions are carbon dioxide, methane, nitrous oxide, and other chemical compounds that trap and hold heat in the atmosphere by absorbing infrared radiation.

greenhouse effect is the holding of the heat of the sun within the earth's atmosphere.

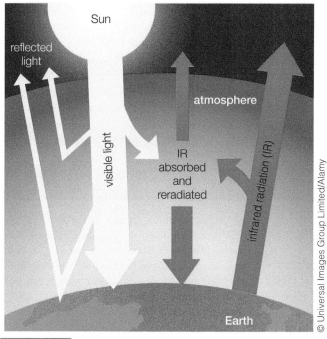

© Universal Images Group Limited/Alamy

FIGURE 14.7 Greenhouse gases contribute to the greenhouse effect.

According to NASA, since the start of the Industrial Revolution more than 200 years ago, the burning of fossil fuels and other human activities have led to an unprecedented buildup in GHGs. Human activities have increased the level of CO_2 by more than 25% in just the past half-century resulting in an increasingly higher **global mean temperature (GMT)**. This phenomenon is commonly known as **global warming** and is one of the most perplexing problems facing governments worldwide.

NASA scientists have concluded that increases in CO_2 resulting from human activities have thrown the earth's natural carbon cycle off balance, increasing global temperatures, and changing the planet's climate. **Tech Note 14.2** describes statistics about the unprecedent rise in GHGs that have been released over the past ten years by scientific institutions around the globe.

global mean temperature (GMT) is the area-weighted global average of the sea surface temperature over the oceans and the surface air temperature over land at 5 ft (1.5 m) above the ground.

global warming is the upward trend in the GMT.

Tech Note 14.2

Scientists Warn About the Impact of Increased GHG Emissions

In 2009, climatologists at the United Nations' Annual Climate Conference warned that catastrophic damage to life on earth will occur if GHG emissions rise to 2°C (3.6°F) above the preindustrial GMT set between 1850 and 1900.

In 2012, Dr. Faith Birol, the then Executive Director of the International Energy Agency (IEA) in Paris, warned that the upward trend in global warming was perfectly in line with a temperature increase of 6°C (10.8°F) by 2050, which is three times the threshold of 2°C (3.6°F) above the preindustrial GMT set at the UN Annual Climate Conference in 2009.

In 2018, the NOAA Global Climate Summary (**https://www.ncdc.noaa.gov/sotc/global/201813**) reported that the GMT had increased to roughly 0.7°C (1.26°F) above preindustrial levels. This means that the GMT had risen at an average rate of 0.07°C (0.13°F) every decade since preindustrial times. However, the main concern was that the rate of increase each decade (0.17°C/0.31°F) since 1981 was more than twice as great as the average rate since preindustrial times.

In 2019, the Global Carbon Project, a group of scientists who monitor the global carbon cycle, reported that almost 37 billion metric tonnes of carbon emissions were added to the atmosphere. That is five metric tonnes for every person on the planet.

In November 2019, several climate experts in Germany published a commentary in *Nature* (**https://www.nature.com/articles/d41586-019-03595-0**) warning that acceleration of ice loss and other effects of climate change have brought the world "dangerously close" to abrupt and irreversible changes.

Based on the most recent rates shown in Tech Note 14.2, the world is not on track to reduce GHGs between 50% and 85% by 2050 to prevent the global temperature from rising too much too fast because of the greenhouse gas effect and may well be on the verge of a climate emergency. This begs the question "Does our society have the capacity to endure in such a way that all 9 billion people expected to live on the planet by 2050 will be able to maintain a basic quality of life?"

The answer is uncertain—and hotly debated among scientists and experts who are extremely alarmed by global warming and climate change and those skeptics who outright deny that these phenomena exist. The debate may be resolved to some degree by data provided by climate change satellites described in **Tech Note 14.3** that are presently orbiting the earth.

Tech Note 14.3

Satellite Data May Help Resolve the Climate Change Debate

Japan's **Greenhouse gases Observing Satellite (GOSAT)** measures CO_2, Co_4 (methane), and N_2O (nitrous oxide). GOSAT is a joint effort promoted by the Japan Aerospace Exploration Agency (JAXA), National Institute for Environmental Studies (NIES), and Ministry of the Environment (MOE).

NASA's **Orbiting Carbon Observatory (OCO)** program with OCO spacecraft designed to make precise measurements of CO_2 (carbon dioxide) in the earth's atmosphere. In May 2019, the third generation OCO-3 was launched on the International Space Station. The missions of these GHG observatories are helping scientists reduce uncertainties in forecasts of how much CO_2 is in the atmosphere and improve the accuracy of global climate change predictions.

---

parts per million is a measure of small concentrations of pollutants in a solution of solid or gas and is a common unit of measure of CO_2 levels. 1,000 ppm is equivalent to 1%.

According to the National Oceanic and Atmospheric Administration (NOAA), the outdoor annual mean growth rate of CO_2 has steadily increased from 316 ppm (**parts per million**) in 1958 to 408.27 ppm in December 2019 (**Figure 14.8**). To put this into perspective, the atmospheric CO_2 level has risen 78% over the past 60 years at a rate that is roughly 100 times faster than previous natural increases in years during the ice age and current global average. This means that current CO_2 levels are significantly higher than at **any point** over the last 800,000 years (Lindsey 2019). **Figure 14.9** shows the differences in CO_2 levels across countries worldwide as reported by GOSAT. **Figure 14.10** shows the influence of all major human-produced greenhouse gases from 1979 to 2018 including a disturbing 43% increase in the last 30 years.

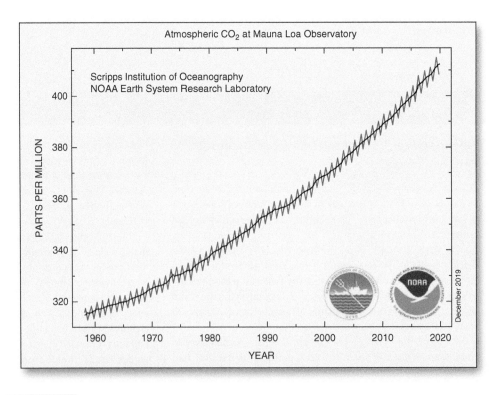

FIGURE 14.8 Annual mean growth of CO_2 from 1958 through 2019.

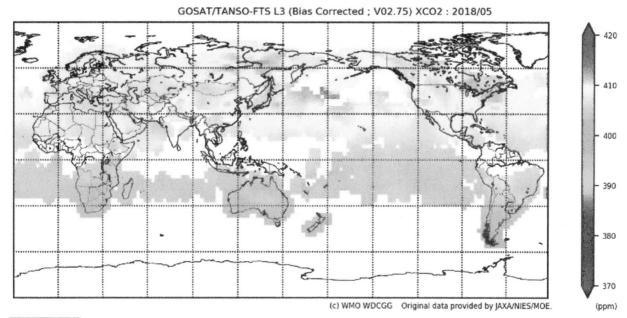

FIGURE 14.9   Differences in monthly averages of CO_2

Source: From https://gaw.kishou.go.jp/satellite/file/0053-9001-1001-08-08-9999 ©2019 WMO World Data Centre for Greenhouse Gases; Original data provided by JAXA/NIES/MOE

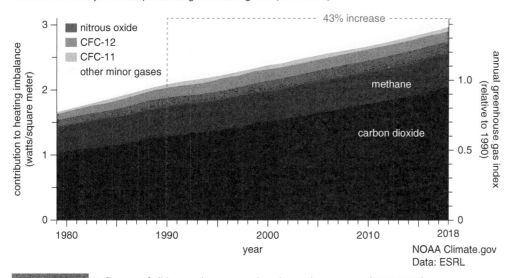

FIGURE 14.10   Influence of all human human-produced greenhouse gases (1979–2018).

The Link between ICT and Climate Change

It is widely accepted that ICT production and use are large contributors to the negative effects of global warming. For example, individuals and companies have become "gadget crazy" using electronic devices from smartphones to IoT for hours on end every day. The production and operational energy of IT devices, along with the operational energy for the supporting IT infrastructure has contributed significantly to the rise in GHG with millions of metric tonnes being emitted daily around the globe. For example, most employees are being provided with one or more desktop, laptop, display, and mobile device. More and more products have IoT capabilities. More processes are being automated daily. People access YouTube to watch hundreds of millions of hours and generate billions of views. Millions of people spend many hours every day on electronic devices carrying out their work activities, researching, and playing games. Statistics about LinkedIn, Twitter, and other social media services show phenomenal growth as the number of smartphones grows beyond the population of the planet.

No one sees CO_2 being emitted from their Androids or iPhones. But wired and mobile networks enable limitless data creation and consumption—and these activities increase energy consumption. Quite simply, the surge in energy used to power data centers, cell towers, base stations, and recharge devices is damaging the environment and depleting natural resources. It is critical to develop energy systems that power our economy without increasing global temperatures beyond 2°C.

Analysis conducted in a recent study at McMaster University in Canada (Belkhir and Elmeligi, 2018) reported:

- At the current rate, the IT sector's carbon footprint of roughly 1.5% in 2007 could grow to more than 14% by 2040 because of increased use of tablets, smartphones, apps, and services and the exponential growth of the IT industry. To help, rather than worsen, the fight against climate change, the IT sector must manage its own growing impact and continue to reduce emissions from data centers, communicate networks, and the manufacture and operation of main consumer devices.

- Among all devices, trends suggest that by 2020, smartphones will be the most damaging devices to the environment. While smartphones consume little energy to operate, 85–95% of their emissions impact comes from production, including the smartphone's chip and motherboard that are made up of precious metals that are mined at a high cost to the carbon footprint.

- The IT infrastructure accounts for most of the IT industry impact growing from 61% in 2010 to 79% in 2020. Embedded in this number is the impact of data centers, which grew its contribution to the overall carbon footprint from 33% in 2010 to 45% in 2020.

In addressing climate change concerns before the U.S. Senate in 2018, Dr. Birol outlined four large-scale shifts in the global energy system that are contributing to a reduction in global warming. Three of them are directly IT-related. The four major trends are:

- Rapid deployment and falling costs of clean-energy technologies
- Growing electrification of energy
- Shift to a technology-enabled service-oriented economy
- Resilience and growth potential of U.S. shale gas and tight oil resources

Climate Change Mitigation

carbon footprint is the amount of carbon dioxide and other carbon compounds emitted due to the burning of fossil fuels by a person, group, organization, or country.

climate change mitigation is any action to limit the magnitude of long-term climate change.

The first step in mitigating climate change is for organizations to assess their **carbon footprint**. They can do this by measuring the current level of GHG emissions produced by the manufacture and use of their products or services.

There are no easy or convenient solutions to carbon emissions from the fossil fuels burned to power today's tech dependencies. But there are pathways to solutions, and every consumer, organization, and nation can play an effective role in **climate change mitigation**.

For example, everyone can start to switch to low-carbon renewable energy sources such as geothermal heat, wind power, solar power, hydroelectric power, wave power, and biomass (ethanol, biodiesel). There have been encouraging successes in this area and IT has enabled them. For instance, in smart offices automatic light controls and HVAC levels can be adjusted by movement and space usage to optimize energy use. Conference rooms can be linked to room scheduling programs that dynamically boot up technology and adjust lighting to conserve energy.

Deloitte's Center for the Edge in Amsterdam (**https://www.bloomberg.com/features/2015-the-edge-the-worlds-greenest-building/**) is the most sustainable office building in the world. It creates more than enough solar power from solar panels on its own and neighboring roofs to meet all its energy needs. It also makes its employees' time at work more enjoyable and increases the company's overall efficiency. Employee smartphones are used to tailor healthy environments for its workers and reduce energy use. A company-developed app helps employees find the best place to work based on their personal preferences and adjusts heat and lighting to each worker's preference, making time lost due to climate control and distraction a thing of the past. They even get the right coffee blend and add-ins when they use smart coffee machines that recognize individual employees when they approach.

Just as technology is helping reduce carbon emissions in your surroundings at home and at work, technology companies are working with automobile manufacturers to improve air quality and decrease global warming. Gas-powered cars produce approximately 20% of all U.S. carbon emissions. The use of **electric vehicle technology** to develop hybrid and electric cars can significantly reduce this high level of GHGs. As a result, automobile manufacturers are moving away from producing gas-powered cars to a develop a zero-emissions transport market through the production of hybrid and all-electric cars. Most of us can quickly name several hybrid car manufacturers and know about electric car manufacturer, Tesla, but it might surprise you that there are 40 automobile manufacturers throughout the world that make electric vehicles (EVs).

State and federal governments are doing their part to support the zero-emissions transport market by subsidizing the production and sale of EVs to the tune of billions of dollars, but regulatory pressure alone will be insufficient to reach this goal. Right now, EVs are a niche product for the wealthy. Two-thirds of them are owned by households with an annual income of $100,000 or more. To make a difference EVs will have to become much more affordable. Hyundai, Kia, and Toyota have recently unveiled hybrid cars for around $30,000. Hopefully this better pricing will significantly increase demand by environmentally conscious consumers around the globe. To help make owning and operate an EV even more attractive Volkswagen just announced a self-driving robot that can autonomously recharge the EV at home. The bot is accessed through a smartphone app to give an EV a 50-Kw boost. With a command from the app the bot goes to the car, plugs in, handles the charging process and returns to a base station. As of March 2019, there were 5.6 million EVs on the road. That is a 64% increase from the same time in 2018 and the second consecutive year that the zero-emissions transport market has seen significant growth. To make a difference, industry experts forecast we need 125 million EVs on the road worldwide by 2030.

Network service providers also must reduce energy use to decrease their carbon footprint. The Internet is the largest network in the world. It produces a huge amount of GHGs required for the manufacture and shipping of servers, computers and smartphones and in powering and cooling them throughout their useful life and in transmitting the data they carry. For example, one Google search produces from 0.2 to 7 grams of CO_2, an e-mail has an estimated carbon footprint of 4 grams of CO_2 and a large attachment has a footprint of up to 50 grams. To deal with these challenges, wired and wireless service providers and companies are upgrading their networks to next-generation, all-IP infrastructures that are optimized and scalable. The network must provide sustainability in traffic transport and deliver services more intelligently, reliably, securely, efficiently, and at the lowest cost. For example, Alcatel-Lucent's High Leverage Network (HLN) can reduce total cost of ownership (TCO) by using fewer devices, creating an eco-friendly choice for service providers. Fewer devices mean less power and cooling, which reduces the carbon footprint. HLN can also handle large amounts of traffic more efficiently because the networks are intelligent, sending packets at the highest speed and most efficiently. Investments in research and development (R&D) to reduce the amount of carbon emitted by power stations for mobile networks are paying off.

Formal Climate Change Initiatives and Agreements

Along with tax incentives and subsidies to targeted industry sectors, several local and international groups have developed initiatives to guide the use of technology to achieve sustainability goals. Several reports and initiatives that focus on ways in which technology can be used to help mitigate the global climate crisis are discussed next.

The **Global e-Sustainability Initiative (GeSI)** rings together leading information and communication technology (ICT) companies, including telecommunications service providers and manufacturers, as well as industry associations and nongovernmental organizations committed to achieving sustainability objectives through innovative technology. Its members include

49 companies around the globe including Accenture Strategy, AT&T, Bell, T-Mobile, Deutsche Telekom, EPI Consulting, and Telstra.

The Climate Group's SMART 2020 Report was the world's first comprehensive global study of the IT sector's growing significance in global warming. By 2025, it is estimated that the value of the machine-to-machine (M2M) connections markets will reach $30 billion. M2M includes wired and wireless machine-to-machine connections such as IoT, M2M modems, routers, mobile point-of-sale modules, and wireless beacons used in the healthcare, utilities, retail, security/surveillance, energy, and agriculture sectors. One benefit of machine-to-machine connections is that they can relay data about climate changes that make it possible to monitor emissions.

The SMART 2020 Report provides an overview of the ICT industry's role in addressing global climate change and facilitating efficient and low-carbon development. The role of ICT includes emission reduction and energy savings not only in the sector itself, but also by transforming how and where people work. The most obvious ways are by substituting digital formats—telework, videoconferencing, e-paper, and mobile and e-commerce—for physical formats. Researchers estimate that replacing physical products/services with their digital equivalents would provide 6% of the total benefits the ICT sector can deliver. Greater benefits are achieved when ICT is applied to other industries. Examples of those industries are smart agriculture, smart waste management, smart building design and use, smart logistics, smart electricity grids, and smart industrial motor systems.

To assist organizations in developing sustainable development programs to reduce their carbon footprint, governments in many countries are providing tax incentives and standards to encourage energy conservation. For example, the International Chamber of Commerce (ICC) has committed to supporting the UN Framework Convention on Climate Change (UNFCCC) in accelerating the transition to a sustainable low-carbon future and in the UK, The Prince of Wales' Corporate Leaders Group on Climate Change have continually lobbied over the past 15 years for more aggressive climate legislation within the United Kingdom, the European Union, and internationally. Currently, over 40 countries across Europe, North America, Asia, Australasia, and South Africa offer GHG reporting programs within which they have established carbon footprint standards and private consulting companies exist to help organizations identify their current major emission sources and identify opportunities for future savings.

The **Paris Climate Pact** is the most far-reaching international climate change regulatory initiative that has been embarked on. On November 4, 2016, this landmark international climate agreement that sets nation-by-nation limits on GHG emissions was signed in Paris by representatives from 195 countries. The terms of the agreement will take effect in 2020. It is anticipated that the Pact will have a significantly positive impact on the global economy and be a rallying point for sustainability initiatives in industries around the world. Large polluting nations like China and India have already begun introducing stricter regulations in accord with the Paris Climate Pact. Even though the United States is one of the world's largest per capita carbon emitters, in November 2019, U.S. President Donald Trump formally notified the United Nations that the United States was backing out of the Pact and would begin the one-year process to withdraw. His announcement came amid widespread public protests and warnings from noted environmental scientists that his actions threaten to undermine the global effort to combat the climate crisis. Australia—another significant carbon emitter—also threatened to withdraw but to date has not followed through on its threat.

Beyond Climate Change

ICT is helpful when natural disasters occur. It can monitor the progress of storms and send out warnings and efficiently distribute instant communications to first responders, news reporters, families, and friends. Innovative technologies can also be used to help put out fires and one ICT innovation can be used to quickly replace destroyed homes. New Story (**https://newstorycharity.org/**), a housing non-profit company, and Icon (**https://www.iconbuild.com/**), a construction technology company, are working together to quickly build houses for people who are displaced or destitute. Using the Vulcan 2 printer, Icon has developed 3D Printing robotics, software, and advanced materials capable of 3D printing entire communities with up to 2,000 square foot homes in a way that is quicker, produces less waste, and costs less than traditional homebuilding methods. For example, a 500 square foot 3D-printed home can be built in approximately 24 hours. In the past two years, New Story and Icon group has built more than 2,700 houses in Bolivia, El Salvador, Haiti, and Mexico. In addition to helping those suffering because of natural disasters, New Story's grand vision is to put an end to global homelessness for the more than 1 billion people who currently live without access to adequate shelter.

Social responsibility in the supply chain is also a sustainability issue that can be addressed through ICT. For example, Provenance, a UK-startup, uses blockchain technology and smart tagging to trace the origins and journey of yellow and skipjack tuna from catch to consumer to ensure socially responsible practices are being followed in the supply chain. In other industry sectors, mobile apps and drones are making it easier to map and better understand the sustainability of our oceans. Certification programs delivered using technology are guiding companies in developing a diversity of sustainability initiatives.

Unfortunately, there are numerous financial and political reasons why countries will not even consider using the latest technologies to reduce or eliminate dependency on fossil fuels. For example, Carbon Dioxide Capture and Storage (CCS) technology captures carbon emissions from manufacturing processes, compresses the carbon dioxide into a liquid, and pumps the CO_2 underground to store it deep below the surface of the earth. This type of technology has yet to be seriously considered or adopted because of the enormous costs involved and the government policies that would have to be put in place to regulate it.

ICT and Sustainability in Developing Countries

Developing countries are faced with several unique and particularly disturbing health, social, and economic sustainability issues impacted by climate change and can benefit from the use of ICT solutions. These include access to clean water and sanitary conditions, food security, and unsustainable agriculture.

Access to Clean Water and Sanitary Conditions   No person or community can

function effectively without access to safe water and sanitation. In developing countries, nearly one million people die each year from water, sanitation, and hygiene-related diseases. This means more than six times the population of the United States live without a water connection. The United Nations estimate that by 2030 the global population will suffer from a 40% shortage in water resources needed for drinking, washing, cooking, and maintain sanitation systems. Because of this, one in nine people worldwide in developing countries like Brazil, India, Africa, Indonesia, and the Philippines must spend time finding and carrying water instead of working, going to school, or caring for their families. The lack of clean drinking water is of particular concern in Africa where it is one of the greatest causes of disease and poverty. Imagine having to walk over a mile to get water or wait in line for an hour to get one jerry can full. But your job's not over. At that point you must carry the equivalent of a 40 lb. weight the mile or more back to your home. Access to safe water can save lives and turn time spent into time saved, unlocking educational and economic opportunities, and improving the health of millions resulting in annual economic losses of more than $260 billion.

Clean water and personal hygiene go hand in hand. It's hard to believe that more people have a smartphone than have toilets! Approximately one-third of all the people in the world have no access to a toilet. That means two billion people in developing countries, 10% of whom defecate in the open, must spend time several times a day searching for a place "to go." This leaves them open to disease, compromises their safety, and undermines their self-worth.

On a national level, both concerns pose a huge social and economic problem for both the country and the organizations trying to do business there. These unsanitary conditions result in the deaths of one million people each year and an annual loss in time and income of $260 billion dollars. Providing access to water and sanitary conditions enables communities to flourish economically and gives people back their time, improves their health and education, and restores their dignity.

Fortunately, world health organizations are stepping in to help. Sustainability Goal 6 (SDG 6) of the UN Development Program (**http://www.undp.org/content/undp/en/home/ sustainable-development-goals/goal-6-clean-water-and-sanitation.html**) is "Clean Water and Sanitation" and commits to ensuring the availability and sustainable management of water and sanitation worldwide, including an end to open defecation by 2030.

ICT is playing a pivotal role in reaching this goal by combining physical infrastructure, data management, and communication technologies in new and innovative ways. For example, ICT can enhance engineering technology that delivers and maintains water and sanitation facilities and manage the water itself taking a data-driven approach. Especially important technologies that are transforming the quality of life in developing countries are artificial intelligence (AI) and the Internet of things (IoT). IoT is driving improvements in healthcare, sanitation, water access and quality, natural resource management, and resilience to climate change. AI is providing developing countries with expertise that was previously unavailable to them. Some examples of how ICT is being used to address lack of clean water and sanitation problems include:

- Water sensors are helping measure urban air pollution in developing cities.
- Interconnected water flow gauges and software modeling help warn locals and authorities about impending floods.
- Surveillance drones are helping nations map and monitor their natural resources.
- The Rainforest Alliance is using AI technology for training and raising awareness among its users who benefit from the expertise that is embedded within it.
- In Somalia, network sensors and satellite imaging are being used to measure groundwater levels and provide decision makers with a clear picture of a water system capabilities.
- In Kenya, the Ministry of Health has implemented an online, real-time monitoring system of maps and reports to show national progress toward the goal of communities to become "open defecation free."

Just as climate change affects water availability, rising sea levels can contaminate coastal groundwater with saltwater and depletions in groundwater, reservoir levels, and water availability impact food security and health. **IT at Work 14.3** describes the efforts of a Canadian company to increase the water quality of our oceans around the world and reduce poverty at the same time.

IT at Work 14.3

The Plastic Bank Uses Blockchain Technology to Turn Plastic Waste into Currency for the Poor and Save Our Oceans.

Blockchain waste management is an up-and-coming field that is saving companies millions of dollars and helping protect the environment at the same time. The World Bank Group estimates that waste generation will reach 2.2 billion metric tonnes of rubbish by 2025. Much of the waste is disposable plastics, including plastic bags, water bottles, coffee cup lids, and straws. Since the middle of the 20th century, it is estimated that 8.3 billion metric tonnes of plastic have been produced and 60% of it has ended up in landfills. Landfills are toxic hubs that leak poisonous materials into the ground and nearby water sources polluting the water and negatively impacting the greenhouse effect.

Spending precious time finding ways to recycle didn't make sense to residents in developing countries who spend hours every day trying to get enough food to eat, seek out private places for sanitation activities, find a place to live, and stay healthy. Recently, two Canadians, David Katz and Shaun Frankson, came up with the idea for The Plastic Bank (**https://plasticbank.com/**), an economic development program to reduce pollution and poverty and increase the safety of seal life by keeping vast quantities of plastic waste out of our rivers and oceans. The Plastic Bank sets up locally run plastic waste collection centers where participants in communities with no or insufficient recycling facilities can sell their plastic waste by type or weight. Collectors earn cash, digital tokens, or vouchers they can use to acquire daily essentials as well as pay for healthcare and school fees. The digital credits linked to smart contracts in a blockchain-based app are available to those who have mobile phones. This gives destitute families with no access to a traditional bank account with a means of depositing and growing their money.

The Plastic Bank is currently offering collection centers in disenfranchised communities throughout Haiti, Brazil, the Philippines, and Indonesia. In the Philippines the Plastic Bank has partnered with Shell Oil Company to create Plastic Bank markets at 1,000 gas stations throughout the country and plans to expand this venture to Indonesia, Ethiopia, and India in the near future.

Other companies in other countries are partnering with the Plastic Bank to promote its efforts and make it an even greater success. For example, Marks & Spencer (UK) and Henkel (Germany) pay extra to use recycled plastic from the Plastic Bank in their products that are labeled "Social Plastic" to help their customers see they are helping people in developing countries and keeping plastic out of our oceans.

Their efforts are also indirectly being promoted through a European Commission-funded project supported by the UN that is calling for consumers to buy only electronic and electrical products made with recycled plastic and for manufacturers to redesign products to improve recyclability and integration of recycled plastics in new products. Philips and Whirlpool are among the first firms to get on board providing The Plastic Bank with more outlets for the plastic waste it collects.

This simple innovative sustainability concept is producing amazing results. To date, the Plastic Bank has collected more than 17 million pounds (8 million kilograms) of plastic—that's the equivalent of nearly 400 million 16 oz. (500 ml) water bottles, 1.5 billion coffee cup lids, and 500 billion drinking straws. Along the way, it has improved the lives of more than 4,200 families living in poverty, significantly reduced pollution by plastic waste in several developing countries and is saving our oceans.

Sources: Compiled from Mok (2018), Smith (2018), NFK Editors (2019), Peshkam (2019), POLYCE (2019), and Sharma (2019).

The Current State of Food Security Without adequate clean water, agriculture suffers and access to adequate nutritious food is at put at risk (**Figure 14.11**).

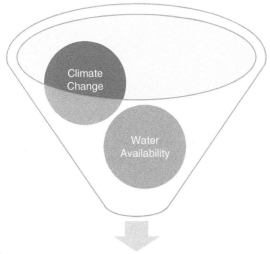

Lack of Food Security

FIGURE 14.11 Relationship between climate change, water availability, and lack of food security.

Most of us don't have to think about where our next meal is coming from, but according to a 2019 report (**http://www.fao.org/state-of-food-security-nutrition/en/**) published by the UN's Food and Agriculture Organization (FAO) approximately 26% of the world's population are moderately or severely insecure about their ability to find food to sustain them. That's almost 2 billion people—mostly in developing countries—who have little or nothing to eat and this number is rising. **Food security** is a complex sustainable development issue. It is linked to health problems through malnutrition and negatively impacts a country's economic development, environment, and trade.

The FAO specifies three different levels of food security (**Figure 14.12**). A household is considered food secure when its occupants have an adequate supply of good quality food. People are moderately food insecure where they are uncertainties about their ability to consistently obtain good quality food and people suffer from severe food insecurity when they don't have enough food to sustain a healthy, active life for the entire household.

Food security is when all people in a household always have access to enough safe and nutritious food and can maintain healthy and active lives.

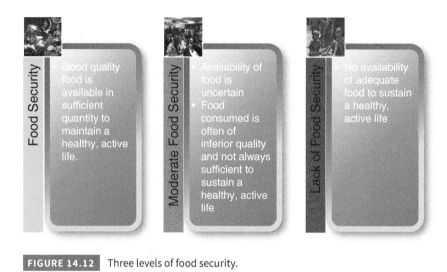

FIGURE 14.12 Three levels of food security.

Figure 14.13 illustrates the distribution of moderate and severe lack of food security around the world. Africa, Latin America, and Asia are the three continents that are most adversely affected. Food insecurity is minimal in North America and Europe.

Percentage shown is of each country's total population

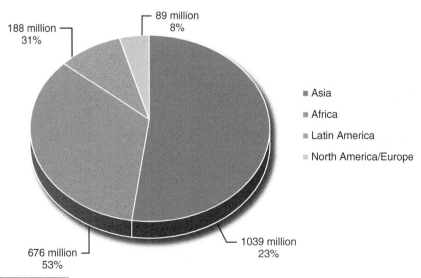

89 million
8%

188 million
31%

676 million
53%

1039 million
23%

- Asia
- Africa
- Latin America
- North America/Europe

FIGURE 14.13 Distribution of moderate and severe lack of food security around the world.

The people who suffer most from lack of food security live in Sub-Saharan Africa and South Asia **(Figure 14.14)**. These people are in constant fear of starvation. The food insecurity situation is most critical in Africa where the level has risen steadily since 2015. Food shortages around the world can be caused by a lack of farming skills such as crop rotation, or by a lack of technology or resources needed for higher yields.

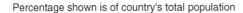

Percentage shown is of country's total population

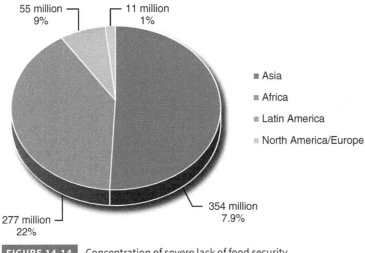

55 million
9%

11 million
1%

■ Asia

■ Africa

■ Latin America

■ North America/Europe

354 million
7.9%

277 million
22%

FIGURE 14.14   Concentration of severe lack of food security.

ICT can be used in several ways to help with the food security crisis. For example, the use of ICT to provide farmers with access to agricultural information and extension services, enables them to improve agricultural production and profitability. ICT can also improve market efficiency, provide jobs, and encourage the adoption of healthier practices and more effective risk management. Smartphones make it easier for rural farmers and traders to access financial services by providing a mechanism for farmers and traders to transfer money electronically. As a result, the cost of sending and receiving money can be dramatically reduced and transactions costs are lower. This in turn translates into lower grain prices that enable households to save money and buy more product. Some examples of ICT-supported food security initiatives that have helped developing countries include:

- Sugar cane farmers in Kenya increased their average yield by almost 12% as a result of receiving personalized SMS on their smartphones advising them to complete certain tasks in the fields.

- Farmers in Uganda increased their crop revenues by as much as 55% when they received price information via radio.

- Food was made more affordable for consumers in Niger when grain prices were reduced by 10–16% after grain traders started to use smartphones to call them to search for price information over larger areas and see their grains in more markets.

- In Africa, to increase human and animal welfare, provide regional and local food security and conserve the environment, the Infonet-Biovision Information Platform (www.infonet-biovision.org) provides farmers and rural communities with validated information and knowledge from local experts and international scientists on crop, animal, human, and environmental health.

- An African business to business learning network (www.linkinglearners.net) supports local entrepreneurs in Kenya, Uganda, and Tanzania to teach them how to operate commercial access enterprises. The project links small farmers with other key players in the market supply chain from producer to consumer.

ICT also plays a particularly key role in food security in both ongoing and disaster situations in rural areas. Currently, ICT is used by governments and international organizations like the World Health Organization (WHO) to map and monitor world food supplies and act as early warning systems when disasters strike. For example, geographic information systems (GIS) are used to map agricultural productions and establish comprehensive databases of food shortage that enable the storage and analysis of statistical data. GIS are particularly useful in food emergency response.

Barriers to ICT Acquisition, Implementation, and Use in Developing Countries

In most communities in developing countries, especially in rural areas, local access to ICT equipment, facilities, and highly skilled human resources are a challenge. These limitations can be further complicated by the legal issues associated with ICT adoption, operation, and use.

Lack of Technical Infrastructures Electricity and communication networks are essential prerequisites to ICT adoption and development. Unfortunately, these basic of an ICT infrastructure are often in short supply in developing countries. For example, low Internet bandwidth and availability can hinder effective application of ICT and make reliable and responsive access to the Web and online resources difficult. In addition, penetration rates of smartphones can be exaggerated and aggregating country statistics across rural and urban areas can make important differences in the adoption of ICT. For example, in Brazil, while 83% of households are reported to have smartphones, the rate drops to 53% when only households in rural area are measured. Since cost can be a severe limiting factor in developing countries, open source hardware and software are good options as a starting point for improving technical infrastructure. Beyond this, governments can provide attractive incentives to encourage private sector companies to participate in building new infrastructures or improving existing ones.

Inadequate STEM (Science, Technology, Engineering, and Math) Education Low literacy levels and education, particularly in the STEM subjects, poses a barrier to the use of ICT and the spread of useful information. Although many developing countries have university exchange programs and agreements with their counterparts in developed countries to ease the flow of knowledge many participants fail to return to their country after graduation, causing a brain drain. To decrease its dependence on education programs and technology providers in highly developed countries, developing countries must encourage the creation of technically skilled human resources by providing widely available and effective STEM-based academic curriculum and extension programs. By providing future generations with the skills necessary to confront and respond to the realities and complications of ICT developing countries will be able to more effectively address the different types of sustainability issues discussed in this chapter.

Scarcity of ICT Policies and Regulations It can lead to complications when legal decisions need to be made in ICT privacy, copyright, and security breach disputes. Enforcement can also be an issue. In some cases, a simple legal trial might take much longer than it would take in a developed country and the outcome might be easily manipulated by bribery or threats. This lack and/or unpredictability of legal recourse creates a level of risk that can easily deter external and internal investors. To address the inadequacy of rules and regulations, a quick solution is for a country to learn about, adopt, and customize rules and policies from developed countries. An example of this related to sustainability rules and regulations can be seen by the number of developing countries who are represented in international agreements such as the Paris Climate Pact or have become active members of the ICC. Another way is to provide training programs to decision makers, law enforcement officials, judges, and lawyers to make sure they have a working understanding of ICT and its application before they are faced with adjudicating ICT cases. Governments need to invest significant resources in designing polices to ensure that the best possible information is made available to facilitate ICT adoption and implementation.

Taking a People-First Approach to Technology

It is becoming more and more obvious that a people-*first* approach to IT is the key to any organization's digital success. People hold the power to shape and apply technology to create positive change, improve lives, and transform business and society locally and globally. Going forward, to improve the quality of work life around the globe the biggest ICT innovations will not be in the technology tools themselves, but in how they are designed with people, profit and planet in mind. Taking a **people-first approach** by empowering people with more human technology will allow organizations to improve performance by redefining their relationship with customers and employees from provider to partner. This will require organizations to change the way they develop their business models and provide technology that support them in their efforts to promote social responsibility.

> **People-first approach** ensures that technology meets the needs of users by involving the users at every stage of systems development.

For individuals, carefully evaluating how they are currently using ICT and becoming more mindful and conscious about the way they use ICT in the future should result in significant improvement in each of the six aspects of their quality of life. For organizations focusing on the needs and expectations of its employees, consumers, and partners, to avoid **tech-clash** will help them reap greater social, environmental, and economic benefits of a significantly more productive and efficient workforce and create a more viable planet.

> **Tech-clash** is the love/hate relationship technology users experience when they perceive the business value of technology is not aligned with their personal values, expectations, and needs.

Sustaining Business in a Post-COVID-19 World

The COVID-19 pandemic has made ICT more relevant than ever before as organizations depend on innovative technologies to help them stay afloat during lockdowns and quarantines. The use of digital payments, telehealth, AI, and robotics, for example, has accelerated sharply during 2020 to help businesses stay open and reduce the spread of the virus to make organizations and society as a whole more resilient.

To sustain business during and after the COVID-19 pandemic, companies will have to embrace more and more of these disruptive technologies. For the past 20 years, Accenture has published its *Technology Vision* that identifies five key IT trends that are expected to impact business and society in the next three years. In 2020, Accenture departed from its usual practice of issuing a single report and released a second report to factor in the short-term and long-term impacts of COVID-19 on technology innovations (Accenture, 2020; Daugherty, 2020).

A comparison of the technology trends highlighted by Accenture's *Technology Visions 2015, 2017,* and *2020* exposes an increasing need for companies to defuse *tech-clash* and focus on a *people-first* approach in developing, implementing, and using technology post coronavirus (see **Table 14.7**).

TABLE 14.7   **Comparison of Accenture's Top Five Technology Trends 2015, 2017, and 2020**

Technology Vision 2015	Technology Vision 2017	Technology Vision 2020
Internet of Me	Artificial Intelligence as the new User Interface	The I in Experience
Outcome Economy	Design for Humans	AI and Me
Platform Evolution	Ecosystems as Macrocosms	The Dilemma of Smart Things
Intelligent Enterprise	Workforce Marketplace	Robots in the Wild
Workforce Reimagined	The Unchartered	Innovation DNA

To achieve this goal, Accenture's *Technology Vision 2020* identifies five key trends companies must address to defuse tech-clash by developing new forms of business value driven by stronger, more trusting relationships with employees, consumers, and partners and overcome business disruptions due to COVID-19. These five future IT trends are discussed next.

TREND 1: The I in Experience

COVID-19 has transformed the role and heightened the importance of digital experiences as people engage in more and more e-commerce transactions, some for the first time ever. When companies use a black-box approach to customize the customer experience, customers feel out of the loop and out of control. The black-box approach currently taken by companies needs to be completely revamped. To be successful in the future, companies will have to build personalized, interactive, and shared virtual communities to allow customers to create their own meaningful digital experience.

TREND 2: AI and Me

Before COVID-19, the piloting or adopting of AI was already a high priority. In the future, AI should be an even higher priority. AI needs to be used not to just get work done. For example, Insilico Medicine, a Hong Kong-based biotech company has repurposed its AI platform to form a partnership between researchers and technology by using a "huge Lego system" of machine learning techniques to speed up the drug discovery process in their discovery and development of a market-ready COVID-19 drug (Field, 2020). Investing in AI and other tools that enable a true partnership between humans and AI will allow business to reimagine their work and workforce in the future.

TREND 3: The Dilemma of Smart Things

Companies must consider how they can introduce new features and repurpose smart devices to fight the COVID-19 pandemic. For example, repurposed smart health devices like smart thermometers and operating systems that track the physical proximity of smartphones to alert users who may have been exposed to the virus, can help identify symptoms, monitor patients, and collect huge quantities of data to help researchers and governments conduct contact tracing. However, they must also consider privacy issues related to data collection, storage, and use, and companies and governments will need to ensure they operate within strict privacy guidelines to maintain customer confidence.

TREND 4: Robots in the Wild

COVID-19 is strengthening the case for robotics and automation. As more people stay home and distancing becomes the new normal, robots are more critical in business and society than ever. This "contact-less" solution is already helping frontline workers fight the virus, and anti-virus robots that can sanitize surfaces and scan for fevers among patients and the public are being enabled by ultraviolet bars and infrared cameras. For example, in China ZhenRobotics Corp. has developed RoboPony, a six-wheeled, 27-inch high bright yellow robot, that is being used to patrol malls to identify customers without masks, hand out sanitizer, and broadcast anti-virus information (Associated Press, 2020) and in Thailand ninja robots are being used to monitor patients' fevers and allow doctors to communicate with patients remotely (Dangprasith and Suwarumpha, 2020). Among other applications, robots are also being used successfully to deliver food and other products to people in lockdowns and quarantines, and drones are being used to perform ground and air disinfection in the battle against the spread of the coronavirus. These technologies create a high demand for workers who are highly skilled in teleoperations and virtual reality to operate robots in newly created pandemic-related roles.

TREND 5: Innovation DNA

Accenture's Innovation DNA trend includes three different areas: mature digital technologies, scientific advancements, and emerging technologies. Current emerging technologies are referred to by the acronym of DARQ (distributed ledgers, artificial intelligence, extended reality, and quantum computing). In the wake of COVD-19, these DARQ technologies are taking on greater importance. For example, Applied VR is partnering with Red One Medical to offer VR stress management programs to frontline works (31) and HACERA's MiPasa project is a blockchain-based open data hub developed through a collaboration between the World Health Organization, IBM, Microsoft, Oracle, and other technology companies so that government agencies and international health organizations can quickly identify COVID-19 carriers and hotspots (van Hoek and Lacity, 2020). These types of partnerships will be necessary to help companies combine innovation strategies so they can change quickly and continuously as the pandemic evolves and to position themselves to meet new needs and build new capabilities when the pandemic is past.

COVID-19 is causing the greatest upheaval in our lifetime. It is not only severely impacting the world's economies and disrupting growth and innovation in companies around the globe but is also intensifying the need for even more innovative technologies like those described above. As the world changes faster than ever before, companies are responding to the need to be more flexible including one high-end apron company that changed its operations over to produce protective face masks within 24-hours (Segran, 2020) and General Motors and Tesla that temporarily shut down their American automotive capacity to collaborate in repurposing their production lines to manufacture ventilators to meet a critical ventilator shortage in the early days of the pandemic (Bomey, 2020). Moreover, the pandemic has highlighted the fact that if companies want to sustain their business disruptive technologies are *not an option*. They are *a requirement* to effectively protect and connect employees, consumers, and business partners. To meet the challenges of the COVID-19 pandemic, companies will need to remain standfast in creatively combining new innovation strategies and forming new partnerships to invent new products and services and redefine themselves through technology throughout the COVID-19 pandemic and beyond.

Questions

1. What is the greenhouse effect?
2. Why do some experts warn that carbon emission reductions of 45% are necessary by 2030? How does the use of mobile devices contribute to the level of GHGs?
3. What is ICT's role in global warming?
4. What are the three major sustainability issues in developing countries?
5. How can developing countries benefit from being sustainable?
6. What are the three major categories of barriers to ICT adoption in developing countries?
7. Which continents are most at risk from lack of food security?
8. How is blockchain technology being used to reduce poverty and help clean up our oceans?
9. Why is it important for organizations to take a *people-first* approach to IT?
10. What is the next biggest challenge companies currently face with respect to ICT and sustainability amid the COVID-19 pandemic?
11. What disruptive technologies could our company use to address the challenges of the COVD-19 pandemic?

Chapter Summary

LO14.1 *Describe* the three basic tenets of business and IT ethics and how IT-related unethical behavior impacts business, employees, customers, shareholders, and the civil rights of protected classes.

The three basic tenets of business and IT ethics are responsibility, accountability, and liability. This means that when interacting with others, individuals, organizations, and countries must engage in ethical behavior centered around anticipating and accepting the consequences of their decisions and actions, assigning responsibility for actions taken and requiring the right to recover damages for actions committed by others. In the workplace, a code of ethics, ethics and compliance programs, and ethics training are effective tools that help in the encouragement and enforcement of ethical behavior. Unethical behavior can lead to very serious consequences that can cause a company time and money in trying to repair their reputation, cost millions of dollars and even prison time, and adversely affect its sustainability. The production, development, and use of IT can involve unethical behaviors such as risky behavior built into mobile apps, exploitation of AI, dangerous distractions, additive manufacturing dilemmas, and computer-related fraud. IT can also negatively impact the civil rights of protected classes. Discrimination through recruiting ads placed on social media platforms and negligent hiring have become major problem when companies microtarget their ads to exclude protected classes based on age, gender, and race.

LO14.2 *Discuss the three facets of sustainability and how ICT impacts profits and the six elements of quality of life in developed countries before and during the COVID-19 pandemic.*

The three pillars of sustainability are profits, people, and planet. Interactions among the three pillars center around fair trade (profits and people); eco-efficiency (profits and planet); and environmental justice (planet and people). More than one-third of organizations report a profit from sustainable activities, such as producing and selling sustainable products, conserving energy and water, and engaging in sustainable, responsible, and impact investing.

The six elements of quality of life that technology can impact are communications, relationships, work-life balance, healthcare, education, and travel. While ICT can allow people to communicate faster anytime/anywhere and enable employees to work remotely to boost productivity and efficiency, ICT can also distort communications and encourage off-the-cuff, impulsive, and emotion-based decisions.

With respect to relationships, working remotely saves employers time and money, but it has also made it more challenging for companies to establish and maintain close relationships with its employees, customers, vendors, and suppliers. ICT can also discourage employee-to-employee engagement that sometimes result in health issues.

Social and personal time and work–life balance can suffer because of ICT. Many people live and work in a state of continuous partial attention as they move through their day—loosely connected to friends and family through various apps on mobile and wearable devices. This digital distraction and loss of focus can lead to loss of productivity.

The impact of technology on health is not always positive. Major innovations have led to improved cures for disease, innovative medical equipment, orthotic devices, and drugs and telemedicine that is particularly beneficial for patients who live in rural and undeveloped areas. Unfortunately, ICT has also been shown to lead to mental health issues including technology addiction and attention deficit syndrome.

Education and ICT is a good fit. New technologies enable anytime/anywhere learning that caters to several different learning styles. Knowledge and experience can also be captured and used to educate new hiring and less-experienced existing employees. On the flip side, when ICT replaces the work of a human being less employment opportunities exist, and human talent can get lost.

ICT has severely disrupted the travel and tourism industry particularly in the ways that companies interact with their customers. A new generation of expedient online self-service platforms operated by the airlines, rental car companies, and on-demand startups like Airbnb and Booking.com have made people more independent and customizable wearable devices are providing travelers with a more personalized travel experience. ICT has also helped reduce traffic congestion, save money and natural resources, and reduce pollution, accidents, and stress levels.

Amid the COVID-19 pandemic innovative technology and flexibility are key to helping companies sustain themselves and protect and connect their employees, consumers, and partners during and beyond the pandemic.

LO14.3 *Explain how ICT production and use is impacting climate change and the two main sustainability issues in developing countries and the barriers to improving them.*

Natural disasters are increasing in intensity and frequency and all are associated with climate change caused by a steady increase in fossil fuel use and GHGs causing outside temperatures around the world to rise to dangerous levels. ICT is both a detractor and a supporter of climate change. It has contributed to climate change because of the increased energy use in the production and use of ICT and ICT innovations are helping to address the fallout from climate change. Several government incentives and initiatives have been crafted to help with the global warming crisis including the Paris Climate Pact and the SMART 2020 report. In developing countries, the main sustainability issues are access to clean water and sanitary conditions and lack of food security. ICT is helping in numerous ways to address poverty, hunger, lack of personal hygiene, and excessive amounts of waste. Unfortunately, barriers such as lack of technical infrastructures, inadequate STEM education, and a scarcity or ICT policies and regulations are thwarting those efforts.

Key Terms

Assuring Your Learning

Discuss: Critical Thinking Questions

1. How can internal controls help to prevent fraud?

2. How do companies allow themselves to become targets for insider fraud?

3. What are the benefits of prosecuting an employee who has committed fraud against the company?

4. What are three examples of strong internal controls?

5. Why will companies and recruiters continue to engage in social recruiting?

6. Why is microtargeting a major issue in online recruiting ads?

7. Visit two or more social media sites and review information that people have posted about themselves—or their friends have posted about them. What types of protected class information did you find? Give examples.

8. When organizations source their hiring to recruiting firms, how might that increase or decrease the risk of social media discrimination?

9. What three actions can a company take to protect itself against being charged with social media discrimination?

10. What three actions can a candidate take to protect him/herself to increase their chances of being hired?

11. Discuss the ethical issues of anytime–anywhere accessibility.

12. Discuss three ways that IT affects travel.

13. What health and quality-of-life issues are associated with social networks and a 24/7 connected lifestyle?

14. How does the use of mobile devices contribute to the level of GHGs?

15. What is ICT's role in global warming?

16. What are the major sustainability issues faced by developing countries?

Explore: Online and Interactive Exercises

1. Find out if your company has a written code of ethics or code of conduct that guides ethical behavior at work and protects your rights. Write a short essay explaining your findings.

2. Social media discrimination and negligent hiring are serious considerations for employers.

   a. Research recruiting service providers and vendors. Select two of them.

   b. Review the website of each service or vendor.

   c. Describe the features they provide to defend against negligent hiring.

   d. Do each of them protect against age, gender, and religious discrimination? Explain your answer and give examples.

3. View the video at https://www.businessinsider.com/i-quit-social-media-for-one-month-it-changed-my-life-facebook-instagram-snapchat-twitter-millennial-2018-1 (4:18).

   a. What was your reaction to Emma Flerberg and her views on quitting social media?

   b. Could you do what Emma did? Explain.

   c. What other ways can you think of to cut down on your dependence on technology?

   d. How do you think quitting social media for one month would change your life?

4. Visit the Nokia website: https://www.nokia.com/blog/nokia-looks-zero-emissions-digital-society/.

   a. Read about how Nokia is advocating for a zero emissions digital society.

   b. Describe what the company has done to make others aware of this issue.

   c. Explain how, by how much, and when the company hopes to reduce emissions from its facilities.

   d. What do you think is Nokia's most significant contribution to sustainability?

5. Visit https://www.nature.org/en-us/get-involved/how-to-help/carbon-footprint-calculator/.

   a. Calculate your carbon footprint.

   b. Was your carbon footprint higher or lower than you expected? Explain.

   c. Name three ways in which you could reduce your carbon footprint.

6. Visit Zimperium's website at https://get.zimperium.com/07-31-19-mobile-threat-report-webinar-archive/. Sign up and watch their On-Demand Seminar: State of Enterprise: 2019 H1 Mobile Threat Report. Write an opinion essay on what you heard in the webinar. Include answers to the questions: Why are mobile devices the new favorite attack target? What threats are trending across devices and networks? Relate two of their 2019 mobile threat stories.

7. Visit https://www.cnn.com/2020/01/22/tech/cruise-origin-gm-honda/index.html and watch the video about Honda and GM's new AVs. What is your reaction to this revolutionary automobile design? Would you own a fully self-driving car? Who do you think this type of automobile would benefit? Explain.

Analyze & Decide: Apply IT Concepts to Business Decisions

1. Find and research a major corporate fraud.

    a. Identify the company and explain when and how the fraud occurred, who was involved, and what damages were sustained.

    b. Describe how the fraud was detected.

    c. Describe any red flags associated with the fraud.

    d. Visit **https://www.sas.com/en_us/software/fraud-management.html** and explain how SAS fraud management could have helped prevent the fraud.

2. A technology company hired to perform an information security audit accidentally finds a link embedded within the company's website that leads to information regarding another vendor's product embedded within the organization's site. Should they inform their client? Explain.

3. In your opinion, what is the meaning of *responsible conduct* with respect to the use of social media for screening purposes?

4. Do you agree with the FTC's rule that states that searches by hiring companies into how you spend your personal time, hobbies, and the like do not violate your privacy? Explain.

5. Clerks at 7-Eleven stores enter data regarding customers' gender, approximate age, and so on, into a computer system. However, names are not keyed in. These data are then aggregated and analyzed to improve corporate decision making. Customers are not informed about this, nor are they asked for permission. What problems do you see with this practice?

6. Discuss whether cognitive overload is a problem in your work or education. Based on your experience, what personal and organizational solutions can you recommend for this problem?

Reinforce: Ensure Your Understanding of the Key Terms

Solve the online crossword puzzle provided for this chapter.

Web Resources

More resources and study tools are located on the student website. You'll find useful Web links and self-test quizzes that provide individualized feedback.

Case 14.2

Business Case: Spies vs. Pirates—La Liga Fined Over Mobile App That Spied on Illegal Match Screenings

In June 2019, La Liga, the Spanish premier soccer league was fined a whopping $280,000 by Spain's data protection agency (AEPD) for violating Europe's General Data Protection Regulation (GDPR). Users were outraged to discover that La Liga's app had done more than just show a minute-by-minute commentary of its soccer games. Instead, La Liga had spied on its customers to identify illegal match streamings and the spy mode function was not mentioned in the app's description. On the flip side of the coin, La Liga brought its first criminal prosecution case against the 600 bars throughout Spain that were illegally streaming its soccer games.

The Case Against La Liga

When unwitting fans who hadn't read the Li Liga's app permissions word for word found out they had been recruited to out their favorite local bars they took to social media to vent their anger and their case was taken up by the Spanish Data Protection Agency (AEPD). Frustrated by its loss of revenue from illegally rebroadcast games, La Liga had programmed its mobile Android app to listen in on fans to find bars that were illegally streaming the games. As a result of La Liga's inappropriate monitoring of fans' Android smartphones, 600 bars and restaurants were identified and accused of pirating games. To monitor its app users' smartphone microphones and locations without their approval, La Liga had used its inhouse developed software Marauder to identify illegal streaming of their soccer games. In so doing La Liga violated Article 5.1 of the GDPR that requires that personal data be processed lawfully, fairly, and in a transparent manner. Marauder imperceptibly identified bars playing league games pairing it with geographical information to verify the bar had paid a licensing fee for the content or was showing it illegally. La Liga officials claimed they had expressly asked for user opt-in, but this didn't appear to be the case. By not alerting fans every time that the app remotely switched on their smartphone microphone to record their surroundings, La Liga had violated the transparency requirement of the regulation. La Liga also violated Article 7.3 of the GDPR that requires that when consent is being used at the legal basis for processing personal data users should have the right withdraw their consent at any time. La Liga's app did not do this. The clear verdict was that La Liga had spied on its customers.

In defense of the bar owners, the motivation to illegally rebroadcast games lie in the extremely high fees charged to commercial venues for sports-based packages. For example, Mediapro, a large sports rights broker, reportedly paid $150 million to broadcast La Liga games in bars, restaurants, and hotels during the 2018–2019 season. Individual viewers were also feeling the pinch. Many people watch illegal broadcasts in Spain because most of the games are only televised on pay TV, which is expensive.

The Case Against the Data Pirates

To protect their intellectual property, La Liga filed its first criminal court case that could result in "data pirates" spending a minimum of 4 months in prison plus payment of substantial damages. Being paid for their intellectual property is important to La Liga because they are competing heavily for television rights with the UK Premier Soccer League that typically gets the most lucrative television deals in European soccer. Not only does the UK league have a much larger subscriber base—about 10 million more than La Liga—but it also has far fewer illegal streamings, which translates to a much higher revenue stream. This puts the UK league in a much better position to pay the high fees associated with purchasing television rights.

In defense of La Liga, the mobile app identifications from smartphone owners watching a game at a public venue resulted in the detection of 19,000 illegal streams and 60 cases of sub-contractors who were selling or aiding access to its content. Studies by one anti-piracy group claims that as many as 20% of all Internet users in Spain watch games through illegal broadcasts.

It's no wonder that La Liga takes data piracy very seriously. Overall, La Liga estimates it has lost approximately $450 million in revenue from the piracy of intellectual property and continues to do so at a rate of approximately $186 million a year. To identify the data pirates La Liga has a team of 100 inspectors that made 80,000 visits in one season alone to ensure bars were paying the correct public broadcasting fees. La Liga also enlisted the help of Google, Facebook, and Twitter to find and block unauthorized streaming of its soccer matches. La Liga also works with several international anti-piracy groups and even joined forces with other sports leagues and the United States government to fight the problem.

The Outcome

At the end of the day, when the AEPD weighed up the impact of data privacy against that of data piracy, it was the protection of its citizens' personal data that won out. In the meantime, La Liga is appealing the decision made against them by the AEPD and the case brought by La Liga for the theft of intellectual property is still pending.

Questions

1. Why did La Liga fans file a complaint with the AEPD?
2. Why did La Liga file a lawsuit against 600 bars throughout Spain?
3. Why does La Liga consider data piracy to be a very serious problem?
4. When the AEPD weighed up the impact of data privacy versus data piracy in whose position did it favor?
5. Did you agree with the AEPD decision? Explain.

Sources: Compiled from Associated Press (2017), Anonymous (2019), Feldman (2019), Jones (2019), Khalid (2019), Lomas (2019), and Telecompaper (2019).

Case 14.3

Video Case: IT Ethics in the Workplace

In the digital age, most organizations are tracking employee activity in all kinds of ways to get more productivity.

Some are using keyloggers to measure keystrokes or using programs that can tell supervisors when a keyboard has been idle for 15 minutes. Others use keywords to flag which websites employees visit—and block ones that aren't related to work—or are checking employees' e-mails and instant messages to make sure that they don't contain inappropriate or proprietary material.

Indeed, nearly every aspect of work is now measurable in some way: Hours are tracked via security badges and fingerprint scanners, locations are monitored using GPS, and certain employee activities are captured by digital camera and video.

While it's clear that employers *can* measure nearly everything employees do, the question for many is whether they *should* measure employee behavior. To find out, it's important for companies to have a clear sense of what they hope to accomplish—and to be forthcoming

and transparent in their communication with employees. When employee monitoring is done poorly, businesses may find that what they hoped to gain in productivity is undermined by what they lose in engagement and trust.

Visit YouTube and search for the video *"Ethics in the Workplace to IT – Team 8."* Answer the following questions.

Questions

1. Why do you think employers monitor their online behavior at work?
2. Name the policies the company has put in place in regard to ethics in the workplace.
3. What monitoring technologies does the company use to keep track of websites employee access?
4. Do you think it's ethical for employers to monitor websites that employee access?
5. Which is more expensive—firing an employee or putting policies in place for employees to follow?

IT Toolbox

The Ten Commandments of Computer Ethics

Commitment to ethical conduct is expected of everyone who interacts with IT, whether they are IT professionals or users. The Computer Ethics Institutes Institute offers the Ten Commandments of Computer Ethics to help reinforce ethical behavior. The commandments were created as a set of standards to guide and instruct people in the ethical use of computers. The International Information System Security Certification Consortium (ISC) uses the commandments as a foundation for its own ethics rules. They are an excellent foundation upon which to model your technology-related ethical behavior.

1. Thou shalt not use a computer to harm other people.

2. Thou shalt not interfere with other people's computer work.

3. Thou shalt not snoop around in other people's computer files.

4. Thou shalt not use a computer to steal.

5. Thou shalt not use a computer to bear false witness.

6. Thou shalt not copy or use proprietary software for which you have not paid.

7. Thou shalt not use other people's computer resources without authorization or proper compensation.

8. Thou shalt not appropriate other people's intellectual output.

9. Thou shalt think about the social consequences of the program you are writing or the system you are designing.

10. Thou shalt always use a computer in ways that ensure consideration and respect for your fellow humans.

Print this out, post it somewhere you can see every day, and let it serve as a tool to guide your online behavior to enhance your work and social interactions.

References

Accenture. "COVID-19: Post-Coronavirus Technology Trends." 2019. Available from https://www.accenture.com/us-en/insights/technology/tech-vision-coronavirus-trends. Accessed on August 11, 2020.

Anonymous. "La Liga Fined EUR 250,000 for Using Smartphone Microphones to Detect Illegal Feeds." *Telecompaper*, June 11, 2019.

Associated Press. "RoboPony: Chinese Robot Maker Sees Demand Surge Amid Virus." *New York Post*, March 20, 2020.

Associated Press. "La Liga Gets Tough on Piracy of Its Content." *The New York Times*, April 8, 2017.

BBC News. "Facebook Accused of Job Ad Gender Discrimination." *BBS News—Technology*, September 2018.

Belkhir, L. and Elmeligi A. "Assessing ICT Global Emissions Footprint: Trends to 2040 & Recommendations." *Journal of Cleaner Production*, Vol. 177, pp. 448–463, 2018.

Bomey, N. "GM, Tesla Tackle Ventilator Shortage Amid Coronavirus Pandemic." *USA Today*, March 22, 2020.

Bontrager, S. "Does Technology Actually Improve Quality of Life?" *ST112 A2018, A Colby Community Web Site*, February 7, 2018.

Britz, K. "Sustainable Banking at RBS." Accessed from https://www.rbs.com/rbs/news/2017/02/building-a-more-sustainable-bank-.html on January 13, 2020.

Building Sustainability. "RBS: The Royal Bank of Scotland." *Building Sustainability,* 2019.

Campbell, A. "Facebook, Amazon and Hundreds of Companies Post Targeted Job Ads That Screen Out Older Workers." *Vox, May* 31, 2018.

Campbell, A. "Job ads on Facebook discriminated against women and older workers, EEOC says." *Vox*. Available from https://www.vox.com/identities/2019/9/25/20883446/facebook-job-ads-discrimination accessed on January 2, 2021.

Dangprasith, P. and Suwarumpha, L. "Thai Hospitals Deploy 'Ninja Robots' to Aid Virus Battle." *Medical Press,* March 19, 2020.

Daugherty, P. "Technology Vision 2020: We, the Post-Digital People—Can Your Enterprise Survive the 'Tech-Clash'?" 2020. Available from https://www.accenture.com/us-en/insights/technology/technology-trends-2020 accessed on August 6, 2020.

Davies, H. "Royal Bank of Scotland & The Financial Crisis: Ten Years On." *Lecture at King's College London*. 2020. Accessed on January 13, 2020 from https://www.rbs.com/rbs/news/2018/09/chairman_howard_davies_looks_back_at_the_financial_crisis.html

DeSilver, D. "Working from Home was a Luxury for the Relatively Affluent Before Coronavirus–Not Any More." *World Economic Forum*, March 2020.

Dreyfuss, J. "Here's How Employers Are Using Tech Tools to Keep a Close Watch on Their Remote Workers." *CNBC Technology Executive Council*, June 24, 2020.

Farr, C. "A Bunch of People in Tech Are Setting Resolutions to Spend Less Time Using Tech." *CNBC*, January 1, 2020.

Field, H. "Inside a Start-Up's Pivot to Have AI Fight Coronavirus." *Protocol*, March 26, 2020.

Feldman, J. "Massive La Liga Fine Just the Beginning of Sports' Media's Newest Battle." *Sports Illustrated*, June 14, 2019.

Fetherolf, A., Allen, B., and Romer-Friedman, P. "Older Workers Open up New Fronts in Campaign to Stop Age Bias by Hundreds of Major Employers Who Have Hidden Job Ads from Older Workers on Facebook." *CWA Press Release*, May 29, 2018.

Fountain, H. "Climate Change Is Accelerating, Bringing the World 'Dangerously Close' to Irreversible Change." *The New York Times*, December 5, 2019.

Gerein, K. "A New Year's Resolution for Albertans; Be Less Awful to Each Other on Social Media." *Edmonton News*, December 31, 2019.

Global Workplace Analytics. "Global Work-from-Home Experience Survey Report." 2020. Available from https://globalworkplaceanalytics.com/whitepapers accessed on August 11, 2020.

Gruenberg, M. "Facebook Settles CWA, ACLU Lawsuit on Bias vs. Women, Minorities." *People's World*, March 21, 2019.

Harker, W. "12 Ethical Principles for Business Executives by Michael Josephson." LinkedIn, August 7, 2014.

Hayes, L. "More Than Half of Employers Have Found Content on Social Media that caused them NOT to hire a candidate." *Career Builder*. Available from http://press.careerbuilder.com/2018-08-09-More-Than-Half-of-Employers-Have-Found-Content-on-Social-Media-That-Caused-Them-NOT-to-Hire-a-Candidate-According-to-Recent-CareerBuilder-Survey accessed on January 2, 2021.

Help Net Security. "Blacklisted Apps Increase 20%, Attackers Focus on Tax-Branded Key Terms." *Help Net Security*, October 25, 2019.

Horn, A. "RBS: We Are Building a More Sustainable Bank." *3BL Media*, February 27, 2018.

Jones, S. "La Liga Fined Over App That Spied on Illegal Match Screenings." *The Guardian*, June 12, 2019.

Josephson, M. "12 Ethical Principles for Business Executives." *Global Leadership Bulletin*, January 13, 2015.

Kandel, E.R. *In Search of Memory*. New York, NY: W. W. Norton & Company, 2006.

Kitch, A. "State and Federal Efforts to Reduce Distracted Driving." *National Conference on State Legislatures*, 26(23), June 2018.

Khalid, A. "La Liga Fined €250K for Using Its App to Catch Illegal Soccer Streams." *Engadget*, June 11, 2019.

Kuligowski, K. "Distracted Workers Are Costing You Money." *Business News Daily*, May 7, 2019.

Luism75. "12 Ethical Principles for Business Executives." *Ethics Education*, December 3, 2019.

Lindsey, R. "Climate Change: Atmospheric Carbon Dioxide." *NOAA—Climate.gov*, September 19, 2019.

Lomas, N. "La Liga Fined $280K for Soccer App's Privacy-Violating Spy Mode." *TechCrunch*, June 12, 2019.

Mabonga, M. "Moses Kuria Promises to Deactivate Social Media, Quit Alcohol as New Year Resolution." *TUKO*, January 1, 2020.

Malley, L. "5 Resolutions to Improve Your Social Media Strategy in the New Year." *Business 2 Community*, December 27, 2019.

McDevitt, J. "CWA Files Landmark Age Discrimination Lawsuit." *Liberation*, December 23, 2017.

McRae, R. "Bioprinting Human Organs: Saving Life or Redefining It?" 2016. http://blogs.kentplace.org/bioethicsproject/2016/02/08/bioprinting-of-organs-what-does-this-mean-forour-future-and-how-should-we-regulate-it/.

Mok, K. "Plastic Bank Using Blockchain Tech to Monetize Plastic Waste." *TheNewStack*, June 28, 2018.

NHTSA. "Distracted Driving" 2018. Available from https://www.nhtsa.gov/risky-driving/distracted-driving accessed on January 2, 2021.

NFK Editors. "The Plastic Bank—Treating Plastic Like Money." *News for Kids*, June 5, 2019.

Nguyen, N. "The ACLU Is Charging Facebook with Gender Discrimination in Its Targeted Ads." *BuzzFeedNews*, September 19, 2018.

Ojala, S. and Pyorio, P. "Mobile Knowledge Workers and Traditional Workers: Assessing the Prevalence of Multi-Locational Work in Europe." *Acta Scoiologica*, Vol. 61, Issue 4, pp. 402–418, 2018.

Peshkam, M. "How Blockchain Can Win the War Against Plastic Waste." *INSEAD Entrepreneurship Blog*, July 24, 2019.

POLYCE. "Reducing, Reusing Europe's 2.5 Million Tonnes of E-Waste Plastic Each Year." *SciTechDaily*, December 30, 2019.

The Creative Group. "The Benefits of Using Social Media for Recruiting Employees", *Robert Half Company*. Available from https://www.roberthalf.com/blog/management-tips/the-benefits-of-using-social-media-for-recruiting-employees accessed on January 2, 2021.

Romer-Friedman, P. "Age Discrimination in Facebook Ads." *OG*, May 31, 2018.

Segran, E. "How Your Business Can Help Fight Coronavirus: One Brand's Pivot to Making Masks." *Fast Company*, March 23, 2020.

Sharma, T. K. "Winning the Plastic War with Blockchain." *Blockchain Council*, August 28, 2019.

SHRM. "COVID-19 U.S. Business Index". 2020. Available from https://www.shrm.org/about-shrm/press-room/press-releases/pages/shrm-releases-covid-19-us-business-index-.aspx. accessed on August 11, 2020.

Smith, R. "Blockchain Waste Management: One Man's Rubbish Is Another One's Treasure." *CoinCentral*, July 31, 2018.

Stetler, B. "Tune out the Noise, Plus other New Year's Resolutions from Media and Tech Executives." *CNN*, January 2, 2020.

Telecompaper. "La Liga Prosecutes Over 600 Bars for Illegal Streaming." *Broadband*, March 15, 2019.

The Zebra. "Texting and Driving Statistics 2019." *The Zebra*, January 2, 2019.

Vanian, J. "ACLU, Labor Union, Allege Facebook's Ad Targeting Discriminates by Gender." *Fortune*, September 18, 2018.

Volkov, M. "Ethics, Profits, Sustainability and Stakeholders: An Update on a Familiar Relationship." *Corruption, Crime and Compliance*, March 21, 2019.

Valentino-DeVries, J. "AARP and Key Senators Urge Companies to End Age Bias in Recruiting on Facebook." *ProPublica*, January 8, 2018.

van Hoek, R. and Lacity, M. "How the Pandemic Is Pushing Blockchain Forward." *Harvard Business Review,* April 27, 2020.

Withers, I. "RBS Embarks on First Takeover since ABN Amro Deal That Broke the Bank." *The Telegraph*, March 27, 2018.

4G networks Digital or IP networks that enable relatively fast data transfer rates.

5G networks They are designed to support the escalation in mobile data consumption, with users demanding higher data speeds and traffic volumes expected to increase by hundreds or even thousands of times over the next 10 years.

6G networks The coming generation of broadband technology. Work is already underway on the development of 6G mobile telephone networks. 6G will be able to use higher frequencies than 5G networks and provide substantially higher capacity with much lower latency. 6G is not expected to be available before 2030.

Acceptable use policy A document that lists the constraints and practices a user must agree to for access to a corporate network or the Internet.

Access control It is the major line of defense against unauthorized insiders as well as outsiders. It is a security technique that dictates who is authorized to use an organization's computing resources.

Active data warehouse (ADW) The technical ability to capture transactions when they change and integrate them into the warehouse along with maintaining bath or scheduled cycle refreshes.

Ad hoc or on-demand reports They are unplanned reports. They are generated to a mobile device or computer *as needed*. They are generated on demand to learn more about a situation, problem, or opportunity.

Administrative controls Deal with issuing guidelines and monitoring compliance with an organization's security guidelines.

Advanced data analytics The examination of data using sophisticated methods and techniques to discover deeper insights, make predictions and/or generate recommendations.

Advanced persistent threat (APT) A prolonged and targeted cyberattack in which an attacker gains access to a network and remained undetected for a period of time.

Adware A software that embeds advertisements in the application. It is considered a legitimate alternative offered to consumers who do not wish to pay for software.

Affinity analysis A data mining technique that discovers co-occurrence relationships among activities performed by specific individuals or groups.

Agile A very flexible iterative, incremental systems development methodology that overcomes the disadvantages of the waterfall model.

Agility Being able to respond quickly.

AJAX technologies Include JavaScript, extendable markup language (XML), document object model (DOM), hypertext markup language (HTML), XMLHttpRequest, and cascading style sheets (CSS).

Always-on supply chain An integrated set of supply networks characterized by a continuous, high-velocity flow of information and analytics creating predictive, actionable decisions to better serve the customer 24/7.

Anything-as-service (XaaS) A broad category of increasingly diverse services offered over the internet via cloud computing instead of being provided locally, or on site.

Application defense controls Safeguards that are intended to protect specific applications.

Application programming interface (API) An interface that defines the boundary where two separate systems meet. Acts as a software gateway that programmers can use to pass data back and forth between two or more applications, platforms, or websites by allowing software, content, or websites to "talk" to each other in a way they both understand without extensive programming.

Applications portfolio A list of major, approved information system projects that are also consistent with the long-range plan.

Artificial general intelligence (AGI), also known as "strong" AI, essentially future applications that will be on par with human capabilities.

Artificial intelligence (AI) The theory and development of computer systems that can perform tasks normally requiring human intelligence, such as visual perception, speech recognition, decision making, and translation between languages.

Artificial narrow intelligence also known as "weak" AI, essentially current applications.

Artificial super intelligence (ASI) essentially, future applications with capabilities that surpass what humans are capable of.

Atomicity It means that any modifications to the database (insert, update, delete) are either completely made or discarded.

Attack vector A path or means by which a hacker can gain access to a computer or network server in order to deliver a malicious outcome.

Audit An important part of any control system. Auditing can be viewed as an additional layer of controls or safeguards.

Augmented analytics The use of machine learning and AI in BI tools to automate data preparation and help users discover and share insights.

Augmented reality A technology that superimposes a computer-generated image onto an image of the real world to provide information or entertainment.

Backdoor Also a difficult-to-detect malicious computer program used to provide an attacker with unauthorized remote access to a compromised PC by exploiting security vulnerabilities and works in the background hidden from the user.

Back-office operations They support accounting, inventory management, and shipping processes in the fulfillment of orders.

Balanced scorecard A strategic management methodology for evaluating performance based on both financial and nonfinancial metrics.

Bandwidth of a media is the maximum amount of bps that can be transmitted over the media and it varies by media type.

Bar code A machine-readable code consisting of numbers and a pattern of thick and thin lines that can be scanned to identify the object on which the code appears.

Barriers to entry Economic obstacles to market participation such as a fixed cost that must be incurred by a new entrant into a market that existing market participants have not had to incur.

Baseline A specification of the project plan that has been formally reviewed and agreed upon. It should be changed only through a formal change control process.

Batch processing Occurs when data are collected over a period of time and processed together at a predetermined time, such as hourly, daily, or weekly.

Behavioral feasibility Assessing the skills and the training needed to use the new IS.

Big data An extremely large data set that is too large or complex to be analyzed using traditional data processing techniques.

Biometric controls They have been integrated into e-business hardware and software products.

Biometric input devices They measure the unique physical characteristics of a person, typically for use in security devices designed to only allow access to specific individuals. Examples of commonly used visual biometric inputs include recognition of fingerprint, retina, iris, and facial features.

Bits per second (bps) The speed at which data are transferred over a network.

BitTorrent A communication protocol for P2P file sharing used to distribute data and electronic files over the internet, such as movies and music.

Biz-tech ecosystem It demands that business treat IT as an equal partner and IT steps up to the mark.

Blacklisted app A malicious app that mimics a reputable, highly downloaded app.

Blockchain A distributed ledger represented by a sequential chain of data blocks that records transactions, establishes identity of the user, and establishes contracts.

Blogging platform A software application used to create, edit, and add features to a blog. *WordPress* and *Blogger* are two of the most popular blogging platforms.

Blogs Websites (or sections of a website) where people or organizations regularly post content.

Bluetooth An open wireless technology standard for transmitting fixed and mobile electronic device data over short distances.

Botnet The term botnet is derived from the words ro**bot** and **net**work. Botnets are typically used to send spam and phishing e-mails and launch DDoS attacks.

Bounded rationality The idea that rationality is limited by the tractability of the decision, cognitive limitations of the mind and time available to make the decision.

Brainstorming A group problem-solving technique in which group members offer up spontaneous ideas for discussion to stimulate creative thinking and develop new ideas.

Brand advocates Regularly portray the brand or company positively in their online writing and social media posts.

Breach of privacy The loss of, unauthorized access to, or disclosure of personal information.

Business case A presentation or document that outlines the justification for the startup and funding of a project.

Business continuity The ability of a company to maintain essential functions during, as well as after, a disaster has occurred.

Business continuity plan A roadmap that guides the maintenance of normal business functions or restores them quickly when there has been a major disruption. The plan covers business processes, assets, human resources, business partners, and more.

Business driver A condition, process, resource, or rationale that is vital for an organization to thrive.

Business impact analysis (BIA) Estimates the consequences of disruption of a business function and collects data to develop recovery strategies.

Business intelligence (BI) A set of tools and techniques for acquiring and transforming raw data into meaningful and useful information for business analysis purposes in the forms of reports, dashboards, or interactive visualizations.

Business–IT alignment Refers to applying IT in an appropriate and timely way that is consistent with business strategies, goals, and needs.

Business model A company's core strategy for making a profit. It defines the products and/or services it will sell, its target market, costs associated with doing business, and the company's ongoing plans for achieving its goals.

Business need A gap between the current state of a business and its goals.

Business objectives The goals of an organization and the building blocks of a strategy.

Business process A series of steps by which organizations coordinate and organize tasks to get work done within and across their different business functions.

Business process management It consists of methods, tools, and technology to support and continuously improve business processes.

Business process reengineering The radial redesign of core business processes to achieve a dramatic improvement in productivity, cycle times, and quality.

Business strategy Sets the overall direction of an organization and defines how it will achieve its mission, vision, and organizational goals.

Bus network configuration It has a main channel to which nodes or secondary channels are connected in a branchlike structure.

Capital budgeting The process of analyzing and selecting investments with the highest return on investment (ROI) for the company.

Carbon footprint The amount of carbon dioxide and other carbon compounds emitted due to the burning of fossil fuels by a person, group, organization, or country.

Centralized database Stores all data in a single central computer such as a mainframe or server.

Change data capture (CDC) These processes capture the changes made at data sources and then apply those changes throughout enterprise data stores to keep data synchronized.

Channel conflict Competition between a manufacturer's distribution partners who sell through different channels. Channel conflict can occur at the wholesale, retail, or internal sales department level.

Circuit switching Occurs when there is a dedicated connection between a source and destination.

Citizen data scientist An employee in an organization who can use advanced data analytic methods and techniques and software to create data models but has not been formally trained as a data scientist.

Civil rights The rights of citizens to political and social freedom and equality.

Click-through rates (CTRs) Percentage of people who click on a hyperlinked area of an SERP or Webpage.

Client The name used for a computer on a network.

Climate change The most pressing sustainability issue that is currently capturing the attention of environmentalists and other scientists relative to sustainability of the earth.

Climate change mitigation Any action to limit the magnitude of long-term climate change.

Cloning Duplicating the electronic serial number (ESM) of one phone and using it in second phone, the clone. This allows the perpetrator to have calls and other transactions billed to the original phone.

Closed-circuit television (CCTV) With the growing network of security cameras and closed-circuit television (CCTV) feeds, the amount and availability of image and video data is growing exponentially.

Cloud computing A model of networked online storage where data are stored in virtualized pools generally hosted by third parties.

Cloud data warehouse (CDW) A database delivered in a public cloud as a managed service that is optimized for analytics, scale, and ease of use.

Cloud service Services made available to users on demand via the Internet from the servers of a cloud computing provider instead of being accessed through an organization's on-premises servers.

Cloud service agreement (CSA) Also referred to as cloud service-level agreements (SLAs), the CSA or SLA is a negotiated agreement between a company and service provider that can be a legally binding contract or an informal contract.

Cloud storage services They provide users with the ability to save documents and other kinds of electronic media on servers connected to the Web. This makes it possible for users to access their data from multiple devices and to share files with other individuals.

Cloud strategy A complex strategy to source scale and delivery IT capabilities on demand without physical location, labor, or capital restrictions in addition to on-premise systems.

Code of ethics A set of principles and rules used by individual and organizations to govern their decision-making process, as well as to distinguish right from wrong.

Cognitive computing The technology that uses machine learning algorithms.

Cognitive overload Occurs when too much information or too many tasks are assigned or undertaken, resulting in an inability to process the information.

Coherence The ability of a quantum computer to maintain information in qubits that are in a state of superposition (the "in-between 0 and 1" state that qubits can represent).

Cold site It provides office space but requires the customer to provide and install the equipment needed to continue operations.

Collaboration platforms Based on Web 2.0 technologies, they help team members communicate and coordinate an increasing amount of digital activity as the campaign grows.

Collaborative filtering Makes recommendations based on a user's similarity to other people.

Collaborative robots, also known as **Cobots.** They work together with human workers to accomplish a task or set of tasks.

Collection analysis module Creates utility indexes that aid in providing search results.

Communication How, when, and with whom to communicate.

Comparative advantage A country's ability to produce goods or services more efficiently and inexpensively than another.

Competitive advantage When an organization differentiates itself by charging less and creating and delivering better quality products or services than its competitors.

Competitive forces model, also called the **five forces model** A simple but powerful strategic planning tool for understanding the strength of an organization's competitive position in its current environment and in the environment into which it's considering moving.

Computer-aided design The use of computer systems to assist in the creation, modification, analysis, and optimization of a design.

Computer-aided manufacturing The capability of a computer system to process, store, and display large amounts of data representing part and product specifications.

Computer-aided software engineering (CASE) tools Software used to automate systems development.

Computer-integrated manufacturing (CIM) Integration of manufacturing operations by integrating people, technology, and manufacturing processes.

Computer networks Set of computers connected together for the purpose of sharing resources.

Computer-related fraud The use of computers, the Internet, and other IT devices to defraud people or organizations of resources.

Computer vision A field of artificial intelligence that trains computers to see using deep learning and cameras to identify objects in images and video and take appropriate action based on that information.

Consistency It refers to leaving all data in a consistent state at the end of a transaction to maintain the integrity of the database.

Constant time series A time series in which the mean value of the time series is constant over time.

Content-based filtering Recommends products based on the product features of items the customer has interacted with in the past.

Content marketing A strategic marketing approach focused on creating and distributing valuable, relevant, and consistent content to attract and retain a clearly defined audience—and, ultimately, to drive profitable customer action.

Contract hackers They are available for hire or complete hack attacks can be bought.

Cookie A small piece of data sent from a website and stored in a user's Web browser while the user is browsing a website.

Core business processes They include accounting, finance, sales, marketing, human resources, inventory, productions, and manufacturing.

Corporate governance A structure of rules, practices, and processes used to control and operate a company.

Corporate procurement It deals with the transactional elements of buying products and services by an organization for its operational and functional needs.

Crawler control module A software program that controls a number of "spiders" responsible for scanning or crawling through information on the Web.

Crawler search engines Rely on sophisticated computer programs called spiders, crawlers, or bots that surf the Internet, locating Web pages, links, and other content that

are then stored in the search engine's page repository.

Critical infrastructure Systems and assets, whether physical or virtual, so vital to a country that the incapacity or destruction of such systems and assets would have a debilitating impact on security, national economic security, national public health or safety, or any combination of those matters.

Critical path The shortest time possible to complete all tasks required to finish the project. A delay of any task on the critical path will delay the project.

Critical success factor An element that is necessary to ensure the success of an organization or project, that is, access to adequate financial resources, clear definition of goals, realistic calendar of tasks and activities.

Critical task Each task or activity on the critical path.

Cross-functional business process They occur when different departments within the same organization work together to achieve a common goal.

Cross-functional business system It integrates the end-to-end activities of an entire business process and cross-departmental boundaries.

Crowdfunding Raising funds for a project from the public, or *crowd*, via the Web.

Crowdsourcing A model of problem solving, production, and idea generation that marshals the collective talents of a large group of people that use the Web.

Cryptojacking A way that cybercriminals can make money with minimal effort.

Customer-centric An approach to doing business that focuses on providing a positive customer experience at and after the point of sale to drive profit and gain competitive advantage.

Customer experience Describes the cumulative impact of multiple interactions over the course of a customer's contact with an organization.

Customer lifetime value (CLV) The value a customer contributes to the business over the entire lifetime of their relationship with the company.

Customer relationship management The process of choosing the most suitable and efficient approach to making and maintaining interactions with customer and clients.

Cyberattack An actual attempt to expose, alter, disable, destroy, steal, or gain unauthorized access to a computer system, infrastructure, network, or any other smart device.

Cyber security The discipline dedicated to protecting information and systems used to process and store it from attack, damage, or unauthorized access.

Cyberthreat The method used to commit a cyberattack that seeks to damage data, steal sensitive data, or disrupt digital life in general.

Cycle time The period to complete one cycle of an operation or to complete a function, job, or task from start to finish.

Dashboard An easy-to-read, often single-page, real-time user interface, showing a graphical presentation of the current status and historical trends of an organization's key performance indicators to enable instantaneous and informed decisions to be made.

Data Describe products, customers, events, activities, and transactions that are recorded, classified, and stored.

Data analytics Technique of qualitatively or quantitatively analyzing a data set to reveal patterns, trends, and associations that often relate to human behavior and interactions, to enhance productivity and business gain.

Data as a service (DaaS) An information provision and distribution model in which data files (including text, images, sounds, and videos) are made available to customers over a network by a service provider.

Database Collection of data sets or records stored in a systematic way.

Database management system (DBMS) Software used to manage the additions, updates, and deletions of data as transactions occur, and to support data queries and reporting. They are online transaction-processing (OLTP) systems.

Database query language Refers to any computer programming language that finds and retrieves data from a database and information system by processing user queries.

Data breach The *successful retrieval* of sensitive information by an individual, group, or software system.

Data center A large group of networked computer servers typically used by organizations for the remote storage, processing, or distribution of large amounts of data. A data center can also refer to the building or facility that houses the servers and equipment.

Data deduplication These processes remove duplicates and standardize data formats.

Data discovery The process of using BI to collect data from various databases and consolidate it into a single source that can be easily and instantly evaluated.

Data entity It is anything real or abstract about which a company wants to collect and store data.

Data governance The overall management of the availability, usability, integrity, and security of data used in an enterprise.

Data integrity Refers to the maintenance of data accuracy and validity over its life cycle including the prevention of unintended modification or corruption.

Data lake A single store of structured, semistructured, and unstructured enterprise data stored in its natural format.

Data latency The elapsed time (or delay) between when data are created and when they are available for a query or report can significantly impact database performance.

Data management The management of the flow of data from creation and initial storage to the time when the data become obsolete and are deleted.

Data mart A small-scale data warehouse that supports a single function or one department.

Data mashup The integration of two or more data sets from various business systems and external sources without relying on the middle step of ETL (extract, transform, and load) into a data warehouse or help from IT.

Data mining The process of using software to analyze unstructured, semistructured, and structured data from various perspectives, categorize them, and derive correlations or patterns among fields in the data.

Data privacy The right to self-determine what information about you is made accessible, to whom, when, and for what use or purpose.

Data product A technical function that encapsulates an algorithm and is designed to integrate directly into core applications.

Data science A multidisciplinary field that uses domain expertise, scientific methods, programming skills, algorithms and statistics to extract knowledge and insights from structured, semistructured, and unstructured big data sets to predict future behavior and prescribe actions.

Data security refers to the protection of data from malicious or unintentional corruption, unauthorized modification, theft, or natural causes such as floods. The purpose of data security is to maintain data integrity.

Data silo Stand-alone data stores. Their data are not accessible by other ISs that need it outside that department.

Data structure A specialized format for organizing and storing data. General data structures include, file, record, table, tree, and so on.

Data tampering A cyberattack during which someone enters false or fraudulent data into a computer, or changes or deletes existing data.

Data validity involves tests and evaluations used to detect and correct errors, for instance, mistakes that might occur during data entry in fields such as customer name and address.

Data virtualization The process of abstracting, transforming, merging, and delivering data from disparate sources to provide a single point of access.

Data visualization The process of representing abstract business or scientific data as images, diagrams, graphs, or animations that can aid in understanding the meaning of the data.

Data warehouse A central depository of integrated data from one or more disparate sources.

Decision optimization Process of calculating values of variables that lead to an optimal value of the event under investigation.

Decision support system A knowledge-based system used by senior managers to facilitate the creation of knowledge and allow its integration into the organization.

Declarative language A high-level programming language that allows the user to express what they want without specifying how to get it, thus separating the process of stating a problem from the process of solving it.

Decoherence It is caused by things like vibrations, temperature changes, and electromagnetic waves, to which current quantum computers are extremely sensitive.

Deep learning A subset of machine learning and artificial intelligence that employs artificial neural networks. These artificial neural networks are computer algorithms that loosely replicate the function of neurons in the human brain and are capable of learning from large, structured and unstructured data sets.

Deliverables Tangible or intangible goods or services produced in a project and intended to be delivered to a customer..

Descriptive data analytics Create a summary of historical data to yield useful information and possibly prepare the data for future more sophisticated analysis.

DevOps A set of processes that encourages collaboration between system developers, operators, and testers.

Digital advertising Banner ads and graphic ads that appear on websites willing to host advertisements from online display networks like Google Ads or Yahoo.

Digital business model Prescribes how businesses make money and meet their goals using digital technology, such as websites, social media, and mobile devices.

Digital dashboard A static or interactive electronic interface used to acquire and consolidate data across an organization.

Digitization The process of transforming any kind of activity or information into a digital format that can be collected, stored, searched, and analyzed electronically—and efficiently.

Direct e-commerce It involves organizations selling their products or services directly to other organizations from their own private website or one managed by a third party.

Direct procurement Involves organizations procuring materials to produce finished goods.

Direct-to-consumer (D2C) marketplace It is composed of businesses that ship their products directly to consumers without using wholesalers, distributors, or other middlemen that play a role in other retail channels.

Dirty data Poor-quality data that lacks integrity and cannot be trusted.

Discrimination A biased or prejudicial treatment in recruitment, hiring, or employment based on certain characteristics, such as age, gender, and genetic information, and is illegal in the United States.

Distributed database Stores portions of the database on multiple computers controlled by a database management system (DBMS) within a network in a client-server configuration.

Do-not-carry rules Employees can bring only "clean" devices to workplace and are forbidden from connecting to the company network while off premises.

Drill down Searching for something on a computer moving from general information to more detailed information by focusing on something of interest, for example, quarterly sales—monthly sales—daily sales.

Drone A flying robot that can be remotely controlled or fly autonomously through software-controlled flight plans working with onboard sensors and GPS.

Durability It requires that a completed transaction, once committed, becomes part of the database and is not reversible.

Eco-efficiency Involves the creation of more and better goods and services while using fewer resources and creating less waste and pollution.

E-commerce or "electronic commerce" The buying and selling of goods and services on a computer network, such as the Internet or the World Wide Web.

Economic feasibility Determines if the project is an acceptable financial risk and if the company can afford the expense and time needed to complete the project.

Economic order quantity (EOQ) Inventory model used to decide when to order and how much to order.

Edge computing Part of a distributed computing topology where information processing is located close to the edge—where things and people produce or consume the information.

Edge service A term that refers to a cloud service that integrates back-to-core internal systems that correct and share data with enterprise systems.

Electronic content A collection of documents, records, and unstructured data available as a broad range of digital assets, such as audio, video, flash, multimedia files, and so on.

Electronic data interchange Electronically communicating information such as purchase order and invoices.

Electronic document Any paper, electronic form, file, email, fax, contract, lease, and so on actively being worked on.

Electronic document management The electronic storage, maintenance, and tracking of electronic documents and electronic images of paper-based information.

Electronic document management system A software system for creating, organizing, storing, and retrieving different kinds of electronic documents.

Electronic funds transfer (EFT) A transfer of funds from one bank account to another over a computerized network.

Electronic record Any document that has been made final and is no longer meant to be altered.

Electronic records management Establishes policies and standards for maintaining diverse types of records.

Electronic records management system (ERMS) This system consists of hardware and software that manage and archive electronic documents and image paper documents; then index and store them according to company policy.

Embedded BI The integration of self-service analytics tools and capabilities within commonly used business software apps.

Employee development A joint endeavor between employee and employer to update the existing skills and knowledge of an individual employee.

Entanglement It describes the case where two things are connected, such as two entangled coins, such that when one lands on heads, the other lands on heads, and vice versa.

Enterprise architecture (EA) A conceptual blueprint that defines the structure and operation of an organization's strategy, information, processes, and IT assets.

Enterprise cloud A special case of using cloud computing for competitive advantage through cost savings, increased speed and agility, and vastly improved collaboration among business partners and customers.

Enterprise content management The capture, storage, retrieval, and management of a diverse set of digital assets including documents, records, emails, electronic communications, images, video, flash, audio, and multimedia.

Enterprise content management system (ECMS) Captures, preserves, and manages structured and unstructured a wide variety of digital assets and secures them digitally in compliance with policies.

Enterprise data mashup Combination of data from various business systems and external sources without relying on the middle step of ETL (extract, transform, and load) into a data warehouse or help from IT.

Enterprise data warehouses (EDWs) Data warehouses that integrate data from many different databases across an entire enterprise.

Enterprise knowledge management Any solution or system that deals with organizing data into structures that create business knowledge out of existing assets while ensuring its security and managing access.

Enterprise knowledge management (EKM) system An information system used to capture, organize, and create knowledge to enhance organizational processes.

Enterprise resource planning Business process management software that allows an organization to use tightly integrated applications to manage business and automate business processes related to services, technology, and human resources.

Enterprise risk management It is a risk-based approach to managing an enterprise developed by the Committee of Sponsoring Organizations of the Treadway Commission (COSO).

Enterprise search utilities Enable acquisition of knowledge management and access to internal records that can be of value to the group.

Enterprise social platform A private, company-owned social media software app that promotes social connectivity and collaboration with an organization and enhances productivity and employee satisfaction.

Enterprise systems Cross-functional and interorganizational systems that support the business strategy.

Environmental justice Focuses on the fair treatment and meaningful involvement of all people regardless of race, color, national origin, or income with respect to the development, implementation, and enforcement of environmental laws, regulations, and policies.

E-procurement The reengineered procurement process using e-business technologies and strategies.

E-sourcing It refers to many different procurement methods that make use of an electronic venue for identifying, evaluating, selecting, negotiating, and collaborating with suppliers.

Ethical behavior Acting in ways consistent with the accepted values of society and individuals.

Ethics The values and customs of a particular group that identify what is considered right and what is considered wrong.

Eventual consistency Means that not all query responses will reflect data changes uniformly and operates well at a low latency.

Exabyte One quintillion bytes (1,000,000, 000,000,000,000 bytes), which is the equivalent of 1,000 petabytes of data or 7 trillion online video clips. Five Exabytes is equal to all words ever spoken by humans.

Exception reports Generated only when something is outside the norm, either higher or lower than expected.

Executive information system (EIS) A strategic-level information system that helps executives and senior managers analyze the environment in which the organization exists.

Expert system (ES) A branch of AI that has been developed to solve complex problems in a specific discipline with greater speed and information processing capabilities than a human expert.

Extensibility The ability to get data into and out of the cloud service. These cloud service challenges need to be addressed before deciding on sourcing solutions.

eXtensible Business Reporting Language (XBRL) Makes it possible for the reports to be read by any software that includes an XBRL processor.

External service provider It delivers IT services to customers outside the organization.

External transactions Business transactions that originate from outside the organization, for example, from customers, suppliers, regulators, distributors, and financing institutions.

Extract, transform, and load (ETL) Data enter databases from transaction systems. Data of interest are **extracted** from databases, **transformed** to clean and standardize them, and then **loaded** into a data warehouse. These three processes are called ETL.

Extranet A WAN that can be logged into remotely via the Internet to facilitate communication with clients and vendors.

Extreme programming A pragmatic systems development to Agile development that emphasizes business results first and takes an incremental approach to building software, using continual testing and revision.

Facial recognition systems A special application of AI-enhanced image and video search that can identify people by matching a person's image to images or video from security cameras and CCTV feeds.

Fair trade Means pricing products and services in an affordable and equitable manner, providing employees with decent working conditions in all locations, and offering fair terms of trade to farmers and workers in developing countries.

Fault tolerance The ability of a computer or a network to keep working despite the failure of one of its components.

Feature engineering Identifies elements in organization data that would be helpful training an AI application to identify cases of suspected money laundering activity.

Financial Accounting Standards Board (FASB) It establishes financial accounting and reporting standards for public and private companies and not-for-profit organizations.

Financial misrepresentation It occurs when a company has intentionally deceived one or more other parties.

Financial planning and budgeting systems They help companies create and manage budgets, improving the organization's ability to monitor performance and quickly identify departures from planned financial activity when they occur.

Five Forces Model A simple but powerful strategic planning tool for understanding the strength of an organization's competitive position in its current environment and in the environment into which it's considering moving.

Flexibility Having the ability to quickly integrate new business functions or to easily reconfigure software or applications.

Fog node The physical device where fog computing is deployed. Examples are servers, routers, or switches.

Folksonomy A system of classifying and organizing online content into categories by the use of user-generated metadata such as keywords.

Food security When all people in a household always have access to enough safe and nutritious food and can maintain healthy and active lives.

Formal process A process that has documented and well-established steps. For example, order taking and credit approval processes.

Fraud A nonviolent crime in which fraudsters use deception, confidence, and trickery for their personal gain.

Fraud risk management A system of policies and procedures to prevent and detect illegal acts committed by managers, employees, customers, or business partners against a company's interests.

Free trade A policy by which a government does not discriminate against imports or interfere with experts by applying tariffs to import or subsidies to exports.

Frequency The capacity of a transmission media.

Front-office operations Operations involve order fulfillment activities visible to the customer, like sales and advertising.

Fulfillment as a service It typically involves contracting with a third-party business to handle the tasks associated with fulfilling orders received by a retailer. FaaS companies employ sophisticated technology to manage inventory, warehousing, and complex logistical operations to deliver retail orders (and returns) with increasing speed and efficiency.

Functional Business System (FBS) An IS designed to improve the efficiency and performance of a specific functional area within an organization.

Fuzzy logic Mathematical logic that attempts to solve problems with an open, imprecise range of data that can allow accurate conclusions.

GAAP Financial Reporting Taxonomy A list of over 15,000 computer readable tags.

Gantt chart A horizontal bar chart that graphically displays the project schedule.

General controls They are established to protect the system regardless of the specific application.

Geocoding The process of reading input text such as an address and converting it to output in the form of a latitude/longitude coordinate.

Geographic information system (GIS) A computer-based tool that captures, stores, manipulates, analyzes, and visualizes geographic data on a map.

Geospatial data Data that has an explicitly geographic component, ranging from vector and raster data to tabular data with site locations.

Globalization The free trade of goods and services across national borders and cultures as the interdependence of nation's economies grows driven by people, technology, information, and cash flow.

Global mean temperature (GMT) The area-weighted global average of the sea surface temperature over the oceans and the surface air temperature over land at 5 ft (1.5 m) above the ground.

Global warming The upward trend in the GMT.

Goal seeking The ability to calculate backward to obtain an input that would result in a set output.

Go/no-go decision A determination to proceed with or abandon a plan or project.

Goods-based comparative advantage A situation in which a country can produce goods for a lower opportunity cost than other countries.

Gray hat Person who may violate ethical standards or principles, but without the malicious intent ascribed to black hat hackers.

Greenhouse effect The holding of the heat of the sun within the earth's atmosphere.

Greenhouse gas (GHG) emissions They are carbon dioxide, methane, nitrous oxide, and other chemical compounds that trap and hold heat in the atmosphere by absorbing infrared radiation.

Hacking Broadly defined as intentionally accessing a computer without authorization or exceeding authorized access. Various state and federal laws govern computer hacking.

Hacktivist Short for hacker-activist or someone who performs hacking to promote awareness for or otherwise support a social, political, economic, or other cause. Hacking an application, system, or network without authorization, regardless of motive, is a crime.

Hardware Any physical device used in a computerized IS.

Hash A function that takes an input value and outputs a unique fixed-size hexadecimal number that is the cryptographically created key for the data.

Hashtags Terms proceeded by a hash sign (#) that people use to associate their message with a topic or theme.

Hot site It has all the necessary equipment including office space, furniture, communications capabilities and computer equipment. It also includes staffing to manage and monitor the equipment.

HR compliance The process of defining policies and procedure to ensure lawful employment and work practices in line with the company's human capital resource goals.

HR planning, control, and management The continuous process of systematically forecasting future human resource requirements and determining the extent to which existing human resources can be most effectively utilized to meet those requirements.

Hub A hardware device where data from many directions converge and are then sent out in many directions to multiple devices in a network. Hubs are commonly used to connect segments of a LAN.

Human resource information systems (HRIS) It provides a centralized repository of employee master data that the HR management group needs for completing HR processes.

Human resource management A field that deals with employment policies, procedures, communications, and compliance requirements.

Hybrid recommendation engines They develop recommendations based on some combination of the methodologies such as content-based filtering, collaboration filtering, knowledge-based and demographic systems.

Hybrid search engines They combine the results of a directory created by humans and results from a crawler search engine, with the goal of providing both accuracy and broad coverage of the Internet.

Immediate consistency Means that as soon as data are updated, responses to any new query will return the updated value.

Inbound logistics Refers to receiving inventory.

Income statement Summarizes a company's revenue and expenses for one quarter of a fiscal year or the entire fiscal year. It is also known as a P&L (profit and loss) or earnings statement.

Indexer module Creates look-up tables by extracting words from the Web pages and recording the URL where they were found.

Indirect procurement Acquisition of products for daily operational needs.

Inference engine The component of an expert system that applies rules and information processing methods to information in the knowledge base.

Informal process A process that is typically undocumented, has inputs that may not yet been identified, and are knowledge-intensive.

Information Data that have been processed, organized, or put into context so that they have meaning and value to the person receiving them.

Information management The process of collecting, storing, managing, and maintaining data that is accurate, timely, reliable, valid, available, unique, and relevant to an organization.

Information systems (ISs) A combination of information technology and people's activities using the technology to support business processes, operations, management,

and decision-making at different levels of the organization.

Informed user A person knowledgeable about information systems and IT.

Infrastructure as a service (IaaS) A way of delivering servers, storage, networks, workload balancers, and OSs as an on-demand service.

In-house development Systems are developed or other IT work is done in-house by IT developers, IT operators, IT project managers, etc.

Insider fraud A term that refers to a variety of criminal behaviors perpetrated by an organization's employees or contractors against an employer.

Insider threats Cyberattacks carried out by people inside an organization. Insider threats and misuse of privileges threats are a major challenge largely due to the many ways an employee or contractor can carry out malicious activities.

In-store tracking In-store shopping experiences can be optimized through mobile technology that can track a customer's movement through a retail store. This is analogous to e-commerce sites that track the pages a customer looks at to better understand consumer interests and to make decisions about website design.

Integrated CASE tools Used in the all stages of the SDLC from requirements gathering to testing and documentation.

Integrated change control processes Help to manage the disruption resulting from requested changes and corrective actions across the project life cycle.

Intellectual capital The collective documented and undocumented knowledge of individuals in an organization or society that can be exploited for some money-making or other useful purpose.

Intellectual property A work or invention that is the result of creativity that has commercial value, including copyrighted property such as a blueprint, manuscript, or a design, and is protected by law from unauthorized use by others.

Intelligent personal assistant (IPA) IPA software is typically designed to help people perform basic tasks like turning on/off lights and small appliances, activating household alarm systems, and searching the Internet for music, videos, weather, and other types of information.

Interface To connect to and exchange data with apps and systems.

Interference A third concept that describes the way that something can increase (constructive interference) or decrease (destructive interference) the behavior of another thing.

Internal service provider It delivers IT services to a single business unit in its own organization.

Internal transactions Business transactions that originate within the organization or that occur within the organization, for example, payroll, purchases, budget transfers, and payments (in accounting terms, they are referred to as *accounts payable*).

Internet of Things (IoT) Network of physical objects or "things" embedded with electronics, software, sensors, and network connectivity that enables these objects to collect and exchange data.

Internet Protocol (IP) Method by which data are sent from one device to another over a network.

Internet Service Provider (ISP) An organization that provides services for accessing, using, or participating with the Internet.

Intranet A computer network like the Internet except access is restricted by the intranet's owner, and users must sign into the intranet with a username and password. Many companies create intranets for their employees and business partners.

Intrusion detection systems (IDSs) As the name implies, an IDS scans for unusual or suspicious traffic. An IDS can identify the start of a DoS attack by the traffic pattern, alerting the network administrator to take defensive action, such as switching to another IP address and diverting critical servers from the path of the attack.

Intrusion prevention system (IPS) An IPS is designed to take immediate action—such as blocking specific IP addresses—whenever a traffic-flow anomaly is detected.

Inventory control system An IS that controls stock or inventory management.

IP address A unique identifier for each device that communicates with a network that identifies and locates each device. An IP address is comparable to a telephone number or home address.

IPOS The cycle of inputting, processing, outputting, and storing information in an information system.

Isolation It makes a transaction separate from and independent of any other transaction.

IT architectures Guide the process of planning, acquiring, building, modifying, and interfacing with deployed IT resources in a single department within an organization.

IT infrastructure An inventory of the physical IT devices that an organization owns and operates. It does NOT include the people or process components of an information system.

IT resilience The ability to protect data and apps from any planned or unplanned disruption to eliminate the risk of downtime to maintain a seamless customer experience.

IT service management (ITSM) A strategy by which IT systems are offered under contract to customers and performance is managed as a service to achieve greater business–IT alignment and smooth business processes and operations.

IT services The application of business and technical expertise to enable organizations in creating, managing, optimizing, and accessing information and business processes.

IT sourcing The strategy used to acquire and maintain IT systems and IT services including in-house development and outsourcing options.

IT steering committee A team of managers and staff that represents various business units that establish IT priorities and ensures that the IT department is meeting the needs of the enterprise.

IT strategic plan A formal document that details how the IT department will provide, support, and ensure ongoing business operations.

IT strategic planning The process of defining an organization's strategy or direction in adopting, implementing, using, and disposing of its IT assets.

IT strategy A plan of action to create an organization's IT capabilities for maximum and sustainable value in the organization, goals, and objectives and specifies the necessary financial requirements, budgets, and resources.

Joint Application Development (JAD) A team-oriented technique used in the planning and analysis stages of the SDLC to collect business requirements.

Just-in-time inventory management Minimizing holding costs by not taking possession of inventory until it is needed in the production process.

Kanban A technique used for managing the creation of parts of a system with an emphasis on continuous delivery while not overburdening the development team.

Key performance indicators A set of quantifiable measures used to evaluate factors that are critical to the success of an organization.

Keywords Keywords used in content should be selected for their ability to help search engines match the information with a user's intent or the context of the search.

Knowledge Adds understanding, experience, accumulated learning, and expertise as they apply to a current problem or activity, to information.

Knowledge base It contains all the information (facts) the system has about the discipline or domain for which it was designed.

Knowledge management (KM) The process of creating, sharing, using, and managing knowledge and information in an organization to make the best use of the knowledge.

Known known Something that we know, and we know that we know it.

Known unknown Something we *don't* know, and we know we *don't* know it.

Lagging indicators They confirm what has happened. They evaluate outcomes and achievements.

Latency-sensitive apps Apps that are expected to respond quickly to specific events.

Law enforcement agency (LAE) It attempts to discover specific objects in this data using manual search methods would face a daunting if not impossible task.

Lean manufacturing system It streamlines efficiency and processes by connecting production line machinery and warehouse management systems to maximize productivity.

Legacy systems They are older information systems that have been maintained over several decades because they fulfill critical needs.

Legal and organizational feasibility This analysis looks at the company's policies and politics, including impacts on power distribution and business relationships.

Lessons learned An important document created to review the project. It is created during project closing.

Limited memory machines AI applications in the limited memory category utilize a combination of programmed rules and memory of recent events to determine the correct action.

Linear regression A statistical method that analyzes and finds relationships between a dependent variable and one or more independent (or explanatory) variables. Simple linear regression has one explanatory variable. Multiple linear regression has two or more explanatory variables.

List skills API It has a bi-directional interface that updates lists each time users make Shopping list or To Do requests.

Local area network (LAN) A group of computers and other devices that share a communication line or wireless link to server within a limited geographic area.

Logical design It lists and describes all the information resources (data and processes) and the scope of duties and responsibilities of consumers of the information involved in the operation of the new system. It is business focused and always precedes physical design.

Logistical infrastructure It refers to the organization of a complex system of facilities, equipment, transportation, and other requirements necessary for the delivery of goods and services from the point of origin to the point of sale to the end user.

Logistics It entails all processes and information needed to efficiently move products from origin to destination.

Long-range IT plan Aligns with strategic-level business planning.

Low-code development platform Software that provides developers and non-developers with an intuitive graphical user interface instead of a traditional computer programming environment to create apps.

Lower CASE tools Used in the design, implementation/testing, and support/maintenance stages of the SDLC to automatically generate code, test for functionality and defects, monitor implementation, and perform software maintenance activities.

LTE The fastest and most consistent cellular technology.

LTE-A A version of LTE cellular technology that more closely follows the IEEE 802.11ac wireless network standard.

Machine learning Scientific algorithms that identify patterns in big data to learn from the data and create insights based on the data.

Machine-to-machine (M2M) technology Enables sensor-embedded products to share reliable real-time data via radio signals.

Malware Refers to hostile or intrusive software, including computer viruses, rootkits, worms, trojan horses, ransomware, and other malicious programs used to disrupt computer or mobile operations, gather sensitive information, gain access to private computer systems.

Management information system (MIS) A general-purpose reporting system whose objective is to provide managers with scheduled reports to track operations, monitoring, and control.

Man-in-the-middle They occur when cyber criminals insert themselves between two parties in a transaction with the intention of stealing data.

Manufacturing execution systems They manage, monitor, and synchronize the execution of real-time, physical processes involved in transforming raw materials into intermediate and/or finished goods and execute work orders with production scheduling and enterprise-level systems.

Marketing management The process of planning and executing the creation, pricing, promotion, and distribution of ideas, goods, and services to create market exchanges that satisfy customers and organizations.

Marketing management system Used to systematically collect and report accurate data obtained through market research, survey, and customer feedback.

Marketplace e-commerce Where product or service information is provided by multiple third parties and transactions are processed by one marketplace operator.

Mashup A general term referring to the integration of two or more technologies.

Master data The term used to describe business-critical information on customers, products and services, vendors, locations, employees, and other things needed for operations and business transactions.

Master data management (MDM) Integrates data from various sources or enterprise applications to create a more complete (unified) view of a customer, product, or other entity.

Master file A collection of records describing one of the main entities in a database, such as customers, products, employees, and vendor. It is usually periodically updated.

M-commerce or "mobile commerce" The buying and selling of goods and services using mobile devices (such as a smartphone) and a telecommunications or computer network.

Medium-term IT plan More closely aligns with managerial- or administrative-level business planning.

Mega trends Forces that shape or create the future of business, the economy, and society.

Metadata Information that describes other types of data. For example, metadata attached to a file would describe the nature and format of the data in the file, making it easier for some programs to use.

Meta-search engines Compile results from other search engines. For instance, Dogpile generates listings by combining results from Google and Yahoo.

Microblog A blog that consists of frequent, but very brief posts containing text, pictures, or videos. Twitter is perhaps the most well-known example of a microblog.

Micropayments Involve relatively small sums of money.

Microtargeting A marketing strategy that uses consumer data and demographics to create targeted subsets or market segments.

Milestone Periodic "flags" used to manage the project work effort, monitor results, and report meaningful status to project stakeholders.

Millennials Term used to describe people born between the early 1980s and the early 2000s.

Mindmapping A creative and logical method of note-taking that maps out ideas on a graph.

Mission Defines the organization's purpose and what it hopes to achieve.

Mobile biometrics They can significantly improve the security of physical devices and provide stronger authentication for remote access or cloud services.

Mobile browser A Web browser that is optimized to display Web content effectively on a small mobile device such as a smartphone.

Mobile commerce The buying and selling of goods and services using mobile devices (such as a smartphone) and a telecommunications or computer network.

Mobile location-based marketing A marketing strategy that uses information from a mobile device's GPS or customer's mobile check-in on a social network to determine the content of marketing communications they receive on the device (e.g., advertisements, coupons, special offers).

Mobile marketing A variety of activities used by organizations to engage, communicate, and interact over Wi-Fi and telecommunications networks with consumers using wireless, handheld devices.

Modern BI Allows users to product reports and analysis on-the-fly and share data with other users to make decisions and optimize business results.

Moral hazard The risk that a party to a transaction has not entered into a contract in good faith or has provided misleading information.

Natural language processing (NLP) A technology that allows users to interact with computers using their natural language instead of a predetermined set of commands and syntax structures.

Natural language search tools Creation of a semantic representation of the query in which words from questions like "How many countries are there in Europe?" are extracted.

Near-field communication (NFC) Enables two devices within close proximity to establish a communication channel and transfer data through radio waves.

Negligent hiring The hiring of an employee when the employer knew or should have known about the employee's background, which, if known, indicates a dangerous or untrustworthy character.

Net neutrality A principle that Internet service providers (ISPs) and their regulators treat all Internet traffic the same way.

Network A combination of lines, wires, and physical devices connected to each other to create a telecommunications network.

Network data model A data model that allows multiple records to be linked to the same parent.

Network effect From the field of economics, the network effect explains how the perceived value of a product or service is affected by the number of people using the product or service.

Network interface card (NIC) A circuit board or chip installed in a computer to enable it to connect to a wired or wireless network.

Not Only SQL (NoSQL) A non-relational database query language.

Object-oriented (O-O) An iterative systems analysis and design methodology that emphasizes modularity and reusability.

Object-oriented database management system A data model that supports the modeling and creation of data entities as objects that contain both data and the relationships of those data

Offshoring The practice of acquiring and maintaining IT systems and IT services from external third-party providers located in a different country from the company sourcing the systems and services.

Omnichannel retailing A business strategy that provides customers with a seamless and integrated experience across multiple retail channels such as in-store, online, mobile, and other sales and product distribution channels.

On-demand economy The economic activity created by technology companies that fulfill consumer demand through the immediate provisioning of products and services.

Online analytics processing (OLAP) The analysis of complex data from a data warehouse.

Online marketplaces Websites that provide a platform for multiple retailers to promote and sell product and services, usually for a fee, commission, or other type of remuneration. Popular examples include Amazon, eBay, and Etsy.

Online transaction processing (OLTP) system A database design that breaks down complex information into simpler data tables to strike a balance between transaction processing efficiency and query efficiency.

Onshoring The practice of acquiring and maintaining IT systems and services from external third-party providers located in the same country as the company sourcing the systems and services.

The Open Group Architecture Framework (TOGAF) is a useful IT strategy tool that is currently being used by more than 60% of Fortune 500 companies to align IT goals with overall business goals to improve business efficiency.

Opportunity cost The benefit that is missed or given up when an individual, business, or country chooses one alternative over another.

Optimizing The process of finding an alternative that is most cost effective or produces best achievable performance under given constraints by maximizing desired effects and minimizing undesired effect.

Order fulfillment Set of complex processes involved in providing customers with what they ordered on time and all customer services related to on-time delivery of a product.

Outbound logistics Refers to shipping inventory.

Outsource relationship management (ORM) company Companies that provide automated tools to monitor and manage the outsourcing relationships.

Outsourcing Involves the development and maintenance of IT systems or IT services by an external service provider who is a third-party supplier or vendor.

Outsourcing contract A legal document that specifies what work will be handled by a third party, project deliverables, the schedule within which project deliverables will be delivered, and the consequences of non-performance.

Packet A piece of a message that is collected and reassembled with the other pieces of the same message at their destination. To improve communication performance and reliability, each larger message sent between two network devices is often subdivided into packets.

Packet switching Occurs when data or voice is transferred in packets.

Page repository A data structure that stores and manages information from a large number of Web pages, providing a fast and efficient means for accessing and analyzing the information at a later time.

Parallel conversion A process in which the old system and the new system operate concurrently for a specified period of time.

Parts per million A measure of small concentrations of pollutants in a solution of solid or gas and is a common unit of measure of CO_2 levels. 1,000 ppm is equivalent to 1%.

Patch A software program that users download and install to fix a vulnerability.

Payload Code that is dropped on the system that performs any or all the following functions: facilitates the infection or communicates with the command and control server or downloads more code. In doing so, the payload carries out the purpose of the malware.

Pay-per-click (PPC) ads Paid search listings are often referred to as pay-per-click advertising because advertisers pay search engines based on how many people click on the ads.

Peer-to-peer (P2P) Allows shared access to files and peripherals without the need for a central server in a network where each computer can act as a server for the others.

Peer-to-peer (P2P) marketplace Business model based on exchanges that occur between two individuals.

Peer-to-peer network A mechanism that is used to boost the security of the blockchain.

People Any person involved in developing, operating and using an IS.

People-first approach It ensures that technology meets the needs of the users by involving the users at every stage of systems development.

Periodic report Created or run according to a preset schedule. Examples are daily, weekly, and quarterly.

Phased conversion Introduces components of the new system, such as individual modules, in stages.

Phishing Using a fraudulent communication, such as an e-mail, to trick the receiver into divulging critical information such as account numbers, passwords, or other identifying information.

Physical controls Protect physical computer facilities and resources. This includes protecting computers, data centers, software, manuals, and networks. They provide protection against most natural hazards as well as against some human hazards.

Physical design It transforms business requirements into a specific technological solution by identifying all physical servers and major technical components that will be used to support the desired business outcome.

Pilot conversion Introduces the new system in one location, or with one group of people, to test it out. After the new system works properly, it is rolled out to the entire organization.

Platform as a service (PaaS) A computing platform that enables the quick and easy creation, testing, and deployment of Web applications without the necessity of buying and maintaining the software and infrastructure underneath it. It is a set of tools and services that make coding and deploying these applications faster and more efficient.

Plunge conversion   The old system is cut off and the new system is turned on at a specified time. This type of conversion is the least expensive, but it is the riskiest if the new system does not work as planned.

Portfolio   The entire set of projects within a department or organization.

Postmortem   A method for evaluating project performance, identifying lessons learned, and making recommendations for future projects.

Predictive data analytics   The process of using data analytics methods and techniques to model and make predictions about unknown events from data.

Predictive model   The model is based on several factors likely to influence future behavior and predicts at some confidence level the outcome of an event.

Predictive modeling   A process that uses data mining and probabilities to forecast outcomes to create a statistical model to predict outcomes.

Prescriptive data analytics   Finding the best course of action among various choices given the known parameters.

Privacy paradox   The disconnect between how important people say their online privacy is versus how they actually behave in real life.

Private cloud   It delivers cloud computing services over the Internet or a private internal network to only select users instead of the general public.

Private SNSs   Use social technology to create a community restricted to members selected by the SNS's owner.

Procedures   Documentation containing directions on how to use the other components of an IS.

Production and operations management   It is responsible for processes that transform inputs into value-added outputs.

Production and operations management system   It assists in the operation, planning, execution, and ongoing management of an organization.

Program   A set of related projects.

Program management   Involves overseeing and controlling a group of related projects and focused on current project.

Project   It is a well-planned sequential series of tasks to achieve a result. Projects have a defined beginning and end, a scope, resources, and a budget. Projects are approved before they are funded and allocated resources.

Project management   Application of knowledge, skills, tools, and techniques to project activities to meet project requirements.

Project management office (PMO)   An organizational group responsible for coordinating the project management function throughout an organization.

Project management technology quotient (PMTQ)   A person's ability to adapt, manage, and integrate technology based on the needs of the project or the organization.

Project portfolio   A group of unrelated projects that list major resource projects, including infrastructure, application services, data services, and security services, that are consistent with the long-range plan.

Project portfolio management (PPM)   A strategic-level initiative that closely aligns with the business strategy and future goals and provides oversight of project and program managers.

Projects   Temporary endeavors undertaken to create a unique product, service, or result within a given timeframe.

Project sponsor   A person or organization that approves and/or supports the allocation of resources for a project, defines its goals, and evaluates the success of the project at completion.

Proof of concept (POC)   A vendor demonstration of a product to see how or how well it works.

Proof-of-work   A mechanism that is used to boost the security of the blockchain.

Protected class   A group of people with characteristics that cannot be targeted for discrimination and harassment such as age, race, disability, gender, marital status, national origin, genetic information, and religion.

Prototype   A working model of a system or part of a system usually built to demonstrate it to users, who can test it, and request rework as necessary.

Public cloud   It is based on the standard cloud computing model in which a service provider makes resources, apps, or storage available to the general public over the Internet either free or on a pay-per-usage model.

Pure network applications   They are developed expressly for use by two more devices that help transfer data and communicate across a network.

Pure play e-commerce retailers   Retailers that only operate online (the Web) and do not use other channels such as mobile or in-store retailing.

Quality management system (QMS)   A formalized integrated system that documents processes, procedures, and responsibilities to achieve quality policies and objectives to consistently meet customer requirements while also satisfying regulatory and development requirements.

Quality of life   The general well-being of individuals and societies, including physical health, family, education, employment, wealth, safety, religious beliefs, and the environment.

Quality of service   A network's ability to achieve maximum bandwidth, optimize network performance elements like latency, error rate, uptime and downtime, and control and manage network resources by setting priorities for specific types of data on the network.

Qubits   A kind of switch used in quantum computers that can hold any value between 0 and 1, e.g., 0, .2, .5, .7, 1.

Query   Ad hoc (unplanned) user request for specific data.

Query interface   Location where users enter words that describe the kind of information they are looking for.

Query predictability   The greater the number of ad hoc or unpredictable queries there are, the more flexible the database needs to be. Database or query performance management is more difficult when the workloads are so unpredictable that they cannot be prepared for in advance.

Query processing capabilities   Database queries are processed in real time and results are transmitted via wired or wireless networks to computer screen or handheld devices.

Quick response (QR) code   A two-dimensional barcode usually in a square structure with information stored in a black and white geometric symbol.

Query response time   The time it takes to respond to a user query. The volume of data impacts response times to queries and data explorations. Many databases *pre-stage data*—that is, summarize or precalculate results—so queries have faster response rates.

Ransomware   A type of malware that is designed to block access to a computer system until a sum of money has been paid.

Rapid Application Development (RAD)   An interactive process used throughout the SDLC continuing until the system is completely developed and all users are satisfied with the outcome.

Rapid prototyping   An iterative process used to quickly create an early sample, model, or release of a system to test a concept or process.

Reactive machines   They are designed for one task and are unable to learn new tasks or even develop ways of performing their task better.

Real-time processing Also referred to as online transaction processing (OLTP)—occurs when transactions are processed as they occur to keep account balances and inventories up to date and ensure the system always reflects the current status of the data.

Really Simple Syndication (RSS) A technology that allows users to receive updates and shared information from websites in a standardized way. These updates can be in the form of blog posts, news, or video and audio recordings.

Recommendation engines They proactively identify products that have a high probability of being something the consumer might want to buy.

Regulatory compliance systems They are designed to help organizations understand what regulations, policies, and obligations are applicable to them locally and globally to manage changes to applicable financial, data, environmental, and health and safety regulations.

Reinforcement learning The computer learns by trial and error.

Relational data model An approach to managing data using a structure and language that involves the use of data tables to collect groups of elements into relations.

Remote access trojan (RAT) A form of trojan horse that creates an unprotected backdoor into a system through which a hacker can remotely control that system.

Remote wipe capability Needed in the event of loss or theft of a device. All major smartphone platforms have a remote erase capability and encryption option.

Request for proposal (RFP) A document issued by an organization to request third-party bids for products, solutions, and services.

Resilient distributed dataset (RDD) A fault-tolerant, immutable, and distributed collection of objects that can be processed in parallel across a cluster.

Responsibility matrix Lets everyone know who is responsible for completion of tasks.

Responsiveness Means that IT capacity can be easily scaled up or down as needed, which essentially requires cloud computing.

REST API The Representational State API is used to build Web services that are lightweight, maintainable, and scalable. It provides a way to access resources in a particular environment.

Retrieval/ranking module Determines the order in which pages are listed in an SERP.

Reverse supply chain A series of activities required to retrieve a used product from a customer to either dispose of it or reuse it.

Ring network configuration One in which each computer is connected to two adjoining computers to form a closed circuit.

Risk A situation involving exposure to danger.

Risk mitigation The action taken to reduce threats and ensure resiliency.

Risk register Lists all known risks and their source, an estimation of unknown risks, and the response to be taken to each risk.

Robotics The branch of technology that deals with the design, construction, operation, and application of robots.

Rogue application monitoring It is used to detect and destroy malicious applications.

Rootkit A set of software tools that enable an attacker to gain control of a computer system without being detected.

Router links computers to the Internet to enable users to share a network connection. It acts like a dispatcher, choosing the best paths for data packets to travel from their source to their destination based on IP addresses.

Rules-based decision-making Decision-making that helps novices make decisions like an expert.

Safety stock Extra inventory used as a buffer to reduce the risk of stockouts. It is also called buffer stock.

Sales management It involves sales procedures and tasks from the generation of leads and quotes and moving to customer conversion, purchases, returns, and support.

Sales management systems They combine different sales procedures and tasks to provide a detailed overview of a sales team's work on different products, services, location, and customers to accelerate the tracking of sales flow and help an organization achieve its sales targets faster.

Satisficing A decision-making strategy that involves searching through available alternatives until an acceptable solution is found. It is a composite of the words "satisfy" and "suffice."

Scalability The ability of the system to increase in size to handle data growth or the load of an increasing number of concurrent users, that is, scalable systems efficiently meet the demands of high-performance computing.

Scope The body of work that needs to be completed within a project to achieve a desired outcome.

Scope creep The accumulation of small changes that by themselves are manageable but in aggregate are significant.

Scrum A framework that consists of small self-organizing, cross-functional Scrum Teams who work together to produce small pieces of a system iteratively and incrementally in sprints to maximize opportunities for feedback.

Scrumban An agile systems development methodology that combines certain aspects of Scrum and Kanban originally designed as a way to transition from Scrum to Kanban.

Search engine An application for locating Web pages or other content (e.g., documents, media files) on a computer network. Popular Web-based search engines include Google, Bing, and Yahoo.

Search engine marketing (SEM) A collection of online marketing strategies and tactics that promote brands by increasing their visibility in SERPs through optimization and advertising.

Search engine optimization A strategy of "optimizing" an organization's website so that it will be positively evaluated by the search engine's ranking algorithm and appear at the top of SERPs organic or unpaid listings.

Search marketing The umbrella term that refers to two different strategies for influencing how a website will appear on SERPs: search engine optimization and search engine marketing.

Self-aware machines Not only create representations of things in their environment, but also of themselves.

Self-service analytics A form of BI that enables and encourages managers and other users to perform queries and generate reports with nominal IT support.

Semantic search engines Designed to locate information based on the nature and meaning of Web content, not simple keyword matches.

Semantic technologies Semantic Technologies include artificial intelligence (AI), natural-language-processing (NLP) and other emerging technologies that enable computers to understand the meaning and context of words and languages that appear online. This greatly increases the power and effectiveness of search engines and other web-based applications designed to communicate with written or spoken language.

Semantic Web An extension of the World Wide Web that utilizes a variety of conventions and technologies that allow machines to understand the meaning of Web content.

Semantic Web search Takes advantage of content tagged with metadata. Search results are likely to be more accurate than keyword matching.

Sensor fusion Combining data from different sources so that the result is less uncertainty than would exist if the separate data sets were used individually. Also known as multisensor data fusion.

Sentiment analysis A widely used approach to understanding consumer attitudes and emotions in the era of social media that uses natural language processing, text analysis, computational linguistics, and biometrics to systematically identify, extract, and quantify affective stages and subjective information.

Server A central repository of data and various programs that are shared by users in a network.

Service-based comparative advantage countries compete based on the the creation of large-scale exportable business, financial, and entertainment *services* including call centers, knowledge portals, medical transcription services, electronic publishing, telemarketing and help desks.

Service-level agreement (SLA) A contract between a service provider and its internal or external customers that document services the provider will furnish and defines the service standards the provider is obligated to meet.

Service portfolio Refers to the complete set of services managed by a service provider.

Service relationship The degree of cooperation between a service provider and service customers, vendors/suppliers, and regulatory agencies including service provision, service consumption, and service relationship management.

Shadow IT The use of IT-related hardware or software by an individual or a department without the knowledge of the IT department within the organization. Also known as stealth IT.

Shared service provider It provides IT services to different business units in its own organization.

Sharing economy An economic system in which goods or services are shared between private individuals, either free or for a fee, typically arranged through an online company or organization.

Short code It works like a telephone number, except that it is only five or six characters long and easier to remember.

Short message service (SMS) A technology used to send and receive text messages on mobile devices via a telecommunications network.

Showrooming The practice of examining products in a traditional retail store, sometimes with the help of a salesperson, and then purchasing the product online.

Signature A unique value that indicates the presence of malicious code.

Smart city On a broader scale, the IoT can be applied to things like "smart cities" that can help reduce waste and improve efficiency. Applications include water distribution, traffic management, waste management and environmental monitoring designed to remove the discomfort and issues with city living such as traffic congestion, noise and air pollution and personal safety.

Smart grid A combination of smart meters, wireless technology, sensors, and software creates the smart grid that allows utility companies to accurately track power grids and cut back on energy use when the availability of electricity is stressed.

Smishing Similar to phishing, but the fraudulent communication comes in the form of an SMS message.

Social bookmarking tools Allow users to tag Web content with keywords of their choosing.

Social commerce Refers to a wide range of strategies and tactics used by business organizations to engage with consumers on the Web and social media apps to influence their purchasing behavior. This includes advertising, promotion, content marketing, organic (unpaid) interactions with consumers, and so on.

Social engineering Experts believe that one of the greatest cybersecurity dangers over the next few years will involve a hacker's clever use of deception or manipulation of people's tendency to trust, be helpful, or simply follow their curiosity on social media. This phenomenon is called social engineering.

Social media A collection of Web applications based on Web 2.0 technology and culture that allows people to connect and collaborate with others by creating and sharing digital content.

Social media discrimination Occurs when a potential employer or recruiter uses social networking websites to research a person's character, behaviors, and social circles and treats them less favorably than another person based on the information they gather.

Social media optimization Refers to strategies designed to enhance a company's presence on social media sites.

Social–mobile–analytics–cloud (SMAC) The concept that the convergence of four technologies is currently driving business innovation and digital transformation.

Social monitoring services A fast-growing sector in the social technology field. Monitoring applications allow users to track conversations taking place on social media sites.

Social network It is defined by a user's connections and interactions with other people. Users can have different types of social networks, such as family connections, connections of friends, school connections, professional connections, and so on.

Social networking service (SNS) An online platform or website that allows subscribers to interact and form communities or networks based on real-life relationships, shared interests, activities and so on.

Software A set of machine-readable instructions (code) that makes up a computer application that directs a computer's processor to perform specific operations.

Software as a service A widely used software licensing and delivery model in which software is licensed to users on a subscription basis and is centrally hosted.

Software-defined data center A way to dramatically configure and provision apps, infrastructure, and IT resources, allowing a data center to be managed as a unified system.

Software-defined WAN (SD-WAN) Managed by one central app that efficiently distributes network traffic across a WAN over the Internet or cloud-based private networks.

Source code generator Automatically generates common application source code in any computer programming language, for example, BASIC, VB, PHP, ASP.NET, SQL, C#, Java Script.

Spam Malicious software that enables attackers to search, sort, and compile a list of e-mail addresses, generate random addresses, insert fake headers into message, and use multiple mail servers simultaneously to broadcast unsolicited messages to unsuspecting recipients.

Spear phishing A type of phishing that targets select groups of people who have something in common. They can work at the same company, bank at the same financial institution, use a specific Internet provider, or attend the same church or university.

Spiders Also known as crawlers, Web bots, or simply "bots," spiders are small computer programs designed to perform automated, repetitive tasks over the Internet. They are used by search engines for scanning Web pages and returning information to be stored in a page repository.

Sprint A set period of time during which specific work has to be completed and made ready for review in agile software development. Traditionally, a sprint lasts 30 days.

Spyware A tracking software that is not designed to intentionally damage or disable a system. For example, an employer may install spyware on corporate laptops to monitor employee browsing activities, or an advertiser might use cookies to track what Web pages a user visit in order to target advertising in a marketing campaign.

Standalone network applications They were originally developed for use on a single device and their functionality retooled to allow them to run on networks.

Standard operating procedures (SOPs) A set of written instructions on how to perform a function or activity. SOPs provide the framework for complex processes to be managed more effectively.

Star network configuration One in which each computer is directly linked to a central computer and indirectly to each other.

Statement of work (SOW) Written as a definitive statement, which means that it defines the project plan but does not offer any options or alternatives in the scope.

Stealth IT Also known as shadow IT, defined above.

Stockouts Inventory shortage arising from unexpected demand, delays in scheduled delivery, production delays, or poor inventory management.

Strategic technology The potential to make significant impacts on an organization's long-term plans, programs, and initiatives.

Structured decisions They are relatively straightforward and made on a regular basis, and an IS can ensure that they are done consistently.

Structured query language (SQL) A standardized query language for accessing databases.

Subscription-based retailing Where a customer subscribes to receive a regular parcel of goods, usually on a monthly or quarterly basis.

Sunk cost A cost that has already been incurred and cannot be recovered.

Superposition The ability to be in two places at once.

Supervised learning Analogous to providing the machine with a teacher, however the "teacher" is really the part of a data set containing the correct answer.

Supply chain Starts with the acquisition of raw materials or the procurement (purchase) of products and proceeds through manufacture, transport, and delivery—and the disposal or recycling of products.

Supply chain management (SCM) Efficient management of the flows of material, data, and payments among the companies in the supply chain, from suppliers to consumers.

Sustainability The ability to create and maintain conditions that enable humans and nature to exist in productive harmony to support present and future generations.

Sustainable development An initiative to create long-term stakeholder value through implementing a business strategy focused on doing business in an ethical, social, environmental, cultural, and economically responsible way.

Sustainable, responsible, and impact investing (SRI) An investment strategy that considers environmental, social, and corporate governance (ESG) criteria to generate long-term competitive financial returns and positive societal impact.

Switch A controller that enables networked devices to talk to each other efficiently by transmitting data packets based on IP addresses. It connects the computers, printers, and servers within a building or a company to create the network. It is more sophisticated than a hub.

Synchronous communication Dialogue or conversation that takes place in real time, without the long delays between exchanges that occur, for instance, in e-mail or discussion board conversations.

Systems development A set of activities, methods, best practices, deliverables, and automated tools to creating and maintaining IT architecture and software.

Systems development life cycle (SDLC) A multiple-stage approach used by IT professionals to develop high-quality ISs from planning and analysis through support and maintenance.

Tactical adoption approach Incremental approach to deploying cloud services that results in apps and services that are patched together to create end-to-end business processes.

Tactical IT plan aligns with operational-level business planning.

Tech-clash The love/hate relationship technology users experience when they perceive the business value of technology is not aligned with their personal values, expectations, and needs.

Technical feasibility Determines if the required technology, IT infrastructure, data structures, analytics, and resources can be developed and/or acquired to solve the business problem.

Technology platform The operating system and computer hardware used as a base upon which other applications, processes, or technologies are developed.

Technology solutions as a service (TSaaS) It combines software, hardware, networks, and telecommunications to provide specialized technology solutions that allow companies to adopt new technologies and transform their business.

Technology stack The multiple layers of hardware, software, network connectivity, and data analytics capability that comprise a technology platform.

Template A sample document that demonstrates required/suggested formatting and already has some details in place.

Terms of service (TOS) agreement A formal listing of the policies, liability limits, fees, user rights and responsibilities associated with using a particular service. Users are typically required to acknowledge they

have read, understand, and agree to the TOS before they are allowed the service to use.

Text mining The process of deriving high-quality information from text aided by software that can identify concepts, patterns, topics, keywords, and other attributes in the unstructured data.

Theory of mind machines Machines in this category are capable of developing representations of their environment and other agents or things in the world.

Time-series regression model Estimates the direction a variable is trending over time.

Time-to-exploitation The elapsed time between when a vulnerability is discovered and when it is exploited.

Traffic shaping The ability to prioritize and throttle network traffic.

Transaction A single logical unit of work that accesses and possibly modifies the contents of a database.

Transaction mechanism A set of logical operations used to help ensure integrity and concurrency and eliminate multiplicity.

Transaction processing system An information system that collects, monitors, stores, processes, and distributes specific types of data input from ongoing transactions.

Transmission control protocol/Internet protocol (TCP/IP) TCP/IP is the most widely used and most widely available protocol suite. It is a layered architecture where each layer depicts the functionality of the protocol.

Trended time series is a time series in which the mean value of the time series can fluctuate by season.

Trial run When a vendor product or service is tested in a pilot study or limited area of the business to confirm its usefulness to the company.

Triple bottom line A process by which companies manage their financial, social, and environmental risks, obligations, and opportunities.

Triple constraint The combination of the three most significant elements of any project: scope, time, and cost. It is also known as the iron triangle.

Trojan horse A program that appears harmless, but is, in fact, malicious.

Tweet A brief 140-character message or post broadcast on Twitter, a microblogging service.

Twittersphere Universe of people who use Twitter, a microblogging service.

Unethical behavior An action that is not considered morally right or proper carried out by a person, a profession, or an industry.

Unknown unknown   Something we don't know, and we don't realize we don't know it.

Unstructured data   Data that either does not have a predefined format or is not organized in a predefined manner. Unstructured data is typically text, although it may also contain some dates and numbers.

Unstructured decision   Decision that depends on human intelligence, knowledge, and/or experience—as well as on data and models to solve.

Unsupervised learning   The machine is on its own to identify patterns and structures in the data used to categorize things.

Upper CASE tools   Used in the planning and analysis stages of the SDLC to perform repetitive activities such as gathering requirements, diagramming processes, and presenting them in an organized way.

Use-case description   A text-based list of actions or steps that detail the interactions between users and the system needed to achieve the goal of the system.

Use-case diagram   A graphic depiction of the major elements (use cases) within a system and it environment.

Use-case model   A list of actions or steps that define the interactions between a user and system to achieve an expected outcome.

User-generated content (UGC)   Content created by users on social media in contrast to traditional media—TV, radio, and magazine**s**.

User interface   The expert system component that interacts with a user.

Value-added reseller (VAR)   Customizes or adds features to a vendor's software or equipment and resells the enhanced product.

Value chain model   identifies where the greatest value exists in an organization and how that value can be increased.

Value driver   It enhances the value of a product or service to consumers, creating value for the company. Advanced IT, reliability, and brand reputation are examples.

Vendor management organization (VMO)   A business unit with an organization that is responsible for evaluating suppliers of goods and services and overseeing regular interaction and long-term relationships with vendors.

Virtual machine (VM)   An emulation of a computer system based on computer architectures and provide functionality of a physical computer.

Virtual private network (VPN)   A service that allows safe and private network access by routing connections through a server and hiding the online actions.

Virtualization   It allows the sharing of a single physical instance of an IT resource or app among multiple customers and organizations.

Virus   Infects apps like Microsoft Word where it executes instructions once opened before transferring back control to the app.

Vishing   Again, similar to phishing, but the fraudulent communication comes in the form of a voice or voicemail message encouraging the victim to divulge secure information.

Voice biometrics   An effective authentication solution across a wide range of consumer devices including smartphones, tablets, and TVs.

Voice over IP (VOIP) networks   They carry voice calls by converting analog (voice) signals to digital signs that are set as data packets.

Volatility   The database needs adequate processing power to handle the volatility of the data. The rate at which data are added, updated, or deleted determines the workload the database must be able to control to prevent problems with the response rate to queries.

Vulnerability   A gap in IT security defenses of a network, system, or application that can be exploited by a cyberthreat to gain unauthorized access.

Wardriving   The act of searching for Wi-Fi wireless networks by a person in a moving vehicle using a laptop or smartphone.

Warm site   Provides a fully equipped physical data center, but it has no customer data.

Waterfall model   A sequential, predictive systems development methodology that is simple to use and understand, but inflexible.

Web 2.0   A term used to describe a phase of World Wide Web evolution characterized by dynamic Webpages, social media, mashup applications, broadband connectivity, and user-generated content.

Web directories   They list Web pages organized into hierarchical categories.

Whistleblower   An employee, supplier, contractor, client, or any other individual who has and reports insider knowledge of illegal activities occurring in an organization.

White hat   Computer security specialist who breaks into protected systems and networks to test and assess their security.

Whitelisted app   An approved app or executable file that is permitted to be present and active on a computer system.

Wide Area Network (WAN)   A communication network that spans a large geographic area.

Wi-Fi   Connects computers and smart devices to a network via a single access point like a router.

Wi-Fi hotspot   A wireless access point that provides Internet access to mobile devices like laptops and smartphones.

Wiki   A social media content management application that allows teams to collaborate on the creation of Web pages.

WiMAX   Stands for worldwide interoperability for microwave access and was developed to overcome the short-range limitations of Wi-Fi.

Wireless local area network (WLAN)   Typically extends an existing wired LAN by attaching a wireless AP to a wired network.

Wireless router   A device that works as a router to forward data between network devices and serves as both a wireless access point and a router.

Wireless transmission media   A form of unguided media that does not require physical links between two or more devices.

Wireless wide area network (WWAN)   Has a wider range than a local area network and can cover a group of buildings.

Work automation   The term used to describe replacing a human worker with a robot.

Work breakdown structure (WBS)   A list of tasks that identify all work or activities that need to be performed, the order in which the work will be performed.

World Wide Web (WWW)   A network of documents on the Internet, called Web pages, constructed with HTML markup language that supports links to other documents and media (e.g., graphics, video, audio).

Worm   Doesn't attach itself to a host, like a virus, but these self-contained programs can replicate themselves across computers and networks.

Zero-day exploit   Malicious software that exposes a vulnerability in software or hardware and can create complicated problems well before anyone detects it.

Name Index

Subject Index